Social Psychology

Visit the *Social Psychology,* Companion Website at **www.pearsoned.co.uk/dickerson** to find valuable **student** learning material including:

- Multiple choice questions to test your learning
- Essay questions and guided answers to help you prepare for exams
- Interesting podcasts, in which the author gives an overview of each chapter as well as discussing the important points and key debates
- Links to relevant sites on the web
- Interactive online flashcards that allow you to check definitions against the key terms

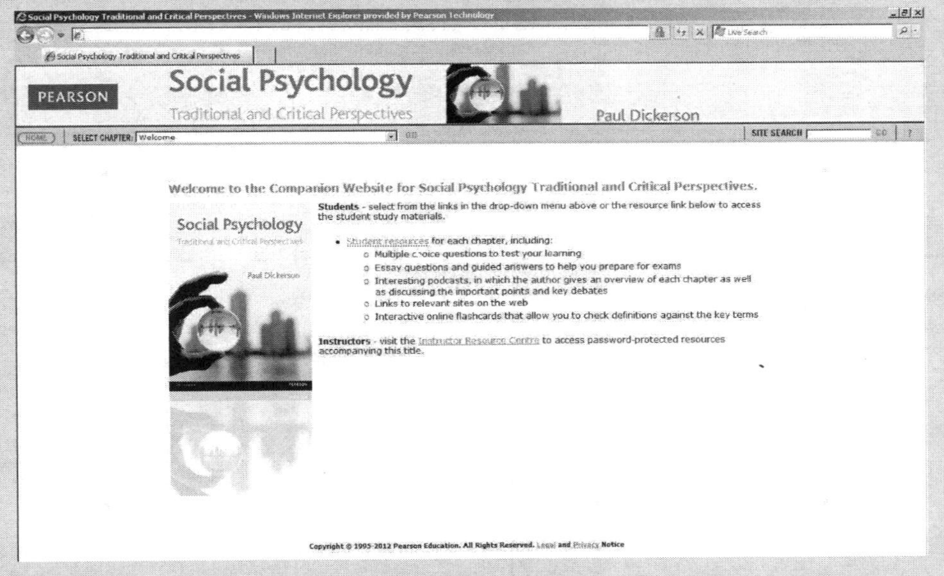

PEARSON ALWAYS LEARNING

Paul Dickerson

Social Psychology: Traditional and Critical Perspectives

With Contributions by Rory Coughlan, Ph.D.
Second Custom Edition for Trent University

Taken from:
Social Psychology: Traditional and Critical Perspectives
by Paul Dickerson

Cover Art: Courtesy of PhotoDisc and Getty Images.

Taken from:

Social Psychology: Traditional and Critical Perspectives
by Paul Dickerson

Pearson Learning Solutions, 501 Boylston Street, Suite 900, Boston, MA 02116
A Pearson Education Company
www.pearsoned.com

Printed in Canada

5 6 7 V0RB16 15 14

000200010271726869

LF

ISBN 10: 1-269-62480-6
ISBN 13: 978-1-269-62480-0

Brief contents

Praise for *Social Psychology: Traditional and Critical Perspectives*

"Finally, a textbook of social psychology that does justice to the different strands of contemporary work. It is sophisticated, scholarly and bang up to date. It is also very clearly written with an engaging style that brilliantly overviews a range of sometimes difficult ideas. Dickerson is able to cover the traditional work in a way that does its complexity justice, while also covering different strands of new and critical psychology showing how they deal with those more traditional issues. Debates and controversies are effectively illuminated and its historical introduction is wide-ranging and incorporates the latest thinking. It is organized in a way that is student friendly with learning outcomes, boxes and annotated web resources. In my view it is the best contemporary introductory textbook in social psychology."
Professor Jonathan Potter, Loughborough University

"Many textbooks have the feel and appeal of telephone directories: crammed full of information but with little insight into researchers' personal and theoretical commitments or how these shape the production of social psychological research. Dickerson's text is exceptional in every respect. It explores the key topics at the heart of the discipline and does so in a manner that conveys a clear sense of how they may be conceptualised and investigated from very different standpoints and perspectives. The result is a text that eschews a standard formulaic approach and which brings to life the diversity and controversy in contemporary theory and research. There is a breadth and depth of perspective which allows insight into the vitality of the discipline and why it so engages its practitioners. To have achieved this in a textbook is remarkable."
Dr Nicholas Hopkins, University of Dundee

"This is no ordinary textbook: Dickerson brings a fresh and critical reading of social psychology's central topics by placing readers in the box seat of both classic and new research in the discipline. Instead of the conventional and 'potted' versions of classic experiments that have come to define social psychology, Dickerson brings them to life by providing nuanced detail much of which has been lost or forgotten over the years. The reader is provided with a sense of 'being there' in the experimental moment, an invaluable learning resource for students. This is thoughtfully contrasted to critical and discursive approaches that challenge taken-for-granted concepts and methods."
Professor Martha Augoustinos, University of Adelaide

"This is a ground breaking text, and an important marker in the history of social psychology. Paul Dickerson offers us the first attempt to integrate both traditional and constructionist/critical inquiry into a single, coherent account of the field. Lively and unusual, it invites students into dialogue as opposed to the usual spoon-feeding."
Professor Ken Gergen, Swarthmore College, USA

Contents

Supporting resources

Visit **www.pearsoned.co.uk/dickerson** to find valuable online resources

Companion Website for students

- Multiple choice questions to test your learning
- Essay questions and guided answers to help you prepare for exams
- Interesting podcasts, in which the author gives an overview of each chapter as well as discussing the important points and key debates
- Links to relevant sites on the web
- Interactive online flashcards that allow you to check definitions against key terms

For instructors

- Testbank of question material
- PowerPoint slides to use in lectures
- A downloadable Instructor's Manual to accompany the book

Also: The companion website provides the following features:

- Search tool to help locate specific items of content
- E-mail results and profile tools to send results of quizzes to instructors
- Online help and support to assist with website usage and troubleshooting

For more information please contact your local Pearson Education sales representative or visit

www.pearsoned.co.uk/dickerson

List of figures and tables

Figures

Tables

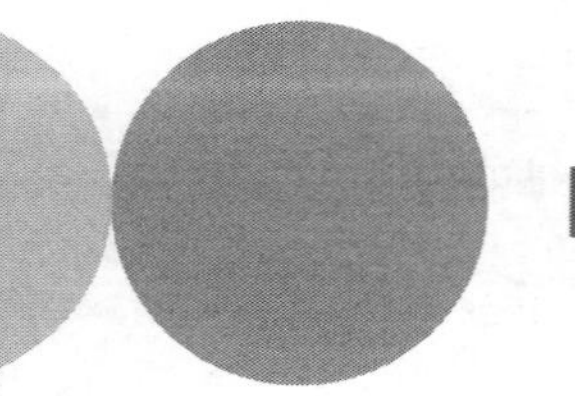

Preface

For much of my academic career in psychology it has felt like there have been two parallel worlds. First, there is the world of debate and uncertainty, research findings that are questioned and challenged and theoretical perspectives that smash against each other. Then, there is the world of the textbook. In this more serene world, knowledge seems to accumulate in an ordered and orderly fashion–new findings emerge that add to what has gone before and the terrain of social psychology seems more knowable, predictable and safe. In the lecture room, I would appeal to students using the words of Umberto Eco: 'switch on your critical faculties' – wanting them to critically evaluate, debate and question all of the research findings and theoretical perspectives that they encounter. I had become disenchanted with psychology textbooks because they did not (admittedly a crude and unfair generalisation here) seem to support this vital means of engaging with social psychological literature.

Alongside this concern was a second, related issue. I was aware of certain literatures that received little or no attention in many social psychology texts. Discourse and conversation analytic research, for example, while an important presence within social psychology conferences and various academic journals, was – in my opinion – often relegated to more specifically focused texts (some of which are brilliant). One danger of this was that both the fundamental challenges that these different perspectives might raise and the specific empirical findings they offered was, potentially at least, less immediately available and somewhat marginalised.

It was as if these – and various other questioning or critical perspectives – were the optional condiments to the 'mainstream' social psychology meal. If you were lucky, you might get a taste of these, but, then again, you might not. I did not want these very diverse perspectives – which, in different ways, challenge how we go about social psychology – to be treated like embarrassing relatives, barred from attending some family event. If their presence makes for some discomfort, questioning some implicit consensus, rubbing up against other viewpoints, challenging and being challenged, then it may not be an attractive scene of serenity and order, but it is *vibrant, alive* and a place where genuine *engagement, argument* and *thought* are both possible and necessary.

To get a feel for some of the energy and debate within and around social psychology, it is important to read original papers and books and go beyond overly narrow disciplinary boundaries. Going to the original source gives a completely different and much more rewarding sense of engagement than does simply relying on second-hand accounts. Unless you feel that you have the special gift of being able to contact the world of deceased psychologists, you will probably never get a chance to chat with Sherif, Tajfel, Festinger, Ichheiser and Allport and many living social psychologists might refuse or ignore your invitation to a dinner party – but you *can* do the next best thing and read what they have to say in their own words. I have, in this text, tried to convey something of the detail of certain key studies, but you can take this much further.

Going beyond disciplinary boundaries involves reading the work of those who might not consider themselves to be psychologists. I fully understand if some of you need to sit down now and take some medication to recover from the shock of this assertion. I would urge you, though, to be investigative and curious – follow any leads you may have, even if that takes you into the seemingly unfamiliar territory of sociology, anthropology, linguistics or philosophy. In this text, I have drawn on the work of those who often do not appear in social psychology texts – Foucault, Butler, Sacks and Goodwin (among many others) – yet their work raises important and profound issues for the very 'core' topics of social psychology, such as self, relationships and communication. It is a shame to miss out on their insights just because they appear to be wearing the badge of a group we don't normally associate with.

This book, then, is ambitious as, rather than producing impressively long lists of people who have contributed to social psychology, it tries to get you started in engaging with original sources, critically evaluating them and drawing on different literatures to question, challenge or reframe implicit or explicit assumptions. On the one hand, this involves paying some careful attention to the detail of what original authors have argued in their empirical and theoretical papers. On the other, it involves drawing on different literatures, often marginalised or ignored within social psychology, to question or challenge what may be familiar ways of thinking. If this book succeeds, you might well wind up disagreeing with much of it, but it will, I hope, have offered you some encouragement to make social psychology your own, to read it and read around it, to think and argue with it and, perhaps above all, enjoy it! I do hope your time with social psychology *is* enjoyable, as well as engaging and fulfilling, and that this book adds to your experience.

Paul Dickerson
January 2012

Guided tour

Box 2.1 FOCUS
Classic research: An empirical investigation into self-attitudes (Kuhn & McPartland, 1954)

Kuhn and McPartland (1954, p. 68) drew on Mead's idea of 'the self as an object which is in most respects like all other objects' and his understanding that 'an object is a plan of action' to suggest that a framework for thinking about self consistent with Mead can be developed by thinking in terms of 'self-attitudes'. Kuhn and McPartland's (1954, p. 69) classic paper was concerned with developing a test of 'self-attitudes' and these are the instructions that they gave to their participants:

> There are twenty numbered blanks on the page below. Please write twenty answers to the simple question 'Who am I?' in the blanks. Just give twenty different answers to this question. Answer as if you were giving the answers to yourself, not to somebody else. Write the answers in the order that occur to you. Don't worry about logic or 'importance'. Go along fairly fast, for time is limited.

'sub-consensual' statements refer to 'groups, classes, attributes, traits or any other matters *which would require interpretation by the respondent to be precise or to place him relative to other people*'. Kuhn and McPartland suggest that 'student', 'girl', 'husband', 'Baptist', 'from Chicago', 'pre-med', 'daughter', 'oldest child' and 'studying engineering' are examples of consensual statements, while 'happy', 'bored', 'pretty good student', 'too heavy', 'good wife' and 'interesting' are sub-consensual.

Kuhn and McPartland found that, while there was substantial variation across participants, people tended to use more consensual, 'more directly socially anchored' statements, suggesting that this component of their self-definition was more salient. Kuhn and McPartland's work further suggested, where participants had group affiliations that were more 'differentiating' (applying

Focus boxes highlight classic and contemporary research studies so you can read about them in more detail.

Box 2.2 TRY IT OUT
Role relationships and identity

Take a moment to list about a dozen different roles and relationships that you are involved in – sister, daughter, partner, student, member of specific clubs or societies, employee, parent, best friend with X, close friend of Y and so on.

List these different roles and relationships in a column on a sheet of paper and, next to each, note some traits that describe how you experience yourself in these roles and relationships – pride, togetherness, caring, isolation, inhibition, confidence, for example.

What you have listed as traits are some of your sub-identities. Now, look through the traits and see if there are any that keep coming up or are particularly important to you (perhaps they arise in interactions with those who are currently most significant in your life). These recurrent and salient traits are your generalised attributes.

Now abstract from these generalised traits the few that are absolutely most important. Some of them may be almost impossible to detach from specific roles – such as 'loving parent', 'devoted partner'. In these cases, note both the role *and* trait.

What you now have is your core identity. This should be relatively stable, though it can change if, for example, there are certain significant changes in roles and the interactions they entail.

Have a look at what you have. Do these self-descriptions make sense to you? Do they feel like you? Do you think that the role relationships really do shape your sense of who you are? Do some of your salient traits create a

Try it out boxes suggest activities to help your understanding of key concepts.

external, unstable and specific causes and our failures to internal, stable and global causes.

Critical evaluation of self-serving bias

The self-serving bias, while largely supported by meta-analyses (Mezulis et al., 2004) may not adequately account for significant discrepancies – most notably (but not exclusively), those who are depressed show a reversal of the bias. Work on the ASQ and self-schema allows for the idea that people can have different types of self-bias, not all of which are 'self-serving'.

In addition to the issue of individual differences in attributional style, cross-cultural differences in the extent of the self-serving bias have been identified. Mezulis et al. (2004) note that the self-serving bias is far more prevalent among US samples (and, to a lesser extent, Western participants generally) than it is among Asian samples. This raises the issue that the self-serving bias may not only be a matter on which there is some individual difference but also on which there is cross-cultural variation. The idea that we attribute our successes to ourselves and our failures to others or situations may, then, reflect a specific cultural perspective rather than a universal feature of our attribution process.

Problems with the internal–external distinction that has been referred to throughout this chapter have a particular resonance with regard to the self-serving bias. According to the self-serving bias, we will attribute our successes to internal causes and our failures to external

attributions about self as an interactional phenomenon may enable a more subtle understanding of the ways in which actions such as exoneration or blame are accomplished within specific sequences of interaction.

Critical recap

Self-biases

1 There may be variations in the self-serving bias across individuals (for example, depressed people may exhibit a self-defeating bias) and cultures (for example, the bias may be much stronger in US rather than Asian samples).

2 The internal–external distinction may be too crude to identify the types of attribution that would be self-serving.

3 The self-serving bias provides a clear case where it seems sensible to focus on attribution talk and what that talk *does*, rather than inner mental activity.

Reflective questions

1 *Can you think of one person you know who exhibits the self-serving bias and one who shows a much more self-critical way of making attributions for their successes and failures?*

2 *Have you ever noticed people seemingly not take full credit for their successes in conversations? How do you make sense of this?*

Critical recaps help you to critically evaluate the literature, while **Reflective questions** encourage you to think beyond the text.

Box 2.6 KEY RESEARCHER
Professor Ken Gergen: constructions of self

How did you become interested in issues of social construction and the self?

Early in my career I believed that the proper aim of research was to illuminate or understand human social behaviour. This meant observing carefully, using accurate recording devices, deploying large numbers of subjects, employing statistical analysis and, ideally, using experimental methods. However, after years of reading, writing and reflecting, I have come to see this entire set of assumptions as deeply flawed. This is in spite of the fact that all these assumptions continue to be broadly shared within the field of social psychology.

To briefly summarise my orientation today, I have come to see that in carrying out research we don't 'find' out about social behaviour so much as we 'create' it. That is, we interpret the world of observation in the terms we alone? Why should people everywhere not have voice in defining, describing or explaining the nature of social life? Second, the concepts we use in describing and explaining are far reaching in their implications. For example, we now have a long history of calling certain people's actions prejudiced, aggressive, conforming, obedient, morally underdeveloped, cognitively deficient, and so on. These terms are scarcely neutral. They are terms of moral judgement and political in consequence. In effect, in spite of claims to scientific neutrality, when people are exposed to the 'knowledge' that science generates, they are subtly informed about the nature of the good. Methods of research also carry moral and political implications. Methods that involve observing others from a distance, carry far different political implication than those holding that knowledge emerges from active dialogue with others.

Key researchers within social psychology give their perspectives, allowing you an insight into their work.

Box 1.6 IN THE NEWS
How can we explain aggressive behaviour?

The news story illustrated here concerns three people who were killed in Melbourne in what reports suggested was a gang-related attack. How can social psychology make sense of incidents such as this? Should we think in terms of what makes people aggressive or the things that encourage or trigger aggressive behaviour? Should we think about the attack as being related to the influence of being in a gang or perhaps the perpetrators' identity as gang members? As well as considering what might cause the event itself we could also ask, how do people make sense of incidents such as these – how do we work out the causes of such violent behaviour? Is our thinking shaped by stereotypes that we might hold about gangs or a 'crime family boss'?

Three people were shot dead on a bloody day in Melbourne amid fears that the execution of a crime family boss had sparked a new gangland war

Source: © Newspix/Tim Carrafa

Each of these questions that we can readily ask about real-world events relates to key topics in social psychology – aggression, group behaviour, attribution (how we think about causes) and stereotypes. As mentioned above, this should not be viewed as a one-way street, in which social psychology provides its definitive, unilateral 'answers'.

In the news boxes feature relevant events that have been in the news, so that you can evaluate the relevance of social psychology for 'real world' contexts.

Review questions

1 *How do you think that people can decide between ego theory and bundle theory? Is such a choice necessary or important for social psychologists?*
2 *From a symbolic interactionist perspective, how might acquiring a new role result in some change in identity?*
3 *What is meant by the 'dynamic self-concept'?*
4 *What does the literature suggest are the consequences of a discrepancy between my perceived actual self and my ideal self?*
5 *Why might we reflect on who we are?*
6 *How might consumer behaviour relate to issues of self-regulation and identity?*
7 *What empirical evidence is there to suggest that people act in terms of their social identity?*
8 *What are the problems with an individualised conception of self? What are the alternatives?*
9 *What do discursive psychologists make of people's contradictory talk about themselves?*
10 *Why might people use category descriptions in talk about self and others?*
11 *How might ideas about self-formation and/or subject positions be relevant to the social psychology of self and identity?*

Review questions at the end of each chapter help you to think back over what you've read and check your understanding.

Recommended reading

Anderson, C. A., & Bushman, B. J. (2002). Human aggression. *Annual Review of Psychology, 53*, 27–51. An important outline of the general aggression model.

Berkowitz, L. (1990). On the formation and regulation of anger and aggression: A cognitive-neoassociationistic analysis. *American Psychologist, 45*(4), 494–503. Len Berkowitz's outline of his developing perspective on aggression.

Billig, M. (1995). *Banal Nationalism*. London: Sage. Billig's social constructionist critique of much of our understanding of groups and national identity.

Brown, R. J. (2000a). *Group processes* (2nd ed.). Oxford: Blackwell. Rupert Brown's clear and authoritative overview of inter- and intragroup research, with a particular focus on social identity and self-categorisation theory.

Livingstone, A. G., & Haslam, S. A. (2008). The importance of social identity content in a setting of chronic social conflict: Understanding intergroup relations in Northern Ireland. *British Journal of Social Psychology, 47*, 1–21. A social identity study within the context of a situation of chronic real-world conflict.

Useful weblinks

http://homepage.psy.utexas.edu/homepage/Group/BussLAB/publications.htm David Buss' website with resources and publications relating to evolutionary psychology.

http://psychclassics.yorku.ca/FrustAgg/ A classic paper based on a symposium on the frustration–aggression hypothesis.

www.psychology.iastate.edu/faculty/caa/recpub.html Craig Anderson' publications. This site features many downloadable papers relating to the general aggression model.

www.zimbardo.com/zimbardo.html Philip Zimbardo's website – includes links to publications addressing aggression and deindividuation.

http://portal.st-andrews.ac.uk/research-expertise/researcher/sdr/publications A great resource for publications (many downloadable) by Steve Reicher.

www.sussex.ac.uk/psychology/people/peoplelists/person/92858/ A great resource for publications by John Drury, with a particular emphasis on crowd psychology.

www.sussex.ac.uk/migration/profile95042.html Recent

Recommended reading and **Useful weblinks** give you guidance so you can explore the topics further.

Guided tour of the companion website

Social Psychology is accompanied by an interactive website, where you can learn more about the topics, test your knowledge and find links to other interesting sites.

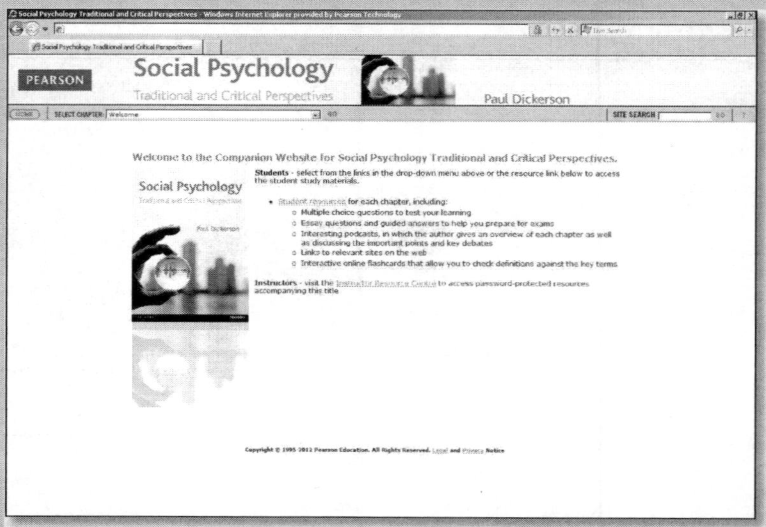

Listen to the author talk about issues and debates in social psychology in the **podcasts** for each chapter.

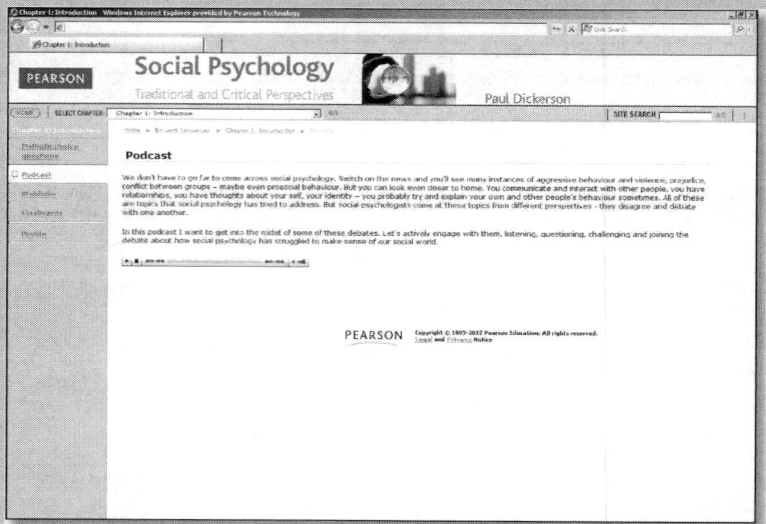

Explore the **weblinks** to other useful and interesting sites on social psychology and topics related to the chapters.

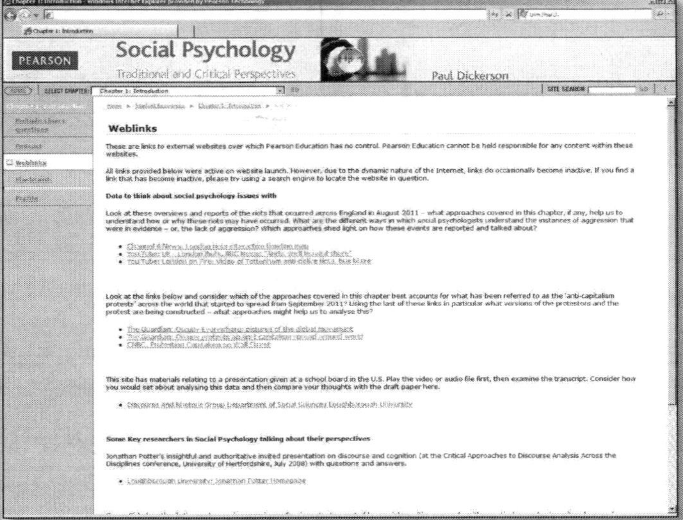

Test yourself and prepare for exams with each chapter's **essay questions** and **multiple choice questions**.

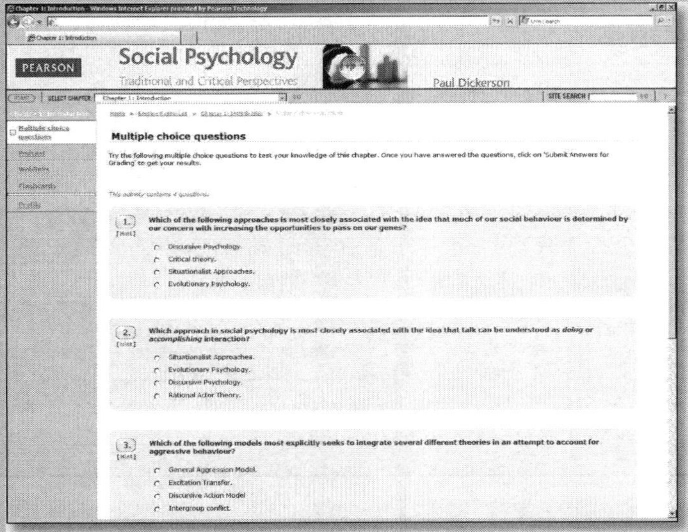

Revise with the **interactive flashcards** and test yourself on key definitions.

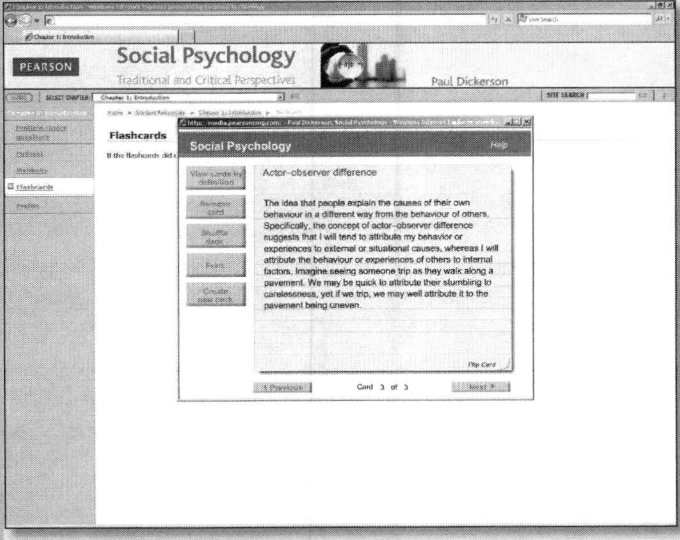

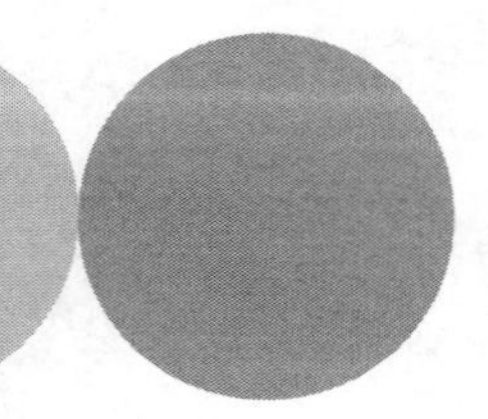

Author's acknowledgements

'I don't really like psychology textbooks', I rashly blurted out on the phone.

This text started with me having a moan. I was maligning psychology textbooks for not covering some of the literature that I thought they should and for not demonstrating the sort of critical evaluation psychology lecturers always assert is one of the hallmarks of good, well-written essays. My criticism was perhaps a little unfair, but from these sentiments this text was born. Sentiments can remain just that, though, and might never amount to anything. These acknowledgements are a brief tribute to some of those who enabled something to emerge from these unlikely beginnings.

If you look at the spine of the book you might think that there is one name, but look again – as well as Dickerson you will see the name Pearson. This does not simply indicate a company founded by Samuel Pearson in 1844 – it tells you that there is a team of people without whom this book would remain some loose, half-baked idea in the author's head. These people – of whom I will single out just a handful of individuals – enabled the metamorphoses that resulted in the book in front of you.

I am indebted to the recipient of my moaning about textbooks, Pearson's academic sales manager Gale Capper, who, rather than seeking to exit the conversation with 'Mr Grumpy' passed on my details to senior acquisitions editor Janey Webb. Janey was initially assisted by Catherine Morrissey and subsequently Jane Lawes and I am grateful to both Catherine and Jane for their invaluable mixture of humour, encouragement and diligence and very recently Neha Sharma (editor) for bringing warmth & enthusiasm to this project. To be a brilliant senior acquisitions editor takes an unlikely combination of skills, such as being able to encourage blue sky thinking while ensuring that the technical and practical aspects of producing the text are not lost, enabling free-flowing creativity without compromising the requirements of structure and format and, above all, being able to listen with depth and sensitivity and offer advice that is wise and insightful. I am enormously grateful to Janey Webb for having all of these qualities in abundance and – based on an exchange of over 300 e-mails, numerous phone calls and several meetings – I have come to the conclusion that she is always right.

If one metamorphosis was to turn half-formed ideas into a credible text, a second was to turn the text into an attractively presented book. I am grateful to Kevin Brown for his resourcefulness in making my greedy wish-list of images a reality. I owe thanks and considerable sympathy to copy-editor, Michelle Clark, and proofreader, Julie Jackson, who may well be the people who have read this text more times and more carefully than anyone else on the planet. What extraordinary tenacity, attention to detail and patience! I would also like to acknowledge the ongoing work of Jodie Marshall and Hayley McCarthy who have brought insight and inspiration to the development of the companion website, and Oli Adams and Maddy Kershaw for the vision and creativity with which they are approaching the marketing of this text. I am once again filled with a sense of good fortune and gratitude that, driving the whole myriad processes involved in producing this book, managing editor Joe Vella was so adept at making things happen, brilliantly attending to not just the big picture but also every single detail within it and in keeping everyone, including myself, on track.

Writing a book like this does not occur in a vacuum, but, in various ways, intersects with other aspects of life. During the writing of this text I have worked at Roehampton University – a place where I began lecturing nearly two decades ago. I am enormously grateful to all my friends at Roehampton, fellow staff and students who, together, have provided the necessary mixture of interest, encouragement and, perhaps above all, tolerance that have made this task possible. I am also grateful to the wider academic community and would like to acknowledge the very genuine improvements that each of the reviewers below initiated.

Dr Christopher Cocking, London Metropolitan University
Professor Susan Condor, Lancaster University
Dr Pippa Dell, University of East London
Dr Roberto Gutierrez, Anglia Ruskin University
Dr Nicholas Hopkins, University of Dundee
Ms Lisa Lazard, University of Northampton
Professor Alan Lewis, University of Bath
Dr Kesi Mahendran, The Open University
Dr Chris McVittie, Queen Margaret University
Professor Jonathan Potter, Loughborough University
Dr Stephanie Taylor, The Open University
Dr Val Tuck, Newcastle University
Dr Caroline Wesson, University of Wolverhampton
Dr Sue Widdicombe, University of Edinburgh

I would also like to thank each of the contributors to the Key researcher features in the book – Mick Billig, Ken Gergen, Liz Stokoe, Martha Augoustinos, Charles Antaki, Jane Piliavin, Rupert Brown and Chuck Goodwin. Their work has been an inspiration for me and their contributions add enormously to this text. I would additionally like to single out Geoffrey Stephenson, Jonathan Potter, Derek Edwards, John Rae and the late Gail Jefferson, who, in markedly different ways, have shaped my stance with regard to social psychology.

Last and foremost, I turn to those most difficult to acknowledge because, despite writing 300,000 words of this text, words fail me. I would like to thank my sisters, Ann, Jane and Beth and my mother for their steadfast loving interest and support and my wife and children for the important part they played in writing this book. When this book began, my daughter – Miriam Sita Dickerson – was born and my son – Joshua Krishna Dickerson – was three years old. I worked on the text mainly between midnight and 4 a.m. in the weekdays and in the daytime for at least some of most weekends. This meant that Joshua, Miriam and my darling Suba would cope not only with my absence at weekends but also with the side-effects of my sleep deprivation during the week! I am deeply grateful to Joshua and Miriam for the various ways in which they have helped with the writing of this book. Finally, I cannot adequately thank Suba for her constant loving support and encouragement – from prompting me to write the book in the first place to continually enabling and sustaining me throughout the task itself. I would like to end by stealing the words of Sebastian in Shakespeare's *Twelfth Night*: 'I can no other answer make but thanks, and thanks.'

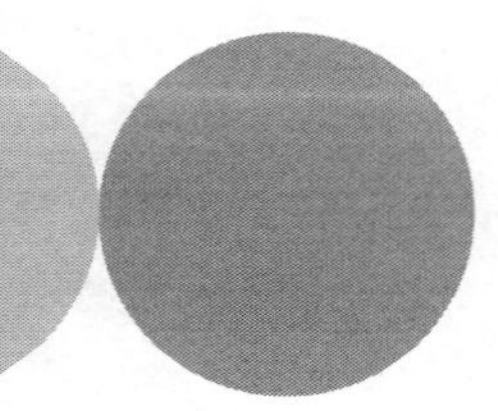

Publisher's acknowledgements

We are grateful to the following for permission to reproduce copyright material:

Figures
Figure 2.4: After 'Self-discrepancy: A theory relating self and affect', *Psychological Review*, 94, 319–340 (Higgins, E. T., 1987); Figure 2.6: After 'When a better self is only a button click away: associations between materialistic values, emotional and identity – related buying motives and compulsive buying tendency online', *Journal of Social and Clinical Psychology*, 26(3): 334–61 (Dittmar, H., Long, K. & Bond, R., 2007); Figure 3.6: After 'Equity and sexual satisfaction in dating couples', *British Journal of Social Psychology*, 22: 33–40 (Traupmann, J., Hatfield, E., & Wexler, P., 1983); Figure 6.3: Adapted from 'The theory of planned behaviour', *Organizational Behavior and Human Decision Processes*, 50: 179–211 (Ajzen, I., 1991). Copyright © Elsevier 1991; Figure 9.3: From 'Human aggression', *Annual Review of Psychology*, 53: 27–51 (Andersen, C. A. & Bushman B. J., 2002).

Photographs
The publisher would like to thank the following for their kind permission to reproduce their photographs:

Page 3: Reuters / Amr Abdallah Dalsh; 18: Newspix / Tim Carrafa; 31: Press Association Images / AP Photo / Joe Skipper; 39: Getty Images / Mark Thompson; 75: Getty Images / Dominic Lipinski / AFP; 84: Rex Features / Patsy Lynch; 111: Rex Features / Lehtikuva OY; 128: Press Association Images / Fredrik von Erichsen / DPA; 133: Rex Features; 151: Getty Images / Stefan Postles; 174: Getty Images / Mike Flokis; 182: Getty Images / Georges Gobet / AFP; 187: Press Association Images / AP Photo / Khalid Mahmoud; 205: Alamy Images / Blend Images; 213: Media Wales Ltd; 225: Press Association Images / Polfoto; 236: Press Association Images / Andrew Milligan / PA Archive; 249: Corbis / Bettmann; 265: Photoshot Holdings Limited; 302: Press Association Images / Martin Rickett / PA Wire; 309: Getty Images / William West / AFP; 314: Getty Images / An Fu / ChinaFotoPress; 325: Reuters / WikiLeaks / Handout; 346: Wesleyan University Press from *The Robbers Cave Experiment* by Muzafer Sherif, et al. (Wesleyan Univeristy Press, 1988). Copyright © 1988 by Muzafer Sherif and reprinted by permission of Wesleyan University Press; 353: Guardian News and Media Ltd; 373: Reuters / Darrin Zammit Lupi; 375: Press Association Images / AP Photo; 391: Photolibrary.com; 398: Paul Ekman Group, LLC / Paul Ekman, PhD; 407: Rex Features / Chris Lobina;

Cover image: Getty Images

Every effort has been made to trace the copyright holders and we apologise in advance for any unintentional omissions. We would be pleased to insert the appropriate acknowledgement in any subsequent edition of this publication.

Socially Constructing Dichotomy: A Materialist Exploration of Modern Meta-Categorizational Systems among Colonial Cultures.

Rory Coughlan, Ph.D.

Associate Professor of Social Psychology, Trent University

There has not been a universal assumption in philosophy that categories should necessarily be discretely dualistic. In fact, although much rarer nowadays owing to western colonialism, many cultures devised distinctly non-dualistic and non-dichotomous systems of categories. Of the few still existing today, some North American indigenous, Buddhist and Vedic configurations exemplify a more holistic interpretation of embodied existence. From the earliest fore-bearers of the western tradition, dualistic categorizational systems have underpinned socially constructed political, economic and cultural arrangements. However, it will be argued here that it is the realm of material and social practices that shape meta-categorizational and philosophical systems and these systems are reinforced because of their continuing relation to the predominating form of material practices (Marx 1846/1963; Volosinov, 1973). How each culture arranges its political and economic practices in relation to what the natural and cultural world affords them to survive, becomes the starting point for the shaping of ideas, narratives, myths and religions that that culture will devise to explain themselves to each other. In other words, the practices that each culture engages in to ensure survival will be the springboard for ways of thinking about the relation between that culture and the world at large.

Ancient classical conceptions

In the western tradition stemming from the classical Greek period forward, the predominant cultural project has been the acquisition of natural resources and the subjugation of “other” peoples by means of firstly military and later by ideological domination. Philosophical considerations and the meta-categorizational systems that are utilized in guiding societies are linked to the overall material practices of the culture and are reinforced through the use of the linguistic tools of communicative interaction (Duranti, 1997; Volosinov, 1973). The material, economic, ideological, and communicative practices appear to be seamless, and while they are interpenetrated, material and economic forces set the foundation as cultures attempt to describe who they are and what they believe in. Every culture starts from a point of rationalizing what they must do to remain a viable people and to create a certain amount of solidarity in informing individual members of the culture about who they are and why they are involved in their particular socio-economic practices. In other words, activity in creating a system that provides sustenance to a people will be formative in the narratives, stories, myths, religions and meta-categorizational systems that every culture creates (Marx & Engels, 1846/1963). Societies that are predominantly “warrior” in terms of their socio-economic activity tend to find dichotomization a natural description of their reality and useful in their continuing societal project concerning the otherization, victimization and/or domination of “others” and/or the natural world. Today we know this as imperial or colonial practices.

In the various early pre-classical Greek divinities there was a sense of a non-chaotic universe that was holistic. Mythical figures represented an undivided natural-supernatural continuum where the natural world, the world of humans and the world of the Gods were often practically indistinguishable. This mythic/natural holism was gradually eroded by late Homeric conceptions and the classical Greek tragedian tradition in which the human character and human actions were seen to largely determine the fate of humanity (Tarnas, 1991). As Greek society evolved and became more concerned with a project of colonial domination and exploitation, there was a move to the gradual separation and dichotomization of philosophical categories (Spetnak, 1984).

In certain earlier Greek renditions of this dualistic separation, the ordering principle was mythical or supernatural, while in others the ordering principle was considered to be material and governed by chance or blind necessity (Finley, 1966). Parmenides, theorizing that ordering principles were superior and changeless, concluded that "true" reality is separate from expression in human affairs. This formulation set the conditions for the separation of being/becoming; appearance/essence; rational/irrational and truth/perception that became the grist for later philosophizing about the nature of embodied natural existence. Anaxagoras also greatly contributed to a fundamental dualism when he postulated the separation of "nous" (or mind) from the rest of the natural order and posited this "quality" as superior and as giving form and motion to the universe (Tarnas, 1991). In much the same fashion, what I am referring to as “agency” in human affairs has been contested and categorically reassigned throughout European intellectual history. It has been a concept that has been elusive because it has been expressed through different concepts such as “will”, “hubrus” and “grace”, for example. However, the general trend has been to dichotomize the universe. Important concepts such as those concerned with a self/environment continuum have suffered from this gradual process of abstraction, making concrete contextualized explanation of humans and their activities and intentions, extremely problematic. We have taken the dualistic meta-categorizational system as a natural, all-pervading - the way the world “just is” - rather than consider that ideas and arrangements of relations between categories are socially constructed and based upon the socio-economic practices of cultures during a particular stage of development.

The Pythagorean table of opposites created out of a philosophy that was a blend of the mystical and rational-mathematical continued the direction of oppositional explanation and expanded the gulf between the natural and the mythical. The Sophist tradition assumed the explanatory high ground temporarily, positing that as all explanations are divergent and therefore (as Protagorus expounded) "man becomes the measure of all things." In this turn we have an early contemplation of the subjective/objective divide that forms a major pillar of modern western dualism that has endured, continuing to ensnare scientific and particularly, psychological scholarship to this day (Tolman, 1994).

Opposed to the subjective relativism of sophistry, the critical occupation of humanity according to Socrates is the discovery of knowledge through virtue. Although one must accept that he may well be the unwilling accomplice in Plato's rationalization of his own philosophical system, Socrates is reported to venture that to know virtue one must discover the "essence" that is the determining principle and which animates examples of virtue that we see in everyday experience (Church, 1956). The separation of pure essence from everyday examples was further reinforced by Plato's separation of transcendent "forms" (to which the soul is closely related) from mundane experience in which the soul is embodied (Finley, 1966).

The dualism of Plato was exaggerated by the political as well as intellectual crises of his day that furthered the separation and dichotomized categories of the "philosopher" versus the "common man"; the mind and soul as opposed to matter and ideal “forms” versus the phenomenal world. Although fundamentally considered "rationalist" in character, the foundation of Plato’s rationalism was universal and divine and it was also similar to modern conceptions in that rationality was discussed in terms that defined this concept in opposition to "irrationality" or "necessity". The irrational was associated with nature, instinctual desire, the body and matter, whereas the rational was associated with mind, the transcendent and spirituality (Keller, 1985). The dichotomization of the soul/mind from necessity/nature was furthered by the predominantly political idea that freedom is expressed only by the "guardian classes" of society in their bid to overcome the slavery of their biological embodiment (Arendt, 1958). In addition to the bifurcations discussed above, classical Greek systems internalized the dichotomous categories of male/female, high/low social castes, abstraction/contextualization and an early contemplation of individual/society, all of which have been formative in the evolution of western categorizational mechanisms . Aristotle further contributed to the dichotomous world view as he reassigned Plato's "soft" dualism of gender in his system by widening and hardening the distinction (Eisler, 1987).

Medieval variations of dualism

Roman stoicism developed out of Plato's idealistic dualism, and this in turn exerted a strong influence over formative Christian theology (Synnott, 1993). Seneca followed in this dualistic tradition, although his opposition between body and soul was not as emphatic as Epictetus' outright condemnation of the body and worldly nature as inimical to spirituality. Marcus Aurelius spoke of the divide between the higher and lower aspects of humanity, viewing death as a "release from impressions of sense . . . and from service to the flesh." The Christian configuration of dualistic categories was (and continues to be) decidedly Platonic but somewhat variable in terms of the relative strength of the opposition with regard to particular dualistic categories. For instance, the Christian view of the body (as opposed to spirit) has been historically somewhat ambivalent, depending on the view of particular theorists (Tarnas, 1991). Saint Paul gives a different rendition of the place of the body depending on whether it is considered physical or spiritual (as in the case of the redeemed body in the afterlife). The

Pauline view of the physical body, in connection with biology is not quite as negative as in Plato's characterization. Certain sections of the New Testament describe holy miracles that intercede in human affairs and particularly in aid of physical needs, a tradition that today finds expression in liberation theology. Origen, however was an extreme fundamentalist and considered the body (and especially sensuality) to be an enemy of the soul. He was so convinced of the perception of the danger from sensuality to his spiritual existence that he castrated himself in an effort to save his soul from eternal damnation (Chadwick, 1966). John Chrysostom (circa 400) was also adamant concerning the enmity between the body ("a whited sepulcher") and soul, but later moderated this position saying that the body could be useful but only in relation to a remembrance of "Him who framed it." Augustine, who probably had the greatest effect on Christian doctrine was more in the mellow of Chrysostom's latter view of the body, referring to it as "a revelation of the goodness of God" but still considered it to be a separate and inferior category in relation to the spirit. In general, the mythical aspects of Greek life that fostered pluralistic and indeterminate characteristics of mythical figures became transformed to Christian oppositional archetypes that were fixed and deeply antagonistic to each other.

Later, Thomas Aquinas rejected aspects of both Platonic dualism and Aristotelian materialism and developed a theology of body/soul unity and bodily resurrection. At the same time, however, he magnified the male/female divide and probably greatly institutionalized the misogynous dichotomy of woman, nature and evil as opposed to man, spirituality and reason (Ranke-Heinemann,

1990). Undoubtedly the institutionalization of gender and body/soul oppositions led in part to, among other cruel and oppressive practices, the horrors experienced throughout the Inquisition.

The dualistic vision of early Christian belief as derived from Plato; Aristotle; Judaism; Pauline theology; Gnostic dualism, Zoroastrianism and Neoplatonism reinforced each other in Christianity after Augustine. Dominant elements of Judaism that found expression in Christianity included the experience that evil pervaded man and nature and that both were deeply alienated from the divine. Particularly Judaic elements finding a renewed expression in Christian theology, included the strict adherence to law, the attempt to separate and preserve the faithful minority from the contamination of "others" and the expectation of apocalyptic punishment (Tarnas, 1991). All of these ordering mechanisms were deeply dualistic and reinforced the Christian dichotomous categorizational constellation.

<u>Modern scientific dualism</u>

Whereas in early Christian formulations reason was very much tied to the mundane phenomenal world, being considered inferior to the realm of the divine, it was eventually to replace God as the superior category and final appeal in the modern world-view. The dawn of the modern era led to changes in some dichotomous hierarchical polar opposites, including a new emphasis on some previously relatively weak oppositions (e.g. individual/society) but many of the old oppositions remained. The changes were related to the emergence of a new social class in the continuing project of domination and the new social practices that advanced the power of this pre-industrial mercantile class including further attempts at colonial empire-building.

These changes to the hierarchical dichotomous system that emerged in the modern era facilitated the growth of new political and economic forms based on monetary capital that challenged the ancient philosophical systems. One of the fruits of these massive changes from feudalist authoritarianism to the beginnings of industrial capitalism was the radical conception of "the individual". This newly minted modern individual was now partly freed (should he be a member of elite society) from some of the stifling encumbrances of medieval relations. Later into the industrial age ordinary peasants also needed "freeing" thereby facilitating their mobilization in the new economic reality. The practical requirements of a mobile labour force in early industrialization led to the gradual demise of the centuries-old agrarian collective identity and this change in economic practices led to the modern conception of a more individualized sense of identity.

In connection with a gradual change from a feudal collective sense of identity to more modern individualist conceptions, the advent of Protestantism was important. Protestant Christianity represented a re-evaluation of the relationship between the divine and each individual human soul that disempowered the Roman church and its functionaries as necessary via mediums for human redemption. The Protestant focus on individual relations between man and God gradually led to a belief that it was incumbent upon the individualized believer to demonstrate their God-fearing nature through various forms of application, including work. However, the majority of the fruits of such work, if consumed in a decadent fashion, could be viewed as spoiled with the possible risk of censure owing to an incursion into sinful activity. Thus, Protestant individuals demonstrated their worthiness by amassing wealth and power and attempted to extend the reach of Christianity in much the same way as their Catholic brethren, by the domination of non-Christian 'others". As the industrialization of western economies became dominant, both personal and socio-economic relations assumed an individual ontology based on the metaphor of market relations. By the mid-20th century such instrumental relations based on the logic of the marketplace became internalized to an extent that this radical reformulation of individual identity had become almost invisible.

> However, once these new "radical" forms are in place, and people are brought up in them, then this individualism is greatly strengthened, because it is rooted in their everyday practice, . . . it comes to seem the only conceivable outlook, which it certainly wasn't for their ancestors who pioneered it.
>
> (Taylor, 1991, p. 58).

Industrial capitalism, Protestantism, and the growing superiority of logical methods reinforced each other in forms of discourse and action to transform the old dualistic systems into a slightly amended version that suited the new secular pre-industrial and industrial economic and political projects. Science became the legitimating organ in the social actions and social relations of the modern era, including the individualist narrative of social relations constructed to reflect the necessity of the appropriation of individual labour.

> . . . an assertion of knowledge always legitimates certain kinds of actions and certain kinds of institutions. If something is known, in the sense of known to be true, then we are supposed to act on the basis of it, and if we do not then we are being foolish, irrational and disruptive. Thus an assertion of knowledge is always an assertion about proper social actions and social relations.
>
> (Wright, 1992, p. 6)

Galileo had earlier declared that the use of mathematical reason would unravel the mysteries of an atomistic nature and lay the foundation for the science of mechanical physics and the essential principles of scientific methods. He entrenched the concept of primary and secondary qualities as a major dualistic divide and argued that judgment concerning nature should be made considering only the quantifiable "objective" qualities (such as size, shape, weight, motion and number) and that secondary qualities (being subjective) should be given far less credence. Descartes contributed to the separation of these qualities, in a form that inverted Galileo's formulation. Through a combination of skepticism and mathematics, he proclaimed the essential hierarchical division of the world to be the primary indivisible rational thinking consciousness (*res cogitans*) and the material, secondary and divisible object of consciousness (*res extensa*). Thus, although the main thrust of this separation was considered to be a division of soul (later understood by others as mind) from all material substance including the body, the more lasting and formidable separation (especially for psychology) was between the subject of experience and the objective world. This would divide sensation from perception and would be consolidated by the philosophers following in the empirical tradition such as Locke, Hume, and Berkeley as practically indisputable.

From here there arose a division of the new "rational" methods. One that followed in the empiricist tradition of Bacon, Hobbes, Locke and Mill that devoted attention and gave predominance to the objective world, and a rationalist tradition stemming from Descartes, that gave primacy to the ordering principle of rational ideas. It is paradoxical that the empiricist tradition that flourished in Britain (and was a reaction to the Cartesian position of the primacy of the internal ordering principles) only solidified the subjective/objective divide by emphasizing the primacy of the opposing pole of this division. Therefore, empiricism rather than countermanding the rationalist position, empiricism actually consolidated Cartesian dualistic principals. The combination of both schools reinforced the modern notion that the individual should be considered the site of rational knowing and the foundational unit of future scientific rumination and analysis.

> Mind-body dualism certainly was not new, but now linked to a subjectivized philosophy it attained levels of abstruseness not previously encountered. A second important result, obviously linked to the first, was a fundamental <u>individualism</u> which made

> the individual mind, not the collective mind or universal logos, the foundation of all certainty. A third important result, owing more to the context of the new science in which the philosophy was developed than to the philosophy itself, was a pervasive mechanicism.
>
> (Tolman, 1994, pp. 5-6)

> The fruit of the dualism between rational subject and material world was science, including science's capacity for rendering certain knowledge of that world and for making man master and possessor of nature. In Descartes vision, science, progress, reason, epistemological certainty and human identity were all inextricably connected with each other and with a conception of an objective, mechanistic universe. Upon this synthesis was founded the paradigmatic understanding of the modern mind.
>
> (Saul, 1992, p.84)

The Christian dichotomies of spirit/matter and God/natural world were transformed into mind/matter, subject/object, man/nature, individual/social and the rational-scientific methods versus the irrational, intuitive and emotional. While Cartesian rationalism suggested and affirmed the conception of man as opposed to and dominant vis-a-vis nature, modern empiricism solidified the divide. The development of the modern version of dualism by Descartes was to have a lasting effect on the development of scientific systems and would prove to be extremely problematic for the development of psychology. His system is often discussed in terms of the legacy of mind/body dualism but the most problematic divisions were the separation of subject and object. This is a restatement of the classical Greek dichotomy of essence and appearance encoded as the separation of sensation and perception in psychology by the mainstream representationalist theories of perception where human perception of their environment is tragically separated from the "true" objective world. Truth then is constituted as only coming into being if separated from embodied human perception. In this way Descartes contributions reinforced distinctly Platonic formulations of essentialism – the idea that "purity" or "truth" can only exist independent of human material life. Thus instead of humans seeing themselves "in" their environment and intricately related and involved in it, humans are conceived as not only individuals but individuals outside of the environment – outside of and facing the environment as a problem to be solved. The otherization of all environments as separate and opposite of subjective individually competitive persons allows the domination and destruction of the environment. Thus we have a philosophical narrative that gives "freedom" to industrialists to destroy the environment that human beings actually rely on to sustain all life on the planet.

Scientific knowledge has always contained and legitimated hidden and specific cultural values and commitments (Danziger, 1990; Putnam, 1981; Rorty, 1979; Tolman, 1994). These values, meaning-constellations and commitments are rooted in the concrete societal projects and are encoded through social relations in the discourses of cultural systems (Volosinov, 1973). Meanings are locally contested within discursive fields, with the power to control a particular field residing in claims to a specific reading of rational scientific knowledge, embodied in the social relations and writings of disciplinary and professional institutions (Dant, 1991; Scott, 1990; Shapiro, 1988). The regularities of hegemonic or powerful discourses are rooted in social practice and because versions of knowledge cannot operate reflectively on the context within which they emerge, it is unlikely that they can remain unaffected by the power relations that permeate the political and historical processes of the social project of which it claims to analyze (Dant, 1991; Foucault, 1984; Weedon, 1987).

> It attempted simply to break the captive logic of arbitrary power and superstition with reason and scepticism. Now, that same self-justifying has asserted itself within the new system. It took us four and a half centuries to break the power of divine revelation only to replace it with the divine revelations of reason . . . yet to argue against reason means arguing as an idiot. The structures of argument have been co-opted so completely by those who work the system that when an individual reaches for the words and phrases . . . he finds they are in active use in the service of power.
>
> (Saul 1992, p. 36)

The evolution of western culture up to and including the establishment of the modern scientific world view provided the essential features of the dichotomous constellations that have molded experience and expressed themselves in conceptions of aspects of embodied existence. The addition of the individual/social and the reordering of the rational/irrational bifurcated categories interacted with the older, but continuously utilized bifurcations of mind/body; male/female; essence/appearance; culture/nature and class divisions to constitute a constellation of assumptions and research strategies in scientific investigation. The old is replicated in the new system because the cultural/societal projects of colonialism, imperialism continue unabated in modern industrial society and the constellation of ideas that underpinned the older systems of "warrior" societies are still useful today.

Although it may well be true to look at the rising predominance of science as a revolution in epistemology, culture and eventually economic systems, *at the meta-theoretical level it was merely a further evolution and continuance of a system of dualistic categorization linked to the dominant social project of dominating other cultures and/or nature*. The predominant cultural project of the domination of nature and "otherized" cultural systems remained the same but the future continuance of this project would now hinge on the utilization of scientific methods as the means to achieve these goals. At the meta-categorizational level, little would change except of course the foundation of this epistemological rationalization (Coughlan, 1995).

Mainstream psychology and the sub-discipline of social-psychology, being integral to the modern industrial project, inherited the assumptions of the natural science paradigm and conflated this particular model of scientific investigation with science "per se". As a result, mainstream social-psychological research has assumed the meta-categorizational system of dualism in its more modern Cartesian version, as well as a specific form of this organizational principle by abstracting the individual from the naturally occurring concrete relations of culture and social interaction. These assumptions have hampered the creation of a meaningful system of social-psychological scholarship that is adequate to explain the realities of everyday experience. Further, mainstream social-psychological formulations were (and continue to be) contextualized by extra-scientific, economic necessities of procuring funding and garnering status for practitioners. The usual funders/purchasers of scientific research are more interested in practical applications in social engineering. Thus a great deal of social-psychological research was far more interested in the prediction and control of both outcomes and individuals. Consequently, the production of psychological knowledge actually tends to hamper the emancipation of ordinary people from modern systems that are often perceived as antithetical to personal needs, goals and desires. Most modern social-psychological research has tended to follow in the footsteps of the parent discipline by assuming theoretical orientations that are ill equipped to explain personal agency or intentionality and instead often become complicit in the development of technologies that actively seek to limit experiences of personal agency. The problems of the internalization of these principles into mainstream North American social psychological research will be discussed in greater detail in the following chapter.

The Cartesian Blind Alley: Problematic Psychological Narratives of Perception, Communication and Intentionality

Rory Coughlan, Ph.D.

Associate Professor of Social Psychology, Trent University

This chapter will continue the discussion of dualism as a meta-categorizational system in western thought and deepen the understanding of this influence on the development of modern social-scientific systems by focusing on a critique of a major foundation of modern psychology: mainstream theories of perception. Dualism as expressed in mainstream perceptual theories has far reaching effects on scientific notions of self and agency in psychology and by extension, social-psychology.

Dichotomization is a major meta-categorizational foundation of many scientific and extra-scientific cultural products in western industrialized nations. The breadth of general acceptance is owing in part to the mainstream perceptual theory which is built upon: dualistic pre-cursors to modern scientific systems. Modern scientifically supported versions of dualism stemming from Descartes and as expressed in mainstream representationalist perceptual theory are major determinants of the vacuum of coherent theoretical explanation in the areas of "self" and "agency". The overall meta-categorizational system of western dualism, along with the modern expression of this in the foundations of psychology cannot be seen as disconnected from inadequacies in the development of modern socio-cultural systems and the consequences that appear as problems in the expression of personal agency in industrial economies.

The modern context

The beginning of a new millennium has brought a similar sense of pessimism and powerless similar to that felt at the turn of the last century. In industrial western nations as well as the third world many people have grave doubts concerning the ability to enact changes to personal circumstances. External social, political and cultural occurrences seem to constrain rather than galvanize a sense of competence. In the global village, power is wielded from ever more remote distances and consequently is increasingly perceived as debilitating to many people's sense of personal agency. While the majority are unable to identify the source of an increasing physical/spiritual/moral anomie, many critical social and political commentators (for example, Saul, 1995; 1999; Townsend, 1999; Foucault, 1984, Harvey, 1990) trace this feeling of uncertainty and experience of dwindling horizons for personal action to the simultaneous demise of the democratic nation state and the dawn of a "coporatist new world order". This substantial evolution of late capitalist culture is a development John Ralston Saul has referred to as the dawning of an era of the "New Medievalists" (Saul, 1995). His point here is that we are entering a period where personal agency is being steadily eroded by the privatization and commodification of public services and indeed actual human existence itself. This undermines the general public interest in many cases and is linked to an increasing sense that the public sphere is no longer able to address the interests of the ordinary person. This is supported at a philosophical level by various “postmodern” viewpoints that tend to be little more than a rationalization for a restatement of autocratic governance common to pre-democratic medieval culture.

In Saul’s view, global “corporatism” represents a substantial threat to personal agency worldwide. Residents of the industrialized world are forced to increasingly scramble to reorganize their lives to rapidly changing economic and political conditions and are further hampered by the dissolution of the mediating influences of social welfare policies to support a generalized entitlement and security (Saul, 1995; Harvey, 1990). People are finding that they are working longer hours than was current 20 years ago with fewer or no benefits. More energy is expended on basic survival chores leaving little time for community, or reflection on national or global problems. Desperately poor communities especially in the third world are further rent asunder by internecine warfare. Even in the relatively stable industrial world, communities have fractured and devolved into collections of fearful and instrumentally related, competitive individuals (Harvey, 1990). A culture of fear is reinforced by the corporate media, and being suspicious of others, many have been convinced to seek both shelter and an impoverished sense of agency in passive, consumerist-inspired recreation (Beaudrillard, 1994; Palmer, 1990). In late industrial culture we have been taught to be fearful of social and personal intimacy. The inability to act co-operatively has led to a general malaise of disaffection with society leading to a retreat into subjectivized nihilism and the faux intimacy of mediated or virtual communion (Beaudrillard, 1994).

Considering the near impossibility of trying to change things for ourselves, or to form communities that can conceive of working co-operatively towards some shared vision of change, most are coerced to retreat to one of the few legitimate positions left for expression: recreation linked to passive consuming, as individuals (Baudrillard, 1994; Saul. 1995; Palmer, 1990). At the legal level we are free to dissent in industrial democracies, but increasingly the field of discourse is accepted as one of the only legitimate avenues for the expression of agency (Foucault, 1984; Horrocks & Jevtic, 1996; Baudrillard, 1994). As long as motivated people expend their energy in discussing new or better conceptions of designing human socio-political-economic systems in a "talking-shop" model, dissent is accepted. It is when such ideas threaten the hegemonic systems of industrial capitalism that entrenched elites become alarmed. Postmodern philosophies of various shades and stripes have both described this trend and reinforced its acceptance (Harvey, 1990; Norris, 1990). Real avenues of political activism or even academic and scientific non-conformity are being removed from the menu of available courses of action as states increasingly abandon the funding of formerly public institutions to the corporate sector. The enlightenment ideal of the progression of freedom and justice has thus become truly idealistic in that, at best, discourse concerning these matters has replaced and become mistaken for broad-based consensual activity towards a realization of actual solutions to practical societal inadequacies (Norris, 1990; Harvey, 1990). Most have already left the running of all important aspects of their lives to bureaucratic and corporate organizations. For the few who remain in the fray; their acceptability as "respectable" social commentators rests on their self control in not allowing individualized, radical discourse to lead to organized social action (Reicher, 1996; Michael, 1996). The message many academics have generally internalized is that, for us, discussion is sophisticated but concerted collective action may be regarded as suspicious on both scientific and political grounds (Reicher, 1996). Such work to help actualize a material embodiment of "the just society" often meets with disapproval from political figures as well as possible sanction from administrative bodies in our universities.

Much of "postmodern" philosophy and some discursive variants of social constructionism are attempts to overturn elements of inequality in the "modernist' project and to explore the cultural embeddedness of some of our more repressive institutions (Berger & Luckman, 1966; Shotter, 1993). However correct their criticisms concerning modern industrial scientific and economic systems might be, in general their programmes have reinforced the notion that resistance is primarily found in altering individualized discursive forms. Amendment at this idealistic discursive level is promoted along with the vain hope that such alternative discourse will be reflected in actual personal, social and societal events, at a later date. This postmodern discursive resistance to inequality is a variant of trickle-down economic theory used as a metaphor for a theory of social development. This co-option of critical philosophy to neo-liberalist ideology by the use of such metaphors and the resultant impotence of resistance to "corporatist" domination cannot be over-emphasized. In actual fact, the focus on purely individual discursive events (as opposed to social action) results in a focus way from serious modernist societal goals such as equity and justice. The postmodern move to valorize discourse has led to a change of focus to play (as opposed to purpose), chance (as opposed to design), surface appearance (as opposed to depth) and indeterminacy (as opposed to determinacy). The substitution of action-oriented modernist programmes with postmodern subjectivized relativist accounts merely reflects the experience of anomie inherent in late industrial society (Harvey,1990).

At a deeper level the advent of postmodern and subjectively oriented discursive social science is consistent with the move from a predominantly production oriented to a consumerist society. The replacement of objective modernist with subjective postmodern narratives provide a rationale for such changes within the capitalist paradigm and does not represent a true break with the traditional aims of industrial capitalism (Tolman, Coughlan & Robinson, 1996). The emancipatory value of the broad group of postmodern accounts is extremely limited because of their unacknowledged reinforcement of discursive events as a reality unto themselves and their reliance on metaphors of consuming recreation as the predominant template. Desire and fantasy were always a part of cultural life but late capitalism has exploited the standardization and commodification of fantasy as the <u>predominant</u> engine to increased value production in the global economy.

> The production that now counted was the production of new needs, wants and desires in order to fuel consumption. It was in

> this context that play replaced purpose, with corresponding emphasis on anarchy, chance, exhaustion, performance, indeterminacy and non-interpretation. Attention was directed to desire and fantasy.
>
> (Tolman, Coughlan & Robinson, 1996, p 129-30)

The results of postmodern attempts at broad-based emancipation via fantasy were never really viable. Such programmes were flawed from their very outset because of their acceptance of the radical separation of individual consumers of texts from concerted co-operative practical action. The move from modernist to post-modernist individualized narrative "accounts" serve as a consolidating force for the late industrial period and actually work to inoculate oppressive systems from egalitarian efforts. Postmodern individualized narratives function to side-track social emancipatory activity into subjectivized, disconnected and ultimately vain individual discursive re-interpretation as an alternative to organized acts of resistance.

Such ideas could not succeed without broad social acceptance of certain ideas concerning "human nature." Our problems in mounting a defense against such a postmodern construction may well be in large measure owing to a pre-disposition in current thought to accept that humanity is naturally comprised of independent competitive and consuming individuals. Such individuals who exist in a society that operates mechanically, instrumentally, and selfishly and who are convinced by socialization in such societies to be passive, will tend to accept this model of human nature and social relations as true and immutable. In the current state of affairs, where a majority of the denizens of modern industrial cultures feel themselves to be socially disempowered and have therefore retreated to express their desires and personal agency in the malls, sports arenas and T.V. rooms, there is a willingness to accept the truth of individual passive subjectivity as natural. This lived reality of individuals as passive reactors to stimuli from the environment is parallel to and informed by the striking resemblance of classical traditional theories of human nature, the relation of consciousness to the world and by implication, mainstream “representationalist” theories of human perception.

These models and narratives of the relation of humans to their environment and the explanation of human experiences of perception seem reasonable because modern western cultural forms have continually reinforced this belief. These models developed because of their connection to and applications within historical contexts. They matured and became practically irresistible because they were in harmony with the overall predominant societal project of industrial capitalism. The tragic separation of human consciousness from action in the world, from other members of the human community and even from aspects of our own selves owes a great debt to the history of dualistic systems of categorization and in particular to the Cartesian dichotomous version. Traditional representationalist theories of perception are fundamental expressions of Cartesian dualism and this is linked to the acceptance of humans as passive being seen as a natural fact.

Representationalism and cognitive psychology

The three moment scheme (Input-Central Processing Mechanism-output) which characterizes representationalist theories of perception is a direct descendent of the Cartesian dualist concepts as described in article XVI of *The Passions of the Soul*. The entire system is characterized as constituting a one-way mechanical causative chain. The information necessary to the system is input in the form of sensations and the Central Processing Mechanism (CPM), related to the actions of the soul, is constrained by its own nature but most importantly by sensory data. The soul becomes part of the mechanical network leaving it vulnerable to be replaced as the brain as the site of central processing in later renditions common in cognitive science (Tolman & Robinson, 1997). This three moment mechanically organized scheme of representation radically separates the realms of sensation and perception leading to subject/object dualism which forms one of the fundamental assumptions of all modern mainstream psychological and social-psychological investigative practice.

According to this model, subjective experience concerning the separate outside world is only in terms of the play of nervous energy. Not only are the realms of subjective experience and objective world split apart but the experience of radically isolated individuals becomes the primary focus of psychological (and by extension) social-psychological practices. Inter-subjectivity is relegated to a secondary, problematic concern. The current experience of modern individualism then becomes a natural, rather than a culturally embedded, fact of existence. In mainstream social-psychology, as mentioned previously, the additional complication of social life is tackled with a qualitatively similar toolbox of methods that are generalized from psychological theories assuming representationalism. Thus, internalizing Descartes' scheme, all mainstream theories and methods have reinforced a conception of relations that is congruent with the modern industrial and consumerist project. Cartesian formulations in social-psychology have seriously undermined any coherent explanation of the reality of experienced volitional activity, inter-subjective meaning creation and the evolution of culturally saturated institutional systems.

The combination of subject/object dualism and mechanical causation has led to a general assumption in most schools of mainstream psychology, that the world is forced upon us, constraining our actions to be merely reactive to the environment while at the same time we are separated from this "objective" world. The combination of the three-moment scheme and the one-way mechanical causation severely restricts any coherent explanation of agency for people endeavouring to order their life in terms of their own needs and desires. The Cartesian derived, three moment perceptual scheme has led to insubstantial and problematic descriptions of the relation of individuals to their cultural life as well as some unparsimonious mechanical theories of communication which similarly fail to adequately reflect actual interactive discursive behaviour.

> A subject-object dualism only makes sense to the ordinary mind when it is supported by mechanical causation and representationalism . . . which does indeed correspond to our

> actual abstraction and isolation as individuals in bourgeois society. Causality and representation help this appear natural.
>
> (Tolman & Robinson, 1997)

The problem remained that while it seemed so natural to assume this Cartesian explanation of perception that tragically isolated the individual subjective experience from the world, later scientific rumination laid bare some troubling contradictions. Future explanations of the connection of human consciousness with a now separated world would either have to be extremely convoluted and unparsimonious or they would have to attempt to artificially conflate the objective sphere into the subjective or the reverse via some form of reduction.

Acceptance of representationalism means that we can only have an indirect experience of the physical and social environment. This leads to some logical quandaries in terms of the application of this paradigm, in psychological practices. If we are to accept the indirect realist account, then what credence can be given to psychological observations? The mainstream psychological gaze is at logical odds with the representationalist theoretical framework within which it operates. The inconsistency appears when the assumption of indirect realism is applied to the subject in a psychological investigation but to make conclusions acceptable as rigorous science, it must be abandoned in terms of the investigators' perceptions (Katz & Wilcox, 1984).

Behaviorism

Behaviorism is a grand example of attempts to artificially overcome this duality by conflating the subjective realm into objective behaviour, but with little success. Cognitive aspects of an organism were translated to be seen only in terms of bodily movements. For example, thinking was studied in terms of supposed laryngeal movements and personality as a general tendency to react to stimuli (Heidbreder, 1933). The rejection by behaviorism of the existence of consciousness for all practical purposes is however, not always clear. Some behaviorists denied its existence altogether while others asserted that regardless of whether it existed or not, it was not amenable to scientific psychological investigation. Either way, mental processes were considered not to be the concern of psychological investigation whereas external behaviour was (Talyzina, 1981). The second view can be recognized as a reintroduction of Cartesianism into the behavioristic system. The active participation of the organism in choosing to construct its future through "consciousness" was viewed as threatening scientific objectivity and excluded from investigations as it disrupted the aim of scientific psychological research which was objective prediction of behaviour (Lethbridge, 1992).

In Skinner's version of the behaviorist project, the mind was viewed as "a fiction" (Skinner, 1971). The set of assumptions he worked with which postulated that behaviour is shaped by its consequences states that behaviour before the process of operand conditioning, is a randomly emitted phenomenon (Skinner, 1953). A "self" is a repertoire of behavior appropriate to a given set of contingencies which cannot choose to act on the world: instead the world causes actions in the organism (Skinner, 1971). Thus, this position is one that cannot conceive of a coherent theory of self let alone an explanation of intentionality or agency (Lethbridge, 1992). Human behaviour is reactive rather than active: it always merely responds to and is determined by externalities. According to this view, the fact that we experience consciousness and something approaching agency does not mean that material stimulus events do not cause our behaviour. Such things, as are experienced are "diversions": collateral by-products of the play of stimuli on our biology and history of S - R chains and are "epi-phenomena". Yet, there is no explanation of why, how or when this epi-phenomenon emerges or what its function might be!

The organism (meaning any organism) was considered passive. Behaviour would be emitted in response to various forms of stimulation and it was assumed that it would be an objectively predictable response. Thus, this reductionistic variant of Cartesian psychology was not only antithetical to the study of consciousness and agency but completely abandoned these topics in its framework. Theirs was an unsuccessful strategy of overcoming dualism that conflated subjectivity into behaviour in a mechanical externally oriented arrangement that preserves individualism (Talyzina, 1981, Lethbridge, 1992).

In its favour, at least behaviorism did not always replicate the representationalist aspect of Cartesianism. Many in the field held to a direct realist, unmediated account of perception. However, even in this attempt the project was to be unsuccessful as later investigators were forced to reintroduce the CPM in the form of various layers of "intervening variables". While attempting to explain consciousness in terms of stimulus-response chains and operand conditioning, many behaviorists couldn't dispose of or explain the differing constitution of particular organisms in particular environments. It was generally agreed that there were no marked differences between one organism and another. The view that the same psychological laws apply equally to all species meant that they failed to understand the evolutionary aspects of qualitative change and ignored the marked differences that human cultural life engenders (Razran, 1971). The return of this middle term, or a set of intervening variables of course looked very similar to the CPM and returned us again to a Cartesian dualism.

From behaviorism to cognitivism

As a revolt against the spartan, reductionistic and mechanical dualism of behaviorism, both cognitive and humanistic psychology reconfigured a different model of the appropriate object of psychological investigation (Lethbridge, 1992). However both models would assume Cartesian representationalism and would both fail in offering any coherent account of agency or inter-subjective engagement. While behaviorism attempted to artificially dispose of the gulf between subjective experience and objective world via a reduction, it would seem that such a separation was something that appeared to be somewhat revolutionary and actually embraced by cognitivism. The only possible explanation for such a claim can be that psychology suffers from an extremely serious memory malfunction. Fodor's, classical use of computational models tries to hide the Cartesian scheme by the use of slightly different terminology but he explicitly points to the radical separation of the physical world and individual subjective experience. He reaffirms the divide by claiming two descriptive levels that arise by the artificial separation of the world and sensation (at the sense receptors) which mechanically convert sensations into arbitrary neural codes. These are later decoded into representations using certain "processing qualities" of the neurological C.P.M., to produce perception. The assumption is that the senses are provided with an impoverished description of the world and that the inadequate data can only form an image or representation of the original input data by the intervention of various cognitive "modules". Sensations merely record this impoverished data by registering energy as intensity, frequency, wavelength etc. There is a great reliance on memory to make sense out of static energy to add depth perception, locomotion, movement and meanings from static images or representations of the world. It is assumed that memory is used to fill in the discrete momentary snapshot of the stimulation of sense organs which is devoid of information concerning time (hence movement) and the dimensional arrangement.

> In the case of organisms as in the case of real computers, if we get the right way of assigning formulae to the (psychological) states, it will be feasible to interpret the sequence of events that <u>causes</u> the output as a computational <u>derivation</u> of the input.
>
> (Fodor, 1975, p. 74)

The reductionism of cognitivism is opposite to that of behaviorism in that the mental realm is assumed but activities are separated and said to be accomplished by means of the use of appropriate “modules”. The self is not really addressed but we can consider that cognitive psychology also treats it as an epi-phenomenon of the interaction of these various cognitive compartments, if not in theory, at least in practice. Metaphorically, the person is transformed into an interaction of computer machine parts which has a tendency to reify processes by their connection to structures assumed to be in the brain. Again, without a reasonable rendition of the self there is little chance that a coherent model of human agency will be revealed. The self is portrayed as a passive structure or schema that integrates all the self related information, perhaps an “executive module”. Cognitive psychology has much to say about abstracted and separated self-concepts but has very little to offer concerning “self”, itself. In other words while cognitive psychology discusses how we form impressions or ideas about the self it comments little or nothing on how, why, where, when or what the self is. As with behaviorism, the cognitive model is reductionistic, mostly mechanical and radically separates the individual from the inter-subjective reality of active life for a cultural species.

> Qualities of active agency, will, consciousness and so on are merely contingently present if they are present at all.
>
> (Lethbridge, 1992, p.25)

We have no direct access to the world only access to our neurological representations. In this view, meaning is not something that can be approached directly but only apprehended in subjective experience, something in the back of our individual brains. This unparsimonious explanation of human consciousness not only reproduces the same minefield of contradictions as earlier forms of dualism, it does not explain the lived experience of humans as existing as agents in the world. There is no explanation of how we experience choice in relation to physical, biological and cultural constraints. The utility of this version of self, supported by the metaphors of computational industrial machinery actually produces an impoverished "image" of both individuals and societies that is consistent with the aims and practices of late capitalist industrial society.

Self-efficacy and locus of control

There were a few mainstream psychological attempts to explain human agency but at most they labeled constructs and only succeeded in describing limited aspects. These attempts side-stepped theoretical problems because the subject of agency is problematic for both behaviorism and cognitive science. They are standpoints that are ostensibly outside the general thrust of these mainstream systems but were accepted as important contributions because while they didn't affirm any theoretical system they neither denied nor constructed a new paradigm. Bandura's concept of self-efficacy occurred at a transitional phase between behaviorism and cognitivism. Bandura (1977) defines the concept of 'self-efficacy" as an appraisal of whether one perceives an ability to successfully cope with a particular situation or not. Self-efficacy appraisals are considered to have emotional and cognitive aspects and these reactions were posited as having an impact on the initiation of “coping behaviours”. Bandura (1986), Litt (1988) and Haney & Long (1995) all agree that estimations of “self-efficacy” are different to “control appraisal”. In their view, self-efficacy appraisals mediate the appraisal of perceptions of the ability to exercise control over a situation and any consequent coping behaviour. The literature includes the investigation of hypothesized links between perceptions of self-efficacy and abilities in performing physical performance tasks.(Feltz, 1988; McAuley, 1985) career tasks (Stumpf, Brief & Hartman, 1987) as well as health behaviours (Ewart, Taylor, Reeses & Debusk, 1984). In all studies it was found that those who were measured to have higher self-efficacy performed better. Experience with particular situations was associated with greater self-efficacy, perceptions of control and success in the performance of laboratory tasks. Higher levels of perceived control and self-efficacy are inversely linked with somatic anxiety and positively related to perceptions of task satisfaction (Haney & Long, 1995). This research confirmed other investigations in this area demonstrating that perceptions of low self-efficacy and control tends to be associated with a “disengagement” coping strategy whereas perceptions of high self-efficacy and control tends to be associated with an “engagement” coping strategy. By disengagement it is meant that participants tended to cope with certain tasks by the use of various avoidance strategies and that engagement requires behaviours that are consistent with concentrating on the assigned task. However, such research regarding self-efficacy assumed rather than demonstrated construct validity and defined its usefulness by correlating it with other assumed constructs and measuring the effects on external correlates. There was no attempt to explain the genesis or by what means such appraisals take place nor how this phenomenon is connected to existing theoretical systems. Instead, discussions of this version of perceived agency were limited to the creation and labeling of the construct and an empirical appraisal of predictive viability in situations where agency was defined as the individualized ability to react to experimenter-defined situations in laboratories.

The kinds of beliefs that people hold about their own sense of personal control and the ability to act in their own interests have profound effects on their adaption to major life changes. (Langer, 1983; Lefcourt, 1983;) One of the only ways this has been investigated in general cognitive terms is under the rubric of "locus of control" (Rotter, 1966; 1975; Parks, 1985). This concept is defined in relative terms as an orientation regarding environmental and personal circumstances as either under personal control or dependent on external circumstances. Rotter & Mulry (1965) discussed how expectancies for control influence a person's choice of performance situation. Using this construct they found that those who were measured to identify with an internal locus of control preferred skill testing situations whereas those with an external locus of control were more at home with chance tasks. This was supported by Strickland (1978) and again later by Sandler, Reese Spencer & Harpin (1983) who both agreed that people are more motivated by situations that are congruent with their personal beliefs about the degree of control they generally perceive. Those who perceive little agency in their life in general are comfortable with situations that also restrict such control. In addition, Rothbaum, Weisz & Snyder (1982) argue that a general orientation to give up power to others or the situation (external locus of control) tends to be reinforced over time and leads to generalized defensive and reactive behaviour strategies. This construct has often been used in an attempt to account for health behaviours. Patients' perceptions of illness and disability have been related to coping styles (Johnson & Sarason, 1978; Kobasa, Maddi & Kahn, 1982; Lefcourt, 1983; Strickland, 1978; Sullivan & Reardon, 1985), the effects of social support on a sense of control when ill (Albrecht & Adelman, 1987; Lefcourt Martin & Saleh, 1984; Sandler & Lakey, 1982), the success of recovery through rehabilitative medical intervention (Abella & Heslin, 1984; Schlenk & Hart, 1984) and the communicative strategies that increase or mitigate against perceived control over health behaviour (Brenders 1989).

As was the case with Bandura's concept of self-efficacy, the concept of locus of control was an attempt to address the reality of choice but without any coherent connection to any existing systems. For the most part the conceptualization of the subject of cognitive psychology meant that agency was a phenomenon viewed as at best, peripheral to the purview of investigation. Such a definition of the field of cognitive science avoided the problematic theoretical issue of building a coherent explanation of agency upon the foundation of a representationalist perceptual theory, which because of its construction of organisms as primarily passive, all but precludes the possibility.

Humanistic psychology, self and agency

Humanistic psychology evolved as a reaction to the bleak mechanicism of behaviorism and although it could be viewed as an opposite pole in most aspects, there was a similarity in that both schools emerged in an effort to reconfigure psychology on a less inadequate basis than their predecessors (Murphy and Kovach, 1972). Behaviorism was a reaction to the introspectionism of nineteenth century structuralism whereas humanistic psychology was a reaction to the extreme objectivism of behaviorism. In turn, the Humanist project attempted to re-establish a subjectivist point of view, albeit at a higher level. The Humanistic movement in psychology was a protest against banishment of the particularly human experience of meaning-creation, values and intentions from psychological inquiry (Murphy & Kovach, 1972). Rather than the structuralist project of examining the separated contents of consciousness, the humanistic paradigm was interested in the experiences of people conceived holistically (Lethbridge, 1992). The problem with this reaction was that is was merely the "flip-side" of behaviorism and was itself an equally one-sided reconfiguration of the object of psychological investigation, now conceptualized as separated subjective experience. While criticizing behaviorism for its biological reductionism, the Humanist movement posited that humans are "hard-wired" towards the exercise of certain constructs such as "self-actualization". Commentators have seen such humanist constructs as essentialist (and Platonic) characteristics and at a fundamental level cannot be conceived as anything but another version of a psychology that at base rests upon biological reductionism (Lethbridge, 1992). This being so, we can clearly see that this project was equally unable to derive a coherent explanation of agency (other than being driven by an unexplained innate drive towards self-actualization) or of inter-subjectivity.

Problems in humanistic conceptualizations were noted by followers and others relatively quickly. Schisms ensued and in general this movement was accused of being unscientific. In the 1980's it became complicit in a cross-polination with New Age philosophizing regarding the supernatural. In its later stages it fulfilled much of its detractors' prophecies as it deteriorated into a philosophical rationalization of a mix of upper-middle class bourgeois values, integrated with quasi-religious navel-gazing as an apologia for competitive material acquisitiveness and instrumental social relations. Self and self-actualization were conceived of as harmonious to the aims of industrial culture and thus reinforced the tenets of individualist subjectivism. In fact these later "new-age variants" not only accept individualized and narcissistic identities and social relations as a natural fact, they provides a rationale for why they should be actively sought, as goals in and of themselves.

All three of the aforementioned positions (behaviorism, cognitivism and humanistic psychology) are one-sided in their approach to psychological investigation (Lethbridge, 1992; Parker & Spears, 1996). None of these systems can sufficiently address the individual in terms that preserve the natural contexts of consciousness, inter-subjectivity, cultural and biological constraints. All have used some form of reductionism in their systems, all assume and reinforce dualistic configurations that stem from Cartesian dichotomous philosophy and the representationalist explanation of perception (Parker & Spears, 1996). Therefore, all have reinforced an understanding of the abstract individual. Both behaviorism and cognitive science have also conceived of the individual as reducible to separated, operationally defined variables which has led to the mainstream North American impoverishment of social-psychological investigation. Instead of empowering the "individual" according to the rationale of the rhetoric, the individual living person has suffered a conversion into a data-point: an abstract, disembodied and meaningless existence that is perfectly compatible to the scientifically rationalized bureaucratic project of intervention and manipulation (Danziger, 1990). The reductionist and dualistic assumptions carried over from the parent discipline and the application of methods tied to these Cartesian models has meant that there is no adequate understanding of the self, personal agency or inter-subjective and cultural relations.

> If the mind is to be understood as a domain of skills and techniques that renders the world meaningful to the individual then our conception of the mind as a Cartesian entity sealed into its own individual and self-contained subjectivity must be revised
>
> (Harre and Gillett, 1944 p. 22).

<u>An alternative conception in the Western tradition</u>

There are several ways to reconceptualize the relation between the individual and the physical and social/cultural environment but I will touch briefly on one possible western escape from dualism that can be constructed by a combination of a scientifically amenable theory of perception and a dialectical social theory. A more logically tenable perceptual foundation for explaining our concrete experience in the physical and socio-cultural world is offered by James J. Gibson. Gibson (1986) offers a non-dualist realist perspective that explains how meanings are appropriated from the relationship of the organism and environment and assumes rather than denies the agency of the organism. This ground-breaking work is a great step away from Cartesian representationalist perceptual theory and has opened up a possibility for superseding dichotomous Aristotelian laws of identity, non-contradiction and excluded middle by providing the foundation for an extension into social relations if melded with a dialectical social ontology. The mixture possesses real possibilities for overcoming the problems of dualism, individualism, mechanicism and reductionism.

In *The Ecological Approach to Visual Perception* (Gibson,1986) the focus is primarily, but not exclusively on vision. He firstly attempts to explain that in order to talk about perception one should approach the subject using the appropriate level of analysis applicable to the lived experience of particular organisms. From the point of view of scientific logic based upon the methodology of reductionism, this would seem truly radical. The world to a particular organism is related to that organism and rather than talk about how the senses can be analyzed into separate components and thereby respond by neurologically encoding abstract sensations he prefers to talk about perceptual organs as his unit of analysis. These organs “pick-up” information that exists in the light (and other mediums) that are transmitted from objects in the environment to the matrix of perceptual organs. Gibson realizes that although one can analyze reactions to stimuli at the level of separated physical energies, it is not helpful for understanding how each perceptual organ actually works as a unit to use the information (Ben-Zeev, 1981). Rather, it is more helpful to conceive each perceptual organ (the eye, hearing etc.) as actively working together to gather the information through both exploratory and performatory activity.

Information is about complex structures in the world and specifies an environment to an animal. For traditional, including cognitivist theorists, the sensations are impoverished and need active processing by the mind to arrive, indirectly, at a derivative image of the world. In contrast, Gibson approaches the problem at a more appropriate psychological level stating that we appropriate information about our environment directly, or to put it another way, "stimulation specifies the environment and no elaboration is necessary" (Michaels & Carello, 1982). An evolutionary perspective is utilized accepting that although the world existed before the evolution of organisms, the perceptual organs evolved along with both the organism and the world. Perceptual organs developed to utilize information that exists in the environment (or the aspects of the world that is appropriated and relevant to the particular species of animal). As animals are active and are chiefly interested in events, perceptual organs co-evolved to track events in both space and time and also to utilize information about movement of the organisms and movement of structures.

Whereas Gibson's ecological theory of perception overcomes the radical separation of the individual from their environment and the duality of sensation and perception, the separation of the individual perceiver from the social/cultural sphere can be accomplished if we meld Gibsonian perceptual theory with two levels of dialectical social theory. The combination of a non-dualist theory of perception and non-dualist social theory have far reaching consequences in helping explain personal agency in coherent scientific terms.

The human species is unlike others because although other organisms may occasionally avail themselves of the use of tools, such usage is rarely if ever generalized to the point that tool use becomes a dominant activity. For humans, our environment although based on the pre-existing "natural" world, is now continually changing at the hands of tool-using humans in a vast number of ways. Thus, our use of these tools has long been a dominant form of existence. Natural substances are converted to artificial materials for a vast variety of uses, many of which have enriched and simplified human existence. However, human technological advancement has also created some problematic side-effects that make human existence more difficult and insecure. It is not that there are two separated environments of the "natural" existing unchanged and the artificial, changed by the human dominant form of tool use. Again, Gibson avoids the normal traditional separation of untouched natural world from the artificial constructed and amended environment of humans. We are nature, in that it is "natural" for humans to change the environment that we inhabit, and create a hybrid non-separable meaning system that is the relation between individual humans and the socially mediated, physical-cultural environment. It is a natural phenomenon of humans to form societies, create languages and design institutions and therefore this cultural environment is also "natural."

This social extension of Gibson can be accomplished by utilizing aspects of Activity theory (especially the work of Leont'ev and Vygotsky) and a further extension to explain power and constraints on personal agency as discussed by German Critical Psychology and in particular, Klaus Holzkamp. Both Activity Theory and German Critical Psychology are constructed using non-dualist dialectical logic and share a further common foundation in Marxist social theory. They both follow naturally from Gibson's rudimentary exploration of socially contextualized individual perceptions.

According to Gibson (a view that is shared by Marxist social theorists) we are born as humans into a world that has undergone several thousand years of transformation by an evolving system of cultural traditions and socially embedded symbolic systems that are accompanied by all the artifacts of this development. Human culture, including systems of symbolic interaction, values, ethics, morality and productive relations have created changing meanings in relation to shifts in the choice of particular social, economic and ideological tools. This development both constrains and opens-up the development of our changing cultural intentions and their expression in activity. Our action, which is mediated socially, adds a new dimension and both increasing levels of complexity as well as constraints to the possibility of the appropriation of "affordances".

Human infants do not just passively accept information about the environment nor do they be become little Robinson Crusoes and actively explore as individuals. This aspect is extremely important in Mead's (Concrete Social Behaviorism) and Vygotsky's explanations of how individual consciousness evolves as a consequence of action that is mediated by inter-subjectivity (Mead, 1977, Vygotsky, 1978). Children are introduced to the present crystallization of cultural meanings about the human-environment relationship carried in language and social relations. Although there exists a certain latitude in generating relations to the physical/cultural environment, values act as constraints on what will be perceived as sanctioned, legitimized or what may become a dominant relation. Not only is our environment transformed in the way of artifacts (Heft, 1989) but our horizons of the possible or legitimated modes of activity are also transformed and constrained because we are introduced to them through socially mediated, culturally embedded activity (Mead, 1977; Vygotsky, 1978).

Marxist psychological formulations share a common ontological position of explaining the development of social relations, belief, and values with reference to and springing from activity. In a sense, Marxist social ontology needs the basis of Gibsonian direct perception as much as Gibson's non-dualist perception cries out for coherent extension, expansion and perhaps completion, at the levels of both social meaning creation and institutionalized societal relationships. They share enough in common to help complete one another.

Lev Vygotsky has been associated with a school of Marxist psychology developed in the Soviet Union which has now blossomed throughout much of

Northern Europe and particularly throughout Scandinavia. Activity theory could be thought of as a descendent from the writings of Vygotsky and Leont'ev (1979; 1981)forming a loose affiliation of approaches to social psychological functioning. (Tolman, Coughlan & Robinson (1996). Vygotsky's outline of the concept of the culturally embedded relation of active learning and socialization, the zone of proximal development, contributes greatly to the continuation of a non-dualist perspective (Vygotsky, 1960, 1978, 1986). Much like Wittgenstein, Vygotsky believed that the meaning of linguistic forms can be objectively approached when we look at their use. While Wittgenstein leaves his accounts open to being used in some very relativist narratives (as he implies elsewhere regarding a separation of the world of symbols and material) Vygotsky grounds his system most definitely in the realist perspective. Active appropriation of material needs leads, in his view, to the development of linguistic abilities and this changes human capabilities to relate to each other and to relate to their environment through the explanatory medium of symbolic interaction as a form of tool. Much like the Gibsonian insight of tool use in overturning the sharp distinction between the animal and its environment, linguistic systems are seen as tools that develop out of concrete social action. Such a view can also bolster the Gibsonian contradiction of the notion that consciousness (and by extension, perception) is a wholly private and individual experience. Information concerning affordances (the relations between organisms and their environment) are available to all who share the same biology and in the case of humans, the same or similar cultural socialization. The meaning exists in the relation of (in this case) the human organism and its cultural-natural niche. Language develops from practical activity in the world and the appropriation of what the world affords. Thus, language developed from human social action is used to help develop individual consciousness of self, affordances and personal agency. Language is a crystallized carrier of legitimate social activities, intentions and therefore values. The younger members of society enter into this culturally mediated world of action by mastering the linguistic codes in a Zone of Proximal Development (Vygotsky, 1978). The linguistic code organizes action in what is perceived by the culture as legitimate forms and the use in social interaction is the first phase of organizing the younger member's appropriation of available cultural affordances. There is no private code in which representations or images of the reality are shaped in the mind. The so-called "inner language of representation" does not exist. The symbolic appropriation of the meaning of individuals' relation to the physical/cultural environment is firstly a social phenomenon, rooted in activity. Through social institutions, a zone of proximal development is created in the interaction of neophytes with more skilled members of a culture. Through this zone and the appropriation of cultural affordances, the social is internalized and thus becomes the individual's mode of symbolic appropriation that is experienced as private or subjective consciousness.

There is no dualism between inner representation and a social linguistic system and no dualism of social linguistic system and the activity of appropriating affordances. Here, what is considered to be the private language of "thought" is not strictly speaking, inner or private, in the sense it is closed off or an individualized subjective experience. What is now (for want of a better word) “inner” owes its existence to and is non-different to what is “outer” in the social space and what is in the social space is a linguistic crystallization of affordances appropriated though activity.

Vygotsky’s zone of proximal development and the appropriation of social and cultural norms and values from the linguistic mediation of activity explains how younger members of cultural groups take ownership of cultural knowledge and develop an individual experience of conscious awareness. This argument is saved from becoming merely a reduction of personal subjectivity to socialization by the understanding that individual and social levels are again in constant dialectical relation. The point is that this dialectical relationship is also <u>unsymmetrical</u> in that while crystallized cultural meaning <u>leads</u> and may well constrain individual subjectivity in the process of socialization, it does not determine. Meaning creation is a constant process of dialectical negotiation between individuals and between themselves and their culture.

While there is an implied notion of cultural values as constraining the appropriation of affordances, in the Vygotskian perspective, a fuller account is given by the German critical psychologist Klaus Holtzkamp (Tolman, 1994). Ideological values and societal relations, as mentioned before are crystallized in language because language is a social tool that aids in the activity of the appropriation of affordances. In class societies that are comprised of hierarchically arranged strata, whereby certain members have a wider horizon of opportunity for action than others, there is somehow a differential in the perception and utilization of affordances. In Europe, where there has been a considerable history of continually reproducing class sub-cultures, social meanings, vertically layered legitimate forms of action and even the use of linguistic codes can be seen to be quite different from one class or geographical region to another. Is it that those who find themselves at the top of the hierarchical class structure are somehow superior because they are able to maintain their superior ability to appropriate a greater variety of affordances or is there something which is effectively blocking the same appropriation to those who are less powerful? In bourgeois industrial culture, those who own the means of production seem to have a greater ability to avail themselves to choices of action and thus to reproduce their power and enriched living conditions ever more. As Marx (1932/1977) commented, those who own the means of production also control the means for the production of ideas that suit their own ends. In other words “the ruling ideas are always the ideas of the ruling class”.

Over time certain ideas are encoded in language and in the constellation of legitimate social institutions that govern the generation of meanings in a culture. Those who wish to be admitted to be seen as legitimate in the eyes of institutions developed by the elite of a certain culture, must accept the social meanings, linguistic codes and legitimacy of these institutions. This includes, (in the case of western medieval and industrial cultures) a certain tolerance for unequal distribution. By the reproduction of these class relations through the socialization process of one generation by the previous one, certain members of society will always be subject to a limited field of action befitting their place in the lower regions of the hierarchy of social relations. Thus, they will be precluded from the ability to legitimately choose from a variety of courses of action that are open for others.

They will experience or endure, in Holzkamp's words, "restricted action potence." In order to be part of the activities of society and by sharing in a linguistic code that is amended to both reflect and constrain their particular place in the economic activity of a society, they must submit to some restriction on their choices of action. In Gibsonian terms they will fail to perceive or fail to feel competent to act on certain affordances that others take for granted. By agreeing to certain limitations on their freedom to avail themselves of certain action possibilities they agree not to see themselves as legitimate appropriators of particular types of affordances, and this sacrifice gives them a limited entrance to the broad system of legitimated cultural activities. The price of entering into society through linguistically mediated social institutions is a culturally socialized failure to perceive or act on certain affordances or action possibilities. In other words, affordance horizons can be either enlarged or curtailed by means of the internalization of social meaning systems learned through linguistically mediated interactions and activity. These are related to socially and ideologically mediated class based systems of activities.

Holzkamp has extended the discussion of linguistic and ideological tools as the means that evolving societies utilize to construct and enforce unequal relations. Agency can be constrained by physical, biological and by ideological means but these means are always in relation to, and are set in motion by, the dominant cultural and economic systems operating within a society. Agency is necessary to the appropriation of the cultural-natural world by an individual but this agency (also seen as affordances and action possibilities) can be restricted depending on ones relation to the predominant forms of production and reproduction. Ones' subjective experience or consciousness can become fully harmonized with an unequal culture so that the situation ceases being experienced as in opposition to ones interests, needs and desires. In such a situation the acceptance of this "false consciousness" (Marx, 1932/1977) precludes many forms of resistance to win back the extinguished action possibilities.

In reality, even those who have become acculturated to relinquish many of their own interests and to identify with institutions that are oppressive, have at least a minimal experience of discomfort and as a consequence often seek to rectify the situation with minimal forms of resistance. However, in sophisticated industrial society even the forms of resistance have slowly been co-opted. This is where (as mentioned previously) postmodern discursive philosophy has unconsciously conjoined and reinforced consumerist interests to remove people from the world of co-operative action to extend their possibilities, to a separated world of individualized, subjective, discursive narrative. Play, superficiality, indeterminacy, individuality, difference, relativism are all to be celebrated and preferably in a form that sustains the consumerist market economy. Thus, the paths of resistance left legitimately open to most, only further compounds actual alienation. This disrupts the perception of and actions in relation to certain physical/cultural affordances and constrains many from achieving potential action potence and the potentiality of personal agency. Agency is the perception of the actual relations between the individual and their physical/cultural niche and is therefore rooted in intersubjectivity and promoted by unimpeded co-operative relations.

The model of the individual as constructed by the technology of mainstream psychological formulations, by constant use over a considerable period can function ideologically to inform, through socialization, all succeeding generations of people that such a reality it is a natural “fact” rather than a culturally constructed norm. The "individual”, so reconstructed as abstracted from social and cultural contexts, is also abstracted from the real potential of individual agency and latent power that is rooted in the concreteness of intersubjectivity and communicative interaction. (Harre & Gillett, 1994). The real potential power as individuals can in actuality be accomplished by understanding that an individual exists primarily in relation to a community of shared values, social commitments and interdependent goals. However, by the deployment of the rhetoric of particular versions of science in which social-psychology is deeply implicated, we now tend to surrender real potentiality for enfranchisement in exchange for passivity. The construction of a disoriented, anomic and neutralized human identity composed primarily of qualities that can be made to respond to bureaucratic intervention and an existence of marginalized compliance is a model that psychology and social-psychology have largely reinforced and legitimated through the scientific enterprise.

The personal resistance that can be deployed in this impoverished atmosphere tends to be inversions of predominant modes of conduct (seen as anti-social schisms or sub-cultures) self-destructive reactions (as in various means of escape through substance abuse). Other legitimated forms of resistance include harmlessly escapist behaviour (as in an addiction to sporting events or other trivia), a purely rhetorical discursive resistance (as in the re-narration of subjugation or abusive life events in terms more complementary to self-esteem) and/or in forms harmonious to the predominant economic interests through the purchasing and consumption of products or services. There exists a tendency to believe that we can emancipate ourselves if we make a few adjustments and make the commitment to redouble our efforts to harmonize ourselves with the forces that are in actuality, often opposed to our interests in expressing unrestricted agency. The kinds of problems that many people suffer as a result of restrictions on their ability to be agents are construed by western institutions (supported by mainstream renditions of psychiatry and psychology) as resulting from deviant individual maladjustment and crises of personal belief rather than as evidence for the inadequacy of the current social paradigm. Mental suffering is conveniently defined as a possibly treatable individual, biological or behavioural malfunction rather than as an often understandable, if not reasonable, reaction to perceptions that the available menu of legitimate culturally-mediated affordances are at odds with the individual's reasonable needs and desires (Parker & Spears, 1996).

This extension of the Gibsonian direct perceptual perspective by elements of Vygotsky's and Holtzkamp's Marxist-based explanations of social psychological function is, as yet, quite cursory. Further and more careful explorations of the utility of conjoining these aspects to fully socialize Gibson's concepts needs to be accomplished in later ruminations. However, the utility of Gibson's relational system in overcoming the snares of logically incoherent and unparsimonious explanations that stem from Cartesian and traditional cognitivist accounts of perception cannot be overstated. The further elaboration of non-dualist systems will perhaps contribute to improved theoretical explanatory schemes but more importantly, lead to an extension of agency and emancipatory action (Hayes, 1996). Agency is not a private internal experience but a social phenomenon. As such it can be supported or hidden and distorted by cultural systems and harmonious conceptions of psychological functioning.

This chapter has outlined how mainstream representationalist theories of perception have drawn on the meta-categorizational system of dualism, particularly the scientifically legitimated version stemming from the writing of Descartes. The acceptance of mainstream perceptual theories has problematized the understanding of agency as well as seriously undermining the explanatory potential of social psychological formulations in general. The following chapter will trace the development of social psychology following from the assumptions of the parent discipline that is based upon the acceptance of a dualistic theory of perception. The discussion of this development will be contextualized by the predominant socio-economic goals of western industrial culture in which social psychology has been heavily implicated.

A Theoretical & Methodological Morality Play: The Surveillance Society and the Creation of a Distinctly "unsocial" Social Psychology of Manipulation, Prediction and Control

Rory Coughlan, Ph.D

Associate Professor of Social Psychology, Trent University

Man is a credulous animal and must believe in something. In the absence of good grounds for belief, he will be satisfied with bad ones.

(Bertrand Russell)

Previous chapters have outlined how dualism has been a foundational ordering principle in western society from at least the classical Greek period forward to the present. While the rationale has changed during the past two thousand years from mystical beliefs of one sort or another to science, at a meta-categirizational level it is merely a predictable evolution. Dualism as a philosophical system has continued because of its usefulness for cultures whose predominant societal project is based upon the domination of nature or other peoples. The scientific basis of the dichotomization of the world stems from Cartesian divisions and this has been assumed and reinforced by representationist models of perception.

Social-psychology has internalized the Cartesian framework and has additionally assumed the hidden anthropology of the isolated individual further reinforcing the dichotomy between individual behaviour and all forms of social interaction (Tolman, 1994: Jackson, 1988). In addition to primarily treating social aspects as stimuli and then examining individual behaviour as the result of social stimuli, social psychological knowledge has generally been used to predict and control individual behaviour (Danziger, 1990; Lethbridge, 1992). Catering to state and corporate institutions' consumption of such knowledge products has provided the discipline with its primary raison d'etre (Danziger, 1990). Personal agency or intentionality becomes a problematic concept not only because of the assumption of theoretical assumptions antithetical to a coherent explanation but because the extra-scientific societal context of knowledge production and consumption make explication of agency an under-funded, unprofitable and (given the morays of the main consumers of such knowledge) an undesireable subject of investigation. This present chapter will outline a contextualized history of the development of mainstream North American social-psychology and discuss the philosophical, scientific and socio-economic conditions that have shaped the discipline.

Social psychology as a sub-discipline of psychology, inherited the philosophical incongruences of the parent with respect to dualism. This has caused many commentators and critical social scientists to question the ongoing project of research and to posit that social psychology is flawed at a basic level because of a general lack of relevance in relation to the actual needs and experiences of normal people (Jackson, 1988; Parker & Spears, 1996). This crisis of relevance stems in great measure from the unsolved problems of dualistic systems of categories in mainstream psychological science (Tolman, 1994; Lethbridge, 1992). These categorizational systems have seriously hampered coherent explanations of psychological phenomena as experienced in everyday life and are particularly evident in the representationalist theory of perception that in turn has solidified the hidden anthropology of the isolated individual. Investigatory methods based on the ideological foundation of individualism have seriously undermined coherent explanations of cultural phenomena such as human collective agency and communicative interaction (Harre & Gillet, 1994: Shotter, 1993: Strong, 1984)

Modern mainstream social psychology, particularly in North America, has evolved an identity that is deeply intertwined with the hegemony of the objective natural-scientist tradition that takes physics as its model. The lingering philosophical issues that have made the research of psychological phenomena problematic (such as the relation between sensation and perception, individual experience and culture, process and structure and a myriad of other thorny issues) have been partially obscured by the appropriation of the mainstream North American model of scientific psychological investigation that sidesteps these fundamental uncertainties. Questions that have been the central concern of psychological thought from the dawn of western philosophical investigation remained unsolved when they were hidden from view with psychology's break with departments of philosophy in the late 19th century. Considered a branch of philosophy for the early years of its modern academic life, precisely because the investigation of consciousness and the psyche intrinsically revolved around such difficult philosophical questions, psychology was abandoned by departments of philosophy in many European schools. At about the same time psychologists wanted to embrace a “truly” scientific stance to investigation: one that assumed and built upon the tenets of natural scientific methodological orthodoxy. This change was hastened by the fact that the fledgling discipline could not yet exist independently but had to look for another suitable mentor-discipline. The changes faced by the emerging discipline were different depending on the particular cultural and economic arrangements in different countries but eventually North American cultural hegemony prevailed, leading to a redefinition of psychological subject matter that used the natural science methodological toolbox.

Similar to other culturally constructed phenomena, social psychological investigative practices use categorizational principles that function in and rationalize the over-arching social projects of industrial society. The choice of investigative subject matter and the methods utilized in their investigation are those that can provide knowledge understandable and/or useful within the paradigm of western industrial and consumer culture (Jackson, 1988; Danziger, 1990). Even at an early stage in the development of the discipline it can be shown that extra-scientific, economic and cultural concerns interacted with logical and scientific matters to produce the particular form and direction that psychology and social psychology would take in the years ahead

(Danziger,1990).

In England, the redrafting of the political, economic and social landscape occurred earlier and with more ease than anywhere else in Europe. The Tudors stripped ecclesiastical institutions of many of their traditional power as early as the middle of the 16th century. The middle classes gradually became more expert in exerting their economic and political muscle and by the 19th century an industrialized society was a *fait accompli*. The scientific and philosophical underpinnings of the new industrial order did not owe its existence to the pitiful state of the University system in Britain. Both Oxford and Cambridge, the only two until the founding of the University of London in 1838, were peripheral to the rising dominant scientific paradigm owing to their ecclesiastical conservatism (Littman 1979). Loose associations of "amateurs" outside the elitist university system were undertaking the important scientific work. Most scientific work therefore was completely within the paradigm of an emerging "radical" industrial ideology. While higher education in England became largely irrelevant to hegemony of industrial culture, the same was also true in France. In both nations (and especially in France) research and teaching were separated entities thus there was no development of an organized self-perpetuating system of research (Littman 1979).

The German situation, in contrast, was more organized. Universities combined teaching and research and therefore science developed along institutional lines within the University system (Barnes and Feldman 1980). The niche that German higher education had garnered and the idealist tradition that evolved therein was due to an entirely different political atmosphere that slowed the development of industrialization. Whereas in England those challenging the old order were also working in the vanguard of scientific practice, science in Germany was conducted within an existing system that placed a high value on a plurality of philosophical considerations. Therefore, academic practitioners tended to adopt a less negative reaction to a more traditional established regime. The philosophical idealism that flourished in the German socio-political milieu that encouraged romantic and nationalist reactions to the industrial project maintained a more skeptical position towards an all-encompassing embrace of a radical, empirical individualism.

Unlike England and France, who had long since solidified their national identity, Germany in the first half of the 19th century was a loose affiliation of states and principalities that felt overshadowed by both Austria and France. In England, the void left by the failing medieval systems were filled by an understanding of a "freedom from authority" while in Germany freedom could be achieved by a collective effort to establish a German speaking nation-state. The attempt to create a freedom through a nationalistic collective enterprise solidified the adoption of a less individualistic version of scientific inquiry (Blumenthal, 1975). For instance, Johann Gottfried Herder made the distinction between the primary community of a shared culture formed through language and the secondary bond founded upon power or contract (Danziger 1983). The idea that a shared cultural identity is primary and that the individual is a product of the "cultural spirit" was highly influential in the birth of a unified Germany and was reflected both in artistic and intellectual development.

For psychology in Germany, unlike the British empiricist tradition, it was not enough merely to collect data from experimental situations: a more encompassing form of explanation was necessary. The German philosophical tradition that included Leibniz, Kant, Fichte, Hegel, Schelling and Herbart expounded persuasive arguments against an abstract, one-sided psychological materialism dominant in British Empiricism (Robinson 1982). From the German philosophical standpoint the empiricist and "associationist" psychological model of Lock seemed incompatible with findings concerning the totality of conscious experience. The formulation of Leibniz that postulated the necessity of a receptive and creative mind in the production of ideas seemed far more plausible. The influence of the idealist tradition was evident in the German model as exemplified by Wundt's psychological publications, from the beginning (Robinson 1982).

Although important, historians have until recently overlooked the fact that Wundt explicitly stated that experimentation could never amount to the sole legitimate method in understanding human psychological functioning (Danziger 1980). According to him, experimental psychology should only be considered a minor, secondary enterprise because the most important aspects of the human psyche, such as higher mental processes cannot be adequately investigated without the construction of a predominantly social-anthropological method (Rappard, 1979, Danziger, 1980). His conception of "Volkerpsychologie" which would investigate these higher mental and peculiarly cultural processes (such as memory, cognition, etc.) owes a great debt to Herbart whose model of the relationship between intra-personal and interpersonal processes is similar to some 20th century versions of systems theory. His indebtedness to Herbart in this connection is through the writings of Lazarus and Steinthal who modified the Herbartian position into one that was amenable to psychological explanation (Danziger, 1983). Wundt did not see the use of historical and comparative methodology in Volkerpsychologie as being any less objective or scientific than experimental methods. So opposite were Wundt's formulations to the British tradition, that he posited *volition to be a primary psychological category* and reflex activity to be a special adaptive evolutionary development from volitional action.

Certainly the importance of volition is deeply involved with ethical issues, one of the reasons Wundt envisaged that psychology should remain a sub-discipline of philosophy. Unfortunately, the success of psychology's growth resulted in its eventual abandonment by philosophy in German universities. As more psychologists were given chairs within philosophy, a revolt was ignited resulting in the birth of psychology as a separate discipline. Because of the relative newness of psychology as an academic field and without an amiable tie to the larger and respected departments of philosophy, the orphaned infant of psychology needed to look to, and formed an unsuitable allegiance with the natural sciences (Danziger, 1990). This would have far-reaching future affects on the conceptualization of the subject matter and methods considered appropriate in the investigation of psychological phenomena.

The Leipzig laboratory attracted many students from the United States. However Americans would find it difficult to understand the tradition of idealism in Germany because their culture was based upon very different philosophical foundations. The American constitution was, and continues to be heavily influenced by laizzer-faire, liberal economic philosophy and particularly the empirical individualist philosophy of John Locke. Many of those who returned home to the U.S. from Leipzig were not able to transcend their own ideological and cultural blinders. Experiences of the German model were filtered through empiricistic assumptions, leading to the development of an individualist version of psychology that is prevalent in North America today. Even leaving aside the immense barriers of culture and language, Wundt's most influential students were responsible for the virtual disappearance of his system by means of sheer willful misrepresentation. This tendency for recasting in accord with one's own cultural values was exemplified by Titchnerian attempts to manipulate and recast Wundt's psychological formulations and harmonize them with the additive, elementalist inductive assumptions which form the foundation of North American scientific orthodoxy grounded in the philosophy of Mill. Boring, Titchener's student, compounded the erroneous view by declaring Wundt's system to be a version of mind/body dualism combined with a very narrow anti-voluntaristic system of mental chemistry (Blumenthal 1980). Boring's view fully harmonizes and recasts Wundt's conceptual programme so that it appears that the individualist paradigm of British and North American science can be portrayed as a seamless and uncontested pedigree emanating forward from the first experimental psychological laboratory. In fact, nothing could be further from the truth.

The particular philosophical and ideological environment of continental European rationalism bred a psychological project with a particular object of investigation, allied investigative techniques and a particular harmonious mode of experimental interaction. The transplanting of psychology into the totally different ideological atmosphere of North America had far-reaching effects on the development of all these aspects of psychological investigation. Whereas, the German intellectual climate evolved through a three-stage development (reminiscent of Comte's evolutionary schematic) that started with theological allegiances, followed by a period of intense philosophical pluralism out of which science evolved, North American intellectual endeavours evolved from a two-stage development that skirted any serious experimentation with pluralities in philosophy.

In the United States everything was geared to the appropriation and domination of the natural and cultural world. North American cultural and economic systems refined the concept of humanity as individually autonomous, competitive, rational, self-directed individuals (Moscovici, 1985). Although there was some resemblance to classical intellectual pursuits, it was the world of industry that increasingly shaped the development of the universities and the direction of scientific inquiry. Psychology, transplanted from Europe, had to adapt to an atmosphere that demanded economic rationalism. Forced to prove itself in the marketplace of knowledge products if it was to survive and garner status for its practitioners, any alliance with philosophy and the investigation of subjective experience was likely to doom psychological scientific practice to a rapid demise. (Danziger, 1990). Not only were philosophical ruminations generally viewed as unscientific, but unnecessary, unproductive and perhaps even subversive.

The different approaches to the new industrial order and the history of each nation-state led to different understandings of the nature of the relation between individual consciousness and society, the object of investigation for the emerging discipline of psychology and the legitimacy of scientific methods that should be utilized. As discussed in Chapter 2, the different conceptions of meaningful, scientific theoretical systems led to a division of psychological approaches. In North America and in Britain psychological practices followed from the empiricist tradition of Bacon, Hobbes, Locke and Mill gave predominance to the objective world and an individual that was to be conceptualized as a receptacle of separated variables. This model, later paved the way for the legitimation of the measurement of abstracted aspects of individuals, in mass aggregate studies which was a project that was seminal in assuring the continuance of the discipline. In the competitive market-oriented culture of North America, the knowledge products resulting from the mass measurement of society would make psychology a useful tool in the evolution of industrialism and garner funding and status for it' practitioners (Danziger, 1990)

In continental Europe, but especially in Germany, a rationalist tradition continued that stemmed from Descartes, giving primacy to the ordering principle of rational ideas. As was noted previously, it is paradoxical that the empiricist tradition that was a reaction to the Cartesian position regarding the primacy of the internal ordering principles only exacerbated the division between subjective and objective aspects by emphasizing the opposing pole. Empiricism and rationalism together actually consolidated the Cartesian notion that the individual is separated from the world and should be considered the seminal unit of psychological analysis. In addition, it led to the development of a perceptual theory of representationalism, which radically divided sensation from perception. This duality has been a major stumbling block to an understanding of everyday human experiences, including coherent explanations of individual consciousness, human agency, communicative interaction and the relation between individuals and cultural institutions.

The vast majority of mainstream psychologists today do not recognize themselves to be "Cartesian" because they rightly proclaim that they do not support the separation of mind and body. However, substance dualism can be shown to be a relatively unimportant facet of Descartes system and that the lasting relevance for psychological practices is greatly misunderstood. As previously discussed in chapter 2, Descartes gave two differing renditions of perception: one in article XXXV of The Passions and another in The Optics (Tolman & Robinson, 1995). The problematic dualism for psychology, and which deepens the substance dualism given by Descartes in The Passions, is the radical separation between the experiencing subject and the objective world. According to the more sophisticated discussion of these matters, we are tragically separated by the play of nervous energy and we can experience little of the true qualities of the "world outside". It is these assumptions of dualism as described in The Optics that has led modern psychologists to generally subscribe to the three-moment scheme of perception (Input - central processing module - output). In addition, the components are generally connected by a process of one-way mechanical causation. This is the first example of and reference point for modern representationalist theories of perception.

At a meta-theoretical level another important duality stemming from the acceptance of Cartesianism was imported into psychology and from there affected the development of social-psychological investigation. This was the further separation of scientific and philosophical realms under positivism. According to this doctrine, science alone supplies the only rational explanation of the world and is defined in opposition to "anti-rationalism" common to many strands of philosophy (Boeselager, 1975).

This movement started with Comte in the 1830's, was influential into the mid 1940's evolving through some different versions during this time. In general, this appeal to science was seen as a "positive" move out of the philosophical stalemate engaged in by "the negativists" involved in the doldrums of metaphysical and philosophical debate. Such ruminations were seen to be ensnaring "real" progress towards the social good. In later developments of positivism, the combination of J.S. Mill's inductive empirical model and Spencer's sometimes totalitarian evolutionary positivism resulted in the acceptance that science should be limited to empiricism and neutral on any moral or metaphysical issues (Kolakowski, 1972).

After several reformulations, later particularly virulent versions emerging in logical positivism claimed that a divide should be drawn between language (considered a fitting object of scientific investigation) and objects and experiences. In an effort to overcome the duality caused by the barrier of the senses, this school had created another duality by erecting a formalist barrier of language. Although different members of the Vienna Circle proffered differing views, the position eventually adopted sought to unify scientific inquiry. This unification was thought to be accomplishable with the reduction of chemistry and biology to physics and the reduction of psychology to neurophysiology (Feigl, 1969). This reformulation had a lasting affect on psychology as it introduced yet another source of dualistic foundations providing a foundation for behaviorism, particularly in the way important subjects such as cognition and imagination were negated as fitting areas for investigation. In the scientific project of behaviourism, everything could (at least theoretically) be reduced to behaviour.

Additionally, positivism had a further and longer lasting affect on social-psychological investigatory practice as it provided a template for scientific research that could exclude all “unscientific” moral and ideological considerations. It helped to create the myth of an “objective”, value-neutral scientific experiment by hiding the extra-scientific, economic and cultural embeddedness of investigative practices. This belief helped promote the discipline to view itself as removed and above the ordinary messiness of everyday life, thus allowing scientific social psychology a privileged position from which to make objective observations. It is this conceit, among other problems, which incurred the wrath of critical psychologists and other commentators throughout the 20th century.

In North America, during the early twentieth century, "social" was prefixed to individual psychological processes and social psychology was born as a sub-discipline (Jackson, 1988). Social actions were approached as being just a continuation of the types of processes that explained individual actions, only there were some further complications that required qualitatively similar explanations with the help of abstract and reductionistic research methodology (Billig, Condor, Edwards, Gane, Middleton and Radley, 1988). North American experimental social psychology combined the individualistic paradigm of Locke and Mills with a harmonious base in certain continental European conceptions rooted in "crowd psychology". In the nineteenth century, Sighele and Le Bon theorizied on the divide between the "rational" individual and the irrational emotional automaton that individuals apparently appeared to be transformed into, when part of a crowd (Danziger 1992). It is interesting to note that Le Bon saw the crowd as partaking in activities that were contrary to "their most obvious interests", as individuals. This particular view can perhaps be at least partially explained by the relatively sheltered social position of philosophers and scholars at this historical juncture. Academics and philosophers were considered part and parcel of an elite, whose interests were opposed to the predominantly proletarian composition of crowds within industrial cities and their rising discontent with the economic status quo. As Europe became more urban and living circumstances deteriorated in industrial cities, the under-privileged became increasingly militant in support of their claims for just treatment. It is quite understandable that such commentators would see "the crowd" as “irrational” and needing diffusion and control by those whose interests are supported by the predominating system of social relations. It must have been confusing to these commentators that such irrationality witnessed in crowds was so opposite to the more usual observation of “rational” acquiescence to their “betters”, when common people were approached alone.

Later, Moede derived many of his ideas for experimental work from these conceptions and attempted to measure this assumed contrast between individuals and individuals in groups, in artificial laboratory situations (Danziger, 1992). This conceptualization of social life harmonized nicely with the North American individualist paradigm. At Harvard, F.H. Allport continued this model in laboratory experimentation, measuring performance of individuals in completing what were to become, the prototypical "meaningless" tasks. The future thrust of the sub-discipline could be encapsulated by his statement that “There is no psychology of groups which is not essentially and entirely a psychology of the individual.” (Allport, 1924).

Experiments of this type, measuring abstracted "variables" in experimental situations came to be accepted as <u>the</u> way to conceptualize and investigate social relations. Social relations were generally viewed as merely the action of individuals as stimuli to each other. To exert the necessary controls and to reduce as much “error variance” as possible these studies were increasingly carried out in artificial situations, comparing only a minimum of operationally defined behaviours at any one time. Using methods common in the parent discipline, social-psychology adopted the method of operationalizing and abstracting variables that were amenable to quantification. According to the mainstream view, social psychologists regard their discipline as an attempt to understand and explain how the thought, feeling and behaviour of individuals are influenced by the actual, imagined or implied presence of others (Allport, 1985). The promotion of the "rational" individual as a receptacle of measurable “variables” became a template for a conception of social life. The dubiousness surrounding the confrontation of the "irrationality" of social processes is evident in the large body of investigation within the paradigm of social influence or conformity (Coughlan and Johnson 1991). Here it seems most obvious that social psychological investigative practices and theoretical assumptions are conceptualized in terms of the effect of social stimuli as generally corrupting influences on individuals. In addition, the contextualization of the investigation of social interaction by the predominant socio-economic culture helped to define social relations merely in terms of instrumentality. Conceptions of social relations were being gradually impoverished by the extension of cultural metaphors that applied an “exchange value” logic to human interaction and this too was internalized by theoretical narratives of social-psychological explanatory paradigms .

The end of World War II and the defeat of the Fascist and Nazi project which relied heavily on the scientific "discovery" of general laws of behaviour in order to manipulate a collectivist conformity, created a backlash in North American social science. Given this context, it was for very good reasons that the post-fascist North American social scientific project mounted a critique on the irrationality of organized collective behaviour and reinforced the individualistic tenor already existing in North American culture. It is paradoxical to note that the individualist reaction to the evils of fascist conformity would be used for practical purposes of prediction and control of individuals living in a mass society. The group was conceptualized as opposed to the individual with the tacit assumption that it was the group that created a negative influence, corrupting the higher rational nature of the individual in a one-way process. (Coughlan and Johnson, 1991; Stephenson, Bavelas, Coughlan and Johnson, 1993).

> Of all the attempted unitary explanations of human social behaviour, suggestion and imitation are the most direct ancestors of contemporary social psychology. The problem of social influence. . . is pervasive throughout (social psychology); in fact it has been proposed that social psychology is the study of influence.
>
> (Jackson, 1988, p.19)

Social aspects were generally seen as yet another form of stimulus, devoid of context, history, culture and function. From this point forward, the mainstream of North American social-psychological practice continued within this paradigm, assuming the anthropology of the isolated individual and constructed ways to measure elementalized behaviours as separated "variables" (Solano, 1989; Sampson, 1988; Senn 1989; Tolman, 1994). The norms of a certain kind of experimental practice were now equated with the essential nature of the social reality to be investigated (Danziger, 1992).

In a socio-economic climate that relied heavily on individual competitiveness, labour mobility, efficiency and productivity, social-psychology could find itself a valued identity by catering to the knowledge needs of bureaucratic agencies by finding ways to engineer a conformity of individualism (Danziger, 1990). A collateral result of this client-producer relationship was a general atrophy in knowledge that might promote collective efforts of resistance and emancipation. An industrial mass society needed mass information to improve bureaucratic control and the "efficiency" of the economic system. If psychology could build a scientific model that included the prediction of human behaviour, its success would be assured. It was these needs, which provided a market for the disciplines of psychology and social psychology and psychological research was reorganized in order to harmonize psychological knowledge products to suit the needs of the cultural and economic marketplace. Discussions concerning the meaningful explanation of the genesis and reality of consciousness, especially social consciousness was considered secondary, mostly irrelevant and in some quarters, probably subversive. Knowledge that assumed the identity of humans as individuals and could measure certain attributes of individuals, en masse, could produce technologies that measured predictability that augmented bureaucratic control. In the overall social project of the appropriation of natural and human resources, such technologies could demand wealth and status for its practitioners (Danziger, 1990).

Out of several existing models of psychological investigation it was the Galtonian statistical model that would fit the bill in terms of providing a way that individuals could be reified, compared, standardized and measured (Danziger, 1990). This led to the relative increase in data that was derived from aggregate studies of individuals' scores on abstract "variables" (rather than single-subject investigations), and the generation and application of sophisticated statistical comparisons. It is ironic that the model of psychology that adopted an understanding that legitimated the individual as <u>the</u> unit of investigation, ended up with a measure of abstracted <u>decontextualized</u> mean scores and deviations on particular operationalized behavioural variables. The living individual subjects disappear in this reformulation. Most of the important facets of individuals are now "controlled" within the experimental design or parcelled out as "random error". Increasingly, research data were generated from questionnaires that internalized this model. Primarily, their use was at first designed for the benefit of military and educational bureaucracies and later governmental and corporate institutions increasingly used such methods. (Danziger 1990, Jones, 1985).

While mainstream North American psychology increasingly identified its interest with the success of the relationship with bureaucratic institutions those on the front-line in industry were making startling discoveries. Taking subjectivities into account in the mass production process helped to ameliorate workplace social problems that were interfering with the efficiency of the accumulation of industrial capital (Taylor & Brown, 1979). In this regard, the work of W. Edwards Denning demonstrated that the improvement of quality in the manufacturing process depended upon the acknowledgment of the centrality of co-operative relations among industrial workers. Such workplace co-operative relations were found to be linked to worker self-esteem which was an important facet in the attempt to maintain high production quotas along with the manufacture of products of a uniformly high quality. His findings are in direct contradiction to the elementalized mass-industrial production-line methods typical of Taylorism. However, these findings did not greatly affect social-psychological theoreatical models or research methodology. Even in industrial psychology, the goal remained to gather information concerning the external correlates of such findings rather than an explication of underlying inter-subjective processes that explained such phenomena (Taylor & Brown, 1979, Coughlan, 1995).

> We have lost contact with ourselves, and our own natural being, and are driven by an imperative of domination that condemns us to ceaseless battle against nature both within and around us . . . with its sharp sense that human beings had been triply divided by modern reason - within themselves, between themselves, and from the natural world.
>
> (Taylor, 1991, p 94)

Social psychologists, at least those who are historically minded, now refer to the 1970s as a period of crisis. There are differing explanations of the roots and validity of the criticism and reappraisal that took place after what has been called social psychology's "Golden Age" from 1947 to 1970 (Apfelbaum, 1992). This period of expansion after World War II resulted in the creation and demarcation of different fields, each busily collecting data and guarding intellectual “property”. Only a few practitioners were engaged in attempting to develop coherent theoretical frameworks that could make sense of the enormous expansion of knowledge claims generated by predominantly empirical experimental and quasi-experimental research programmes (Jackson, 1988). While it would seem a practical necessity that individual investigators should concentrate on a manageable area (Buxton, 1985), this had a tendency for the separation of schools of thought and for each new school to focus on certain aspects, while ignoring important scientific findings in other schools (Hilgard, 1987). The development of a coherent field of scientific knowledge should require more than “mere fact gathering nor isolated hypothesis testing but thoughtful systematic approaches” (Hilgard and Bower, 1966).

> The absence of a single scientific system that would embrace and combine all of our contemporary knowledge in psychology results in a situation in which every new factual discovery . . . that is more than a simple accumulation of details is forced to create its own special theory and explanatory system. In order to understand facts and relationships investigators are forced to create their own psychology - one of many psychologies.
>
> (Vygotsky, 1956, p 57-58).

This "piecemeal" or "jigsaw puzzle" approach to creating the discipline and the claim to scientific respectability, in the minds of many critical psychologists, eventually started to crumble under the sheer weight of unconnected and often divergent conclusions. Social psychology, by the late sixties, was also roundly criticized from both within and without for the growing divergence between the existing theoretical frameworks and the new realities of the post-war social and sexual revolutions as well as for other epistemological, methodological and ethical incongruencies (Jackson, 1988; Leary, 1989). Critical voices were attempting to save the discipline from a relevancy crisis that stemmed in part from the construction of a self-serving "angelic" public relations persona that attempted to deflect any criticism (Hurtig & Pichevin, 1986). It was certainly an important progressive move that ethical shortcomings in research practices were addressed vigorously. However, such improvements were made at the expense of a more comprehensive re-evaluation of underlying methodological and theoretical concerns. Eventually, with the end of the 1970's, the crisis was happily consigned to the past with the mainstream of the discipline claiming the crisis averted, even solved. Many problematic areas highlighted in this decade (e.g. relevance issues, individualistic methodology) were swept under the rug, and in the view of many critical voices, the underlying conditions of the relevancy crisis remained intact (Jackson, 1988, Danziger, 1980). Apart from peripheral critical voices, the mainstream re-embraced the abstracted individual as the natural unit of analysis and the continuation of psychological measurement in terms of abstracted operationalized variables continued unabated.

In the case of North American mainstream social science the use of the label "value-neutral" regarding these empirical practices was reinforced. Results provided by designs that assumed the anthropology of the isolated individual tended to be understood as positive "evidence" of the reductionist, individualistic and hierarchical nature of both physical and social reality (Solano, 1989). However, theoretical assumptions and methods accepted as bona-fide in terms of these assumptions, along with the results of such designs, can and often do, form a self-perpetuating tautology. Such circular logic can perpetuate itself because it is seldom recognized that the same ideology can be present in the theoretical foundations of all these stages of the investigative process. If one believes that the social experiences are essentially concerning the the mutual stimulation of individuals who are receptacles of discrete behavioural, cognitive, emotional and personality variables this will be assumed in the methods used to test this assumption. It should be no surprise that the results will tend to support this belief. Over time, continued reproduction tends to promote this invisibility (Foucault 1984, Dant, 1991). However, more critical commentators on the periphery of the discipline have described this self-referential system as "the shame of social-psychology" (Folger,1987).

The final stage in the harmonizing of psychological investigation with the modern industrial project was the appropriation of the history of science. Particular "histories" of psychology were offered for consumption in which the values of industrial culture were inserted into the narrative either as the culmination of technical progress or the culmination of the progression of the work of a succession of great "heroic" technicians (Jackson, 1988). Thus, these particular narratives obscure the relatively recent plurality and relative equality of psychological systems, choices of objects of investigation and methods. To many mainstream practitioners, a study of the history of social psychology can be justified only if it shows the relevance of historical backgrounds to present-day foregrounds. Certainly this was Allport's (1985) view and one which has received more than a smattering of support. Such views have had an unfortunate influence on the teaching of the history of psychology and psychological theories at the undergraduate level, especially since this subject is often considered a luxury during these times of economic rationalization and cost-cutting in higher educational facilities.

The result is that the social embeddedness of scientific inquiry has become hidden from view and the particular methods used in particular projects have become the <u>only scientifically defensible methods.</u> The study of concrete culturally embedded consciousness was generally replaced with the investigation of behaviour (in its raw form or later translated as connected to inferred cognitive structures), biological and/or physiological aspects of perception or brain functioning. As important as these types of investigation are, the natural scientific paradigm and the accredited methods linked to this tradition are not completely adaptable to the wholly different subject matter of an intrinsically cultural organism, without producing knowledge that is incomplete. Redefining the subject matter of psychological and especially social-psychological phenomena to be consistent with the toolbox of available methods as imported from natural science, more often than not impoverishes the kinds of questions that can be asked as well as limiting practical applicability in the field of human need satisfaction.

Human psychology exists at the intersection of biological, physiological, individual and cultural realms and to do justice to this unique object of investigation, we need to carefully preserve the natural relations and inter-penetratedness of these co-constituting aspects without using technologies that simply reduce to one or another of these terms. The potential explanatory power of social-psychological investigation has remained largely unfulfilled, owing to the continuing attempt to simplify the subject matter to make it amenable to the inherited toolbox of methods. Instead of broadening discussion to investigate the insufficiency of predominant conceptions of the subject matter of psychology and tackling the underlying mismatch of subject matter and methods, mainstream practitioners erroneously conflate the particular model of scientific investigation that assumes reductive methods, with science itself. This has serious repercussions in terms of the sufficiency of social-psychological formulations to provide reasonable discussions of personal agency and communication, both of which are largely beyond the reach of presently accepted reductionistic and operationalist, variable models of investigative practice. In addition, the complicity of social psychology in projects to discover knowledge that would be of greatest interest to institutions of social control tends to make it more unlikely that any coherent conception of agency would take shape because of the discipline's commitment to prediction. The immense emancipatory potential of social-psychology is thus mostly neutralized as the sub-discipline has become unwittingly complicit in the agenda of dominant extra-scientific and especially socio-economic interests that are not especially supportive of the ordinary persons' desires to gain greater insight and control over their lives.

The dualistic foundations of mainstream North American psychology, in particular representationalist models of perception, have provided the template for theoretical and methodological developments in social-psychological formulations. These foundations have been reinforced and have interacted with other dichotomies, most notably the separation of individual from cultural and socio-economic aspects. These contexts have been artificially separated from an abstract operationalized model of the individual conceived as a container of discrete variables. These conceptions bare little resemblance to actual human experiences. The allegiance of mainstream North American social psychology to dichotomization has interacted with extra-scientific commitments of the sub-discipline to consumers of its knowledge products to create an impoverished model of socialness that is primarily focused on the prediction of individual behaviour for the benefit of elite factions in society. This model is not only insufficient to explain the phenomenon of social and cultural behaviour, it actually mitigates against a coherent account of human agency and an emancipatory psychology. The following chapter will extend a discussion of the influence of dualistic trends by tracing holistic and dualistic aspects of conceptions of health and medicine. This historically contextualized discussion will show that as medicine has evolved into a predominantly scientific enterprise it also tended to internalize and reinforce a basic Cartesian antipathy between mind and body. In addition, the professionalization of scientific medicine also tended to preserve the power of practitioners while simultaneously abrogating the agency of patients in their desire to gain information and to act in their own health interests.

Social Psychology

1

Introduction

Learning outcomes

By the end of this chapter you should have an understanding of:

- what is meant by 'critical thinking' and 'critical literature'
- one 'conventional' account of the emergence of social psychology
- a critique of that conventional account
- an understanding of how Kuhn's work on paradigms is relevant to thinking about the interpretation of data within social psychology
- an understanding of some of the issues that Billig's work regarding 'fictional things' raises for social psychology
- an understanding of why differences between social psychologists are not readily settled by an empirical investigation
- an awareness of some of the key approaches to social psychological issues within the field
- an ability to contrast what some of these approaches might bring to our understanding of a particular topic within social psychology.

On 25 January 2011, a wave of popular protest began in Egypt. It is thought that it was, in part, influenced by the 'Tunisian revolution', which saw the overthrow of the Tunisian president. Protests, sometimes referred to as the 'Arab Spring', spread throughout several countries in North Africa and the Middle East, including Bahrain, Libya, Syria and Yemen. These momentous, historically significant events pose a challenge for social psychology – what can social psychology add to our understanding of these phenomena?

Source: Amr Abdallah Dalsh/Reuters

People celebrate in Egypt on 8 February 2011, following protests – known as the '25 January revolution' – that resulted in the overthrow of President Hosni Mubarak's regime.

We might wonder whether there was some shift in attitudes that precipitated the protests or, if they have not changed, how the attitudes came to be expressed in the form of demonstrations on a scale not seen before in these countries. We might wonder, too, if the protesters' identities are relevant – are their actions related to some shared 'Arab' identity, for example, that made the occurrences in one 'Arab' country relevant to others? While many of the protests were peaceful, what can we make of aggression on the part of protesters and government police, army and security forces – should we explain it in terms of inner drives, the immediate situation or wider ideological issues? Finally, what are we to make of the 'social influence' that appears to be at work? How is it, for example, that some Libyan pilots followed orders to attack Libyan protestors, while others defected after receiving such orders? Even the way in which these events are explained and made sense of can be investigated in terms of social psychological topics.

Events such as these can be useful in getting us to think about some of the core topics within social psychology – the sorts of topics addressed in this text. We need not be limited to these, though – we could think about all types of things we notice and experience in our everyday lives, things that will not make it on to the news, but are perhaps important precisely because they are such common occurrences, and we could ask what understanding social psychology provides. As we turn to social psychology, however, we should perhaps ask questions not only in terms of, 'What has social psychology got to say about this?' but also of social psychology itself. That is, we should not only use social psychology to cast light on events we seek to understand but also use these events themselves to question and perhaps trouble what the multiple perspectives within social psychology have to offer.

Introduction

As you read and think about social psychology, you may find that it answers all of the questions that you have about why both news and everyday events occur as they do. You may find within its very varied ideas enough to make sense of it all and satisfy your desire to understand 'Why?' Equally, you might not. That second reaction, which may involve disappointment, perhaps disenchantment, is worth cherishing. If you feel that social psychology does not quite address the issues or does not provide an adequate understanding, is contradictory or does not even identify the issues that should be addressed, you might be onto something. Thinking in this way could be an important part of your critical engagement with social psychology – who knows where it could lead you?

This sort of critical thinking about social psychology is exactly what this book tries to empower you to do. That is, it seeks to encourage you to engage with each topic in social psychology with an understanding of some of the different perspectives that may be relevant and an ability to question and challenge the ideas that are presented – including what you might think of as the author's own perspective. The book covers areas that are typically regarded as the key topics of social psychology – so there are chapters dealing with the self and identity, relationships, attribution, attitudes, stereotypes, prosocial behaviour, social influence, aggression and intergroup conflict, plus communication and interaction. It endeavours to engage with these, perhaps familiar, topics in a *critical* manner.

Chapter overview

This introductory chapter aims to start to equip you for your critical engagement with social psychology. It does not try to turn you into a critical (or any other sort of) social psychologist, but it does seek to give you some different ways of thinking about social psychology and its development and an awareness of different perspectives within the discipline.

The chapter starts by reflecting on the two different ways in which this text aims to be critical: first, this book introduces literature that challenges much of traditional social psychology and is sometimes described as *critical literature;* second, it seeks to encourage *critical thinking* about all of the social psychological literature that it reviews.

Like many introductory chapters in social psychology texts, a fairly conventional account of how social psychology has emerged will be given. In this account, social psychology is positioned as emerging from the success of experiment-based psychology – forging its particular concern in terms of the, largely experimental, investigation of how people perceive and make sense of their social worlds. In contrast to most texts, however, this conventional understanding is then radically questioned and an alternative understanding outlined. This alternative approach, informed partly by Billig (2008), pays attention to the neglected aspects of the famous founding figures of psychology in general and social psychology in particular. It also brings on to centre stage those who rarely receive recognition for their contributions to thinking about psychological and social psychological issues. Listening to these neglected voices in this way gives critical ideas a more central and well-established place within social psychology, making engagement with them a matter of necessity rather than choice.

The issue of why social psychologists do not agree with each other is addressed. Some attention is given to Kuhn's work on paradigms to illustrate the idea that certain commitments – for example, to particular meta-theoretical perspectives – can guide how we define the issues, collect the data and interpret the findings. This makes it relatively unlikely that the research will question the very commitments through which it was conceived, executed and interpreted. Attention is also given to Billig's (2011) work on 'fictional things' – which questions some of the ways that social psychologists create or 'call into being' entities, concepts (such as schemas, deindividuation and social categorisation), that can come to be treated as 'real' entities. Some of these ideas are illustrated first by reference to research into majority and minority influence and then through a relatively detailed review of a vividly debated piece of (televised) research by Reicher and Haslam (2006a, 2006b) about which Zimbardo (2006) expressed serious misgivings.

Having considered the issues of disagreement at a somewhat abstract level, albeit illustrated with specific cases, attention is given to some of the specific types of theoretical commitments that are relevant to social psychology. Ten different – though interrelated – streams of thought within social psychology are briefly touched on. These ideas are not neatly packaged and equivalent to each other in form or scope, neither are they each relevant to the different topics addressed throughout the text. They do, however, illustrate some of the sorts of ideas that have informed several specific social psychological theories and reoccur across different topics in social psychology. Getting an initial grasp of some of these differing perspectives provides a useful key for unlocking a number of debates right across the discipline. Following this, there is a very brief overview of the scope and aims of this book.

1.1 Two aspects of being critical

As mentioned above, this text endeavours to encourage two (interconnected) ways of being *critical* in or of social psychology: critical in terms of the type of ideas and literature that we draw on and critical as a practice – a questioning way of engaging with the ideas and research that we encounter.

Critical literature

It is worth emphasising that social psychology does not simply comprise *a* traditional literature and *a* critical literature. This book tries to do justice to some of the many different perspectives that inform social psychology – some of which we could think of as more 'traditional', others more 'critical'. These terms 'traditional' and 'critical' are far from perfect, but are used here to recognise that a range of (critical) social psychology literature has developed raising questions unasked in other (traditional) social psychological research. For some critical psychologists, such as Parker (1999), there is an interest in seeking to identify what sorts of ideas, understandings and assumptions are dominant or *privileged* in psychology and what ideological or other power-related work these accounts *do*. For others, such as Edwards and Potter (1992), there is perhaps less of an overt interest in the power-related implications of assumptions in psychology. Instead, there is more attention paid to challenging the ways in which questions about how the social world works have been reduced to individual cognitive processes rather than interactional language practices. Both perspectives – and others that also might be classed as 'critical' for the sake of this text – raise challenges about fundamental assumptions, methodological practices and interpretations of data within much of psychology – particularly, in terms of our current concerns, experimental, social psychology.

For critical psychologists, ideas and assumptions held by psychologists – even, perhaps especially, those which seem to be agreed on by most – need to be exposed, considered against alternative ideas and have their implications identified. One example of this is the notion that the individual is, or should be, the main focus of psychological and social psychological accounts of human behaviour. Social psychology is a particularly interesting example of this 'individualism' as, while it explicitly or implicitly claims to be about *social* phenomena, it often winds up – as Billig (2008) and Greenwood (2004a, 2004b) note – somewhere inside the individual's head. Thus, social psychological theories often emphasise how the *individual perceives* the social world and depict this as being at the root of their behaviour in interaction with others. These 'individualising' social psychology theories could be understood as reflecting assumptions – for example, about behaviour being rooted in the perceiving mind of separate individuals – that are present in both much of social psychology and in many Western cultures in general.

Many critical social psychologists – including Prilleltensky (1989) and Fox (1985) – note that psychology's individualising theories about human behaviour – particularly what becomes defined as 'negative' human behaviour, such as aggression – often draw attention away from societal issues. If the *individual's social cognitions* are to blame for social ills, then, implicitly, it is they *and nothing else* that need to change. This approach implicitly endorses the status quo – any existing inequalities in economic and political power are able to carry on without even a passing comment as the 'problem' to be fixed is located not in power relations, nor political or economic disadvantage, but in the individual's mind. For many critical thinkers, social psychology is not being politically neutral or apolitical if it focuses attention on the individual rather than social factors; instead, it is merely being politically naïve. From this perspective, not referring to or not recognising the influence that issues of power and inequality have on people's lives does not remove that influence – it just leaves it unchallenged and, implicitly, endorsed.

Critical social psychologists – though differing from each other in many important respects – often emphasise an alternative take on social phenomena. Thus, in place of individual cognition we find – as Billig (2008) exemplifies – an emphasis on the ways in which our thoughts are tied to and shaped by their cultural and historical context. Rather than our attitudes, beliefs, stereotypes (and other cognitions) being spontaneously created by individuals in cognitive isolation, they are understood as interlinked with the surrounding understandings and debates of the time and culture in which they are manifest. Similarly, critical social psychologists – such as Sampson (1988, 1993) and Gergen (2009a, 2009b) – challenge the idea that self is best thought of as a separate entity and the primary cause of human behaviour, considering the way in which the other and the relation with other *is* who we are. Some of these ideas and their historical roots in the development of social psychology are considered below, but, for now, it is worth noting that this is no 'merely academic' debate (if that term can ever be used) – at the very least it has profound consequences for how we think about our lives as well as every single topic in this book.

Critical thinking in social psychology

It is not uncommon to be asked to do critical thinking in social psychology. You might have already encountered essay titles that require you to 'critically discuss' or 'critically evaluate' certain aspects of psychology, but it is not always clear what this means or how to go about it.

One way of thinking about it is to recognise that, in your everyday life, you almost certainly already engage in some forms of critical thinking. Think about the last time you had a discussion with someone where you genuinely disagreed with their point of view – when you argued about ideas and the evidence for those ideas. Even with seemingly trivial decisions, such as deciding which mobile phone to buy, you may have to weigh different ideas about the various attributes of each phone and perhaps evaluate some of the claims that are made. Perhaps watching or listening to politicians, you are aware of not taking all that they say at face value – you might even question some of the statistical evidence that they cite to support their claims. In all of these ways, and numerous others, you are already doing some of the sort of critical thinking that is relevant for social psychology. Whenever we evaluate claims, weigh evidence and consider counter-arguments, we are, at some level, doing critical thinking.

With social psychology, you might not feel inclined or empowered to question and challenge in quite the same way as you do when you have an argument with a friend, weigh up a purchasing decision or listen to a politician. First, you might not want to – you may want answers about why relationships fail and why people are sometimes aggressive rather than an appreciation of different perspectives on these issues. This approach however, fails to recognise that the clash of ideas is a feature of social psychology. The different theories within each topic in social psychology do *not* fit together neatly like a jigsaw – instead, they contradict and challenge one another. Also, it takes debate to be a negative when it could be viewed as one of the most positive features of the discipline. The fact that social psychology involves debate suggests there is some vibrant intellectual activity involved – the discipline is alive. Thales of Miletus, who was an ancient Greek often taken to be the founder of Western philosophy, used to say, 'Here's my teaching take it and improve upon it' – that is, he encouraged critical thinking about the ideas he gave rather than rote learning of them. The debates within social psychology afford us something of the same opportunity to join in the thinking about the discipline. By joining in the debate we become part of the development of ideas within social psychology.

A second barrier to critical thinking within social psychology is that, while willing, we may not feel able to debate. Again, this idea tends to assume that social psychology is rather more consensual than it actually is – realising something of the debates in the discipline, both historically and in the present, can be quite empowering for those wishing to join in the debate. At this stage, you might point to the empirical base within social psychology and ask, 'How can I question that?' The development of social psychology involves just that sort of questioning of both theories and empirical data – some of which starts with a sense of struggle with the ideas or data presented. Indeed, the discipline of social psychology has developed from people struggling with the existing ideas and trying to forge something better. You may at first feel that questions about ideas in social psychology are like blocks to your understanding – obstacles that have to be cleared up so you can get on with the business of learning – but another way of thinking about them is our questioning *is* our learning. If we can stay with our questions, let them develop, see where they take us and use them to open up debates with different perspectives, then they are a fantastic resource for deepening our understanding and being a participant in social psychology rather than just an onlooker.

1.2 The emergence and development of social psychology – a conventional history and some unconventional problems

There are many different ways of presenting the emergence and development of social psychology. One fairly common version is outlined in Box 1.1 before alternative understandings are considered.

In Box 1.1 social psychology is seen as emerging following, and as a consequence of, the work of Wundt (who wrote *Principles of physiological psychology* and founded a psychological laboratory) and McDougall (who wrote another text entitled *An introduction to social psychology*). A combination of the behaviourists' interest in the external environment and the gestalt psychologists' interest in perception is seen as helping to identify the broad concern of social psychologists with how individuals perceive their social world and the empirical investigation of topics relevant to this concern.

Wundt is typically portrayed as initiating modern psychology through his development of experimental methods to investigate aspects of mental processing. Wundt wrote the highly influential textbook *Grundzüge der physiologischen psychologie* (*Principles of physiological psychology*) in 1873–1874 (1904) and established arguably the first laboratory specifically designed for the study of psychology in Leipzig in 1879.

Wundt's psychology – often referred to as *physiological psychology* – managed to combine two fields that many of his contemporaries were concerned with – namely, physiology and philosophy. In physiology, there was a concern with how we can best understand sensations, the nervous system and the brain. In philosophy there was a particular interest in issues such as how we arrive at a knowledge about the world and how we can best understand the nature of consciousness.

Wundt is typically depicted as pioneering an empirical programme for addressing these issues that relied on experiments: 'The introduction of the experimental method into psychology was originally due to the modes of procedure in physiology' (Wundt, 1897, cited in Manicas, 1987 p. 63).

McDougall's publication of *An introduction to social psychology* in 1908 is sometimes seen as the time when social psychology became a recognised subdiscipline within

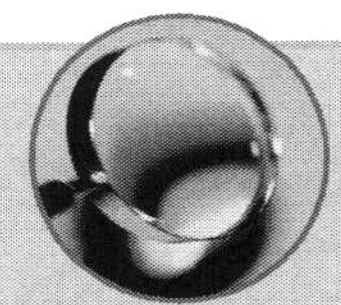

Box 1.1 FOCUS
One understanding of the emergence of social psychology

One understanding of how social psychology emerged from psychology is given here. The suggestion is that Wundt provides the broad context of experimental psychology, out of which McDougall starts to carve social psychology. The specific social perception interest is depicted as emerging from the confluence of behaviourism and gestalt psychology.

Wilhelm Maximillian Wundt
Wundt established experimental psychology as a discipline with his major psychology text *Principles of physiological psychology* (1904 [1873–1874]) and the first dedicated psychology laboratory (1879).

William McDougall
McDougall published what is sometimes considered to be the first social psychology textbook – *An introduction to social psychology* (1908).

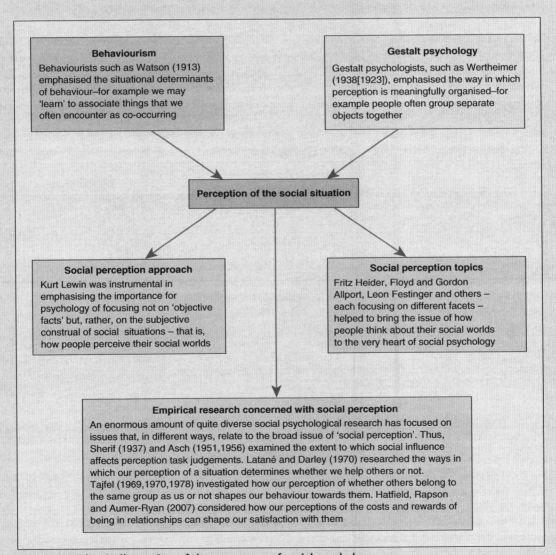

Figure 1.1 A 'typical' overview of the emergence of social psychology

psychology. McDougall's specific attention to instincts in his text certainly did not chart the course for subsequent social psychology (as it was to remain a relatively small part of social psychology in the future). Also, his interest in eugenics, understandably and perhaps rightly, did much to estrange him from others (except during a brief spell in the 1920s and 1930s when eugenics became popular). Mc Dougall, however, can be understood as offering some continuity with Wundt's empirical approach to the discipline and an important counterpoint to behaviourism – particularly as represented by Watson (who is briefly discussed below).

The specific focus of much of current social psychology on social perception can be seen as linked to the gestalt psychologists' interest in the meaningful organisation of perception. One example of this is found in Wertheimer's (1938 [1923]) work, which considered how individual elements can come to be apprehended as grouped in various ways, often – as in Box 1.2 – based on proximity, with proximal elements being perceived as forming some distinct 'whole'. Gestalt psychologists' attention to the way that stimuli are meaningfully organised in the process of perception tended to consider highly simplistic physical phenomenon and some papers – such as Wertheimer's (1938[1923]) classic – did not present any empirical data to support their argument.

What is sometimes depicted as a complementary emphasis came from behaviourist psychology. Pavlov's (1927) research with dogs suggested that a neutral stimuli (a bell) could be conditioned to trigger a target response behaviour (salivation) if it was repeatedly presented with a stimuli (such as food) that automatically brought about that target response behaviour. Watson and Rayner (1920) took the idea that, by repeated pairing, one stimuli could come to have a very similar effect to another quite distinct stimuli in their notorious experiment with a child referred to as 'little Albert'. Little Albert was 'taught' to be afraid of a fluffy white rabbit after having heard a loud noise each time he was exposed to the rabbit.

In this way, behaviourism could readily demonstrate 'evidence' for its own success – for example, showing that a fear response had been learned using the principles of classical conditioning. This empiricism appeared all the more scientific given behaviourism's commitment to identifying causal links between highly specific variables. This scientific, empirical emphasis was an attractive feature of the behaviourist perspective for North American academics – especially when coupled with its message of individual self-determinism – as, by arranging the environment, individuals could be enabled to do or achieve all manner of things. These appealing features of behaviourism led to it being the dominant North American approach in psychology until the 'cognitive revolution' of the late 1950s.

The social psychology that emerged from the confluence of behaviourism and gestalt psychology had a particular interest in empirical – and especially experimental – data concerned with social perception. In different ways, these concerns can be seen as important in the work of Fritz Heider, Floyd and Gordon Allport and Leon Festinger, among others. One figure who particularly exemplifies this attention to individuals' perceptions of their social environment is Kurt Lewin.

Lewin (1943, p. 308) gave the following illustration of the importance of the perceiving individual: 'If an individual sits in a room trusting that the ceiling will not come down, should only his "subjective probability" be taken into account for predicting behavior or should we also consider the "objective probability" of the ceiling's coming down as determined by engineers? To my

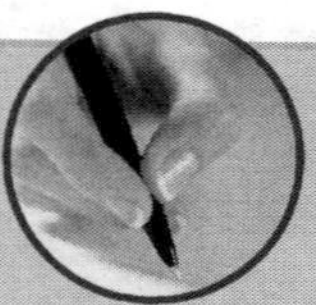

Box 1.2 TRY IT OUT
Gestalt theory

The image in Figure 1.2 is adapted from Wertheimer (1938 [1923]). What do you see when you look at this image?

Figure 1.2 A stimulus image used in gestalt experiments

Figure 1.2 could be seen as 12 dots with spaces, but perhaps you saw it as 4 groups of dots – each group containing 3 dots.

One of the interests that gestalt psychologists had was how we tend to group objects that we perceive – that is, how our minds organise the raw perceptual stimuli in certain meaningful ways, such as looking for patterns and groups. The whole issue of dot perception may seem disconnected from the concerns of social psychology, but imagine combining this interest with how social phenomena are perceived – for example, when do people start to perceive other individuals as belonging to and sharing the presumed characteristics of a particular social category or group?

mind, only the first has to be taken into account.' In other words, what is crucial to understanding human behaviour is the way in which individuals *perceive* their social environment.

Lewin's commitment to the idea that individuals' behaviour can be best understood by considering how they perceive their environment can be seen as something of a manifesto for much of subsequent (particularly US) experimental social psychology. Lewin was much more interested in *social* perception than any other form of perception and the idea that, at the heart of social behaviour, is individuals' perceptions of social phenomena has been of considerable influence in social psychology. Thus, social psychologists have been interested in the ways in which individuals can come to perceive other individuals as belonging to a certain category or group, such as 'protesters', 'fundamentalists', 'activists'. Furthermore, social psychologists have been interested in the ways in which, once placed in a category or group, individuals can come to be perceived as sharing certain attributes the individual perceivers associate with that category or group, such as 'troublemakers', 'people of integrity', 'a threat to others'. These perceptions of the social world can be seen as having consequences for the ways in which people behave and respond to each other. Thus, much of social psychology can be seen as concerned with this broad question of how individuals think about their social world.

1.3 Rethinking the development of social psychology

The above outline of the emergence of social psychology – and related versions of this – can often be found in introductory chapters of social psychology textbooks. Just because this history is something of a commonplace, however, does not mean that it cannot or should not be criticised – perhaps quite the reverse. One striking note in the above outline is its almost triumphal tone – social psychology has emerged, bringing the empirical rigour of psychology to questions of social importance – but this can, and should, be challenged. This history of what was gained through social psychology's pedigree can be juxtaposed with consideration of what has been lost. One element of this is the thinkers of relevance to social psychology whose work has been 'lost' or at least neglected. A second strand is that some of those who do make the social psychology 'hall of fame' have aspects of their work ignored, neglected or relegated to only minor significance. These missing figures and neglected ideas will be considered below, along with some reflection on the challenge that they offer to current social psychology.

Figures missing from social psychology

There are many names that could be mentioned to make the point that conventional histories of social psychology are limited. These might include the Greek philosopher and 'father of Western philosophy', Thales of Miletus, or the Islamic psychologist, Ibn-Sina (Leahey, 2004).

A refreshing perspective on psychology's 'hidden roots' has been developed by Billig (2008) that brings the debates between Locke, Shaftesbury and Reid in the late seventeenth and early eighteenth centuries to centre stage. At that time, and between these characters, we find ancient issues about how science should be conducted being argued about with urgency, just as modern concepts of science were being formed and the topics of 'human understanding' and 'human characteristics' were becoming mainstream. In the various debates between Locke, Shaftesbury and Reid, Locke could be seen as laying down something of the topic area for much of what followed in psychology (including social psychology), as well as its overarching – or meta-methodological approach.

Locke was particularly concerned with 'the mind' (the processes of cognition rather than the physiology of the brain) and was a significant figure in developing the idea that the mind, and the ideas within it, are 'examinable' objects of study. Arguing strongly against the notion of innate ideas, Locke made the case that the mind builds knowledge about the world through experience, which, for Locke, involved a relatively passive and accurate process of perception. Locke's work, focusing as it does on processes within the mind (such as memory and perception) and his emphasis on the shaping role of experience (if not his conception of perception as extremely passive), can be seen as of great importance to contemporary psychology. Locke's influence does not end there. He also advocated a strong empiricist position, arguing that we should advance our scientific knowledge about the mind through observation or experiment – the evidence thus collected should speak for itself concerning the facts of the issue(s) under investigation. Moreover, for Locke, this empiricism should involve approaching questions about the mind in terms of the relationships between discrete measurable bits, rather than trying to apprehend some whole or contemplating issues and variables not amenable to objective, verifiable measurement.

With Locke, then, we have seemingly another figure – perhaps even another 'founding father' – contributing to our previous picture of the development of social psychology. In considering the two other thinkers who responded to the work of Locke, however – Reid and Shaftesbury – we find not just other names but also other ideas that rupture any simple map charting the march of scientific progress in psychology in general and social psychology in particular. As Billig (2008) notes, with Reid, we find that Locke's concept of 'ideas' within the mind as being 'real', researchable objects 'of the mind' is challenged. Reid's rejection of 'cognitivism', along with his idea that language should be considered in terms of what it does (rather than as a mere reflection of some underlying 'cognitive reality') provides a markedly different agenda for psychology. For Billig (2008, p. 6), Reid – so often forgotten in histories of psychology –'strikingly anticipates the view of language which was seemingly created anew in the mid-nineteenth century and which is currently so influential in discursive psychology today.'

Similarly, with the often forgotten figure of Shaftesbury, we find ideas of contemporary critical relevance. Billig (2008) characterises the differences between Locke and Shaftesbury by reference to the two dominant philosophical and lifestyle positions of ancient Greece: epicureanism and stoicism. Cast in these terms, Locke is an epicurean committed to atomism – the idea that, to understand complex phenomena, such as the mind, we need to break them down into their smallest, simplest, measurable parts (the 'atoms', as it were, of the issue we are seeking to investigate). Shaftesbury, a stoic, by contrast, criticised this approach arguing, 'If you search for ever smaller units, you will come up with discoveries of increasing triviality.' (Billig, 2008, p. 101).

The 'lost' ideas of Shaftesbury, then, present a holistic approach to the world in general and the human world specifically – the emphasis being on understanding the *whole* person rather than their tiniest conceivable constituent bits. Furthermore, each person was approached not as a separate, self-contained entity but, rather, as an interconnected part of a larger social whole. For Shaftesbury – and subsequent thinkers from Bakhtin to Gergen, Sampson and Billig – a crucial aspect of each person, in being an interconnected part of a social whole, is the practice of *dialogue*; our sense of self, our thoughts and our very capacity for thought itself being rooted in *interaction with others*. This presented – and still presents today – an important challenge to dominant approaches to understanding the human.

As Billig (2008) argues, many of the themes central to the concerns of what has become known as 'critical psychology' are not recent reactions to the steady scientific progress of mainstream psychology – rather, they stem from a deep-rooted, alternative understanding that questions many of the assumptions which came to be seen as representing 'mainstream' psychology. Implicitly, and sometimes explicitly, much of psychology and, indeed, 'social' psychology has assumed the proper objects for study are the simplest measurable variables within the individual minds of separate, self-contained and essentially asocial beings (see also Box 1.3). These assumptions can be seen as legitimising a programme of study in which controlled experiments dissect ever smaller measurable units with limited, if any, serious attention to the inseparable importance of social context and social interaction. Critical

Box 1.3 KEY RESEARCHER
Professor Michael Billig: critical psychology

What things helped or hindered your research?

I was very fortunate in having a great teacher, Henri Tajfel. Henri was one of the most important British social psychologists. He was interested in exploring the 'normal' aspects of prejudice, how ordinary aspects of thinking can lead us to hold prejudiced and stereotyped views of other groups. I was immensely lucky to be an undergraduate at Bristol University, while Henri was there as professor of social psychology. He was an inspiring figure, who influenced just about every British social psychologist of my generation. When I finished my undergraduate degree, Henri employed me as his research assistant to run the first 'minimal group' experiments. These explored how just putting people into groups could lead them to develop a group identity. Henri persuaded me to stay on in Bristol and do a Ph.D. Without his guidance, I would never have become a social psychologist – or, indeed, an academic. So, it was the luck of being in Bristol at that time and having such a brilliant and generous teacher that led me to academic work.

How did you become interested in critical psychology?

Again, I can cite the influence of Henri Tajfel. Many social psychologists are very narrow in their perspective, believing that experiments alone provide 'scientific' data and that social psychologists should primarily be interested in social psychology. Henri wasn't

Box 1.3 continued

like that at all. He believed that if you are genuinely interested in social psychological questions – such as, 'What are the foundations of prejudice?' – then you must read widely. Sociology, anthropology and above all history have as much, even more, to teach us as social psychology. If you only study social psychology, then you will not even understand social psychology properly.

So, I have always tried to read widely. Over the years, I have found that social psychology which is narrowly based on experiments is unsatisfactory. It fails to tell us how culture and history influence the way we think. As a result, I became less impressed by mainstream social psychology and increasingly drawn to less conventional ways of doing social psychology. These less conventional methods and theories are often loosely called 'critical psychology', although there is a rich variety of different sorts of psychology that have been grouped under the label.

Tell us about your work in this area.

My work has covered a variety of topics. I have studied extreme right-wing prejudice – this involved interviewing members of fascist groups. I have also examined nationalism, attitudes towards monarchy, psychoanalytic theory and humour. In recent years I have been broadly associated with those psychologists who believe that the study of language holds the key to the study of human thinking.

Above all, I have enjoyed reading about the past. Most of my work has had a historical dimension – this includes my work on nationalism and my work on psychoanalysis was bound up with exploring how Freud came by his ideas. Recently, I have been looking at the historical roots of some ideas of critical psychology that critical psychologists often assume to be very modern, but which have a long history. It is often humbling to realise that ideas which we think are daringly innovative and very up to date were around hundreds of years ago. That is one reason why I wrote my book *The hidden roots of critical psychology* (2008). It tells of a story about how the origins of certain ideas about thought and language have been forgotten and how some very critical ideas about thinking have their origins in a most 'uncritical' figure – the third Earl of Shaftesbury. The great thing about history is that it is full of surprises.

What do you recommend to people wanting to start to research this topic?

I have been very fortunate and possibly more than a little selfish. I have always researched whatever has caught my interest, regardless of whether it is 'proper' psychology or not. I even at one point wrote a short book about the history of rock 'n' roll. I would advise any young researcher to be similarly selfish – just be curious, take risks and follow your own intuitions. If you're not interested in exploring something, then the chances are that you won't find anything interesting. Most of what we do isn't particularly important – we're not medical researchers looking for cures to diseases – so the best we can do is to try to be interesting ... and for that, we must ourselves be interested – indeed, interested almost to the point of obsession.

alternatives, represented in the work of Shaftesbury, Reid and others, and considered throughout this book, propose several radically different historically and culturally situated takes on social psychology, in which the ideological context of the person becomes important, the person is understood as constituted in and through interaction and language is seen as constructing reality and 'doing interaction', rather than merely being a secondary reflection of underlying, measurable, atomistic mental processes.

Neglected ideas of key figures in social psychology

The second 'lost' part of the simplified picture of the emergence of social psychology provided above concerns some of the forgotten contributions of those psychologists who are otherwise remembered. Here attention will be paid to Wundt and McDougall.

It is well known and widely reported that Wundt advocated, developed and institutionally established experimental approaches in psychology, yet he argued that this experimental approach should be supplemented with Völkerpsychologie – a psychology concerned with language, myth and custom. For Wundt, the complex mental processes involved in social psychological phenomena are best served by a quite distinct framework that does not use experiments on individual subjects to get at individual mental phenomena but, rather, approaches the cultural and historical context of social communities. As Greenwood (2004b) notes, Wundt here can be seen as directly drawing on Lazarus (1851, cited in Greenwood, 2004b), who coined the term Völkerpsychologie, and, in turn, Vico (1975 [1725], 1975 [1744]) and Herder (1969 [1784]), who particularly emphasised the importance of cultural and historical factors. Greenwood (2004b) notes that Wundt's students who returned to the USA 'almost completely ignored Völkerpsychologie'.

McDougall's (1920, p. 10, cited in Greenwood, 2004b, p. 127) overtly social emphasis befell a similar fate. McDougall had argued, 'the thinking and acting of each man [sic], insofar as he thinks and acts as a member of a society, are very different from his [sic] thinking and acting as an isolated individual'. For McDougall (echoing some of the concerns of Durkheim, 1898), the social behaviour that social psychology seeks to understand cannot simply be reduced to the sum of individual psychological processes. From this perspective, then, if we conceptualise our objects of study as the isolated individual and their cognitions and design experiments to inspect the self-contained individual and their specific, separate mental processes we are missing the *social* processes we are proporting to study.

Greenwood (2004b, p. 101) suggests that some of the subsequent neglect of the cultural, historical and social emphasis of Wundt and McDougall (among others) can be seen as a reaction to the 'illegitimate "reification" or "personification" of social psychological phenomena'. That is, partly because some authors (such as LeBon, 1896) had written of the 'group mind' and the crowd forming a 'single being' with 'mental unity' – ideas that were subsequently seen as 'discredited' – there was a reaction against any emphasis on social psychology as being distinct from individual psychology. Floyd Allport (1924, p. 366, cited in Greenwood, 2004b, p. 200) put the case in the following terms: 'there is nothing in social psychology that is not logically explainable at the level of the individual.' As a result, Greenwood argues, American social psychology in particular became much more individualistic in focus, sometimes neglecting overtly social topics, such as group research, and leaving to one side the ideas of Wundt, McDougall and others that social phenomena might not be reducible to mere individual psychological processes or researchable in terms of isolated and decontextualised, experimental data.

Rethinking critical thoughts about social psychology

These lost figures and neglected ideas in oft-reproduced histories of the emergence of social psychology are much more than interesting historical asides. By reconnecting with figures such as Shaftesbury and Reid and the neglected social and contextual emphasis of Wundt and McDougall, we find ideas that radically critique the assumptions and practices of present-day social psychology. Current ideas among various strands of critical psychology can be seen to raise just the sorts of concerns found in these hidden parts of social psychology's legacy. Rediscovering social psychology's 'family tree' in this way shows that its heritage is richer and more varied than it often seems and contains within it the seeds to question the idea that we should convert social issues into easily measurable, cognitive entities in the mind of the isolated individual.

These critical perspectives equip us to tackle a question such as 'How can we understand aggression?' without presuming that the answer will be delivered by simply another experiment concerned with trying to explain aggression in terms of decontextualised perceptions, cognitions and actions of an individual. Instead, they raise the issue that the social, historical and ideological contexts in which real, non-laboratory acts of aggression occur may be of importance. Such critical perspectives also enable us to investigate the ways in which interactions between people may be crucial for understanding the emergence, justification and condemnation of aggression. They encourage us to explore the ways in which identities are built by people who might be victims, perpetrators (or both) of specific acts of real-world aggression. Finally, these critical perspectives open the possibility of analysing the sort of language that is used to talk about targets – and perpetrators – of specific, culturally and historically located aggressive acts. In this way, a more critical history of the emergence of social psychology does not narrow down our approaches to social psychological issues; instead it opens up the terrain to different ways of framing the question, researching the issues, and thinking and debating about the data we encounter.

1.4 Why can't social psychologists agree with each other?

In reading this book you may get a sense that there is very little solid ground in social psychology. It may seem that, with each topic, there is lots of disagreement and debate and very little agreed on fact. This can be unsettling and frustrating, especially if you turn to a text such as this to provide a straightforward, factual answer to your social psychology questions. However, the disagreements and debates in social psychology are perhaps one of its greatest assets. Social psychology is at the centre of crucial debates in psychology – and the social sciences in general. It is here, in social psychology, that the fundamentals of how we should understand the person, human interaction, the research process and the knowledge that we generate are most vividly and thoroughly debated.

By reading social psychology, you are walking into a live debating chamber where you can and should participate.

Despite this positive spin on debate in social psychology, it may seem somehow unsatisfactory that there is so much of it. You may feel that social psychologists should sort out their differences and come to some kind of agreement. Perhaps some carefully designed series of empirical studies could determine where the truth lies – that is, research itself might show which ideas are true and which are false. Alternatively, you might hope for some unified theory that somehow encompasses all of the differing and seemingly contradictory ideas in social psychology and explains how they interrelate. You might see your role in studying social psychology as sifting through the evidence to find the approach that is true – or at least the one most supported by the available evidence. These understandings are laudable – they demonstrate some awareness of the debates in psychology and an attempt to engage in them. They do, however, run the risk of underestimating just how fundamental certain debates are and overestimating the extent to which the empirical facts of research 'speak for themselves'.

It is worth noting that debates in social psychology could be thought of as operating at different levels, as some debates are between specific theories that agree on many fundamental questions, but differ in certain specific details about what causes people to think and interact as they do. Thus, as we will consider in Chapter 6, we could debate that, in trying to persuade someone, it is *who* is doing the persuading or *what* their persuasive message is that counts. If, instead, we take the position that it is both the persuasive person *and* the message that are important, we could debate precisely how these potentially causal factors (or independent variables) combine and under what circumstances, if any, one is more important than the other. Other debates are much broader and reflect different positions that are not localised to a specific topic, such as persuasion but, instead, affect the way we research and understand several or perhaps even all aspects of social psychology. Thus, some social psychologists might adopt a perspective in which the thoughts of the individual about their social world are taken as the central focus for social psychology, while others might place primary emphasis on features of the environment, structures of power and inequality or talk and interaction.

Kuhn's paradigms

One way of understanding these big, trans-topic, meta-perspective debates is provided by Thomas Kuhn's (1996) work on 'scientific revolutions'.

Kuhn's work reflects on big changes in theoretical positions within natural science research – the sorts of shifts we get pre and post Copernicus or from Newtonian to quantum physics. Kuhn provides a way of understanding not just how one perspective can come to replace a previously dominant one but also, crucially, how, in empirical research, the evidence does *not* simply 'speak for itself' when deciding between perspectives. Thus, for Kuhn, ongoing research in scientific communities is not an 'observer-independent' accumulation of self-evident facts, but, rather, a process guided and made sense of by particular *paradigms*.

'Paradigm' is the term Kuhn uses to capture the frameworks that guide how research should be conducted and how the data collected should be interpreted or made sense of. Our paradigm will shape (and is evidenced in) the questions that we ask, the methods we use and the meanings we give to the data we generate (see Box 1.4).

Box 1.4 TRY IT OUT
Thinking in paradigms

Have a look at the image in Figure 1.3 – what is it?

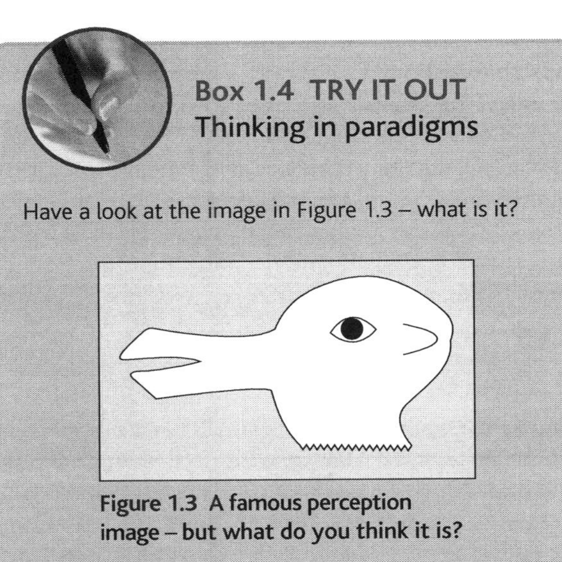

Figure 1.3 A famous perception image – but what do you think it is?

Look at the following words: *swan goose mallard.*

Now look at these words: *hare bunny lop-eared.*

Does this lead to a different interpretation of the ambiguous image?

You may find this effect works best on a friend or friends where you can ask them what they think the image is – having previously primed them with either the waterfowl words or the rabbit and hare words. Indeed, your friends may be delighted and surprised by your demonstration and explanation of this powerful and instructive image. If the people you try this on have already encountered this image, there are numerous websites devoted to optical illusions

Box 1.4 continued

(see for example: www.optical-illusion-pictures.com/ambig.html).

The important point that this particular image illustrates (and the reason Kuhn himself referred to it) is that one's interpretation of the ambiguous drawing is shaped by expectations that you come to it with. If we approach the drawing having thought in terms of waterfowl, then we are likely to interpret the image as that of a duck facing to the left. If instead, we come to the image primed with thoughts of hares and bunnies, then we may see the face of a rabbit with its ears back facing to the right. The same stimulus drawing appears different when our thoughts, expectations and, indeed, our assumptions are changed.

For Kuhn, it is because empirical research is unavoidably shaped by paradigmatic assumptions that communities of scientists do not radically revise their fundamental assumptions with every piece of research. Instead, research is conducted and interpreted consistently in line with fundamental perspectives. If anomalies do become apparent, these are first made sense of within the existing framework and it is only after they become overwhelming that the entire sensemaking system is changed and a new paradigm emerges.

As Potter (1996) notes, Kuhn is not criticising scientific research and suggesting that it should operate in a paradigm-free or paradigm-neutral manner – this is seen as impossible and not particularly desirable. For Kuhn, any attempt at research implies a particular set of commitments to specific issues to be addressed and methods for doing so. Furthermore, it will generate data that has to be made sense of and, therefore (even if implicitly), a paradigm is at work. Far from 'the facts speaking for themselves,' what we might think of as 'the facts' could be thought of as being generated by, and interpreted within, a tradition of research where, typically, other traditions exist, or will come to exist.

Billig's fictional things

Billig (2011) highlights the way in which much of the technical terminology found within social psychology actively constructs 'fictional things' – things such as 'schemas', 'social categorisation' and 'deindividuation' – the presence of which can only be inferred. In some ways, these are *theories as descriptions*. Deindividuation, for example, is part of a *theory* of a psychological response to external conditions of anonymity, but it becomes, or can become, *a thing that is described*. There is a shift in the epistemological status here from a theoretical postulate to – as Billig (2011) argues – a thing the existence of which becomes increasingly taken for granted. Drawing on Vaihinger, Billig (2011, p. 15) suggests that, 'there are problems when we confuse the imagined world of our fictional things with the world that we are trying to use these fictions to understand'.

One can imagine, for example, how theories about interpersonal attraction can start to create a language through which the phenomenon is viewed and then the data is examined with reference not to the original human phenomenon to be explained, but the landscape of fictional things that the researcher is committed to – perhaps populated by 'excitation transfer', 'reproductive fitness', 'assortative mating' or 'market forces'. The reification of these fictional things is perhaps implicated in some of the ways in which researchers may reinterpret findings, such that they fit their overarching theoretical commitments. In these cases, results are sometimes not allowed to upset, displace, reform or question the existence of those things that the researcher created, is committed to or has come to view as perhaps 'more real than the things that ordinary people recognize in the social world' (Billig, 2011, p. 15).

Data collection and theoretical assumptions

A brief example of how different perspectives can shape the way that data is collected and interpreted can be found in the development of the idea of 'minority influence' (see Figures 1.4a and b in Box 1.5). Moscovici and Lage's (1976) and Moscovici, Lage and Naffrechoux's (1969) relatively novel concept that the minority can influence the majority, led to some rethinking of Asch's famous conformity experiments (discussed in detail in Chapter 10). Asch (1951, 1956) had found that having several experimental collaborators (confederates, 'C') call out the wrong answer in an obvious visual task could generate wrong answers from the real (or naïve, non-confederate, 'N') participants. That is, sometimes the naïve participant would copy the confederates who called out obviously wrong answers – seemingly because the minority (the one naïve participant) desired to conform to the majority (the six or so confederates).

Moscovici et al., rather than understanding Asch's findings as highlighting how ubiquitous conformity is, understood them as (at least in part) reflecting the experimental design used. If all but one of the apparent participants were confederates – employed by the experimenter

Box 1.5 FOCUS Majority and minority influence

Asch's (1951, 1956) experiment involved several confederates (people covertly working with the experimenter) who deliberately called out incorrect answers for some visual perception tasks. The experiment focused on the extent to which the naïve participant (who did not know that the others were working with the experimenter) was influenced by the confederate majority.

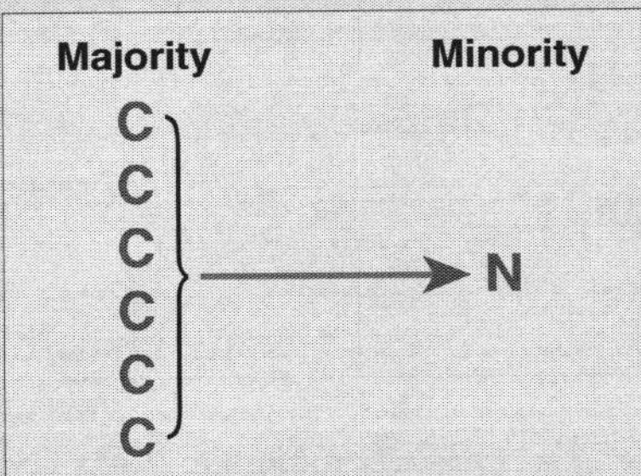

Figure 1.4a A majority exerting an influence on a minority

Moscovici and Lage's (1976) and Moscovici, Lage and Naffrechoux's (1969) experiments involved investigating whether a minority – two confederates – could exert some influence on the judgements of a larger number of naïve participants.

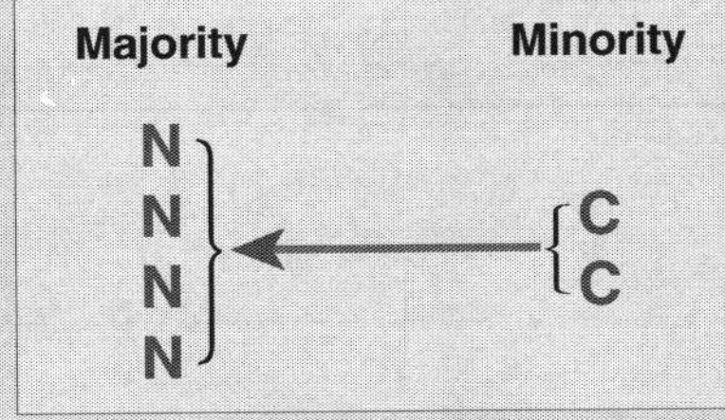

Figure 1.4b A minority exerting an influence on a majority

and instructed to periodically call out the same wrong answer – then the only effect one is likely to find is conformity (the experiment is not able to measure possible minority influence because the majority are experimental confederates who are giving pre-scripted responses). Moscovici et. al.'s different perspective, which emphasised minority influence, led not only to a questioning of some interpretations of Asch's experiment but also to questioning the way that the design of the experiment closed off certain issues from investigation. Specifically, it did not enable consideration of the influence that the minority might have on the majority.

Moscovici et al.'s experiment also involved visual perception tasks (albeit less clear-cut ones), but, crucially, a *minority* of participants were confederates with the *majority* being 'real' or naïve participants. Moscovici et al. found that, designing the experiment in this way, the minority were found to influence the majority – a possibility that could not occur within Asch's experimental design.

Asch's and Moscovici et al.'s experiments illustrate not just different theoretical understandings of social influence but also the broader issue that the way in which we collect our data – in this case, the design of the experiment – may shape, limit or, in some cases, predetermine what we may find.

The idea that research findings may not resolve debates because they can be interpreted in markedly different ways is evidenced throughout this book. Social psychological research findings have often attracted controversy concerning what the findings actually mean. In later chapters, we will have the opportunity to consider many such controversies, including whether or not Argyle, Alkema and Gilmour (1971) established that non-verbal communication can be more powerful than verbal (Chapter 11), Locksley, Borgida, Brekke and Hepburn's (1980) experiment found gender stereotypes to be redundant (Chapter 7) and Huesmann and Eron (1986) found that televised violence had a causal impact on violent behaviour across cultures (Chapter 9). For now, however, another piece of research that has generated significant debate will be considered – Reicher and Haslam's (2006a, 2006b) BBC prison study. As the name of the study suggests, this research is somewhat unusual in that some of the data generated formed a programme – *The Experiment* – that was broadcast by the BBC in May 2002.

Making sense of Reicher and Haslam's BBC prison experiment

Before briefly discussing Reicher and Haslam's field experiment (that is, an experiment set in a real or simulated 'non-laboratory' context), it is worth noting that the results stood in stark contrast to one of the most famous social psychology field experiments of all time, – Zimbardo's (1969) Stamford prison experiment (SPE).

Zimbardo's study (which is considered more fully in Chapter 10) involved undergraduates in a mock (but quite convincing) prison, undertaking the roles of either guards or prisoners. Zimbardo found that the roles had a profound effect on behaviour. For Zimbardo in the SFE, prisoners and guards assumed the roles of their respective positions of prisoner or guard and acted consistently with the norms associated with those roles – compliant and authoritarian respectively. Being in a group, wearing the relevant uniform and being given the associated power (or lack of power) was enough, according to Zimbardo to give rise to acts of tyranny and acquiescence to that tyranny.

In Reicher and Haslam's (2006a, 2006b) study, similarly, participants were divided into two groups – 'prisoners' and 'guards' – and lived for eight days in a mock prison, the prisoners being locked in three-person cells for some of the time. All participants were made aware that they were being filmed for research purposes and that some of the film would be broadcast by the BBC. In addition to video data of the participants, Reicher and Haslam also collected data using a variety of psychometric tests that were intended to assess social identification, compliance, self-efficacy and depression, among other variables.

During the experiment, the prisoners appeared to be somewhat compliant with the guards' regime for the first three days. During this phase, the prisoners were made aware that, for one time only, the prisoner who was deemed to be best behaved would be 'promoted' to become a guard.

From day four onwards, the prisoners were found to increasingly challenge the guards' authority – for example, insisting (successfully) on having the same smoking rights as the guards.

On day six, some prisoners broke out of their cells and occupied the guards' quarters. For two days following this, the prisoners and guards decided to carry on with the experiment, but as a single self-governing commune (rather than as two communities of prisoners and guards).

On the eighth and final day, some, who were disaffected by the commune, sought to impose a new authoritarian guard structure. This prompted the experiment to be terminated, amid fears that this may contravene the ethical guidelines for the study.

So, Reicher and Haslam's (2006a, 2006b) study involved the prisoners challenging the guards and asserting themselves rather than – as Zimbardo found – merely complying with the tyranny of the guards' rule.

Reicher and Haslam's (2006a, 2006b) study criticised both the empirical basis of Zimbardo's study and what they saw as the rather negative view of groups that emerged from it. With regard to the study itself, they argue that Zimbardo's instructions to the participants may have distorted the findings. Some instructions may have given the prisoners the sense that they could not leave the study, which, Reicher and Haslam suggest, could have resulted in 'role confusion' and reduced the likelihood of them developing some common identity as prisoners who might challenge the guards. Reicher and Haslam suggest that other instructions, given to the guards, may have led the guards to behave in a way that they might not have done had they not received those instructions. Reicher and Haslam saw their study as an opportunity to collect data in a different way without what they saw as potentially 'distorting' interventions or 'leading' instructions given to participants. They also collected additional data, from the psychometric tests.

Reicher and Haslam's interpretation of their research

Reicher and Haslam interpreted the results of their study as providing support for social identity theory. In particular, as soon as there was an impermeable boundary between the prisoner group and the guard group (when the possibility of 'promotion' was removed), the prisoners formed a cohesive social identity (as measured using the psychometric instruments and observed in their talk and behaviour). For Reicher and Haslam, if the prisoners had merely identified with their role of 'being a prisoner' (as Zimbardo suggested they did in the SPE), they would have been far more compliant, talking and behaving consistently with that prisoner role. According to Reicher and Haslam, however, the prisoners in their BBC study had generated a strong sense of belonging to this *specific* prisoner group. The identity of this group was far more resistant than some generic notion of being a 'powerless prisoner' and the participants engaged in collective and individual acts of resistance which were consistent with this identity. Reicher and Haslam thus argued that their BBC study provided convincing empirical evidence for a social identity theory account of tyranny and resistance. From this perspective, rather than groups being part of the problem that leads to role identification and tyranny, groups can be the very means of resisting tyranny. Where groups are able to form a collective identity, they are able to challenge and resist tyranny; where such group identity fails to emerge, then tyranny can flourish, unchallenged.

Zimbardo's interpretation of Reicher and Haslam's research

The same empirical study has been interpreted in a markedly different way by Zimbardo (2006). In a strongly worded criticism of their research, Zimbardo does not merely provide a differently nuanced interpretation of their data – he entirely dismisses its scientific merit.

For Zimbardo, the research lacks validity, there are issues with the sampling of participants, it does not provide an environment in which role theory can be adequately tested and the results have been misinterpreted. These issues will be considered in more detail when we revisit this study in Chapter 10, but, for now, we can note just three of the features that Zimbardo considers especially problematic.

First, the experimenters designing in a 'promotion possibility'. Zimbardo sees this as making the simulation entirely unlike any prison (it is rare to find a prison in which prisoners can become guards), which, in turn, could be understood as interfering with the sense of role identification that participants in a more realistic simulation (with no opportunity to become a guard) might experience.

Second, Zimbardo raises problems about the impact that the experimenter's regular use of psychometric measures might have had on the participants – again, raising problems for the realism of the study and, in turn, the role identification of participants. Third, Zimbardo argues that the participants' awareness that they were being filmed raised their self-awareness and, therefore, inhibited certain psychological processes (such as the loss of awareness of oneself as a responsible individual) that Zimbardo saw as important in giving rise to aggressive guard behaviour in the SPE.

Why psychologists interpret Reicher and Haslam's research in different ways

For our current purposes, there are four particularly relevant aspects to this debate about what can be made of Reicher and Haslam's BBC prison study.

The first point is that one reason it is hard to design an experiment that will finally resolve a debate within social psychology (for example, in very crude terms here, between the relative importance of role theory and social identity theory) is that some of the design choices reflect theoretical commitments. Thus, for Zimbardo (2006), one important part of testing the influence of being assigned the role of prisoner or guard was how the norms associated with that role were adhered to. Therefore, an important feature of Zimbardo's study was familiarising participants (the guards in particular) with a sense of what behaviours are permitted or expected of guards. This was problematic for Reicher and Haslam (2006a, 2006b) because they saw it as somewhat predetermining the participants' behaviour, giving them less scope to develop their own norms and identities. Conversely, an important feature of Reicher and Haslam's BBC study was determining the ways in which social identity was at work in the prisoners' behaviour. This led to a manipulation of the permeability of the boundary between the two groups (allowing for a promotion from prisoner to guard and then withdrawing it) and using psychometric tests to assess their group identifications. While this allowed Reicher and Haslam to comment on boundary permeability and expressed group identification, it raised problems for Zimbardo. Zimbardo saw the 'promotion' as a 'game show gimmick', making the study unrealistic and less amenable to scientific analysis. The regular psychometric testing was also seen as quite unrealistic and likely to constantly reorientate participants to the fact that they were in an experiment rather than a prison. These issues, for Zimbardo, made it less likely that the sort of role identification that typically occurs in realistic, non-permeable, role situations would occur in the BBC study.

Second, as we saw when considering the work of Kuhn above, the same data can be made sense of in different ways, each interpretation reflecting the theoretical commitments of the researchers. Thus, the prisoners' rebellion was interpreted by Haslam and Reicher as reflecting their development of a strong social identity that enabled them to collectively oppose the tyranny of the guards. By contrast, Zimbardo interpreted the rebellion as reflecting the particular personalities involved combined with an environment (with the regular experimenter interventions and the awareness of cameras) that made the prisoners very self-conscious and, therefore, likely to act in ways that reflected their own personality traits. The lack of a prisoners' rebellion in Zimbardo's SPE is interpreted by him as their identification with their subjugated prisoner role. By contrast Haslam and Reicher interpret this same phenomenon as a reflection of the specific interventions and instructions by Zimbardo that inhibited the development of a social identity among the prisoners.

In considering this debate between Zimbardo and Reicher and Haslam, you may wonder if the best solution is just to design the most 'realistic' prison study. This, too, is more problematic than may first appear to be the case. Some of the deviations from reality that, for example, Reicher and Haslam were accused of were, from their perspective, important as they enabled them to investigate issues concerning group boundaries and group identities. Furthermore, there may be different constructions of what is more typical, or real, of the situation that is being replicated – in this case, a prison. For example, for Zimbardo the very general principles given to participants about their roles could be seen as replicating just the sort of exposure to protocols that guards would ordinarily encounter and they were subsequently invited to draw up their own specific rules. Reicher and Haslam, by contrast, interpreted these instructions as merely 'leading' the participants to behave in a particular way and undermining their spontaneous development of a group identity with its associated norms for group members' behaviour.

A final issue to be touched on here concerns the different way in which the filming of participants was handled in Zimbardo's SPE and in Reicher and Haslam's BBC study. In both cases, the participants were filmed, but in Zimbardo's SPE, they were unaware of this at the time, whereas participants in Reicher and Haslam's BBC study were made fully aware in advance that they would be and, indeed, wore microphones throughout. As was the case in Reicher and Haslam's study, most studies would be required by the relevant ethics committee to obtain consent for the filming in advance of it taking place (whether broadcast or not). For Zimbardo, awareness of the cameras is massively significant as it distorts the results – it makes participants self-conscious and, therefore, much more immune to the effects of being in a group and assigned a specific role. Indeed, Zimbardo goes so far as to argue that the effect of the knowledge of being filmed is so profound that, in real-life prison contexts, being aware of being filmed would be a very useful tool for moderating otherwise potentially tyrannical behaviour on the part of guards.

The above discussion does not seek to adjudicate on the Reicher and Haslam v. Zimbardo debate but, rather, use it to illustrate that debates between different theories in psychology might not be easy to resolve by just 'collecting the facts'. People working from different theoretical perspectives may have quite different ideas about the sorts of data that need to be collected in order to investigate their ideas, they may have different sensitivities regarding what empirical details would support or undermine research findings and may interpret any data that *is* collected in different ways. Having spent some time illustrating the idea that debates between perspectives are inevitable and not readily resolved (see also Box 1.6), some key theoretical approaches relevant to social psychology are briefly sketched next and drawn on in explaining specific social phenomena.

Box 1.6 IN THE NEWS
How can we explain aggressive behaviour?

The news story illustrated here concerns three people who were killed in Melbourne in what reports suggested was a gang-related attack. How can social psychology make sense of incidents such as this? Should we think in terms of what makes people aggressive or the things that encourage or trigger aggressive behaviour? Should we think about the attack as being related to the influence of being in a gang or perhaps the perpetrators' identity as gang members? As well as considering what might cause the event itself we could also ask, how do people make sense of incidents such as these – how do we work out the causes of such violent behaviour? Is our thinking shaped by stereotypes that we might hold about gangs or a 'crime family boss'?

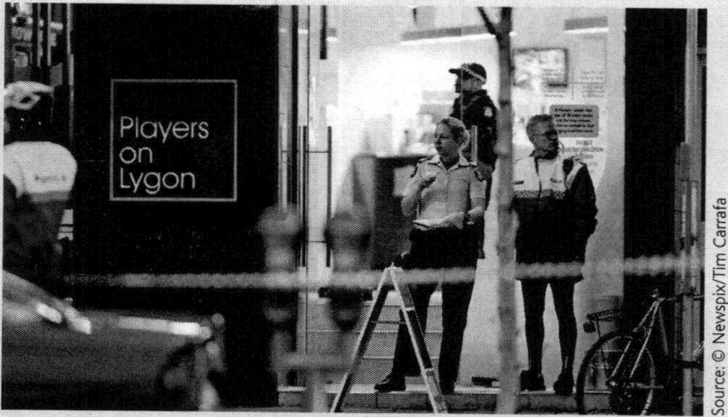

Source: © Newspix/Tim Carrafa

Three people were shot dead on a bloody day in Melbourne amid fears that the execution of a crime family boss had sparked a new gangland war

Each of these questions that we can readily ask about real-world events relates to key topics in social psychology – aggression, group behaviour, attribution (how we think about causes) and stereotypes. As mentioned above, this should not be viewed as a one-way street, in which social psychology provides its definitive, unilateral 'answers'. Instead, it is important to recognise the debates within each social psychological account and the troubling, unsettling nature of the issues that 'real-world events' can pose for the sometimes too neat and narrowly framed answers that social psychology is ready to give.

1.5 Some different 'streams of thought' within social psychological research

Below, ten perspectives or 'streams of thought' that play a part in social psychological research are briefly outlined. Referring to them as 'streams' is an attempt to get away from the notion of a simple, fixed categorisation scheme – these are ideas that move or change and can mix with each other in various ways. They are broad – some 'streams' encompass several markedly different ideas – and overlap – often two or more of them are present within a single piece of research. They do not necessarily each contribute to all of the topics considered in this book, nor do they adequately capture the full breadth of ideas at work in social psychology, but, for each of the topics considered, some of them will be relevant. The ten are briefly defined below before being illustrated.

1 *Situationalist.* This refers to an extremely broad range of research that is concerned with the ways in which situations can shape the cognition and/or behaviour of a person, people or some form of group. From a situationalist perspective, our thinking and behaviour is shaped (or at least partly shaped) by factors 'outside of ourselves'.

2 *Rational actor.* Research concerned with the idea that our behaviour is (or should normally be) rational, usually driven by our perception of what will benefit us. Research drawing on this tradition tends to either present rational decisionmaking and action as the norm or as an *idealised model* of individual behaviour that is often modified in practice by the operations of errors and biases.

3 *Social cognition.* Research that treats our thinking within a social context or about aspects of our social world as an important focus in itself and uses it to explain aspects of our thoughts, feelings and/or behaviour. Social cognition research has been particularly concerned with some of the cognitive and behavioural consequences of our thinking patterns, such as how thinking of people in terms of the category (or categories) we perceive them as belonging to may be at work in prejudice.

4 *Group.* This captures the markedly different traditions of research that have been concerned with collections of people who could be referred to (by others and themselves) as a group or a crowd. This research encompasses some diametrically opposed positions, such as whether group and crowd behaviour should be thought of in terms of a loss of control or a shift to a different sort of group-identity form of control.

5 *Evolutionary.* Research concerned with the idea that we act in terms of what will benefit us or has benefited our ancestors in evolutionary terms.

6 *Cross-cultural.* The markedly different research approaches that in some ways draw on the idea that how we think and act may be informed by the culture we are in or have been exposed to.

7 *Social representations.* A varied collection of research concerned with shared understandings or belief structures through which people make sense of the world. This can include examining the ideas, representations and metaphors they draw on in so doing. Some social representations work has emphasised their link to groups, with social groups being thought of as sharing certain representations of reality. Another interest in social representations work has been the ways in which ideas may change over time – sometimes drawing on and transforming 'expert' understandings in their representations.

8 *Ideological.* The different research approaches that are concerned with various 'dominant' sets of ideas or constructions within society and particularly how issues of power relate to these. One strand of this work considers the way in which highly *individualised* understandings of self may serve to maintain the status quo – for example, a person's unhappiness being understood as a problem of *the individual* and requiring that they and not other societal arrangements need to be changed.

9 *Discourse analytic/discursive.* Different approaches that are concerned with how talk constructs reality, attends to issues of its own veracity and *does* things. The things that talk does might be *interactional,* such as managing issues of accountability or orientating to interactional concerns or (in the case of some *discourse analytic* research) *ideological,* such as constructing power-relevant identities.

10 *Conversation analytic.* Research that is principally concerned with how talk, body movement, gaze or gesture can be understood in terms of what it is doing *within its sequential environment* – that is, where it is placed within an interaction.

Situationalist

Zimbardo's approach, considered above – with its emphasis on the prison guards' roles and situations that promote anonymity, shaping their aggressive behaviour – provides one example of a broadly situationalist approach to understanding issues within social psychology. From this perspective, to understand human social behaviour, we need to consider the environment – usually the immediate social environment (or features of it that are thought to be psychologically significant) – within which the behaviour occurs.

Situationalist ideas are at the heart of a great deal of social psychology. For example, Zajonc (1968) emphasised that we will be attracted to those we often encounter, while Asch (1956) and Milgram's (1963) conformity and obedience experiments in different ways considered how others (peers and an authority figure respectively) can exert social influence on us, shaping our behaviour.

The situation or the environment that is seen as crucially shaping behaviour could be one or more other people, it might be those features of the situation that promote anonymity or certain situationally relevant roles. In addition – and crucial for situationalist approaches to aggression – the situation would include stimuli that we are exposed to, such as images that could be understood as cuing aggression. Ideas that media violence may legitimise or otherwise encourage acts of aggression could be understood as a classic instance of situationalism – it is the situational stimuli (in this case, violence in the media) that are understood as giving rise to a subsequent violent act on the part of the media consumer.

While a heterogeneous range of research has been identified under the banner of situationalism, there is a common thread in that the work referred to here stands in contrast to other approaches that have emphasised cognitive perception, social forces and instincts. Situationalism captures something of the spirit of much of social psychology, which seeks to move our gaze away from either the individual or macro social forces and, instead, concentrate on those variables that are made present in the immediate setting. It is perhaps no surprise that his approach emerged particularly out of experimental research, much of which involved manipulating the environment in which participants found themselves and examining the possible impact of those situational (and other) manipulations.

Rational actor

An alternative – and in some ways less clearly identifiable perspective – emphasises not so much the situation but, rather, 'rational thinking' on the part of the person whose behaviour we are trying to understand. To some extent this stream of thought within social psychology has been shaped by the development of rational choice theory in economics (Simon, 1950).

In some social psychological research the concept of 'rationality' is utilised to depict an *idealised model* of human thought or action – how we *could* think and act if unconstrained by biasing or distorting factors. Thus, Kelley's (1967) covariation model of causal attribution depicts the person as making an attribution (working out the cause of an event) in an entirely logical, rational manner.

In other aspects of social psychology, the 'rational actor' appears to inform some (if not all) specific theories about how we *actually do* think and act. Thus, in Darley and Latané's (1968) study of prosocial (helping) behaviour, people intervened in cases where their interpretation of the situation made the potential rewards of helping outweigh the potential costs (an approach further developed by Dovidio, Piliavin, Gaertner, Schroeder, & Clark's, (1991) arousal: cost – reward model). This notion of our behaviour being shaped by our assessment of the costs and benefits of different courses of action is at the heart of exchange and (to a slightly lesser extent) equity models of relationships – (Hatfield, Berscheid, & Walster, 1976; Hatfield, Rapson, & Aumer-Ryan, 2007) in which our relationship contentment is understood as being related to our perceptions of the rewards and costs of the relationship for us and our partner.

Some models of human behaviour draw on the idea of the human as essentially a 'rational actor' as one part of a model, where that rationality may be pitted against other influences. Anderson and Bushman's (2002) development of the general aggression model provides an illustration of this. This model of aggression incorporates several different approaches, but of particular relevance to our current concern is the identification of an appraisal and decision process that determines whether the individual engages in thoughtful or impulsive action. The general aggression model has a place for the 'rational actor' – the person may accurately appraise or reappraise the situation and choose thoughtful, non-aggressive action. In other cases, however, the 'internal state of the individual' (such as having an extremely high level of arousal) may lead to irrational, spontaneous and aggressive behaviour.

Social cognition

A particularly influential strand within social psychology has emphasised the specific way in which the individual perceives and processes information about the social world. To some extent this strand within social psychology can be seen as having been influenced by the so-called 'cognitive revolution' in psychology – when, in the late 1950s, several influential publications (Broadbent, 1958; Chomsky, 1959; Miller, 1956; Newell, Shaw

& Simon, 1957) played a significant role in emphasising the importance of cognitive processes within psychology. 'Social' cognition paid particular attention to aspects of our cognitive processing of distinctly social phenomenon. So, rather than, for example, consider the way in which the physical environment is perceived or how many bits of information can be stored in memory, *social* cognition applied an interest in cognitive processing to social topics, such as how we think about ourselves and others.

Social cognitive approaches developed ideas regarding fundamental cognitive elements – for example, *schemas* (cognitive structures representing our information and misinformation about a person, object or event). Crucial aspects of psychology, such as our self concept, prejudice and group behaviour, came to be explained by reference to the relevant guiding schema. Furthermore, social cognition approaches developed models that emphasised process (inner, cognitive processes) rather than just observable responses. Whereas behaviourism was content to examine the extent to which the response covaried with particular stimuli, the social cognition approach attempted to model the hidden inner processing that it saw as mediating the relationship between an observable stimulus and observable response. Social cognition approaches, therefore, sought to describe what we did with our cognitive perceptions of reality.

A particularly important strand within social cognition has been the *cognitive miser model*, which emerged in the 1980s. The model constructed our thinking – that is, our social cognitions – as limited in terms of effort and capacity and, therefore, as involving schema-based processes to reduce the need for thinking effort. Stereotypes (being understood as a particular, rigid type of schema) are an example of this. According to the cognitive miser model, stereotypes are drawn on to save thinking effort and are maintained – even in the face of contradictory information – so as to reduce the thinking effort of changing them wherever possible.

While the cognitive miser model is still influential within social psychology, an additional model – the motivated tactician – has joined it. The motivated tactician brings motivation centre stage once again, in that the social perceiver is seen as having at his or her disposal a number of quite different thinking strategies and choosing one on the basis of 'goals, motives and needs' (Fiske & Taylor, 1991, p. 13). Additionally, it can be noted that issues of both neuroscience and culture are increasingly important for current social cognition research. As Fiske and Taylor (2008, p. 21, cited in Abell & Walton, 2010, p. 688) note, 'As social cognition outgrows its original Western (North American and European) boundaries and simultaneously reaches into the brain, it extends its cultural reach as well'.

Group

The situationalist, rational actor and social cognition approaches outlined so far have a somewhat individualistic flavour to them. Each, albeit in quite different ways, tend to emphasise the individual responding to situations, making rational decisions or cognitively processing the social world. Yet, an important strand within social psychology throughout its history has addressed the idea that group behaviour may, in gestalt terms, be different from the mere 'sum of individual behaviours'.

The idea of the group has been crucial to social psychology in many different forms. Some research has paid attention to within or intragroup processes, Asch's (1951, p. 56) conformity research being one notable example. Other research has focused on different forms of interaction between groups, Sherif's (1966, 1967) summer camp studies examining the ways in which group relations are shaped in part by whether their goals are mutually compatible or not.

One particularly important aspect of research has concerned groups and identity. Some research, perhaps starting with LeBon (1896), has stressed the way that individuals may lose something of themselves in a crowd situation. Zimbardo (1969, 2007) refined and developed this broad theme when articulating the idea of deindividuation – the loss of awareness of self as an individual that can occur in situations where the individual is anonymous, especially in a group context. This work has typically approached groups and crowds as releasing destructive and impulsive behaviour that is no longer under the control of the individual and their sense of themselves as a distinct individual.

Another markedly different group approach to groups and identity has emphasised not the loss of identity that may occur in groups but, rather, the *change* of identity, from personal to group or social identity. This work, shaped by Tajfel (1970, 1978), Turner, Hogg, Oakes, Reicher and Wetherell (1987) and Brown (1978) draws attention to the ways in which individuals come to categorise themselves as members of a certain group and the influence that a group identity can have on their behaviour – particularly intergroup behaviour. Some work has developed an understanding of the ways in which group behaviour may, in turn, shape group identity (Drury and Reicher, 1999, 2000) and the ways in which social identity may relate to deindividuation (Postmes & Spears, 1998).

Evolutionary

Evolutionary ideas have been so influential in psychology that the term 'evolutionary psychology' is sometimes employed to describe evolutionary approaches to a broad sweep of psychological concerns. 'Evolutionary social psychology' has emphasised the extent to which our social behaviour can be understood as consistent with instincts found in many intelligent species. This work may be best introduced by considering three aspects of social psychology that it has particularly contributed to – aggression, altruism and attraction.

With regards to aggression, Lorenz (1966) argued that we have an inherited 'fighting instinct', which comes from the evolutionary needs for the fittest males to win the rights to mate with females so as to pass on the strongest, best-adapted genes. More recently, Hilton, Harris and Rice (2000) note that males' tendency to aggress against other males rather than females reflects evolutionary concerns with aggressing against possible competitors for mates. By contrast, male aggression against a female could be understood as potentially decreasing mating opportunities (the females possibly rejecting males who may threaten them or their offspring).

Likewise, certain instances of prosocial behaviour (especially involving help given to family members) can be interpreted, as Hamilton (1964, cited in Brown, 1986, pp. 91, 92) suggests, as a means of gene pool protection: 'Because animals that are related will share genes, it is theoretically possible for an individual to preserve its genes, not through itself, by behaving altruistically with respect to kin.' Burnstein, Crandall and Kitayama (1994) suggest that these concerns with maximising the propagation of our own genes explain their reported results that human participants reported a preference to help those to whom they are most closely genetically related.

Evolutionary understandings of attraction have reported on discrepancies between what males and females 'look for' in a potential mate. Some of the reported findings suggest that males are more concerned with youth and females with wealth in potential opposite sex mates (Buss, 1989; Chu, Hardaker, & Lycett, 2007). These differences have then been explained in terms of concern with maximising the opportunity for successful mating (hence males seek females with maximum likelihood of fertility) and rearing of young (hence females seek males who will provide the best resources for their offspring).

The evolutionary perspective, then, tends to explain various facets of human social behaviour not in terms of social perception or social forces but, rather, common instinctual drives within each individual.

Cross-cultural

Cross-cultural research certainly does not cohere into one perspective within social psychology – it is drawn on by researchers whose theoretical commitments range from social constructionism to social cognition. Cross-cultural issues have been at the heart of heated debate in social psychology – for example, between Eckman, who emphasised the importance of universal aspects of facial displays and recognition of emotions, and Russell, who argued that these were not universal but culturally specific. One area where cross-cultural research has a particular resonance is that concerned with the self and identity.

Markus and Kitayama (1991) draw attention to the different self-representations found in Eastern and Western cultures. Eastern cultures are associated with more emphasis on *interdependent* self-representations (self-schemas that emphasise the properties of the self in contrast to others), while Western cultures are associated with more *independent* representations of self (self-schemas that emphasise relations with others). The significance of this for Markus and Kitayama (1991) is all the more pronounced as they argue that this results in Western individuals having their behaviour and responses shaped by different (more independent) self-representations than their Eastern counterparts (for whom interdependent self-representations have more influence).

Sampson (1993) drew a similar East–West distinction in terms of understanding self. He drew on a range of cross-cultural research to show both the vast differences in terms of how fundamental aspects of self are construed in Eastern and Western cultures and question the assumptions that he argued permeate much of psychology.

Sampson argued that the predominant Western – and psychological – view of self was that of a 'self-contained individual', whereas the dominant view in much of the non-Western (particularly non-English-speaking) world is described as a dialogic, relational or ensembled individual. While the self-contained individual is defined by contrast with others and as the primary agent in their lives, the relational self is defined in concert with others and was not considered the 'chief agent' in determining their lives. For Sampson these ideas do not lead to a nuanced understanding of the ways in which representations of self differ or which type of representations are most influential – instead, they raise fundamental questions about our everyday and professional, psychological assumptions regarding how the self should be understood, ideas which are developed in the work of Gergen (2009a, 2009b).

Before running away with the idea that all social psychologists – regardless of other allegiences – are happy to draw on cross-cultural differences, it is worth noting that some have sounded a word of caution. Vignoles, Chryssochoou and Breakwell (2004), for example, raised the issue that representations of the person may be much more diverse than broad cultural assertions appear to suggest. Similarly, Jaspal and Cinnirella's (2010) research raises the issue that people can be found to have complex, contradictory identities – an observation that, again, may problematise ideas that draw on the notion of a relatively homogeneous culture.

Social representations

Social representations are shared, or collective, beliefs – sometimes thought of as 'commonsense' theories or broad understandings that circulate in society. Some social representations literature emphasises the cognitive as well as the societal dimensions to these representations, defining them as 'constellations of beliefs, social practices and shared knowledge that exist as much in individuals' minds as in the fabric of society' (Moscovici, 1973, cited in Morant, 2006, p. 817).

Through its emphasis on broad, collective understandings, social representations research has provided a stance that challenges, and supplements, approaches that are tied to individual perceptions and understandings of social reality. Two areas of this contribution that are touched on here and developed in respective chapters of this text are *attributions* and *attitudes*.

While most attribution research has been concerned with detailing the means by which individuals arrive at judgements regarding causes of behaviour (such as why someone did what they did), social representations brings more widely held explanatory systems into focus. Thus, beliefs such as Christians being blamed for the great fire of Rome and Jews for the bubonic plague are examples of widely held, historically located social representations in which terrible events were attributed to specific, identifiable groups of people. Examples of genocides in the twentieth century reveal, graphically, the pernicious power of such shared understandings, with, for example, Jewish and Tutsi people being blamed for national discontent in Germany in the first few decades of the twentieth century and in Rwanda in the 1990s, respectively.

Similarly, while much research on attitudes has conceptualised it in individualistic terms, social representations broadens this to encompass shared or social understandings of the social world. One example of this, which is developed in Chapter 6, is Moloney and Walker's (2002) research on representations of organ donation and transplantation. By drawing on the concept of representations, they are able to situate individual stances on organ donation and transplantation within wider understandings concerning medicine and 'the gift of life'. This not only adds to an understanding of the shared network of beliefs and understanding associated with a specific 'attitudinal position' regarding organ donation but also enables an appreciation of the contradictory or dilemmatic aspects of those positions. Through the lens of social representations, we can go beyond individual cognition and see something of the culturally held frameworks of understanding and the complex and inconsistent stances on a specific topic (in this case, organ donation) that these enable.

Ideological

As noted above, social representations research provides a framework for moving beyond individual acts of cognition to a consideration of how beliefs and understandings might be more widely held. This work overlaps considerably with what might be thought of as *ideological* approaches to social psychology. Two quite distinct aspects of this will be touched on here – work that is, in various ways, inspired by Marxist understandings and that draws on Foucault's ideas.

Historically, Marxist ideas have had a significant impact on psychology. As Hepburn (2003) notes, there have been several 'anti-fascist Jewish Marxist radicals', such as Max Horkheimer, Erich Fromm and Theodor Adorno, who fled the Nazis in the 1930s. One particularly important strand of research within this tradition concerned the ways in which fascism – which was related to an individual's 'authoritarian personality' – could have emerged from the ideological superstructure of late capitalism. That is, 'late capitalism gave rise to an authoritarian state, an authoritarian culture and an authoritarian personality' (Hepburn, 2003, p. 54) – an idea that links societal structure with personality and, in turn, with support for tyrannical societal regimes.

Another important strand of research, shaped by Marxist concerns but separate to the Frankfurt School, is the work of Prilleltensky (1989) and Fox (1985). Prilleltensky and Fox provide important, wide-ranging criticisms of psychology in general and social psychology in particular – a recurrent element of which is their highlighting of the *individualising* emphasis of psychology. From this perspective, not only is social psychology's conception of the self individualistic – with economic and power relations being treated as irrelevant – but also the individualism is reflected in social psychology's dominant explanations for social behaviour. Thus, aggression between groups, for example, is understood (perhaps by reference to the individual's social perception or immediate situation or biological imperatives) without reference to the possible issues of injustice or inequality that may form an important rationale for the aggressive action. Work from a broadly Marxist perspective suggests that, in attempting to side-step issues of power and ideology, psychology's individualising tendency has adopted the ideological position of supporting the status quo. From this perspective, whatever social ills we are trying to explain, it is not society or power relations that need to change but, rather, the individual.

Foucault's work is drawn on particularly in Chapters 2 and 10. Foucault provides a radical challenge to many ideas within social science. In the case of social psychology, he introduces both the importance of institutional practices and disciplinary constructions of reality without succumbing to an overly simplified 'top-down' model of power. Foucault gives a sense of how available frameworks for talking and thinking about phenomena – discourses – do not simply reflect but, rather, construct our sense of our selves and our worlds.

A particularly important aspect of Foucault's work for social psychology is the complex ways in which each person is involved in their own 'subjectification'. That is, the ways in which persons make themselves *subjects* – constituting or *constructing themselves* and making themselves *subject to* regimes of power. This provides a radically different way to understand issues of self and identity – introducing the idea that we may form our identity through positions, subject positions, which discourses make available. Similarly, social influence need not be depicted as simply the operation of external forces on the individual. Instead, how the individual subjects themselves – *even in the very process of constructing their individuality* – comes into view.

Discourse analytic/discursive

In briefly outlining certain aspects of Foucault's work that are important for our thinking about social psychology above, mention was made of *discourses*. There the term was used to refer loosely to constructions of reality – versions of any aspect of reality. This interest in constructions of reality and the ideological relevance they have is an important concern for much of discourse analysis. A second concern, in what is often termed *discursive psychology*, has paid particular attention to how people *do* things – particularly interaction-orientated things – in and through their talk. Running through both of these strands of research is a concern with the ways in which the versions of reality that are produced do not only do ideological and interactional work but may also be self-warranting, attending to their own epistemological, or truth, status.

Attention to power-infused constructions of reality has focused on constructions where issues of power imbalance may be especially important. Thus, there has been considerable work done in the area of discourses concerning ethnicity and race (van Dijk,1993; Wetherell & Potter, 1992) and relating to masculinity, femininity and sex (Gill, 1993; Wilkinson & Kitzinger, 1995). In briefly illustrating the second of these concerns it can be noted that Anderson (2008a, 2008b, 2008c), Edley and Wetherell (1997) and Wetherell and Edley (1999) have analysed some of the versions of masculinity that men adopt in constructions of themselves in talk – for example, how they construct being 'male', 'heroic' and a 'new man'. Koborov and Thorne (2009) have examined young women's constructions of relationships in a context that particularly values romantic accounts and Evans, Riley and Shankar (2010) the sexual subjectivities that women might occupy in a highly sexualised contemporary society.

Potter (2010) notes that discursive psychology has its roots in previous discourse analytic research that was interested in ideological themes or ways in which features of the world are constructed in talk (interpretative repertoires) and relied largely on interviews for data to analyse. The term 'discursive psychology' was deliberately used to signal a new strand of work that developed an interest in the sort of interactional work done in everyday life. Thus, real-world data (broadcast talk, print media and everyday talk of all forms) came to be the data that was turned to. The analysis of this data was particularly concerned with both highlighting the sorts of interactional work accomplished in talk and using this to develop a critical response to cognitively orientated psychology (and social psychology in particular), so this work has provided a critical take on many of the topics addressed in this text. Potter (2010) notes the ways in which discursive work now continues to engage with the 'problems of cognitivism', while also contributing to a better understanding of institutional practices and everyday interactions.

Discourse analytic and/or discursive work is important for each of the chapters in this text, developing as it does a challenge, particularly to cognitively inspired approaches to social psychological topics. Discourse analysis and discursive psychology might not – and perhaps should not – provide a 'last word' on each topic (if, as Billig, (1987) notes such a thing were ever possible), but they do in different ways highlight many of the implicit assumptions within social psychological research and provide a different way of conceptualising and researching each topic.

Conversation analytic

Conversation analysis overlaps considerably with the concerns of discursive psychology and, indeed, is acknowledged as an important source of inspiration for discursive psychology (Potter, 2010). Conversation analysis has its roots in a series of lectures given in the mid to late 1960s by Harvey Sacks. In these lectures, Sacks outlined a radical rethink regarding how we might make sense of talk and interaction. He took advantage of what was the comparatively young technology of readily available audio recording equipment to record a wide variety of material, including group therapy sessions, everyday phone calls (taking advantage of the shared or 'party' line used in California at the time) and calls to a suicide prevention centre. From this last source, Sacks noticed something in the following interaction (Extract 1.1).

Extract 1.1

Op: Go ahead please.
A: This is Mr Smith (B: Hello) of the Emergency Psychiatric Centre, can I help you?
B: Hello?
A: Hello.
B: I can't hear you.
A: I see. Can you hear me now?
B: Barely. Where are you, in the womb?

Source: Sacks (1995, p. 7)

The interaction proceeds without B giving his or her name (a concern at the centre at that time) and subsequently resists doing so. This seemingly unremarkable slice of interaction suggested that B's 'mishearing' (whatever its ontological status) was somehow linked to resisting giving his or her name.

This observation could, as Schegloff (1995, p. xviii) suggests, be seen as the birth of conversation analysis because, 'there is the distinctive and utterly critical recognition here that the talk can be examined as an object in its own right.' That is, Sacks was interested in *talk action* – not talk as a reflection of something else (such as underlying cognition), but talk as *doing action in interaction*. He also was sensitive to the remarkably detailed organisation of talk in interaction – details easily missed (such as the apparent mishearing) showed the fine-grained ways in which participants organise their talk. This organised action was also understood as being inextricably linked to sequential placement. What any utterance was doing could only be *understood* by examining its placement in the turn by turn sequence of interaction. Also, what any utterance *did* was occasioned by, and made possible through, the surrounding interaction sequence.

Sack's (1995) and Sacks, Schegloff and Jefferson's (1974) work also originated the idea of membership categorisation devices – that is, how people use category descriptions to do interactional work. In everyday interaction, people regularly employ category descriptions such as 'old', 'male', 'female', 'mother', father' to categorise certain members of society. Rather than seeing these categories as reflecting either the reality of categories in our world, or, the structure of an individual's perception of the world, however, they are seen as forms of talk that accomplish interactional work, partly because of the implicit associations that these categories have – the sorts of relationships, other categories and associated behaviours that are taken to normatively cohere with the category in use.

Conversation analysis thus has a vast relevance for how we make sense of any talk. In this text, the discussion of self, attraction and relationships, explanation, attitudes and communication and interaction draw on conversation analytic research. In each of these cases, particular attention is given to the way in which talk can be understood as sequentially contingent action. To highlight just two illustrations from this work, Stokoe and Edwards (2010) illustrate the sort of exonerating work that seemingly 'neutral' category use may orientate to (see Chapter 2), while Goodwin (1995, 2003) draws on his development of conversation analytic work concerned with body movement, gaze and gesture to investigate how a person with a severely impaired lexicon can engage in complex communication through the sequential placement of their gaze, gestures and speech fragments.

1.6 About this book

As the title suggests, this book is concerned with drawing on different perspectives within social psychology in order to acknowledge debates that exist in the discipline and encourage you to join in with them. The title creates a dichotomy between 'traditional' perspectives on the one hand and 'critical' perspectives on the other – this is to signal the range of different literatures that are engaged in here and emphasise the exhilarating clash of ideas that emerges when they are brought together. It is worth noting, however, that 'traditional' may sound both pejorative (suggesting that these perspectives are somehow 'out of date') and, at the same time, somewhat endorsing (suggesting that they are well established). Both of these value-laden interpretations are best avoided. As you will see when reading this book, there is well thought out, insightful, relevant and 'up-to-date' literature that could be seen as non-critical or 'traditional' and, as this chapter has argued, the issue of how 'well established' critical ideas are can be debated. One aim of this book is to do justice to the contribution that this body of work continues to make in social psychology while at the same time encouraging engagement with challenges to it.

As mentioned earlier in this chapter, this book also makes use of 'critical literature' – that is, the diverse body of literature which in different ways questions various assumptions about how we approach topics, conduct research or even write about social psychology. Examples of this fundamental questioning start in the very next chapter where, alongside literature that has sought to understand cognitive processes implicating self and identity, the whole issue of what we take to be 'self' is opened out for debate. The critical literature is often, though not always, introduced towards the end of each chapter. This simply reflects that the critical literature is usually a comment or perspective on the material that has gone before, so it is easier if that 'target of the criticism' is outlined first. The 'critical' literature is not meant to be a sort of trump card to close the debate wherever it is produced, but, instead, is intended to expose assumptions and implications and open out issues for debate. Where possible, some of the issues and limitations of this literature will be addressed also. As Billig (1987) reflects, just because something might appear as a 'last word' in a chapter should not be taken to mean that it is in any sense the 'last word' on the issue – the debate can, and should, continue.

It is worth having a quick look through the chapter titles that are coming up: Self and identity, Attraction and relationships, Attribution, Explanatory talk, Attitude change and persuasion, Stereotypes and prejudice, Prosocial behaviour, Aggression and intergroup conflict, Social influence and intragroup processes and Communication and interaction. Some of these titles perhaps hint that something slightly 'different' from the usual coverage will be involved – 'explanatory talk' and 'communication and interaction' both (correctly) suggest that some sort of discursive and/or conversation analytic research will be covered in those chapters. The other chapter titles appear much more conventional – the sorts of titles that you might find in many social psychology textbooks. If you look beyond the titles, however, you will find in each of them that dual-sided critical approach referred to earlier in this chapter. In addition to covering both classic and contemporary 'traditional' literature, each chapter will raise critical reflections regarding the literature covered and will introduce critical literature that opens out for debate some of the unexamined assumptions of what might be called more 'mainstream' contributions.

This chapter started with the observation that momentous events in the news and everyday occurrences in our daily lives might make us turn to social psychology for answers. Social psychology might not have simple, uncontestable, singular answers to these questions, but, in some ways, this is part of its appeal. The fact that social psychology is so full of debate does indicate that it is developing, emerging, alive in some sense. The scope for debate and critical thinking within social psychology also gives you the wonderful possibility of being an *active* participant in the discipline, rather than a mere passive consumer of 'empirical' (or any other form of) 'truth'. If this book succeeds, it will support you in becoming more aware of the debates, more willing and able to critique the ideas and research that you encounter and more empowered in your *active, argumentative* and *critical engagement* with social psychology.

Summary

- This chapter began by outlining 'critical thinking' – as a way of describing a questioning, argumentative engagement with social psychology – and 'critical literature' – a term used to refer to literature that questions many of the fundamental and often implicit assumptions within social psychology.
- The chapter has provided an account of the emergence of social psychology that emphasised its experimental lineage and concern with issues broadly associated with social perception.
- This depiction of the emergence of social psychology was problematised in terms of the forgotten contributors to social psychology and the ignored aspects of those contributors who were acknowledged. Attention to these forgotten and ignored contributions was seen to position 'critical' ideas much more centrally within social psychology.
- The chapter addressed some of the ways in which what we might take to be 'the data' does not simply 'speak for itself'. Kuhn's work on paradigms and Billig's work on 'fictional things' was drawn on in developing these ideas.

- The chapter drew on research by Reicher and Haslam (2006a, 2006b) and Zimbardo's (2006) critique of this work to illustrate some of the ways in which debates within social psychology may not be readily resolved by further empirical research.
- Finally, this chapter outlined ten key approaches within social psychology – illustrating some of the ways that, even within a single topic in social psychology, markedly different approaches may be drawn on. These differing approaches were seen to provide not simply different answers to an agreed on, consensual understanding of a given topic but, rather, markedly different ways of explaining, researching *and* constructing the issues themselves.

Review questions

1. *What do you understand by 'critical' thinking and 'critical' literature in social psychology?*
2. *What are the problems, if any, with conventional accounts of the emergence and key focus of social psychology?*
3. *What is Billig (2011) referring to in his argument about 'fictional things' within social psychology? Can you think of some examples?*
4. *Why is it that social psychologists cannot readily settle their differences by conducting an empirical study to test their different ideas? Can you think of an example to illustrate your ideas?*
5. *Drawing on the social cognition, group and evolutionary approaches above, how might social psychologists make sense of aggression?*
6. *Drawing on the situationalist and rational actor approaches above, how might social psychologists explain prosocial behaviour?*
7. *What sorts of issues do you think cross-cultural and ideological work could raise regarding these explanations of aggression and prosocial behaviour?*
8. *Drawing on the social cognition, group and social representations theories above, how might social psychologists understand someone speaking in a prejudiced way about members of a particular ethnic group? What do you think discourse analytic/ discursive psychology or conversation analysis might suggest?*

Recommended reading

Abell, J., & Walton, C. (2010). Imagine: Towards an integrated and applied social psychology. *British Journal of Social Psychology, 49*, 685–690.

Billig, M. (2008). *The hidden roots of critical psychology: Understanding the impact of Locke, Shaftesbury and Reid*. London: Sage. A delightful, thoughtful and thought-provoking book that encourages us to rethink many assumptions we might have about the emergence of psychology and critical thinking within it.

Corcoran, T. (2009). Second nature. *British Journal of Social Psychology, 48*, 375–388.

Greenwood, J. D. (2004a). What happened to the social in social psychology? *Journal for the Theory of Social Behaviour, 34*, 19–34. A briefer version of the interesting and important argument developed in Greenwood's book below.

Greenwood, J. D. (2004b). *The disappearance of the social in American social psychology*. Cambridge: Cambridge University Press. An impressively detailed examination of how social psychology came to have a somewhat individualistic focus.

Kuhn, T. S. (1996). *The structure of scientific revolutions*, (3rd ed.). Chicago, IL: University of Chicago Press. The third edition of Kuhn's landmark work.

Leahey, T. H. (2004). *A history of psychology: Main currents in psychological thought*, (6th ed.). Upper Saddle River, NJ: Prentice Hall. An engaging and thoughtful treatment of some of the history of psychology and how we might understand current fault lines within the discipline.

Articles relating to a debate concerning contemporary discursive psychology:

Potter, J. (2010). Contemporary discursive psychology: Issues, prospects and Corcoran's awkward ontology. *British Journal of Social Psychology, 49*, 657–678.

Papers that relate to the lively debate between Reicher and Haslam and Zimbardo:

Reicher, S., & Haslam, S. A. (2006a). Rethinking the psychology of tyranny: The BBC prison study. *British Journal of Social Psychology, 45*, 1–40.

Reicher, S., & Haslam, S. A. (2006b). Rethinking the psychology of tyranny: The BBC prison study. *British Journal of Social Psychology, 45*, 55–63.

Zimbardo, P. (2006). Commentary – on rethinking the psychology of tyranny: The BBC prison study. *British Journal of Social Psychology, 45*, 47–53.

Useful weblinks

www.bbcprisonstudy.org This site gives a useful overview with behind-the-scenes material relating to Reicher and Haslam's (2006) prison study.

http://psychclassics.asu.edu or **http://psychclassics.yorku.ca** This is a wonderful website with a fantastic collection of some of psychology's most famous publications – particularly strong on what might be considered 'mainstream' literature prior to 1960.

www.socialpsychology.org A useful site for searching for and locating social psychologists and websites – has a US emphasis.

www.discourses.org A great resource for much of Teun van Dijk's discourse analytic research with some excellent downloadable publications, presentations and courses, plus links to other important sites.

www.dennisfox.net/critpsy Dennis Fox's website is a great resource for thinking about critical perspectives in psychology.

www.davidsmail.info/introfra.htm David Smail's website has good resources that support his argument – psychological distress cannot be understood without reference to 'how power is distributed and executed in society'.

www.radpsynet.org/index.html The radical psychology network site, which has an impressive range of resources aimed at challenging the status quo in society and in psychology in pursuit of social justice.

www.youtube.com/watch?v=WJlx8CI-rRg This is an entertaining talk by Prilleltensky who makes the case that social factors and ideologies (rather than just genetic or intra-psychic factors) are crucial for well-being.

www.psych.lse.ac.uk/psr The site for an open access journal *Papers on Social Representations*. It publishes an impressive variety of papers reflecting developments in social representations theory and its applications.

www.bbc.co.uk/radio4/programmes/formats/documentaries/all This archive of Radio 4's documentaries often contains features of relevance to social psychological concerns.

Self and identity

Learning outcomes

By the end of this chapter you should have a critical understanding of research concerning some of the different perspectives on self and identity – in particular:

- debates concerning whether or not there *is* a self
- ideas about the importance of situational factors in thinking about self and identity
- work that has tried to understand self and identity by reference to self-schemas
- ideas about the internal, cognitive aspects to self and identity
- ideas about the way self and identity are shaped by group membership
- critical challenges to dominant, mainstream ways of understanding *what self is*
- interactional perspectives concerned with what self and identity talk *does* in interaction.

On 19 February 2010 Tiger Woods made a very personal public apology following revelations regarding his extra-marital affairs:

Source: AP Photo/Joe Skipper/Press Association Images

Tiger Woods, apologising at a press conference after his affairs became public knowledge

> The issue involved here was my repeated irresponsible behavior. I was unfaithful. I had affairs. I cheated. What I did is not acceptable, and I am the only person to blame. I stopped living by the core values that I was taught to believe in. I knew my actions were wrong, but I convinced myself that normal rules didn't apply . . . I was wrong. I was foolish. I don't get to play by different rules. The same boundaries that apply to everyone apply to me . . .
>
> I've had a lot of time to think about what I've done. My failures have made me look at myself in a way I never wanted to before. It's now up to me to make amends and that starts by never repeating the mistakes I've made. It's up to me to start living a life of integrity . . . People probably don't realize it, but I was raised a Buddhist, and I actively practiced my faith from childhood until I drifted away from it in recent years. Buddhism teaches that a craving for things outside ourselves causes an unhappy and pointless search for security. It teaches me to stop following every impulse and to learn restraint. Obviously, I lost track of what I was taught.

Woods talks about who he is in a way rarely seen in public figures. He talks about both his core values and spiritual practices, learned from his mother, and how his recent behaviour has been discrepant from these. Tiger Woods also talks about his behaviour making him look at himself in a way he 'never wanted to before'. The statement provides both some sense of an account of why he did what he did – referring to his misplaced sense of entitlement – and an extended apology – 'I was wrong. I was foolish.'

In this statement, issues of self and identity are absolutely central – the statement directly addresses the question 'Who is Tiger Woods and how are we to make sense of who he is in the light of his recent behaviour?' The distinction between manifest behaviour (having affairs) and core values (Buddhism) suggests that the latter is somehow more enduring and more 'true to who he really is'. The statement gives a sense of Tiger Woods struggling with his self-concept – seeing things about himself he does not like and wanting to change them. The statement also suggests that part of talking about who we are can involve explaining ourselves or accounting for our behaviour in certain ways. Indeed, even if we see the statement as revealing very little about what Tiger Woods *really* thinks or feels, it still provides an example of how talk about self *does* things – it accounts, explains, agrees with criticism, apologises – or, at least, can be used to try to do these things.

This chapter addresses some of the ways that we can understand how the self and identity have been understood, ranging from work on the importance of the self-concept and group identity to work on the actions that are enacted through talk about self. The very different perspectives covered in this chapter suggest that we need go no further than ourselves to find some of the most intense and far-reaching debates within social psychology.

Introduction

Think of some of the times when you describe who you are. You might use words and photographs when describing how popular, interesting and fun you are on a Facebook page. Perhaps you mention your 'good sense of humour', kindness and sociability when describing yourself to a potential partner – for example, in a 'lonely hearts' advertisement. You may make some claims about yourself in conversation – 'For me, friends come first', 'I can't stand hypocrites', 'I'm not the sort of person to just give up like that.'

Stop for a moment and think about how you describe *who you are* in these sorts of settings. Are they the *real* you or is that somewhere else? If the real you lies elsewhere, where is it – is it your self-concept? Should we think about the real you in terms of the groups that you belong to and identities that you have as a member of these groups? Is the real you somehow shaped by the culturally available ways of thinking about yourself – for example, as a certain type of male or female? Should we pay attention to what you are *doing* – exonerating yourself, blaming others, for example – when you are talking about the sort of person you are? It is precisely these questions that open up the social psychology of the self and identity.

Chapter overview

This chapter starts by briefly reflecting on two classic questions concerning self: 'Is there a core self?' and 'Is our identity socially situated?'

The first of these questions opens up a long-standing debate about how we can understand whether there is a 'self' over and above the individual's collection of experiences. The second addresses the extent to which our sense of who we are is derived from sources outside of ourselves, in particular our perceptions of others' perceptions of us.

Two particularly important strands of work concerned with cognitive approaches towards self within social psychology are then reviewed. The first of these focuses on schema theory – an approach that brought self back to centre stage within social psychology by addressing the ways in which our collections of information (and misinformation) about self are consequential for our processing of social stimuli. The second strand of cognitive work is research that has paid particular attention to issues of self-affect and self-esteem. This diverse assemblage of research briefly reviews some of the important contributions to thinking about issues of how we reflect on self (self-awareness), how we make judgements and feel about self (self-esteem) and how we seek to control or modify who or what we are (self-regulation).

The chapter then addresses research that has examined social identities – social identity theory and self-categorisation theory, both of which challenge the emphasis on a stable, core individual self found in much of the work on schema, affect and esteem. By contrast, social identity theory and self-categorisation theory argue that self is not always experienced in terms of personal identity (for example, what is or is not 'me'). Instead, these theories emphasise that self can be experienced in terms of a shared, group or *social* identity, where the attributes associated with a group one identifies with, 'us' (as opposed to those of an *outgroup* 'them'), become more salient.

This concern with social identity leads to a wider critique of much of the social psychology of self, which, from some perspectives, has adopted a rather individualistic focus. Historical and cross-cultural analysis is drawn on in support of the idea that the currently predominant concept of self within Western cultures in general – and much of psychology in particular – can be challenged. A theme developed here is that less individualistic ways of thinking about self are not only available, but also our ways of thinking about self are *consequential* for how we think about societal problems and their solutions.

The final part of the chapter addresses two areas that are less frequently represented in social psychology textbooks – identity talk in interaction and Foucault and identity formation. In considering identity talk in interaction, attention is given to some of the sorts of interactional things that may happen when people talk about self – such as how apparently contradictory versions of self may be produced to deal with specific and changing interactional contingencies.

Last of all, the chapter briefly reflects on Foucault's radical contribution to thinking about self and the ways in which his work has enabled much subsequent research – which has drawn on his notions of *discursive formations* and *subject positions*.

2.1 Historically important questions about self and identity

This chapter starts by highlighting two important questions about **self** and **identity**. The first of these concerns whether or not there is a 'core' self over and above conscious experiences and the second is whether our sense of who we are – or our identity – is socially created or not. In examining the debate about whether or not there is a core self, the starting point will be the ego theory versus bundle theory debate, which was especially prominent in the eighteenth century. This debate, however, perhaps provides a starting point for some contemporary, radical questioning about the individualised concepts of self and the ideologies of self that are addressed later in this chapter.

The second question is whether our identity is socially created or not. This question is explored by considering some symbolic interactionist work on identity, ranging from the work of Mead at the beginning of the twentieth

Self As with *identity*, a term used in this chapter where the literature being considered uses it. Self is difficult to define – not least because of the different ways in which it is used in social psychological literature. At its broadest, self can be thought of as referring to any aspect of who or what the individual is – or is considered to be.

Identity Identity and *self* are used in this chapter in a way that is consistent with the literature being reviewed, much of which tends to emphasise one term rather than the other. Identity broadly refers to anything that can be considered a 'representation' of self such as talk or thoughts about who one is.

century to more recent research addressing the ways in which role relationships and possessions may shape our identity. The issues addressed here have some resonance with research on schemas and self (which includes consideration of how interactions may activate self-schemas – sometimes referred to as schemata) and research on social identities (which particularly develops the idea of shared, group-based identities), both of which are addressed later in this chapter.

Is there a core self?

One crucial debate regarding self-concerns whether self is best thought of as comprising some essence beyond the millions of individual conscious experiences we have – every thought and sensation – or whether there is nothing more than a collection (or bundle) of such experiences. These two positions are clearly illustrated in the quotes below. The first is from Thomas Reid (cited in Blackmore, 2003, p. 96):

> I am not thought, I am not action, I am not feeling: I am something which thinks and acts and feels.

Reid was an eighteenth-century Scottish philosopher who suggested that, in addition to our conscious experience – and behaviour – there is some *essential self* that is the agent or subject. This self experiences our experiences and undertakes our actions. It is quite possible that this perspective (known as **ego theory**) sounds like common sense – it may well reflect the views of ourselves or others that there is a real 'self' over and above each mental experience that we have had. Consider for a moment, however, an observation made by another eighteenth-century Scottish philosopher, David Hume (cited in Blackmore, 2003, p. 96):

> I never catch *myself* at any time without a perception, and can never observe anything but the perception.

Hume is suggesting that there is no separate self that can be grasped beyond a constant flow of conscious experiences. We can contemplate our thoughts, our feelings, our intentions, our attitudes and our motivations – even our very sense of self – but each time we are encountering yet another conscious experience rather than anything that stands outside of or separate from consciousness. This idea that there is no self beyond our collection of mental experiences is known as **bundle theory** – according to which we are just a bundle of mental experiences.

The very term 'bundle' could give the impression of some form of disintegrated consciousness, jumping haphazardly from one conscious experience to another. William James (1890) was especially important here, in developing the notion of a 'stream of consciousness'. For James, thought is 'sensibly continuous' – that is, it *feels continuous*. Our sense of conscious continuity – the very lack of jumping from one conscious experience to another – need not, therefore, be immediately attributed to the stable, underlying self of ego theory but could be a result of our experience of a 'stream of thought, of consciousness or of subjective life' (James, 1890, p. 239).

It is worth stopping for a moment and asking 'ourselves' a few questions. Who owns your phone, your car, your body? You might respond, 'I do!', but what 'I' are you referring you – is it your body, your brain, your thoughts?

One more recent theorist, Dennett, suggests that the way we talk and think as though there is a separate me 'inside' us is important. For Dennett, it is this way of constructing our worlds – with some 'self' at the centre – that gives us a sense of having some unified, coherent, essential self. Dennett suggests that we have a stream of conscious perception – but a web of narratives tying these together to form a sense of self – or selves. According to Dennett, then, it is our narratives, or representations of self, that create the sense that there is a self separate from our conscious experience. 'Our tales are spun, but for the most part we don't spin them; they spin us. Our human consciousness, and our narrative selfhood, is their product, not their source' (Dennett, 1991, p. 418, cited in Blackmore, 2010, p. 120).

At the start of this chapter we had the example of Tiger Woods' personal statement accounting for his actions. In his statement, he produced narratives of core values (his spiritual values), the way that behaviour inconsistent with those values is problematic ('what I did is not acceptable') and his agency and responsibility for his behaviour ('only I am to blame'). These ideas that there are core values underneath our behaviour reflecting our true self, our behaviour should be consistent with these values and is accountable when it is not and we are (or should be) responsible for the actions we undertake are all very widespread versions – or, in Dennett's terms, narratives – of self.

Dennett's work, therefore, endorses the bundle theorists' idea that we are a stream of conscious mental

Ego theory The idea that there is some essence beyond our conscious experiences – we are more than just the bundle of our stream of conscious experiences – and this something is *self*.

Bundle theory The idea that what we are is simply the totality of our conscious experiences, with no essential self lying beyond this stream of consciousness.

experiences, but also the idea that we feel we are more than this. In developing the idea of narratives of self that give rise to a sense of 'having' a core, real, underlying self that accounts for our behaviour, Dennett addresses issues related to social constructionist perspectives on self and identity considered later in this chapter.

Is our identity socially created?

This idea that our identity is linked to our interrelations with others draws on symbolic interactionist work that has deep roots in social psychology. Cooley (1902/1922) argued that self is intrinsically tied to society: 'a man [sic] is bound into the whole of which he is a member, and to consider him apart from it is quite as artificial as to consider society apart from groups' (Cooley, 1902/1922, p. 38). (see Box 2.1 for classic research partly inspired by Cooley and Mead).

Mead (1934) developed this theme to consider the ways in which our sense of self ('me') is at least partly contingent on how we experience others' conceptions of us through our interactions with them. From this perspective, our sense of self is both malleable – it can change as our interactions change – and social – it depends on interactions with others. In a meta-review of research into

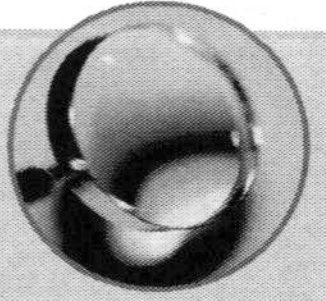

Box 2.1 FOCUS
Classic research: an empirical investigation into self-attitudes (Kuhn & McPartland, 1954)

Kuhn and McPartland (1954, p. 68) drew on Mead's idea of 'the self as an object which is in most respects like all other objects' and his understanding that 'an object is a plan of action' to suggest that a framework for thinking about self consistent with Mead can be developed by thinking in terms of 'self-attitudes'. Kuhn and McPartland's (1954, p. 69) classic paper was concerned with developing a test of 'self-attitudes' and these are the instructions that they gave to their participants:

> There are twenty numbered blanks on the page below. Please write twenty answers to the simple question 'Who am I?' in the blanks. Just give twenty different answers to this question. Answer as if you were giving the answers to yourself, not to somebody else. Write the answers in the order that occur to you. Don't worry about logic or 'importance'. Go along fairly fast, for time is limited.

The 'twenty statements test', as it became known, was administered to 288 undergraduate students at the State University of Iowa in 1952. Students were given the instructions either orally or in writing and had 12 minutes to complete the test.

Kuhn and McPartland (1954) were interested in the distinction between what they referred to as 'consensual' and 'sub-consensual' statements in participants' responses. Sometimes this distinction is glossed in terms of 'group' versus 'individual' self-descriptions, but this is not exactly what Kuhn and McPartland were saying. For them, (1954, p. 69), 'consensual' statements 'refer to groups and classes *whose limits and conditions of membership are matters of common knowledge*, i.e. consensual' and, by contrast, 'sub-consensual' statements refer to 'groups, classes, attributes, traits or any other matters *which would require interpretation by the respondent to be precise or to place him relative to other people'*. Kuhn and McPartland suggest that 'student', 'girl', 'husband', 'Baptist', 'from Chicago', 'pre-med', 'daughter', 'oldest child' and 'studying engineering' are examples of consensual statements, while 'happy', 'bored', 'pretty good student', 'too heavy', 'good wife' and 'interesting' are sub-consensual.

Kuhn and McPartland found that, while there was substantial variation across participants, people tended to use more consensual, 'more directly socially anchored' statements, suggesting that this component of their self-definition was more salient. Kuhn and McPartland's work further suggested, where participants had group affiliations that were more 'differentiating' (applying to fewer members of the immediate population), they were more likely to make reference to them. Thus, members of religious groups that are less prevelant in a given population (in the Kuhn and McPartland, 1954, p. 74) study these included 'Roman Catholics, Jews and members of small sects') should 'carry religious references more saliently in the self-conception'. Kuhn and McPartland provide some evidence for this.

Kuhn and McPartland's work provided an influential test of self-definitions and findings that not only address symbolic interactionist concerns about the way in which self comes to be defined but also, to some extent, anticipated future social identity and self-categorisation work about the ways in which self-definitions in terms of group affiliations can become relevant for individuals.

Box 2.2 TRY IT OUT
Role relationships and identity

Take a moment to list about a dozen different roles and relationships that you are involved in – sister, daughter, partner, student, member of specific clubs or societies, employee, parent, best friend with X, close friend of Y and so on.

List these different roles and relationships in a column on a sheet of paper and, next to each, note some traits that describe how you experience yourself in these roles and relationships – pride, togetherness, caring, isolation, inhibition, confidence, for example.

What you have listed as traits are some of your sub-identities. Now, look through the traits and see if there are any that keep coming up or are particularly important to you (perhaps they arise in interactions with those who are currently most significant in your life). These recurrent and salient traits are your generalised attributes.

Now abstract from these generalised traits the few that are absolutely most important. Some of them may be almost impossible to detach from specific roles – such as 'loving parent', 'devoted partner'. In these cases, note both the role *and* trait.

What you now have is your core identity. This should be relatively stable, though it can change if, for example, there are certain significant changes in roles and the interactions they entail.

Have a look at what you have. Do these self-descriptions make sense to you? Do they feel like you? Do you think that the role relationships really do shape your sense of who you are? Do some of your salient traits create a relatively stable 'core identity' for you?

how self-perceptions relate to others' perceptions of self, Shrauger and Schoeneman (1979) argued that, rather than seeing themselves as others *actually* saw them, people saw themselves as they *thought* others saw them. That is, if we perceive that others think of us in a certain way (eccentric, egotistical and forgetful, for example), then it is that which will inform our sense of self rather than what they *really* think of us (such as generous, intelligent and humorous).

The idea that our sense of self is dependent on social factors may raise the question, if our sense of self is so dependent on interactions with others, then why do we have a sense of continuity? It is worth thinking about these issues in the light of your own thoughts regarding your identity. To do this, grab a pen and paper (or any electronic equivalent) and try the exercises detailed in Box 2.2.

Rossan's (1987) research examined the structure of identity using new and expectant mothers as the specific sources of data. From a series of interviews with these women, Rossan examined the ways in which new and prospective interactions (with maternity staff and the newborn infant) and altered interactions (with a partner, friends and family) could shape these mothers' identity. Rossan argues, however, that, while we may be involved in many interactions, not all of these will change our sense of identity and those that do are likely to affect our outer **sub-identities** rather than our inner **core identity**. Thus, Rossan distinguishes our underlying, continuous sense of self – our core identity – from the more peripheral and varied sub-identities, which reflect the varied interactions (particularly those involving roles) that we engage in. In between the inner and peripheral aspects of identity, Rossan posits that there are certain recurrent facets of identity or 'generalised traits'.

Critical review of historically important questions about self and identity

Is there a core self?

Bundle theory appears to go against the sense that we have of an underlying or core self. This feeling that there is some 'I' is central to how we organise our lives yet it is challenged as no more than a fiction, perhaps created by language.

Ego theory, by contrast, endorses the common perception that there is some core or essential self, but is this merely endorsing a cultural presupposition and, if there is a core self, has anyone satisfactorily defined it?

Sub-identity A relatively specific identity arising from a specific role relationship. See also *core identity*.

Core identity A person's relatively stable sense of who they are, being formed from recurrent features of several *sub-identities*. This can change according to symbolic interactionist ideas, but is likely to change less readily than a sub-identity.

James' work on stream of consciousness provides a way of understanding how we may have a sense of continuity of conscious experience without necessarily presupposing a self.

Dennett's work suggests that we need to pay attention to the narratives of self, as it is here that our sense of self is constructed. This work, however, and all of the literature considered in the ego theory – bundle theory debate has the difficulty of not being readily related to empirical research. This not only means that it is not easily validated against existing research findings but also that it does not readily inspire future relevant research. The very different lines of research that are reviewed in the rest of this chapter do little to address the question of a core self as outlined by the ego theory – bundle theory debate, leaving it largely as a theoretical rather than empirical question.

Is our identity socially created?

Symbolic interactionist work challenges the idea of self as decontextualised, suggesting that self cannot be understood without considering the impact other people and objects can have on an individual's identity. Instead, self is made sense of in terms of a network of relationships that can inform how people come to make sense of who they are. Furthermore, rather than being either relatively fixed or entirely fluid, an individual's identity is understood as having elements of both continuity *and* change – the constants and variants in our *outer* world shaping our *inner* sense of identity.

Symbolic interactionist work, however, can seem to imply a causal link – usually flowing from other people (and how they perceive and interact with the individual) to the individual's sense of their identity. It is, of course, possible to ask (as Billig, 1987 suggests we do of any plausible idea), is the reverse also possible? Thus, it may be that our identity could cause us to get into 'identity-supporting' roles (our identity shaping our exposure to social factors supporting our sense of who we are). Similarly, it could be that we distort our perceptions of how others see us, such that they are consistent with our pre-existing self-image. In each of these ways, the causal arrow from external sources to identity is challenged by considering identity as driving social encounters and social perceptions rather than merely being their consequence.

Questions can also be asked about the way in which data that appears to support **symbolic interactionism** is interpreted. Imagine, for example, a piece of research in which a person perceives that others think of them as being caring and confident. Subsequently, they report (whether in interview or questionnaire) that they perceive themselves as caring and confident also. Discursive and conversation analytic research, considered below, can offer a different way of understanding the empirical data. For example, constructing others' views of us as the same as our own may make our views more consensual and less accountable.

> **Symbolic interactionism** A collection of approaches particularly concerned with the ways in which a sense of self is socially based, being dependent in various ways on the perceptions made by others and interactions with them.

More generally, from a conversation analytic and discursive perspective, issues can be raised concerning whether attention should be on some 'inner' identity (albeit caused by outer relationships) or on the outward 'doing' of identity. As is outlined below, for discursive and conversation analytic research, attention is given to how identity is constructed in interaction and what those constructions do depending on when and where they are placed in interaction.

Critical recap

Historically important questions about self and identity

1 On the one hand, bundle theory may seem counter-intuitive – that is, it seems to contradict our sense (or at least a 'Western' sense) of having some essential self. On the other hand, bundle theory's lack of fit with common sense may have little to do with whether it is true or not and, instead, point to how common sense itself is constituted.

2 Ego theory is, in contrast to bundle theory, more consistent with certain commonsense views in asserting that there *is* a self beyond the mere collection of our conscious experiences. Ego theory, however, typically lacks a clear and compelling specification of what self is.

3 More generally, the empirical basis for any claims regarding these historically important claims about self is limited – and perhaps inevitably so.

4 Symbolic interactionist work provides a different perspective, in which – rather than attempting to define self in the abstract – *context* – especially the context of the network of relationships between self and others – becomes all important. From this perspective, our sense of who we are is realised, accomplished and defined in relation to others. The implication that relationships shape identity could be challenged, however, by considering if the opposite is just as reasonable (Billig, 1987) – that is, perhaps one's sense of identity shapes how and with whom one relates.

5 A still more radical challenge is offered by discursive and conversation analytic research. From this perspective, we could approach talk about self not in terms of what it reveals or conceals about a 'real' self but, rather, in terms of *what that talk does as and where it occurs in the interaction.*

Reflective questions

1 *Do you consider that there is more to you than the sum of all of your experiences? If so, what is that additional something?*

2 *Can you think of any objects you own that are somehow related to your sense of who you are? If so, how do these objects inform your sense of identity?*

2.2 Schemas and self

If you were to write down what you thought the 'social psychology of self' had investigated, it is quite likely you would come up with something that reflects some of the concerns of research on schemas and self. It is in this stream of research that we find attention being paid to our ideas and concepts of self and how these shape our thinking about self and others. The research on schemas and self does not stop with a simple deterministic idea of a single self-concept shaping our cognitive processing, however. Instead, it encompasses the idea we have different conceptions of self that are dynamic, being activated and shaped by factors within ourselves as well as by interactions with others. The picture becomes still more complex when we consider the ways in which our cultural context can shape how we think of our own self – the difference typically being drawn between Western independent and Eastern interdependent conceptions of self.

Schematic dimensions

One important aspect of social cognitive thinking about self concerns the idea of *schematic* and *aschematic* dimensions.

This idea relates to the notion that we have **self-schemas** – information, misinformation and associated affect about self. This work owes some debt to Tajfel's (1969) more general contribution to **categorisation**, in which he argued for the importance of category-based thinking. Tajfel noted that category-based thinking speeds up our cognitive processing (we can quickly identify dangerous others or situations, for example) and therefore has developed partly out of its utility in terms of our survival. Category-based thinking, however, while expedient, is often inaccurate, leading to distortions and errors as we see the category-based attributes rather than the individual detail.

In developing work on schemas, Markus (1977) was paying attention to the crucial, yet somewhat neglected social psychology of self, drawing on the idea that collected bodies of information (and misinformation) were an important part of how self was cognitively represented.

Take five minutes to write down how you would describe yourself. Your description might refer to how you dress, the music that you are into, sporting interests, political or religious beliefs.

Those dimensions that we draw on when describing ourselves have a particular importance and are referred to as **schematic**; those dimensions we do not draw on in describing ourselves are **aschematic**. That is, we are schematic on those dimensions important to us in defining who we are and we are aschematic on dimensions not important to us in defining who we are.

The relevance of schematic and aschematic dimensions is that they influence how we process information about self and others. Schematic information is thought to be easier and faster to process than aschematic information (Druian & Catrambone, 1986). If 'fashionable' is an important aspect of how you describe yourself, for example, then you will more quickly process information relating to that, whether it relates to yourself or others. Thus, if you are presented with self-descriptors relating to fashion, you will quickly respond to them if you are schematic on the dimension of fashion (Markus & Sentis, 1982, cited in Fiske & Taylor, 1991). Think of how quickly you might fill in a self-description survey or questionnaire when it relates to those aspects of yourself that are important to you, but, when the items seem less relevant to how you think about yourself, you may struggle with them more.

These dimensions on which we are schematic not only speed up and ease our processing of schema-related information but also shape how we perceive and judge others. That is, 'people tend to judge others on dimensions that are personally important to themselves' (Markus & Wurf, 1987). If you are very politically active – and see yourself as such – this dimension will be important when you meet others – that is, you will think about them (at least partly) in terms of their political activity (or lack of it). Furthermore, you may well draw inferences from your judgements of people on the dimensions with some (perhaps misplaced) confidence – for example, thinking that a person who is not politically active must be apathetic, selfish or

Self-schema The collection of ideas that a person holds about themselves; tends to be used by cognitive social psychologists.

Categorisation In the cognitive social psychology literature, this refers to the way in which we think of people (and things) in terms of common groupings or categories.

Schematic (aschematic) Issues and topics that are relevant (irrelevant) to our *self-schema*.

uninformed (Markus & Wurf, 1987). In these ways, the very dimensions we reference when we think about self may be important – shaping how we process information and make inferences about both self and others.

Dynamic self-concept

An important strand of social cognitive thinking about self has been the development of the idea of the **dynamic self-concept** (see Figure 2.1). This argues that the **self-concept** is both an important determiner of **cognition** and behaviour and is open to change and development – and we need to pay attention to the way in which the working self-concept at any one time draws on just some of the pool of possible self-representations available to the individual. Markus and Wurf (1987, p. 301) describe the move from a static understanding of self-concept to a dynamic one in these terms: 'What began as an apparently singular, static, lump-like entity has become a multidimensional, multifacted dynamic structure that is systematically implicated in all aspects of social information processing.'

As Figure 2.1 illustrates, the *working self-concept* describes those range of schemas from the pool of possible self-representations that are activated or made salient at any given time. In the example depicted, an individual is asked a question about their work in a tutorial. Two highly relevant self-representations are then made salient in that situation and become part of the working self-concept.

A key feature of the dynamic self-concept is the idea that it, rather than being singular, involves a collection of 'self-representations' (including self-schemas). From that collection, certain self-representations are likely to be salient (cognitively accessible and dominant) at any one time. This subset of self-concepts that are salient at a given moment is referred to as the **working self-concept**. This depicts the 'in the moment' relationship between working memory, and, the intrapersonal and interpersonal processes, that research on the dynamic self-concept suggests.

Dynamic self-concept The idea that a self-concept has consequences for cognition and behaviour, is fluid and open to change.

Self-concept The version or idea about self that someone holds. It is very similar to self-schema (but is not only used by cognitive social psychologists).

Cognition Thinking or mental processes.

Working self-concept The currently active or salient collection of self-concepts – the idea being that these are just a selection from a wider pool of all possible self-concepts.

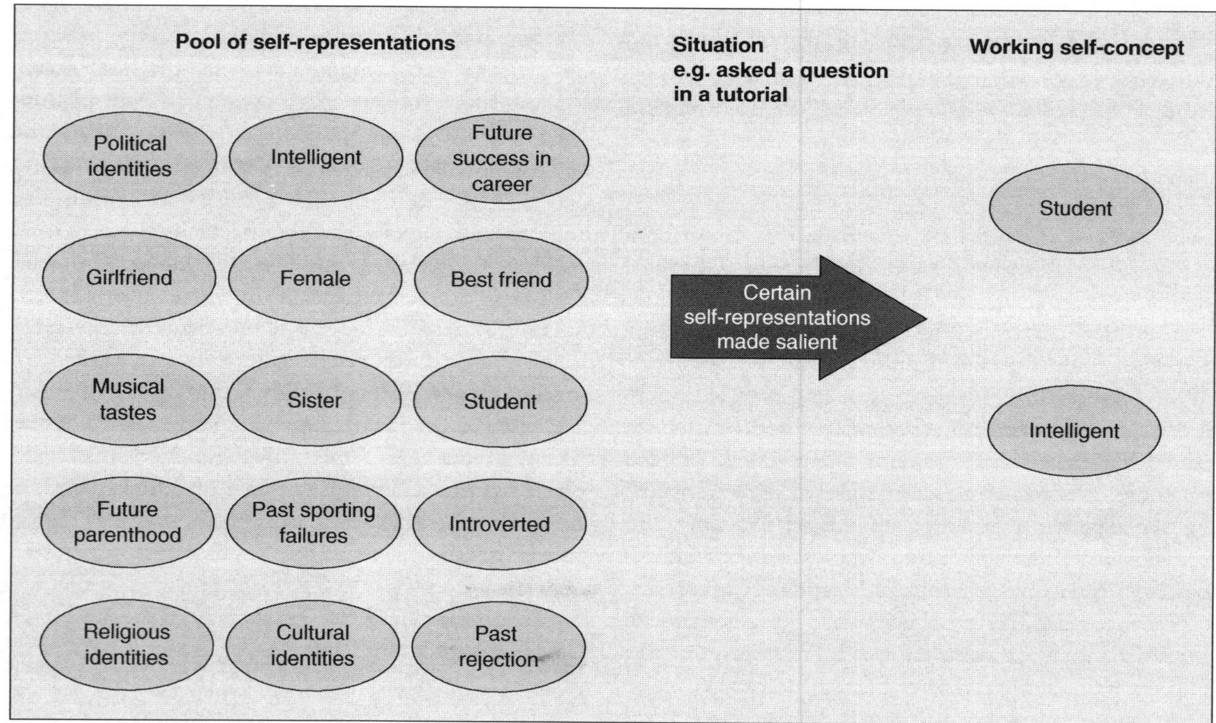

Figure 2.1 Dynamic self-concept – the working self-concept is drawn from a larger pool of potential self-representations

In Markus and Wurf's model, the working self-concept is comprised of a selection of self-concepts drawn from a wider pool of all available self-concepts. This pool of self-concepts is described as including not only *actual* but also *possible* selves: 'the selves one would like to be or is afraid of becoming' (Markus & Wulf, 1987, p. 302). Think for a moment about a sportsperson trying to motivate themselves to train hard on a cold, dark morning. Thinking about the possible future self, as an Olympic champion, such that it becomes a part of the current working self-concept, may be a powerful motivator for their present behaviour. Similarly, fears about what we may become can also shape our motivations and behaviours. A smoker envisaging himself becoming seriously ill with lung cancer can shape current behaviour that he perceives as relevant – as a consequence, he may quit smoking, for example. Together, actual and possible selves form a large array of potential self-concepts, a small number of which will form the working self-concept at any one time and thereby shape our cognitive and behavioural responses.

Markus and Wurf (1987) argue the repertoire of active self-representations that get to form the working self-concept can be selected automatically or deliberately. Thus, in some cases, something in the situation may make certain self-concepts salient. For example, being at a football match may bring one's self-concept of being a supporter of a particular team into the working self-concept (see Box 2.3). In some cases (as indicated above) the individual deliberately draws on certain self-concepts – if you are about to sit an examination, you might deliberately think about your past successes and your knowledge of the topic to help give yourself confidence.

Some of the ways in which self-concepts relate to intrapersonal behaviour have already been indicated – envisaging myself as an Olympic champion may help to motivate me when I have to run round the track on an icy morning, contemplating getting cancer may make me quit smoking. As well as our motivations, our **affective state** may be influenced by the working self-concept – seeing myself as failing, unsuccessful or socially isolated may evoke negative affect, such as sadness or anger. A similar influence can be found from working self-concept to interpersonal behaviour. If my working self-concept includes social ease and competence, for example, I may perceive and interact with strangers at a party quite differently from when my working self-concept is flooded with concepts of being socially inept and fearful.

The model of the working self-concept also allows for it to be influenced to some extent by intrapersonal and interpersonal behaviour. One such influence is that affective states may make certain self-concepts more salient. Have you ever noticed that when you are feeling down, negative self-concepts are more salient than positive ones? When we are in a negative affective state, we typically have negative views about ourselves. Some of this could be understood as a result of a negative working self-concept producing negative affect, but the reverse is also possible – negative affect, such as feeling down or depressed, may make affectively consistent self-concepts more salient. That is, we may *think* negatively about ourselves because we are *feeling* negative. This suggests the possibility of a reinforcing relationship between a working self-concept and affect – a negative self-concept may evoke negative feelings that may make negative self-concepts more salient and so on. Similarly, our interactions with others may not only be shaped by our self-concept but also be shaping our working self-concept. Experiencing people as interested in us and enjoying our company may evoke self-concepts of being socially competent; by

Box 2.3 TRY IT OUT
The dynamic self-concept

Look at the individuals in this photograph of Northern Ireland football fans. How important do you think that their identity as fans of Northern Ireland is for each of them? Do you think that the identity of being a fan becomes more important for these individuals at certain times and places and, if so, why?

Source: Mark Thompson/Getty Images

Northern Ireland football fans displaying symbols of their salient group identity during a football match

Affective state A person's emotional state or feelings at a given time.

contrast, experiencing people as being negative and disinterested towards us may promote self-concepts of having poor social skills. In both cases, the experience – or, indeed, perception – of interpersonal interaction can be seen to shape our working self-concept.

These ideas suggest that the working self-concept is less static than may have previously been thought – that is, it not only dynamically influences cognition and affect within the individual but also shapes how the person perceives and behaves towards others. Furthermore, rather than being fixed, it is somewhat more fluid – open to the possibility of change. Markus and Wurf (1987, p. 318) note how this model of a dynamic, mutually influencing self-concept differs from many other measures, which present a relatively fixed snapshot as *the* self-concept: 'The stability of the self that is implied by such measures may belie significant malleability or fluidity that occurs as individuals respond to information that challenges their view of themselves.'

Culturally located self-schemas

If Markus and Wurf (1987) can be thought of as extending schema theory to encompass a more *dynamic* self-concept, then Markus and Kitayama (1991) extended it to allow for a more *culturally located* one. They argue that our cultural context shapes which attributes we treat as most relevant for our self-schema and has an impact on our schema-related cognitive processing. The big cultural dividing line that Markus and Kitayama (1991) draw (which is similar to Sampson and Gergen's work, considered below) is between the West (with its *independent* conception of self) and the East (with its *interdependent* conception of self). The Western, independent view of self involves self-representations such as 'I am creative', which emphasise 'individual desire, preference, attribute, or ability' (Markus & Kitayama, 1991, p. 226).

Markus and Kitayama (1991, p. 227) argue that:

> For those with independent construals of self, it is these inner attributes that are most significant in regulating behaviour . . . Such representations of the inner self are thus the most elaborated in memory and the most accessible when thinking of self . . . They can be called *core conceptions, salient identities*, or *self-schemata*.

By contrast, while people in cultures with an interdependent view of self may attach *some* importance to individual attributes or aspects of the 'inner self', conceptions of self in relation to others are more important. An attribute such as 'being confident' may be an important part of self in both an independent and interdependent framework for understanding self. For those with an independent understanding of self, however, it is a property of the individual, regardless of whom they are relating to. For those with an interdependent understanding of self, it may be that a much more socially situated self-concept – such as being confident with friends – is at work.

Markus and Kitayama (1991) further argue that these different **self-construals** are consequential for processing stimuli, affective response and motivation – each of these is addressed in turn below. With regard to processing stimuli, Markus (1977) argued that people respond differently to self-schema-relevant stimuli – for example, showing increased sensitivity, attention and speed of processing. For those with an independent construal of self, the self-schema from which the working self-concept is drawn is likely to be defined in terms of inner attributes, which, to a greater or lesser extent, differentiate the individual from others. For those with an interdependent construal of self, the self-schema will include self in relation to others. This suggests that the processing of stimuli relating to significant others could differ according to the individual's culturally informed understanding of self. The more that a person adopts an interdependent view of self, the more they will respond to stimuli concerning significant others as if they are a part of the self – with just the sort of heightened sensitivity, attention and speed of processing that is associated with self-related stimuli.

Markus and Kitayama (1991) also argued that **affective responses** will differ depending on whether an independent or interdependent construal of self is at work. For those with an independent self-construal, positive affect may be generated by having a sense of autonomy, expressing attributes, having inner attributes acknowledged and rewarded and achieving in competition with others. For those with an interdependent self-construal these individualistic sources of satisfaction are likely to be of lesser importance and positive interpersonal relationships are likely to be of increased importance.

Finally, with regard to motivation, Markus and Kitayama (1991) argue that, while independent self-construers will be motivated to express their self-defining inner attributes, their interdependent counterparts will be motivated to increase relatedness or connectedness. In practice, as Markus and Kitayama

Self-construal Almost synonymous with self-concept – the ways in which an individual construes or thinks about self.

Affective response The emotional responses or the feelings that a person may experience.

acknowledge, this can mean that the same end – such as studying at a particular university – is worked towards, but the driving motivation differs – self-achievement versus doing it for one's family, for example.

Critically reflecting on schemas and self

The work on schemas and self outlined above has attempted to understand the ways in which our cognitive representations of ourselves have consequences – particularly in terms of cognitive processes such as perception, our feelings or affective responses and our motivations. Research by Markus and Wurf (1987) challenged the notion that self-concepts were static and, instead, suggested that, at any one time, there was an active or working self-concept that could be comprised of different self-construals or self-schemas.

Cross-cultural work by Markus and Kitayama (1991) provides a critical stance on much cognitive and other research regarding self-concepts. Whereas previous research had often presumed that the operation of a self-concept was the same across cultures, Markus and Kitayama suggested it differed in important respects. According to Markus and Kitayama (1991), in some cultures, the predominant construal of self is as an independent individual, while, in others, the person has a more interdependent understanding of self. Markus and Kitayama note most psychological research has implicitly or explicitly assumed that the participants would have an independent view of self, not considering the fact that (especially in non-Western cultures) other, more interdependent understandings of self may prevail.

Certain criticisms can be raised, however, regarding both self-schema research and the cross-cultural development of this work. Even work that overcomes the limits of presuming a singular understanding of self by drawing on cross-cultural differences tends to suggest that, while, there are differences in fundamental understandings of self *between* cultures, there is substantial agreement *within* cultures. Vignoles, Chryssochoou and Breakwell (2004) suggests that we should not presume such homogenised understandings of self within any one culture.

Onorato and Turner (2004) suggest that – notwithstanding the idea of a 'working self-concept' – the model of self that schema theory develops is stable rather than truly dynamic. As is outlined below when considering social identities, social identity theory and self-categorisation theory encompass the idea of a radical shift from thinking about self in personal terms to thinking about self in social terms. For Onorato and Turner (2004), then, self should not be equated with the personal, because self is not always thought about in personal terms – instead, genuinely social conceptions of self and the transition from personal to social identities (and vice versa) need to be incorporated into any model of self-representation.

The challenge to concepts of self within schema research is also raised by research that questions individualised and context-free concepts of self and develops interactional and ideological perspectives (see below). These issues are touched on in critiquing self, affect and esteem research below and in the sections that follow. For now, though, it is worth considering that the cognitive stance towards understanding self is concerned with content and processes that have a predictable, causal relationship between relatively abstract variables. It is possible to contrast this with radically different alternatives – for example, my representations of self could be conceptualised as discursive resources, drawn on in interaction to do sequentially sensitive interactional work.

Thus, a derogatory representation of self – for example, 'I am so hopeless with names' – might best be thought of in terms of what it is used to do in a given interaction (perhaps account for not recalling someone's name). Stripped of the context in which this representation is used, it becomes instead a standalone object – one that we feel we can understand in itself, one we can then abstract and perhaps join with others in some content- and context-free model of self-schemas.

Interactional work therefore presents a challenge to schema theory (and to research on self, affect and esteem below) to think of representations of self in a different way. Schema-type representations can be understood not so much in terms of what they tell us about the hidden, interior world of cognition but, rather, how they (partly because they can be treated by others in interaction as having this relatively stable cognitive reality) are used wherever they are spontaneously produced to do specific sorts of interactional work.

Critical recap

Schemas and self

1 Schema theory and the idea of a working self-concept challenge the notion that a self-concept is static.

2 Cross-cultural cognitive research has challenged the idea that the operation of a self-concept is a culture-free universal.

3 Even within cross-cultural cognitive research, there is a tendency towards presuming that – at least at the level of a specific culture – people will all share a somewhat homogeneous understanding of self.

4 Onorato and Turner (2004) suggest that, even with a working self-concept, schema theory presents a relatively static, rather than truly dynamic, concept of self.

5 Schema theory develops a relatively individualised and context-free concept of self.

6 Interactional approaches suggest that cognitive social psychology's interest in underlying cognitive entities be replaced with observable interactional practices.

Reflective questions

1 *What challenge does cross-cultural research raise regarding our understanding of how self-construal shapes cognitive and affective processes?*

2 *Can you think of an example of how your concept of a future possible self has shaped your current behaviour?*

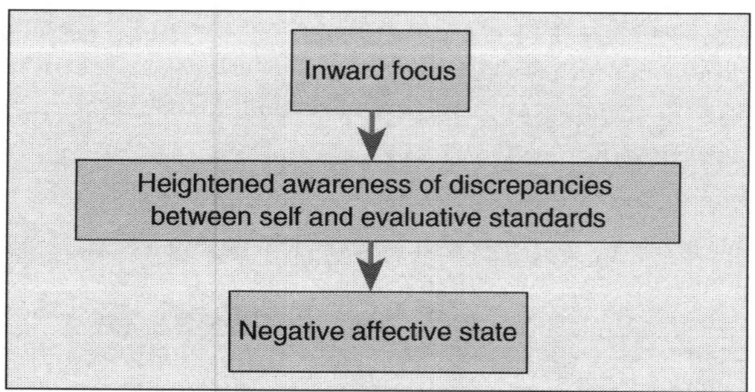

Figure 2.2 Attentional focus as a determiner of affective state (after Duval & Wicklund, 1972)

2.3 Self, affect and esteem

Schema theory developed an influential approach to understanding aspects of how the information (and misinformation) that individuals have concerning themselves can be consequential. It was important partly because it marked psychology's engagement with a topic (self) that had not been centre stage for much of the twentieth century. Schema theory has, however, sometimes been seen as rather too focused on the information-processing aspects of self-representations at the expense of considering emotional responses (or affect) and our self-esteem. Here, three important strands of research that touch on the issue of self and affect are considered. First, we will consider the relationship between being aware of self and the individual's affective state. Second, we will review some of the important contributions to our understanding of how we compare and contrast ourselves with others – and the impact that has on our self-esteem. Third, we will briefly touch on research into how we may control (or regulate) self – in particular, the role that affect has in our failure to do so.

Self-awareness and affective state

Research into self-awareness and affective state (or mood and emotions) has tended to suggest that a negative affective state is associated with heightened self-awareness. Duval and Wicklund (1972) suggested that we can become aware of ourselves as an object – just as you might be aware of this book or the room you are in. This heightened self-focus can increase awareness of how self fails to meet evaluative standards, leading to negative affect. Here, then, the causal arrow goes from heightened self-focus to a negative affective state of sadness (see Figure 2.2).

Look at the model developed from Duval and Wicklund's (1972) work in Figure 2.2 and imagine that you were going through the stages outlined. First, you are perhaps alone and reflecting on things that are relevant to self – for example, 'Why didn't I get invited out with the others?' In this state you may start to compare yourself to 'self as you feel you want to be' or 'as you feel you ought to be' – for example, you might think, 'I should be getting invited out. I wish I was more popular.' This reflection can, as Wildschut, Sedikides, Arndt and Routledge's (2006) comments on Duval and Wicklund suggest, be understood as linked to concerns with self-regulation (which is returned to below) – that is, our concern with controlling aspects of self-behaviour. In terms of the current example, you may examine yourself with a concern for what you can change about how you behave – so as to avoid negative experiences in the future. Your reflection on how you fall short of your ideal self, in turn, according to Duval and Wicklund, brings about negative affect (feeling sad or depressed, for example).

The exact reverse of this has also been investigated – namely, how mood states might give rise to certain types of attentional focus (Sedikides & Green, 2000). This research has suggested that sadness, particularly that which has been brought about by some personal setback or loss, instigates an avoidance of the outside world and a corresponding inward-focused attention as the implications of the event that provoked the state of sadness are contemplated. The reverse is the case for happiness, which, the literature suggests, encourages an outward and other focus as the individual seeks stimulation from and contact with the external environment (see Figure 2.3).

Again, it is worth thinking through an example as you consider Figure 2.3. Imagine that you are feeling a bit

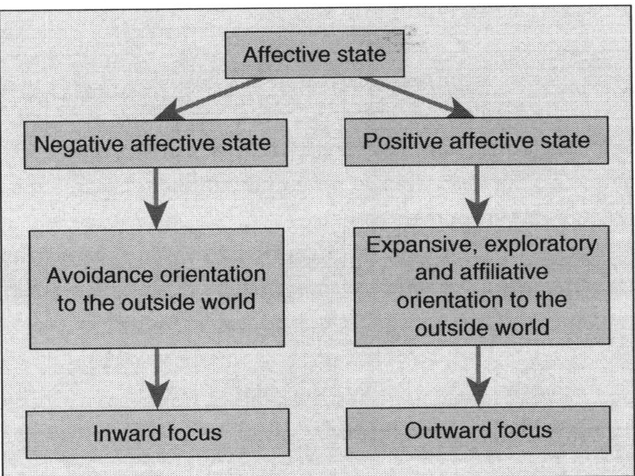

Figure 2.3 Affective state as a determiner of attentional focus (Sedikides & Green, 2000)

low – maybe you invited someone to meet up in the evening and they declined your invitation and this has made you feel sad. This negative affective state – feeling sad, in this case – leads to what Sedikides and Green (2000) refer to as 'avoidance orientation to the outside world'. The clearest example of this is the way in which an individual who feels sad might withdraw from, or avoid contact with, other people. In our example, it may be that you decide not to meet up with anyone that evening but stay in on your own. This avoidance orientation, according to Sedikides and Green (2000) results in an inward focus. In this state of sad affect and avoidance of the outside world, you become aware of and focus on your self.

The other path that Sedikides and Green (2000) identify starts with positive affect. Perhaps you have invited someone out and they have accepted. Imagine how this might make you feel more sociable – you may strike up conversations with the person you have invited out or others, you may well find that you are more actively engaged with the outside world. In turn, in this happy, positive affect scenario, you may find that you are more focused on others – for example, what they are saying in talking with them – and pay rather less attention to your own inner feelings. That is, you may find that you have an outward rather than an inward focus.

Self-comparison

An important aspect of the Duval and Wicklund's (1972) model of self-awareness above is the comparison between self and some 'ideal' standard. It was suggested that negative affect could be a consequence of an increased awareness of discrepancies between self and this ideal. Research by Higgins (1987) seeks to refine this observation by distinguishing two forms of discrepancy – each resulting in a specific type of negative affect. For him, the discrepancies are not just between a possible, desirable and an actual self, but, instead, between *either* a perceived *actual* self and what the individual thinks self *ought* to be, or, between a perceived actual self and the individual's *ideal* self (the self they would ideally like to be). Higgins, then, suggests that we should beware of presuming that 'what we ought to be' and what *ideally* 'we would like to be' are synonymous – instead, they are distinct and bring about different affective responses.

As Figure 2.4 suggests, the actual–ought discrepancy leads to social anxiety, while the actual–ideal discrepancy leads to depression. That is, where we have representations (from self or significant others) concerning our duties, responsibilities or obligations ('ought') that we perceive our *actual* self as failing to fulfil, we will experience fear, threat and restlessness (what Higgins refers to as agitation-related emotions). By contrast, where we experience a discrepancy between our actual self and our own (or significant others') hopes, wishes or aspirations – our *ideal* self – then we will experience a different range of negative emotions, such as disappointment, dissatisfaction and sadness (what Higgins refers to as 'dejection-related' emotions).

The picture of self-comparison offered so far is both inward-focused and rather bleak – it involves contrasts with better possible *selves* and, consequently, results in negative affect as we become aware of discrepancies between who we think we ought to be or would ideally like to be and who we actually are. These internal comparisons (where we compare our self with an

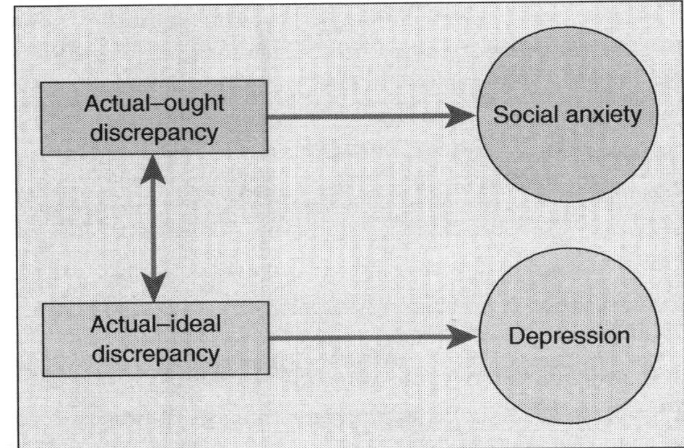

Figure 2.4 Affective consequences of perceived discrepancies, actual–ought discrepancy and actual–ideal discrepancy.

Source: Higgins, E. T. (1987). Self-discrepancy: A theory relating self and affect. *Psychological Review*, *94*, 319–340. Reproduced with permission from the American Psychological Association.

imagined self) may, as touched on earlier, be linked to self-regulation concerns – we may be motivated to identify how we can change, modify or control our behaviour so as to better realise the self that we feel we ought to be or would ideally like to be.

Sedikides (1993) conducted a series of experiments that sought to clarify the relative importance of some of the different purposes that our reflections on self may serve. He considered three possible motives that an individual may have for reflecting on who we are – self-assessment (to find out more about self), self-verification (to confirm what the individual already thinks they know about self) and self-enhancement (to feel good about self). Participants were informed that asking themselves questions was 'a good way for people to find out about themselves' (Sedikides, 1993, p. 323) and required to select questions from a list presented to them or, in a subsequent experiment, generate their own questions about self. Participants were also required to answer these questions.

Sedikides examined what sorts of questions participants selected or generated and the sorts of motivations for self-reflection that these appear to indicate. Sedikides argued that participants chose and generated questions for themselves, the answers to which meant they came out rather well (reflecting concerns with self-enhancement), even if the questions would not help them confirm what they already thought about self (self-verification), nor find out about self (self-assessment). For Sedikides, the questions selected and generated revealed that participants are particularly motivated by self-enhancement concerns, then self-verification and, last and least, with assessing or finding out about self.

This concern with self-enhancement raises the question how might we maintain a positive self-image when there are others whom we may recognise as being more successful than us? If we really perceive ourselves to be the best at everything, then all of our contrasts with others would be *downward* – that is, with 'inferior' others. These downward contrasts (unless they actually challenged our sense of superiority) would be self-enhancing, giving us a sense of our positive attributes. In the real world, however, things are not quite so straightforward for most of us. This raises the question how do we manage to maintain a positive self-evaluation in a social context where, clearly, some people are *'better'* than us, at least on some attributes. Tesser's (1988) self-evaluation maintenance model suggests that it is important to recognise that sometimes we can actually *gain* self-esteem from observing the success of others – a process referred to as *social reflection*. We might, for example, gain esteem from having a circle of friends at university who are talented in various ways. According to the model, however, we could find ourselves responding to successful others with an upward **social comparison** – where we compare ourselves with another person (or other people) in a given domain (or on shared dimensions). Thus, we might compare their 'popularity', 'intelligence', 'attractiveness' or 'humour' with our own – potentially threatening our self-esteem rather than enhancing it.

Tesser's (1988) model suggests two important factors that determine whether we engage in social reflection or social comparison: first, if the domain in which the person is successful is irrelevant for us and, second, whether or not we feel certain about our own abilities.

Considering relevance first, if the domain in question is not important to us – for example, your friend is a talented ballet dancer, but you have never wanted to even attempt ballet – then we may be more likely to engage in social reflection, enjoying that sense of having talented friends. If the domain *is* important to us, however – for example, your friend is performing brilliantly in social psychology while you have struggled to perform at a minimal level – then we may engage in social comparison, potentially undermining our own self-esteem.

Our certainty in our own abilities plays an important part also, perhaps unsurprisingly. If we feel certain in our own abilities (perhaps we recognise that we have a warm, engaging way of being with others or are good at music or statistics), then we are more able to engage in social reflection, experiencing the success of others as self-enhancing. If, by contrast we are uncertain of our own abilities, then, unfortunately, the success of others poses a threat to our already vulnerable self-esteem – and we may compare our abilities in the domain in which the other person (or people) are more successful than us in a negative way.

According to Tesser (1988), not quite all is lost, even if the domain of another's success is important to us and we are uncertain of our own abilities. He notes that we could engage in four strategies to maintain our self-esteem even when we are faced with an upward comparison. These are illustrated below, using as an example your friend is performing as well as you wish you were in social psychology:

1 *Exaggerate the ability of the successful target:* 'She is just out there on her own – unusually gifted, a rare genius.'
2 *Change the target of comparison:* 'I am doing the same or better than a lot of other people.'

Social comparison Comparisons made between the attributes of one's own self and those of others in a given domain (or on shared dimensions), such as comparing your own intelligence with that of someone else.

3 *Distance self from the successful target:* 'I don't feel that close to her – I wouldn't really call her a friend.'
4 *Devalue the domain or dimension of comparison:* 'She may be good at social psychology, but there are many more important things in life than social psychology – like having friends!'

The strategies that Tesser (1988) outlines serve to mitigate the effects an upward social comparison might have on our self-esteem. Strategies 1–3 lessen the relevance of comparing with *that* target person – because they are not normal (strategy 1), because there are others against whom one can compare (strategy 2) and/or because they are no longer as important and relevant as a point of comparison (strategy 3). The final strategy addresses not the target person but the target domain (or dimension of comparison) perceiving it as less important than other domains or as unimportant.

Tesser's (1988) self-evaluation maintenance model, while usefully distinguishing different responses to others' success and strategies for maintaining self-esteem, does also beg the question – is our social comparison and social reflection thinking always conscious and deliberate? Stapel and Blanton (2004) addressed exactly this issue, suggesting that sometimes comparisons with others can be 'triggered outside of conscious awareness' and, once triggered, the comparison process may be more spontaneous than deliberative. They suggested that people who were subliminally exposed to an image (the image being presented so quickly that they are not aware of having seen it) could unconsciously start a process of comparison that appeared to have a measurable effect on their perceived self-esteem. Thus, participants who were exposed to a subliminal image of Einstein reported lower perceived self-esteem than those exposed to an image of a clown – the difference being explained by the presumably upward comparison with Einstein (superior intelligence) leading to lower self-esteem. Stapel and Blanton (2004) therefore made the case that sometimes there may be rather less choice about whether we do or do not start the process of comparison and perhaps less strategic manipulation of that process once it has started than Tesser (1988) suggested.

While Stapel and Blanton (2004) introduced the idea of *unconscious and spontaneous* comparisons with others – their emphasis was on *contrast* effects – how upward comparisons (with 'superior' others) may lower self-evaluations and downward comparisons (with 'inferior' others) may raise self-evaluations. That is, they did not consider anything comparable to Tesser's 'social reflection' in which the perceived success of others enhanced rather than depleted self-esteem. Blanton and Stapel (2008) developed on this work to suggest that unconscious and spontaneous processing need not only involve *contrasts* between self and other. Instead, *assimilation* may be triggered unconsciously and developed spontaneously also. They use the term assimilation to refer to the way in which the perceived worth, value or esteem that the perceiver sees in others is drawn into their own sense of worth, value or esteem. If we are assimilating, then perceiving a 'superior' other (like Einstein) means that we increase our own self-esteem because the target of our perception (Einstein) is somehow seen as part of us.

Blanton and Stapel (2008) draw on and develop Blanton's (2001) three selves model, suggesting it is the representation of self that is activated, which is important in determining whether there are contrast effects (where the 'superiority' of others lowers our self-esteem) or assimilation effects (where the 'superiority' of others raises our self-esteem). For Blanton and Stapel (2008), it is the self-representation that is activated by the social context that is all important. If the social context activates the *personal self* – our sense of ourselves each as a separate individual – then this is likely to lead, spontaneously and unconsciously, to contrast effects. If the social context activates the *possible self* – our sense of what we might become in the future – this is likely to lead, spontaneously and unconsciously, to assimilation effects. Finally, if the social context activates the *collective self* - our sense of self arising from our membership of meaningful groups – this is likely to lead, spontaneously and unconsciously, to assimilation effects.

Blanton and Stapel (2008) are suggesting something quite far reaching regarding how we might respond to seemingly 'superior' and 'inferior' others. They are arguing that our responses may be unconscious and spontaneous rather than just conscious and deliberate and may lead to contrast or assimilation effects *depending on the representation of self that the social context makes relevant.* Their work mobilises many different aspects of the social psychology of self, drawing on Markus' future possible self-schema work (considered above) and the social identity and self-categorisation theory of Tajfel (1978) and Turner, Hogg, Oakes, Reicher and Wetherell (1987), considered below.

Self-regulation issues

The literature reviewed so far suggests that perceived deviations from 'standards' or points of comparison are important, some of the literature suggesting that individuals will take steps to focus on 'positive' aspects of self and derive 'positive' comparisons with others. **Self-regulation** research addresses the ways in which we do not simply manage the process of self-reflection or comparison (for example, by focusing on comparisons that enable a positive self-evaluation) but also manage our *selves*. Research in self-regulation addresses some of the ways in which we may seek to – or face restrictions on – changing how we are so as to better meet perceived 'standards'.

DeWall, Baumeister, Mead and Vohs (2011, p. 2) define self-regulation as, 'altering one's own responses so as to bring them into line with standards for socially desirable thoughts, feelings, and behaviours.' These standards might relate to our sense of 'ought' or 'ideal' and may be shaped by comparisons and contrasts with 'superior' others. The important point from a self-regulation perspective is that self *does* or at least *can* take steps to control its behaviour to better meet its desired goal. What self-regulation focuses on, therefore, is not simply cognitive data or affective responses but *actual or intended control over or modification of one's own behaviour* (such as control of emotions, eating behaviour, exercise). The literature addresses not just the facilitation of self-regulation but also its inhibition – that is, it considers what helps and hinders individuals in their endeavour to exercise control over aspects of their thoughts, feelings and behaviours. Self-regulation is touched on in Chapter 6, where we consider future planned action – here attention is given to the role of affect in the process of self-regulation.

Self-regulation has attracted a considerable amount of research attention, spurred on by findings that point to its significance. Wirtz, von Kanel, Mohiyeddini, Emini, Ruedisueli, Groessbauer and Ehlert (2006), for example, point out that, among people with hypertension, there is a higher incidence of low emotional self-regulation and low perceived social support than among those whose tension is within a 'normal' (or 'non-clinical') range. While it may be going a step further than the data allows to suggest that lower self-regulation actually causes clinical conditions, the very association could be seen as indicative of the clinical significance of self-regulation.

What is particularly relevant to our current concerns is the way that self-regulation may be related to affect (see Figure 2.5). Baumeister, DeWall, Ciarocco and Twenge (2005) conducted a series of experiments in which they used manipulations designed to evoke feelings of social exclusion (such as leading them to anticipate a lonely future or informing them that no one wanted to work with them). They found that, compared to control conditions, participants who were exposed to 'social exclusion' manipulations were less able to consume a 'healthy but bad-tasting beverage', ate more cookies, quit sooner on a frustrating task and performed less well on an attention-related task. These effects were found to be ameliorated by either offering a cash incentive or increasing the participant's self-awareness. This work suggests that affect (and awareness) can be intricately tied to observable manifestations of self-regulation – in these cases, behaviours that were particularly associated with healthy and unhealthy eating. The potential impact of this work is enormous – if affect genuinely shapes the extent to which we can regulate our behaviour, then it becomes important to support people's affective state, such that they are able to engage in those aspects of self-regulation which are 'beneficial'.

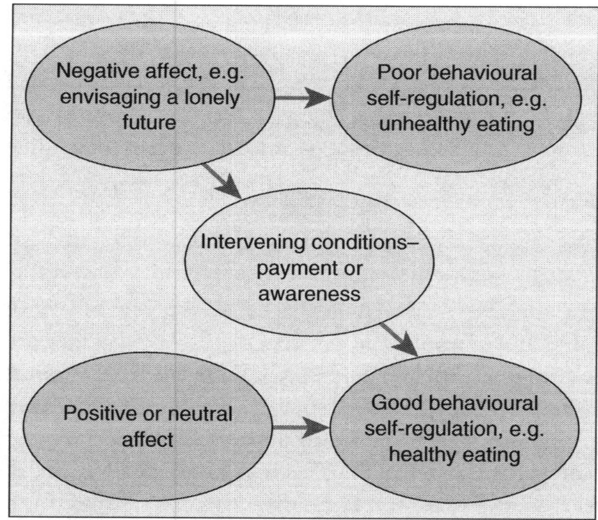

Figure 2.5 Self-regulation and affective state (based on Baumeister, DeWall, Ciarocco & Twenge, 2005)

In Figure 2.5, positive (or neutral) affect is depicted as being associated with 'good behavioural self-regulation' – in this case, engaging with healthy eating. Negative affect is depicted as being associated with poor behavioural self-regulation – unhealthy eating – unless there are some intervening conditions, such as payment or promoting self-awareness, both of which may alter the affective experience.

Ideal self and regulating affect as motives for compulsive buying

Before leaving our consideration of self, affect and esteem, it is worth briefly considering how many of the issues touched on here can come together in instantaneous, impulsive behaviours. One example of this is

Self-regulation The means by which we manage or regulate ourselves – particularly our behaviour and our emotions.

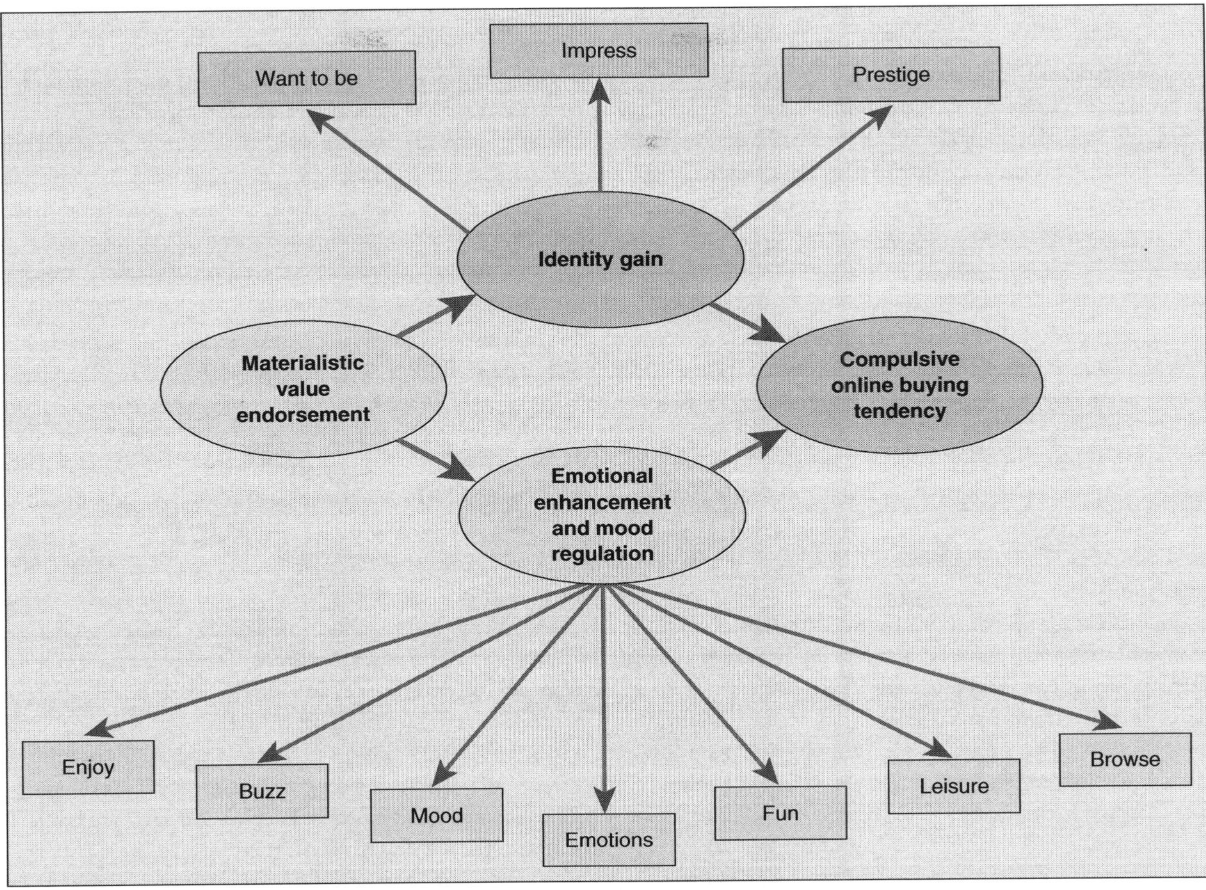

Figure 2.6 Motivations for compulsive online shopping (based on Dittmar et al., 2007)

Source: Dittmar, H., Long, K., & Bond, R. (2007). When a better self is only a button click away: Associations between materialistic values, emotional and identity-related buying motives and compulsive buying tendency online. *Journal of Social and Clinical Psychology*, *26*(3), 334–361. Reproduced with permission from the Guildford Press.

provided in Dittmar, Long and Bond's (2007) model of compulsive online shopping (see Figure 2.6).

Dittmar et al.'s model defines a materialistic value orientation as attaching importance 'to the ownership and acquisition of material goods in achieving major life goals' (Richins, 2004, cited in Dittmar et al., 2007, p. 336). This is coupled with the belief that 'the acquisition of material goods is a central life goal, prime indicator of success, and key to happiness and self-definition' (2007, p. 336). Compulsive shopping is defined as comprising an irresistible urge to buy, a loss of control over buying behaviour and continuation in buying despite adverse consequences for the lives of those with this compulsion.

Dittmar et al.'s (2007) model suggests that a materialistic value orientation can give rise to compulsive shopping by means of two distinct types of buying motives. On the one hand, there are identity-related buying motives and, on the other, emotion-related buying motives. Some of the ideas touched on in this section – about concepts of an ideal or sought after self – can be involved in identity-related buying motives. Thus, individuals may come to think that they can attain, or start to attain, aspects of their **ideal self** by making a certain purchase or, in acquiring a certain possession, they will improve their social image. Once this link is made between the purchase decision and some form of ideal or sought after image, then there is a strong identity motivation to make the purchase.

Emotional buying motives can be linked to an individual's attempt to 'regulate or repair' their emotions. In this way, the buying behaviour may be linked to a means of regulating or managing, not one's behaviour, but one's mood. Once the purchase decision is linked to positive moods – especially where it is felt that these might manage or replace negative affective states – then there is a strong emotional buying motive for the purchase.

Ideal self A representation of a self that one desires to be.

Figure 2.6 depicts a number of affective responses that may be linked – or appear to be linked – with a purchasing decision for the individual.

Dittmar et al.'s (2007) model thus suggests that a discrepancy between our perceived 'actual' and 'ideal' self and a desire to replace our negative affect with positive emotions can provide the grounds for compulsive purchasing – particularly in cases where our values lead us to associate purchasing and acquisition with our 'ideal self' and positive affective states. Dittmar et al. manage to hint at the potential influence of ideology (through considering the importance of materialistic values, even though there is a focus on individual difference in materialism in their model) and they incorporate both identity-based motivation (our drive to be more like our 'ideal' self) and self-regulation issues (specifically our methods for managing our emotions).

Dittmar et al.'s (2007) model outlines the way in which materialistic values can lead us to believe that purchasing something will address our affective needs (for example, replacing our negative mood with a positive mood) and our identity needs (for example, enabling us to be closer to our 'ideal' self). Emotion and identity thereby become important motivators in compulsive (online) buying behaviour.

Critically reflecting on self and affect

The research addressed above has endeavoured to develop increasingly sophisticated models of self – models in which affect moves to centre stage in thinking about self. There is likely to be a resonance between the ideas reviewed here and everyday experiences of self – we may have a sense of how our mood relates to self-reflection, how we compare ourselves to others or ideal standards and how we attempt to regulate our behaviour or our feelings. Questions can be raised, however, about the methodology and theory involved in this work.

Methodologically, the research reviewed makes considerable use of questionnaires in order to measure affective states, concepts of actual and ideal self and behaviour. It can be noted that considerable effort is taken to ensure that the measures are – within the parameters of current psychological practice – valid and reliable, new measures typically being validated against older, more established ones. If self is a relatively robust, cognitive phenomenon that people can, and typically do, report honestly, then this might not be such a problem – but what if this is not the case? People may not be able or willing to report honestly on a singular self – self might be much more multifaceted or variable than this suggests. There might not be some relatively fixed cognitive core to people's self-representations. People's responses on sets of questionnaires may thus proffer a sort of 'laboratory logic' – some coherence that is a product of the measurements used in the context in which they are used. Even where actual behaviour is examined, this tends to be within the confines of the laboratory setting. Again, it is worth reflecting that, if self is nuanced, subtle and fluid, then self and self behaviour revealed in the highly unusual setting of questionnaire completion and laboratory scrutiny may form a somewhat distorted picture.

Onorato and Turner's (2004) criticism of self-schema theory also applies to much of the research considered here. They argued that schema theory and 'social cognition models more generally' see the self-system as relatively stable and contrast this with the highly dynamic properties of self-categorisation theory. As will be seen, self-categorisation and social identity theory develop a self-system that encompasses the radical shift from thinking about self in personal to social terms (and vice versa).

The notion of self that is at work in the research considered here and research on self and schema tends to be both individualised and decontextualised. That is, it implies self can be thought of, made sense of and researched largely alone, without necessarily involving others and without needing to invoke any wider context. These ideas are critiqued in each of the sections covered below – starting with the critique that social identity theory and self-categorisation theory develop regarding the importance of social self, continuing with research that problematises individualistic notions of self and finally reaching the radical critiques provided by interactional and Foucaultian perspectives on self.

For now, it is worth just considering one specific example concerning where our ideas regarding our 'ideal' self might come from. While some of the models considered here have hinted at wider cultural considerations (such as Dittmar's concern with materialistic values), the emphasis of most of the work in this field is on how our 'ideal' self is formed from representations held by self and/or significant others. What is missed in this picture is the way in which wider social forces could be at work. Think for a moment about how, without millions of people around the world holding an ideal of a youthful appearance (principally for women), the cosmetics industry would lose billions of dollars each year. More widely still, it could be that there are power-serving ideologies at work to give each of us both some sense of 'failing to reach our "ideal"' and needing to consume food, exercise regimes, life coaching, social psychology textbooks, holidays, cosmetics, clothes, electronic ephemera, furniture, cars, houses and so on in order to move closer to that 'ideal self'. Keep these ideas in mind when we critically review individualised conceptions of self below.

Critical recap

Self, affect and esteem

1 This research has endeavoured to develop sophisticated models of self that incorporate affect.

2 The reliance on questionnaires and laboratory-based observations can be questioned in terms of what they tell us about how people see themselves and how they act outside of these unusual questionnaire-filling, laboratory-observed contexts.

3 Self – and its various representations, ideals and associated emotions – may not be as simple and easy to report on as much research assumes.

4 Onorato and Turner (2004) suggest that, like schema theory, the models considered here generally see the self-system as relatively stable, which they contrast with the highly dynamic properties of self-categorisation theory.

5 The research addressed here implies that self can be thought of in individualised and decontextualised ways – ideas that are critiqued in each of the sections below.

Reflective questions

1 *Can you think of one time when comparisons with successful others have lowered your self-esteem and one time when they increased your self-esteem?*

2 *What problems can you identify regarding the ways in which the research considered here has conceptualised and researched self?*

2.4 Social identities

In reviewing research on schemas and self some attention was paid to the concept of categorisation, particularly as developed in Tajfel's (1969) classic paper. Tajfel's development of his categorisation work was not solely, or principally, concerned with *individual* identities, however. Instead, it particularly focused on group or **social identities**. This work examines some of the ways in which we come to develop a sense of ourselves as a member of a group – our *social* identity – and the ways in which this social identity shapes our thoughts and actions (see Box 2.4).

The idea of group membership being important to our sense of identity was, as noted above, an issue addressed by the symbolic interactionist work of Mead (1934), but a significant development in the social psychology of group-related identity came from an innovative and highly influential series of experiments initiated by Tajfel. Tajfel's classic **minimal group** experiments (detailed in Box 2.5) examined the ways in which participants appeared to think of themselves in terms of group membership and act in terms of that group membership – even in cases where the group was seemingly meaningless in objective terms.

Tajfel's experiments are striking because the groups involved did not reflect pre-existing affiliations – they were not concerned with fans of particular sporting teams or members of political, religious or activist groups. In fact, Tajfel went out of his way to examine the very least important sorts of groups imaginable – the schoolboys in his experiments were told that they were 'high estimators' or 'low estimators' (following a task where they had to estimate the number of dots quickly flashed on a screen) or that they were fans of either Kandinsky or Klee – abstract artists they were unlikely to have heard of (see Box 2.5).

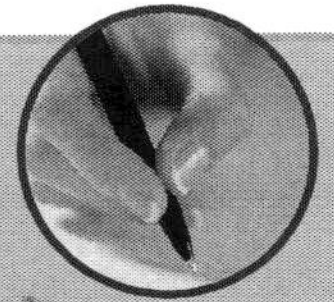

Box 2.4 TRY IT OUT
What are your social identities?

Think for a moment about the last time you recall watching 'your' football team play a match or 'your' country compete at the Olympics or 'your' political, religious or activist organisation being involved in a televised debate.

In this situation, did you get a sense of a 'group' (or shared) identity being involved (did you feel that you shared some group or social identity with the person or people you were watching)?

If you had some sense of a shared group (or social) identity, do you think that this shaped your responses to their 'performance'?

Social identity Our sense of ourselves as being a member of a group or groups – our shared, collective or group identity.

Minimal group A group that has a minimal basis for being thought of as a group, usually created by social psychologists who deliberately use the most spurious basis for distinguishing one minimal group from another. The minimal group will, however, have some characterising label (such as high estimators, Kandinsky group) and members will be made aware that they belong to that specific group and not another named group.

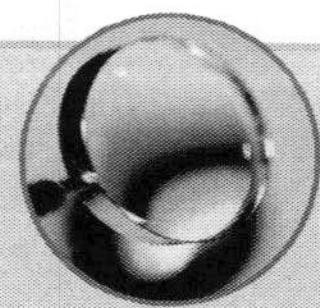

Box 2.5 FOCUS
Classic research: minimal group experiments (Tajfel, 1970)

Schoolboys from Bristol in the United Kingdom aged 14 and 15 were shown art by painters they were unlikely to have heard of before – namely, Kandinsky and Klee. They were asked to record their preferences.

These were analysed and the boys were assigned to either the Kandinsky or the Klee group, purportedly on the basis of their preferences (although, in fact, they were randomly assigned). Each group (which comprised eight members) had to complete a series of reward matrices that they were told would determine the payment (in tenths of a penny) that other boys (not themselves) would receive for participating in the research.

The matrices had two pieces of information: randomly allocated numbers for the boys (which made the process anonymous) and the names of the groups that they had been allocated to (Kandinsky or Klee). In the example shown in Table 2.1, a schoolboy belonging to the Kandinsky group is asked to choose one column determining payment for a Kandinsky member and a Klee member.

Table 2.1 Matrices of Kandinsky and Klee groups

No. 23 Kandinsky	11	12	13	14	15	16	17	18	19	20	21	22	23
No. 34 Klee	5	7	9	11	13	15	17	19	21	23	25	27	29

If a Kandinsky group member wanted to reward exactly the same amount to boy 23 from his group and boy 34 from the Klee group, he would choose the column in which both received 17 (tenths of a penny). If the boy wanted maximum rewards for his group – and maximum joint rewards – he would choose the column with 23 for Kandinsky and 29 for Klee. If, however, he wanted maximum difference in favour of the Kandinsky group, he would choose 11 for his group and 5 for the Klee group.

Across a series of experiments with meaningless or minimal groups, Tajfel found that participants made choices that showed concern about there being a difference in favour of their own groups, even when this meant that their group received a smaller total reward.

As Box 2.5 shows, Tajfel (1970) found that even in the most minimal of groups, the very fact of being identified with a group can shape our behaviour in favour of the group we belong to (the **ingroup**) and against the other group (the **outgroup**). In each of the different forms of minimal groups (high/low estimators, Kandinsky/Klee), Tajfel found that participants displayed some bias towards the ingroup. What is especially interesting here – and in subsequent social identity research – is that participants displayed a preference for giving their group more rewards than the other group – *even when this meant a lower absolute amount was received by their group*. Thus, the ingroup bias that Tajfel identitifed revealed that participants were concerned with a *positive differentiation in favour of the ingroup*, making decisions in which the ingroup received more than the other group rather than just concerning the total ingroup reward. This finding is striking, given the minimal nature of these groups, but it is also found in non-minimal, meaningful groups. Brown (1978) conducted research with groups of workers at an aircraft engineering factory, the groups involved were 'toolroom', 'production' and 'development'. Through a series of interviews and matrices, Brown found that members of these groups were concerned with *positive ingroup difference* rather than *absolute reward*. An example of this is found in how members of the toolroom group responded to the matrix shown in Table 2.2 concerning what they felt the weekly wage should be.

In this decision task, each member of the toolroom group was confronted with a choice – should they opt for

Ingroup A group to which we belong or perceive ourselves belonging to.

Outgroup A group to which we do not belong or perceive ourselves belonging to.

Table 2.2 Toolroom and production salary matrices

Toolroom group	£69.30	£68.80	£68.30	£67.80	£67.30
Production and development group	£70.30	£69.30	£68.30	£67.30	£66.30

equality (£68.30 for each group), the maximum reward for their own group (£69.30 for the toolroom group and £70.30 for the others) or maximum positive difference in favour of their own group (£67.30 for the toolroom group and £66.30 for the others). Brown (2000a, pp. 316, 317) notes that, 'Toolroom were virtually unanimous in choosing the extreme right-hand pair ... this meant a sacrifice of as much as £2 per week in absolute terms in order to establish a £1 differential over the other groups.'

In both meaningless and meaningful groups, there is evidence that group members use their group identity – their sense of belonging – as a basis for decisionmaking. In cases where the decisions could potentially affect them as well as cases where they will not, people have been found to act in favour of their own *ingroup*. This ingroup favouritism takes the form of a particular concern with positioning their own group favourably with respect to other groups, even when this means lower absolute rewards.

These experiments are foundational for social identity theory and have been used to argue that people can think of themselves in terms of their group or social identity and, when this identity is salient, it will inform not just decisions but all manner of cognitions, emotions and behaviours. The findings about decisions that maximise positive *ingroup* difference have been understood as indicating that when our social identity is activated we are motivated to see our group (whichever group identity is salient) in terms of positive differences from other groups – 'positive distinctiveness'.

A second concern in social identity theory is the way in which, when we think about ourselves in terms of our group or social identity, we will tend to act consistently with that identity and the behaviours that we associate with it. This perspective has been used to understand a massive range of intergroup behaviour, from helping others who are perceived as having a common group identity to conflict with those who are perceived as belonging to a different group.

Self-categorisation theory

Turner, Hogg, Oakes, Reicher and Wetherell (1987) developed this theory, focusing on the ways in which an individual can switch in their self-categorisation – that is, they can change the category that they currently assign themselves to. The potential scope of self-categorisation theory is vast – Turner et al. seeing it as consistent with but 'more general' than social identity theory, as it attempts to explain categorisation switches not only at a group (or intermediate) level but also at a superordinate level (concerning the individual's identity as a human being) and the subordinate level (dealing with categories relating to individual differences, such as personality types).

In discussing self-categorisation theory, Onorato and Turner (2004) note the contrast that it provides with the work on self-schemas discussed when considering research on self, affect and esteem above. Thus, Onorato and Turner (2004) cite and critique Gaertner, Sedikides and Graetz's (1999) view that self-schemas are, 'monuments of stability. They remain stable across time ... and across situations' (Gaertner, Sedikides & Graetz, 1999, p. 5, cited in Onorato & Turner, 2004, p. 259). For Onorato and Turner (2004), the notion of a relatively fixed, stable self-representation is problematic precisely because self can be experienced not only in terms of 'personality' or 'individual differences' – instead, people can think of themselves in terms of *personal identity* (personal self) or *social identity* (collective self). For self-categorisation theory, then, 'self-perception is highly variable and context-dependent' (Onorato & Turner, 2004, p. 257).

With regard to the current focus on group or *social* identities, self-categorisation theory contributes to an understanding of how people switch from thinking about themselves in personal terms to thinking about themselves in group terms and it emphasises that individuals not only categorise themselves but come to think of themselves in terms of attributes associated with the relevant group – that is, they *self-stereotype*. For Turner et al. (1987) and Onorato and Turner (2004), the switch from personal identity (where the individual is concerned with 'me' versus 'not me' categorisations) to social identity (where 'us' versus 'them' categorisations become the focus) can occur in situations where the social identity is made more salient than the personal identity. An individual choosing their snack for the train, answering their phone and then getting ready to board a train may be thinking about themselves as an individual, but the presence of fellow football supporters on that train, wearing team colours, chanting team songs, may cause the individual's social identity as a fan of that team to become so important it *replaces* the concepts the person had about themselves as an individual. For Turner et al. (1987), the individual may start to think about themselves in terms of the stereotypes they hold about supporters of that football team.

Onorato and Turner (2004) found that, when participants were instructed to think about themselves in personal terms – 'describe yourself as an individual' – then personal identities and attributes became salient. When people were encouraged to think about themselves in social terms however – 'describe yourself as a woman in contrast to men' – then people tended to respond consistently with the salient social identity – even when this contradicted their personal self-schema.

Social identities and behaviour

Research drawing on social identity and self-categorisation theories has detailed something of the impact that an activated social identity can have on a person's behaviour. As described in Chapter 8, Levine, Prosser, Evans and Reicher (2005) conducted research that suggested football fans – who were encouraged to think of their identity as a supporter of their team – are more likely to help an injured person wearing their own team colours than someone dressed neutrally or in a rival team's shirt.

A similar influence of social identity on behaviour was found in research by Livingstone and Haslam (2008) (discussed in Chapter 9). Their investigation within the context of chronic conflict in Northern Ireland suggested that the more important an individual's group or social identity was to them, the more their attitudes and behavioural intentions would reflect intergroup hostility.

These examples of social identity research can be interpreted as offering support for the idea that a person's social identity can shape their attitudes and behaviour in either a positive or negative direction. Where the person has an opportunity to help a member of their own group (or another group with whom their group enjoys harmonious relations), then salience of group identity appears to promote helping behaviour. By contrast, where there is intergroup conflict, then attitudes and behaviour towards a member of the antagonistically related group has an increased likelihood of being negative.

Critical reflections on social identities

Social identity research argues that a crucial aspect of our sense of self is our group (or social) identity – that is, our sense of ourselves as a member of a group. Social identity theory suggests that we are motivated to feel good about our own group by seeking to differentiate our group from others in ways that enhance our perception of our own group. Furthermore, according to social identity theory, in situations where our group membership has been made relevant, much of our group-referenced behaviour – for example, towards members of our own and other groups – will be shaped by our group (or social) identity.

Some work provides a challenge at least for overly simplistic interpretations of these ideas. Working within a social identity framework, Hinkle and Brown (1990) argue that the idea of seeking positive evaluative comparisons between one's own group and others may be less universally true than is often presumed. Hinkle and Brown refer to those groups who, in particular circumstances, rely on comparisons with other groups for their sense of group identity as having a 'relational' social orientation. They also note, however, that some groups, in a given context, do *not* rely on such comparisons for their sense of identity – they refer to these groups as being 'autonomous'. Drawing on Hinkle and Brown (1990), Mummendey, Klink and Brown (2001, p. 161) argue that favouring the group one identifies with and being biased against other groups, 'should be most noticeable under conditions which promote a relational orientation or among group members who habitually favour such an orientation.' Thus, football fans may relate to rival fans in a way that shows considerable ingroup bias during or following a football match between the two sets of supporters. By contrast, religious groups may not use other groups as an important point of reference in establishing a sense of their own group identity or for guiding their relationships with members of other faith groups. From this perspective, social identity theory provides a more context-dependent set of predictions about intergroup behaviour, seeking to differentiate one's own group and showing that ingroup bias *can* occur, but in circumstances where the situation and the group combine to create a relational orientation, rather than being true of *all* groups at *all* times.

Some social identity research has suggested that identity might not only shape behaviour but may also, in turn, be modified by that behaviour – a perspective that has become known as the 'elaborated social identity model' (ESIM; Drury & Reicher, 1999; Reicher, 1996). Drury and Reicher (2000) provide an illustration of this in their empirical study of a protest about the building of a major road that would have a significant impact on a community in a London suburb. In their interviews, they found that people reported not only that their social identity as 'village' members shaped their action but also their act of protest and confrontation with the police changed how they thought about themselves. As a consequence of their antagonistic encounter with the police, some participants in the protest developed a more radicalised identity, supporting increasingly confrontational tactics as the protest developed and having a changed sense of themselves as more radical citizens after the event. The elaborated social identity theory model therefore accepts that a person's social identity can shape their behaviour. The model, however, adds that the direction of influence can be reversed, so behaviour, such as interactions with other groups, can itself change the social identity.

Some questions can be raised concerning the empirical basis for social identity theory. Most of the minimal group experiments have obtained very mild ingroup favouring effects rather than a marked reaction against an outgroup. Indeed, minimal groups can themselves be criticised as they – unlike all 'real' groups – have no meaning and no history, raising the question, can such experimentally contrived groups really inform us about meaningful, interconnected 'real-world' groups? To believe they can is to presume that some abstract underlying 'intergroup process' is relevant to both experimental studies and real-life groups and, at some level, aspects of its operation are insensitive to whether a group is 'real' or created in a laboratory. Where social identity theory *does* draw on real-life groups, there is, again, often some presumption of what Billig (1995) refers to as 'generic' group processes. That is, specific, culturally and historically located groups in interaction with one another are thought to reveal context-free or generic processes relevant to *all* (or nearly all) groups. The quest for generic processes that operate across such vastly different groups can lead to the real relevance of the specifics of context and interaction being ignored or marginalised.

Social identity theory and self-categorisation theory can also be subject to the same discursive and conversation analytic criticisms outlined above with regard to cognitive approaches to understanding self. Thus, from a conversation analytic and a discursive perspective, issues can be raised about the idea that 'identity' should be understood as a relatively stable cognitive entity. As has been noted above, by shifting to a concern with how people construct identities in interaction, attention is given to how people use identity talk to do things such as blame others or account for their own behaviour. From this perspective, the interest is focused not on analysts' models of the social–cognitive processes involved in identity or self-related interactions but how *people themselves* use the resource of talk about self and identity to 'do interaction' in concert with others.

Critical recap

Social identities

1 Some work within the social identity tradition (such as Hinkle & Brown, 1990) has questioned the idea that concerns with positive differentiation from other groups and ingroup bias will be true for all groups at all times.

2 Work on the elaborated social identity model (Drury & Reicher, 2000) suggests that, while identity can shape behaviour – particularly group-related interactions – those interactions can, in turn, shape and reshape identity.

3 Questions can be raised about the empirical basis of much social identity theory – both regarding the use of unrealistic minimal groups and the attempt to divine general intergroup processes from highly specific instances of intergroup data.

4 Discursive and conversation analytic research suggests that talk about shared identity can be examined in terms of how people do things in interactions with and through such talk.

Reflective questions

1 *In what way does the elaborated social identity model differ from social identity theory?*

2 *Do you belong to any groups that you feel are important for your sense of identity? If so, how has your identification with the group shaped your behaviour – has it had consequences for your attitudes or behaviour towards other groups?*

2.5 Critiques of individualised concepts of self

Some of the work considered so far in this chapter appears to go beyond the idea of self and identity as being phenomena that are entirely within the head of the isolated individual. In considering schemas and self, we looked at the way that interpersonal interaction is an important factor in activating certain schemas and their content may be shaped by cultural factors. When we considered social identities above, attention was paid to the importance of group or social, rather than just individual, identity. As we shall see below, however, for some researchers, social psychology – including these approaches – suffers from a narrow, individualistic conception of self. Examining the different ways in which self has been conceptualised across cultures and throughout history has led some researchers, such as Sampson, to suggest that Western society has a uniquely individualised notion of self that, as Gergen (1973, 1991, 1994, 2009a, 2009b), Fox (1985), Prilletensky (1989) and Smail (2002, 2004, 2006a, 2006b) note, perhaps unwittingly, informs much of psychology. This individualised psychology – according to Gergen and others – has very significant implications for how we relate to others, how we 'do' psychological interventions and whether or not we see 'societal wrongs' as necessitating changes in 'society' or individuals.

Drawing on a range of cross-cultural research, Sampson (1988, 1993) investigated the common assumptions about self within English-speaking communities within the UK, USA and Australia, as well as other communities, such as the Chewong of Malaysia, Maori and Japanese and Chinese communities. Sampson reported differences between the Western English-speaking communities and other – often indigenous – communities across the world, arguing that the former hold to a certain 'self-contained individualism', while the latter have a more relational understanding of self (Sampson has referred to this as 'ensembled individualism', and the 'dialogic self'). These differences are summarised in Table 2.3.

Sampson suggests that **self-contained individualism** is the dominant framework for thinking about self in English-speaking cultures – not just as an everyday or 'folk' psychology but also for most of academic psychology itself. From this perspective, self is seen as markedly separate from others, having a 'sharp boundary that ends at one's skin' (Perloff, 1987, cited in Sampson, 1988, p. 16). There is no perceived difficulty with distinguishing self from other, as each are understood as clearly bounded individuals. From this perspective there is a clear distinction between self and other – self being understood as a distinct collection of attributes associated with a biologically separate, individual being. Furthermore, self is perceived as being under personal control – for example, we each understand our own behaviour as being (principally) under our own control – we are responsible for what we do. Finally, the conception of self – who or what self is – is defined in contrast to (not in conjunction with) others – for example, I think of my attributes in terms of what makes me *different* from others rather than the *shared* attributes or identities that we might have.

Sampson (1988, 1993) argues that a markedly different concept of self – **ensembled individualism** or the **dialogic** or **relational self** – is found in many other cultures. In this way, the more relational conception of self is not a marginal oddity but, cross-culturally, a more widespread conception of self. From this perspective, the self–other boundary is more fluid and not simply defined by the biological individual. As Sampson (1988, p. 17) – referring to the work of Howell (1981) – notes,

Self-contained individualism This predominant Western understanding of the individual – also the perspective that is most common in psychology – stands in contrast to the three terms indicated below and stresses self as being separable from others.

Ensembled individualism This refers to a view of the individual person widely held in non-Western (and particularly non-English-speaking) cultures. According to ensemble individualism, a 'self' includes others and relationships with others and cannot be so readily separated from them as self-contained individualism assumes.

Dialogic self This term is used here almost synonymously with ensembled individualism and the relational self and contrasts with self-contained individualism. Where it does differ from ensembled individualism and the relational self is that it suggests dialogue between people in interaction is where self is constructed.

Relational self As with the previous two definitions, this offers a view on an interdependent, interconnected self, in which self necessarily includes us 'in relation' to others.

Table 2.3 Sampson's distinction between self-contained individualism and dialogic understandings of self

	Self-contained individualism	Ensembled individualism/ dialogic/relational self
Self – other boundary	Firm (a clear distinction between self and others)	Fluid (a less clear boundary between what is self and other)
Control over the person's life	Personal (self in control)	Field (others or the situation in control)
Conception of self	Excluding (defined by contrast with others)	Including (defined in conjunction with others)

'The Chewong of Malaysia, for instance, do not distinguish sharply between person and nature.' What is a clear boundary from certain (largely English-speaking) Western perspectives is less clear from other (relational) perspectives on self. Similarly, Sampson, drawing on Smith (1981), notes that the Maori understand control in a way that differs from self-contained individualism: 'the individual was not considered the chief agent determining his "own" life, nor was he considered to be altogether responsible for his experience' (Smith, 1981, cited in Sampson, 1988, p.17). Sampson (1988, p. 17) challenges the notion that self *has* to be understood in terms of contrast and exclusion by illustrating the Japanese perspective: 'the Japanese consider the idea of an individual who is defined completely apart from the environment to be a very foreign notion.'

The debate about whether or not there is a self beyond the sum of our mental experiences relates to another issue concerned with when and where the idea of self emerged – that is, how and when did people come to think of the individual self? One attempt to address this within psychology came in 1987 when Roy Baumeister published a paper entitled 'How the self became a problem.' In the paper Baumeister examined how historical research suggests that it was only around the sixteenth century we find the concept of a unified single human life or 'self' emerging. Baumeister notes that, prior to this time, people's frame of reference was much more anchored in their station in life – their role and their community, both of which were relatively fixed. With increased mobility from the sixteenth century onwards, however, the individual biological being became *an* important and, eventually, *the* important frame of reference in people's lives.

In a further illustration of this inclusive conception of self offered by relational views of self, Sampson (1993) refers to Maloo exchange, citing the example of a common form of greeting, in which when one person offers praise for having done something, the other replies acknowledging their part. The example Sampson gives is that the greeting 'Well done the trip' might be met with 'Well done the staying home'. While this could be seen as merely a polite format, Sampson invites us to see the way in which the response recognises the actions (or seeming inactions) of the other in 'their own' endeavours. Thus, 'the trip' might only have been possible because of *both* the going by one person *and* the staying home by the other. From this perspective, the doing of something is not an act of a lone individual for which they alone are responsible, but, rather, is necessarily a joint venture involving others. Seeing actions in this way arguably involves a conception of self in which 'others' are at the very heart of what one *does* and, indeed, what one *is*.

Sampson's outline of self-contained individualism and relational understandings of self seeks to identify several assumptions about how self has been conceptualised in English-speaking, Western societies – including within academic psychology. It endeavours to illustrate widespread alternative conceptions of self that show an alternative version of how self can be understood. Furthermore, Sampson makes the case that this perspective of self as relational, with its more social and inclusive version of self, does not marginalise or mitigate against the realisation of the 'core cultural values' of freedom, responsibility and achievement but, instead, actually enhances the possibility of their realisation.

Gergen (2009b, p. 83) also criticises what he refers to as the 'ideology of the self-contained individual'. One strand of Gergen's criticism is that social constructionism provides a stance from which versions of the world – however culturally familiar they may be – can be opened up to being questioned. In the case of the social psychology of self and identity, social constructionism not only questions the prevailing (in Western cultures) perspective of self-contained individualism but also – through its focus on language – points to the possibility that our selves and identities are more social than we might readily acknowledge.

Consistent with this social constructionist position, Bakhtin's (1981 [1935], 1986 [1952]) work has been drawn on to suggest that our very sense of self can be understood as located not in our separate selves but in our interactions with others (Dickerson, 1997b; Sampson, 1993; Shotter, 1995). That is, it may be our interactions that create our very sense of an 'inner' world. Think, for example, about being in a conversation where you are being very open and honest. If you are asked how you feel, you might not just relay some already formulated cognitive state. Instead, you might construct that apparently 'inner' state there and then – *in* and *for* the interaction taking place. Some aspects of social constructionist perspectives on self and identity are developed later in this chapter.

A second strand of Gergen's (2009b, p. 84) argument against self-contained individualism is concerned with ethics – specifically, viewing people as separate individuals may encourage the pursuit of individual self-interest without regard to the interests of others who are seen as different, separate or alien to self. 'If what is most central to me is at the outset you are fundamentally "other" – an alien who exists separately from me.' For Gergen, then, our philosophy of self shapes the way in which we make sense of the other – that seeing others as separate from me feeds in to an isolation from and a distrust of these separate others. Furthermore, believing that individuals are principally responsible for their actions leads to a certain form of moral judgement – found not just in everyday explanations of others' behaviours but also in the explanations offered and supported by institutions and, indeed, by academic psychology itself.

It may appear that Gergen's case here is relying on a challenge to the ethics implied by self-contained individualism rather than some more familiar academic evaluation of its theoretical and empirical merits and shortcomings, but his focus on conduct is not by accident. Gergen (2009b, p. 81) produces a reworking of what – in the light of social constructionism – the scholar's task is, or should be considered to be: 'The scholar's task is not to "get it right" about the nature of the world, but to generate understandings that may open up new paths to action.' For Gergen, then, the ideology of self-contained individualism is not just an abstract theoretical issue – it has implications for the way in which institutions, disciplines and all of society treat each other. Psychology is there in this mix – as Fox and Prilleltensky (1996) note (see above). Psychology's individualising perspective can be understood as legitimising certain ways in which institutions and members of society in general may understand and respond to others.

Individualising psychology

Gergen (2009b, p. 87) (see Box 2.6 and note that we shall return to his work when considering the individual

Box 2.6 KEY RESEARCHER
Professor Ken Gergen: constructions of self

How did you become interested in issues of social construction and the self?

Early in my career I believed that the proper aim of research was to illuminate or understand human social behaviour. This meant observing carefully, using accurate recording devices, deploying large numbers of subjects, employing statistical analysis and, ideally, using experimental methods. However, after years of reading, writing and reflecting, I have come to see this entire set of assumptions as deeply flawed. This is in spite of the fact that all these assumptions continue to be broadly shared within the field of social psychology.

To briefly summarise my orientation today, I have come to see that in carrying out research we don't 'find' out about social behaviour so much as we 'create' it. That is, we interpret the world of observation in the terms we bring to the research. When we begin to study attitudes, social cognition or prejudiced thinking, for example, we take for granted their very existence. We will both frame our research and interpret the results in these terms. In the same way, people in other cultures might launch research into *atman* or *liget*, or indeed, religious traditions might determine the purity of one's soul. Each community creates a world in its own terms. In effect, once we have purchased a given 'lens for looking' we can 'shed light' on the 'phenomena' that are created by the lens. But without the lens, there is no 'it' to be studied.

This is no small matter. Why, at the outset, should one small group in the West, labelled social psychologists, presume that it should construct the world in its terms alone? Why should people everywhere not have voice in defining, describing or explaining the nature of social life? Second, the concepts we use in describing and explaining are far reaching in their implications. For example, we now have a long history of calling certain people's actions prejudiced, aggressive, conforming, obedient, morally underdeveloped, cognitively deficient, and so on. These terms are scarcely neutral. They are terms of moral judgement and political in consequence. In effect, in spite of claims to scientific neutrality, when people are exposed to the 'knowledge' that science generates, they are subtly informed about the nature of the good. Methods of research also carry moral and political implications. Methods that involve observing others from a distance, carry far different political implication than those holding that knowledge emerges from active dialogue with others.

Ultimately there is no way of stepping outside of ethics and politics in our research. We are never neutral, even when we cannot comprehend the ways in which we are not. Thus, the major challenge for research is not to 'get it right' about the nature of the social world, but to contribute to the kind of future that one believes to hold promise for humankind. This challenge includes selecting the kinds of concepts or theories that your research will construct as 'real', the topics created as important and the kinds of methods employed. In my view, decisions about all these matters are best made in dialogue, and not from a singular, or isolated, perspective or set of values.

Box 2.6 continued

Tell us about your work in this area.

My work as a social constructionist began in the early 1970s when I published an article 'Social psychology as history' (Gergen, 1973). There I proposed that research findings in social psychology do not accumulate in the same way as the natural sciences. Simply put, because as people learn about social psychological findings, they may be moved to change their behaviour. This is especially so because the terms of description in social psychology are value loaded. If people know about the research on obedience to authority, they may become less obedient; if they are aware of conformity research, they may try to be less conforming, and so on. In this sense, social psychological research doesn't contribute to general laws of human behaviour, so much as it reflects and creates current social conditions. The response to this publication were so lively and resistant that I was moved to explore more deeply current developments in philosophy, sociology, history and anthropology. Among the results were my scholarly book, *Realities and relations: Soundings in social construction*, and later my book for students, *An invitation to social construction*.

With these ideas in place, I began to explore issues in the conception of self. If the ways in which we conceive of ourselves (rationality, emotions, motives, etc.) are social constructions, then how are we to account for our contemporary constructions? This interest led, for one, to enquiry into the social construction of the person in history and culture (Gergen & Davis, 1985; Graumann & Gergen, 1996). Later I became fascinated with current changes in society. In particular, it seemed to me that with the development of new communication technologies – and resulting immersion in relationship – the presumption of a 'true self' was eroding. It is no longer 'I think, therefore I am', but 'I communicate, therefore I am'. The results of this exploration were featured in my book, *The saturated self*. Most recently I have attempted to show how the very concept of self depends on a process of collaborative action (co-action). Independent minds do not come together to form relationships, but it is out of relational process (co-action) that the very idea of an independent mind emerges. Further, if we place the highest value on sustaining and enriching the relational process, there are enormous implications for practices of education, research, therapy, organizational development, and more. These ideas and practices are explored in my book, *Relational being: Beyond self and community*.

How does your approach compare and contrast with others?

As you might imagine, constructionist views are highly controversial. Most traditional social psychologists simply reject them, not because they have knock-down arguments to the contrary, but because they challenge their commitment to 'search for truth'. At the same time, there are increasing numbers of social psychologists whose work is informed by constructionist ideas. Psychologists engaged in discourse analysis, action research, narrative analysis, critical psychology, indigenous psychology, dialogic process, theoretical analysis, and processes of meaning making, for example, are all attempting to reshape and enrich the field.

What things helped or hindered your research?

Most helpful have been like-minded scholars in the field. From a constructionist standpoint there is not 'one right way' to think or to carry out research. As a result there is an enormous amount of creative work being carried out. Through active interchange with this growing community, one is inspired; one is continuously learning and growing. Also, I strongly emphasise reading outside the field of psychology. Not only is it important for the field to stay abreast of ideas in adjoining fields such as anthropology, sociology and philosophy but if one's work is to have any significant value, it should speak to issues of concern to the society. The greatest hindrance to enquiry is tradition - as represented in educational curricula, journal practices, research funding, and the separation of fields of study. This does not mean destroying the existing traditions of empirical psychology. For the constructionist, empirical research can make a contribution to society. The danger is in the belief that this is the only or best form of enquiry.

And finally - considering research in this area, what do you recommend to people wanting to start to research this topic?

Two things I like most about constructionist enquiry are that it encourages young scholars 1) to follow their passions and 2) to join in the dialogues of the field. In the first case this is to invite enquiry that really matters to you, and in the second, to realise that your voice can count in generating the future. However, these opportunities are enormously facilitated by teachers who share a constructionist perspective. Otherwise one may find oneself imprisoned by traditional conventions.

versus relational self below) develops a similar critique of the dominant **individualist perspectives** on self:

> Because we believe in self-contained individuals who think, feel, weigh evidence and values, and act accordingly, we also inherit a handy way of understanding bad action – weirdness, crime, harassment, bigotry and so on. In all cases we are led to suspect a fault in the internal functioning of the individual . . . Individuals cause problems and individuals must be repaired – through therapy, education, imprisonment, and so on.

Gergen's thoughts here raise numerous issues about how everyday understandings operate and – through both promoting and uncritically importing these everyday understandings – how institutions concerned with treatment and punishment of 'individuals' as well as both psychiatry *and psychology itself* also operate.

It is worth, as Smail (1978) suggests, reflecting on the ways in which psychology frames issues such that the individual is central, the individual *has the problem* to be fixed, the individual *contains the causes* of the problem and the individual should be the *target for change*. In a vivid illustration of this Smail (1978) invites us to consider a man who is experiencing considerable anxiety arising from his work. Psychology might locate the cause of such distress as within the individual person, possibly associated with their perceptions of themselves and others, and thus, the solution may be framed as necessitating a change within them also, perhaps involving some adjustment to their perceptions. However, before we feel too comfortable with our psychological understanding of the individual and *his* anxiety problem, now consider that the year is 1944, and the work setting is Auschwitz II, Birkenau – the notorious extermination camp and centre for the so called, 'final solution'. Suddenly our previous individual framing seems inadequate and actually a potentially dangerous distraction from the *'real'* – broader, societal – issues at stake.

In a similar fashion, Fox and Prilleltensky (1996) have developed a critical perspective on psychology which challenges the idea that the individual self should be the focus of analysis. Drawing on a Marxist perspective, wider issues – such as the means by which the social, economic and political status quo is maintained – become central. For Fox and Prilleltensky (1996) this wider, societal perspective is not just relevant for obviously extreme cases – it is *always relevant*, even in societies where individuals may have the (*false*) conscious experience that they have substantial freedom and choice in their life. Whilst Fox and Prilleltensky are often accused of being 'ideological' by 'mainstream' psychology – they argue that mainstream psychology is itself ideological – it just adheres to a different and *unacknowledged* ideology. As Hepburn (2003, p. 57) notes, Fox and Prilleltensky suggest that: 'mainstream camps . . . don't realize that their own individualist position is equally ideological. Adopting an individualist stance blots out any recognition of social factors.'

As Gergen, Smail, and Fox and Prilleltensky suggest, it could be that psychology's assumptions regarding self-contained individualism force our attention to the *individual in isolation* and blind us to the idea that our experiences and behaviours cannot be sealed off from the contexts within which they emerge.

Critical reflection on critiques of individualised concepts of self

The research on individualising versus relational self considered above brings to mind some of the earlier criticisms of mainstream psychological perspectives on self considered earlier. Work presenting a relational perspective is typically influenced by social constructionism – which enables conceptualisations of what self *is* to be understood as versions of the world for which others are available. An important resource in developing this argument has been the conceptualisations of self that can be found in different cultures – in particular, the marked contrast to dominant Western (and psychological) notions that self can be thought of as a separate, self-contained individual. If there are constructions of self that are radically different from the dominant versions that we encounter – in Western cultures and mainstream psychology – then these dominant versions of self can be seen as constructions for which alternatives are available. We can then move on to the ethics of different versions of self – that is, psychology could take into account what ends are served by a relational versus an individualising version of self.

One issue with the way in which the case for a relational or dialogic self has been advanced is that it often relies on depictions of cultural perspectives that suggest a homogeneity of cultural perspectives on self. It should be noted that the case for a specific cultural perspective is not solely made by reference to illustrations of specific cultural ideas or practices – Sampson (1993) draws on some cross-cultural survey data as well. Whichever form of data is presented, however, the impression is typically given that members of the culture concerned share one relatively unified understanding of self. Aspects of this could be challenged from the social constructionist perspective itself. If multiple versions of self are available, why should there be a cultural consensus regarding

Individualist perspectives This refers to ways of understanding self that emphasise self as an individual rather than self in relation to others.

which one of two versions (self-contained individual versus ensembled self) are adhered to? Furthermore (as Chapter 6 illustrates), social constructionism has been drawn on to criticise the notion of relatively fixed attitudes and beliefs – if the flux-like nature of positions is applied to ideas about self, then even locating a stable view within one individual becomes problematic.

Discursive psychology and other perspectives that develop the idea that apparently stable, cognitive entities – such as beliefs and attitudes – are not as fixed as is often supposed, stress the way in which they are *locally realised*. Thus, our beliefs and attitudes may be formulated in specific ways to do certain types of interactional work within specific sequences of interaction. It could be that even our perspectives on self could be approached as locally accomplished. Thus, the idea that the individual person is responsible for 'their' actions – rather than being a relatively fixed cultural reference point – might be both aligned with, and not aligned with, even by a single person in a single interaction, depending on what interactional business is at hand. For example, if I am exonerating someone from blame, then the idea that the environment shapes the actions of self could be drawn on, whereas personal responsibility could serve the purpose of blaming someone. The point is that seemingly fundamental aspects of how we construct self could be investigated in terms of how they are locally realised. In so doing, we might find variation in versions of self that can be made sense of in terms of the *specific interactional work that these versions of self do*.

A related issue is that the data used to make the case – typically surveys and brief ethnographic vignettes – do not give the detail of talk and interaction that is often associated with social constructionist research. While discursive psychology and other forms of discourse analysis make extensive use of transcripts of talk, there are relatively few sustained examples of this in the literature that develop a critique of self-contained individualism. It could be that if more attention was given to constructions of self as accomplished in interaction, then the issue of versions of self being built to do interactional work (such as blaming and exonerating) would be developed.

Critical recap

Critiques of individualised concepts of self

1 Do cultures have relatively agreed on – or homogeneous – understandings regarding whether self is 'self-contained' or 'relational'?

2 Discursive and conversation analytic research suggests that ideas about self (as self-contained or relational) might be fluid – constructed in the moment to do specific actions in interaction.

3 Questions can be raised about the empirical basis for some of the claims made. From a discursive and conversation analytic perspective, examining self-talk in the sequence of talk in which it arises enables an investigation of the precise interactional work such talk may be orientated towards.

Reflective questions

1 *What are the consequences for psychology and in everyday situations of having a relational rather than a self-contained understanding of self?*

2 *Have you ever come across any cross-cultural differences regarding how aspects of self are understood – such as the extent to which the individual is seen as separate and self-contained or relational?*

2.6 Identity talk in interaction

In the previous section, the idea that self could be thought of as relational was juxtaposed with self-contained individualism, one argument being that certain culturally informed understandings of self could shape both everyday and psychological notions of self. The conversation and discourse analytic research reviewed here could be seen as taking up the baton of a relational approach to self – in that, with this research, the emphasis is on what self or identity talk does *in interaction*. It should be noted at the outset, however, that many of the researchers who have been interested in what identity talk does in interaction have not developed – nor been particularly concerned with – issues of how we should come to think about the nature of self. Thus, the research considered here focuses on identity *talk* – such as talk about who we (and others) are or are not and what sorts of interactional work that talk does.

In reviewing research on identity talk in interaction, three different, though interconnected, strands will be addressed: contradictory constructions of identity, membership categorisation devices in talk about self and others and how our talk *does* knowledge identity work.

The first of these– contradictory constructions of identity – examines some data in which speakers appear to produce contradictory versions of their identity. The point developed here is such 'contradictions' can support an analysis that attends to what each version of the speaker's identity is *doing* where and when it is uttered.

The second issue – membership categorisation devices in talk about self and others – examines the way in which talk about self and others makes use of categories. In the work considered here, these categories are examined in terms of what interactional work the category talk does *at that specific place in an interaction sequence*.

Finally, this section considers how talk can draw on and make relevant our knowledge identities – for example, our position of superior knowledge – about the matter that our talk refers to. This seemingly abstract concern is examined with reference to a grandmother talking with a friend about her grandchild. The data shows that knowledge identity (in this case, the grandmother's superior knowledge) can be invoked in subtle yet consequential ways for the interaction.

Contradictory constructions of identity

An early interest in discourse analytic research within social psychology was the contradictory aspects of people's talk about themselves. Potter and Wetherell, in their classic *Discourse and social psychology* (1987), illustrated their discussion of the implications of discourse analysis for social psychology with extracts from interviews with middle-class white (Pākehā) New Zealanders regarding 'Polynesian immigrants'.

In one of the interviews, a participant gave the following description of their stance on the issue of immigration: 'I'm not anti them at all you know … '. Stop for a moment and think – what do you expect to hear next?

Do you think this utterance will be followed by talk that you would describe as celebrating racial and ethnic diversity or something more prejudiced. Interestingly, although this talk overtly expresses a 'tolerant' attitude and, thereby, positions the speaker as 'tolerant' or 'not prejudiced' against Polynesian immigrants, it is probably no surprise that what follows next in Extract 2.1 has, by contrast, a more prejudiced tone.

Extract 2.1

Respondent: I'm not anti them at all you know, I, if they're willing to get on and be like us; but if they're just going to come here, just to be able to use our social welfares and stuff like that, then why don't they stay home.

Source: Potter and Wetherell (1987, p. 47)

As Potter and Wetherell note, we encounter problems if we try to locate a specific singular attitudinal position – or, indeed, speaker identity – from this passage of talk. The talk seems to encompass both tolerance *and* prejudice. What Potter and Wetherell propose is that, rather than try to use the talk to get to the *real* thoughts, feelings or identity of the speaker, we could, instead, consider what the talk is *doing*. Focusing on the action orientation of the talk – what the talk *does* – the first part of talk, which denies prejudice, could be seen as a *disclaimer* – that is, a piece of talk designed to deal with potential negative inferences based on the subsequent talk.

Let's go back to the exercise above – when you contemplated what sort of talk might follow 'I'm not anti them at all you know … '. Now it is possible that the use of 'them' could signal some potentially negative or at least distanced stance from the group referred to – and may have given you a clue as to what sort of talk was to follow – but, even without this clue, you may have inferred there could be some prejudicial subsequent talk. The fact that we can make such inferences from these sorts of generalised, non-discriminatory initial statements suggests disclaimers are not just an artefact of this speaker or these interviews, but are a relatively common phenomenon in prejudiced talk. For our current concerns, this extract illustrates an alternative to taking identity-relevant talk as telling us about the singular inner essence of the speaker – instead, we can see what identity talk *does* at specific points in interaction.

A further illustration of contradictory constructions of self is found in the discursive psychological work of Dickerson (1996). In a series of interviews concerning audiences' understandings of and responses to television news, Dickerson interviewed one participant who described himself as 'not really into politics' (see Extract 2.2).

Extract 2.2

(*Note:* Line numbers from the original)

30 L I'm not really *into* politics
31 rea[lly in the sense of err watching and sort of err
32 P [no
33 L studying it or whatever you know

Source: Dickerson (1996, p. 63)

Looking rather crudely at the above talk, this extract conjures an identity of a participant who has limited interest in politics and this is evidenced in his behaviour – he does not 'watch' or 'study' it. It is possible that 'watching it and studying it or whatever' could be characterising a particular type of 'studious' watching, which is being denied. Nonetheless, this passage in isolation gives the sense of some limits to the participant's engagement with the very focus of the interview. Now check the Extracts 2.3–2.5 from the same interview with the same participant.

Extract 2.3

(*Note*: Line numbers from the original)

5 L errmm >I think programmes like *Question Time* are
6 quite revealing< (1.0)
7 P yeah
8 L when whe [when they *actually*
9 P [yeah
10 L (0.5) and and *Walden* as well I I like watching *Brian*
11 Walden's sort of interviews

Source: Dickerson (1996, p. 65)

Extract 2.4

(*Note*: Line numbers from the original)

1 L I watch (0.5) the the *Nine O'clock News* I watch the *Ten*
2 *O'clock News* as well

Source: Dickerson (1996, p. 65)

Extract 2.5

(*Note:* Line numbers from the original)

(Following a discussion about party political broadcasts)
1 L I usually sort of sit down listen (0.5) to all parties
2 listen to what they've got to say

Source: Dickerson (1996, p. 65)

In the above series of extracts, a markedly different participant identity emerges. Here he seems (literally) very switched on to televised politics, many contemporary and past UK political news and discussion programmes being mentioned (*Question Time, Walden, Nine O'clock News, Ten O' clock News,* party political broadcasts).

Dickerson (1996) argues that, faced with these contradictory constructions of the participant's 'viewer identity', the analyst could attend to *where* the different versions of self are produced and *what they do*. It can be noted that producing a wide repertoire of televised programmes

TRANSCRIPTION KEY

Symbol	Meaning
.	Preceding talk is falling, stopping
,	Preceding talk as falling/rising (continuing intonation)
?	Preceding talk is rising
!	Preceding talk is animated
↑	Following talk goes up suddenly
↓	Following talk goes down suddenly
:	Preceding sound is lengthened
(word) (text in brackets)	Uncertain transcription
( )	Transcription gloss
((word))	Transcription comment
[[	Overlap or co-occurrence of talk or actions of two people – square brackets mark points where overlaps occur
Word (underlining)	Spoken with emphasis
WORD (capitals)	Spoken with increased volume
(0.5)	Pause – timed to nearest tenth of a second
(.)	Pause – can't be timed (less than 0.2 seconds)
[text] [text]	Adjacent lines overlap
<text>	Talk spoken at slower pace than surrounding talk
>text<	Talk spoken at faster pace than surrounding talk
<text	Word starts suddenly
°hh or .hh	Inbreath
hh	Outbreath
H____	Gaze at person, indicated by the first letter of their name – in this case, Helen
..H__	Full stops (in non-vocal transcription lines) indicate gaze moving towards specified gaze target – in this case, H
H , , ,	Commas (in non-vocal transcription lines) indicate gaze falling away from prior gaze target – in this case, H

Note: The transcription key in the table above is informed by the system developed by Gail Jefferson (see Jefferson, 2004, for an overview and guide). The system has been extended by Goodwin and others (for example see Goodwin, 1986, 2003) to capture non-vocal aspects of interaction.

that are watched positions the participant – potentially at least – as politically informed and sufficiently resourced to engage in an interview about viewing televised politics. Imagine, by contrast, a participant first agreeing to talk about their viewing of televised politics and then, once the interview has started, denying that they watch any – the interviewee might potentially be held accountable for agreeing to take part in the interview in such circumstances. Displaying what one does watch and is aware of, by contrast, gives the interviewee a certain legitimacy as an interviewee.

Extract 2.6

(*Note:* Line numbers from the original)

12 L I think it's *basically* a bit of a *sham*
13 really (0.5)
14 P yeah
15 L because umm (1.5) yuheh (0.5) li like
16 I said you you got *three* different parties all sa[ying
17 P [yeah
18 L what they *believe* (0.5)
... ((lines 19–25 omitted))
26 L because they are sort of coming round to say what
27 we're saying in the first place so [it's a *point to us*
28 P [yeah
29 L it just sort of (0.5) it makes a bit of a sham of it
30 I think of it's (0.5) I'm I'm not really *into* politics
31 rea[lly in the sense of err watching and sort of err
32 P [no
33 L studying it or whatever you know [but err it just
34 P [sure
35 L seems err (0.5) they're all as silly as each other

Source: Dickerson (1996, pp. 62, 63)

Extract 2.6 shows where the 'I'm not really into politics talk' occurs. Rather than being uttered into some context-free void, it can be seen as placed at a specific point in the interaction. Having been asked about what he makes of political argument, he expresses that he thinks it is 'a bit of a sham' (line 12), a point he returns to in line 29 ('it makes a bit of a sham of it'). Interestingly, after this reiteration of a point previously stated, we find that L constructs his identity as relatively disinterested in politics. One reading of this, as Dickerson (1996) suggests, is that constructing one's identity as politically disinterested can be a means of accounting for the scope of the responses given. This may be of heightened relevance as the interviewer does not close down the topic, keeping it open for more to be said on what the interviewee thinks about political debate. By constructing his identity of political disinterest at this point in the interview, the interviewee can be understood as providing an account of the limits of what he has said and what he may add to it – how can someone who is 'disinterested' be expected or required to say any more?

These two snapshots of discursive psychological work on contradictory constructions of identity suggest three thoughts for our current concern with identity talk. First, attempts to locate a singular attitude or speaker identity are problematic – while this project may seem possible with questionnaire responses or small snippets of talk, as soon as we engage with extended passages of talk, we find contradictions. Second, these contradictions can be made sense of by examining the surrounding talk context – that is, the *sequences of interaction* in which they emerge. Third, from this perspective, speakers' talk about themselves can be approached not in terms of what it *reveals* but what it *does*. From the perspective of discursive psychology (and conversation analysis), what talk does is understood in interactional terms – that is, the interest is in what *interactional work* (justifying, exonerating, blaming) is done *in* and *through* the talk.

Membership categorisation devices in talk about self and others

One strand of research emerging within conversation analysis concerns the way in which people use categories in their interactions. This strand of research was first developed by Sacks in his 1964 lecture entitled 'The MIR membership categorization device' (Sacks, 1995) and subsequently returned to in lectures entitled '"Hotrodders" as a revolutionary category', '"We" category bound activities', 'Being "phoney"' and, most famously and frequently, 'The baby cried. The mommy picked it up.'

Sacks noticed that, in regular, everyday interaction, when people have 'first conversations' – conversing for the first time – there are certain characteristic questions, especially at the beginning. We have all had such first conversations where we have asked and been asked, 'Where are you from?', 'What do you do?' Sacks was interested in the way he could conceptualise these questions – in abstract terms, what are these questions getting at? What are they doing? Sacks became interested in the way in which these interactions indicated that people use sets of *categories* – categories that can classify people, for both describing self and others – to do things in interaction.

Sacks refers to sets of categories such as 'sex, age, race religion, perhaps occupation' (1995, p. 40). These are not called ***membership* categorisation devices** (MCDs) for nothing – they are not an official list from a government census or from academic sociology, but the sets of categories that people use in their everyday interaction. Sacks argues, 'Now, I haven't made up these categories, they're Members' categories'. This, like most of Sack's observations, is no throwaway comment: it is a crucial feature of conversation analysis that it is concerned with how people interacting *themselves* display what is necessary to understand what they are doing in interaction. That is, rather than relying on our own academically informed (or otherwise) ideas about people, identity or interaction we can inspect what they themselves treat as relevant in the interaction. In terms of our current concerns, then, it is not for us to speculate about or pronounce on what categories people use and what using these categories will do, but, rather, to take these issues to the data to see what categories people *are found to use* and what work these can be *discovered to do* in specific sequences of interaction.

One frequently occurring action undertaken in conversation concerns *accountability* – blaming or implying blame and denying blame or exonerating. All sorts of talk, whether everyday (such as friends or family chatting over a meal) or institutional (politicians being interviewed, a medical consultation or a courtroom cross-examination, for example), people frequently produce talk that holds someone or other to account and/or exonerates themselves or others. In Box 2.7 there is an example of MCDs being used to do precisely this.

Extract 2.7 is a transcript of the aftermath of an encounter between Gordon Brown, then UK prime minister, in the 2010 general election campaign and a member of the public – Mrs Duffy. Although Gordon Brown's language was somewhat milder than certain other instances of politicians being recorded completely unawares (compare, for example, the expletives used by John Major (UK prime minister in the 1990s) when describing fellow members of his cabinet and former US president George W. Bush's likening of a journalist to a specific bodily orifice, the incident sparked enormous media interest. What is of particular interest here is that certain categories for describing people are used by Gordon Brown: 'that woman', 'bigoted woman' – Mrs Duffy: 'ordinary woman' – and the media commentator, Nick Robinson: 'life-long supporter', 'anybody with concerns about immigration' and 'bigot'.

These category descriptions could be made sense of in quite different ways. One approach would be to see them as reflecting the way that the world is – that is, we could look for and measure how bigoted people are, for example (Adorno's F scale, referred to in Chapter 7, attempted to get at something similar). Alternatively, the categories could be approached in terms of the cognitively based perceptions that people hold of each other. From this perspective, rather than reflecting the world, they are seen as revealing our ways of thinking about the world – our cognitions about the people we encounter. Work relating to stereotypes (covered in Chapter 7) considers this cognitively based approach to categories. The idea of MCD provides a third alternative – these categories that describe our own and others' identities can be examined in terms of *what sorts of interactional things they do* and how they come to do what they do.

Applying these ideas to Extract 2.7, we see that Gordon Brown, having negatively characterised his encounter with Mrs Duffy ('disaster'), goes on to answer the question, 'What did she say?' not by quoting or paraphrasing her words but drawing on a category to which he assigned her – 'bigoted'. The category here implies something of the sorts of words that might have been uttered by Mrs Duffy without actually detailing them – one can infer from the category alone what sorts of things might have been said. The category also does something else: describing someone as 'bigoted' implies they have unacceptable views that they can be held to account for and any negative encounter with someone so described is implicitly the fault of that person. By using the category 'bigoted', then, Gordon Brown implies culpability on the part of Mrs Duffy for both having such views and any negative aspects of the encounter.

In Extract 2.8, Mrs Duffy can be seen to challenge the way in which she was described by providing an alternative MCD – 'ordinary woman'. First, the two categories 'bigoted' and 'ordinary woman' can be understood as, to some extent, mutually exclusive. By laying claim to belonging to the category 'ordinary woman', Mrs Duffy is challenging being categorised as 'bigoted'. Furthermore, arguing that she is an 'ordinary woman' normalises her and her talk, making her less accountable as it is far harder to hold someone to account by constructing them as 'ordinary' rather than 'bigoted'. This normalisation is further underscored in Mrs Duffy's characterisation of her talk as being the sorts of questions that 'most people' would ask. By self-assigning to the category of 'ordinary woman' and questioning like – and, implicitly belonging to the category of – 'most people' Mrs Duffy positions herself and her comments as normalised, not remarkable and not accountable.

In Extract 2.9, the BBC's political editor Nick Robinson provides a characterisation of Gordon Brown's utterances that hold *him* – rather than Mrs Duffy – to account. That is, while Brown's use of an MCD ('bigoted') suggested

Membership categorisation devices (MCDs) The categories that people use to do interactionally relevant work.

Box 2.7 IN THE NEWS
Category-based descriptions

The extracts opposite come from the UK general election campaign of 2010. Extract 2.7 is a recording of the then Prime Minister Gordon Brown speaking, unaware that he was being recorded. Extract 2.8 is the response of the person he was speaking about and Extract 2.9 a television journalist's appraisal of the incident.

Extract 2.7

(*Note:* Transcribed by author. Gordon Brown being recorded unawares following a meeting with a member of the public (Mrs Duffy))

Brown That was a disAster(.)
(.)
should never have put me with that woman
(.)
Whose idea was that?
Aide I don't know I didn't see her
Brown Sue's I think
(.)
Just rid(.)iculous
Aide Not sure they'll go with that one
Brown They will go with that one
Aide What did she say?
Brown Uhh (.) everything (.) she was just a sort of
(.) BIGoted woman

Source: *BBC World News America* broadcast (28 April 2010)

Extract 2.8

(*Note:* Transcribed by author. Mrs Duffy's response on hearing that Gordon Brown had called her 'bigoted')

Duffy↑ Why has he come out with words like that (.)
he's↑ going to lead this country and he's
calling an (..) ordinary woman who's just
come up and asked him↑ Questions that most
people would ask him

Source: *BBC World News America* broadcast (28 April 2010)

Extract 2.9

(*Note:* Transcribed by author. The BBC's political editor's comments on what became known as the 'Duffygate' incident)

Robinson Now >if I ever< (.) retire get round to
writing a book called (.) er (.)'How to win
an election the easy way'(.) I sus↑ pEct Matt
(.)that I will not include in it (.) the
proposal that you take one of your life-long
supporters >and one who (.) likes you at the
end of meeting< (.) insult her personally (.)
and in the process suggest >anybody with
concerns about immigration< (.) is a bigot

Source: *BBC World News America* broadcast (28 April 2010)

that *Mrs Duffy* was accountable, this report holds Gordon Brown to account for using that category to describe her. In his comments, Nick Robinson ups the stakes on Gordon Brown's comments by describing Mrs Duffy as 'a life-long supporter' – this category arguably makes Gordon Brown's criticisms more accountable than had she been described as 'a life-long critic'. It can be noted that this phenomenon of using categories implying increased accountability for Gordon Brown's comments was widely used during many reports on the incident (elsewhere Mrs Duffy is described as a 'widow' and 'pensioner' – categories implying a certain duty of care from others and underscoring the person's 'victim' status). Furthermore, Nick Robinson challenges Gordon Brown's ascription of the category 'bigot' – by implying that he has used it to characterise someone who simply raised 'concerns about immigration'.

Here, then, Mrs Duffy is categorised as someone who did not deserve to be criticised by Gordon Brown (life-long supporter) and implicitly as having unremarkable (rather than bigoted) concerns about immigration. In this way, Gordon Brown has been held accountable for using a category 'bigoted' against his own supporters and being 'trigger happy' in assigning Mrs Duffy to that category for merely being 'like anyone' raising concerns about immigration.

Another less famous, though equally vivid, illustration of the use of MCDs is found in the work of Edwards (2006) and Stokoe (2009), who investigated (among other settings) the ways in which categories are used by suspects in police interrogations.

In Extract 2.10, S, aged 15, is being interrogated by the police regarding the accusation that he assaulted his neighbour. At two points in the extract, S refers to his neighbour (the alleged victim of assault) in terms of a category 'old' (line 3) and 'old bloke' (line 20). When confronted with some category in talk like this, it is possible to ask, 'Why this category?' and 'Why here?'

Extract 2.10

1 S Yeh I did walk towards 'im
2 (0.6)
3 S Cos I walked towa:rds 'im >an' I says< 'If you weren't old
4 then I woulda wha:cked yuh.'
[8 lines omitted]
13 P You've headbutted 'im. You've lunged forward an'
14 [headbutted 'im.
15 S [No::: no I ain't at a:ll.
16 (0.3)
17 S Unless y'cn ge' any proof then:
18 (1.5)
19 S I'v- (.) headbutted 'im↑wha'↑w'd ↑I↑wanna↑headbutt
20 an old bloke fo:r.
21 (2.0)
22 S Shtupi:d.

Source: Stokoe (2009, pp. 88, 89)

It is worth noting that the neighbour might have been categorised in many different ways – for example, as a man, a neighbour; he could also have been categorised in terms of ethnicity, occupation, physical attributes, nationality, regional identification, sporting allegiances, to mention just a few. This range of possibly accurate category descriptors for the victim of the alleged assault can highlight the interactional relevance of the category descriptors that *are* used. Thus, the categories that *are* used – 'old' and 'old bloke' – can be seen not as *determined* by the objective reality of who the neighbour is but, instead, understood as *designed to do some* **interactionally relevent work.**

Stokoe (2009) notes that invoking this category to describe the neighbour here within the setting of a police interrogation and in a sequence in which he is being accused (lines 13 and 14) is part of doing a denial. By characterising the neighbour as 'old' and 'old bloke', S makes use of some maxim that hitting certain categories of people is sanctionable – this could include young children, physically vulnerable others, as well as those described as elderly. The category 'old' and 'old bloke', then, is invoked to characterise the neighbour and thereby problematise the very notion that someone – especially someone like S, who perceives them as old – would assault them. As Stokoe and Edwards note, the denial that S produces here is a general denial of ever 'whacking' or wanting to 'whack' those who S describes as being 'old'. That is, S is producing some dispositional claim that he 'does not whack old people *in general*' as part of his denial that he has 'whacked' this particular neighbour.

Work on MCDs has examined how we invoke categories – not as some cognitive, sensemaking or simplifying framework, but, rather, as an interactional resource. The categories that we draw on when talking about self and other do *interactional works* – often things such as exonerating ourselves, blaming others or corroborating our version of events.

Invoking knowledge identities in interaction

Another important strand of research developed within conversation analysis concerns the ways in which our talk

Interactionally relevant work The things done by talk (such as accounting, blaming and exonerating) that are relevant or consequential for the interaction.

mobilises certain knowledge identities – often concerning the speaker's superior knowledge about the topic of the talk.

In order to get a sense of what is at stake here, consider the following scenarios.

- You are a parent and a stranger tells you how to stop your child from crying.
- A 'friend' who has never studied psychology points out aspects of psychological theory that you 'have not fully grasped'.
- A stranger approaches you and tells you what has been happening and will happen in your love life.
- A stranger approaches you and your partner and offers advice on 'how to improve your relationship'.

In each of these cases, we may feel that the person has no right or entitlement to speak in this way – specifically, we may feel that we have better access to the necessary knowledge because of our identities as parent, psychology student and the only one able to know and decide about our intimate relationships. In a related set of scenarios, however, things could feel quite different.

- A doctor advises us on our child's crying.
- A lecturer points out aspects of psychological theory that we have not fully grasped.
- A psychic we choose to consult tells us about our love life.
- A counsellor we consult with our partner advises us about our relationship.

In each of these examples, exactly the same talk could (but need not necessarily) be produced without us questioning the speaker's entitlement to talk on those matters or in that way.

So, what are we to make of the idea that we can sometimes be affronted by someone's talk if it suggests a certain knowledge (or **epistemic**) **identity** and other times find it unproblematic?

One way to think about this is that it suggests a twofold relationship between (knowledge-implicative) talk and identity. First, certain identities (such as parent, doctor, tutor, psychic or counsellor) suggest various entitlements to speak on certain issues in certain ways in certain sequences of interaction. Second, certain spates of talk (offering parenting advice, critiquing work and advising on love life) make relevant and denote certain knowledge-relevant identities. Conversation analytic research has addressed the idea that, by examining utterances – within the sequences of interaction in which they occur – we can find speakers explicitly and implicitly invoking identities that are relevant for their 'rights to knowledgably speak' on a given matter (their epistemic authority).

Extract 2.11

(*Note:* Transcribed from Martin Bashir's interview with Princess Diana)

```
Bas  Some people would find th(h)at (.)
     difficult to reconcile:
Di   mhm (.)well: (.)
     that's th(h)eir problem:
     (1.0)
     I know what it fe(h)lt like
```

Source: Panorama, BBC1 (November 1995)

In Extract 2.11, Princess Diana has earlier presented a version of events that is treated here as contestable by the interviewer, Martin Bashir – he refers to 'some people' finding her account 'difficult to reconcile'. In response to this, Diana warrants her version of events by referring to her access to her own feelings. Here, Diana's identity as the one who actually experienced what she went through is drawn on to corroborate her version of events. In this case, the directly claimed identity of being the person who has experienced the reported events serves to provide epistemological authority for the account that she has given.

Extract 2.12 is a short passage from a phone conversation between two friends. In it, they discuss the grandchild James, but can you tell from this brief transcript whose grandchild he is – Jenny's or Vera's?

In Extract 2.12, neither Jenny nor Vera directly claim an identity that entitles them to speak in a certain way about James. Instead, examining the talk reveals practices

Extract 2.12

```
Jen  [Yeh James's a little divil ihhh↑ heh heh [.huh
Ver                                             [That-
Jen  .hh[h He:-
Ver     [James is a little bugger [isn'e.
Jen                               [Yeh- Yeah=
     =[(he eats)ev'rythi]ng.
Ver  =[Mindju 'eez good] Jenny. 'e wz misheevious
     but w- 'e wz good.
Jen  Oo 'e wz beautiful here [wuz↑ n't 'ee=.
Ver                          [↓Yes.
```

Source: Raymond and Heritage (2006, pp. 696, 697)

Epistemic identity An identity that is relevant to a knowledge state about a given target. This is particularly relevant where there are different epistemic identities for people involved in an interaction, such as a grandmother talking about her own grandchild with a friend.

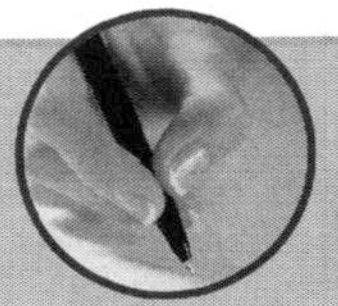

Box 2.8 TRY IT OUT Knowledge identities in interaction

Think of a situation in which someone is telling you about the characteristics of your intimate partner, best friend, child or close relative – someone who (in conventional terms) is not as close to them and should not expect to be as knowledgeable of them as you. When they share their description of *your* partner, best friend, child or relative, what are you to do – simply agree or somehow produce talk that asserts your identity of greater epistemic authority on the matter? How might you assert your identity of having greater epistemic authority through your talk – without confrontationally claiming, 'I know them better than you do'!?

by both Vera and Jenny that make relevant and sustain the identity of grandparent for just one of them.

A brief discussion of some aspects of the extract will be given here – for a more extensive discussion, see Raymond and Heritage (2006). Before we get into the analysis – and, indeed, reveal who the grandmother is – try the exercise in Box 2.8.

In lines 1 and 3 in Extract 2.12, we can note that Jenny has made a statement – an assessment – about James: 'James's a little divil'. Jenny's assessment is met by another assessment from Vera, 'James is a little bugger isn'e'. Both of the assessments appear to be in agreement with one another, but do you notice how the second is somewhat competitively – or even contrastingly – positioned? As you have probably guessed, Vera is James' grandmother, caught in the position outlined in Box 2.7 – that is, being in receipt of an assessment of someone about whom she has greater epistemic authority.

We can note a general feature of Vera's talk that follows Jenny's assessment and the specific means by which it manages to do what it does. In general terms, Vera's talk looks like a first **assessment** itself – it has the appearance of someone making the first statement about James rather than 'responding to' a prior assessment. Raymond and Heritage (2006) draw attention to two features of Vera's talk that could be easily missed – her use of a tag question, 'isn'e', and her use of the name James (even though this has been used in Jenny's talk immediately prior to Vera's).

The tag question sets up Vera's talk as a first pair part – a question – that is ordinarily expected to receive a response (questions and responses being types of talk that are typically paired together, or, **adjacency pairs**). In this way, although Vera's talk comes after Jenny's talk and is, in that sense, in second (or, crudely, responsive) position, by adding the questioning tag, 'isn'e', she is now initiating a question–response sequence, with her question being the first pair part of the question–response adjacency pair.

Raymond and Heritage (2006, p. 694), refer to this use of a tag question as being, 'a practice for asserting epistemic primacy in second position assessments'. Also, although there is no need to reference James by name – his name and only his has been mentioned and he is the only referent in the talk – Vera does so. Raymond and Heritage (2006, p. 694) argue that, in doing so, 'Vera effectively disregards Jenny's just prior reference to him, and by extension, her utterance.'

Raymond and Heritage (2006, p. 677) then note the quite sophisticated ways in which people 'make relevant and consequential specific identities in particular courses of action'. From this perspective, then, our identities have relevance for what we are entitled to speak about. While we may directly claim our epistemic authority, there are, as Raymond and Heritage (2006) note, quite subtle ways in which our talk can assert, or otherwise make relevant, our epistemically consequential identities.

Reflecting on self in interaction

Discursive and conversation analytic research pays some attention to 'real' instances of interaction – typically working from transcripts of interactions between people – sometimes in a research interview, but increasingly for discursive work and almost exclusively for conversation analytic work 'real' (non-researcher-generated) interactions.

Some criticisms of discursive and conversation analysis come from researchers who, in some respects, adopt a similar position. Some social constructionists who are concerned with ideology criticise discursive psychology and conversation analysis for their lack of attention to the ideological or power-infused consequences of talk.

Assessment Used in the conversation analytic literature to mean evaluative descriptions of any aspect of the world.

Adjacency pairs Paired turns of talk that typically come together, such that one part of the pair is usually uttered (or are treated as being expected) in response to the first part of the pair. Common examples include greetings and greeting responses ('Hi' – 'Hi') and questions and question responses ('Do you have the time?' – 'Yes, it's seven minutes past ten.')

From this perspective, by being concerned with micro, interactional aspects of what constructions of self and identity do, we may lose sight of how certain versions of self may have consequences for how power operates in society. Thus, our attention may be drawn to what someone's construction of self does immediately (for example, accounting for what they have or have not done or said) rather than how that same construction sustains injustice and inequality or undermines attempts to address it.

Similarly, Billig (as noted in Chapter 1) raises concerns regarding the extent to which conversation analysis in particular can seem to engage in very careful microscopic analysis of the turn-by-turn organisation of talk without sufficient attention being given to the context in which that talk is produced. Thus, the specifics of the historical and political context and the nature of the relationship between the people who are interacting could be missed, yet be crucial to understanding what a given instance of identity-relevant talk is actually doing.

Finally, from the point of view of realist social psychology, both discursive psychology and conversation analysis are actually offering a different (and, from that perspective, unpallatable) version of social psychology. Some social psychologists want the discipline to enable some degree of prediction – and, in some cases, control – regarding human behaviour. From this perspective, being able to generalise about processes involved in the way that someone's sense of self operates and being able to hypothesise and test ideas about causal relationships between variables such as someone's social identity and their intergroup behaviour is just what they expect from social psychology. From this perspective, the idea that we cannot easily 'get around' someone's interactionally located constructions of self and identity, there may not be some stable cognitive 'essence' of self or identity and we should instead examine what self and identity talk does in interaction is not just a different theoretical point of view, it is delivering a version of science and psychology that they do not want.

Critical recap

Identity talk in interaction

1 Conversation analytic and discursive research has been criticised for being ideologically naïve or apathetic – pursuing the interactional work that self and identity talk does at the expense of leaving the power-relevant consequences of identity talk to one side.

2 Some criticisms have been made regarding the extent to which discursive and conversation analytic research may focus too narrowly on specific extracts of talk without paying sufficient attention to the broader social, political and historical context in which the talk occurs and the relationship between those who are talking.

3 For some social psychologists, the idea of approaching self and identity in terms of constructions designed to do particular types of interactional work is too far removed from their vision of what social psychology is or ought to be about.

Reflective questions

1 *From a discursive and conversation analytic perspective, what questions should guide our investigation of talk about self?*

2 *Think about some examples of how you have talked about self today (for example, 'I'm no good at maths'). Try to examine your talk in terms of what it did in the interaction and how it managed to do what it did.*

2.7 Foucault and self-formation

It is difficult to adequately represent Foucault's contribution to thinking about self. First, Foucault's contribution to these issues is found throughout his work. He stated that an understanding of how we are made subjects was at the very core of his work: 'the goal of my work during the last twenty years has not been to analyse the phenomena of power, not to elaborate the foundations of such an analysis. My objective, instead, has been to create a history of the different modes by which, in our culture, human beings are made subjects' (Foucault, 1982, cited in Rabinow, 1984, p. 7). Second, Foucault's very considerable legacy involves several strands of argument, which are often too distinct to meaningfully pull together into one neat package, yet too closely interwoven to treat as entirely separate concerns. Yet, he is too important, too profound and, indeed, too unsettling to ignore. Rabinow's (1984) outline of three strands of Foucault's thinking about the self as subject are outlined below, with the acknowledgement that these can only be a partial and imperfect gloss – giving, as it were, the aroma of some themes in Foucault's work, in the hope that some may turn to Foucault for the full meal.

Rabinow, drawing on Foucault, refers to three 'modes of objectification of the subject' in Foucault's work. These are the practices and discourses that shape how human beings can come to be 'selves' and what sorts of 'selves' they can be. The three modes are: 'dividing practices', 'scientific classification' and 'subjectification'.

The first of these modes – 'dividing practices' – is the practices that use division to objectify the subject. Foucault's *Discipline and punish* (1977) and *Madness and civilisation* (1967) provide classic examples of this – both examining how it came to be that people would be classified as criminal or good, insane or sane. The divisions entail the operation of both some form of knowledge/power – such as psychiatry or law – and the practices of apprehending, examining, diagnosing, judging and treating or punishing, which it justifies and informs. The implications of social (and, in some cases, physical) exclusion are not only relevant for those assigned to stigmatised categories (such as 'insane' and 'criminal') but also to how we all come to see ourselves.

A related concern is the second mode, of 'scientific classification'. Foucault's *The order of things* (1970) considered some of the ways in which modes of enquiry – particularly the various 'human sciences' – should not be read as simply producing an increasingly accurate picture of the individual person 'as they really are', but, rather, as developing historically located constructions of what it is to be human. Some strands of this thinking can be seen in the work of Baumeister (1987), considered above, who explored the way that aspects of our current, highly individualistic perspectives, with individualised notions of self, have emerged historically. For Foucault, self as an individual subject or 'man' is not some axiomatic starting point that gives rise to human sciences – instead, it is 'an invention of recent date', in part a consequence of those human sciences. As Foucault (1970, p. 387), poetically notes, if the arrangements that gave rise to modern conceptions of 'man' were to change, 'then one can certainly wager that man would be erased, like a face drawn in sand at the edge of the sea.'

The third mode – 'subjectification' – refers to the ways in which the person, rather than being at the mercy of the practices of division and scientific classification, is actively engaged in their own 'self-formation'. It is perhaps worth noting that this element of thinking is present in some of Foucault's work that deals with both 'division' and 'scientific classification'. Thus, *Discipline and punish* (1977) not only reveals the operation of dividing practices such as surveillance as effected by an external authority, but also how this can become a mode of self-subjugation by self-surveillance and the operation of conscience.

Foucault's (1978, 1985, 1986) three volumes entitled *The history of sexuality* provide a particularly detailed consideration of 'the **subject**'. In the second volume, Foucault (1985, p. 6) notes that his previous work had addressed issues concerning 'the games of truth (*jeux de verite*)' exemplified in scientific knowledge and how these interact with 'power relations' exemplified by practices of punishment and sanction. Foucault (1985, p. 6) reports that he now, 'felt obliged to study the games of truth in the relationship of self with self and the forming of oneself as a subject'.

This vast project was pursued in the light of an investigation of 'the history of desiring man'. In this way, Foucault opened up not just how the self is defined from 'outside' or 'above' – by science or systems of power or the interplay of power and knowledge – but also *how subjects comes to see themselves in a certain way*, such as mad, ill, criminal, living, speaking, labouring and desiring individuals. This development of Foucault's thinking has been particularly important in thinking about 'subject positions', discussed next.

Subject positions

Foucault's work has been drawn on to suggest that our identity is informed – or even *formed* – by the various **subject positions** that **discursive formations** make available. Think for a moment of all the different ways in which a person might be a male or female, for example. This could be something other than just cognitively held stereotypes – it could be that, in a given society or culture, there are various 'ways of being' a man or a woman.

Benwell and Stokoe (2010) provide an example of this in an analysis of the talk of three female friends (see Chapter 3 for related analysis). In their illustration of this approach, they argue that 'gendered subject positions' could be seen to be at work – with the females, at times in their talk, enacting a passive female subject position and constructing males as active. Thus, at one point, one female says to the other two, 'it's up to him when he's available, to ask me out' (Benwell and Stokoe, 2010, p. 64). This talk can be understood as positioning self as passive and – in this respect at least – relatively powerless

Subject As used by Foucault, this term refers to the modern individual and is deliberately used to suggest that the individual is not free, but, instead, tied to their own sense of who they are as well as being subject to others.

Subject positions These are the various selves that we might inhabit – the different ways of being a person within a given socio-historical context.

Discursive formations These are culturally and historically located constructions of all aspects of our social world.

and dependent on the male's actions. This approach to analysis has been important, particularly for researchers interested in the ways in which subject positions may provide identities that can create or maintain inequalities of power – sometimes, as in the above example, depowering the very person who is adopting a particular subject position.

Some more recent research (including Benwell and Stokoe, 2010) has been keen to avoid an overly simplistic understanding of subject positions. Benwell and Stokoe (2010, p. 64) touch on this in noting that, 'the positions are variable and fluctuating often within one turn at talk'. Baxter (2002) develops a related idea, suggesting that many attempts to appropriate Foucault's work underestimate the flux-like nature of self and the discourses that produce it. For Baxter (2002, p. 829), Foucault's work points to a self that is, 'constantly positioned and repositioned through discourse.' From this perspective, individuals can be thought of as 'unfixed, unsatisfied, . . . not a unity, not autonomous, but a process, perpetually in construction, perpetually contradictory, perpetually open to change' (Belsey, 1980, p. 132, cited in Baxter, 2002, p. 830).

Baxter (2002) thus suggests, much work that has drawn on Foucault has *correctly* considered the way in which versions of identity – who or what we are or can be – are tied to power-infused discourse. According to Baxter (2002), however, there has often been insufficient recognition of *Foucault's own understanding of power*. In the first volume of *The history of sexuality*, Foucault (1978, p. 93) produces a list of propositions concerning what power is and is not – for example, 'Power is everywhere; not because it embraces everything , but because it comes from everywhere.' Relatedly, Foucault (1978, pp. 94, 95) argues, 'power comes from below; that is, there is no binary and all-encompassing opposition between rulers and ruled', adding this does not mean it can be reduced to the choice or decision of 'an individual subject': 'let us not look for the headquarters that presides over its rationality'.

In this way, Foucault problematises both simplified 'top-down' models of power and notions that power should be thought of in terms of the choices and decisions of individuals. Instead, Foucault's conception is more subtle and complex and the individual subject is at the heart (rather than just the receiving end) of power-infused discourse: 'not only do individuals circulate between its threads; they are always in the position of simultaneously undergoing and exercising this power. They are not only its inert or consenting target: they are always also the elements of its articulation'. (Foucault, 1980, p. 98, cited in Baxter, 2002, p. 829). As Baxter notes, power – and the discourses and identities that interact with it – are much more diffuse, flux-like and subject to negotiation and change than certain approaches that claim to draw on it might suggest.

Critical reflection on Foucault and self-formation

One criticism of the ideologically informed approaches to self considered above is that much of it appears to be very top-down, with the impression that the individual self is a relatively powerless pawn, pushed around by powerful identity prescribing discourses. This view has been challenged by Baxter (2002) and others who have suggested that, while true of some research, it represents a misappropriation of Foucault's work, which, instead, develops a more subtle and less top-down understanding of self, discourse and power.

A related, though more methodologically-focused criticism, is that research concerned with ideology and self has often not been particularly attentive to the data itself. Antaki (1994, cited in Dickerson, 1997b, p. 529) argued that some research provides 'culturally thick' readings of 'empirically slim' slices of data'. This criticism does raise the issue as to whether or not data can be more systematically engaged with in research that is concerned with ideological aspects of self and identity.

Wetherell (1998) provided an illustration of one way of trying to combine a critical interest in ideology with a (conversation analytic) concern with the detail of the data. It could be argued, however, that going to the data is not the objective benchmark for overturning theoretical assumptions and predilections (Billig, 1999a) as even what data is looked at and the framework for making any sense of it is a reflection of theoretical commitments (see Chapter 1 for further discussion of these issues).

Critical recap

Foucault and self-formation

1 Some criticism has been made concerning the top-down nature of research into ideology and self, but this may reflect a misappropriation of Foucault's ideas rather than a problem inherent in considering ideology and self.

2 Some are concerned with the lack of reliance on data, though others have countered that selecting, examining and making sense of data is itself reliant on certain sets of theoretical assumptions.

Reflective questions

1 *What issues does research concerning ideologies and the self raise regarding social psychology's implicit and explicit assumptions about self?*

2 *Can you think of any examples of people adopting an identity or way of being that could be interpreted as directly or indirectly serving some sort of ideological function?*

Summary

- This chapter started by outlining a classic question: 'Is there a core self?' The debate between ego theory and bundle theory was outlined – with the former suggesting there is a self beyond the sum total of our experiences and the latter that there is not. It was noted that some bundle theorists have drawn on social constructionist ideas, suggesting our sense of there being a solid, essential self may not reflect reality, but may, instead, be a construction linked to our ways of talking and interacting with regard to 'self'.

- The second question that was addressed concerned whether or not our identity is socially situated. In considering this issue, some classic symbolic interactionist work was briefly touched on. This work paid attention to the ways in which perceptions of others' views of self could be important in shaping the individual's identity.

- Schema theory was outlined and it was shown how (according to the understanding of self it offers) our ideas about who we are – our schemas and self-concepts – have implications for our cognitive processing, our feelings and our motivations. One strand of research developed these core ideas by suggesting that it is useful to distinguish those self-concepts that are active at any one time (the working self-concept) from the total pool of how self can be construed. A second strand of research developed a cross-cultural sensitivity to schema theory, suggesting that cultural values concerning independence and interdependence will shape the impacts that particular types of schema content have on cognition, motivation and affect.

- The idea of affect was pursued in further detail by examining self, affect and esteem. The research described considered whether certain affective states led to increased self-awareness or vice versa. It also addressed the ways in which our sense of self may relate to the ways in which we think about others in relation to thinking about ourselves (for example, comparing ourselves with others). Attention was also given to the contribution of research that has addressed the ways in which we manage or regulate ourselves and how this may relate to concepts of who we are and who we could or should be.

- The chapter also addressed social identity theory and self-categorisation theory – two approaches that challenge both the idea of a stable, core self and, especially, the emphasis on the individual self found in much of the work on schemas, affect and esteem. Social identity theory and self-categorisation theory emphasise how our *social* rather than just our *personal* identities can be made salient and how, once activated, these social identities can be crucial for understanding our perceptions and behaviour.

- The individualised conception of self – which some have argued is dominant within both Western culture and psychology – was outlined by drawing on work that provides an historical and cross-cultural contrast to this understanding of self. Some of the consequentiality of thinking about self in individualistic, self-contained terms and the possibility of alternative, relational ways was touched on.

- In looking at self in interaction, the chapter considered the way in which talk about self or identity can be approached in terms of *what it does in interaction*. This is clearly illustrated in the case of the seemingly contradictory constructions of self that can be made sense of by considering not which version is true, but, rather, what the different constructions of self *actually do in interaction* as they are uttered. Research concerning the use of categories in talk and talk that is relevant to people's knowledge identities was also reviewed, from the perspective of how attention to the detail of the talk, in its sequential location, enables us to understand what these forms of self-relevant talk *do* at the precise place that they occur in interaction.

- The chapter ended by briefly outlining Foucault's profound contributions to thinking about self. Foucault's work opens up ways of thinking not only about how scientific disciplines and institutional practices help to constitute self but also how the person can be actively engaged in their own self-formation. These ideas, which are touched on at points throughout this text, have phenomenal reach across the social sciences. Here, one fragment – the concept of 'subject positions' and its relevance in critical thinking about self and identity – was briefly illustrated.

Review questions

1. *How do you think that people can decide between ego theory and bundle theory? Is such a choice necessary or important for social psychologists?*
2. *From a symbolic interactionist perspective, how might acquiring a new role result in some change in identity?*
3. *What is meant by the 'dynamic self-concept'?*
4. *What does the literature suggest are the consequences of a discrepancy between my perceived actual self and my ideal self?*
5. *Why might we reflect on who we are?*
6. *How might consumer behaviour relate to issues of self-regulation and identity?*
7. *What empirical evidence is there to suggest that people act in terms of their social identity?*
8. *What are the problems with an individualised conception of self? What are the alternatives?*
9. *What do discursive psychologists make of people's contradictory talk about themselves?*
10. *Why might people use category descriptions in talk about self and others?*
11. *How might ideas about self-formation and/or subject positions be relevant to the social psychology of self and identity?*

Recommended reading

Allegranti, B. (2011). *Embodied performances: Sexuality, gender, bodies*. London: Palgrave Macmillan. A thoughtful, critical and innovative reflection on profound issues related to our sexual, gender and embodied identities.

Benwell, B., & Stokoe, E. (2006). *Discourse and identity*. Edinburgh: Edinburgh University Press. An insightful overview of many different ways in which self and identity have been understood – particularly helpful for understanding conversation analytic, discursive and ideologically orientated perspectives.

Blackmore, S. (2010). *Consciousness: An introduction* (2nd ed.) London: Hodder Education. An engaging overview of key theories regarding consciousness – particularly useful for its review of ego theory versus bundle theory.

Brown, R. (2000a). *Group processes* (2nd ed.) Oxford: Blackwell. Rupert Brown's clear and accessible outline of research on group and intergroup processes – particularly helpful for understanding social identity and self-categorisation approaches.

Edley, N., & Wetherell, M. (1997). Jockeying for position: The construction of masculine identities. *Discourse & Society*, *8*(2), 203–217. An engaging illustration of the social construction of masculinity.

Gergen, K. (2009a). *Relational being: Beyond self and community*. Oxford: Oxford University Press. Ken Gergen's engaging and important outline of a relational understanding of self and its radical challenge to individualistic orthodoxies within much of psychology and many Western cultures.

Hepburn, A. (2003). *An introduction to critical social psychology*. London: Sage. An impressive overview of many key issues in the various forms of critical social psychology.

Honess, T., & Yardley, K. (Eds.) (1987). *Self and identity: Perspectives across the lifespan*. London: Routledge & Kegan Paul. An edited book that contains some useful outlines and empirical illustrations of symbolic interactionist approaches.

Sacks, H., & Jefferson, G. (Eds.) (1995). *Lectures on conversation analysis*, Vols. I and II. Oxford: Blackwell. Harvey Sack's lectures outlining all aspects of conversation analysis. These lectures are where conversation analysis emerged and developed from and they have a marked sense of fresh and profound ideas being formed in the moment.

Sampson, E. (1993). *Celebrating the other: A dialogic account of human nature*. Hemel Hempstead: Harvester Wheatsheaf. Ed Sampson's engaging outline of alternative understandings of self that challenge the dominance (culturally and in psychology) of self-contained individualism.

Useful weblinks

The following websites provide a great resource for research publications relating to specific academics and include a number of downloadable references.

www.psych.lancs.ac.uk/people/JackieAbell.html Publications by Jackie Abell that have a particular emphasis on constructions of national identity.

www.sussex.ac.uk/migration/profile95042.html Publications by Rupert Brown addressing social identity theory issues.

www-staff.lboro.ac.uk/~ssde/index.htm Discursive and conversation analytic publications and other resources by Derek Edwards.

www.dennisfox.net Publications and links relating to 'critical' work by Dennis Fox.

www.swarthmore.edu/x20607.xml Publications by Ken Gergen on social constructionist work.

www.sscnet.ucla.edu/soc/faculty/heritage/publications/publications/Heritage_Publications.html Conversation analytic publications by John Heritage.

www-staff.lboro.ac.uk/~ssjap/JP%20Articles/jparticles.htm Discursive publications and a variety of related resources by Jonathan Potter.

http://portal.st-andrews.ac.uk/research-expertise/researcher/sdr/publications Publications by Steve Reicher addressing a wide range of aspects of group behaviour.

www.davidsmail.info/index.htm 'Critically' focused publications by David Smail.

www.abcgallery.com/M/magritte/magritte54.html One of several of Magritte's paintings that juxtaposes an image of a pipe with the inscription 'Ceci n'est pas une pipe' ('This is not a pipe'). Foucault and Magritte had a quite extensive exchange about these pictures, which among other things, raise the issue that all forms of representations (which might include pictoral, verbal or other representations of ourselves) may be seen as *merely representations*. This raises the question whether there are any representations of self, such as responses to questions about who we are, self talk, etc. that are more than just representations.

3

Attraction and relationships

Learning outcomes

By the end of this chapter you should have a critical understanding of research concerning:

- evolutionary perspectives on attraction
- how misattribution of arousal may be relevant in attraction
- the idea that people are attracted to and select partners with similar attributes to themselves
- the idea that people tend to be paired with others who have a similar 'market value'
- research concerning the importance of perceived fairness – and unfairness – in relationships
- how explanations for a partner's behaviour can be consequential for the relationship
- how constructions of gender and sexuality may involve culturally available discourses
- how constructions of gender and sexuality may do interactionally relevant work
- some of the limitations, shortcomings and assumptions to be found in research on relationships.

On 29 April 2011, Catherine Middleton married Prince William. The event was viewed by perhaps a billion people around the world. Much of the commentary on this event illustrates some of the themes that are relevant to the social psychology of attraction and relationships. Some reports about the couple concern what it is that attracted them to one another – was it physical attraction, a shared university experience and what role did wealth and social standing play, if any? Does it matter that Catherine Middleton was, prior to the wedding, a 'commoner' rather than part of the aristocratic elite? Other comments have addressed what might make the relationship 'work' for them in the light of other royal weddings that have sometimes resulted in separation and divorce. This raises issues concerning what it could be that results in relationship satisfaction – and dissatisfaction.

More radically, we can ask whether this wedding and the way it is referred to and reported produces a particular way of making sense of relationships – does it privilege certain forms of relationship, such as heterosexual, dyadic, romantic relationships involving institutional and legal recognition as 'marriage' above all other types of relationship? Does it create or sustain a particular version of 'romantic' relationships, of what it is to be male and female within a relationship or how we should understand and recognise as legitimate certain forms of sexuality and sexual identity?

These issues – ranging from what makes people experience attraction to another through to what makes people in a relationship experience it as satisfying to the very way in which we construct relationships and sexual identities within them – are addressed in this chapter.

Source: Dominic Lipinski/AFP Getty Images

The wedding of Catherine Middleton and Prince William: How important are issues of physical attraction, wealth, social standing and similarity in making sense of their relationship? Do spectacular and widely reported weddings such as these sustain certain ways of making sense of romance, gender, sexuality and relationships?

Introduction

The social psychology of relationships tries to address issues that can be vividly real for anyone who is in, or wishes to be in, a relationship. If you have ever wondered about why people experience attraction to one another or what makes for a happy and contented relationship, then social psychology, if not exactly providing 'the' answers, does at least raise such questions.

It may be worth reflecting for a moment on your own personal feelings about those answers. You might find that evolutionary perspectives make you reflect on your own appeal in the seemingly cold process of mate selection. Ideas about attraction based on perceived similarity might also give you little comfort – what if others do not perceive you as similar or your current partner seems very dissimilar to you? The evolutionary idea that partners tend to be similar because they have the same value in terms of the sum of their 'appealing' and 'unappealing' traits and attributes may lead you to worry about your own 'market value'. Furthermore, you might not feel drawn to the high-adrenalin activities that are sometimes associated with attraction, according to excitation transfer theory. Ideas that relationship satisfaction depends on cold calculations of equitable rewards in relation to inputs may go against your ideas about how people make sense of their relationships. Finally, if you like a sense of certainty about your world, then encountering social constructionist work – which suggests that ideas about masculinity, femininity, sexuality and relationships can be approached as versions of the world for which alternatives are available – may be an unsettling experience.

The issues addressed in this chapter are designed to give you an overview of the field and encourage your critical engagement with it. If the literature creates some sort of negative reaction in you, then there may be some merit in using this to motivate your own thinking about the material – what is it that seems uncomfortable or wrong and why? Just because this is a heavily researched area in social psychology does not close the door on your critical engagement with it – quite the reverse. *Because* it is important within social psychology and everyday life, it is perhaps more incumbent on all of us to take time to think through the answers the literature tries to provide and the questions it raises.

Chapter overview

This chapter addresses the two interlinked topics of attraction and relationships. First, attention is given to factors that have been identified as important in attraction, including evolutionary perspectives on what males and females 'look for' in prospective (heterosexual) mates. This literature argues there are sex differences in preferences of heterosexuals for opposite-sex partners that can be made sense of in evolutionary terms. Specifically, the literature that is covered addresses the idea that both males and females are concerned with maximising their chances of having offspring who are genetically related to them, but this common drive leads to differences in partner preferences between them. In reviewing this literature, questions are raised about the extent of empirical support available and the treatment of apparently contradictory evidence.

Having sketched out a broad meta-theoretical approach to attraction, our attention shifts to an overarching issue that has been examined from a number of different theoretical positions: similarity and attraction. One important strand of research that is reviewed addresses the idea we are attracted to those whom we perceive as having similar attitudes to us – an idea both critiqued and developed over several decades within social psychological literature. Particular attention is paid to research that attempts to review different explanations for the premise that similarity appears to be important in intimate relationships – pitting 'assortative mating' (the idea we seek out those who are similar to us) against 'market forces' (the idea we wind up with people who have a similar level of appeal as a potential mate).

The final tranche of attraction literature that is reviewed concerns arousal, specifically excitation transfer theory, which suggests that attributing an aroused state to a potential target of attraction can lead to feelings and actions consistent with attraction to that target. As will be seen, this research raises the intriguing possibility that people aroused for reasons not linked to attraction can come to construe that arousal as brought about by a potential target of attraction and, as a consequence, experience and act consistently with being attracted to them.

Having reviewed some of the key literature concerned with attraction, the chapter next addresses work that has sought to understand relationships – in particular, research seeking to ascertain the factors likely to determine the level of satisfaction experienced. One of the most important contributions to this area is the interrelated exchange and equity theories, which see the level of relationship satisfaction as the output of a calculation of the costs, benefits and amount invested in the relationships. Among criticisms raised concerning this approach is evidence partners are concerned with overall characteristics of the relationship and the idea that those couples who perceive a large burden of costs for few benefits might actually do so because they are already dissatisfied with the relationship rather than the dissatisfaction arising from such a perception.

Attribution theory – which is developed in Chapter 4 – is also considered, with particular reference to the idea that the way in which a person explains their partner's behaviour (especially their partner's negative behaviour) can shape concurrent and subsequent reports of relationship satisfaction.

The final area of research examined touches on aspects that are often outside of the remit of social psychology texts and concerns the constructions of relationships. Here two quite different aspects of the construction of relationships are briefly considered. First, some research that illustrates the way in which culturally available frameworks for making sense of relationships is considered. Here, attention is given to the sort of ideological work that such constructions might accomplish. Second, research that addresses the more local interactional work of constructions of relationships is touched on, considering what is being done interactionally by means of talking about relationship matters.

Finally, the chapter addresses some of the shortcomings of research on attraction and relationships, such as its rather narrow heterosexual focus, in which attention is almost exclusively focused on romantic, opposite-sex, dyadic relationships. Some of the methodological shortcomings of the research reviewed is also looked at – encompassing the ways in which experimental, questionnaire and interview data has been collected and interpreted. Also, mention is made of the relative neglect of interaction itself as the site where relationship work is done in and through talk.

3.1 Attraction

The work on attraction considered here addresses specifically attraction that we might consider to have a sexual or intimate component. Most of the research has focused on heterosexual attraction – sometimes developing a theory that could, in principle, apply to gay, lesbian and other relationship configurations and sometimes, either implicitly or explicitly, only addressing highly specific forms of relationship (such as dyadic, heterosexual relationships in which there is the possibility of procreation).

The first of the broad areas of literature considered here – drawing from evolutionary approaches – tends to be framed to address this more narrow configuration of relationship forms, with particular attention being paid to the ways in which male–female differences in desired partner attributes reflect concerns with maximising the possibility of the successful transmission of one's genes. The second area, which considers the role of similarity in attraction (suggesting that we are attracted to those we perceive as being similar to us or repulsed by those we consider different), is perhaps more broadly framed. One specific attempt to make sense of this similarity effect (the idea that people appear to have partners who are similar to them) settles on an explanation that, again, draws on evolutionary ideas – specifically, concerning our 'market value' as potential mates. The final area of literature to be considered here attempts to combine the physiological and psychological components of attraction by examining the ways in which states of arousal – and the ways in which we make sense of them – are vital determinants of our attraction towards potential partners.

Evolutionary approaches to attraction

From the perspective of evolutionary psychology, attraction is instrumental. People are attracted to potential mates who have attributes that, for their ancestors, have been associated with maximising the possibility of their genes being passed on. This is most obviously achieved by having offspring that survive to sexual maturity and then themselves have offspring. These preferences – for mates with 'offspring maximising attributes' (or **reproductive fitness**) – will themselves be passed on through generations of offspring.

It is worth just noting the elegant efficiency of this idea before moving on to look at the details. Preferences for certain attributes associated with reproductive fitness in a mate will be passed on only to the extent to which they *actually do result in the production of offspring*. That is, the evolutionary process selects the genes of those parents who have astute – reproduction-relevant – preferences for their sexual partners. If a male and female have preferences related to actual reproductive fitness (such as for mates of an age that they can produce offspring), they are more likely to produce offspring, their genes will be passed on through them and – as a component of those genes – so will their mate preferences. If a male and female have preferences that are *negatively* related to reproductive fitness (such as for mates beyond the age at which they can reproduce offspring), they will have fewer, if any, offspring and their genes – including their mate preferences – will *not* be passed on.

It should be noted, as mentioned above, that overwhelmingly this research focuses on male–female heterosexual relationships that have the potential to result in offspring biologically related to the partners. This point will be revisited later, but, for now, it is worth noting that all references to male and female preferences refer to heterosexual preferences in cases where there is a prospect of genetically related offspring being produced.

One of the most important studies in this area was undertaken by Buss (1989). This was a massive study involving a survey of 10, 047 adults in 37 cultures across 33 countries. The countries involved spanned the continents of Africa, Asia, Europe, the Americas and Oceania and sometimes involved different cultures within a single country – South Africa 'whites' as well as 'Zulu'; Israeli 'Jewish' as well as 'Palestinian' and Canadian 'English' as well as 'French', for example. Drawing on ideas based on evolutionary theory, Buss hypothesised that certain differences in mate selection (or **sex-linked preferences**) should exist between males and females (see Figure 3.1) and these fell into three broad groupings.

First, females are understood as the sex investing most in reproduction in humans – that is, at a physical level alone, the effort and impact of having children is far greater for women than for men. This, in evolutionary terms, might result in females being 'selected' (by the

Reproductive fitness The extent to which a potential mate is likely to maximise the chance of passing on one's genes to future offspring. Someone with high reproductive fitness is more likely to be able to have offspring (and thereby pass on genes) than someone with low reproductive fitness.

Sex-linked preferences Within the context of the research considered here, this refers to the idea that what is thought to be desirable in a mate is linked to the sex of the person making the judgement. This strand of evolutionary psychology suggests that men and women have different positions regarding ideal partner attributes and this difference can be explained in evolutionary terms.

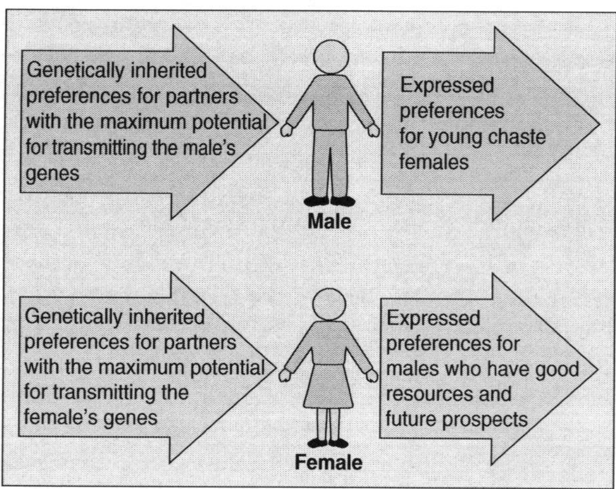

Figure 3.1 Evolution-based hypothesis for male–female differences in partner preferences (based on Buss, 1989)

process of evolution) to exert stronger preferences about mating partners. Chu, Hardaker and Lycett (2007 p. 1292) draw on Trivers (1972) to suggest that, because of this asymmetry in costs of reproduction for males and females, females 'should be more choosy in selecting a potential mate'. This – taken together with the idea that men are, nonetheless, invested as parents – should result in females selecting male mates who 'have the ability and willingness to provide resources related to parental investment such as food, shelter, territory, and protection' (Buss, 1989, p. 2). Buss, (1989, p. 2) suggests that, 'Among humans, resources typically translate into earning capacity'. Thus, he hypothesised that females would attach greater importance to 'good financial prospects' and 'ambitions and industriousness' in their partners than males would in theirs.

Second, females, rather than males, can be understood as having a more highly specified age range in which they are maximally fertile. This, according to Buss, results in males placing particular emphasis on aspects of female potential mates that are indicative of current or current and future fertility. Furthermore, Chu et al. (2007, p. 1292) argue that 'the main limiting constraint on male reproductive success is access to females', from which they infer 'males should be sensitive to cues of female fertility'. For Buss, (1989, p. 2) 'smooth skin, good muscle tone, lustrous hair, and full lips – and behavioural indicators of youth – such as high energy level and sprightly gait – have been hypothesised to provide the strongest cues to female reproductive capacity ... sexual attraction and standards of beauty are hypothesised to have evolved to correspond to these features.' Thus, males were hypothesised to place greater emphasis on the physical appearance and age (with a preference for youth) of potential partners.

Third, because certainty of parenthood is almost entirely a male concern – females confirming that they are the biological parent through the act of birth – males rather than females should value female chastity. The idea here is that males with a preference for female chastity should have more success in ensuring that their genes are passed on – through *their* children (and not others) being born to their sexual mates. This should result in males expressing greater preference for chastity in their mates – or potential mates – than females.

These hypotheses were tested by having participants provide details about themselves, including 'the age at which the respondent preferred to marry, the age difference the respondent preferred to have between self and spouse, who the respondent preferred to be older (self or spouse), and how many children were desired' (Buss, 1989, p. 5). In addition, participants were required to *rate* on a 4-point scale (from indispensible to irrelevant/unimportant) 18 characteristics, including, 'good financial prospect', 'good looks', 'chastity: no previous sexual intercourse' and 'ambition and industriousness'. Finally, participants were required to *rank* 13 characteristics, including, 'good earning capacity' and 'physically attractive' in terms of 'their desirability in someone you might marry' (Buss, 1989, p. 5).

Buss (1989) found some level of support for these hypotheses. Compared to males, female participants across most cultures showed a significantly greater preference for mates who have 'good financial prospects' and – to a lesser extent – those who are described as 'ambitious and industrious'. While, compared to females, male respondents across most cultures reported a significantly higher preference for physically attractive mates and those who were younger than themselves. Rather less supported was the idea concerning chastity – here there was significant cross-cultural variation, leading Buss (1989, p. 12) to suggest that 'cultural differences, ecological differences, or mating system differences exert powerful effects on the value attached to chastity.'

Evaluating evolutionary psychology's perspective on human relationships

Leaving aside predictions concerning male preferences for 'chaste' females, Buss (1989) reports substantial cross-cultural support for his hypotheses. The idea that males are particularly concerned with appearances and females with resources is, in itself, hardly new. Of the many popular expressions of this idea, Marilyn Monroe's portrayal of Lorelei Lee in *Gentlemen Prefer Blondes* provides some particularly vivid examples. Thus, in accounting for her intention to marry for money, Lorelei Lee quips; 'Don't you know that a man being rich is like a girl being pretty? You wouldn't marry a girl just because she's pretty, but my goodness, doesn't it help?' What Buss (1989) did was to provide empirical evidence that substantiated the idea that these preferences were linked to evolutionary ideas – particularly the evolutionary psychology of Trivers (1972) and Hamilton (1964). Indeed, both the findings of Buss (1989) and the data collected have been a significant influence in evolutionary psychology. Consistent with Buss (1989), Stone, Shackleford and Buss (2008) found that, in countries where poor health was relatively widespread, there would be particular preference for partners who displayed good health. Furthermore, Shackleford, Schmitt and Buss' (2005) reanalysis of Buss' (1989) data confirmed that the attributes – such as physical attractiveness and resources – emerging as central to attraction in the original study were of central importance in their identification of four universal dimensions of human mate preferences. Indeed, Buss (2006, p. 502) claims that 'The study of human mating is one of the true "success stories" of evolutionary psychology.'

Not all findings have confirmed what this version of evolutionary psychology might predict, however. Stone et al. (2008) found only modest support for the idea that resource acquisition would be more highly valued in countries where there were fewer resources. Still more problematic, despite predictions that females should be 'more choosy' and particularly concerned with resources (or resource acquisition potential), Chu et al. (2007) found that females showed a consistent preference for attractive males *of medium status rather than high status*. Furthermore, Buss (1989, p. 13) found that the most important dimension for males *and* females were not resources or physical attractiveness: '*Both* sexes ranked the characteristics "kind-understanding" and "intelligent" higher than earning power and attractiveness in all samples'. These issues are considered in further detail below.

Confer, Easton, Fleischman, Goetz, Lewis, Perilloux and Buss (2010) argue that well-designed studies in evolutionary psychology do offer the possibility of falsification – that is, having their hypotheses disconfirmed by the data – and they cite some examples of this. Some of the findings considered above, however – being unpredicted and, to some extent, disconfirming of hypotheses – should perhaps have led to further questioning of the evolutionary approach to relationships than appears to have been the case. The finding in Buss (1989, p. 13) that the attributes 'kind-understanding' and 'intelligent' were more important than others for men and women across all cultures could have caused substantial pause for thought, but, instead, was seen at the time as 'suggesting that species-typical mate preferences may be more potent than sex-linked preferences'. Subsequently, Shackleford, et al. (2005, p. 456) drew parallels between these attributes and two of their four universal dimensions of human mate preferences. In this new outline of universal dimensions of human mate preferences, one of these attributes – intelligence – rather than being an unexpected finding, was construed as confirming what evolutionary psychology would expect: 'consistent with previous work ... women around the world value dependability, stability, education, and intelligence in a long term mate more than men do.'

Similarly, Chu et al. (2007) finding that females showed a consistent preference not for the predicted attractive males *of high status*, but, instead, for *attractive males of medium status*, might be considered problematic in terms of what we would expect based on Buss (1989), Shackelford et al. (2005) and Buss (2007). Chu et al. (2007), however, interpret these findings in a way that is consistent with the 'meta-theory' of evolutionary psychology. Thus, Chu et al. (2007) consider that males who are rated high-status and highly attractive might be rated as less desirable because they are more likely to cheat or their high status may mean they invest less in raising offspring.

These issues regarding the extent to which the data ever questions any premise of evolutionary psychology raise the issue that, in some senses, while specific predictions and hypotheses may be challenged, the theoretical framework from which they emerge is less open to question. In this sense, evolutionary psychology as a meta-theory is somewhat more like a paradigm that not only provides sets of expected relations between variables but also ways of interpreting and understanding even those data that appear – on the surface – to contradict it.

If evolutionary psychology is some form of paradigm through which relationships can be understood, then questions can be asked concerning how it has been applied to this domain and what, if any, alternative frameworks might be available for understanding these results. One issue to emerge here is that, because evolutionary psychology is something of a meta-theory, it may not only support a range of potentially contradictory findings (as referred to above) but also fail to specifically identify particular expected results. Put another way, in some cases there is something of a leap from global theory to specific hypotheses and prediction. For example, Buss (1989, p. 2), having discussed features of skin tone, hair and lips related to youth (see above), continues: 'sexual attraction and standards of beauty are hypothesized to have evolved to correspond to these features.' It is not entirely clear, though, how specific features deemed beautiful across cultures or culturally specific – which might involve the facial structure, size of eyes and position of cheekbones, for example – can be thought of *just* in terms of their indication of age.

Similarly, there can be something of a leap from the ancestral basis of the presumed mate preferences – and what are taken to be their modern-day counterparts. Thus, while resources may – in terms of our ancestors – have been a matter of life and death, Buss (1989, p. 2) translates these into modern-day resources that might be more associated with lifestyle: 'Among humans, resources typically translate into earning capacity. Females, more than males, should value attributes in potential mates such as ambition, industriousness, and earning capacity that signal the possession or likely acquisition of resources.' According to evolutionary theory, then, a heterosexual woman may be attracted to a wealthy male not because of the opportunities for exotic holidays and designer shopping that this affords, but, rather, because his wealth means any offspring they might have will have a better chance of survival and, in turn, the opportunity to produce offspring. In many cultures, however, there may be little correlation between resources and chances of survival or propagation of offspring. Are female preferences for mates with resources to be understood as something carried over from contexts where resources *were* closely related to opportunities for passing on genes or as related to current *lifestyle preferences* available within their specific culture?

This last example raises a further point that other explanatory frameworks might account for the findings appearing to support evolutionary psychology. Confer et al. (2010) are at pains to point out that culture need not be seen as an *alternative* to evolutionary accounts of human behaviour. Indeed, for Confer et al., evolutionary theory should have an impact on culture. Culture may, however, provide an alternative explanation for differences in mate preferences that do not necessitate speculations about their evolutionary basis. Furthermore, culture may open up the meanings that preferences have for humans rather than an evolution-framed meaning that they must have to be made sense of in evolutionary terms.

Looking at the first of these, one important aspect of culture is the ways in which access to resources is distributed within a society – particularly between men and women. It may be that the different levels of access that men and women have to resources in a society may explain some differences in male–female mate preferences *without* invoking evolution-relevant concerns. Thus, females' preference for mates with resources can be made sense of in terms of who has power and control over resources – there might not necessarily be evolution-relevant concerns driving the process behind the scenes.

With regard to cultural meanings, Wheeler and Kim (1997) argue that people hold stereotypes about physically attractive people. Both Korean and American students, while showing some cultural differences, associated the traits of being socially skilled, friendly and well-adjusted with photographs of people who were rated as physically attractive. This research suggests that, for human participants, an attractive mate may be preferred for a range of culturally defined reasons rather than simply because of those meanings identified as being relevant to evolutionary processes of mate selection.

Critical recap

Evolutionary approaches to attraction

1 A number of studies have reported results that do not entirely support evolutionary psychology's hypotheses.

2 It is possible to question the extent to which evolutionary theory is – or perhaps should be – falsifiable. To what extent does it reinterpret unanticipated findings to fit the evolutionary psychology meta-theory?

3 Evolutionary psychology raises the issue regarding how central explanations based on survival and propagation of genes should be for understanding non-survival, non-gene transfer-related behaviour. Thus, are issues of survival relevant for making sense of preferences for mates with resources in contexts where this is *not* strongly correlated to survival or the chances for passing on genes?

4 Should we consider the cultural meanings that mate preferences may have? That is, should we take into account not just what people look for in a mate but also the *meanings* that this may have for them – for example, the positive associations with potential mates judged to be attractive?

5 Evolutionary psychology makes sense of the claim that females rate male resources as particularly important without considering the relative access that males and females might have to resources in a culture. If access differences for males and females are taken into account, then the female preference for mates with resources can be made sense of without invoking evolutionary psychology's ideas about the child-rearing investment for men and women.

6 Finally, is this approach – which is relevant only for relationships that have a prospect of producing genetically associated offspring – a relevant framework for understanding all human relationships?

Reflective questions

1. *Do you think there are consistent male–female differences in what is looked for in a partner?*
2. *How important do you think genetic considerations are for people who are in, or seeking, relationships?*

3.2 Similarity

Research concerned with similarity attempts to explain two interrelated phenomena – that we are attracted to those we perceive as similar to us and, within existing dyadic relationships, the partners tend to be similar to each other.

This very premise concerning similarity could of course be questioned: are we attracted to 'similar' others, are existing partners 'similar' to one another, how is the similarity defined and could the inverse (that we are attracted to 'different' others) be made just as plausible? From a different perspective, one might consider whether or not some other variable, such as propinquity (see Box 3.1), is at work – that is, perhaps similar people are more likely to live nearer each other and be in greater contact and it is this relatively high level of contact which leads to attraction. For most of the research here, however, the premise positively linking similarity and attraction is subscribed to.

The first of the approaches considered below draws on balance theory, which suggests that we experience a

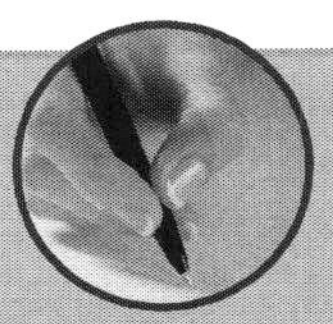

Box 3.1 TRY IT OUT
Propinquity research

One of the earliest approaches to understanding attraction in social psychology is the idea of propinquity. Simply put, your closest friends could well be those who are closest – in terms of where they live – to you.

Festinger, Schachter and Back (1950) asked participants to name their three closest friends in a large student housing complex (with 17 buildings, each with 10 apartments). Festinger et al. found that 65 per cent of friends lived in the same building. Considering the findings within each building, 44 per cent of next-door neighbours were described as 'close friends', but only 10 per cent of those who lived at the opposite end of the hall.

One important approach to understanding the propinquity effect is the idea that mere exposure increases liking, (Bornstein, 1989; Bornstein and D'Agostino, 1992). Moreland and Beach (1992) drew on this idea to account for the findings of their field experiment. They had non-interacting female research confederates attend class between 0 and 15 times (out of a total of 15 sessions). Student liking for confederates was positively correlated with attendance, meaning that those confederates who attended most and were thus seen the most were most liked; those who attended least were liked least.

Draw a map of where you live during term-time, placing your location at the centre. Now mark on the map where your friends and acquaintances live. Is there any indication that your best friends live closer to you than those who are more distant acquaintances? Now repeat the exercise with your non-term-time address (if this is different) – are the results the same?

Many of the propinquity experiments involved judgements made in student accommodation where there was some degree of similarity between people living closer and further away (at the very least, all were students at the same university and, in most cases, they were all of a similar age). When we apply propinquity to more varied – or less homogeneous – populations, however, we may find that the effect is diminished because the network of 'similar' others is geographically dispersed.

Some propinquity research has relied on very minimal relationships – such as the liking for a non-interacting co-present 'student' in Moreland and Beach's (1992) research. Can this usefully inform our understanding of meaningful relationships?

If there *is* a propinquity effect, is it simply that proximity increases social contact, without which there is no relationship (good or bad), or is there some liking effect that occurs from repeated exposure?

state of cognitive consistency in those situations where we like those whom we agree with, so, if we find ourselves agreeing with someone's attitudes, we are likely to experience some form of attraction towards them. Bryne's development of these ideas to form a 'law of attraction' is also addressed, along with approaches that emphasise the importance of self – for example, suggesting we like similar others because they resemble self or we are really concerned with the extent to which others positively evaluate us. Finally, particular attention is given to Wood and Brumbaugh's (2009) research, which has sought to address why partners may tend to be 'similar' and seeks to evaluate the evidence for partners choosing similar others ('assortative mating') and for partnerships cohering from individuals who have a broadly equivalent desirability as a mate ('market value').

Balance theory

Heider's (1958) **balance theory**, which is touched on again in Chapter 6, suggests that we are motivated to achieve a state of balance, so we like those with whom we share similar attitudes and dislike those with whom we lack this common stance. If we find that we have similar attitudes to someone, then we will be motivated – out of a desire for cognitive consistency – to like that person, with the reverse being the case should our attitudes differ from theirs. At the heart of balance theory we find that there is a propensity to like others to the extent that our views are aligned with theirs (see Figure 3.2).

It is perhaps easiest to picture how this theory works with issues that we might feel strongly about and other people with whom we are relatively newly acquainted. If, for example you are a committed vegetarian and someone you have recently met discloses that they too are vegetarian, it is likely that your shared attitude will confirm or increase your mutual liking. If, by contrast, this person invites you to their favourite steak house, shows a derogatory stance towards vegetarians or reveals that they work as a butcher, then the potential spark of liking towards them may be extinguished.

At one level, balance theory makes intuitive sense – we have probably all experienced some form of increased liking for someone who has revealed that their attitude towards a particular person or issue is the same as our own. As soon as we start to increase the complexity of the triangles illustrated in Figure 3.2, however, by, for example, considering that person 'O' may reveal a *range* of attitudes – some similar and some dissimilar to our own – the issue about how this predicts our liking becomes much more complicated.

One attempt to deal with this shortcoming of balance theory in its original form was developed by Byrne (1971) in what he referred to as a 'law of attraction'. He argued that it is the *totality* of aligned and non-aligned attitudes that needs to be considered. From this perspective, if we examine all of the attitudes that two people have, we find that liking between them is positively correlated to the proportion of shared attitudes that they have – as that proportion increases, so does the mutual liking. For Byrne, then, we are attracted to others to the extent that we have shared attitudes across different issues. This stance has received some cross-cultural support (Singh & Ho, 2000).

Similarity and self

An alternative to balance theory's emphasis on cognitive consistency as an explanation for similarity being positively associated with attraction is evidenced in Jones, Pelham, Carvallo and Mirenberg (2004). They conducted archival research, which suggested that there was a significant matching between people sharing the same surname prior to marriage. The authors explained this in terms of an egotistical preference for others resembling self, although other factors, such as connections between the families involved, may have played an important role.

Further studies by Jones et al. (2004) partly addressed this, suggesting that participants in experiments had greater liking for other participants whose experimental code numbers resembled their birth date or who appeared to have a surname that shared letters in their own name or even those whose numbers had been subliminally paired with their own name.

A problem with these additional studies, however, is that they involve ratings of liking in such an unusual environment of relationships between barely acquainted co-participants in experiments. In such a strange situation, rating 'liking preferences' in this way may be a

Balance theory A theory that suggests we seek consistency between our liking of people and common targets of our attitudes. We are in balance when we agree with those we like and disagree with those we dislike. From this perspective, similarity between partners can – in part – be understood as a consequence of having greater liking for those with similar attitudes towards things.

In the following arrangements, **P** is the perceiver whose attitudes we are considering, **X** is the attitude target–the person, entity, experience or phenomenon about which we have an attitude– and **O** is another person. In these examples, consider that you are P, the person whose attitude we are interested in. A '+' indicates liking for the other person or the attitude target, '–' indicates disliking for the other person or the attitude target.

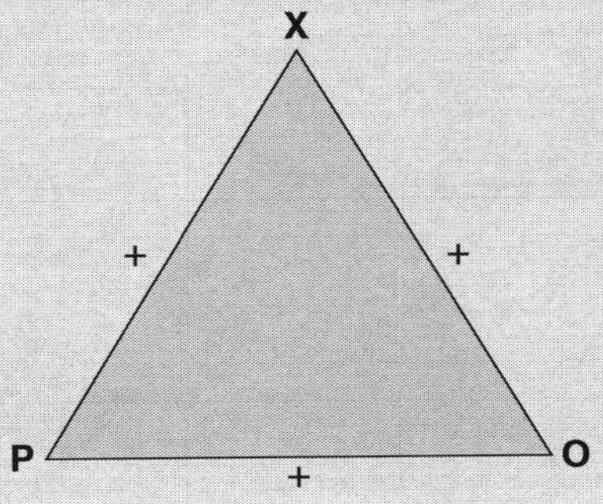

Balanced arrangement: *you agree with someone you like*–for example, you both like the attitude target

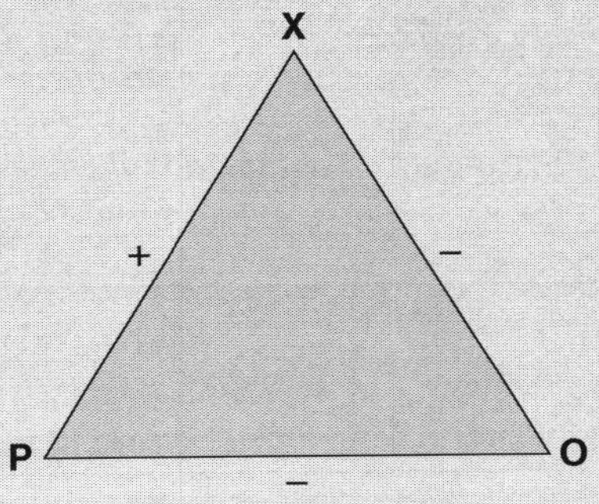

Balanced arrangement: *you disagree with someone you dislike*–for example, you differ from their disliking of the attitude target

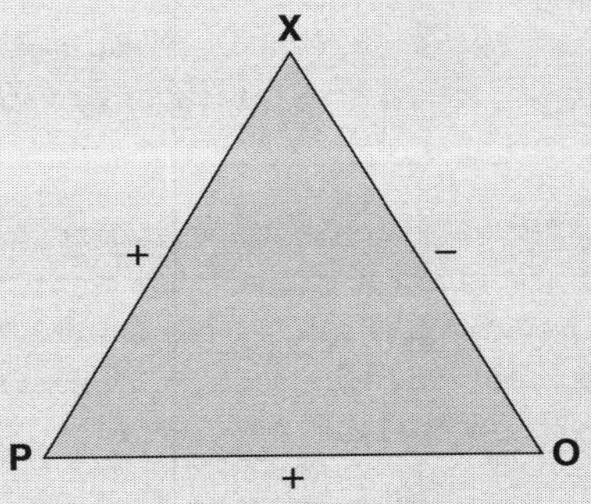

Unbalanced arrangement: *you disagree with someone you like*–for example, you differ from their disliking of the attitude target

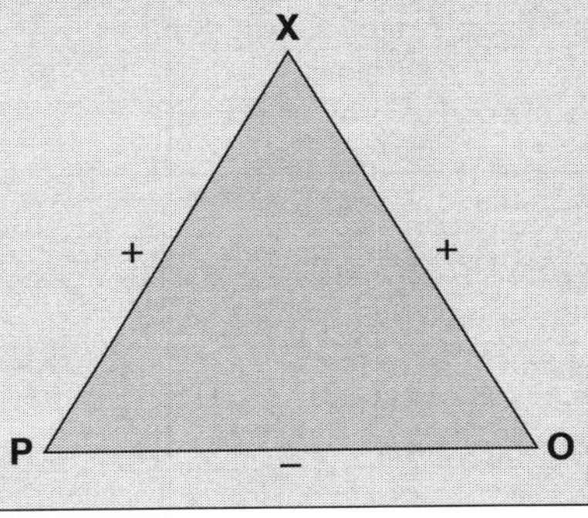

Unbalanced arrangement: *you agree with someone you dislike*–for example, you both like the attitude target

Figure 3.2 An illustration of Heider's (1958) balance theory

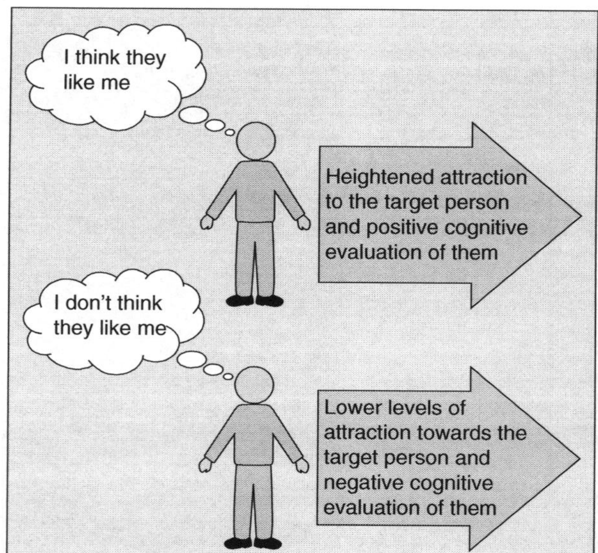

Figure 3.3 Effect of the perceived evaluation of self by others on attraction and cognitive evaluation of them (based on Singh et al., 2007)

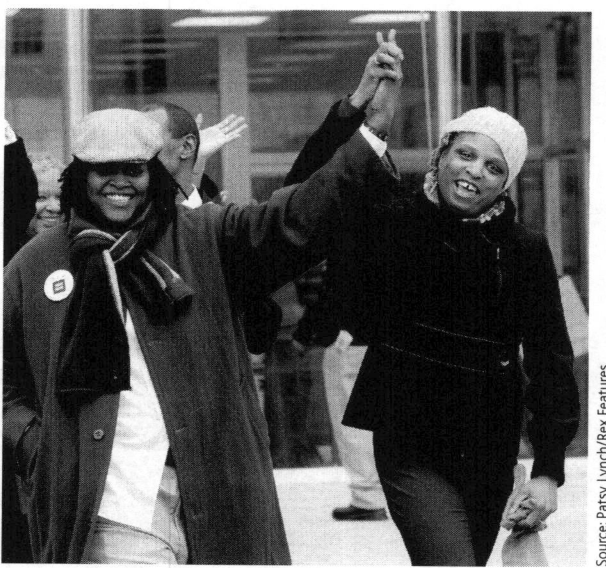

Source: Patsy Lynch/Rex Features

Which of the theories covered might make sense of this recently married couple's attraction? What information about them would we need to know in order to make an informed judgement?

means by which some sort of sense is made of the environment (see criticism of the minimal group paradigm in Chapter 2). Questions can be raised, therefore, about the extent to which the findings generalise from this extremely unusual experimental procedure to 'real-world' experiences of attraction.

Research by Singh, Ho, Tan and Bell (2007) also suggests that self is important in thinking about similarity and attraction – but in a quite different way (see Figure 3.3). Their research confirmed that perceiving others as having similar attitudes to ourselves can indeed have a direct and important effect on attraction. For Singh et al. (2007), however, the perceptions that an individual has of *how they are* ***personally evaluated*** *by the other person* has a more powerful effect on attraction than perceived similarity. According to Singh et al., being positively evaluated by another can activate a level of attraction and positive cognitive evaluation of them (rating them as possessing desirable traits) that makes it different in both magnitude and type of effect to merely encountering shared attitudes.

Riela, Rodriguez, Aron, Xu and Acevedo's (2010) cross-cultural research had results that were sympathetic with the idea that similarity in itself may be less important than perceiving liking of the other for oneself. In a first study, Riela et al. (2010) asked white Americans and Asian Americans to write 'narratives of their falling in love experiences'. They found that 'liking of each other' and 'familiarity' were the foremost factors across all participants. Riela et al.'s (2010) second study (involving participants living in the USA and China) again had **reciprocal liking** emerge as the most important factor in 'falling in love' with 'similarity' much lower for participants in both the USA and China.

Why do people have sexual partners who are similar to themselves?

The literature considered above has focused on the idea that people choose others who are similar to them. This idea has two components – first, that people tend to have friendships and especially partners who are similar to them and, second, that this similarity is due to each partner's choice of a similar other. Wood and Brumbaugh (2009) note that, while there is substantial agreement in the literature about the fact people tend to have sexual partners who are quite similar to themselves, there is disagreement concerning *why* this is the case.

Personal evaluation The way in which an individual believes that they are perceived by another. In the context of this literature, the focus is on how being perceived in a positive or negative way affects attraction towards and cognitive evaluation of the person whose evaluations are being considered.

Reciprocal liking Mutual liking between two people. In the context of this literature, the interest is in how such mutual liking is an important factor in attraction.

Wood and Brumbaugh (2009) note that some of these explanations could be glossed as '**assortative mating**' – that is, people 'prefer and seek out different types'. From this perspective, those who have a certain characteristic like to select sexual partners who also have – or appear to have – the same characteristic. Thus, if someone can be described as 'agreeable', they will seek out others who are 'agreeable'. Byrne (1971), discussed above, as well as Klohnen and Luo (2003) and Buston and Emlen (2003), represent this 'assortative' approach to partner selection.

An alternative explanation is that similar people are paired because they have the same *market value* in terms of the combination of desirable and undesirable characteristics. This '**market forces**' explanation suggests that two people might share a characteristic – such as agreeableness – because these characteristics can be similarly rated in terms of desirability in sexual partners (Buss & Barnes, 1986; Geary, Vigil & Byrd-Craven, 2004). If agreeableness is highly sought after in sexual partners, then it will be highly valued. Those who have (or are perceived to have) the characteristic of agreeableness will have a higher market value, will attract more partners and can, thus, select partners who also have this highly valued characteristic. By contrast, those lacking this – or other – highly valued characteristic will attract fewer partners, 'forcing them to settle for less desirable mates (in this case other disagreeable individuals)' (Wood & Brumbaugh, 2009, p. 1226). In order to examine this debate in more detail, we will now take a closer look at Wood and Brumbaugh's (2009) research.

For Wood and Brumbaugh (2009), distinguishing between the two theories outlined above rests largely on discerning the extent to which there is agreement about which characteristics are attractive. If there is substantial consensus about which features are desirable in a sexual partner, then – for them – that lends support to the market forces explanation for similarity. That is because, if there is high consensus, then the idea of certain characteristics having a market value is much more possible – the more everyone values a given trait, the more sought after and valuable that trait is and the more readily it can be assigned a desirability value. Similarly, if there is substantial consensus about which traits are positive, then any one person's desire for a mate with particular qualities is no longer specific to them – everyone wants the same qualities in their sexual partner as everyone else. Finally, if there is a high consensus for desirable qualities, then it is likely that those who have the most highly desirable characteristics will be more successful at competing for mates who also have these highly desirable characteristics.

Using the procedure described in Box 3.2, Wood and Brumbaugh (2009) sought to clarify the extent to which there is consensus on the desirability of certain features in potential sexual partners, arriving at a 'consensus correlation' as a measure of agreement (the closer to 1.0, the greater the consensus).

They found some evidence of consensus – particularly for men. Thus, heterosexual men had a consensus correlation of 0.62 and homosexual men a consensus correlation of 0.57. Consensus correlations were lower for women – at 0.44 for heterosexual women and 0.48 for homosexual women.

Wood and Brumbaugh also sought to identify *which* features men and women agreed on as being desirable in the photographs they rated (referred to as *targets*). It should be noted that, in their discussion of this aspect of their findings, Wood and Brumbaugh pay considerably more attention to opposite-sex ratings of participants who described themselves as heterosexual than they do to the ratings made by those describing themselves as homosexual.

Wood and Brumbaugh (2009, p. 1235) note that (with regard to males who self-describe themselves as heterosexual), 'Men showed strong general preferences for female targets who were seen as feminine, curvaceous, seductive, thin, well-groomed, trendy and confident.' They (2009, p. 1235) further add that, 'Men also demonstrated small general preferences for female targets who looked sensitive, classy and intelligent.' More generally, Wood and Brumbaugh (2009, p. 1235) suggest that male raters – *regardless of sexuality* – showed a 'strong consensual concern for physical characteristics'.

Wood and Brumbaugh note in passing that, because of these consensual concerns among males with physical characteristics, the objects of male desire (heterosexual women and homosexual men) are likely to experience 'body image' issues. With regard to the preferences of

Assortative mating The idea that people seek out partners who share certain characteristics with themselves. From this perspective, similarity between couples is a consequence of each partner seeking out and selecting another who shares similar traits to themselves.

Market forces In the context of this literature, the idea that people have a certain 'market value' as a potential mate. Similarity between couples can thus be explained in terms of them having similar traits because those matched traits have the same market value.

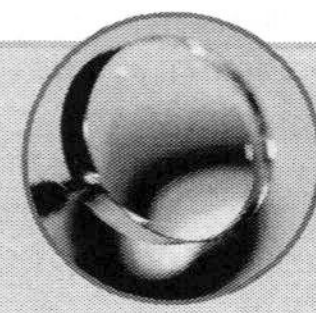

Box 3.2 FOCUS
The experimental procedure used by Wood and Brumbaugh (2009)

Wood and Brumbaugh (2009) used an online survey they called 'The online attraction test' to collect their data. The research process involved the following steps.

1 They obtained 98 male and 98 female photographs from a website that invited people to submit photographs to be rated for physical attractiveness by others.

Wood and four undergraduate research assistants independently rated each photograph using the following dimensions:

Deviant/countercultural, Sensitive/soft-hearted, Formal/classy, Intelligent/smart, Seductive/suggestive (v. modest), Well-groomed (v. unkempt), Confident, Trendy/stylish/urbane, Masculine (v. feminine), Toned (for male photographs), Curvaceous (for female photographs), Smiling (to what extent is the person in the photograph smiling), Under- v. overweight

2 There was a check on the extent to which the raters agreed with each other in their ratings of the photographs on these characteristics.

3 The photographs were made available online so that those viewing the website could rate each photograph using the following questions: 'How *attractive* do you find this person?' and 'How interested would you be in *dating* this person?' For each question, participants were invited to respond on a ten-point scale, ranging from 'not at all' to 'very'. Online participants also completed a few brief questions concerning themselves, such as their sexual orientation.

4 Wood and Brumbaugh (2009) then sought to assess the desirability of each trait they had rated the photographs on (that is, deviant, sensitive, formal, classy, intelligent and so on) by investigating the relationship between a photograph's rating on each characteristic and the participant's desirability rating for that photograph. This is a complex procedure, but imagine, for example, that photograph 91 was rated (in step 2 above) as very high for 'trendy' and another photograph, say number 73, was the same in all respects, except it was rated as very low for 'trendy'. If participants (in step 4) rate photograph 91 (the 'trendy' one) as much more attractive than photograph 73 (the 'non-trendy' one), then this suggests that the quality of 'trendiness' is found to be attractive. This procedure was completed for all participants with all photographs and the extent of the agreement on what was found to be attractive was analysed. The study sought to establish both which features were rated as attractive (is trendiness attractive, for example) *and* the extent to which there was consensus among participants on these attractiveness judgements (do participants tend to *all* rate trendiness as attractive, for example).

heterosexual females, Wood and Brumbaugh (2009, p. 1235) report that; 'Women demonstrated the strongest general preferences for male targets who looked confident, seductive, well-groomed and toned.'

Wood and Brumbaugh (2009) interpret these results as offering support for the idea that there *is* consensus regarding what traits are desirable in sexual partners – albeit strongest when males are doing the rating – and, thus, some support for the market forces explanation for similarity. That is, because heterosexual males consensually seek women who are 'feminine, curvaceous, seductive, thin, well-groomed, trendy and confident', there will be competition for mates who are judged to possess these characteristics and those heterosexual males who themselves have the most desirable characteristics are likely to be more successful than those who don't. Thus, because heterosexual females consensually seek males who are judged to be 'confident, seductive, well-groomed and toned', it is males judged to have those qualities who are likely to be most successful. This results in a potential matching (in heterosexual relationships) of 'feminine, curvaceous, seductive, thin, well-groomed, trendy and confident' females with 'confident, seductive, well-groomed and toned' males.

It can be seen that *some* (though not all) of these characteristics are the same (confident, seductive, well-groomed) and some have been treated as the equivalent in the opposite sex (curvaceous and well-toned). So, if we find that (heterosexual) partners appear similar in that both are confident, well-groomed and seductive and have equally appealing 'sex-typed' bodies, Wood and Brumbaugh interpret this as a function of the fact that these features are consensually desirable. According to this perspective, what we are seeing in cases of similar partners is not the consequence of each partner's individual taste, but, rather, their *equivalent market value*.

Evaluating Wood and Brumbaugh (2009)

Wood and Brumbaugh's procedure was devised partly as a response to what they saw as the failings of previous attempts to investigate what people found to be attractive. They note that, in much previous research, participants are asked to report what they find attractive – sometimes along with items to measure their own characteristics. Such self-reports may be distorted to manage a positive impression – people may not want to appear 'shallow' and so may report that they find 'intelligence' and 'sensitivity' attractive regardless of whether or not they actually do, for instance. To avoid this problem, Wood and Brumbaugh got participants to reveal their preferences by rating the attractiveness of different photographs (not reporting what characteristics were attractive to them). They also liked the standardisation that their procedure gave them – that is, each participant was faced with exactly the same set of male or female photographs to rate for attractiveness. Think how this differs from, say, a speed dating situation (whether simulated or 'real'), in which people could present themselves slightly differently to different potential partners. Unlike a photograph, using real people introduces the problem that the target (about whom judgements of attractiveness will be made) will not appear *identically* to each participant. If you introduce people who have had any previous contact, the problems get worse, according to Wood and Brumbaugh, because, now, people's rating of attractiveness or desire to meet the target person again might be coloured by explicit or implicit rejection that they have previously experienced. For example, I might find someone very attractive, but rate them as less attractive and not want to meet them again not because of their attributes, but because of their actual or feared treatment of me.

There are a number of issues that can be raised about Wood and Brumbaugh's research, but, here, just four broad areas will be considered: issues concerning the use of pre-rated characteristics, the presumptions about these characteristics, a somewhat narrow understanding of sexuality and implicit assumptions regarding the nature of human interaction.

First, with regard to the use of pre-rated characteristics, there are issues concerning which attributes were selected and how these were used. Noticeably absent from the list of attributes on which the photographs were rated by Wood and four undergraduate assistants (see Box 3.2, step 1) is any reference to judgements of wealth or resources, which, in the literature – especially the evolutionary literature (much of which is drawn on by Wood and Brumbaugh) – is a particularly important attractive attribute for males to be perceived as having in judgements made by heterosexual females. Perhaps one reason it was not considered is that photographs were not thought to readily portray this attribute, but this leads to the question of how many of the other attributes might be 'read into' the presented photographs by participants. Even leaving aside the characteristics of intelligence and sensitivity (on which Wood and his assistants had relatively low inter-rater reliability), it is highly questionable that the online participants responded to these photographs in terms of the 11 other attributes that Wood and his assistants rated them as having.

Second, when presented with a set of scales regarding 13 distinct characteristics for each photograph, it is not necessarily a problem – particularly for psychologists and undergraduate psychology students, who may be familiar with the process – to complete them. This may, however, tell us very little about the ways in which characteristics are made sense of either by participants or in everyday life. Thus, these 13 attributes might not be identified, responded to, evaluated for attractiveness or treated as discrete, quantifiable characteristics by participants. Instead, their responses to the target photographs might be more on the basis of some less readily atomised (broken into 13 discrete characteristics) attractiveness judgement.

Third, although Wood and Brumbaugh (2009) refer to findings regarding heterosexuals and homosexuals – which many researchers do not – they can be challenged in terms of their approach to sexuality. Evident in the summary of their work, all participants had to describe themselves as *either* homosexual *or* heterosexual – very much reifying the binary opposition of these two forms of sexuality (see Box 3.2). Along with this, there is some evidence of an arguably stereotyped view of sexuality under the guise of what 'various researchers' have discovered (2009, p. 1230) 'various researchers have found that homosexual men look largely similar to heterosexual men in their heightened preference for casual sex and concern for physical appearance, whereas homosexual women are similar to heterosexual women in their heightened preference for intimacy and long-term relationships'.

Fourth, and finally, this research – like most attraction research – trades on an implicit understanding that human interaction is relatively unimportant in the process of attraction. Thus, attraction between real interacting people is treated as though it can be understood in terms of the presumed mechanisms revealed in relatively asocial situations – such as an individual looking at photographs online. Here, the isolated asocial observer is thought to reveal fundamental mechanisms of attraction that can be read into real-life encounters between people. The assumption is that important context-free mechanisms necessary to explain the process of attraction are found *within the observer in isolation* and interaction between people itself adds nothing – or nothing particularly important – to our understanding of the process of interpersonal attraction.

Critical recap

Similarity

1 Some of the early approaches to similarity and attraction relied on highly simplified models (such as balance theory) that were not reflective of the complexity of human relationships and not subjected to serious empirical investigation.

2 Some attempts at the empirical investigation of relationships have relied on experiments in which trivial 'relationships' between experimental co-participants are investigated. These may tell us little about meaningful, non-experimentally contrived relationships.

3 Some research has suggested that perceived evaluation has a more powerful effect on attraction than perceived similarity.

4 Non-heterosexual relationships are often ignored, marginalised or made sense of in rather derogatory terms.

5 Much of the research approaches attraction as an asocial process of one person's reaction to a static, non-interacting other – like someone seeing and responding to a photograph. Encounters between living people typically involve some form of talk or other behaviour from more than one person and some form of interaction (however minimal) between them.

Reflective questions

1 *Think of some couples you know. In what ways are the partners in each couple similar or different? If there is a marked similarity between partners within each couple, why do you think that is the case?*

2 *How would you design a study to determine whether similarity between partners (if it exists) is due to selection of matched traits and attributes or equivalent 'market value'?*

3.3 Attribution of arousal

Imagine that you are meeting a stranger of the sex that you are more attracted to (or either sex if both are equally attractive to you). Let us suppose that this person wants to meet you on one of two bridges. One of these bridges is a low, solidly built bridge – the sort that people and cars cross hundreds of times a day without thinking about it. The other is quite different, it is an experience – it sways precariously some distance above the ground. Now, it is likely that being on the bridges themselves will make you feel differently – the low, solid bridge might not evoke many strong feelings, but the high swaying bridge could certainly get your pulse going a little, even if you are not particularly bothered about heights. Then, you meet the stranger. Do your bridge-induced feelings influence how you feel about them? How about if there are no bridge-induced feelings on the low bridge, but, for the high bridge, your heightened state of **arousal** or **excitation** shapes how you understand your feelings about meeting the stranger (see Figure 3.4).

These ideas, which form part of the **excitation transfer** theory (see Figure 3.4), also relate to research covered in the chapters on prosocial behaviour (Chapter 8) and aggression and intergroup conflict (Chapter 9). According to the theory, aroused states can be mislabelled and then the **misattributed or mislabelled arousal** can shape future behaviour. For example, a participant who experiences increased excitation as a consequence of

Arousal, excitation These are both used in the literature referred to above to describe states of heightened nervous system activation that include both pleasurable and aversive states. In terms of the literature reviewed here, there is a commonality at a physiological level across the seemingly different states of fear, sexual arousal and other adrenaline-related experiences. For the physiological state to have meaning, it needs to be labelled or attributed to some specific cause.

Excitation transfer This term describes the process of *misattributing* and/or *mislabelling* a state of arousal or excitation, as described below. More specifically, this term denotes a model within social psychology that has sought to explain phenomena such as aggression, prosocial behaviour and relationships.

Misattribute(d) or mislabel(led) arousal In terms of the above literature, these terms refer to a process that may take place once a state of arousal has been experienced – and usually when the initial stimulus (or cause of it) is no longer present. Our labelling of what we are feeling and/or what caused us to feel it is where we make sense of our arousal or excitation. If we undergo a frightening experience and then have some lingering state of arousal, we could mislabel that arousal as sexual attraction and attribute it to a person we happen to be with.

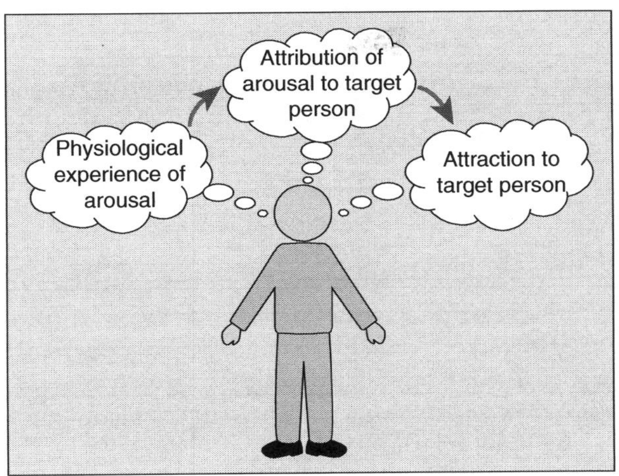

Figure 3.4 The excitation transfer theory account of attraction

riding a bike and is then insulted by a stranger could note their arousal (actually due to cycling), but mistakenly label it as annoyance at the offensive stranger and, therefore, infer that they are mightily offended and act accordingly – seeking some form of revenge. In our bridge case, we have something similar, but possibly involving feelings of attraction rather than aggression. It could be that those who experience heightened arousal attribute that arousal to their attraction to the stranger they happen to meet when in that (bridge-induced) state.

Dutton and Aron (1974) investigated precisely this phenomenon. Working with certain heterosexist assumptions, they had male participants meet a female experimenter on either a very ordinary – non-exciting – bridge or a precarious, high, swaying bridge. They did a brief 'on the bridge' survey and, as is often the case in these 'meeting strangers on the bridge to answer survey questions'-type encounters, the experimenter offered the participants her phone number. The measure of attraction that Dutton and Aron (1974) used was the proportion of participants on each bridge who actually called the experimenter. It will probably come as no surprise that more of those who had met the experimenter on the bridge that swayed precariously high up phoned than those who had met her on the low bridge.

There are, however, a number of problems with this research that are worth briefly noting. First, there is a presumed heterosexuality of participants – not all of the male participants can be assumed to be primarily attracted to females. Second, the idea that calling the experimenter was equated with being attracted to her is difficult to substantiate. This idea seems to involve importing the presumption of an everyday rhetorical commonplace – calling equates with sexual interest – into a quite different context that does not appear to involve people meeting with any expectation of a potential sexual element to the encounter. Third, the explanatory framework of relabelling arousal appears to make a substantial leap from the empirical evidence itself. Thus, more participants might call the researcher when they met them on the high bridge for a variety of reasons that have nothing to do with relabelling the arousal as sexual interest on their part. Participants might call because they are aware that the experimenter has put in more effort to arrange this unusual encounter – possibly out of town, possibly with participants' travel expenditure paid – but evidently with more effort on the experimenter's part even in terms of just getting on to the bridge. That is, there could be a sense of 'owing' the experimenter more when they went to the trouble to set up such a difficult and unusual meeting. There could be a recall factor. We might forget many people and promises to call them, but less so if we meet them on a precarious, high, swaying bridge – the distinctiveness of this experience may help our prospective memory in that we actually remember to call because the experience was a very vivid one.

There could even be a sexually motivated account that has nothing to do with relabelling arousal states. Participants could misconstrue the effort of the experimenter to come on to the dangerous bridge to meet them as some sort of interest in them – an attribution that is less readily available when they have merely met them on a conventional bridge. The point here is that there is quite a jump (no pun intended) from the observed phenomenon – a significantly greater proportion of participants making a call when they meet the experimenter on the more precarious bridge than on the low bridge – to the interpretative framework that has been imposed; other alternatives could fit the same observed phenomenon.

Other research that has proported to support the misattribution of arousal hypothesis includes Cohen and Waugh (1989) and Meston and Frohlich (2003). Cohen and Waugh (1989) had an observer stand (hopefully not too creepily) in a vantage point where they could observe couples as they left different sorts of films at the cinema. The observers noted the physical displays of intimacy between the couples and, in particular, how these related to different sorts of films. They reported that couples leaving 'suspense' thrillers displayed higher levels of holding hands and touching than couples leaving other films (such as dramas and comedies). This was interpreted as support for the idea that the higher levels of (film-induced) arousal they had experienced as a result of the film they had seen led to behaviour that was consistent with heightened *sexual* arousal – suggesting a possible misattribution of arousal.

Meston and Frohlich (2003), in their inventively entitled study 'Love at first fright', found partial support for excitation transfer, but their work also highlight some of the potential limitations with research in this area. They approached males and females who were either about to ride or had just ridden a rollercoaster. The rollercoaster ride was treated as the arousing stimulus in this research and self-reported indicators of arousal (heart rate, breathing and perspiration) largely confirmed this, tending to be higher after the ride.

Meston and Frohlich (2003) asked participants in the pre-ride group and those in the post-ride group to rate the attractiveness of a photograph of either a male or female target (previously rated as being of average attractiveness). In all cases, participants were presented with a photograph of a member of the opposite sex. In addition, participants were asked to rate the attractiveness of the person with whom they were about to ride or had just ridden with (that is, their seatmate). A further factor that was measured was whether participants' seatmates were romantic partners (such as girlfriend, boyfriend, lover, fiancé, husband or wife) or not.

Meston and Frohlich (2003) found that, for people seated with a non-romantic partner, ratings for the attractiveness of the photograph were higher among the post-ride group than the pre-ride group. Assuming for a moment that all relevant differences between these groups were randomly distributed, this is consistent with the idea that the ride was arousing. That is, the arousal could be understood as being misattributed to the photograph and, thus, the photograph was judged to be more attractive than for those in a state of lower (pre-ride) arousal. This finding was not replicated for those participants who were romantically attached to their seatmate. Meston and Frohlich had, in fact, predicted this to be the case – expecting that those with a romantic partner would attribute their arousal to their partner rather than the photograph, leading to higher ratings of attractiveness for romantic partners (in the post-ride group) but not higher attractiveness ratings for the photograph. The post-ride group, however, actually showed *lower* ratings of seatmate attractiveness in *all* conditions – that is whether male or female and whether the seatmate was a romantic partner or not. Thus, the only support for excitation transfer was the higher attractiveness ratings for a photograph in the post-ride group (as compared to the pre-ride group) by participants whose seatmate was not a romantic partner.

Meston and Frohlich (2003) consider the fact that their unanticipated finding – lower ratings of seatmate attractiveness in the post-ride group – could be a function of the specific arousal stimulus that was used in their study. Thus, it could be argued that having a rollercoaster ride as the arousing stimulus could have a negative impact on appearance, possibly increasing the likelihood of a somewhat dishevelled look, countering the attractiveness-enhancing effect of misattributed arousal. Their findings do raise a number of issues concerning research into excitation transfer effects on attractiveness ratings, however. Is the 'arousing' stimulus arousing, is there really a process of misattribution of arousal and should attractiveness ratings be considered as involving some form of situated construction rather than a report on an intra-psychic judgement?

First, there is the issue concerning knowing whether or not the 'arousing stimulus' is, in fact, arousing. Meston and Frohlich (2003) note, administering physiological tests of arousal to the same participants before and after their rides would not only be difficult logistically but also draw attention to the idea that the research was concerned with arousal. Their use of self-reported arousal states for pre- and post-ride participants was no doubt easier to administer, but it, too, may have drawn attention to the issue of arousal and, additionally, introduced the issue of the extent to which self-reported arousal indicators accurately reflect arousal. Also, the between groups approach raises the possibility of there being differences between the groups that may account for the findings.

Second, even if it is clear that the arousing stimulus *has* been arousing, it is difficult to confirm whether or not the aroused state is actually *misattributed* (to the photograph or seatmate in this case). Indeed, it could be that the more obviously arousing the stimulus, the more salient it is as the cause of the aroused condition – for example, participants who are aroused following a bungee jump may be very clearly aroused but also acutely aware that doing the bungee jump has aroused them. In such cases, while there may be some confidence in having participants who are aroused, there may be less likelihood of that arousal being misattributed to the attractiveness of other people, for example. More broadly, regardless of the salience of the arousing stimulus, there is an issue about how one can actually confirm that a misattribution has taken place – indeed, there may be other explanatory frameworks to account for the findings. Meston and Frohlich (2003) themselves consider the possibility that participants who showed higher levels of attraction in the post-ride group may have experienced 'anxiety relief' – that is, the generally more positive mood after one has successfully emerged from an anxiety-inducing experience.

Third, Meston and Frohlich's (2003) findings draw attention to the issue of the social process involved in ratings of attractiveness. It can be noted that *all* seatmates were rated as more attractive than the photograph (even though this had been pre-rated as 'average'). This was especially the case were the seatmate was a romantic partner (here, ratings of seatmate attractiveness were at the top end of the scale). Ratings of the attractiveness of the photographs, by contrast, were not only lower generally but also tended to be particularly low when rated by participants who were romantically attached to their seatmate. These findings hint at the possibility that, rather than simply reporting a quantifiable, knowable, intra-psychic attractiveness judgement, participants asked about attractiveness – whether of a photograph or a seatmate – were involved in a more delicate social process. At its simplest, someone with a romantic partner who rates that partner as unattractive and photographs of strangers (of the sex, or sexes, they are attracted to) as highly attractive may be held accountable for those ratings. The process of rating may therefore reflect concerns with these interactionally sensitive aspects of being asked to judge attractiveness rather than simply reporting a private, internal judgement.

Critical recap

Attribution of arousal

1 Excitation transfer theory involves a number of assumptions about difficult to observe intra-psychic processes – arousal, attribution and attraction. It is possible to question empirical data regarding each of these: are participants aroused by the stimulus, have they misattributed it and is their level of attraction consistent with the theory?

2 In some cases, we might query whether the participants have had an arousing experience or not. In other cases, perhaps the experience is obviously arousing but seems unlikely to be misattributed – for example, our arousal after a bungee jump is readily attributed to the *jump* rather than misattributed to the stranger we are seated next to *after* the experience.

3 In excitation transfer research, increased attraction has been measured by participants making a phone call to a member of the research team, observed intimacy between couples after leaving a film and self-reported attraction. It is quite possible that several of these phenomena may be explained without reference to arousal. Phoning a researcher could reflect a heightened state of obligation, duty, indebtedness or recall rather than increased attraction. Intimacy after 'frightening' films may reflect reassurance rather than increased attraction. Also self-reported attraction may be sensitive to the specific situation in which the measure is taken – for example, in the presence of a romantic partner – rather than be a pure representation of an intra-psychic phenomenon.

4 Even where increased attraction *has* taken place following an arousing event, can we be sure that it is due to the misattribution of arousal? It may be that post-arousing situations involve some positive mood state such as 'post-anxiety relief' rather than a state of arousal being misattributed.

5 Finally, like so much of the social psychology of relationships, there is a focus on not just romantic relationships but also one particular form – the (male–female, heterosexual) romantic relationship. This is most acute in research that blatantly presumes the participants are heterosexual.

Reflective questions

1 *Can you think of a situation when you have experienced arousal for one reason (such as being in a dangerous situation) and then had that arousal influence your behaviour outside of the immediate arousing environment?*

2 *To what extent do you feel that excitation transfer experiments reflect phenomena that people experience outside of the laboratory?*

3.4 Exchange and equity theories of relationships

The research considered below addresses not solely how people come to form relationships but, additionally, aspects of relationships that are already in existence – specifically, what factors determine the level of relationship satisfaction. Two approaches are considered here – exchange theory and equity theory – and attributional approaches are discussed in the next section.

Exchange and equity theories offer very similar accounts of relationship satisfaction – in which satisfaction is the output of a calculation, one that one partner undertakes in terms of the rewards and costs (and, in the case of equity theory, the investments) associated with being in the relationship. Exchange and equity theories suggest that people are satisfied with relationships in which they calculate that they benefit fairly or, in some cases, over-benefit from it.

According to exchange and equity theories in cases where people perceive that they under-benefit in the relationship, then they will be less satisfied.

Research on attribution is concerned with relationship satisfaction and factors that may determine this, too, but focuses on attributions about partner behaviour. Individuals who explain their partner's negative behaviour in 'partner-enhancing' ways – for example, emphasising external, temporary causes and the partner's lack of responsibility for their behaviour – will experience relationship satisfaction. By contrast, those who explain negative partner behaviour in much more 'partner-blaming' ways (such as emphasing that the negative behaviour is brought about by internal permanent characteristics of the partner) and that the partner is responsible for their behaviour, will have lower reported levels of satisfaction.

It is worth noting that these three approaches emphasise, what is, potentially at least, rational cognitive processing of information as being at the heart of understanding relationship satisfaction. For these approaches, the output of the cognitive calculation shapes the level of satisfaction – a causal prediction that is questioned below.

Exchange theory

Exchange theory offers what may seem to be a fairly unromantic understanding of relationships. The idea of the individual as a **rational actor** is very evident – that is, we enter relationships and stay in them if we judge that there is a net profit from doing so. We calculate the profit (or loss) to us of being in a particular relationship by assessing the rewards and costs to us (rewards − costs = profit) and whether or not we believe we can get a better deal (that is, more profit or less loss) elsewhere.

Homans (1958), Thibaut and Kelley (1959) and Kelley and Thibaut (1978) argue that people stay in a relationship only if the profit (or pay-off) is greater than that which they believe they can obtain elsewhere. The rewards can be monetary – suggesting that Groucho Marx's quip – 'Will you marry me? Do you have any money? Answer the second question first?' – has an element of truth to it.

Rewards associated with a relationship can include less easily quantified positive elements, too such as friendship, companionship, status, fun, spiritual, sexual and/or personal fulfilment. Similarly, the costs can be equally broadly defined – financial, time, effort, enduring unappealing aspects of the person and/or the profits associated with alternative relationships that may be sacrificed in order to enter or stay in this relationship. For exchange theory, with two partners approaching the relationship in this way (that is, seeking maximum profit), it is most likely to survive if there is (or appears to be) an equivalence of profit for each partner. If it tilts too far in favour of one, then the other may perceive that their own profit has suffered and they could get a better profit in another relationship.

Imagine a situation in which someone is looking through details of prospective partners received from a dating agency. It is likely that the prospective partners each describe themselves almost as appealing commodities. They might refer to their high income and important job, include a flattering photograph and highlight their socially desirable characteristics (good sense of humour, interest in travel and sociability). They are perhaps less likely to highlight their financial desperation, include a photograph of themselves waking up after a particularly demanding night or refer to their impending court case for an alleged assault. In these descriptions, then, the prospective partners are each maximising their apparent values and minimising any apparent costs for those who might consider starting a relationship with them.

This behaviour on the part of prospective partners – of highlighting apparent rewards and minimising apparent costs of a relationship – could be seen as a way in which they act as if exchange theory is true. That is, the prospective partners act as if those who will see their details and decide whether or not to date them will do so just as exchange theory suggests, by working out the profit, or loss, associated with selecting that potential partner.

Alternatively, imagine someone already in an intimate relationship ending it to begin another intimate relationship with someone else. For equity theory this decision would arise if the person concerned calculates that the profits associated with the new relationship outweigh those of the current one.

These examples suggest that there is a certain 'commonsense' appeal to aspects of exchange theory, but note that both of them are about the possible *initiation* of a relationship more than behaviour within an existing relationship. If we try to transpose the factors relevant for the initiation of relationships with factors relevant *within*

Exchange theory The idea that our motivation to enter and remain in relationships is driven by our assessment of the profit (rewards − costs) of doing so. Our behaviour is thus driven by seeking to maximise our profit. Profit, in this context, can include any perceived net benefits, not just financial ones.

Rational actor The idea that human behaviour can be made sense of in terms of individuals rationally pursuing what they perceive to be their own self-interest.

established relationships, such as deciding whether or not to move in together, have a civil partnership, get married or divorced, the simple rewards minus costs formulae seems somehow inadequate.

The nature of the empirical support for exchange theory further underscores these problems and does little to answer the challenge that it is limited as an account for 'real' relationships. Many of the studies supporting exchange theory have used variations on business games between strangers in a laboratory setting. Often these involve participants having to choose how much help to offer other players in the game. Findings typically support exchange theory in so far as participants appear to choose to help to other players to the extent that they have been helped (Wilke & Lanzetta, 1970). The issue that this raises concerns the external validity of these findings – that is, how much do these relatively inconsequential decisions made in one-off encounters with strangers tell us about the behavioural choices people make in prolonged, meaningful relationships?

There are reasonable grounds for thinking that these differences between 'real' relationships and their laboratory simulation – in terms of consequentiality, longevity and meaningfulness – will profoundly limit the extent to which conclusions from game-based laboratory studies can inform our understanding of participants' consequential relationships with significant others. In this way, exchange theory may provide a framework for understanding human behaviour – with its emphasis on people seeking to maximise their profit – that is, perhaps, more adequate for understanding *transactions* (such as sales negotiations) rather than *relationships* (whether friendship, familial or intimate). It could be argued, then, that the metaphor of *exchange* provides the limitations of the model as a means of understanding relationships. In so far as we are concerned with simple relationships of exchange (such as buying and selling transactions), then, the calculation of profit is arguably highly relevant. What has less credibility and support is the idea that calculation of profit remains the *central* feature for understanding complex, intimate and meaningful relationships.

Equity theory

A related perspective – which could be seen as overcoming some of the limitations described above – is provided by **equity theory**. Equity theory shares a sense that people have a concern with the costs and benefits involved in a relationship, but, arguably, develops a more sophisticated model, taking into account not just isolated transactions but also ongoing relationships. Hatfield, Berscheid and Walster's (1976) outline of equity theory reveals some similarity with exchange theory. Thus, 'proposition 1' states that 'Individuals will try to maximise their outcomes (where outcomes equal rewards minus costs)' (Hatfield et al., 1976, p. 2). This is returned to below, but, for now, it can be noted that this idea of people being driven by a concern with maximum positive outcomes echoes exchange theory, albeit with slightly different terms.

The other propositions of equity theory, however, show that it differs in several important respects – most notably in the concept of fairness or equity. Propositions 2a and 2b state that societies develop norms of fairness – or equity – and teach them to their members. For equity theory, then, while there is an acknowledgement of people's basic concern with pursuing maximum possible profit or outcome, they have also been inculcated in the value of fairness or equity. As a consequence, proposition 3 states that, 'When individuals find themselves participating in inequitable relationships, they become distressed. The more inequitable the relationship, the more distress individuals feel' (Hatfield, et al., 1976, p. 6). Consistent with this is the final proposition – proposition 4 – stating the consequence of inequity and giving it a vital role as a motivator for relationship-relevant behaviour: 'Individuals who discover they are in an inequitable relationship attempt to eliminate their distress by restoring equity. The greater the inequity that exists, the more distress they feel, and the harder they try to restore equity' (Hatfield et al., 1976, p. 6).

Having outlined the four propositions of equity theory, it is worth examining the equity calculation that lies at its heart. Whereas exchange theory considered that people simply calculated their profit (rewards minus costs), equity theory distinguishes *outcomes* from *inputs*.

For equity theory, outcomes are the positive and negative things one receives or gets from the relationship – they are the 'positive and negative consequences that a scrutineer perceives a participant has incurred as a consequence of his [sic] relationship with another' (Hatfield et al., 1976, p. 3). Outcome rewards could include financial gain, status, companionship, personal, sexual or spiritual fulfilment. Outcome costs could include negative aspects of being in that relationship, such as unappealing demands, characteristics or habits of the other person.

Equity theory The idea that people are motivated by a concern with both maximising their outcomes (like exchange theory) and (unlike exchange theory) with fairness. The concern with fairness is understood as a particularly important issue for understanding partners' satisfaction or distress within a relationship.

Inputs are seen as what one brings to the relationship: 'the participant's contributions to the exchange, which are seen (by a scrutineer) as entitling him [sic] to rewards or costs' (Hatfield et al., 1976, p. 3). Inputs include the assets that the person brings to, or invests in, the relationship. These might include the money and status the person brings and the time, help and support they give. Inputs also include the liabilities that the person brings to the relationships, such as their demands on the other person and unappealing characteristics and habits.

It can be noted that outcome costs and input assets can overlap to some extent. So, if you give lots of money to the relationship, this is an outcome cost (one outcome of the relationship is that it costs you a lot of money) and an input asset (you are bringing lots of money to the relationship). In empirical studies of relationships, the distinction between inputs or contributions (assets and liabilities) and outcomes (rewards and costs) is made by the participants, usually in quite global terms. Thus – as Box 3.3 illustrates – participants are typically asked to report how their relationship 'stacks up' on a scale that ranges from 'I am getting a much better deal than my partner' to 'My partner is getting a much better deal than I am'. What makes this an equity scale is that participants are instructed to consider what they and their partner get out of the relationship in relation to *what they each put in to the relationship*. It is worth noting that measures of perceptions of the relationship are also often (but not exclusively) global, including items such as 'How satisfied are you with your relationship' with a scale ranging from very dissatisfied to completely satisfied.

Notwithstanding the issues about the difficulty of distinguishing between certain outcome costs and input assets, the attempt to differentiate outcomes and inputs enables equity theory to emphasise the importance of *entitlement* and *fairness*. By including perceptions of what an individual and their partner *bring* to the relationship, equity theory highlights the notion that people not only seek a net benefit in terms of net outcomes (outcome rewards − outcome costs) but also what they are *entitled to* in terms of their inputs and what is *fair* or *equitable*. In Adam's (1965) formula – see Figure 3.5 – the net outcome (outcome rewards minus outcome costs) is *divided* by perceived *input*. The more a person feels they contribute to the relationship (input), the more they feel they deserve to receive in terms of outcomes/inputs.

The wealthy, high-status, beautiful, intelligent, wonderfully good-natured partner may thus feel *entitled* to a good deal in terms of net outcomes (rewards − outcome costs). Someone with very high perceived inputs may feel entitled to very high net outcomes. The partner who perceives that they bring liabilities – an unattractive, unpopular, unpleasant person with lots of complications (perhaps they are about to begin a long custodial sentence) – may feel they are entitled to less generous net outcomes.

Equity theory further posits that these calculations are undertaken for *both* partners. So, the relative benefit as

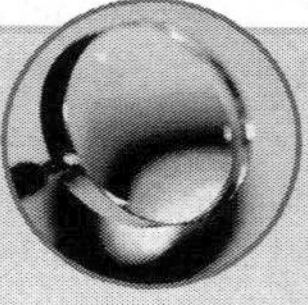

Box 3.3 FOCUS
A typical measure of perceived equity taken from Traupmann, Hatfield and Wexler (1983)

Considering your relationship as a whole, what you put into your dating relationship compared to what you get out of it ... and what your partner puts in compared to what (s)he gets out of it, how does your total relationship 'stack up'?

+3 I am getting a much better deal than my partner.
+2 I am getting a somewhat better deal.
+1 I am getting a slightly better deal.
+0 We are both getting an equally good ... or bad ... deal.
−1 My partner is getting a slightly better deal.
−2 My partner is getting a somewhat better deal.
−3 My partner is getting a much better deal than I am.

This extract illustrates the instructions given to participants in a typical piece of research concerned with equity in dating relationships.

Example 1: A relationship that is perceived as equitable

$$\frac{\text{Net outcomes (person A)}}{\text{Inputs (person A)}} \qquad \frac{\text{Net outcomes (person B)}}{\text{Inputs (person B)}}$$

Let us suppose that person A quantifies their outcome rewards as 40 and their outcome costs as 10 (a net outcome of 30). Person A quantifies their own input as 10. Person A further quantifies the outcome rewards for their partner, person B, as 8 and the outcome costs for B as 2 (a net outcome for their partner, person B, of 6). Person A quantifies their partner's input as 2.

$$\frac{\text{30 (Net outcomes A)}}{\text{10 (Inputs A)}} \qquad \frac{\text{6 (Net outcomes B)}}{\text{2 (Inputs B)}}$$

For person A, the result – what one might call the proportionate benefit – of the relationship is 3 ($30 \div 10 = 3$). Person B seems to be getting far less from the relationship (net outcome of 6), but, when input is considered, they also have a proportionate benefit of 3 ($6 \div 2 = 3$). The relationship, although involving very different absolute values for outcomes, is equitable when inputs are considered. Because A makes 5 times the input to the relationship, they are entitled to 5 times the net outcome.

Example 2: A relationship that is perceived as inequitable

Person C quantifies their own outcome rewards as person A above – a net outcome of 30 – and their own input as person A above – 10. Person C perceives their partner (person D) as also having a net outcome of 30, but with the same input as person B – 2.

$$\frac{\text{30 (Net outcomes C)}}{\text{10 (Inputs C)}} \qquad \frac{\text{30 (Net outcomes D)}}{\text{2 (Inputs D)}}$$

At first glance, the net outcomes are more equivalent here – both C and D have net outcomes of 30. Look, though, at the impact of the input. Because C has an input that is five times greater than D, in order to arrive at the same proportionate benefit from the relationship C would need to perceive that they receive five times the net outcome benefits of D. In Example 2, D's equivalent net outcome is very inequitable when inputs are taken into account, resulting in a proportionate benefit of 3 ($30 \div 10$) for C and a massive 15 ($30 \div 2$) for D.

Figure 3.5 Illustrations of equity calculations based on Adams (1965)

a proportion of input is crucial. If you have ever heard people talking of their relationships in terms of., 'After all I've done – this is all I get!', 'It's not fair!', 'I do everything, and for what?', then you are witnessing equity at work (admittedly, this may be of limited comfort if you are the target of these complaints).

If you were assessing the equity of your relationship, you would calculate your net outcomes ÷ inputs and the same for your partner (see Figure 3.5). As noted above – and in contrast to exchange theory – equity theory is concerned with benefits that are *proportionate to the perceived inputs of each partner*. Those who perceive that they input more than their partners will also feel they are entitled to more positive outcomes than their partners are, so it is the *proportionate* benefit (net outcomes ÷ inputs), rather than the outcomes alone, which need to be equivalent for equity to be achieved.

Throughout this discussion, reference has been made to *perceived* rewards, costs, outcomes and inputs. As Hatfield et al. (1976, p. 4) argue, 'Ultimately equity is in the eye of the beholder.' The values in these formulaic expressions of equity calculations, then, are never intended to represent any 'objective' reality, but, rather, the *psychological reality* – or that is, current perceptions of the equity of the relationships for the people making the equity calculations. There are also psychological consequences arising from equity calculations. Those who feel that the relationship is equitable – proportionate benefits being equivalent – will feel most contented, those who feel relatively over-benefited will feel guilt, while those who feel relatively under-benefited will feel anger.

Hatfield et al. (1976) note that people can take steps to adjust the actual or perceived equity of their relationship. Using the somewhat objectionable example of a 'Ghetto black', they suggest that someone who feels under-benefited, for example, can lower their input or seek to increase their outcomes (or the reverse if over-benefited). Alternatively, the person may achieve 'psychological equity' by changing the value that they attach to the inputs and outcomes – the person who initially felt guilty about over-benefiting can restore a sense of equity by reconsidering that their inputs are greater than they first thought or their outcomes are less positive and the person who felt angry at their under-benefiting could do the reverse. In this psychological restoration of equity, no behaviour is changed in terms of input or outcome, but the *perception of the value* of inputs and outcomes has changed.

What does perceived equity do for a relationship?

As Figure 3.6 illustrates, some equity research has reported that couples who perceive themselves as equitably treated have the highest relationship contentment (Traupmann et al., 1983). From this perspective, being under-benefited can be associated with feelings of anger, while being over-benefited can cause guilt (Hatfield, Utne, & Traupmann, 1979, noting that it was particularly female participants who experienced guilt at perceiving that they 'overbenefited').

This often-cited idea makes intuitive sense and has received some level of empirical support. Hatfield, Walster and Traupmann (1979), in a relatively rare example of longitudinal research in this area, found that participants who reported that their relationship was 'fairly equitable' when first approached were more likely to be in an intact relationship and believe that the relationship had a future three and a half months later. Other research – especially concerning the relationship between perceived inequity and negative emotions – has been more equivocal.

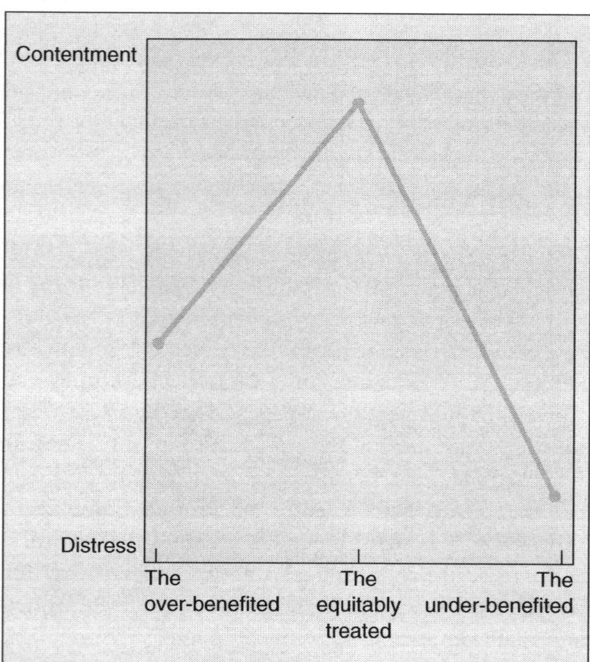

Figure 3.6 A depiction of the *typical* relationship between perceived equity and satisfaction (from Traupmann, Hatfield & Wexler, 1983)

Source: Traupmann, J., Hatfield, E., & Wexler, P. (1983). Equity and sexual satisfaction in dating couples. *British Journal of Social Psychology*, *22*, 33–40. Reproduced with permission from the British Psychological Society.

Figure 3.6 illustrates the relationship between perceptions of equity (on the x axis) and distress–contentment (on the y axis). The figure suggests those who perceive that they are equitably treated also report greatest levels of relationship contentment, with those who perceive that they are over-benefiting reporting considerably less satisfaction (more dissatisfaction). The highest levels of dissatisfaction are reported by those who perceive that they are under-benefiting in the relationship.

Traupmann, Petersen, Utne and Hatfield (1981) found that participants who reported they were equitably treated in their relationship also reported being the most contented in their relationship. Yet, close inspection of their findings reveals that the results for men were not significant and the idea that perceived over- and under-benefit gave rise to guilt and anger respectively received, at best, only partial support. Instead, Traupmann et al. (1981) found that women, in contrast to men, experienced markedly higher levels of guilt when over – rather than equitably – benefited. However, Pillemer, Hatfield and Sprecher (2008), in their study of women aged 50 to 82 who were in an intimate relationship, found that it was those who reported being *over-benefited* – not equitably benefited – who reported the highest levels of happiness and satisfaction with their relationship. Aumer-Ryan, Hatfield and Frey (2007) found that, while their participants in the USA reported most satisfaction when they rated their relationship as equitable, Jamaican participants reported greatest satisfaction when they reported that they were over-benefiting. Finally, Austin and Walster (1975) argued that individuals will sometimes be more concerned with equity across the *totality* of their relationships (am I generally receiving fair rewards, not over- or under-benefiting) rather than being concerned with equity *within* each relationship.

Evaluating equity theory's approach to relationships

Equity theory was developed partly to replace – or at least supplement – the notion of maximising gain with a concern for fairness when we consider our rewards and input our partner's rewards and input. The idea that this calculation is important in relationships can be questioned, as well as the notion that our perceived equity can determine our relationship satisfaction. Finally, it is worth briefly reflecting on the very idea that we can separate out 'equity' and 'satisfaction' as real, identifiable, differentiated cognitive phenomena.

One criticism sometimes raised regarding equity theory is that we only start to weigh our inputs and outcomes – and those of our partner's – at times when the relationship is in some sort of crisis. Thus, the process of calculation is, from this perspective, not a reflection of the *typical* pattern of thinking about relationships.

This idea is partly incorporated into the work of some of the leading equity researchers, Hatfield, Rapson and Aumer-Ryam (2007), who suggest that concerns regarding fairness or equity in the relationship and the process of calculating outcomes and inputs might be relevant at different stages within a relationship (they suggest initiation and deterioration) rather than being consistently relevant throughout. This criticism does, though, raise the issue regarding what is happening in the data that is collected in most equity research. Are some respondents reporting calculations they have rehearsed many times as they brooded over their deteriorating relationship, which could be reflective of their global sense of the relationship? Are others being asked to do calculations from scratch, ones they have not done before, and, thus, are independent of the general sense of the relationship they had prior to being involved in the research?

These last points also relate to the problems with claiming causal links between perceived equity and relationship satisfaction. Most research has required participants to complete scales relating to their relationship happiness, contentedness or satisfaction at the same time as they report their sense of relationship equity. Very few studies have – like Hatfield, et al. (1979) – involved any longitudinal dimension. In fact, even in their longitudinal research, there is the reflection that they are still dealing with correlations between satisfaction and perceived equity and there are limits regarding the sorts of causal claims to be made about such data. It is possible that people's reports on perceived fairness and their reported happiness are part of a stance they have towards their relationship.

Research on relationship satisfaction undertaken by Buunk, Oldersma and De Dreu (2001) suggests that it is not simply a calculation concerning one's own relationship in isolation, but, in various ways, men and women's relationship satisfaction may be related to perceptions of *others'* relationships. Men's satisfaction, particularly, related to their perception that their relationship was superior and the assumption there are relatively few unhappy relationships. Women's satisfaction related to relationship superiority, but less markedly so than for men and, for women, relationship satisfaction was found to be related to the perception that most others were happy with their relationship. This work suggests that attempts to understand relationship satisfaction by reference to calculations regarding relative rewards and investments alone, without consideration of other relationships, gives an incomplete and inaccurate picture of the processes involved.

Wong and Goodwin's (2009) qualitative study also raises questions concerning how relationship satisfaction is thought about by individuals in relationships. In qualitative research across three cultures – the United Kingdom, Hong Kong and Beijing – Wong and Goodwin (2009) found that there was an emphasis on the importance of 'a stable relationship with the spouse', 'spousal support', 'partnership with the spouse' and 'stable family finance'. The cultural differences that emerged included 'companionship' being more important for UK participants and 'harmonious marital relations' being more important for Hong Kong respondents. Taken together, these issues might, indeed, be construable as ingredients that inform equity-based calculations, but some of them are suggestive of something slightly different – perhaps a concern with an overarching 'characterisation of the relationship' rather than a calculation of the benefits and costs of its individual constituent features in the light of profit or fairness concerns.

Aumer-Ryan et al.'s (2007) finding that Jamaican participants experienced more satisfaction when overbenefiting and US participants experienced more satisfaction when there was perceived equity might not reflect actual cognitive experiences outside of the research interview, but, instead, different cultural ways of expressing that the relationship is good within the interview. Thus, it is possible that the Jamaican participants were able to express how good their relationship was not just in responses to the satisfaction scales, but also by making clear how much their partner does for them – over and above what might be expected. Likewise, US participants might have expressed their sense of being in an 'ideal' relationship by reporting that it conformed to the US cultural ideal of being a fair or equitable relationship.

This idea that participants' responses might reflect a stance towards the relationship and a concern with the reporting of that stance within the research process also touches on the issue of the extent to which equity and satisfaction are discrete, cognitive phenomena. When people complete scales about perceived equity and relationship satisfaction, they are treated as giving – or at least potentially giving – a relatively accurate reflection of some inner state of perceived equity and some other inner state of perceived relationship satisfaction/happiness/contentedness. Do participants in this novel social process of responding to interview questions or questionnaires do something different, though? Participants suddenly finding themselves having to answer questions about perceived equity and perceived happiness may wind up producing accountably sensible responses, reporting satisfaction in relationships that they have just described as equitable and dissatisfaction when they have only just reported how under-benefiting from the relationship they feel they are. These response patterns produce findings that appear to suggest perceived equity is associated with relationship satisfaction, but, may, in fact, reflect aspects of the social process of data-gathering in which participants display concern with producing answers that orientate to issues of consistency.

Relatedly, it may be even outside of the research environment, it is helpful to not be wedded to the notion that perceived equity and satisfaction are relatively stable, separable cognitive phenomena. Think, for example, how, in an argument, one way of doing being unhappy, discontented or dissatisfied is to announce the perceived inequity of the relationship. Rather than being two distinct, separate, relatively stable cognitive entities, they may be aspects of a singular, rhetorically charged stance regarding the relationship that are constructed within interactions to do things such as complain or appreciate.

Critical recap

Exchange and equity theories of relationships

1 Exchange theory was seen as narrowly focused on maximising profit and as having relatively little to say about existing relationships.

2 Equity theory sought to address these limitations in exchange theory and introduce the idea that people are concerned with *fairness* or *equity*.

3 There are problems with trying to establish a causal link – for example, the extent to which studies have demonstrated that perceived equity has *caused* relationship distress – rather than just co-occurred – can be questioned with it.

4 If exchange and equity are understood as processes concerned with the individual's relationship without reference to perceptions of others' relationships, then an important aspect of thinking about relationship satisfaction may be missed.

5 Cross-cultural research has challenged the idea that there is a *universal* concern with fairness or equity.

6 It is possible to question whether perceived equity and relationship satisfaction are actually separable, real, relatively stable cognitive entities or not.

Reflective questions

1 *Are you aware of yourself or others having calculated the outcomes in relation to inputs for self and a partner in a relationship? What were the circumstances of this calculation?*

2 *Drawing on cases you are familiar with, do you think that equity calculations reflect the state of a relationship, determine it, both reflect and determine it, or neither reflect nor determine the relationship?*

3.5 Attribution

Imagine for a moment a relationship in which one partner engages in a behaviour that is perceived as problematic. Suppose that one of the partners spends a lot of time on social networking sites such as Twitter and Facebook – so much so that their partner experiences this as a negative aspect of their behaviour. The crucial issue for attributional approaches (as will be touched on in Chapter 4) is not what the behaviour is or even why the partner engages in it, but, rather what ***attributions*** their partner makes about that behaviour.

From an attributional perspective, the explanation for partner behaviour – particularly negative partner behaviour – can be understood as both reflecting and shaping the relationship. So, in a healthy and successful relationship, the behaviour might be perceived as merely reflecting that the partner is currently under a lot of stress and needs to use these sites to 'chill out' a little. In a more conflictual relationship, the behaviour may be understood as being much more endemic – perhaps reflecting dispositional qualities of the partner, such as 'he/she is always like that'. Furthermore, in conflictual relationships, the behaviour may be interpreted as showing more intentionality – showing deliberate disregard for the partner, for example: 'he/she knows I do not like it but carries on deliberately' (see Box 3.4).

Attributions The way in which behaviours are explained in terms of what caused them. If I think that my partner's bad mood is caused by their stress at work, then I have made an attribution regarding the cause of their bad mood. Some attribution literature suggests that attributing negative partner behaviour to certain types of causes – for example, causes 'external' to the partner – is associated with the health and longevity of the relationship. More specifically, if – as in the above example – negative partner behaviour (bad mood) is attributed to an external cause (stress at work), then the relationship is, it is argued, more likely to flourish.

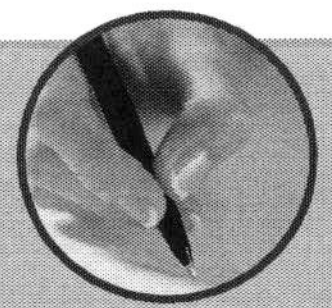

Box 3.4 TRY IT OUT Attributions and relationships

Use YouTube to find a video clip of a relationship or couples therapy session (such as: www.youtube.com/watch?v=fQBZlgmebwY&feature=related). Are attributions, particularly regarding 'negative partner behaviour', at work in either maintaining or resolving trouble in the relationship?

In support of this perspective, Stander, Hsiung and MacDermid (2001) found that marriages rated as 'conflictual' had a higher incidence of distress-maintaining attributions. The partner's negative behaviour in a distress-maintaining attribution is understood as a consequence of something about that partner (rather than their situation) and recurrent (rather than exceptional) and likely to affect other areas of their life (rather than just one small element). In addition, the partner is understood as deliberately or intentionally bringing about the 'negative' behaviour, thereby not only attributing the cause of the behaviour to relatively enduring features of the partner but also attributing responsibility to the partner (see Figure 3.7). Similarly, Fincham, Harold and Gano-Phillips (2000) reported that heterosexual marital attributions at the time of the study were related to marital satisfaction 6 and 18 months later.

Figure 3.7 illustrates the idea that attributions concerning partner behaviour (particularly negatively valued behaviour) shape relationship satisfaction.

With attribution research of this nature, there is an issue regarding whether the attributions about a partner's behaviour cause high or low partner satisfaction or simply *reflect* it. Thus, if I blame my partner's insistence on watching a programme that I cannot stand on their selfishness, does that *cause* low satisfaction or merely *reflect* some level of partner dissatisfaction?

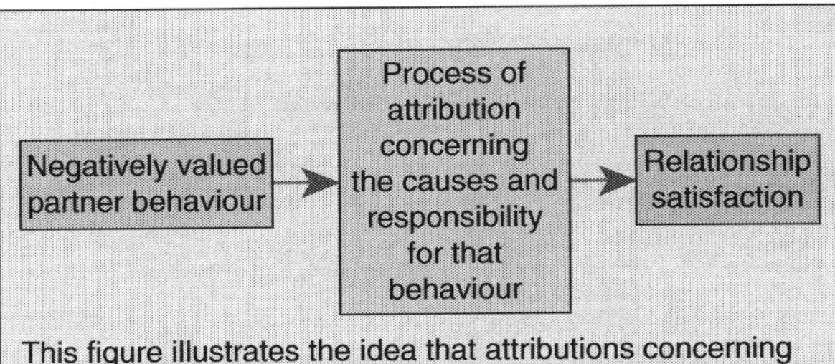
Negatively valued partner behaviour
Process of attribution concerning the causes and responsibility for that behaviour
Relationship satisfaction
This figure illustrates the idea that attributions concerning partner behaviour (particularly negatively valued behaviour) shape relationship satisfaction.

Figure 3.7 Attribution and relationship satisfaction

Likewise, it is possible to question whether we walk around with cognitively formed objects called 'attributions' or our attribution talk is constructed in the moment to do certain rhetorical work, such as blaming or exonerating. When we say 'It's your fault – you just wouldn't listen', should we think of this as principally a report of a cognitive calculation that we have just completed or as some argumentative work, such as blaming the person we are talking to?

Critical recap

Attribution

1 Somewhat similarly to perceived equity, attribution research suggests that our cognitions about our relationship (in this case, our causal explanations) have an influence on how we perceive our relationships.

2 The issue of causality – raised with regard to equity theory – is relevant for attribution theory also. That is, it is not easy to make the case that attributions regarding partner behaviour shape relationship distress or satisfaction.

3 It is also possible to question (as Chapter 5 does) whether we should think of explanations in terms of cognitive calculations existing 'in our heads' or as constructed in talk as doing interactional work (agreeing, blaming, accounting and so on).

Reflective questions

1 *Have you ever noticed how partners explain each other's behaviour? Think for a moment of two different partnerships – one that you consider particularly successful and one more conflictual.*

2 *How do you think negative partner behaviour would be explained in these two different relationships? What consequences would these different explanations have for the relationship?*

3.6 Constructing relationships

Most social psychological research into relationships has sought to understand them as psychological phenomena. As this chapter has shown, attention has been given to what factors (usually within the person) will be most likely to result in the psychological experience of attraction and what psychological phenomena are associated with relationship satisfaction. The research considered below does not simply provide different answers to these questions – it asks different questions. One of these questions is concerned with the discourses or culturally available ways of constructing relationships: how does culture construct (or make available) ways of being in relationship – that is, what are the culturally available ways of thinking about oneself as in a relationship? Another question is what happens locally, in interaction, when we do 'relationship talk': how do we construct relationships in our talk and what sorts of things do those constructions do? These different questions, left to one side in much of social psychology, have become increasingly important in a range of discourse analytic research and social theory and are touched on below.

Cultural constructions of gender and relationships

Some research into the construction of relationships has been particularly concerned with the **available discourses** through which gender and sexuality can be constructed. Such research often seeks to identify the dominant or predominate versions of what it is to be female or male, gay or heterosexual and the implications of these discourses and, indeed, the binary oppositions (such as female–male, gay–straight) themselves. Some research is concerned with the ways in which these discourses embody and perpetuate power-implicative ideas or ideologies by, for example, privileging being male or being heterosexual and denigrating or depowering other modes of being.

Some examples of these selectively privileging constructions are found in work that has considered constructions of sexual desire. Fine (1988, cited in Milnes, 2010) argues that female sexual desire is often denied by constructions of it as merely 'passive' or 'reactive'. Similarly, Holloway (1984, p. 89, cited in Milnes, 2010) describes the construction of the male sex drive as 'active, driven and uncontrollable'. As Milnes (2010) argues, these constructions of male and female sexuality serve to enable a sexual 'double standard', legitimising or excusing male – but not female – promiscuity. It is worth noting that these constructions are not just thought to be abstractly floating around, but drawn on and used in specific, concrete situations. Think, for example, of the phrase, 'boys will be boys' being uttered about a male's promiscuous, inappropriate or aggressive behaviour. This phrase suggests that blame should be withheld, the behaviour mitigated or even exonerated, due to it being inevitably associated with being male. It is, incidentally, telling that in many English-speaking communities, there is no real equivalent exonerating phrase for females.

Research by Boonzaier (2008) considered some of the constructions of gender and sexuality that were drawn on in interviews with couples in which there had been some history of abuse of the female by her current male partner. One of her findings was that male perpetrators would often position themselves as, in some sense, the victims – sometimes as having been emasculated by their partner's dominance or their economic or social power or having a difficult past experience that resulted in their own aggressive behaviour. For example, one male perpetrator of violence referred to the consequences of moving from his own flat to his partner's house: 'she would often use the fact that I was in her house and stuff like this which made me feel, not insecure but I was in a sense emasculated' (Boonzaier, 2008, p. 191). Another participant referred to his own upbringing, in which he witnessed his father using violence against his mother: 'My father used to hit my mother and all that stuff. But, um in the end actually we grew up believing that it was right. The husband must hit the wife, that is how we grew up' (2008, p. 195).

These constructions can be seen as having a twofold relevance: first, they can be seen as culturally recurrent ways of making sense of male violence that, to some extent, appear to mitigate against blame directed to the male and, second, they can be seen as seeking to exonerate the individual male who draws on them. That is, these recurrent discourses that are articulated in specific instances of talk can be understood as having both **ideological** and **interactional implications.**

Available discourses The culturally available constructions about how things are – or how or who we can be. In the context of the work outlined here, consideration was given to how a culture might have certain constructions or versions of how to be a man or woman or how to have a certain sexuality.

Ideological implications In the current context, these are the power-relevant implications of a given construction. Thus, certain constructions of 'being female' have emphasised a relative passivity in contrast to 'active males'. Versions of the world or constructions such as these could be understood as having power implications – empowering men at the expense of depowering women.

Interactional implications These are the implications within an immediate interaction. Constructing gender, sexuality and relationships in a certain way may do things that are relevant for my immediate interaction – for example, doing agreement, blaming, exonerating.

Constructing gender and relationships in interaction

Research that is concerned with the construction of gender and sexuality has also addressed how these constructions are used to do interactionally relevant work. Here, the emphasis is not so much on the ideological or power-infused implications of the talk at a cultural level, but, rather, on the immediate things that are being done with and through the talk *in the interaction* in which it occurs.

A particular concern with the discursive and conversation analytic work that has developed this interactional interest in construction is the way in which what the talk does is not simply a feature of its 'standalone' meaning, but, rather, it does what it does by virtue of its sequential location. This suggests that, rather than abstract pockets of talk from the sequences in which they occur, we should analyse them *in situ* – their sequential environment (the specific sequence of talk in which they are located) being an important aspect of what they can be understood to be doing. One particularly relevant strand of this research (which was touched on in Chapter 2) has considered the way in which categories are used to do interactional work in sequences of talk.

In his analysis of couples therapy sessions, Edwards (1998) investigated some of the work that the categories 'girls,' and 'married women' might do. One example of this is found in Extract 3.1, which is a transcript of part of the talk of a female and apparently heterosexual client, Connie. In the therapy session, Connie's male partner has reported having difficulty with her allegedly 'flirtatious' behaviour. In Extract 3.1, Connie has been asked (by the counsellor) to describe typical nights out with female friends. Her partner is then asked to repeat it and Connie then describes it again – this redescription is given below. Immediately after this extract, Connie goes on to say that the quiet pub she is describing represents the 'type of place' her and her friends would go to 'Ni:ne out of ten times'.

Extract 3.1

(*Note*: Line numbers from the original. Female client (with the pseudonym 'Connie') is talking throughout.)

1846 (...) when I go out with the gir:ls, it's a:ll married
1847 Women talking about our ki:ds or somebody rin:gs (.)
1848 'hh they have a pro:blem, y'know (.) d'you fancy go-"
1849 (.) that's uh-the gir:ls night out
1850 (...) ((several turns omitted here))
1851 When I go out with people it's normally a crowd of
1852 married women, (.) which Jimmy knows each and every
1853 one of them.

Source: Edwards (1998, p. 29)

Looking at this brief extract, there are certain categories for describing people or *membership categorisation devices* (see Chapter 2) at work. Notice how the extract uses the membership categorisation devices 'girls' and 'married women'. As Edward's (1998) notes, Connie uses this second telling of her typical nights out with female friends to deal with the objections that her partner Jimmy has raised about them. Connie uses the phrase 'girls' night out' – a very widely used phrase for going out with a group of female friends and the phrase that Connie used in her earlier talk about nights out – but here she describes the 'girls' as 'married women'.

Think for a moment about the idea of a night out with 'girls' and a night out with 'married women' – the shift in category seems to imply something quite different. Connie also specifies some category-consistent activities that the 'married women' engage in, such as, 'talking about our kids'. Furthermore, rather than being some *unknown* grouping of 'married women', the members of group are further specified as known by Jimmy: 'Jimmy knows each and every one of them'.

Now, bear in mind that this telling and retelling of these nights out with female friends is not in some 'neutral' environment (if that could ever exist) – it is in a counselling session where the male partner, Jimmy (who is present as Connie talks), has objected to Connie being flirtatious on these nights out with female friends. Connie's respecification of the 'girls' as 'married women' could be understood as orientating to Jimmy's allegations that Connie engages in objectionable flirtatious behaviour. The category 'married women' and the behaviour of 'talking about our kids' can be understood as being built to rebut criticisms that Connie is engaged in flirtatious behaviour. If 'girls' night out' might have left open the possibility that flirtatious behaviour was involved, nights out with 'married women' talking about their children seems to counter that interpretation. As Edwards (1998, p. 30) notes, the category 'married women' is not used simply because it may accurately describe who these females are or how Connie perceives them but, instead, 'Its use attends to local, rhetorically potent business in their talk.'

The use of membership categorisation devices to construct relationships in a way that addresses immediate interactional concerns has also been addressed by Stokoe (2010a, 2010b, 2010c, 2012/in press; see also Box 3.5). In Extract 3.2, two friends – Sophie and Emma – are talking as they get ready to go out for the evening.

Box 3.5 KEY RESEARCHER
Professor Elizabeth Stokoe: Social interaction and relationships

How did you become interested in research that addresses issues of relevance to relationships?

I have a longstanding interest in relationships in a very broad sense – in ways that contrast with the more traditional social psychological research in this area. That means, rather than focusing on discrete (romantic) relationship phenomena, like initial attraction, liking, love or mate selection, I am interested in how people interact with each other in the settings of their everyday lives. Building and negotiating relationships – be they temporary and fleeting or longstanding and permanent – is an omnipresent feature of social interaction. And much of my interest is data-driven, in the conversation analytic tradition. This means that any topic for research emerges from fairly open-minded initial analyses of naturally occurring interactional data. So, I have been interested in neighbour relationships, relationships between friends, relationships that are played out in institutional and domestic settings and so on.

Tell us about your research into this area.

The majority of my work on relationships has been on possibly one of the most understudied yet mundane relationships we have – with our neighbours. It is interesting that such relationships never appear in the myriad texts on 'interpersonal relationships' in social psychology. I have studied what happens when neighbours fall out and how they formulate complaints about each other to mediators, council officers and the police. In describing neighbour relationship problems, people simultaneously construct what it means to be a good neighbour and the spatial regulation of their relationships that happen 'on the doorstep', 'over the fence' and 'in the street' (Stokoe & Wallwork; 2003). The neighbour relationship is both distant and intimate: while interactions generally take place at the boundaries of private space, sharing boundaries means that people nevertheless get to know some of the intimate routines of their neighbours' lives (Stokoe, 2006; Stokoe & Hepburn, 2005). In addition to neighbour relationships, I have also investigated initial dating with people on speed dates and looked at how they elicit relationship history talk (Stokoe, 2010a). I found that presenting one's romantic biography can be a difficult business, especially if one falls into the 'never married' category. Finally, I have examined friendship relationships and am currently working on the ways friends talk to each other about romantic relationship troubles.

How does your approach compare and contrast with others'?

As I explained above, I do not typically write under a 'personal relationships' banner, although it is clear that conversation analytic research has a lot to tell us about relationships. I may collect data in which relationships issues become the topic for talk, as well as the thing being managed between participants.

Typically, studies of personal relationships get conducted in the laboratory, on the self-report questionnaire or in the interview. Indeed, because personal relationships are just that – *personal* – they are often thought to be unstudyable outside of the research setting (Feeney, 2006). Largely missing in the wider relationships literature are studies of actual encounters between people–their initial interactions or daily conversations in which they maintain, negotiate and progress their relationships. It is, by now, an old criticism of social psychology that it has often failed to study people in the natural settings of their social lives. Instead, researchers remove people from such settings and extrapolate findings gathered from survey reports, experiments, observations or experiential accounts to generate theories about sociological, communicative or psychological processes (Baxter & West, 2003; Gottman & Driver, 2005; Kruger & Fisher, 2008). Despite years of criticism, social scientific knowledge of *personal* relationships remains based obstinately in data gathered from *impersonal* settings. In contrast, any conversation analytic study of relationships will be grounded in real-life social interaction. For example, Mandelbaum (1987, 2003) and Pomerantz and Mandelbaum (2005) have investigated the way 'coupleness' is displayed in collaboratively built narratives, as well as how people make relevant and hold each other accountable for membership of particular relationship categories (Benwell & Stokoe, 2006; Fishman, 1978; Staske, 1996, 1998; Stokoe, 2008). In a series of studies of Relate marriage guidance counselling interaction, Edwards (1994, 1995, 1998) showed how event descriptions

Box 3.5 continued

may be 'scripted' in ways that characterise parties' motivations and dispositions for doing things and manage blame and accountability for those events. More recently, conversation analysts have looked at how people display affiliation and disaffiliation in conversations between friends and family members and what happens when parties become misaligned (Drew & Walker, 2009; Stivers, 2008; Traverso, 2009).

What things helped or hindered your research?

Having access to large data corpuses means that researchers can build collections of relationship-relevant interactional phenomena across different settings. Although conversation analysis is generally categorised as a qualitative method, one nevertheless needs to collect multiple instances of the action under investigation, to examine possible patterns and practices. Funding helps one build datasets; it is also useful to be part of a wider community of researchers who can share data (when ethical approval for such sharing is granted). So, for example, my current interest in relationship troubles advice sequences will draw on my own datasets (for example, friends talking, students interacting in tutorials, police interrogations) and others available to conversation analysts (for example, domestic telephone calls). I can then track down stretches of talk – sometimes momentary, but still very rich – in which talk about romantic relationships and responses to such talk – are part of a larger interaction.

What points of interest would you like to explore in the future? / What further questions would you like to explore in the future?

As I mentioned above, I am interested currently in the way people talk with friends about relationships and the gendering of advice given (for example, 'that's men for you!'). With Bethan Benwell, with whom I have worked many times (Benwell & Stokoe, 2006) and Frederick Attenborough (Attenborough & Stokoe, 2012), I'm also working on our shared datasets of university tutorial interaction as well as students interacting in other institutional and domestic settings. We are interested in the ways in which university topics crop up while students chat at home or online or in the corridor, and how talk about 'the social' crops up while they undertake educational activities in the classroom.

And finally, what do you recommend to people wanting to start to research this topic?

I think my main recommendation would be to get involved with a community of like-minded researchers and work with them as you build both datasets and your analyses thereof. At Loughborough, I am fortunate to be a member of the Discourse and Rhetoric Group, whose weekly data and discussion meetings help to develop and finesse analytic and theoretical skills and share ideas and possibilities as research develops. I would also recommend building up collections of naturally occurring data in different settings and seeing what it has to offer you, rather than start by imposing your interests on the materials. The data will often take you to more interesting places.

Extract 3.2

((music thumping in the background, clinking glasses and drinking))

S An' then 'e didn't get in, (0.5) so then I saw 'im on the
Saturday.
(0.2)
S .hh an' once I left 'is though 'e was like
'e didn't say anything t'-
E Oh::::
(0.2)
E That's me:n.= that's what James was like: (.) on
Sunday::

Source: Stokoe (2012/in press)

In Extract 3.2, Sophie is describing her boyfriend's behaviour: 'then 'e didn't get in', 'e didn't say anything t'. As Stokoe notes, these descriptions (which are cut off rather than fully specified) can be understood as making a complaint about Sophie's boyfriend's lack of contact and communication with her. What is interesting for our current concerns is Emma's talk in lines 8 and 9: 'That's me:n. = that's what James was like: (.) on Sunday'. Here the categorical description 'men' is not simply stating that James can be categorised as a man but also doing interactional work between these two females. Emma's talk in lines 8 and 9 does what Stokoe refers to as a 'categorical upshot' – using a category (men) in an utterance that captures what can be derived from what has been said previously.

Emma's talk does some form of recognition of the behaviour or the type of behaviour that Sophie describes as being 'typical' of men. As Stokoe (2010, p. 21) argues, the category 'men' 'encompasses a host of unspecified, but locally understandable, meanings of what "men" are like.' In this instance of relationship talk, Emma uses an MCD ('men') to align with Sophie's complaint. This alignment is, as Stokoe notes, both strengthened and evidenced by Emma's reference to another exemplar of 'what men are like' – namely, her own boyfriend, James. As well as aligning with Sophie's complaint, Emma's use of the MCD could be seen as exonerating Sophie from any responsibility for her boyfriend's lack of contact – it is explainable not by anything that may have happened between them, nor indeed by her having wound up with an unusually unresponsive boyfriend, but, rather, by virtue of the category to which he is assigned – 'men'. Assigning a friend's boyfriend (even when he has been complained about) to some form of 'typical man' category could be delicate work, but any overly derogatory connotation of this may be addressed by drawing parallels with one's own boyfriend's behaviour.

Thus, Emma's talk in lines 8 and 9 uses an MCD to align with Sophie's complaint, placing the blame for lack of contact on the boyfriend – not as some unusually unresponsive person, but as typical of the category 'men'. This category claim is strengthened and any overly derogatory connotations attended to by Emma's reference to her own boyfriend's similar behaviour. Emma's talk about 'men' and about her relationship, can be seen as designed to do certain types of interactional work, aligning, exonerating, empathising – work that is relevant not just to her friend in a global sense but also the precise issues at hand at a specific point in the sequence of interaction.

In Extracts 3.1 and 3.2, category descriptions have been used – such as 'girls' 'married women' and 'men' – in talk about relationships. The category descriptions that we find, however, do not simply report the world as it is or as it may appear to be to the speaker – they construct the world, its relevant categories and what these categories mean in a certain way (see also Box 3.6). Furthermore, using category devices to construct the world in a certain way does not occur in a 'neutral' environment – instead, such talk (indeed all talk) can be understood as a site where action is taking place, such as where people are responding to complaints about them (Extract 3.1) or about someone else (Extract 3.2). In these specific contexts – which are realised in and transformed through the specific talk at specific places in sequences of interaction – talk about relationships and the categories used in such talk does work such as exonerating, aligning and empathising. These are not reports on what is involved on a 'girls' night out' or what 'men are like'; they are instances of delicate interactional work. In this way, these instances of talk about relationships are not simply *referring to* relationships, they are actually *doing* relationships. That is, the relationship talk we have considered (like all talk) can be conceptualised as doing

Box 3.6 FOCUS
Professor Judith Butler – gender as performative

We are probably used to the commonsense idea that our gender and sexuality are features of who we are that shape how we behave in various ways. So, our interactions with others, what we wear, how we shop, what we eat and drink, our gestures, our intimate behaviour and our talk could (from this perspective) all be seen as the causal consequence of these relatively fixed aspects of ourselves. In her (1999, p. xv) foreword to *Gender trouble*, Butler refers to the way in which our very expectation that there is some solid, knowable, graspable essence of sexuality and gender produces, 'that which it posits as outside of itself'. From this perspective, then, cultural discourses – or ways of thinking about gender and sexuality – may lead us to anticipate some external, verifiable, essence of gender (and sexuality), which, in turn, brings into being our very sense of these (often binary) categories: female–male, homosexual–heterosexual. Rather than see these as cultural constructions, however, we tend to see them as 'natural facts', 'essences' or 'essential truths'.

One crucial strand of Butler's work concerns the way in which gender is not the fixed 'internal' feature we might presume it to be. Butler (1999, p. viii) asks the following question: 'Does being female constitute a "natural fact" or a cultural performance, or is its "naturalness"

Box 3.6 continued

constituted through discursively constrained performative acts that produce the body through and within the categories of sex?' This question is loaded with meaning, but, for our current concerns, what it opens up is the possibility that gender is more verb than noun – something done, in process, enacted rather than being a fixed preformed entity.

A second strand of Butler's work – of particular relevance to thinking about relationships – is her attention to the way in which certain forms of sexual practices and relationships become recognisable and, in some cases, legitimate, whereas other forms may be conceivable and practised but not available, in the sense of a person being able to have a liveable life or a recognised identity through them. One way of thinking about these issues is that there are often socially available binary oppositions for different modes of being: male–female, married–not married, homosexual – heterosexual. The forms of being and relationship that most trouble these oppositions are those that cut across the oppositions, those that cannot be defined in their terms. Butler (2004, p. 108) refers to the 'nonplaces where recognition, including self-recognition, proves precarious if not elusive, in spite of one's best efforts to be a subject in some recognizable sense.' Butler's work takes us from a presumption that our lexicon of sexuality and relationships reflects 'how things are' and helps us to consider that they may be part of what enables people to be in certain ways – both making available and delimiting who, what and how we can be.

relationship-relevant work, having implications for the relationship between those who are interacting there and then.

Critical recap

Constructing relationships

1 One strand of the research considered above is concerned with common, culturally available constructions of gender and relationships and considers something of the ideological – or power implicative – impact that these constructions may have.

2 Another strand of research considered above focuses on the interactional work that constructions of gender and relationship may do, such as exonerating self from blame, aligning with fellow interactants or blaming a non-present person.

3 As seen in Chapters 1 and 2, ideologically orientated talk can be criticised for sometimes adopting a relatively homogenised view of the discourses that people draw on in their talk and its reliance on *a priori* theoretical positions rather than careful scrutiny of data extracts.

4 Interactionally orientated research is sometimes criticised for being overly concerned with empirical data at the expense of bringing a theoretically informed perspective to the analysis. Similarly, interactional work is seen by some (ideologically concerned constructionists) as approaching data as value-free, neutral and speaking for itself rather than recognising the researcher's active role in constructing 'reality' – including 'empirical reality'.

Reflective questions

1 *What ideas – if any – do you hold about relationships and how they should be? Where do these ideas come from and what implications do you think they could have?*

2 *When was the last time you talked about relationships with a friend who was not your partner? Do you think that your constructions of relationships were related to interactional tasks, such as agreeing, justifying, blaming, exonerating and so on?*

3.7 Reflections on research on attraction and relationships

One issue that has been touched on at various points in this chapter is the narrow understanding of relationships that is often present in the literature. One aspect of this narrowness is evident in the focus on romantic relationships at the expense of most other forms of relationship. A second aspect is much of the literature has produced theories that marginalise forms of relationship which are not heterosexual. In some cases, this marginalisation is implied by the scope of the theory. Thus, some evolutionary literature is principally relevant for relationships where there is the possibility of procreation. In some cases, the actual methodological

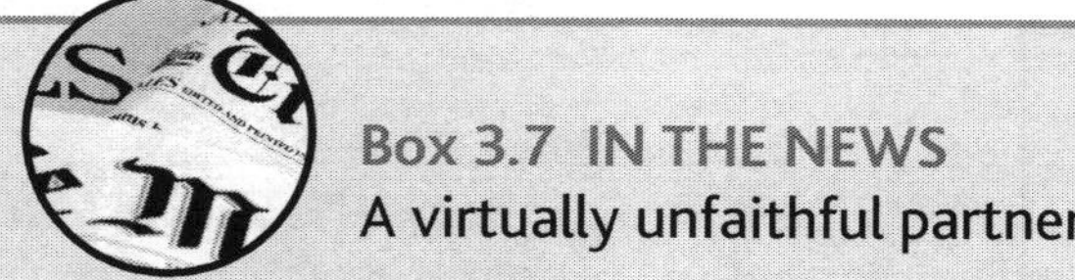

Box 3.7 IN THE NEWS
A virtually unfaithful partner

In 2010, a woman filed for divorce from her husband because she had found him in an intimate embrace with another woman. This news story would be unremarkable were it not for the fact that the embrace was between her husband's avatar and another avatar within the online virtual reality game *Second Life*.

The woman filing for divorce described her husband's behaviour as follows: 'I caught him cuddling a woman on a sofa in the game. It looked really affectionate.' News reports on the case further revealed that the couple had met through their avatars on *Second Life* and the husband had previously been involved with prostitutes, again within the Second Life game.

This news item raises important questions regarding how we think of relationships. First, there is a tendency for research to focus on face-to-face encounters rather than virtual contact – think, for example, about how propinquity research (see Box 3.1) might be challenged by virtual contact that is not geographically restricted. Second, the research raises the issues of how a partner's physical and virtual behaviour could both become relevant and accountable within a relationship. That is, in some relationships, a partner may make judgements – for example, about issues of equity – not simply on the basis of the physically manifest actions of their physically embodied partner but also on the basis of what they may have their avatar do in a virtual world.

A third issue, relating to some of the work by Judith Butler (see Box 3.6, earlier in this chapter) is that, this news story raises something about the way in which we may operate within worlds of available, recognisable and legitimate relationships. Think how technology here appears to make some new form of relationship possible, though we might question the extent to which such relationships are recognised as legitimate. Butler's (2004, p. 205) comments on the 'ambivalent gift of legitimation' (used in a different context) may apply here: 'This is a field outside the disjunction of illegitimate and legitimate; it is not yet thought of as a domain, a sphere, a field; it is not yet either legitimate or illegitimate, has not yet been thought through in the explicit discourse of legitimacy.'

procedures used and/or the interpretation of results presumes that participants are heterosexual by, for example, measuring attraction behaviour by examining male participants' responses to a female confederate or researcher. Much of the literature frames a particular form of heterosexual relationship as the totality of relationships, with no apparent contemplation of other forms of being in relation to others. The growth of online interaction – particularly that which is mediated by virtual world platforms (see Box 3.7) – raises further issues about the adequacy of our frameworks for conceptualising relationships.

A second issue is that experimentally generated data has often relied on using laboratory-generated 'relationships' in order to understand meaningful relationships outside of the laboratory. It is possible to question how much a relationship with strangers who will probably not be seen again in an unfamiliar experimental context will reveal about meaningful or potentially meaningful encounters or relationships.

A third issue is the way in which participants' meanings and understandings have been assessed. Some research has attempted to 'objectively define' stimulus materials, by, for example, having the experimental team rate in advance the attributes that can be read into a series of photographs – participants' responses are then decoded as being in response to these experimenter-attributed qualities. This approach has problems with regard to the presumption that one can guess the basis on which others are responding to a given stimulus. Other approaches, however, that solicit participants' judgements, attitudes, behaviours and evaluations using questionnaires and interviews also have problems – they typically presume that the participants are, in some sense, 'neutrally' or impartially reporting on things as they are. That the responses reflect some reality that lies elsewhere – for example, the responses on a questionnaire may be taken to represent the 'real' feelings and behaviours of the participants. An alternative perspective is that such responses may not report a reality that resides elsewhere but rather be constructions in the moment that may 'do' particular sorts of work as they are expressed.

Finally, much of the research on attraction and relationships appears to downplay the importance of human interaction – both in terms of the theories that are developed and the ways in which data are interpreted. With regard to the ways that theories are developed, much of these – particularly concerning attraction – do little to take account of what might happen in interactions between people. The theories – sometimes like the empirical procedures they are derived from – often present a picture of a static reaction, such as to a photograph, rather than an interaction between two people. With regard to empirical data in interviews and 'everyday data', participants could be understood as doing interaction at the very point that they may seem to be reporting on relationship-relevant material. From this perspective, then, people are not just talking about relationship issues that lie elsewhere, but, rather, in and through their talk, they are doing relationships there and then.

Summary

- This chapter has considered several different perspectives on attraction and relationships.
- From an evolutionary perspective, attraction can be made sense of in terms of each partner trying to maximise the chance of having offspring who are genetically related to them. From this perspective, men and women will prioritise different partner attributes to reflect their differing needs in terms of maximising their chance of successfully passing on their genes. Among issues raised was the point that sometimes seemingly contradictory evidence has been reinterpreted, such that it remains consistent with the evolutionary 'meta theory' and the question that ideas derived from species seeking to maximise chances of survival might not readily map on to human judgements that seem to reflect lifestyle preferences.
- Some research claims that attraction can be made sense of – at least some of the time – in terms of misattributed arousal. That is, an experience of excitation brought about for other reasons (such as fear) may be incorrectly attributed to a potential target of attraction and that target may, in turn, appear more attractive. Questions were raised about the assumptions regarding mental calculations that the theory entails and the measures of attraction that many studies have used.
- Some research appeared to confirm the idea that people often appear to partner relatively 'similar' others. Research into this area, however, was found to rely, in some cases, on abstract, simplified models of attraction and, in other cases, on highly trivial, minimal 'relationships' formed between participants in an experiment. It was further noted that research in this area often marginalised non-heterosexual forms of relationship and had a view of relationships that had little place for interaction between people.
- Equity theory developed the idea that people are concerned with a sense of fairness between their inputs and outcomes and those of their partner. Initial claims, however, that partners have a preference for equity – and will report greater relationship satisfaction when this is the case – was not consistently supported. Sometimes people appear just as happy or happier when they report being 'over-benefited' in the relationship. The idea that our equity calculations form an important part of our relationship satisfaction was also questioned with (among other criticisms) the idea that careful analysis of inputs and outcomes might *reflect* a problem with relationship satisfaction rather than *cause* it.
- Research that considers the construction of relationships was examined. From this perspective, attention is given to the way that relationship-relevant issues (such as gender) are constructed and the sorts of things those constructions might do. One focus within such work is on the culturally available frameworks for making sense of relationships and the sorts of ideological work that they accomplish. A second approach considers what constructions – such as the use of categories to describe 'men' – might do more locally within the immediate interaction. This second approach develops the idea that relationship-relevant talk (and, indeed, all talk) can be understood as not just reporting on relationships (or other issues) but also actually *doing* the business of relationships between the participants within the interaction.
- Finally, some attention was paid to shortcomings across the literature, with a particular focus on its tendency to narrowly focus on romantic heterosexual relationships, its reliance on trivial laboratory relationships or naïve acceptance of participants' questionnaire or interview responses at face value. Furthermore, it was noted that the lack of attention to interaction in much research meant that the very way in which talk between people can *do* relationship is often overlooked.

Review questions

1 *How does evolutionary psychology explain purported differences in male and female partner preferences?*

2 *How can misattributed arousal led to increased attraction?*

3 *What are the limitations of excitation transfer research?*

4 *How does evolutionary psychology explain instances of partner similarity?*

5 *What alternative explanations for partner similarity are there besides the idea of 'market value'?*

6 *What is the evidence that people are concerned with relationship fairness?*

7 *What should be made of cross-cultural differences regarding the apparent importance of equity in relationships?*

8 *What is meant by the idea that certain gender constructions – for example, passive femininity and active masculinity – have ideological implications?*

9 *How can relationship talk do interaction or interactional work?*

Recommended reading

Buss, D. M. (2005). *The handbook of evolutionary psychology*. Hoboken, NJ: Wiley. An overview of evolutionary psychology from one of its foremost proponents.

Butler, J. (2004). *Undoing gender*. Abingdon: Routledge. A thoughtful and thought-provoking critical discussion of issues concerned with gender and sexuality.

Confer, J. C., Easton, J. E., Fleischman, D. S., Goetz, C. D., Lewis, D. M., Perilloux, C., & Buss, D. M. (2010). Evolutionary psychology: Controversies, questions, prospects, and limitations. *American Psychologist*, *65*, 110–126. A review of evolutionary psychology's contribution to psychology.

Edwards, D. (1998). The relevant thing about her: Social identity categories in use. In C. Antaki & S. Widdicombe (Eds.), *Identities in talk* (pp. 15–33). London: Sage. An insightful investigation of the ways in which certain gender-related categories are used to do interactional work in a relationship counselling environment.

Goodwin, R. (2008). *Changing relations: Achieving intimacy in a time of social transition*. Cambridge: Cambridge University Press. A sophisticated overview of relationship research, with a particular emphasis on issues of culture and social change.

Hatfield, E. (2005). *Love and sex: Cross-cultural perspectives*. University Press of America. A review of cross-cultural research on relationships.

Hatfield, E., Berscheid, E., & Walster, G. W. (1976). New directions in equity research. In L. Berkowitz & E. Hatfield (Eds.), *Advances in experimental social psychology, Vol. 9: Equity theory: Toward a general theory of social interaction*. (pp. 1–42). New York: Academic Press.

Pillemer, J., Hatfield, E., & Sprecher, S. (2008). The importance of fairness and equity for the marital satisfaction of older women. *Journal of Women and Aging*, *20*, 215–230. A study into the relevance of equity ideas for a population who are often under-researched in the social psychology of relationships.

Stokoe, E. (2012/in press). 'You know how men are': The anatomy of a categorical practice. *Gender and Language*. 6(1). A paper that brilliantly illustrates the use of membership categorisation devices in talk about gender.

Useful weblinks

www.youtube.com/watch?v=Q50nQUGiI3s A French documentary featuring extensive interviews with Judith Butler.

www.theory.org.uk/ctr-butl.htm A great resource for approaching the work of Judith Butler.

www.culturefirst.com Robin Goodwin's website, with references and downloadable publications.

www-staff.lboro.ac.uk/~ssde/index.htm Derek Edward's publications – a number of which are downloadable.

www.elainehatfield.com Elaine Hatfield's website, with a large number of downloadable publications.

homepage.psy.utexas.edu/homepage/Group/BussLAB/publications.htm David Buss' website, with many downloadable publications and other resources.

Attribution

Learning outcomes

By the end of this chapter you should:

- understand how attribution theory has developed
- understand the main models of causal reasoning
- understand the main approaches to attribution bias
- be aware of how the models of causal reasoning and attribution bias might relate to aspects of everyday life
- be aware of important critiques of specific approaches to research into causal reasoning and attribution bias
- be aware of important critiques of underlying assumptions in attribution research.

On 31 December 2009, a 43-year-old gunman, dressed in black, shot 5 people dead before turning the gun on himself. The incident began with Ibrahim Shkupolli shooting his ex-girlfriend and ended in him opening fire on shoppers and finally himself at the Sello shopping centre in Espoo, west of Helsinki. Witnesses to the events at the shopping centre reported that he appeared to be firing at random. These horrific events had a particular resonance in Finland as they were the third mass shooting in 25 months. On 11 November 2007, an 18-year-old student, Pekka-Eric Auvinen, of Jokela High School in Tuusula, Southern Finland, had entered his school with a hand gun and killed 8 people, injuring a further 10 before killing himself, while, in September 2008, Matti Juhani Saari shot and killed 10 students at the Kauhajoki School of Hospitality north of Helsinki.

Source: Lehtikuva OY/Rex Features

Police vehicles and ambulances outside the Sello shopping centre in Espoo, Finland, following an incident in which a man opened fire on shoppers killing five people before turning the gun on himself. How should we explain events such as these?

In the wake of these horrific events, questions were asked in Finland, and throughout the world, about how such tragedies could occur. Were they connected to the high prevalence of gun ownership in Finland – where recent figures suggest that more than 12 per cent of the population own one or more firearms? Should the incidents be linked to the extreme outlooks of the gunmen involved, two of whom (Pekka-Eric Auvinen and Matti Juhani Saari) made Web postings prior to the incidents in which they revealed violent attitudes and ideologies. Were they due to their mental instability or, perhaps, the breakdown of their interpersonal relationships – Ibrahim Shkupolli having had a restraining order taken out against him by his ex-girlfriend prior to him opening fire on her and others.

Shocking events such as these often leave us puzzled regarding what could possibly cause someone to act in this way. Attribution theory seeks to explain how we calculate the cause or causes of events. It is worth emphasising that, with attribution theory, the target is not the initial event itself, so it does not address why these three men killed others, both known and unknown to themselves. Instead, it focuses on how people observing these disturbing events might try to work out a possible cause for the behaviour. It should be noted that attribution theory considers our attempts to locate causes for events is not limited to horrific events featuring in the news, but would extend to potentially any event or outcome where the location of a cause is felt to be relevant.

Introduction

The focus of this chapter – attribution – may, at first glance, look unfamiliar. We are used to talking and hearing about stereotypes, prejudice, aggression, relationships and, indeed, most of the topics of the chapters in this book. By contrast, 'attribution' falls a little less frequently from our lips, perhaps suggesting to us that it is more technical, perhaps even that it is more limited in its applicability to everyday aspects of our lives. However, attribution theory is *potentially* relevant any time we try to work out what caused something to happen. If we fail an exam, break up with someone or our friend acts in an unfriendly way towards us and we try to explain these occurrences, then attribution theory could be (perhaps, in its own terms, should be) relevant for describing how we work out the cause. If we consider how often we are concerned with questions regarding why things happen – whether the focus is on our own immediate life, the lives of those we know or even wider events – then something of the potential scope of attribution theory comes into focus.

From its beginnings, research in attribution theory has emphasised that we are all particularly concerned with finding causes for negative or unexpected behaviours or events. Thus, the examples given above – failing an examination, the breakdown of a relationship or falling out with a friend – are all instances that might evoke a search for causes on our part and are all *negative* events. In trying to find a cause, we may – according to much of the classic work in attribution – have a particular interest in identifying whether the cause or causes are within the person (internal) whose behaviour we are trying to explain or outside of them – external. I might therefore ask if my friend ignored me because of something outside of them (perhaps someone said something unpleasant to them) or something within them (they might just be in a bad mood). In this way, attribution theory draws some parallels between everyday thinking and the work of psychologists – in both cases, there is a process of trying to work out what might have brought about a given outcome (the event or behaviour to be explained).

Chapter overview

This chapter starts by considering some of the founding figures in attribution thinking within social psychology – particularly Heider and Ichheiser. Here it is noted that they developed some of the concepts central to subsequent attribution theory – although, in the case of Ichheiser, often this was not acknowledged.

Heider's (1958) work conceptualised attribution as a cognitive process that is particularly attuned to calculating whether causes of events to be explained are internal or external and which could be subject to bias – that is, our causal reasoning may fall short of pure, unadulterated rational thinking. Ichheiser (1943a) contributed to the idea of attribution bias – particularly our tendency to explain things in terms of personal dispositions, such as, 'He shouted because he has a bad temper'. Ichheiser also developed the largely neglected idea that culturally located ideas or *ideologies* shape our attribution process – an idea that poses a challenge to an area of research overwhelmingly concerned with just cognitive processes *within the individual*.

The chapter then turns to some of the classic attribution research of Jones and Davis and Kelley. Jones and Davis' work is shown to reflect concerns with both a consideration of the processes of causal calculation and the way in which these processes may be biased – particularly in cases where we consider that the behaviour to be explained has some form of negative impact on us. Kelley's two models of the attribution process are then considered. First, Kelley's enormously influential 'covariation model of causal attribution'. This depicts a thorough, logical, idealised form of causal calculation, placing rationality at the centre of the process. Second, Kelley's 'configuration model', which he suggested might be used where people are unable or unwilling to use the much more comprehensive process depicted in his covariation model.

One criticism of these classic approaches to attribution is that they fail to consider or fully articulate the ways in which the process of working out the cause of something to be explained may deviate from pure rational reasoning – that is, how it may be biased. The chapter next considers three prominent biases, which have received considerable attention in the literature: fundamental attribution error, actor–observer bias and self-bias (sometimes described as 'attributions for success and failure').

The first of these concerns a generic bias towards attributing events to be explained to dispositions – that is, causes within the person rather than the situation. Thus, we might explain someone's unexpected outburst in terms of their bad temper rather than the stressful situation in which they found themselves. Actor–observer bias gets at the idea that we might tend to explain our own behaviour in ways that emphasise the situation, such as, 'I got tongue-tied because of the pressure', and others in terms of their dispositions, such as, 'They got tongue-tied because they are not very articulate.' Self-bias concerns the ways in which we might explain our own success and failure in quite different ways – perhaps attributing our success to some disposition within ourselves, such as, 'I passed the exam because I am capable', and failure to the situation, such as, 'I failed the exam because the paper was unfair.' As is noted in this chapter, however, this pattern may be reversed when the person explaining their behaviour is depressed or otherwise has a negative self-image.

Having considered three prominent biases, the chapter then considers issues that have received rather less attention in social psychology – intergroup bias and societal attributions. Intergroup bias concerns the ways in which we might explain behaviours relating to groups that we see ourselves as belonging to and other groups. So, explanations for 'our' group's (ingroup) actions may differ from those that we have for the actions of other groups (outgroups). For example, explanations for the success of a team that we support (such as skill, ability, effort) may differ from those we produce to explain a rival team's success (such as luck, foul play, incompetent officials).

In considering societal attributions, this chapter returns to some of the issues touched on at the very beginning of the chapter when the work of Ichheiser is first considered. Here, we look at the idea that our ways of explaining why things happened need not be reduced to just cognitions within the individual – whether rational or biased – but could be shaped by our wider cultural environment. Some historical and cross-cultural examples are drawn on to illustrate how the ideas or ideologies we are exposed to may shape the explanations that we produce.

In discussing the different approaches to attribution and attribution bias, some attention is given to real-world examples, typically from items that have been in the news, where issues of attribution seem especially relevant. In addition, specific applications of attribution work with regard to intimate relationships are reviewed. According to this work, our attributions concerning our partner's behaviour – especially their negative behaviour – can have an influence on our relationship with them. If, for example, we explain our partner's loss of temper in terms of the stress they are under at the moment, we may relate to them in a different way than if we explained it in terms of an enduring character trait. Together, these illustrations of the potential relevance and application of attribution work may support a deeper understanding of different attribution approaches, but, ideally this will not mean a passive acceptance of each idea covered – but rather an engaged questioning of the literature.

It is probably worth noting that attribution (and explanation, addressed in Chapter 5) can be among the more conceptually demanding topics within social psychology. Here, we are forced to think about our framework for understanding causes of behaviour – a task that may seem reflexive, intangible and not immediately related to our everyday concerns. If you have a sense of being confused or overwhelmed, try to remember these two things: first, you are not alone and, second, your confusion may actually be a response to problems with the way in which issues have been conceptualised within this topic. Issues of attribution and explanation are central to so much of the process of understanding, blaming and accounting in our society; from weighing the motive in a criminal case to making sense of the shortcomings and misdemeanours of a friend or partner. Grasping how attribution and explanation have been approached in social psychology can be like gazing at a huge but dimly lit stained-glass window – we might struggle to make out what we are looking at, but, if we stay with it long enough, we may find ourselves inspired and uplifted.

4.1 Founding figures of causal attribution

Before outlining some of the classic models of causal attribution, it is worth considering two of the founding figures of causal attribution – Heider and Ichheiser. We should note a couple of points about these two figures. First, although we are treating them as founding figures here, it would be wrong to suppose that, prior to them, no one had given a moment's thought to how people work out causes of phenomena or give an **explanation** or **exonerating explanation** of them (indeed, this was a concern of a number of ancient Greek rhetoricians). Second, one of these figures, Ichheiser, features far less prominently than the other – nearly every social psychology textbook chapter on attribution theory will mention Heider; far fewer will refer to Ichheiser. Here, the contributions of both figures are outlined before moving on to some of the foundational theories of Jones and Davis and Kelley. It can be noted that much of the attribution work that we consider throughout this book tends to draw selectively on Heider's ideas and leaves Ichheiser almost entirely alone. By having an awareness of Heider and Ichheiser early on, though, you will be in a better position to question the work that follows – in particular, pointing out the narrow framework used to approach attribution and the huge areas of this vast topic that have been left unexplored.

Fritz Heider

An important strand of Fritz Heider's approach was to consider what attribution does for us – that is, how it meets some basic human need that we have. For Heider, the process of finding a cause, or **attribution**, is concerned with making the world more orderly and controllable for the social perceiver. Finding the cause or causes of behaviour was understood by Heider (1958, p. 79) as a basic human process rooted in our fundamental desire for predictability and control over events:

> It is an important principle of common-sense psychology, as it is of scientific theory in general, that man (sic) grasps reality, and can predict and control it, by referring transient and variable behaviour and events to relatively unchanging underlying conditions, the so-called dispositional properties of his world.

Explanation The process of communicating an attribution – such as telling someone why you can't come to their party.

Exonerating explanations Explanations that account for why we did something others might not approve of, or we did not do something others wanted us to do – 'I would have tidied the place, but I had to make an important call', for example.

Attribution The process of identifying a cause or causes for an outcome – for example, my thinking about why I got a low grade for my last essay.

According to Heider (1958), then, we might seek to explain why we failed an exam, experienced the breakup of a relationship or had our debit or credit card declined so that we can avoid those unpleasant **outcomes** in the future. Likewise, we may want to explain why our presentation was successful, why people enjoyed our party or why someone we are attracted to was so fascinated when we talked about all of the places we have visited in our life, so that we can bring about these happy outcomes again.

For Heider, readers of this book could be seen as having a double interest in accurately identifying the cause of any behaviour. First, as students of psychology (or 'scientific' psychology as Heider puts it) and, second, as 'lay' people (or 'commonsense' psychologists) in the social world. Heider suggested that the motivation for making attributions might differ between 'lay' people ('commonsense' psychologists) and professional ('scientific' psychologists). While 'lay' people are motivated to make attributions out of a personal concern with maximising positive and minimising negative experiences, Heider suggested that these personal motivations were absent for 'scientific psychology'. Despite this motivational difference, however, Heider (1958, p. 82) argued that there was a marked parallel in elements of the attribution process for 'commonsense' and 'scientific' psychologists: 'In common-sense psychology (as in scientific psychology) the result of an action is felt to depend on two sets of conditions, namely, factors within the person and factors within the environment.' That is, in both everyday thinking and professional psychological thinking, there is a concern with whether the cause of a behaviour is within the **person** or **actor** **(internal)** – or the environment **(external and situational)**. Thus, in everyday terms, we might ask if our exam success was due to us (person) or the exam was easy (environment). Likewise a classic debate in psychology has asked if infants learn to speak because of nature (person) or nurture (environment).

Heider (1958) further argued that the *process* of making an attribution in everyday 'commonsense' thinking is similar to that used in professional 'scientific' psychology. Both commonsense and scientific psychologists make their calculations on the assumption that, 'The cause of a difference resides within the variant condition' (1958, p. 69). In other words, in seeking to establish the cause – as everyday thinkers or scientists – we identify which specific factors covary with the behaviour (or outcome) we are trying to explain. That is, we try to locate which factor or factors are present when the outcome to be explained is present and absent when the outcome is absent. Imagine, for example, that you experience success in cognitive psychology exams each time you write practice exam answers and failure when you do not – the outcome (exam success) covaries with an identifiable potential cause (writing practice essays). Once we spot something that covaries with the outcome, we are trying to explain (writing of practice essays covarying with exam success), then we are likely to identify that covariant (writing practice essays) as the cause. This reasoning process is, as Antaki (1994) notes, the basis of the hugely popular statistical test analysis of variance (ANOVA), as well as providing the framework for one of the most influential models of causal reasoning – Kelley's covariation model of causal attribution.

For Heider (and subsequent researchers such as Kelley), everyday causal reasoning is seen as dependent on the same basic principles that scientists (and, more specifically, experimental psychologists) are presumed to use in identifying causes. The fundamental assumption here is that, in our everyday thinking, we are all like scientists – naïve scientists. The idea that we are all like naïve scientists has an influence beyond attribution theory, as we shall see in Chapter 5, but, for now, it is worth noting that this concept had a vital influence on the development of key theories in attribution and formed the backdrop for the contrasting idea that we are sometimes less rational and objective or *biased* in our causal reasoning.

As Antaki (1994) notes, these strands of Heider's thinking do not fully develop his overarching concern with what he referred to as a 'commonsense' psychology – that is, the ways people make sense of everyday life. Couched in these terms, Heider's (1958) remit could have stimulated and encompassed work that went far beyond an interest in a mechanistic approach to the cognitive unit parts involved in causal calculations. What has become Heider's legacy, however, is a narrower focus on the cognitive mechanics of thinking often expressed in an abstract algebraic formula. Heider's work within the field of attribution inspired subsequent work that tried to capture the private cognitive processes by which people

Outcome The happening, behaviour or event for which a cause is sought – for example, my friend seems to act coldly towards me, I have failed an exam, I did not laugh at the comedian.

Internal, actor and person These terms identify the cause as being *within* the person doing or experiencing the behaviour to be explained – my boyfriend is jealous because of their personality, I failed an exam because I didn't revise, for example.

External and situational These terms identify the location for the cause as outside of the outcome to be explained – for example, I was nervous in the interview because of the spotlight pointed at my face and the aggressive style of questioning.

calculated (correctly or incorrectly) the causes of behaviour (and, to a lesser extent, events).

Gustav Ichheiser

Of equal – or perhaps even greater importance – though, as noted above, typically overlooked – is the rather more radical figure of Gustav Ichheiser.

Ichheiser was quite critical of social psychological research in general. First, he argued (similarly to Billig, 1987) that social psychologists busied themselves in researching issues that suit their particular understanding of a 'precise investigation', leaving other seemingly less amenable issues to one side. Second, he (1943b, p. 204) argued that social psychologists lacked critical awareness of the 'psychological presuppositions rooted in the ideological background' of the society to which they belonged.

From this perspective, then, social psychologists' focus on just those issues that readily fit their narrow, atomised understanding of the social world is *self-perpetuating* – as conceptions or issues which blatantly do not fit this perspective are not adopted or investigated. This situation is made worse when the issue of ideological blindspots are considered. Thus, for Ichheiser, social psychologists are not only blinded to non-atomised ways of doing social psychology but also unwittingly biased by the assumptions that are present within the ideologies of their culture.

This culturally informed perspective – which may have contributed to Ichheiser's marginalisation within social psychology – informed his understanding of attribution specifically. Ichheiser identified a **bias** that people have towards making dispositional (or person) attributions and, in this way, he foreshadowed the subsequent work on attribution bias. Ichheiser (1943b), though, took these ideas to a more critical conclusion as, for him, this bias was not simply a cognitive phenomenon located in the mind of the individual but, rather, could be understood as a result of the 'ideology of our society'. In this way, Ichheiser, early in the development of attribution theory, not only developed ideas about attribution bias but also, by locating them within a culture's ideology, took a critical stance with regard to other more individualistic and cognitive accounts of attribution. This more societal conception of attribution is returned to at the end of this chapter.

Edward Jones and Keith Davis' (1965) correspondent inference theory

Edward Jones and Keith Davis' (1965) **attribution** model – correspondent inference theory – picks up on Heider's concern with whether the cause of what we are trying to explain is within the person or not. Specifically, Jones and Davis address the ways in which we think about an instance of behaviour we are trying to explain and what, if anything, this can tell us about the dispositions of the person who brought the behaviour about. In developing their ideas, Jones and Davis also touched on the idea of attribution bias, which is returned to later in this chapter.

For Jones and Davis, in our attributions we attempt to infer a correspondence between the behaviour we are trying to explain and features of the person (or actor) undertaking the behaviour (their dispositions and intentions). Imagine living in a room on campus next to someone who has a drum kit that they practise on regularly late at night. We might find ourselves forming an image of the person based on their behaviour – Jones and Davis highlight how we work from manifest behaviour to construe attributes of the actor.

As our neighbour bangs out the same rhythm again at 2 a.m. each night, we might find ourselves thinking first about the observed effects of their actions (keeping us awake or interrupting our activities, such as night-time reading of social psychological literature). Jones and Davis suggest that we need to be satisfied that the behaviour is intentional in order to start to consider the dispositions of the person. Thus, we need to be sure that the person has the ability to bring about the action (if the drumming occurs when our neighbour is out, asleep or in a straightjacket, then some other attribution is made relevant).

We also need to be sure that our neighbour knows the consequences of their actions. If they sincerely believe that their room is fully soundproofed or the other residents are not present at 2 a.m., then we cannot read much into their behaviour. If, however, we think that the drumming is brought about by our neighbour and they know it is heard by many other people on the campus, then we are in a position to draw up a mental picture of the characteristics or dispositions that this night-time drummer may have.

Bias Aspects of our thinking that are not rational nor objective, but, instead, influenced by our cognitive limitations or, our motivations to think in a certain way – such as blaming my failure on others so that I can feel good about myself.

Attributional This is often used to refer to research concerned with the impact and applications of attributions – such as how attributions can affect our close relationships and how therapeutic techniques have been developed in the light of attribution research.

In order to work out the dispositions of the actor that might account for their behaviour, we may consider the differences between the consequences of their chosen behaviour and the consequences of other non-chosen alternatives. In the example of the night-time drummer, this is the difference between drumming loudly at night and not drumming, or drumming quietly, or drumming at other times of the day or drumming elsewhere.

It is the non-common effects or the different effects of quite similar alternative courses of action that we treat as especially revealing about dispositional attributes. In attribution literature, this is often illustrated by reference to choices about where to study. The fewer differences there are between two universities being considered, the more confidence we can have in the unique feature of the university that is chosen and in what this tells us about the actor choosing the university. We could, likewise, consider that the choice made by our drummer neighbour to drum specifically at night tells us something about their attitude to the sleep of themselves and others – 'they are the sort of person who presumes, if they are awake, it doesn't matter how much noise they make'.

Our attributions to disposition are also more certain when the behaviour is not socially desirable – we may be able to say far less about them when considering the way they turn up on time for lectures or are polite in the canteen as these are socially desirable behaviours that can be understood as being brought about by some combination of the situation and generally held norms of behaviour. The socially undesirable night-time drumming, however, is likely to be perceived as contrary to socially desirable behaviour and, therefore, more revealing of individual dispositions (noisy, selfish).

Correspondent inference theory and bias

As Hewstone (1989) notes, perhaps the most important contribution of Jones and Davis' correspondent inference theory is the early identification of certain attribution biases that it provided. Work on attribution bias more generally is discussed below, but, here, Jones and Davis' specific contribution will be considered as it is an integral part of their theory. Before doing so, though, it is worth briefly noting that biases are understood in the attribution literature as any identifiable factors other than 'the facts' that can affect the way in which an attribution is made or the outcome of an attribution. Some authors as Hewstone (1989) notes, are keen to distinguish between *motivational* and *cognitive* biases – motivational biases are understood as arising from the interests, intentions or objectives of the perceiver, whereas cognitive biases are thought of as information-processing issues or limitations.

Jones and Davis (1965) identified two motivational biases – *hedonic relevance* and *personalism*. Hedonic relevance concerns the positive or negative impact that the behaviour to be explained has on the person making the attribution – if the behaviour affects us, we are more likely to explain it in terms of a corresponding disposition of the person undertaking the behaviour than if it doesn't. Have you ever listened to a friend talking about problems with their partner? Perhaps the partner does not get along with your friend's family or they are too talkative, shy, indiscrete, negative or lax about personal hygiene. From Jones and Davis' perspective, because of the direct relevance of their partner's behaviour, your friend is likely to make dispositional inferences – that is, attribute the behaviour to dispositions of their partner rather than situational or circumstantial factors. Likewise, our attributions for behaviours that affect us (our neighbour playing the drums or our friends getting into a bad mood) are likely to be dispositional – that is, we will attribute the behaviour to a corresponding disposition within the person undertaking the behaviour.

Jones and Davis argue that this tendency to dispositional attributions is especially strong where the person making the attribution perceives the behaviour to be not just relevant to them but specifically directed at them. Jones and Davis used the term 'personalism' to capture this phenomenon. If we feel that our partner's complaint, our neighbour's noise or our lecturer's sarcasm are directed at us, then we are more likely to understand the complaining, noisy or sarcastic behaviour as corresponding to some disposition within our partner, neighbour or lecturer. Thus, feeling that a given behaviour is personalised or 'aimed at us' (what Heider (1958) came to call 'target attribution'), especially when behaviour is negative, makes a dispositional (within the person) attribution more likely.

Critical evaluation of Jones and Davis' model

Hewstone (1989) raises questions about the emphasis on intent and non-chosen behaviour in their model, as well as the more general issue of whether or not trait attributions should be considered equivalent to causal calculations.

With regard to intent, Jones and Davis treat this as a precondition for making an inference that things correspond when, in fact, a number of dispositions (such as forgetfulness and clumsiness) are usually understood to be non-intentional. This questions the centrality of intent in general and the range of contexts for which correspondent inference theory is relevant.

The theory also emphasises the idea that perceivers consider both chosen and non-chosen behaviours in attempting to make an attribution. It might be the case, however, that we do not consistently contemplate non-chosen behaviours (even if we knew what these were or could do so by conjecture) – we may attend much more to what has been done rather than the various alternatives of what *might* have been done.

More generally, correspondent inference theory does little to outline how we might calculate and choose between alternative causes of a behaviour – for example, whether the behaviour was brought about by something to do with a circumstance, situation or the person themselves. It may be that the way in which we undertake trait attributions (working out the extent to which a behaviour corresponds to a disposition of the person doing the behaviour) may be quite different from the way in which we make a causal attribution (working out what the cause of a behaviour is or where the cause is located).

Jones and Davis' model outlined both the rational questions that might be considered in making a dispositional inference about a given behaviour and the factors which might lead to a bias in this process. In this way, Jones and Davis' work has been something of a template for subsequent work – much of which has focused on identifying either the rational process that is used (or ideally is used) in making attributions or the biases that distort such rational reasoning. Jones and Davis' work approached attribution as a combination of rational processing and biases located within the heads of individual perceivers – a perspective shared by much subsequent work, but questioned, particularly by the discursive and conversation analytic perspectives described below.

Critical recap

Edward Jones and Keith Davis' (1965) correspondent inference theory

1 Is intentional choice behaviour always so central to our attribution thinking? If we try to explain someone's behaviour, will our causal reasoning always entail some deduction of their intention based on the choice that they made between alternative courses of action?

2 Do we really consider what people might have done but did not do – that is, alternatives to the behaviour we are trying to explain that were *not* chosen?

3 Does the correspondent inference theory really tell us about causal reasoning?

Reflective questions

1 *Can you think of a time when you made inferences about a person based on a decision that they had made?*

2 *Think of a case when someone behaved in a way that had an adverse effect on you. Did you attribute the behaviour to some cause within that person?*

4.2 Harold Kelley's covariation and configuration models

Kelley's (1967) covariation model of causal attribution

Perhaps the most famous of all models of attribution – and one of the easiest to misunderstand – is what Harold Kelley (1967) called his *covariation model of causal attribution* (Figure 4.1). This was not Kelley's only model (his simpler configuration model is discussed below also), but this was arguably the most influential of all the models of attribution. Much of the work that followed – whether supportive or critical of the covariation model – treated it as *the* dominant approach to attribution in social psychology. What makes it tricky, and thus requires some care as we consider it, is that many people (and even some texts) fail to clearly distinguish the different reasoning dimensions (*consensus*, *distinctiveness* and *consistency*) that lie at the heart of Kelley's covariation model. If you can make use of the examples given to ensure that you have a clear sense of these three dimensions, you will have mastered some of the most slippery concepts within traditional social psychology.

Of the two models he developed, Kelley himself saw covariation as an idealised model of how we can and should make attributions when we have sufficient information, time and motivation and the configuration model as a less thorough but realistic description of how we often do make attributions. For Kelley (1972, p. 152), then, the covariation model can be understood as 'an idealized model and not descriptive of most everyday, informal attributions'.

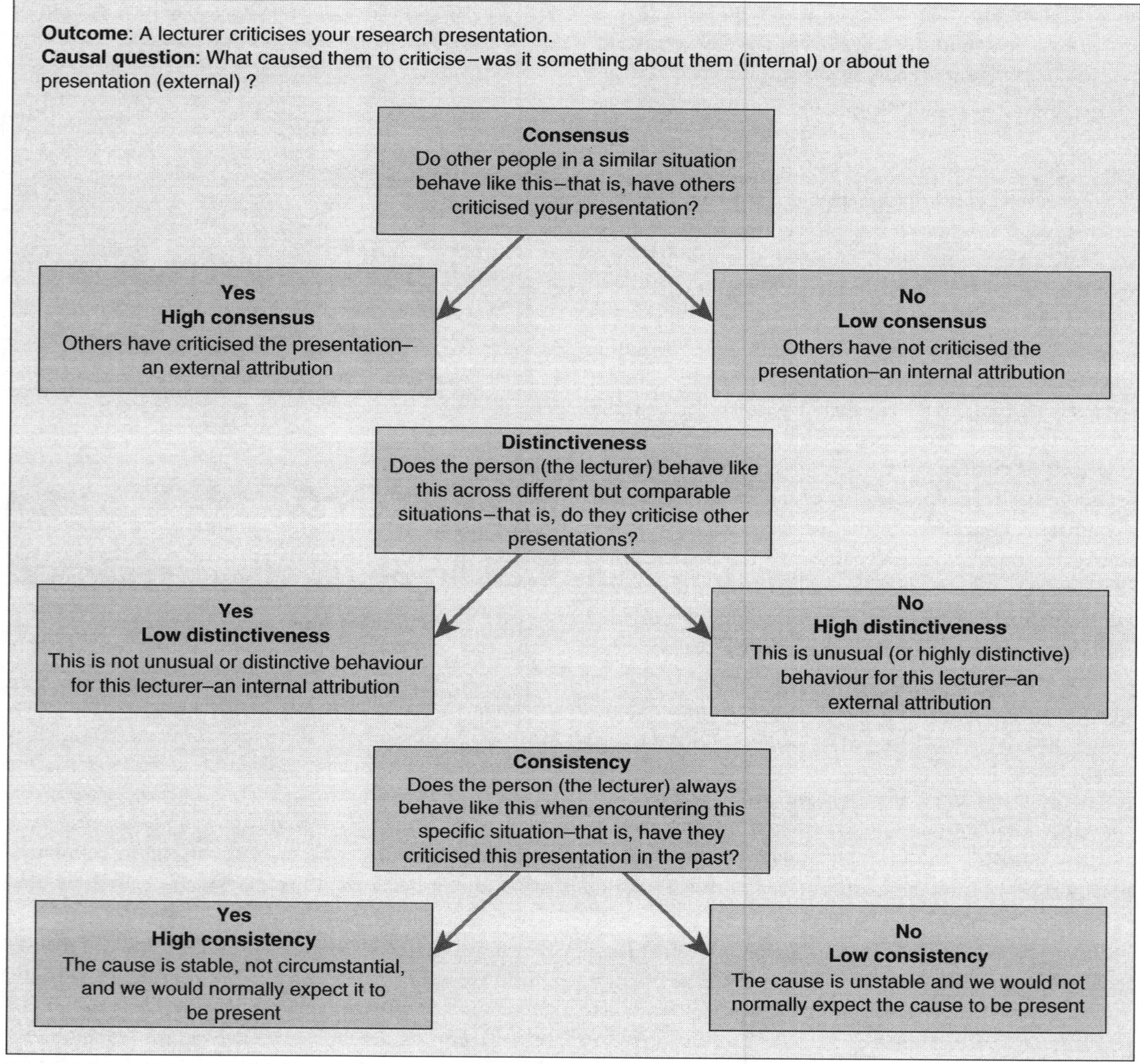
Outcome: A lecturer criticises your research presentation.
Causal question: What caused them to criticise–was it something about them (internal) or about the presentation (external) ?
Consensus
Do other people in a similar situation behave like this–that is, have others criticised your presentation?
Yes
High consensus
Others have criticised the presentation–an external attribution
No
Low consensus
Others have not criticised the presentation–an internal attribution
Distinctiveness
Does the person (the lecturer) behave like this across different but comparable situations–that is, do they criticise other presentations?
Yes
Low distinctiveness
This is not unusual or distinctive behaviour for this lecturer–an internal attribution
No
High distinctiveness
This is unusual (or highly distinctive) behaviour for this lecturer–an external attribution
Consistency
Does the person (the lecturer) always behave like this when encountering this specific situation–that is, have they criticised this presentation in the past?
Yes
High consistency
The cause is stable, not circumstantial, and we would normally expect it to be present
No
Low consistency
The cause is unstable and we would not normally expect the cause to be present

Figure 4.1 Kelley's (1967) covariation model of causal attribution

Key to Kelley's (1967) model – and linked to the concerns of Heider, considered above – is the motivation to identify whether the causes of the phenomenon we are seeking to explain lie within the person or the situation (see Box 4.1).

Consensus, distinctiveness and consistency

Kelley's covariation model sought to identify and concisely express precisely the reasoning process that we (ideally) use to identify whether the cause of a behaviour or occurrence is something to do with the person (or people) or the situation. Kelley's model of causal reasoning also provides for a third (and often overlooked) possible attribution – that is, to the specific circumstance in which the person (or people) finds themselves.

Kelley followed Heider in suggesting that identifying the broad location of the cause – internal to the person or external to them – was a crucial goal of our attribution reasoning. Kelley also subdivided the category of external to distinguish *stimulus* (a recurring feature external to the person) from *circumstance* (something specific to this instance of the behaviour). For Kelley, we all (ideally) follow a causal analysis that is similar to that of an empirically orientated scientist – we investigate the outcome (behaviour or occurrence) to be explained to identify the factors that seem to be linked to it (or with

Box 4.1 IN THE NEWS
The Hillsborough tragedy

To understand Kelley's covariation model, it is worth considering a specific historical event in which attributions were made that distinguished between causes lying within the person or actor (the one doing or experiencing the thing to be explained) or within the stimulus or environment (all potential causes outside of the actor). The Hillsborough tragedy of 1989 provides one such example.

On 15 April 1989 at Hillsborough football stadium, a crush occurred that resulted in 96 deaths. The disaster had a particularly widespread resonance as it was shown live on BBC television's sports programme *Grandstand*, which was broadcasting the football match. Witnesses at the stadium and television audiences watched with bewilderment and horror as fans, who were crushed into a fenced enclosure, climbed over the fence to the pitch, while others were pulled to safety by neighbouring supporters. The pitch began to fill with fans gasping for breath, injured and carrying out the bodies of the dead.

Following the tragedy, the majority of commentators highlighted situational causes – the opening of additional entrance gates immediately prior to the match, the failure to direct fans away from one central enclosure, the dangers of standing terraces and the existence of high security fences. Some individuals, however, with policing responsibility that day attributed the tragedy to the fans themselves – emphasising their drunkenness, blaming them for opening an additional gate (a claim later retracted) and, in some cases, blaming fan behaviour for the existence of high fences in the first place. A tabloid newspaper at the time notoriously vilified some of the fans' behaviour during the tragic event, implying that the awful outcome was, to some extent, brought about by the fans (or sections of the fans). If we think of the fans as a group, rather than separate individuals, then a minority of commentators explicitly or implicitly attributed the causes of the tragedy to the actors or group of fans rather than situational factors.

It is easy to see how the issue of where we locate the cause – within the actor(s) or within the situation – has a major effect on how we respond to the outcome. If we see the tragedy as principally brought about by something to do with the fans themselves, then it is they (and not any feature of the situation) who need to change. If we make an internal attribution, then we will not necessarily feel that there should be changes to stadium design or crowd management.

The tragic events of Hillsborough led to a public inquiry (under Lord Justice Taylor). The inquiry concluded that mistakes in police control and problems with stadium design were the primary causes of the tragedy, while consumption of alcohol by a small section of the crowd was acknowledged as a minor aggravating factor. As a consequence of both the tragic events and the Taylor report, all major stadiums across the country were redesigned to remove standing areas and become all-seater stadiums. Thus, the attribution (by the Taylor report) to situational factors led to a major redesign of the external physical setting provided at many football stadiums so as to remove features of the situation that were present at Hillsborough.

which it covaries). This procedure is often referred to as an analysis of variance (ANOVA), which is a statistical procedure for identifying the covariation of causal variables and outcomes.

Imagine that you give a research presentation (one you have given previously) and a lecturer criticises it. Given this negative occurrence you might want to know what brought this criticism about – is it something to do with the person or actor whose behaviour you are trying to explain (the lecturer), the stimulus or environmental features they encountered (the research presentation) or in the specific circumstances at that time?

If you have information about how others have responded to the research presentation, how the lecturer has responded to other research presentations and (ideally) how they have responded to this presentation on previous occasions, then you are in a position to undertake what Kelley calls a 'full dress', or thorough, causal analysis. That is, you can consider how the occurrence of the outcome varies across people (do others act this way when encountering the same stimulus?), across stimuli (does this person act this way across different but comparable stimuli?) and time and modality (does the person always act this way when encountering this specific stimulus?).

These dimensions – known as consensus, distinctiveness and consistency – are defined below. In examining them, it is worth re-emphasising that Kelley (1972, p. 152) understood them as 'an idealised model and not descriptive of most everyday, informal attributions'. That is, they are how we *should* locate the cause of the outcome or behaviour we are trying to explain, but we might not have the knowledge and/or motivation to undertake such a causal calculation.

Defining consensus, distinctiveness and consistency

Consensus, distinctiveness and consistency can be thought of as three questions that are asked regarding the nature of the cause (see Figure 4.1, earlier).

- **Consensus** Do other people in a similar situation behave like this (or have this experience)?
- **Distinctiveness** Does the person (do the people) always behave like this (have this experience) across different but similar situations?
- **Consistency** Does the person (do the people) always behave like this (have this experience) when encountering this specific situation?

It is worth considering how consensus, distinctiveness and consistency information might be used to work out why the lecturer criticised our research presentation.

Reasoning with consensus, distinctiveness and consistency

Continuing with our example, if others heard your research presentation and they all criticised it, then there is a high consensus for the specific instance of criticism by the lecturer that we are trying to explain. Kelley argues that high consensus is consistent with an external attribution, so we might find we attribute the criticism to the stimuli – if everyone criticises the presentation it must be something about the presentation (perhaps there is a problem with the content, the organisation of ideas or the clarity with which the ideas were conveyed) which caused or gave rise to the criticism. If, by contrast, others do *not* criticise the presentation – perhaps they even praise it – then the criticising behaviour has low consensus, so we are likely to attribute it to some feature of the lecturer (the lecturer might be a very critical person, they might use criticism to get the best out of their students).

We might also consider whether the criticising behaviour is something unusual for this lecturer or a recurrent behaviour. That is, does the lecturer regularly criticise research presentations (low distinctiveness) or is this something of a one-off (high distinctiveness)? If we see the behaviour as unusual or highly distinctive for them – for example, in the past, we have never heard them make a critical comment about a research presentation – we are more likely to consider that something about the stimulus – the presentation – must account for this unusual display of critical behaviour. If, by contrast, we regularly hear this lecturer criticise presentations, then we are more likely to attribute the cause of this low distinctiveness behaviour as something about them (they are critical or they use criticism as a pedagogical tool, for example).

'Distinctiveness' can be a somewhat slippery concept because rating a behaviour as high in distinctiveness is really saying its occurrence (at least for the person concerned) is low and vice versa. Thus, if a behaviour is high in distinctiveness, that means the person rarely does the behaviour; if a behaviour is low in distinctiveness, it means they often do it. It is perhaps worth thinking through some of your own examples to hang this concept on – that shy person you know who had a sudden outburst of exuberance was engaging in behaviour that stands out or is distinctive from the background of their normal behaviour, but, for the confident exhibitionist, the same behaviour merges in with the rest, indistinct from all their other exuberant behaviour.

Finally, *if* we have information about how the person has responded to the stimulus in the past, then we might consider the consistency of the behaviour. That is, we may ask has the lecturer always criticised this presentation? If the lecturer has encountered this presentation in the past and praised it, then the criticism is low in consistency. Where behaviour is identified as having low consistency, then we can find ourselves leaning towards a circumstantial attribution (sometimes called an *unstable* attribution). A circumstantial attribution means that we consider the behaviour to be explained was brought about by something or some things *not usually present but present on this specific occasion* (for example, the mood that the lecturer was in on that specific occasion or something about how we gave the presentation on this specific occasion). If, however, the lecturer has criticised this presentation each time they have encountered it, then we may deduce that the cause is non-circumstantial (or stable). Where we make a non-circumstantial attribution, we are deducing that the behaviour is brought about by some feature of the lecturer (person or actor), presentation (stimulus or environment) or combination of the two that we would *normally expect to be present*.

Consistency, again, is a tricky concept and perhaps easily confused with distinctiveness, so it is worth thinking about it for a moment longer. Consistency gets at just how sure we can be that this person will behave like this when encountering this stimulus – do they always act like this when they encounter this stimulus? It may be worth thinking through an example from your own experience. Perhaps you know someone who has in the past enjoyed watching a certain TV show. If they enjoy watching the latest episode, then their enjoyment of the latest episode is high in consistency (or stable); if they do not enjoy watching it, then their non-enjoyment is low in consistency (or unstable).

Consistency can be still more confusing when we think about the sorts of causes it points to. With consensus and distinctiveness, the high or low rating each point to a cause that is either internal or external – for example, high consensus and high distinctiveness point to an external cause; low consensus and low distinctiveness point to an internal cause. With consistency, however, the high or low ratings do not help to determine whether the cause is internal or external, but rather something about the *temporal quality* of that internal or external cause – is it transient just here, on this occasion, but not necessarily likely to be present on other occasions (such as mood, performance) or is it usually present (an enduring characteristic of the person or stimulus, for example)?

In this way, consistency works with consensus and distinctiveness not to further clarify whether the cause is internal or external, but, rather, to identify what type of internal or external cause is the most likely candidate. If, for example, we are trying to explain a behaviour and consensus and distinctiveness are low (pointing to an internal cause), consistency information can help us decide between the person's mood and their personality characteristics as likely causes. If, by contrast, consensus and distinctiveness are high (pointing to an external cause), consistency information helps us to decide whether the cause is a recurrent, stable property of the stimulus or just something about how the stimulus happened to be on this particular occasion.

Using consensus, distinctiveness and consistency together

In the examples above, we considered consensus, distinctiveness and consistency in isolation, whereas Kelley's model considers how they operate together.

It is possible to distinguish two broad ways in which consensus, distinctiveness and consistency might combine. The first is to point in unison to a single causal locus – that is, to either an internal or an external cause. The second, is to an interaction between some combination of person, stimuli and circumstance.

The most straightforward cases occur when both consensus and distinctiveness point to the same broad internal or external location for the cause. Thus, when consensus and distinctiveness are high, a stimulus or external attribution is indicated; if consistency is also high, then this cause is likely to be a recurrent feature of the stimulus (how it always is); where consistency is low, then the cause is likely to be some transient feature of the stimulus (how it was on this occasion). Where consensus and distinctiveness are low, a person or internal attribution is indicated; if consistency is also high, then the cause is likely to be some recurrent feature of the person (such as their characteristics); if consistency is low, then the cause is likely to be some feature of how the person was on this particular occasion (such as the mood they were in).

More complex possibilities arise when we consider that consensus and distinctiveness might not combine straightforwardly – that is, both being high or both being low. It should be noted that these cases are not just theoretical possibilities – much of the time, the behaviour or occurrences we seek to explain might be less clear-cut than some of the examples given above. That is, in our everyday lives, we might think that a particular person laughs at a comedian, is afraid of the dog, ignores us or enjoys the latest episode of a TV show because of something about the person *and* the stimulus. Alternatively, it may be that our calculation indicates it could be *either* the person *or* the stimulus.

These possible combinations are discussed in some detail by Brown (1986), but, here let us look into this a little more. If our *solemn* friend *always* laughs at a comedian who *no one else* finds funny (high distinctiveness, high consistency, low consensus), then our attribution would be to a person–stimulus interaction – that is, to *both* something within the person *and* something within the stimulus. It is as if our friend and the comedian have found in each other something they could not find elsewhere – the unappreciated comedian has at last found someone who will laugh at his jokes and our friend has at last found someone who can make her laugh. Some quality of the comedian is ideally suited to our friend's particular sense of humour – so, both the features of the comedian *and* of our friend are necessary for the behaviour (laughing at this comedian) to occur. Alternatively, if our other jokey, laugh-a-minute friend always laughs at a comedian who everyone laughs at (low distinctiveness, high consistency, high consensus), then we could attribute the laughing to *either* our friend *or* the comedian – either being sufficient to cause the laughter.

In considering these causal combinations, it is possible to distinguish between outcomes (or behaviours to be explained) that are perceived as rare, complex or unusual and those that seem commonplace, straightforward and everyday. Our solemn friend laughing at a comedian no one else finds funny is an example of an unusual behaviour to be explained (low consensus and high distinctiveness) as it is unusual that the comedian made *anyone* laugh, particularly our friend who rarely laughs. When we are confronted with these sorts of events to explain, Kelley's covariation model suggests that we may arrive at explanations that involve an interaction between person and stimulus – that is, both something within the person and the stimulus are necessary for this to occur. By contrast, when we try to explain unsurprising behaviours or events (high consensus and low distinctiveness) – such as our jokey friend laughing at a comedian everyone laughs at – then we may arrive at a less specific attribution in which person, stimulus and the combination of the two are each sufficient to explain the behaviour.

In the examples above, the covariation process (which entails addressing questions of consensus, distinctiveness and consistency) leads us to an attribution in which there were either multiple necessary causes (more than one factor had to be in place to allow this unusual behaviour to occur) or multiple sufficient causes (any causal factor out of several would account for the behaviour). It is exactly these issues that Kelley addressed with his configuration model (see Box 4.2).

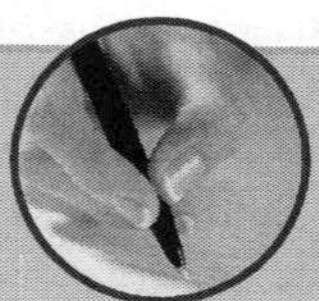

Box 4.2 TRY IT OUT Kelley's configuration model

Think of one extremely easy, predictable accomplishment that you have achieved and one that was incredibly difficult and perhaps unexpected.

Now, imagine that you have to work out what enabled these things to be accomplished, but try to stop yourself as you are about to do so.

Are you expecting a different mix of causes for the easy and difficult accomplishments?

Do you imagine that more things have to contribute together for the difficult thing to have been accomplished?

These are exactly the issues that Kelley's configuration model attempts to describe – that is, the different mix, or configuration, of causes we consider relevant when explaining easy and difficult outcomes. If it is perceived as a difficult outcome, then more causes are expected to be necessary; if it is perceived as an easier outcome, then any one cause is probably perceived as sufficient.

Kelley's (1972) configuration model

As was noted above, Kelley did not consider his covariation model capable of describing how we typically or ordinarily go about making attributions, but, rather, how we *endeavour* to do so, given all of the necessary information. He argued that, in some cases, we might not have the information or the motivation to engage in the fully fledged process of causal attribution – for example, we might not know the details regarding the consensus, distinctiveness or consistency of the behaviour we are trying to explain. In these cases, we might use a far less precise tool that, none the less, gives us some sense of the overall shape or configuration of the causal factor or factors. Thus, Kelley's configuration model (see Figure 4.2) is about the way in which we look for a *broad* fit between the outcome we are trying to explain and the possible cause or causes that may have brought it about (we have a **causal schema**). In particular, Kelley distinguishes between rare, unusual, exceptional things that we are trying to explain and much more common occurrences – for those exceptional occurrences, a number of different contributory causes may have been *necessary*; for the commonplace occurrences, any one cause may have been *sufficient*.

The configuration model suggests that, in cases where we cannot (or do not want to) answer the questions concerning consensus, distinctiveness and consistency, then we might, instead, use our sense of the complexity or unusualness of the behaviour or outcome we are trying to explain to provide some rough blueprint regarding

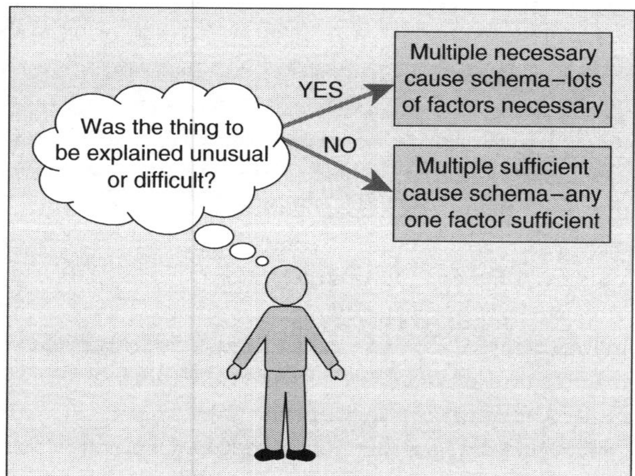

Figure 4.2 Kelley's (1972) configuration model

Causal schema Kelley (1972, p. 151) defined this as 'a general conception that a person has about how certain kinds of causes interact to produce a specific kind of effect.' It is the person's sense of what sort of causal arrangement might explain the thing that they are trying to explain.

the configuration of the causes. Where we perceive that the outcome to be explained is extremely rare or difficult, then we might infer multiple causes are *necessary* to bring it about (we have a **multiple necessary cause schema**). Imagine playing Andy Murray in a friendly tennis match and beating him. For this exceptional occurrence (unless you are an internationally renowned tennis player yourself), lots of factors must have been on your side – your game must have been at its best and Murray's at his worst and the surface, equipment, weather and, perhaps, even the umpire's decisions must have all been to your advantage. In other words, lots of causal factors would have been *necessary* for this amazing result to come about. Likewise, an unusual occurrence – such as our friend bursting into tears when challenged in a seminar – may be attributed to the nature of the challenge as well as stresses that our friend was experiencing at the time. In both these cases, more than one factor is necessary to allow the outcome to occur.

By contrast, where we perceive that the behaviour or outcome to be explained is commonplace, occurs regularly or is unsurprising, then we might infer that any one of several causes is *sufficient* to bring it about (we have a **multiple sufficient cause schema**). Thus, our victory in a tennis match with our seven-year-old nephew can be easily accounted for – our age, experience, strength or skill relative to his readily explains how we came to beat him. We don't need to start considering combinations of causes like we did when we imagined beating Andy Murray in a match. That is, it doesn't take much for this outcome to occur – any one factor is sufficient. Likewise, in the example used above, our jolly friend laughing at a great comedian can be explained by the personality of our friend or the quality of the comedian – that is, either is *sufficient* to cause the laughter.

Kelley's configuration model, then, suggests that an assessment of the difficulty and/or unusualness of the thing to be explained determines the sort of arrangement – or configuration – of causes that are anticipated. The more unusual or difficult the thing to be explained, the more causal factors are anticipated as necessary; the easier it is, the fewer causal factors are seen as being necessary.

Critical evaluation of Kelley's covariation and configuration models

Having outlined Kelley's covariation and configuration models in some detail, it is worth considering a number of criticisms that have been made. Some of the criticisms considered below – particularly those concerned with our everyday reasoning – set the scene for literature that addresses the idea of attribution bias, which is considered in the next section. Certain other criticisms – concerning experimental procedures, the internal–external distinction and the cognitive emphasis – remain an issue for much of the research that followed Kelley.

Attribution experiments differ from everyday causal reasoning

If you are a participant in a covariation experiment, life (at least as far as your causal reasoning needs are concerned) is very convenient – you are given the information (and nothing but the information) that you need to use the covariation model. In everyday life, by contrast, you rarely have just the relevant causal information you need and nothing else. When we're making attributions about people we know well, there may, in fact, be too much information to sift through, whereas when it's people we *don't* know well, there may be too little. In addition, in everyday life, the information that we have is not prepackaged in the dimensions of consensus, distinctiveness and consistency, these may be things we can calculate, but they are only presented to us already answered if we are taking part in an attribution experiment.

If the information confronting participants in an attribution experiment is so different from that which we encounter in everyday life, that we may have cause to doubt whether the experiments truly reveal processes which extend beyond the laboratory. That is, perhaps we do use the covariation model when we are presented with information about consensus, distinctiveness and consistency and nothing else, but, in the everyday world, the amount of information we have or its lack of fit with these dimensions may mean our attribution process is quite different.

Staying with the idea that attribution experiments are highly unusual situations, it is worth considering when – if ever – we do causal reasoning about hypothetical characters (such as our friend and the comedian) because we have been asked to by a stranger. It is likely that this would only occur in a test or in an experiment, whereas real reasoning situations may arise out of some context of sequences of interaction between people (this aspect of everyday explanation is discussed in detail in Chapter 5). No one asks me to start reasoning about the causes of abstract characters' behaviour in my everyday life, but I might well come to make causal judgements

Multiple necessary cause schema This is a schema in which many causes are anticipated as being needed to explain an unusual or difficult to achieve phenomenon.

Multiple sufficient cause schema This is a schema in which any one of a number of possible causes are anticipated as being adequate or sufficient to explain a regular or easy to achieve phenomenon.

or require causal explanations in some interaction with a partner who promised they would call and never did. Unhinged from any form of interactional context, it is possible to ask, should we expect participants' attribution behaviour in experimental settings to be consistent with everyday contextually located attribution behaviour?

Internal versus external causes

The idea that our causal reasoning is directed towards arriving at an internal or external cause is common not just to the work of Kelley but also much of the attribution bias work that followed although, as Box 4.3 suggests, some research has considered the importance of other dimensions, especially in relation to the consequences of attributions. This issue is addressed more thoroughly in the next section, but, for now, let us look at whether our causal reasoning is essentially complete when we arrive at either an internal or external attribution. You can test this by trying to think of something you or a friend have tried to find a cause for (relationship difficulty, low grade for an essay or behaviour of a close friend).

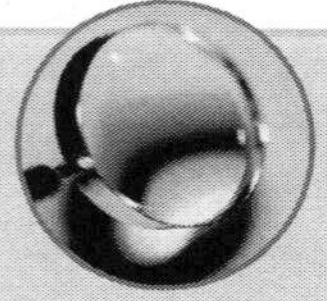

Box 4.3 FOCUS
Applications of attribution theory: attribution and relationship satisfaction

Some social psychologists are particularly interested in the ways in which people explain their partners' behaviour (especially their negative behaviour) as it may be related to how satisfying or distressing that relationship is. According to attribution research, the type or style of attribution matters. For example, whether we attribute what we perceive as their negative behaviour to something about them or their situation can reflect or even shape relationship satisfaction.

Some of the early work in this area focused on whether the attributions made were internal or external. Jacobson, McDonald, Follette and Berley (1985) suggested that where negative behaviour by one's partner, was attributed to the partner, it was associated with relationship distress, whereas, when it was attributed to external factors, it was associated with relationship satisfaction. Fincham, Beach and Nelson (1987), Fincham, Beach and Baucom (1987) and Fincham and O'Leary (1983) developed a more complex picture. They found that 'distressed couples' (who were in marital therapy) attributed hypothetical negative partner behaviour to not only *internal causes* but also more global ones (a cause or causes that will affect many areas of their relationship) than did non-distressed couples. The 'non-distressed' couples, by contrast, made internal, global attributions for hypothetical positive partner behaviour. Fincham (1985) found similar results (with 'distressed' couples attributing negative partner behaviour to internal and global causes) when hypotheticial negative behaviour was replaced with participants' recollections of real instances of negative partner behaviour.

Research in the field of attribution and intimate relationships has increasingly supplemented the internal–external dimension (and stable–unstable, controllable–uncontrollable and global–specific dimensions) with a measurement of responsibility attributions. Stander, Hsiung and MacDermid (2001) argued that couples in conflictual marriages make 'distress-maintaining' attributions. These 'distress-maintaining attributions' involve not only attributing negative partner behaviour to internal, stable and global causes (for example, attributing negative behaviour to internal character flaws rather than a 'bad day') but also seeing the partner as *responsible* (that is, they can be appropriately blamed or held to account) for the negative consequences of their actions.

Davey, Fincham, Beach and Brody (2001) also argue that responsibility attributions are crucial. For them, causal attributions affect marital outcomes, with responsibility attributions *mediating the effect*. Imagine a person dealing with the scenario in which their partner arrives home late from work. The attributed cause could be that they did not notice the time, but this same cause could be made sense of in quite different ways when we consider the attribution of responsibility. One (blaming) attribution of responsibility could be to assume that the partner did not notice the time because they only think about themselves. Another (exonerating) attribution of responsibility would be to assume that they did not notice the time because they were working hard to succeed for the benefit of both themselves and their partner. The responsibility attribution is linked to the causal attribution, but introduces highly blame-relevant issues of partners' intention and motivation for their behaviour. Partners who can be seen not only as bringing about negative behaviour and consequences but also *intending* to do so may be seen as much more blameworthy than those whose negative behaviour can be explained in terms of positive motivations or, at least, with a lack of malicious intent.

Box 4.3 continued

Fincham, Harold and Gano-Phillips' (2000) cross-lagged analyses suggested that there was a reciprocal causal influence between marital satisfaction and attribution for negative partner behaviour. That is, marital satisfaction at time 1 seemed to be associated with partner attributions 6 and 18 months later and partner attributions with marital satisfaction 6 and 18 months later. Those couples who had higher marital satisfaction at the beginning of the research not only made more positive partner attributions concurrently, they also were more positive 6 and 18 months afterwards. Likewise, those couples whose initial testing revealed more positive partner attributions were found to have greater marital satisfaction 6 and 18 months later. Fincham et al. thus argue that partner attributions can both *shape and be shaped by* marital satisfaction.

It is possible that just knowing whether the cause is in the person (internal) or the stimulus (external) is enough, but, quite likely, that we really want to know much more than that. Thus, perhaps the relationship difficulties are due to something about me, but I want to know what (is it my jealousy, untidiness or obsession with extra-terrestrial life forms?). Likewise, the low grade for the essay might be due to me, but is it my lack of effort or lack of ability? Furthermore (as is discussed later in this chapter), it may be that, in making attributions, we are often concerned with issues of intention and responsibility – who, if anyone, is *responsible* for a given outcome – rather than just causal locus.

It could be argued that Kelley was providing an outline of the first steps in our causal reasoning – that is, the covariation model might describe how we narrow the cause down to internal or external, after which we can get into identifying specific causes. If the identification of specific causes is our key concern, however, do we really engage in a causal reasoning process to identify the internal or external locus of the cause in the first instance?

Analysis of variance (ANOVA) as a description of everyday attributional reasoning

With the covariation model, Kenny (1985) notes, Kelley used ANOVA not just as a framework for himself, to investigate how variables covary with outcomes, but, rather, as a proposed description of how people think. That is, Kelley didn't just use ANOVA as a *researcher's* tool to analyse the combinations of causes that brought about an outcome to be explained but, rather, he argued that people in their everyday thinking undertake an analysis of variance *themselves*. For Kelley, then, we are all like scientists – for anything we seek to explain, we consider what it covaries with and from that we work out the causes or combinations of causes which have brought it about.

It is worth asking whether the covariation model has made some sort of presumption here that everyday causal thinking is akin to one particular version of 'scientific' thinking. Indeed, Kelley's covariation model is often described as presenting the everyday person (or 'lay' person) as a scientist (sometimes 'naïve scientist'). Subsequent research on attribution bias (considered in the next section) is one of the challenges to this image of lay person as scientist – it suggests that we do not ordinarily engage in such dispassionate and rigorous thinking as the covariation model suggests.

In fairness, as mentioned above, Kelley did see the covariation model as an idealised model, not descriptive of most everyday, informal attributions – but this does beg the question as to what the model attempted to describe and how it was felt this related to the world of everyday causal thinking. Furthermore, one might question whether scientists themselves are actually quite so dispassionate, logical and objective – that is, the very notion of scientific thinking as some form of objective, idealised version of thinking can itself be challenged (see Potter, 1996, for a useful summary of this work).

Analysis of the configuration model's ability to identify causes in all cases

Kelley's configuration model, at one level, addresses the concerns regarding whether an analysis of variance accurately describes our everyday causal reasoning – it suggests that we might, instead, opt for a simpler schematic sense of what causes (or combinations of causes) are necessary or sufficient to bring about the outcome to be explained. There is, however, something quite provisional about the reasoning process that it describes. If the identification of an internal or external locus for the cause lacks specificity, then this is perhaps even more the case for the configuration model, which identifies the broad shape of the causes (are many needed or are any sufficient) rather than their location.

To return to the thought experiment above, if we think of anything we have tried to explain, we might stumble across situations where we have considered that lots of causes must have been necessary or any would have been sufficient, but such considerations might not take us very far in working out the *specific* cause or causes. Kelley could counter-argue that, in those cases where multiple causes are sufficient or multiple causes are necessary, then identifying or selecting one *single* cause is either difficult or inaccurate. Where multiple causes are sufficient, then the outcome to be explained could have been brought about by any of a *range* of causes or causal combinations – it might be extremely difficult to pin down individual causes. Where multiple causes are necessary, then identifying *single* causes would be inaccurate as some combination is necessary – indeed, it might be that, rather than us having to decide between several possible causes, some combination of them would have been necessary to bring about the outcome to be explained.

In this way, Kelley's configuration model may have a particular relevance in certain extremes of outcomes to be explained – that is, extremely commonplace (multiple sufficient – MS – causes) and extremely unusual or difficult (multiple necessary – MN – causes). For all outcomes in between these extremes, however, – and, indeed, even for some cases that might attract a MS or MN configuration – we may want to identify the specific cause or causes at work. If this is the case, then the configuration model may not capture the actual process that we engage in when we seek to identify specific causes.

Subsequent work on bias

As mentioned above, Kelley's covariation model (and, to a lesser extent, his configuration model) depicted a rational process of causal calculation in which the lay person was (or at least had the potential to be) like a scientist sifting through the evidence in order to locate the cause of the outcome to be explained.

Even early empirical confirmations of Kelley's work, such as McArthur (1972), raised the issue that there could be deviations from this rational ideal – specifically, participants were thought to 'underutilise' consensus information. Indeed, much of the important work to emerge after Kelley's covariation model sought to identify various forms of biases that might interfere with the rational, objective analysis of causal evidence.

Cognitive entities or actions

As will be touched on elsewhere in this chapter (and developed more fully in Chapter 5) there is a debate concerning whether attributions (particularly attribution talk) are best thought of as cognitive entities occurring in our heads or actions in their own right. Imagine, for example, some of the types of attribution talk (or explanations) we might produce or hear in everyday situations. We may have to say why our essay was late, or why the house was such a mess or why we couldn't meet up last night. These examples of explanations *could* be approached as mere expressions of our underlying cognitive calculation of causes, but an alternative is to understand them as discursive or interactional *actions* – talk that *does* something. In the examples given here, the explanations might reduce the blame for (or exonerate) the speaker – for example, 'sorry I couldn't hand in my essay on time/tidy up/come to the film last night – I had a family emergency'. In this way, the emphasis on attributions as being about private thinking events can be challenged by a range of perspectives (account giving, discursive and conversation analytic) that leave to one side questions of possible thinking processes and emphasise the action of the explanatory talk itself.

Critical recap

Harold Kelley's covariation and configuration models

1 Experiments confirming Kelley's covariation model may be very unlike everyday contexts in which attributions are made and may, thus, lack external validity.

2 The internal–external distinction is treated as the central concern for perceivers making attributions. The distinction may be less meaningful and important than Kelley's covariation model has suggested.

3 While ANOVA is undoubtably an influential tool in psychological research, is it useful as a framework for understanding everyday thinking?

4 Kelley's configuration model addresses concerns about the complexity and rigour of a full covariation analysis, but it suggests that the attribution process may result in a relatively vague sense of the causal matrix that brought about the outcome to be explained.

5 The process of making attributions may entail more bias than either the covariation or the configuration models suggest.

6 Attributions could be reconstrued not as cognitive entities but rather as explanatory talk that does things (such as blame or exonerate) in interaction.

Reflective questions

1 *Have you ever carefully worked out whether the cause of someone's behaviour was within them or the situation?*

2 *If you have carefully worked out the location of a cause of someone's behaviour, was your process similar to that outlined by Kelley?*

4.3 Attribution biases

So far in this chapter the emphasis has been on causal reasoning as a largely rational process. Yet, even in the work we have covered so far (Heider, Ichheiser and Jones and Davis), there has been some indication that rational reasoning processes may not give the whole story. This idea that our reasoning deviates from following purely logical processes in working out causes is captured in the notion of **attribution bias**.

Below, some consideration is given to several of the most influential of these biases and some evaluative comments concerning each of them: the fundamental attribution error, actor–observer differences, self-biases and intergroup biases. It is worth noting that work on attribution biases should not be thought of as a single, unified theory. Research on each bias has tended to develop independently of others and, while there may be shared assumptions across the different attribution bias literatures, there are also some contradictions between them.

Box 4.4 TRY IT OUT
The fundamental attribution error

In order to think through the fundamental attribution error, it is worth considering everyday situations where it seems to be, at least potentially, present.

Think through a time when you were especially nervous about meeting someone for the first time – a situation in which you were worried about how you would come across.

Why were you particularly concerned about the possibility of making a bad impression in this situation?

As you reflect on this, you may consider the understanding that the idea of the FAE provides. Part of our concern in such situations may be that others (especially those who have limited prior information about our behaviour) might judge any negative aspects of our behaviour (awkwardness, faux pas, lack of humour) as reflecting our characteristics rather than as being brought about by the situation itself. That is, we may well fear that they will rush to make judgements about who we are as people based on how we come across in that situation.

The fundamental attribution error

One of the most influential ideas concerning attribution bias is the **fundamental attribution error** – called 'fundamental' because it has been thought of by some as influencing so much of our causal reasoning.

Crucial to the fundamental attribution error (FAE) is the distinction between causes that are thought of as being within the person (internal) and those seen as outside of the person (external, see Box 4.4). The idea of the 'fundamental attribution error' is that 'attributers' (anyone trying to make an attribution) tend to overestimate personal or dispositional factors and underestimate external or situational factors in explaining any given behaviour.

The term 'fundamental attribution error' is associated with Ross (1977), but captures a phenomenon identified by Heider (1944, 1958) and Ichheiser (1943a) and empirically demonstrated in a number of experiments – most notably Jones and Harris (1967).

In Jones and Harris' (1967) experiment, participants were required to rate the attitudes of speechwriters (how pro- or anti-Fidel Castro they were) by reading speeches that others had written. Half of the participants were told that the speechwriters had choice about whether they wrote a pro- or anti-Castro speech and the other half were told that they had no choice. In the choice condition, naturally participants judged that the authors of pro-Castro speeches must have pro-Castro attitudes, while the authors of the anti-Castro speeches must have anti-Castro attitudes. Interestingly, though, even in the no choice condition – where participants were told that the speechwriter was told to write either a pro- or an anti-Castro speech – participants still largely (though not quite as much as in the choice condition) judged the attitude of the speech's author on the basis of whether the speech was itself pro- or anti-Castro. It is as if the situational constraint of being told the type of speech to write was not fully taken into account and the presumption was made that the speech must at least partially reflect the true attitude of the speechwriter.

This illustration of the FAE is similar to those occasions when we might presume that, because an actor plays

Attribution bias Distortions or errors that occur in the process of making an attribution.

Fundamental attribution error A specific bias towards making attributions to internal causes – that is, causes thought to be 'within' the person whose behaviour (or experience) we are trying to explain. An example would be to attribute someone's examination failure to their lack of effort or ability (internal causes) rather than to the difficulty of the paper (an external cause).

a character with a certain disposition – perhaps warm, happy and cheerful – they will have these attributes in real life. Here – as in Jones and Harris' experiment – we may be underestimating situational constraints on behaviour – in this case, being required to act in a certain way.

In another experiment, Ross, Amabile and Steinmetz (1977) randomly assigned subjects to be either questioners (who were told to set difficult questions) or contestants (who were told to answer them), then required observers and contestants to rate how knowledgeable the questioners and contestants were. You may well be able to guess who came out best – the questioners. It is as if the situational factor – the questioner's massive advantage of being able to set difficult questions on an area of their own choice – was overlooked. Instead, the fact that the questioner knew the answers to their own questions better than the contestant was explained in terms of the personal qualities of each (in particular, that the questioner was more knowledgeable than the contestant).

The FAE, then, is a description of a pervasive tendency to overestimate personal and underestimate situational factors in making attributions (see Box 4.5). Accounts as to why this error may be present include cognitive, motivational and societal perspectives.

Cognitive explanations for the FAE emphasise information-processing constraints – that is, the ways in which our cognitive limitations may give rise to the error. One example of this is salience. We may, as Rholes and Pryor (1982) suggest, notice and focus on the person rather than the situation. A second example is what Peterson (1980) calls the 'dispositional shift' – we may emphasise dispositional factors more the longer we

Box 4.5 IN THE NEWS
Tragedy at Love Parade

On Saturday 24 July 2010 at the Love Parade music festival held in Duisburg, Germany, 19 people died (subsequently rising to 21) and more than 500 people were injured. The deaths and injuries occurred amid scenes of massive overcrowding, with over a million festivalgoers attending and access to the venue being restricted through a narrow tunnel, which, at one point, appears to have had its exit closed while festivalgoers were instructed to go back. In protests soon after this tragic incident, people held banners asking, 'Who is to blame?'

Source: Fredrik von Erichsen/DPA/Press Association Images

Festivalgoers seek to escape the crush at the Love Parade music festival in 2010, which claimed the lives of 21 people. Should this tragic event be understood in terms of features of the situation or the festivalgoers themselves?

Attempts by eyewitnesses, commentators and officials to explain this tragedy have varied somewhat in emphasis, but have frequently addressed the issue of 'Who is to blame?' Some accounts have emphasised the planning of the event – for example, choosing to hold it at a relatively small venue despite police warnings. Other explanations point to the errors made by police and security forces on the ground – closing the tunnel exit when it was already overcrowded, instructing festivalgoers to turn around and seemingly being unwilling – or unaware – of the need to help as the situation became more serious. Still others have referred to panic within the crowd.

A theme running through many of these attempts to explain the tragic events at Love Parade is the idea that someone or some people – whether the Mayor of Duisburg, police and security chiefs, those attempting to climb out of the crowd to safety or the festival organisers – should be held accountable.

The idea of the FAE is that seeking to blame people (which may or may not be appropriate in the tragic events at Duisburg) is a recurrent propensity – so much so that people will be inclined to find who can be blamed even when an 'objective appraisal of the evidence' points to the situation rather than the person.

leave it before making an attribution. In both cases, it is our own limitations in coping with the full spectrum of information available to us that leads us to tend to overemphasise dispositional information at the expense of situational information.

An alternative explanation for the FAE is provided by Lerner (1980). Lerner's account for the FAE emphasises that we are motivated to hold certain beliefs – particularly about who is to blame when bad things happen to people. For Lerner, there is a pervasive preference in most societies for believing individuals are to blame for the bad things that befall them. Put in motivational terms, we are motivated to make attributions that support the idea of a just world – where we can avoid bad things happening to us by not making the same mistakes (or being the same people) as those who have bad experiences. Thus, if someone has a serious medical condition – such as AIDS or cancer – we may take some (misplaced) comfort from attributing their condition to something to do with them (such as their physiology, genes, lifestyle, diet or habits) because then we can see that it may be less likely to happen to us or at least more under our control. Given that attributions are conventionally understood to be occasioned more by 'bad' than 'good' outcomes, the belief in a just world may mean many of attributions for negative outcomes result in dispositional factors being identified as causes.

A further account for the FAE suggests that it may reflect cultural beliefs. Nisbett and Ross (1980, p. 31) picked up on possible cultural influences linking the FAE to 'the world view of the so-called Protestant ethic'. Some cross-cultural research has suggested that the FAE is either not present or less markedly so in other (particularly Eastern) cultures. Also, Miller (1984) contrasted a sample of US schoolchildren with Hindu Indian children. In the US sample, the older the child was, the more they reported *dispositional* factors as accounting for hypothetical events. In the Indian sample, the older the child was, the more they emphasised *situational* causes for the same hypothetical events. This research suggests – in common with Lerner – that beliefs may give rise to the FAE and further indicates that these beliefs and the extent to which they support the FAE will vary across cultures.

Criticisms of the FAE

In thinking critically about the FAE it is worth considering not just problems inherent in the original model but also how it has been understood in subsequent work. First, as Hewstone (1989) notes, Ross (1977) referred to the overestimation of dispositional causes and the underestimation of situational ones, *not a complete elimination of situational factors in favour of dispositional ones.* Some subsequent work, however, has tended to treat the error as being an absolute category shift from situational to dispositional – thereby losing something of the subtlety of the original formulation, which allowed for differences in the emphasis placed on dispositional and situational factors.

A further criticism concerns the demand characteristics of some of the key experiments – certain features of the experiments may themselves account for much of the phenomenon observed. Hewstone (1989) drawing on Funder (1987) and Block and Funder (1986) notes that participants in experiments such as Jones and Harris (1967) might be quite sensibly presuming that the sentiments expressed in the speech about Castro are supposed to be treated as being of some use in calculating the attitudes of the author of the speech. That is, the experiment itself may set up an expectation that participants should always use sentiments expressed in the speech to inform their judgements – the alternative would be to take the somewhat self-assured stance of treating this information as irrelevant for the condition where participants were informed that the author of the essay had no choice. In these unusual experimental conditions, where participants need to make a judgement on an issue for which, logically, there is no discriminating information, participants may well feel that they are required to make use of any indicators, however flawed.

The cross-cultural research referred to above not only suggests possible explanations for the FAE (in terms of cultural beliefs), it also questions just how *fundamental* it is. That is, if the FAE is understood as reflecting beliefs specific to particular (Western) societies, then it may be far less universal than some have taken it to be. Choi, Nisbett and Norenzayan (1999) argue that the FAE (in which people make an erroneous attribution to person dispositions) is a subset of a more general preference for internal attributions (or 'correspondence bias'). For Choi et al., both the FAE and the more general correspondence bias are not universal but culturally relative. Participants in certain cultures (particularly East Asian cultures such as China and Korea, but, potentially, including Hispanic cultures such as Puerto Rico) were found to be less likely to show a bias towards internal attributions for behaviour than European Americans. Choi et al. (1999, p. 47) argue that the cultural difference is not due to an 'absence of dispositional thinking' on the part of East Asians, but, rather, 'a stronger "situationism" or belief in the importance of the context of behavior in east Asia'. Such cultural data raises the issue that some psychologists may be guilty of ethnocentric thinking, which presumes phenomena that appear to be present in their own culture apply universally across all cultures.

In the light of cross-cultural research that questions the universality of the FAE, some researchers have suggested that the error be reconstrued. Menon, Morris, Chiu and Hong (1999) investigated attributions made by East Asians (Japanese and Chinese) and North Americans in newspapers and hypothetical vignette studies (where participants imagined a specific event occurring) across three studies. In all three studies, while North Americans showed a preference for making attributions to individuals (thereby being consistent with the FAE), East Asians showed a preference for attributions to collectives (or groups of people).

For Menon et al. (1999), these findings may lead to a modification rather than rejection of the idea of the FAE. They suggest that, rather than there being a pervasive tendency to make attributions to stable properties of the actor, there may be a pervasive tendency to make attributions to *stable properties,* the details of which are informed by culturally shaped theories of agency. Thus, in certain Western contexts, the *dispositions of the person* may be perceived as the stable property whereas, in certain Eastern societies, the *properties of the situation or groups in which the individual actor is found* may be perceived as stable. For each culture, then, the universal or pervasive bias is to make an attribution to those factors that are perceived as stable – even though what these are will vary from culture to culture.

Finally, research on the FAE shares with research on causal reasoning considered above an emphasis on the internal/external dichotomy and attributions as cognitive entities rather than resources used in talk in interaction that do things (such as blame and exonerate).

Critical recap

The fundamental attribution error

1 Some research has paid little attention to Ross' (1977) reference to the FAE being about the *overestimation* of dispositional causes and the *underestimation* of situational ones. Instead, some research has treated the FAE as suggesting that there is an absolute replacement of situational causes with dispositional ones.

2 To some extent, many of the experiments reporting the FAE may have been measuring demand characteristics. That is, features specific to the experimental setting may have led participants to presume that they should respond in a particular (bias-exhibiting) way.

3 Cross-cultural research raises the question as to just how universal or fundamental the FAE is. It also raises the possibility that the dispositional bias identified in the FAE is really a subset of a bias for stable attributions. That is, there may be a bias towards making attributions to causes that are believed to be stable, but what is believed to be stable (that is, a person, group or situation) will vary across cultures.

4 The emphasis on attribution as a purely cognitive phenomenon can be questioned by approaches that pay attention to what attribution talk can be found to do in interaction.

Reflective questions

1 *Think of a recent item of news that focused on any aspect of human behaviour. What explanation for this behaviour do you have?*

2 *Do you think that you tend to make more internal or external attributions? Why do you think you come up with the sorts of attributions that you do?*

Actor–observer differences

As the outline above illustrates, the FAE error identifies a dispositional bias thought to be prevalent in attributions generally, the reach of this claim being questioned by cross-cultural research (among other criticisms). The idea of **actor–observer difference** (sometimes called the self–other difference) is that we do indeed have a tendency to emphasise internal causes, but only when we are accounting for the behaviour of others – a different bias is present when we are making sense of our own behaviour. That is, according to the actor–observer difference, we explain our own actions in terms of the external causes – such as aspects of the situation in which we found ourselves at the time – while we explain those of others by reference to internal, dispositional factors (see Figure 4.3).

Actor–observer difference The idea that people explain the causes of their own behaviour in a different way from the behaviour of others. Specifically, the concept of actor–observer difference suggests that I will tend to attribute my behaviour or experiences to external or situational causes, whereas I will attribute the behaviour or experiences of others to internal factors. Imagine seeing someone trip as they walk along a pavement. We may be quick to attribute their stumbling to carelessness, yet if *we* trip, we may well attribute it to the pavement being uneven.

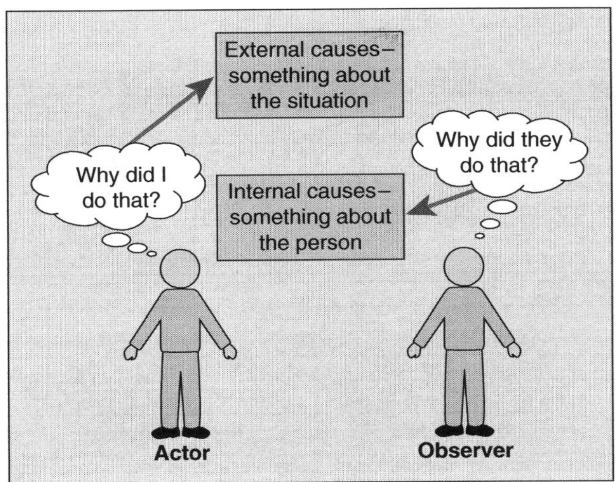

Figure 4.3 The actor–observer difference

The actor–observer difference suggests that the person doing the behaviour to be explained (the actor) is biased to external (within the situation) causes, while an onlooker (observer) is biased towards internal (within the actor) causes.

Have you ever had a situation like this. I once got up from a meal in a restaurant and belatedly noticed that my jacket had knocked over a friend's camera, which fell to the floor and broke. Should the cause of the broken camera be attributed to my clumsiness or my friend's choice of placing it on a small ledge behind me? What is important is not the objective 'truth' of the cause, but, rather, the different explanations that I (the actor) and others (observers) who observe my behaviour will give. According to actor–observer theory, I will explain this outcome in terms of where the camera was placed (on such a tiny ledge) or any other feature of the situation (the person who talked to me as I stood up, the cramped layout of the restaurant and so on), whereas my friend, his partner (who owned the camera) and everyone else in the restaurant will attribute the outcome to my clumsiness.

One explanation for actor–observer differences is in terms of the different amount of information we have about our own behaviour and that of others (Nisbett Caputo, Legant and Maracek, 1973). Imagine being in an interview situation and finding yourself tongue-tied. We know how articulate we normally are and can see the situation as bringing about this lack of verbal fluency. For the interviewers, however, it is possible that this is pretty much all they have to judge us on, so they may be more likely to attribute our lack of fluency to some dispositional factor within us. It is possible to imagine this judgement changing if someone were to get to know us and see our behaviour across a range of settings. Indeed, according to Nisbett et al. (1973) greater knowledge of another is associated with an increase in situational attributions for their behaviour.

An alternative account for the actor–observer difference is it is our perceptual focus that is important – put simply, we blame (or attribute to) what we see. Actors see the situation (and, rarely, themselves), while the visual field of observers may well be dominated by the other person (the actor). To return to the interview situation, I see the intimidating panel of people looking solemnly at me across the table as I try to speak. In simple perceptual terms, the situation is far more salient for me (the actor whose awkwardness we are trying to explain) than it is for the interview panel, but, while I am unseen by myself, I am very visible to others gazing at me. This possibility was investigated in a series of experiments by Storms (1973); (see Box 4.6).

As Box 4.6 illustrates, Storms' experiments suggested that, to some extent, introducing a new visual perspective could have an impact on the attributions that actors and observers make. Imagine having a romantic encounter via a Web cam and finding yourself running out of things to say, trying to be humorous but finding that your repertoire of 'knock, knock' jokes gets nothing but a bored and disapproving response. The findings of Storms suggest that the basic bias in which actors emphasise situational causes more than observers is due to the visual perspective. In this case, I see the person I am trying to impress giving monosyllabic responses to everything I say and they see someone fumbling incoherently before launching into a series of jokes designed for 10-year-old children. If my Web contact was to see how *they* appeared during the interaction, then, according to Storms, they would place an increased emphasis on situational explanations for my behaviour (specifically, seeing themselves, they may realise that they played an important part in my fumbling.

The notion that we blame or make attributions to what we see is simple and makes intuitive sense, but it is worth considering two issues. First, the results of Storms' experiments are not quite as straightforward as is sometimes suggested – *all* participants rated dispositional factors as the most important; it didn't matter whether they were actors or observers or whether they had experienced visual reorientation or not. So, if we were hoping that visual reorientation could radically reverse causal thinking, we might be disappointed. What the reorientation does do is result in a *changed emphasis* on situational causes – seeing a different visual perspective makes actors rate situational causes as having lower importance and

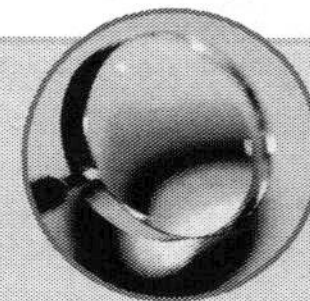

Box 4.6 FOCUS
The experimental procedure used by Storms (1973)

Storms' research process involved the following steps.

1 Two participants, who were strangers, were filmed as they talked with each other for five minutes.

2 The participants then had to rate the behaviour (in terms of friendliness, talkativeness, nervousness and dominance) of themselves and their conversational partner. They were next required to make an attribution regarding the extent to which this behaviour was due to personal characteristics (defined as personality, traits, character, personal style, attitudes, mood) or characteristics of the situation (being in an experiment, the 'getting acquainted' situation, the topic of conversation, the way the other participant behaved).

3 Two observers who were not involved in the interaction also rated the behaviour of a prespecified target actor and were asked to make an attribution concerning the causes of that person's behaviour.

4 In a further condition, Storms changed the visual perspective of actors and observers. Prior to making an attribution for their own behaviour, participants were shown a videotape of themselves.

5 Observers of the interaction who had been told to watch one of the two participants in the conversation were now shown a videotape of the other person in the conversation (the one with whom their target person had been told to interact).

6 This amounted to a visual reorientation as the actors got to see themselves prior to making an attribution and the observers, who were told to watch and rate a specific actor, now saw an aspect of the actor's situation – that is, the person with whom their actor was interacting.

Storms found the following:

1 In the baseline (non-video) condition, people tended to explain their own behaviour with more emphasis on situational factors (such as the other person, the setting and so on), whereas observers explained their target's behaviour with more emphasis on internal, dispositional features of that person.

2 Storms also found that his visual reorientation (showing people a videotape of themselves or someone whom they had not been watching) changed those attributions. Actors having seen a videotape of themselves gave (slightly) increased dispositional attributions and decreased situational attributions (when compared to those not seeing the videotape). Observers being shown the situation of their target actor rated dispositional factors as less important and situational factors as more important than those observers who were *not* shown the videotape of the person with whom their actor was interacting.

Storms concluded that the videotape provided a visual reorientation – showing people a visual perspective they would not ordinarily, see. Ordinarily, actors do not see themselves and, if they are shown film of themselves, then they attribute their behaviour (slightly more) to aspects of themselves and emphasise the situation less. Observers focusing on one actor do not ordinarily see too, much of the other actor, so, if they are shown film of the other, then they make more of a situational and less of a dispositional attribution. In very crude terms, it is as if, according to Storms, we blame – or attribute to – that which we see.

observers rate them as having higher importance than those who do not experience visual reorientation.

Second, it is worth considering just how well Storms' findings account for aspects of our everyday experience. Brown (1986, p. 188) provides a specific illustration of his thinking about Storms: 'I keep trying to check its findings against my own experience. There is one sort of experience in which the findings of the experiment seem to point to the wrong conclusion, and that is what happens at the movies.' Brown notes that when we watch films, we often find that we have a visual perspective dominated by a character who is a victim. Putting aside for a moment the idea that films may differ from real life or even social psychological experiments, according to Storms (1973), visual perspective is the important factor. Indeed, Storms (1973, p. 170) suggests, 'Under some circumstances actual role as actor or observer is unimportant, and visual orientation is totally determinative of attributions.' We would expect, therefore, that, seeing the victim onscreen, we might be inclined to have a decreased situational account for their misfortune. As Brown notes, however, rather than deemphasising situational causes of the victims' plight, we rely very much on them – attributing the suffering that the victim experiences to their situation, particularly the other characters they encounter, even though these others may have far less screentime and be less visually salient. For Brown (1986), the crucial factor is not *visual* perspective but *psychological* perspective – precisely the issue addressed by Regan and Totten (1975).

Dennis Regan and Judith Totten (1975) – empathic attribution

Like Storms, Regan and Totten (1975) were concerned with how observers might make biased attributions, but their experiment suggested that visual perspective was not enough. Instead, for them, it is not just *what we see* that affects what we blame – or how we attribute – but also *where our empathy lies*. If we empathise with the person whose behaviour we are trying to explain, we will explain their behaviour differently from those cases where we do not empathise – we will make an **empathic attribution**.

In Regan and Totten's experiment, participants were asked to watch a video of two women in a 'getting acquainted' conversation. Some participants (the 'observer set') were instructed to 'pay close attention to all aspects of the target's behaviour, to watch what she did and listen to her conversation, carefully observing all aspects of her behaviour' (Regan & Totten, 1975, p. 853). Others (the 'empathetic set') were not given any specific directions about where to look (although the target person was more visually salient in all conditions), but were, instead, given the following instruction: 'While you are watching this "get-acquainted" conversation, please try to empathize with Margaret, the girl on the left side of the screen. Imagine how Margaret feels as she engages in the conversation. While you are watching the tape, picture to yourself just how she feels in the situation. You are to concentrate on the way she feels while conversing. Think about her reaction to the information she is receiving from the conversation. In your mind's eye, you are to visualize how it feels to Margaret to be in this conversation. After the tape is over, you will be asked about Margaret's behaviour.' (Regan & Totten, 1975, pp. 852–853). All participants were then required to rate the behaviour and the importance of personal and situational characteristics in causing it in just the same way as participants in Storms (1973) discussed above.

Regan and Totten found that those participants who received the empathetic orientation instructions were more likely to provide situational attributions and less likely to provide dispositional attributions than those who merely received the observation instructions. The effect of empathetic instructions was such that, while mere 'observers' rated dispositional factors as more important than situational factors, for 'empathisers', this was *reversed*, with situational factors being rated more important than dispositional factors.

Source: Rex Features

Rodney King being attacked by the LAPD while on the ground. Were attribution biases at work when the first jury acquitted the officers involved?

These findings suggest that empathetic observers make attributions similar to those of the actors themselves – that is, to some factor within the situation in which the actors find themselves. Regan and Totten saw their results as confirming Jones and Nisbett's information-processing perspective, empathetic *processing* (rather than any different information) being crucial in shaping the type of attributions that observers make. Regan and Totten further note that Jones and Nisbett (1972) had speculated observer empathy could lead to their attributions being similar to those of actors themselves – a remarkably accurate summary of what Regan and Totten subsequently found.

On 3 March 1991, a bystander videotaped Rodney King (see photo above – he is pictured on the ground) being severely beaten by members of the LA Police Department. In their first trial in 1992, the police officers were acquitted (though they were subsequently found guilty at a federal trial for civil rights violations).

Regan and Totten's research may have some relevance to aspects of the Rodney King *v.* LA Police Department case of 1992. In April 1992, four members of the LA Police Department were acquitted of beating Rodney King. What was surprising about this decision was that the incident had been recorded in detail on a

> **Empathic attribution** This is the idea that if we feel empathy for another person, our attributions for their behaviour will be different. Specifically, we will make more external or situational attributions (meaning that our attributions for their behaviour take a similar form to what the actor–observer difference bias suggests is typical of our attributions for our own behaviour).

camcorder – the film clearly showing that King received 15 baton blows and approximately 41 kicks while lying on the ground. King's injuries included a damaged leg and a fractured skull.

Many factors could be considered to have brought about this unexpected verdict by the jury – not least that the case was moved by the LAPD defence lawyers to Simi Valley, a white middle-class community, and the final jury contained no black members at all. Some of the language used by defence attorneys within the trial, however, has a resonance with the empathetic manipulation of ideas of Regan and Totten, emphasising the feelings of the police officers over the evidence of the videotape: 'These are not Rob cops, ladies and gentlemen, they hurt, they feel pain, they bleed and they die just like everyone else ... You can play the video all you want. Backwards, forwards, slow motion – it'll be available for you as a piece of evidence. I've seen it enough and I think you have, too' (from defence attorney Michael Stone's summation). These 'instructions' from the defence counsel to jurors (along with others urging them to view the incident not through the eyes of the camera but through the eyes of the police officers who were at the scene) could be seen as similar to the empathetic instructions that were used for participants who were about to watch a video in Regan and Totten's research.

In both cases, video viewers were given instructions for viewing that involved visualising how things seemed to the target actor on the film. For Regan and Totten, this resulted in situational accounts for the actor's behaviour and, in the LAPD trial, while attribution was not measured, the jury's not guilty verdict, which exonerated the LAPD, was certainly consistent with a *situational* rather than dispositional account on the part of jurors.

Criticisms of actor–observer differences

Much of the research reviewed has emphasised possible causes of the actor–observer difference, but, as Watson (1982) notes, the effect is perhaps best thought of as self–other (or actor–observer) differences in *situational attribution*, with smaller, if any, effects in dispositional attributions. That is, the actor (self) will tend to place greater emphasis or importance on just the situational causes of their behaviour compared to observers (others). Conceptualising the effect in these terms makes it somewhat less of a radical bias that completely reverses 'normal' causal reasoning.

Regan and Totten's empathetic instructions did seem to result in some reversal in causal reasoning (albeit at a relatively modest level of statistical significance), but there could be reasons for caution in thinking about what brought about these results. It is possible that the experiment may have had certain demand characteristics – that is, the participants receiving the empathetic set of instructions were told to, 'Imagine how Margaret feels as she engages in the conversation. While you are watching the tape, picture to yourself just how she feels in the situation. You are to concentrate on the way she feels while conversing. Think about her reaction to the information she is receiving from the conversation'.

Immediately after the empathising instructions, participants were told that they would be asked questions afterwards. It could be that it was the participants' endeavours to be good participants that led them to make situational attributions for Margaret's behaviour – that is, making situational attributions may be the logical way of demonstrating that you really have followed the instructions. If this is the case, it is a much more 'experiment-specific' effect that has been found and it has little to do with the activation of some generic form of empathetic processing (of the sort we might expect to be available for activation in non-experimental settings).

A more radical challenge comes from Malle, Knobe and Nelson (2007). Malle et al. note that a meta-analysis of 173 studies in 113 articles yielded very low effect sizes (−0.015–0.095). First, Malle et al. noted that the presence or absence of any actor–observer difference varied across the studies reviewed. Some of the variance was methodological – for example, the bias was evidenced more frequently in studies where free response explanations were used (where participants communicated what they thought the cause was) rather than rating scales (where participants were asked to complete scales that rated the internality and externality of the cause). The bias was more evidenced where participants were asked to produce free response explanations for known others rather than strangers. Furthermore, the meta-analysis revealed that the actor–observer difference was only present for negative outcomes and not just absent but actually *reversed* if positive outcomes were being explained. Thus, we are more likely to explain our own success in terms of internal causes and others' by reference to external causes (see under Self-serving bias below).

Malle et al.'s critique goes further than raising questions about effect size and methodology – it questions the framework for thinking about actor–observer difference itself. They offer an alternative to the actor–observer model of attribution, namely the *folk–conceptual* theory of explanation. Malle et al. (2007, p. 495) note that the traditional actor–observer literature would class '[I/she] yelled at him because .. he broke the window.' and '[I/she] yelled at him because .. it was so hot' as both being situational attributions. By contrast, the folk–conceptual theory argues that it is important to distinguish *reason explanations* (which refer to or imply beliefs and desires) from *causal history explanations* (which refer to what brought the outcome about, but not the reasoning, planning or choice of the person). Explaining yelling 'because (we believe) someone has broken something' versus 'because of the heat', while both 'situational' in the classic actor–observer framework are conceptually distinct in folk-conceptual theory. For Malle et al., it is this difference – between *reason explanations* and *causal history explanations* – that is fundamental to the actor–observer difference. Malle et al. argue that, in explaining our own behaviour (actor's self-attributions), we use more reasons and fewer causal history explanations than we do when explaining the behaviour of others (observer attributions). In this way, Malle et al.'s *folk-conceptual* theory replaces the actor–observer model's emphasis on internal versus external causal attributions with a framework that distinguishes intentional reasons, plans and choices from unintentional occurrences.

Critical recap

Actor–observer differences

1 The actor–observer difference may be less radical than it may at first appear. That is, it could be thought of as suggesting that, in attributions concerning our own behaviour, we place more emphasis on situational causes than on our attributions for the behaviour of others.

2 Regan and Totten's (1975) findings could be explained in terms of the demand characteristics of their experiments.

3 Meta-analyses (Malle et al., 2007) suggest that the findings are far from robust and vary considerably according to the specific methodology employed.

4 Malle et al. (2007) provide an alternative account for self–other attributions, which replaces the internal–external distinction of traditional actor–observer difference theory with a reason–causal history one.

Reflective questions

1. *Have you ever had a situation where you performed badly at something and felt others who saw this did not take account of the difficult situation that may have led to this outcome?*
2. *Have there been times when you have interpreted someone else's behaviour in terms of external rather than internal causes?*

Self-biases

The biases that we have examined so far – FAE, actor–observer difference and empathic bias – have looked at biases as having a uniform effect, acting in the same way whatever the outcome we are trying to explain might be. The self-biases develop a different approach. Rather than suggesting that we will always make a certain type of attribution for our own behaviour, they suggest our attributions will vary depending on whether we are trying to explain our successes or failures.

Self-serving bias

The most well-known 'self-bias' is the **self-serving bias** (see Figure 4.4). This bias gets at the idea that our attributions about our successes may differ from our attributions about our failures. With self-serving and other self-biases, one crucial question is asked of the thing to be explained – is it a success or a failure? At its simplest, the self-serving bias suggests that people generally attribute their successes to internal dispositional characteristics (their skills, qualities and effort) and their failures to situational factors (other people, the setting).

Some very clear examples of this bias can be found in the talk of politicians. It is no surprise, therefore, that an early illustration of this by Kingdon (1967) drew on the talk of US politicians. Kingdon interviewed successful and unsuccessful politicians five months after various elections, asking them to summarise what led to their success or failure. Dispositional factors such as hard

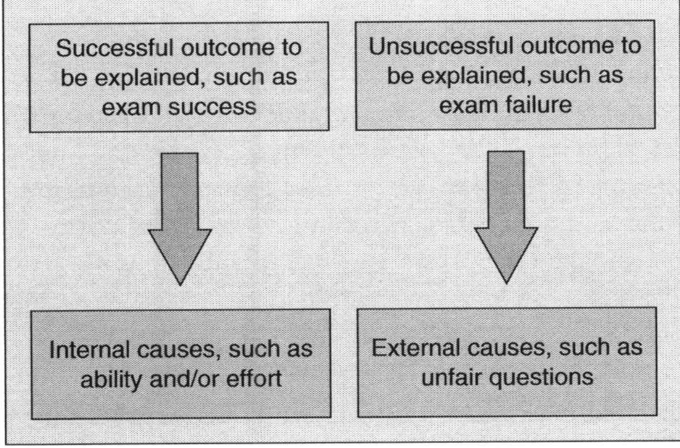

Figure 4.4 The self-serving attribution bias

Self-serving bias A distortion in the attribution process affecting our attributions for our own behaviour and experiences. The self-serving bias suggests that we will tend to explain our successes in terms of internal causes (such as attributing our exam success to our ability and effort) and our failures in terms of external factors (attributing our exam failure to difficulty of the paper or the external stresses in our life, for example).

work, personal service and their own building of a reputation featured as important reasons given by successful politicians. For unsuccessful politicians, aspects of their opponents, lack of money and national and state trends were cited among the important causes of their failure.

There has been some debate concerning whether the self-serving bias should be thought of as containing both a self-protecting bias (attributing my failures to external factors) and a self-enhancing bias (attributing my successes to internal factors). Some researchers (Miller & Ross, 1975) have suggested that there is support only for the self-enhancing bias and this bias can be explained as a consequence of cognitive factors (for example, we plan, seek and perhaps even expect success and, when we achieve it, we are more likely to attribute the fruition of our plans to factors within our self than if the outcome was unplanned, unsought and unexpected). Others, such as Zuckerman (1979), have suggested that there is a self-protecting bias as well as the self-enhancing bias. Zuckerman further suggests, rather than merely being a consequence of the sort of cognitive factors outlined above, that there are important motivational reasons for the self-serving bias – that is, we are motivated to maintain our self-esteem by the attributions for success and failure we make. Yet, those suggesting that cognitive and motivational accounts are somehow mutually exclusive may, as Hewstone (1989) suggests, be misguided as, first, both processes may be present in attribution bias and, second, the processes may be, to some extent, interdependent (with each process containing elements of the other).

Mezulis, Abramson, Hyde and Hankin (2004) conducted a meta-analysis of 266 studies that addressed the issue of self-serving bias. They found the average *d* was 0.96 – indicating a large bias that was present in 'nearly all samples'. While Mezulis et al. confirmed the importance of a self-serving bias, they found there was some variation for the bias according to the age, culture and psychopathology of participants. Thus, the bias was more markedly present for children (8–11 years) and older adults (over 55 years) than for other age ranges. It was more present among US samples, than Western samples generally and least present among Asian samples – a finding that suggests the bias may be linked to beliefs, ideologies and practices among different cultures and subcultures. Finally, samples of studies involving participants with psychopathology were found to have a less marked bias than samples without psychopathology. Further details on these results reveal that the bias is particularly attenuated where the specific psychopathology is depression – a finding that echoes earlier work on the attributional style questionnaire detailed below.

The 'attributional style questionnaire' (ASQ), (Peterson Semmel, von Baeyer, Abramson, Metalsky and Seligman, (1982) seeks to identify relatively persistent patterns of causal reasoning that are understood as characteristic of individual personality. These styles of attribution include biases that are 'self-serving' as well as ones that may reflect a negative self-concept – such as a **depressive attributional style**. The ASQ focuses in particular on how people explain unpleasant or aversive events.

For each hypothetical event, participants are asked to rate the cause using a seven-point scale. Thus, the cause is rated as internal (totally due to me) or external (totally due to other people or circumstances), stable (will always be present) or unstable (will never be present again) and global (influences all situations in my life) or specific (influences just this particular situation). Someone with a self-serving bias might attribute aversive events to a cause or causes that are external to themselves and may further rate these causes as unstable and specific (and, therefore, unlikely to have much impact on their life in general). Someone with a depressive attributional style, by contrast, may still have a bias in their attribution, but this may be reflected in making attributions for aversive events to internal, stable and global causes. Thus, if the stimulus item is 'you have looked for a job but have not found one', while someone with a self-serving bias might attribute their hypothetical lack of success to temporary problems in that area of employment, someone with a depressive attributional style may attribute it to their own lack of ability.

It is easy to see how attributional style has been thought of as a mechanism for perpetuating our self-concept – that if we blame temporary circumstances for our misfortune, then our sense of self-worth need not be diminished, but if we blame ourselves, then our attribution has reinforced a negative self-concept.

Work on attributional style has usefully extended the notion of self-serving bias to consider that it is possible to have biases related to self-concept that might not be self-serving. Furthermore, the work has drawn on dimensions of causality that include how stable and global they are perceived to be as well as how internal and external – an issue that is discussed in more detail below. As Hewstone notes, however, some research (Cutrona, Russell, & Jones, 1985) has suggested that there may be very little consistency in attributional style across situations – that is, its value as a relatively stable personality characteristic

Depressive attribution style The inverse of the self-serving bias. A bias in which people making an attribution blame themselves for negative outcomes and credit others (or situational factors) for positive ones.

has been challenged. Furthermore, the ASQ instrument itself may be criticised for focusing on attributions for *hypothetical* events – that is, I may be asked to make attributions for events that I have never experienced or I do not ever envisage experiencing.

Taken together, work on the self-serving bias and attributional style has usefully identified that our attributions may be influenced by aspects related to our self-perception. One way of conceptualising this is provided by the idea of schema (Fiske & Taylor, 1984, 1991). Schemas are understood as structures of information (and misinformation) that we have about any feature of our social world, including ourselves and other people. Stereotypes are but one type of schema (as Chapter 7 suggests, they are a rigid form of role schema). Our attributions about ourselves may be consistent with our schema. So, if we have a positive self-schema, then we may make attributions consistent with the self-serving bias, such as attributing successes to internal, stable and global causes and blame to external, unstable and specific causes. If we have a negative self-schema, then our attributions may be reversed – that is, we might attribute our successes to external, unstable and specific causes and our failures to internal, stable and global causes.

Critical evaluation of self-serving bias

The self-serving bias, while largely supported by meta-analyses (Mezulis et al., 2004) may not adequately account for significant discrepancies – most notably (but not exclusively), those who are depressed show a reversal of the bias. Work on the ASQ and self-schema allows for the idea that people can have different types of self-bias, not all of which are 'self-serving'.

In addition to the issue of individual differences in attributional style, cross-cultural differences in the extent of the self-serving bias have been identified. Mezulis et al. (2004) note that the self-serving bias is far more prevalent among US samples (and, to a lesser extent, Western participants generally) than it is among Asian samples. This raises the issue that the self-serving bias may not only be a matter on which there is some individual difference but also on which there is cross-cultural variation. The idea that we attribute our successes to ourselves and our failures to others or situations may, then, reflect a specific cultural perspective rather than a universal feature of our attribution process.

Problems with the internal–external distinction that has been referred to throughout this chapter have a particular resonance with regard to the self-serving bias. According to the self-serving bias, we will attribute our successes to internal causes and our failures to external ones, yet some internal factors are far more self-serving than others. Thus, attributing my exam success to my ability is more self-enhancing than if I attribute it to having made a lucky choice of topics to revise. Likewise, attributing my failure to a temporary illness is far more ego protective than attributing it to my lack of ability. In all cases, internal attributions have been made, but the category 'internal' is too crude to identify what type of attribution would actually be self-serving for success or failure.

Finally, the lack of attention to the action that attributions can accomplish in talk is again particularly apparent with regard to the self-serving bias. Self-serving attribution talk can be seen as accomplishing clearly identifiable interactional work, such as exonerating the speaker and blaming others. If, for example, I attribute my relationship failure to factors that I am not responsible for – such as characteristics of my former partner – then my talk exonerates myself and blames my former partner. Thus, rather than just conceptualising cognitive and motivational causes for an inner mental bias, the self-serving bias can be seen as something that is regularly done in talk itself. As will be discussed in Chapter 5, approaching attributions about self as an interactional phenomenon may enable a more subtle understanding of the ways in which actions such as exoneration or blame are accomplished within specific sequences of interaction.

Critical recap

Self-biases

1 There may be variations in the self-serving bias across individuals (for example, depressed people may exhibit a self-defeating bias) and cultures (for example, the bias may be much stronger in US rather than Asian samples).

2 The internal–external distinction may be too crude to identify the types of attribution that would be self-serving.

3 The self-serving bias provides a clear case where it seems sensible to focus on attribution talk and what that talk *does*, rather than inner mental activity.

Reflective questions

1 *Can you think of one person you know who exhibits the self-serving bias and one who shows a much more self-critical way of making attributions for their successes and failures?*

2 *Have you ever noticed people seemingly not take full credit for their successes in conversations? How do you make sense of this?*

Intergroup biases

So far, two of the main biases considered (the actor–observer bias and the self-serving bias) have suggested that our attributions will be biased by *who* it is that we are making an attribution about – specifically, if they are self or other. **Intergroup bias** (see Figure 4.5) takes this idea much further and considers that our perception of the identity of the person or people about whom we are making an attribution can bias our processing. Specifically, it concerns the way in which our sense of the *group* that the person (or people) belong to can shape our attributions.

Imagine a scene after a football match in which both sets of fans talk about the game. It is quite likely that each group of fans will be more predisposed to praise their own team than the opposing team. In those instances where the fans make attributions regarding the successes of the rival team, these might well be explained away (by poor refereeing or luck, for example) whereas successes by their own team may be attributed to characteristics of their team (such as their ability).

This hypothetical example illustrates that our attributions for the actions of those we perceive as belonging to the same group as ourselves (ingroup) may differ from our attributions for the actions of those we perceive as belonging to a different group (outgroup). The issue of ingroups and outgroups is addressed in more detail in Chapters 2 and 9, but, for now, it is worth noting that a 'group' could be any collection of people seeing themselves it as such and recognised as being a group by at least one other (Brown, 2000a). The 'ingroup' is a group that we identify ourselves as being a member of, while the 'outgroup' is one that we do not perceive ourselves as belonging to.

Taylor and Jaggi (1974) developed a model of 'ethnocentric' attribution, which suggests that 'positive' behaviours by ingroup members will be attributed to internal factors, while positive behaviours by outgroup members will be attributed to external factors, the attribution pattern being reversed for negative behaviours – that is, ingroup members' negative behaviour being attributed to external factors and outgroup members' negative behaviour to internal factors. Pettigrew (1979) developed this framework, noting that negative events by an outgroup member will be attributed to 'personal, dispositional causes' often seen as 'innate characteristics' of the group. By contrast, outgroup success will be attributed to factors such as 'luck' or the situation. In some cases, outgroup success will be attributed to effort (that is, a factor less consistently present than ability) and sometimes to 'the exceptional case' (someone who is

Intergroup bias The idea that our attributions for group-relevant outcomes (or things to be explained) may be shaped by our sense of our own and others' group identities. We might, therefore, attribute the success of a football team we support differently (perhaps to the skill of the group) from the success of a rival team (where luck or poor refereeing may be emphasised).

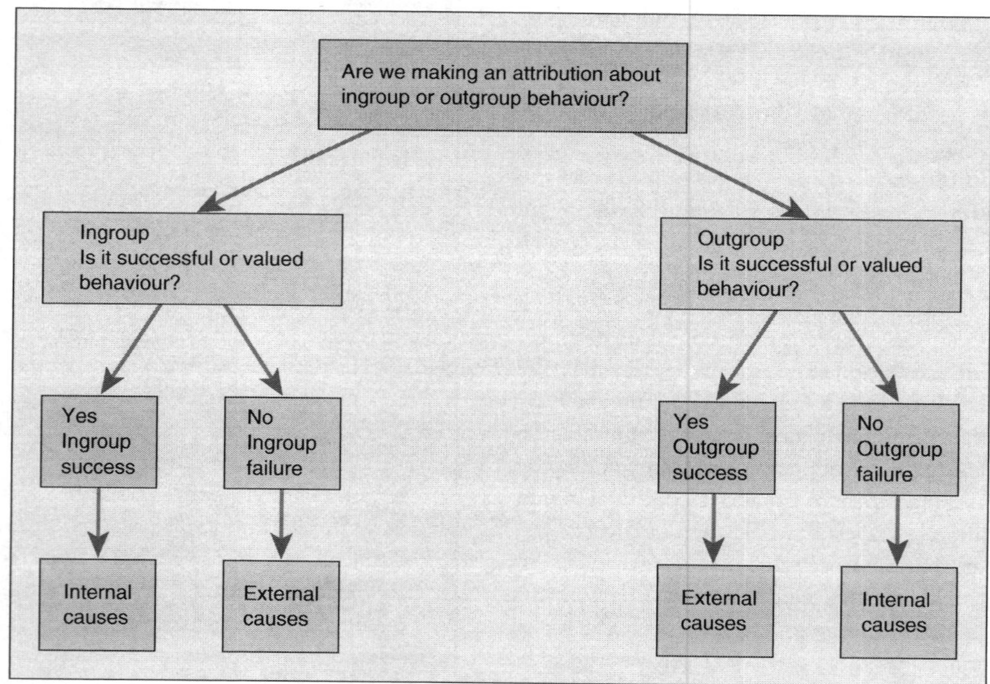

Figure 4.5 Intergroup attribution bias

not seen as representative of the outgroup). If you see your national football team or members of your country's Olympic team succeed against international competition, then you might – according to Pettigrew (1979) – attribute this to their skill and effort rather than luck, cheating or mistakes made by officials. By contrast, when representatives of another country beat those of your own, you may start to make attributions to luck, foul play or incompetent officials.

It is important to note that these biased intergroup attributions can be understood as maintaining the presumed negative view of the outgroup and positive – or relatively positive – view of the ingroup. For example, by attributing the negative or unsuccessful behaviour of outgroup members to some stable feature of their group, a derogatory view of the outgroup can be maintained. Similarly, if we attribute outgroup success or other positive behaviour to factors outside of them (luck, situation) or unstable internal factors (special effort), then we need not incorporate these positive aspects into our views about that group. What do we do, though, in cases where an outgroup member engages in positive behaviour or has success that cannot be explained away? In these cases, we might, according to Pettigrew (1979), Hewstone (1989) and Brown (2000a), reconsider whether the successful outgroup member or members are really representative of the group, whether they really belong to that group or whether the group itself should be rethought, perhaps splitting the big outgroup into smaller subtypes.

While wary of oversimplified versions of intergroup bias, Hewstone (1988, 1989, 1990) developed a model that integrates these ideas and outlines the ways in which intergroup attributions may maintain – or reduce – intergroup conflict. For Hewstone, the negative views of outgroup members could be understood as stereotypes – these are considered in some detail in Chapter 7 – but, for now, they can be thought of as ideas about members of a given category that a person or people hold (in this case, it is the negative ideas held by ingroup members about outgroup members). Merely having an outgroup member display positive or successful behaviour might well fail to challenge the derogatory outgroup stereotype because it will be attributed in such a way that the behaviour is seen as untypical (it was due to features of the situation, circumstance or luck or the person was not typical). By contrast, instances of outgroup behaviour that do confirm a derogatory outgroup stereotype will be attributed in such a way that they are understood as being typical (due to the characteristics of 'that type' of person) and, thus, reinforce the negative stereotype.

According to Hewstone (1989), the only real hope of challenging the negative expectations or stereotype and thereby reducing intergroup conflict depends on not only exposing group members to experiences of positive outgroup behaviour but also enabling them to see such behaviours as typical (and negative behaviours as untypical). Attribution plays a crucial role in this process as Hewstone (1989) suggests that intergroup encounters need to support the ways in which people make sense of outgroup members' behaviours so as to counteract the effects of intergroup bias and promote a positive change in outgroup stereotypes.

Attributions and sex stereotypes

The above work has emphasised the ways in which intergroup attributions may be consistent with stereotypes that can be resistant to change, even in the light of disconfirming evidence. Broadening the picture from more narrowly defined groups to the very widest of categories into which people can be placed – male–female – it is possible to see the issues identified above (with stereotypes shaping attributions) as being relevant in attributions made about male and female behaviour.

Suppose that someone holds the following sex stereotypes: 'men are less competent at childcare than women' and 'women are less competent at DIY than men'. Imagine that this person observes events that seem to confirm this stereotype – a man struggling to control his children or a woman having difficulty assembling some flat-pack furniture. Encountering these stereotype-consistent phenomena, the observer is likely to attribute them to internal and stable causes (the competence of the person in doing this type of task). If, by contrast, the observer saw a woman struggling to control her children or a man having difficulty assembling flat-pack furniture, then the attribution might be external and unstable – the mood of the children at that time or the poor furniture instructions.

Deaux (1976) considered the influence that sex stereotypes might have on attributions for success and failure for men and women. Deaux's review of attribution (published during a period when certain sexist practices in the USA and UK came under increasing criticism) highlighted extremely sexist attributions for success and failure among both men and women. Male success was found to be attributed to ability and female success to effort or luck. Likewise, male failure was attributed to lack of effort or bad luck, while female failure was attributed to low ability. For Deaux, these stereotyped attributions went *beyond* issues of outgroup perceptions – they were found to be true for both males and females and were also *sometimes* true for people's attributions about themselves (Deaux & Farris, 1977).

Försterling, Preikschas and Agthe (2007) also found differences in attributions for success to be partially dependent on the sex of the target person (whose success was being explained) and the attributer (providing the attribution). For them, the crucial factor was not the presence of gender stereotypes but, rather, whether the person whose success was being explained was the same sex as the person making the attribution, or the opposite sex, and whether they were perceived as attractive or not. Thus, Försterling et al. (2007) found that 'derogatory' attributions for success (such as attributing it to luck) were given by women (and gay men) to attractive women and unattractive men and by heterosexual men to attractive men and unattractive women. By contrast, 'glorifying' attributions for success (such as ability) were given by women (and gay men) to attractive men and unattractive women and by heterosexual men to attractive women and unattractive men.

Försterling et al. (2007) note that the findings (which they refer to as the *sexual attribution bias*) are consistent with evolutionary psychology, in that they may be explained in terms of our concerns with selecting and competing for a 'good mate'. In this way, they question the idea that stereotype information about outgroup or ingroup members can adequately account for attributions of success for same- and opposite-sex targets. Instead of attributions being shaped by stereotypes, Försterling et al. suggest it is evolutionary concerns that shape how we make attributions for same- and opposite-sex success.

Critical review of intergroup biases

The research on intergroup bias does broaden attribution theory from thinking about attribution entirely in terms of individuals – one individual making an attribution about their own or another individual's behaviour. Instead, the idea of intergroup bias allows for the idea that people might make attributions in terms of their own and others' perceived group membership, bringing issues of group identity and group stereotypes into the picture. Furthermore, the intergroup bias research, touched on here, while concerned with the internal–external distinction, does place some emphasis on other dimensions – particularly stability. That is, while much of the previous research in attribution bias was concerned with whether causes were internal or external (often to the exclusion of other dimensions), the intergroup bias research acknowledges, for example, that an internal and stable attribution (such as skill) may function very differently from an internal and unstable attribution (such as mood or unusual effort).

Some of the potential criticisms of intergroup bias were touched on when we considered literature concerned with attributions and sex stereotypes. Coming from quite different perspectives, the work of both Deaux (1976) and Försterling et al. (2007) questioned whether attributions – at least as far as gender is concerned – can be made sense of in terms of the group membership of the one making the attribution and their target (the person about whom they are making an attribution). These diverse perspectives suggested that people may make stereotyped and/or negative attributions about groups to which *they themselves belong* rather than only make derogatory attributions for members of an outgroup. This finding is interpreted by Deaux as a societal prevalence of sex stereotypes (rather than being mediated by one's own sex category membership) and by Försterling et al. as displaying people's concern with reproductive threat and opportunity (rather than outgroup stereotype preservation).

Additionally, it could be suggested that, while intergroup bias research does broaden the dimensions via which causes are thought about, with its emphasis on stability as well as the external–internal dimension, it does not fully address other meaningful ways in which attributions are distinguished. One important aspect of this is the idea of responsibility. In many cases, simply deciding that a cause of an outgroup member's failure is internal and stable may not support a derogatory stereotype if our specific attribution appears to absolve them of responsibility (they failed because of a long-term medical condition, for example). Thus, as with the other approaches to attribution and attribution bias considered in this chapter, causal location (even when enhanced by consideration of stability) may be emphasised at the expense of the (sometimes more meaningful) dimension of *responsibility*. The importance of considering attributions of responsibility has been particularly important in some of the research (Davey et al., 2001; Stander et al., 2001) concerning attributions and intimate relationships.

Furthermore, and in common with the approaches considered within this chapter so far, the intergroup bias literature tends to construe attributions as essentially cognitive processes. Thus, although intergroup bias research acknowledges that attribution can have an effect on important social issues, such as intergroup relationships, they are still seen as essentially private mental processes that are informed by and, in turn, sustain other mental processes such as stereotypes. It is as if attribution is packaged within some sort of 'individual cognition' container, its relationship to the outside world being mediated by perceptions about group membership and stereotypes concerning the ingroup and outgroup.

Alternative approaches are developed by work concerned with explanations in interaction – reviewed in Chapter 5 – and in the discussion of societal and ideological attributions in the next section. If attributions are approached not purely as matters of individual cognition but, instead, constructions or versions of the world, then we can start to ask what it is that the attributions (or any talk of relevance to attribution) actually *do*. In Chapter 5 this idea is developed in terms of discursive and conversation analytic work, with particular attention being given to the sort of interactional work that 'explanatory talk' might do (such as how our explanations might enable us to decline an invitation). In the next section, this is developed by reference to what sort of *ideological* work attribution talk might do. These different approaches point to a shortcoming not just in research concerned with intergroup bias but also attribution and attribution bias work more generally, in that its concern with documenting cognitive activity has arguably occluded consideration of the social, interactional things that attributions themselves actually *do*.

Critical recap

Intergroup biases

1 Some work concerned with sex stereotypes has questioned the extent to which attribution is determined by whether or not the target of the attribution is seen as a member of the ingroup or the outgroup.

2 As with most of the approaches considered in this chapter, limited attention has been given to the issue of responsibility – that is, the extent to which others are actually perceived as being *responsible* or accountable for having brought about a particular outcome to be explained.

3 Again, in common with most of the approaches considered in this chapter, the emphasis on attribution as an individual cognitive process can be challenged by approaches that attempt to consider what attribution talk does in interactional and ideological terms.

Reflective questions

1 *Have you ever experienced difficulty in admitting that a team you support – or a group you identify with – failed because of their own shortcomings?*

2 *Have you encountered examples of explanations of behaviour that are consistent with sex stereotypes?*

4.4 Societal attributions

At the beginning of this chapter, two founding figures of attribution theory were referred to – one, who has been much cited in attribution literature, was Heider; the other, somewhat neglected figure, was Ichheiser. As was mentioned above, some of Ichheiser's ideas became important themes in much of the attribution work that followed. For example, he was the first social psychologist to note the bias people show towards dispositional (or person-blaming) attributions, which has been developed in work on the FAE. Ichheiser's ideas differed significantly from most of the attribution research that has been considered in this chapter. Ichheiser, unlike most of those who followed, emphasised the importance of the 'ideology of society'. While most of the approaches considered in this chapter have emphasised cognitive processes within the individual – from the rational causal reasoning of Kelley's covariation model to the distorted processes of the self-serving bias – Ichheiser pointed to the importance of *socially shared ideas* or *ideologies*.

Ichheiser saw what became known as the FAE as a reflection of an ideology within society that emphasised self-determination – that is, people achieving (or failing) on the basis of their individual, personal qualities such as the amount of ability they possess and the amount of effort they expend. In this way, the bias towards dispositional causes was not to be located simply within the heads of individuals without reference to their societal context but, rather, was seen as a reflection of prevailing ideologies, which were seen as shaping the way in which people thought about causes. As Hewstone (1989) notes, Ichheiser himself tracked a change in prevailing ideologies. For example, in 1949, Ichheiser noted fewer person-blaming attributions for unemployment with an increased emphasis on social conditions. In this way, Ichheiser highlighted that, rather than being fixed frameworks for thinking, the ideologies informing the sorts of attributions that are made shift themselves as the societies in which they are located undergo change. Here, the idea of shared or societal attributions that may change will be explored, with particular reference to the concept of *social representations*.

Social representations

This idea of socially shared understandings that change over time has been developed in Moscovici's work on **social representations**. Related to Durkheim's (1898) concept of *representations collectives* Moscovici's (1976, 1988) concept of social representations captures the idea of shared frameworks for making sense of the world at a given time by a given group (or groups) of individuals. For Moscovici this was not a simple top-down indoctrination, but something far more subtle, in which

Social representations The definition of this term is the subject of some debate and discussion, but, broadly, is used to refer to socially shared understandings that may change over time or differ for certain groups. One concept that could be thought of in these terms is 'mental illness' – an idea that has been defined in incredibly different terms across time and cultures, yet, within some groups has certain shared or consensual properties.

communications between individuals was seen as a key means by which such representations originated and developed. Moscovici (1988, p. 214, cited in Hewstone, 1989, p. 207) notes that, as sets of ideas for making sense of the world, social representations frequently encompass attributional or explanatory elements:

> Social representations ... concern the contents of everyday thinking and the stock of ideas that gives coherence to our religious beliefs, political ideas and the [mental] connections we create ... They make it possible for us to classify persons and objects, to compare and explain behaviours and to objectify them as parts of our social setting.

One element of Moscovici's work on social representations noted the way in which certain ideas became shared or social representations. Moscovici (1976) investigated the ways in which ideas about psychoanalysis spread through French society and how they were *represented*. Thus, Moscovici found that technical psychoanalytic terms such as 'complex' were reported as being used by large numbers of school pupils and even larger numbers of students in making sense of other people's behaviour. What began as a set of ideas used by psychoanalysts for explaining and making sense of patients' behaviour had become a more socially distributed representation of those ideas, with all of the possible change and modification to those original ideas that the word 'representation' implies.

Moscovici's work spawned an enormous amount of 'social representation' research in which a wide variety of data sources (interviews, questionnaires, newspapers, diaries, letters, books, pamphlets and broadcast media) were drawn on in quite different ways to examine shared or social understandings about the world. Herzlich and Pierret (1987), in their bibliographic research, examined the ways in which representations were drawn on to make sense of plagues and epidemics – often placing the specific ailment of concern within a wider explanatory framework, such as being a punishment for moral decay and tracing the shifting representations of illness and medicine over time. Jodelet (1991) conducted interviews with local people living close to a community care scheme involving 'mental patients' in a small French town. Jodelet notes the way in which particular representations of madness are formed by the local community – representations that made sense of their own reactions to the 'mental patients' whom they find in their neighbourhood.

The idea of shared or social representations also provides, as Hewstone (1989) illustrates, a potential framework for thinking about many of the most notorious instances of misattribution in history. Thus, we find Christians blamed for the great fire of Rome, Catholics blamed (for a time) for the fire of London, Jews blamed (by many) for the bubonic epidemic and for all of Germany's problems in the 1930s and, in the 1990s, Tutsis blamed (by the Hutus) for problems in Rwanda. These last two examples, involving Germany and Rwanda, give some sense of the sinister power that these collective ideas can have – in both cases, the blamed group became victims of a terrible genocide. From horrific historical events, there appears to be some sense in which versions, or representations, of reality that involve making attributions to particular groups are associated with persecution and even genocide against those groups.

In addition to these extreme cases, there are many other instances of prejudice that could be approached in terms of social representations. Look at this passage from a book about the history of London (Wilson, 2004, p. 11).

> Those who inhabit this place are, some of them *holders* of British passports, but increasingly not. In the last ten years London has witnessed the phenomenon of 'asylum seekers' on a scale unrivalled by any other city in the world. Hundreds of thousands of Londoners are now visitors who have arrived without sanction in the city from Eastern Europe and elsewhere. Their arrival has been coincident with a colossal increase in crime, and a near crippling of such resources as council-owned housing, hospitals and schools. There also has been, in the last half-century, a huge legal immigration to London by British passport holders from the West Indies, from Pakistan, India, Bangladesh, Africa and the Far East.

With regard to the concerns of this chapter, it is not difficult to see the way that there is a strongly implied association with some broad brush assertions of various social ills, including strains on resources and an increase in crime. While crime and the lack of sufficient social resources are not directly attributed to 'asylum seekers' or 'visitors . . . from Eastern Europe and elsewhere', there is an implication that they are (at least partly) to blame. It is also possible to see how the above passage is consistent with certain ideas found in social representations theory. First, it is possible to contemplate how views about asylum seekers and immigrants from Eastern Europe could be developed and distributed through conversations within a community. Second, while the specific target here is, primarily, 'Eastern European' immigrants, it is easy to imagine how this could be other religious and ethnic groups at different times – perhaps Catholics, Jews or Muslims or people from Ireland, Asia, Africa or the West Indies. That is, aspects of the representation could change over time. Third, and perhaps most fundamentally, it is, unfortunately, possible to see how such ideas could be understood as shared by a group (or groups) of people.

The above extract and those in Box 4.7 also serve, however, as an illustration of certain limitations with social

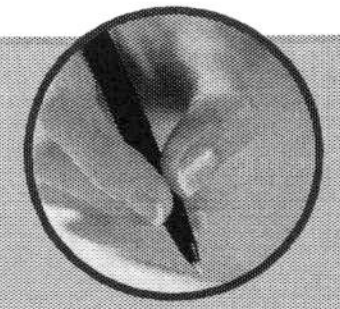

Box 4.7 TRY IT OUT
Thinking about social representations

Look at the two pieces of racist text below – one produced by the British National Party (BNP), the other, a post to an online discussion forum (both are reproduced as they appeared in the original).

With Extract 4.1, look at the way in which some versions of the way things are and what has caused them are being built up.

With Extract 4.2, can you see how here – and in many online communities – constructions of reality are debated? How does this link to the social representations work (and its criticisms) discussed in this chapter?

Extract 4.1

The scale of the crisis
Britain's existence is in grave peril, threatened by immigration and multiculturalism. In the absence of urgent action, we, the indigenous British people, will be reduced to minority status in our own ancestral homeland within two generations.

The disastrous effect of mass immigration on British society
There is no escaping the fact that the admission into this country of large numbers of foreigners has, inter alia, created a poorer, more violent, uncertain, disorientated, confused, politically correct, ill-educated, dependent, fractured society.

Source: BNP manifesto (2010)

Extract 4.2

Post
I really can't believe you guys won't support a party that wants to stop all none western immigration, simply because they have a few Jews in their ranks. Jews are not all the same, some Jews are only Jewish by birth and are Atheist. The way I see it voting for a party like this can't be any worse than voting for the current ultra left wing Marxist party that Denmark currently have.

I honestly think most people on here refuse to support a party like this, for the sole reason that they might have re-establish their views on Jews in general 😮

Even if they are only stopping immigration of useless immigrants and deporting unemployed ones, that is still less immigration which is a good thing. If it stops political correctness being so dominant that is another good thing, less race mixing propaganda etc. People aren't just gonna wake up one day and be ultra right wing, we need to ween them off it.

A response
Personally, I'm a little undecided on that. At the end of the day Jews are just another group of immigrants, non-western ones on top; on the other hand, opposing the chosen ones is for now really not a good idea, as long as the media machinery is mainly in their hands. So it's maybe just tactics.

And indeed DF (Danish People's Party) is the only party in Europe that so far could put fierce restrictions on immigration. But when there is a development like with EDL (English Defence League) where loyalty to Israel is greater than to England, or like TEA party where they invite Rabbis, there really is a line where one should accept "the occasional Jew" methinks. It's one thing not to start with chasing them, but swearing loyalty to Israel makes a nationalist party look really bad too.

And you shouldnt let you blind by the notion they are "atheists". This is no precondition for that they believe in their chosen status, nor does this make them less "Jewish". A Turk doesnt become less Turkish just because he's christian or atheist either, right? Just saying 🙂

Source: Popular online discussion forum on the topic of the Danish People's Party

representations theory identified by Billig (1991) and Potter (1996). Billig (1991) argues that, from a rhetorical perspective, attention should be paid to the ways in which constructions, such as the above passage, do the job of criticising and negating counter positions. That is, constructions such as these are not isolated from alternative, contradictory versions of reality but, instead, vie with them and are expressed and developed in contra-distinction to them. Look, for instance, at the way that the above extract by Wilson appears to marshal evidence for its apparently anti-Eastern European immigration stance. Rather than a bland statement of position, an *argument* is developed. In emphasising the argumentative dimension of such stances, Billig (1991) develops Moscovici's own definition of 'social' as referring to the idea that, 'representations are the outcome of an unceasing babble and a permanent dialogue between individuals' (Moscovici, 1984, p. 950, cited in Billig, 1991, p. 74). For Billig, the 'babble' and 'dialogue' very much involve argumentation and negation.

In a related vein, Potter (1996) notes the way in which social representations work underestimates the extent to which the representations (or constructions of reality) are constructed to do certain things within particular contexts. Staying with the above passage, it is possible to note the distinction that appears to be drawn between the legal immigrant and those 'without sanction' and between those who hold British passports and those who do not. Rather than being against *all* immigration at *all* times throughout London's history, the author appears to be problematising something much more specific – namely, recent, predominantly Eastern European, immigration. One thing (among several) that such contrasts may do is position the author's stance as rather more precise, targeted and, thereby, *reasonable* than it might appear if they were to be blatantly against all immigration to London across the last 2500 years. Thus, in this passage – and still more evidently in conversations – it is possible to see the way in which what might be thought of as *social representations* are not simply expressions of monolithic stances on an issue but, rather, constructed in much more subtle, nuanced and sequentially sensitive ways to do things (particularly of an interactional nature) such as blame, exonerate, agree, justify and so on. These issues are developed further in Chapter 5, where approaches to explanatory talk are examined.

Critical recap

Societal attributions

1 Billig (1991) raises the issue that social representations theory does not always adequately articulate the argumentative nature and argumentative context of social representations. For Billig, rather than being isolated, social representations are socially located and positioned – defined and shaped in part by their very contrast to and argument with other (perhaps contradictory) versions of the world.

2 While Moscovici referred to the importance of the interactional context from which representations arise, this sense of interactional context – and the work that social representations can do in such contexts – is, according to Potter (1996), typically underdeveloped in social representations literature. Thus, for Potter there should be more attention to where representations occur in interactional sequences and what sort of interactional work they can be found to do when and where they occur.

Reflective questions

1. *Look at an example of prejudiced talk or writing (such as Box 4.7). Are there any shared representations that appear to be mobilised?*
2. *Staying with the example of prejudiced talk or writing, in what ways might the representations be shaped by their argumentative or interactional context?*

4.5 Critical review of attribution research

The internal–external distinction crucial to Kelley (and a large proportion of other attribution research) can be questioned. First, we might ask whether arriving at the attribution of internal or external actually tells us what we want to know. Is it a satisfying answer to our search for a cause in itself – that is, do I really just want to know whether a cause is internal or external? Alternatively, does an attribution to internal or external factors enable me to identify the specific cause or causes that brought about the outcome to be explained? Both of these possibilities seem problematic when considered in the light of specific examples. It might be that I know my exam failure is something to do with me, but what I might want to further clarify is whether it is due to my lack of ability or effort. I might know that my friend is upset because of something about her, but I am likely to want to know what that something is. Considering such examples may cause us to question whether just deducing that a cause is internal or external is enough and wonder if more attention needs to be given to the process of identifying the specific cause, or causes, for a given outcome.

A second problem with the internal–external distinction concerns the way in which they have been treated as opposite ends of a single continuum. That is, internal and external have been thought of as negatively correlated – the more a cause or causes have been thought of as being 'within the person', the less they have been presumed to be 'within the stimulus'. As Hewstone (1989) notes, this thinking is reflected in studies that measure perceived causality using either a single scale labelled internal at one end and external at the other or treat a measure of internality as a negative measure of externality (and vice versa). Hewstone (1989), drawing on and citing Solomon (1978), suggests that internality and externality should be treated as separate.

A third, related, problem is whether the distinction between internal and external is meaningful. Imagine that your friend switches from studying psychology to law. Quite naturally, you might want to know why she has turned her back on such a wonderful discipline. If your friend answers, 'Law is a very lucrative field', you might attribute her decision to the money available to those qualified in law (an external cause). Suppose, however, your friend answered, 'I want to earn a lot of money.' In this case, her decision might be attributed to the motivations and ambitions of your friend (internal causes). This suggests that sometimes the internal–external distinction is an artefact of the specific way in which causality is expressed – that is, the distinction between external and internal causes might lie in the words that report causality, not in some truth separate from those words.

A fourth concern is that, in many cases, simply knowing whether a cause is within the person or outside of them is insufficient – we might want to know who or what is *responsible* for the behaviour (or outcome) we are trying to explain. If you arrange to meet a friend and she leaves you waiting, without any explanation, for hours in the cold, you might well want to know what caused her to not turn up. Now imagine that you call her up and discover it is something to do with her – that is, it could be she is seriously ill, had a severe accident, was just feeling too lazy to bother or had forgotten all about meeting up. It is quite likely that we would be concerned with whether she was responsible (that is, was it her fault) rather than simply was it something in her, or her, environment.

A fifth problem with attribution research is that many of the classic experiments used provide an extremely unusual context for causal reasoning. Think, for example, of McArthur's (1972) experiment in which participants were presented with snippets of information about a fictitious character – for example, 'John laughs at the comedian', 'John always laughs at comedians' – and then asked to respond by making a judgement as to whether John's laughing was something to do with John or the comedian. It is possible that, within the framework of this experiment, participants produce the 'logically correct' response, but it is equally the case that this situation does not correspond very much at all to the sorts of causal reasoning phenomena that it purports to describe. Thus, these classic experiments involve causal reasoning being initiated because a stranger asks the participants to work out the cause. Furthermore, the participants are given bits of information (and only those bits) that correspond to specific attribution models (such as Kelley's covariation model) and, finally, the participants are asked to express their causal thinking simply in terms of some predefined dimension or dimensions (such as internal–external). The vast differences between many classic attribution experiments and the sorts of real-world instances of causal thinking they attempt to simulate may, therefore, pose problems with regard to the external validity of these experimental findings.

A sixth problem with some of the attribution work considered above is its cultural specificity. This was particularly evident in the case of certain attribution biases – for example, the FAE was found to be culturally specific rather than universal. The issue that this implicitly raises, however, is the extent to which other – or, indeed, all – research considered in this chapter should be seen as to a greater or lesser extent culturally relative.

A seventh problem with attribution research is the relatively little attention that has been given to societal levels of attribution. Despite Ichheiser outlining the importance of this issue at the inception of attribution research within social psychology, there has been relatively little attention to the ways in which there may be widely shared, culturally available 'readymade' attributions or, perhaps, ideological frameworks that shape how individuals explain important, shared aspects of their social worlds.

Finally, questions can be asked about the commitment to detailing unobservable cognitive processes within the individual found in most of the work considered in this chapter. From the perspective of some of the discursive and conversation analytic research developed in Chapter 5, attention could move to explanatory talk not as something that stands in a specific relation to 'underlying cognition' (such as reflecting, shaping or distorting it) but, rather, the place where the action of explanation is being done and being seen to be done.

Critical recap

Attribution research

1 The interal–external distinction, crucial to much of attribution theory, has been questioned. Many of these challenges hinge on the issue of whether this distinction is informative or not (does it help the attributer locate the actual cause or does it provide enough causal information in itself?) and meaningful (can internal and external causes be neatly distinguished?). Some recent attribution research has introduced other dimensions, such as how global or specific a cause is, or considered responsibility rather than whether the cause is 'within the person' or not.

2 A further challenge was raised concerning empirical studies of attribution. Many of the classic studies (such as McArthur, 1972) involved eliciting causal judgements in situations unlike any that participants would ever encounter outside of the social psychology laboratory.

3 Research that has examined attribution across cultures (often focusing on attribution bias) has suggested that the universalist understandings in much of attribution research may be misplaced.

4 Finally, questions can be raised concerning the way that most researchers have conceptualised attributions as private mental events. Many social psychologists treat attributions as created afresh in the minds of individual perceivers, paying little attention to seemingly shared or recurrent aspects of attributions within a given society or group. Similarly, conceptualising attributions as 'essentially cognitive' processes has taken attention away from the sort of interactional and rhetorical work that attribution-relevant talk may *do*.

Reflective questions

1. *Think of the last time you made an attribution or had one communicated to you. Which of the approaches considered here best describes what was involved?*
2. *Look through a newspaper for one or two stories where attributions are relevant. How many of the approaches covered in this chapter can you draw on in making sense of what has happened?*

Summary

- This chapter addressed the issue of attribution by first examining the classic contributions of Ichheiser, Heider, Jones and Davis and Kelley to understanding the process of causal reasoning. It then considered the different ways in which deviations from the reasoning process, or attribution bias, have been approached, considering the FAE, actor–observer differences, self-biases and intergroup biases. Finally, the chapter addressed issues raised in the early work of Ichheiser, regarding societal attributions.
- The chapter started by reviewing the work of two founding figures of attribution research in social psychology – the oft-quoted Heider and the oft-neglected Ichheiser. It was noted that Heider was important in that his work sketched out both the importance of the causal reasoning process and how that process is typically geared to calculating whether the cause of an event or behaviour to be explained lies within or outside of the person. In addition Heider's work was seen as envisaging the possibility that the causal reasoning process could be subject to bias.
- Ichheiser's work was seen as addressing aspects of causal thinking that have been neglected until comparatively recently. Ichheiser not only argued that people had a tendency to produce dispositional (or internal, person-blaming) attributions – an idea developed in work on the FAE – but also that this bias was based in cultural ideologies (rather than simply being distortions within the mind of an individual).
- The FAE describes the way in which there is a tendency for individuals making attributions to attribute the behaviour or event to be explained to causes within the person rather than the situation. Typically, this is presented as a distortion from the process of accurate reasoning that occurs within the mind of an individual. More recent research suggests that this bias varies considerably across cultures, which, in turn, lends some credibility to Ichheiser's idea that it is linked to cultural ideologies.
- The actor–observer difference bias suggests that observers of an actor's (anyone doing an act to be explained) behaviour produce different attributions from those of the actors themselves. Some work in this area suggested a perceptual basis to this bias – we blame what we see. So, actors see the situation, observers see the actor and both make attributions accordingly. Work on the empathic bias suggested that when observers sympathise with actors, they tend to produce situational (rather than dispositional, person-blaming) attributions.
- The self-biases that were considered included both the self-serving bias, which suggested that individuals tend to attribute success to themselves and failure to aspects of the situation (including other people). It was noted, however, that there can be a depressive attributional style in which the opposite pattern is found – that is, success being attributed to external causes and failure to internal ones. Research also

suggested that the internal–external distinction was often further amplified by other dimensions, such as how global–specific and stable–unstable the causes were perceived to be. Thus, depressed people were found to not only attribute negative outcomes to internal causes but also these causes were perceived as global (affecting many areas of the person's life) and stable (always present).

- Intergroup bias research suggests that – particularly concerning behaviour or outcomes that have some evaluative meaning (being judged as either successful or unsuccessful) – people will tend to make ingroup-enhancing attributions – attributing their own group's successes and failures in much the same way as the self-serving bias suggests for individual successes and failures. Conversely, attributions concerning the successes and failures of other, or outgroups – particularly those from whom the ingroup members seek to distance themselves – will be judged more harshly, with successes and positive behaviour being attributed to factors other than stable properties of the group, while outgroup failures *are* likely to be attributed to stable features of the group. Work concerned with changing derogatory outgroup attributions have suggested that it is no good merely exposing people to positive outgroup behaviour or successes – these need to be seen as *brought about by stable features of that group* in order for a more positive outgroup stereotype to emerge.

- Work on societal attributions provided a means of considering shared or collective understandings that inform explanations about certain social phenomena or categories of people. On the one hand, it was noted that this perspective – often informed by social representations theory – usefully extends beyond the limits of individual cognition, providing a framework for making sense of widely held ideologies or understandings informing attributions. On the other hand, it was also noted that the theory of social representations can be challenged for paying relatively little attention to the argumentative and interactional contexts in which the representations are manifest.

Review questions

1. *What research is most consistent with the ideas that Ichheiser developed?*
2. *What are the limitations of Jones and Davis' correspondent inference theory?*
3. *What factors does Kelley identify as important for attribution calculations?*
4. *How do these factors differ from each other?*
5. *How universal is the FAE?*
6. *Why might our attributions for the behaviour of those we observe differ from those for our own behaviour?*
7. *What is meant by empathic attribution?*
8. *What different forms do self-biases take?*
9. *What does attribution research suggest regarding challenging and changing derogatory outgroup stereotypes?*
10. *What does the idea of societal attribution contribute to our understanding of how attributions work?*

Recommended reading

Brown, R. (1986). *Social psychology* (2nd ed.). New York: Free Press. Exemplary coverage of the key research in attribution and attribution bias.

Choi, I., & Nisbett, R. E. (1998). Situational salience and cultural differences in the correspondence bias and actor–observer bias. *Personality and Social Psychology Bulletin*, *24*, 949–960. An interesting cross-cultural investigation into the extent to which participants make use of information about situational constraints in explaining another person's behaviour.

Försterling, F., Preikschas, S., & Agthe, M. (2007). Ability, luck, and looks: An evolutionary look at achievement ascriptions and the sexual attribution bias. *Journal of Personality and Social Psychology*, *92*, 775–788. An evolutionary alternative to ingroup-serving attribution bias in accounting for male/female attributions regarding male/female success or failure.

Hewstone, M. (1989). *Causal attribution: From cognitive processes to collective beliefs*. Oxford: Blackwell. This book provides thoughtful, intelligent coverage of much of the material presented in this chapter.

Hewstone, M. (1990). The 'ultimate attribution error'? A review of the literature on intergroup causal attribution. *European Journal of Social Psychology*, *20*, 311–335. A useful, authoritative overview of literature concerned with intergroup attributions.

Malle, B. F., Knobe, J., & Nelson, S. (2007). Actor–observer asymmetries in behaviour explanations: New answers to an old question. *Journal of Personality and Social Psychology*, *93*, 491–514. An important paper that critiques traditional understandings of the actor–observer difference bias.

Mezulis, A. H., Abramson, L. Y., Hyde, J. S., & Hankin, B. L. (2004). Is there a universal positivity bias in attributions? A meta-analytic review of individual, developmental, and cultural differences in the self-serving attributional bias. *Psychological Bulletin*, *130*, 711–747. A significant meta-analytic study that broadly supports the idea of self-serving bias while highlighting its variation across different populations.

Sedikides, C., Campbell, W. K., Reeder, G. D., & Elliot, A. J. (1998). The self-serving bias in relational context. *Journal of Personality and Social Psychology*, *74*, 378–386. An interesting paper that suggests limits to the self-serving bias when investigated in terms of close dyadic relationships.

Seligman, M. E., Abramson, L. Y., Semmel, A., & von Baeyer, C. (1979). Depressive attributional style. *Journal of Abnormal Psychology*, *88*, 242–247. A seminal paper that developed the idea of attribution style, such as the sorts of attributions made about successes and failures being associated with depression.

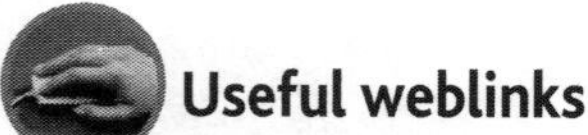

Useful weblinks

Word of warning – there are numerous websites that address aspects of attribution covered in this chapter, but do please check for their accuracy!

www.sv.uit.no/seksjon/psyk/floydartikkel2.html An interesting biographical piece concerning Ichhieser.

http://psychclassics.yorku.ca This website is an excellent resource for downloading original classics, and some more obscure papers, by leading psychologists (including Heider and Ichheiser).

http://cogweb.ucla.edu/Discourse/Narrative/Heider_45.html A brief account and demonstration of the work of both Heider and Simmel (1944) and Michotte (1962) concerning perceptions and imputed attributions regarding the movement of geometric shapes.

www.fastcompany.com/1657515/a-theory-called-a-fundamental-attribution-error A brief video that takes a simple but entertaining look at the FAE.

www.psych.lse.ac.uk/psr An online journal, *Papers on Social Representations*, which is an excellent resource for current developments in social representations.

Explanatory talk

Learning outcomes

By the end of this chapter you should:

- understand some of the key approaches, which argue that causal reasoning can be affected by verbal representations of the outcome (or event) to be explained (attributional semantics and critical linguistics)
- understand the idea behind the conversational model that the cognitive process of attribution is both triggered and constrained by the explanation-eliciting question
- understand the account-giving literature, distinguishing between real and communicated explanations and the features of 'successful' communicated explanations
- understand approaches that have emphasised how explanations undertake actions within specific sequences of interaction (discursive and conversation analytic approaches)
- be aware of how these approaches might relate to aspects of everyday life
- be able to use each of these approaches to provide some critique of other perspectives in attribution and explanation
- be able to critically evaluate the approaches covered in this chapter.

While running for election in July 2010, Australia's Prime Minister Julia Gillard became embroiled in a controversy concerning her former bodyguard, Andrew Stark. Questions were raised in the media and by the opposition party regarding the revelation that Mr Stark sometimes attended meetings of the Australian National Security Committee in place of Julia Gillard. Look at the way the issue is addressed in the following example of newspaper coverage (*Sydney Morning Herald*, 31 July 2010) and in a statement by Julia Gillard.

Source: Stefan Postles/Getty Images

Australian Prime Minister Julia Gillard, who found herself having to explain why former bodyguard Andrew Stark had deputised for her at meetings of the Australian National Security Committee

> **Gillard sent bodyguard to meetings**
>
> Prime Minister Julia Gillard has been accused of sending a former bodyguard and junior staff member to attend highly sensitive security meetings on her behalf.
>
> In another damaging leak for Labor, sources have told *The Weekend Australian* that when Ms Gillard was deputy prime minister she regularly failed to attend Cabinet's National Security Committee meetings.

In the wake of this controversy Gillard made the following statement about Mr Stark:

> Mister Andrew Stark was a member of the Australian Federal Police for twenty-one years. And I think it is offensive to him, it's offensive to me and I believe it would be offensive to hardworking police right around this country to somehow conclude that a man who spent twenty-one years in the Australian Federal Police as a police officer doesn't know anything about security.

The press report and the statement by Gillard both illustrate several aspects of how explanations can be used that are addressed in this chapter. The press account of what took place could be understood as holding Gillard to account – that is, the very description of events appears to not only describe – but also suggest – that Gillard has a case to answer, that in some way she is to blame. In this example of press coverage, Gillard is depicted as actively doing the sending ('Gillard sent') and the blameworthy nature of what she did is implied by describing the person deputising (Mr Stark) as a 'bodyguard' and the meetings as 'highly sensitive'.

Gillard's statement shows another side of explanations – that is, how talk can be used to give an account, justify or exonerate. Gillard does this in part by characterising Mr Stark not as a 'bodyguard' but 'a member of the Australian Federal Police for twenty-one years'. Gillard's characterisation arguably makes Mr Stark's deputising appear more legitimate and she explicitly refers to the criticisms themselves as 'offensive'.

Introduction

This chapter investigates exactly this two-sided nature of explanations – how they are used to blame and excuse or exonerate. Some of the literature is concerned with quite explicit examples of blaming and exonerating – for example, where a direct accusation and a direct denial or justification is involved. Other literature considers the way that blaming and exonerating can be done in the very descriptions that are used, just as we can see in the descriptions of Mr Stark above – one description implying blame, the other implying justification.

It is worth noting that the relevance of explanations includes, but also extends far beyond, political debate. If you have ever had to explain why you were late, missed someone's birthday party or invited a disturbingly deluded person that you met on holiday to come and stay for a week, then you may have been involved in the issues of explanation that this chapter covers. The research considered here echoes some of the issues touched on in earlier chapters regarding what talk (and written accounts) *do* rather than what it might *express* – with the specific focus here being what it does with regard to blaming and exonerating from blame. There is a distinction, then, between being mainly concerned with what 'thinking processes' or cognitions people are engaged in and focusing on what sorts of things people are *doing* when they talk (such as exonerating and blaming). This difference picks up on a major distinction between approaches to social psychology that are concerned with individual cognition (such as the main attribution theories covered in Chapter 4) and discursive and conversation analytic approaches (which are touched on later in this chapter).

Chapter overview

In the previous chapter, we considered some of the key ways in which social psychology has tried to understand how we make attributions for events. One criticism of the work reviewed is that much of it concentrates on attribution as essentially a cognitive phenomenon – the words involved are understood as being relatively unimportant. This emphasis on getting at the 'underlying' cognition tends to mean that, in many experiments, the words are treated as neutral conduits of 'underlying' thought and not worthy of any special attention themselves. There is little thought in such research about how the words or sentences used might shape attribution judgements. Similarly, there is scant consideration of what attribution talk looks like outside of the laboratory – that is, how people actually do the business of communicating an attribution or explanation or, indeed, requesting one of someone else. Attribution (or explanatory) talk is thus treated as something like the flotsam rising and falling with the (cognitive) wave – from this perspective it is the 'underlying' cognition that is important, not the particular forms that a given instance of attribution talk might take. The work considered in this chapter suggests that the attribution talk or explanatory words used and the interactional context in which they are used are vitally important. The work to be reviewed here falls broadly into six areas: attributional semantics, critical linguistics, conversational model, accounts, discursive psychology and conversation analysis.

Attributional semantics research considers the ways in which our very description of the event or behaviour to be explained (such as John laughed at the comedian) might imply one cause (in this case, John) more than others merely because of the implication of the specific verb used (in this case, 'laughed') in the sentence. For attributional semantics, then, verbs vary significantly in terms of whether they imply causal responsibility for the first noun phrase (in this case, John) or the second (the comedian) – changing the verb can change the causal implication. Some work within the field of critical linguistics has had a similar interest in sentences that imply causal relationships. Rather than examining the causal implications of verbs, however, critical linguistics has paid particular attention to the positioning of the noun and verb within sentences that describe actions or occurrences. Thus, 'The dog frightened John' is thought to implicate the dog as causing John's fear more than the passive alternative 'John was frightened by the dog', in which John (who is mentioned before the dog) is somewhat implicated. Critical linguistics research endeavours to show the potentially profound implications of this observation when we consider, for example, how our news is communicated.

The conversational model considers the way in which the calculation of causality and the communication of explanations is initiated and shaped by the 'cause-eliciting question' that precedes it (for example, 'Why did he push him?'). For the conversational model of attribution, our typically everyday attributions arise in conversations in which we are asked to provide an explanation. The 'cause-eliciting' question not only starts the attribution process, getting us to think what the cause is, but also gives a steer to the attribution process.

One strand of this thinking draws on attributional semantics work in considering what causal implications the verb used may have, such as 'push'. Another strand of this considers how the 'cause-eliciting question' may shape what potential causes are considered. For example, 'Why did he push him?' creates an explicit contrast between 'he' (the one doing the pushing) and 'him' (the one receiving the push). Over and above constraints created by the specific wording of the 'cause-eliciting question', the conversational model further considers how a general concern with making relevant cooperative contributions to conversations will shape the response that is made – an issue discursive psychology and conversation analysis, albeit in a markedly different manner, seek to address.

Some of the research into explanatory talk has sought to identify different types of *accounts* or exonerating explanations and consider what determines how effective they are. Such work has suggested, for example, that if I attribute some failing on my part (such as arriving late) to causes that are outside of my control (such as, 'there was a huge traffic jam caused by an accident'), this might be more effective in exonerating myself than referring to causes under my control (such as, 'I didn't feel like rushing').

Discursive psychology is also concerned with the ways in which explanations *do* things – such as giving an account for one's behaviour – but it becomes something much more radical. First, for discursive psychology, *all talk does interactional work*. Even our talk that seems to be merely descriptive ('It's been non-stop today') can do interactional work, such as exonerate (accounting for why I did not do something) or blame (holding someone else to account for not helping out). Second, the surrounding talk context is crucial in shaping what it is that a given piece of talk does – in other words, the action any talk does is both tailored to and shaped by the sequential context in which it occurs. Third, from a discursive psychology perspective, these observations, regarding how people do things with their talk in interaction, support a wider critique of the cognitive centric approach found in much of social psychology (and in psychology more

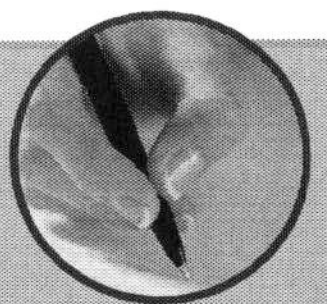

Box 5.1 TRY IT OUT
Explaining behaviour

What is the last explanation you gave for something that you did? If you think carefully, it may have taken a somewhat subtle form – you might have explained a purchase by commenting on the merits of the thing that you bought, for example. Keep your example in mind as you look through the different approaches in this chapter.

What is the last explanation that you came across in the media? Did you hear or read about a politician explaining or justifying a policy decision? Was it a celebrity talking about a personal decision? Again, keep this example in mind as you consider the different approaches in this chapter.

generally). Conversation analysis is somewhat less concerned with developing a critique (especially a social constructionist one) of psychology, but it very much shares with discursive psychology a concern with what *all* talk – including that which we might gloss as 'explanatory' – is doing in *sequences of interaction*.

Many of the concerns outlined above might seem 'merely academic', in the narrowest use of that term – different approaches colliding with each other but seeming to have limited connection to our 'real' everyday lives – but stop for a moment, look at Box 5.1. Aren't you using and encountering 'explanatory talk' even today?

As you go through this chapter, some of the material is complex and intricate, but try to keep a clear sense of how – at least potentially – there is something very profound being discussed here that, from radically different perspectives, tries to shine a light on things we hear and things we say every day of our lives.

5.1 Attributional semantics

The focus in 'classic' attribution research addressed in Chapter 4 was on developing models of cognitive causal reasoning processes and biases. These models sought to describe how an individual comes to think about where the cause of an outcome (or thing to be explained) may lie. If we reflect for a moment on our everyday lives, however, we may be aware of the way in which we often engage in causal reasoning when others have given us some information (see Box 5.1). Every time we watch the news, read a newspaper or have a friend tell us about something that has happened, we are dealing with *other people's descriptions* of events and behaviours. If our friend informs us that, 'Sita shouted at Doreen', then we might start thinking through what caused Sita to shout. What **attributional semantics** suggests is that the very way in which that, seemingly straightforward, description is constructed (and, in particular, the verb used) will shape how we come to think about the cause.

To illustrate these ideas further, it is worth returning to the headline used at the beginning of this chapter, shown in Extract 5.1.

Extract 5.1

Gillard sent bodyguard to meetings
Prime Minister Julia Gillard has been accused of sending a former bodyguard and junior staff member to attend highly sensitive security meetings on her behalf.

Source: *Sydney Morning Herald* (31 July 2010)

In discussing the coverage concerning Gillard's former bodyguard at the beginning of this chapter, it was noted that the press account could be thought of in terms of how it appears to hold Gillard to account. Thus, Gillard is described as 'actively doing' the 'sending' of the former bodyguard – 'Gillard sent' rather than 'deputy duties were undertaken by Mr Stark'. Both of these alternatives could be understood as describing the same event, but the point – from an attributional semantics perspective – is that there is something about the first version ('Gillard sent') that implies the causality lies with Gillard. This description of events appears to not only describe but also suggest that Gillard has a case to answer – she is in some way accountable. The blameworthy nature of what she did is implied by emphasising both Gillard's role in actively sending and in characterising the person deputising (Mr Stark) as a 'bodyguard' and the meetings as 'highly sensitive'.

Because attributional semantics is concerned with the ways in which these simple descriptive sentences might affect our attributions, the research methods employed involve presenting participants with different types of

Attributional semantics An area of attribution research that is concerned with the ways in which our verbal descriptions can have causal implications. A particular emphasis of attributional semantics research has been on the identification of the different sorts of causal implications that different verbs may have.

descriptive sentences (or sentence stems) and eliciting their causal explanations. This enables researchers to analyse what sorts of attributions are associated with different forms of descriptions. A detailed illustration of this type of research is presented in Box 5.2, where the research methodology of Ferstl, Garnham and Manouilidou (2011) is summarised.

As Box 5.2 indicates, the sentences that are focused on take the following form: noun phrase 1 (such as 'Tony') verb (such as 'telephones') noun phrase 2 (such as 'George'). It can be noted that these sentence stems (as used in most attributional semantics work) involve an active rather than passive verb – that is, 'Tony telephones George because' rather than 'George is telephoned by Tony because', 'Vita thanked Mattewus because' rather than 'Mattewus was thanked by Vita because' or 'Desmond admired Sita because' rather than 'Sita was admired by Desmond because'. The potential significance of active compared to passive forms of sentences is considered below when we discuss critical linguistics approaches, but, for now, we can note that attributional semantics concentrates largely on simple, active verb sentences in an effort to detect what influence the verb itself might have on implied causality.

These sentence fragments or sentence stems (ending in 'because') enable the participant to complete the sentence with an attribution. The focus of work in attributional semantics is on the way in which the choice of verb in these simple, active verb sentences can influence the cause that participants use to complete the sentence. These sentences typically have one name then a verb followed by a second name. Each name is referred to as a 'noun phrase' (as names are proper nouns), the one before the verb being referred to as 'noun phrase 1', the one after the verb as 'noun phrase 2'.

By presenting participants with sentence fragments of this type to complete ('NP1 verb(ed) NP2 because ... '), a wide array of verbs has been investigated and categorised in the light of empirical results. Each 'test' verb is simply inserted into the NP1 verb(ed) NP2 formula – so, Joshua *thanked* Abbey because, Joshua *telephoned* Abbey because, Joshua *admired* Abbey because. As noted in Box 5.2, Ferstl et al. (2011) took particular care about the way in which typically male and typically female names were used: each sentence stem had one male and one female name. This procedure enabled easier classification of the participants' responses (most participants completed the stem with 'because ... *he*' or 'because ... *she*'). In addition, by using a counterbalanced design (in which each of the verbs was presented with both male noun phrase 1, female noun phrase 2, as well as, female noun phrase 1, male noun phrase 2) Ferstl et al. (2011) were able to investigate possible gender effects.

Using this type of methodology (though typically without the care Ferstl et al. have shown with regards to gender), attributional semantics work, collectively, has provided some measure of empirical support for what Rudolph and Fosterling (1997) refer to as the 'verb causality effect' – that is, the way in which verbs differ in the causality that they imply. Crinean and Garnham (2006, p. 637) argue that implicit causality inferences 'constitute part of the meaning of the verb' – that is, our comprehension of verbs includes a semantic, or 'meaning', understanding of the causal factor(s) that they imply. Thus, the verb 'blame' includes, as part of its meaning, 'a causal imputation to the person blamed' (2006, p. 637).

Since Garvey and Caramazza's (1974) initial work, attributional semantics research has sought to develop an increasingly comprehensive and precise description of the ways in which different verbs – far from being 'neutral descriptions' – can imply certain types of cause. As noted above, much of this research has used simple sentence stems, usually structured as 'noun *verb(ed)* noun', such as, 'Sita *laughed* at Angus'. Across nearly 40 years of research, many of the findings could be interpreted as offering some support for the basic idea that 'verbs matter' or that they have attribution-relevant connotations. Brown and Fish (1983), Au (1986), Crinean and Garnham (2006) and others have categorised large numbers of verbs as tending to elicit either noun phrase 1 attributions or noun phrase 2 attributions. Verbs such as 'lied to', 'confessed to', 'apologised to', 'helped' 'telephoned', are all examples of NP1 verbs – that is, participants presented with sentence stems such as 'Rebecca lied to Miriam because ...' or 'Sita helped John because ...' typically completed the sentence by reference to factors to do with NP1. By contrast, verbs such as 'detested', 'resented', 'honoured' and 'thanked' are all examples of NP2 verbs and participants presented with sentence stems such as 'Venky detested Siobhan because ...' or 'Lance thanked Jamie because ... ' completed the sentence by reference to factors to do with NP2.

Attributional semantics research has offered something quite distinct from the classic attribution research considered in Chapter 4. It takes seriously the possible importance of verbs in the descriptions of what was done or what happened that often precede our causal reasoning. In so doing, it pays attention to the way that representations of reality – at least in terms of the selection of verbs used in describing phenomena – can be consequential. It is worth reflecting, however, on the potential limitations of the research detailed below. Some of these limitations suggest that additional issues are incorporated

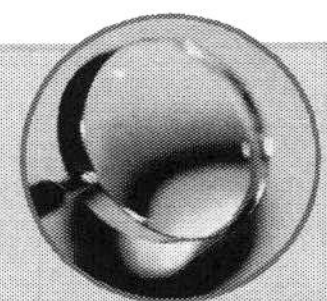

Box 5.2 FOCUS
Researching implicit causality in English verbs (Ferstl, Garnham, & Manouilidou, 2011)

Ferstl et al. (2011) provide a clear demonstration as to how the implicit causality of specific verbs can be researched. Their research used the following procedure.

1 A number of verbs were identified – largely drawn from previous studies concerned with attributional semantics.

2 This pool of verbs was edited down to exclude verbs that had very low frequency of use or 'odd' connotations, which led to verbs such as lull, awe, boggle, afflict, elate and disgruntle being excluded.

3 The chosen verbs were classified according to how many characters long they were, frequency of usage (using the CELEX database) and valence (how positive or negative they were judged to be by 12 participants).

4 In addition, the verbs were divided by the researchers into linguistic categories – 'activity verbs' (such as 'kiss') and 'psychological verbs' (such as 'love'). These categories of activity and psychological verbs were subdivided.

- Activity verbs were treated as having a definite thing being done by a person – an *agent* – to another person or thing – a *patient*. Activity verbs were further subdivided into Agent Patient (AgPat) verbs, such as 'carry', and Agent Evocator (AgEvo) verbs, such as 'praise'. Both of these verb types involve some action performed by an agent, but, in the first (AgPat) case, the 'carrying' is, or appears to be, *done to* some other person or thing; in the second (AgEvo), the 'praising' appears to be *evoked by* some person or thing.
- Psychological verbs were treated as states of *experience* and were subdivided into Experiencer Stimulus (ExpStim) verbs, such as 'love', and Stimulus Experiencer (Stim Exp) verbs, such as 'upset'. Both of these psychological verbs involve an experiencer and some corresponding stimulus (person, thing or occurrence). In the first (ExpStim) case, however, the 'loving' is, or appears to be, something that the experiencer *directs towards* some stimulus; in the second (StimExp) case, the 'being upset' is, or appears to be, brought about by the stimulus.

5 The categories of verbs identified in step 4 were used to inform an analysis to check whether the different types of verbs were balanced in terms of valence, frequency and word length. This was found to be partially the case, meaning that the unequal distribution of verb length and frequency of usage had to be borne in mind when making sense of the results.

6 Each verb was used to build a sentence stem – each including one male and one female noun phrase (the noun phrases used in this study were proper nouns – a male and a female name). Clearly gendered names were used, resulting in sentence stems such as, 'John (noun phrase 1) admired Mary (noun phrase 2) because ...' or, 'Mary admired John because ....'

7 A total of 96 participants completed a Web-based questionnaire that consisted of sentence stems such as, 'John admired Mary because ....' The participants were asked to type in 'sensible completion of these sentences, similar to the short examples provided to them (e.g., 'The lion ate the zebra, because ... it was hungry', Ferstl et al., 2011, p. 129).

8 The results were then analysed to see if the reason given clearly indicated that the cause was to do with the noun phrase occurring before the verb (noun phrase 1) or after it (noun phrase 2). In 91.2 per cent of cases, participants responded with a gendered pronoun, 'he' or 'she', thereby enabling their response to be 'automatically' scored as noun phrase 1 or noun phrase 2. Two raters were then used to decide for each of the remaining cases whether the respondent had indicated that the cause was within noun phrase 1, noun phrase 2 or 'other' (which included responses seeming to imply both noun phrases as the cause). This process resulted in 94 per cent of responses indicating either noun phrase 1 or noun phrase 2.

9 The results examined the extent to which linguistic categories (identified in point 4) were associated with particular types of noun phrase selection. That is, they enabled examination of the extent to which different types of verb *in themselves* implied a causality for the noun phrase which came before it (noun phrase 1) or after it (noun phrase 2). In addition, this study, unlike some attributional semantics research, examined the effects of gender (that is, are particular types of verbs attributed more to either the male or female noun phrase in the sentence stem) and verb valence (that is, does whether the verb is positive or negative influence whether it is attributed to noun phrase 1, or noun phrase 2).

into an analysis of verbs' implied causality. For example, Ferstl et al. (2011) raise the importance of considering gender effects alongside verb effects. Other research, such as Fowler's (1991) critical linguistics, provides a different emphasis – focusing not so much on the idea that different verbs have different causal implications, but, instead, on the effects of the order in which noun phrases occur within the target sentence. More fundamental problems concern the utility of 'stripped-down' sentences and the lack of attention to how causally implicative talk is *used to do things* in everyday life. These latter criticisms are so radical that they suggest not so much to an *amendment* to attributional semantics research, but, rather, to its *abandonment* in favour of the detailed study of actual instances of 'causally relevant' talk and what is done in and through such talk.

Critical review of attributional semantics

Gender of participant and noun phrase

Ferstl et al.'s (2011) research, outlined in Box 5.2, offered some partial support for the idea of implicit 'verb causality' – one part of their findings identifying that certain verbs tended to imply causality within either noun phrase 1 or noun phrase 2. Their research, however, also raised questions about whether other factors – specifically, gender – may be even *more* important. They found that the sex represented in the noun phrase was consequential and male and female participants responded differently to it.

Ferstl et al. (2011) found that men showed an 'own-gender effect' – that is, men tended to make more 'male' attributions when they completed the sentences and this occurred whether the male in the sentence was in noun phrase 1 or noun phrase 2 position. So, confronted with a sentence stem such as, 'Jasmine shouted at Gareth because'..., male participants would be more likely to see the cause of the shouting as within Gareth *(selecting the male, regardless of whether it forms the first or second noun phrase)* than female participants would. By contrast, female participants were found to show a noun phrase order effect, *choosing more noun phrase 1 causes* (and fewer noun phrase 2 causes) than men. Female participants encountering the same sentence – 'Jasmine shouted at Gareth because ... ' – would be more likely to select a cause within 'Jasmine', not because the name is female but because it forms the *first* noun phrase in the sentence stem. Furthermore, both male and female participants tended to attribute negative verbs (such as 'hit', 'kill') to men and positive ones (such as 'cuddle', 'welcome') to women, *regardless of where they were located in the sentence.*

Ferstl et al. (2011) note that these findings do raise problems for interpreting implicit causality simply in terms of lexical properties of the verbs themselves, as Crinean and Garnham (2006) suggest. If the causal biasing was entirely explainable in terms of the verb meaning, then the sex of the participant and the sex of the noun phrases should not make a difference. Because Ferstl et al. (2011) found the sex of the participant and the noun phrase *did* make a difference, they suggest that some other processes are at work – they refer specifically to cultural stereotypes about men and women.

Noun phrase positioning

As was mentioned earlier, much attributional semantics research has tended to make use of highly simplified sentences – noun phrase 1 *verb(ed)* noun phrase 2 (such as, 'Terhi *shouted* at Ragnor') and so on. Not all sentences take this simple active verb form, however. Any active sentence could be transformed into a passive form, such as 'Ragnor *was shouted at* by Terhi'. This switch from an active sentence structure to a passive one might seem irrelevant, but, for critical linguists such as Fowler (1991), it is crucial.

From this perspective, whatever implications the verb within a sentence might have, it is the **noun phrase positioning** that is seen as vitally important. Because we are so used to active sentence structures (such as 'Sean *called* Helen'), we tend to interpret noun phrases on the left (or in noun phrase 1 position) as having agency – that is, as bringing about (or at least contributing to) the thing we are trying to explain. Fowler (1991, p. 78) drawing on the work of Halliday (1985), suggests that 'there seems to be a schema for English which assumes that the left-hand noun-phrase (NP1) refers to an agent unless or until there is evidence to the contrary'(parentheses added). If we encounter a passive sentence structure, such as 'Helen was called by Sean', then, even though the semantics point to Sean being active, we may find ourselves tending towards seeing the cause as *within* Helen, simply because her name comes first in the sentence.

This may seem somewhat abstract and unimportant, but it *is* important for critical linguists such as Fowler as choosing to construct sentences in active or passive forms implies both causality and responsibility and can have

Noun phrase positioning This refers to the position that nouns have within (usually quite simple) sentences. Some research within this field has suggested that changing the order of nouns can change the causal implications of the sentence. Thus, a passive sentence such as, 'Student shouted at by lecturer' may suggest that the first noun (the student) at least partly brought it on him- or herself, whereas the active alternative, 'Lecturer shouted at student' might imply that it was entirely the lecturer's fault.

substantial ideological implications, with, for example, passive formulations being used to exonerate those in positions of power from blame. Fowler discusses how sentences in headlines and newspaper reports, such as 'A boy of five was shot', can do some sort of exonerating work for the authorities involved because they suggest that there might be something about the boy that gave rise to the shooting, without explicitly stating it.

Fowler's critical linguistics approach, then, provides an alternative to attributional semantics work because it highlights that, if the verb presentation changes, so, too, do the implied attributions. Furthermore, Fowler is keen to build from implied causality an understanding of what is being done by the choice of active or passive presentation (in news headlines in particular). For Fowler, this is approached in ideological terms – in particular, he is interested in how sentences that use passive forms of verbs are used to exonerate those in power.

It can be noted that others, such as Edwards and Potter (1992, 1993) and Antaki (1994) below, share an interest in what is being done in constructions of relevance to causes and responsibility, but, for them, the concern is less with the ideological implications of transitivity and more with the interactional work that is accomplished by virtue of where such talk occurs in sequences of interaction.

The utility of 'stripped-down' stimulus sentences

As has been noted above, attributional semantics research has endeavoured to map the causal implications of verbs themselves using very simple **stripped-down stimulus sentence** forms. While this may, in the eyes of attributional semantic researchers, enable a clearer focus on the implications of the verb alone, it does differ markedly from how we might encounter sentences describing causally relevant phenomena in everyday life.

Think for a moment about where you might encounter a sentence such as, 'John telephoned Mary ... 'on its own. It is extremely likely that each time we come across such a sentence *outside of a psychological experiment* there would be, or we would seek, more surrounding context. Thus, if we are told 'John telephoned Mary ... ', our concerns may include, 'What do we know about John and Mary?', 'What was the nature of the call?' and 'Why are we being told this (or what is being done in our being told this)?' and 'What is the content and reason for the call?' Issues of why we are being told will be dealt with very shortly when we consider the pragmatics of causal talk, but, for now, it is worth considering how any further contextualising information, such as information about who 'John' and 'Mary' are and what the call was about, changes the attributional implications.

Edwards and Potter (1992, 1993) note that, in the stripped-down form used in psychological experiments, we might well attribute the cause of the telephoning itself to the person who engages in the physical action of making a telephone call. As Edwards and Potter (1992, 1993) note, however, if further details are added (of the sort we would know or seek to know in a real-life informing about the call), we can change the picture markedly. Thus, to borrow an illustration from Edwards and Potter, if we add, 'Having received Mary's message to call her urgently on his ansaphone, John telephoned Mary', we can clearly distinguish the grammatical agent physically responsible for the act of telephoning (John) from the factors responsible in the situation for bringing about the phoning action (in this case, Mary). It is possible to envisage many variations that might highlight John or Mary or a combination as responsible for bringing about John's act of telephoning Mary.

Edwards and Potter (1992, 1993) argue that this situational responsibility – who is responsible for bringing about the conditions giving rise to the action – *is of more importance* to people talking about such behaviours than any abstracted causal inference associated with the verb's meaning in isolation. Thus, although attributional semantics researchers might emphasise that they want to find the pure causal implications of verbs – and may even concede other factors might be usefully added to reflect the complexity of everyday life – Edwards and Potter argue, rather than having a primary role in considerations of cause and responsibility, 'grammatical role agents' or the causal inferences inherent in the verb are overshadowed by the far more important consideration of responsibility. We are less interested in who has conducted the gross physical act than who or what can be seen as responsible for bringing this about – real-life talk about actions demonstrates our concern with information that is relevant to the issue of *responsibility*.

A further concern is the way in which the identities of the noun phrase characters may overwhelm any effect of the verb itself. Ferstl et al. (2011) highlighted the way in which, when gender information was manipulated, it became a relevant means by which participants calculated the cause of the target behaviour. Often in sentences we encounter, however, we will know – or seek to know – more than simply the gender of the protagonists and

Stripped-down stimulus sentences This refers to the made-up sentences given to participants in experiments without any surrounding context in order to assess the causal implications of the verb, the noun and/or the sentence structure. The phrase is usually used to highlight how different these experimental conditions are from the way in which causal sentences and explanations are encountered in non-experimental contexts.

these details will be important in calculating issues of cause and responsibility. If we switch the unknown fictitious characters we encounter in attribution semantics experiments for people we know or have heard of, any 'causal inference' property of the verb may well be overwhelmed.

Try, for example, completing this sentence:

> Name1 (person whom you find somewhat obnoxious) blamed
>
> Name2 (person of whom you are particularly fond) because ...

or:

> President Bush blamed the environmentalists because ...

or, perhaps a still more extreme example:

> Hitler blamed the Jews because ...

According to the results derived from the typical attribution semantics studies, 'blame' is an NP2 verb and we should complete the sentence in terms of causes associated with or located within the second person referred to – that is, in the above cases, our close friend, environmentalists and Jewish people respectively. Yet, the sentences suggest that it is easy to consider a range of noun phrase details that overwhelm any supposedly *pure effect* of the verb itself.

What is being done in causal talk?

It has been suggested above that considerations of the verb's definitional causal implications are secondary to who or what is deemed situationally responsible for the act (or experience) being considered. For example, we are less concerned with who the verb implies is the agent of phoning or the stimulus of praise than with who can be understood as responsible for it in the specific situation.

There is another consideration, however, that may be of even more immediate concern in real-life instances where we encounter (or even produce) the sorts of stimulus sentences that are crucial to attributional semantics research. If we are told, 'John telephoned Mary', assuming we know who the characters are, we are likely to consider why we are being told this – what is being done by the act of telling us this – and design our response in the light of this. It is possible to envisage a number of broad actions that the sentence might be designed to accomplish.

Imagine that you hear the sentence, 'John telephoned Mary' from a romantic partner. It may be delivering news or a prelude to a story. Perhaps John and Mary have a potentially romantic relationship and the phone call is a breakthrough event. It could be exonerating John for something that he had been held accountable for. For example, he may have been rightly or wrongly blamed for not phoning Mary, but now it can be reported that he has made the required call, so the blame ends. The sentence could be blaming John. Perhaps Mary is an ex-girlfriend and he swore to his current partner that he would not contact her. Then, the act of phoning is something that, as far as his current partner is concerned, he can be held accountable for. It may be that 'John telephoned Mary' is a means of holding you to account for not having made a similar call to your partner. Perhaps John is being held up as a model partner who called his partner Mary to wish her well prior to an important interview, while you have fallen short of John's high standards and made no such call to your partner in similar circumstances. Perhaps 'John telephoned Mary' addresses an argument that you were having in which you, correctly as it turns out, argued that John had made the call while your partner denied that the call had taken place. Here, the sentence is an acknowledgement that you were indeed right in the position you took.

It is possible to think up many more such examples, but the crucial point is this: in real-life usage, the sentences found in attributional semantics research are uttered *to do certain sorts of actions* and this is of vital importance to the participants in that interaction. As someone being told 'John telephoned Mary', you need to know whether *you* are being blamed or informed, whether *John* is being chastised or praised – without this knowledge you cannot know how to respond to the sentence. The possibility of considering how people might use various 'noun phrase – verb – noun phrase' sentences is completely shut off in experiments where participants are merely presented with a stream of decontextualised stimulus sentence stems to be completed in a testlike (rather than interactional) setting.

As Edwards and Potter (1992, p. 88) note, 'In all of the verb semantics studies of attribution, inferring the cause of an event takes no account of the speaker's action in describing it as so caused. The event is merely given, taken as true, so that the attribution of responsibility is for the event, not for the sentence.' This attention to what is being done is at the heart of the discursive action model that Edwards and Potter (1993, p. 23) develop: 'The approach we recommend here is that causal attributions, both inside and outside the laboratory, can fruitfully be studied as social acts performed in discourse and not merely as cognitions about social acts which happen to be expressed within conversations.'

If we want to consider how participants actually use these simple sentences and make sense of them when used, then perhaps the best port of call is everyday talk itself, where we can see when they are drawn on and what they are treated as doing by co-participants. Approaching causal talk in this way involves treating it as *action-orientated* – designed to do specific interactional work (such as informing, blaming, exonerating, acknowledging) and *sequentially sensitive* (accomplishing what is does by virtue of where it comes in a sequence of interactions). These considerations will be returned to when we look at discursive and conversation analytic work concerned with causal talk in Section 5.4. For now, it can be noted that attributional semantics work has been an important attempt to stress the link between talk (even talk that is not explicitly causal) and attribution, but some of its alleged shortcomings have been potentially addressed in two further fields of study that will be briefly reviewed next – the conversational model of causal attribution and the account-giving literature.

Critical recap

Attributional semantics

1 Ferstl et al. (2011) suggest that the gender of the protagonists in a stimulus sentence and the gender of participants are both highly consequential for causal judgements. They also suggest that the effects of noun phrase gender and participant's gender are often greater than any effect of the verb alone.

2 Work within the critical linguistics tradition (Fowler, 1991) has paid particular attention to the ways in which the order of the noun phrases can be important. Such work has suggested that noun phrases 'on the left-hand side' of a stimulus sentence are potentially causally implicated. The connotations of noun phrase positioning might be to reinforce any effect from the verb itself, but might mitigate or even reverse such an effect. As such, for critical linguists, the relative failure of attributional semantics literature to consider noun phrase positioning means that vitally important, causally implicative grammatical material is being overlooked.

3 Attributional semantic experiments, as we have seen, fail to consider the impact of noun phrase details. We perhaps only ever get the 'uncontaminated', 'pure' single sentences in these sorts of attribution experiments. The preoccupation with the causal implications of verbs alone may differ markedly from the everyday use of contextual detail when considering who is responsible for the action being considered. In real life, more detail is likely to be present (or sought if it is not present) and it may be more important for judgements of cause and responsibility than the attribution implications of the 'pure verb'.

4 In real life – rather than in decontextualised encounters with stimulus sentences – descriptive talk itself will be made sense of in terms of *what it is doing* or orientating to (Edwards & Potter, 1992, 1993). That is, if we are presented with a descriptive sentence, we will be particularly concerned with why we are being told this, what is being done by being told this and what we might do ourselves via our response. These key concerns, while crucial to how we engage with descriptions, cannot be examined in experiments where descriptive sentences appear devoid of any sequential context.

Reflective questions

1 *How would you design an attributional semantics experiment?*

2 *What would you expect to find?*

5.2 Conversational model of attribution

One issue with the attribution theory work considered in Chapter 4 and the attribution talk considered so far is that it seems disconnected from the everyday context in which attributions and explanations are actually used. Attribution theory focuses on the (private) cognitive event of making an attribution, not its communication. The attributional semantics work above takes a step towards the everyday context by giving some sense of how the words used in describing an outcome to be explained may shape our causal thinking. Thus, attributional semantics has a relevance for thinking critically about attribution experiments – such as how the verbal presentation of stimulus may itself shape the causal reasoning process. It also has a relevance for everyday contexts in which a verbal representation of the outcome to be explained is encountered – the most obvious example of this being news reports, particularly newspaper reports. In this way, while attributional semantics work has relied heavily on experimental data, it has conceptualised the importance of the descriptive words used in shaping actual instances of attribution, rather than trying to describe a generic content-free causal reasoning process. What attributional semantics does, then, is encourage us to consider the particulars of specific instances, not just a global template of the reasoning or biasing processes at work in all cases of attribution.

Attribution semantic work, however, could still be seen as disconnected from many everyday instances of attribution talk. Think for a moment of a specific instance when you made an attribution statement – what was said? It is likely that, first, you will find it hard to think of an instance when your talk matches the sort of attribution talk that is implied in much of the research considered so far. Thus, you probably can't think of many instances in which you said, 'John laughed at the comedian because of something about John'. As we shall see later, actual instances of 'attribution-relevant talk' may be much less formulaic than that.

Second, your attribution talk was probably fitted into some sort of interaction context. It is unlikely that you marched up to someone at a bus stop and announced, 'John is frightened about the dog because of something about the dog'. If you did suddenly announce an attribution to an unsuspecting stranger, your behaviour would probably be marked as odd in some way as it breeches social conventions – an issue that Garfinkel (1967) was particularly interested in. Instead, our attribution talk typically occurs where there is some other talk to which it relates. For example, the person we are talking with may ask us a question to which we respond to with an attribution. For example 'Why's the place such a mess?', to which we might reply, 'Because the phone's been ringing non-stop!' The **conversational model** approach considered here picks up on certain aspects of how attributions are made and communicated in the context of interactions. For now, we can note, and leave to one side, the point that the subsequent approaches – particularly the discursive and conversation analytic approaches – strongly criticise the extent to which the conversational model really engages with everyday attribution talk and interactional contexts (Antaki, 1994).

For the conversational model, attributions are thought of as being produced in a conversational sequence – typically forming a response to a prior question that asks for an explanation (see Figure 5.1). Thus, if someone asks, 'Why are you late?', 'How come you got up so late?' or 'Why are you speaking with your eyes shut?' the person to whom the question is addressed will typically make an attribution in their response, such as, 'The traffic was dreadful', 'I was up late reading a new social psychology textbook' or 'It helps me to concentrate.' As Antaki (1994) notes, the conversational model of attribution developed by Lalljee (1981) and Hilton (1990, 1991) describes the cognitive processes of attributions as being 'triggered' by such prior questions. Indeed, as we shall consider later, the model *only* accounts for attributions that are given as a response to some prior request. It therefore excludes what Antaki refers to as monologue explanations – where the speaker presents and explains a case themselves.

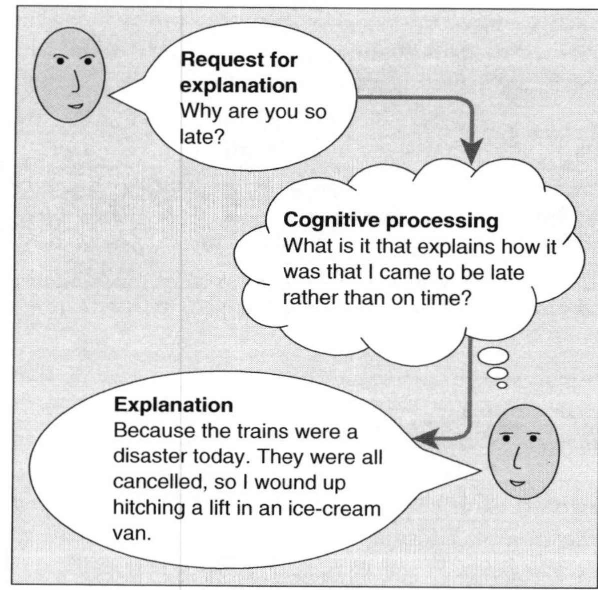

Figure 5.1 The conversational model of causal attribution

The conversational model, while distinct from attributional semantics in its conversational emphasis, does incorporate the general idea (central to attributional semantics research) that the attribution process may be shaped by the way in which the event, or outcome, to be explained is described. Thus, the description of the outcome to be described (in the question that elicits an explanation) is thought to constrain, influence or shape the subsequent attribution and explanation. As Antaki (1994) notes, some of the work in the conversational model goes further still and imports attributional semantics research wholesale, understanding verbs as having just the same sort of attribution-implying effect as the attributional semantics research considered above. For the conversational model of attribution, however, the influence of outcome description is not limited to choice of verb – one particularly important factor is the implicit or explicit contrast in the explanation-eliciting question.

Conversational model An approach to attribution that emphasises the way requests for explanations may shape the explanations they elicit. One particular focus has been on the implict (sometimes explict) contrast between the actual and possible states of affairs that are being asked about – for example, the question, 'Why are you late?' requires an explanation that is relevant for lateness, but not punctuality. Researchers in this field tend to make use of hypothetical sentences rather than the careful examination of sequences of interaction.

The conversational model notes that requests for explanations *themselves* contain some implicit (or explicit) contrast between the specific event or outcome to be explained and other possible alternatives. Thus, when we are asked why we are late, the contrast is with a state of affairs where we are *not* late. Although not explicitly stated, the question, 'Why are you late?' implicitly contrasts being late with being on time – it's as if we are asked 'Why are you late rather than on time?'

The conversational model argues that our response picks up on the specific, implicit (or explicit) contrast within the question. That is, the causal reason we give has to be a factor which is present for the case to be explained and not present in the contrast case. This discriminatory factor is referred to as a 'counterfactual'. The very question, 'Why are you late?' sets up the need for a response that fits and identifies some such counterfactual – a potential causal factor accounting for what came about (our lateness) and not present when we are on time. So, our response, 'I was up late last night' might not be a sufficiently discriminating counterfactual if we are *always* up late, but might fit very well if this is a factor that co-occurs with (and only with) our being late. Indeed, the counterfactual identified in explanatory talk is typically the unusual, abnormal or surprising factor that might reasonably explain the outcome. Thus, the recipient of a request for an explanation for lateness will pay little attention to factors common to all days and, instead, select a potential cause that is 'unusually present' in the case of being late.

The conversational model has so far suggested everyday causal attribution work can be seen to occur where a request for an explanation is made that makes or implies a contrast between the event to be explained and other contrastive possibilities. The person giving the explanation undertakes a cognitive search through factors that could potentially bring about the event to be explained and identifies those that are counterfactuals – present for the event, but not the contrastive possible events. Before a specific counterfactual is offered, however, there is what Antaki (1994, drawing on Hilton, 1991) refers to as a 'quality control filter'. This proposed filter is Grice's (1975) 'conversational cooperative principle'.

Before outlining this, let's just think for a moment about the way in which your explanations of the event could differ, depending on who you were talking to. With a close friend or partner, for example, you may have such a shared pool of knowledge, you can formulate your explanations in ways that might make no sense to others but do to them. Imagine, for example, your partner asking, 'Why's the rubbish been taken out of the bin?' Replying, 'It was you know who' may be perfectly informative, given a shared understanding as to the 'who' being alluded to. If, however, the question was asked by some unknown person who was in the process of collecting the bin, this response may fail to be sufficiently informative and clear.

For Grice (1975), all of our conversational utterances are expected to adhere to the principles of being informative and clear, as well as relevant and true. That, is while we can be uninformative, obscure, irrelevant and untruthful, to keep the conversation running smoothly, we need to meet these cooperative requirements. Thus, Hilton suggests that, in communicating our explanations, we assess them, shaping and reworking them as necessary so they meet Grice's maxims of conversational cooperation.

The conversational model has, to some extent, both cognitive and interactional dimensions. Cognitively, the process of causal reasoning is itself understood as essentially a mental event. In terms of the interactional element, the explanation is seen as located within and triggered by the conversational context – with the explanation typically following a request. Thus, the attribution calculation process is seen as initiated by a request for an explanation. Rather than having interactional features also shape something of the communicated explanation, the explanation request is seen as providing implicitly (or explicitly) some sense of the contrastive possibilities, the non-occurrence of which needs to be accounted for in the explanation given. Furthermore, Gricean maxims of conversational cooperation are thought to help mould the specific form in which the explanation will be communicated. In this way, the conversational model can be seen as providing some advance on much previous work in which attribution was understood simply in terms of inner cognitive calculations and distortions. The issue of how the attribution process related to the real world of social interactions that was largely ignored and undertheorised in most attribution approaches has been integrated into the conversational model. The idea that explanations may be responsive or orientated in some way to prior talk is a concern developed in research using discursive and **conversation analysis** approaches. As is outlined below,

Conversation analysis Easily confused with the conversational model because of its name, but very different. Conversation analysis is a term used to describe an approach that cuts across several disciplinary boundaries and involves the careful analysis of real-world sequences of interaction with an emphasis on the ways in which people build interaction conjointly – with each turn of interaction both orientating to and reshaping the immediate sequential context.

however, from a discursive and conversation analytic perspective, there are major problems with the rigid, cognitively driven way in which the conversational model articulates the relationship between explanation and explanation-eliciting prior talk.

Critical review of the conversational model of attribution

Additional determinants

First, it is worth noting – as Antaki (1994) does – that the conversational model does not recognise the full range of 'syntactic determinants' that the event description might contain. That is, while the conversational model lays great emphasis on the ways in which the talk that solicits an explanation can shape or constrain that explanation by implicit or explicit contrast cases or by the verb used, it does not consider how these potential determinants might be affected by other aspects of grammar or syntax.

One example of this was considered above in our discussion of the critical linguistics perspective. Fowler (1991, drawing on Halliday, 1985) suggested that noun phrases occurring very early in the sentence (left-hand noun phrases) were implicitly more active causal agents than those placed later in the sentence. Thus, 'Why was the boy attacked by the gang?' implies some potential feature of the *boy* as being relevant in the subsequent explanation, whereas 'Why did the gang attack the boy?' can be heard as perhaps highlighting features of the *gang* as more relevant. Thus, from the stance of critical linguistics, where there are two possible nouns that could be causally relevant (here 'boy' and 'gang'), the noun phrase positioning in the explanation-soliciting sentence may have bearing on what the explanation focuses on. Here, the noun phrase positioning may not be just relevant, it may undercut what the verb might be expected to imply in terms of attributional semantics – for example, 'attack' might be expected to suggest a causal agency on the part of the person from whom the 'attacking' behaviour issues, but placing 'boy' first in the sentence may imply that the boy might reasonably be the focus of the explanation.

Requests for an explanation are not always followed by an explanation

Inspecting actual sequences of everyday interaction reveals that where causal questions do occur, they are not always responded to by explanations in the way that the conversational model of attribution suggests. An example of this is provided in Extract 5.2.

Extract 5.2

(A broadcast of a news interview, JG, *asks a question of the interviewer*, IR)

(*Note:* Transcription simplified)

JG I'm asking you *why* you dis*tort*ed those facts (0.2)
IR Well we didn't distort them

Source: Heritage and Greatbatch (1991, p. 105, cited in Antaki, 1994, p. 35)

Following the conversational model of attribution, we might expect that JG's question would trigger IR to make an attribution. Thus, IR's response might be expected to be the identification of some explanation for the distortion of the facts. Instead, however, IR does not produce an explanation fitted to the outcome description within the question stimulus ('you distorted those facts'). Far from producing an explanation that is matched to the information contained in the question, IR challenges the description of the outcome to be explained itself.

Occurrences such as these, where the presentation of the outcome to be explained is challenged, are not unusual and, often, quite key to disputes within interactions. We can note that, first, instances such as this raise problems for the conversational model's idea that explanation-seeking questions will prompt explanations in response.

A second, and more fundamental, issue, which is developed in Edwards and Potter (1992), is that this extract problematises the idea that we can have a straightforward, non-problematic description of the facts awaiting explanation. Instead, as we shall see later, Edwards and Potter argue that the facts can be variously constructed – that is, there are many different ways of describing the phenomena we present. These different possible versions presented are not neutral, but serve particular interests – that is, our description of facts is used to do specific work in interaction, such as blaming, exonerating, agreeing or disagreeing. Finally, rather than being separate from the process of causality, they may often imply issues of responsibility and accountability themselves. In the above extract, the description 'you distorted those facts' does a blaming, it holds the interviewer, IR, to account for some sanctionable behaviour.

Explanations are not always preceded by a request

Examining everyday interaction also reveals that explanations are not always preceded by causal questions (see Extract 5.3).

In Extract 5.3, B makes some slightly critical comments regarding another person – 'she still has that silly chatter about 'er'. B provides an explanation for these

Extract 5.3

B I like 'er very much.
B But she still has that silly chatter about 'er.
A Mm hm,
B That is like a
(1.0)
B Oh, I'm not much of a teaser
(1.0)
B Well now this is my fault. I don't like teasing.
A Mm, hm,
B And I know People love it.

Source: Pomerantz (1984, p. 94)

comments in terms of B's own attributes – 'Oh, I'm not much of a teaser', 'Well now this is my fault. I don't like teasing'. As is evident above, however, both the item to be explained and the explanation are provided by B, rather than being produced in response to a request for an explanation by A. This is not only problematic for the conversational model in its very occurrence – according to which, explanations should not be volunteered but requested – but it also raises a fundamentally different perspective on explanations within everyday interaction. Instead of seeing explanations as being orientated to issues identified by prior questions, explanations can be understood as orientating to whatever is occurring within the sequence of interaction. In the above extract, for example, we can note that B's explanation is a self-deprecating remark: 'Well now this is my fault. I don't like teasing'. This is produced in an interactional context where B's criticism of another person's 'silly chatter' does not elicit agreement on the part of A. B's self-deprecating explanation may thus be a useful device for orientating to potential disagreement with earlier assessments that the speaker has made.

Extract 5.4 further illustrates a non-requested explanation. This time, the setting is a televised political interview.

In Extract 5.4, three statements can be identified that appear to be explanations of one form or another (lines 7 and 8, 10 and 11 – 14). Contrary to the conversational model of attribution, none of these explanations appears to occur after an explicit request. Furthermore, rather than being constrained by what has been said by the other conversational participant previously and orientating to Gricean maxims of cooperation, the explanations are used to dispute what has been said by the other participant and advance an alternative construction of events. Each explanation is, very briefly, considered below.

The first explicit explanation can be found in lines 7 and 8 – 'no:> er ↑let's be honest about it< let's:: (0.5) in this: period (0.5) mister Ma↑jor's called this: election (0.5) not me'. Here, the explanation is provided alongside the event to be explained – calling the election. This talk, which explicitly disputes the prior talk of the interviewer, constructs the calling of the election as the event to be explained, whereas the previous turn at talk by JS concerned the consequences of concentrating on 'this one single issue'. EL's explanation also sets up an explicit contrast between two possible causes of the calling of the election – 'mister Major' 'not me'.

This first explanation, then, was not triggered by a prior question, constrained by its syntax or conversationally cooperative. Instead, it constructed an event to be explained (calling the election) and provided an explanation that accomplished a blaming (of Major), an exoneration (of the speaker, EL) and was framed as providing an alternative version of events to that presented in the prior talk of JS ('no:> er ↑let's be honest about it<').

Extract 5.4

(*Note*: Modified slightly)

JS >Mister ↑Major says< that (0.3) by er:: (0.4) s:o concentrating on this
<one single issue> you are o↑bliterating (0.5) ex↑tinguishing (0.5)
what people understand of the rest of the government's achievements
[erm] in the ↑end >this is going to come home to haunt you in=
EL [not true]
JS =your own seats<
(0.7)
→ EL no:> er ↑let's be honest about it< let's:: (0.5) in this: period
→ (0.5) mister Ma↑jor's called this: election (0.5) not me (0.6) now this
is an (0.4) [an opportunity]
→ JS [>opposition that] caused it though<=
EL =HHHH hehh nonsense:: (0.6) heh >am I responsible for the fact that
→ we're forty points behind (.) I tell why we're forty points behind<
→ because we promise tax cuts at the General Election and we've
→ increased taxes [↑because]

Source: Channel 4 News broadcast, 23 June 1995, Jon Snow interviewing Edward Leigh – transcription from Dickerson (2001, p. 208)

The second explanation (line 10: '[>opposition that] caused it though<=') follows not a request for an explanation but, rather, the explanation just considered above. This second explanation, again, is not triggered and constrained by the prior talk, nor is it conversationally cooperative with it. Instead, it follows the immediately prior explanation (which exonerates EL) with an alternative explanatory framing (which holds EL to account). The second explanation does not dispute the idea that Major literally called the election, but does dispute the implication that this can be used to blame Major and exonerate EL by constructing the opposition (which EL was central to) as the prior cause – the factor that caused the election to be called.

Here, then, in direct contrast to the conversational model of attribution, providing an explanation is not found to cooperatively close a question–explanation interactional exchange. Instead, the explanation itself becomes the topic of dispute and is orientated to by the construction of an alternative explanation.

The third explanation occurs in lines 11–14: '=HHHH hehh nonsense:: (0.6) heh >am I responsible for the fact that we're forty points behind (.) I tell why we're forty points behind< because we promise tax cuts at the General Election and we've increased taxes [↑ because]'. This explanation, again, does not follow any request on the part of the conversational co-participant, but is offered as a direct challenge to the previous explanation.

Explanation number three constructs the event to be explained as the Conservative Government being 'forty points behind' (the then opposition party, Labour) in the opinion polls. It constructs the cause as broken promises by 'we' (the Conservative Government). This construction of being 'forty points behind' as the issue to be explained can, again, be seen as a rhetorical strategy for disputing the previous explanation that EL was to blame for the opposition that caused the election to be called.

Now, implicitly, 'being forty points behind' is positioned as the prior cause that (according to EL) caused the opposition of EL, which, in turn (according to JS), caused the election to be called. In attributing 'being forty points behind' to the broken promises of the Conservative Government (which EL was a part of only in so far as he was a Conservative member of Parliament), EL exonerates himself from blame and places it on the Government instead. Here, then, the construction of the issue to be explained and the explanation are more readily seen as rhetorical or disputational moves – orientated to the issues of blame and exoneration rather than cognitive calculations, triggered by a request, constrained by the description of the thing to be described and orientated to conversational cooperation.

Making explanations relevant and giving explanations are sequentially located activities

From a conversation analytic and discursive perspective, the conversational model does not pay attention to *what explanations do* within *specific sequential positions*. The conversational model points to context in a minimal respect – noting how explanations are triggered and, to some extent, constrained by the explanation-eliciting question that precedes them. From a conversation analytic and discursive perspective, however, this relies on rigid and narrowly specified frameworks (regarding 'explanation-eliciting questions' and 'explanation') and on a hypothesised cognitive process linking the two.

From a conversation and discursive perspective, talk that might make explanatory talk relevant can take a vast number of different forms. For example, what might appear to be mere descriptions can make an explanation extremely relevant: 'This place is a mess!', 'It's gone midnight!', 'You have done nothing but complain all night.' What this talk does and makes relevant can be examined without recourse to cognitive processes. Instead, the sequence itself can be examined to see how such talk is treated by subsequent turns at talk. These may well reveal some form of explanation or account being given or address the relevance or expectation that an account might be given. This means that what we may find in a subsequent turn may take many forms rather than being a prototypical 'explanation' constrained by the explanation-eliciting question. For example, 'I was trying to find your necklace!', 'You are always checking up on me!', 'I don't have to put up with any more of this!' All of these utterances show that they are responsive to what the preceding talk has made relevant, yet are not narrowly constrained by that talk in the way the conversational model suggests.

Critical recap

Conversational model of attribution

1 As Antaki (1994) notes, there may be other factors, such as the syntax of the explanation-eliciting question, that 'constrain' the explanation given. Thus, the form that the question takes, whether it is passive – 'Why was X attacked by Y?' – or active – 'Why did Y attack X?' – could 'constrain' the type of explanation that is received.

2 Sometimes, as Antaki (1994) notes and Heritage and Greatbatch (1991) illustrate, requests can be followed by other types of action than explanations – for example, objecting to the basis of the question or posing an alternative question suggesting that people may not be constrained in the way that the conversation model suggests.

3 Data analysed by Pomerantz (1984) and Dickerson (2001) illustrate that explanatory talk may be offered without being preceded by an explanation-eliciting question.

4 Discursive and conversation analytic research provides a different way of conceptualising what sort of prior talk might make some form of explanatory work relevant – this was seen to be much wider than explicit requests for an explanation. Similarly, discursive and conversation analytic work is sensitive to the different ways in which subsequent talk can display its orientation to the relevance of 'explanatory work', which may involve an explicit or implicit explanation or some other type of action altogether (such as challenging the prior talk or holding the other person to account in some way).

Reflective questions

1 *Can you find an example of one explanation that does and one which does not appear to be preceded or shaped by an explanation-eliciting question?*

2 *What criticisms do discursive and conversation analytic work raise regarding the conversational model?*

5.3 Account-giving literature

In considering attributional semantics and the conversational model above, it is possible that the discussion seems a little abstract – removed from our everyday concerns with explanations. We may not be regularly aware of or concerned with the causal implications of verbs or the way in which explanation-eliciting questions shape our explanations. We are, however, very likely to be aware of having given reasons and/or excuses for things that we have done or not done.

The account-giving literature seeks, whether successfully or not, to provide some meaningful understanding of the types of accounts (or explanations) that we use in our talk and comment on the perceived effectiveness of those accounts. Here, then, we might find – or hope to find – the type of explanatory talk that we could well be quite conscious of using – those reasons and excuses we give for all of our shortcomings. Also, we might hope to find some sort of 'psychologically informed guidance' regarding which of our accounts would actually be most effective.

Imagine turning up late for a date or a job interview or forgetting a birthday or an anniversary or promising to pick up some groceries for a friend and then not doing so – all of these are examples of behaviour we might be required to explain. We can probably think of many times when we have explained ourselves for such misdemeanors or omissions: 'Sorry I'm late the traffic/transport/journey/psychic energy was terrible', 'Sorry about your birthday, it has been so stressful at work/college/home/rehab'. Thus, when we have engaged in what Antaki (1994) calls 'sanctionable behaviour' – undesired behaviour for which others might seek an explanation – we typically find ourselves excusing, justifying or otherwise exonerating ourselves – that is, *accounting* for that behaviour. The explanatory talk is our account for our behaviour.

Accounts can also be given for unanticipated behaviour – that is, others might require or expect us to explain how we managed to stay awake through every single social psychology lecture or display real interest when our uncle showed us the 400 photographs that he took of a colleague's wedding. In fact, it may well be that *most* of our explanatory talk concerning our own behaviour is in the form of an account. We probably do not very regularly say things such as, 'I laughed at the comedienne because her timing was great' or 'I was frightened of the dog because of something about me', but, even if we did, it is hard not to hear these utterances as, in some sense, providing an account. That is, the fact that we voice a cause implies the behaviour referred to somehow *needs* to be explained – it perhaps implies there was something inappropriate or unexpected about the laughter or fear.

One important strand of research in the accounts literature has concerned the types of account talk that can be found. Scott and Lyman's (1968) classic paper provided one of the first of many taxonomies of accounts. For them, 'excuses' were understood as quite distinct from 'justifications'. Excuses deny agency or actor responsibility – 'I didn't mean to forget, I suffer from stress-related amnesia' – whereas justifications accept responsibility, but give reasons for the act – 'I was thinking of you. You said you wanted to forget about your birthdays from now on.' Semin and Manstead (1983) further specified the different subtypes of excuses and justifications (with some changes and additions to Scott and Lyman's taxonomy), but kept the same basic split between the responsibility-denying excuses and the 'good reason'-giving justifications.

A second strand of research – which Antaki (1994) refers to as 'pencil and paper studies' – has attempted to investigate what factors are associated with higher or lower ratings of effectiveness or acceptability of the different excuses and justifications. Studies such as Mehrabian (1967), Blumstein, Carssow, Hall, Hawkins, Hoffman, Ishem, Maurer, Spens, Taylor and Zimmerman (1974),

Schlenker and Darby (1981), Hale (1987) and Holtgraves (1989) investigated the effectiveness of exonerating statements by presenting participants with hypothetical scenarios concerning an offence being committed (such as handing in an essay late, corrupt political practice) and various excuses and justifications offered to account for them. Participants would typically be asked to rate the effectiveness or acceptability of the excuses and justifications given.

A third strand of research entails experimental enactment of the offence and the excuse or justification. In this research, a confederate commits an offence against the participants (who are usually secretly monitored) and then offers an excuse or justification. Thus, participants might experience a confederate pushing into a photocopier queue (Langer, Blank, & Chanowitz, 1978) or turning up late (Weiner, Amirkhan, Folkes, & Verette, 1987) and then receive one of the several variants of excuses and/or justifications that are being investigated.

Some of this research has led to attempts to conceptualise the features of effective excuses for certain classes of offence. The specific exoneration uttered by the confederate is treated as less important than the *broader type of excuse or exoneration* that it is thought to represent. Likewise, the specifics of the offence are treated as less important than the *broader class of offence* that it is taken to represent.

Shaw, Wild and Colquitt (2003) conducted a meta-analysis that investigated the effectiveness of **excuses versus justifications** in an organisational context. This review of previous research pitched Scott and Lyman's (1968) two main types of account – excuse and justification – against each other. Was it more effective (particularly in an organisational context) to provide an account that denied agency or responsibility (an excuse) or an account providing reasons for the action taken (a justification)? Which sort of account would work best if, for example, someone was late for a meeting – an excuse, 'There was an accident and all the roads were blocked', or a justification, 'I thought I would give you a few moments to think things through before we met.'

Shaw et al. (2003) found that excuses tended to be more effective. As Hareli (2005) notes, however, these findings may confound account *type* (excuses and justifications) with account *quality*. Hareli argues that it may be easier to come up with higher-quality excuses than justifications and it may be *this* quality of an account that is all-important rather than whether it takes the form of an excuse or a justification.

Weiner et al. (1987) provide one approach to tackling the content of an account in a little more detail than its gross categorisation as either an excuse or justification (see Box 5.3). To get a clear understanding of their work, it is worth thinking for a moment about various social *faux pas* – such as turning up late, or not at all, for a meeting – perhaps with a friend or acquaintance. Think of the various reasons for lateness or non-arrival you have been given by people in the past and the reasons you have given. It is very likely that these communicated accounts include things such as transport – 'You would not believe the trains/traffic/buses' – or illness – 'I must have been coming down with something, I felt so awful' – or pressing other commitments – 'My mum and dad dropped by out of the blue and I couldn't get out of it'.

These examples suggest that the accounts we typically communicate (and have others communicate to us) tend to downplay responsibility and choice. By contrast, if we reflect on the various 'real' reasons for our own lateness or non-appearance, other causes come into the frame – 'I didn't really want to go' or 'I just forgot all about it'. It is probably the case that these reasons are often true (for ourselves and others), but are less frequently communicated (see Figure 5.2).

Weiner et al.'s first experiment (see Box 5.3, Figure 5.3a) investigated precisely this issue of **communicated accounts versus real reasons** Participants were

Figure 5.2 Communicated accounts versus 'real' reasons

Excuses versus justifications Excuses deny agency ('it was not my choice or fault' – for example, an excuse for arriving late at a dinner party could be, 'The train was late'. Justifications, by contrast, accept responsibility and give a rationale for the action, so a justification for lateness could be, 'I thought it would be nicer for you if people staggered their arrival – some coming early and some, like myself, later.'

Communicated accounts versus real reasons This distinction is between the explanation (or account) that is given – for example, the reason that you *said* you were unable to pop round for a coffee when asked by the shifty-looking stranger at the bus stop (for example, 'Too busy right now') – and the real reason you declined the invitation (for example, they gave you the creeps).

asked to describe a recent time in which they had given a reason for being late, not turning up or failing to do something expected of them. In one condition, participants were asked to report on a case where the reason given was true, while, in another condition, they were asked to report on a case where they had given a false reason (and report on what the true, non-communicated reason was). Ratings of the reasons (given by independent raters) suggested that there was a distinction to be drawn between communicated reasons (whether true or false) and non-communicated reasons. That is, the accounts people gave to others (which Weiner et al. represent with the prototypical 'My car broke down') tend to be external (although, sometimes, the internal account of illness is given) are usually uncontrollable and almost always unintentional. That is, they do not reside in the person (illness being the notable exception here), are not within the person's control and do not reflect any intention on the part of the person. By contrast, concealed reasons – that is, 'real reasons' where a false reason was communicated (which Weiner et al. represent with the prototypical, 'I did not want to go') – are nearly always internal, controllable and, usually, intentional. Participants' responses indicated that they felt these internal, controllable and intentional reasons, if communicated, would be detrimental to the impression given, make the wronged party angry and damage the social bond between them.

A follow-up experiment – in which participants were asked to imagine being on the receiving end of various accounts – provided some corroboration for this idea that the wronged party might react more negatively to internal, controllable and intentional accounts than external, uncontrollable and unintentional ones (see Box 5.3, Figure 5.3b).

The accounts that evoked the highest anger ratings were ones in which the 'wrongdoer' reported a preference (such as, 'I did not want to go') and were rated by the participants themselves as internal, controllable and intentional. Accounts that evoked the lowest anger ratings included illness and transportation problems. Interestingly, in this follow-up study, illness ('I had the flu') was rated by participants as being an external rather than an internal cause.

It should be noted that participants in this experiment were asked to presume all of the accounts were true, whereas, in real life, if we have doubts about the truthfulness of an account it is perhaps more likely that the account in question refers to external, uncontrollable and unintentional causes than admitting to a preference. Furthermore, in this experiment, participants were reporting how angry they would feel in *hypothetical* circumstances.

Concerns about the retrospective dimension to the first experiment and the hypothetical aspect of the second were addressed in two further experiments. In the third experiment, (see Box 5.3, Figure 5.3c), a confederate (who was understood by genuine participants to be a fellow participant in an experiment on 'first impressions') arrived 15 minutes late. Across different conditions, the confederates either gave an external, uncontrollable and unintentional account ('The professor in my class gave me an exam that ran way over time and that's why I'm late. I had to run all the way here'), an internal, controllable and intentional account ('I was talking to some friends I ran into in the hall and that's why I'm late. I figured it would be no problem') or no excuse. Findings suggested that those giving the external, uncontrollable and unintentional excuse evoked more positive emotions, were rated as having more positive traits and the participants expressed more desire for future contact. Those offering the internal, controllable and intentional account were rated similarly to those who said nothing at all.

In the final experiment, (see Box 5.3, Figure 5.3c) accounts were offered by participants to other participants, albeit with some direction from experimenters. Thus, the experiment was designed such that one participant would be late in meeting the other. The late participant was asked to 'do a bit of acting', giving either a bad excuse that would evoke anger, a good excuse, any excuse or no excuse for their lateness.

Recipients of the excuse then completed a 22-item questionnaire on their emotional reactions, the presumed traits of the late participant and their desire to see them again.

Findings indicated that participants in the 'any excuse' condition gave similar accounts to those in the 'good excuse' condition – that is, when asked to make up any excuse, participants tended to give what was perceived to be a good excuse. These 'good excuses' differed from 'bad excuses' in several respects – most notably in not referring to free choice at all and seldom citing negligence as a reason. By contrast, negligence and free choice were the most popular accounts given in the 'bad excuse' condition. Participants who received the accounts rated their own emotions and desire to see the fellow participant again more positively and judged the traits of their co-participants to be more positive in the 'good' and 'any excuse' conditions and lower in the 'bad excuse' conditions.

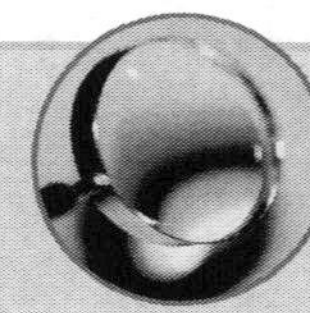

Box 5.3 FOCUS
Overview of Weiner et al.'s (1987) experiments

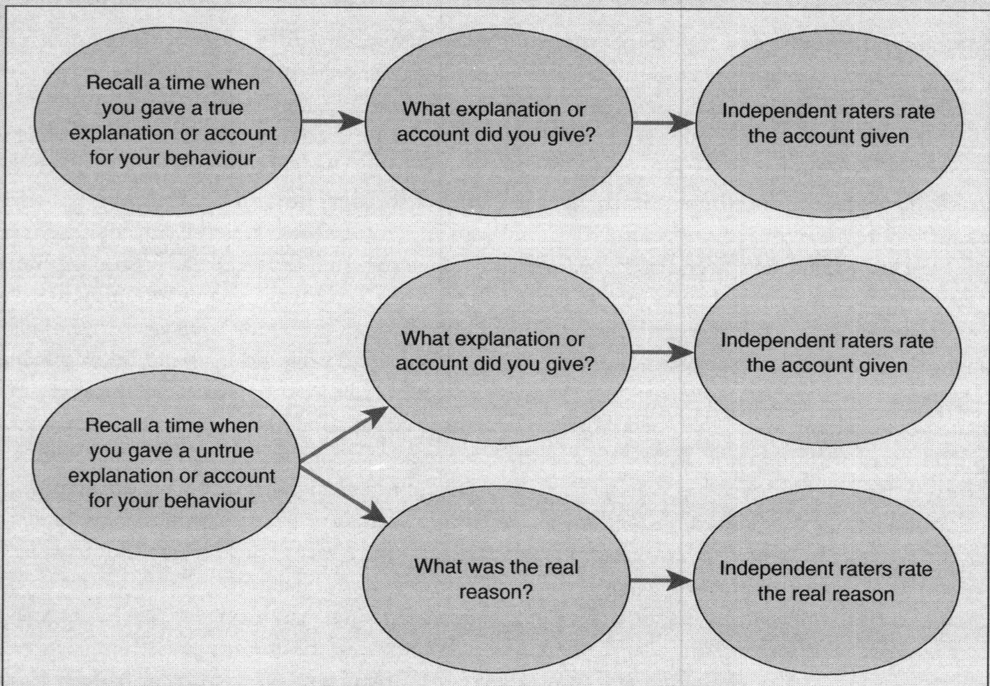

Figure 5.3a Experiment 1 – recollections of true and untrue explanations or accounts given in the past

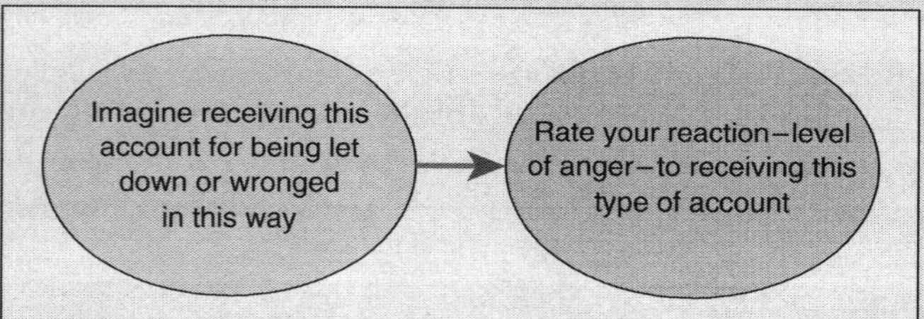

Figure 5.3b Experiment 2 – participants record their reactions to different types of account in hypothetical scenarios

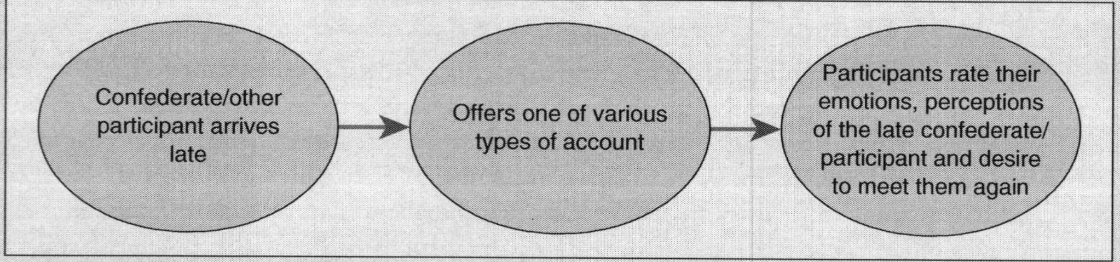

Figure 5.3c Experiments 3 and 4 – a confederate arrives late and offers different types of account (or none at all) and the participants rate their reactions

Critical review of the account-giving literature

The account-giving literature in general and Weiner et al.'s (1987) work in particular can be seen as emphasising how explanations given for ourselves – or accounts – are used. In contrast to certain more abstract concerns of models of causal reasoning or descriptions of cognitive, motivational, societal or linguistic biases, the account-giving literature places centre stage the notion that, in many cases, reasons are given to do exonerating work by someone who is expected to account for their 'wrong' or unexpected behaviour.

In addition, Weiner et al. exemplify research within the account-giving literature that has moved beyond simply comparing excuses with justifications. It is possible, however, to question the extent to which research has engaged with aspects of the quality of the accounts' content and the importance of the context of the surrounding talk for accounts.

Quality of the accounts' content

Weiner et al. (1987) thus move beyond the excuse–justification dichotomy, but still rely on characterising accounts on broad dimensions – for example, 'effective' 'good' excuses were distinguished from 'ineffective' 'bad' excuses on the basis of their appeal to external, uncontrollable and unintentional causes. For Weiner et al., it is enough to know that an excuse refers to external, uncontrollable and unintentional causes – 'Someone snatched my assignment from me on the way to class' – for it to be judged an effective, good excuse. Hareli (2005), however, raises problems with this idea. For him, it is the content and quality of that content (does it appear to be true, reasonable, normative and appropriate?) that is all-important.

Offering unlikely or inappropriate excuses would not be perceived as effective, even if they had the features of appealing to external, uncontrollable and unintentional causes. Thus, the external, uncontrollable and unintentional excuses that *are* effective are a subset of accounts that already pass the criteria of appearing to be true, reasonable, normative and appropriate. Claiming that I do not have an important essay 'because aliens snatched it from me unexpectedly in the night' is certainly appealing to external, uncontrollable and unintentional causal factors, but is unlikely to be an effective excuse because it would not be perceived as true, reasonable, normative or appropriate. For Hareli, these criteria of quality are more fundamental and take precedence over both crude classifications, such as excuses versus accounts, and more refined distinctions, such as the different types or dimensions of excuses.

Context of the surrounding talk

Crucially, also from a discursive perspective, to understand how such talk is used, hypothetical scenarios, scripted enactments or staged encounters are of limited use when genuine sequences of interaction are taken to be central. For discursive psychology and conversation analysis, looking at how accounts are given in actual sequences of talk shows them as doing what they do by virtue of where they occur in a specific sequence of interaction. The experimental, account-giving literature implicitly approaches accounts as isolatable, context-free utterances and they do, or do not do, effective account-giving *regardless of where they occur in any sequence of talk*.

This perspective ignores the idea developed in discursive psychology and conversation analysis that we can only understand what any specific utterance does in interaction by investigating it in terms of its placement or position *within the sequence interaction in which it occurs* – that is, it is in and through the sequences of interaction that all interactional actions (including exonerations) are accomplished.

Furthermore, from a discursive perspective, exonerating talk need not always be as self-evidently exonerating as the accounts literature suggests. Thus, mere descriptions can often be constructed to exonerate. 'It's been non-stop today' may not be framed as an overt account for not having done something that was expected, but this description – if placed after some implicit or explicit complaint – may orientate to issues of exoneration. Talk context, therefore, may shape our judgement of what is, or is not, an account.

What counts as an account or explanation?

A third issue with Weiner et al.'s (1987) research and, indeed, most account-giving literature, is that it tends to have a narrow understanding of what sort of talk can give an account (or explanation). Accounts that are researched tend to have the surface form of an account – 'I couldn't come on time because . . .' One of the points developed in the discursive psychology research outlined below is, even talk that does not have the surface form of an account – for example, apparently descriptive talk, assessments, evaluations and many other apparent forms – can *do* the work of accounting. Thus, saying, 'I hate that bus service!' may just as effectively account for lateness as, 'I was late because there were several buses that were cancelled.'

Critical recap

Account-giving literature

1 Account-giving research has paid attention to the attributional type of account that is given and how this is linked to effectiveness (such as uncontrollable, external and unintentional accounts tend to be more successful). As Hareli (2005) suggests, however, the actual quality of the account (its apparent truth and reasonableness) is often more important than its attributional typology.

2 Account-giving research tends to focus on the account-giving utterance without considering its context. From a discursive and, especially, a conversation analytic perspective, it is the *interactional sequence* that may make it relevant for an account to be given. Furthermore, whatever is *done* by a piece of talk where an account is relevant is done by virtue of *where it is* in the sequence of interaction.

3 Account-giving literature tends to focus on a narrow range of overtly accounting-type talk. Discursive and conversation analytic work shows how even talk that does not appear to be giving an account may be doing just that – because what is done is an *interactional achievement* rather than a property of an utterance on its own.

Reflective questions

1. *Have you found that accounts you have given differ in systematic ways from your real reasons? What sorts of differences are there?*
2. *Do you think that the type of account (external, uncontrollable and unintentional, for example) or the quality of account (whether it appears to be true, reasonable, normative and appropriate) is most important in terms of its positive impact on the recipient?*

5.4 Discursive and conversation analytic approaches

These approaches to attribution theory – considered in Chapter 4 – could be thought of as carving up the social world in a certain way. The classic approaches to attribution theory distinguished 'events' or 'outcomes' to be explained, 'causally relevant information' (such as about consensus, distinctiveness and consistency), 'cognitive calculations' and 'reported attribution'. If we are trying to make sense of an event to be explained (such as why I failed an exam), causally relevant information (such as everybody failed) will be drawn on to calculate and communicate the cause (for example, I may calculate and explain my failure as being due to the difficulty of the exam).

Classic attribution studies focus on describing the cognitive causal attribution process. While this cannot be seen directly, it is argued that it can be inferred from the ways in which reported attributions vary with the causally relevant information presented. Thus, observing that reported attributions are more likely to be external when there is attribution-relevant information suggesting high consensus leads to the inference that the cognitive calculation of attribution involves the processing of consensus information.

Attribution bias work introduced the notion we might systematically distort our perceptions or causal calculations, such that our perception may differ from 'the world as it really is', but held that the reported attribution was an unproblematic window on to the outcome of our attribution processing, enabling us to model how information and biasing factors shape the process of making an attribution. In all cases, verbal representations of 'events', 'causally relevant information' and 'reported attributions' were taken as neutral reflections of how things are or are perceived. That is, descriptions of events to be explained and causally relevant information are typically treated as uncontroversial givens, simply reflecting reality as it is or as it is perceived by the individual making an attribution. Likewise, explanations are treated as uncontroversial reflections of the underlying cognitions of the person making an attribution. From this perspective, we need never ask how else an event might be described or what is being done by describing it in one particular way. Furthermore, we need not consider how causally relevant information might be drawn on, evidenced or undermined in an argument about causes. Finally, if our explanations simply reflect our causal calculations, we need never contemplate the *interactional work that communicating an explanation might accomplish.*

Some of the approaches covered in this chapter have already provided a challenge to elements of this perspective by, for example, suggesting that the description of the event to be explained may *itself* make some causal inference. Thus, attributional semantics and critical linguistics considered the verb and the noun phrase positioning in a sentence that describes the event to be explained as potentially making causal inferences. The conversational model argued that the attribution process is triggered by a prior question that solicits an explanation and the description of the event in this question may also influence and, indeed, constrain the subsequent explanation.

To some – rather limited – extent, then, some of the work considered in this chapter moved away from the idea that the description of events to be explained was an entirely unproblematic (or at least unconsequential) reflection of reality and started to consider how the description might impact the causal reasoning process. Likewise, the account-giving approach has considered the ways in which explanations may do interactional work – in particular give an account for – that is, exonerate or justify – potentially accountable behaviour. Thus, my explanation that the bus was late might exonerate me from blame for my late arrival at a meeting. In this way, the account-giving approach provides some – again, arguably limited – sense of explanations *doing* interactional work rather than merely reporting inner cognitive calculations.

Discursive psychology draws on everyday instances of talk to argue in a much more far-ranging manner that all of our verbal representations are constructions of reality – versions for which other alternatives are available – and that these constructions do interactional work in sequences of interaction. From this perspective, then, the descriptions of the events to be explained, 'causally relevant information' and attributions or explanations themselves are all, unavoidably, constructions of reality that do or accomplish things in interaction, such as blaming, exonerating, agreeing and disputing. According to discursive psychology, examining actual, everyday attribution talk reveals that descriptions of events, talk about causally relevant information as well as overt explanations can all be seen as constructed in the light of what actions participants are engaged in and these constructions, far from being givens, are often justified and disputed in conversation.

From a discursive psychology and a conversation analytic perspective, participants *do* things with their talk and they describe, explain, make inferences about events and hold each other to account for their talk in the business of accomplishing interactional work.

Next, various strands of research that draw on discursive psychology are addressed, with particular attention being given to the ways in which seemingly descriptive talk can do explanatory – or explanation-relevant – work. Then, we will consider conversation analytic work that has explored the sequential placement and relevance of explanatory talk.

Discursive psychology and the explanatory relevance of 'descriptive' talk

The commitment to everyday interaction in discursive psychology is not a lazy criticism of experimental social psychology as being 'unlike real life'. Instead, for discursive psychology, certain key factors that are orientated to in real attribution talk – **the explanatory relevance of 'descriptive' talk** – simply are not present in laboratory attempts to measure or describe attribution processes. In real sequences of talk, participants are not neutral or disinterested – as they might be regarding fictitious characters who are, or are not, frightened of a fictitious dog. Instead, as Edwards and Potter (1992, 1993) note, they have a stake in the interaction at hand. In everyday interaction, participants are *doing interaction* (agreeing, disputing, exonerating, accounting, blaming, excusing, inviting, refusing, noticing) in and through their attribution talk. Furthermore, in everyday contexts, the attribution talk occurs in a real *sequence* of talk – not following the presentation of some stimulus or some hypothetical conversational question, nor even some scripted or staged enactment of various types of account. That is, actions in interaction are underway and the attribution talk does what it does by virtue of occurring where it does in the sequence of talk.

Below, extracts from a rape trial testimony, interviews with men who had been involved in domestic abuse, political debate about the responses to climate change and other broadcast data are examined in order to briefly consider the interactional work that is accomplished in talk. It should be noted that the distinction below between event description, causally relevant factors and explanation are not given to reify these categories, but, rather, show how discursive psychology reworks these traditional ways of carving up the social world. The focus on inner cognition – central to traditional attribution work – is replaced in discursive psychology with an interest in *what construction of reality* is produced in talk and *what that construction does*.

For discursive psychology, then, event description, causal information and explicit explanation are all constructed and contestable versions of the world that are *used to do interactional work*, some of which is directly concerned with issues of accountability, blame and exoneration, which are central to attribution.

Constructing events

Drew (1998, cited in LeCouteur & Oxlad, 2011, p. 7), a conversation analyst, made a powerful, cogent case for the work that seemingly merely descriptive work does,

The explanatory relevance of 'descriptive' talk This refers to the way in which simple descriptions can *do* interactional work, such as accounting for or holding someone else to account for why something was or was not done. Thus, 'It's so untidy in here!' may hold someone to account for the mess, while, 'It's been non-stop since you left!' may account for the untidiness.

which, actually, very neatly presents discursive psychology's interest in description as action in interaction:

> Insofar as descriptions are unavoidably incomplete and selective, they are designed for specific and local interactional purposes.

Drew thus notes descriptions are never simple – reports that reflect how the world is – nor are they reflections of how the individual thinks about or perceives the world. Instead, for Drew, descriptions are produced and produced in the specific form they take to *do* certain sorts of interactional work. An excellent example of this is found in Drew's analysis of the cross-examination of an alleged victim in a rape trial (see Extract 5.5).

Extract 5.5

(*Note*: The extract below is taken from a rape trial. In the trial testimony, the alleged victim is being cross-examined by the defendant's attorney regarding events on the night of the alleged attack)

A Well yuh had some uh (p) (.) fairly lengthy
conversations with thu defendant uh: did'n you?
(0.7)
A On that evening uv February fourteenth?
(1.0)
W We:ll we were all talkin
(0.8)
A Well you kne:w. at that ti:me. that the
defendant was. in:terested (.) in you (.)
did'n you?
(1.3)
W He: asked me how I'(d) bin: en
(1.1)
W J- just stuff like that

Source: Drew (1992, p. 478)

In Extract 5.5, from a rape trial analysed by Drew (1992), the attorney can be heard to produce descriptions of events on the evening of the attack that mark up the intimacy between the alleged victim, the witness (W), and the defendant. Thus, in lines 16 and 17 we get 'fairly lengthy conversations', in line 19 the date, 'February fourteenth' (St Valentine's day), and, in lines 23–24, a description of the witness's state of knowledge about the defendant – 'Well you kne:w. at that ti:me. that the defendant was. in:terested (.) in you'.

These descriptions by the attorney, far from being a neutral setting out of the facts, can be understood as contestable versions of events that have implications for understanding how the alleged attack should be characterised and explained. The descriptions by the attorney then imply that W participated in some level of (at least) emotional intimacy with the defendant on a day when romance is notably celebrated and that this proceeded with W's knowledge of the defendant's (implicitly romantic) interest in her.

These descriptions, then, rather than being factual starting points for making attributional calculations are, instead, directly concerned with the guilt or innocence of the defendant. The descriptions offered by the defendant's attorney imply that the event the trial concerns might not be accurately described as rape and rather than the defendant being responsible for a sexual attack, W may have consented to any physical intimacy that did occur.

This attribution-implicative **constructing of events** is not directly disputed (W does not use what Drew, 1992, terms 'overt correction markers') – instead W produces an alternative description that characterises the events in a different way. The attorney's 'lengthy conversations' (lines 16 and 17) is responded to in with; 'We:ll we were all talkin' (line 21), and the attorney's, 'Well you kne:w. at that ti:me. that the defendant was. in:terested (.) in you' (lines 23 and 24) was responded to with, 'He: asked me how I'(d) bin: en (1.1) J- just stuff like that' (lines 27–29). By placing her descriptions of what happened directly after the attorney's, W implicitly positions them as '*alternative* versions designed to qualify and *replace* the versions initially produced by the attorney' (Drew, 1992, p. 491). What is important to note is that these alternative descriptions do attributional work also – the details produced are used to characterise the events in a way that suggests a non-intimate relationship and, therefore, implicitly, an absence of consent on the part of W to intimate physical contact.

The important point for our purposes here is that what on the surface may seem to be mere descriptions of details of events are specific versions that are constructed to undertake particular interactional work. Thus, events are not 'givens' but formulated or constructed in talk, the constructions are contestable and different versions of an event may serve quite distinct rhetorical purposes – such as exonerating or blaming. As Edwards and Potter (1992, p. 119) argue, 'these formulations of facts are not merely "given" and unproblematic bases for inference, but are

Constructing events This refers to the idea that events may be talked about or constructed in different ways and any one version can be investigated in terms of the sort of interactional or ideological work that it may do.

constructed and dismantled by participants themselves, a rhetorical process inseparable from the drawing of inferences.'

Membership categories as explanations

The issue of **membership categories** was introduced in Chapter 2. There, reference was made to the ways in which invoking recognisable categories in talk can be seen as attending to the interactional work at hand. Thus, a young man accused of assaulting another man was found to invoke the category 'old man' to not only describe the alleged victim but also problematise the allegation itself. By describing the other person as an 'old man', the action of hitting is implicitly less well fitted – 'old men' are associated with increased vulnerability and being recipients of behaviours that do not include assault. Merely invoking the category, then, may make 'hitting' more problematic as a description of what happened.

Extract 5.6

Interviewer: And have you thought about why you behaved abusively that day?
Nick: Yeah because she picked up a hitchhiker.
Interviewer: So what did that mean to you? Was that sort of scary (.) that she shouldn't have done that?
Nick: Yeah.
Interviewer: Something could have happened to her?
Nick: No (.) she shouldn't have done that. That's just commonsense ya know? A, a single girl in a (.) in a car picking up a male hitchhiker. That's stupid.

Source: LeCouteur and Oxlad (2011, p. 13)

Extract 5.7

Interviewer: Thinking back, can you describe to me the first time you were abusive towards an intimate partner and what led to it?
Jim: Uhh um probably, I don't know (.) probably about twelve months or so ago when it first started. It just ah it was over er because I'm a tidy person and I don't like to leave things too untidy for too long and yeah I tend to jump up and down a little bit over that. So yeah, so that'd probably be the main one yeah. Just because I'm a tidy person and she likes to just do it whenever she wants to do it.

Source: LeCouteur and Oxlad (2011, p. 20)

LeCouteur and Oxlad (2011) use the framework of membership categories to examine interviews with males who attended counselling sessions concerning their involvement in domestic violence. What is of interest for our current concern, and developed much further in their analysis, is the way in which merely invoking a membership category can be part of the way in which these males justify, mitigate or otherwise make more reasonable their violent behaviour. Extracts 5.6 and 5.7 illustrate these points.

In their analysis of Extracts 5.6 and 5.7, LeCouteur and Oxlad (2011) note the ways in which the categories in play work to minimise or account for the violent behaviour that the interviewee was or had been engaged in. In Extract 5.6, 'Nick's' description of a time when he physically abused his partner makes use of the categories 'a single girl' and 'a male hitchhiker'. These gendered categories are presented together not as a compatible pair, but, rather, to draw attention to the alleged transgression – 'a single girl' implicitly *should not* pick up a 'male hitchhiker'. As LeCouteur and Oxlad (2011) note the use of the indefinite article 'a' invokes 'a standard relational pair' – that is, it makes this incident just one example of a wider maxim about how 'a single girl' should relate in those cases where they encounter 'a male hitchhiker'. It can additionally be noted, as Edwards (1998) develops, the very category 'girl' is loaded with interactionally relevant implications – in this case, it perhaps underscores the vulnerability of the female in the presence of the male (not 'boy') hitchhiker.

In Extract 5.7, the male uses a category to describe themselves in explaining their violent behaviour – 'because I'm a tidy person'. This category description is detailed in an interesting way. First, as LeCouteur and Oxlad (2011) note, the detail avoids providing a problematic specification where 'Jim's' concern with tidiness is portrayed as unreasonable or obsessive – 'I don't like to leave things too untidy for too long' – and – the reaction he describes does not specify violence – 'I tend to jump up and down a bit'. Here, then, the category presents a means of accounting that emphasises a reaction born out of reasonable concerns. It can be further

Membership categories The categories that people use in their talk to do interactionally relevant work.

noted that 'jump up and down' is a far from neutral description – it provides a way of both encompassing a physical aspect to Jim's reaction and, yet, seems to minimise its menace – sounding like a child having a tantrum rather than a man physically attacking a woman.

LeCouteur and Oxlad (2011) provide an analysis in which both description and membership categories are invoked to do interactional work. The categories considered in these two extracts each provide something of an explanation for the male's violence, accounting for it as a reaction to the wrongs of their victim, positioning it as understandable not by the crude tool of explicit justifications and denials, but the more nuanced, sophisticated and implicit work of the categories themselves.

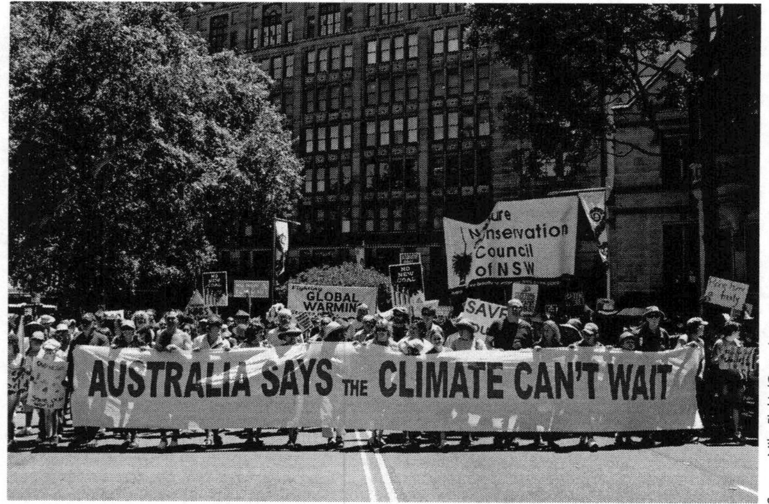

Source: Mike Flokis/Getty Images

Australians giving a very clear and direct message about climate change. How, though, has talk about the national interest been drawn on in arguments about climate change in Australia?

Constructing 'the national interest'

Kurz, Augoustinos and Crabb (2010) draw on work by Dickerson (1998) and Reicher and Hopkins (2001), which identifies the importance of reference to 'the national interest' in political talk. As Kurz et al. (2010, p. 604) note, Dickerson (1998) argued that such talk could be seen as undertaking action on both an ideological and an interactional level – promoting certain ideological agendas while 'attending to local interactional concerns such as exoneration and blaming'.

Kurz et al. (2010) examine the ways in which talk about 'the national interest' has a rhetorical potency. Some of this may be due to it having a sort of 'trump' status – somewhat like a 'commonplace' or stance that all within a given community might reasonably be expected to agree with or support. In addition to this – as Kurz et al. (2010) note – the national interest is also rather vague and can be specified in markedly different ways. These two factors make it a compelling and flexible rhetorical resource – one that can out trump most other appeals and be specified in such a way that it can be invoked to support quite contradictory positions.

As Kurz et al. (2010) note, in Extract 5.8, lines 17 and 40, Howard invokes the idea of 'Australia's interest' and the 'long-term interests of the Australian economy' quite explicitly in accounting for the government's stance with regard to the environment. Australia's national interest is given as the explanation for not ratifying Kyoto (a United Nations protocol aimed at tackling causes of

Extract 5.8

7	Rudd	how can a
8		government that is full of climate change sceptics=
9	Unknown	=ohh:=
10	Rudd	=be part of the climate change solution.
11	Various	Hear hear
12	Speaker	>The Honourable the Prime Minister<
13	Unknown	°Hear hear°
14		(0.5)
15	Howard	Well Mister Speaker it is true that um (0.2) we ah haven't ratified
16		Kyoto because ah (0.4) .h to ratify Kyoto would not be=in
17		Australia's ↑interest
		((19 lines omitted))
37	Howard	so Mister Speaker (0.3) I <u>am</u> I am a sceptic yes. (0.6) I'm sceptical
38		Mister Speaker (0.3) at the capacity of the Australian Labour Party
39		(0.5) to provide an <u>answer</u> to this great challenge (0.3) .h that
40		<u>doesn't damage</u> the long-term interests of the Australian economy.
41	Various	Hear hear

Source: Kurz et al. (2010, p. 610)

Extract 5.9

(*Note*: Originally from *Hansard* (7 November, *24*), adapted here from Edwards and Potter (1992). This and Extract 5.10 concern a political controversy in the UK in 1988 when journalists reported that Nigel Lawson, then chancellor, had been accused of suggesting abandoning universal benefit for old people, irrespective of need, which he denied. The journalists countered that if it was not true, then why had so many of them come to the same erroneous interpretation?)

Mr Lawson	[] Let me say that the only announcement I have to make – the only change I have to inform the house of – is the one that I informed the house of today. This is a matter which I hinted to certain journalists on Friday They misunderstood what I was saying – [Laughter.] There is no [Interruption]
Mr Speaker	Order. This kind of laughter and these interruptions take up a great deal of time. Many Hon. Members want to ask questions about this matter
Mr Lawson	.- and as a result went in for a farrago of invention but that is no reason for the Hon. Member to take it out.

Source: Edwards and Potter (1992, p. 114)

global warming, which Rudd subsequently ratified on 3 December 2007). Here, then, the national interest is invoked to provide an explanation that can justify what might otherwise appear to be overwhelming international – let alone ethical and moral – imperatives for Australia to ratify Kyoto. The national interest here works in a manner similar to what Billig (1991) refers to as 'rhetorical commonplaces' – shared, commonly held stances that are often appealed to as a rhetorical move as they are difficult to dispute in themselves (thus, it is hard to argue that one should work against the national interest).

In the latter part of Extract 5.8, line 40, as noted Howard appeals to Australia's interests – here slightly more narrowly framed as 'the long-term interests of the Australian economy'. Rather than denying scepticism, Howard reconstrues it as a virtue, arising out of concern for Australia's national interest and targeted on threats to that national interest. In this extract, then, Howard does not deny the charges of non-ratification or scepticism, but, rather, aligns them with defending the national interest. His account or explanation for his government's decision regarding Kyoto and its stance more generally is that it is in the national interest. This defence simultaneously explains or accounts for the government's decision and stance and holds the opposition, Labour, party to account for not aligning with the Australian national interest.

Causally relevant 'information'

Classic attribution experiments have often entailed presenting 'facts' relevant to a calculation of attribution in order to establish how these relate to reported causal judgements and what the intervening cognitive calculation entails. Following Kelley's covariation model of causal attribution, these causally relevant 'facts' often include information about distinctiveness, consistency and consensus. Edwards and Potter (1992, 1993) use Extracts 5.9 and 5.10 to provide a discursive rethinking of consensus that challenges the idea that such (apparently) causally relevant information is indisputable, attribution-determining, factual information that informs our cognitive causal calculation.

Extract 5.10

Mr Lawson	I am grateful to my Hon. Friend. In fact, the statements, as I said – the statements that appeared in the press on Sunday bore no relation whatever to what I in fact said. What I have said to them [the reporters] is that, while we were absolutely, totally committed to maintaining –
Ms Clare Short	They will have their shorthand notes.
Mr Lawson	Oh yes, they will have their shorthand notes and they will know it, and they will know they went behind afterwards and they thought there was not a good enough story and so they produced that.

Source: Edwards and Potter (1992, p. 116)

Extracts 5.9 and 5.10 concern a political controversy from the UK in 1988 in which ten journalists reported that the then UK chancellor of the exchequer, Nigel Lawson, had floated the idea of abandoning 'universal benefits for old people irrespective of need'. This interpretation was subsequently denied by Lawson, in response to which the journalists raised the question as to how and why so many of them (high consensus) could have arrived at the same erroneous interpretation.

In Extract 5.9, Lawson provides a construction of the high consensus as a 'farrago of invention' – here, the agreement among the journalists is reworked by Lawson as a form of collusion arising from their misinterpretation of what he was saying. In Extract 5.10, the evidence of 'shorthand notes' is marshalled by an opposition MP as being a reflection of what *did* take place, so can determine which version of events is correct – did the journalists agree because that's what the chancellor said or because they colluded? Lawson responds by reworking the shorthand notes as evidence that they would have known what he said but also as potentially tampered with in the process of journalistic collusion that he constructs. In Extract 5.10, then, the collusion is explained in terms of the vested interests of the journalists by constructing what might be assumed to be a common journalistic motivation – the need for a 'good enough story' – and, hence, could account for the fact that ten journalists produced the same interpretation of what Lawson said.

In Extracts 5.9 and 5.10, we see the way in which this 'real-world' consensus information differs from the consensus information of most attribution experiments. In experimental settings, the consensus is presented as an unproblematic, factual constituent of reality, ready to be perceived and processed. Indeed, as Edwards and Potter (1992, 1993) note, the truth or epistemology of 'causally relevant' information cannot possibly become an issue

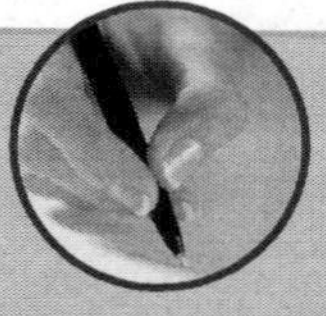

Box 5.4 TRY IT OUT
The explanatory relevance of 'descriptive' talk

Look at this brief extract from a discussion broadcast on BBC Radio Four's *Today* programme on 14 August 2007. See if you can identify the way in which features of classic 'causally relevant information' are drawn on to warrant and question the different cases being argued in this multiparty interview.

Extract 5.11

(Key to Speakers: SM = Sarah Montague TD = Dr Theodore Dalrimple PW = Peter Wayne)

SM Well (.) Doctor Dalrimple you hear there a personal experience challenging the views that you're outlining in your book >which are your PERSonal views<

TD Well they are but they're based also on experimental views for example in the 1930s it was established that (.) people withdrawing from opiates were unable (.) er to distinguish reliably er between eh injections of water and injections of erm of er opiates in order to relieve their symptoms (...) so it is well known and again there is experimental evidence about this that demonstrates that they are inclined to exaggerate their symptoms

SM Peter Wayne is champing at the bit now to come back in (.) because everything you've said there seems to have angered him

PW I mean this seems to be absolutely typical of the attitude of the prison doctors that I've experienced over the years (...) this this this man is is is against the UKDP Commission for Drugs, the RSA Drugs Commission Report this year, the BMA, the Royal College of Psychiatrists, the Retox National Focal Point (.) all three major political parties (.) the er Advisory Committee for the Misuse of Drugs, the Home Office Affairs Select Committee these are (.) these are establishment organisations not loony fringe

SM And what are they saying?

PW They are saying heroin is a very very serious medical condition and the police are backing it up as well Doctor Dalrimple Ken Jones err Chief Constable of Sussex er President of the Association of Chief Police Officers-=

SM =Allright we've got (.) we've got the list now (.) so back to you Doctor Dalrimple

Source: BBC Radio Four's *Today* programme (14 August 2007)

for participants who are told that 'everyone laughs at the comedian' or 'everyone is afraid of the dog'. Inspection of 'real-world' arguments about causally relevant information, however, suggests that what might have been presumed to be unproblematic, 'out there to be discovered and processed', causally relevant information can be reconceptualised as another feature which can be constructed as it is in the course of argument and counter-argument. It may also go further than that, however. It may be that, even leaving to one side explicitly argumentative talk, perhaps *all* of our causally related talk is 'interested' – that is, it reflects and orientates to specific interactional interests that we may have (most obviously our talk might be exonerating ourselves from blame and blaming another). From this perspective, all talk about causally relevant information can be examined to see how the 'information' is constructed to undertake specific interactional tasks (see Box 5.4 for an illustration of this). Far from being a *neutral* report on things as they are, talk constructions of consensus, distinctiveness and consistency are resources for us to accomplish *interested* interactional work.

Conversation analysis and the sequential relevance and placement of explanatory talk

The conversation analytic approach picks up on many of the critical themes raised so far – in particular, it emphasises the action orientation of talk and the importance of interactional sequences. That is, for conversation analysis, it is important to approach talk in terms of what it is doing and where in a sequence of talk it is doing it. Indeed, it is the location of an utterance at a precise point in a sequence that enables it to do what it does. From a conversation analytic perspective, there would be little point in relying on prespecified categorisation schemes that tell us what implications causal understanding of a verb or verb form might have because this takes attention away from *what is being done here and now in the interaction* as the account-relevant talk is being uttered. Typologies of excuses and justifications and judgements of their effectiveness in certain categories of situations are also problematic. While they usefully emphasise some of the work that account talk may do, they judge this on the basis of a gloss of the target utterance content alone rather than considering precisely *what* was said and *where in the talk sequence it was uttered.*

As noted above, a sentence such as 'John telephoned Mary' may be found to imply that John is the causal agent, but, if uttered in an interaction, the person to whom it is addressed may be more concerned with *what it means in interactional terms*. Thus, the addressee may need to work out what is being done in being told this – are they being blamed ('He did, why didn't you?'), being given a story preface prior to being told more about John and Mary ('I know newsworthy stuff about John and Mary that I am about to tell you'), being given an account of something they did or didn't do ('It was fine that I didn't call because John passed on the message anyway when he called Mary'). What should come next? What is made relevant by the prior talk is a key concern for people in any form of talk and, for analysts, it is this talk that can shed light on what the prior talk did or was treated as doing.

Likewise, the precise details of *what is said and where it is said* may be more important than a crude sense of the type of account and its fitness for this type of situation. Indeed, participants use interaction context – including the talk that comes before the account-giving utterance – to work out what is being said and what is being done with what is said. This completely redraws any typology of accounts as inadequate because they attempt to separate the account utterance from the very talk context that enables it to do account-giving work. Without prior talk context, the utterance, 'Do you know how many calls I've had today?' looks like a question (or interrogative) rather than an account, but, if it were to follow a co-participant saying, 'This room was tidy when I left', then it can be heard to do a different sort of action (exoneration). It is the talk or interaction sequence, then, that is crucial to what is being done by any specific utterance rather than any sense of what that utterance does in isolation. In real interaction (as compared to certain experiments), utterances (other than openings and closings) almost never just appear all on their own; they follow prior talk and are followed by subsequent talk.

A useful framework for understanding what conversation analysis can offer to our understanding of explanations, or accounts, is provided by Antaki (1994), who developed the idea of 'explanation slots'. 'Explanation slots' captures the idea that, often within an interaction, it will be relevant for one participant or another to 'explain, justify or warrant' something that they have done, are doing or are about to do. The 'slots' are these places in the talk where it is relevant to do the explaining, justifying or warranting. The thing being explained, justified or warranted might be an action (or inaction) outside of the conversation itself (why I arrived late for the lecture) or something that is being done here and now in the talk (why I am refusing, or about to refuse, your kind offer to come and live with me, rent-free, for six months).

Antaki (1994, p. 75) distinguishes between explanation slots that are created by one speaker for another from those that are 'created and filled by the speaker him or her self'. In the first type, one person is 'casting something about another speaker as requiring explanation' (for example, 'It's nearly 3 p.m., the lecture was due to start at 9!') In the second type, the 'explanation' is not implicitly or explicitly requested by the other speaker, but made relevant by the potentially problematic (dispreferred) or unexpected nature of what the current speaker is doing or is about to do (such as, 'Err well ... I would love you and your uncle to come and stay for six months but it's just my landlord is very strict about that sort of thing'). In this second type, the speaker producing the explanation is doing so because it accounts for what they themselves are saying (or doing) in the interaction. Thus, my refusal of your invitation to come and stay at my place needs to be accounted for, so I spontaneously provide an explanation. A further brief illustration of these types of explanation slots is given below (much more extensive coverage can be found in Antaki, 1994 – see also Box 5.5).

Explanation slots set up by prior speaker

Antaki (1994, p. 76) notes a fundamental principle of conversation analysis – namely, that the speaker 'expects what is said is appropriate to what is going on'. That means merely reporting (or doing a 'noticing' of) the patently obvious can invite the co-participant to account for it. Thus, when we hear someone report to us, 'the laundry is not done', 'this place is a mess', 'the washing up is still there', we treat it as doing **interactionally relevant work** beyond being a statement about observable physical realities. In responding to such noticings, participants often provide an account for the thing that has been 'noticed'.

Here, in Extract 5.12, as Antaki (1994) notes, the 'noticing' of a 'redundant' piece of information by S makes it relevant for the addressed party (C) to provide an account for what has been noticed – in this case, why she did not get an ice-cream sandwich. The explanation that is given in the last line, then, can be seen as brought about by what is happening in the interaction, rather than just the remote private cognitions of C. That is, the talk of S has made it relevant for an account to be given by C and C provides this explanation at just the moment (or at precisely the sequential position) that it has been made relevant for her to do so.

Providing an account following a noticing is something that we have probably all done without necessarily realising it. Some noticings may make an exonerating explanation relevant – for example, 'This room is in a terrible state', 'The washing-up hasn't been touched', 'The laundry pile is still there', 'The bin still hasn't been taken out'. Other noticings might make some form of account relevant but not necessarily an exoneration – such as 'You've shaved your left eyebrow off', 'You've got a new television', 'You're wearing a large pointed hat'. Responses to such noticings might well explain the remarked-on feature but not necessarily attempt to justify or exonerate it.

In each case, we can note, first, that, in our interactions, we treat talk as relevant to our ongoing interaction and, thus, see the voicing of a redundant fact as a means of spotlighting some feature of our world to be talked about – and often accounted for or explained. Second, the explanation that is provided does not just randomly pop out of the mouth of the speaker, regardless of what is going on in the interaction. Instead, it is carefully placed at precisely that position where it has become interactionally relevant. These observations lend weight to the idea that our explanations can be understood as being *interactionally occasioned* – brought about by what is done in the interactions where they are uttered rather than being primarily private cognitive calculations.

Extract 5.12

(*Note*: Simplified transcript).

[Door squeaks]
S Hi Carol=
C =H[i::
R [CA:ROL,HI
→ S You didn't get an *ice*-cream sandwich
C I know, hh I decided that my body didn't need it

Source: Antaki (1994, p. 76, cited in Schegloff, 1988, p. 128).

Explanation slots set up by current speaker

The second class of explanation slots that Antaki (1994) identifies concerns those set up by the 'explainers' themselves. As mentioned above, an important feature of these 'current speaker explanation slots' is they can be found to occur when the speaker has done or is about to do something in their talk that is, in some sense, accountable (makes relevant the giving of an account). Antaki identifies many different forms that these explanation slots may take, including declining an invitation, disagreement with an assessment, accounts for speaker-initiated actions and sequence-closing talk. Here, we shall just consider declining invitations.

Interactionally relevant work The things done by talk (such as accounting, blaming and exonerating) that are relevant or consequential for the interaction.

Box 5.5 KEY RESEARCHER
Professor Charles Antaki: conversation analysis

How did you become interested in conversation analysis?

I started out as a traditional sort of social psychologist, earning my PhD stripes at the excellent (but now sadly defunct) MRC Social and Applied Psychology Unit at Sheffield University. But something was gnawing at me, even as I was plotting my experiments and shuffling through my response sheets.

What did people's answers to my 'response items' mean? In fact, why was I giving people questionnaires and asking them abstract questions anyway? I began to wonder if I might be missing something. It dawned on me that I could actually drop all the paperwork and actually go and see what people were doing in real life.

Well, it turned out that watching and recording what people did in everyday life wasn't really the done thing among psychologists at the time (not much has changed, I regret to say). Desperate to join (what they thought was) the scientific crowd, psychologists were busy, as I had been, bringing people into the laboratory and more or less beating the everyday life out of them.

How does your approach compare and contrast with others'?

What, then, to do? Back in the late 1980s, I began to hear about a mysterious procedure called 'discourse analysis'. I started to understand that language wasn't just a form of information transmission (I ask the questions, you give me the answers on my questionnaire). Language was a way of doing things – people make promises, offer jobs and pass laws, by using words in certain ways at certain times. I stumbled across the pioneering book *Discourse and social psychology* by Jonathan Potter and Margaret Wetherell and that crystallised all that was wrong with laboratories and checklists. They offered an exciting way forward, working with language as used in everyday life. A marvellous book and one that made me take the decisive step out of the laboratory.

A bit later I was drawn, as are many ex-discourse analysts worried about a bit too much theory and a bit too little actual observation, to the extraordinary world opened up by the sociologist Harvey Sacks. His posthumous *Lectures on conversation* (1995) were a riveting mix of people-watching and hard-nosed, detailed analysis of everyday life. They still are. If you can find a copy of the book, plunge in and see for yourself how the familiar can be made unfamiliar, and then put back together again.

Tell us about your work in this area

Now my home base is in conversation analysis. That's the very close and painstaking study of interaction, of any sort: talking to the doctor, say, or making arrangements to go to the cinema or guiding a pilot through fog. In my own research, I've looked at how people argue, how people with intellectual impairments get across their feelings to careworkers and how psychotherapists handle their clients' problems (and vice versa). Talk does things; conversation analysis (CA) uncovers what and how. CA works with recordings of interaction – usually nowadays in video and increasingly from multiple viewpoints. You carefully transcribe what's going on (which can take many hours, but brings you up very close indeed to the raw data) and you start to discover patterns of practice, rules of conduct, exceptions, deviations and all the things that allow people to transact their business with each other. It's hard work, but it's intensely satisfying – and if you're a born people-watcher, there can't be a better way to do psychology.

And, finally, what do you recommend to people wanting to start to research this topic?

If the idea of the close analysis of interaction interests you, here are a few things to whet your appetite and get you going on a reading list.

- Robin Wooffit's *The language of mediums and psychics: The social organization of everyday miracles* (Ashgate, 2006) reveals the conversational means that mediums use to persuade us that they are in touch with the dead. Fascinating.
- Wayne Beach's *A natural history of family cancer: Interactional resources for managing illness* (Hampton Press, 2009) is a sustained analysis of a family's phone conversations as they confront the death of one of their members. A scholarly yet humane and moving account.
- Tanya Stivers' *Prescribing under pressure: Parent–physician conversations and antibiotics* (Oxford University Press, 2007) helps solve the puzzle of why doctors prescribe so many antibiotics – to no one's medical benefit. Stivers' sophisticated analysis reveals how parents get what they think their children need.

Of course, surveys and experiments have their place in social psychology, but, if you want to go where the action is – what people do with each other, for each other and to each other – then there's no real substitute for taking your camera out and recording them. Bring the tapes back, pull up a chair and look carefully: social life is exquisitely choreographed and one of the psychologist's most rewarding jobs is to understand the steps in the dance and how it swirls people around the stage.

When invitations, requests and offers made by one party in a conversation are accepted by another (to whom they are made), the acceptance is typically delivered promptly, without any inserted talk, qualifications or explanations. An example of this is found in Extract 5.13.

Extract 5.13

(*Note*: Transcript simplified from the original)

Gladys I have the paper here I thought you might like to have it
Emma Thank you

Source: Potter (1996, p. 59)

Things are markedly different, however, when the invitation, request or offer is declined, as in Extract 5.14.

Extract 5.14

(*Note*: Transcript simplified from the original)

1 B Uh if you'd care to come over and visit a little while
2 this morning I'll give you a cup of coffee
3 A hehh
4 Well
5 that's awfully sweet of you,
6 I don't think I can make it this morning .hh uhm
7 I'm running an ad in the paper an-and uh I have to
8 stay near the phone

Source: Potter (1996, cited in Atkinson & Drew, 1979, p. 58)

As Potter (1996) notes, the acceptance turn varies in form from the decline turn. The immediate, brief, unqualified and unexplained acceptance of Extract 5.13 is a consistent feature of acceptance turns more generally. Extract 5.14, in which an invitation is declined, has a number of distinctive features. Interestingly, we are so intuitively aware of these that, even without knowing about conversation analysis at all, we would probably know by lines 3 or 4 (and almost definitely by line 5) that a decline was coming. In Extract 5.14, A might have made a more direct decline (a straight 'No' at line 3), but, instead, the decline (line 6) comes after a delay (in this case, the vocalisation 'hehh' delays the start of A's talk). This is followed by 'well', which marks the turn as 'dispreferred' – in this case, indicating that a rejection is likely. In line 5, A produces an appreciation of the invitation prior to what Potter (1996) notes is a softened or hedged decline – 'I don't think I can make it' (rather than a blunt 'No'). Along with the decline – but entirely absent from the acceptance – we get an account or explanation.

The account that is given in an invitation, request or offer decline has certain regular features that can be found in Extract 5.14. Thus, the explanation presents A as being in a position of appreciating the invitation (implicitly or explicitly suggesting that they *want* to accept) but *having to* decline because constraints mean that they are *unable* to accept. The reasons given do not imply blame (or that a further account is needed) for either party, nor do they make B accountable for issuing the invitation in the first place. Imagine these alternative declines: 'I could make it but I don't want to', 'I can't make it because you give me the creeps', 'I am trying to avoid you', 'I just can't be bothered', 'I'm too tired', 'I've told you before I am never free on Thursday and I am violently allergic to coffee'.

It is possible that these – or at least some of these – might be the sorts of reasons for declines that the decliner could share with others (for example, 'I am *so* trying to avoid him, he gives me the creeps'), but they are unlikely to be voiced to the person issuing the invitation, offer or request. If we were to talk about issues we have with the person doing the invitation or our lack of motivation as a reason for declining, then it is likely that we would be held to account for why we find the person inviting us creepy ('What do you mean?') or why we can't be bothered ('Why not?'). In this case, the very account that we have provided has merely left us with something harder to explain or account for than the decline itself. In fact, the spiral of accounting could continue until we found some reason that does not open up further issues to be accounted for – that is, it should not impute blame to either party and should not question the appropriateness of the invitation, offer or request in the first place.

Where these predictable structures are breached (such as our explanation blames the other person – 'You are so boring' – or makes their invitation accountable – 'Will you stop bothering me') – there is either something further to be accounted for – ('Why did you say that?') – or the relationship itself is likely to be in jeopardy. The fact that explanations used to decline offers, invitations and requests typically avoid implying blame or accountability has a distinct interactional advantage. It does the work of declining without topicalising the decline or the explanation given, so enabling the interaction to move on rather than get caught up on unresolved issues to be explained or accounted for. Furthermore, the normal format for declining requests, offers and invitations can do so without undermining future possible interactions between the parties.

In fact, it is our intuitive grasp of these practices that enables us to use them each time we decline an offer or invitation and recognise them when they are produced in response to offers, invitations and requests that we ourselves make. Just think of all of the times you have declined an offer, invitation or request – however reasonable or unreasonable the object of our decline we tend to use the same format. Thus, if someone we hardly know from our social psychology lecture makes an unreasonable request ('Could me and Joe just come and stay at yours for a few months, just until we find something'), the *content* of our refusal will be specific to the request ('... Err, ... well ... that would be great, it's just that the landlord is really strict about it – he says my studio flat is just for one person – he doesn't like me having anyone stay over'), but the *format* or *structure* will be replicable across numerous declines.

Conversation analysis does not provide us with another hypothetical model of our causal reasoning, nor a list of factors that might bias our thinking in specific ways. Instead, it – like several other approaches considered above – provides a means of understanding explanatory or account-giving talk. With the exception of the discursive psychology approach (with which conversation analysis overlaps considerably), however, it differs markedly from each of the other 'language-focused' approaches. The method of presenting stimulus material common to all classic and attributional semantics work does not allow for the possibility of investigating how attributions operate interactionally. That is, if we present participants with a stimulus sentence for them to complete the causal clause of or to calculate cause, then we are seriously limited in what we can actually observe happening. It is only by investigating sequences of interaction that we can see how talk emerges that makes some form of explanatory work relevant and, correspondingly, how subsequent talk addresses the fact that some sort of 'explanatory' work has been made relevant. See Box 5.6 and have a try yourself.

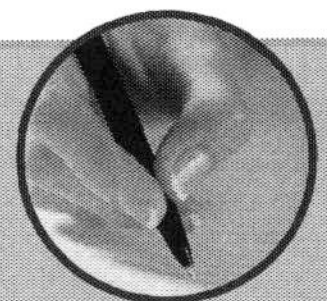

Box 5.6 TRY IT OUT Thinking about real-world explanations

Find a bit of 'everyday' data – it might be from the Internet or news media – watch or listen through it a few times. Are issues of relevance to explanation present? Do the approaches considered in this chapter shed light on what is going on?

Critical review of discursive and conversation analytic approaches

The discursive psychological contribution to thinking about explanatory talk highlighted the way that talk which may *appear* descriptive can do important work of relevance to explanation. Merely describing situations can give an account or make it relevant for others to do so, while references to membership categories may in themselves give account, exonerate or explain behaviour. Explicit constructions of reasons for behaviour – such as the national interest (see Box 5.7) – can be seen as constructed, detailed in order to address specific interaction contingencies. Finally, the very ingredients identified by classic attribution studies as crucial for causal reasoning – such as consensus – can, instead, be seen to reappear as rhetorical resources drawn on to warrant (or undermine) claims that are made or positions that are adopted.

From a conversation analytic perspective, discursive psychological research can overemphasise content features at the expense of giving attention to sequential placement. This problem is particularly related to methodologies that have, in some discursive literature, relied on interviews. Thus, if the focus is on the importance of relatively context-free, abstractable content (such as how people talk about a certain ethnic group or sexuality), then interviews appear a perfectly acceptable means of generating such data. The data thus generated may well have relatively long passages of interviewees talking about the content topic of interest (the ethnic group or sexuality) and the interactional orientation of such talk may be less readily apparent. This may, in turn, shape or even limit the understanding of what the talk is doing *to those things that can be observed in such data*. In this way, issues of accountability and warranting (which may well be a concern in interview interactions), as well as wider ideological concerns, may be emphasised at the expense of other types of interactional work (such as sequence initiation, closings) that are perhaps more readily apparent in everyday, non-interview data. These concerns, as Potter (2010) suggests, are perhaps more relevant for certain forms of discourse analysis and the emergence of discursive psychology arguably marked a movement towards more systematic engagement with everyday data and the full range of interactional concerns at work in interaction.

The conversation analytic research investigated here drew particularly on the idea of explanation slots. This conceptual framework brings home both the sequential locatedness of talk that orientates to explanatory concerns and the relevance of conversation analysis to our thinking about explanations. It may be, however, that caution

Box 5.7 IN THE NEWS
Accounting for political decisions

In the Irish elections of 2011, the ruling Fianna Fail party experienced its worst defeat in nearly 80 years, coming third behind Fine Gael and the Labour Party.

In deciding to leave office as the head of Fianna Fail party, Brian Cowen gave the following explanation in a press conference on 22 January 2011. Which of the approaches considered in this chapter (and Chapter 4) provides the best way of understanding this account? Does the type of data (political interview) or the way it is presented here (a monologue) shape your decision in any way?

Source: Georges Gobet/AFP/Getty Images

Brian Cowen waves goodbye as he steps down as Prime Minister following the Irish elections of 2011

Extract 5.15

At this crucial time (.) when decisions and choices have to be made (.) by the people (.) about the
future of our country (.) the focus should be on what pOlicies the political parties are offering (.)
rather than on the narrow focus of personality politics (.)
I am concerned (.) that >renewed internal criticism of my leadership of Fianna Fail is deflecting
attention< from these important debates therefore taking everything into account and having
discussed the matter with my family I have decided on my own council to step down as ((two
syllables)) of Fianna Fail and leader of Fianna Fail (.) my intention now is to concentrate fully on
government business and on implementing fully the recovery plan

Source: www.bbc.co.uk/news/world-europe-12259346

is needed here also. If we were to misinterpret this work, we might wind up marching through data 'looking for the slots', thereby missing the precise interactional work being orientated to in the sequence of data at hand. Likewise, we might mistakenly develop some form of mechanistic idea about how an explanation slot 'triggers' an 'explanation', failing to recognise either that talk in interaction is far more nuanced than this suggests or an 'explanation' may have been treated as accountably relevant even in sequences where it was not overtly present. Finally, we may be seduced by the psychological ballast of the term 'explanation', feeling that it is something solid and knowable as well as being orientated to in talk. It may, however, prove insufficiently fine-grained to attend to the highly specific interactional work within specific sequences of interaction.

It should perhaps, finally, be noted that these critical reflections have not come from a neutral position – if such a position were ever possible – but, rather, from a largely conversation analytic set of concerns. It is, however, possible to critique this work – and these criticisms – adopting quite different voices.

Researchers committed to ideological issues may – perhaps correctly – criticise the restricted focus of the material presented here. The discursive material considered was much more orientated to interactional concerns than ideological ones. Explanations may have a distinctly ideological dimension that is quite different from the sort of nuanced interactional shaping that has been addressed in much of the work considered here.

Much of the work considered earlier in this chapter had explicit or implicit commitments to cognitive processes. In some cases, this provided a bridge between the explanation work considered here and the theories of attribution considered in Chapter 4. From the stance of this work, jettisoning cognitivism may be a costly sacrifice that does not do justice to the concerns these researchers have. For such researchers, turning to discourse or conversation analysis would mean a focus on talk at the expense of their cognitive interests and commitments and involve work that is either unhinged from empirical evidence or restricted to a narrow range of concerns with what is demonstrably done in the data.

Critical recap

Discursive and conversation analytic approaches

1 The work covered here highlights the sort of explanatory work that talk – even 'descriptive' talk – can do.

2 The conversation analytic work in particular (and some aspects of discursive work) highlight the importance of examining talk in the sequences of interaction in which it occurs.

3 Some discursive approaches can, to some extent, be criticised for emphasising content at the expense of sequential location.

4 From a different, more ideologically orientated perspective, the research considered here may pay insufficient attention to the relationships between ideological concerns and explanatory talk.

5 The critique of cognitivism may itself be problematised as dropping social psychology and its concerns with cognition in favour of various forms of linguistic analysis.

Reflective questions

1 *Are you aware of your own, or others, 'descriptive talk' doing explanation-relevant work?*

2 *How important do you think interaction sequences are for understanding explanatory talk?*

Summary

- This chapter began by considering the contribution of attributional semantics to the issue of explanatory talk. Attributional semantics emphasises the ways in which our description of an event or behaviour to be explained can imply causality in itself. As was detailed above, this research has tended to concentrate on relatively simple sentences comprised of two noun phrases and a verb, such as 'David (noun phrase 1) laughed (verb) at Doreen (noun phrase 2)'. For attributional semantics, different verbs have different causal implications – some imply causal responsibility for the first noun phrase (in this case, David) and some the second (Doreen). The related area of critical linguistics suggests that the positioning of the noun and verb within the sentence is crucial rather than just the specific verb used. Thus, 'Doreen frightened David' is thought to implicate Doreen as causing David's fear, whereas the passive; alternative, 'David was frightened by Doreen;' –implicates David in his own fear reaction. One criticism of the research covered was that it may have underestimated the importance of the noun phrase itself. Thus, swapping the gender-implicative noun phrases round (Doreen was frightened by David) or describing Doreen as a comedienne (David laughed at the comedienne) could result in quite different implied attributions.
- The conversational model considers the importance of the explanation-eliciting question (such as, 'Why are you so late today?') in shaping the calculation of causality and the communication of explanations. The conversational model seeks to position explanations within interactions in which they are requested, suggesting that the eliciting question not only prompts the fact of attribution and explanation but also shapes its content. Through its reference to the interaction context in which explanations are produced, the conversational model is seen as touching on aspects that are addressed in discursive and conversation analytic approaches to explanation-relevant talk. It was also noted, however, that the model provides an approach to interaction that is somewhat mechanical, cognitively focused and does not do justice to the local, turn-by-turn organisation of talk in interaction.
- The third perspective considered above is the literature concerned with account-giving. This research has endeavoured to identify different types of accounts or exonerating explanations and identify the features of successful and unsuccessful accounts. Some research has suggested that accounts emphasising external, uncontrollable and unintentional causes ('I couldn't make it because of the terrible fire') increase the chances of them being successful, but other research has suggested this is only in a subset of cases where the explanation offered appears to be true, reasonable and of the sort which would normatively account for the behaviour being explained (thus, if there evidently was no fire, the earlier explanation would be unsuccessful, whatever its attributes in terms of the type of cause it highlights). Some discursive and conversation analytic research has considered how accounts are given, but the focus here has been how these are constructed and sequentially located in 'everyday' or 'real' interactions (where the sequential context becomes far more self-evidently

relevant) rather than in strange, dramatic vignettes played out in experimental simulations.

- Discursive psychology and conversation analysis were both shown to pay attention to the idea that talk – all talk – even mere description – *does* or can do interactional work, including explanation-relevant work, such as accounting for behaviour. One aspect of this that is developed is the way in which 'mere descriptions' can give, or make it relevant for others to give, explanations. A second aspect is the way in which sequential context becomes important in making explanatory talk relevant and in shaping what any piece of talk *does* (for example, whether a piece of talk becomes an explanation of some form or not).

Review questions

1 *How might verbs or sentence order have specific attributional implications?*

2 *Are there ways in which noun issues – such as the gender of the protagonists in hypothetical stimulus sentences – can influence the attributional implications of a sentence?*

3 *In what ways do explanation-eliciting questions shape subsequent explanations?*

4 *What are the key differences between the conversational model of attribution and conversation analysis?*

5 *In what ways might our communicated explanations be found to differ from our real ones?*

6 *What criticisms have been raised concerning account-giving research?*

7 *How can mere description do explanatory work?*

8 *In what ways are explanations related to sequential context?*

9 *Which approach do you think best describes everyday instances of explanatory talk?*

Recommended reading

Antaki, C. (1994). *Explaining and arguing: The social organisation of accounts*. London: Sage. A lucidly written and engaging review of explanation with a clear articulation of the relevance of conversation analysis for thinking about these issues.

Drew, P. (1992). Contested evidence in a courtroom cross-examination: The case of a trial for rape. In P. Drew & J. Heritage (Eds.), *Talk at work: Social interaction in institutional settings* (pp. 470–520). Cambridge: Cambridge University Press. A fascinating, if disturbing, investigation of some of the interactional work done in 'descriptions' of events by an alleged victim and cross-examining barrister during a trial for rape.

Edwards, D., & Potter, J. (1992). *Discursive psychology.* London: Sage. The text that first used and defined 'discursive psychology' a well-argued and eminently readable discursive account of several psychological topics, including attribution and explanation.

Edwards, D., & Potter, J. (1993). Language and causation: A discursive action model of description and attribution. *Psychological Review, 100*(1), 23–41. An important paper presenting an impressively clear and well-argued case for a discursive approach to what we might gloss as 'attribution and explanation'.

Ferstl, E. C., Garnham, A., & Manouilidou, C. (2011). Implicit causality bias in English: A corpus of 300 verbs. *Behavior Research Methods, 43*(1), 124–135. A detailed investigation of the implicit causal implications of verbs.

Hareli, S. (2005). Accounting for one's behavior: What really determines its effectiveness? Its type or its content? *Journal for the Theory of Social Behavior, 35,* 359–372. A useful critique of much of the account-giving literature.

Kurz, T., Augoustinos, M., & Crabb, S. (2010). Fighting the 'climate change election': A discursive analysis of Australian political rhetoric around climate change. *British Journal of Social Psychology, 49*, 601–625. A fascinating investigation of ways in which the 'national interest' is constructed and arguments concerning Australian policy in relation to environmental issues.

LeCouteur, A., & Oxlad, M. (2011). Managing accountability for domestic violence: Identities, membership categories and morality in perpetrators' talk. *Feminism and psychology, 21*, 5–28. An insightful examination of the use of membership categories in the accounts given by perpetrators of domestic violence about episodes of violent behaviour.

Weiner, B., Amirkhan, J., Folkes, V. S., & Verette, J. A. (1987). An attributional analysis of excuse-giving: Studies of a naive theory of emotion. *Journal of Personality and Social Psychology, 52*, 316–324. An important and fascinating experimental investigation of excuse-giving.

Useful weblinks

www.qualitative-research.net/index.php/fqs/article/viewArticle/745/1612 An online paper that makes good use of some of Antaki's (1994) application of conversation analytic considerations to the issue of explanatory talk.

The following sites provide a great resource for the research publications relating to specific academics and include a number of downloadable references:

www-staff.lboro.ac.uk/~ssca1/antaki1.htm Charles Antaki's conversation analytic publications and related resources.

www-staff.lboro.ac.uk/~ssde/index.htm Derek Edwards' discursive and conversation analytic publications.

www.sussex.ac.uk/profiles/194001 A list of publications by Evelyn Ferstl, some of which address the idea of the implicit causality of verbs.

research.haifa.ac.il/~shareli/ Hareli's publications, addressing various aspects of social emotions.

www-staff.lboro.ac.uk/~ssjap/index.htm Jonathan Potter's discursive publications and related resources.

The following websites might be worth looking at as potential sources of data – you could look at the video clips with some of the ideas covered in this chapter in mind.

www.bbc.co.uk/news/world-europe-12259346 An interview with the outgoing Irish Prime Minister Brian Cowen.

www.youtube.com/watch?v=mEsF6WPd-wA US cabinet meeting regarding the BP oil spill.

www.youtube.com/watch?v=rzOz2KXdmo8 Town hall meeting concerning the BP oil spill.

www.youtube.com/watch?v=FL3pfF97uWQ&feature=related Town hall meeting concerning the BP oil spill (contains strong language).

www.youtube.com/watch?v=Ng1bth8g7YM A public meeting about the proposed abolition of the Forestry Commission in the UK.

6

Attitude change and persuasion

Learning outcomes

By the end of this chapter you will have a deeper understanding of:

- different ways of thinking about attitudes
- ideas about the numbers of components that attitudes have
- the ways in which attitudes have been measured
- how attitudes relate to behaviour
- critical perspectives on attitudes
- how attitude change can be seen as caused by a preference for consistency
- what factors researchers have identified as making persuasive attempts successful
- how researchers have investigated the relationship between these factors
- rhetorical and discursive approaches to attitude change and persuasion.

A particular focus of the chapter is the critique of the literature that is reviewed and the consideration of rhetorical and discursive positions. By the end of this chapter you will be able to:

- critically review much of the literature that is covered
- compare and contrast the 'traditional' and 'critical' approaches to attitudes and attitude change.

In September 2005, the Danish newspaper *Jylland-Posten* published a controversial cartoon featuring the prophet Muhammad. The publication and subsequent reprinting of it by Norwegian, French and German newspapers led to waves of protests across many parts of the world. As well as some peaceful demonstrations and boycotts (such as the one pictured here), there were violent clashes and attacks on Danish and Norwegian embassies in India, Indonesia, Afghanistan, Syria and Lebanon, among other countries. The protests throughout the world resulted in a number of deaths – 15 people being killed in Nigeria alone in 2006. There were calls for the cartoonist to be killed and a reward of $1million was offered to whoever did so. The reaction lasted for years after the initial publication, with some people arguing for publication freedom and others for greater respect for religious leaders.

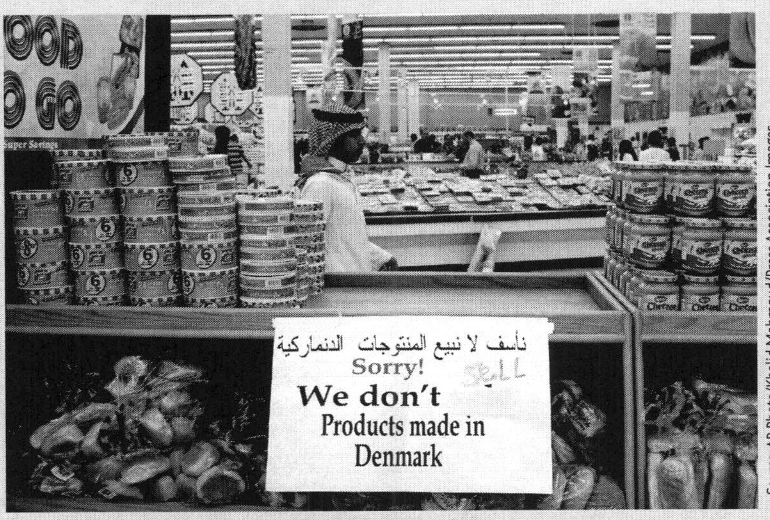

نأسف لا نبيع المنتوجات الدنماركية
Sorry!
We don't
Products made in
Denmark

Source: AP Photo/Khalid Mahmoud/Press Association Images

A Saudi shop refuses to stock Danish products in response to the publication of a controversial cartoon regarding the prophet Muhammad. Can the social psychology of attitudes help us to understand the intensity of people's feelings on this issue?

This cartoon controversy exemplifies very marked attitudinal stances towards an issue. People not only held differing opinions regarding the publication of the controversial cartoon but also, in many cases, the attitudes people had seemed to be associated with very intense behavioural responses.

The apparent power of attitudes in this case to shape behaviour may cause you to question whether or not attitudes always have such an influence on the behaviour of people who hold them. You might also wonder whether the attitudes involved in this series of events could be modified or changed by some persuasive effort, or whether they are too entrenched or resistant to change? Perhaps still more fundamentally, what do we mean by 'attitudes' and is this the best way of understanding what is going on in this and other cases where we are trying to understand human decisions and reactions?

Introduction

The news story referred to above provides a very dramatic introduction to thinking about attitudes and persuasion. If, however, issues of attitude and persuasion were just restricted to such intense responses, then it probably would not be as central to social psychology as it is. One key reason for the popularity and prominence of attitudes and persuasion within social psychology is the breadth of its relevance – issues connected to attitudes and persuasion saturate our worlds. Our reactions to all the different media we encounter – almost every conversation, perhaps every decision – could be examined through the lens of attitude and persuasion. No wonder, then, that attitudes and persuasion are often taken to be the single most researched area within social psychology.

Chapter overview

This chapter starts by reflecting on some different ways that we might think about attitudes. The dominant approach within social psychology has understood attitudes as measurable, quantifiable, individual stances towards a target (which might be any aspects of our world – people, animals, things, events or experiences). This is briefly contrasted with an alternative rhetorical approach that challenges the focus on thoughts, or cognitions, within individuals and, instead, emphasises the way we have attitudes on issues that are up for debate and how they are shaped by the argumentative context in which they arise. Related discursive work is briefly outlined that suggests we should examine what attitude talk does, rather than the traditional concern with notions of 'underlying' cognitions, evaluations, beliefs or intentions.

After this initial outline of such radically different approaches to attitudes, two more narrowly framed debates are addressed by considering the number of components (such as affective responses, cognitive responses and behavioural intentions) that comprise an attitude. Also, some consideration is given to the ways in which attitudes might best be measured, including both explicit measures (such as the Thurstone, Likert and semantic differential attitude scales) and implicit measures (such as speed of response to different stimuli flashed on a computer screen).

The chapter then addresses a crucial focus of research that has spanned several decades – namely, the extent to which attitudes relate to behaviour. In discussing this literature, attention is given to both research that has identified problems with the link – arguing attitudes are poor predictors of behaviour – and which attempts to improve their predictive power. One particularly important argument, which is central to the *theory of reasoned action* and the *theory of planned behaviour*, is that the specificity of the target behaviour should be matched to the specificity of the attitude measured. This research suggests that, for example, my attitude to *environmental issues in general* might be a poor predictor of whether or not I actually recycle my cornflake boxes, but my attitude to *recycling itself* should be a much better predictor.

Before moving to the issue of attitude change and persuasion, the area initially touched on at the start of the chapter will be revisted by addressing (in more detail) rhetorical and discursive critiques of attitude research. Particular attention is given to discursive work that has emphasised the importance of considering the surrounding talk context (or *sequential context*) in which attitudes are expressed, so as to examine the *interactional work* attitude talk does. From this perspective, talk that might have the form of 'expressing an attitude' can be examined in terms of what it is doing in the interactional environment in which it is uttered. Thus, saying, 'I love carrots' could be *doing* appreciation, agreement, disagreement or prefacing some carrot-related anecdote – the sequential location of this utterance would shape the sort of interactional work that it does.

Having addressed various strands of research concerned with attitudes, the chapter then addresses issues of how attitudes might change. The first approaches to be considered are concerned with internally generated change – specifically, with how our motivation to be *consistent* can lead to us changing attitudes to make them consistent with other attitudes that we have (*balance theory*) or our behaviour (*cognitive dissonance theory*). Attention then turns to some of the models of persuasion that attempt to describe how and under which circumstances people can be persuaded by others to change their attitudes. The Yale Communication and Attitude Change Program (which commenced because of US 'propaganda needs' during World War II) developed a taxonomy of source, message and audience factors that might most predictably result in successful persuasion. These 'ingredients of persuasion' are considered, along with the *elaboration likelihood model,* which attempts to describe the circumstances under which one set of factors (such as the *source of a message*) will become more important than another (such as the *message content*).

Finally, rhetorical, discursive and conversation analytic research, which raises problems for traditional approaches to attitude change and persuasion, is briefly touched on. One issue developed here is how talk is constructed such that it *appears to be true* – that is, the talk itself (or 'the message') may be designed in such a way that it warrants or substantiates the claims or arguments being made. Thus, in real instances of persuasive communication, we might find speakers talking about other people who endorse what they are saying (such as, 'all leading scientists agree with me on this'). How claims such as this may construct reality in a way that backs up what the speaker is saying is addressed in this final section.

6.1 Different ways of thinking about attitudes

Most textbook chapters on the topic of attitudes and attitude change start with a definition – sometimes acknowledging the differences between one-, two- and three-component definitions – and then, having established some broadly common ground, move on to consider how attitudes relate to behaviour and when and how they change. This chapter, too, considers the one-, two- and three-component definitions of attitudes, but also goes further. It considers some of the issues that rhetorical and discursive psychology raise for our understanding of attitudes – it will be seen that these perspectives are a radical challenge to traditional perspectives.

Rather than getting the definition out of the way so we can move on, the very different perspectives considered here provide different understandings of not only how we should conceptualise 'attitudes' but also how we should research them and what we should be looking for in that research. It can be noted that consideration of how attitudes relate to behaviour and how they come to change are typically informed by a 'traditional' understanding of what attitudes are – as broadly stable cognitive structures – whereas a concern with what attitudes *do* – in ideological terms and in interaction – are informed by rhetorical and discursive approaches to what attitudes are.

Traditional approaches to attitudes

Stop for a moment and think about the last chat you had with a friend. Chances are, at least one of you expressed your liking or disliking for something or someone – you might have complained about someone, or raved about something you experienced or are about to experience. It seems our lives are full of these responses, stances, evaluative positions with regard to almost everything and everyone that we encounter. These positions – your positive or negative responses to people, things and events – are your attitudes. At least, that is how social psychologists have traditionally approached the topic. From this traditional perspective, then, attitudes are our positive or negative judgements, evaluations or responses concerning people, events or objects.

The fact that you love your mobile, can't stand being ignored and feel sick at the thought of invasive research on animals are, in traditional terms, *attitudinal positions* that capture how you feel about certain *attitudinal targets* (anything about which you can hold an attitude). This places attitudes firmly in the head of the individual, with each of us 'containing' a collection of attitudes about the person sitting next to us in a lecture theatre, the food served up in the canteen, the TV show we watched last night or what we think of the current government. There is certainly some debate within the traditional perspective as to whether our definition of attitudes should include behaviour and thoughts (see one-, two- and three-component models below), but there is fundamental agreement that attitudes are essentially *mental objects* – that is, things located within the mind of the individual.

Allied to this is an emphasis on attitudes as being quantifiable (see Section 6.3). That is, from a traditional perspective, one can measure attitudes either by providing statements of (predetermined) varying strength for people to agree or disagree with (see Section 6.3, about the Thurstone scale) or providing a statement against which they plot the strength of their agreement or disagreement (see Section 6.3, about the Lickert Scale below). These measures can then provide a numeric representation of the strength of someone's attitude. Approaching attitudes as measurable and quantifiable in this way have been foundational assumptions for an enormous amount of research that has sought to understand (among many other issues) how attitudes can be most accurately measured, how they relate to behaviour and what is most likely to make an attempt at persuasion successful. This breadth of research should not be taken as confirmation that the assumptions are correct, however, nor should it stop us from questioning whether thinking of attitudes as being mental objects that are quantifiable is the best way of understanding what attitudes are. Indeed, just as it is wise to ensure that a skyscraper has good foundations, so, too, the vast edifice of research resting on these assumptions about attitudes should encourage us to stop and reflect on them and consider alternative understandings.

Rhetoric and attitudes

One such alternative understanding is provided by Billig's (1987, 1991, 1996) **rhetorical approach** to attitudes. Billig's social constructionist work has been partly informed by a careful thinking through of some of the understanding about the art of persuasive talk – or, rhetoric – that emerged in ancient Greece.

Many social psychologists would reject such ancient work on the grounds that the ideas were not tested in controlled experiments or that they pre-date modern understandings of the human mind – it may be worth noting your own reaction to finding that a current social psychology textbook is referring to ideas that are nearly 2500 years old! One advantage of investigating ideas that come from a different time and place in our current setting, however, is that, *precisely because* they emerge from a culture with very different sets of assumptions from our own, they might have insights our 'common-sense' everyday understandings and assumptions blind us to. Thus, our own cultural biases may make us expect to find measurable, mental objects within the individual that cause behaviour – indeed, this may be so much a part of how we see the world that it is hard to imagine how or why we should question it. Billig demonstrates how a careful engagement with certain ancient ideas can provide a refreshing contemporary critique of current social psychology.

In particular, Billig has drawn on concepts developed by a contemporary of Socrates called Protagoras (it is from his name that we get the word 'protagonist'). Among many pithy and insightful statements about life and argument, Protagoras is reported to have said that, 'for every question there are two sides to the argument exactly opposite to one another'. For Billig, this brilliantly captures just

Rhetorical approach In the context of the literature considered here, this refers to Billig's work, which emphasises how attitudes are argumentatively shaped, being formed on matters that are up for debate and designed to argue against other stances on these argued-about issues.

what it is we come to have an attitude about and what form that attitude takes. That is, Billig argues an important way of approaching attitudes is to think of them as questions or issues that are 'up for debate' or controversial. Few of us count among our attitudes our stances towards notions regarding the causes of rain or the rotation of the Earth around the Sun, but these were positions of argument and stance – or *attitude* – in the past. In more recent history, it is possible to see how attitudes about the cold war, nuclear power, unilateral nuclear disarmament, damage to the ozone layer, melting ice caps or 'man-made' climate change can become more salient during times when these issues become matters of debate and controversy. That is, we seem to have attitudes about things that are being debated or *argued about at the moment* – when those things are no longer controversial, then perhaps we less obviously have an attitude regarding them.

This makes the *topics* of attitudes (the issues we have attitudes about) much more socially situated – but Billig goes further and argues that *the very expression of our strong views* (our attitude talk or evaluations) is shaped by the context of argument out of which they are forged. That is, from Billig's rhetorical perspective, attitudes cannot be adequately conceptualised as relatively fixed mental objects within the mind of the individual that can be neatly captured by a number on a scale (such as rating someone as having a '5' for strongly agreeing with the sentence 'Stem cell research should no longer be funded'). Instead, whenever we produce attitude talk – or make an evaluation (such as, 'I can't stand people who moan about mobile phones') we are not just expressing an evaluation but also *doing so against counter-positions*. That is, the way in which we express our strong views or make our evaluations is shaped by the fact they arise out of issues which are controversial.

This is all the more evident when, instead of one-sentence snapshots, we let people talk in more detail about their views. Here, we may find apparent contradictions in what they say. For example, the person who is against people who complain about mobile phones may concede that they themselves do not like phones ringing when they are watching a film. These apparent contradictions point to the sort of argumentative (or rhetorical) work that evaluations do (conceding I recognise limits to the public use of mobile phones may make my position that generally people shouldn't complain about mobile phone use seem more reasonable and convincing and me seem less of a crazed techno-freak, for example). This approach to attitudes as being held on topics of current controversy and attitude talk, or evaluations, being designed to argue against counter-positions will be returned to later in this chapter.

The traditional perspective – with its emphasis on attitudes as quantifiable mental objects – can also be contrasted with discursive social psychology (which is closely related to Billig's rhetorical approach). As has been detailed in previous chapters, discursive social psychology – particularly as developed by Edwards and Potter (1992, 1993) – is critical of social psychology's attempt to conceptualise and explain all aspects of social behaviour in terms of what is taking place in the mind of the individual. That is, discursive social psychology criticises the ways in which social psychology has approached many of its objects of study (whether self, attribution, attitudes, stereotypes or groups) as being essentially *cognitive entities in the mind of the individual*. From the traditional perspective, attitudes, too, are mental phenomena – ones that might predict our behaviour (see Section 6.4) and might themselves change as a result of the effects of external persuasion on our thinking or our own desire for consistency between our thoughts (see Section 6.6).

Discursive psychology provides an approach to the topic of attitudes that reformulates the object of study as *attitude talk* itself. Whether the analysis is of a speech made by an Australian Prime Minister (Augoustinos, LeCouteur, & Soyland, 2002) or everyday talk about food preferences (Wiggins & Potter, 2003), the focus is on *what is said* rather than any thoughts, feelings or other mental features. In a discursive approach to attitude talk, or evaluations, there is a particular interest in *what the talk itself might do* (rather than how it is caused by, or relates to, the thoughts of the speaker). Discursive psychology then sees attitude talk or evaluations as action-orientated, accomplishing or doing things in interaction – that is, it is understood as '*practical* rather than *abstract* or *theoretical*' (Wiggins & Potter, 2003, p. 520).

As will be seen below, the discursive perspective would make sense of a specific piece of 'attitude talk', such as 'I hate being rushed' or 'That bus service is rubbish' as *doing* something in the interaction where it is uttered. The utterance 'I hate being rushed' might not tell us about some fixed mental evaluation of 'being rushed' that the speaker has, but could be a means by which the person saying it can object to or resist some attempt to hurry them. Similarly, 'That bus service is rubbish' need not be simply seen as an abstract evaluation of the bus service in question, but could be a means by which someone arriving late explains, or accounts for, their lateness. Alternatively, saying, 'That bus service is rubbish' could be a means by which someone demonstrably sympathises with the negative bus experience of someone else – perhaps a friend who has just reported waiting for hours for a bus. In these examples, the talk has not been traced back to some measurable, relatively fixed 'attitudinal mental entity' that is thought to have caused the words to be said. Instead, these examples show how talk can be investigated in a different way – by considering *what it might do in the interaction* in the light of where and when it is uttered.

6.2 How many components does an attitude have?

Social psychologists have often disagreed about whether attitudes are comprised of different psychological parts – or components (see Figure 6.1). For some – who have a one-component view of attitudes – the attitude is best thought of as being a feeling, or affective, response to a given issue. Others see attitudes as being comprised of separable thinking (cognitive) and feeling (affective) parts and, thus, suggest a two-component view of attitudes. Finally, others incorporate behaviour into their definition of attitudes.

One-component view

Thurstone (1931) – whose scale is considered below – defined attitudes in terms of just one component: the person's 'for or against' feeling-response to a 'psychological object'. From this perspective, attitudes are understood as feeling-judgements – positive or negative – regarding anything about which an attitude could be held (any experience, object, person, other being and so on).

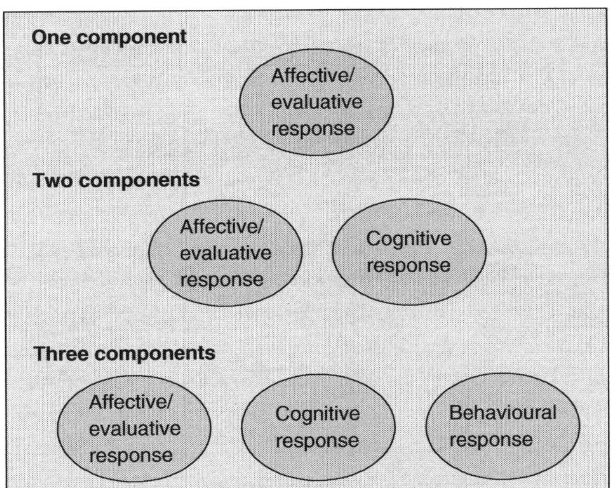

Figure 6.1 One-, two- and three-component understandings of the structure of attitudes

You might have strong feelings about the controversial Danish cartoons and the responses they evoked (see above) or you might feel strongly about human or animal rights or environmental issues. In all of these cases, you might find that you have some feeling-response, some like/dislike reaction.

This feeling-response has subsequently become defined as the *affective* component and future models (two- and three-component models) have kept the affective component while adding the cognitive and behavioural components respectively.

Two-component view

Allport's (1935) review argued that the affective response or evaluative component was insufficient as a definition of attitudes and cognitive elements should be introduced. In other words, if we want to know someone's attitude(s) regarding a target issue, we should ask them not only what they feel but also what they think about that issue. If you think again about an issue you have strong feelings about, there may be cognitive elements alongside affective ones. If you have strong feelings about taking action to protect the environment, you may well have related thoughts or cognitions – perhaps including what will happen to the Earth if no action is taken.

Evidence for two (or more) components to attitudes has often sought to suggest some combination of the following points. First, that the cognitive and affective dimensions are coherent – that is, they relate to each other sufficiently to suggest they can be treated as a coherent entity. Second, that, while coherent, they are distinguishable – that is, they can be seen as measuring aspects of attitude which are meaningfully different. Finally, that the two components have good predictive validity with regard to attitude-relevant behaviour – that is, they tell us something about how people will behave.

Bagozzi and Burnkrant (1979) examined scales reporting affective and cognitive responses on the topic of 'being religious' with data originally collected by Fishbein and Ajzen (1974). Bagozzi and Burnkrant found that factor analysis of the data suggested a two-component model (which included responses on cognitive scales) was more coherent than a one-component model (which relied just on responses on affective scales).

Verplanken, Hofstee and Janssen (1998) found evidence to suggest that, while coherent, cognitive and affective dimensions could be seen as meaningfully distinguishable. In their research, they asked participants what they *felt* and what they *thought* about certain brand names and countries and found that there was evidence for both cognitive and affective dimensions to attitudes – with affective components being more accessible than cognitive components.

With regard to predicting behaviour, Bagozzi and Burnkrant (1980) researched college students' attitudes and actual behaviours regarding 'personal participation in political activities'. With this data they found that introducing a measure of cognitions about personal participation in student protests led to an *improved prediction of actual behaviour* compared to just relying on the affective response.

Advocates of the three-component model argue that the prediction of future behaviour is better still if a third component – which includes aspects of behaviour (such as past behaviour and/or intended behaviour) – is included as well.

Three-component view

Proponents of the three-component model of attitudes embrace the affective and cognitive responses considered above and add a third ingredient: *behavioural* responses. Ajzen (1998, p. 244) – one of the most prominent advocates of the three-component model – refers to the third component as *conative*, which he defines as, 'behavioural inclinations, intentions, commitments, and actions with respect to the attitude object'. *Behavioural intentions* – that is, how the person plans or intends to behave with regard to the attitude target – have been a particularly important focus in much research concerned with a three-component model of attitudes.

Ouellette and Wood (1998) argue that both past behaviour and behavioural intentions are vitally important in predicting future behaviour. For unusual or difficult future behaviour, it may be our behavioural intentions that are especially important – thus, our *intention* to do a presentation on some research findings might importantly predict our behaviour (especially if we do not regularly do such presentations). For more routine behaviour, it may well be that our *previous practice* is a good predictor of future behaviour – for example, if we regularly text a friend each time there is a 'newsworthy' event concerning our partner, then this may predict the likelihood of texting them when our partner suddenly announces that they are going to move in with us.

Reflecting on components of attitudes

Often the issue of how many components an attitude has is presented with little or no commentary on it – students are expected to learn the definitions like the meanings of symbols in the highway code. These definitions, however, do merit some reflection – not just regarding 'which one is best' but also about the assumptions, blindspots and further questions that we are confronted with when considering these definitions of attitudes.

First, the two- and three-component models both have cognitive and affective components and may imply that both of these factors operate on individuals in shaping their attitude-relevant behaviour. Trafimow, Sheeran, Lombardo, Finlay, Brown and Armitage (2004), however, suggest that this is too simplistic, arguing that some people will be more under affective control and others under cognitive control. In this way, Trafimow et al. (2004) insert a personality factor as a mediating variable in between the attitude structure and attitude-relevant behaviour – the personality of the individual determining whether affective or cognitive components will better predict their attitude-relevant behaviour.

Second, from a different perspective, we could note that, while a large amount of research – for example, Breckler (1984), Millar and Tesser (1990) and Haddock, Maio, Arnold and Huskinson (2008) – emphasise the distinction between affective and cognitive components, some research has problematised it in various ways. Eagly, Mladinic and Otto (1994), for example, argue for a *synergistic relation* between affect and cognition, suggesting that they cannot exist in a pure, separate form, 'uncontaminated' by each other – our thoughts (or cognitions) *are bound to* influence our feelings (affect) and vice versa.

From yet another perspective, it can be noted that much of the research relies on responses to a semantic distinction between words concerned with feelings (such as, 'I dislike X', 'I enjoy X') and words concerned with thoughts (such as 'I think X is unwise,' 'I think X is valuable'). In some cases, the preface 'I think that ... ' versus 'I feel that ... ' is used in an attempt to distinguish measures of cognitive and affective components. If people seem to respond by having a coherent set of affective responses to an attitude target that differ from their coherent set of cognitive responses, we can ask whether the differences found using this approach are *real* differences between distinct psychological objects or merely reflect how participants cluster together certain types of words when requested to report their 'attitudes'. Relatedly, Potter (1998), taking a rhetorical approach, argues that, instead of focusing on the meaning of abstract sentences (such as 'I think spending cuts are necessary') presented in isolation to participants, attention should be given to *how and where participants themselves* use such utterances within sequences of interaction.

Third, with regard to the three-component model of attitudes, it is possible to question whether behavioural intentions and past behaviours should really be conceptualised as being part of the structure of attitudes. The problem is not their predictive efficacy – Ajzen (1998) and Ouellette and Wood (1998) suggest that these aspects of the 'behavioural component' of attitudes *improve* predictions of attitude-relevant behaviour – but, rather, the theoretical justification for their inclusion. Does thinking of 'past behaviour' as 'part of the structure of attitudes' run the risk of being a sort of 'cognitive imperialism' where non-cognitive elements (past behaviour, habit) are implicitly incorporated into what is traditionally thought of as an essentially cognitive structure (attitude)? Does including 'behavioural intention' (especially if it is highly specific) become almost tautological? It may be true but uninsightful to say that my intention to take the dog for a walk is a good predictor of my act of taking the dog for a walk, for example. See Box 6.1 for some other ideas that will be referred to in the rest of this chapter.

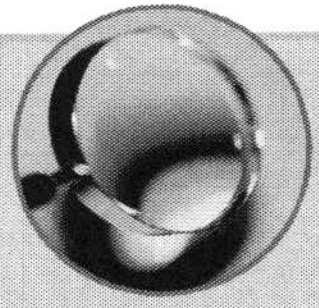

Box 6.1 FOCUS
Breast or bottle?

Between the 1930s and early 1970s across much of Europe, Australasia and North America, government-backed campaigns tried to persuade parents to use commercially available formula milk for their babies rather than breastmilk (the dates varied from country to country, bottle-feeding campaigns beginning much earlier in the USA than in New Zealand). Formula was subsequently portrayed as scientifically advanced, medically approved and nutritionally complete.

From the 1970s onwards, there was a marked shift in public policy that was subsequently endorsed by a joint WHO and UNICEF statement in 1991 on the benefits of exclusive early breastfeeding. Precisely the same countries that had been advocating formula were now trying to persuade parents that breastmilk was superior – *it* was now the medically approved and nutritionally advanced option. In addition, it was also depicted as both immune-boosting and natural.

From the perspective of some attitude researchers, there is some tentative evidence that the persuasive campaigns had some effect. Prior to the promotion of formula, breastfeeding was very prevalent, with 70 per cent of mothers initiating breastfeeding of their newborn infants in the USA in 1915. Breastfeeding was found to decline, however, while formula was being promoted (reaching a low point of 22 per cent initiating breastfeeding in the USA in 1972) and increased after the persuasive campaigns switched to advocating breastmilk (reaching approximately 62 per cent initiating breastfeeding in the USA in 1997).

In 2001, the WHO recommended breastfeeding exclusively for the first six months of an infant's life – a recommendation that the UK and a number of other countries (though not the USA) complied with in 2003.

A further twist to the global pattern of fluctuating advice and practice emerged in 2010, when research published in the *British Medical Journal* began to question if breastfeeding exclusively may be linked to iron deficiencies and increased risk of allergies and coeliac disease, leading the UK government to review its recommendations.

This example illustrates a number of features that will be drawn on throughout this chapter.

1. Governments sometimes use persuasive campaigns to endeavour to change people's behaviour by changing their attitude rather than passing legislation that either forbids or requires certain behaviour. That is, the campaigns are based on a presumed link between people's attitudes and their behaviour (see Section 6.4).
2. The campaigns that were developed (both for and against formula feeding) emphasised the expertise of those making the case. Speaker, or source, expertise has been an important strand of research into persuasive communication (see Section 6.6).
3. The above example illustrates a change in the prevailing understandings, beliefs and attitudes at a societal level – that is, historically, understandings and attitudes (at least in so far as behaviour is a guide to them) were found to change. This emphasis on a shared societal belief or attitude has been conceptualised in both rhetorical work and work on social representations (see Section 6.5).

Box 6.1 continued

4 The attitudinal positions that were advocated can be seen as argumentatively or rhetorically organised – that is, each campaign was shaped to not only promote one position (such as bottlefeeding) but also to critique the counter-position at that time (breastfeeding). In this way, attitudes can be understood as occupying a position in a debate with the opposite point of view and are thus culturally located stances rather than merely being cognitive entities abstracted from any wider contextual setting (see Sections 6.4 and 6.5).

5 The language of the persuasive attempts can be analysed in itself. Thus, the ways in which positions are aligned with 'scientific advances', being 'medically approved' and the 'latest scientific evidence' can be seen as ways in which the talk orientates to issues of making itself appear to be true, or, warranting. Likewise, the talk of 'modern', 'advanced', 'immune-boosting', 'mothers' milk' and 'natural' can be analysed in terms of the versions of reality that it produces, such as how it constructs the responsibilities and identities of mothers, the idea of what is natural and how this relates to medicine, science and commerce (see Section 6.7). It is worth noting that Crossley (2009) investigated the ways in which rhetoric about being and doing what is 'natural' played an important part in conversations that mothers had concerning breastfeeding.

Critical recap

How many components does an attitude have?

1 Some research suggests that, while there may be cognitive and affective components to attitudes, their effect is not uniform and individual differences need to be taken into account. Thus, people will differ in the extent to which they are influenced by cognitive or affective dimensions of attitudes.

2 The distinction between cognitive and affective components of attitudes may be problematic. From one perspective, the two components may be thought of as psychological objects that are bound to influence each other. From a very different perspective, the reliance on abstract representations of affective and cognitively based attitude positions in isolation may be challenged. Does this tell us about *real, separate* psychological entities or replace genuine investigation of how positions are constructed in interaction with an abstract test of semantic associations?

3 It is possible to question the extent to which past behaviour and intended behaviour should be conceptualised as a component of attitudes.

Reflective questions

1 *Think of an issue that you have a different attitude towards than one or more of your friends. Do you think your attitude is based on cognitive or affective dimensions? How about your friend's attitude?*

2 *When was the last time you expressed a strong attitude, such as, 'I can't stand X!' Would someone need to know the context in which it was said or can the attitude be understood from the utterance alone?*

6.3 How attitudes and behaviour are measured

Methods of measuring attitudes are often presented as relatively unproblematic and sometimes as restricted to three very well-known attitude scales – the Thurstone, semantic differential and Likert scales, with the Likert and semantic differential scales being the most frequently used in contemporary research. These scales are presented below and illustrated in Box 6.2, but, along with discussing potential problems with the individual scales, consideration is also given to the problem with explicit scales and the relative merits and demerits of implicit measures of attitudes. Finally, some issues with measuring the 'attitude-relevant behaviour' are also addressed.

Attitude scales

The **Thurstone scale** (as seen in Box 6.2) involves presenting participants with a number of attitudinal statements on the issue about which researchers are seeking to measure people's attitudes.

These statements are created by, first, listing 100 or so statements relevant to the issue. They should represent a range of attitudinal positions regarding the attitude topic being investigated. The statements are given to approximately 100 people to rank order them as to whether they are strongly or mildly pro or anti the issue in question. The

Thurstone scale An attitude scale that involves the participants selecting preweighted statements they agree with on a given topic. Unlike the other popular scales, the participants do not have to indicate their position on a linear scale (such as the extent of their agreement or disagreement).

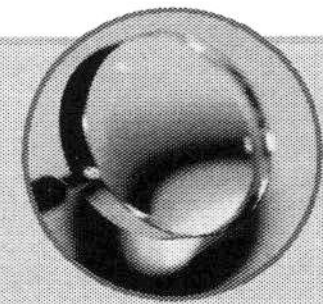

Box 6.2 FOCUS
Illustrations of three different attitude scales

Thurstone scale
Tick the statements that you agree with.

China should listen to the demands for autonomy raised by representatives of Tibet. ❑

China should not be forced into actions regarding Tibet that are against its own interest. ❑

It is crucial that the world takes all necessary action to force China to free Tibet. ❑

It would be worth representatives of China and Tibet meeting to discuss issues that concern them. ❑

Any interference by the outside world regarding Tibet is an act of aggression against China. ❑

Semantic differential
Indicate the position on each scale that best reflects your feelings about each item.

China's actions in Tibet are
Completely justified - - - - - - -- - - *Not at all justified*

China's actions in Tibet have been
Positive -- - *Negative*

China's actions in Tibet have been
Good - *Bad*

Western concerns regarding China's actions in Tibet are
Completely justified - - - - - - - - - - *Not at all justified*

Likert scale
Indicate the position on each scale that reflects the extent of your agreement or disagreement with each statement.

China's actions regarding Tibet are a matter for the Chinese alone.
Agree strongly - - - - - - - *Disagree strongly*

China has improved the life of people living in Tibet.
Agree strongly - - - - - - - *Disagree strongly*

Western concerns about Tibet are completely hypocritical.
Agree strongly - - - - - - - *Disagree strongly*

investigator assigns a value to each statement based on the median ranking that each statement receives.

Approximately 20 statements that show a high level of agreement are selected from the 100 statements to represent the range of attitudinal positions that may be adopted regarding the attitude topic. Participants whose attitudes are being measured, are asked to tick each statement that they agree with. Their attitude position is taken from the median of all the scale scores that the person agrees with.

Semantic differential scales (see Box 6.2) involve the presentation of a sentence stem, such as 'Drastically cutting public expenditure is …', with a response scale that has terms (often single-word adjectives) on either end – for example, 'good .... bad'. The scales provide an opportunity for the respondent to indicate not only which term better describes their attitudinal position, but also the extent to which it depicts their position, typically using a

Semantic differential An attitude scale that requires participants to indicate where they are positioned on scales labelled with mutually incompatible adjectives at opposite ends to each other.

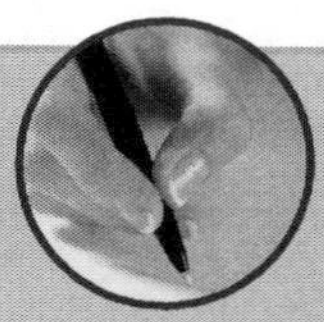

Box 6.3 TRY IT OUT
Measuring attitudes

Using a Likert scale, measure the strength of your agreement or disagreement with the statements listed below. Do you have clearly defined attitudes about some items more than others? Can you identify anything about the items you feel most and least strongly about – for example, are they topics of wider social controversy or debate, do the statements reflect one side of an issue that is being, or can be, debated (Billig, 1987, 1991)?

Unilateral nuclear disarmament is necessary for world peace.
Agree strongly - - - - - - - Disagree strongly

Immigration has been beneficial for my country.
Agree strongly - - - - - - - Disagree strongly

Same-sex marriages are a positive social development.
Agree strongly - - - - - - - Disagree strongly

It is right that people should pay the full cost of their university education.
Agree strongly - - - - - - - Disagree strongly

five- or seven-point scale. Placing your tick or cross in the middle of the scale is taken to mean that both terms are equally agreed or disagreed with, while placing it immediately next to one term indicates that term is very strongly agreed with.

The **Likert scale** (see Boxes 6.2 and 6.3) has characteristics of both the Thurstone and semantic differential scales. Similarly to the Thurstone, the Likert scale presents attitude statements to the participants for them to respond to – for example, 'More needs to be done to protect the environment.' The participants are, however, required to express the extent of their agreement or disagreement, usually using a five- or seven-point scale. The scales are typically labelled along these lines – 'agree strongly, agree somewhat, neither agree nor disagree, disagree somewhat, disagree strongly' (the order may be reversed to address response biases).

Issues with the Thurstone, semantic differential and Likert scales

The Thurstone, semantic differential and Likert scales considered above have each been criticised in several respects. Here, attention will be paid to the scaling of attitudes using the Thurstone scale, the issue of neutral responses for semantic differential and Likert scales and the issue of self-presentation and demand characteristics with all three scales. In developing this third issue, the idea of implicit attitudes and their measurement will be addressed.

As can be seen in Box 6.2, the Thurstone scale is the only measure of the three considered in which the respondents do not assign themselves to a point on a scale. For the semantic differential and Likert scales, it is the respondents filling in the scales who puts their marks on a point between two adjectives (semantic differential) or measure of agreement scale (Likert) to identify the valance (or positive/negative direction) and strength of their attitudes, but the Thurstone scale gives responsibility for that to the researcher. Rather than the respondents indicating where they are on an issue, it is the preassigned weightings that are used.

On the one hand, it could be argued that this may overcome any small element of self-presentational bias – that is, not seeing the weighting given to the statements may, at least in theory, enable respondents to answer without being overly concerned with the position that they are seen to adopt on an issue. On the other hand, however, the procedure presumes that some preassignment of attitudinal weightings is possible for a range of statements and the respondents' own positions can be judged as the midpoint (median) of the various (attitude-weighted) statements that they have agreed with. Can statements be neatly assigned an uncontentious attitude weighting, though, and, even if they can, are respondents' 'real' attitudes the midpoints of statements that they agree with? In other words, the Thurstone scale opens up the issue that position of the respondent on the attitudinal scale is not directly measured but assigned, using a procedure with certain questionable assumptions.

While the semantic differential and Likert scales overcome the issue of assigning respondents to an attitudinal scale position, they have a problem that arises from requiring participants to indicate their own positions on these scales. One difficulty is that, while responses at each end of the scale may (though not inevitably) be indications of a clear attitudinal position, responses in the middle of the scales may be open to different readings. This is particularly evident in cases where a semantic differential

Likert scale An attitude scale that requires participants to indicate the extent of their agreement or disagreement with attitude-valanced statements – that is, they are required to mark on a scale their agreement or disagreement with distinct attitudinal positions.

scale uses labels that are not semantically opposite – for example, imagine being required to describe a tutor using this scale:

Kind .... Wise

Imagine that you placed your tick in the middle and someone had to make sense of it. Does the tick in the middle mean that you perceive the tutor as both kind *and* wise or as neither kind *nor* wise. Kaplan (1972) refers to this problem as the 'double definition of the neutral category'. The person choosing the midpoint might be communicating that they want to endorse *both* of the scale items (sometimes this is referred to as ambivalence) or *neither* of them (sometimes this is referred to as indifference). The situation might appear to be resolved when the scale is labelled with seemingly opposite terms – as with these examples from Box 6.2:

Semantic differential

China's actions in Tibet have been

Positive .... *Negative*

Likert

China has improved the life of people living in Tibet.

Agree strongly .... *Disagree strongly*

Even with this case, however – and others for which the scale's ends appear to have mutually exclusive labels – it is possible to consider the way in which the midpoint could have more than one meaning. With the first example above, the midpoint could signify that the respondent feels China's actions are neutral – *neither* positive nor negative – or that they are both positive *and* negative. These are quite different positions. In one case, the actions are neither black nor white – somewhere in between positive and negative – in the other, the actions may be complex, involving both very markedly positive and very markedly negative elements. Likewise, the midpoint on the 'agree' scale in the second example above may indicate *neither* fully agreeing *nor* disagreeing or *both* strongly agreeing with the idea that some actions have improved the lives of people living in Tibet *and* strongly disagreeing that other actions have improved the lives of those living in Tibet.

Implicit association test

An issue that relates to all three scales is they are quite explicit about what they measure. In many cases this might not be a problem – you might be quite happy to disclose your attitudes about music, academic subjects, activities you enjoy, perhaps even politics and religion – but what about attitudes likely to be less favourably received? Imagine asking people to reveal their liking or disliking for different ethnic groups. It is possible that even those whom we might consider to be prejudiced may not reveal their prejudice. There may be some element of self-presentation (see Chapter 2), with people concealing their 'true' attitudes so as to appear in a more positive light. In recent years, many attitude researchers have become interested in measuring not just *explicit* attitudes – like the scales above attempt to do – but also *implicit* attitudes.

The most popular **implicit attitude measure** is the implicit association test (IAT), developed by Greenwald, McGhee and Schwartz (1998). In order to understand this test it is worth thinking about a computer keyboard. Imagine having to press either the 'A' key on the left side or the '5' key on the number pad on the right side. Now let us suppose that, on the screen, different stimuli appear – perhaps words or images that you had to respond to quickly but accurately using either the 'A' key or the '5' key.

Let us suppose that some stimulus words (happy, peace, crash, rotten and so on) are presented and you have to categorise them, hitting the 'A' key if they are pleasant and the '5' key if they are unpleasant. Imagine that you are a Korean participant and are presented with names and you have to decide whether they are Japanese or Korean surnames (Youn, Kawa and so on, for example), hitting the 'A' key if they are Korean or '5' if they are Japanese. Now it starts to get interesting. How about the screen showing a mixture of names and words – you now need to hit the 'A' key for both Korean names and pleasant words and the '5' key for Japanese names and unpleasant words. Finally, there is a reversal of this – you are again shown a mixture of words and surnames, but now it is the 'A' key for pleasant words and Japanese surnames and the '5' key for unpleasant words and Korean surnames.

This experimental procedure is complex, but the idea behind it can be readily grasped. We are likely to be faster on tasks that require us to perform the same action – pressing the same key, in this case – when that action has a shared or consonant meaning for us. Do you think that the Korean participants in Greenwald et al.'s (1998) experiment were faster when the same key ('A') was used

Implicit attitude measures These are indirect measures of attitudes that are thought to avoid problems anticipated if a more explicit (such as a self-report) measure were to be used. Implicit attitude measures are often used where it is thought the participants might be reluctant to admit their 'real' attitudes – for example, research into prejudice. Often reaction times to stimuli presented on a computer screen are used for this sort of measure.

to mean 'pleasant' and 'Korean' or when it was used to mean 'unpleasant' and 'Korean'?

If the key has some shared meaning that can readily be grasped, then it is easy to respond with it, but, when it is used to represent things that do not fit together for us, it slows us down. The Korean participants were faster when 'pleasant' and 'Korean' were combined on the same key (a compatible combination for them) and slower when 'pleasant' was combined with 'Japanese' (an incompatible combination for them). The reverse was true for Japanese participants. This difference in speed of response can, of course, be measured and is often known as the IAT effect (measured in milliseconds by subtracting the 'compatible' from the 'incompatible' combinations).

The IAT has stimulated something of a renaissance in attitude research – being drawn on in quite different ways to understand the link between attitudes and behaviour (considered further below) and to provide a more sophisticated conceptualisation of people's attitudinal positions. Some work following the development of the IAT has emphasised the difference between implicit and explicit attitudes – for example, suggesting that implicit attitudes predict spontaneous behaviour (such as where there is no opportunity or motivation to think about the behaviour), while explicit attitudes predict deliberate behaviour.

Dovidio, Kawakami and Gaertner (2002) found measures of implicit prejudice better predicted spontaneous prejudice in interaction than explicit measures did. Other work, such as Spence and Townsend (2007), by contrast, stressed that implicit and explicit measures get at different aspects of a single attitude construct and both are predictive with regard to the same target behaviour.

Finally, some work has sought to draw on both implicit *and* explicit measures to arrive at a more fine-grained attitudinal typology. Son Hing, Chung-Yan, Hamilton and Zanna (2008) drew on the IAT to suggest that, instead of simply categorising people as high or low in prejudice on the basis of their explicit attitudinal responses, integrating explicit and implicit measures allows for a more complex conceptualisation in which people can be high or low on implicit prejudice and high or low on explicit prejudice. These combinations allow for four quite distinct prejudice subtypes that overcome the simplicity of earlier high–low prejudice conceptualisations.

The use of implicit measures in general and the use of the IAT for measuring implicit prejudice specifically has attracted criticism, however. Arkes and Tetlock (2004) raised questions regarding what they refer to as the 'inferential leaps' in the interpretation of IAT results. First, they question whether the seemingly prejudiced responses are not so much a reflection of the individual's level of prejudice but, rather, cultural associations. Thus, if Korean respondents appear to more readily associate Korean surnames with the concept of pleasant, this may reflect something at a cultural rather than an individual level. Indeed, individuals who do not agree with the stereotype may still be aware of it and it may thus influence associations measured by the IAT.

Second, they question whether the affective negativity can be understood as arising from prejudiced attitudes or other, non-prejudiced associations. Arkes and Tetlock (2004, p. 258) ask whether an association of a group – for example, black Americans – with negative evaluative terms might (in some cases) reflect 'guilt, shame, embarrassment, or social anxiety that might plausibly accompany interracial relationships in a society trying to overcome a long, grim history of interracial tension.' In other words, the negative association might not be a consequence of the individuals' negative evaluation of the group, but, instead, their awareness of the link between the target group and prejudice, mistreatment and tension.

Finally, Arkes and Tetlock (2004, p. 267) ask whether those who use the IAT are too ready to brand participants as prejudiced purely on the basis of their reaction times: 'it is misleading to bemoan the very high proportion of participants who exhibit prejudice, unless the speaker clarifies that prejudice merely means a relative difference in RT (reaction time) and not any necessarily racial animus.'

Measuring behaviour

Before moving on from our consideration of attitude measurement it is important to note that even the seemingly straightforward 'attitude-relevant behaviour' may pose issues in terms of its measurement.

Imagine for a moment that you, like Eliot, Armitage and Baughan (2007), are concerned with how attitudes relate to behaviours – that is, will someone's attitude about speeding while driving relate to their actual driving behaviour? How do you measure actual speeding behaviour? Many studies would use self-reports of speeding behaviour, so you might present the participant with some stimulus, such as, 'I often speed on my way to work', but would this really reflect what the participants actually do? Elliott et al. used both self-reported behaviour and observation of behaviour in a driving simulation (issues concerning this measure will be touched on later).

Eliot et al.'s (2007) research raised questions regarding whether or not observations (notwithstanding their limitations) tended to confirm self-reported behaviour. What Eliot et al. found was that they did not, thereby

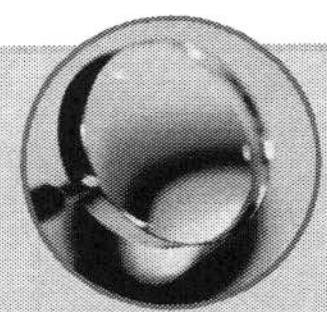

Box 6.4 FOCUS
Are attitudes an artefact of the procedures used to measure them? (Puchta & Potter, 2002)

Puchta and Potter (2002) analysed focus group interviews in an attempt to understand something of the apparent contradiction between the arguments made in discourse and rhetorical studies and the apparent evidence from more traditionally framed attitude research. While discursive and rhetorical research has suggested that attitude (or evaluative talk) is variable, constructed to *do* interactional and argumentative work, various 'attitude' studies appear to find evidence of 'enduring underlying attitudes'.

Puchta and Potter (2002) argue that the 'freestanding individual opinions' produced in focus groups are a product of the ways in which the focus group interactions are conducted by the moderator. That is, moderators encourage participants to produce 'abstract', 'freestanding' (or context-free isolatable) attitudes and ignore those elements of talk (such as refinements, qualifications, self-contradictions) that do not conform to this freestanding format. Thus, the product of focus group research – freestanding, isolatable, context-free attitudes – can be seen as a direct result of the practices that occurred within the group.

Puchta and Potter (2002) make the broader point that, just because certain forms of attitude (such as freestanding ones) can be the product of research, it does not mean that is how attitudes *really* are. It could be – as in the case of the focus group research that they investigate – that the means of data collection – (the interactions, instructions, specifications and scope for participants' responses) shape the form attitudes arising from such research appear to take. By examining the process of their production, Puchta and Potter (2002) seek to provide a means of questioning certain dominant conceptualisations of attitudes – the latter being shaped by the data collection processes involved.

identifying problems regarding how behaviour is actually measured in attitude research. The question that this discrepancy raises is what measure of behaviour should be used – self-report or observation?

It might seem that observation of actual behaviour is the obvious choice – surely that is the 'true' behaviour, whereas self-reporting involves some sort of distortion from that 'truth'. Even observation may be problematic, however, as some behaviours might not easily be observed. Imagine, for example, being interested in whether or not people respond violently during heated arguments. How would you go about observing someone's behaviour in the context of such an argument? Would you film someone non-stop until a heated argument occurred (which would be difficult practically and ethically) or would you try to create a heated argument (which might not be realistic). Both options seem far from ideal.

As noted above, even Eliot et al.'s (2007) measure of speeding raises questions as they used a driving simulator, which we might well expect to yield different speeding-relevant behaviour from that of *actual* driving. The issue, however, is still not readily resolved, even if *actual* speeding-relevant behaviour could be observed as the mere fact of observation would be likely to change the target behaviour (see Box 6.4).

Critical recap

How attitudes and behaviour are measured

1 The Thurstone scale relies on preweighting items presented to participants, with each participant's position being inferred from their responses to these items. The process of preweighting and inference can be criticised as insensitive to the individual participants' own understandings and meanings with regard to the target of the attitude.

2 Both semantic differential and Likert scales use scales (typically with five or seven points) on which participants can indicate the strength of their attitudes. For both scales, however, responses in between the two ends of each scale are open to contradictory interpretations. Does a midpoint response mean *disagreement* with both of the ends of the scale (neither) or *agreement* with both of them?

3 Explicit measures of attitudes may *all* be problematic when certain non-socially desirable attitude stances are relevant. Thus, explicit measures may be limited by self-presentational concerns when attitudes regarding certain topics are being investigated.

4 Implicit measures of attitudes may have an alternative set of problems – for example, concerning the extent to which the measure (typically reaction time) actually tells us about the attitude being investigated. Do differential reaction times that suggest negative attributes may be associated with specific ethnic groups tell us about individual attitudes or culturally formed associations? This, in turn, raises a big issue concerning whether we should, in fact, think of attitudes in terms of individual stances or wider culturally informed positions.

5 Measurement of behaviour is frequently assumed to be relatively straightforward, but some research identifies inconsistency where different measures are used (self-reported behaviour is not always the same as observed behaviour, for example). Even observation of behaviour is far from perfect, as the mere act of observing may well change the target behaviour itself.

Reflective questions

1 *Which of the measures of attitude do you consider to be the strongest and weakest? What are the reasons for your answers?*

2 *Choose a particularly important 'attitude' that you have (or could be thought of having.) Would any of the above scales and measures adequately capture it?*

6.4 Attitudes and behaviour

The issues considered so far concerning the components of attitudes and the measurement of them are typically a secondary concern in social psychological research into attitudes. One of the main issues for nearly a century has been how attitudes relate (or fail to relate) to behaviour. This issue is not a concern for social psychologists alone but also political parties, businesses and governments, all of whom are interested in influencing our voting, consuming and other socially relevant behaviour. For behaviour that cannot easily be controlled by legislation, the idea that it relates to attitudes provides a basis for interventions that change or shape attitudes. Thus, politicians, businesses and governments might attempt to get people to vote for their party, buy their product or engage in some preferred behaviour by targeting their attitude in the hope that this, in turn, will shape their behaviour.

The idea that attitudes relate to behaviour seems obvious and almost intertwined – your voting activities and purchasing behaviour, for example, seem unavoidably linked to your attitudes. This presumption was dealt a serious blow by LaPiere (1934), however.

LaPiere began his research by touring the USA with a Chinese couple, visiting 66 hotels, caravan parks and tourist homes and eating in 184 restaurants – a research programme, the like of which, sadly, may prove difficult to fund these days. LaPiere and the Chinese couple were refused service once in more than 170 service encounters.

Six months later LaPiere sent a questionnaire that sought to establish the attitude (perhaps more accurately, behavioural intention) of the places they had visited. In response to the question, 'Will you accept members of the Chinese race as guests in your establishment?' a stunning 92 per cent (of the 128 establishments that replied) said they would not, only 1 per cent they would and 7 per cent indicating it would depend on circumstances.

LaPiere's study raised serious questions regarding the method and theory of attitude and behaviour research. Methodologically, issues were raised about how attitudes and behaviours were measured. One example of this is the **levels of specificity** of the measurement of both attitudes and behaviours. Thus, as noted below, while specific behaviours might relate poorly to general attitudes, they might relate better to measures of specific attitudes. In the context of LaPiere's study, perhaps asking about attitudes concerning this specific Chinese couple (sending a photograph and details of who they would be arriving with, for example) would yield different results that would better relate to actual behaviour.

Theoretically, LaPiere's study raised questions about how the relationship between attitudes and behaviours was conceptualised – the simple, commonsense link was problematised and some more complex models were developed that built in specificity and a range of moderating factors which might affect the link between attitudes and behaviour. In between LaPiere's study and some of the dominant models of attitudes developed between 1975 and 1991, however, a radical suggestion was made: perhaps social psychology should *abandon* the concept of attitudes altogether.

In 1969, Wicker wrote a review of 42 attitude studies that reported attitude–behaviour correlations. These studies measured attitudes (using questionnaires) and

Levels of specificity In the context of this literature, the term refers to a concern that the specificity of the attitude measure and the behaviour measure are compatible – that is, either both are highly specific or both are quite general.

overt behaviours that were taken to be directly related to the expressed attitude. In a hypothetical world of perfect predictability, the correlation coefficient would be 1.0. Such correlations are never found – if they were, they would be viewed with great suspicion – but the higher the number is (between 0.0 and 1.0), the stronger the correlation and the more closely the measured attitudes are related to the measured behaviour. So, what was the mean correlation that Wicker found across these studies? Was it a remarkable 0.7 or above or a respectable 0.5? It was neither. Wicker found a mean correlation of 0.15. It does not take a great deal of statistical knowledge to recognise that, as it stands, 0.15 is quite a weak correlation. Wicker (1969, p. 64) argued that, 'taken as a whole [it] is considerably more likely that attitudes will be unrelated or only slightly related to overt behaviours than that attitudes will be closely related to actions.'

Wicker's (1969) paper and his call to abandon the concept of attitudes, as Eagly (1992) suggests, formed part of what became known as the 'crises' in social psychology. If attitudes could not be found to be reliably correlated to any measurable behaviour (let alone predict it), then the construct of attitudes could be abandoned and, with it, not only a crucial area of social psychological research but also a conception of the person as shaped by measurable cognitive entities.

In the wake of Wicker's research, two distinct strands can be discerned. One strand kept to the idea of attitudes and more broadly a somewhat cognitive approach to social psychology and concentrated on refining the ways in which the relationship between attitudes and behaviours was conceptualised and measured. The theory of reasoned action and theory of planned behaviour considered below represent particularly important milestones in this tradition. Another strand, which perhaps found its fullest expression with rhetorical and discursive psychology, developed a radically different conceptualisation of attitudes and, indeed, social psychology.

Martin Fishbein and Icek Ajzen's (1975) theory of reasoned action

Martin Fishbein and Icek Ajzen (1975) developed an extremely important and influential model of the relationship between attitudes and behaviour that addressed or attempted to address some of the issues regarding poor prediction of behaviour raised by Wicker (1969). Figure 6.2 shows their model – the theory of reasoned action.

As Figure 6.2 suggests, the model identifies three core factors that determine attitude-related behaviour. First, there is the '*attitude*' towards the behaviour – that is, the individual's positive or negative feelings about performing a behaviour, comprising both the individual's beliefs about the consequences of the behaviour and an evaluation of the desirability of those consequences. Second, there is the **subjective norm** – the individual's perception of what people who are important to him or her think about the target behaviour and how motivated the individual is to comply with those perceptions.

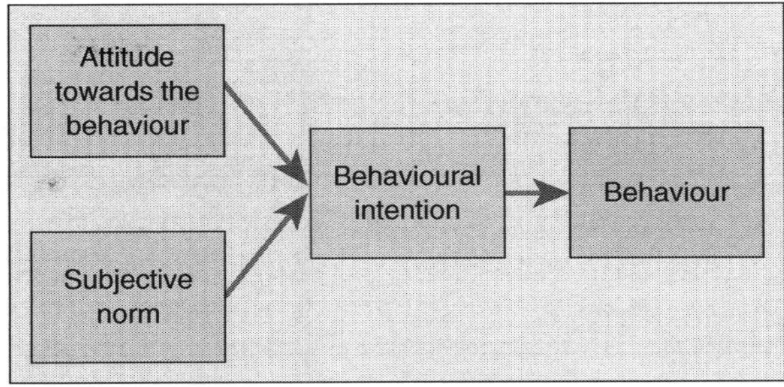

Figure 6.2 Fishbein and Ajzen's (1975) theory of reasoned action
Source: Fishbein, M., & Ajzen, I. (1975). *Belief, attitude, intention, and behavior: An introduction to theory and research*. Reading, MA: Addison-Wesley. Reproduced with permission from Pearson Education, Inc.

Perhaps most important for our current concerns, the theory of reasoned action introduced a crucial mediating variable between attitudes and behaviour – the **behavioural intention.** It was argued that this was a better determinant of actual behaviour than attitude alone. The behavioural intention was described as the decision to engage in a particular action and this was understood as shaped by a highly specific attitude – that is, the attitude towards the specific behaviour about which a decision is being taken.

According to Fishbein and Ajzen's (1975) theory of reasoned action shown in Figure 6.2, if we want to know whether or not a friend's pro-environmental attitude will mean that they engage in a specific act of recycling their waste, then we need to consider something much more specific. We need to take into account their attitude towards the specific action of recycling and the perceived attitudes of their significant others – their partner, family, best friend – towards the behaviour in question and our friend's motivation to comply with these (subjective norms). For Fishbein and Ajzen (1975), this will influence

Subjective norm The individual's perception of what people who are important to him or her think about the target behaviour and how motivated the individual is to comply with those perceptions.

Behavioural intention The decision to engage in a particular action.

their intentions to recycle and this, in turn, will be a strong predictor of the target recycling-relevant behaviour.

Fishbein and Ajzen (1974, 1975) and Ajzen (1988) argue that much of the apparently poor prediction of behaviours from attitudes rests on a problem of differential levels of specificity in measures of attitude and behaviours – that is, a general pro-environmental attitude might not predict specific pro-environmental behaviours (such as recycling), but might be better at predicting **aggregated behaviours**. Our friend's pro-environment attitudes and subjective norms might predict their behavioural intentions and actual behaviour across a wider spectrum of 'green' behaviour (our friend might not recycle, but cycle everywhere, never take a flight, always turn the heating down, only buy local organic foods and insist on renewable sources of energy for their electricity).

Fishbein and Ajzen's (1975) model is often known as an 'expectancy value' model and, more specifically, as the theory of 'reasoned action'. Expectancy value is the idea that the attitudes are formed by a scrutiny of the consequences of behaviour – it is our appraisal of the outcomes or the positive or negative consequences we expect that produces for us an attitude towards engaging in a specific behaviour. Likewise, it is this evaluation of outcomes that guides our intention to behave in a specific way.

The model is referred to as the theory of reasoned action precisely because it emphasises behavioural intentions as determined by careful, reasoned weighing of perceived outcomes. The assessments that we make of the outcomes of a behaviour might be erroneous. We may be inaccurate in our perception of subjective norms – for example, we might think that our partner wants us to place their notebook in the recycling bin when they do not. Likewise, our attitude-relevant beliefs may prove to be incorrect – for example, we might believe that our recycled waste will be reused locally and later discover that it will be transported many thousands of miles. For this model, however, it is our perceptions that guide our behaviour, not the 'objective truth'. Furthermore, our behaviour is still reasoned in that it is our reasoning through – *with the information that we have as we perceive it* – about likely outcomes that is the basis for our behavioural intentions and subsequent behaviour.

Ajzen's (1985) theory of planned behaviour

Ajzen (1985) introduced an important development that has largely superseded the theory of reasoned action. As Figure 6.3 illustrates, Ajzen's theory of planned behaviour has several of the ingredients found in Fishbein and Ajzen's (1975) theory of reasoned action (see Figure 6.2).

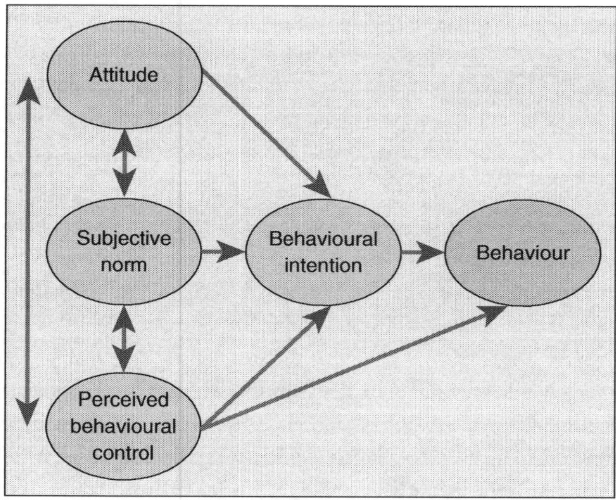

Figure 6.3 Ajzen's (1985) theory of planned behaviour

Source: Ajzen, I. (1991). The theory of planned behavior. *Organizational Behavior and Human Decision Processes*, 50, 179–211. Reproduced with permission from Elsevier Science.

The theory of planned behaviour still has behavioural intentions that are shaped by attitudes and subjective norms, but more emphasis has been placed on the possibility of interaction between these elements (note the two-way arrows in Figure 6.3) and, crucially, it introduced the novel element of **perceived control**. Indeed, perceived control is *so* important in the theory of planned behaviour that it not only influences behavioural intentions but is also depicted as having a direct effect on behaviour (which is not mediated by behavioural intentions).

Perceived control is how easy or difficult the behaviour is thought to be by the individual themselves. Our friend may have pro-environment and even pro-recycling attitudes and a partner and many significant others in their lives who are perceived to encourage recycling behaviour, but these motivational factors may not result in a specific intention to recycle if the friend thinks of recycling as too difficult for them to do. For example, we may catch our friend saying, 'I would love to recycle, but I am too busy to sort through my waste' and then, according to the theory of planned behaviour, we might not expect their behaviour to reflect their attitudes.

Aggregated behaviours A collection of comparable behaviours – for example, all environmentally friendly behaviours (such as recycling, energy consumption, not burning fossil fuels, steps to reduce carbon footprint) – rather than just one (such as recycling). The emphasis on aggregated behaviours is thought to be important where the attitude being measured is at a relatively broad level.

Perceived control This refers to how easy or difficult the target behaviour is thought to be by the individual.

According to Ajzen's (1985) theory of planned behaviour (see Figure 6.3), our friend's target behaviour, such as their completion of an essay, is not only predicted by their attitudes and subjective norms (as in Fishbein and Ajzen's theory of reasoned action discussed above) but also, crucially, and potentially directly, by their perceived behavioural control. Thus, even though our friend may expect consequences they positively value (attitudes) and may perceive that important others want them to complete their essay (and those others have opinions they are motivated to comply with), their sense of behavioural control could still be a vital determinant. If, for example, their attitude and subjective norm suggest that they will intend to complete their essay, their sense that the task is too difficult for them could change their behavioural intention or even stop them from completing the essay *despite their intention to do so.*

Applying Ajzen's theory of planned behaviour

Schifter and Ajzen (1985) undertook research that applied the theory of planned behaviour to the issue of weight loss over a six-week period. A total of 83 female undergraduate psychology students were recruited to the study. Initially, the participants were weighed and completed various questionnaire scales. The questionnaire items sought to measure the key components of the theory of planned behaviour – that is, attitudes, subjective norms, perceived control and behavioural intention. 'Attitudes to weight loss' was understood as the participants' favourable or unfavourable evaluations of losing weight and trying to lose weight over the next six weeks, such as, 'For me to reduce weight in the next six weeks would be good ... bad ... desirable ... undesirable ... harmful ... beneficial.' 'Subjective norms' was understood as the participants' perceptions of what others who are important to them were perceived as feeling about the participants' weight loss over the next six weeks. Subjective norms were measured by questionnaire items asking if most people who were important to them would think that they 'should ... should not' lose weight and try to lose weight over the next six weeks and whether they would 'support ... oppose' their weight reduction over the next six weeks. 'Perceived control' was understood as the ease or difficulty of losing weight – that is, the extent to which participants felt their actions could effect weight loss over the six-week period. Items measuring perceived control included asking participants about the 'likelihood, if you try, you will manage to reduce weight over the next six weeks'. 'Behavioural intentions' was understood as the desire or intention to reduce weight over the next six weeks and was measured using items such as 'I intend to reduce weight over the next six weeks' and 'I have decided to lose weight over the next six weeks'.

Schifter and Ajzen (1985) investigated the relationships between attitudes, subjective norms and perceived control and behavioural intentions and found that, together, the regression coefficient was a highly significant 0.74. Even on its own, 'attitude' was found to have a 0.62 regression coefficient with behavioural intentions. When actual weight loss (that is, how many kilos of weight were lost after six weeks) was considered, the picture changed in two important respects. First, the regression coefficient for 'attitude' and 'actual weight loss' was 0.1, even 'behavioural intention' and 'actual weight loss' gave a modest regression coefficient of 0.25. It can be noted – as Schifter and Ajzen (1985) do – that, with weight loss, they are measuring not simply 'behaviour' but, rather, 'behaviour-related outcome'.

Thus, it may be that behavioural intention and, indeed, attitude have higher regression coefficients with weight loss behaviour than with actual weight loss, where factors independent of the participants' behaviour and control such as metabolism might play a part. Indeed, most other attitude studies are concerned with the relationship between attitudinal factors and target behaviours, not subsequent outcomes. Second, perceived control became particularly important – it was the single factor that had the strongest association with actual weight loss (yielding a modest but significant regression coefficient of 0.41) and, combined with behavioural intention, the correlation increased slightly to 0.44.

Schifter and Ajzen, then, provided some support for the theory of planned action and their results could be understood as affirming the importance of perceived control in particular. For Schifter and Ajzen, perceived control is important not just as a factor that influences our behaviour by shaping our attitudes and our behavioural intentions but also as a factor which has an important direct independent influence on our actual behaviour. For Schifter and Ajzen, perceived control is important because of both its subjectivity and the objectivity from which it is, in part, derived. Subjectively, it is our sense of control that is an important determinant of our behaviour – how we feel about the ease or difficulty of the behaviour, for example, is crucial. Schifter and Ajzen also argue, however, that perceived control gives useful information about things as they really are – that is, the presence or absence of real constraints are reflected in perceived control. In Schifter and Ajzen's study – albeit with its unusual focus on behavioural outcome (weight loss) – perceived control not only told us about motivationally relevant information (how participants felt about the ease or difficulty of the behaviour and outcome) but also told us something about whether or not there were other constraints (time, money, opportunity, metabolism) that would affect weight loss.

Reconceptualising and modifying Ajzen's theory of planned behaviour

It is possible to roughly distinguish two concerns in research that relate directly to Ajzen's theory of planned behaviour. One strand raises questions about how variables – in particular, 'perceived control' – are conceptualised. A second strand introduces additional variables or moderating factors into the model.

Looking first at attempts to reconceptualise perceived control, Terry and O'Leary (1995) suggest that internal control-related perceptions – for example, my perceptions of what I can or cannot do or self (or self-efficacy) – should be distinguished from my perceptions of external constraints or perceived control over the behaviour. Similar distinctions occur in a range of subsequent research, including Kraft, Rise, Sutton and Røysamb (2005).

Kraft et al. investigated attitudes and subsequent self-reported behaviour regarding regular exercise and recycling drinking cartons among 112 undergraduate students at Bergen college. In this research, the concept of perceived control was reconfigured in terms of a combination of both perceived confidence (which relates to efficacy) and perceived control (which incorporates perceptions of external constraints). Items such as, 'If I wanted to, I would not have problems in succeeding to *perform behaviour* over the next two weeks' were thought to measure perceived confidence, while items such as, 'I have full control over *performing behaviour* over the next two weeks' were thought to measure perceived control.

Kraft et al. (2005) argued that the distinction between perceived *confidence* and perceived *control* is consequential for the predictive efficacy of the theory of planned behaviour. Perceived *confidence* was found to predict subsequent self-reported exercise (but not recycling), whereas perceived *control* was found to predict subsequent self-reported recycling (but not exercise). For Kraft et al., then, the variable of perceived control as conceptualised in the theory of planned behaviour conflates two separable elements – efficacy (the individual's ability to do the behaviour) and opportunity (the opportunity for the behaviour to be executed). Kraft et al. argue that the influence of these elements of efficacy and opportunity varies according to the behaviour in question, some behaviours being far more influenced by efficacy and some by opportunity. By developing the model to incorporate these separate elements, it can better account for behavioural intentions and behaviour.

Cooke and Sheeran's (2004) meta-analysis of 44 studies investigated seven potential moderating factors – accessibility, stability, direct experience, involvement, certainty, ambivalence and affective–cognitive consistency. They argued that each of these factors moderated and improved the attitude–behaviour correspondence, apart from involvement. Thus, our attitudes better predict our behaviour where the attitudes are readily accessible, stable, certain, low in ambivalence and high in consistency across our thoughts and feelings about the behaviour. Furthermore, where we have direct experience of the attitude-related behaviour, our attitudes will better predict our behaviour. This last factor – prior behaviour – has received attention in a number of studies, including Fazio and Williams (1986), who linked it to accessibility, and Sheeran, Aarts, Custers, Rivis, Webb and Cooke (2005), who were particularly concerned with habit (see Box 6.5).

Sheeran et al.'s (2005) study of drinking behaviour confirmed the idea that prior, habitual behaviour can be an important influence on our behaviour. They found that participants responded differently to stimuli that were linked to drinking depending on whether they had a drinking habit or not. For those with a drinking habit, merely presenting questions about socialising (and other 'goals' that are sometimes related to the behaviour of drinking) was enough to result in heightened levels of subsequent 'drinking behaviour'. By contrast, participants who did not have an established drinking habit did not show

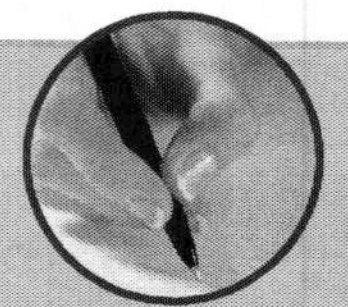

Box 6.5 TRY IT OUT
Good intentions, bad habits

In order to appreciate Sheeran et al.'s (2005) study, it is worth thinking for a moment of some New Year's resolutions – perhaps you or someone you know resolved to stop smoking, drinking, eating jelly babies or sending texts during lectures. Things might go well with our resolutions for the first few days, hours or, perhaps, minutes, but – as we all know from bitter experience – some repeated or habitual patterns of behaviour seem hard to break. Soon we find ourselves smoking, drinking, eating jelly babies and sending texts.

heightened drinking behaviour as a result of exposure to the same stimulus questions about socialising (and other drinking-related 'goals'). It should, however, be noted that, in Sheeran et al.'s (2005) research, the dependent variable 'drinking behaviour' was measured in initial studies by speed of response to the word 'drinking' in a verb identification task and, subsequently, by the participants' choice of a voucher for beer/wine or tea/coffee. Notwithstanding issues about how the dependent variable of 'drinking behaviour' was operationalised, their research suggests that past behaviour – particularly habitual behaviour – may predict, or at least be associated with, subsequent behaviour once goals relating to the behaviour are activated.

Ajzen (1991) was somewhat ambivalent about the role of past behaviour and habit, arguing that much of the influence past behaviour has on a given behaviour can be understood as mediated by factors already within the theory of planned behaviour. Thus, our past engagement may well shape or, indeed, reflect our attitude (having undertaken the behaviour – especially repeatedly – may be related to our liking of it) and our perceived control (if I could do the behaviour in the past, then I may perceive that I can do it again). Our past behaviour may also reflect our perception of a behaviour-supporting subjective norm (if I undertook the behaviour previously, clearly my perception of the subjective norm was either sufficiently supportive to enable me or not sufficiently prohibitive to stop me). Ajzen (1991) is somewhat sceptical about any independent influence of past behaviour on present behaviour. He is therefore reluctant to embrace it as another independent variable alongside attitude, subjective norm and perceived control, but does suggest that it would be 'premature' to draw definite conclusions.

Mohiyeddini, Pauli and Bauer's (2009) investigation of people's intention to exercise identified an intriguing moderating factor that may have been assumed to be already present in the attitude component of both the theory of reasoned action and the theory of planned behaviour – that is, the *emotional appraisal of the behavioural intention.*

Mohiyeddini et al.'s research suggests that, rather than being simply another facet of the attitude component, *emotional appraisal of intention to exercise* is a separable component. They measured *emotional appraisal* by asking participants to rate their feelings when 'thinking about their intention to exercise the following day' using the items 'alert, energetic, unhappy and downhearted'. The inclusion of the emotional appraisal of behavioural intention was associated with an increase of 17 and 20 per cent respectively of self-reported exercise frequency and exercise duration behaviour variance explained over the basic theory of planned behaviour.

Source: Blend Images/Alamy

Many people have positively disposed attitudes and intentions regarding exercise, but what factors determine whether or not they will act upon these?

For Mohiyeddini et al., behavioural intention remained the most important factor in predicting exercise behaviour, but it was considerably stronger when emotional appraisal of behavioural intention was also taken into account.

Critical recap

Attitudes and behaviour

1 Wicker (1969) found such low correlations between attitudes and behaviour that he suggested the attitude concept should be abandoned.

2 Fishbein and Ajzen (1975) produced a rebuttal to Wicker by arguing that, in assessing the correspondence between attitudes and behaviour, the level of specificity must be considered – general attitudes, such as being pro-environmental issues will have a good correlation with aggregated environmentally related behaviours (for example, support for Friends of the Earth and Greenpeace, recycling, low energy use, low carbon-emitting transport choices and so on), but cannot be expected to correlate highly with each specific strand of behaviour. To find better correspondence with specific behaviours, we need to consider attitudes to that specific behaviour.

3 Fishbein and Ajzen (1975) and Ajzen (1985) can themselves be criticised for moving some distance from the sort of attitude–behaviour correspondence that many researchers were initially interested in (Eagly, 1992). That is, it may be more interesting to know how our attitudes to the environment might impact our voting or consumer behaviour rather than to have to settle for an impact on aggregated pro-environmental behaviour. Likewise, knowing that our attitude to buying organic fruit is likely to correspond closely with our decision to buy organic fruit may tell us, or appear to tell us, less than expected behaviours inferred from more broadly based attitudes.

4 Some researchers have critiqued the theory of planned behaviour, suggesting that it should be modified, revised or rethought in the light of moderating factors such as habitual behaviour (Sheeran et al., 2005). Ajzen (1991) acknowledges the possibility of modification, but argues that, in many cases, the impact that moderating factors – such as past behaviour – have is precisely as a result of the variables already identified in the theory of planned behaviour model.

5 From a discursive social psychology perspective (Potter, 1996, 1998; Potter & Wetherell, 1987), the entire conceptualisation of the correspondence between attitudes and behaviour is mistaken. Rather than conceptualising attitudes as essentially unitary cognitive concepts that form – or should form – important causal antecedents of our behaviour, we could understand 'attitudes' as evaluative practices in their own right. That is, attitudes need not be considered in terms of how they relate to *a separable phenomenon of action* – we could investigate *how attitudes themselves do or accomplish certain interactional actions*. My spontaneous expression of an attitude in everyday life may do a blaming, an exoneration or an agreement, it might start or end a conversation. These are all actions – not caused by or corresponding with a separate mentalistic 'attitude', but accomplished in the 'attitudinal' or 'evaluative' talk itself. Each of these actions and any number of other talk actions are not pre-specifiable from the utterance alone, but, rather, it is the precise sequential placement of any given utterance that enables it to undertake specific work or do certain types of action.

Reflective questions

1. *Does your behaviour reflect your 'attitudes'? Can you think of one case where it does and one where it does not? How can you account for the differences?*
2. *Which – if any – of the models considered above (and the challenges to them) provides the best way of thinking about the relationship between attitudes and behaviour?*

6.5 Critical perspectives on attitude research

Most of the research considered so far, while offering different answers to the questions regarding how many components an attitude has, how they might best be measured and how they relate to behaviour, shares something of a common conceptualisation of attitudes. As mentioned at the beginning of this chapter, attitudes have tended to be conceptualised as (broadly) mental or cognitive entities located within the mind of the individual. The rhetorical and discursive challenge to this understanding of attitudes was briefly touched on earlier, but it is worth considering in a little more detail some of the different strands of research that have challenged the individualistic and cognitivist assumptions of most attitude research. Here, some of the research that has emphasised attitudes as social rather than purely individual and as action-orientated rather than purely expressive will be considered.

Attitudes as social rather than purely individual

As mentioned earlier, Billig's rhetorical approach laid great emphasis on the social context of attitudes, underscoring that we actually have attitudes about what are, *in our time and social context*, controversial issues. Billig (1996, p. 206) argued that, 'all attitudes are situated in a **wider argumentative context**. This becomes apparent if we ask what it is that individuals have attitudes about … people hold attitudes about controversial issues' (bold added).

This emphasis on the social dimension of what might be termed 'attitudes' is found in a number of quite distinct 'critical' research traditions. For example, in developing his theory of social representations, Moscovici drew on Durkheim's (1898) idea of a 'representation collective' partly to challenge the markedly individualistic focus in psychology. Moscovici's theory of social representations sought to emphasise–with relevance to many areas of psychology–the importance of shared, or social, understandings of the social world. Thus, what we might take to be 'our' individual attitudes can be thought of in terms of the extent to which they arise from, reflect and are sustained and challenged by *shared* or *social* understandings or *representations* of the social world.

Our interactions in the social world (which Moscovici, 1985, sometimes referred to as 'unceasing babble') are seen as the source and sustenance of our understandings, or representations – hence, they are *shared* or *social*. When we report 'our attitude' on a given topic, then

Wider argumentative context The idea that attitudes can be considered in terms of their relation to the sorts of things that are argued about or debated at a given place and time. This is suggestive of a move from attitudes as simply the cognitive and/or affective products of individual minds operating in isolation from one another.

we are reporting something that is fundamentally *social* rather than fundamentally individualistic. Once formed, our representations of the social world are *talked about* – they are agreed with and challenged by others. Thus, our social encounters will help to shape whether we maintain, modify or change our representations. Here, the idea of attitudes as social (rather than purely individual) is illustrated by some research that draws on both Moscovici's social representations *and* Billig's rhetorical and argumentative approaches.

Maloney and Walker (2002) note that, while people often report that they are in favour of organ donation – saying that they strongly support the idea of vital organs being taken from the bodies of the recently deceased to save the lives of others who have experienced some form of organ failure – actual participation in organ donation schemes is low. Rather than conceptualising this in terms of an attitude–behaviour discrepancy (and thereby linking to the concerns considered above), Maloney and Walker wanted to investigate how organ donation and transplantation have been socially understood. They note that, while initially being a medical possibility, then a procedure understood only by the medical profession, it (like many social representations) came to be a more widely distributed representation. Thus, organ donation and transplantation came to be 'understood in non-medical terms, imbued with non-medical beliefs, values and knowledge' (Maloney & Walker, 2002, p. 300).

Maloney and Walker sketch some of the representations of organ donation and transplantation in Western Australia over the last few decades. For example, representations in the late 1960s and early 1970s are characterised as 'medical' with a mechanistic conception of the body and an emphasis on the pivotal role of the transplant surgeon (and relegation of the donor to being a 'spare part'). They suggest that in the early 1980s another representation developed in which it was 'anchored in the non-medical world' (2002, p. 300), specifically focusing on the donor and donor's family as transplants were represented as 'the gift of life from a donor to the recipient' (2002, pp. 300, 301). For Maloney and Walker (2002, p. 301), these different representations form a 'representational field' that has, at its centre, 'two conflicting images – a "gift of life" and the "medical removal and replacement of body parts"'.

It can be noted in passing that, within social representations research, there is some debate about the extent to which representations are coherent and stable. Guimelli (1998) argues that it is important to distinguish 'core' from 'peripheral' elements of a representation – suggesting that there will be coherence and stability with the 'core' elements – those fundamental to the representation – but there may be more fluidity and change with elements that are not so central to the representation. Maloney and Walker, however, suggest that social representations *can* accommodate *conflicting core images* – suggesting, specifically, that *both* images of organ donation and transplantation referred to above ('gift of life' and 'medical removal and replacement of body parts') may coexist within social representations of donation and transplantation.

In their focus group interviews, Maloney and Walker found that participants situated their pro-organ donation talk in 'the non-medical world'. Extract 6.1 illustrates this position.

Extract 6.1

I am also in favour [of organ donation] because it is a service to humanity and it is giving life ... Because you are, of course, dying so it is better off that you save someone else's life, like a gift for society. (Man, Group 1).

Source: Maloney and Walker (2002, p. 309)

Coming from the predominantly individualistic perspectives considered earlier, this talk could be seen as the individual's expression of their own attitude. We could whip out our attitude scales, give the individual an attitude score and think about how or why the individual's attitude may (or may not) relate to their individual behaviour. What Maloney and Walker offer is something quite different. The individual participant's articulation of an attitude is not snatched from the wider framing he or she gives it; instead, it is examined *within* that framing. Extract 6.1 shows the overtly attitudinal fragment of talk 'I am also in favour . . .' is justified and expanded on in subsequent talk. Maloney and Walker (2002) make the case that this justification and expansion situates the participant's talk (and their 'attitude') within a wider, shared, *social representation* – specifically, within the image of donation and transplantation as a 'gift of life'.

Maloney and Walker also found that pro-donation positions were qualified and these qualifications were situated in the other image comprising the social representation of donation and transplantation – that of the 'medical removal and replacement of body parts' (see Extract 6.2).

Extract 6.2

Thinking of them as a hunk of meat, like a piece of sheep or something. That is how doctors think. (Man, Group 2).

Source: Maloney and Walker (2002, p. 309)

Here, then, we do not find individuals pitted against each other, each with their own different specific stances on this issue of donation and transplantation. Instead, those who express pro-donation stances also qualify their position. This complex, seemingly contradictory positioning is, in itself, something of a problem for those who seek to conceptualise attitudes as relatively stable, measurable, individual positions regarding a specific attitude target (in this case, organ donation and transplantation). Furthermore, and of particular importance for our current concerns, these articulations of attitudes are not simply understood as purely individual positions, but, rather, as situated within representations – *social* representations. The participants' talk was, thus, intricately linked with the broad representation of donation and transplantation that Mahoney and Walker identified as emerging and developing within Western Australia at different historical points – and which, for them, contains contradictory images ('gift of life', 'medical removal and replacement').

Reflecting on social representations

The extent to which the theory of social representations is consistent with discursive and rhetorical concerns has, as Maloney and Walker (2002) acknowledge, been a matter of debate. From a rhetorical perspective, Moscovici's notion of a 'thinking society', while admirably challenging the individualistic focus of psychology, is too static and cognitive and should be replaced by what Billig (1987) calls an 'arguing society'. The 'thinking society' reifies cognition, positioning it as the true phenomenon of interest and implying something consensual and uniform about its content and form ('society thinks X'). Billig's concept of the 'arguing society', by contrast, prioritises the act of argumentation (rather than 'thinking') and highlights the contradiction and dilemmas entailed in having and expressing what are traditionally termed 'attitudes' or 'opinions'.

From a discursive perspective (Edwards and Potter, 1992; Potter, 1996; Potter and Wetherell, 1987), social representations can seem a blunt and heavy instrument for the moment-by-moment interactional contingencies that participants in an interaction attend to. Analysis of everyday interactions can reveal considerable contradiction and nuance in the constructions people produce in their talk and these can be seen as *action-orientated* – constructions that *do* things in interaction. That is, rather than invoking large, monolithic representations, people in interaction appear to construct in the moment, for the moment, versions of the world that *do* interactional work (for example, doing a compliment or complaint, agreement or disagreement, starting or ending an interaction).

Maloney and Walker's (2002) research does not address all of these concerns – the data extracts, for example, are presented without sufficient argumentative context to be clear about how any one argument is shaped to deal with those voiced by co-present others. Similarly, the lack of surrounding talk context makes it impossible to identify actions that are accomplished or become relevant across the sequences of interaction from which the extracts are taken – and, therefore, difficult to be confident about the sort of interactional work being done by the speaker in isolation in the data presented in each extract. Notwithstanding these criticisms, however, Maloney and Walker's research does offer some potential grounds for, if not rapprochement, then at least discussion between these different traditions.

Maloney and Walker's (2002) development of Rose, Efraim, Gervais, Joffe, Jovchelovitch and Morant's (1995, p. 4) idea of social representations as comprising a field in which there is 'contradiction, fragmentation, negotiation and debate' overcomes some concerns about representations being depicted as highly consensual, singular positions on a given issue. Finally, Maloney and Walker (2002) make some attempts to tie their analysis of these contradictions within the social representation of donation and transplantation to argumentative processes at work in their focus groups – a concern that relates to the action orientation of attitudes touched on below.

Attitudes as action-orientated rather than purely expressive

In addition to providing a critique of highly individualistic conceptions of attitudes, some critical work has challenged the idea that 'attitudes' are singular, underlying, cognitive entities. Much of this currently predominant emphasis on underlying cognitions developed alongside governmental concerns with public opinion (see Box 6.6).

Discursive psychology has developed a particularly sustained critique of these ideas, challenging the notion that there are mental entities, 'attitudes', that are 'really' or 'fundamentally' mental objects 'beneath' or 'behind' our talk and need to be measured (using various 'reliable and valid' attitude scales). Potter (1998) provides a neat contrast between attitudes as *'preformed'* and attitudes as *'performed'*. While traditional conceptions of attitudes cast them as pre-existing, *'preformed'*, mental formations that are sometimes articulated in talk, discursive psychology is interested in how they are *'performed'*, or *done*,

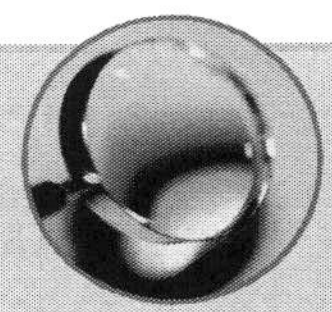

Box 6.6 FOCUS
A science of democracy (Rose, 1998)

Nikolas Rose (1998) provides a compelling account of the ways in which the development of the social psychology of attitudes and persuasion has been intricately interconnected with government (particularly government in the USA) concerns regarding an accountable basis for the exercise of power. For example, in the USA in 1929, Herbert Hoover established 'The President's Research Committee on Social Trends', which commissioned major attitude studies in order to undertake, 'a complete impartial examination of the facts ... to help all of us see where social stresses are occurring and where major efforts should be undertaken to deal with them constructively ... The means of social control is social discovery and the wider adoption of new knowledge' (Cina, 1976, p. 36, cited in Rose, 1998, p. 127). This description of the committee's remit reveals, more generally, the different facets of governmental concern with a 'scientific democracy'. Citizens had their individual attitudes measured and recorded and the aggregate of these scores, on the one hand, informs attempts to exert social control by government and, on the other, provides a means of justifying the decisions taken *in terms of democracy*.

This second point is worth dwelling on for a moment. First, the mere act (or even promise) of measuring and aggregating 'individual opinions', or attitudes, in and of itself can be a means by which governments appear to be 'listening to the will of the people' – a stance almost synonymous with being a democracy. Second, framing decisions that have been made, or are to be made, in terms of such surveys of public attitudes, such as, 'we did X because of public opinion' appears to be exercising power in a way that reflects the will of the people – enabling a government to be seen as *doing democracy* and, thus, having those decisions insulated from question and challenge. The scales of Thurstone and, subsequently, Lickert (who, as Rose notes, in 1939 worked in a research organisation funded by the government in the USA) became vital 'scientific' means by which individual people could be turned into measurable aggregates of opinion, against which decisions could be made and justified.

The 'attitude'-related research became still more intensive during World War II, with extremely influential programmes of research (see Hovland in Section 6.6) being funded so as to develop better propaganda. For now, however, it can be noted that, in helping to serve up a 'science of democracy', social psychologists, such as Allport (1937, cited in Rose, 1998), argued against the 'fallacies and blind alleys' of research concerned with the 'collective mind' and approaches that emphasised the group (rather than the individual) more generally. The technology of measuring and aggregating individual attitudes delivered something serviceable for democratic governments – and resulted in some form of breaking up of the concept of the importance of the collective or group. People were understood, and investigated, via a highly individualistic 'social' psychological lens, where their individual attitudes were measured and society was understood as a statistical aggregate of individual positions on various issues.

in talk – that is, **attitudes as action-orientated versus expressive**. Rather than looking for some central, underlying cognitive core attitude that is relatively stable over time, from a discursive point of view, we can examine the actions orientated to, made relevant and accomplished *in the very moment of articulating 'attitudes'*.

An enormous amount of discursive psychological research has outlined the ways in which constructions produced in talk can be understood as *performing* or *doing* action. As Potter (2010) notes, this concern with what is being done in talk has been one of the core arguments of discourse analytic and, subsequently, discursive psychological research. An important strand of early, often interview-based, discourse analytic research was the repertoires, or ways of constructing social reality, that were drawn on in talk. This work enabled examination of many ideologically relevant issues, such as the subtle forms that racism may take (by 'sympathetic', but

Attitudes as action-orientated versus expressive This distinction is between an understanding of attitudes in terms of what they do (particularly in interactional terms) and what underlying cognitive and affective states they express. Thus, if someone says 'I hate being late!' should we think about that as a stand-alone expression of some underlying cognitive or affective reality - or in terms of what sort of interactional work it could be doing (perhaps chivvying others along) at the moment and in the interactional context where it is uttered?

depowering and excluding, descriptions of other ethnic groups, Wetherell & Potter, 1992) and the justification of sexist practices (by constructing differences between men and women, Gill, 1993).

As Potter (2010) notes, more recent engagement with 'real-world' data brought renewed focus to the ways in which talk (including 'attitude talk') can be examined in terms of what is being done interactionally. This concern itself has broadened from an emphasis on how people deal with with issues of accountability in their talk (see Chapter 5) to encompassing a vast range of actions in interactions, much of which is inspired by conversation analytic research (Potter, 2010, provides a brief but effective summary of this).

Here, the discursive psychological emphasis on what talk does is illustrated by brief reference to Wiggins and Potter (2003). This paper is particularly relevant to our consideration of attitude talk because it pays special attention to when and where, and with what action relevance, participants themselves treat talk as being a 'subjective' 'attitude' rather than an observation of 'objective' fact. It should be noted that the data was collected by an audio recording of 'real' (which, in this case, means it would have occurred even if the researcher had not been carrying out this research) mealtime interaction (see Extract 6.3).

Extract 6.3

Doris	that was lovely Lau: ↓ra [thank ↓yo:u
Bill	[because eh-
Beth	it is [love↓ly
Laura	[>did you enjoy that< there is
	[some >d'you want<
Bill	[she ↑ said-
Laura	there's a bit mo:reif you ↓want (0.6) >there's
	a bit< more [↑sauce?

Source: Wiggins and Potter (2003, p. 522).

In Extract 6.3, Beth, Bill and Doris have just eaten a meal that Laura has cooked. As Wiggins and Potter (2003) note, the praise for the meal from Doris – 'that was lovely' (line 1) – and Beth – 'it is [love↓ly' (line 3 – is framed not so much in terms of a subjective evaluation, such as 'I enjoyed that', but, rather, as an objective report on how the meal was. By contrast, the person in receipt of the compliment (Laura) recasts the 'objective' descriptions of Doris and Beth as 'subjective' – '>did you enjoy that<' (line 4). Framing compliments as reflecting things as they are could make them appear somewhat more wholehearted than framing them more explicitly as attitudinal stances. Thus, while 'that was lovely' and 'I enjoyed that' are both compliments, arguably the former gives Laura more praise than the second, in which the appreciation of the food is implicitly at least partly to do with the particular tastes of the individual speaker. For those consuming the food, then, there is some benefit in constructing appreciation as an objective description rather than a subjective, attitudinal evaluation. By contrast, the recipient of the praise (Laura in Extract 6.3) might avoid the potentially boastful actions of confirming an objective description – 'yes it was' – or offering an assessment upgrade – 'it was stunning' – and, instead, recast the praise as the subjective, attitudinal stance of the individuals 'did you enjoy that'. Extract 6.3, then, suggests that constructing praise as a subjective, evaluative, attitudinal stance on the one hand or an objective description of the world on the other is not a neutral reflection of the praise's ontological status (that is, what it is), but, rather, a discursive move – a construction of reality that performs some specific sequentially sensitive action.

Wiggins and Potter (2003) suggest that constructing talk as attitudinal or as an objective description of reality attends to *interactional* concerns – rather than being a reflection of distinct cognitive entities. There is a systematic preference that everyday talk reveals to construct, for example, proffered compliments and accounts as non-attitudinal and received compliments as attitudinal. This systematic structure suggests that the construction of a piece of talk as an attitude or something else is tied up with the specific action that is being accomplished through that talk. From this perspective, then, whether we construct something as an attitude is part of the way in which we accomplish actions in interaction.

Critical recap

Critical perspectives on attitude research

1 Traditional perspectives have depicted attitudes as formed by psychological processes. Billig's work questions this arguing that 'attitudes' might be less individualistic than lay conceptions and traditional social psychological research presumes them to be. We have attitudes about the very things that are up for debate. There is a dilemmatic or argumentative dimension to holding strong opinions rather than them being simple, static entities that can be captured using scales.

2 When actual talk is investigated (either in relatively open-ended interviews, in institutional or everyday settings), variations or contradictions are often found. From a discursive perspective, this variation usefully illustrates the sort of work that the 'attitude talk' or evaluations are doing. By investigating what evaluations are produced at specific places in the sequence of interaction, we can better understand what it is that they are doing. This focus on the action done by the talk provides an important criticism of traditional approaches to attitudes as mental objects.

Reflective questions

1 *Note some of the ways in which you and others 'do' appreciations – for example, during a mealtime when someone has cooked for others. How are 'evaluative' and 'objective' assessments (see Wiggins & Potter, 2003) used?*

2 *What attitudes do you hold that reflect positions held by others, rather than being purely individual? Are these associated with issues that are controversial or debated in some way?*

6.6 Attitude change and persuasion

So far, this chapter has focused on how we might describe, measure and think about attitudes and how we can understand their relationship (or lack of it) with behaviour. An enormous amount of research, however, has sought to understand a distinct aspect of attitudes – that is, how and when they may change and what forms of persuasion may be most effective in bringing this change about. So, first, consistency theories – specifically, balance theory and cognitive dissonance theory – are briefly outlined. Second, some of the key research on persuasion is considered, focusing, in particular, on Hovland's list of ingredients for effective persuasion and Petty, Cacioppo and Goldman's (1981) elaboration likelihood model of persuasion. Then, in the next section, some discursive critiques of persuasion research are outlined.

Consistency theories

One approach to attitude change that we looked at in Chapter 3 attempts to describe the way in which we change our own attitudes to avoid an uncomfortable sense of inconsistency. If you have ever felt disappointed when someone you were getting to know and like reveals an attitude that differs markedly from your own, then you have experienced exactly the sort of discomfort that Heider was interested in. Imagine, for example, that you meet someone, get to like them, when, suddenly, out of the blue, they reveal that they can't stand repeats of your favourite television programme – the sitcom *Friends.* For Heider, this is an unbalanced situation in which 'P' – that, is the perceiver whose attitudes we are considering, who, in this example, is you – feels positive towards the other person, 'O', yet has a different attitude towards a mutual object, 'X' (the TV show *Friends*). We could also be in an unbalanced relational triad if we found ourselves agreeing with someone we disliked. Thus, if 'P' has a negative attitude towards 'O', but they have a common attitude towards a mutual object, 'X', this, too, could cause the same discomfort of inconsistency.

It is out of these situations of inconsistency, when the triad of 'O', 'P' and 'X' is unbalanced, that we are motivated to change our attitude to either the other person or the mutual object to restore balance. Thus, we are motivated to agree with those we like and disagree with those we dislike or, to like those we agree with and dislike those we disagree with. Attitude change therefore arises from the internal motivation to achieve balance or consistency across our perceptions of these relational triads (see Chapter 3 for further details of balance theory).

As you think through examples of balance theory, it may strike you that the theory works best if we consider very tentative attitudinal positions. For example, if we have only just met 'O' (the other person in Heider's model) and they reveal something unpalatable for us – perhaps that they enjoy bullfights – we could change our attitude towards them if we have strong animal rights attitudes. Alternatively, it could apply perhaps, in some finely balanced cases, such as when two people we very much like become sworn enemies, leaving us feeling that we have to choose to remain friends with only one of them.

While balance theory offers an account that makes some intuitive sense, one criticism concerns whether (even in its own terms) the simplification of considering just three elements can ever meaningfully reflect real-world attitude change. Thus, it may be that our attitude towards a mutual object (such as a television programme) is unlikely to be swayed by the fact that a friend of ours has a different view as we might know many other people who share our attitude. Likewise, it would perhaps be rather odd if we suddenly dissociated from a friend just because they reveal that they like a neighbour whom we find irritating, or dislike ballroom dancing when we love it. Again, with each person we know, there are so many combinations of known similar and dissimilar attitudes it is hard to imagine how the revelation of any one factor might change our attitude towards them.

Festinger's (1958) cognitive dissonance theory also suggests that attitude change can arise out of a preference for internal consistency, indeed, for Festinger, this is a strong, biologically based motivation to avoid inconsistent cognitions. For Festinger, like Heider, attitudes can change where there is an internal dissonance or inconsistency. For Festinger, however, the source of such dissonance need not arise from triadic relations but, rather, from any two inconsistent or potentially inconsistent cognitions. Thus, if I have positive and negative cognitions about smoking (such as thinking positively about the experience, but negatively about the consequences of smoking or having the cognition that I know I smoke with the cognition that I know it is bad for me), then I may be motivated to reduce my dissonance. I might change my behaviour (stop smoking) or my thoughts about the consequences ('It won't happen to me') or I might justify my behaviour ('I need to smoke just while I am in the middle of these exams') or even reinterpret my behaviour ('I am not *really* a smoker because I smoke infrequently/I smoke small amounts/I smoke 'light' cigarettes').

A fascinating example of Festinger's cognitive dissonance theory is developed in his (1956) book *When prophecy fails,* written with Riecken and Schachter. This book documents a participant observation study of an apocalyptic cult, the members of which believed that aliens were to save cult members at a specific time and date, whisking them to safety, while the non-believers perished in a flood. Through what cult members thought of as contact with spiritual beings, instructions were given for the group to be ready for the aliens to give them a lift to safety on 17th, then 21st and, finally the 24th of December. As you have no doubt deduced, the aliens did *not* arrive (although at least one group member reported seeing a 'spaceman' wearing a white helmet and white gown) and neither did the prophesised flood.

What is interesting, from a cognitive dissonance theory point of view, is that the disconfirmations lead not to an abandonment of the beliefs (and associated attitudinal positions) but, rather, to their modification. Suddenly, it becomes the case that the cult followers' actions have averted the full scale of the disaster. Rather than live with inconsistency (beliefs and associated attitudes disconfirmed), the cognitions are modified, such that the cult members were right in their *predictions,* but their faithful action has changed the course of events and saved the world.

In a classic experiment, Festinger (1958) found that people who performed a boring task for a significant reward maintained a low rating of the task's intrinsic appeal. In Festinger's terms, they need not experience dissonance as there was an external reason for their compliance with the task – they were paid well – so they need not revise their attitudes ('It was boring but at least I was paid'). Those who found that they complied with the experiment and performed a boring task for very little reward, however, were found to subsequently rate the task as more intrinsically interesting. In Festinger's terms these participants experienced dissonance – they had done something extremely boring when they need not have – and, due to the dissonance that resulted, they revised their attitude, viewing the task as less boring ('perhaps the task was not so boring after all').

These research findings – and cognitive dissonance theory in general – have attracted criticisms that focus particularly on whether or not too much speculation is placed on presumed cognitive dissonance to make sense of observable behaviour. That is, we cannot see the participants' dissonance, raising the question as to whether or not this hypothethised mechanism is present or necessary in accounting for such findings. Bem's (1972) self-perception theory, for example, suggests that people do not undergo the discomfort of dissonance, but merely report their own attitudes by observing the evidence (as they might observe other's behaviour and make inferences about their attitudes). From this perspective, people observing that they themselves completed a boring task, but were paid, could infer that they completed it for extrinsic reasons or because of external forces (to get the money), leaving them with a rating that they found the task boring. If, by contrast, they observe that they completed a boring task for little or no financial (or other) reward, then they may infer that there must have been something about the task that was satisfying or appealing and, therefore, they may infer that they feel more positively disposed to it.

An alternative criticism arises from impression management (Tedeschi & Rosenfeld, 1981). From this perspective, participants do not undergo a rethink to deal with dissonance, nor do they dispassionately observe their behaviour and make inferences about their attitudes. Instead, they are concerned with *how they appear to others.* Participants who were paid well can credibly rate the task as boring – their behaviour makes sense because of the financial reward they received. What about participants who received little or no reward, though? If they report that the task was boring, then how can they explain the fact that they did the task? Could others perceive them as being a pushover – people who will comply with any sort of request? By rating the task as intrinsically interesting, these participants make their behaviour seem sensible and accountable – something that will not give a negative impression to others.

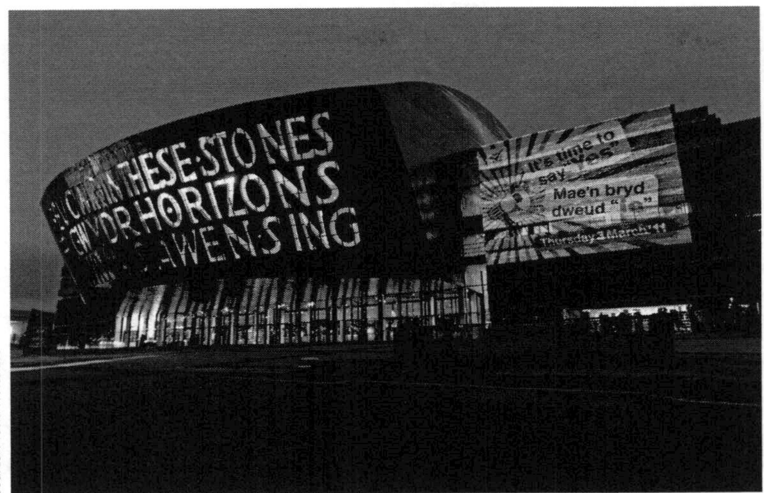

Source: Media Wales Ltd

The Yes for Wales group projected glowing images with the words, 'It's time to say yes' on to the Senedd, Wales' Millennium Centre, Millennium Stadium, National Museum of Wales and Cardiff Castle 28 February 2011. Do messages like this persuade people? If something else is needed, what is it?

Ingredients of persuasion

A markedly different programme of research on attitude change was concerned not with how change was brought about through an internal quest for consistency but, rather, through external attempts at persuasion. Much of this work springs from the Yale communication and attitude change programme. It was developed, as Billig (1987, 1996) notes, out of the US military's perceived need for propaganda in World War II. Specifically, the US government approached Hovland to identify how to create effective propaganda for convincing US service personnel that the war with Japan may last longer than envisaged (subsequently this proved not to be the case).

Hovland, Janis and Kelley's (1953) research programme (which started in the 1940s, giving rise to a large number of publications in the 1950s) identified a number of factors that were thought to be consequential for persuasion – some of these concerned the source of the message (expertise, credibility, likeability), some the message itself (numbers of arguments, strength of arguments, inclusion of counter-arguments) and others the audience (is the audience initially pro or anti the message to be communicated, how many years of schooling have they had?) The findings, which emphasise the components of source, message and audience, have sometimes been captured in the phrase 'who says what to whom' – 'who' being the source, 'what' being the message and 'whom' being the audience or other recipients of the persuasive attempt.

Perhaps the most promising component proved to be the message source, but, before considering this, it is worth briefly touching on some key findings regarding the message itself and the audience. Research on the persuasive message has suggested, for example, that more supporting arguments can lead to jurors having an increased certainty of guilt (Calder, Insko & Yandell, 1974). Furthermore, 'strong' arguments (which marshal substantial evidence or are perceived as logically coherent) are (not entirely surprisingly) deemed more effective than arguments judged to be 'weak' (Axsom, Yates & Chaiken, 1987), though as O'Keefe and Jackson (1995) note, researchers not only have differing explanations for this phenomenon but also have yet to agree upon a credible and convincing means of measuring 'argument quality'. Regarding the audience, McGuire (1968) argued that increased self-esteem and intelligence was associated with increased comprehension, but decreased yielding – that is, confident and intelligent audiences might better understand the message, but they may be more resistant to persuasion.

One particularly important piece of research arising from Yale's work was Hovland and Weiss' (1951) investigation of the importance of 'source credibility'. They sought to understand the effect of high- versus low-credibility sources of a communication. Participants received an essay and were informed that it was written by a specific source – these sources were varied between participants to include highly valued, credible sources and low-value, less credible sources. One group of participants received an essay arguing about the practicality of building an atomic-powered submarine and were informed that it had been written by the esteemed US physicist Richard Oppenheimer, while another group received the same essay, but were told that it came from a much less credible source for the US participants at that time – the Russian newspaper *Pravda*. As Billig (1987, 1996) notes, Hovland and Weiss summed the results from high-credibility sources and did the same for low-credibility sources. Hovland and Weiss found that highly credible sources were more persuasive (by measuring subjects' reported attitudinal positions), on average, than those with low credibility.

This finding became axiomatic for subsequent research and, indeed, interventions regarding persuasion – sources had to be credible to be persuasive. It is worth noting, however – as Billig (1987, 1996) points out – this summary of Hovland and Weiss does gloss over important variations within the results. Thus, they found that, when audiences were exposed to a message about the future of the cinema, the low-credibility source had more persuasive effect than the high-credibility source. Billig, notes that, while it would have been interesting to explore this inconsistent and intriguingly counter-intuitive finding, Hovland and Weiss (like most social psychologists faced with inconsistent results) largely brushed it under the carpet and concentrated on aggregate results.

A range of subsequent research developed Yale's interest in source, message and audience as components in effective persuasion. With regard to the source of a persuasive message, Maddux and Rogers (1980), for example, suggested that, for a source to be persuasive, it was not just expertise that was important but also *relevant* expertise for the specific message. For Maddux and Rogers, presenting someone as an expert in sleep made their message about how much sleep we need each night much more persuasive than if they were described as an (equally acclaimed) expert in another area. Chaiken (1979) found that undergraduate students deemed more attractive were more persuasive – both in questionnaire measures on attitudes and in getting fellow students to sign a petition – although attractiveness here was possibly confounded with other factors as the more attractive student communicators were also found to have higher grade point averages, more positive self-concepts and better communication skills than less attractive ones. Brock (1965) suggested that similarity to the audience could lead to more effective persuasion. In this case, strangers who presented themselves as similar 'in their levels of consumption of paint' to customers in a store were better able to influence their purchasing decisions than those who said they consumed different quantities.

Eagly, Chaiken and Wood (1981) drew on ideas in attribution theory to develop an important cognitive account of calculations regarding source credibility. For them, what is crucial is the attribution that audiences make regarding the message. Audiences ask of any persuasive message, 'Can it be attributed to the situation?' (that is, is it merely what the audience wants to hear), 'Can it be attributed to source bias?' (that is, is it a reflection of the sources' own knowledge or vested interests) and 'Is it due to the entity?' (that is, is it an accurate reflection of how things are).

As Fiske and Taylor (1991) suggest, the attributional analysis of source characteristics can be illustrated by considering a pro-environmental message. Imagine, for example, you were to hear a pro-environmental message reporting evidence of the damage done by burning fossil fuels and the need to switch to sustainable sources of energy. If this message was delivered by the president of Greenpeace, speaking to members of Greenpeace, you might readily attribute the message to the speaker's own 'biases' (their knowledge and vested interests) or to the situation (the attempts of the speaker to please the audience). In this situation (leaving to one side any stance you may have regarding the issues yourself), the message may be less persuasive than it could have been. If, by contrast, the message was from the president of an oil company, speaking to the shareholders of that company, then it is less easy to dismiss the 'anti-fossil fuel' message as being due to either source bias or situational factors. Instead, in this situation, we might sit up and take notice and make an entity attribution – that is, we may consider that, perhaps, it is the way that the world is that has resulted in the message content, rather than distortions arising from speaker or circumstance.

Dual process models of persuasion

Some of the work arising from Hovland et al. (1953) and outlined above can give the sense of being a list of ingredients – any of which might add to persuasive effectiveness. It is perhaps not surprising that Hovland et al. (1953) developed their work in this way as, during the Second World War (when much of their research was conducted), the government wanted usable findings of this nature – they wanted a list of what makes for effective propaganda.

During the 1980s, an approach to persuasion was developed that attempted to systematise these findings to some extent, addressing the issue of when, for example, an audience might be particularly concerned with the source of the message (who is saying it) and when they may be more concerned with the message content (what is said). Dual processing models were developed describing a parallel process wherein audiences for a given message might process it in such a way that they are particularly attentive to the source of the message, or to the message itself. The crucial determinant that came into focus was the audience's (pre-message) level of engagement with the message topic.

The **dual processing models** suggested that if the message topic is important or relevant to us, then we are motivated to hold the 'correct' attitude and, thus, more likely to think about the message. If the arguments in the message give rise to more pro-persuasion message thoughts when

Dual processing models Models that describe two different processes for responding to a persuasive attempt, one of which (such as the central or systematic route) typically entails greater involvement with the message itself and the other (such as the peripheral or heuristic route) more attention to the source.

we engage with them, then we will be persuaded. Thus, if I am keen to buy a mobile phone and laptop package, then I might pay particular attention to an advertisement about the advantages of a particular product and, depending in part on the quality of the arguments presented, my thinking about this message afterwards may persuade me to purchase that package. If, by contrast, the topic is not important or relevant to us, it is the quality of the source (rather than the message) that is crucial in determining whether we are persuaded or not. I might, therefore, have a more favourable attitude towards a product that is unimportant to me and I do not feel motivated to think about merely because it was endorsed by a famous footballer, rock star or psychologist.

Petty et al.'s (1981) elaboration likelihood model (and others, such as Chaiken's, 1980, heuristic systematic model) depicts precisely this sort of dual processing (see Figure 6.4). For Petty et al. (1981), the variables of message, source and audience formed part of a dual process model – audiences might process a communication using the central route (paying attention to the message content, such as how convincing the arguments are) or they might process rather less carefully using the peripheral route (where surface-level features, such as the perceived source characteristics, become the important determiner of persuasion).

For Petty et al., the crucial determinant is audience involvement in the message topic – where audiences are involved and the message is highly personally relevant to them, then they will be persuaded on the basis of the quality of what is said, but where they are not involved and the topic is not personally relevant to them, then they will merely attend to features of the source, such as whether or not the source is intrinsically expert (or, in other research, credible, trustworthy, likeable or attractive).

Petty et al.'s research involved college students being presented with arguments concerning a major new exam for college students. They were told either that they themselves would have to sit the exam (of high personal relevance) or it would only come into effect in ten years' time (of low personal relevance). The quality of the message arguments was either high (logically coherent, drawing on relevant evidence to support them) or low (unsupported by evidence) and the message was attributed to a source that was either highly expert (the prestigious Carnegie Commission on Education) or low in expertise (schoolchildren).

Petty et al.'s research found that, when students were told that they would have to sit the exam themselves (of high personal relevance), the source's expertise did not have any significant impact on the extent of their attitude change, but the quality of the message condition did – with greater attitude change occurring when the message quality was high. Where students were told that the exam would be introduced in ten years' time (of low personal

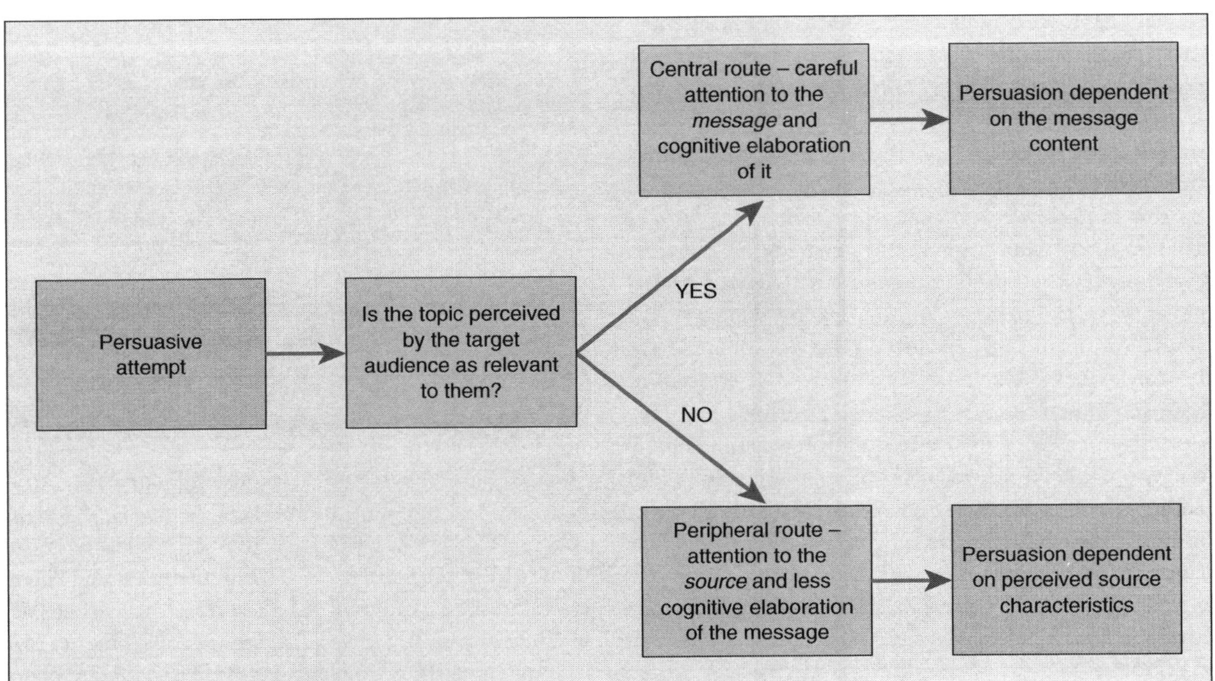

Figure 6.4 Petty, Cacioppo and Goldman's (1981) elaboration likelihood model of persuasion

relevance), it was the source's expertise that appeared to become the important determinant of the extent of the attitude change, not the message quality.

Petty et al.'s research does suggest that, when the persuasive message is highly relevant, the message becomes relatively more important than the source, whereas in cases of low personal relevance, the reverse is true. It is possible to question, however, whether we are really so motivated to find the truth when things are highly relevant for us. Indeed, it may be that when things are particularly important or relevant for us, we have strong vested interests in a particular position and it is this which brings about a **cognitive response**. If your university proposed to close the library and, instead, share a library facility with another institution many miles away or double all of its fees or convert all student accommodation to a conference-only facility, you might be motivated to find out the truth about whether the change is an improvement or not, but you might also be inclined to forcefully oppose these proposals. Eagly and Chaiken (1993) and Jain and Maheswaran (2000) develop this line of criticism, suggesting that, in some cases, we may be motivated to hold or arrive at certain conclusions rather than objectively evaluate the information we are exposed to. Far from adopting a detached, rational processing of the evidence, we might be more inclined to justify our stance and argue against alternative positions where issues really do matter to us.

A further issue, detailed in Dickerson (1997a), is that, in this and most research into persuasion, the characteristics of the source of the message are unproblematically assigned by the experimenter – the participants are simply told that 'the essay comes from Oppenheimer', '*Pravda*', 'an expert on sleep', 'the Carnegie Commission' or 'schoolchildren'. In real-life persuasive communications, who the source or sources for a message are can be *part of the rhetorical work that is being orientated to.* That is, those who might try to persuade us will often cite others, either quoting their talk or referring to their general endorsement of the persuasive message. Two implications spring from this. First, the depiction of how persuasive talk (with its complex use of sources) happens in real life is not accurately portrayed in many experiments. Second, source characteristics can be reconceptualised not as unproblematic givens that an audience will instantly recognise, but actively orientated to and constructed in the talk and argument of those who seek to persuade us.

Cognitive response In the context of this literature, the amount of cognitive involvement with the message content in a persuasive attempt.

Critical recap

Attitude change and persuasion

1 Some of the initial research on persuasion seemed orientated to governmental concerns with usability.

2 Dual process models of persuasion attempted to outline when either the source, or the message, might be of more concern to audiences.

3 Research on persuasion has relied on unproblematic conceptions of the independent variables. Thus, source and message characteristics have been emphasised in the work of Hovland et al. (1953) and integrated into Petty et al.'s (1981) work. By investigating real-world persuasive attempts, however, it is possible to see that some features, such as source characteristics, are constructed in the talk. That is, rather than being static, unproblematic givens – as they are in social psychological experiments – in 'real-world' persuasion attempts, these source features become *part of what is constructed and argued about.* In other words, the separation between source and message that has been so important in traditional social psychology may prevent us from understanding how it is often within the messages themselves that source characteristics are constructed and disputed.

Reflective questions

1 *Can you think of a time when someone attempted to persuade you regarding an issue that you felt was important? Do you think that you paid particular attention to either the source or the message? Were you open to persuasion?*

2 *Watch or listen to politicians talking (for example, on a news programme) – what means of persuasion do they seem to employ?*

6.7 Rhetorical, discursive and conversation analytic approaches to 'persuasive talk'

Much of the research considered above is concerned with persuasion in terms of the measurable effects of certain classes of variables. With this literature, there is more than a little sense of the government-sponsored interest in attitudes and persuasion touched on earlier (see Box 6.6 above). It is easy to see how a causal model (for example, detailing what causes persuasion to be effective) with context-independent specifications of variables (detailing factors that are not tied to the topic or context of persuasion, such as 'expertise') would be the ideal sort of finding for those eager to have something 'applicable'.

The work considered here, though, is markedly different – it does not seek to measure the effectiveness of persuasive talk or any other form of talk. Neither does it seek to identify context-independent variables that are important in persuasion talk. Instead, it looks at how talk in a range of different contexts may attend to issues concerning its own veracity and how this may be addressed in the *detail* of the talk. Here four different, though overlapping, concerns will be touched on, each concerned with features of the detail of talk that attend to issues such as the warranting of that talk – that is, what is done in talk that makes the claims made appear true and/or the position adopted in the talk appear justified.

Extract 6.4

I had ear plugs in my ears
'cz I couldn't stand all the noise
I had (.) dark glasses on
>because I didn't want
to see anybody<
an' I was standing right there
on the platform (0.7) waiting
for this damned train to come (.)
all of a sudden
(2.3)
I (.) began to feel as total
Totally (.) absolutely (.)
Insubstantial that is
I had no bodily feeling whatsoever

Source: Wooffitt (1992, pp. 117, 118)

Constructing talk as reflecting 'out there' reality

One particularly important contribution that conversation analytic, discursive and rhetorical approaches have made to the study of persuasion is detailing how positions that are advocated are constructed as real or true – what Potter (1996) refers to as the 'out-there-ness' of accounts. Some conversation analytic work has been particularly informative in outlining some of the features of accounts that orientate to issues of warranting or the apparent truthfulness of what is said. Some compelling examples of this come from the work of Wooffitt (1992, 2007), who found that people telling of psychic experiences (where issues of the truth and accuracy of the claims made may be especially relevant) use certain routine formats that warrant their talk. One such format is to talk about the routine, mundane context *before* the unusual or paranormal experience occurred. An example of this is given in Extract 6.4.

As Wooffitt notes, in Extract 6.4, the speaker begins the account of a 'paranormal' experience by describing what has happened immediately prior to it. Importantly, in these accounts of what was happening, they do not report looking for or expecting any paranormal activity – thus, the speaker above reports wearing earplugs and dark glasses and waiting for a train, not, 'I was just reading a book about out-of-body experiences and was trying to think what it would feel like, when, all of a sudden ...'. Similarly, the paranormal experience is not given in a stripped-down way, the mundane context is not removed – the speaker here does not begin with, 'I had no bodily feeling whatsoever'.

The format that is used in Extract 6.4 is to construct the 'paranormal' experience as bursting unexpectedly into a largely mundane context. One way in which this serves to warrant the account is that it positions the occurrences as *in the world* rather than in the mind of the individual – they are encounters constructed as coming to the individual rather than being a consequence of the individual's own motivations, preoccupations or world-view. This device, which Wooffitt (1992) refers to as 'I was just doing X when Y', is particularly effective as a means of placing the occurrence in an **'out there' reality** rather than as something looked for or brought about by the speaker (see Box 6.7).

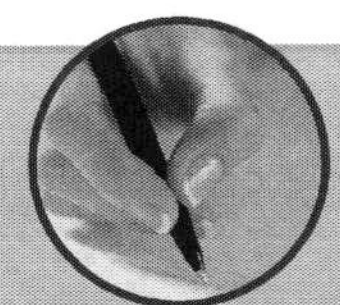

Box 6.7 TRY IT OUT
Constructing talk as reflecting 'out there' reality

Can you think of a situation where you told of something unlikely that occurred? Are there features of the way in which you told your story that relate to the 'I was just doing X when Y' format referred to above? How about when you have heard friends or relatives report incredible occurrences – are these structured using this (or other formats) that make them seem more 'out there' phenomena rather than being brought about by the speaker?

'Out there' reality Within the current context, this refers to the ways in which speakers may try to construct their talk or stance as a reflection of the 'real world' rather than a subjective or partisan stance for which equally credible alternatives exist.

Constructing talk as being against or beyond the speaker's own interests

A feature of talk that is offered in contexts where the **speaker's own interests** or stake are considered to be important is the way in which it attracts the charge that the speaker 'would say that wouldn't he or she?' (Edwards & Potter, 1992). Sometimes – as in the case of news interviewers – the speaker may be concerned with achieving neutrality. Clayman (1992) noted that news interviewers need to robustly challenge the positions taken by politicians (and others) while always appearing to both interviewees and audience to be impartial or neutral. The fact that interviewers can do this and are only exceptionally held to account for a position taken in an interview rests, in part, on the ways in which they cite others' talk to produce challenges to the claims that their interviewees make – the interviewer becomes the mere animator of ideas expressed by others.

Dickerson (1997a) drew on these ideas when considering the ways in which politicians may orientate to the potential charge that they are merely expressing their own vested interests when they cited others as supporting the ideas, claims and positions that they are putting forward. By doing this, speakers can claim the endorsements of experts, even when their own perceived expertise might be in doubt. Furthermore, they can deal directly with the accusation of vested interests by citing the endorsement of people we might presume to be opposed to them. This can be seen in Extract 6.5.

Extract 6.5

(*Note:* The following extract is taken from the second presidential debate of 15 October 1992. Bill Clinton's response is to a question put by a member of the studio audience. Line numbers from the original)

BC (0.5) I ask (.) everybody to look at my
(.) economic ideas nine Nobel prize winners and over
five hundred economists and hundreds of business
people >including a lot of Republicans said< this is
the way you've got to go

Source: Dickerson (1997a, p. 41)

Bill Clinton constructs those who endorse the economic plans he is advocating in terms of their expertise (Nobel Prize winners, economists, business people) and with reference to consensus ('nine', 'five hundred', 'hundreds'). In addition to this, Clinton, then a Democratic governor, specifically constructs 'a lot of Republicans' as supporting him. From one perspective, if they really *are* supporting him, they might not be Republicans (or, perhaps, no longer Republicans, having been Republicans in the past), but, for Clinton to construct endorsers of his claims as being from the opposing party, directly addresses the issue of vested interest. If Clinton had argued that numerous *Democrats* supported him, the audience could readily dismiss his claims and the Democrats' endorsement as merely reflecting their own vested interests, but, when *Republicans* are cited, this is less readily done.

This idea of the source being constructed as a rhetorical resource is evidenced in Extract 6.6. Here, a former Conservative minister (Michael Heseltine) is attempting to quote another source (Dick Marsh) as supporting the ideas that he is putting forward. While he is attempting to do this, a member of Parliament from another political party (Tony Benn, then a Labour member of Parliament) challenges how the cited source (Dick Marsh) is constructed. A snippet of this interaction is given in Extract 6.6.

The debate between Michael Heseltine and Tony Benn illustrates that seemingly unproblematic source characteristics can, instead, be understood as to-be-constructed-resources. That is, the identity of a cited source is something that can be – and is – attended to in persuasive talk. Dick Marsh *was* a member of the Labour government who then became a Conservative peer. For Heseltine (a Conservative minister), it is more rhetorically effective to construct Dick Marsh in terms of a Labour identity as then Dick Marsh's criticisms of Labour policy and support for the Conservative's position are less easily dismissed as merely reflecting his own party political interests. For Tony Benn (a Labour MP), by contrast, emphasising Dick Marsh's *current* affiliation as a Conservative peer undermines Heseltine's case by hinting at a vested interest behind Marsh's cited criticisms of the former Labour government.

In this way, both Heseltine and Benn are orientating to the idea that people speaking *against* their vested interests are more believed than those speaking *for* their vested interests. The resource that they are using to do so, however, is their differing construction of a specific individual source – the source is being discursively constructed to do the job of producing counter-interest endorsement (by Heseltine) or undermining such claims by constructing them as

Speaker's own interests In the current context, this refers to the ways in which speakers construct the interests of themselves and others (particularly those they find themselves arguing with). Speakers may position their own talk as unconnected to or even running counter to their own vested interests, while constructing the talk of their argumentative opponents as simply a reflection of their opponents' own self-interest.

Extract 6.6

(*Note:* The following extract is taken from *Question Time* (a discussion programme in which members of the audience put questions to a panel largely comprised of politicians representing mainstream party political perspectives in the UK) broadcast in October 1992 after news of the UK government's controversial pit closure programme was released. This was a particularly interesting time in UK politics as it was then that a crucial switch in the popularity of Labour and Conservatives was noted in opinion polls, with Labour becoming more popular than the Conservatives. Line numbers taken from original.)

Key to speakers

PS = Peter Sissons (Chair)

TB = Tony Benn (Labour politician)

MH = Michael Heseltine (Conservative Cabinet Minister)

SA = Studio audience.

MH	>may I just
	quote him?< and it is Hansard the twentieth of October
	nineteen ninety two the speaker Dick Marsh in the
	House of Lords
TB	a Tory (1.0) he's a Tory
SA	(laughter approximately 1.5 seconds)
MH	[Dick Marsh
PS	[>you served in a Cabinet with him?<
MH	Dick Marsh (.) Dick Marsh
	[was the Labour Minister when this
TB	[a Tory
SA	(laughter throughout the following exchange)
MH	[apparent triumph of the Labour Party=
TB	[he's a Tory
TB	=he's a Tory
MH	apparent triumph=
TB	=he's a Tory
MH	apparent triumph=
TB	=he's a Tory
PS	wham wh why did why did you why
	did you [se
TB	[well I
	want everyone to know they might not know that he's a
	Tory (0.5) go on

Source: Dickerson (1997a, p. 45)

reflecting the sources' own party political interests (by Benn).

In real-world contexts, then, source characteristics, rather than being simple, factual features of the world to be straightforwardly noted, are rhetorically charged – who they are constructed as being is a crucial part of making an argument for or against a persuasive message. Investigating real-world data suggests that source characteristics are open to different constructions and the construction of a source that a speaker produces can be used as a rhetorical device to do particular work (such as warrant or undermine a claim being made). In this way, rather than a source being something that is separable from what is said (the message), it is constructed in and through what is said. Being able to cite and construct sources who support a speaker's position is one important means by which the speaker can usefully attend to challenges that the speaker's talk merely reflects their own vested interest.

Invoking commonplaces, rhetorically self-sufficient arguments and categories in talk

A third collection of research, while not exactly a coherent strand, can be assembled under the loose heading of **invoking commonplaces, rhetorically self-sufficient arguments and categories in talk**. What is at work here is the way in which the talk can imply and build on common understandings about the way the world is.

Billig (1991) draws on Aristotle and other ancient Greek masters of rhetoric in sketching out the importance of 'commonplaces'. These, often moral, maxims reflect and rely on certain commonly shared values (among the community in which the argument is being made). In the context of courtroom rhetoric, for example, ancient Greek authors suggested that the defence appeal to the commonplace of mercy, the prosecutor to the commonplace of justice. Using commonplaces involves mobilising a shared position or stance ('Everyone must be treated fairly'), such that the audience come to think of the specific case being argued about *in terms of the commonplace appealed to*. The relevance of this work reaches far outside of the courtrooms of ancient Greece – modern-day political debate, for example, is replete with appeals to commonplaces: 'We can't carry on living beyond our means', 'We can't stand by and watch as atrocities happen', 'We have to look after the most vulnerable'.

Invoking commonplaces, rhetorically self-sufficient arguments and categories in talk This refers to some of the different ways that talk may draw credibility or warrant itself through an appeal to common understandings about the way the world is.

In a similar vein, Wetherell and Potter (1992) note some of the ways in which clinching, or rhetorically self-sufficient arguments (such as 'Everyone should be treated equally', 'Injustices should be righted', 'You can't turn back the clock', 'You have to be practical') were used as Pakeha (white majority) New Zealanders sought to warrant or justify their position in talking about racial inequalities in New Zealand. What is particularly noteworthy – and the reason commonplaces and rhetorically self-sufficient arguments are so often invoked – is that they can be used to support directly contradictory positions. As Billig (1991) notes, justice and mercy are both commonplaces, yet may suggest completely different positions are adopted on a given issue. Likewise, 'Injustices have to be righted' and 'You can't turn back the clock' could warrant diametrically opposed stances towards dealing with injustices of the past. This breadth of contradictory commonplaces and rhetorically self-sufficient arguments means that, whatever position is being argued, it is likely that there is some 'common ground' that can be appealed to.

Summers (2007) investigated the way in which rhetorically self-sufficient arguments concerning 'equality', 'human rights', 'democracy', 'the interests of the majority' and 'the interests of children' were invoked in arguments in Western Australia concerning legislation regarding lesbian and gay rights. One particularly interesting aspect of Summers' research is the way in which *the same arguments* (for example, concerning the rights of children) were appealed to in support of contradictory positions.

Extracts 6.7 and 6.8 both involve an appeal to the rights and interests of children. In Extract 6.7, the appeal is used to argue *against* any attempt to increase adoption rights for lesbian and gay citizens, whereas in Extract 6.8, the appeal is used to argue *for* an increase in their adoption rights. Extracts 6.7 and 6.8, then suggest that not only are their different commonplaces or rhetorically sufficient arguments to support contradictory positions but also these very arguments themselves may be sufficiently ambiguous that *a single one* may be invoked to support contradictory positions.

Fogarty and Augoustinos (2008) found a similar attention to 'children's interests' in arguments recorded during the public hearings of the Australian Public Inquiry into Child Custody. They further note that categories themselves (such as 'parent', 'mother', 'father') can be invoked to do rhetorical work. Thus, rather than merely being 'neutral' descriptions, the categories are mobilised and elaborated in the work of making an argument. This issue of categories being mobilised to warrant or corroborate a case being made was illustrated in Chapter 2 – and repeated here in Extract 6.9 – from Stokoe and Edwards (2009).

The issue of interest here is that the suspect, accused of headbutting another person, invokes a category – 'an old bloke' – in the act of his denial. Here, then, two competing versions of events are at work – that of the police officer – 'You've head butted 'im' (line 13) – and the suspect's denial – '[No::: no I ain't at a:ll' (line 15). The category 'old bloke', far from being a neutral description of the alleged victim, is, instead, rhetorically constructed, such that it problematises the police officer's version of events and substantiates the suspect's denial.

What is particularly intriguing here is the ways in which the mere invocation of the category can be seen to do important work. This shares something of the idea of common ground that was considered above – there is some reliance on, and implication of, the unlikelihood of this suspect performing that act on someone characterised in terms of that category. Seen in this way, what could

Extract 6.7

(*Note*: John Day (Liberal member for Darling Range), 6 December 2001. Line numbers from the original)

The demands of adults who argue that
they have a right to adopt children regardless of their situation should not be
paramount. We will lose sight of our responsibilities as a Parliament and as a
community if we put the rights of adults before the rights of children in this
respect

Source: Summers (2007, p. 848)

Extract 6.8

(*Note*: Inane Guise (Labour member for Wanneroo), 5 December 2001. Line numbers from the original)

The adoption of
children should be based on the best interests of children, not on the sexual
orientation of the adopting parents.

Source: Summers (2007, p. 850)

Extract 6.9

(*Note*: This is from a recording of a police officer's (P) interview with a suspect (S). Line numbers are from the original)

P You've head butted 'im. You've lunged forward an'
[head butted 'im.
S [No::: no I ain't at a:ll.
(0.3)
S Unless y'cn ge' any proof then:
(1.5)
S → I'v- (.) headbutted 'im ↑wha' ↑w'd ↑I ↑wanna ↑head butt
→ an old bloke fo:r.

Source: Stokoe and Edwards (2009, p. 106)

so easily be dismissed as 'mere categories' can themselves be crucial rhetorical resources – perhaps being all the more rhetorically powerful *because* they can operate in an implicative, relatively unspecified manner.

The discursive, rhetorical and conversation analytic approaches sketched here have moved some way from the government-sponsored agenda that drove much of early attitude and persuasion research. With the work considered here, there is attention to data found in real-world (not created by the researcher) contexts rather than that which is experimentally generated or produced at the prompting of questionnaires – or researcher-initiated interviews. In leaving the laboratory, such research has also left the idea of operationalising relatively abstract, context-free variables (such as speaker 'expertise' and 'topic relevance' for the audience). Rather than looking for the operation of abstracted variables – and seeing details as mere flotsam to be cast aside – the approaches considered here pay careful attention to the details of talk that is designed to warrant or corroborate claims made or positions adopted and to the context of that talk. Such an approach does not produce a causal model of what leads or does not lead to persuasion, but it does – at its best – endeavour to describe what is going on in actual, real-world instances of 'persuasive talk' and the intricacies and subtleties that such talk entails.

Critical recap

Rhetorical, discursive and conversation analytic approaches to 'persuasive talk'

1 Those working within an experimental tradition may have problems with discursive and rhetorical approaches. They could be seen as not addressing the very questions that the field hopes to address, such as the ways in which we might better predict human behaviour or how we might better influence or persuade people. From this perspective, discursive and rhetorical psychology may be thought of as having a somewhat deconstructionist agenda, providing criticism but not a better method to address the questions that are important, for the traditional concerns of social psychology.

2 Discursive and rhetorical psychologists would acknowledge that there is a different agenda and discursive approaches do not provide answers about predicting future behaviour or generic factors to ensure effective persuasion. The approach they offer, however, opens alternative questions about how attitudes are actually used and how persuasion is really done – questions that, far from being trivial, reflect a concern with the reality of attitudes and persuasion in everyday life.

Reflective questions

1 *Try finding examples of people talking about unusual experiences – for example, alien encounters or paranormal experiences on YouTube. Do they use some of the devices touched on here? Do these (potentially) lend their accounts more credibility?*

2 *Look at a newspaper and see if you can identify commonplaces in a couple of articles that seem to advocate a particular opinion or stance on an issue.*

Summary

- This chapter first outlined some different ways of thinking about attitudes. The idea of attitudes as measurable, quantifiable, individual stances towards an attitude target was contrasted with rhetorical and discursive approaches (Billig, 1987; Edwards and Potter, 1992). It was noted that rhetorical and discursive approaches criticised the individualistic and cognitive focus of traditional attitude research, suggesting instead a sensitivity to argumentative context and attention to what attitudes do in interaction.
- The chapter then considered different positions regarding how many components comprised attitudes and how attitudes (and attitude-related behaviour) might best be measured. Here, consideration was given to both attitude scales and implicit tests of attitudes. Ideas about the process of measurement shaping the form in which attitudes were found were also touched on.

- The issue of the extent to which attitudes relate to behaviour was addressed, starting with Wicker's (1969) review casting doubt on the utility of the attitude concept. Two prominent responses to this challenge were provided in Fishbein and Ajzen's (1975) theory of reasoned action and Ajzen's (1985) theory of planned behaviour – both of which addressed the issue of attitude specificity (specific attitudes predict those specific behaviours) and introduced additional variables to better understand how and when attitudes may predict behaviour.
- Critical perspectives on attitudes were considered that highlighted social and action-orientated understandings of attitudes. Here, an example of social representations research was touched on in illustrating something of the way that attitudes can be conceived of as social rather than simply individual positions or representations. Discursive work was drawn on to illustrate some of the ways in which attitudes and the articulation of evaluation (or 'attitude') can be understood as accomplishing action in interaction.
- The chapter then moved from attitudes to attitude change and persuasion, first addressing some of the literature concerned with consistency. This included Heider's (1958) balance theory, which suggested we are motivated to ensure that we agree with those we like and disagree with those we dislike (and will change our attitudes to achieve this balance where necessary). Also, Festinger's (1958) cognitive dissonance theory, which suggested that we may sometimes change our attitudes where we have experienced it as being inconsistent with our behaviour, was touched on.
- Work on the ingredients of persuasion by Hovland et al. (1953) was outlined as was Petty, et al.'s (1981) elaboration likelihood model of persuasion, which attempted to describe under what circumstances an audience would pay particular attention to either the source of a message or the message itself.
- Finally, rhetorical, discursive and conversation analytic research, which raises problems for traditional approaches to attitude change and persuasion, was addressed. This included Wooffitt's (1992) work on formats used by speakers to position their talk as reflecting true 'out-there' experiences. Attention was also given to the ways in which sources can be constructed and commonplaces and categories invoked in a manner that attends to rhetorical issues (such as warranting the speaker's talk).

Review questions

1 *What are the problems with explicit scales that try to measure attitudes?*

2 *What issues are raised by implicit measurement of attitudes?*

3 *Should attitudes be understood as individual cognitive evaluations or as wider social phenomena?*

4 *What does it mean to say that attitudes are action-orientated or that they do things in interaction? How can a preference for consistency lead to attitude change?*

5 *What did Hovland et al. (1953) identify as the key variables in determining the effectiveness of persuasion?*

6 *According to the elaboration likelihood model, what factors will make a persuasive attempt successful?*

7 *What does it mean to say that source characteristics are constructed in the persuasive talk itself? What consequences might this have for thinking about persuasion?*

8 *What is meant by invoking commonplaces and how can this be relevant for thinking about persuasion?*

Recommended reading

Ajzen, I. (1991). The theory of planned behaviour. *Organisational Behaviour and Human Decision Processes, 50*, 179–211. A seminal publication that outlines Ajzen's theory of planned behaviour.

Augoustinos, M., LeCouteur, A., & Soyland, J. (2002). Self-sufficient arguments in political rhetoric: Constructing reconciliation and apologising to the stolen generations. *Discourse and Society, 13*, 105–142. An excellent demonstration of a critical discourse approach to the analysis of a political speech. Attends to the issue of collectively shared linguistic resources and how these are mobilised in a way that has a power relation consequentiality by, for example, largely justifying the status quo.

Augoustinos, M., Walker, I., & Donaghue, N. (2006). *Social cognition: An integrated introduction*. London: Sage. Clearly outlines and very usefully integrates experimental, social representational and discursive approaches to attitudes. Makes important links to group processes.

Billig, M. (1987). *Arguing and thinking*. Cambridge: Cambridge University Press. A hugely important book that, along with Potter and Wetherell (1987), helped to introduce a discursive, and here specifically, rhetorical perspective to thinking about social psychological topics and literature. See also revised edition (1996).

Billig, M. (1991). *Ideology and opinions: Studies in rhetorical psychology*. London: Sage. An excellent overview of a series of studies that makes the case for a rhetorical approach to attitudes and opinions and for a social psychology that embraces ideology and argument as key concerns.

Dickerson, P. (1997a). 'It's not just me who's saying this . . .': The deployment of cited others in televised political discourse. *British Journal of Social Psychology, 36*, 33–48.

Eliot, M. A., Armitage C. J., & Baughan C. J. (2007). Using the theory of planned behaviour or predict observed driving behavior. *British Journal of Social Psychology, 46*, 69–90.

Fishbein, M., & Ajzen, I. (1975). *Belief, attitude, intention, and behavior: An introduction to theory and research*. Reading, MA: Addison-Wesley. A landmark publication outlining the theory of reasoned action.

Fiske, S. T., & Taylor, S. E. (1991). *Social cognition*. (2nd ed.). New York: McGraw-Hill. Provides a clearly conceptualised overview of the social cognition accounts of attitudes, attitude change and persuasion.

Hepburn, A. (2003). *An introduction to critical social psychology*. London: Sage. Provides a clear and carefully argued outline of a range of critical theoretical positions. With regards to the current chapter, illustrates the ways in which discursive research into 'attitudes' about gender can be linked to feminist ideas.

Mohiyeddini, C., Pauli, R., & Bauer, S. (2009). The role of emotion in bridging the intention–behaviour gap: The case of sports participation. *Psychology of Sport and Exercise, 10*, 226–234. A well-argued paper making the case for emotion variables being incorporated into the theory of planned behaviour model.

Petty, R. E., Cacioppo, J. T., & Goldman, R. (1981). Personal involvement as a determinant of argument-based persuasion. *Journal of Personality and Social Psychology, 41*, 847–55. An important paper providing an empirical demonstration of the elaboration likelihood model of persuasion.

Potter, J. (1996). *Representing reality: Discourse, rhetoric and social construction*. London: Sage. An excellent overview of the contribution of discursive psychology to understanding how reality is constructed, with a particular emphasis on how constructions are designed to orientate to their own apparent truthfulness.

Potter, J. (1998). Discursive social psychology: From attitudes to evaluations. *European Review of Social Psychology, 9*, 233–266. A clear and thoughtful outline of the ways in which discursive social psychology reconceptualises 'attitudes' and how they might be researched.

Potter, J., & Wetherell, M. (1987). *Discourse and social psychology: Beyond attitudes and behaviour*. London: Sage. A landmark book that, more than any other publication, presented and developed discursive ideas as an approach to social psychology.

Weatherall, A., & Walton, M. (1999). The metaphorical construction of sexual experience in a speech community of New Zealand university students. *British Journal of Social Psychology, 38*, 479–498. Illustrates some of the interest that some researchers within the discursive psychology paradigm have in the specific words that are used when people construct their opinions.

Wiggins, S., & Potter, J. (2003). Attitudes and evaluative practices: Category vs. item and subjective vs. objective constructions in everyday food assessments. *British Journal of Social Psychology, 42*, 513–531. An excellent empirical demonstration of the action orientation of everyday assessments. Includes some useful critiques of traditional approaches to conceptualising and measuring attitudes.

Useful weblinks

The websites given below provide a great resource for publications and other downloadable resources relating to the work of specific academics.

http://people.umass.edu/aizen/publications.html Icek Ajzen's theory of planned behaviour publications and related resources.

www.lboro.ac.uk/departments/ss/depstaff/staff/potter.html Jonathan Potter's discursive social psychology publications and related resources.

www.psy.ohio-state.edu/petty Richard Petty's publications regarding persuasion experiments.

http://psy-publications.group.shef.ac.uk/staff/paschal-sheeran.html An overview of Paschal Sheeran's publications addressing behaviour change and other attitude-related issues.

http://psych.nmsu.edu/faculty/trafimow/pubs.html#articles A list of publications by David Trafimow.

www.radpsynet.org/docs/index.html Some useful links to radical psychology people and publication excerpts.

www.lboro.ac.uk/departments/ss/depstaff/staff/publications/wilkinson.htm Sue Wilkinson's social constructionist and feminist publications.

The following websites can be examined in terms of the rhetorical work being done:

Sylvia Browne – UFO experience

www.youtube.com/watch?v=xL9eVL-gynU&feature=related
www.youtube.com/watch?v=b1V9ewLNY50&NR=1

Texan UFO abductee speaks

www.youtube.com/watch?v=_Fif4fk-_34&feature=related
www.youtube.com/watch?v=lZKn00lBqgY

Interview with an American medium

www.youtube.com/watch?v=ODNWpiETzdI&NR=1&feature=fvwp

Colin Fry – sixth sense

www.youtube.com/watch?v=Y1WNIns16uE&feature=related
www.youtube.com/watch?v=zRFW3yFn0L4&feature=related
www.youtube.com/watch?v=UdlAFVmbwao&feature=related
www.youtube.com/watch?v=BHit4hJRKVA&feature=related

7

Stereotypes and prejudice

Learning outcomes

By the end of this chapter you should have a critical understanding of:

- what stereotypes are
- research findings relating to how stereotype content has changed
- Asch's contribution to how stereotypes are formed
- what the illusory correlation suggests about the formation of stereotypes
- Allport's contribution to ideas about prejudice and categorisation
- Tajfel's development of categorisation
- how schemas have been thought to shape thinking
- Billig's criticism of categorisation-based approaches to understanding prejudice
- Locksley's work questioning the resilience of stereotypes in the face of disconfirming information
- how ideas about schemas and stereotypes have developed
- the contribution of discourse analysis to our thinking about prejudice.

In 2001, the Danish People's Party's Youth Organisation ran a campaign in the form of posters and other printed advertisements that depicted a female Muslim alongside text that attempted to link a tirade of negative assertions to 'multi-ethnic' society in general. The poster read:

> Your Denmark? A multi-ethnic society with: Mass rapes, Crude violence, Insecurity, Suppression of women, Forced marriages.

Source: Polfoto/Press Association Images

Pia Kjaersgaard addressing Denmark's right-wing Danish People's Party, which she leads. How can we understand the prejudice against immigrants and minority ethnic groups that is often associated with such parties?

The poster ends with the question, '*Is this what you want?*' before urging the reader to join the Danish People's Party's Youth Organisation – 'Do something – be a member of The Danish People's Party's Youth Organisation - a Danish future.'

The above example represents prejudice in its most explicit and abhorrent form. An extreme right-wing party producing anti-Islamic and anti-multicultural propaganda. This captures part of what the social psychology of stereotypes and prejudice attempts to explain, raising the issue of how derogatory stereotypes are explicitly used in prejudice and the way in which constructions of denigrated groups are deployed for specific purposes (in this case, to further the cause of the Danish People's Party).

Stereotypes and prejudice can be seen as important in far less explicit instances of racism as well, however. On 16 July 2009, a man was seen attempting to force his way into a house in Cambridge, Massachusetts. A neighbour witnessing this called the police. The police arrived and arrested the man. This event sounds unremarkable, but became hotly debated in the USA after President Barak Obama referred to it as demonstrating 'stupidity' on the part of the police and that the issue of race still haunts the USA.

The man who 'broke in' was a leading African American scholar, Professor Gates, returning to his own home after a trip to China, having misplaced his keys. A white officer arrested him, in his own home, despite evidence that he lived there. How did the break-in come to be interpreted as a crime by neighbours of Professor Gates? Did neighbours simply report what they saw or was their seeing shaped by Professor Gate's colour? Was Professor Gates' ethnicity a factor in him being arrested while in his own home? Was Barak Obama himself being prejudiced in his comments about police stupidity? Was Barak Obama accurate in saying that the issue of race still haunts the USA?

These are just the issues that this chapter seeks to address. Research into stereotypes has questioned what stereotypes people hold, to what extent they are used and how they might shape the ways in which we make sense of other people's behaviour. The idea of rigid stereotypes has been a dominant framework for understanding the social ill of prejudice. This chapter also considers the ways in which this framework has been challenged by work suggesting that stereotypes are less powerful than previously thought, that they are more fragmented and, that to understand prejudice, we are better off looking at how people talk about themselves and others than trying to impute the stereotypical thinking processes involved.

Introduction

The words 'prejudice' and 'stereotypes' are sometimes used synonymously. We might think of the prejudiced person as holding certain negative stereotypes and these being the basis of prejudice. In this chapter, while there is considerable overlap in the use of these terms, there is an important distinction that highlights some of the different research in this area. The term '**stereotype**' is used to refer to the idea of underlying cognitive structures (schemas) that shape our judgements about other people (and, indeed, ourselves) – research that explicitly addresses stereotypes, then has some interest in underlying cognition. 'Prejudice' is used to refer to both judgements made relatively quickly, or in advance of

> **Stereotype** A type of role schema that is relatively rigid. Once a person being perceived has a stereotype applied to them, then, however accurate or inaccurate it may be, our perception is likely to be significantly affected by the content of that stereotype.

comprehensive information about the other, and to talk that can be understood as implying such judgements. In this way, research that addresses prejudice may vary in the extent to which it emphasises underlying mental structures – it may wholeheartedly embrace stereotypes, combine stereotypes with other factors or avoid any reference to underlying cognition at all. The chapter aims to highlight something of these very different approaches to understanding the social judgements that people make about others.

Chapter overview

This chapter first reviews work that has focused on stereotype content – that is, what traits people associate with different groups – in particular ethnic groups. Some of the earliest work on stereotypes examined just this, with the Princeton trilogy of studies mapping changes in ethnic stereotypes across a 34-year period. In the light of this work and subsequent research by some, attention is given to reflecting on not just how stereotypes might have changed but also *why* they might have changed or *what shapes* their change.

The chapter first considers cognitive approaches to understanding the formation of stereotypes, drawing on Asch's work on impression formation and work known as the illusory correlation. Asch (1946) contributed to an understanding of how people forming impressions of others might combine different traits that they perceive the person to have. The illusory correlation emphasises that categories might be 'paired', 'associated' or 'correlated' with certain attributes if they are perceived as sharing certain features – including scarcity, thus minority groups can become paired or correlated with minority behaviour, such as crime.

A crucial aspect to work on prejudice and stereotypes is the contribution of Allport (1950, p. 54) and Tajfel (1969) to thinking about categorisation. Particular attention is given here to the way that Allport and Tajfel both described categorisation as a universal thought process that enables humans to cope with potentially overwhelming stimuli, but gives rise to prejudice. Billig's (1985, 2002) criticism of this approach to categorisation is addressed, particularly with regard to its emphasis on the universality of categorisation and the inevitability of prejudice.

This chapter then examines how stereotypes (and other schema) can be seen as shaping cognitive processing – that is, how they might affect what we notice and remember and how we evaluate social stimuli. This work suggests that stereotypes and other schema might save thinking effort, but, in turn, can be distorting and self-perpetuating (we might not notice or remember contradictory evidence). Attention is given to Billig's (1985, 2002) criticism of the categorisation basis of the schema approach – particularly the ideas that such categorisation actually describes how we think or that this type of thinking could ever save thinking effort.

Locksley, Borgida, Brekke and Hepburn's (1980) and Locksley, Hepburn and Ortiz's (1982) research, which appeared to raise questions about how easily stereotypes might be abandoned, is also reviewed. Criticisms of Locksley's method and the interpretation of her results are covered. In the wake of Locksley, some different ideas about how schemas are used and the importance of subtypes rather than global categories emerged, so these are considered, as well as more radical, discursive criticisms that question the cognitive emphasis of most research into stereotypes and prejudice.

The last key approach to be reviewed develops this alternative to a cognitive perspective on stereotypes and prejudice by examining how prejudice talk is organised. In reviewing discourse analytic perspectives on prejudice, attention is given to early work examining features of talk that appear to minimise for the speaker the accusation that they are being racist or prejudiced, such as Potter and Wetherell's (1987) work on disclaimers, as well as more recent attempts to consider the collaborative aspects of prejudiced talk, such as Condor, Figgou, Abell, Gibson and Stevenson (2006). This work is evaluated in the light of both cognitively based social psychology (that finds it insufficiently cognitive and causal) and conversation analysis (that finds it sometimes lacking a sensitivity to the sequential placement of utterances).

7.1 Stereotype content

Research into stereotypes and prejudice within social psychology encompasses not just different answers to shared questions but also, often, very different questions. The first tranche of research that we will review concerns not how stereotypes work or what they do but, instead, the actual **stereotype content** and especially the extent to which this content changes over time. See also Box 7.1.

The Princeton trilogy

One early approach to examining prejudice was found in a series of three studies known as the 'Princeton trilogy'.

Stereotype content This refers to research that has been concerned with the specific characteristics (intelligent, aggressive, antisocial, gregarious) people attribute to different groups or categories of people. Research within this tradition has paid particular attention to the ways in which the stereotype content associated with certain groups changes over time.

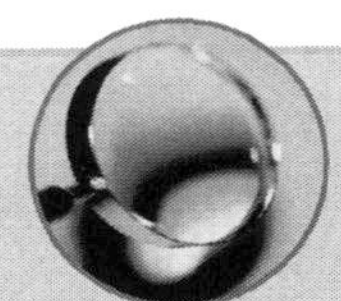

Box 7.1 FOCUS
Key thinker: Walter Lippmann

The concept of *stereotypes* is traditionally attributed to Lippmann's (1922) classic *Public opinion*. Lippmann, so the story goes, introduced the term – previously used to describe a printing process – to depict an important way in which we think about our social worlds that is captured in the phrase 'pictures in our heads'. That is, we have preconceived 'pictures in our heads', fixed like the type used to print books. As Newman (2009) points out, these assumptions are misplaced. He suggests that the word was used in a similar way to how 'cliché' is used today. For example, in 1910, the phrase 'stereotyped businessman' was used. Lippmann's contribution in terms of the development of the word was to broaden its use to include mental representations.

Some of Lippmann's work makes uncomfortable reading. One might expect, as a Jew himself and someone who inspired research among those strongly opposed to prejudice, that he might reflect ethnically tolerant, liberal and inclusive values – instead, as Newman (2009) points out, we find some apparently anti-Semitic material and criticisms of forms of democracy that give too much power to the cognitively limited 'average person'.

Lippmann (1922) provides a somewhat multifaceted take on stereotypes, treating them as organising bodies of information/misinformation (like schemas), considering how emotionally charged they are (like psychodynamic approaches to stereotypes) and, in places, implying a central role in the cultural shaping of stereotypes. To stay with that last point for a moment, in some (though not all) passages Lippmann's (1922, p. 55, cited in Newman, 2009, p. 11) actual treatment of the concept of stereotypes suggests a far less individualistic and cognitive focus than had become dominant in the field: 'In the great blooming buzzing confusion of the outer world we pick out what our culture has already defined for us, and we tend to perceive that which we have picked out in the form stereotyped by our culture.'

With Lippmann, then, while we may be wise to recognise shortcomings in aspects of his social and political outlook, we can still acknowledge his emphasis on mental representations and the ways in which his understanding of stereotypes was unusually broad, encompassing the organisation of cognition, emotion and the influence of society.

The trilogy comprises research by Katz and Braly (1933), Gilbert (1951) and Karlins, Coffman and Walters (1969), each of which attempted to measure the ethnic and national stereotypes of Princeton students.

In the original Katz and Braly (1933) study, students were presented with a list of 84 adjectives (such as intelligent, materialistic, ambitious, superstitious, lazy, happy-go-lucky, musical, mercenary) and asked to select the five that best described ten different ethnic groups (including European Americans, Japanese, Jews and Black Americans). Gilbert (1951) and, subsequently, Karlins et al. (1969) replicated Katz and Braly's (1933) research, thus providing not only a snapshot of national and ethnic stereotypes within each time period, but also the possibility of investigating *changes across those time periods*. The data, then, provides the opportunity to investigate the adjectives attributed to the various ethnic and national groups, the extent to which there was a consensus in attributing certain adjectives and how stereotype content and consensus changed over time. Just take a moment to reflect on how you imagine the descriptive adjectives selected by these Princeton students changed across the three time periods – 1933, 1951 and 1967. How do the results in Table 7.1 relate to that you expected?

One finding is that the participants tended to give more favourable ratings to the category 'European Americans' in the first two time periods (1933 and 1951), but this was less evident in the last time period (1967). The change in 1967 is considered below, but, for now, we can note that the participants displayed – at least initially – some sort of favourable evaluations of their own group. These research findings are consistent with social identity theory – considered in more detail in Chapter 2. Social identity theory suggests that we make sense of self and others (at least in part) by reference to perceived group membership and are motivated to perceive positive (own group- or ingroup-favouring) differences between our group and others. To a large extent, in Karlins et al.'s research, the framework for thinking in group terms is built into the task – participants being required to make judgements solely on the basis of ethnic group labels – but, however 'artificial' this may seem, the responses of

Table 7.1 Most commonly selected adjectives attributed to different ethnic groups (top two selected, three included if these were equally prevalent; Karlins et al., 1969)

	1933	1951	1967
Americans	Industrious, intelligent	Materialistic, intelligent	Materialistic, ambitious
Japanese	Intelligent, industrious	Imitative, sly	Industrious, ambitious
Jews	Shrewd, mercenary	Shrewd, intelligent	Ambitious, materialistic
African Americans (label used at the time was 'Negros')	Superstitious, lazy	Superstitious, musical	Musical, happy-go-lucky
Chinese	Superstitious, sly, conservative	Loyal to family ties, tradition loving	Loyal to family ties, tradition-loving
English	Sportsmanlike, intelligent	Tradition-loving, reserved	Conservative, sophisticated
Germans	Scientifically minded, industrious	Scientifically minded, industrious, extremely nationalistic	Industrious, scientifically minded
Irish	Pugnacious, quick-tempered	Quick-tempered, very religious	Quick-tempered, extremely nationalistic
Italians	Artistic, impulsive	Very religious, artistic, pleasure-loving,	Passionate, pleasure-loving
Turks	Cruel, very religious	Cruel, very religious	Aggressive, physically dirty

the participants (in 1933 and 1951) suggest that these groups were treated as meaningful and, furthermore, the judgements made were somewhat ingroup-favouring. It can be further noted that, for social identity theory (and particularly the closely linked self-categorisation theory), this propensity to perceive and evaluate in terms of group membership extends beyond judgements of others to include judgements about self. Thus, Turner, Hogg, Oakes, Reicher, and Wetherell (1987) refer to *self-stereotyping* – that is, we can be found to perceive self as well as others in terms of the stereotypes that we have about the groups we assign ourselves and others to.

A second finding in Karlins et al. is the ways in which the attributed characteristics for these ethnic groups varies to some extent across the three time periods. Table 7.1 indicates something of this, though it is worth noting that the variation is generally moderated by some elements of continuity – for example, previously used attributes often become less prevalent rather than disappear altogether. To pick just three brief examples, look at the attributed adjectives for 'Japanese' in 1933. The adjectives 'intelligent' and 'industrious' seem very positive – clearly very much more so than the 'imitative' and 'sly', which were the most commonly selected to describe the Japanese in 1951. For the category 'Jews', the shift was in the opposite direction – here, a somewhat negative start in 1933 ('shrewd' and 'mercenary') is replaced in 1951 by 'shrewd' and 'intelligent'. Stereotypes for 'Germans' show an element of consistency, being described as 'scientifically minded' and 'industrious' across all three time periods, but, in 1951, the term 'extremely nationalistic' became much more prevalent.

At the risk of oversimplifying these results, it is possible to make some sense of them by considering the way in which historic events may have had an impact on the perceptions of different ethnic groups. The momentous historic event between 1933 and 1951 was, of course, World War II – the USA being involved in combat with Japanese and German troops. It is easy to interpret the more negative descriptors of Japanese and German people as related to groups who, a few years prior to the study, had been national enemies. By contrast, in the years immediately after World War II, as the horror and scale of the Holocaust became apparent, it is easy to envisage a sympathy towards Jews and a distancing from anti-Semitism.

A third finding concerned the extent to which participants adhered to a rigid stereotype. The picture here is somewhat complex. Karlins et al. (1969) note that, in 1951 – as compared with 1933 – stereotypes appeared to be less uniform – more adjectives being typically chosen to describe each ethnic group. While Karlins et al. anticipated that this trend would continue, the final study (1967) showed a more uniform stereotype across all groups except for African Americans (label used at the time 'Negros') – becoming very slightly less uniform – and Germans – who stayed the same. What Karlins et al. (1969, p. 9) did find, however, was participants had volunteered responses that suggested they were not happy to apply stereotypes – for example, one participant left the following comment: 'I must make it clear that I think it ludicrous to attempt to classify various ethnic groups. . . . I don't believe that any people can accurately be described as having, in total, certain characteristics.' This echoed the same reluctance that Gilbert et al. had found in their 1951 study and Karlins et al. (1969, p. 9) concur with them that 'college students have become more "sophisticated" and "objective" about making generalizations of other groups'. Thus, on the one hand, there is evidence that suggests stereotypes were more uniform in the 1967 study compared with earlier studies, while, on the other hand, comments in both 1951 and 1967 suggest some participants questioned the whole idea of applying stereotypes to ethnic groups. Some of these issues are returned to when we consider stereotypes and disconfirming stimuli below.

Critical reflection on the Princeton trilogy

One problem with the Princeton studies is, when the results are cited, there is the danger that they are referred to as the stereotypes *Americans* held of different ethnic groups when, in actual fact, the participants comprised just *Princeton University students*. Karlins et al. (1969, p. 2) note that, in 1951, the Princeton students were not solely 'well-to-do' and 'privileged' but, instead, 'represented much more of a cross-section of American youth'. Furthermore, in Karlins et al.'s (1969) own study, they report on care being taken to ensure that the proportions of participants from state-funded and fee-paying schools (90:60) reflected the overall profile of students at Princeton at the time of the research. Despite this, the participants were not representative even of Princeton University students, let alone the American public. Karlins et al. (1969, p. 3) also note, without further comment, who was removed from the study: 'On the basis of anonymous questionnaires at the end we eliminated foreign subjects, Negro subjects, and those who indicated familiarity with the Katz and Braly study.' The terminology 'Negro' and the lack of justification for the exclusion both seem problematic looking back at the study some 40 years after its publication (although there is perhaps some scope to debate how pejorative the term 'Negro' was in 1960s America). Though not specifically referred to, there is also the implication that the group called 'Americans' not only excluded African Americans but also all of the other groups about whom ethnic stereotypes were sought – so, Jews, Japanese, Chinese, English, German, Irish, Italian and Turks are all treated as 'other ethnic groups' about whom the 'Americans' stereotypes were sought. This suggests that the group of Princeton students described as 'Americans' were a very narrow cross-section of American society in terms of their ethnicity as well as socio-economic and educational background.

There is also an issue regarding what is meant by the category labels used in the research. For example, when asked about perceptions of Americans, the implication is that participants were supposed to think of others in the USA, *excluding* African Americans, Jews, Chinese (and each of the other ethnic groups detailed). When asked about perceptions of those ethnic groups identified, such as 'Negros', 'Jews', 'Chinese', presumably it was anticipated that participants might include those 'Negros' 'Jews' and 'Chinese' who had US citizenship (and were therefore legally 'American'). This problematises any sense of a rigid boundary between the ethnic groups – for example, Karlins et al. may have conceptualised Americans as completely separate from 'Jews' (even though the USA had frequently been the country in which the largest number of Jews lived). This conceptual confusion makes interpretation of the stereotype content trickier as it is difficult to know precisely *whom the participants had in mind* when responding to these ambiguous category labels.

Madon, Guyll, Aboufadel, Montiel, Smith, Palumbo and Jussim's (2001) research considered below raises the issue that methodological features may have had an impact on these complex results. Each of the Princeton studies used the same ethnic labels, which included increasingly outdated descriptions such as 'Negro' and reflected a range of groups that may have been more relevant in 1933 than 1967 (no reference is made to 'Hispanics', for example). Furthermore, the adjectives presented for participants to select from, despite being partially amended in 1951 and 1967, still included some antiquated terms – the presence of outdated terms, or the absence of some more current descriptors, could in itself have had some impact on the uniformity and, indeed, content of the stereotypes.

The Princeton trilogy revisited

Madon et al. (2001) replicated the Princeton trilogy with three follow-up studies. In their first follow-up study they used the same list of 84 adjectives as was used in the Princeton trilogy – this clearly had the advantage of replicating the earlier studies more exactly, but the potential disadvantage that the adjectives used in 1933 may be different from those of the late 1990s and, even where the same descriptors are used, their meaning may have shifted over time. Madon et al.'s (2001) second study addressed this by including not only the original 84 adjectives but also more recent sets of adjectives, including Gough and Heilbrun's (1983) list of adjectives and other descriptors and 68 'free responses' from a preliminary study in which participants were asked to list up to 3 attributes for each group. In their third study, Madon et al. (2001) got 19 'white undergraduates' to rate the favourableness of the stereotypes used for each national and ethnic group for the Princeton trilogy and Madon et al.'s second study.

Madon et al.'s first study (the replication of the Princeton trilogy) also contrasted the responses of European American psychology students (which reflect the ethnic composition of participants in the Princeton trilogy) with non-European American psychology students (who described their identity as Asian, Latino, African American, Native American or 'other'). Perhaps surprisingly, Madon et al. (2001, p. 998) note that the results for European Americans and non-European Americans 'indicate remarkable similarity between the stereotypes endorsed by the European and non-European American samples'. Madon et al. reflect that this could be an artefact of the (possibly) outdated attribute list. A second issue to note in passing is that the category 'non-European American' may not be particularly meaningful. At face value at least, it is a very heterogeneous group, with ethnic identities within this group spanning three continents (Asia, the Americas and Africa).

In their first study, Madon et al. contrasted the current responses of European American students with the findings in 1933, 1951 and 1967 to see if (and how) the attributed descriptors for the ethnic and national groups had changed and whether there was more or less agreement or consensus among participants in their responses (that is, did they have a similar level of agreement in their descriptions of the ethnic and national groups to previous years). Again, somewhat surprisingly, in this first study, stereotype content was reported as not significantly changing for most ethnic and national groups. Tests of whether or not the agreement exceeded chance achieved significant results for all groups except for stereotypes held about the Japanese (where there was a not significant agreement between the current findings and those of 1933) and for African Americans, where stereotypes showed the most marked change. Indeed, stereotypes about African Americans differed significantly from each of the three studies comprising the Princeton trilogy.

In terms of content, it can be noted that, while 'musical' was still the most commonly attributed characteristic for African Americans in Madon et al.'s (2001) study, it was closely followed by 'loyal to family ties'. The descriptor 'loyal to family ties' failed to feature in attributed characteristics for African Americans in the 1933, 1951 or 1967 studies and was not selected to describe Americans in any of the studies.

Madon et al.'s (2001) first study additionally found that most stereotypes had similar levels of consensus across time – that is, participants across the four time periods tended to have similar levels of agreement with each other for a given ethnic or national group. Thus, participants choosing characteristics that they felt described Jews, for example, tended to agree with each other to the same extent (even if content varied slightly) in 1933, 1951, 1967 and Madon et al. (2001). Some stereotypes were more consensual in Madon et al. than they had been in one or more previous studies (those for Chinese, Japanese and Turks) and one stereotype was less consensual (that for African Americans). In their replication of the Princeton trilogy then, Madon et al. (2001) found largely – though not entirely – significant agreement in the content of stereotypes and levels of consensus among participants for the characteristics they attributed to the ten ethnic and national groups across the four time periods. The most notable exception to the impression of replicated findings appears to be with regard to stereotypes for African Americans, which were less consensual than in previous years and the most different in content. The more general picture of both content and consensus of stereotypes remaining relatively consistent was questioned by Madon et al. (2001) as possibly being an artefact of them using the same (potentially outdated) list of adjectives as had been used since Katz and Braly (1933).

In their second study – which used the additional descriptors referred to above and a rating scale asking participants the extent to which each characteristic described each group – the results were somewhat different. First, African American and European American participants, while generally endorsing similar stereotypes, revealed more disagreement than in the first study. Second, with regard to consensus, Madon et al. (2001) report more change in the second study (with its inclusion of more contemporary descriptors) than was found in the first study. Of particular note, while stereotypes for African Americans and the English were less consensual, stereotypes for Americans, Chinese, Japanese and Turks were more consensual than was found in one or more of the Princeton trilogy studies.

In terms of stereotype content, agreement with the Princeton trilogy findings only exceeded chance for the stereotypes held about the Irish – for all other ethnic and national groups, agreement was not significant. This picture of change over time differs dramatically from

Table 7.2 Most commonly selected adjectives attributed to different ethnic groups by European and non-European participants (From Madon et al., 2001)

	European American participants' judgements	Non-European American participants' judgements
Americans	Diverse	Diverse
Japanese	Scientifically minded, disciplined	Loyal to family ties
Jews	Very religious, wealthy	Proud
African Americans	Listening to a lot of music, noisy	Musical, tough
Chinese	Disciplined	Loyal to family ties
English	Competitive	Egotistical, proud, liberal
Germans	Liking to drink beer	Liking to drink beer
Irish	Liking to drink beer	Liking to drink beer
Italian	Loyal to family ties	Macho
Turks	Very religious	Cultural

what was found in the first study, where only stereotypes relating to African Americans changed significantly over time. The inclusion of additional, more contemporary, descriptors shaped the results enormously, as these were often chosen over and above the 84 originally used when describing each ethnic or national group. For example, by far the most frequently selected attribute used to describe Americans was 'diverse' – an option not available in the 1933, 1951 or 1967 studies. A summary is provided in Table 7.2.

Madon et al. (2001) concluded that the results of the second study revealed genuine change in stereotypes over time that was not detected by the 'outdated attribute list' (which was used in the original 1933, 1951 and 1967 studies as well as Madon et al.'s first study).

Summarising and characterising these changes in stereotype content is difficult – even attempting to say whether each group has a more favourable or less favourable stereotype than they had previously is tricky. Also, individual attributes may be difficult to assess in terms of how positive or negative they are. Thus, it may be that 'noisy'(attributed to African Americans in Madon et al.'s research) is more negative than 'happy-go-lucky', but then 'happy-go-lucky' does sound a little condescending. Likewise, characterising Americans as 'diverse' might appear very positive, but this reading might reflect certain broadly 'liberal' value assumptions in favour of diversity. Similarly, one can ask whether 'liking to drink beer' – a descriptor used of the Irish and Germans – is a positive (sociable, relaxed) or a negative (drunk, time-wasting).

Madon et al.'s (2001) response to this was to present the stereotypes from the three original Princeton studies and their own second study and ask 19 American psychology students to rate them for favourableness. In this way, each of the ten ethnic and national groups received favourableness ratings for each of the four time periods (1933, 1951, 1967 and Madon et al.'s second study). Overall findings suggest that the participants considered the most recent time period (Madon et al.'s second study) to have the most favourable stereotypes. The three groups judged to have less favourable stereotypes were Americans (who were perceived as having less favourable stereotypes in Madon et al.'s second study than in the 1933 and 1951 studies) and the English and Germans, who were perceived as having less favourable stereotypes in the current study than in any earlier studies.

Generally, then, with the exceptions noted above, Madon et al.'s participants in their third study judged that stereotypes had become favourable. Before we rush off to crack open the champagne, however, Madon et al. note several reasons for being cautious about our response to these findings. First, although stereotypes had been judged by 19 American participants to be generally more positive, this does not tell us how the various ethnic and national groups themselves might feel about the current content of the stereotypes held about them. Furthermore, even seemingly neutral or positive stereotypes could engender discrimination in certain contexts – for example, being judged as 'liking a drink' may be seen as a negative in certain employment situations. Second, there is some suggestion (in the first and second studies) that there is greater agreement among the current American participants about the content of stereotypes than previously. This greater consensus could amplify any potentially negative stereotype content because higher consensus means that more people hold the same stereotype about a given ethnic or national group. If the greater agreement among Madon et al.'s participants reflects a more widespread increase in consensus, then both positive *and* negative stereotype content will be more universally subscribed to by the population.

Third, some increases in perceived favourableness have been uneven, so the perceived favourableness of stereotypes held concerning African Americans, while more favourable in Madon et al.'s second study than in the 1933 and 1951 studies, was not found to be significantly different in favourableness from what was measured in 1967. Finally, the list of ethnic and national stereotypes was deliberately the same in 1951 and 1967 as it was in the original Katz and Braly (1933) study, to enable comparison of the stereotypes held for each ethnic and national group. Madon et al. reflect on the fact that, had other – more 'topical' – ethnic or national groups been selected, the results might well have been different.

At a simplistic level, the Princeton trilogy illustrated that, to some extent, if one's country is at war, or has recently been at war, then the national and ethnic groups with whom there is or was conflict might well be perceived in terms of more negative stereotypes. Similarly, as patterns of immigration change, so, too, might the targets of negative, immigrant stereotypes. Likewise, world events, such as acts of terrorism identified with a specific ethnic, national or religious group, may, similarly, be associated with certain ethnic or national groups being subjected to negative stereotypes. Any claim about more favourable stereotypes has to be tempered with the question 'About whom?' because the categories of ethnic or national (or other) groups used might not reflect those who are currently the prime targets of negative stereotypes.

Madon et al.'s research raises some important issues for our thinking about research into stereotypes. First, it suggests that findings about stereotype content can be affected by the stimulus materials that are used – using an out-of-date list of adjectives may yield different findings from more contemporary alternatives. Second, it suggests that levels of consensus or agreement about stereotype content – in this case, regarding different national and ethnic groups – can change over time. Third, it suggests that stereotype content itself can change over time. Fourth, in their reflections on whether or not stereotypes have generally become more positive, Madon et al. suggest that cultural topicality may play a role – that is, minority groups salient within a given culture at a given time may attract negative stereotypes.

These issues point to the possibility – not specifically explored in Madon et al. – that stereotypes may operate at more than just an individual level. It may be cultural or social changes that alter the language we use in describing different groups of people. Cultural or social changes may be linked to changes in the consensus and content of stereotypes. Likewise, cultural and social changes may be linked to which groups are currently associated with the most negative stereotypes. This idea of seeing stereotypes as something potentially wider than private, individual cognitive phenomenoa is returned to in our discussion of discursive approaches below. For now, some of the foundations of research in this area and the development of a **stereotype process** perspective (where the emphasis is on how stereotypes affect our thinking processes) need to be examined.

Stereotype content model

Cuddy et al. (2009) developed an approach they called the *stereotype content model*. This model suggests that, across ten very different countries (seven European and three East Asian), there are discernable common principles concerning the content of societal stereotypes. More specifically, despite the cross-cultural variation in participants, there was a near universal trend to derogate groups to which they did not see themselves belonging (outgroups) as either lacking 'warmth' or 'competence'. Furthermore, these attributes of 'warmth' and 'competence' were directly related to the perceived 'status' and 'competition' of these outgroups. Stereotypes held about groups that were perceived as less competitive were more likely to include 'warm' as an attribute, while stereotypes held about groups perceived as high status were more likely to include 'competent'.

Cuddy et al. (2009) argue that the stereotype content model thus identifies universal principles regarding what will determine aspects of stereotype content (perceptions of status and competition determine judgements of warmth and competence). Their (2009, p. 25) stereotype content model, however, allows for cross-cultural variation in what that content is – because of variation in the perceptions of warmth and competence of a given outgroup, 'Our research suggests that everywhere, a group's stereotype follows from perceived status and competition with other groups. However, culture influences group status and perceived group competition. Hence, specific group's stereotypes vary cross-culturally.'

Critical review of stereotype content research

It is worth briefly considering two criticisms of stereotype content research that relate to other approaches considered in this chapter. The first of these relates to the concern that the cross-cultural – or pan-historical – perspective

Stereotype process This refers to research that considers the ways in which having a stereotype shapes cognitive processes such as encoding, retrieval and evaluation.

has led to a somewhat blunt sense of the context in which stereotypes might be found to operate. The second, from a very different perspective, raises the issue that the more important focus from a social psychological perspective is on the cognitive processes related to the operation of stereotypes.

With regard to the first point, two of the studies considered above – the Princeton trilogy and Madon et al. (2001) – suggest that, despite varying levels of consensus at any one time, there is typically sufficient agreement in stereotype content to be able to talk about the stereotype held by a specific group in a given era about a culturally, nationally or ethnically defined target group. Cuddy et al. (2009), though less concerned in documenting the change in stereotypes over time, sought to identify the processes through which culturally informed perceptions of other groups might shape aspects of stereotype content. Thus, all of the research reviewed that has addressed content has, on the one hand, sought to show how certain contextual features are important – for example, the historical era, the intergroup relationship – but, on the other hand, seems insensitive to more local understandings of context. Thus, it could be argued that stereotypes can vary enormously within cultures, groups and even individuals – from the discursive perspective considered later in this chapter, stereotypes should be considered in terms of the argumentative or even sequential context in which they occur. That is, stereotypes could be looked at as tailored to the specific talk context in which they occur rather than as relatively uniform, cognitive structures that are shared by groups or ethnic groups within a particular era.

The second issue is that social psychologists investigating stereotypes should really explore the sorts of cognitive things that they do rather than their content. To some extent, this perspective reflects a view held by a number of social psychologists with a particular interest in cognition that focusing on cognitive processes reveals mechanisms that explain the individual's thought, emotion or action and such processes (when fully articulated) will, unlike stereotype content, be relatively stable and universal features of human cognition. This second criticism is addressed below when considering cognitive approaches to the formation and operation of stereotypes and schemas.

Critical recap

Stereotype content

1 Some of the early Princeton studies in particular had a very narrow range of participants.

2 The meanings of some of the ethnic labels presented to participants in the Princeton studies could have been ambiguous – for example, were participants supposed to include US citizens when judging the category 'Jews' and were they supposed to include Jews when judging the category 'Americans'?

3 The adjectives used shaped the results found – antiquated descriptors seemed less likely to reflect possible changes in perceptions.

4 Many of the studies imply some agreement about homogeneous stereotypes for given ethnic groups at a given time – this may not do justice to the variety that is within even a select group of participants.

5 The issue of how culture and/or ideology might shape stereotype content is not developed.

6 The focus on content may not suit the agenda of cognitive social psychologists.

Reflective questions

1 *Can you identify a stereotype (perhaps concerning an ethnic, religious or national group) that seems to have changed in content over time?*

2 *Why do you think that the content of this stereotype has changed?*

7.2 Cognitive approaches to the formation of stereotypes

In the above section, we reviewed some of the research concerned with the content of stereotypes, but this begs the question as to how such stereotypes are formed in the first place. Some of the research considered above implied some societal factors – resulting in different stereotype content at different points in time and place. The approaches outlined below take a more individualistic perspective and consider some of the ways in which processes within the individual's cognition may be linked to the formation of stereotypes.

Solomon Asch's model of impression formation

An early attempt to consider the mental processing involved in judgements about others is found in the work of Solomon Asch (1946). Asch was particularly interested in how people form impressions of others – and, specifically, how the perception of individual traits is combined into some form of overall impression.

Think for a moment about someone you have got to know over the last few months. It is possible that you could list certain attributes (as you perceive them), yet may well still have some overall sense of the person – 'They're really nice', 'They're a bit self-centred'. Even our description combines different traits – 'They are a bit shy, but warm and friendly when you get to know them' – and there is often some sort of unified impression that we have.

Over a series of 12 studies, Asch requested that participants form an impression of a hypothetical person described by a list of personality traits they had been given. As you have no doubt already worked out, different groups of participants received different lists of personality traits. If you were a participant in Asch's research, you might have received a description of this hypothetical person as being 'intelligent, skilful, industrious, cold, determined, practical and cautious'. In your own words, how might you describe the impression that you have of this person – based on these adjectives? Other participants had a similar list – 'intelligent, skilful, industrious, warm, determined, practical and cautious'. Again, imagine being a participant and write in your own words the impression that you have of the person so described.

You have probably noticed that one of the seven adjectives was changed in the second list – 'cold' was changed to 'warm'. Did that one adjective change result in a different impression for you?

In Asch's findings, swapping certain adjectives such as cold and warm had a big impact on participants' reported impressions. It may be worth just thinking about anyone you would describe as 'cold' and then reflecting on any positive traits they may have – do you have an overall negative impression of the person?

Asch developed two models to account for how we form unified impressions from separate bits of information about others. One of these models is the *algebraic model*, which suggests there is some mathematical respect for the separate values of the individual traits that we are aware of and these are combined to form an overall impression of the person. In the example above, 'cold' can be understood as an extremely negatively valued trait and will quite likely lead to an overall negative judgement, even when combined with more moderately positive traits, such as 'intelligent' and 'skilful'.

The other approach that Asch developed was the *configural model*. It suggests that the individual elements do not remain unchanged when they are combined together – instead, just like herbs and spices thrown into a cooking pot, the individual flavours (or impressions) combine with one another and each is changed in the process. For the configural model, we form an overall impression of others and – in some ways similar to work on cognitive dissonance – we reappraise potentially discrepant elements to make them consistent with our overall impression.

The configural model would make sense of Asch's findings by suggesting that 'cold' and 'warm' are particularly influential in our overall impression formation and, once we have our impression, other attributes, such as 'intelligent' are reappraised in the light of this. Consider for a moment the self-descriptions used in so-called 'lonely hearts' columns where people describe themselves in the hope of friendship and/or intimacy with others. One of the most commonly used descriptors is GSOH (good sense of humour). Think of the impression that this gives on its own. Does it change when you combine it with 'warm'? How about when you combine it with 'cold'?

It is quite likely that, while 'warm' did little to change the feeling of 'humour' combining it with 'cold' suggests that the 'humour' is perhaps of a cutting, sarcastic and cynical type – that is, the very impression of humour itself changes through its combination with other traits (in this case, cold). The configural model, further, suggests that, if there is some discrepancy between traits, people will find ways of resolving them. So, if someone is described as being 'helpful and selfish', we might resolve it by considering that they are helpful when it suits them or they help in order to get something.

The configural model suggests that the whole (impression) is not simply the sum of its parts and there is something more active or dynamic at work than simply adding up the individual elements of an impression. For the configural model, individual trait information not only shapes the impression we form but also that impression, in turn, shapes how we think about each individual element and how we make sense of any apparent contradictions. This idea of an active, social cognition in which a drive for a unified and organised impression shapes our mental processing formed a crucial element of what became the dominant approach within the area of social cognition considered below – *schema theory*.

The illusory correlation

Before considering schema theory, it is worth noting another approach that has been understood by some (Hamilton, 1979; Hamilton & Gifford, 1976) as an important basis for stereotyping. This approach – *the illusory correlation* – describes a bias in our perception that means we sometimes perceive links or correlations that are not actually present. Chapman (1967) noted that, when participants were presented with word pairs (such as lion–tiger, lion–eggs and bacon–eggs), some of the pairings would be perceived as occurring more frequently than others – even though there were the same numbers of each pairing. Chapman noted that if words could be thought of as having some associative meaning – that is, if our previous experience leads us to see them as belonging together (such as with lion–tiger, bacon–eggs), then they will be perceived as co-occurring more (or being more highly correlated). Word pairs that lack this sense of belonging together (as with lion–eggs) will be perceived as occurring less frequently. Furthermore, words having *paired distinctiveness* – that is, sharing some distinctive property unrelated to meaning – for example, being the two longest words – would also be perceived as co-occurring more frequently than those word pairs which did not share a distinctive feature.

The link to stereotypes becomes apparent when we think not of word pairings but characteristics and categories – that is, the ways in which certain attributes may be perceived as correlated with particular social groups. Associative meaning is a less frequently researched area and becomes somewhat circular as an account for stereotype formation. Thus, the idea that certain categories are associated with particular attributes and we form stereotypes by perceiving a correlation between the category and attribute seems to explain one association (between stereotype attributes and category) by reference to another (the associative meaning between attributes and category).

A more fruitful line of research has investigated how paired distinctiveness can work to explain negative stereotypes of minority group members. Hamilton and Gifford (1976) suggested that minority group members, by virtue of their minority status and reduced contact with majority group members, can be found to be perceived as less prevalent by the majority group. Similarly, out of the whole range of behaviours we encounter, certain negative ones may also be perceived as less prevalent. The minority category and the negative behaviour may thus be paired just because they are perceived as *similarly distinctive* or low in prevalence. In this way, an ethnic group may be associated with criminal or antisocial behaviour simply because both are rarely encountered by majority group members.

In a 'meta-analytic integration' of previous studies examining paired distinctiveness, Mullen and Johnson (1990) found that the effect, while typically moderate in size, was consistently present. They further note the way in which the illusory correlation is accentuated when the behaviours – or attributes – are negative and the person perceiving the relevant group is cognitively stretched (for example, being required to remember a large amount of material).

Johnson, Mullen, Carlson and Southwick (2001) suggested that affect plays an important role in the illusory correlation. They have thus challenged the prevailing idea that the illusory correlation is an information-processing bias, free from motivational and affective influences. Instead, for them (2001, p. 343), affective responses to the relevant group, in turn, shape perceptions of correlations: 'If a positive affective response is associated with a group, a low estimate of the number of undesirable behaviours performed is likely. If a negative affective response is associated with a group, a higher estimate of the number of undesirable behaviours is likely.' These affective responses were found to be shaped by the emotional intensity with which data about behaviour was presented – the more emotionally intense the description of behaviours, the more marked the positive or negative affect and, in turn, the greater the illusory correlation effect. Following Johnson et al.'s (2001) model, one can imagine certain emotionally intense tabloid treatments of violent crime, for example, leading to more negative affect towards (negatively perceived) minority groups and accentuating the illusory correlation.

Criticisms of cognitive approaches to the formation of stereotypes

With Asch's approaches in particular, it is possible to question whether we really – outside of certain social psychological experiments – actually perceive people in terms of collections of adjectives. Instead, our perceptions of others could be understood as being more affective in nature or more informed by global impressions (such as schemas, considered below) from which individual dimensions cannot be so readily or meaningfully isolated. The illusory correlation can be critiqued for its largely cognitive–mechanistic approach – although Johnson et al. (2001), with their emphasis on affective components, provide some redress for this.

All of the work considered above can be critiqued by adopting a perspective that is much less concerned with cognition in isolation (Billig, 1987, 2002). Indeed, even the work on stereotype content considered above suggests that aspects not purely restricted to individual cognition are at work in shaping the content of stereotypes – such as group processes and cultural influences. If stereotypes are approached as constructions of reality, then we can start to consider the ways in which prevailing ideologies shape not only the content but also the topicality, importance and consequentiality of stereotypes.

To take a sweeping and horrific example, all acts of genocide in the twentieth and twenty-first centuries have involved some form of denigration and dehumanisation of the victims – these may be best approached as linked to an overarching justifying ideology rather than the coincidental co-occurrence of lots of individual cognitive calculations. In other cases, we may be less concerned with societal denigrations of specific groups and more interested in specific constructions of other groups as they occur in conversation. From this perspective, the local context of talk becomes incredibly important in shaping the occurrence, form and placement of what we might call the 'stereotype'.

These perspectives that approach stereotypes as constructions of reality not only challenge the idea that they arise from cognition in isolation, but also encourage us to consider what these stereotyped constructions actually do – at an ideological and interactional level. Thus, we can ask how denigrating an outgroup might justify actions taken against them. Alternatively, we can inspect precisely where in a conversational sequence a stereotypical construction is used and what it might do within that specific interaction, at that moment, by occurring exactly where it does in the sequence (for example, it might be a means of doing agreement or disagreement, it might exonerate or hold to account). See Box 7.2 to explore the formation of stereotypes and prejudice further.

Box 7.2 IN THE NEWS
A disconfirmed stereotype?

One of the most widely viewed video clips of all time, with well over 100 million Internet hits, is of a 47-year-old Scottish woman singing a song on a UK talent show (*Britian's Got Talent*). Susan Boyle's rendition of 'I dreamed a dream' (from the musical *Les Misérables*) achieved dramatic worldwide attention and quickly became YouTube's fifth most popular clip.

Perhaps the most striking thing about the clip and the reason it aroused such interest, is that Susan Boyle's appearance and demeanour seemed to give little clue as to the power and beauty of her voice. If you watch this clip – www.youtube.com/watch?v=9lp0IWv8QZY&feature=fvw – it is apparent that the judges and audience seemed to expect very little of the performance and responded with some disbelief as she talked about wanting to be a professional singer like Elaine Page. Even more striking is the shocked reaction of the judges, the show's hosts and the audience alike once Susan Boyle started to sing.

Source: Andrew Milligan/PA Archive/Press Association Images

Susan Boyle, who achieved considerable success following her debut on ITV's *Britain's Got Talent* show. Many people seemed surprised by her ability. Why did her demeanour lead people to expect that she could not perform as well as she did?

The clip vividly illustrates that ideas about people can be quickly formed on the basis of the initial visual impression they create and these ideas may be completely wrong and often have no logical basis – what is the rationale for a good singing voice being related to a certain type of appearance? It also, arguably, reveals that, in some circumstances, prejudgements or prejudices based on visual impressions can be abandoned in the light of evidence to the contrary.

This next clip – www.youtube.com/watch?v=b2xiAQCTy2E&feature=related – also features Susan Boyle and further illustrates issues of relevance to thoughts about prejudice and stereotypes. The clip shows Susan Boyle's behaviour following her performance in the final of *Britain's Got Talent*. The day after this, she was admitted to the Priory Hospital amid some mental health concerns.

What is noteworthy for our current concerns is the way in which aspects of her behaviour following her performance – where she does a chopping gesture to her neck and subsequently raises her skirt slightly on exiting

Box 7.2 continued

the stage – were interpreted after she was admitted to the Priory. One commentator on BBC Radio Four's *Today* programme (1 June 2009) cited these behaviours as evidence of mental health issues.

In the light of research concerning prejudice and stereotypes, it is interesting to consider if the knowledge of her admission for some form of mental health treatment led to these potentially ambiguous behaviours being interpreted as signs of some form of mental health problem. It may be worth watching the clip and asking if what these behaviours are could be characterised in different ways (could they be interpreted as reflecting humour, 'showmanship', eccentricity or awkwardness instead of mental health problems?) and how knowledge of her admission to the Priory could shape the way in which they are made sense of.

Critical recap

Cognitive approaches to the formation of stereotypes

1 The procedure adopted by Asch and the attempt to explain the combination of discrete variables may not reflect situations that are encountered outside of the social psychological experiment.

2 Both Asch's work and the illusory correlation could be seen as very mechanistic accounts of human cognition.

3 The work of Asch and the illusory correlation give an impression of stereotypes forming devoid of any social context – even though earlier work on stereotype content strongly suggested some social dimension was involved in this process.

Reflective questions

1 *What sort of negative (or positive) correlations do you think are supported in the mass media?*

2 *Can you think of an example where social context appeared to be important in the formation of stereotypes?*

7.3 Categorisation and prejudice

At the heart of the social psychology of stereotypes and **prejudice** is the idea of **categorisation** – that is, the grouping of individual people, things, events, experiences (stimuli) into categories. Here, particular attention is paid to the work of Allport and Tajfel, both of whom helped to develop what became foundational for later work.

Gordon Allport

Gordon Allport's work on categorisation arose to some extent in response to Adorno, Frenkel-Brunswik, Levinson and Sanford's (1950) notion of the *authoritarian personality*.

Writing shortly after the end of World War II, Adorno et al. wanted to explain how fascism had become so widespread in Germany in preceding decades. In attempting to understand why people might become fascists, Adorno et al. framed the question in terms of individual predispositions – that is, they wanted to know, what are the features of certain individuals that might make them susceptible to fascist ideas? Drawing on their extensive survey and interview work, they identified a set of characteristics – or a personality 'type' – that they referred to as the 'authoritarian personality'.

Adorno et al. identified nine attributes of the authoritarian personality. Of particular relevance to our current concerns is one subcategory, 'stereotype', which describes 'the disposition to think in terms of rigid categories'. For now, it can be noted that Adorno et al. (1950) tackled prejudice as part of a concern about psychological factors that predispose individuals to fascism and identified rigid categorisation as one part of the psychological profile of these individuals.

Allport (1954) argued that categorisation was a hallmark of prejudiced thinking. Occasionally, as Billig

Prejudice Any instance in which judgements about another are made in advance of adequate scrutiny of the relevant facts (particular attention is given to racist and sexist forms of prejudice). While many researchers would see stereotypes as being the cause of prejudice, the term 'prejudice' (unlike stereotypes) does not make a presumption about the importance of various types of cognitive activity. Thus, many researchers drawing on approaches that are not cognitively orientated (for example, discourse analysts) might refer to prejudice rather than schemas or stereotypes.

Categorisation The process of perceiving events, objects and people as belonging to various categories. The focus in this chapter is on the allocation of people to different categories, such as ethnic categories, sex categories and occupational categories.

(1985) notes, Allport implied that prejudice could be seen as a consequence of a particular style of rigid categorical thinking on which individuals differ – similar to Adorno's understanding of rigid categorisation as a personality characteristic of prejudiced people. More generally, Allport saw a universal tendency to be prejudiced because we all, of necessity, engage in category-based thinking. Thus, Allport (1958, p. 21, cited in Billig, 1985, p. 80) argues, 'Man has a propensity to prejudice. This propensity lies in his normal and natural tendency to form generalizations, concepts, categories, whose content represents an oversimplification of his world experience.'

Allport here identifies some key ingredients for subsequent cognitive perspectives on prejudice and stereotypes. First, he presents prejudice as a byproduct of a thinking style that is universally shared. Second, he identifies categories and their associated generalisations and concepts as at the heart of prejudiced thinking. Third, Allport, writing well in advance of a more wholehearted 'cognitive turn' in psychology, notes that prejudiced ideas involve a simplification (indeed, oversimplification) of the environment. Subsequent work continued to emphasise that category-based generalisations were a common style of thinking – largely because they simplified the stimulus in the environment – and this category-based thinking led to cognitive distortions, including prejudice.

Henri Tajfel

Henri Tajfel's work, as Billig (2002) notes, can also be understood in part by considering who and what he was arguing against. Tajfel 's nemesis was the 1973 Nobel Prize-winning biologist (who largely devised the field of ethology) Konrad Lorenz.

In recent years, Lorenz has been criticised for his support of the Nazi party. Along with just over half of biologists who remained in Germany in the 1930s, Lorenz joined the Nazi party. More damning than this, though, was his work and comments prior to and during World War II in particular, which at times seemed to voice active support for Nazi ideology. Some, though not all, scholars felt Lorenz showed sufficient contrition in later years to be able to assume an active – and, indeed, prominent – position in post-war biology.

Quite apart from any issues with Lorenz's earlier support for the Nazis, Tajfel took issue with the specifics of his theory. He was not happy with Lorenz's ideas of instinct – irrational, biologically based impulses – being used to explain human behaviour and, specifically, aggression. For Lorenz (as discussed in Chapter 9), humans, like other animals, have an aggressive instinct but lack the biologically based inhibitory mechanism found in other species.

Tajfel argued that Lorenz's instinct approach suggests that there is something universal and invariant about the cause of aggression and so cannot readily explain the variation – or waxing and waning – of either social conflict or individual acts of aggression across contexts.

Second, as Billig (2002) notes, Tajfel found a moral–political problem with Lorenz's approach. If all aggression is a result of an underlying instinct, then, by implication, nothing can be done about it. Furthermore, abhorrent ideologies that justify the very worst forms of racist oppression may find some witting or unwitting support in those aspects of Lorenz's work suggesting prejudice and the desire to favour one's own race is part of the human condition. In summary, as Billig (2002, p. 173) notes, 'Tajfel's assertion of a common rational humanity was an argument against a counter-position' – specifically, this was Lorenz's 'blood-and-guts model for social phenomena' (Tajfel, 1981, p. 128, cited in Billig, 2002, p. 173).

Rather than simply critique Lorenz's approach, Tajfel developed an alternative understanding that became a major development in cognitive approaches in social psychology. For Tajfel, categorisation, not instinct, was the key to understanding prejudice and the conflict that often arose from it. Tajfel (1959) argued that people are readily influenced by category labels. Introducing labels to a wide range of perceptual judgement tasks will result in a distorted perception in which the perceiver exaggerates the differences between stimuli from different categories and minimises differences between stimuli within any one category (an issue explored further in the discussion of minimal group research in Chapter 2).

For Tajfel, categories are important because we have too much sensory information to deal with all the details concerning all the stimuli we are exposed to. Categories provide a way of arranging our perception of the world to simplify it, making it manageable and meaningful – once a stimulus is categorised, it can be thought of in terms of its category rather than its individual attributes. This simplifies the world, meaning that we do not have to process all of the information we are exposed to, but this comes at a cost – in simplifying and thinking in terms of generalised category attributes, we also distort the world.

Tajfel's (1957, 1959) categorisation ideas also stood in contrast to earlier work on perception bias. Bruner and Goodman (1947) had conducted research that suggested participants' estimates as to the size of unfamiliar coins would be biased by information as to their value – coins that were said to be more valuable would often be judged to be larger. Tajfel (1957) suggested that something more subtle yet potentially more significant was at work. For him, what was at work was an *accentuation* effect – that is, in cases where value really did provide information about size, the size estimates were exaggerated or accentuated. If participants were exposed to coins that were more valuable and larger, the extent to which they were judged to be larger than a smaller, lower-value coin would be accentuated. As well as introducing the idea that accentuation was at work, Tajfel (1957, 1959) also emphasised the importance of superimposed categories (high value versus low value) rather than continuums (gradations of value) on judgements about physical properties such as size. It is this grouping into categories and the effect that such categorisation has on judgements and decisions that was absolutely key to Tajfel's work.

This issue was developed in Tajfel and Wilkes' (1963) study where participants were first exposed to eight lines that slightly differed from one another in length – line 1 being the shortest and line 8 the longest (see Figure 7.1). Participants were then required to make repeated judgements regarding the length of each line.

Tajfel and Wilkes were particularly interested in the differences in the estimates for lines 4 and 5 – two 'middle-length' lines. In one condition, each of the shorter lines (lines 1–4) was presented with a letter 'a' and the longer lines with the letter 'b' while in the control condition, no category labels were used. Participants were requested to make judgements about how long each individual line was either with or without a category assignment ('a' or 'b') for each line.

You can probably guess the results. In the category label condition, the differences between the estimates of lines 4 and 5 were greater than in the control (no category label) condition. Tajfel and Wilkes (1963) found that, by categorising the lines into 'a' and 'b' – in this case, where the categories were meaningful (that is, they were related to the size of the stimulus lines) – the differences between stimuli belonging to the two categories were accentuated by the participants. Just adding the category information had an impact on their judgements about length.

Corneille, Klein, Lambert and Judd (2002) conducted replications of Tajfel and Wilkes' (1963) line length estimate study, in which they manipulated the unit of measurement that participants were asked to use – that

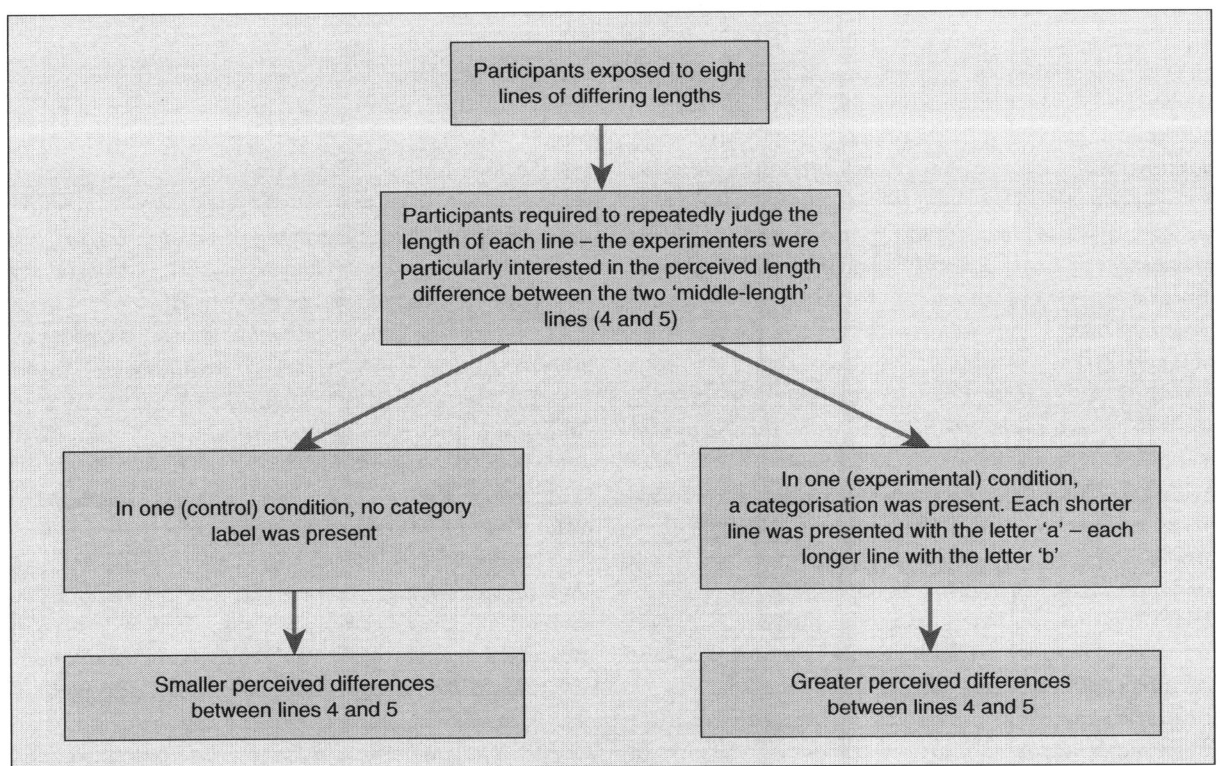

Figure 7.1 How categories affect judgements about perceived differences in line length (Tajfel & Wilkes, 1963)

is, some were asked to estimate in inches and others in centimetres.

As you read this, think about the unit of measurement you are least familiar with (inches or centimetres) and use it to estimate the width of this book. It is in this sort of situation, where we are less certain about the judgements we have to make, that we are – according to Corneille et al. – most likely to rely on category-based information. Thus, participants making judgements using unfamiliar units showed more distortion due to category labels than those who made judgements using familiar units.

From this quite specific empirical finding, Corneille et al. (2002, p. 380) argue; 'in conditions of subjective uncertainty, people preferably use categorical information to define themselves and others.' Thus, Corneille et al. suggest both an applicability of categorisation and also a limit. From this perspective, categorisation is important where there is uncertainty, but, as certainty increases, the impact of category labels decreases.

Tajfel's ideas about categorisation are important for social psychology because they extend beyond perceptions of physical stimuli to our social perceptions. Thus, if we superimpose category labels on other people, then those labels will enable us to make quick judgements, but, in so doing, will simplify and distort our perceptions of them.

In order to get some sense of category-based judgements, imagine for a moment that your job was to take calls for a popular live radio phone-in programme and decide which callers should discuss their point on air with the host of the radio show. Let us suppose that you receive hundreds of calls during a show, but can only select a few to be broadcast. In speaking to hopeful callers, you need to make quick judgements about who should and should not be selected for broadcast based on what they say in the first few seconds of talking. Because the show is live, your selection is particularly important – if you choose wrongly, callers' broadcast might be offensive, libellous, deceptive, irrelevant or boring. In this situation, carefully evaluating each caller on individual merit may be too difficult to do, given the volume of calls you have to deal with, so using categories might make your judgements more expedient. Thus, being able to use their first few words to decide if the caller is a bigot, crank, expert, bore or fraud, means that all of the information and misinformation that you have about those categories can then be invoked in order to decide whether or not you should put them through.

In the example above, the use of categories to make quick judgements seems not particularly vital (it helps the production of a radio show) and not very consequential for those being categorised (they either get on air or they do not). Tajfel's work, however, suggests that categorisation is a vital adaptive process and is highly consequential, explaining, among other things, prejudice.

Tajfel and Forgas (1981, p. 114, cited in Billig, 1985, p. 84) refer to the 'segmentation of the environment in terms of groupings' as being the 'sine qua non condition of survival'. That is, categorising people, objects and events into different groups is – for them – not just a useful adaptation but absolutely crucial. It is easy to imagine that, for our cave-dwelling ancestors, fast judgements about threats to our survival would be, literally, a matter of life or death – in that situation, an unfamiliar creature or person would require a snap judgement to be made concerning the threat that they might pose.

Tajfel's work suggests that categories come to the rescue here because simply assigning the unfamiliar to a category with known attributes – for example, as belonging to a certain tribe or animal type – means that we can know whether they are friend or foe. Thus, confronted with a stranger, for example, my quick categorisation of them into a tribe or other grouping gives me the information I already have about members of that tribe or grouping and may tell me if they are a friend or an enemy.

Tajfel (1981, p. 141, cited in Billig, 1985, pp. 83, 84) also noted 'the importance of the adaptive cognitive functioning of Man [sic] in the causation of prejudice'. That is, while categorisation is seen by Tajfel as the pre-eminent adaptive cognitive function, it comes with a substantial sting in its tail – it is at the root of prejudice. As Tajfel demonstrated in perceptual judgement tasks, categorisation leads to the accentuation of differences between groups and the attenuation of differences within groups. This phenomenon is sometimes referred to as the *in-category or ingroup homogeneity effect* and the *inter-category or intergroup heterogeneity effect* – that is we tend to minimise differences *within* groups or categories, but exaggerate differences *between* them (see the discussion of intergroup differentiation in Chapter 9). Categorisation, then, can be seen as directly implicated in prejudice. The very word 'prejudice' is derived from the Latin *prae* (before) and *judicium* (judgement), suggesting just the sort of judgement in advance that the categorisation process involves. Think for a moment of different sorts of prejudice you have come across – racism, sexism, homophobia, ageism. We can see how, with each of these, there is a category at work and it is the assumptions made about members of these categories that is prejudicial. From this perspective, a person who is being racist, for example, can be seen as having certain negative category-based assumptions about certain ethnic groups and applying these assumptions to those he or she perceives as belonging to the group. The process of categorisation, then – so crucial for human survival – is drawn as the arch villain in acts of prejudice, simplifying the complex social world but distorting it and allowing for negative assumptions to be attributed to people merely because they are perceived as belonging to a given category.

Criticisms of Allport's and Tajfel's categorisation approaches

Allport's work has some tension between treating prejudice as a matter of individual difference – a personality trait (in this he is similar to Adorno) – and, as is found in most of his work, understanding prejudice as a consequence of a universal tendency for category-based thinking (in a similar way to Tajfel).

Billig (1985, 2002) argues that both Allport and Tajfel treat categorisation as a necessary form of thinking with prejudice being an unavoidable consequence. From this perspective, then, human thought becomes characterised in terms of its propensity to categorise and prejudice is seen as understandable in terms of the categorisation process alone. Furthermore, rather than being a morally accountable choice, prejudice becomes almost excused as just an inevitable consequence of our universal need to use category-based thinking. Thus, Billig (2002, p. 177) notes that, for Tajfel, 'we must use categories in our thinking, and categorisation predisposes us to prejudgement'.

Billig (2002) argues that, while Tafel's work takes a markedly different perspective from that of Lorenz – emphasising social perception rather than instinct – it, too (along with Allport), treats prejudice as inevitable. This idea that categorisation and therefore prejudice is inevitable raises for Tajfel the very objections that he made of Lorenz's work. As we saw above, Tajfel argued that Lorenz's 'blood and guts' account did not explain the waxing and waning of hostilities (most obvious in the peaks and troughs of widespread human conflict). For Billig, this same charge can be made of Tajfel's categorisation approach, which is described as an invariant adaptive human capacity that will inevitably lead to prejudice. This, in turn, raises similar moral and political objections to Tajfel's work. If prejudice is a consequence of a fundamental way in which our cognitions are organised, then who can be held responsible for their prejudice? Furthermore, the idea that categorisation is adaptive is dangerously close to the sort of justification of prejudice that fascists draw on and, at the very least, runs the risk of making prejudice excusable.

It is important to be clear that Billig is by no means accusing Tajfel of supporting prejudice – indeed, arguably, unlike Lorenz, it appears that it was his very objection to prejudice that was an important spur to his own research. Billig does, however, make the case that, unwittingly, Tajfel's radically different cognitive account of prejudice can – through its emphasis on categorisation as both a fundamental cognitive process and an important cause of prejudice – have similar implications for our ideas about the inevitability and justification of prejudice.

Billig (2002) raises the issue that, although much of Tajfel's work suggests categorisation is the inevitable and central factor in prejudice, his work does (in places) also suggest being prejudiced is more than just the consequence of category-based thinking: 'if a man [sic] is prejudiced, he has an emotional investment in preserving differentiations between his own group and 'others'' (Tajfel, 1969, p. 134, cited in Billig, 2002, p. 179). Although it is not made clear what the emotional investment is, this does suggest something other than the mere mechanical operation of categorical thinking. As Billig (2002) notes, the apparent intensity and wilfulness of prejudice that we witness in many cases of aggressive prejudice does seem at odds with the idea that it is 'merely a category mistake' – the reference to emotional investment may, in some sense, acknowledge this, but is in need of more explicit development.

In a related vein, Billig notes that Tajfel does not use categorisation to explain the most extreme forms of 'prejudice' or 'genocidal eliminationist' thinking witnessed in the Holocaust. In these extreme cases, the idea of invoking a sort of cognitive inevitability caused by categorical thinking seems ludicrously reductionist. Here, instead, Tajfel's own reference to depersonalisation and dehumanisation (Billig 2002, p. 181) seems much more apt and relevant. Billig (2002) argues, however, that when we turn to horrific genocides throughout history, such as the Holocaust, we find that depersonalisation and dehumanisation operate not through isolated cognitions of lots of individuals but, rather, through a shared ideology about the persecuted group. These ideas regarding ideology and prejudice are picked up later in this chapter, but, for now, we can note two things. First, that Tajfel himself saw some sort of limit on the applicability of categorisation as an explanatory tool and pointed to depersonalisation and dehumanisation. Second, as Billig (2002) suggests, depersonalisation and dehumanisation can be approached in terms of the ideologies of which they are a part and, viewed in this way, they stand in contrast to approaches to prejudice that emphasise individual cognition.

Critical recap

Categorisation and prejudice

1 Allport's work has sometimes vacillated between portraying prejudice as a personality type and as a universal process.

2 Allport (most of the time) and Tajfel present categorisation as a universal process, with prejudice as an inevitable consequence. Billig (1985, 2002) has demonstrated that both aspects of this assumption can be challenged. Is prejudice universal? Is prejudice *inevitable*?

3 Billig (1985, 2002) notes that when we consider the most extreme versions of 'prejudice' (the word itself problematically understating the phenomenon), it seems that much more than mere categorisation is at work.

Reflective questions

1 *Do you think that categorisation is an inevitable part of the human condition?*

2 *Does the mere presence of a category affect your judgements? Does it explain prejudice?*

7.4 Schemas and cognitive processing

In the previous section, we considered some of the debates concerning whether or not categorisation is an important process and how it might be important for understanding prejudice. Here, we develop the idea that categorisation is important in prejudice – focusing on the category-based information and misinformation (or schemas) that people often draw on in perceiving, remembering and making judgements about others (see Figure 7.2). The schema-based research that is considered here is particularly concerned with the idea that our cognitive processes are shaped (or biased) by our schema-based expectations and this, in turn, can perpetuate our schemas.

This idea that category labels can shape or distort what we perceive is particularly important in social cognition research. The idea is that we have a great deal of *a priori* thoughts about any given type or category of stimulus – they could be about types of people, places, objects, events or experiences. Once a stimulus (an individual person, for example) is assigned (by us, them or others) to a particular category, then the **schema** – all of the information and misinformation we have about that category – can be drawn on. In the work considered here, attention will be paid to the ways in which schemas shape our cognitive processes – with a two-fold consequence.

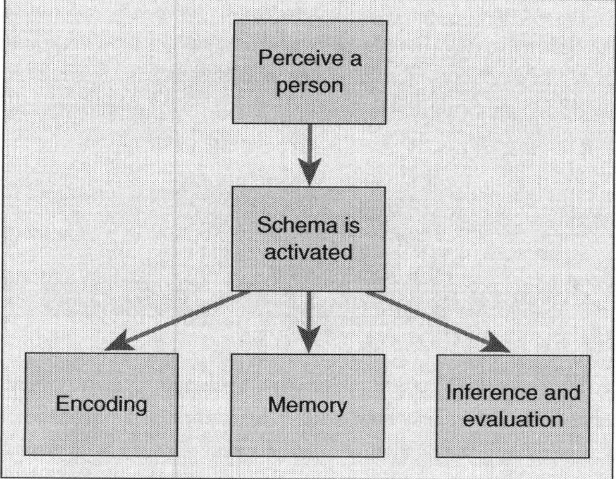

Figure 7.2 How an activated schema can influence the cognitive processes of encoding, memory, inference and evaluation

First, schemas are thought to influence our encoding, memory and judgements, such that we do not need to spend as long with each new stimulus we encounter and, thus, thinking effort is saved. This perspective has become known as the **cognitive miser** paradigm – a perspective that suggests we are inclined to save thinking effort. Schemas (and stereotypes in general), it is argued, enable us to save thinking effort by replacing detailed individual thoughts about each stimuli we encounter with more general, category-based information. Second, because of our relative inattentiveness to individual stimuli when we have a schema to draw on, we make schema-induced errors – that is, we misremember or incorrectly evaluate because our thinking has been guided by our schemas rather than the evidence in front of us.

In our discussion here, we will keep the focus on person perception, particularly stereotypes, while

Schema A cognitive structure that represents the information and misinformation we have about any form of category. This chapter focuses in particular on those that relate to social positions known as *role schemas*. The role schemas considered include both *achieved roles*, which involve and reflect some choice (such as job, educational status, sports groups, political or religious affiliation), and *ascribed roles* that do not (such as age, sex and ethnicity). Some work examined considers the ways in which, once a person being perceived has been categorised, the relevant schema then has an influence on the thinking about that person.

Cognitive miser An important idea concerning what schemas are used for that stresses their function in saving (or being miserly with) thinking effort on the part of the person using them.

acknowledging that schema theory is designed to explain the ways that pre-existing ideas can be relevant to any stimulus that we might categorise. Stereotypes are understood as being just one type of schema – that is, a particularly rigid form of role schema.

If you are being introduced to someone at a party and you are told that he or she is a television presenter or a psychiatric patient or a convicted criminal, then the label might influence your thinking about the person. You could still apply a label even if the person you are meeting is not introduced in this way – his or her appearance may lead you to apply a category (for example, regarding age, sex, ethnicity, religion, sexuality, political allegiance or wealth). It could even be as a result of the person's talk or behaviour that you apply – or perhaps adjust – some seemingly relevant category (educated, nervous, boisterous, paranoid, slimy, warm, for example).

Thus, the category assignment might come about in a number of ways – via a label assigned by another (the case in most experiments in this field), appearance or manifest behaviour. Whatever way category assignment occurs, as soon as we encounter someone whom we believe belongs to a given category, there is the possibility that the preformed information and misinformation we have about the category – our schema – can distort our thinking about the person. Thus, as soon as we have the label 'psychotic', whatever the person in front of us then does or does not do, all of our preconceptions associated with psychotics may shape our thinking about that particular individual we see. It is as if we now have two sources of information about the person in front of us – the individual and our category-based thoughts and ideas.

Later, we discuss ideas about how people, in perceiving others, might deal with possible tensions between their category-based preconceptions and contradictory evidence from the person in front of them, but, for now, let us, first, consider how schemas, such as stereotypes, might be activated and, second, the ways in which – once activated – they might shape our encoding memory and inference and evaluation.

Which schema will people use?

Fiske and Taylor (1991) suggest that some types of schemas are more likely to be used than others. Notably, people make more use of *role* schemas – lecturer, clown, politician – than *trait* schemas – extrovert, shy. They suggest that role schemas are more immediately available categories that we use to segment our social worlds – we can probably think of fellow psychology students and lecturing staff much more quickly than 'people who are very extrovert'. Furthermore, Fiske and Taylor (1991, p. 143) argue that role schemas could be seen as more informative: 'There are simply too many ways to be extroverted (e.g. like a comedian, a politician, or a bully), but there are apparently fewer ways to fulfil a concrete role schema, such as being a politician.' Thus, features of role schemas – such as how easily and frequently they are used to categorise our social worlds and their perceived informativeness – arguably make us particularly disposed to make use of this type of schema.

A second feature that can determine the schema we use is the physical cues – particularly the visual cues presented by the target person. As Fiske and Cox (1979) suggest, visual cues have been found to be particularly important in person perception in general and can be informative about sex, age, ethnicity and attractiveness. Indeed, physical cues may be indicative of socio-economic status and, possibly, occupation (for example, a person's clothing, uniform, demeanour) and, thus, it is little surprise that they are seen as particularly important at activating schemas.

A third determinant of the specific schema to be activated is whether not we are primed for it. Thus, if we frequently use a certain schema or have recently used it, we are more predisposed to using it again. Imagine watching a football match, then, on the way home, you witness someone punching another person. We might categorise the offender in many different ways – sex, age, apparent social class and so on. If, however, we had just watched a football match, football team allegiance (for example, supporting the opposing team) might be especially primed and, therefore, a key schema that we would draw on as we witnessed the violence. Thus, primed as we are, we may see this as an attack by, specifically, a supporter of one of team on a supporter of another, rival team.

How schemas shape encoding

Imagine that you are about to meet someone for the first time – perhaps a friend's new partner – and are given some information about them. Is it possible that having such information would shape how you take in, or encode, information about them? Let us imagine that you are told that they have sympathies with far-right political groups and you do not. Now, it is possible that you might hold a fairly rigid schema, or stereotype, about such far-right supporters. Holding this stereotype about a group you consider quite distinct from you – far-right political supporters – may lead you to think of the friend's partner across a narrow range of attributes. That is, without the stereotype (or with one you are more sympathetic towards), you might have a far less preconceived idea about what they are like, but, with this stereotype, you have a less complex, narrower concept of what they will be like. Thus, even before we have started to have cognitions about what the friend's partner does or says, it is as if we are predisposed to process the incoming information in a particular way.

Linville (1982) and Linville, Fischer and Salovey (1989) found that young people have less complex conceptualisations of 'the elderly' than they do of 'other young people'. Thus, they required fewer dimensions to describe those categorised as 'elderly' (a group to which they do not see themselves belonging) than those for 'young people' (a group to which they do see themselves belonging).

Linville's (1982) and Linville et al.'s (1989) research suggests that stereotypes of an outgroup (a group to which the perceiver does not see themselves as belonging) are narrower than of the ingroup (a group which the perceiver does see themselves belonging to). Related to this, outgroups tend to be perceived as being more similar to each other than do ingroups – who are perceived as more varied. This phenomenon is known as the *outgroup homogeneity effect*. As Fiske and Taylor (1991, p. 123) note, 'Minimising the variability of members within an outgroup means that they are not being recognised as distinct individuals as much as they would be if they were perceived as ingroup members.'

The issue of how we process information that is inconsistent with our stereotypes will be returned to, but, for now, we can note that literature concerned with the cognitive impact of schemas and stereotypes suggests it tends to be processed more slowly than stereotype-consistent information (Fiske & Neuberg, 1990).

To continue our example of meeting a friend's partner who, we are informed, is a supporter of the far right, if when we meet them they strike us as not looking, sounding or behaving like a supporter of the far right, we may be slower at taking in this schema-inconsistent information. In fact, the very phrase 'taken aback' suggests that very unexpected encounters and occurrences can slow down or interrupt our normal cognitive processing. If the person comes across as warm, sensitive and caring, we may be slower, less automatic, in our processing of their schema-inconsistent words and actions.

Various studies measuring participants' reaction times to schema-inconsistent information suggests the operation of just this process. For example, Klatzky, Martin and Kane (1982) found that mismatches between someone's attributed role (such as athlete or farmer) and their appearance resulted in slower participant reaction times. Dovidio, Evans and Tyler (1986) found that 'white' participants had faster reactions to negative and stereotypical traits when they were presented as 'could ever be true of' individuals described as 'blacks' than for individuals described as 'whites'. Even when the negative stereotype was rejected by the white respondent, the automatic, negative stereotype shaped the speed of processing, such that schema- (or stereotype-) consistent information facilitated faster responses.

How schemas shape memory

Imagine that you attend a party, meet someone and get talking. It is quite likely that you will ask them about what they do. Let's suppose that they say they work in the fashion industry. After you return home and your mind wanders back to meeting this person, what will you remember about them?

Being told that they work in the fashion industry might shape your recall towards schema-consistent information. Thus, you might recall how snappily they were dressed, suddenly you can picture their carefully manicured nails, you might remember how much they talked about shopping. If, by contrast, they had told you that they were a taster for a chocolate company, you might think about what they chose to eat, how they ate it, you might recall their complexion or how they talked about food. It is possible, therefore, that, out of all of the possible things we might remember about people, our schemas structure our recall, such that schema-consistent information is more readily retrieved than other details.

In Cohen's (1981) research, participants watched a video of a lady enjoying a birthday dinner with her husband. Half of the participants were told that she was a waitress and the other half that she was a librarian. The video showed her drinking beer, watching TV, wearing glasses and listening to classical music – presumably not simultaneously. Which bits of information do you think the different participants (those told she was a librarian versus those told she was a waitress) recalled? Take a moment to write down your responses.

Of those participants who were told that she was a waitress, a greater proportion recalled her drinking beer and watching TV above the other details. Those told she was a librarian recalled her wearing glasses and listening to classical music more than the other activities.

If you did not guess the results of this research correctly, then do not worry – it might mean that these particularly outdated stereotypes no longer apply as perhaps they once did. It could mean something else, however. Perhaps you spotted the idea that (when this research was done) participants might have expected a librarian to be more likely to be into classical music and a waitress to be more likely to drink beer. Having spotted this, you might also have thought that, sometimes, it is the inconsistencies that are more likely to stand out. That is, if I have an expectation that a librarian will not drink beer or that a waitress will not listen to classical music, then, surely, I will notice and remember this more than the other more expected, schema-consistent behaviours.

This point raises the question about the extent to which recall is driven to be consistent with schemas. An alternative to the idea of consistency is *relevance* – that is, we do not just recall what endorses our schemas but also recall things that are in some ways relevant to it. Being relevant could mean that it endorses our schema or contradicts it – in both cases, the stimulus has something to say with regard to the schema.

The extent to which stereotypes actually distort recall has been debated in recent years. Some researchers argue that stereotypes *do* promote stereotype-consistent responses to memory-type tasks, but not because of a distorting effect on the recall process (Cook, Marsh, & Hicks, 2003; Macrae & Bodenhausen, 2000; Sherman & Bessenoff, 1999). From this perspective, stereotypes are drawn on to fill in the gaps where people fail to remember. Imagine that you are helping serve refreshments at a friend's party where you do not really know the guests. You are bringing a tray of drinks to a table and really cannot recall who wanted the real ale, the low-calorie cola and the dry sherry. It is possible, in this context, that you might make a judgement based on your stereotypes about the bearded man, young female and older female seated at the table. In doing this, you would be aware that you were making a probabilistic judgement using your category-based expectations. You would not treat this as *actual* recall, so you would not visualise them actually having made the specific orders you have just guessed at. If this approach is correct, then stereotypes do have some effect on recall responses, but it is limited.

From this perspective, people who draw on stereotypical information when they are required to recall something *know* that they are doing so – they are aware they are making a judgement based on expectations associated with the relevant category rather than actual memory. A crucial consequence of this is that people drawing on expectations based on stereotypes should be less confident that their responses are correct than they are when they rely on actually recalled information.

An alternative perspective is provided by Dodson, Darragh and Williams (2008), who argue that stereotypes shape the recall process itself (rather than just provide the basis for guesses when people realise that they do not remember). Drawing on Tulving's concept of *synergistic ecphory*, they (2008, p. 461) argue that; 'the experience of recollection is assembled from activated trace information and from information in the retrieval cue and retrieval environment.' In other words, the process of recall is not a simple retrieval of a memory trace (which may be decayed or intact) but, instead, it is open to influences from the context in which the recall is made.

Some evidence for this general approach is found in research that has examined the impact of 'leading questions' on recall. This research has found that, when a question about some prior event is worded in such a way that it implies a given state of events, the recall of those responding to such questions is affected (Loftus, 1975; Loftus & Zanni, 1975). In one study, participants were shown a film clip from *Diary of a Student Revolution* in which eight demonstrators disrupt a class. Participants who were asked, 'Was the leader of the 12 demonstrators who entered the class male?' recalled significantly greater numbers of demonstrators being present (in a test one week later) than those who had been asked, 'Was the leader of the 4 demonstrators who entered the class a male?' (Loftus, 1975, p. 555). Dodson et al. (2008) argue that stereotypes can be found to similarly distort actual recall. In making their case, they note that Hicks and Cockman (2003) found that participants who made stereotype-consistent errors in recall tasks were highly confident about their responses. If stereotypes merely informed guesses (in cases where people are aware that they do not actually recall), then participants should be less confident about their responses. The high level of confidence in stereotype-consistent recall errors suggests that the stereotypes do distort actual recall rather than merely inform guesses.

How schemas shape inference and evaluation

A few years ago on the London Underground, the Metropolitan Police ran a poster campaign. The image they used had what appeared to be a white uniformed police officer chasing an Afro-Caribbean male. The smallprint below the image asked the reader to think about what they thought was going on in the picture – was the white police officer chasing the Afro-Caribbean man because the latter had just committed a crime? Another interpretation was offered – the white police officer was in pursuit *with* the black male, who was an undercover police officer, and both were trying to apprehend a third person, not in the image.

Extract 7.1

A The real point is whether he is willing to stay in some stagnant position or take a little risk and get ahead.
B But you're forgetting that the company will probably fold.
A You're just too damn conservative. With an attitude like that you'll never get ahead.
B What do you mean by that?

Source: Duncan (1976, p. 593)

The idea of the poster was that our schema-based ideas might lead us to infer things that are not true. The same could be true of our interpretations of ambiguous behaviours.

If you had been a participant in Duncan's (1976) classic study, you would – after quite lengthy, and largely bogus, instructions – find yourself observing two other students interacting. What you would have observed was a disagreement that centred on whether some hypothetical person should take a new job or stay where they were. The exchange included the words in Extract 7.1.

Then you would have seen one of the students (B) shoving the other student (A) and been required to rate the interaction. Depending on the experimental condition you were assigned to, you would either have witnessed a black or white student doing the shoving and a black or white student being shoved.

The results of the actual study make somewhat depressing reading. In each of the six cases where the protagonist (doing the shoving) was black, the shove was most typically characterised as 'violent behaviour' and attributed to the protagonist. In four of the six cases where the person doing the shoving was white, the shove was most frequently characterised as 'dramatizing'. In one case, 'aggressive behaviour' was the most frequently chosen label and, in another, 'dramatizing' and 'aggressive behaviour' were equally endorsed. Across all cases, when the person shoving was white, the behaviour was attributed to 'something about the situation'. Thus, black protagonists were much more likely to have their shoves described as 'aggressive behaviour' than white protagonists, who were much more likely to have their shoves described as 'playful' or 'dramatizing'. Furthermore, black participants were much more likely to have their shoves attributed to *themselves*, while white participants were much more likely to have their shoves attributed to the *situation*.

Duncan (1976, p. 597) interpreted his results more in the light of attribution theory than stereotypes, although he does acknowledge the relevance of stereotypes and categories: 'It would appear that the black man is imbued (stereotyped, categorized, etc.) with such salient personality properties (e.g., given to violence) that these traits tend to engulf the field.' The development of schema theory, however, provides a way of understanding Duncan's findings that is consistent with the ideas in the above quote, but, from the perspective of schema theory, more specific and more part of an integrated cognitive–social psychology framework. From this perspective, then, the evaluation of the 'ambiguous shove' was likely to have been guided by one of two different schemas: a schema about young white college males (which did not particularly associate violence with this category) and a schema about young black college males (which did associate violence with this category). When asked to interpret something that was potentially ambiguous (the shove), it is as if the schema disambiguated the target behaviour for the participants, enabling stock schema (mis)information to inform an interpretation of what had taken place.

Critical review of categorisation, schemas and cognitive processing research

The schema and cognitive processing research considered here rests on the idea of categorisation. We shall critique this next before going on to consider other problems with the approach. Particular attention is paid to the problems that arise when we try to use categorisation and schema theory as a way to understand prejudice.

Problems with categorisation

Explaining prejudice in terms of a relatively automatic and inevitable process of categorisation has been extensively critiqued by Billig (1985, 2002). Billig (1985) argues that, when we examine in detail the process of applying and maintaining category-based prejudices, we discover the thinking involved is more varied, flexible, active and involves more effort than those who explain prejudice as an automatic consequence of categorisation suggest.

Billig (1985) characterises the thinking required to maintain a prejudice as involving just the *opposite* process to that of categorisation – that is, *particularisation*. Billig arrived at this term by using the dialectical strategy of reversing claims for the way phenomena – such as psychological processes – work, to see if the opposite held true. Thus, we have particularisation – thinking about what differentiates a particular stimuli (the target of our thought) from other stimuli category or categories. The precision of the term particularisation is arguably less important than the point that thinking is more varied than being simply category driven and maintaining and using categories involves cognitive effort.

Imagine, for example, a woman whom we might consider particularly prejudiced against people who have recently arrived in the UK from Eastern Europe. Now suppose that a family from Poland move in next door to her. We could sketch in a few more details for our characters. Let us suppose that both the family from Poland and their prejudiced neighbour comprise a husband and wife and two young children, the children of both families attending the same school, both considering themselves Christian and attending a church regularly.

The prejudiced woman actually belongs to a number of the same categories as the Polish mother next door, so, to maintain her prejudice requires that she select from all the possible categories the category 'Eastern European' and apply that to her neighbour. We can note already that this is not an automatic, mechanical process, but involves selecting and applying one particular category from a number of alternatives. To really keep being prejudiced, the *shared* categories have to be made sense of in some ways – especially those that could suggest some shared values or outlook. So, the Polish neighbour's Christianity could be seen as different in its form, basis, practice or sincerity from the prejudiced woman's (for example, 'They don't believe the same things we do'). Thus, the shared category of 'Christian' has been differentiated into 'Polish Christianity' and the 'Christianity' of the prejudiced neighbour. Additional thought, then, is required to tackle evidence that contradicts any negative category-based assumptions that are held.

Let us suppose that the prejudiced neighbour takes the position that people from Eastern Europe cannot be trusted. If the Polish neighbour then does something trustworthy, such as handing back a purse that fell out of the prejudiced neighbour's handbag, then further thinking will be required to maintain her derogatory views about Eastern Europeans. The honest act could be differentiated from similar acts by people who are not from Eastern Europe, the prejudiced neighbour using some cognitive effort to reinterpret the act in line with her prejudice – for example, 'She did that to try and convince me she's honest, but I am not falling for it!'. The prejudiced person could, instead, engage in thinking effort to see people from Poland as the exception to her general prejudice against people from Eastern Europe. Alternatively, this *particular* Polish neighbour could be seen as the exception to the general category-based prejudice against Eastern Europeans. The point is that, to really maintain category-based prejudice *requires thinking effort* and that thinking is not adequately described as entirely category-based.

Problems with categorisation and schemas as an approach to understanding prejudice

One key problem that Billig (2001) identifies with drawing on schemas and categorisation processes to explain prejudice is that it pays insufficient heed to content. Here, Billig is not advocating further detailing of the somewhat monolithic ethnic group stereotype at different historical periods that Karlins et al. (1969) investigated, but, rather, the sort of ideological content that is often wrapped up in specific prejudiced positions. For Billig, to investigate prejudice, the best thing we can do is examine prejudiced talk. In advocating this, Billig (2002, p.179) sees the *talk* as the prejudice, rather than it being a mere expression of a prejudice held elsewhere (for example, in mental representations): 'The hatred is not separate from the discourse. To hate is not merely, or principally, to feel something at a bodily or visceral level – but to believe and to utter particular sorts of things about others' (Billig, 2001).

Investigating actual instances of prejudiced talk would, from Billig's (1985, 1987, 2001, 2002) perspective, make it clear that prejudiced constructions are not isolated acts of individual cognition, but, instead, argumentative positions that orientate to counter-positions. Indeed, novel arguments and novel situations 'might elicit novel previously unformatted responses' (1985, p. 99). Thus, prejudice is seen as accomplished in talk that, in turn, may construct negative stereotypes, which somehow take into account alternative (for example, *less* prejudiced) positions.

One simple illustration of an argument emerging in a changing situation is the way in which Billig (1985, p. 99) found that high levels of unemployment led to not just more racist talk but also talk specifically interweaving a prejudiced position and the new, or at least topical, issue of widespread unemployment: 'there'd be more jobs if there were less blacks'. Some discursive work considered below likewise emphasises constructions in specific interactional contexts, but places perhaps more emphasis on what those constructions do by virtue of where they appear in sequences of talk.

Can self-perpetuating stereotypes ever be adaptive?

As was indicated in the discussion of Tajfel's (1969) research, categorisation has been positioned as a universal adaptive process, enabling quick judgements to be made in life-or-death situations. If, however, stereotypes shape our encoding, memory and evaluation to a very great extent, then they might no longer be adaptive since they insulate the individual from perceiving the world as it actually is. This not only presents a somewhat odd understanding of the individual as rather cut off from social reality but also raises the issue that, for stereotypes to be so resistant to disconfirming evidence, could make them more of a hindrance to survival than an adaptive response.

Critical recap

Schemas and cognitive processing

1 Billig (1985, 2002) has raised the question, does the category-based thinking at the heart of the idea of schemas actually describe how we think?

2 Billig (1985, 2002) has also questioned if categorisation actually saves thinking effort.

3 Billig (1985, 1987, 2001, 2002) has suggested that prejudice could be understood as an argumentative position rather than an isolated cognitive act.

4 If stereotypes are as self-perpetuating, as some schema work suggests, then it is possible to question if they are actually adaptive to a 'real' – rather than distortedly perceived – environment.

Reflective questions

1. *Can you think of an example where your memory or evaluation of a person was shaped by the schema that you applied to them?*
2. *Can you find an example of prejudice talk or text in which you can identify the position or positions that it is designed to argue against?*

7.5 Stereotypes and disconfirming stimuli

One particularly important area for research into stereotypes concerns what the individual social perceiver does – or, indeed, should do – when they encounter some evidence that appears to contradict their stereotype. One facet of this concerns how we might judge an individual when, on the one hand, we have some category-related expectations, but, on the other hand, their behaviour seems to contradict these expectations. If, for example, you have a strong belief that academics are absent-minded and encounter an academic who remembers a request you made some weeks ago, there is a contradiction between your stereotype (of absent-minded academics) and the behaviour of the individual academic you are perceiving.

The work considered in the previous section suggested that what we notice and remember and how we interpret behaviour might stop us from perceiving a contradiction in the first place. If, however, we perceive that this individual academic has been markedly *not* absent-minded, yet our stereotype suggests that absent-mindedness is extremely prevalent in the category 'academic', we have a contradiction. We could ask what happens to our general stereotype about academics in the light of this contradiction – how is it changed or revised? We could also consider how the category membership might be revised – is this person *really* an academic or a particular 'different' subtype of academic? For now, however, let us keep the contradiction and consider how it might affect our thinking about this specific individual.

The dilemma, then, is, if we have to judge whether or not this individual is absent-minded, should we use our category-based prevalence, the individual's behaviour or both? Some social psychology research suggests that we tend deal with these dilemmas by putting our category-based expectations to one side and focusing on the individual's behaviour. This seems like good news, but, from some perspectives, this could be seen as a flawed way of dealing with two contradictory bits of information.

To get at this idea, it is worth considering medical diagnosis for a moment. Imagine that you are a doctor in the USA and you have a male and a female patient (let's call them Tom and Nancy), both presenting symptoms that are on the borderline of being attributed to arthritis. In the USA, arthritis is nearly twice as prevalent among women as it is among men. If the symptoms are absolutely identical for your two patients, who is more likely to have arthritis?

An eighteenth-century statistician, Thomas Bayes, addressed just this sort of issue, developing a formula that suggests how individual information (that is, what we perceive about the specific target stimuli we are judging)

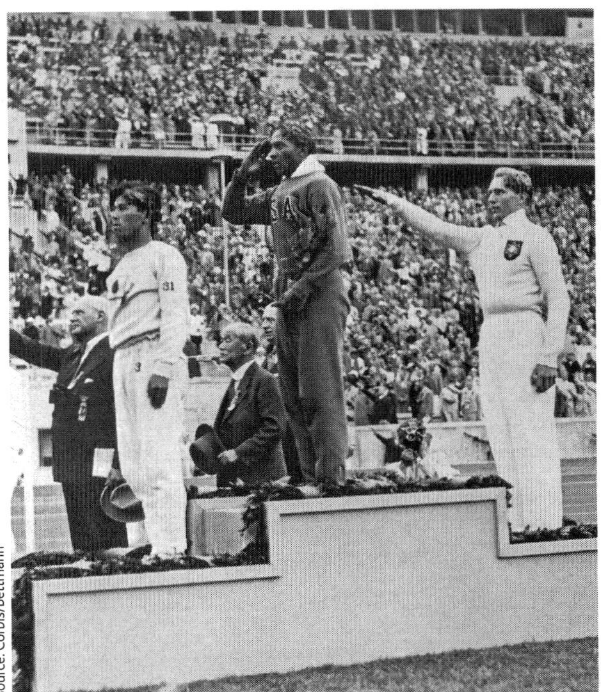
Source: Corbis/Bettmann

When Jesse Owens won four gold medals at the 1936 Berlin Olympics, he disconfirmed some racist stereotypes associated with the idea of 'Aryan superiority'

and **base rate** information (our information concerning the category-related prevalence) should be combined. For our present example, Bayes' formula suggests how the stimulus information (the symptoms Tom and Nancy present) might be combined with the category-related prevalence (the greater prevalence of arthritis among females than among males). The simplified bottom line, according to Bayesian statistical theory, is that we should take into account *both* the base rate (the category-related prevalence) *and* the individual, stimuli information. The critical point in social psychology is that, typically, people underutilise the base rate information.

It is worth briefly noting that some treatments of base rates focus predominantly on statistical information about prevalence presented to participants (Kahneman & Tversky, 1973; Tversky & Kahneman, 1980, 1981, 1983) and, therefore, are examining the use or non-use of base rates and so are much more precise and potentially more reliable than impressions of prevalence derived from stereotypes. In the highly influential series of studies conducted by Locksley et al. (1980, 1982), however, the base rate information that participants did or did not use did not come from statistics that the experimenter had presented to them. Instead, they merely indicated the sex of the person to be judged and presumed that this would make some base rate information available to them. They had established that, at the time of their research, there was a stereotype concerning men and women and assertiveness. Specifically, they found, when asked, both men and women reported that, typically, men are more assertive than women, with an estimated proportion of 7:3 (seven assertive males to every three assertive females). Just by indicating the sex of a person, the stereotype itself should provide a base rate of assertiveness being more than twice as prevalent among men than women.

Participants in Locksley et al.'s studies were presented with scenarios describing the behaviour of fictitious characters and required to rate how assertive they judged the character to be. By giving a name to the characters in the scenarios (Tom or Nancy) participants in these studies had two pieces of information – the sex of the target person and the description of their behaviour. The behaviour described in these scenarios was designed to be either relevant or irrelevant to the issue of assertiveness and the character within them was varied to be either male or female. Two examples are given below (cited in Brown, 1986, p. 598).

> **Scenario 1: Target person engages in relevant behaviour**
> The other day Nancy (or Tom) was in a class in which she (or he) wanted to make several points about the readings being discussed. But another student was dominating the discussion so thoroughly that she (he) had to abruptly interrupt this student in order to break into the discussion and express her (or his) own views.
>
> **Scenario 2: Target person engages in irrelevant behaviour**
> Yesterday Nancy (or Tom) went to get her (or his) hair cut. She (he) had an early morning appointment because she (he) had classes that day. Since the place where she (he) gets her (his) hair cut is near the campus, she (he) had no trouble getting to class on time.

You can probably get a sense of the research design that Locksley et al. used now. Groups of participants were presented with a scenario about Nancy or Tom (male or female) and the scenario was either relevant to estimating Tom or Nancy's assertiveness (Scenario 1) or not (Scenario 2). The dependent variable for this study was

> **Base rates** Expectations concerning the frequency with which any attribute might occur in a specific category, such as what proportion of males and females might be thought of as 'assertive'? Base rates may be based on information or misinformation given to or discovered by the person making the judgement or on ideas about the prevalence of the attribute based on the schemas that they hold – for example, the person's sex schema may suggest what proportion of males or females can be described as being assertive.

participants' judgements regarding the assertiveness of the characters described and was measured by asking them 'How likely/probable is it that Nancy (or Tom) is assertive?'

What is particularly interesting is how participants responded when – as in Scenario 1 – the question was about a female (Nancy), who has just been described as engaging in stereotype-disconfirming behaviour (being assertive). In this scenario, participants could rely on the stereotype alone (and make a judgement that Nancy is not highly likely to be assertive) or on the scenario-based information alone (and judge that Nancy is likely to be assertive) or on some combination of both. If you had to make the judgement and you had the admittedly unpalatable situation of not having this book in your hand, how would you respond? How do you think the participants responded?

The participants' ratings regarding the likelihood of Nancy being assertive was taken as a clue to the information that they relied on. The more assertive Nancy was judged to be, the more, it would appear, that participants had relied on the information contained in the scenario rather than stereotypical ideas. The less assertive Nancy was judged to be, the more participants were understood to have relied on their stereotype. Locksley et al.'s findings – which caused quite a sensation – were that, in those cases where the participants had disconfirming evidence in the form of a scenario describing female assertiveness, then *they relied entirely on that evidence and appeared to abandon the stereotype* (see Figure 7.3). The radical sense of these results is easily lost as we look back on them decades later, confident that we would *always* judge on the individual evidence, but, at the time, the findings raised serious questions about how stereotypes had been understood. If stereotypes were so weak that they were abandoned the moment contradictory evidence presented itself, then perhaps they were far less important (at least in the case of sex stereotypes) than social psychologists had thought.

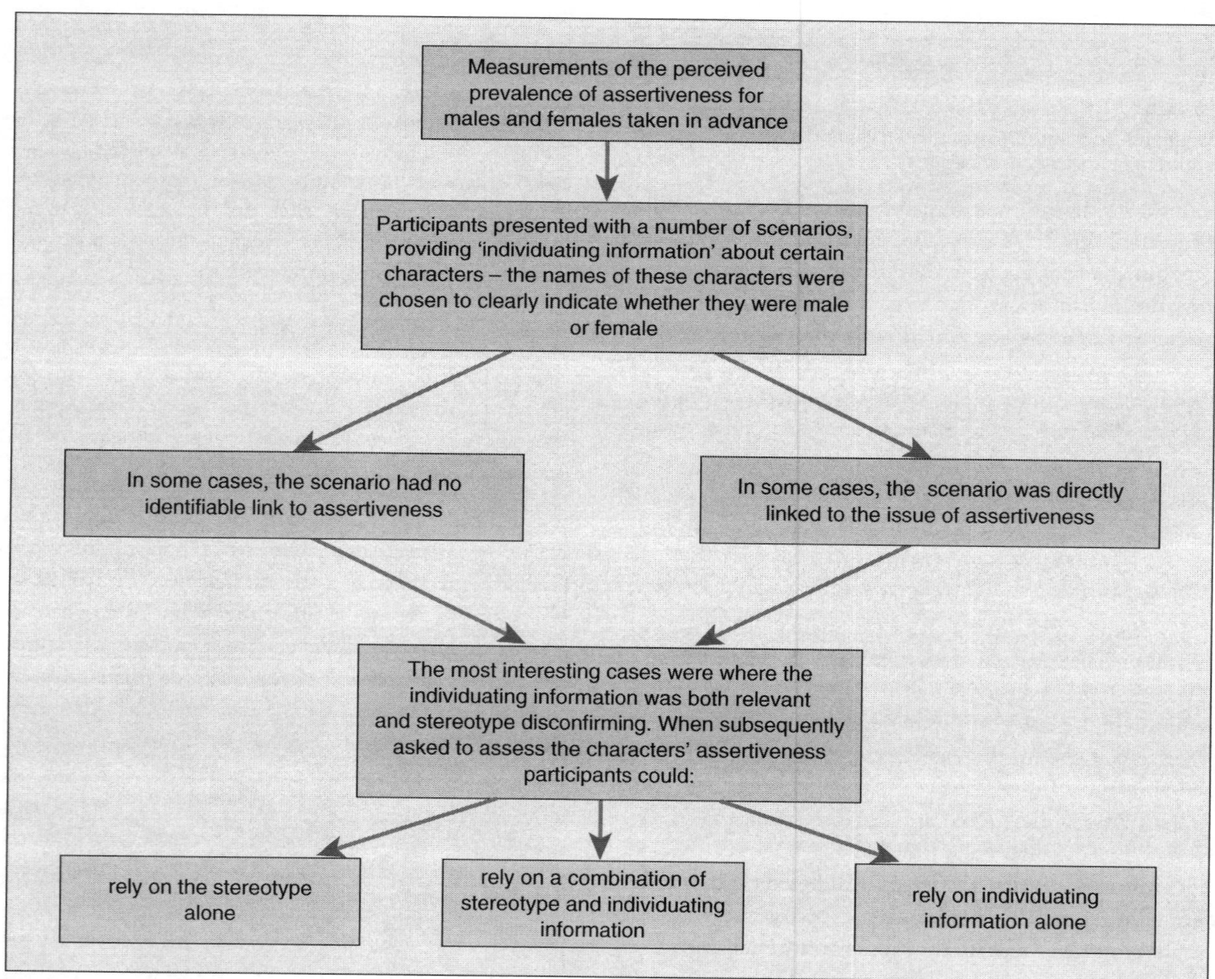

Figure 7.3 Locksley et al.'s experiments on the use of stereotype-disconfirming information

Critical reflection on Locksley et al.'s experiments

Before looking at some of the consequences that Locksley et al.'s results may have for our thinking about stereotypes, it is worth considering some critical issues concerning potential methodological limitations and the interpretation of their results.

First, we can note that the stereotypic trait used – 'assertiveness' – may have been present as a component of sex stereotypes at the time of Locksley et al.'s research but may have been less entrenched than some other stereotypical traits.

Second, the instances of assertive behaviour that participants were presented with in the study did not leave much scope for doubt or different interpretations. These scenarios of assertive behaviour could be seen as being what Fiske and Taylor (1991, p. 136) refer to as, 'unambiguously judgement relevant, to the point of redundancy with the judgement'. That is, the scenarios that depicted assertive behaviour described behaviour so unequivocally assertive that participants may have had little scope to refer to underlying stereotypes about assertiveness. The point here is that real-life contradictions of stereotypes might be more subtle than the blatant contradictions used in Locksley et al.'s study.

Third, the judgement made about the assertiveness was entirely inconsequential for the participants. In this respect it is unlike much of everyday life, where our judgements may be consequential, or we may have to argue about or justify them. Thus, in everyday life, one can imagine certain sales and marketing positions requiring assertiveness – in such situations, employers may make such judgements in quite a different way from the inconsequential judgements following experimental scenarios detailing fictitious behaviours performed by fictitious characters.

Fourth, the scenarios used present behaviour that is less complex and contextualised than everyday behaviour. There is less scope to selectively attend to this behaviour or recast it than there may be in complex, socially contextualised, real-life behaviour. Again, therefore, it is unclear how much the judgements elicited tell us about how people deal with the very different form of information we get in real-life scenarios. Staying with complexity for a moment, a key argument concerning stereotypes and schemas in general is that they are designed to simplify our processing of the complex – indeed, overwhelming – nature of everyday life. Experimental scenarios that actually take all of the complexity away, arguably, create a special situation where there is a reduced need for stereotypes because the information is already simplified.

Finally, there are important concerns regarding whether Locksley et al.'s research *really* reveals the participants' concerns with social desirability rather than the abandonment of sex stereotypes. In developing this point, Brown (1986, p. 607) first notes that, if we believe people put aside their stereotype whenever they meet someone who contradicts it, then 'that would be tantamount to claiming that there is not now and has not been discrimination on the basis of race, sex, and nationality, which is of course absurd. Instead, Locksley et al.'s, findings are interpreted by Brown (1986, p. 607) as being 'socially desirable nondiscriminating responses'. In this way, Brown suggests that participants would have quickly worked out just what the study was getting at and given responses that downplay any gender prejudices they might have.

Rethinking stereotypes in the light of Locksley et al.

Notwithstanding some of the criticisms of Locksley et al.'s studies discussed above, the research can be seen as having raised some questions concerning how stereotypes have been thought about and if there are problems with the idea that stereotypes are mechanically imposed on stimuli regardless of contradictory evidence. Though not all directly inspired by Locksley et al., the three positions outlined below give three ways in which stereotype and prejudice research has developed post-Locksley et al.

Increased emphasis on subtypes

It may have struck you that, with Locksley et al. (1980, 1982) and, indeed, much of the research concerned with stereotypes, the focus is often on relatively crude categories, such as black and white, male and female. Some work has emerged that suggests the importance of looking at smaller categories – subcategories or subtypes – within these overarching dichotomies. Eckes' (1994) research suggests that, instead of looking for the confirmation or disconfirmation of global stereotypes about males or females, attention should be paid to subtypes.

Ecke's research began by asking undergraduates at a German university to describe in diary form the 'types of' people they met over a two-week period using a label (of one or two words) and descriptive characteristics. From this, 16 female and 23 male labels or 'types' were selected and rated on bipolar scales that were derived from the descriptions of traits, attitudes, beliefs, behavioural preferences and physical appearance that participants had used in the initial study. Female types included 'career woman', 'housewife', 'punk', 'women's libber', 'bourgeois', 'trendy' and 'chick'. Male types included 'hippy', 'yuppie', 'punk', 'macho', 'bourgeois', 'trendy' and 'cad'.

Factor analysis of the data revealed that there were identifiable clusters around subtypes for both men and women. Thus, to some extent, rather than monolithic, global sex stereotypes Ecke's work suggests that participants think in terms of other, more complex quite differentiated subtypes. Thus, participants perceived a 'career woman' (rated as 'well-groomed', 'active', 'egoistic', dominant', 'strong' and 'hides feelings') to be quite different from a 'naive type' (described as 'weak', 'dependent', 'silly' and 'shows feelings'). This work suggests that categories are still at work and used by people, but often at a more subtle and fragmented level than the big, overly inclusive categories that a lot of research focuses on.

Selective use of stereotypes

Fiske and Taylor (1991) outline a way in which cognitive processing of others can move from initial categorising to more individually tailored thinking if our initial stereotypes are not confirmed.

Imagine that you are waiting around at an airport and someone sits near to you. Let us suppose that he is male, about 50 years old, wearing a dark, pinstriped suit and talking on a mobile phone. We might, based on these visual cues, immediately classify him as travelling on business. If you do not have the opportunity or inclination to find out any further information about him, then your initial categorisation will remain and you may draw on all the information and misinformation that your schema about businessmen contains. If you do have an opportunity to find out more information, however, you might find out things that confirm your initial categorisation – for example, hearing him talk about the Dow Jones or export tariffs. You might instead, however, discover contradictory information that leads you to recategorise him or find a relevant subcategory. So, imagine, while sitting next to your, apparently, businessman stranger, you overhear his conversation about his charity work or he may speak to you about the charity work he is involved in. This could open up a subtype of businessmen who do charitable work or another category altogether of charity workers. It is also possible, however, that as you find out more information you find it very difficult to categorise this person – perhaps he says things which make you doubt his charitable and business involvement or credentials. In such cases, where we cannot find a category that fits, we may become even more attentive to the particular individual attributes that we perceive in the person. Fiske and Taylor (1991, p. 138) point out, it is at this point that a more elemental, attribute by attribute process can take place: 'Finally, when it is not easy to re-categorize, people will proceed piecemeal, attribute by attribute, through the data.' In this way, Fiske and Taylor suggest that a continuum starts – attempts to categorise, if disconfirmed, can lead to recategorising, which, if too difficult, can lead to a more algebraic or elemental process of forming an impression of the person based on individual attributes.

Attention to contextually located constructions

It was noted in criticising Locksley et al.'s studies that the situation in which participants found themselves was highly unusual – when have you ever been in a room with others and had a brief vignette presented, then had to make a judgement about the person described? This situation is both highly unusual and unlikely to occur in everyday life – but quite common in social psychology experiments. The discourse analytic approach outlined below raises a problem with not only Locksley et al.'s study but also many experimental procedures relating to stereotypes and prejudice.

From a discourse analytic perspective, most research into stereotypes, either implicitly or explicitly, adopts a number of assumptions – that prejudice and stereotypes are essentially cognitively based (for example, the result of schemas), they are held by individuals in isolation and not particularly shaped by or responsive to social context. Discourse analytic research questions each of these assumptions, instead approaching prejudice as constructions in talk, sometimes related to widely held ideologies and orientated to the immediate interaction context in which it is found.

As will be seen in the next section, part of this shift to discourse analytic research depends on a shift regarding how we understand talk. Discourse analysis challenges the notion that talk merely represents or reflects an inner mental world where prejudice and stereotypes can really be found. Instead, discourse analysis presents *talk* as being the place where prejudice *is* and as being about *action*, specifically *action in interaction* rather than just representation.

Critical recap

Stereotypes and disconfirming stimuli

1 Locksley et al.'s (1980, 1982) research could be criticised as investigating a weak stereotype up against very strong disconfirming evidence.

2 The experimental situation meant the judgements that participants made were inconsequential – and potentially unlike many real-life contexts.

3 The information presented to participants by way of simple vignettes is very different from how we encounter information in everyday life – where it is much more complex and potentially inconsistent.

4 Brown (1986) raises the issue that the participants may have produced 'socially desirable non-discriminatory responses' rather than reveal their true judgements.

5 Fiske and Taylor (1991) suggest that the idea of stereotypes should not be abandoned, but seen as more flexibly applied.

6 Eckes (1994) emphasises the importance of sex subtypes, which contrasts with the global sex stereotypes (male, female) that Locksley et al. (1980, 1982) investigated.

Reflective questions

1 *Have you ever modified, completely changed or dropped a stereotype that you once held? Has someone close to you done so?*

2 *What do you think led to that change?*

7.6 Discourse and prejudice

In the majority of perspectives considered above, the emphasis has been on understanding prejudice as somehow related to intrapsychic processes – thus, prejudiced categorisation, stereotypes or other schemas are thought to be fundamental to prejudice. Discourse analysis takes a different perspective – the focus is on prejudice talk itself (which includes what is spoken, written, institutional, broadcast and everyday) rather than on anything within the head of the individual. Thus, rather than approach prejudice as either being something essentially cognitive or caused by something cognitive, discourse analysis looks at prejudice talk to see the ways in which that *does* prejudice. Discourse analysis, then, exposes how the talk accounts for and warrants its claims, justifies prejudiced practice and constructs versions of the denigrated other. See Box 7.3 for an example of a key researcher using this approach in her work.

Orientating to the accountability of appearing prejudiced

One feature that discourse analysts have identified in a range of racist (and more generally prejudiced) talk over the last few decades is the way in which it orientates to the possibility of having to account for itself. That is, the talk is often designed to fend off accusations of being racist or prejudiced (Augoustinos, Walker, & Donaghue, 2006; Condor, 2000; van Dijk, 1993, 2002; Potter & Wetherell, 1987; Wetherell & Potter, 1992).

Disclaimers

Imagine for a moment that one of your friends has introduced you to a friend of theirs and then left the room. While you are chatting, their friend starts an utterance with the words, 'I'm not prejudiced about coloured people, but. . .' How would you feel? What sort of thing would you think they were likely to say next? Think for a moment of the last time you heard someone start a sentence with words such as 'I'm not racist, but . . ., – what sort of talk followed these words?

These statements – which are typically positioned in advance of some stretch of talk and which make a claim against a negative judgement that might be inferred from the talk – are disclaimers. One particularly important form that disclaimers take in the case of prejudice talk is that they are used to deny speaker prejudice in advance of talk that appears to indicate prejudice.

If you heard someone utter the words 'I'm not prejudiced about coloured people' or 'I'm not anti them at all', it is possible that you might take those statements to reflect a low level of prejudice on the part of the speaker, but you might interpret it otherwise. You might, for example, be somewhat shocked by the reference to 'coloured people' or 'them', but, regardless of this, you might anticipate that, in both cases, a denial of prejudice will be followed by prejudice talk. Both of these disclaimers are actually taken from published data, so we need not guess what was said next, as we can see the subsequent talk for ourselves – the second of which is shown here.

The disclaimer 'I'm not anti them at all' was uttered by a white, middle-class New Zealander who was taking part in an open-ended interview reported in Potter and Wetherell (1987, p. 47). Here is the full extract.

> I'm not anti them at all you know, I, if they're willing to get on and be like us; but if they're just going to come here, just to be able to use our social welfares and stuff like that, then why don't they stay home?

This extract shows that the 'I'm not anti them at all' claim can be understood not as revealing some standalone, independent, cognitively based low-level prejudiced attitude, but, instead, as built to do some rhetorical work in the talk. Specifically, these **disclaimers** – which

Disclaimers Utterances that deny the accountability the talk might otherwise entail. Disclaimers often preface potentially accountable talk and provide a way for recipients to interpret what follows.

Box 7.3 KEY RESEARCHER
Professor Martha Augoustinos: stereotypes and prejudice

How did you become interested in research that addresses issues of relevance to stereotypes and prejudice?

As a first-generation Greek Australian growing up in what was typically described as a multicultural nation, I became interested in stereotypes and prejudice from a very young age. Of course, as a child, I didn't necessarily understand and experience these issues through such terms and categories, but I did know that I was different from my Anglo-Australian peers and that this difference mattered. At university I was surprised and delighted that psychology devoted entire theories to understanding stereotypes and prejudice. Although I found most of these approaches interesting, authoritarian personalities, minimal groups and cognitive miserliness all seemed to be lacking, at least from my own experience of these phenomena. Borrowing from poststructuralism and good old-fashioned Marxist social theory (which they still taught in the 1980s), I began to explore what social psychology had to say about ideology, power and discourse, which led me to the work of Michael Billig, Serge Moscovici and, later, Jonathan Potter and Margaret Wetherell. Moscovici's social representations theory was central to my PhD research, but, post PhD, my work became more and more influenced by the turn to discourse in social psychology in the early 1990s.

Tell us about your research into this area

My first research project on stereotypes and prejudice was influenced by Patricia Devine's (1989) landmark study on the automatic and conscious activation of stereotypes and its relationship to prejudice. In between 'flirting' with this literature, which was becoming very influential in mainstream social psychology, I read *Mapping the language of racism* by Wetherell and Potter (1992), which blew me away by its theoretical rigour and empirical insights on the dilemmatic nature and expression of stereotypes and prejudice in everyday talk and formal discourse. That book was an intellectual turning point for me: I abandoned the laboratory and got serious about examining everyday talk and conversation about some of social psychology's central topics, such as social categorisation, social identity, social influence, attitudes, attributions, etc.

In 1998, together with Amanda LeCouteur (who had also become a discourse convert), I was awarded a large grant from the Australian Research Council to examine the trajectory of the 'race debate' that had dominated Australian public discourse since 1995 with the emergence of Pauline Hanson and the far-right party she founded, One Nation. Among other issues, the project investigated: how Indigenous Australians are constructed in everyday conversation (Augoustinos, Tuffin, & Rapley, 1999) and political discourse (LeCouteur, Rapley, & Augoustinos, 2001); argumentative forms and discursive practices mobilised in everyday public reasoning and political discourse on the appropriateness of apologising to Indigenous Australians for historical injustice (Augoustinos, Hastie, & Wright, 2011; Augoustinos, LeCouteur, & Soyland, 2002; LeCouteur & Augoustinos, 2001); and the categorisation and representation of asylum seekers in political discourse and everyday conversation (Every & Augoustinos, 2008; Hanson-Easey & Augoustinos, 2010). Together this body of work has identified patterns of talk, metaphors and argumentative forms that are recurrently drawn upon in both formal and informal discourse in Australia about matters pertaining to race and intergroup relations. It builds a picture of how particular groups are constructed in talk and how these representations serve social, psychological and ideological functions.

How does your approach compare and contrast with others?

Traditional approaches in social psychology treat concepts like attitudes, attributions, stereotypes and prejudice as cognitive entities located in the minds of individuals. Discursive approaches, in contrast, prefer to treat the core topics of social psychology as discursive practices – things that people do in discourse. In everyday talk and social interaction, we describe and categorise issues, people and events in particular ways, provide accounts, build identities, justify, excuse and rationalise our own and others' behaviour, accuse, blame and make attributions. All these phenomena that are the bread and butter of social psychology are accomplished through language and yet social psychology has not taken everyday discourse and talk seriously, preferring to elicit attitudes, stereotypes, attributions and the like

Box 1.3 continued

through contrived laboratory experiments or self-report measures. You don't have to look far to find that these things are naturally occurring in the world – in everyday talk and conversation, in newspaper articles and editorials, in public speeches and political debate, in everyday mundane and formal institutional practices. Rather than treating stereotypes and prejudice as stable cognitive and psychological phenomena that are to be found in the minds of individuals, a discursive approach locates these in shared discursive practices or ways of talking that are flexible, contradictory and dilemmatic.

What things helped or hindered your research?

Although discourse is to be found everywhere, doing discursive research is not as straightforward as it might seem. First, collecting data can be very time-consuming, especially if it is naturalistic and not specifically generated for the purposes of research. Transcription is especially time-consuming and, as such, is relatively expensive compared to the cost of collecting and preparing quantitative data. Second, analysing the data can also be tricky as there are now competing approaches as to how to do 'proper analysis'. The most important thing that facilitated my research was being part of a core group, albeit small, of like-minded academics and postgraduate students at my institution. The Discourse and Social Psychology group (formerly known as DARU) has been a very supportive intellectual environment. I have been especially fortunate to have worked with some exceptional postgraduate students who have produced some excellent work. Support from national and international colleagues has also been crucial.

What points of interest would you like to explore in the future?

As in other Western countries, Australia has witnessed a protracted public debate about the value of multiculturalism as the official government policy of managing cultural diversity and social cohesion. Critics have argued that the values central to multiculturalism have, in reality, resulted in a less cohesive society, encouraging minority groups to remain insular and thus reducing their incentive to 'integrate' into the Australian 'way of life'. Indeed, it has been argued that multiculturalism actually undermines national unity and identity. I am very interested in examining the vicissitudes of this debate in public policy, political discourse, the media and in everyday reasoning and argument. Specifically, I am interested in a detailed discursive analysis of categories such as multiculturalism, social diversity and social inclusion; how they are mobilised in discourse, what meanings they take on and how they are understood and oriented to by various stakeholders.

Finally, what do you recommend to people wanting to start to research this topic?

My recommendation is to read widely and appreciate the varied and sometimes oppositional approaches to understanding stereotypes and prejudice in social psychology. Keep an open mind and don't let artificial disciplinary boundaries get in the way. Most importantly, find a supportive intellectual environment – a mentor, department, school or research group – to support and inspire you!

involve a denial of prejudice that precedes prejudiced talk – can be understood as orientating to the possible accountability issues raised by the subsequent prejudiced talk. That is, in their talk, the speakers may orientate to the possibility of challenge and disagreement by denying – in advance of the controversial content – that it can be taken to indicate an unacceptable, challengeable or accountable position on the part of the speaker.

An extreme example of the use of disclaimers can be found in the talk and literature of some groups that are associated with racist ideologies. In the European elections of June 2009, certain nationalist groups that have been associated with racism (such as the British National Party) specifically positioned themselves as *not* racist, with election literature filled with claims starting with 'because it's not racist to ...', followed by specific and policy commitments such as 'oppose mass immigration'. This practice, evident in interviews with members of the BNP, in which racism and prejudice are denied before then being expressed, illustrates a pernicious way in which disclaimers can be part of speakers' attempts to reposition their prejudice talk as reasonable. It is worth noting that talk which denies prejudice is not just restricted to carefully devised political propaganda, nor even to extremely prejudiced talk, but is extremely widespread. From a discursive perspective, such statements are not reflections of an underlying attitude on the part of the speakers, nor are they 'to be discarded' irrelevancies – instead, they are designed to undertake a certain type of action to deal with the talk context into which they are uttered.

'Sympathetic' denigration

There are other ways in which talk can appear to be *not* prejudiced, yet still denigrate or disempower others. Indeed, the seemingly liberal elements of such talk can be part of the means by which it both denigrates the other, yet appears to be reasonable, tolerant and even liberal. Some examples of **sympathetic denigration** are found in Wetherell and Potter (1992).

In reporting on interviews with Pākehā (white) New Zealanders talking about Maori (Indigeneous) New Zealanders, Wetherell and Potter noted that some seemingly sympathetic talk about Maori culture could, nonetheless, construct the Maoris as separate from the technology, power and progress of Pākehā New Zealand society. Constructing Maori culture as therapeutic or as part of a heritage can be part of an argument that it should be preserved and, at the same time, can position Maori people as not wanting, needing or meriting more power and involvement in aspects of contemporary New Zealand society. Thus, the seemingly sympathetic construction of the preservation of ancient Maori culture and the good that this does can be a sympathetic disempowerment that weds Maoris to the past and gives them no stake in contemporary society.

Likewise, Augoustinos et al. (1999), drawing on a data set of student talk about current race relations in Australia, note that potentially sympathetic talk about problems that the Aboriginal people face can also be denigratory. Extract 7.2 illustrates this.

Extract 7.2

I think too and also when you look at history you look back at the fact that the Aborigines were very very primitive (Mmm) and they confronted our culture that was superiorily [sic] more advanced, the wheel had been invented and whatnot but the Aborigines hadn't seemed to advance past that very primitive stage and whatnot (Mmm). Umm, they had sort of had no modern technologies as such as the British had. Like the British had gunpowder and alcohol and these things, ahh, I think that was another big problem.

Source: Augoustinos et al. (1999, p. 357)

Elements of this talk are sympathetic – referring to the problem for the Aborigines of the situation the speaker describes – but the talk constructs a backward, inferior Aboriginal culture that is contrasted with the superior and technologically advanced British culture. The presence of the seemingly sympathetic dimension to the talk enables the whole extract to be somewhat less accountable. Imagine, for a moment, that the talk was pared down to just a list of claims – 'white British culture was superior', 'Aboriginal culture was very primitive', 'Aboriginal culture lacked modern technology', 'the British had modern technologies' and 'the British had gunpowder and alcohol'. Stripped of any sense of sympathetic telling, the claims are perhaps even more stark and overtly objectionable than when embedded in a narrative about the problems that the Aborigines faced. The element of 'sympathetic telling' makes these claims hearable as less of a rant about white supremacy and, instead, more of a 'reasonable' or 'defendable' or 'not maliciously intentioned' account of problems with the 'Aboriginal situation'.

Appeal to rhetorical commonplaces

The way in which talk is designed to ward off or defend against accusations of prejudice is closely linked to one aspect of the **appeal to rhetorical commonplaces** in prejudice talk. The notion of commonplaces can, as Billig (1996) notes, be traced to ancient rhetorical textbooks concerned with detailing certain recurrent, or common, argumentative points – the sorts of assertions that could be weaved into a wide range of different arguments. Platitudes, clichés and truisms such as 'in helping others we help ourselves', 'a friend in need is a friend indeed', 'charity begins at home', 'if you want respect from others you must first respect yourself', 'people have to learn to help themselves', 'you can't please all of the people all of the time', 'money doesn't grow on trees' are examples of commonplaces.

Billig (1996) develops the notion of commonplaces to encompass both frequently used rhetoric and commonsense folk wisdom shared by both speaker and audience. The idea of these being phrases for a vast range of different arguments points to their dilemmatic and contradictory nature. That is, because they can be used to argue such a wide range of positions, it is easy to see how commonplaces are contradictory with one another (for example, 'too many cooks spoil the broth' and 'many hands

Sympathetic denigration This refers to the ways in which talk may denigrate or disempower others while appearing to be sympathetic towards them.

Appeal to rhetorical commonplaces This refers to the ways in which talk can mobilise points of consensus by seeking to place the position being argued as a natural consequence of adopting some consensual point or commonplace.

make light work' are both commonplaces but directly contradict each other) and can, in many cases, be interpreted to mean different things according to the argument being made.

In arguing that they reflect commonsense folk wisdom, Billig points out that, alongside their contradictory (or dilemmatic) nature, they are also widely shared – and treated as being widely shared, commonsense values and understandings – so stating a commonplace is to arrive at a common ground between speaker and audience.

The idea that prejudice (at least on certain grounds, such as ethnicity) is wrong is, in many cultures, a widely held position or rhetorical commonplace. In referring to the writing of a former far-right, fascist political party, the National Front, and prejudiced talk more generally, Billig (1991, p. 129) argues that prejudice can be both denied and used as a charge levelled at opponents. Billlig argues that, in denying prejudice, 'the speaker not only seeks to deflect criticism, but also lays claim to be a member of the moral community of the unprejudiced. Even the fascist is laying claim to be a member of the moral community of the unprejudiced.'

This appeal to the idea that prejudice is wrong is evidenced in the overt disclaimers considered above ('I'm not prejudiced but ….') and is also reflected in the way in which prejudiced talk avoids the appearance of prejudice. In this way, as Myrdal's (1944, p. 37, cited in Billig, 1991, p. 124) comments on the talk of Southern whites defending discrimination in the USA suggests, 'everybody – not only the intellectual liberals – is thus anxious to locate race prejudice outside himself'. Indeed, locating prejudice outside of the speaker or author themselves can sometimes take the form of specifically accusing others – typically opponents – of prejudice. Billig (1991, p. 123) noted such accusations in racist literature – specifically referring to an article by the National Front that ended with the following charge made regarding its liberal opponents: 'Dare we say it – it is they, not we, who are prejudiced.' Similarly, in an interview (*Today* programme, 8 June 2009) that challenged the BNP leader Nick Griffin about racism in his party (following the election of two BNP representatives to the European Parliament in June 2009), he argued that, 'there's a huge amount of racism in this country … overwhelmingly it's directed against the indigenous British majority'. Likewise, Billig (1991, p. 125) notes that his earlier research involving interviews with working-class white youths in the UK revealed not only prejudice against 'blacks', but also an accusation that it is they, rather than the white speakers, 'who hold the real prejudices'.

Constructions of difference

One aspect of prejudiced talk is the way in which differences can be constructed to justify certain prejudiced talk, action or practices. Gill (1993) illustrates this in her analysis of an interview with a programme controller (PC) that explored the issue of the underrepresentation of women as DJs at the station. Extract 7.3 is from one section of the interview.

Extract 7.3

Int Do you think there are a set of reasons why women are put off from entering the DJ world?

PC (...) Presenters have to have a number of skills. They've got to have ... they've got to be very very dextrous (.) they've got to be very familiar with technical equipment (.) they've got to have a personality they are used to expressing and they've got to have a good knowledge of music as well as having a good personality (.) and those things are *not* as advanced in my view as far as women are concerned as with men. Um (.) um (.) I've got to be able to sit somebody in a radio studio and they've got to understand what they're doing kind of thing as well as being a good broadcaster and women (.) in their whole background are not brought up in that kind of environment.

Source: Gill (1993, pp. 82, 83)

In her analysis of this extract, Gill (1993) notes that – with the exception of 'familiar with technical equipment' – most of the person specifications outlined here are more likely to be associated with stereotypes of females (dextrous, good at expressing themselves) than with stereotypes of men. This in itself points to the larger issue that **constructions of difference** in real talk may not simply involve reading off a list of stereotypic attributes but can, instead, be seen as a much more active process.

In Extract 7.3, the differences between men and women are constructed not to simply share some inner stereotype about what men and women can and cannot do but, rather, justify why the station employs no female DJs. That is, the construction of difference is not a neutral reading of some separate cognitive stance but an active doing – in this case, justification – tailored to a specific

Constructions of difference This refers to the ways in which differences – in this case, between groups of people – can be built up and used in talk. One example is the way in which constructions of gender differences can be used to justify inequality between men and women.

Extract 7.4

Cliff: That's- one thing people say, I mean I- I haven't um b-been much to London, I've only been, you know down to stay for a couple of weekends and so forth. People were saying that London's changed an awful lot over the past-
Mrs A: Don't go there.
Mrs B: Don't go back. Don't go back. We don't go back.
Cliff: Yeah? Why not, what's- what's- (.) people say it's changed but in what- what- what way?
Mrs A: I'm not – I'm not prejudiced, a-about [coloured] people=
Mrs B: [No, no]
Cliff: Uhuh?
Mrs A: =But, when you've been living in a house, we lived in a house for nearly 50 years, and you had neighbours, Pakistani neighbours=
Cliff: Uhuh?
Mrs B: =Frying all their stuff
Mr B: What's wrong with the Pakis?
Mrs A: No-
Mrs B: No, [listen to her!]
Mrs A: [Nothing wrong with them]
Mrs B: Wait, wait, wait.
Mrs A: They were very friendly
Mrs B: Yes
Cliff: [Uhuh?]
Mrs A: [But], they weren't us.

Source: Condor et al. (2006, pp. 455, 456)

interactional context in which the low number of female DJs was an issue. Specification of differences (in this case, between men and women) does the specific task of justifying why they might be – or appear to be – treated differently.

Interactional context of the talk

The disclaimer considered at the beginning of this section – 'I'm not – I'm not prejudiced, a- about coloured people' – is taken from data reported in Condor, Figgou, Abell, Gibson and Stevenson (2006). The data, to some extent, crosses the distinction between interview and everyday talk because it was generated by one of the researchers ('Cliff') asking questions of two couples who already happened to be chatting together over their garden fence. Extract 7.4 above was kicked off by Cliff asking about how London may have changed in recent years.

Condor et al. (2006, p. 455) note in passing that the above extract could be considered 'a textbook case of a "modern" form of "racist discourse"' – in which Mrs A pre-empts accusations that her talk is racially prejudiced by starting with the disclaimer, 'I'm not – prejudiced, a-about coloured people'. They go on to further note, however, that the **interactional context** of this sequence of talk can be seen as a collaborative undertaking for the different participants present. First, they note that the parties to the talk treat certain ways of talking often associated with prejudice as being permissible – Mrs A is not held to account for her use of the term 'coloured people', nor is Mr B for his use of the term 'Pakis'. Second, they note the use of agreement markers (from Mrs B). Third, while Mrs A's claim to not being prejudiced is, somewhat playfully, challenged, her right to carry on speaking on this topic (her right to the floor) is made available by the actions of the others, who generally do not produce competitive talk. Where some *potentially* competitive spate of talk *does* occur (Line 16, Mr B's 'What's wrong with the Pakis?') it is treated as an unwelcome interruption (Line 18, Mrs B's 'No, [listen to her!]'). Condor et al. (2006, p. 457), note, then, that this prejudiced talk, rather than being the achievement of one person, is, instead, 'sustained, and in fact worked up, through the effective support of interlocutors' – that is, it is collaboratively accomplished.

Condor et al. (2006) further reflect that this collaborative dimension to prejudiced talk may have only become apparent because of the way in which the data had been collected. Quite evidently, data derived from one-to-one interviews could reveal aspects of the way in which prejudice talk is designed (for example, disclaimers are often found in such interviews), but would give no opportunity to see prejudice as a joint accomplishment between people in interaction. Condor et al. not only recorded a group of people, but a group already talking together (rather than being brought together for the sake of research). These features may have brought them closer to recording how prejudice talk is actually done in everyday settings rather

Interactional context This refers not to the physical setting but, rather, the sequence of vocal and non-vocal communication. Thus, any single utterance could be analysed in terms of its place within a sequence of interactions.

than a more limited understanding of how prejudice talk is done in overtly 'research interview' settings.

Critical review of discourse and prejudice

Criticisms could be made of research using discourse analysis to understand prejudice from some markedly different perspectives.

From a social cognitive perspective, the approach offered by discourse analysis merely describes the forms that prejudice talk takes – such as how it orientates to criticism or rebuttal. Cognitive social psychology has sought to use an understanding of mental structures when developing causal models to explain what gives rise to prejudice (or any other phenomenon being studied). For social psychologists from this tradition, discourse analysis leaves unaddressed an articulation of cognitive causes and processes as part of an account of why people are prejudiced. As has been noted in Chapter 5, discourse analysis takes a radically different stance towards understanding talk and the role of cognition in social psychological theory. It is because of these philosophical differences that there is no cognitive causal element in discourse analytic research – if there were, it would be inconsistent with discourse analytic principles and its discourse analytic credentials would be called into question.

A second criticism from within discursive psychology and the related approach of conversation analysis is that much of the research has relied on interview data. Potter and Hepburn (2005) provide a more detailed discussion of these issues, but, for now, one key point will be briefly highlighted. From a discursive and conversation analytic perspective, when people are interviewed, then, whatever the interviewer does and however minimal their contribution is, participants will – to a greater or lesser extent – *attend to that in their talk*. This is probably most evident in one-to-one interviews where the interviewer proceeds through a pre-prepared list of questions. Here, it is obvious that the interviewer is shaping the interaction and the interviewee is giving responses that orientate to 'being interviewed'. There is no way out for the interviewers, however, – they will be part of the collaborative talk even if they are silent. For example, silence may be orientated to by interviewees as indicating a problem with what they have just said. The problem, then, is that, from a discursive and a conversation analytic perspective, talk is always some form of collaborative action. Trying to look at the talk of one person by interviewing them is like trying to watch one person waltz, arm wrestle or do synchronised swimming – the phenomenon that you wanted to explore will be changed because you have tried to remove its collaborative nature. Unlike these examples, however, in interviews, the interviewees cannot extract themselves from the collaborative process – they unavoidably become part of the collaborative construction and trying to strip this away – by being silent, for example – just makes the interaction even more unusual than everyday life.

A tension, then, still exists between wanting people to talk on a particular topic (or reveal how particular types of talk are done) – for example, prejudice – and wanting to just have naturally occurring everyday talk. Condor et al. (2006) arguably established a good compromise in their interview with people already talking, but the interviewer was still part of the process – clear from his topic-initiating turns (Lines 1–4 and 7 and 8) through to his minimal continuers (Lines 11, 14, 23), quite apart from any non-vocal aspects (nods, shakes, eye gaze placement, gesture, body orientation) and any point in the interaction where the absence of talk, body movement, gaze or gesture was notable.

A third, related criticism from a conversation analytic perspective (which informs the work of some discursive psychologists) is that much of the research has paid relatively little attention to the sequential organisation of talk. This is most obviously the case where we find segments of talk taken from the specific sequential context in which they were found and analysed as 'standalone' objects. Thus, van Dijk (2002) produces a useful taxonomy of actions that are found in prejudice talk, such as *apparent denial* – 'We have nothing against blacks, but …' – *apparent empathy* – Of course refugees have had problems, but …' – and *reversal or blaming the victim* – 'Not they, but we are the real victims' – but to analyse these or any related discursive moves without reference to the sequence is to change them. That is, what a given piece of talk does can be understood as not residing in the form of words used but, rather, those words placed where they were in the conversational sequence. If we investigate such utterances where they occur, with surrounding talk context, then we are making available to ourselves the resources that the participants themselves had to use and make sense of the words used; if we do not, then we may make misplaced suppositions about what such talk is actually (rather than hypothetically) used to do.

A fourth criticism, developed in the work of Condor and Figgou (2011) is that, while many discourse analytic studies adopt an anti-individualist stance in terms of their theoretical position, they are often individualistic in their method. Thus, discursive and rhetorical research that focuses on the interaction-orientated work of individual speakers is seen by Condor and Figgou as displaying a methodological individualism – often having a narrow focus on individuals in the way in which data is gathered and analysed. The 'collaborative cognition' perspective that they develop seeks, instead, to understand prejudice in terms of emergent, collaborative cognition. From this perspective, prejudice may occur in the midst of people talking and thinking together about issues of relevance to prejudice. According to this approach, others are not merely co-present but are *co-participant* in constructing the positions regarding issues of prejudices that may emerge, which, for Condor and Figgou, represents a genuine movement away from the limits of an individualistic approach.

Critical recap

Discourse and prejudice

1 From the perspective of cognitive social psychology, discourse analytic approaches do not get at the underlying cognitive causes of our behaviour – in this case, prejudice.

2 From a discursive and conversation analytic perspective, there are limitations to using interview data in trying to get at an understanding of prejudice in non-interview settings.

3 From a conversation analytic perspective, much of the research does not pay sufficient attention to how the talk does what it does by virtue of where it is positioned in the sequence of interactions.

4 Questions can be raised regarding whether discursive and rhetorical research may, perhaps unwittingly, be individualistic in its attention to how constructions are deployed by individuals, for individuals (albeit in an interactional setting).

Reflective questions

1 *Consider an example of prejudice talk – do you think it should be understood in terms of what the talk is doing or as revealing underlying, cognitively based stereotypes?*

2 *How would you design a study to investigate prejudiced talk?*

Summary

- This chapter began by reviewing some of the very earliest research into stereotypes, which investigated the content of stereotypes – albeit the content of a very select group of Princeton University students' stereotypes. Perhaps the most interesting thing to emerge from this research was not so much that stereotypes change but what those changes might tell us. Some consideration was given to the idea that socially shared perceptions of ethnic groups that can be influenced by national and intergroup relations, can shape the current content of a given stereotype.
- The work of Asch (1946) and the later work by Hamilton and Gifford (1976) on the illusory correlation both gave a much more cognitive – rather than societal or intergroup – understanding of how stereotypes are formed. These approaches, however, have been criticised as being somewhat mechanical – more recent approaches, such as Johnson et al. (2001), suggest, for example, the importance of affect and motivation in the illusory correlation.
- Allport (1950) and Tajfel (1969) undertook extremely influential work that laid out the categorisation basis for subsequent cognitive social psychology work on stereotypes and prejudice. Their approach depicted categorisation as adaptive – enabling us to cope with being exposed to too much stimuli for us to process – and universal – being a characteristic feature of our thought. The work on schemas and cognitive processing was built on this categorisation basis and outlined how schemas could save thinking effort – but distort reality, give rise to prejudice and be self-perpetuating. Billig's (1985, 2002) work was seen to criticise the fundamental basis of this work by questioning if categorisation *did* describe our thinking process adequately and if categorisation *could*, in fact, save thinking effort as well as whether prejudice *can* and *should* be excused as a mere consequence of a universal thinking style.
- Locksley et al.'s (1980, 1982) research also raised problems for research into stereotypes. Their research showed an apparent underutilisation of stereotype-based 'information' whenever relevant individual information was present. Responses to Locksley's studies both criticised her methodology and interpretation of results and resulted in modifications in theories about the use of stereotypes and other schema (modified versions were less deterministic and more concerned with the importance of category subtypes than huge, global categories).
- Some work, however, took a markedly different approach. Discourse analysis could not be seen so much as a way of researching or understanding stereotypes – the notion of stereotypes presumes cognitive structures that discourse analysts might wish to question – but, rather, prejudice. From the earliest, pioneering development of discourse analysis within social psychology (for example, Potter & Wetherell, 1987), attention has been paid by discourse analysts to the ways in which prejudice talk is organised. This is found to include ways in which there are features built into the

talk that appear to address possible challenges (about the speaker being prejudiced or distorted, for example) before those challenges are actually voiced. The work of Condor et al. (2006) raised the issue that, given the right research methodology – one that allowed for more 'natural' interaction within a group of people known to each other – the collaborative nature of prejudice talk can be seen.

- The work reviewed in this chapter then raises questions about whether we approach stereotypes and prejudice as involving broad social dimensions – which the early content work implied – or individual acts of cognition. It encourages us to question just how important categorisation is in our thinking and whether or not it saves us thinking effort and automatically give rise to prejudice. The material here also gives us cause to think about the balance between the evidence before us and our schemas and stereotypes. Is our thinking profoundly shaped by stereotypes or can the evidence before us break through and challenge and change them?

- Finally, what sort of social psychology do we want? Do we want cognitively based models that attempt to explain why we do, think or say what we do? Alternatively, do we see talk as a crucial place where the prejudice actually *is* – and want a better understanding of how prejudice is accomplished by people in talk in interaction? Our responses to these issues may well be informed by our experience and the data reviewed, but, equally, it too may be shaped by our philosophical, psychological and empirical positions and commitments. We might not just wind up where the evidence takes us on these issues, we might make sense of that evidence in the light of our position.

Review questions

1. *What evidence is there to support the idea that prejudice should be thought of in terms of the broad social context in which it is found to occur?*
2. *What are the arguments for the idea that categorisation is inevitable?*
3. *What arguments does Billig develop to question the idea that categorisation is inevitable and that it explains prejudice?*
4. *What is the evidence for the idea that schemas can shape cognitive processes such as encoding, memory and evaluation?*
5. *What did Locksley et al. find about how participants dealt with stereotype-disconfirming information?*
6. *Name one criticism of Locksley et al.'s studies.*
7. *In what ways have stereotypes been rethought since the time when Locksley et al. conducted their studies?*
8. *In what ways might stereotypes – or the expression of them – do things, interactionally or ideologically?*
9. *What evidence has discursive psychology offered for the idea that prejudice can be examined in terms of what the prejudice talk does in interaction?*
10. *Which approach or combination of approaches do you think best explains prejudice? Do any give a realistic sense of how prejudice may be challenged or changed?*

Recommended reading

Billig, M. (1985). Prejudice, categorization and particularization: From a perceptual to a rhetorical approach. *European Journal of Social Psychology, 15*, 79–103. The classic paper that challenged the idea of categorisation as providing an adequate account of prejudice.

Billig, M. (1991). *Ideology and opinions*. London: Sage. A very readable collection of essays that develop a rhetorical approach to understanding prejudice.

Billig, M. (2002). Henri Tajfel's cognitive aspects of prejudice. *British Journal of Social Psychology, 41*, 171–188. A sensitive reappraisal of Tajfel's work and the social identity theory legacy.

Brown, R. (2010). *Prejudice: It's social psychology* (2nd ed.). Chichester: Wiley-Blackwell. An engaging and clear overview of key perspectives on prejudice, with particular attention being paid to social identity and related approaches.

Cuddy, A. J. C., Fiske, S. T., Kwan, V. S. Y., Glick, P., Demoulin, S., Leyens, J. P., Bond, M. H., Croizet, J. C., Ellemers, N., Sleebos, E., Htun, T. T., Kim, H. J., Maio, G., Perry, J., Petkova, K., Todorov, V., Rodriguez-Bailon, R., Morales, E., Moya, M., Palacios, M., Smith, V., Perez, R., Vala, J., & Ziegler, R. (2009). Stereotype content model across cultures: Towards universal similarities and some differences. *British Journal of Social Psychology, 48*, 1–33. An important cross-cultural investigation of the content of outgroup stereotypes.

Dixon, J, & Levine, M. (Eds.) (2011). *Beyond prejudice: Extending the social psychology of intergroup conflict, inequality and social change*. Cambridge: Cambridge University Press. A thoughtful and critical rethink of a wide range of research that encompasses different perspectives on prejudice.

Dodson, C. S., Darragh, J, & Williams, A. (2008). Stereotypes and retrieval-provoked illusory source recollections. *Journal of Experimental Psychology: Learning, Memory & Cognition, 34*, 460–477. A paper that addresses the idea that stereotypes can distort actual recall rather than just interpretation.

Fiske, S. T., & Taylor, S. E. (2008). *Social cognition: From brains to culture*. London: McGraw-Hill. A comprehensive review of social cognition literature.

Howitt, D., & Owusu-Bempah, J. (1994). *The racism of psychology: Time for change*. Hemel Hempstead: Harvester WheatSheaf. Psychologists are used to consider racism as something 'out there' in the populations being studied, this book insightfully and engagingly highlights racism within psychology itself.

Madon, S., Guyll, M., Aboufadel, K., Montiel, E., Smith, A., Palumbo, P., & Jussim, L. (2001). Ethnic and national stereotypes: The Princeton trilogy revisited and revised. *Personality and Social Psychology Bulletin, 27*, 996–1010. A detailed empirical investigation into ethnic stereotypes that provides an interesting contrast to the Princeton studies.

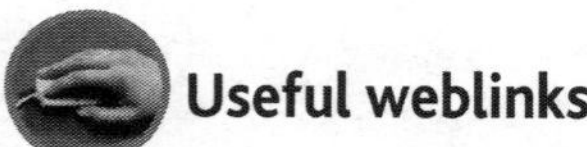

Useful weblinks

The following list of websites provides a great resource for research publications relating to specific academics and include a number of downloadable references.

www.discourses.org/Teun.html Publications – particularly addressing issues of prejudice – by Teun van Dijk.

www.psych.lancs.ac.uk/people/SusanCondor.html Recent publications by Susan Condor that address issues of prejudice and nationalism.

www-staff.lboro.ac.uk/~ssjap/JP%20Articles/jparticles.htm An impressively comprehensive resource for publications by Jonathan Potter.

www.sussex.ac.uk/migration/profile95042.html A listing, with some downloadable papers, of Rupert Brown's important contribution to social identity research.

weblamp.princeton.edu/~psych/PsychSite/ns_fiske.html Recent social cognition publications by Susan Fiske.

www.psych.lancs.ac.uk/people/JohnDixon.html A great resource for downloading John Dixon's work, much of which addresses prejudice.

www.understandingprejudice.org/readroom A resource with relevant academic and other links addressing different forms of prejudice.

The following websites may be useful sources of data for considering the constructions at work in prejudiced talk, the ways in which criticism is managed and the ways in which such talk is positioned as 'reasonable' by those producing it.

www.youtube.com/watch?v=4iKfrY9l2kY&feature=related

www.youtube.com/watch?v=zNVB43xfBRY&feature=fvwrel

www.youtube.com/watch?v=fqtTLIED33s&feature=related

www.youtube.com/watch?v=bQE0QPFoLfs&feature=related

www.youtube.com/watch?v=C3gDnq9E4vw&feature=related

www.youtube.com/watch?v=-jQsTtbR1OU&feature=fvwrel

Prosocial behaviour

Learning outcomes

By the end of this chapter you should have a critical understanding of:

- approaches that emphasise various motivations (such as altruism, rewarding feelings or competition) for engaging in prosocial behaviour
- approaches that link prosocial behaviour to psychological state (such as arousal and positive or negative mood)
- approaches to prosocial behaviour that draw on evolutionary theory (kin selection, reciprocal altruism, group selection)
- research that suggests diffusion of responsibility can inhibit prosocial behaviour
- research that emphasises how our attributions about the causes of a person in need's situation affects our propensity to help (attributional approaches)
- research that approaches prosocial behaviour as linked to views regarding how 'just' or fair the world is perceived to be (the 'just world hypothesis')
- research that attempts to integrate why and when people engage in prosocial behaviour by considering (the arousal: cost–reward model)
- theories attempting to explain different forms of prosocial behaviour (planned, long-term and between known or similar people)
- inter- and intragroup perspectives on prosocial behaviour
- social constructionist challenges regarding how and why behaviours might be constructed as 'prosocial'.

In March 2011, an enormous tsunami hit the east coast of Japan, sweeping away entire buildings, let alone cars and people, in its path. The images of the disaster also showed something of the way in which people helped one another. In some cases, this involved people risking their own lives to help others, such as the schoolteacher who rushed towards the coastal area threatened by the tsunami in order to warn his class of the impending danger or the Japanese emergency workers who, similarly, risked their lives to save others. In other cases, the help took the form of professionals and members of the public undertaking an ongoing commitment to help those who were homeless and destitute.

What this event graphically illustrates is a phenomenon that is sometimes evident in the most desperate of circumstances – helping others, or, *prosocial behaviour*. Social psychologists have been keen to understand what causes it and how we can understand why it is sometimes present and, unfortunately, sometimes absent.

A soldier from Japan's Ground Self-defence Force carries a woman to safety following the catastrophic tsunami in Japan. Does the social psychology of prosocial behaviour enable us to understand this and other instances of helping behaviour?

Source: Photoshoot Holdings Limited

Introduction

Social psychology textbooks can make depressing reading. Any book you choose will have chapters dealing with aggression, prejudice and ordinary people being persuaded or coerced into harming others. Prosocial behaviour stands in contrast to all of that – it is where we start to examine acts that help rather than harm others. In the midst of historical examples of the worst of human behaviour, we also find some of the best. Victor Frankel refers to those in the Nazi concentration camp where he was imprisoned who did not live to tell their story – they went around the camp distributing their meagre food rations, even though this hastened their own starvation. In the midst of the Rwandan massacre, Jean Banzubaze – a Hutu – risked his own life by hiding a young Tutsi in his house and pretending to be the boy's father. During the Yugoslavian civil war, Croatian soldiers forced a Croatian civilian at gunpoint to choose 12 Muslim civilians from a line-up to be executed and decide the means of their death. The Croatian man turned to the armed soldiers and said, 'You should be ashamed of yourselves! These people are innocent. Release them. Let them go home.' He then turned to the Muslim civilians and said, 'I'm so sorry. This is all I can do. I know they will kill me tonight. I wish you all the best.' He was indeed killed that night, but some of the civilians in the line-up survived to report on his altruistic act.

These are quite dramatic, newsworthy examples, but it is worth reflecting on two issues. First, what images come to mind when you think of prosocial behaviour? Do you think of daring feats of heroism – diving into rough seas to save a child from drowning – where there is substantial risk to the one giving help? Perhaps it is the image of helping someone who has collapsed. It may be that you think of helping a sick relative or friend or the regular commitment you make to voluntary work or a charity. Second, what sorts of explanations do you have concerning why and when people do and do not engage in helping behaviour – is it something *within* the person or the situation that is most important?

As this chapter suggests, some of the leading researchers in this field were very directly influenced by news reports and their own experiences, particularly concerning a lack of prosocial behaviour. As you read this chapter, keep in mind the ways in which the images of helping and not helping that we have can shape our explanations for prosocial behaviour.

Chapter overview

The theories reviewed in this chapter divide into three broad categories. First, there are theories that address *why* people engage in prosocial behaviour – the motivations and emotions that give rise to it. Second, there are theories that address *when* people engage in prosocial behaviour – the circumstances, perceptions and calculations that are associated with prosocial behaviour. Finally, there is a theory that attempts to incorporate something of the when *and* why of prosocial behaviour – seeing how issues of arousal can trigger calculations which shape possible instances of prosocial behaviour.

Theories addressing *why* people engage in prosocial behaviour look at motivations that differ in terms of how self-centred they are – some suggest we are motivated out of genuine empathic concern for others (*empathy altruism hypothesis*), others bring more selfish motivations to the fore, such as wanting to feel good (*empathic joy hypothesis*) or look good (*competitive altruism*). Other theories have been concerned with how mood relates to our prosocial behaviour – some emphasising that positive moods promote prosocial behaviour, others suggesting we often engage in prosocial behaviour to escape our negative emotions (*negative state relief model*). Finally, some *evolutionary theories* will be considered, which address the various evolutionary functions that prosocial behaviour may serve.

Theories addressing *when* we will engage in prosocial behaviour are dominated by the idea of *diffusion of responsibility* – which focuses on whether or not bystanders feel personal responsibility to intervene in an emergency by engaging in prosocial behaviour. In most texts, this is epitomised by the Kitty Genovese case in which, it was alleged, 38 witnesses failed to help a victim who was murdered in front of them. This chapter addresses recently available evidence that questions this widespread interpretation of the events. The situational emphasis in some approaches that emphasise diffusion of responsibility work is challenged by approaches (*attributional* approaches) emphasising the potential helper's interpretation of the situation – in particular, the extent to which the victims 'brought it on themselves' – and their sense of fairness concerning the victim's plight and actions to help them (*just world hypothesis*).

The main theory that attempts to address both why *and* when people engage in prosocial behaviour is *the arousal: cost–reward model*. This model argues that a heightened state of arousal – not inherently positive or negative – starts a process of thinking that may lead to prosocial behaviour. That is, in the presence of situations that might make prosocial behaviour relevant (such as when someone has collapsed), bystanders have some level of arousal and this may lead them to weigh up the costs and rewards of intervening. Thus, the model incorporates the *why* factors (which tend to be within the person) and the *when* factors (which tend to be in the situation or the bystander's interpretation of it).

Running through most of the models we have considered – often implicitly – is a particular conceptualisation of prosocial behaviour in which the emphasis is on explaining the ad hoc, direct help offered by one individual to a stranger. This chapter considers some aspects of prosocial behaviour that are missed in this conceptualisation – such as that which is long-term or appears to be shaped by group identity issues. Furthermore, some of the quite diverse ways in which experiments have operationalised – or defined, observed and measured – the seemingly coherent notion of prosocial behaviour are described. Finally, the chapter addresses the idea that how we come to define an instance of behaviour as 'prosocial' may not always be as straightforward as we typically assume – in doing so, this will raise the issue of the ideological context in which we think and talk about prosocial behaviour.

8.1 Why do people engage in prosocial behaviour?

One approach to understanding **prosocial behaviour** is to consider what is it within the person – their feelings, motivations or drives – that results in them engaging, or not engaging, in helping behaviour.

One strand of research taking this approach considers quite a diverse range of possible motivations, some of which appear much more altruistic than others. Thus, on the one hand, there is the idea that prosocial behaviour is driven by a genuine concern for others – best expressed in the *empathy–altruism hypothesis* – while, on the other, at the opposite end of the spectrum, is the theory of people engaging in prosocial behaviour purely for selfish reasons (such as celebrities seeking good publicity) – this is the *competitive altruism hypothesis*. In between these two is the *empathic joy hypothesis*. This, perhaps more morally

> **Prosocial behaviour** Following Dovidio et al. (2006), this is used to refer to a broad range of 'beneficial' behaviours. Usually these behaviours would benefit others, though the person engaging in the prosocial behaviour may also benefit.

ambiguous position, suggests that we help in order to have those positive 'I have just done a good deed' types of feelings.

A second strand of research is concerned not with motivations but, instead, how psychological states – such as one's mood or level of arousal – relates to prosocial behaviour. Is a positive mood more likely to result in prosocial behaviour or a negative one? Does being in a state of heightened arousal increase or decrease the probability of an individual engaging in prosocial behaviour?

The third strand of research, reviewed in the next section, shares something of the concerns of the first, in that it considers the ends to which our prosocial behaviour may be directed, though, in this case, we might not be consciously aware of them. This third strand encompasses a number of differing approaches that cohere around evolutionary theory, emphasising, in particular, that our prosocial behaviour can be understood in terms of the advantages it has for the transmission of shared genes.

As you look through these different approaches, you may reflect on how difficult it is to tease apart the different internal factors – did the person help because of altruism, self-interest, being in a good mood, heightened arousal or because of some evolution-relevant drive? Experiments designed to pinpoint the precise motivation or mood at work in decisions about helping behaviour and surveys aimed at measuring how decisions to help relate to the perceived genetic proximity of the person in need might not provide the unambiguous answers we could be looking for. Use Box 8.1 to think about some of these points.

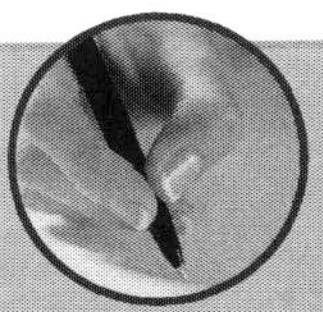

Box 8.1 TRY IT OUT
Motivations and emotions in prosocial behaviour

Stop and think for a moment about the last time that you engaged in some form of prosocial behaviour – it may have been a life-saving act of heroism or, perhaps more likely, something a little less dramatic, such as giving spare change to charity, helping someone cross the road, carrying someone's shopping or helping out a friend or relative in need.

Write down why you think you did it and how you felt before and after helping. How do your answers compare with the theories about why people engage in prosocial behaviour that are addressed in this chapter?

Motivations for prosocial behaviour

The first range of internal factors addressed here are *motivational* factors. It was noted above that the different theories – empathy–altruism, empathic joy and competitive altruism – provide different gradations of selflessness in their explanations of helping behaviour. One concern at work here seems to be whether, by uncovering the motivations for helping behaviour, we can better judge the extent to which prosocial behaviour (both within the specific experiment and more generally) should be thought of as selfish or unselfish. As you consider the research below, try to reflect on the extent to which it informs, first, about the motivation at work and, second, about judgements regarding whether something selfish, or selfless, is at work in prosocial behaviour.

Empathy and altruism

Think for a moment about an example of prosocial behaviour. Do you imagine a situation in which someone helps out a complete stranger – perhaps at some cost to themselves? This is a classic instance of just the sort of behaviour that social psychologists have attempted to explain. Now, consider why people might engage in such helping behaviour. The chances are, one of the first explanations that comes to mind is people help others because they feel empathy for them in their situation – they can envisage what it must be like for them, how they must be feeling, and so are motivated to help (see Figure 8.1a in Box 8.3, later in this chapter). This concern for the well-being of others is the essence of the *empathy–altruism hypothesis* developed by Batson, Duncan, Ackerman, Buckley and Birch (1981).

From this perspective, compassion for others and the desire to help someone in need is the motivating force behind helping behaviour (Batson, Klein, Highberger, & Shaw, 1995; Batson & Oleson, 1991). The empathy–altruism hypothesis has been developed to suggest that, once we feel compassion and a desire to help, then we may even be prepared to face considerable personal cost and risks in order to help the other (Batson, Batson, Todd, Brummett, Shaw, & Aldeguer, 1995).

Batson (1991) acknowledged that there could be other types of prosocial behaviour that have an egotistic motivation – that is, being caused by people's desire to act in their own self-interest. Thus, people might engage in some prosocial behaviour to avoid punishment or gain a reward. Alternatively, people might engage in prosocial behaviour to reduce their own feelings of distress that seeing a person in need can cause – for Batson, this, too, is an egoistic motivation as the bystander's own feelings are paramount. Batson (1991) identifies that genuinely altruistic motivation is behind some prosocial acts – where empathic concern for the person in need generates a genuine altruistic motivation to address the victim's needs and reduce their suffering.

Proponents of this perspective have to surmount a considerable challenge – which Dovidio Piliavin, Schroeder and Penner (2006) identify – that is, evidence has to indicate the presence of an essentially unseeable motivation. There is no easy opt out by simply *asking* people how altruistic their motivation is. Even if one presumes that there *is* a determinable, fixed level of 'altruism' that can simply be reported (and these are major assumptions), then, as Dovidio et al. (2006) further note, self-presentational concerns may mean that people over estimate the 'altruistic' aspects of their motivation.

Batson, O'Quin, Fultz, Vanderplas and Isen (1983) arranged an experiment in which participants who were assigned the role of 'observer' watched, on a TV monitor, a confederate, whom they thought to be another participant, receive electric shocks. The confederate receiving shocks then expressed some distress to the experimenter, relaying an account of a traumatic incident involving electricity when they were a child. The 'observers' were then asked by the experimenter if they wanted to change places with the confederate, receiving electric shocks in their place or for the experiment to be terminated.

As far as the observer participants were led to believe, agreeing to swap places would mean that the other participant (actually a confederate) would not have to endure any more electric shocks. They, however, would no longer merely *watch* electric shocks being administered but would *themselves* receive the shocks.

Participants who were presumed to feel *more* empathy towards the confederate receiving the shocks (because the confederate had been described as similar to the participant) were found to exchange places with the confederate. Participants who were presumed to feel *less* empathy towards the confederate (because the confederate had been described as dissimilar to the participant) were found to choose for the experiment to end rather than exchange places and receive electric shocks themselves in their place. In this way, empathy was understood as the crucial determinant of whether or not participants would undertake costly altruistic behaviour – those participants who decided to accept physical pain themselves in place of a stranger were understood as having greater empathy for the stranger than those who did not.

It is worth reflecting for a moment on certain features of the Batson et al. (1983) experiment and the stories in Box 8.2. The experiment raises some

Box 8.2 IN THE NEWS
A tale of two onlookers

Read through the following accounts of two news stories.

On Thursday 15 January 2009, an 81-year-old woman lay collapsed on a pavement in North London, having been seriously injured as a result of a mugging. Her injuries were so severe that, despite being taken to hospital, she died the next day. Prior to being helped to hospital, she lay on the pavement for ten minutes, calling for help, with people simply walking past. Witnesses reported that they thought the victim had collapsed because she was drunk, rather than having been the victim of a fatal attack.

In a separate incident occurring on 12 July 2009, a person who had collapsed and stopped breathing while competing in the Missoula Marathon immediately received help from two bystanders. One attended to the marathon runner, tilting his head back to open his airway, while the other got help from a Red Cross volunteer. The swift response of the two bystanders and the further help given by the Red Cross volunteer saved the man's life.

Thinking about these two incidents raises the question that research into prosocial behaviour tries to address: why is it that people engage in prosocial behaviour in some situations but not others? As you read through this chapter, try to ask, of each of the theories covered, to what extent does this explain why, as is shown by these two news stories, sometimes people help and sometimes they do not.

important questions regarding how both empathy and **altruism** are defined. First, with regard to empathy, one can understand – perhaps, empathise – that measuring what is taken to be an intra-psychic phenomenon such as empathy is fraught with difficulties. If one were to hand out a questionnaire, then, even if it did accurately measure the participants' empathy towards the 'victim', it would interrupt and quite likely distort the rest of the experiment – at the very least, participants would become very aware that they were in an experiment about empathy, which could in itself change their subsequent behaviour (perhaps this awareness would make them more empathic). If a questionnaire measuring empathy was completed by participants at the *end* of the experiment, then this might merely be completed in a way that is consistent with the prior behaviour. Both Festinger's (1958) cognitive dissonance theory and Bem's self-perception theory (discussed in Chapter 6) suggest that our perceptions of ourselves – which would encompass judgements about our feelings of altruism to a stranger – are shaped to be consistent with prior behaviour.

In Batson et al. (1983), a commonly used proxy for empathy was drawn on – that is, likely perceptions of similarity by giving participants a description of the confederate as someone similar to themselves. To test this, other participants were given descriptions of the confederate as *dissimilar* to them. This was to determine if the more similar they felt the other was to them, the more empathy they would feel.

It is worth considering some of the limitations of using perceived similarity as a proxy measure of empathy. When we think about empathy as being a crucial determinant of prosocial behaviour, we may well envisage helping as not just being limited to those others whom the helper perceives as similar to themselves. Indeed, we might think that some of the greatest acts of altruistic behaviour cut across divisions of gender, age, ethnicity and religious affiliation and seem all the more prosocial because of that.

So, what are we to make of an empathy measured only by perceived similarity? Is this exactly the same 'empathy', working in the same way, as that which is felt and expressed towards dissimilar others or are there two or more different types of empathy? Furthermore, it is possible to question whether the act of kindness towards another perceived as similar is best described as *empathy* – it might be considered as more closely allied to other perspectives on empathy, such as *ingroup favouritism* (where we are more likely to help those we perceive as belonging to groups that are important to us) or even *kin selection* (where we are thought to protect whoever most closely relates to our gene pool).

A second consideration arising from Batson et al.'s (1983) research is how the prosocial behaviour itself was operationalised in this experiment. Participants who were described as engaging in prosocial behaviour chose to swap places with the confederate and receive shocks instead of them. This does indeed sound like prosocial behaviour, at least until we consider the alternative. Those participants who were deemed *not* to have acted in a prosocial way preferred to end the experiment – a choice that meant neither they, nor the confederate, would receive electric shocks. In other words, the difference between the two choices is not whether or not the confederate would receive any more shocks – they would not in either case – but whether or not the participant would receive shocks so that the experiment could continue. Couched in these terms, the participants who elected to continue with the experiment by receiving shocks themselves seemed to be helping the *experimenter* more than the confederate (who would not receive shocks anyway). It is possible that the decision to continue with the experiment (by electing to receive shocks) is, in fact, a better measure of compliance with the *experiment* or, perhaps, obedience to the experimenter (see Chapter 10) than of behaviour designed to relieve the suffering of others.

Batson, Klein, Highberger and Shaw (1995) suggested that altruism may promote certain prosocial behaviours at the *expense* of others. Their experiment required participants to allocate other participants to either a positive reinforcement or a negative reinforcement condition in a work performance experiment – those in the positive condition received a raffle ticket for each 'correct' response; those in the negative condition received an electric shock for each 'incorrect' response. Needless to say, there were no other participants, no electric shocks and no raffle tickets. The question at stake was whether participants who were induced to feel empathetic to a participant that they had to allocate reinforcement to would show preferential treatment, placing them more consistently in the positive reinforcement condition than participants who were allocating reinforcement to those they were not induced to feel empathy for.

Altruisim The word altruism comes from Auguste Comte who distinguished 'altruism' from 'egotistic' helping. This distinction – which, as Batson (1991) and Dovidio et al. (2006) note, is still important today – raises three important issues for thinking about altruism. First, for many researchers, definitions of altruism emphasise the motivation or intent driving the 'helping' behaviour, second, the idea that altruisitic behaviour is driven by the intent to benefit others and, third, that altruistic helping can be contrasted with other (more selfishly driven) helping behaviour.

Batson et al. (1995) found that where empathy had been induced, then concern for the target of the empathy overrode considerations of being fair or even-handed and participants tended to allocate those they empathised with to the positive reinforcement condition. They suggested that empathy produces an altruistic motivation to help the target of the empathy, even if that comes at the expense of other types of prosocial response, such as being even-handed in their allocation decisions.

In the study, empathy was not presumed to be present by means of the manipulation of perceived similarity – as found in Batson et al. (1983). Instead, it was induced by perspective-taking instructions. Thus, participants in their 1995 study (and many related experiments) were required to 'imagine how [the target of the empathy] feels'. This approach arguably overcomes some of the limitations of using similarity as a presumed precondition of empathy and, thus, altruistic motivation – here at least the participant is being instructed to do something that seems consistent with an empathic stance towards the other. It raises another problem, however, which is that the experimental procedure may itself shape participants' behaviour – not through the presence or absence of underlying altruistic motivations, but by raising a sense of the expected or normative behaviour for the participant. That is, receiving instructions to think about how the other feels could steer participants towards preferential treatment as a sort of obedient interpretation of the instructions – or their perceived gist of them – rather than because they prompt any real psychological change, such as arousing empathy and, thus, an altruistic motivation.

Even the measure of prosocial behaviour can be questioned. Is the allocation of participants to positive or negative reinforcement conditions the same as deciding whether or not to swap places with someone receiving shocks (or to end the experiment by refusing to do so) and are these things really related to helping a stranger in an emergency? While we can argue that they are all instances of good, helpful prosocial behaviour, we should note that Batson et al. (1995) found that prosocial behaviour could take different, often contradictory, forms, which were brought about in different ways. Thus, the different forms of prosocial behaviour found in these and other experiments should not be presumed to be the same (and have a uniform cause).

Empathic joy

The empathy–altruism hypothesis model explained prosocial behaviour in terms of the helper's empathy for the person in need of help – the helper's attunement with the victim's feelings being a key aspect of the model.

In the empathic joy model, the helper is somewhat more concerned with the positive emotions – the joy – that making a positive difference to a person in need can bring about (see Figure 8.1b in Box 8.3). Smith, Keating and Stotland (1989) argue that helpers are motivated to help because doing so can provide us with the knowledge that we have had a positive impact on others and this knowledge leads us to experience positive emotions.

Think for a moment about any charity appeals that you can remember, perhaps on television or in some direct mailing. It is very likely that these emphasise not just the need of the people for whom help is sought (which would be sufficient as far as the empathy–altruism hypothesis is concerned) but also the impact that your donation can have. Indeed, many charity appeals will state what positive change can be brought about for a specific amount of money. These charity appeals are trying to make more concrete the positive difference that the act of giving can make, which, from the perspective of the empathic joy model, makes the act of giving more appealing.

Empirical support for the empathic joy model is derived from experiments in which participants who have the opportunity to know the positive impact of their actions have a greater propensity to engage in prosocial behaviour. Smith et al. (1989) conducted an experiment in which a female college student expressed that she might drop out of college because of her experience of isolation and distress. In common with most prosocial behaviour experiments, empathy was manipulated by describing the student as being either similar (empathy condition) or dissimilar (not empathy condition) to the participant. In terms of the empathy–altruism hypothesis, eliciting empathy (by describing the person as similar to the participant) should be enough to bring about prosocial behaviour on its own, but, for Smith et al., a second factor proved decisive – half of the participants were informed that they would receive feedback about what impact their advice had on the student; the other half were informed that they would not find out what happened to the student.

The decision to intervene and offer advice (prosocial behaviour) was found to occur where participants experienced *both* empathy (person in need of help perceived to be similar to the participant) *and* the promise of feedback about the outcome of their helping behaviour. In this way, empathy alone was understood as *necessary* but not *sufficient* to bring about prosocial behaviour – the opportunity to know the impact of the helpful behaviour was a necessary additional factor.

Earlier experiments that seemed to suggest empathy alone was sufficient to bring about prosocial behaviour

Box 8.3 FOCUS
Three models of motivation for prosocial behaviour

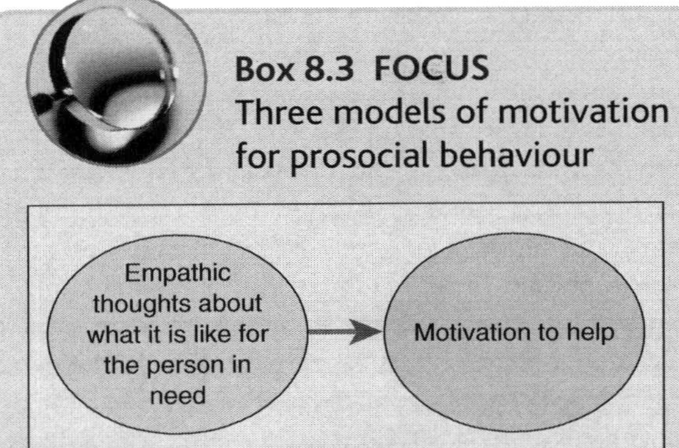

Figure 8.1a The empathy–altruism hypothesis

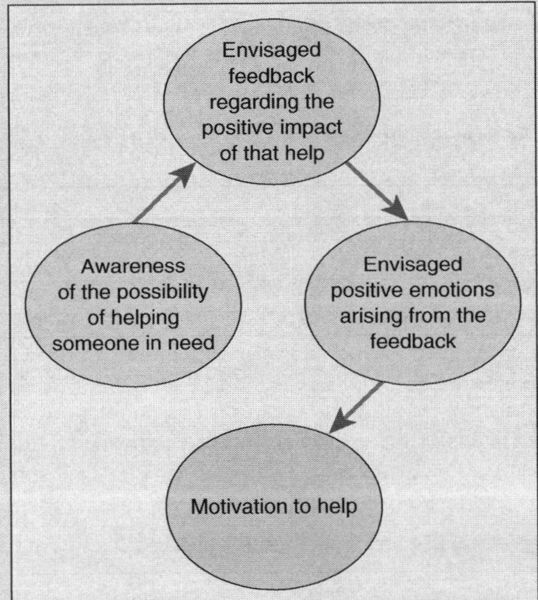

Figure 8.1b Empathic joy

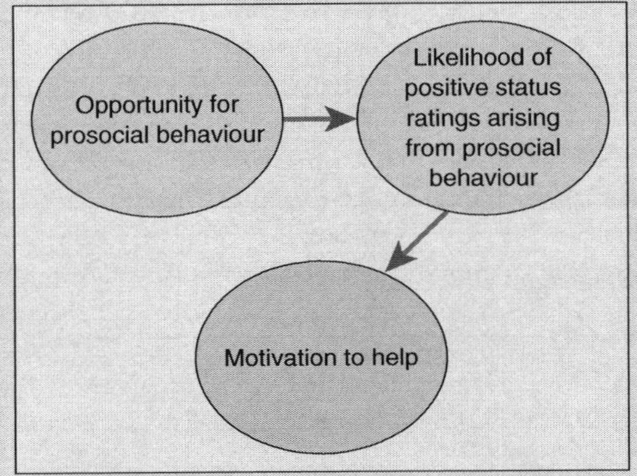

Figure 8.1c Competitive altruism

could – at least in some cases – be understood as providing the impression to participants that feedback about the positive impact of their helping would be given. For example, in Batson et al. (1983) described above, participants might well have anticipated that, by exchanging places with the person who was fearful about receiving electric shocks, they would meet the person and see the relief that their intervention had brought about. That is, the *prospect* of feedback about the positive impact of their helping could be seen as being present in Batson et al.'s (1983) experiment for all participants who contemplated helping, even though it was not identified as a separate variable. What Smith et al.'s (1989) experiment offers is a separation between the act of helping and the prospect of receiving feedback – allowing the discrete impacts of empathy *and* feedback to be measured.

Competitive altruism

An alternative model for why people are motivated to engage in prosocial behaviour focuses on neither empathy nor feedback about the impact of our helping. Instead, it emphasises the potential status associated with engaging in prosocial behaviour (see Figure 8.1c in Box 8.3).

It is easy to conjure pictures of celebrity 'givers' who, far from the widow secretly giving her mite, seem so public in their 'generosity' that one wonders whether they would be so generous and public-spirited *without* the presence of cameras. One parody of this can be found in Steve Coogan's *Knowing me – Knowing you*, in which a fictitious celebrity guest Keith Hunt – initially appeared reluctant as the host, Alan Partridge, asked him about a newspaper report of his generosity to a local charity. After the guest had described his generosity in some detail – adding 'You've got to put a little bit back' – Alan Partridge handed the newspaper article to the guest and thanked him for bringing it in.

The competitive altruism approach suggests that prosocial behaviour – especially if it is costly or difficult – can confer status on the person doing so and it is the prospect of accruing such status that motivates people to help. Support for this idea comes from two empirical findings – first, that those who enagage in prosocial behaviours (such as sharing money with others) receive higher status ratings from observers than those who appear to be less prosocial in their behaviour (for example, sharing less with others) and, second, the prospect of increased status motivates people to engage in prosocial behaviour.

Hardy and van Vugt (2006) conducted an experiment that provided some evidence for the idea that conspicuous prosocial acts confer status from others observing them. They examined whether people were rated more positively when participants rated the status of each other *after* they had made a decision about reward allocation (in which money given to them was to be shared between themselves and the group – comprising themselves and two other participants).

In the condition where participants did *not* know the reward allocations of those they had to judge, then the extent to which the person being judged shared their money (that is, what proportion of the money they chose to allocate to the group rather than themselves) had no bearing on status judgements made about that person. In the condition in which participants *did* know exactly how much each person had contributed to the group and to themselves, however, the status judgements were associated with the generosity of the individual being judged – the most generous being conferred the greatest status and the least generous the lowest status.

Flynn, Reagans, Amanatullah and Ames (2006) suggest that people who are high in self-monitoring (for example, being very attentive to situational requirements and able to alter their behaviour to fit these) can be particularly disposed to being net givers in exchange terms – that is, helping more than they receive help. Flynn et al. (2006, p. 1134) note that, while this could be seen as generous and displaying a commitment to the other person and the relationship with them, 'such generosity may not be entirely altruistic. Instead, high self-monitors may be making these investments in their exchange relations with an expectation of a valuable return – a position of elevated status among their peers'.

Acting in this way, the high self-monitors were not only perceived as more generous, but also conferred a higher status by others. Flynn et al. argue that the high self-monitors have acute status needs that they address by adapting their behaviour to be generous, which, in turn, confers the status they seek.

One potential limitation with Hardy and van Vugt's (2006) study is that it required judgements of others to be made in situations where there was a paucity of information – complete strangers, about whom almost nothing was known, had to be rated. In this somewhat strange experimental situation, the one thing that was known in one of the conditions was the extent to which these strangers had chosen to allocate money to themselves or to the group. It could be argued that the experiment not only created a very unusual situation – where all we know about others we are asked to judge is their giving behaviour – but, also, this unusual situation directly shaped the results. That is, perhaps in situations where there is only one bit of information about others whom we are required to judge, that bit of information will be heavily relied on for the purpose of the judgement. In Hardy and van Vugt's experiment, as giving behaviour was the only thing that was known about the fellow participants, that giving behaviour was heavily influential in the status judgements that were made. Arguably, what Hardy and van Vugt's experiment does not illuminate is how important prosocial behaviour is in status judgements *where other potentially relevant information is available*. Additionally, in their experiment it should be noted that the type of prosocial behaviour involved was not just some neutral, good act – it was prosocial behaviour that directly benefited the people making the status judgement. It is possible that very different types of prosocial behaviour (including those that do *not* benefit the people making the status judgement) might have a different impact on status judgements made by others.

Psychological state and prosocial behaviour

While the research above has considered differing hypothesised motivations for engaging in prosocial behaviour, the research below focuses on mood and arousal. Here, what may appear to be contradictory research findings are discussed – they appear to support both the idea that positive mood is associated with **helping** behaviour *and* the seemingly opposite idea that bad moods are more associated with helping behaviour. The third state to be considered – 'arousal' – has been particularly important in thinking about prosocial behaviour and is returned to at different points throughout the chapter.

Current mood

Think of the last time that you engaged in prosocial behaviour by helping out a stranger – perhaps you gave money to someone or helped someone who was struggling with a heavy suitcase. Were you in a happy or sad mood prior to offering help? If you were in a happy mood, then you may be interested to know that research has supported the idea that being in a positive mood can increase the likelihood of engaging in prosocial behaviour (see Figure 8.2a in Box 8.4). You may be equally interested to know that research has also supported the

Helping Could be understood as, 'an action that has the consequence of providing some benefit to or improving the well-being of another person. The definition of helping is not particularly stringent; as long as the well-being of one or more people is improved by the actions of another' (Dovidio et al., 2006, p. 22).

Box 8.4 FOCUS
Positive and negative moods and prosocial behaviour

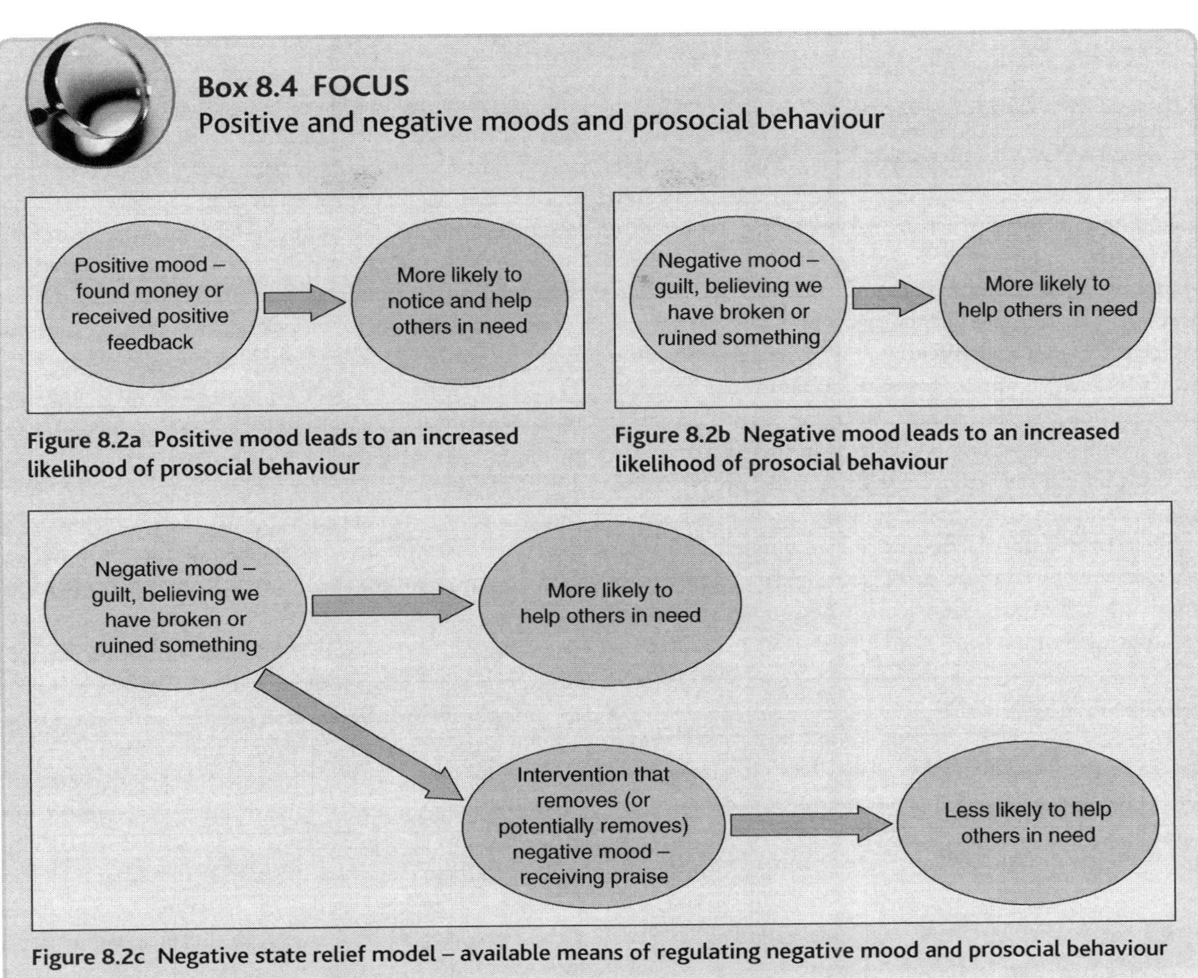

Figure 8.2a Positive mood leads to an increased likelihood of prosocial behaviour

Figure 8.2b Negative mood leads to an increased likelihood of prosocial behaviour

Figure 8.2c Negative state relief model – available means of regulating negative mood and prosocial behaviour

exact *opposite* finding, suggesting that being in a negative mood is *also* associated with an increased likelihood of engaging in prosocial behaviour (see Figures 8.2b and c in Box 8.4).

Positive moods

Experiments examining the effects of positive mood on helping have attempted to induce the required mood in participants by means of a variety of procedures. Allowing participants to 'find' money in a phone box, infusing the surroundings with the aroma of fresh coffee and biscuits and giving participants positive feedback about their performance on a prior task – have all been used to induce a positive mood in participants. After exposing them to such stimuli that are presumed to give rise to a positive mood, the participants' behaviour is then observed in more or less 'staged' scenarios. These are situations that the experimenter creates by arranging objects and people (confederates) in the surrounding environment to make a specific course of prosocial behaviour relevant. This might be to leave a stamped addressed envelope lying on the floor, or have a confederate drop something, or obviously struggle in some way. Participants who found money in a phone box were observed to be more likely to pick up and post a 'lost letter' that happened to be lying nearby (Levin & Isen, 1975). Participants who were exposed to the aroma of coffee and biscuits were more likely to pick up a dropped pen for a passing stranger who just happened to drop it (Baron, 1997). Finally, participants receiving positive feedback regarding task performance were found to notice and respond to a passing female who was carrying so much that she struggled with the door (McMillen, Sanders, & Solomon, 1977).

This last finding is worth reflecting on for a moment, as McMillen et al. (1977) suggest that there is not just an association between good mood and helping behaviour – but also a mechanism by which a good mood can *prompt* prosocial behaviour. Specifically, they argue that, when people are in a good mood, they are more attentive to their environment and it is this *attentiveness* that increases the likelihood of them engaging in prosocial behaviour.

It is quite easy to imagine someone in a terrible mood being so preoccupied with whatever is upsetting them that they are relatively inattentive to the environment – including people in the environment who may need help. In one study, McMillen et al. (1977) found that participants in a good mood (those who were given positive feedback regarding performance on an earlier task) were quicker to show signs of noticing white noise that the experimenters gradually introduced than those in a bad mood (those who were given negative feedback). They also found – using the same method for mood manipulation – that the majority of participants in a good mood noticed and helped a female (confederate) who was struggling to open a door because of the amount of things she was carrying. By contrast, participants in a bad mood typically only helped the confederate when she made a noise to attract their attention.

Negative moods

One problem with the idea that good moods can evoke 'good' or prosocial behaviour is that bad moods seem to do so, too (see Figures 8.2b and c in Box 8.4).

Regan, Williams and Sparling (1972) conducted an experiment in a shopping mall in which a confederate asked strangers if they would take a photograph of him using his camera. Each unfortunate participant had the experience of the camera appearing to break in their hands as they touched it. Half of the participants were reassured by the confederate that it was not their fault and the other half were made to feel that it actually *was* their fault. It is easy to imagine that if we were the naive participant who had apparently just broken a stranger's camera (the confederate), we might feel a degree of guilt about it. Subsequently, in the same shopping mall, the participant comes across someone whose groceries are falling out of their bag (another confederate). Who do you think is more likely to help – the ones who feel heightened guilt about the camera breaking or the ones who were not made to feel that it was their fault?

As you might have deduced – it was the ones who were made to feel that is *was* their fault – who presumably felt more guilt – who were found to engage in a spontaneous act of prosocial behaviour by helping the person with their shopping. In fact, 55 per cent of the participants who were made to feel that the camera breaking was their fault stopped to help with the subsequent falling shopping, whereas, among those who were *not* made to feel responsible, the figure was 15 per cent.

Dovidio et al. (2006) note that, in recent times, the somewhat crude distinction between positive and negative emotions has become more nuanced, with the emphasis being on 'differentiated emotion' – that is, a concern with the specific *type* of emotion rather than the crude categories of positive and negative. From this perspective, prosocial behaviour may be more readily associated with *some* negative states – perhaps guilt and sadness – than others, such as anger or disgust.

One of the most developed models linking negative affect to prosocial behaviour is the *negative state relief model* (see Figure 8.2c in Box 8.4). If we witness someone being harmed, we might feel sad; if we feel responsible for the harm, we may feel guilt. Either of these negative states will – according to the negative state relief model – motivate us to reduce the unpleasant negativity. We are motivated to engage in prosocial behaviour, then, because we believe that doing so will give us relief from our negative mood.

According to the model, negative emotions will not *always* give rise to prosocial behaviour – we may not have an opportunity for prosocial behaviour while experiencing the negative state, have some other mood restorer or come to believe that the prosocial act available to us will not restore our mood. Thus, Cialdini, Darby and Vincent (1973) found that participants who were induced into guilt or sadness (by being made to believe that they had ruined someone's thesis data or watching someone else do so) were less likely to engage in prosocial behaviour if they experienced praise prior to an opportunity to engage in prosocial behaviour. The praise they received was understood by Cialdini et al. to restore the participants' mood and, with the negative state removed (through praise), the motivation to engage in prosocial behaviour to get rid of the negative affect was no longer present. Those who did *not* receive praise showed a significantly higher propensity to engage in prosocial behaviour.

The issue that both positive *and* negative emotional states (if we can use such crude terms) seem able to cause an increase in prosocial behaviour was partly addressed in the work of Manucia, Baumann and Cialdini (1984). They put participants through procedures to induce a sad mood (they were asked to reminisce about two memories of experiences that made them feel sad), happy mood (the reminiscences focused on two happy memories) or neutral mood (no mood induction procedure was used). All of the participants were given a placebo they called 'Mnemoxine', which was presented to them as a memory-enhancing drug. Half were told that it had the side-effect of enhancing whatever mood the participant was *already* in, the other half were not. The measure of the dependent variable – prosocial behaviour – was the number of phone calls that the participants volunteered to make on behalf of a charitable blood donor organisation. When compared to the neutral mood condition, the happy mood led to higher levels of prosocial behaviour – this was true whether they believed that Mnemoxine would make their mood stay the same or not. In the negative mood state, a more complex picture emerged.

Participants who were in the negative mood condition only engaged in higher levels of prosocial behaviour (compared to the neutral condition) *if they believed that their mood could change*. If participants in the negative mood condition were told that their mood was 'fixed' by the Mnemoxine (that is, they believed that prosocial behaviour would not change the negative mood), then they did not engage in higher levels of prosocial behaviour.

Manucia et al. (1984) therefore argue that positive emotions promote prosocial behaviour as a side-effect – people do not engage in it to extend their positive emotions (if they did, then being told that their good mood was fixed by Mnemoxine should have meant they would be less motivated to engage in prosocial behaviour). By contrast, negative emotions prompt action to remove them – prosocial behaviour being one option. If, however, the person in the negative mood really believes that prosocial behaviour will *not* make them feel any better (because Mnemoxine has fixed their emotions), then they are less likely to engage in it.

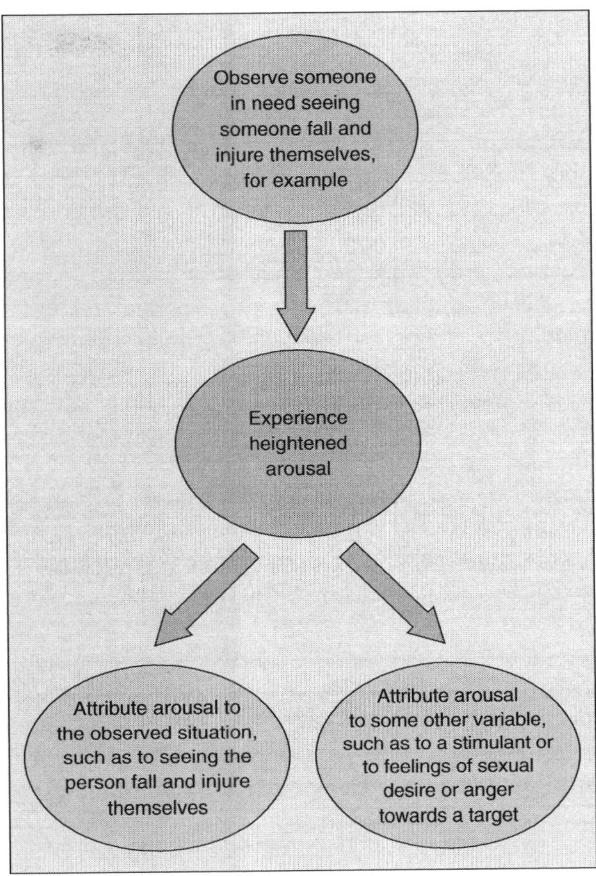

Figure 8.3 Attribution of arousal and prosocial behaviour

Arousal and prosocial behaviour

A different stance with regard to the link between emotion and prosocial behaviour is found in the work of Piliavin, Dovidio, Gaertner and Clark (1981). They move away from a direct interest in positive or negative emotion to consider how witnessing someone in need of our help may affect us. Watching someone else suffer or in need of help often results in the observer experiencing something at a physiological level. Piliavin et al. refer to this basic heightened physiological and emotional experience as *arousal* – this may mirror the pain that the other is feeling. Piliavin et al.'s (1981) *arousal: cost–reward model* is returned to later on in this chapter when considering arousal and decision making in prosocial behaviour, but, for now, the importance of arousal and the way in which the arousal is thought about will be addressed (see Figure 8.3).

Vaughan and Lanzetta (1980) suggest that when watching others receive apparently painful electric shocks, observers will often display heightened arousal and mirror the facial expressions of the person apparently receiving the shocks (as you may have guessed, no one was actually hurt in their experiment). These intriguing findings relate somewhat to work on mirror neurons (Di Pellegrino, Fadiga, Fogassi, Gallese, & Rizzolatti, 1992; Fabbri-Destro & Rizzolatti, 2008; Gallese, Keysers, & Rizzolatti, 2004) which suggests that an observer watching someone undertake an action, or experience something physically, can cause neuron activity in the observer that is similar to what they would experience had they had the physical experience or undertaken the action being observed themselves.

Gaertner and Dovidio (1977) used a placebo pill that they presented (remarkably) as being capable of enhancing participants' ability to receive ESP messages! Half of the participants were informed that the pill would arouse them, the other half were not. Lo and behold, an opportunity for prosocial behaviour presented itself. Out of the blue, they heard something that sounded like a possible emergency involving another participant. Here, then, was an opportunity to help, but – assuming that they believed what they had been told about the placebo – half of the participants might be inclined to attribute their heightened arousal to the pill they had taken, the other half to the overheard situation.

Gaertner and Dovidio found that how participants attributed their arousal was crucial in shaping whether they intervened or not. In the condition where participants were likely to attribute their arousal to some other cause (the placebo) than the possible emergency they overheard, then they were slower and less likely to help (55 per cent eventually responding). If, by contrast, participants attributed the arousal to the overheard event, they were faster and more likely to help (85 per cent responding). Similarly, if people are aroused by something other than the emergency that they witness – yet attribute their arousal to that emergency – then they are more likely to help.

As will be seen below in the discussion of the arousal: cost–reward model, Piliavin et al. (1981) suggest that arousal (and how that arousal is understood by **bystanders**) influences the likelihood of their engaging in prosocial behaviour. Rather than instantly triggering prosocial behaviour, however, the arousal, and its interpretation, is presented as typically giving rise to the bystander's calculation of the rewards and costs of intervening. Thus, if I attribute my arousal to some event I have witnessed that presents an opportunity for prosocial behaviour, then I am more likely to intervene (than if I did not experience arousal or did not attribute it to the event), but I will usually first engage in some form of weighing up the costs and rewards of helping. This cost–reward analysis is discussed below, but, for now, it can be noted that Piliavin et al. (1981) accept that witnessing events inviting prosocial behaviour (such as accidents) can cause such high levels of arousal and acute awareness of the benefits of helping (for example, saving a life), that they may spur people to help without considering the costs.

Critical recap

Why do people engage in prosocial behaviour?

1 These approaches treat emotions or motivations as intrapsychic first causes – that is, prosocial behaviour is seen as driven by what is going on in the mind of the bystander with relatively little attention to the situation or how that is perceived by the bystander. This lack of attention to how the situation – or its perception – may shape behaviour leaves on one side a key emphasis in much of social psychology.

2 Researchers who are interested in the inner motives for prosocial behaviour or the psychological state of bystanders, need to find ways around the fact that such psychological variables are not available for psychologists to simply inspect. This obvious point leads to procedures being used that seek to define, create and measure (operationalise) these psychological variables through the experimental procedure. It is possible to question whether the experiments have successfully created the motivations, or the moods, that they seek to investigate.

3 As will be discussed in Section 8.5, it is possible to question not just how the independent variable (the motivation or psychological state) has been operationalised in the experiment, but also what participant behaviour is taken to be 'prosocial' behaviour in the various experiments we have reviewed.

Reflective questions

1 *What is the first example of prosocial behaviour that comes to mind if you had to think of one? What is it that makes this 'prosocial'? What sort of factors explain why 'prosocial' behaviour was present in this case?*

2 *What factors – other than motivation and psychological state – could be important in determining whether or not someone engages in prosocial behaviour?*

8.2 Evolutionary perspectives on prosocial behaviour

As is seen elsewhere in this text (particularly Chapters 3 and 9), the development of evolutionary psychology has had an influence on several areas of social psychology. Here, some of the main evolutionary perspectives regarding prosocial behaviour are outlined – kin selection theory, reciprocal altruism and group selection theory – but, first, it is worth briefly touching on the overarching framework of evolutionary theory itself.

Evolutionary theory

Evolutionary theory has had a somewhat mixed relationship with the notion of altruism and prosocial behaviour

Bystander Here, bystander is used to refer to anyone who could be considered to be aware of another person in need of any form of helping intervention. Thus, if you observe someone collapsed on a train, struggling with a heavy load or searching for something they have lost, you could be defined as a bystander, whether you know them or not, and whether you help them or not.

in general. In its original form – as found in the work of both Darwin and Wallace – the concept of 'survival of the fittest' seemed diametrically opposed to any form of prosocial behaviour at all, especially altruism. The notion of the survival of the fittest was a means of capturing the idea that those animals best able to successfully compete for food, shelter and mating rights have a higher chance of survival and, therefore an increased opportunity to produce offspring. This suggested that there was a basic evolution-based drive for each animal to strive for their own individual supremacy. If we think back to the definitions of prosocial, helping and altruism considered above in the light of this, it is hard to imagine any evolutionary basis for these behaviours.

The problem with these benevolent behaviours is twofold: first, they seem to involve the opposite of the individual's struggle for supremacy and, second, any genes that might be linked to such behaviour should be less likely to be passed on (as it is the self-serving 'fittest', not the self-sacrificing altruist, who gets the opportunity to have offspring). An evolutionary account of prosocial behaviour, then, needs to provide a way of understanding how such behaviour is functional in evolutionary terms (for example, how it increase the chances of survival and/or genetically related offspring) and how the gene providing the impulse for this behaviour is transmitted to subsequent generations within the species.

Some evolutionary perspectives have attempted to define prosocial behaviour as rather more self-serving than it might at first appear. For Ghiselin (1974, p. 247, cited in Dovidio et al., 2006, p. 40), prosocial behaviour will only occur if it is in the organism's immediate self-interest: 'Where it is in his own interest, every organism may reasonably be expected to aid his fellows ... Yet given a full chance to act in his own interest, nothing but expediency will restrain him from brutalizing, from maiming, from murdering.' In this way, whenever prosocial or helping behaviour occurs, it is *not* altruistic and always driven primarily by the organism's concern with their own individual advancement. A major breakthrough in evolutionary approaches to prosocial behaviour came when the emphasis shifted from the individual organism to the idea of the gene pool.

The idea of individual 'fitness' (or capacity for survival) was replaced by what Hamilton (1964) referred to as 'inclusive fitness' – that is, the successful transmission of copies of the individual's genes to the next generation. This shift meant that the driving mechanism of evolution was not thought of in terms of the struggle for the survival of the individual (whether human or other organism) – instead, it came to be understood as the drive to protect the individual's genes. In other words, rather than the organism being driven by a desperate need for their own survival, we can see that the more fundamental drive is to maximise the chances of their genes (or copies of their genes) being passed on.

Thinking this through in human terms, it is easy to see how – much like the earlier concept of 'survival of the fittest' – the drive to pass on copies of our genes could mean seeking our own survival at the expense of others'. Thus, extremely non-prosocial behaviour, such as killing someone who is perceived as a danger to us or likely to take our opposite-sex sexual partner from us, could be understood as protecting our chances of directly passing on copies of our genes through procreation. Perhaps somewhat counter-intuitively, however, the drive to pass on copies of our own genes can also account for prosocial behaviour – even if, in some instances, that behaviour means sacrificing our own lives. The most obvious example of this is parents risking their lives to save their offspring. Donating organs, diving into a dangerous river, stepping into the middle of a confrontation – these 'heroic' acts make good biological sense if we consider that the parents are putting themselves at risk to maximise the possibility of copies of their genes being passed on through their children. Some of the evidence for this propensity to help relatives (among humans and other animals) is considered next in the discussion concerning kin selection theory. The question as to if and how evolutionary theory might account for helping non-relatives is considered in the discussions of reciprocal altruism and group selection theory that follow it (see Figures 8.4a, 8.4b and 8.4c in Box 8.5).

Kin selection theory

Suppose one night you are just sitting down watching another repeat of *Friends* when you receive two successive texts – both asking for you to come as soon as you can to visit the person texting you in hospital. Let us further imagine that both have a similar severity of illness and that you need to make a choice – you do not have the opportunity to visit both. Now, the crucial bit, one of the people asking you to visit them in hospital is a close relative, the other is a friend. Who would you visit? What if the two texts revealed a different situation and there was the possibility that their lives were in danger if you did not help – who would you choose to help?

It may be difficult to work through these abstract examples – especially when we may be keen to know more details, such as what the specific needs are and what impact our help is likely to have. Nonetheless, from the perspective of **kin selection theory**, all other things being equal, we are predisposed to help our close relatives because they are more genetically similar to ourselves (see Figure 8.4a). Helping our offspring is obviously an immediate way of ensuring that copies of our genes are passed on (which, incidentally, would account for people being willing to help their opposite-sex, sexual partner), but there is significant gene similarity with other close relatives. Kin selection theory suggests that prosocial behaviour will typically be directed towards those who are most closely related to us because, by helping them – especially if our help saves their lives and increases the opportunities for them to have offspring – we are ensuring common genes between us and them are passed on.

Studies of non-human animal species have lent some support to kin selection theory. Thus, as Curry (1988) notes, mockingbirds have been found to show a preference for feeding close relative nestlings – even if they are not direct offspring – over unrelated nestlings. Similarly, Sherman (1985) found that squirrels were much more likely to warn relatives of impending predator threats than they were to warn unrelated squirrels. As Dovidio et al. (2006) note, Sherman (1981) also found that female squirrels were more likely to cooperate in chasing away animals entering another squirrel's territory when the squirrel in need of help was a close relative. These cooperative defences were found to be most likely where the genetic link was strongest (mother, daughter, followed by sisters) and least common where the genetic link was weaker (cousins and non-kin). Studies of non-human species, then, suggest that not only will parents direct prosocial behaviour at direct offspring but they will also be prosocial towards close relatives and the closer (or more genetically similar) the relative is, the greater the likelihood of them being a target of prosocial behaviour.

Burnstein, Crandall and Kitayama (1994) suggested that some similar hierarchy of preference was at work in humans also. They presented participants in Japan and the United States with dilemmas, some of which were similar to the example of receiving two texts considered above. Participants had to choose who to help (close relative, distant relative, non-relative) in everyday and life or death scenarios.

Participants in both the USA and Japan reported that (especially in life or death situations) they would be most likely to help close relatives (such as siblings), then more distant relatives (such as cousins) and, finally, non-relatives. It is worth reflecting for a moment on the fact that, rather than revealing cross-cultural differences (which many studies of US and Japanese participants do), in this study, both the US and Japanese participants revealed the same preference for helping close relatives, suggesting that these prosocial preferences were not simply derived from culturally specific norms.

Burnstein et al. also sought to test the kin selection theory idea that we are less likely to help relatives who are unlikely to produce offspring. Relatives – even close relatives – who were beyond the age when they were likely to have children – were found to be less likely to receive help in life or death situations than younger relatives. This, potentially at least, provides further evidence for kin selection theory – if our helping *is* driven by the transmission of shared genes, then a relative who is extremely unlikely to reproduce (such as a post-menopausal female) should be a less genetically beneficial target for help in a life or death situation than someone who is likely to reproduce.

It might be worth just staying with that last finding for a moment. If, as Burnstein et al. suggest, we have a greater propensity to help close relatives who are more likely to reproduce than those who are not, then we should have a sex preference when it comes to helping elderly relatives. In order to grasp this point, it is worth noting the biological fact that (notwithstanding medical breakthroughs), while both men and women experience a decline in fertility as they age, men can continue to reproduce beyond the age at which most women experience the menopause. Because this is widely known, it should inform calculations that are entirely concerned with the likelihood of transmitting shared genes. Thus, we might expect that this would mean we would be more likely to help our fathers (in life or death situations) than our post-menopausal mothers because – potentially at least – our fathers have a higher likelihood of further transmitting our shared genes through future reproduction. Indeed, we could push the example further and suggest that, according to this interpretation of kin selection theory, we should be more likely to help our elderly uncle than either our post-menopausal mother or our young sister who has had a hysterectomy (unless we believe that advances in medical science may reverse the effects of this in the future).

It is perhaps fair to mention that some versions of kin selection theory suggest that men and women differ in parental certainty – men rather than women may be found to doubt whether a child is really theirs or

Kin selection theory An account of prosocial behaviour that is consistent with evolutionary theory. Kin selection theory suggests that we will show a preference for helping those who are most closely genetically related to us and, thereby, increase the likelihood of our common genes being passed on.

not – and this could, perhaps, reduce the preference for helping male relatives (as there might be less certainty that any children he 'has' are his). Nonetheless, the examples above do perhaps raise a query about whether the preference for helping younger relatives is really solely – or even primarily – concerned with the likelihood of passing on shared genes. If that is our chief concern in life or death helping, then we really should find we choose not just the young, but also those relatives who are able to reproduce – older males rather than older females, those who are reproductively intact rather than those who are not – even if they are more distantly related.

If these preferences are not evident, then it may be that the reported preference for helping younger relatives is not simply due to their perceived reproductive potential but may also be influenced by other factors, such as a Millsian calculation of the good achieved by helping someone who has many years to live compared to someone much closer to death, or a cultural norm linked to that or a response bias to reporting such accountable preferences.

In this way, kin selection theory may rightly identify that we are predisposed to offer help (especially in an emergency situation) to those to whom we are most closely related and it arguably offers a plausible explanation for this predisposition. It could be argued, however, that evidence for the idea we are more inclined to help those who have the greatest probability of passing on our shared genes (due to their reproductive 'fitness') is a little less clear-cut and, perhaps, open to alternative interpretations.

Reciprocal altruism

While kin selection theory provides an account of why animals (including humans) might help their relatives, it does not directly explain help that is directed to non-relatives.

Reciprocal altruism – a term coined by Trivers (1971) – provides an evolutionary rationale for helping that extends beyond those who happen to share some of our genes by suggesting it is adaptive to help *if the helping is likely to be reciprocated* (see Figure 8.4b). Although the term 'altruism' is used, it should be noted that this theory does not suggest there is a 'selfless' motivation behind the action – instead, the focus is on those actions which can be considered to serve the survival of the altruist's gene pool.

Some vivid examples of this are found in large animal groupings, where animals may take turns to help one another. Meerkats on sentry (or look-out) duty are doing something prosocial for the *group*, not just relatives, by checking for predators. Because this act is reciprocated, however, – other meerkats will take turns to be on look-out – the entire group benefits from an increased chance of survival by being warned of any imminent predator threat. Dovidio et al. (2006) note a similar example with emperor penguins. Thousands of penguins are found to huddle together, taking turns to shield the rest of the group from the freezing Antarctic weather.

Reciprocal altruism, then, suggests that such helping is driven by a genetic tendency – that it is beneficial to the groups of animals who engage in it and, because it benefits them, the gene prompting this behaviour is passed on to subsequent generations.

One potential problem for the theory of reciprocal altruism is, as Cosmides and Tooby (1992) note, that (especially with human altruism), when help is given, it is not always instantly reciprocated. Think for a moment of the last altruistic act that you did – perhaps helping someone carry a pushchair up some stairs or giving some money to a good cause. It is unlikely that these acts received some immediate reciprocity of the sort that meerkats and emperor penguins experience. Rothstein and Pierotti (1988) suggest earlier forms of prosocial behaviour that *did* gain immediate reciprocity may have evolved first and then more complex forms (with delayed reciprocity) may have developed from that.

As Dovidio et al. (2006) note, Moore's (1994) notion of emotionally connected behaviours could be at work – that is, if certain altruistic behaviours are unequivocally helpful to the animal engaging in them, then positive emotions might be experienced when engaging in those behaviours and also in associated behaviours. Thus, the genetic tendency to help in cases where that help will be immediately reciprocated could lead to positive emotions for this behaviour, which could generalise to other forms of prosocial behaviour.

The idea that reciprocal altruism is often delayed in human interactions also has an implication for how we judge who is likely to reciprocate our altruism. That is, we may at times need to judge who really will repay our altruism and who will cheat us. Buss (2004, p. 64, cited in Dovidio et al., 2006, p. 51), in line with experimental findings by Cosmides and Tooby (1992), argues that humans have evolved 'psychological mechanisms specifically designed to detect cheaters'. Some, such as Cheng

Reciprocal altruism An account of prosocial behaviour that is consistent with evolutionary theory. Reciprocal altruism suggests that people engage in altruistic behaviour because it increases the likelihood of themselves receiving help at some point.

and Holyoak (1989), agree that the human mind has this capacity, but doubt such complex thought processes can be accounted for solely in terms of evolutionary processes.

From the perspective of reciprocal altruism, it is not enough that humans can spot those who might cheat them by refusing to reciprocate. For it to work as a biologically beneficial behaviour, reciprocity needs to be a widely held value – there needs to be evidence of a strong norm for fair play and reciprocity and sanctions against those who cheat. Anecdotally, it is easy to see evidence for some such norm. Think for a moment about any reality television programmes you have watched – who are the people who have aroused most audience hostility? What did they do to become so unpopular? It is quite likely that cheating and/or hypocrisy were at work – or perceived as being at work – with these unpopular contestants.

This is not just some quirk of reality television, though. In the UK during the summer of 2009, the media were full of news about UK MPs 'cheating' on their expenses claims. The public reaction was one of outrage and it prompted dramatic actions on the part of all of the main party leaders and the first resignation of the then speaker of the House of Commons in hundreds of years. Those who – rightly or wrongly – are perceived as cheating, or as being hypocritical, often evoke negative reactions from the public (sometimes evidenced in being booed, jeered and heckled). Indeed, de Quervain, Fischbacher, Treyer, Schellhammer, Schnyder, Buck and Fehr (2004) found neuropsychological evidence for pleasure among participants who watched a cheater being punished.

People who appear to cheat others or present a false face to them are potentially problematic for the success of reciprocal altruism as an adaptive behaviour because, if we help them, we may not benefit as they may fail to reciprocate. The negative reaction that apparent cheating or hypocritical behaviour receives could be seen as evidence for a norm for reciprocity. While some see this norm as culturally derived, for others it is understood as being genetic and having an evolutionary basis, enabling certain types of helping behaviours to operate in an environment where they will be reciprocated and, therefore, allowing a biological benefit for both recipients and helpers.

Group selection theory

The final evolutionary theory to be considered here is **group selection** theory (see Figure 8.4c). Proponents of this theory argue that groups containing a higher proportion of altruistic group members should benefit and therefore survive better than those groups solely comprised of selfish members. Given that having altruistic members gives an important survival and procreational advantage to some groups, the 'altruistic' groups should benefit at the expense of more selfish groups, leading to an increase in groups including at least some altruistic members.

This perspective, then, suggests that altruistic behaviour can be directed towards members of a group and, because this benefits the group, the group may have an evolutionary advantage, leading to subsequent generations in which altruists are present in groups. As Dovidio et al. (2006) note, proponents of group selection theory now argue that it can fit alongside more individual perspectives (such as kin selection theory and reciprocal altruism) as part of what McAndrew (2002) calls a 'multilevel-selection theory'.

Whether or not evolutionary selection can operate at a group level is open to some debate, as Dovidio et al. (2006) note. One potential problem could be that genes are transmitted, typically, through a single male and female procreating and this dyadic procreation does not allow for some collective 'group gene' to be passed on. Thus, if an altruistic group member sacrificed his or her opportunities for mating as an altruistic act to benefit the group, then that specific altruistic gene is less likely to be passed on, even though it is present within the group.

In this way, group selection theory does usefully highlight that altruistic members can benefit a group, increasing its chances of survival, but it perhaps has more difficulty in accounting for *how altruistic genes of individuals within a group may be passed on*. Notwithstanding debates about the extent to which group selection may take place, group selection theory does usefully highlight an issue that will be returned to later in this chapter (and in Chapter 9), which is, human behaviour often appears to be shaped by group membership considerations. That is, we are perhaps more likely to help common group members (ingroup members) than members of other groups (outgroup members) and – according to group selection theory – there are important benefits in terms of survival arising from this. Box 8.5 summarises the above three evolutionary models of prosocial behaviour.

Group selection An account of prosocial behaviour that is consistent with evolutionary theory. Group selection suggests that, because altruistic behaviour increases the probability of survival for groups where it is found, those groups where it is present are more likely to successfully pass on their pool of genes (including genes associated with altruistic behaviour).

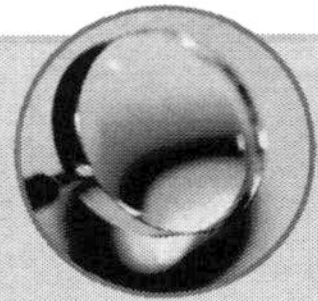

Box 8.5 FOCUS
Three models of evolutionary perspectives on prosocial behaviour

Kin selection theory

Kin selection theory draws attention to the ways in which the choice of target to be helped is consistent with the helper's self-interest (in evolutionary terms). Specifically, it suggests that we will show a preference for helping those who are most closely genetically related to us and, thereby, increase the likelihood of our common genes being passed on.

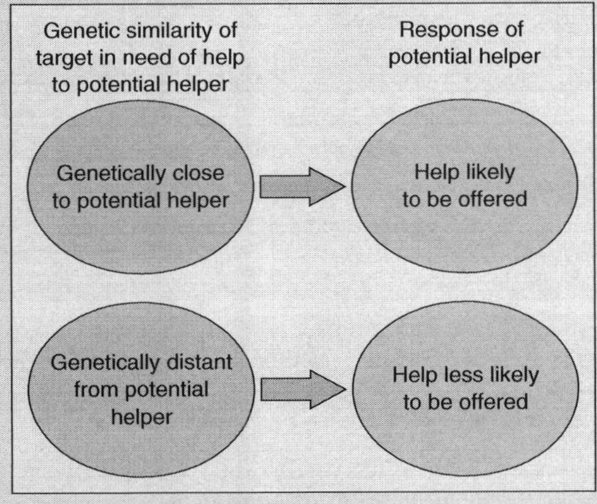

Figure 8.4a Kin selection theory

Reciprocal altruism

Reciprocal altruism explains altruistic behaviour as being offered because, by doing so, it is more likely to be reciprocated. Because of norms of reciprocity, through the act of helping, the helper increases the likelihood of themselves receiving help at some point.

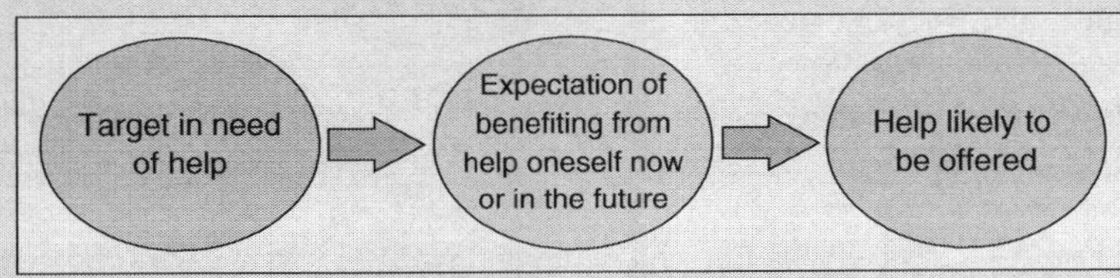

Figure 8.4b Reciprocal altruism

Group selection

Group selection provides an account of how the gene for altruistic behaviour is likely to be passed on. This theory suggests that, because altruistic behaviour increases the probability of survival for groups where it is found, those groups where it is present are more likely to successfully pass on their pool of genes (including genes associated with altruistic behaviour).

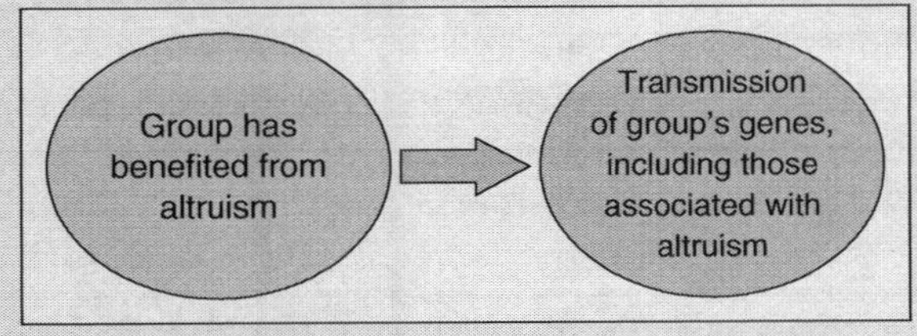

Figure 8.4c Group selection

Critical recap

Evolutionary perspectives on prosocial behaviour

1 It is possible to question evolutionary theories regarding how well they account for help given beyond those who might be identified as tied by bonds of kith and kinship.

2 Evolutionary theories arguably provide some explanation for why people might be more willing to help those with whom they share a large percentage of genes than those with whom they do not. They can each be challenged, however, regarding the extent to which they explain different propenstities to help *within* any category of genetic 'closeness' – for example, why are complete strangers sometimes helped and sometimes not, even though they are equally unrelated to the helper? Evolutionary theories can be challenged regarding whether they provide an account of the very diverse forms of prosocial behaviour or are more applicable to instances where questions of survival are at stake.

3 A number of the studies in this area make use of questionnaires rather than observed actual behaviour. This, then, relies on participants reporting what they have done or would do in various helping scenarios, which raises issues concerning how these reported behaviours or predicted, hypothetical future behaviours relate to predictable propensities to help.

Reflective questions

1. *Are you aware of differences in whom you would select to help in an emergency – where a choice had to be made? Do the evolutionary approaches considered here provide a means of understanding those preferences, in terms of who you would prioritise for help?*
2. *What are the problems with questionnaire-based research designed to identify such choices regarding whom to help?*

8.3 When do people help?

The research considered above focused in different ways on the factors within the person that could shape whether or not helping behaviour might take place. Here, attention shifts to factors in the situation that may be important. Three different approaches to addressing this issue are considered here.

The first approach is the big one – the diffusion of responsibility model developed by Darley and Latané (1968); (see Figure 8.5). This highly influential model broadly suggests that whether or not a person chooses to engage in prosocial behaviour – particularly helping a stranger in an emergency – will depend on whether or not they perceive that others could help instead of them. In situations where the potential helper perceives that there are others who could help, they are less likely to do so themselves.

This research was partly inspired by press coverage concerning a young woman who appeared to be murdered as neighbours looked on without offering help or calling the police. In reviewing the diffusion of responsibility model, some attention is given to the recent evidence that questions how this case has come to be understood. Some attention is also given to Piliavin, Rodin and Piliavin's (1969) research, which develops an alternative understanding of when people help and also serves to refocus attention to aspects of Darley and Latane's work that have been neglected.

A second area of research covered here concerns attributions that the potential helper makes concerning the victim's plight (see Figure 8.6). A particularly important consideration here is the extent to which the person thinks the 'victim' has 'brought it on themselves' – that is, whether they appear to have caused their own predicament. As the literature discussed suggests, believing that the person lying on the ground has fallen because they are drunk (or through some other fault of their own) will give rise to very different emotional and behavioural responses from cases when it is believed the person has had a heart attack or was pushed (not something that is their own fault).

A third aspect of research concerned with people's decisions about when to help moves away from considering how people make sense of the specific situation in front of them and, instead, considers how their more general beliefs about the world may be important. The just world hypothesis suggests that people who have a strong belief that the world is essentially fair or 'just' will have a positive stance towards opportunities to help others – to some extent independent of the particular circumstances of each case (see Figure 8.7). Some research suggests that those

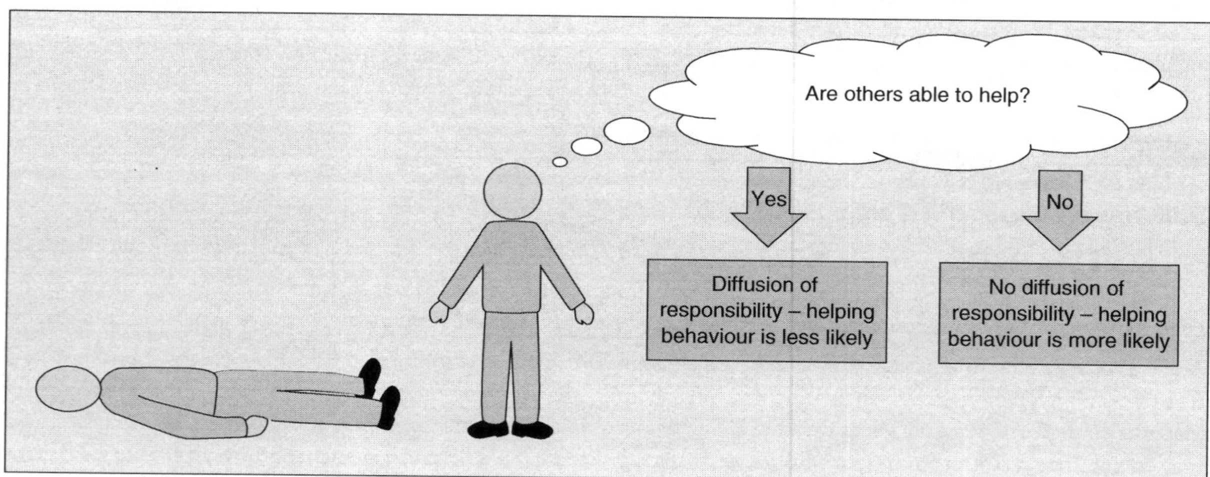

Figure 8.5 Diffusion of responsibility and prosocial behaviour

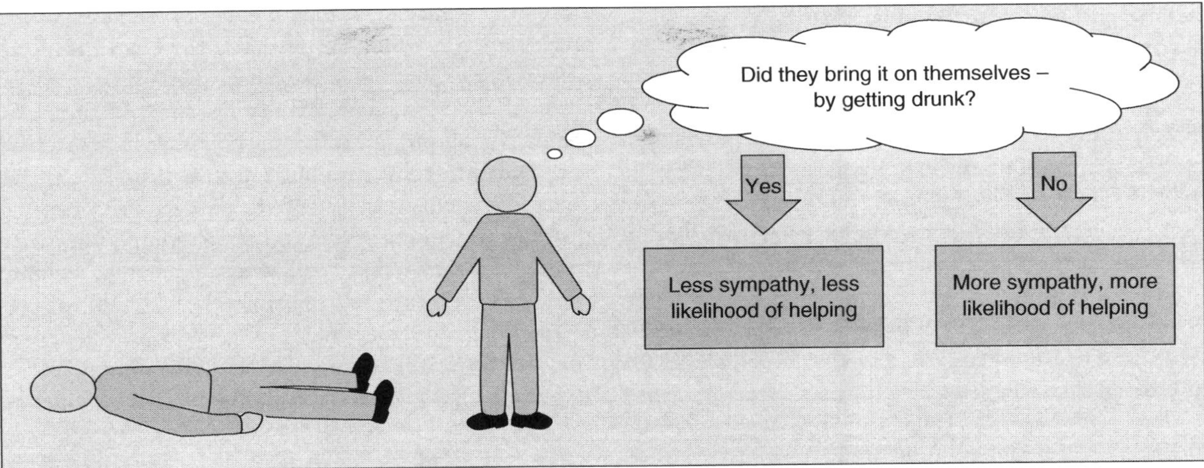

Figure 8.6 Attribution and prosocial behaviour

Figure 8.7 Belief in a just world and prosocial behaviour

who believe in a just world are *more* likely to help others (by being good, they may feel more good things will happen to them), while other research suggests these people may be *less* sympathetic to those who are suffering, believing that, at some level, they deserve it.

The three approaches considered here each emphasise the importance of how the potential helper makes sense of the situation in which help may be required. For diffusion of responsibility, the potential helper calculates the necessity of them offering help themselves; for attribution theory, it is a calculation of the deservedness of help, based on the perceived cause of the person's predicament; for the just world hypothesis, it is a more general stance, driven by perceptions about the fairness, or justness, of the world.

Take a look at Box 8.6 before exploring these theories further.

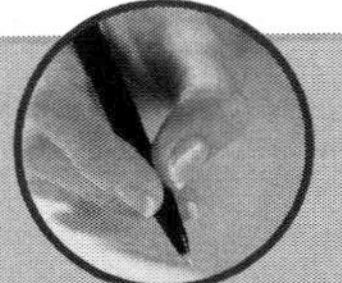

Box 8.6 TRY IT OUT Accounting for prosocial behaviour

Get together with a couple of friends and try to think of times when you have given or received help or have witnessed it.

Think about the answers at two levels. First, how do you each explain the prosocial behaviour that you experienced? Which, if any, of the theories are finding support in your examples? Second, consider how you each tell these accounts of prosocial behaviour. Do you notice anything about how you each talk about prosocial behaviour? Do you do anything to build the importance or 'goodness' of the behaviour you are describing?

Diffusion of responsibility and prosocial behaviour

One of the most famous names in social psychology does not belong to a psychologist but a young woman who was stabbed to death in New York in 1964. A particularly salient feature of Kitty Genovese's murder (see Box 8.7) was that it was prolonged (taking more than half an hour) and it was reported that, in nearby apartments, 38 people watched it happen. In the light of the number of witnesses and the length of the attack, it is still shocking to believe that not *one* person intervened or telephoned the police about the crime.

Darley and Latané (1968) note that media explanations at the time for what became known as 'bystander apathy' included 'moral decay', 'dehumanisation' caused by the urban environment, 'alienation' and 'existential despair'. For Darley and Latané, however, these explanations did not engage with what they saw as the crucial feature of this specific case – namely, that the 38 witnesses would have each been aware that others were also witnessing the events, yet unaware of precisely what those others had, or had not, done. Thus, each witness would know that others were seeing the events also, but would not be quite sure whether they had telephoned the police or not.

Darley and Latané argued that the crucial ingredient in this tragic incident was responsibility for action (such as phoning the police) and the potential blame for inaction (for example, being criticised for doing nothing) was spread out, or diffused, among the many witnesses. That is, because each witness *was aware of others* witnessing the crime, their own sense of responsibility to act was diminished.

When we try to picture ourselves in scenarios like this, we probably wind up being the person who phones the police and possibly intervenes directly to save the young woman's life. Think for a moment, though, of a time when you could have helped someone, but, instead, left it to others to do so. It may be that you thought of the others as being better able to help or your involvement was unnecessary or even counterproductive. We can imagine the witnesses of Kitty Genovese's murder thinking something similar, such as 'someone else is bound to call the police', 'someone else has probably already called the police', 'others might have seen more of this than me – it's best if they call the police', 'I'm quite new here – it's best if someone more experienced tries to help', 'I'm too old to get involved – someone else will be in a much better position to help'. These observations led Darley and Latané (1968) to devise an experiment to see whether an increase in the number of bystanders would make any one bystander less likely to help, or to do so more slowly than if there were fewer bystanders.

In their experiment, the psychology undergraduate participants were informed that the research concerned personal problems in adjusting to college life. If you were a participant, you would first have been ushered into an individual room and (after completing some brief questionnaires) informed that you could communicate with other participants (whom you could not see) using a microphone (to be used when it was your turn to speak) and headphones (which was the only way of hearing each other). You would then have been told that only one participant would be audible to the others at any one time and the experimenter would not listen, but ask questions after your discussion.

The first person to speak mentioned the problems that he had had with adjusting to New York City and to his degree course – he also mentioned, reluctantly, that he was prone to seizures. Then, the other participants spoke, mentioning their issues (in one condition, the person reporting seizures was the only other participant, in other conditions there were either one or four other participants), but no one else mentioned anything as dramatic as being prone to seizures. You would have been the last to speak before it was the turn of the first speaker again – the one who reported having seizures. He would have started speaking quite calmly, but then got louder and more incoherent before the following (somewhat melodramatic) outburst:

> I-er-um-I think I-I need-er-if-if could-er-er-somebody er-er-er-er-er-er-er give me a little-er-give me a little help here because-er-I-er-I'm-er-erh- h-having a-a-a real problem-er-right now and I-er-if somebody could help me out it would-it would-er-er s-s-sure be-sure be good ... because-er-there-er-er-a cause I-er-I-uh-I've got a-a one of the-er-seizure-er-er-things coming on and-and-and I could really-er-use some help so if somebody would-er-give me a little h-help-uh-er-er-er-er-er c-could somebody-er-er-help-er-uh-uh-uh [choking sounds] ... I'm gonna die-er-er-I'm ... gonna die-er-help-er-er-seizure-er-[chokes, then quiet].

Let's assume that you didn't interpret this as someone auditioning to be the victim of an alien attack in an episode of *Star Trek*. In fact, Darley and Latané (1968) note that the reactions of all but two participants (including comments during the 'fit') suggest they were convinced the situation was genuine. Data from the two participants who were less clearly convinced was removed from the analysis. The person who reported being prone to having a seizure seems to be having one. Although we can only hear

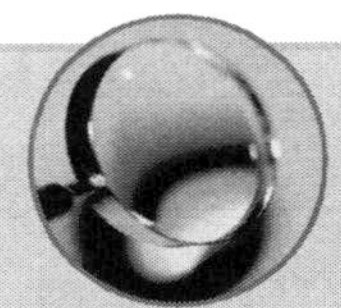

Box 8.7 FOCUS
Rethinking Kitty Genovese

As mentioned above, the Kitty Genovese case of 13 March 1964 became very important in social psychology – here was a real-life example where 38 witnesses appeared to hear and see an attack that resulted in murder, yet did nothing to help and did not even call the police. This case became not only the most vivid illustration of bystander apathy but also shaped subsequent research.

In an interview many years later, Darley described how he and Latané – prior to developing their influential models of bystander apathy – 'met over dinner a few days after this terrible incident had occurred and began to analyse this process in social psychological terms' (Evans, 1980, p. 216, cited in Cherry, 1995, p. 18). Thus, the very question, 'How could this happen?' provided the impetus for new research, as well as being a test against which models of prosocial behaviour and apathy could be judged. More recently, however, the Kitty Genovese case has been rethought in two important ways. First, Cherry (1995) offered a different, contextually embedded, perspective on exactly what the Kitty Genovese case illustrates. Second, Manning, Levine and Collins (2007) argue the version of the case that appears in all social psychology textbooks to date is based on flawed newspaper accounts and trial transcripts suggest the case did *not* illustrate bystander apathy.

Cherry (1995) approaches the case not by abstracting it as a context-free occurrence in which one person was attacked and murdered while 38 people passively watched, but by embedding it in particular social and historical details. Cherry argues that when the Kitty Genovese case is referred to in most social psychology literature, it becomes a vivid illustration of a relatively abstract – or non-particularised – phenomenon – 'people failed to intervene to help a victim'. Thus, certain features of the incident are either ignored or treated as less worthy of attention. One aspect of this is that the occurrence of the attack itself – why this man attacked this woman – is not treated as the issue to be explained but, instead, the focus is almost entirely on the apparent apathy of witnesses to the attack. A second aspect is that the explanatory framework drawn on in making sense of the case within social psychology does not typically make reference to the fact that this was an attack by a man on a woman.

For Cherry, the Kitty Genovese case could be reflected on quite differently. Social psychologists might turn to the case and question what brought about this sexual assault and murder and such reflections may involve considering issues of sex/gender relationships and structures of powerlessness (linked to sex, race, age and class). Furthermore, the lack of intervention by witnesses itself could be made sense of with a similar attention to sociocultural factors. Cherry (1995, p. 19) notes, 'Kitty Genovese and her assailant, Winston Moseley, were living in a society at a time when its members did little to intervene in violence against women.' That is, the apparent bystander apathy in this case could itself be considered not as due to some abstract variable such as 'diffusion of responsibility' but, rather, as linked to societal attitudes to violence against women. Cherry also suggests that, in Kitty Genovese's case, the lack of intervention may have been further compounded by a phenomenon that Shotland and Straw (1976) refer to concerning the fact that interventions are lower in cases where the victim is perceived as knowing the attacker (even if they do not, as in Kitty Genovese's case). Onlookers may have been deterred from intervening not only because of the ways in which male violence towards women is perceived in general, but also because of particular sets of assumptions they may have held regarding intervening in a case of a male attacking a female in what appeared (albeit erroneously) to be a domestic dispute.

Cherry's (1995) challenge to conventional ways in which the case of Kitty Genovese has been understood within social psychology raises important questions for not only how this event has been approached but also regarding the tendency for social psychologists to move from particular details to abstract theories. Thus, Cherry points out that social psychologists typically think about a specific instance in terms which concentrate on context-free variables at the expense of the particular detailed context. In disregarding certain particular details of specific cases, the accounts that are developed in social psychology are often stripped of any reference to sociocultural context – yet, by removing reference to class, gender, sex, historical setting, we could be losing what could be crucial elements for understanding what has occurred. Furthermore, this very process of abstraction may perpetuate the idea that it is both possible and desirable for social psychology in general to strive towards a decontextualised understanding of social phenomena.

Manning et al. (2007) draw on court transcripts relating to the trial of Winston Moseley (Kitty Genovese's murderer), other associated legal documents, as well as a review carried out by Joseph De May (a local historian and lawyer)

Box 8.7 continued

to challenge the conventional account that there were 38 apathetic bystanders who witnessed the murder. It is worth noting that most accounts emphasising bystander apathy in this case are based (directly or indirectly) on the work of two journalists, Martin Gansberg and A. M. Rosenthal. Martin Gansberg wrote an article appearing on the front page of *The New York Times* two weeks after the murder – the article was entitled '37 who saw murder didn't call the police'. This version of events was developed by A. M. Rosenthal (1964) into a short book entitled *Thirty-eight witnesses*. Gansberg (1964, p. 1) describes the 38 witnesses as watching 'a killer stalk and stab a woman in three separate attacks', noting that 'Not one person telephoned the police during the assault; one witness called after the woman was dead.' As Manning et al. note, numerous social psychology texts refer to the Kitty Genovese case and, in doing so, nearly all draw on (to a greater or lesser extent) Rosenthal's and Gansberg's versions of what happened – that is, 38 witnesses watched the attack, there were 3 separate attacks, lasting approximately 30 minutes, only 1 person called the police and that was after the final, fatal, attack.

Manning et al. draw on De May's analysis to challenge all elements of this version of the story of the 38 witnesses to Kitty Genovese's murder – that is, 38 witnesses did *not* 'watch' the attack as some witnesses only *heard* the attack and no one could have watched the attack for the full 30 minutes because the victim and assailant were only visible to potential witnesses for a few moments. Furthermore, there were two – not three – separate attacks, the second of which occurred inside part of the building (and was therefore not visible to most of the witnesses). Finally, the police were called immediately after the first attack (according to witnesses' claims) and Kitty Genovese was still alive when the police arrived at the scene.

Manning et al. further note that, at the trial itself, prosecutors refer to there being just half a dozen witnesses who saw the attack and could be used in bringing the case against Winston Moseley (though they indicate there were at least two other witnesses they did not want to use). Even with the three witnesses who were identified as having the best views of the attack and were called on to give evidence for the prosecution at the trial, there were some reports of seeing an ambiguous situation – for example, witness Frost reports seeing Genovese and Moseley 'standing close together, not fighting or anything' (*People v. Moseley*, 1964, p. 63, cited in Manning et al., 2007, p. 558). Thus, rather than seeing a vicious, unambiguous, prolonged attack, two of the three witnesses refer to something that was, at least at their first glance, rather less clear-cut. As Manning et al. note, the trial transcripts also make it clear that, after being frightened off after the first attack (one of the witnesses having shouted at Moseley to scare him away), Kitty Genovese slowly made her way into the back of her apartment building. The second attack – in the stairwell of the building – could not be seen by any of the trial witnesses and, indeed, only a single witness (not 38) was known to have been able to see both attacks.

The construction of this event in terms of bystander apathy also sits uneasily with evidence from the trial – and from many accounts thereafter – that suggest the police were called early on (even though the year of the attack, 1964, predates the US 911 emergency service and required calling an often hostile local police station) and (as mentioned above) one witness shouted at Moseley, forcing him to abort the first attack. Indeed, in stark contrast to the notion that this case was the antithesis of the good Samaritan story, one resident was reported to have 'immediately phoned the police then rushed to Kitty's side' (Takooshian et al., 2005, p. 67, cited in Manning et al., 2007, p. 558).

For Manning et al. (2007), the evidence discredits the version of the Kitty Genovese case that has been popularised in most social psychology texts and raises a number of issues. First, reiterating one of the points raised by Cherry (1995), perhaps the case was too swiftly construed as one of bystander apathy, at the expense of seeing it as an unprovoked male sexual assault and murder of a female. Second, the way in which an incorrect version of events has been seized on and popularised in social psychology texts could be seen as one example of a broader issue concerning the often uncritical and consensual way in which social psychology textbooks treat the ideas they report. Third, the story of unresponsive bystanders has been used (initially by Latané and Darley, 1970) to situate the idea of apathetic bystanders into a tradition of research that associates crowds with antisocial (rather than prosocial) behaviour. Latané and Darley (1970, p. 4, cited in Manning et al., 2007, p. 560) describing the failure to help as being 'like crowd behaviour in many other emergency situations'. Ironically, this version of events to some extent exonerates the purported 38 witnesses (as individuals) while simultaneously blaming the crowd and the negative impact of crowds in general. This third issue is developed in Chapter 9, where intergroup research is discussed, but, for now, it can be noted that a close inspection of evidence concerning perhaps the most widely cited real-life example in social psychology, seriously questions the accuracy of the popular story and challenges some of the ways in which it has been used for the past 40 years.

him, he appears to be in distress – 'I'm gonna die' – and very specifically mentions the word 'seizure' before falling ominously silent – 'I'm . . . gonna die-er-help-er-er-seizure-er-[chokes, then quiet]'. What do you do?

Again, we probably like to think that we would rush to the assistance of the person who seemed to be experiencing a seizure – perhaps getting help from the experimenter, perhaps helping the person directly.

Darley and Latané report that, in the condition where participants thought that 'they alone knew of the victim's plight', 85 per cent of them reported the seizure before the end of the fit. If the participants believed that there was another person who was aware of the fit, this figure fell to 62 per cent. In the third condition, where participants believed that 4 others were aware of the fit, it was 31 per cent. Darley and Latané ran other variations to see whether the sex of the participant, other bystander or victim had any significant effect and concluded that it did not. Finally, one might imagine that if the participant believed that the other bystander was a 'premedical student' (and therefore medically competent), it would have an effect, perhaps reducing the likelihood of their own intervention, but, again, this did not have any significant effect.

Interestingly, Darley and Latané (1968, p. 382) note that subjects who did not report the seizure were not apathetic or indifferent: 'If anything, they seemed more emotionally aroused than did the subjects who reported the emergency.' Darley and Latané (1968, p. 382) suggest that the non-responding participants did not so much decide *not* to respond but, rather, 'they were still in a state of indecision and conflict concerning whether to respond or not'. They argue that all participants had to weigh the costs of reporting versus not reporting the 'seizure'. For participants who believed that only *they* were aware of the 'victim's' plight, it was relatively easy to resolve the conflict. Thus, the potential costs for these participants of not helping – the distress of the victim, the need for their help and the feelings of guilt they might feel if they did not help – easily outweighed the potential costs of helping – looking foolish by overreacting and disrupting the experiment. For those participants who believed there were others who were aware of the 'seizure', however, Darley and Latané (1968, p. 382) argue that, 'the cost of not helping was reduced and the conflict they were in more acute'. That is, these participants had a more finely balanced cost analysis in front of them and therefore 'vacillated between' action and inaction.

Belief that others were aware of the situation, therefore, did not give rise to callous indifference but, rather, an adjustment in the calculation regarding the costs of intervention versus non-intervention. For Darley and Latané, if bystanders believe that they alone have witnessed the victim's plight, they have a clear sense of the high cost of their non-intervention. If, by contrast, they believe that others are aware of the victim's plight, each bystander will have a reduced sense of the cost of their non-intervention and, therefore, be less likely to intervene. Darley and Latané argue that where other witnesses were believed to be present, then the responsibility for helping and the potential blame for doing nothing was diffused among the observers. Furthermore, in Darley and Latané's experiment – where the other witnesses were not visible – participants could consider that others, unperceived, had already initiated helping action. It is as if those believing that they are solo bystanders witnessing an emergency are saying to themselves something like, 'Oh my, that person needs help, I'd better do something quickly', while those who believe there are other witnesses (as in the popular version of the Kitty Genovese case) experience more vacillation – 'Maybe I should do something, but, then, I'm sure someone else has called the police. Perhaps I should call just in case, but I don't want to be a nuisance and others might have seen more of what happened than I did.'

Darley and Latané's (1968) and Latané and Darley's (1970) research came to be understood primarily in terms of increasing the number of bystanders diffuses responsibility and makes it less likely that any one bystander will accept responsibility for helping. The more general idea that we calculate costs of intervention and non-intervention – though an important element in Darley and Latané's (1968) paper – received less immediate attention in work that drew on their research.

The **diffusion of responsibility** idea is plausible and has a certain resonance in everyday contexts. Have you ever sent a group e-mail asking for assistance, asked for volunteers in a large meeting or seen people walk past someone in need? Where people are aware of others who might help, they do sometimes seem to avoid taking responsibility to help themselves. Increasing the number of bystanders does appear to reduce the sense of responsibility that any one bystander might have for helping and can result in a lower probability of any help being given.

Diffusion of responsibility Within the context of prosocial research, diffusion of responsibility refers to a (theoretically defined) phenomenon of a reduced sense of a personal responsibility to help occurring in situations where the potential helper perceives that others are available to do so. This has been incorporated into models of prosocial behaviour that suggest where people perceive others are available to offer help, individuals will experience their own 'responsibility for helping' to be spread or diffused among these others and, therefore, be less likely to help themselves.

While diffusion of responsibility is very plausible, however, it is worth reflecting on our own experiences of bystander help (or non-help), not just in the more trivial examples referred to above, but in a real emergency situation. One example of this that springs to mind was when I was travelling on a crowded train in South London one day. It was a warm day and the train was absolutely bursting with people. Suddenly, a few metres ahead of me (and, I hasten to add, rather difficult for me to reach in the crowded carriage), a young woman collapsed to the floor. Following Darley and Latané, we might expect that, with a diminished sense of responsibility, no one would help her. Someone, however, swiftly emerged to assist the woman, offer her water and help her off the train (the person was, incidentally, a distinguished conversation analyst, cited in this text, who happened to be travelling in the same carriage). Others, standing close by joined in, offering help and checking that she was all right. Fortunately, the woman was not injured or particularly ill – just faint – but the fact of the swift intervention, despite the presence of many other potential helpers, seems to contradict what would be predicted according to the diffusion of responsibility model.

Rethinking diffusion of responsibility

Research by Piliavin, Rodin and Piliavin (1969) suggests that this experience is not entirely uncommon – that is, even when others are present, help might be forthcoming.

They undertook some research into helping on express trains operating in New York's 8th Avenue subway line as they wanted to investigate helping behaviour outside of the laboratory by using staged enactments of a collapse in front of real onlookers riding the subway. In the study, teams of four students were used, which comprised one male 'victim', one male 'model' who would help after a certain amount of time if no onlookers did so and two female observers. The teams rode on the subway, with the victim collapsing about 70 seconds into his journey and the model ready to intervene after a pre-specified time period.

Piliavin et al.'s study compared the effects of race of the 'victim' ('black' versus 'white'), apparent cause of the collapse (the 'victim' appeared to collapse for no reason and was carrying a cane or walking stick or appeared to be drunk, smelling of and carrying alcohol) and also recorded the numbers of onlookers who were present in that part of the subway train. They also intended to measure the impact of 'models', who were scheduled to help the 'victim' after a certain amount of time following his collapse – the idea being that perhaps seeing someone else helping might affect the behaviour of the onlookers.

Piliavin et al.'s (1969) results were quite striking. In the condition where the 'victim' appeared to collapse for no reason and was holding a cane, help was offered spontaneously (that is, before the 'models' offered any help) by onlookers in 62 out of the 65 trials (95 per cent). Regardless of the numbers of onlookers (which varied from 15 to 120), in the overwhelming majority of trials, at least 1 (and usually more than 1) onlooker intervened to help. The extent of spontaneous helping was so much greater than Piliavin et al. had envisaged, it actually meant that there was little opportunity for them to investigate the impact of the models' behaviour on the onlookers' helping behaviour – usually, the onlookers had already started to help before the models were scheduled to assist.

Overall, the race of both the 'victim' and onlookers played some part in helping – same-race helping tended to be more frequent, especially if the 'victim' appeared to be drunk. The sex of onlookers also appeared to be associated with patterns of helping behaviour, in that the 'victim' (always male) was more likely to receive help from a male, than a female onlooker. It should be noted that, because the data does not report how close to the 'victim' the male or female, black or white onlookers were, it is hard to know if the differences in helping could be a mere function of proximity. Thus, if more males were standing close to the place where the victim collapsed, then that closer proximity may explain their greater propensity to help rather than them being male – that is, being the same sex as the victim.

What really stood out in the results, however, was the importance of the *apparent cause of the collapse* – whether the victim standing with a cane collapsed versus the victim carrying and smelling of alcohol. Where the victim appeared to be drunk, helping fell from 95 per cent (for the victim holding a cane condition) to 50 per cent (in 19 out of 38 trials). This difference cannot be explained away in terms of diffusion of responsibility due to the number of onlookers – the mean numbers of onlookers was actually slightly higher in the 'cane' condition, which should, according to the diffusion of responsibility approach, be associated with *lower* levels of help.

Piliavin et al. (1969) made sense of the results by sketching out the beginnings of a model that drew on aspects of arousal, emotional lability, attribution and a cost–benefit analysis of the decision to help or not help. This model – which became the arousal: cost–reward model, discussed below – integrates issues addressed in our consideration of both *why* and *when* people engage in prosocial behaviour. Thus, Piliavin et al. suggest that seeing an emergency creates emotional arousal in the observer. The observer might label – or interpret – this state in quite different ways that have different implications regarding offering help. Thus, observers might label their arousal as fear, disgust, sympathy or some combination of these. This state of arousal may be reduced by helping or getting help, leaving the scene or construing the 'victim' as undeserving of help – for example, attributing blame for their situation to the victim. The arousal and its label are components – along with an analysis of possible consequences for self and the victim – in the cost–benefit analysis that precedes the decision to help or not help. Thus, following arousal, we may decide *not* to help if we can attribute our arousal to something other than the victim's situation (for example, to our mood or medication), but, if we interpret our arousal as sympathy, then we might consider helping. Our considerations will take into account the benefit to self and victim of intervening and also the costs – if the costs are too high for the perceived benefits, then, despite our sympathy for the victim, we may decide not to help.

What Piliavin et al. (1969) have provided is a caution against a narrow interpretation of Darley and Latané's (1968) work. Some versions of diffusion of responsibility do not sufficiently emphasise that it is not the actual numbers of other bystanders who are able to help that matters but, rather, the individual's *perception* of available, competent others which can give rise to diffusion of responsibility. Furthermore, most work drawing on Darley and Latané (1968) has tended to downplay their emphasis on a cost calculation for prosocial behaviour – that they noted perceptions of other bystanders who might be available to help (which allow for diffusion of responsibility) gives rise to a perception of a reduced cost for not helping. This cost calculation – picked up in the work of Piliavin et al. – is more evidently present in Darley and Latané's original work than in subsequent versions of it.

See also Box 8.8 for an insight into Piliavin's work.

Box 8.8 KEY RESEARCHER
Professor Jane Piliavin: altruism and helping behaviour

How did you become interested in altruism and helping behaviour?

During the 1967–1968 academic year, Irv Piliavin – not yet my husband – was on an NSF (National Science Foundation) career enrichment grant, studying with Bibb Latané at Columbia. Bibb and John Darley had just begun their research on diffusion of responsibility in emergency situations. As a social worker by training, Irv was quite dissatisfied with the artificial laboratory research they were doing and was wondering how one might study this topic 'in the real world'. One day, as he was riding the subway, a drunk fell off his seat to the floor. He was rolling around and nobody was doing anything to help him. Finally, Irv helped him back to his seat, got off the subway and got on a train to Philadelphia. By the time he arrived at my house in that city, he had designed the first of what turned out to be a series of three studies in which we examined factors that influenced whether or not, and how fast, people intervened when a man collapsed in a subway car.

Tell us about your research into altruism and helping behaviour

I have done research in several areas of the larger topic of altruism and helping behaviour.

First, there is the work on emergency intervention. Irv and I developed the arousal: cost–reward theory of helping behaviour based on the first subway study and, as noted above, did two more studies in subways. He then lost interest in the area – it was still too abstract to suit him – and I went off on my own, doing a number of other studies and then writing the book *Emergency intervention* with Jack Dovidio, Sam Gaertner and Russell Clark, published in 1981. This book was organised around the arousal: cost–reward theory, but reviewed all the research we could find on the topic.

While we were writing the book, which took us about four years, I started wondering about what to do next. By this time I was quite committed to the general area of helping and altruism. One day when brushing my teeth and thus looking in the mirror – a technique known to increase self-awareness – I thought, 'You have just finished giving your first gallon of blood. I wonder why you've started doing this. I wonder why anyone would do that'. Hmmm, that sounds like an interesting research project. (I'm sure the fact that my mother, father, and sister were all blood donors was a not unimportant reason). I had been giving blood at a permanent collection facility on the Wisconsin campus (having moved to Wisconsin in 1970), so I decided to start by interviewing the nurses who worked there and a small group of donors who had given at least four times (identified by the nurses). From there I moved to handing out questionnaires to first-time donors and following them through longitudinal research. I published a number of articles with graduate students who were by then working

Box 1.3 continued

with me and, eventually, in 1991, the book *Giving blood: The development of an altruistic identity* with Peter Callero, one of my students. Our central finding was that, over time, some donors developed a role-identity as a blood donor, which sustains their habit of regular donation. We found a number of factors that appeared to increase the likelihood of this happening, which was of great interest to the blood-collection industry. During this time I got very involved with blood industry and government committees. It was an important time, since it was in the early 1980s that it was discovered AIDS was transmissible through blood transfusion.

My most recent research has attempted to contribute to answering the question of whether volunteering and other community participation improves mental and physical health. I have been involved with the Wisconsin Longitudinal Study (WLS) since 2002, when planning began for the 2003 – 2004 wave of that study. The WLS began with a 1/3 random sample of everyone who graduated from a Wisconsin high school in 1957 – a sample of about 10,000 people. Follow-ups were done in 1964, 1975, 1992 and 2004, with amazingly high retention. There is a more recent wave as well. With my students, we also added information about the community participation of the sample members while in high school, based on the 'blurbs' by their pictures in the yearbook. The answer is that, in this sample, as well as in many other studies in the literature, participation *does* improve psychological well-being. In my study, it does not affect physical health, but they were not yet very old in 2004, only on average 64. Since I retired I have not been very actively involved in this research, but I am thinking of getting back into it now that I have been widowed.

How does your approach compare and contrast with others'?

I think I am more eclectic than a lot of people in terms of methodology. I have done participant observation, qualitative interviewing, structured questionnaire research, lab experiments and field experiments. I tend to be led by students into new areas and new theoretical approaches. The role identity model was brought to me by Peter Callero, for example.

What things helped or hindered your research?

Having good students is, of course, central. Second most important is money. Third is good colleagues to critique one's research. I was never very good at getting money. I did get a good-sized grant for the blood donor research, from NIH, and I got a small grant to pursue the work on the WLS. Being married and raising a family does interfere with one's ability to totally commit to a research career. Don't let anyone tell you it doesn't. The good thing is that there is now some understanding within universities that this is the case; and both men and women are now involved in the household work. Not being in a psychology department severely limited my ability to do laboratory research, because of being shut out of the subject pool.

What do you recommend to people wanting to start to research this topic?

If I get back into research again, I would like to pursue the work I began on the WLS. With the most recent wave, there should be a chance to find effects of volunteering on physical health and even mortality. About 10 per cent of the sample has died.

I don't like to give advice to other people. Pick a topic that fascinates you and pursue it. Don't let people talk you out of it. When I was studying blood donation in the late 1970s and early 1980s and I would tell people about it, they thought it was really weird. Why would anyone be interested in that? When AIDS came along, all of a sudden it became important.

Critical recap

Diffusion of responsibility and prosocial behaviour

1 Some interpretations of diffusion of responsibility have sometimes mechanically applied the idea that the larger the number of bystanders, the more any one individual will experience diffusion of responsibility and, therefore, be less likely to help. This underemphasises the crucial role of the individual's perception of competent available bystanders as a precondition for the experience of diffusion of responsibility.

2 Subsequent versions of diffusion of responsibility have underemphasised the cost–reward calculation aspect that Darley and Latané's (1968) original work developed. Diffusion of responsibility was understood as a particularly important means by which the cost of not helping could be perceived as lower (in comparison to similar situations where responsibility was perceived as not diffused).

3 It is also possible to question whether the ways in which participants are aware of others with capacity to help in experimental settings, corresponds to the sort of awareness they would have in real-world settings. In many cases, it is likely that in 'the real world', unlike in an experiment, there is far more ambiguity regarding who else might be available and able to help.

4 As will be referred to later, it is possible to recast diffusion of responsibility as not a cognitive cause for the failure to engage in prosocial behaviour but, rather, a *justification after the event* for a failure to engage in prosocial behaviour. That is, the idea of others being better able to help could be seen as something we produce after the event when we have not helped, in order to justify our lack of helping.

Reflective questions

1. *What are the implications of the Kitty Genovese case being so incorrectly described?*
2. *Can you think of examples based on your own experience that support or contradict the idea of diffusion of responsibility?*

Attribution and prosocial behaviour

In Chapter 4, we considered the idea that the way in which we make attributions about events or behaviours can have important consequences – for example, our explanations about our partner's negative behaviour can have an influence on how we perceive the relationship. Attribution work has suggested that the same is true for prosocial behaviour – the way in which we explain, or make **attributions** about, someone's predicament can shape whether we help them or not (see Figure 8.6). Attributions could be considered as relevant to spontaneous help offered to strangers who appear to be in need or assistance offered to those who ask for help, as well as more planned help, such as giving to specific charities. Our explanations for the plight of the 'victim' may shape our emotional reaction to them (such as our sympathy or anger) – emotions that, as was discussed above, are associated with very different behavioural responses. If our attributions lead us to feel anger at the 'victim', we are far less likely to help than if we feel sympathy. Attribution research provides one way of understanding cases where people have observed someone apparently in need of help and yet simply walked or driven past – dismissing the victim as drunk or somehow having inflicted their misfortune on themselves. According to attributional approaches to prosocial behaviour, if bystanders blame the victim for their plight, they are less likely to help than if they feel that they are in no way to blame for what has happened to them.

Greitmeyer and Rudolph (2003) argue that if the perceived cause of the victim's situation is seen as controllable (by the victim), this may evoke anger, whereas if it is seen as out of their control, they may receive sympathy. Thus, if we think someone 'brought it on themselves', we feel less sympathy for them and are less inclined to help than if we feel 'they could not have done anything to prevent this from happening to them'.

These distinctions are perhaps not as clearly etched into the 'reality of the situation' as we might think. Think, for example, of someone walking home and having their mobile phone snatched from them. Was it partly their fault if they flashed their mobile phone around ostentatiously to everyone in a club shortly before walking alone down a notoriously dangerous unlit alley at 3 a.m.? We may well feel sympathy for someone with cancer, but would we feel less sympathy if it was a clear consequence of their extremely heavy smoking? Weiner, Perry and Magnusson (1988) found that sympathy for a person with AIDS varied with the presented cause of their AIDS. Where participants were informed that the AIDS came about through a blood transfusion, participants had high levels of sympathy; where they were informed that it was due to the person's sexual promiscuity, they had much lower levels of sympathy. Our attributions may partly determine the sympathy that we feel and, therefore, influence the extent to which we volunteer help.

Our attributions may also shape how we respond to requests for help. Imagine that someone asks if they can borrow your lecture notes. Would the likelihood of helping them be shaped by how they account for missing the lecture? Schmidt and Weiner (1988) found that when the request was made by someone claiming they needed eye treatment, it was far more successful than when they said that they missed the lecture because they went to the beach. The first explanation seems to be far less under the person's control than their decision to visit a beach.

Sometimes our attributions and propensity to help may be shaped by the way in which the victim is described. You might notice that charity appeals (perhaps quite rightly) typically present victims in terms of terrible experiences over which they had no control (floods, drought, disease, war), whereas newspapers' depictions of victims they wish to vilify (often asylum seekers) emphasise their culpability and choice. Henry, Reyna and Weiner (2004) conducted a

Attribution This refers to the process of locating a cause for a given phenomenon. In the context of prosocial behaviour, attribution is relevant in terms of how potential helpers make attributions about what brought about the difficulties experienced by 'the potential recipients of help'. If an individual thinks about how it is that a person has fallen to the floor, or that the inhabitants of a country are experiencing starvation, then they could be thought of as making an attribution that might, potentially, shape whether, and how, they help.

study in which the people to be helped were described as either 'welfare recipients' or 'the poor'. Which description do you think was likely to result in more willingness to help? I suspect that you guessed 'the poor' – and you are right. Henry et al. (2004) suggest that the label 'welfare recipients' evokes a stereotype suggesting some personal responsibility for their situation. If the description triggers a stereotype suggesting that the person's predicament is partly their own fault, then (according to attributional approaches) our sympathy and readiness to help will be decreased.

The distinction between 'controllable' and 'uncontrollable' is common in work that draws on attribution to understand when people will engage in prosocial behaviour. It may overcome some of the problems with the internal–external distinction discussed in Chapter 2, but it, too, has problems. The sense of what the cause is may, in some cases, be much more complex than it first appears. Think, for example, of a person dying from cancer needing our help to get out of bed. We might attribute the person's situation to the immediate illness – not being able to get out of bed because of the serious illness, which seems far more out of the person's control than attributing an inability to get out of bed to binge-drinking the previous night. We might, however, frame the cause in terms of an illness brought about by the person's extremely heavy consumption of cigarettes – a cause that seemingly can be controlled and, therefore, feel less sympathy. What, though, if the person grew up in an era when cigarettes were promoted as neutral, or even *good* for people's health, and formed a lifelong addiction as a consequence. Again, the balance tips towards being less controllable. What this illustrates is that, while controllability could be an important factor linked in some way to sympathy and prosocial behaviour, we should be aware that the *construal* of controllability could be more fluid – shaped by how we frame the cause or causes – than some of the attribution literature implies.

A second potential challenge to attributional approaches to prosocial behaviour is whether attributions have causal primacy with regard to prosocial behaviour. That is, although attributions of uncontrollability might be linked to helping behaviour, does the attribution come first or the willingness to help? Imagine you are sitting at home, flicking through a much-loved social psychology textbook, when there is a knock at the door. Someone is trying to get you to make a donation to a young offender's rehabilitation scheme. It is possible that, if you wind up making a donation, you will justify this to yourself and others by talking about the desperate situations that drove them to crime – the poverty, abuse and injustices that were inflicted on them. That is, you might emphasise uncontrollable causes for the young offender's predicament. If, by contrast, you close the door with a curt 'No, thank you', you may find yourself justifying this by reference to the young offender's responsibility for committing crimes in the first place. That is, our accounts for our decisions to help, or not help, may draw on ideas of controllability – for example, whether the people to be helped are responsible for their situation or not – *to justify the decision we have made.*

The just world hypothesis

Closely linked to attributional approaches is the **just world hypothesis** (Lerner, 1980) – this is the belief that the world is just, fair or equitable (see Figure 8.7). The idea here is that people who believe the world to be fair or just will presume that good things happen to good people – and bad things happen to bad people. If you ever find yourself responding to the good or bad fortunes of others with the thought 'they deserve it', then you are responding as someone showing signs of believing the just world hypothesis – that is, the world is fair.

Research in this area suggests that many people interpret the social world with this distorting or biasing presumption, so, if we encounter someone who has just had an incredible promotion, started a relationship with a highly desirable partner or somehow acquired vast and unexpected wealth, we might think about what a hard-working, capable, nice and good person they are. What happens, though, to our perceptions of people who meet with ill fortune? Those who have a strong belief in a just world might see the person who is redundant, seriously ill, who has split up from their partner or who has become bankrupt as in some sense *deserving* their misfortune. Many clichéd expressions capture this sense of deserved misfortune – 'They brought it on themselves', 'What goes around, comes around' or 'They have finally got their come-uppance'.

Believing in a just world seems to have a complex association with prosocial behaviour. Some early research by Zuckerman (1975) suggested that students who had a strong belief in a just world were more likely to engage in helpful behaviours (such as reading to a blind person) just prior to an exam. The idea here is that believing 'good things happen to good people' can bring about certain displays of 'goodness' at certain critical times (such as just before an exam). Other research has suggested that we might help others in

Just world hypothesis This refers to the idea that may be more or less common in certain populations that the world is essentially fair. According to this hypothesis, bad things happen to bad people and good things happen to good people. The just world hypothesis predicts both *not* helping (the onlooker thinks the 'victim' deserves what has happened to them) and *helping* (the onlooker thinks that, by helping, good things will happen to them).

order to sustain our belief in a just world, so, if something potentially unjust has happened to someone (and we believe the world is just), we might help so as to restore a sense of justice to the world. Bierhoff, Klein and Kramp (1991) interviewed those who helped, and a demographically matched sample of those who did not help, at traffic accidents and found that helpers believed more in a just world. Bierhoff et al. interpreted this as a means by which 'believers' could maintain their belief that (ultimately) the world is just.

Before we get the impression that belief in a just world is *always* associated with a higher propensity to engage with prosocial behaviour, however, it is worth noting this is not always the case. While it can result in prosocial behaviour (to make the world more just for undeserving victims), it can – as Miller (1977) suggests – result in denigration of the victim in those cases where we cannot or do not help. Furnham (1995) found that students who had higher levels of belief in a just world had more negative views regarding people with disabilities. As considered above, the just world hypothesis can lead to a sense of people deserving their misfortune, especially if we are unable to do anything to remedy their situation.

Taken together, research into the just world hypothesis suggests that it can affect our prosocial behaviour in contradictory ways. Believing the world to be just can increase our prosocial behaviour if we ourselves are hoping to become more 'deserving' of success or if, through our actions, we can make the world more just, equally, it can decrease it if we perceive needy others as deserving their hardship. As noted above, Miller (1977) offers one way to make sense of this contradiction: if we can easily help, we will (to 'keep' the world just); if we cannot (or it is too costly to do so), we may denigrate the victim to see them as deserving their suffering – rather than our help. The contradictory evidence, however, could cause us to question if belief in a just world actually makes any difference as to whether or not someone engages in prosocial behaviour.

It may be that ideas about a victim deserving help or 'getting their just deserts' are not linked to some sort of fixed belief about the way that the world is, and do not determine whether we help or not. Instead, our reactions regarding what people in need deserve may be a way in which we account for our own decision to help, or not help, or our own position on approving or disapproving of another's help. Taken in this way, the notion of a relatively stable belief guiding our prosocial behaviour could be replaced by an interest in the ways in which *deservedness is drawn on as a resource to explain why we did or did not help* (or approve of help).

Arousal: cost-reward model – An account of prosocial behaviour that suggests the process begins with some observed stimuli (for example, seeing someone in distress) creating a state of arousal, which then leads to a weighing up of the costs and benefits (to self and other) of helping versus not helping.

Critical recap

Attribution and the just world hypothesis and prosocial behaviour

1 Both of these approaches suggest an element of calculation on the part of the bystander as to whether the victim should or should not be helped. It is possible to question whether bystanders actually engage in this sort of mental processing prior to the decision to help or not.

2 The criticisms regarding diffusion of responsibility being a post hoc (after the event) justification for non-intervention is very relevant to attribution and just world approaches also. That is, rather than seeing attributions of responsibility for the victim's predicament or beliefs regarding its fairness (or unfairness) as the cognitive genesis for prosocial behaviour occurring or not, we can reverse the order and see the behaviour as happening and then being made sense of. This issue is returned to in the critique of research into prosocial behaviour near the end of this chapter.

3 Once again, the question of how prosocial behaviour has been defined in the above research raises questions regarding both consistency across studies (quite different behaviours are interpreted as being prosocial behaviour) and external validity (that is, questions can be raised about how well any one experimentally defined 'prosocial behaviour' relates to 'real-world' prosocial behaviour).

Reflective questions

1 *Can you think of a case where attribution may have prevented someone from receiving help?*

2 *Is the just world hypothesis relevant and useful in thinking about prosocial behaviour?*

8.4 Integrating why and when: arousal and decision making in prosocial behaviour

The literature considered so far has tended to concentrate either on motivations for engaging in altruistic behaviour or cognitions about specific circumstances in which help may be required. The work considered in this section attempts to draw on both of these elements as developed in the **arousal: cost–reward model** (see Figure 8.8). This

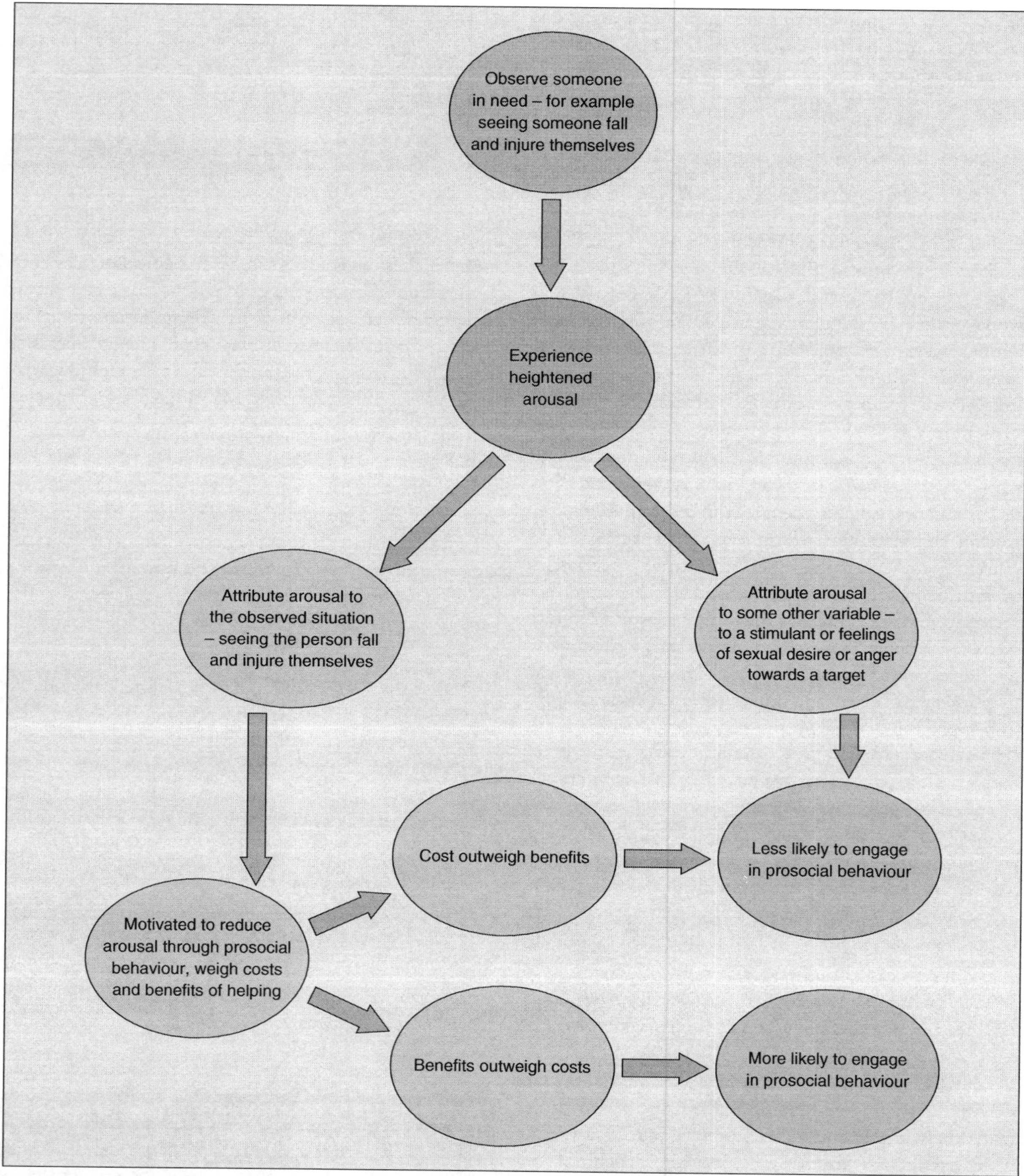

Figure 8.8 A simplified overview of the arousal: cost-reward model of prosocial behaviour

model incorporates the psychological state of arousal, the idea that the attribution of arousal is important, and cost–benefit analysis, which, in turn, incorporates diffusion of responsibility (if others are perceived as able to help, my decision not to help is less costly). In order to understand the arousal: cost–reward model, the component parts of arousal, labelling arousal and weighing of costs and benefits are each examined before reviewing the model as a whole.

The arousal: cost–reward model

Piliavin, Dovidio, Gaertner and Clark (1981) developed the arousal: cost–reward model (Dovidio, Piliavin, Schroeder, & Penner, 2006, provide an updated version of this) – an approach to prosocial behaviour that integrated physiological and cognitive elements (see Figure 8.8). From this perspective, when we observe a situation where someone is in distress, we first have a 'pure' physiological arousal response, we then think about or label this state of arousal and, finally, we evaluate the costs and rewards of intervening. Each of these components is considered in turn below.

Arousal

The physiological element that Piliavin et al. (1981) were particularly interested in was arousal. Thus, rather than focus on positive or negative mood, they identified something at once both fundamental – arousal could be thought of as occurring in many contexts that might make prosocial behaviour relevant – and ambiguous – it could be seen as a component of many different mood states. For Piliavin et al. arousal is most easily measured by heart rate – the higher our heart rate, the more aroused we are assumed to be. They note that our arousal when witnessing someone in distress – particularly if it is some form of emergency – can go through an orientating reaction (where our physiological responses are slowed, including a reduced heart rate).

Our orientating reaction can be understood as a physiological response that enables us to, relatively calmly, make sense of the situation. The orientating action is short-lived and followed by a defence reaction. This is the physiological reaction we probably more readily associate with witnessing someone in distress – our arousal increases and our body gets ready to respond (in crude terms, we are ready for 'fight' or 'flight'). Our level of arousal is often associated with the nature of the event we witness, so, for example, the more severe the event is, the higher our level of arousal (Geer & Jarmecky, 1973).

Piliavin et al. link arousal to the question of why some people might be quicker or more willing to help than others, arguing that increased levels of arousal among bystanders are associated with an increased propensity to help. The more aroused we are (the higher our heart rate, for example) the more quickly we are likely to respond to someone in distress. Gaertner and Dovidio (1977) conducted an experiment in which participants witnessed a woman who appeared to be hurt by chairs that fell on her. Those participants who were fastest to respond also had faster heart rates (and were therefore taken to be more aroused).

Labelling the arousal

Piliavin et al.'s work also draws on Schachter and Singer (1962) to address the ambiguity of states of arousal. Sometimes we might experience heightened emotions, yet exactly what the emotion is can be ambiguous – it is quite common to come across cases of situations where people are unsure whether to laugh or cry. Dovidio et al. (2006) use the example of parents waiting up for a child returning home and how their emotion may change from worry to anger to relief – perhaps we have all experienced this when we have tried to contact someone and become increasingly concerned about their welfare. Rather than some hardwired emotional fact changing, however, it may be that what we have is some form of emotional arousal, plus our labelling of what that is. Dovidio et al. note that it may be something circumstantial – such as being surrounded by frightened or angry people – that leads us to label our arousal as fear or anger.

A strand of this ambiguity that Piliavin et al. are particularly concerned with is the *cause* of the arousal. If we witness someone suffering and experience arousal that we interpret as somehow caused by seeing their suffering – that is, we think 'I am feeling distressed because they are suffering' – then we will be motivated to help or at least carefully consider helping. It is this that will prompt us to move to the crucial decision making stage, in which we weigh the rewards and costs of helping.

Calculating the costs and benefits of helping

The exchange or cost–reward idea may seem a little unpalatable at first – we perhaps do not want to think of our own, or others', prosocial behaviour as having come from some seemingly cold calculation of costs and rewards. It is worth perhaps bearing in mind first that exchange theory represents quite a wide-ranging perspective on human behaviour, which tries to explain not just helping behaviour but also why people enter into (and stay in) any type of relationship (see Chapter 3). Exchange theory is often described as having an economic view of human behaviour because it suggests that much of human behaviour can be understood as an attempt to maximise our gains and minimise our costs – even when we seem to be helping others. Also, the specific components that comprise rewards and costs may not be purely self-serving – there is scope for including feelings about the distress of the other within this model, though we could debate how 'altruistic' these concerns on the part of the bystander really are.

According to exchange theory and cost–reward analysis, our decision regarding whether or not we help is driven by our appraisal of the perceived benefits and costs to us of helping or not helping. If the perceived costs of intervention increase beyond a certain point or the benefits decrease, then we may decide not to help. The exchange approach to prosocial behaviour, as developed by Piliavin, Rodin and Piliavin (1969), Piliavin, Dovidio, Gaertner and Clark, (1981) and Dovidio, Piliavin, Gaertner, Schroeder and Clark (1991), suggests that bystanders assess the costs to themselves for helping and the costs to themselves and the victim of not helping (these could equally be seen as the opposite of the benefits of helping – for example, if guilt is a cost of not helping, the absence of guilt is a reward for helping). Table 8.1 gives some examples of these perceived costs that may inform the bystander's decision to help or not help a stranger who appears to be in need.

In Table 8.1, examples of the costs are organised around the three types of cost that exchange approaches have concentrated on. It is worth bearing in mind that the dominant type of helping situation to which these costs typically refer is one in which help is given to a stranger in some sort of ad hoc way – this differs from helping known others or engaging in planned or long-term helping behaviour. The first of these costs is the most obvious – the personal cost or sacrifice that will be made if the bystander helps as, typically, our help will involve some sort of time and effort, but may involve risk or expense. There can also be what might be thought of as psychological costs associated with how our helping might be perceived – what if we misunderstood the situation or our help was unneeded or ineffectual – or draws attention to ourselves in a way that makes us feel awkward or embarrassed?

Table 8.1 Examples of perceived costs of helping and not helping

Costs to bystander of helping	Costs to bystander of not helping	Victim costs of bystander not helping
Time	Guilt/shame	Internalising victim's continuing suffering
Risk to personal safety	Negative perceptions of others	Distress at witnessing continuing suffering
Expense	Potentially dangerous situation may escalate	Sympathy for the victim's continuing suffering
Effort		
Risk of having misunderstood the situation		
Awkwardness/ embarrassment		
Ineffectual help		

Equally, there are costs for the bystander of *not* intervening – if you have ever not helped a stranger in need and felt bad about it afterwards, you will have experienced these costs. We may feel guilt that we did nothing and distress at the victim's continuing suffering. Our lack of help might mean that a situation escalates – for example, a potential confrontation may become increasingly heated, which could incur personal safety costs as well as the distress of watching the situation deteriorate. Furthermore, if we do not help, we may be negatively judged by others, either at the time or subsequently.

The final costs to be considered are those that take into account the victim's continuing suffering if the bystander does not help. Although these are – as in Table 8.1 – typically referred to as costs for the victim of the bystander's decision not to help, they are, more accurately, costs to the bystander arising from the bystander's awareness of the victim's continuing suffering should he or she decide not to help. That is, these costs – often referred to as *empathic costs* – are the psychological costs to the bystander of thinking about how their decision not to help is allowing the victim to continue to suffer. Witnessing continuing suffering is distressing in itself – it may arouse sympathy and/or we might ourselves start to internalise their suffering, feeling how it must be for the victim to suffer as they do. These empathic costs will be higher if we perceive the victim's suffering as beyond their control, or lower, if we feel that they have brought it on themselves. If we have ever felt terrible seeing a disabled person collapse to the floor, then we have experienced an empathic cost, but contrast in your mind how differently you might feel if the person collapsing was drunk rather than disabled.

These three sets of costs – which could be expanded to include costs to the victim of the bystander's decision *to* help (that is, costs associated with the potential further suffering for the victim of counterproductive help, such as moving someone whose back is broken) – are intended to outline and differentiate factors that influence the bystander's decision about any given instance of prosocial behaviour. Studies designed to investigate exchange theories of prosocial behaviour have often involved experiments that provide some specific opportunity for prosocial behaviour, while the cost associated with engaging in it is varied across experimental groups.

A witty illustration of how costs may inhibit prosocial behaviour is found in Darley and Batson (1973), who wanted to see how helpful students training to be priests would be to a stranger who was slumped in a doorway. The seminarians were each due to give a talk on the parable of the Good Samaritan – the famous story in the Bible about the help given by a member of a despised religious group to a stranger who lay collapsed on the ground, having been robbed.

It was arranged that, as the seminarians passed the stranger, some would be just on time for their talk, others early and still others late. As you may have guessed, it was the early seminarians who stopped to help the stranger – for them, the cost of helping making them late was not a factor. Seminarians who were already late were the least likely to stop and help – some even stepped right over the slumped body to rush to give their talk about the importance of helping strangers!

Latané and Darley (1970), similarly, found that increasing the cost of helping could inhibit prosocial behaviour. In their study, a confederate travelling on a New York subway train asked a member of the public (the unsuspecting participant) for very obvious directions. At this point, another confederate interrupted and gave the first confederate (who had asked for directions) completely inaccurate directions. Latané and Darley arranged it so that, in some cases, the confederate interrupting with false directions had physically intimidated another passenger (also a confederate) and, in other cases, they had not.

Imagine that you are the participant in this study. You are just giving directions to someone who had asked you for them when another person interrupts, to give obviously incorrect directions. Would you correct them and, more to the point, would your decision about whether to correct them be affected by having seen them physically intimidate another passenger. If we do weigh the costs and benefits of our action before engaging in prosocial behaviour, then witnessing the physical intimidation should increase the perceived costs of intervention (risk of personal physical intimidation) and, therefore, decrease the propensity to engage in the prosocial act of correcting the mistaken directions. This is just what Latané and Darley found – increasing the perceived costs decreased prosocial behaviour.

Increasing the perceived needs of the victims however, can increase prosocial behaviour. According to exchange theory, the greater the victim's perceived needs, the higher the empathic costs of not helping. Piliavin and Piliavin (1972) in a further experiment in the already experiment-rich location of New York's subway, had a confederate collapse, bleeding, and, in another condition, a confederate collapse but without bleeding. As you would expect, the blood was not real but appeared to be. Which confederate do you think received more help?

If you thought it was the stranger collapsing and bleeding, you would be correct – they were helped in 95 percent of cases, which is significantly higher than the 65 percent of non-bleeding confederates who received help. The explanation is that the apparent bleeding increased the empathic costs for the bystander of not helping.

If you guessed wrong, then what you may have noted is that the apparent presence of blood could also increase the *costs* of helping – especially in more recent years with the widespread concern about the transmission of illnesses via blood.

The arousal: cost–reward model developed by Piliavin et al. (1981) not only indicates how perceived costs may influence the likelihood of bystanders deciding to engage in prosocial behaviour or not but also highlights the types of behaviour that different combinations of costs might give rise to. In Table 8.2, the high or low costs (to the bystander) of helping form a matrix with the high or low costs (to the victim) of not receiving help. In each cell (labelled A–D for ease of reference), two examples of instances of prosocial behaviour that represent the combination of costs for bystander and victim are given.

In cell A, where the cost to the victim of the bystander not helping is high (risk of death) and the cost of helping is low (involving relatively little effort or risk on the part of the bystander), then help is both likely to occur and be directly given by the bystander. In cell B, the bystander is potentially placed in a dilemma – the help called for by the situation is vitally important to the victim, yet potentially very costly to the bystander. These kinds of situations mean those who help are deemed to be heroic – risking their lives to save a life. In such cases, there may be direct help (bystanders risking their lives to save the victim) or indirect help (letting someone else know, contacting the emergency services) there can also be redefinitions of the situation that address the potential dissonance associated with not helping.

Thus, deciding not to help can make us feel extremely ashamed and guilty (our inaction causes us dissonance), but we can minimise our psychological distress by redefining the situation (perhaps the person in the river is engaging in some sort of prank, the person who has collapsed is 'probably drunk') or deciding that other bystanders are responsible for helping (there are others who 'saw the whole thing' and are better able to help).

In cell C, we have the opposite case – here, the 'victim's' needs are relatively trivial, so if we do not help nothing dreadful will happen, but the helping itself is not costly we do not need to 'put ourselves out'. In these cases, we may help and whether we do or not is perhaps influenced by norms regarding the circumstances (such as giving up our seat for those who are pregnant or elderly).

In cell D, we have the situations that are least likely to evoke help as while helping would be very costly to

Table 8.2 Evaluating the costs and rewards (to the bystander) of helping based on Piliavin et al.'s (1981) arousal: cost–reward model

		COSTS TO THE BYSTANDER HELPING	
		Low	**High**
VICTIM'S NEED	High	**A** **Example:** Throwing a rubber ring that is nearby into a river to save someone from drowning, ***or*** passing medication to someone who would otherwise suffer a heart attack Help is perceived as highly important to the victim and the cost of offering is low. Direct intervention on the part of the bystander is likely	**B** **Example:** Diving into a river to save someone from drowning, ***or*** entering a burning building to rescue a child who is trapped This situation is the most uncomfortable as there is a high price for both helping and not helping. Indirect options might be followed, such as alerting others to the situation – calling emergency services. Sometimes the situation or victim themselves may be redefined to make the bystander feel less responsible for helping
	Low	**C** **Example:** Helping someone with their luggage up some stairs, ***or*** giving up your seat on a crowded train for someone who appears to need it Help is neither costly nor especially important and situational norms, such as helping the elderly, may shape behaviour	**D** **Example:** Diving into a river to retrieve a copy of the *Metro* (free newspaper) that someone has dropped, ***or*** risking missing a flight to pick up something seemingly unimportant that someone has dropped The high cost of giving help and the limited perceived benefit to the victim mean that help is unlikely to be given

us (risking life, considerable effort or expense) and the actual need is fairly insignificant. We would be extremely unlikely to help in these circumstances, possibly even ignoring the 'need'. Indeed, in cases where someone does offer such costly help to meet such little need, the behaviour might appear bizarre, somehow self-aggrandising or romantic, depending on the specific circumstances.

It is worth thinking through any recent examples of what might be broadly thought of as prosocial behaviour, especially times when you intervened in some situation where you had the opportunity to simply observe, without intervening. The clearest example from my own recent experience happened a couple of days ago when I travelled on a bus in my neighbourhood in South London. The bus journey was completely uneventful, until someone got on and refused to pay the bus fare to the driver. A heated altercation between the passenger and driver ensued, with lots of threats and derogatory remarks about each other's mothers. During this time, the bus did not move. I was travelling with my two young children and wanted the shouting to stop, the bus to move and, perhaps most of all, nothing more serious to develop. I went up to the driver and paid him the bus fare. The fare was refused by the driver who said that he now refused to take the passenger as he had become abusive. The altercation was never entirely resolved, although eventually the passenger left the bus with some loose proposal to seek a physical resolution to the disagreement at a later date.

What were the costs of my (unsuccessful) intervention? Most obviously there would have been the bus fare itself (£2). Perhaps more significant were the potential repercussions – my intervention in this heated dispute could have led either or both parties to turn their aggression on me, the fellow passengers might have criticised my intervention and getting involved might have made my children more aware of the dispute and, in turn, they would have been more likely to notice if I received negative attention as a consequence of intervening. The potential benefits of helping included feeling that I had tried what I could, possibly stopping anything worse from developing, possibly providing a means by which the driver could continue driving the bus.

This illustration perhaps shows some endorsement of the arousal: cost–reward model – some decision was made that appeared to take into account the costs and rewards of intervention. Do you notice, however, that this example was unexpected and of the type likely to cause arousal in bystanders, yet not an emergency situation – it allowed for arousal as well as the possibility of a relatively rational appraisal of the costs and rewards of intervention.

The arousal: cost–reward model (see Figure 8.8 earlier in this chapter), to some extent, integrates the work on mood and arousal with the situational perception and decision making approaches – giving a role to the situation as a trigger for a reaction, which is then made sense of that, in turn, may trigger a rational calculation of the pros and cons of intervening. It brings psychological state into the picture (arousal), not as an intrapsychic 'first cause' – like a mood state – but, rather, as a response to some unexpected event where prosocial behaviour may be relevant. It also avoids a deterministic view of the psychological state by emphasising that what the arousal leads to depends on how it is labelled by the bystander. Finally, it depicts the decision to intervene or not as depending on a rational appraisal of the situation.

It is possible, however, to question how many situations simultaneously cause arousal in bystanders and allow for a rational cost–benefit appraisal on the part of bystanders. If situations are very arousing, they may require a more urgent response than the cost–reward element of the model suggests. Similarly, if they allow for a careful weighing up of rewards and costs, then they might not be as intensely arousing in the first place. Furthermore, the cost–reward element of the model suggests that the behaviour results from a rational appraisal of costs and rewards, but is perhaps a little unclear about just how altruistic this is. Thus, Dovidio et al. (2006, p. 86) argue that 'Bystanders weigh the needs of the victim and their own needs and goals and then decide whether helping is too costly in that circumstance', which sounds like there is an altruistic element, but elsewhere describes the model as 'egoistic'. If the model really *does* include 'victim's need' as well as 'bystander's guilt' as the costs of not intervening (which Dovidio et al. suggest), then there is the implication that some combination of altruistic and egoistic considerations are at work – even though the model itself is not explicit about this.

A further criticism of the cost–reward aspect of the model is that, in being a so-called 'economic' model, it carries over assumptions that work reasonably well in economics (where costs and profits can be clear, quantifiable, known factors), but less well in situations where the values are not known or perhaps even unknowable. That is, can bystanders readily weigh the costs and rewards or, at the very least, act as if they can in order to make their decision? In many real-world (non-economic) situations, we might not know the rewards and costs of our decisions, we might not act as if we know and the knowing might not be a meaningful possibility. Finally, as with other models that suggest reasoning precedes decisions to help or not, it could be argued that the model may work as a means of justification after the event rather than the cognitive cause before it. That is, we might draw on the idea of a rational appraisal of costs and rewards to justify why we did or did not intervene rather than calculate this prior to intervening or not.

Critical recap

Integrating why and when: arousal and decision making in prosocial behaviour

1 The arousal: cost–reward model suggests that, prior to a decision to intervene with prosocial behaviour or not, the bystander engages in a calculation of costs and rewards that takes into account costs for the victim of not helping. It is possible to question the extent to which spontaneous help in emergency situations is preceded by such mental calculations.

2 There is some uncertainty with regard to how egoistic or altruistic the model is. This rests crucially on what factors bystanders weigh up when considering costs and rewards.

3 The model carries certain economic decision making assumptions that may be less applicable in non-economic human interactions.

4 It also raises issues about whether the rational basis for intervening or not is best thought of as a device drawn on to justify what we did (or did not do) rather than as a cognitive basis for action.

Reflective questions

1 *Does the arousal: cost–reward model provide a convincing account of real-life prosocial behaviour?*

2 *What changes – if any – would you make to the arousal: cost–reward model?*

3 *Think of a case of prosocial behaviour that you have been directly involved in. Do you think that the arousal: cost–reward model describes what you experienced?*

4 *Which of the models considered so far best explains helping in emergency situations? What about non-emergency helping behaviour, such as volunteering, helping a charity and so on?*

8.5 Critiquing research into prosocial behaviour

It is worth returning for a moment to a point made at the beginning of this chapter. When we think of instances of prosocial behaviour, we often wind up with some sort of direct help offered by one person to a stranger in an unexpected emergency situation, such as helping a person who has collapsed on the floor. This prototypical version of prosocial behaviour is surprisingly dominant in research as well – that is, much of the research on prosocial behaviour conceptualises it in exactly these terms. It is an interesting exercise to quickly review just how much of the literature covered implicitly or explicitly tries to explain this specific type of prosocial behaviour. The problem with this is that other types of prosocial behaviour, though less dramatic, are probably more frequently engaged in, yet receive less attention. Here, we will consider help offered to and solicited from others who are known to or similar to one another, as well as planned, rather than spontaneous, helping. Furthermore, while prosocial behaviour has nearly always been thought about as an interpersonal process – one individual helping another – here we will consider intra- and intergroup aspects of prosocial behaviour.

A second, related, issue is that, even within the research that predominantly focuses on direct one-to-one help given to a stranger in an emergency, there are issues about how the act of prosocial behaviour has been operationalised – that is, what behaviour on the part of the participant is treated as being 'prosocial'. Furthermore, there is scope to question the social construction of 'prosocial' behaviour – should it be a taken-for-granted given or is there an issue concerning how certain behaviours come to be construed as 'prosocial'? These issues receive attention below.

Help given to and received from known or similar others

Some research suggests that where those in need of help are able to choose their helper, there is a preference that is not simply defined by the need itself.

Medvene (1992) examined college students' preferences with regard to who they would turn to when seeking help regarding academic and social problems. Students were able to choose between professionals, students who had been specially trained to offer advice (para-professionals) and other students without training, but who had experienced the same problems and had coped better, worse or the same as the student seeking help. Who would you turn to? Medvene (1992) found that the most commonly selected category – sought out by more than 50 per cent of participants for academic problems, 58 percent for social problems – was a student who had experienced the same problems and coped better. If students had simply selected those most qualified to give expert advice, then professionals should have been the most frequently selected category of helper, but they chose other students who had both experienced the same problem and coped better with it.

Medvene explains these results as a compromise between the students seeking self-improvement (hence, seeking someone who has coped better) and self-image concerns (hence, preferring someone who has also experienced the same problems and would presumably be less likely to negatively judge the student seeking help).

Wills (1992), similarly, found that people might not turn to professionals for help with regard to their psychological problems. Indeed, Wills suggests that people seeking such help are between two and five times as likely to turn to friends, family and other acquantainces rather than professionals (despite their relevant training and expertise). Thus, the choice seems to be governed by not relevant expertise but, rather, the type of relationship between the help seeker and the help giver.

Wills suggests that, in some types of relationships, exchange considerations will be particularly salient – that is, both parties will be aware of when one has given and the other received help and there may be a sense of indebtedness regarding this imbalance. For the person receiving help, this can be uncomfortable. If, by receiving help from some people, I have a strong sense that I 'owe them one', I might prefer to choose help from someone else instead. Wills contrasts these 'exchange' relationships with 'communal' relationships, in which there is less keeping of a tab on who has given what and who owes what to the other and more interest in the well-being of the relationship and each other. Seeking help from those with whom I feel I have a communal relationship may avoid me feeling that I then owe the other person something and this may be more desirable to me *even* if the help giver is less qualified than other possible sources of help.

Planned helping

Much of the emphasis in research has been on spontaneous, ad hoc help, usually given (or not given) in an emergency situation – such as helping a stranger who has collapsed – whereas much prosocial behaviour takes the form of planned, longer-term help that is coordinated by some organisation, such as a charity. Research into **planned helping** activities often distinguishes between the *initiation* of the activity (what makes people start to help in this way in the first place) and the *maintenance* of this prosocial behaviour (what keeps people doing this). With planned helping behaviour – such as supporting or volunteering to help a charitable organisation or giving blood – often elements outside of some direct victim's needs play a part in initiating people's involvement.

Planned helping This refers to the non-ad hoc help that we might offer by, for example, giving our time or money to a charity or providing other forms of regular help to others (such as visiting or assisting them on a regular basis).

Piliavin and Callero (1991) found that having friends or relatives who gave blood greatly increased the likelihood of an individual giving blood themselves (the approval of significant others for the activity has resonances with the idea of subjective norms influencing attitude-related behaviour, as discussed in Chapter 6). Planned helping can also be influenced by wider cultural and historical events. Penner, Brannick, Connell and Webb (2005) found that, after the September 11, 2001 attacks on the World Trade Center and the hijack of two additional planes on 11 September 2001, there was an unprecedented increase in people in the USA registering to volunteer for charitable work (as measured by 'VolunteerMatch. a Web-based resource for placing people with charitable agencies). From the week, in which the attacks happened and the two following weeks, volunteering massively increased to peaking at approximately three times the rate it had been in the previous year.

Jonas, Schimel, Greenberg and Pyszczynski (2002) suggest that when people become aware of their own mortality, they are more likely to endorse a 'cultural worldview', in which helping others is particularly highly valued. It is possible that this – in addition to other factors, such as the increased coverage of the ways in which charitable organisations, such as the Red Cross, helped in the emergency and the perception of increased need itself – had an influence on the sort of premeditated, planned helping which would not be born out in the cases of spontaneous ad hoc help social psychologists have concentrated on.

With regard to the maintenance of prosocial behaviour, Piliavin and Callero (1991) suggest that where the helping behaviour becomes a part of how people define themselves (part of their identity), then it is much more likely to continue. Thus, blood donors for whom giving blood was a part of how they thought about themselves were found to continue donating more than those for whom this prosocial behaviour did not come to form a part of their identity. These specific issues regarding the role of identity in the maintenance of planned prosocial behaviour provide a way of understanding a hugely important aspect of prosocial behaviour, yet are left unexplored in studies that have focused on ad hoc spontaneous prosocial behaviour.

Group aspects of prosocial behaviour

Another strand of prosocial behaviour that is eclipsed by the focus on one-to-one helping is the influence of group membership. One element of this concerns whether some form of unintentional racism shapes the propensity (in the USA) that white participants have to help black individuals. In a review of 31 studies, Saucier, Miller and Doucet (2005) suggest that, while white participants helped both black *and* white individuals to the same extent, there was a significant difference where either the costs of helping were higher or when the situation demanded an instant response. They account for this in terms of 'aversive racism' – the somewhat depressing idea that many white people have a prejudice they do not like to admit to (that is, it is aversive). This prejudice does not lead to discrimination, where it would be obvious to all that prejudice was at work – that is, when there is no good reason not to help – but, as soon as excuses or justifications for not helping are available (such as the effort, difficulty, time or risk involved in helping), then less help is given to black as compared to white individuals. Similarly, in cases where immediate helping action is called for, then the bias towards helping white individuals is apparent because, according to Saucier et al. in such cases there is less opportunity for individuals to suppress their discriminatory biases.

An alternative take on **group aspects of prosocial behaviour** is found in the work of Levine, Prosser, Evans and Reicher (2005) and Stuermer, Snyder and Omoto (2005). Levine et al. conducted an experiment in which they first made participants' football (soccer) team preferences salient by asking them to complete a questionnaire about which team they preferred and then invited them to go to another building to watch a match involving that team, then answer questions about it. These procedures were intended to encourage the participants to think of themselves in terms of their identity as fans of that specific team. What a coincidence – the moment they walked over to the other building, someone who had been jogging appeared to slip and hurt their ankle. The question was, of course, would the participants, who had been made conscious of their football allegiances, help the jogger. Interestingly, it depended on what the jogger was wearing. If the jogger was wearing a rival team's shirt or a neutral shirt, then the levels of helping were pretty low (30 and 33 per cent, respectively). If, however, the jogger was wearing a team shirt that matched the participants' own preferrence, then the level of helping was up to 92 per cent. It should be noted that the similar low levels for the rival team and the neutral (no club) shirt suggest that the participants were not so much punishing rival supporters as helping members of their own ingroup of supporters of a specific football team.

Group aspects of prosocial behaviour This refers to the various ways in which prosocial behaviour may be shaped by our own perceived group identities (for example, our religious, political or activist identities may shape our prosocial behaviour) and/or those of others (for instance, perceiving others as belonging to the same or a different group than us may shape our prosocial behaviour towards them).

In a second study, Levine et al. (2005) made the identity of being a *football* supporter (rather than being a supporter of a different sport or no sport) salient over and above affiliation to an individual club. In this condition, football fans helped collapsed joggers dressed as supporters of their own team most (80 per cent), other football supporters next (70 per cent) and those who did not wear a football shirt least (20 per cent). What is crucial, according to Levine et al., is that where there is a group dimension to opportunities to help, the identity which is active at the time will shape whether or not helping takes place. That is, the group identity that I think about myself as having (football supporter or specific club supporter) will shape whether I help when they are relevant in the helping situation I encounter.

Stuermer et al. (2005), similarly, found that when people had opportunities to help members of a shared group, then group membership was the basis for helping regardless of any interpersonal considerations, such as how much the potential helper liked the individual in need. By contrast, if the person in need did *not* share the same group identity, then the decision to help was much more influenced by interpersonal issues, such as how much the potential helper liked the person needing help.

Taken together, intergroup research on helping suggests that a perception of common group membership can greatly enhance the propensity to help another. The research further suggests that there is a certain fluidity regarding the specific group identity that a potential helper may draw on – the identity that is most prominent or salient at the time will shape the helping behaviour. Furthermore, these intergroup considerations, especially the identification of the person in need as sharing a group identity with us, once made relevant to the potential helper, will often override other considerations regarding whether or not to help.

Source: Martin Rickett/PA Wire/Press Association Images

On 14 May 2008, a Glasgow Rangers fan helps a fellow supporter following riots in Manchester. Do you think that having a shared group identity – as Rangers fans – made it more likely that this person would stop and help? Do you think that fans from the rival team (Zenit St Petersburg) would have stopped to help this injured fan?

Constructing prosocial behaviour

One framework for thinking critically about prosocial behaviour is provided by social constructionism (see Chapter 1). As is argued throughout this book, social constructionism is a perspective that emphasises the 'put together in language' – or *constructed* – aspects of ourselves and our worlds. Hepburn (2003, p. 175) draws on Gergen (1994) to provide a particularly succinct summary of its concerns – two of which are given here:

1 The terms we use to describe ourselves and our worlds are not dictated by their objects.
2 The terms through which we understand the world and ourselves are social artefacts, produced over historical time through exchanges between people within cultures.

Thus, Hepburn notes that social constructionism, particularly as developed by Gergen, questions the very terms we use to describe and understand 'ourselves and our worlds'. From this perspective, then, the 'objects' of study for social psychology (and not just the theories) can be questioned. Rather than seeing, for example, aggression, self or prosocial behaviour as phenomena that are out there, waiting to be discovered, we could see the active work using these terms does. Thus, in a textbook such as this, we could stop and not simply learn a fixed definition just to get on to the 'interesting' ideas about what causes prosocial behaviour, but, instead reflect on how something comes to be defined as prosocial and what is done by constructing a given behaviour in that way. Research sensitive to social constructionist considerations could move away from the exploration of *causes* of the fixed, knowable, 'in the world' reality of prosocial behaviour and, instead, address how, in everyday life, certain forms of behaviour come to be talked about (in specific sequences of interaction) as being or not being prosocial.

Think for a moment of two cases where seemingly prosocial behaviour might become argued about. First, imagine you are watching a televised charity 'extravaganza', with lots of celebrities imploring the public to give money to the charities that are being supported. At some point in the evening, a chief executive from a large financial institution presents a giant cheque (with the company's name very prominently displayed) to one of the hosts of the show. Let us suppose that you roll your eyes and say, 'That's just blatant advertising!', but your partner disagrees and points out the generosity of the gift. In this case, you may start to substantiate or warrant your version of the 'donation', while your partner may warrant theirs. That is, the idea of this donation as being a prosocial act is not a 'fixed truth' or a given – it is a position that your partner adopts and you dispute with an alternative construction. Furthermore, these **constructions of prosocial behaviour** are not context-free reflections on the nature of reality – they are views that reflect argumentative positions and you each have some stake or vested interest (albeit minimal) in constructing the act as being prosocial or not.

Now imagine a second example. You are just about to walk past someone sitting on the ground when you stop to buy a copy of *The Big Issue* (a charity magazine distributed to poor and homeless individuals for them to sell and keep the proceeds). Your partner stops and asks, 'What are you doing?' Now, you could construct your act as prosocial – you might construct it and what motivated it in terms of your concern for the person, their children or the wider cause they represent. You might choose to construct it in terms of the exceptional and rarely encountered nature of this person's specific need. Equally, you could construct it in terms of pragmatics – you wanted them to stop hassling you, get rid of some loose change – or self-interest – you were interested in articles in that copy of *The Big Issue*.

The point here is that a single person talking about their own act could actually draw on lots of different 'true' accounts to explain why they gave money to someone. The version chosen might be determined not so much by reality but what is accomplished by the account that is offered. That is, even though there are many different accounts we *could* give of why we did what we did, we usually arrive at one and that is often shaped to *do* something in interactional terms. Each construction of the act might do something slightly different – for example, the prosocial account might project a kind version of self, the 'exceptional case' version might address issues of using discretion, the pragmatic account might ward off accusations of gullibility and the self-interest account might address issues of financial imprudence. Thus, a single act can be seen as open to multiple constructions and the construction that is given can be investigated in terms of what it does in interactional terms. Explore these ideas yourself in Box 8.9.

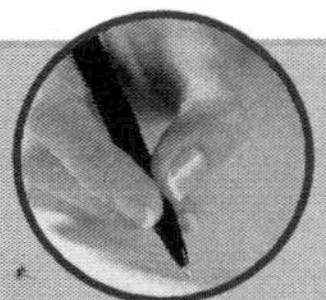

Box 8.9 TRY IT OUT Constructing prosocial behaviour

Look through a couple of newspapers or use an online news service such as Reuters to find two examples of prosocial behaviour (you might need to use other search terms such as 'helping', 'hero', 'altruistic').

Do you think that these examples support an explanation in terms of factors within the person, the situation or a combination of the two?

If you want an additional challenge, consider what sort of ideology these accounts might reflect. Is there an individualism (good/bad individual people) at work, is there a sense of who is entitled to receive help, is there a sense of how 'good' 'helpful' behaviour is defined?

Besides an immediate, argumentative context for constructing acts as prosocial or not, there is a wider, ideological context in which the act can be situated. This is addressed in other chapters (see Chapters 1, 2 and 10) where some of Foucault's contribution to thinking about power and ideology is considered. Here, we can briefly note that, just as we can critically inspect how some people and forms of behaviour can come to be defined as 'sane' or 'insane' – within given cultures and historical periods (Foucault, 1967) – so too, we can critically think about how behaviours may become culturally defined as 'prosocial' or 'antisocial'. Think for a moment about some of the extraordinary acts of courage referred to in the introduction to this chapter – many of these acts were illegal and against the prevailing ideologies, where they occured.

During World War II, many citizens would have considered reporting on Jews who were hiding an act of civic duty and, in some sense at least, prosocial, the Nazi ideology providing a framework for understanding such actions (that would lead to those reported on being murdered) as being 'good', 'just' and 'prosocial'. As Dovidio et al. (2006), note the so-called 'Good Samaritan' laws of Germany in the 1930s required German citizens to report 'enemies of

Constructions of prosocial behaviour This refers to the ways in which we come to define and talk about certain actions as being 'prosocial'. One strand of this is concerned with culturally shared definitions – how do people in a given culture at a given time come to share certain ideas of what is or is not prosocial behaviour? A second strand concerns how we may construct the behaviour of self and others as prosocial or not in our talk and interaction with.

the State' (homosexuals, gypsies, Jews and other groups whom the Nazis decided to persecute) to the SS. Within that specific context, reporting members of these groups was construed (by some) as prosocial behaviour, in that it was deemed to help the German Reich. Now, however, in a very different context, such behaviours would be universally condemned. Similar, ideologically located definitions of helping are present in all genocides – helping someone defined as 'subhuman' or an enemy of the State can be construed as antisocial, disloyal, unpatriotic behaviour, while refusing to help them or reporting them to the authorities can be – and frequently is – valued within the prevailing ideological framework.

Critical recap

Critiquing research into prosocial behaviour

1 Many of the approaches to prosocial behaviour considered above have focused on the cognitions and/or emotions that are involved in determining whether or not people choose to help others. It is possible, however, to question whether individual cognition and affect provide the best ways of making sense of helping behaviour. This emphasis situates prosocial behaviour as an essentially individualistic act, generated by the isolated cognitive experiences of individuals. Such an approach underestimates the relevance of shared, group or, indeed, cultural ways of making sense of who should be helped and what behaviour is deemed 'prosocial' or helpful.

2 In a related vein, research that emphasises cognitive reasoning as the internal determinant of prosocial behaviour may not recognise the sort of interactional work that post hoc explanations can do. Thus, accounts of why I did, or did not, intervene and help could be conceptualised as 'me accounting for my action' in the immediate interaction rather than being simply taken as an accurate reflection of my cognitive activity prior to my intervention or lack of it.

3 A third issue is the forms of prosocial behaviour that have received particular attention in the research reviewed in this chapter. Much of it has focused on stranger help in emergency situations, arguably narrowing 'prosocial behaviour' to a highly specific subset of a much larger whole. While definitions of prosocial behaviour can, and should be, debated (see point four below), they might well extend beyond giving emergency help to strangers. Indeed, it is likely that most of our behaviour is more planned than ad hoc, involves those we know and is within a routine rather than an emergency context.

4 The conceptualisation of prosocial behaviour is further narrowed by the relative inattention paid by many researchers to group aspects of helping behaviour. Some research has highlighted the ways in which helping behaviour may be associated with the group or social identity of the potential helper and of the person in need of help, but thinking of prosocial behaviour as one individual helping another may lead us to underestimate the importance of social identities.

5 A more radical critique can be developed by thinking again about how we come to define something as being 'prosocial behaviour'. From a social constructionist perspective, rather than prosocial behaviour being a real thing 'out there' that we need to carefully observe and accurately define, it is a form or construction of reality. From this perspective it is important to identify what comes to be defined as prosocial behaviour and what sorts of things are done by defining it in those ways – for example, what sorts of behaviour towards what groupings of people are encouraged or discouraged in these construction?

6 Such questions about how we construct prosocial behaviour relate to issues regarding how it has been operationally defined in experiments – that is, what sort of behaviour is treated as 'prosocial' in the literature. A quick review of this chapter reveals an enormous range of explicit (and implicit) definitions. It is worth noting that some studies observe actual behaviour in the laboratory, some in more natural settings (such as on a train or in a shopping mall, where confederates collapse or struggle with their shopping) and some use questionnaires, asking about actual behaviour or future hypothetical scenarios. The actual range of behaviours taken as measures of prosocial behaviour in the research reviewed in this chapter have included; helping a stranger who has collapsed, accepting electric shocks in place of another person, assisting with heavy shopping bags, forwarding a stamped addressed letter left on the floor, sharing lecture notes, offering advice, promising hours of telephone help for a charity and generously sharing money with other participants. These extremely diverse measures of prosocial behaviour raise questions about how they relate to each other. How can one paper critique another if it used a vastly different measure of prosocial behaviour? It also raises the question of whether all (or any) of these relate to specific, real-world instances of prosocial behaviour – or the lack of it – that we are trying to understand and will findings about prosocial behaviour that asked participants to report how they would respond to a family member needing an organ donation really tell us about their help for strangers in an emergency? More radically still, will it actually tell us how they will respond in a genuine organ donation situation or are the reports and questionnaires that elicited the organ donation responses best understood as quite distinct (and, indeed, unusual) opportunities for forms of social action that do not necessarily relate to the *actual* purported topic of their enquiry?

Reflective questions

1 *Can you think of an action that some people might define as 'prosocial', while others would not?*

2 *What are the limitations with the ways in which 'prosocial behaviour' has been implicitly, and, explicitly defined in social psychology?*

Summary

- This chapter addressed the issue of why and when people will engage in prosocial behaviour.
- Theories that attempt to explain why people engage in prosocial behaviour can be divided into those concerned with motivation, those concerned with psychological state and those that draw on evolutionary theory. The motivational accounts for prosocial behaviour include altruistic explanations, such as the empathy–altruism hypothesis (people are motivated to help others who are in need) and more egoistic explanations, such as the empathic joy hypothesis (people help to feel good) and competitive altruism (people help to look good). Psychological state accounts include the idea that we help because we are in a positive mood (it makes us more attentive and positive) and the negative state relief model (we help in order to gain relief from negative mood states). Evolutionary approaches suggest that we engage in prosocial behaviour because doing so has proved adaptive (increasing the chances of common genes being transmitted to future generations).
- These approaches to why people engage in prosocial behaviour can be criticised in several respects. Approaches considering motivation and psychological state are dealing with purported causal factors that are not directly accessible, so the way in which the relevant mood or motivation is defined, induced and measured can be queried. Evolutionary theory approaches have often relied on questionnaires regarding hypothetical prosocial behaviour, which may or may not be informative about *actual* past, present or future prosocial behaviour. All of the approaches to why people engage in prosocial behaviour can be questioned with regard to how precisely they account for the apparent variation across situations.
- Theories that attempt to understand when people engage in prosocial behaviour have suggested that it is linked to the ways in which bystanders perceive and make judgements about the victim and their circumstances. This tradition of research began with diffusion of responsibility (the idea that people might not help if they feel the responsibility for doing so is spread among others). Subsequent attributional approaches emphasise that prosocial behaviour can be linked to our attributions concerning what has caused the predicament of the person we may or may not help. The somewhat related just world hypothesis suggests that our beliefs concerning the fairness or justness of the world (for example, that bad things happen to bad people) will shape our likelihood of helping others.
- These approaches that seek to address when people will engage in prosocial behaviour can also be criticised. First, we can question whether people have the necessary information or are able to engage in the calculations that the models suggest in real-life situations. Second, the ideas covered may work better as justifications after the event than act as cognitive causes of our actions. In other words, I might justify my not giving help in terms of there being others who could help or the victim causing their own problems, or them somehow deserving what has happened to them, but these justifications might arise after my decision to not help rather than before.
- One model – the arousal: cost–reward model – attempted to combine an element of psychological state – arousal – with cognitive processing of the situation, in which the rewards and costs of helping are weighed. From this perspective, arousal that is attributed to the situation of witnessing someone in need can trigger an evaluation of the pros and cons of intervening and, as a consequence of this rational appraisal, the decision to help or not is made. This model was criticised, partly because it applies the notion of economic decision making to non-economic interpersonal processes (where 'costs' and 'rewards' are far less knowable and quantifiable). Furthermore, the arousal: cost–reward model – like the other decision making models – could be seen as a resource used when accounting for why we did or did not intervene *after* a decision has been made rather than determining whether or not help is given.
- The research reviewed in this chapter also raised the question of how prosocial behaviour can be defined. One strand of this is the empirical lack of precision with implicit definitions in empirical studies, which can treat quite different measures as 'essentially' referring to the same 'underlying' prosocial behaviour. A second element of this is the conceptual narrowness of prosocial behaviour – the emphasis being on one stranger helping another in an emergency ad hoc situation. Less well-known research covering help between known or similar individuals, intergroup help and planned helping was also reviewed. A

third element of this was addressed by drawing on social constructionist ideas to question how a given behaviour may come to be constructed as being prosocial or not to attend to interpersonal or ideological issues.

Review questions

1 *What different motivations for prosocial behaviour have been debated in the literature?*

2 *How does mood relate to prosocial behaviour?*

3 *How do evolutionary approaches explain prosocial behaviour?*

4 *What does it mean to say that there are issues concerning how motivations and psychological states are operationalised in experiments?*

5 *What is diffusion of responsibility?*

6 *How do attributions relate to prosocial behaviour?*

7 *How could someone's belief that the world is 'just' shape their prosocial behaviour?*

8 *What is meant by the criticism that some accounts of prosocial decisionmaking might be post hoc justifications?*

9 *What is the arousal: cost–reward model?*

10 *What is meant by attributing the arousal to the victim's situation?*

11 *How do perceptions of costs and rewards shape potential prosocial behaviour?*

12 *What types of prosocial behaviour are there – what has most research focused on?*

13 *What issues does intergroup research raise for traditional accounts of prosocial behaviour?*

14 *What relevance does social constructionism have for our thinking about what prosocial behaviour is?*

Recommended reading

Darley, B., & Latané, J. (1968). Bystander interventions in emergencies: Diffusion of responsibility. *Journal of Personality and Social Psychology, 8*, 377–383. The paper that started much of the social psychology of prosocial behaviour, a classic – treat yourself to reading it in the original.

Dovidio, J. F., Piliavin, J. A., Schroeder, D. A., & Penner, L. A. (2006). *The social psychology of prosocial behaviour.* Mahwah, N.J.: Erlbaum. A wonderfully comprehensive review of a broad spectrum of prosocial behaviour research.

Henry, P. J., Reyna, C., & Weiner, B. (2004). Hate welfare but help the poor: How the attributional content of stereotypes explains the paradox of reactions to the destitute in America. *Journal of Applied Social Psychology, 34*, 34–58. A fascinating investigation into the powerful effect that descriptions of potential recipients of help may have.

Hepburn, A. (2003). *An introduction to critical psychology.* London: Sage. A vital resource for rendering complex critical ideas accessible.

Manning, R., Levine, M., & Collins, A. (2007). The Kitty Genovese murder and the social psychology of helping: The parable of the 38 witnesses. *American Psychologist, 62*, 555–562. An excellent rethink of the Kitty Genovese case.

Piliavin, I. M., Rodin, J., & Piliavin, J. A. (1969). Good Samaritanism: An underground phenomenon? *Journal of Personality and Social Psychology, 13*, 289–299. This is another research classic – read it in the light of Jane Piliavin's reflections in the Key researcher feature earlier in this chapter.

Useful weblinks

www.bbc.co.uk/radio4/science/case_study_20080507.shtml Some useful materials and links relating to the case of Kitty Genovese.

www.wadsworth.com/psychology_d/templates/student_resources/0155060678_rathus/ps/ps19.html Darley and Latané's work on the unresponsive bystander.

www.sagepub.com/vaughnstudy/articles/dair/Saucier.pdf Saucier, Miller and Doucet's (2005) research on discriminatory aspects of helping behaviour.

www.psych.lancs.ac.uk/people/MarkLevine.html A great resource for Mark Levine's publications on social identity and bystander behaviour.

9

Aggression and intergroup conflict

Learning outcomes

By the end of this chapter you should have a critical understanding of research concerning:

- the evolutionary basis of an 'aggression instinct'
- the idea that situations can bring about aggressive behaviour by frustrating our desires
- how situational factors can trigger aggression
- how violence in the media may influence aggression
- the combined effect of physiological, situational and cognitive factors on causing aggression
- how being in a group may relate to aggressive behaviour
- how group identity may relate to intergroup conflict
- the impact of groups' self-interest on intergroup relations
- the limitations of many of the assumptions in the aggression and intergroup conflict literature.

On Saturday 2 January 2010, as he walked through Cruickshank Park, Melbourne, on his way to work in a fast food restaurant, Indian accountancy graduate Nita Garg was stabbed to death. The murder of Nita followed a series of attacks on Indians – particularly Indian students – in Melbourne and other Australian cities.

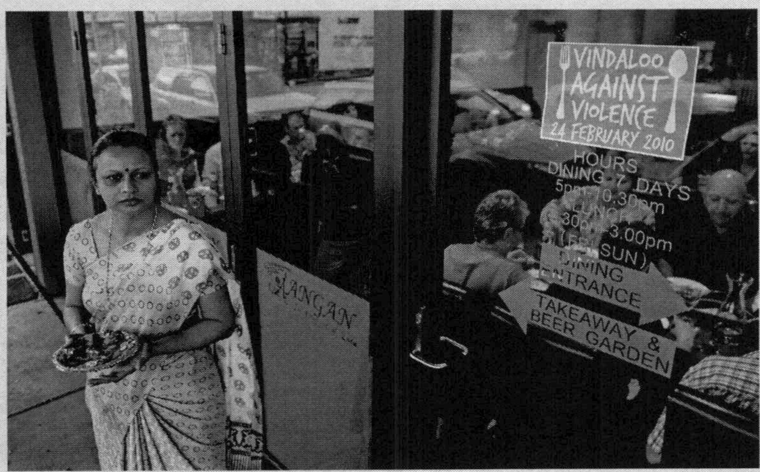

Source: William West/AFP/Getty Images

A scene from Australia's *Vindaloo against Violence* event – a campaign held across Australia (and beyond) to protest against attacks on Indian students living in Australia

How can this event be understood? The Indian media explained it as just the latest example of a wave of racist violence against Indians in Australia that started to become apparent in 2007 – around the time that the numbers of Indian students deciding to study in Australia began to increase. The Australian police and government largely took a different line – describing the crime and other seemingly related attacks as the acts of individual criminals rather than as related to any racism or hostility from groups within the 'white Australian' community towards students from India who live and study in Australia.

The subsequent 'vindaloo against violence' protest was part of a series of protests by a wide cross-section of Australians, international students and others against what they perceived as racist attacks. This incident and the series of attacks on Indian students raises the more general question as to how instances of violence such as this should be understood. Should our starting point be the individual criminal or the groups and group relations that may be relevant?

Introduction

The focus of this chapter – which encompasses both aggression and intergroup conflict – is often apparent in news stories such as the one reported above. Its relevance for me, however, was made sharply apparent in a personal experience of someone coming to see me to explain why their essay would be late. The student told me that her teenage brother had been shot while waiting with a younger relative at a bus stop. Apparently, because he was wearing clothing with certain colours, he was mistakenly identified as a member of a gang belonging to a specific area of South London and was shot by a rival gang member – members of which always wore other colours. Thankfully, the student's brother survived the shooting, but the event was deeply disturbing. Merely by wearing the colours associated with a particular London postcode, a human being became a target to be shot at.

Events such as these raise important issues regarding aggression and intergroup conflict. How should we make sense of such aggression? Is it something about being human that makes us aggressive – do we all have this predisposition – or should we think in terms of individual differences, such as gender or personality? Is there something about the perpetrator's life situation or the immediate circumstances that makes them aggressive? Does violence in music, films and computer games play a part? Should we shift our frame of reference and, instead, consider how aspects of being in a group may be associated with aggression on some occasions?

While social psychology does not pay the same attention to individual pathology or personality characteristics as some branches of psychology (such as personality, abnormal, clinical and forensic psychology), it still encompasses a considerable range of approaches, with emphases that include biologically-based drives, arousal, mass media, processes within groups and intergroup relations. The aim of this chapter is to outline some of the key debates found in these different approaches, thereby encompassing something of the range of social psychological perspectives on the causes of aggression and intergroup conflict.

Chapter overview

This chapter starts by considering aggression in terms of drives and instincts, focusing on Lorenz's (1966) *adaptive theory*, which approaches the drive to aggression as being 'adaptive' – that is better enabling members of the species to survive and propagate their genes.

It then reviews the *frustration–aggression hypothesis* – a perspective that emphasises the importance of frustrating situations (those that stop people from attaining what they wish to) in creating a sense of frustration that results in aggressive behaviour. The effects of 'aggressive stimuli' – for example, images of guns – and unpleasant or 'aversive stimuli' – the experience of pain, for example – are then considered.

Next, attention is given to the idea of *excitation transfer*, which considers the way in which a state of arousal – potentially from any arousing prior stimuli or activity (pornography, exercise, unpleasant prior encounter) – can lead to a lingering state of arousal that can lead to aggression against a target person (especially if the arousal is attributed to negative behaviour on the part of that person).

An attempt to integrate several of these approaches into the *general aggression model* is then considered.

The first of the more specifically group-orientated approaches to be addressed is *deindividuation theory*. Here, early deindividuation theory is considered, which emphasised the idea that being in a large group made people anonymous and, thus, made them lose their identity, which resulted in the release of destructive impulses. We will then consider the more recent *social identity approach* to deindividuation theory, which suggests that being in a group gives rise to not a loss but a change of identity – only resulting in violence if that is consistent with the group identity. The social identity of relations between groups is then considered, which emphasises the way in which intergroup relations (whether involving conflict or not) are shaped by the group identity of those involved. The chapter then addresses the *contact hypothesis,* which has suggested ways in which contact between members of different groups can reduce intergroup tensions. *Realistic conflict theory* is the next approach to be examined. This suggests that where groups have mutually incompatible goals (the success of one resulting in the failure of the other), there is likely to be conflict, whereas when groups have mutual goals (both groups benefiting from and being necessary to attain success), the likelihood of cooperation rather than conflict is increased. Finally, critical issues concerning how social psychology has approached aggression and intergroup conflict are considered.

In many textbooks, acts of aggression and intergroup conflict are treated separately – often occupying separate chapters. It is worth noting that they can indeed prove to be quite distinct phenomena – intergroup conflict may or may not involve aggression and, likewise, aggression may or may not have a group or intergroup dimension. As you read this chapter and consider such a broad range of approaches in social psychology to understanding aggression and conflict, however, you may get a clear sense of the breadth of social psychological perspectives of relevance to both agression and intergroup conflict. In addition, bringing perspectives as different as, for example, the evolutionary or 'adaptive' perspective and realistic conflict theory together may make the debates (for example, between individual drive and intergroup approaches) more readily apparent. Finally, juxtaposing these different perspectives can bring into focus both certain commonalities to seemingly very different approaches (such as how 'aggression' is conceptualised) and highlight some of the potential limitations of these shared assumptions.

9.1 Evolutionary approaches to aggression

Our journey through the social psychology of aggression and intergroup violence will start with some of the approaches that emphasised factors *within the person*. Particular attention will be paid to Lorenz's idea of an evolutionary based *instinct* for aggression. For Lorenz, the instinct to aggress is not entirely negative when viewed in an evolutionary context – on the contrary, it is because this instinct has been so successful in evolutionary terms that we have inherited it from our (successfully) aggressive ancestors. In this way, Lorenz develops a *person-based,* rather than situation-based, understanding of aggression.

Konrad Lorenz

Konrad Lorenz was influenced partly by Freud's (1930) work on the *Todestrieb*, or, *death drive* (subsequently referred to as the *Thanatos*). Freud, noting how some patients re-enacted traumatic events, argued there was a motivating force within the psyche that entailed an attraction to death, destruction and division. For Freud, this drive was not an adaptive instinct – he did not see it as relevant to the survival of our species (in the way reproduction or nurturing are), but a drive that could account for some of humanity's most destructive behaviour. Lorenz echoed Freud's location of aggression as *within* the individual, but, in contrast to Freud, envisaged this as an *adaptive* instinct.

For Lorenz, we experience an urge to aggress because this **instinct** had proved very important to our evolutionary ancestors, helping their survival. For previous organisms, then, aggression was adaptive because it encouraged species to disperse and gave the physically strongest the greatest opportunities to reproduce. Think of a pride of lions in the African savanna being drawn to a highly desirable watering hole. If there are already lions at that watering hole, they may well aggressively chase the newcomers away. This act of aggression encourages the newcomers to disperse more widely, – they will have to find their own watering hole elsewhere and hunt in a separate territory, meaning that there is less competition for the scarce resources of food, water and shelter. Furthermore, aggression over mates – typically between males in a given species – provides a selective opportunity for reproduction. A male ape, for example, may need to challenge another male to have opportunities to mate with a specific female – the physically fittest ape being likely to win the confrontation and have the opportunity, therefore, of passing on a gene pool in which the likelihood of physically stronger offspring is increased. The important point here is that the aggression serves the function of helping the species to survive.

This **adaptive** or **functional** view of aggression is even more apparent when we consider that, according to Lorenz, often it is an aggressive display that is sufficient rather than the causing of actual harm to the other. That is, for many animals, baring their teeth or claws, making an aggressive noise or adopting an aggressive stance is enough to demonstrate physical superiority. Also, in many species, the subordinate animal will display submission by, for example, lying with their neck exposed or stomach facing upwards.

These observations provide a way of understanding how something that could be adaptive for other species is altogether more destructive for humans. First, the needs for dispersal and selective breeding on the basis of physical strength are not crucial to the survival of the human species as technology enables large concentrations of humans to be within small geographic locations and (again, partly due to technology) brute strength does not have a species survival utility. Second, the display rituals in which one animal could display (rather than enact) aggression and the other could display submission are somewhat less available to humans – we have less obvious means of showing aggression and submission. Third, we have technologically advanced implements for doing aggression – thus, knives, guns and bombs enable deadly acts of aggression to be readily executed without any prior display of aggressive intent, making them less amenable to display rituals that avoid actual harm. Finally, some implements for aggression, such as guns and bombs, enable the aggressive act to be undertaken at more physical distance from the victim, again reducing the opportunity for any victim's responses to curtail the harmful act of aggression.

Reviewing evolutionary approaches to aggression

The idea that aggression can be accounted for purely in evolutionary terms, while old has been reinvigorated by a wider emphasis on evolutionary approaches in many areas of social psychology within the last couple of decades. While there may be an elegant simplicity to some evolutionary accounts of aggressive behaviour and perhaps (for some) an appeal in linking social psychological issues to a fundamental aspect of biological science, there are several criticisms that are worth briefly raising.

First, if we have an account that emphasises the instinctive aspects of aggression, we are likely to de-emphasise the idea that there can be meaning or purpose to aggression. From the evolutionary perspective, then, a riot in a deprived neighbourhood would not be read principally as a protest about anything, but, rather, as the consequences of the aggression instinct that we have evolved.

Second, from the evolutionary perspective, it matters little where and when aggression or conflict is manifest – instinct rather than situation forms the explanatory framework. Thus, instances of aggression between two men outside a pub, in a clash between rival football fans, in 'terrorist' activity and military combat are all stripped of contextualising detail and explained in terms of the internal, intrapsychic phenomenon of instinct.

Finally, the evolutionary account draws on the idea of instincts developed specifically for survival and propagation of genes to account for behaviour that is not (and is unlikely to be perceived as) related to survival or genes. Thus, we can question to what extent we can account for a gang-related shooting or a protest that turns violent in

Instinct In the above literature, a genetically transmitted tendency towards certain types of behaviour.

Adaptive, functional In the literature considered above, these terms refer to the idea that an instinct – such as the aggression instinct – has evolved because it had some usefulness in terms of the survival and transfer of genes for our evolutionary ancestors.

terms of an approach in which aggression has an adaptive survival basis. The notion of an aggression instinct tries to bridge that gap – being applicable to survival but more general and, thus, applicable to non-survival situations. Moving towards the notion of a generalised aggression instinct (rather than a survival instinct), however, arguably starts to uncouple evolutionary psychology from the parsimony and logic of evolutionary theory itself.

Critical recap

Evolutionary approaches to aggression

1 The evolutionary approach suggests that it is unlikely that acts of aggression can have a meaning or purpose – beyond that of maximising the likelihood of passing on the aggressor's genes.

2 All circumstances and acts of aggression are treated as equivalent with little attention to the relevance of the context or impact of situational factors.

3 The presumption is that while our propensity to aggress has a basis in issues of survival (of ourselves and our genes) it can apply to instances of aggression that have no conceivable bearing on survival.

Reflective questions

1 *Using a newspaper choose a story reporting of an instance of aggressive behaviour. To what extent does the evolutionary approach outlined above provide an adequate account of this behaviour?*

2 *In what ways, if any, does evolutionary psychology concentrate on genetic concerns at the expense of purpose, meaning and the specifics of context in explaning aggression?*

9.2 Situational approaches to aggression

Frustration–aggression hypothesis

Some of the most important social psychological contributions to understanding aggression stand in sharp contrast to the evolutionary approach considered above. While the evolutionary approach looked 'inside' the person – highlighting, for example, evolutionary based instincts – the approaches that are addressed below consider the way that factors 'outside' of the person – the environment or *situations* – can play a part in aggressive behaviour.

Dollard, Doob, Miller, Mowrer and Sears (1939) developed one of the most famous situational models of human behaviour in the whole of social psychology with their frustration–aggression hypothesis, which emphasised the ways in which frustrating experiences cause aggressive behaviour. Some of the work following this model (in particular, Berkowitz) kept an emphasis on situational factors, but, instead of focusing on frustration, considered the impact of other unpleasant situational factors.

Dollard et al. tried to articulate some of the ways in which the environment could trigger aggression. They sought to frame their account in the most generic terms possible – to find a way of understanding *all* acts of human aggression – yet pinpointing what it was in the environment that would bring these about. Their famous frustration–aggression hypothesis states, 'the occurrence of aggression always presupposes the existence of frustration and, contrariwise, that the existence of frustration always leads to some form of aggression' (Dollard et al., 1939, p. 1). The hypothesis claims that any act of aggression is traceable to some prior **frustration** – an instance when the aggressor wanted something, but was blocked from obtaining it. Furthermore, it claims that any time we are frustrated – that is, when we cannot have something we want – it will result in 'some form of aggression'. Picture a small child wanting an attractive toy from a shelf, but being dragged away, stamping and screaming. It is very easy to see how tantrums can be understood as instances of frustration (wanting something that the parent denies), leading to aggressive outbursts (such as kicking and screaming).

For the frustration–aggression hypothesis, we are all somewhat like the small child – the moment that we are stopped from getting what we want (our goal response is blocked), we will act aggressively. It is worth noting at this point that Miller (1941) repositioned himself regarding the frustration–aggression hypothesis that he had co-authored, Miller felt that, while it was true frustration was a necessary precondition for aggression, it was not sufficient. That is, aggression could *always* be attributed to frustration, but frustration did *not* always result in aggression. This reformulation takes out an element of the overstated claims within the frustration–aggression

Frustration Any situation in which the individual does not get what they want – sometimes referred to as their goal response being blocked.

hypothesis. In this revised version, we are perhaps slightly better behaved children and, each time we burst into aggression, we can find some prior frustrating experience, but each instance of frustration will not result in us acting aggressively. For Miller, frustration can have other consequences besides aggression and, even if it results in an 'instigation to aggression' or readiness to act aggressively, it does not always follow that the aggressive act will be carried out – we might *feel* like hitting someone or shouting at them, yet may restrain ourselves from doing so.

A significant legacy of the frustration–aggression hypothesis has been the emphasis on *environmental* causes of aggression. Whereas earlier approaches had looked within the person, to *inner* instincts or drives, here the emphasis moved out of the person to their (frustrating) environment.

Work that followed the frustration–aggression hypothesis reworked how the environment might result in aggression – on the one hand broadening the range of environmental experiences that might trigger aggression and, on the other, introducing additional factors necessary for aggression. Berkowitz (1962, 1989) argued that it is not *just* frustration that can result in aggression. First, people's *perceptions* of being deprived of what they want are important, rather than *actual* experiences of frustration. Second, *any* **aversive event** can result in frustration. Thus, rather than just focusing on those situations in which our goals are blocked, Berkowitz broadened 'environmental factors' to mean anything we experience as being unpleasant or aversive. From this perspective, *any* unpleasant experience could be a contributing factor to subsequent aggression. This could include being unfairly criticised, insulted, pushed or even being in a long queue or getting uncomfortably hot (see Box 9.1). Berkowitz's conception of environmental causes of aggression, therefore, includes experiences of frustration, but goes beyond them – we now have a vast range of aversive experiences that could result in aggression.

Critical review of the frustration–aggression hypothesis

The frustration–aggression hypothesis is another 'classic' approach to understanding aggression – the main legacy of which has arguably been the subsequent work that has examined environmental causes of aggression. One very obvious criticism of frustration–aggression theory research is the very reductionist flavour of its initial statement that 'the occurrence of aggression always presupposes the existence of frustration and, contrariwise, that the existence of frustration always leads to some form of aggression' (Dollard et al., 1939, p. 1).

Even though Miller subsequently questioned the second of these tenets – that frustration *always* resulted in aggression – the first is, in itself, problematically prescriptive. There is the danger that – like many universal claims – it can only be made to fit the available evidence if the concept (in this case, the definition of frustration) is broadened to such an extent, its utility as a definable variable comes into question.

While the approach did lead to an increased emphasis on situations as causes of aggression, in itself it does little to detail the way that aspects of the environment may give rise to the psychological state of frustration and how that translates into aggression directed at specific targets. Thus, one can still ask what specifically can frustrate an individual and how does that lead to aggression directed at some targets rather than others?

Also, understanding aggression as driven by an intrapsychic drive again takes attention away from any perceived purpose or intention. For the frustration–aggression hypothesis, aggression is understood as initiated by inner drives in response to situational frustrations rather than having the possibility of being purposive or meaningful.

Critical recap

Frustration–aggression hypothesis

1 Even in its modified form, the frustration–aggression hypothesis makes a universal claim that frustration is a *necessary* cause of aggression.

2 Beyond the idea that they may frustrate our desires, there are few specifics on how situational factors may shape aggression.

3 There is little chance of seeing aggression or conflict as purposive or meaningful – instead, it it depicted as a reaction to being stopped from getting what we want.

Reflective questions

1 *Think of one or two instances of aggression that you have witnessed. Were they caused by some form of frustration?*

2 *What do you consider to be the major weaknesses of the frustration–aggression hypothesis?*

Aversive event Any unpleasant experience, which can include frustration, but may also include other unpleasant affect (anger, sadness) or sensations (pain or discomfort).

Box 9.1 FOCUS
Temperature and aggression

Berkowitz's promotion of the idea that any aversive event can increase aggression can be illustrated by research into the effects of temperature on aggression. The idea that higher temperatures are associated with aggression is not new. Bushman, Wang and Anderson (2005) note that nineteenth-century writers such as Leffingwell (1892, cited in Bushman et al., 2005) and Lombroso (1899, cited in Bushman et al., 2005) both advocated that higher temperatures were associated with higher levels of aggression.

In July 2009, as temperatures reached 40°C (104°F) in many parts of China, swimmers struggled for space in a pool – but do temperatures like this lead to increased aggression?

Berkowitz's *negative affect theory* suggests that high temperatures increase levels of aggression because the aversive experience of being unpleasantly hot produces negative affect, which in turn leads to aggression. Anderson (1989) developed a related but slightly amended version of Berkowitz's negative affect theory – *negative affect escape theory*. Anderson's theory suggests that if temperatures increase beyond being comfortable, there will initially be an increase in aggression, but, if they *keep* getting hotter, aggression will actually start to *decline*. Thus, levels of aggression have an inverted 'U' shape when plotted against temperature. He suggests that, at first, the uncomfortably hot temperatures will create negative affect and, therefore, increased aggression – with the highest levels of aggression occurring around 29°C (85°F). According to his theory, however, when it gets even *hotter*, people would sooner take action to escape the heat rather than aggress.

Bushman et al. (2005) note that much of the literature suggesting an inverted 'U' between temperature and aggression fails to take account of the time of day. They report that their data indicated aggression (measured by reported assaults) was much more common between 9 p.m. and 2.59 a.m. than between 3 a.m. and 8.59 p.m. Separating out these two time periods reveals that, in the lower assault time period, temperature has a small positive relationship, with aggression tending to flatten out at around 21°C (70°F). In the peak assault time period, however, – when, by far, the greatest number of assaults occurred – there was a strong positive linear relationship with aggression that did not diminish as temperatures continued to rise, even when that involved temperatures beyond 32°C (90°F). Thus, they suggest that when time of day informs the analysis – and especially when attention is given to the time period when the greatest number of assaults occur – the data supports Berkowitz's negative affect theory of increasing temperature giving rise to negative affect, leading to increased aggression.

Leonard Berkowitz's aggressive and aversive stimuli and aggression

As was noted above, Leonard Berkowitz (1989, 1990, 1993) extended the frustration–aggression hypothesis by emphasising not just *frustrating* situations but also *any aversive situations* as, potentially, being capable of contributing to aggressive behaviour. For Berkowitz (1989) frustrations give rise to aggression *because they are unpleasant* not because they involve frustration (or blocking someone's goals). From this perspective, 'any kind of **negative affect**' (1989, p. 71), whether anger, sadness or depression, can potentially produce aggressive inclinations (though not necessarily aggressive behaviour) – and it is exactly this issue that Berkowitz and others sought to investigate across a series of influential studies.

Most of Berkowitz's work used experimental procedures in which the participant was first 'angered', then exposed

Negative affect Any unpleasant feelings, such as anger, sadness or depression.

to the experimental stimuli before having an opportunity to aggress. Participants were typically angered in one of two ways: in some experiments, they received electric shocks – purportedly from a fellow participant – while, in other experiments, they were treated in a 'patronizing and insulting manner' or heard 'disparaging remarks' made about themselves, either by the experimenter or their confederate. The experimental stimuli sometimes included images or films that were associated with aggression and, thus, thought likely to elicit an aggressive response.

Berkowitz and LePage (1967) found that male students who had received high numbers of electric shocks would subsequently administer higher electric shocks themselves if they saw a gun and a rifle rather than two badminton racquets in the laboratory. Berkowitz (1965) found that angered male student participants who then watched a prize fight film showed more aggression (negative evaluation and number and length of electric shocks) towards a person labelled 'boxer' than they did if they watched a non-violent film.

This research saw the initial provocation as creating the disposition or readiness to aggress and the aggressive stimuli as bringing an association with aggression that elicited an aggressive response. In this way, much of the work of Berkowitz (and others) drew on classical conditioning – stimuli associated with aggression being sufficient to elicit an aggressive response in those inclined (for example, due to prior provocation) towards aggression.

This somewhat automatic effect of aggression-eliciting stimuli was refined in some of Berkowitz's other research. Thus, some work considered how the aggressive stimuli – usually a film – was presented. Berkowitz and Geen (1967) found that provoked male student participants administered greater numbers of shocks to their provoker in cases where they saw an aggressive film in which the aggression was presented as *justified* rather than *unjustified*. This was especially found to be the case where the victim of the aggression in the film had a similar name to the person who had provoked the participant.

Berkowitz and Alioto (1973) found that, given the opportunity to retaliate, angered male student participants (who watched films introduced as *aggressive* and involving *realistic aggression*) administered longer and more frequent electric shocks to their tormentor than did angered participants watching films not introduced in such terms.

These experiments point – albeit tentatively – to Berkowitz's increasing concern with the meaning that participants gave to the aggression that they viewed rather than the automatic associations inherent in the aggressive stimuli themselves. In drawing on and developing this cognitive neo-associationism, Berkowitz (1984, p. 411) argued, 'How people react to the message they read, hear or see depends considerably on their interpretations of the message, the ideas they bring with them to the communication, and the thoughts that are activated by it.' This notion of; 'thoughts that are activated' by stimuli proved a particularly important aspect for Berkowitz's subsequent understanding of the effects of not only aggressive stimuli but also *all* aversive stimuli.

Berkowitz's stance further developed to more explicitly take into account the idea that *any* aversive stimuli could elicit aggressive associations and meanings for the participant. In a study that used female US student participants (rather than the much more frequently used male US student participants), Berkowitz, Cochran and Embree (1981) found that participants who had an aversive experience – immersing and keeping their hand in uncomfortably cold water – could enact higher levels of aggression than participants who kept a hand in water of a more comfortable temperature. It can be noted that the different measures of aggression used in this study, administering noxious noise, and low numbers of rewards did produce slightly different findings. This study illustrates something of the generality of the claim that Berkowitz is making regarding aversive stimuli leading to aggression – that even those stimuli we may not explicitly associate with aggression may lead to it because, at some level, the association between aversive stimuli and aggression is there.

Berkowitz (1990, 1993) came to articulate his position in **neo-associationist** terms (see Figure 9.1), dropping the

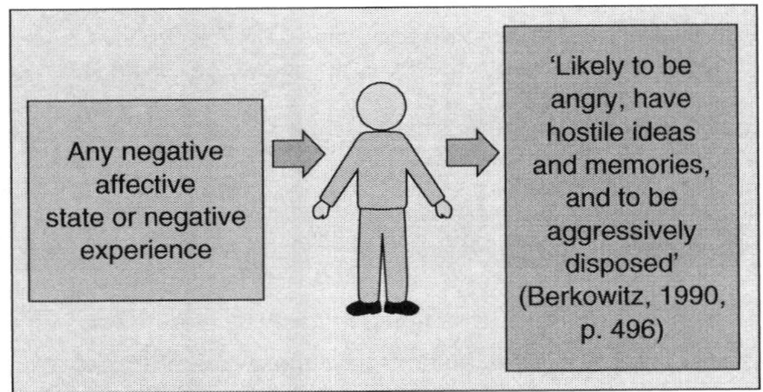

Figure 9.1 Berkowitz's neo-associationist account of aggression

Neo-associationist A theoretical position informed, partly, by behaviourist concerns with associations between environmental stimuli. In the case of the literature considered above, it specifically refers to the idea that negative affect is associated with anger-related feelings and aggressive thoughts and intentions.

'cognitive' prefix. This term was used to refer to the way that we associate all negative affective states and experiences – at some level – with aggressive responses. Thus, Berkowitz (1990, p. 496) argues:

> there is an associative connection between negative affect and anger-related feelings, ideas and memories. It is because of these associations that persons who feel bad for one reason or another – whether they have a toothache, or are very hot, are exposed to foul smells or an unpleasant noise, or are just very sad or depressed – are likely to be angry, have hostile ideas and memories, and to be aggressively disposed. See also Box 9.2.

Berkowitz's research into aggressive and aversive stimuli takes elements of the frustration–aggression hypothesis but broadens the basis for understanding the motivation to aggress and tries to account for why the motivation to aggress will sometimes (but not always) result in actual aggression. In terms of motivation to aggress, the idea of frustration is broadened by Berkowitz to cover *any* unpleasant or 'aversive' experience – so, not just frustrations but such unpleasant experiences as physical sensations (such as being too hot) and interpersonal encounters (for example, meeting an obnoxious person).

Berkowitz also introduced the notion of cues to aggression to explain why aggressive inclinations (caused by an aversive experience) may not always result in aggression. Thus, he addressed another limitation of the frustration–aggression hypothesis, which was its difficulty in accounting for *when* aggression would occur and the seemingly contraindications to the claim that aggressive behaviour would *always* result from frustration. For Berkowitz, **stimulus conditions** – that is, cues to

Stimulus conditions In the above literature, this refers to factors in the environment – such as aversive conditions – that may bring about a given behavioural response – such as aggression.

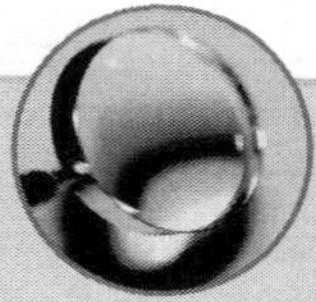

Box 9.2 FOCUS
Media effects research

The work of Zillmann, Berkowitz and others is often referred to in media studies as *effects research*. This is an approach that has focused on the measurable influence that mass media – particularly television, and film have on their audiences. It has been specifically concerned with the behavioural and attitudinal effects on audiences of exposure to images or films that contain various types of aggressive, erotic or pornographic content. Effects research is particularly committed to the possibility of investigating a measurable causal link between the type of media content (for example, aggressive versus non-aggressive) and its effect (aggressive versus non-aggressive attitudes or behaviour).

Typically, but not exclusively, effects research relies on laboratory or controlled field studies that enable the manipulation of the independent variable or media presented to participants (for example, one group of participants see a film defined as 'aggressive', another see a film defined as 'non-aggressive).

As the review of the literature above suggest, effects research has involved a very wide range of measures of 'effects' (or dependent variables) that include an array of observable behaviours, participants' ratings of others and reported attitudes.

Within the context of social psychology, it is effects research that has dominated the field – the work of Berkowitz, Zillmann and so on. Within media research, however, it sits among several other approaches, against which some of its strengths and weaknesses may come into view. Two of these alternative approaches to media research will be briefly considered here – first, critical theory and, second, reception analytic research.

Looking first at critical theory, this has a long history that stretches – in different forms – from the Frankfurt School through to the Glasgow Media Group and the work of Hall. This research has been concerned with the way in which the news media transmit the dominant ideology – that is, ideas about power relations, concerning, for example, industrial, race and sex relations, found to be present in the content of what is broadcast. Sometimes the dominant ideology is overtly present in the broadcast media – for example, strikes are often treated as an example of negative behaviour motivated by selfish concerns. Sometimes the dominant ideology may be more subtly present. For example, ideas of independent females may be incorporated into dominant patriarchal sexist ideologies so that the female's sexual desirability to men is treated as their

Box 9.2 continued

defining feature – the TV show and subsequent film *Charlie's Angels* is sometimes cited as an example of this (Fiske, 1987). From this critical perspective, the emphasis was largely on careful analysis of the content of actual broadcast material, with a view that 'the (ideological) effects of the media could, in effect, be deduced from the analysis of the textual structure of the messages they emitted' (Morley, 1992, p. 7). Thus, while this critical tradition paid careful attention to the details of media content, the media audiences were, as Morley (1992, p. 7) notes 'largely absent' from the analysis.

An alternative perspective was provided by reception analytic research, which sought to consider the way in which media 'consumers' might be considered – at least potentially – as active decoders of media messages (Morley, 1980). They might align with the ideology or content of the media material or they may, to varying degrees, be resistant to or critical of it. Morley's classic *The 'Nationwide' audience* (1980) pioneered this perspective, noting the various interpretative stances taken by different groups of audiences (differing on occupational, social and political identity dimensions). While Morley's research itself can be criticised – for example, it tends to treat members of identifiable socio-economic and political groups as largely having one way of reading or decoding media output – it did pave the way for analyses that reintroduced the audience as important, while still paying attention to detailed ideological content of media material. From this perspective, *effects research* does not do justice to either the ideas or ideology contained in media material or to the active process audiences go through to make sense of and position themselves with regard to these ideas.

These two media perspectives provide a critique of effects research as almost entirely uninterested in the detailed content of the media. Instead, however, it is as if, for effects researchers, the important aspect is the census board classification of the content. For many (though not all) effects studies, it is enough to know that the film contains violence or pornography and the necessary details for the independent variable(s) have been identified. For most effects research, messages in the media about race, class, gender, sexuality or international relations are not treated as important. Instead, it is as if a concern with aggressive behaviour on the part of audiences has completely framed the terms of reference for thinking about media content, resulting in just two factors being emphasised – 'sex and violence' – leaving all other media content (which is less obviously causally linked to individual aggression) unconsidered.

The critical and reception analytic perspectives briefly outlined here are typically absent from social psychology textbooks, yet provide a perspective that suggests detailed scrutiny of media output can reveal crucial messages about how people can or should make sense of themselves and others, how they should relate to one another, how we should understand our nation and its relationships with other nations. Messages such as these can provide frameworks that are relevant to all social issues, including aggression. Thus, the media may give messages about under what circumstances individual acts of aggression may be justified (such as for certain types of betrayal) or what values might supercede those of non-violence (such as loyalty, patriotism).

More broadly, analysis of media content can enable us to consider how aggression may not be confined to *individual effects*. Thus, media messages may justify acts of aggression between groups or nations – for example, the bombing of another country – or provide a perspective from which international relations has to be approached in terms of threats of violence against nations that can be simply understood as 'bad' or 'evil'. The development of reception analytic research adds to this the possibility that attention to media content need not preclude the possibility of active 'meaning making' audiences who do far more than just passively receive the messages transmitted.

aggression in the environment – are crucial determinants of whether or not and when the aggressive inclination will result in aggressive behaviour. According to him, with a cue to aggression (such as watching violence on the media or seeing a violent weapon or act of violence), aggressive inclinations will result in aggressive behaviour; without them they will not.

Critical review of Leonard Berkowitz's aggressive and aversive stimuli and aggression

Berkowitz's research marks not only a serious engagement with situational aspects of aggression but also a turn to an experimentally driven social psychology of aggression. In these two respects (as well as via his specific theory),

Berkowitz has had a profound influence on the social psychology of aggression. Many of the criticisms considered here are – as shall be seen – true of much of the experimentally driven social psychology of aggression and conflict.

First, as will be addressed elsewhere in this chapter, there is a question as to how aggression is defined. This is addressed in much greater detail later, but, for now, two components of this can be considered: an experimental operationalisation of the idea of aggression (what measure of aggression is used in specific experiments) and a theoretical orientation (how the phenomenon that the theory is trying to explain – in this case 'aggression' – is conceptualised).

A second criticism is the way in which the experiments operationalise aversive events and, to some extent, situational cues. As you read back through this section, you might ask how realistic and applicable is it to, for example, administer differing numbers of electric shocks as an aversive stimuli – it may be so highly unusual and unrelated to any non-laboratory experience that it does not tell us about people's responses to more commonly encountered aversive stimuli.

Third, although informed by situational factors, aggression is, again, approached as something concerning individuals who are not in relation to one another (or those relationships only matter in so far as they affect aversive experience and aggressive cues).

Finally, aggression is, once again, approached as reactive to triggers, not as something potentially purposeful.

Critical recap

Leonard Berkowitz's aggressive and aversive stimuli and aggression

1 It is possible to question the ways in which aggression has been conceptualised – that is, what range of behaviours come to be treated as 'aggression' – for example, should this include physical violence, verbal behaviour and/or military action?

2 The operational definitions of aggression (the way in which it is measured in experiments) both here and elsewhere can be questioned. Are they meaningfully related to real-world instances of 'aggression'?

3 The operational definitions of 'aversive stimuli' can also be questioned. How do these relate to the real-world 'aversive' phenomena that they seek to replicate?

4 Aggression has been approached as essentially an individualistic phenomenon, with little attention to the role of other people.

5 As with other research considered, the idea that aggression can sometimes be purposive or meaningful is eclipsed by the idea of it merely being a reaction to or triggered by situational stimuli.

6 It is possible to question how the role of the media has been conceptualised in 'effects research'. Has it been exaggerated? Has there been a narrow focus on depictions of violence at the expense of other, for example, ideological influences that the media may have?

Reflective questions

1 *Look at a recent newspaper. Which incidents come to be called aggression and which of these are treated as a problematic form of aggression? Now try this exercise with a social psychology textbook.*

2 *Are there cultural, ideological or other influences on how we come to define what (problematic) aggression is in psychology and the sorts of causes that we typically consider?*

9.3 Dolf Zillmann's excitation transfer and aggression model

So far, we have considered approaches that either emphasise factors within the *individual* (evolutionary approaches) or the *situation* (frustration–aggression hypothesis, aggressive and aversive stimuli). The excitation transfer and aggression model (see Figure 9.2) suggests that *both* person *and* situation need to be considered when attempting to understand aggression.

Zillmann and Bryant (1974) criticised earlier approaches – in particular, Berkowitz's early work – that had attempted to understand the impact of cues to aggression on aggressive acts. They (1974, p. 738) argue that, while these stimulus–response connections are useful for understanding *animal* aggression, the situation is different for humans:

> the human aggressor ... engages in rather complex considerations which may lead to the inhibition of a spontaneous response ... It appears that because of this human capacity to delay the execution of aggressive activities, general references to past experiences, learning theory, and response hierarchies have limited value in predicting human aggression.

Zillmann's approach – in contrast to this characterisation of some of the research considered above – emphasised

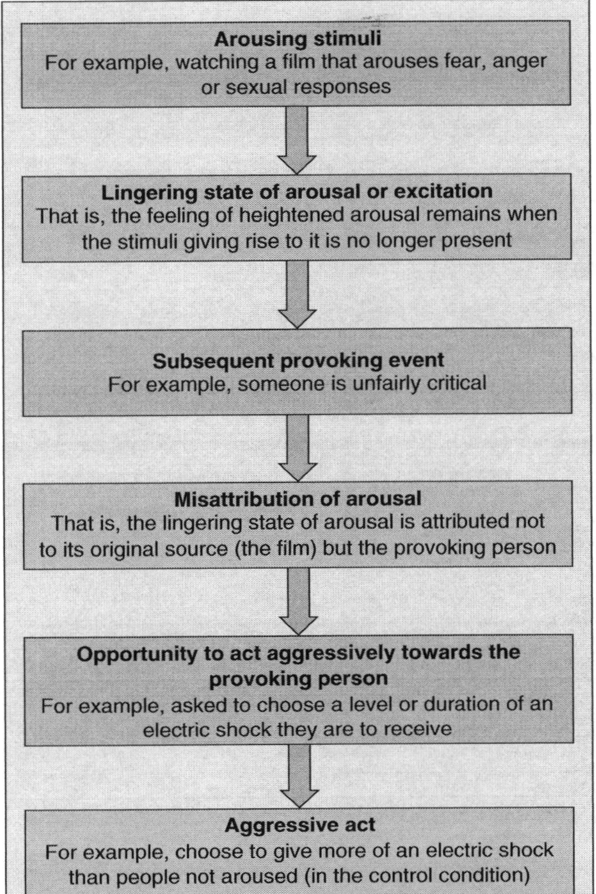

Figure 9.2 The excitation transfer model of aggression

the way in which people **cognitively appraise** their physiological and psychological states of heightened **arousal** or **excitation**.

In this way, Zillmann's (1983) approach brought together environmental, cognitive and physiological elements in accounting for acts of aggression. His excitation transfer approach argues that aggression is preceded by a physiological experience of arousal. For Zillmann, this could be anything that 'excites' the nervous system, such as narrowly avoiding a serious accident, experiencing a sudden shock, encountering some source of sexual stimulation (see Figure 9.2 and Box 9.3) or engaging in strenuous exercise. If we can think of any situation or stimulus that results in our heart rate increasing, then this involves some increase in arousal. Zillmann argued that this feeling of heightened arousal can linger beyond the presence of whatever it was that gave rise to it, so, after nearly experiencing a car crash, nearly getting run over or stopping ourselves from falling down some stairs, the effect of that arousal still remains. If, in this heightened state of arousal (or excitation), we then encounter some provoking situation – for example, another vehicle cuts in front of us, someone bumps into us as they walk past or the person making our latté is incredibly slow and keeps getting it wrong – then we are more likely to act in an aggressive manner, than if the previous incident had not happened.

For Zillmann, it is not just that our state of arousal directly causes a more volatile reaction to these environmental provocations – there is an intervening cognitive process. In our post-excitation encounter, we may **misattribute arousal** perceiving our residual arousal as being caused by the new provoking condition or persona and not the actual arousing situation. Have you ever overheard someone in an argument say something like, 'I'm actually very annoyed about that' or 'You are really starting to annoy me' (there are, of course, many less polite variants on these utterances). Now suppose that those people had experienced a completely separate previous incident (such as a near miss on the road) just moments before. It is possible that, in their current argument, they are making sense of their physiological reactions to the previous incident in terms of the (irritating) person in front of them now. The faster heartbeat and breathing (and other sensations we associate with adrenalin) could be misinterpreted by the person as caused by the *current* conflict and, therefore, heighten the sense of anger and aggression that they feel they have towards that person.

Zillmann (1983, 1996) argues that the physiological experience of excitation has two properties of particular importance for our current considerations. First, excitation responses are not readily associated with a specific emotional state – that is, we cannot readily distinguish exercise-induced, fear, anger or sexual states of arousal. Second, our aroused state may outlast 'the emotional experience with which it was originally associated', resulting in a heightened intensity for 'subsequent emotional experiences and behaviours' (1996, p. 244). As a consequence of this, any state of arousal that we have can be interpreted in several different

Cognitively appraise The process of thinking about and making sense of our (in this case) increased arousal or excitation. This thinking may involve trying to attribute it to a cause.

Arousal, excitation Any experience of heightened nervous system activation – often associated with an increase in heartbeat. Arousal/excitation may include sexual arousal, fear, anger and the effects of exercise.

Misattribute or misattribution of arousal The idea that we might incorrectly make sense of a heightened state of arousal, perceiving it as being caused by something other than what actually had caused it. This is thought to be particularly likely where the state of arousal lingers until the original cause is no longer present but an alternative, credible cause *is* present – the arousal then being misattributed to it.

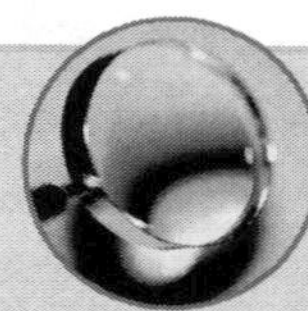

Box 9.3 FOCUS
Does erotica increase or decrease aggression?

Donnerstein, Donnerstein and Evans (1975) attempted to provide a way of understanding the potentially contradictory effects of erotica on aggression. For them, on the one hand, erotica could be understood as giving rise to arousal and arousal is associated with aggression, so thus exposure to arousing stimuli could be seen as increasing the propensity for aggression. On the other hand, erotica could be understood as leading to an attentional shift – the person exposed to it being absorbed in it and less preoccupied with thoughts of retaliation, revenge or other forms of aggression.

Donnerstein et al. suggested that there may be some distinction to be made between mild and strong erotica – mild being associated with attentional shifts and lowered aggression, strong being associated with significantly heightened arousal and increased aggression. Zillmann and Sapolsky (1977) provide partial support for this idea. Their erotic stimulus photographs, which were subsequently identified as only mildly arousing for the participants, were associated with lower levels of reported annoyance by participants who had previously been provoked. That is, participants who were first annoyed and then subsequently exposed to the (mildly) erotic pictures reported that they were less annoyed by the provocation than those who saw non-erotic pictures.

Ramirez, Bryant and Zillmann (1982) provided further support for this distinction between mildly suggestive erotica and much more explicit erotica. They found that suggestive erotic films decreased aggression among male college students in cases of mild provocation and led to no difference (compared with those in a control group who had not seen the films) in cases of severe provocation. By contrast, explicit erotic films led to increased levels of retaliation, regardless of the extent of the prior provocation, although the retaliation was strongest when there had been prior provocation.

As well as degree of explicitness, research has considered the different aggression effect of violent erotic films. A particular concern has been the impact of films where the violence is portayed as having a 'positive outcome' – meaning that the victim of a sexual attack is depicted as subsequently enjoying it (Donnerstein & Berkowitz, 1981).

A related line of research has considered the ways in which erotic material might affect the attitudes of participants towards females. Malamuth and Check (1980) found that male college students who were exposed to violent pornography showed reduced sympathy for victims of rape. Similarly, Mullin and Linz (1995) found decreased sympathy for victims of domestic violence – an effect that they report as lasting for three days after viewing violent erotica, with participants' responses being the same as participants' in the control group, who did not see these films, five days after viewing. Linz, Donnerstein and Penrod (1988) had somewhat more ambivalent findings regarding the effects of repeated exposure to sexually explicit films, while supporting the idea that violent films (which may include a 'mild' erotic element and in which women were the victims) could reduce sympathy for a victim in a re-enacted rape trial and – if films were repeatedly viewed – for rape victims in general.

Another strand of research, by Mulac, Jansma and Linz (2002), found that viewing films judged to be sexually degrading for the women involved had an impact in how men subsequently interacted with women. In particular, viewing such films appeared to result in increased levels of dominance, interruptions and sexually explicit comments and reduced attention to the contributions of females.

ways and, though triggered by a previous event, we may look to current circumstances to make sense of our lingering sense of arousal. If, then, we experience a heightened state of arousal (for example, from narrowly avoiding an accident) and, subsequently, someone provokes us in some way, then these *current* circumstances (being provoked) provide a way of making sense of our experience of arousal. Thus, we may interpret our arousal as our anger at that person who is provoking us (without being aware of the lingering impact of the near accident). In this way, we may get an inflated sense of just how upset and angry we are with that person. This sense that we are outraged with the person can readily spill over into aggressive responses to them – even though they did not contribute to the initial state of arousal. See Box 9.4 to consider how this theory might work in practice.

Donnerstein and Berkowitz (1981) challenge Zillmann's idea that prior arousal results in aggression (when misattributed) and, instead, suggest it is exposure to material that elicits aggressive thoughts, which will result in aggression. They first had their male college participants angered by a male or female confederate who administered a number of mild shocks to them. The shocks were to indicate how negatively the confederate rated an essay that the participants had previously written. The number of shocks given to participants and separate rating responses on five-point scales indicated that the confederate rated the essay negatively. The participants then watched either a neutral film, an erotic, non-aggressive film, an erotic aggressive film with a 'positive victim outcome' (that is, the victim was portrayed as first resisting and then enjoying being sexually assaulted) or an aggressive erotic film with a 'negative victim outcome' (that is, the victim continued to show distress while sexually assaulted). The aggression measure that Donnerstein and Berkowitz used was the level of shock to be administered by the participant to the confederate in a 'learning experiment'.

Donnerstein and Berkowitz (1981, p. 721) argue that, from the perspective of excitation transfer, the research participants who watched a purely erotic film should misattribute their arousal to their prior provocation and, thus, 'regard themselves as highly angry and then behave accordingly'. They did not find this, however. Instead, the *type* of arousing content was important – specifically, it was aggressive films (and especially aggressive films with 'positive victim ending') that resulted in the highest levels of aggressive behaviour, as measured in this experiment. Provoked male participants who viewed an aggressive erotic film acted aggressively towards the confederate who provoked them – if the confederate was female. For the male college student participants who viewed the aggressive erotic film with a 'positive victim ending', however, it did not matter if they were provoked at all – even unprovoked viewers of this film were subsequently aggressive towards a female target.

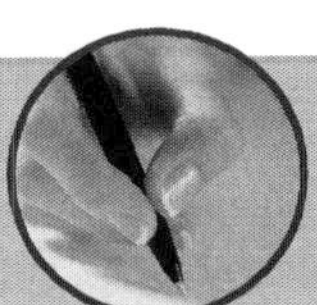

Box 9.4 TRY IT OUT
Arousal and aggression

Can you think of a time when your own experience of aggressive feelings may have been influenced by some event that caused some form of arousal – such as narrowly avoiding an accident, experiencing embarrassment, being anxious about being late? Do you think that these states of arousal might have led to something other than aggressive feelings? Could labelling or attributing the arousal differently shape the extent to which you might feel or act aggressively in these sort of situations?

Critical review of Dolf Zillmann's excitation transfer and aggression model

The excitation transfer account of aggression provides a theoretical combination that is unusually broad for social psychological accounts. Thus, Zillmann and others draw on the physiology of arousal, the sociocognitive process of attribution, as well as retaining (like Dollard and Berkowitz) a situationalist element in his reference to environmental stimuli. The criticisms outlined here address both aspects of the experiments that Zillmann and others present in support of excitation transfer and the theory itself as an account of human aggression.

First, the experiments that are presented as supporting the excitation transfer account of aggression generate the maximum chance of misattributed arousal (for example, meeting an obnoxious person after intense exercise), but can appear contrived and unusual rather than typical scenarios. It is certainly possible to contemplate real-world parallels to these experiments, for example, we might meet someone who irritates us as we leave the gym and scenarios that are (according to the theory) conceptually equivalent (such as being angry at another road user after a near miss when driving.) These scenarios, however, are arguably a small proportion of the total pool of aggressive responses that we might seek to explain. In this way, not only are the experimental situations atypical but also the theory itself – though wide in the theoretical frameworks it draws on – may only be applicable to a few instances of aggression.

A second issue with excitation transfer, which links to criticisms of its account of prosocial behaviour, is if aggression can be thought of as typically involving the cognitive process of the attribution of cause prior to aggressive behaviour. That is, we can question whether the physiological experience of arousal, rather than leading directly to aggression, has an intervening stage involving a cognitive examination of possible causes of arousal.

Third, as with earlier approaches, the emphasis is on the individual psychological (and, in this case, physiological) reactions rather than on any social dimension, such as group membership, relationships or cultural context.

Fourth, in common with the other approaches considered, there are issues with the understanding and measurement of aggression.

Finally, once again, aggression is seen as a largely reactive process rather than being in any sense meaningful. While excitation transfer theory attempts to detail causes of aggressive behaviour, there is no sense of purpose or causes towards which the behaviour might be directed.

Critical recap

Dolf Zillmann's excitation transfer and aggression model

1 The experimental scenarios used to investigate the possibility of the misattribution of prior arousal may relate to a very narrow range of real-world experiences.

2 It is possible to question whether or not, in real-world instances of aggressive behaviour, people actually engage in a cognitive appraisal of the causes of their heightened arousal.

3 The emphasis of excitation transfer theory is, again, on the lone individual aggressor. Relations to others are only considered in so far as they cause frustration or are blamed for the individual's negative arousal.

4 As with other approaches, acts of aggression are seen as reactive – to misattributed states of arousal – rather than purposive or meaningful.

Reflective questions

1 *Have you ever responded aggressively in a situation because of some previous arousing experience, such as narrowly avoiding an accident?*

2 *What are the empirical limitations of the research into excitation transfer?*

9.4 General aggression model

If the excitation transfer model of aggression sought to provide a broad-based account of aggression, then the general aggression model sought to go one (or perhaps several) step(s) further. As is detailed below, the model is complex, including and seeking to incorporate many different approaches to aggression, but, at its core, it rests on the idea that both person *and* situation factors are important in the many different ways in which aggression can be initiated and continued.

Anderson and Bushman (2002) and Bushman and Anderson (2002) developed an account of aggression that, to some extent, seeks to integrate some of the different approaches considered above into a unified process model. The general aggression model (see Figure 9.3) is an account of aggression that incorporates a large number of potential factors which may be associated with aggression, considers the process relationship between these factors and emphasises how the outcomes from any one **episode** of potential or actual aggression can influence future episodes. Each of these features – breadth of factors, interrelationship and effects across episodes, or, **cycles** – is considered in turn below.

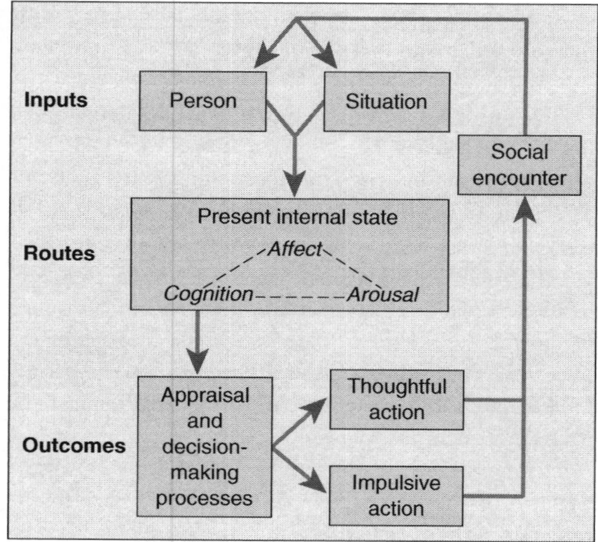

Figure 9.3 General aggression model (from Anderson & Bushman, 2002, p. 34)

Source: Anderson, C. A., & Bushman B. J. (2002). Human aggression. *Annual Review of Psychology*, *53*, 27–51. Reproduced with permission from Annual Reviews.

As Figure 9.3 suggests, the general aggression model seeks to incorporate a comprehensive array of potential causes of aggression. The model not only includes the potential environmental causes of aggression considered above, such as arousing stimuli and aggressive cues, but also incorporates **person factors** and **internal states**.

Person factors include the person as changed by previous episodes of potential or actual aggression (such as desensitisation, considered below), as well as relatively independent person characteristics, such as sex and personality characteristics. With regard to sex, Anderson and Bushman (2002) note that, in addition to socialisation differences, the higher propensity for male physical aggression can be made sense of in evolutionary terms, as

Cycles, episodes of aggression In the above literature, this refers to the idea that an instance of aggression may not end with the aggressive act, but, instead, the aggressive act (and responses to it) may feed into the cognitions and affective response of the person who aggressed (and others) and can result in other aggressive or non-aggressive behaviour.

Person factors Any characteristics of our personality or gender, it can include factors that have been modified by the current or other cycles of aggression.

Internal states Any cognitions and feeling that we may have – for example, anger.

by aggressing, males can then maximise the opportunity to mate and, thereby, pass on their genes.

One of the personality characteristics particularly linked to aggressive behaviour is narcissism – a trait that is defined as being present where individuals have 'inflated or unstable self-esteem' (Anderson and Bushman, 2002; Bushman, Bonacci, van Dijk, & Baumeister, 2003). Where such inflated self-esteem is threatened, then the narcissist has a propensity for aggressive responses towards the person who has threatened their self-esteem (Anderson & Bushman, 2002; Bushman, Baumeister, Thomaes, Ryu, Begeer, & West, 2009). Additionally (as detailed below), the model allows for the internal states of arousal, affect and cognition, as well as an appraisal and decision-making process (which may result in thoughtful or impulsive action), to play their part in determining the type of behavioural outcome arising from each episode. In this way, the factors included in the general aggression model can be seen as encompassing potential causes of aggression that have frequently been addressed separately as situationalist, personality and cognitivist accounts.

In addition to including a very wide range of potential causes of aggression, the general aggression model proposes a way of understanding how these may interrelate that is underspecified by 'mini-theories' about specific aspects of aggression, such as evolutionary psychology, the frustration–aggression hypothesis aggressive cues or excitation transfer. Thus, Anderson and Bushman (2002, p. 35) argue that one of the key strengths of the model is that it provides 'a simpler and more comprehensive understanding of human aggression than is possible using the mini-theory approach so commonly used throughout contemporary psychology.'

The model interrelates different factors both temporally and interactively. Temporally, the model depicts a progression from inputs (person–situation) through routes (the present internal state of the person whose behaviour we are considering) to outcome (appraisal, decision making and, subsequently, action). This behaviour results in some consequential social encounter – something is or is not done viz à viz other people – and this, in turn, feeds into both the person and the situation. Interactively, it is *the interaction* of person and environment that is consequential for the current internal state – likewise, the interconnections between the internal states of arousal, cognition and affect that shape decision making and appraisal and subsequent behaviour. Similarly, it is the resulting social encounter itself that potentially changes, resets or maintains the person and the situation.

Imagine, for example, a man with a history of jealous and aggressive behaviour encountering a situation in which his partner is approached by another man. This interaction of personal dispositions and a 'triggering' situation may lead to a present internal state of heightened arousal and, specifically, anger, as well as 'anger-maintaining' cognitions – 'What does he think he's doing?' 'How dare he?' and so on. This may result in the man making an immediate negative appraisal of the situation – 'that man is trying to take my partner' – which may provoke the decision to retaliate (drawing on past social learning history of violent behaviour and current aggressive thoughts).

The man in this example may lack the resources and inclination to reappraise the situation (seeing it as more innocent or less of a threat) or to decide on other courses of action (doing nothing or acting without aggression). Let us suppose that our hypothetical man aggressively shoves the person who approached his partner. This aggressive action (which could be impulsive if spontaneous or thoughtful if premeditated) creates a resultant social encounter, along with the other man's response or lack of response. If the other man *also* acts aggressively, then this creates a new person–situation input for the next cycle, in which the person is now at least partially changed by the latest episode of aggressive behaviour and encountering someone who is responding aggressively to *them*.

The above example illustrates something of the cyclical nature of the general aggression model – each episode and its resultant social encounter shapes the person–situation inputs for the next episode. This cyclical dimension provides the opportunity to consider moment-by-moment cycles, which enables us to find some way of making sense of how aggression can escalate from aggressive talk to aggressive action for example. Additionally, it enables us to consider the way that cycles of aggression operate over time.

In the above example, the hypothetical man was glossed as having a history of jealous and aggressive behaviour. The general aggression model allows for the idea that the cumulative experience of our cycles of aggressive (or non-aggressive) actions and social encounters shape who we are and who we become. The person, then, who has frequently acted aggressively in previous episodes – possibly over many years – has shaped their own person input variable as having an increased propensity for aggressive action. Having behaved aggressively in a succession of previous episodes (and experienced the resulting social encounters), the person's understanding and perception of the social world – that is, their understanding and interpretations of events (scripts) and people (schemas) and other knowledge structures – are changed. These changed perceptions and understandings – or knowledge structures – increase the likelihood of the person being predisposed towards aggression in future episodes.

The general aggression model also incorporates the idea that not just repeated violent behaviour but also repeated *exposure* to violence (for example, through violent video games, films or *in vivo* experiences of violence) can shape the person's knowledge structures. These knowledge structures – which include attitudes, beliefs, perceptions, expectations, behaviour scripts and sensitivity to violence – in turn, constitute how aggressive the personality is and, thus, the person's predisposition to violence as an input variable (in interaction with the specific situation).

Bushman and Anderson (2002) first got male and female participants to play either a violent or non-violent video game and then complete a 'story stem', which presents the start of a story – about a car collision, someone trying to persuade her friend to come on holiday with her or someone experiencing slow service in a restaurant. Participants were then requested to suggest what happens next by listing 20 things that the protagonist will do, say, think or feel in response to the situation. They note some of the extremely aggressive responses that the participants suggest – threatening to kill the driver who collided with the protagonist's car, dumping the friend who would not come on holiday and taking the friend's boyfriend instead and, in the case of slow restaurant service, hitting the waiter and refusing to pay. Overall, Bushman and Anderson (2002, p. 1683) argued, participants who played a violent video game for 20 minutes showed 'significant increases in expectations that potential conflict situations would be handled aggressively'.

Carnagey, Anderson and Bushman (2007) argue that exposure to violent video games results in a **desensitisation** to violence. They found that male and female participants who played a violent video game – even for just 20 minutes – showed a desensitisation to violence in comparison to those who played a non-violent video game. Thus, participants playing a violent video game had a lower heart rate and galvanic skin response while viewing a film of a real shooting, stabbing or beating.

Bartholow, Bushman and Sestir (2006) found some potential link between repeated exposure to violent video games and measurable brain responses to violent images. Those participants who reported that they frequently played violent rather than non-violent video games had a reduced P300 amplitude (a measure of brain response associated with aversive stimuli) in response to violent images. Bartholow et al. interpreted these results as consistent with the idea of desensitisation – repeated exposure to violence via video games being associated with a reduced reaction to violent stimuli across a number of physiological measures.

Desensitisation The idea that we may – through familiarity – become less responsive (sometimes measured physiologically) to stimuli – such as aggressive images – which we frequently encounter.

Finally, Konijn, Bijvank and Bushman (2007) found that when a video game is realistic and leads participants to feel immersed within it, these problems can be exacerbated as participants may be more likely to identify with violent characters and, in turn, act out aggressive behaviour when the opportunity arises.

Critical review of the general aggression model

The general aggression model aims to integrate several of the ideas covered earlier, including evolutionary theory, situational cues, arousal and cognitive appraisal, as well as incorporate other factors such as personality traits and social learning. Furthermore, while most approaches considered so far seek to explain single aggressive episodes in isolation, the general aggression model attempts to consider both how any episode of aggression results in a new context for immediate behaviour and, cumulatively, becomes part of the person's past experience of behaving aggressively. Thus, each time potential aggression is enacted (or not), the person and their situation is not only changed immediately but also more gradually as their accumulated experiences of potentially aggressive situations are added to.

Despite the apparently broad scope of the general aggression model, however, it – like the approaches above – depicts aggression as individualistic and largely without meaning. Furthermore, as discussed below, questions can be asked about the ways in which aggression has been measured in experimental settings – do they all get at the same phenomenon and relate to the sort of aggression we find in the real world that the model seeks to explain? The model places substantial emphasis on the role of the media in causing aggression – approaching them very much in terms of 'effects theory' (see Box 9.2 for a review of this approach). One problem with the way in which the media are approached within the general aggression model is that – like effects research – there is a somewhat behaviourist emphasis on the negative effects of violent stimulus, such as violent actions visible on screen, rather than on meanings which can be read into the broadcast material. Thus, a film that visually details a fight would be seen as (potentially at least) a cue to aggression. By contrast, non-visual content that supported a violent ideology (for example, implying that certain groups are inhuman and violence against them is justified) might

Box 9.5 IN THE NEWS
Understanding military aggression

On 12 July 2007, American soldiers in an Apache helicopter opened fire, gunning down 12 civilians in Baghdad. What was particularly striking was that the video of the attack (see www.youtube.com/watch?v=lS_NFygheVo) that reveals the soldiers seeming to treat the episode as if it was a video game, with one of the soldiers seemingly celebrating saying, 'Ha ha, I hit 'em' as the civilians were injured.

This incident raises questions about what we understand aggression to be in social psychology. Many texts do not refer to military action at all – or only exceptional incidents, such as the My Lai massacre, but, should our understanding of aggression include instances such as the one above, should it include aggression directed towards other combatants also? If we start to treat incidents such as the Baghdad attack as aggression, then the notion of the effects of video war games may change also. Sites such as America's Army www.americasarmy.com provide both software for war games and recruitment information for joining the US army – this very link between war *games* and the army itself might suggest (rightly or wrongly) that the 'shoot 'em up' mentaility is relevant for and perhaps even encouraged by the US army.

An image from the WikiLeaks video that showed American soldiers in an Apache helicopter shooting 12 civilians. Do video games play a part in shaping the behaviour – and the celebratory attitude – that this video appeared to reveal?

Source: Wikileaks/Handout/Reuters

not be seen as a cue to aggression. If we consider the ways in which the media have conveyed violence-supporting ideologies historically (for example, prior to and during the Holocaust, during the conflict in Rwanda), the idea of focusing on visual depictions of or associations with violence seems narrow and misplaced (see Box 9.5 for a related question for social psychology).

Critical recap

General aggression model

1 As with previous approaches, the general aggression model regards aggression as a phenomenon of the individual – arising from the individual's perceptions of and reactions to the environment.

2 Again, in common with other approaches, aggression is understood as reactive rather than purposeful.

3 The way that aggression has been conceptualised and operationally defined in experiments is again open to question – what range of real-world behaviours are treated as 'aggression' and how do the measures of aggression used in experiments relate to the real-world phenomenon of aggression?

4 The general aggression model takes an 'effects research' perspective with regard to the media – with an emphasis on isolated (and primarily visual) depictions of violence. There may be an overemphasis on the idea that visual depictions of violence can affect subsequent behaviour – and a corresponding underemphasis on the impact of implicit or explicit ideologies regarding aggression.

Reflective questions

1 *Think of an instance of aggression that you know well and try to apply the features of Figure 9.3 to it. How well does it fit?*

2 *What understandings of aggression and causes of aggression, if any, are not encompassed in – or are less emphasised – in the general aggression model?*

9.5 Critical review of how experiments measure aggression and its causes

As Box 9.6 indicates, aggression has been measured in a wide variety of different ways in experimental research into the phenomenon. In a very few cases the **observed actual aggression** measure has been used – Diener (1976) had to stop several of his experimental trials because of the level of pain inflicted on a passive victim and Leyens, Camino, Parke and Berkowitz (1975) raised ethical concerns about their study of actual aggression following violent films shown to children in 'care'. For practical and ethical reasons if nothing else, almost all cases of laboratory research involve measures of aggression that stand in proxy for the actual aggressive behaviour – outside of the laboratory – that the experiment seeks to understand. Thus, researchers are not interested in explaining why people choose to administer electric shocks of a certain intensity to others – almost no one does this outside of an experimental setting – but doing so is taken as a measure of aggressive behaviour that tells us about the real-world actions of mild to severe verbal and physical aggression.

One potential criticism of the measures used is the range of them and the consistency of the results they yield – that is, how can making a **questionnaire evaluation** of someone in a critical way be treated as equivalent to snapping an elastic band in their face and choosing to administer a high level of unpleasant noise to them?

These issues become all the more problematic when we consider that studies attempting to use multiple measures often obtain different findings about the aggression elicited *as a function of the measure of aggression used*. That is, using attitudinal and electric shock measures of aggression for the same participants, experiencing the same conditions, yields different results on the two measures. This suggests that caution is needed before one treats these measures as pointing to a unified, generic construct of aggression.

A related issue concerns the external validity of the measures used. That is, to what extent do experimental operationalisations of potential causes (or independent variables, such as prior provocation, **aversive** stimuli, situational cues and **victim empathy**) and consequences (or dependent variables – that is, aggression) validly represent real-world phenomena? How does the experimental simulation of provocation or the experimental measure of an aggressive response relate to the real-world instances of provocation and aggression that the researchers conducting these experiments seek to explain? Berkowitz and Donnerstein (1982) and Anderson and Bushman seek to address precisely this point, arguing against, what Anderson and Bushman (1997, p. 29) refer to as, 'the overly pessimistic critiques of the value of laboratory aggression paradigms.' They acknowledge that results in and out of the laboratory can be different. For example, the link between temperature and aggression (see Box 9.1) has an average laboratory effect of 'about zero', while the 'weapons effect' does not appear to be significant outside of the laboratory. Prior provocation – crucial to many laboratory studies – has not been effectively used outside of laboratory settings. Furthermore, as Mulac et al. (2002) argue, even when the stimulus is identitical, the contexts of the laboratory and the real-world setting may be incredibly significant. Thus, as they argue, viewing aggressive or erotic (or, indeed, any type of) films is likely to be distinctly different in many important ways when one is a participant in a laboratory experiment and when one is viewing at home, for example.

Anderson and Bushman (1997, p. 44) acknowledge these discrepancies, but argue that the laboratory research and the measures used generally in aggression research can inform us about the core concepts we use to understand aggression:

> It is important to note that real world aggression measures (e.g. violent crime) share few surface features with laboratory aggression measures (e.g. delivery of an electric shock). However, these aggression measures do share the conceptual features of delivering a noxious stimuli to a victim with the intent and expectation of causing harm. As noted by Mook (1983), Berkowitz and Donnerstein (1982), and others, we should expect to generalize our theories. In other words, the conceptual relations among variables are expected to be similar in quite dissimilar situations.

Observed actual aggression This is a measure of aggression in which attention is given to what people would conventionally define as aggression – the direct infliction of physical pain or discomfort on another.

Questionnaire evaluations A measure of aggression that relies on how positively or negatively the participant evaluates someone else (often an experimenter) on a questionnaire.

Aversive Anything that could be perceived or experienced as unpleasant. Some aggression experiments measure it by examining the extent to which a participant will choose to administer a loud and unpleasant (aversive) noise to another person.

Victim empathy The extent to which participants express empathy (usually in questionnaire responses) for victims (often presented as summaries of a case where someone has been the victim of a crime).

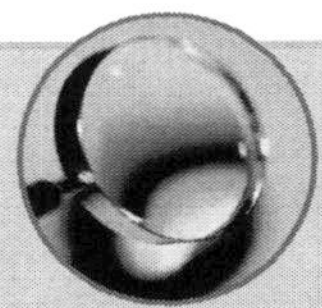

Box 9.6 FOCUS
How aggression has been measured in aggression research

In research that purports to be concerned with aggression as the key dependent variable, aggression has been operationalised (or conceptualised and measured) in a number of different ways – some of which are described below.

Electric shocks

The number, duration and intensity of the electric shocks administered to a confederate in 'learning-style experiments' has been taken as a measure (a scalable measure) of aggression; (Berkowitz & Alioto, 1973; Berkowitz & Geen, 1967; Berkowitz & LePage, 1967; Berkowitz, Lepinski, & Angulo, 1969; Donnerstein & Berkowitz, 1981; Donnerstein, Donnerstein, Simon, & Ditrichs, 1972). Higher numbers of shocks, greater duration and greater intensity were understood to register higher levels of aggressive behaviour.

Aversive noise

The frequency, duration and intensity of aversive noise administered to a confederate has also been taken as a scalable measure of aggression (Bushman, Baumeister, Thomaes, Ryu, Begeer, & West, 2009; Konijn, Bijvank, & Bushman, 2007; Konrath, Bushman, & Campbell, 2006; Zillmann & Bryant, 1974). More frequent, longer and higher levels of aversive noise were understood as registering higher levels of aggressive behaviour.

Observed direct physical aggression

Observed actual aggression has been much less frequently used as a measure. Diener (1980) reported observations of attacking a passive target in a laboratory context. The attacks varied in intensity, but included the use of foam swords, paper balls and elastic bands (which were snapped on the target's face). In a number of instances, Diener felt the aggression had reached such intensity that the experiment had to be halted. Leyens, Camino, Parke and Berkowitz (1975) had observers – in cottages temporarily occupied by children in 'care' – witness instances of physical aggression.

Observed direct verbal aggression

Again, this is less frequently used as a measure of aggression. Leyens et al. (1975) – referred to above – also had the observers note verbal aggression between the children involved. Mulac et al. (2002) examined videotaped male–female interactions following exposure to experimental stimuli, with an interest in interactional dominance, interruption and ignoring of the other's contributions. It should be noted that these were largely treated as significant behavioural effects in themselves rather than chiefly as indicators of an underlying aggressive response.

Questionnaire evaluations

A number of studies have used participants' evaluations of an experimenter, confederate or job applicant as the measure of aggression (Berkowitz & Troccoli, 1990; Ramirez, Bryant, & Zillmann, 1982; Zillmann & Sapolsky, 1977). If participants reported more negative evaluations, such as rating that the experimenter should not be 'reappointed as a research assistant', that was interpreted as aggressive behaviour.

Measures of victim empathy

Some studies have used measures of victim empathy – such as empathy for specific and general cases of rape (Linz, Donnerstein, & Penrod, 1988) or victims of domestic violence (Mullin & Linz, 1995). It should be noted that, similarly to observed, direct verbal aggression (see above), these measures have often been treated as significant behavioural effects *in themselves* rather than chiefly as indicators of an underlying aggressive response.

Combined aggression measures

Some studies have sought to combine different measures of aggression. Donnerstein, Donnerstein and Evans (1975) measured both the liking of the experimenter and the intensity of the shocks given. Berkowitz, Cochran and Embree (1981) used attitudes towards a confederate and the experimenter, aversive noise and the giving of lower numbers of rewards, obtaining differing results across these measures. Berkowitz (1965) used both ratings of the experimenter and the number and duration of electric shocks, finding slightly different results for the two measures.

This idea of conceptual relations between the variables of provocation, aggressive stimulus and aggressive response relies in part on participants making sense of these variables when they encounter them in an experimental setting in the same sorts of ways that people do outside of the laboratory. Thus, the prior provocation might be unusual – for example, receiving electric shocks as negative feedback for an essay – but the meaning participants give to it – 'I'm offended and angered by that' – is thought to override that difference. Likewise, administering high-intensity shocks or evaluating the experimenter in a negative way is also unusual but also might elicit the meaning of revenge and the desire to cause the target harm – 'I' ll teach them!'

What this perspective does not sufficiently consider, however, is the extent to which the meanings that participants arrive at are not just products of generalisable, context-free variables operating on them or within them – provocation, desire for revenge. Instead, these meanings and real-world actions can be understood as much subtler *interactional* achievements or as being *ideologically informed*. In interactional terms, it may be that 'being offended' is arrived at via a sequence involving two or more people in interaction – and it may be subject to reconstrual, not just as a result of the private reattribution or relabelling of the emotion but also because of joint construction in the interaction itself. Similarly, aggressive acts are rarely such detached, context-free operations as pressing a button that will deliver a shock to a non-present other. Instead, **observed direct verbal aggression**, for example, is again, located within and made sense of in sequences of interactions between people and it is there that the actions undertaken are placed and come to have a meaning. A sequential analysis of offence and aggressive behaviour yields a radically different perspective that approaches these not as context-independent states or actions but rather as *only having sense* in a specific context, being *intricately related to the interactional context* in which they are found and as *having meaning in the joint actions of those in interaction.*

A related illustration of this approach, from the perspective of female victims of date rape, is provided by Kitzinger and Frith (1999). They suggest that we need to consider how refusals are done in sequences of interaction – often involving delayed responses and appreciations rather than immediate explicit rejections – to better understand how sexual refusal is done. These refusals are sequentially located accomplishments, so any attempt to take the female response from that sequential context by, for example, looking just at what she says or does not say in isolation, distorts the sequentially contingent nature of her actions. The female's silence or compliment, taken out of sequential context, may be (and in some defence cases *is*) used to undermine the *fact* of her refusal, but the refusal *action* is done *with* and *in* the surrounding sequential context, not independently of it. Somewhat similarly, when 'being provoked' and 'being aggressive' are considered as sequentially located actions, attention needs to turn not to context-free internal or external variables, arousal, attribution of arousal, aggressive stimuli, aggressive cognitions and aggressive action but the *sequences of interaction in the real*, interacting world where what we come to see as 'being provoked' and 'being aggressive' are located.

Observed direct verbal aggression This is a measure of aggression in which attention is given to aggressive and domineering ways of talking and interacting – it includes 'interactional dominance', interruption and 'ignoring others'.

Critical recap

How experiments measure aggression and its causes

1 There are questions regarding how the wide range of measures used for dependent variables and aggression itself relate to one another – and whether or not they yield consistent results.

2 All of the measures can be questioned, regarding their external validity or how they relate to real-world phenomena. Thus, can we treat receiving electric shocks as equivalent to being provoked by someone outside of the laboratory? Can we think of filling in a questionnaire about someone in a negative way as equivalent to hitting them?

3 Some researchers have stressed that, despite surface differences, there is *a conceptual* equivalence between real-world phenomena and their experimental manifestations. Thus, the participants may experience receiving shocks as a form of provocation and giving shocks or filling in a questionnaire negatively as 'getting their own back' at the provoking individual.

4 There has been little attention given to how the meaning given to, for example, a 'provocation' might be informed by interaction between the provoker and the provoked.

5 Similarly, there has been little attention paid to the way in which ideologies concerning the potential target of aggression (for example, the groups that they belong to) and the legitimacy of aggression towards them might inform instances of aggression.

Reflective questions

1 *Which measures of aggression do you feel are the most – and least – valid?*

2 *If you were to design an experiment to examine an aspect of aggression, how would you measure it?*

9.6 Deindividuation

The approaches to understanding aggression that we have considered so far have encompassed both factors *within* the individual person and their *situation*, but little attention has been paid to the sorts of situational effects that the presence of other people may have. Think for a moment about how your own behaviour may be different – perhaps less inhibited – if you are in the midst of a crowd. The idea of deindividuation (see the summary in Box 9.7 near the end of this section) is that situations which alter our sense of ourselves as an identifiable and distinct individual (such as being in a crowd) can result in changes to our sense of self, which, in turn, can allow for the release of aggressive behaviour.

One of the earliest contributions to social psychology addressed just this issue. In his notorious work *The crowd: A study of the popular mind* (1896) – a text drawn on by Mussolini, Goebbels and Hitler – LeBon provided a damning indictment of crowds. For him, crowds inevitably bring out the worst in people. Whereas an individual may be well-behaved and cultivated, placed in a crowd, that same individual, because he or she feels anonymous, is highly suggestible and quickly goes along with the prevailing 'group mentality'. As Brown (2000a) notes, a lasting legacy of LeBon's work is the idea that being in a group situation can provide a state of **anonymity**. This, in turn, is understood as leading to a decrease in personal control over one's behaviour and, instead, a release of destructive impulses. As Reicher (1996) notes, Le Bon's work both ignored the **social context** of the crowd behaviour that he himself referred to and, furthermore, through its emphasis on *irrational* processes, resulted in an approach which did not consider the need for or possibility of finding any *rationale, purpose* or *meaning* for crowd action.

Festinger, Pepitone and Newcombe (1952) drew on several strands of LeBon's thinking in developing the notion of **deindividuation**. Like LeBon's concept of people in a crowd, deindividuation is a state in which people (often because they are anonymous in a group of people) have a reduced sense of both accountability for their own actions and awareness of themselves as individuals. Diener, Lusk, DeFour and Flax (1980) argue that within Festinger et al.'s (1952) formulation was the gestalt idea of the perception of whole figures rather than individual parts. Diener et al. (1980, p. 449) argue that, 'just as visual attention can be directed by the characteristics of visual figures, so one's attention to persons and oneself when one is in a group may be directed by the characteristics of the group.' That is, individuals in groups may experience reduced self-consciousness or self-awareness 'because their attention is directed to the groups in which they are immersed' (1980, p. 449).

The concept of deinidividuation (albeit without the emphasis on the perceptual shift from self to group) took centre stage in ideas emerging from Zimbardo's (1969) series of experiments into the psychological and behavioural consequences of people being placed in situations where they are not individually identifiable – that is, conditions of anonymity.

Zimbardo's deindividuation experiments involved participants who were led to believe that they were taking part in a learning experiment. Participants were given the opportunity to select the duration of apparently real electric shocks that the 'learner' (really a confederate) would receive. In the control condition, participants wore their everyday clothes but also had large name badges. In the 'deindividuation' condition, the participants were made anonymous by wearing a large white gown with a hood – the hood covering the entire head with holes cut out for the eyes and mouth.

In the first experiment, student participants were randomly allocated to either the deindividuated or control conditions. Which group do you think chose to administer electric shocks of a longer duration? Well, you are probably right – the deindividuated participants

Anonymity, anonymous This refers to the external conditions under which a person is not readily identified as an individual and/or their actions cannot readily be attributed to them as an individual.

Social context Often introduced to criticise aspects of deindividuation theory, this refers to the wider setting within which real instances of aggression take place. By considering the specifics of the social context, aggressive behaviour may be seen as having a meaning or purpose in some cases that cannot be appreciated when issues of social context are ignored.

Deindividuation This is used in different ways in the literature (see the above text for a discussion of this), but, generally, denotes a psychological state of decreased awareness of oneself as an individual and/or a lessened sense of accountability for one's own behaviour.

administered shocks lasting approximately twice the duration of those of the control group. This finding was certainly consistent with the ideas of LeBon (1896) and Festinger et al. (1952) – that anonymity was associated with more aggressive behaviour (administering potentially painful electric shocks for a longer period of time).

Zimbardo (1969) argued that the external conditions of anonymity gave rise to the psychological state of deindividuation (reduced awareness of self as an individual and reduced sense of responsibility for one's actions), which, in turn, led to the release of destructive impulses. A subsequent experiment by Zimbardo (1969) involving Belgian soldiers, however, contradicted these findings as the soldiers administered shocks of *shorter* duration when they wore the gown and hood compared to when they wore their uniform.

Despite some attempt to explain the contradictory findings in terms of the soldiers having already been deindividuated by their uniform and being individuated (or reindividuated) by putting on the gown and hood, the results do raise problems. These problems could be operational – that is, how well do the experimental procedures 'stand in for' their real-world corollaries, (for example, does wearing a gown and hood consistently make people feel anonymous, does duration of shock selected consistently reveal aggressive impulses?) The problems could, however, pose a far greater one. That problem is not just with how anonymity and aggressive impulses were operationalised in this specific experiment, but also with the overarching theory of anonymity causing deindividuation, which causes the release of destructive impulses, as such ambivalent results may cause us to pause and question the inevitability of these causal connections.

Diener (1976) raised some qualifications regarding this theory of anonymity bringing about the psychological state of deindividuation and the behavioural manifestation of increased anti-normative behaviour – particularly aggressiveness.

In Diener's experiment, 80 male psychology students were given either an arousing task (throwing rocks and bottles as fast as they could at a concrete wall) or a non-arousing task (painting an ecology sign) to complete and then taken into a darkened room where they were invited to participate in 'fast physical activity' in a room that had a role-player sitting on the floor. Participants were shown newspaper balls, pellet pistols, foam swords, foam bricks and elastic bands, among other materials, that they could use. They either entered the room with two others (one of whom was a confederate who modelled some aggressive behaviour towards the role-player) or alone. Participants were either anonymous to both experimenter and role-player – being told that the experimenter would not learn their names and the role-player could not see them through his protective goggles – or not, with their photograph, name, address, subject of study and home town being inspected by both experimenter and role-player before they entered the room. Additionally, in this latter condition, participants were informed that they would be meeting the role-player later in the day. Unseen observers rated how aggressively participants acted towards the passive role-player during their time in the room. Finally, participants completed questionnaires that attempted to measure how 'deindividuated' they had been when they were in the room with the role-player. The self-reported deindividuation questionnaire asked participants about their self-consciousness, liking for the group, concern for social evaluation and assessed the extent to which they had distorted perceptions of their own aggressive behaviours and the time they spent in the room

Diener certainly found aggressive behaviour – among other actions, participants snapped elastic bands into the face of the role-player. Diener (1976, pp. 504, 505) notes; 'The aggression exhibited by participants in some of the conditions of the present study was surprisingly extreme and certainly fits Zimbardo's (1969) description of deindividuated behaviour as being impulsive and of high intensity.' Diener (1976, p. 505) notes that, in three instances, sessions were abruptly terminated 'because of excessive aggression'. What is noteworthy, however, is that anonymity and deindividuation – as operationalised and measured in this study – were not central determinants of aggression. Diener reports that only prior arousal (throwing bottles and rocks at a wall) produced significantly higher levels of observed aggression – anonymity having no effect and group presence leading to a significant *decrease* in aggression. It can be noted in passing, however, that by far the highest aggression scores were for the condition in which aroused participants were alone and anonymous, suggesting that anonymity may have had some role in observed aggression. Furthermore, Diener's self-report questionnaires designed to measure deindividuation suggested that anonymity did not result in increased deindividuation – only arousal did – and did not significantly correlate with aggressive behaviour.

For Diener (1979) and Diener, Lusk, DeFour and Flax (1980), it was important to return to Festinger et al.'s (1952) emphasis on groups rather than merely conditions that may create anonymity. Thus, Diener (1979) suggests groups that are cohesive, uniform and outwardly focused may be deindividuating. Similarly, Diener et al. (1980) suggest that an increase in group size is associated with lowered self-consciousness (a feature of deindividuation).

Along with the increased emphasis on groups in contributing to deindividuation, Diener (1979) and Diener et al. (1980) raise two other issues: the first concerns how deindividuation can be understood; the second concerns the implications of inconsistent findings regarding the behavioural consequences of deindividuation.

Diener (1979) proposed a definition of deindividuation, saying that it could be thought of in terms of a reduced monitoring of one's own behaviour and reduced awareness of oneself as an individual. He (1979, p. 1169) suggests that this reduced self-monitoring and self-awareness should result in decreased self-regulation and increased disinhibition 'because the person is less aware of behaviour–norm discrepancies and less likely to plan for the future.' Diener et al. (1980) further note, however, that these anticipated associations between apparent deindividuation and disinhibited behaviour are not consistently supported. Diener suggests this requires some empirical thinking regarding how 'disinhibited' behaviour is defined and the operational measures of this construct that are used in experiments. More fundamentally, for Diener et al. (1980, p. 458), the inconsistent results also raise theoretical questions regarding 'how awareness to different aspects of the environment, the group, and the self, relate to deindividuation.' and 'under what circumstances disinhibited behaviour will follow from internal deindividuation.'

This reworking of the concept (as well as the experimental operationalisation) of deindividuation has been present throughout the history of this concept in social psychology. Festinger et al. (1952), drawing on LeBon, coined the term 'deindividuation' to get at the feeling of 'not being scrutinized or accountable when submerged in the group' (Postmes & Spears, 1998, p. 240). For Zimbardo, the idea of anonymity within the group (operationalised largely by clothes that hid the individual's identity) was particularly emphasised. While the extent to which Zimbardo emphasised the group – rather than just anonymity – is debatable, Postmes and Spears argue that he maintained the sense of 'accountability to an audience' found in Festinger et al.'s original formulation.

As seen above, Diener was particularly keen to return to Festinger's emphasis on a shift of perception from self to group and link this to the reduced self-awareness and self-monitoring that he associated with the deindividuated state. Postmes and Spears (1998) argue that these approaches (Festinger et al., Zimbardo and Diener) all share an emphasis on deindividuation as involving a reduced sense of accountability and refer to them as *classical deindividuation theory*.

By contrast – as Postmes and Spears note – the work of Prentice-Dunn and Rogers (1983, 1989) understands deindividuation as simply reduced private self-awareness without any necessary reduction in accountability. From this perspective, the state of deindividuation involves us experiencing a reduced self-consciousness, as if a psychological shift occurs in which there is not a shift to group thinking, but less thinking about ourselves and our behaviour. Think of a time when you felt lost in the moment – caught up in music, dance or laughter. It is likely that this experience was in some ways disinhibiting. For Postmes and Spears, Prentice-Dunn and Rogers' (1983, 1989) research, with its emphasis on reduced *self-awareness* rather than reduced *accountability*, constitutes a significant change from previous research and they refer to it as *contemporary deindividuation theory*.

This issue regarding how deindividuation is understood proved relevant to one strand of Postmes and Spears' (1998) meta-analyses of deindividuation studies. From their review of 60 deindividuation studies (including those by Zimbardo, Diener and Prentice-Dunn & Rogers), they found very limited support for the idea that the psychological state of 'deindividuation' leads to behaviour which can be described as 'anti-normative' and 'disinhibited'. The slender support for aspects of deindividuation theory Postmes and Spears *did* find was that reducing accountability related to an increase in anti-normative behaviour – but, private self-awareness and anonymity did not.

In this way, the meta-analysis supported an element of *classic deindividuation theory* – that reduced accountability can sometimes be linked to increased anti-normative behaviour. Postmes and Spears found little support, however, for either 'disinhibited anti-normative behaviour' or, perhaps more pertinently, the deindividuated state itself. Thus, the very psychological mechanism that was central to both classic *and* contemporary deindividuation theory was challenged. Postmes and Spears argued that, instead, their analyses supported an alternative perspective on apparent deindividuation effects. For them, instances of so-called 'anti-normative' behaviour that *did* arise in settings associated with deindividuation research (such as increased aggression in situations of being in a group and anonymity) could be understood by reconstruing them as reflecting *group* norms. This alternative approach provides one way of making sense of the findings of

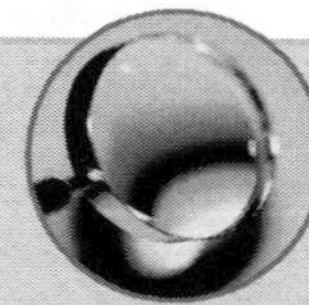

Box 9.7 FOCUS
Summary of classic and contemporary deindividuation theories

1 The individual is in a situation that may involve being in a group and feelings of anonymity.

Figure 9.4a An individual in a crowd experiencing being in a group and anonymity

2 Classic deindividuation theory: they have a reduced sense of personal accountability (Diener, 1979; Diener et al., 1980; Festinger et al., 1952; Zimbardo, 1969). Contemporary deindividuation theory: they experience reduced private self-awareness (Prentice- Dunn & Rogers, 1983, 1989).

Figure 9.4b The individual experiences deindividuation

3 This can result in the release of destructive impulses and/or anti-normative behaviour.

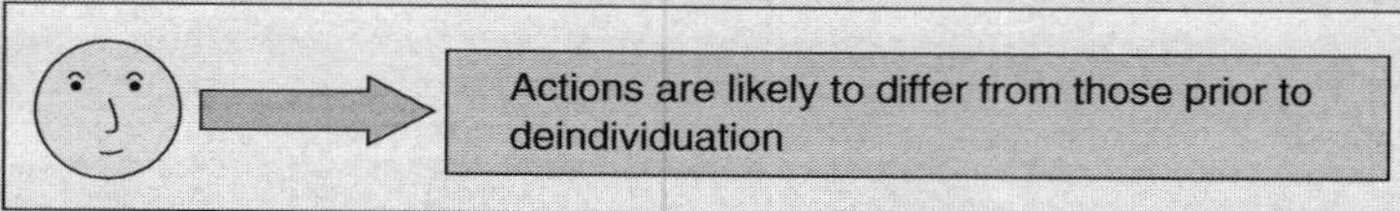

Actions are likely to differ from those prior to deindividuation

Figure 9.4c As a consequence, the individual behaves differently from how their individuated self would behave

Johnson and Downing (see Box 9.9) and is more fully developed in an approach that draws on social identity theory to make sense of 'deindividuation effects' – **social identity deindividuation effects (SIDE)**. See Box 9.7 for a summary of the deindividuation theories that we have looked at so far and Box 9.8 to think a little more about the ideas discussed.

Social identity deindividuation effects (SIDE) Emphasises the way in which situations of group immersion and anonymity can give rise to, not a loss of identity but, rather, a change of identity, with a particular emphasis on the group identities that may become salient in such situations.

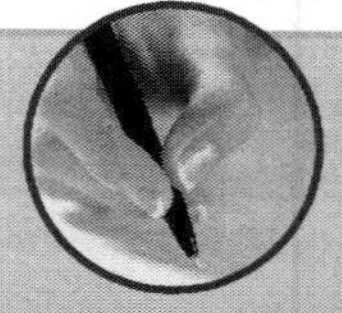

Box 9.8 TRY IT OUT
Deindividuation

Have you ever experienced the feeling of being anonymous in a large group or crowd? Do you think that it changed how you felt about yourself? If so, do you think that you 'lost' or 'changed' your sense of identity? Did you simply become less aware of yourself as an individual or do you think that some shared sense of identity became salient for you?

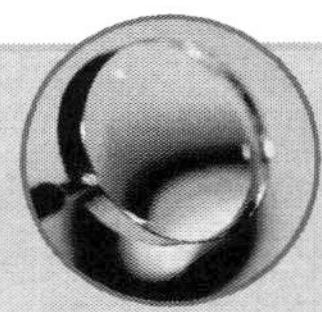

Box 9.9 FOCUS
Anonymity and situational cues (Johnson & Downing, 1979)

Johnson and Downing developed a modification of Zimbardo's (1969) experiments that sought to investigate the extent to which situational norms – rather than the absence of norms – could account for the behaviour of deindividuated participants.

The participants (excluding those in a control condition) were allocated to either one of the two individuated conditions or one of the two deindividuated conditions. In all conditions, the participants wore white robes and had to stand at a console, selecting the level of shock to be administered to a 'learner' in a 'learning' experiment.

In the *individuated* conditions, participants wore large name tags and had their photographs attached to the consoles where they stood. They were also informed that the individual levels of shock they chose could be identified. In the *deindividuated* condition, participants had the name tags and photographs mixed up, so they could not be identified by either, and were informed that the individual levels of shock they chose to administer could not be identified.

Each of the participants (with the exception of those in the control condition) was also allocated to one of the two situational norm conditions. As they were handed the robes to wear, they were told either, 'I'm not much of a seamstress – this thing looks kind of Ku Klux Klanish' or 'I was fortunate that the hospital recovery room let me borrow these nurses' gowns.' This manipulation was designed to create strongly contrasting norms – either one of aggression or prosocial behaviour. This meant that four different conditions could be compared with the control condition to see whether higher or lower levels of shock were selected in each one.

It was found that deindividuation on its own did not lead to an increase in the levels of shock administered – a finding that stands in sharp contrast to the notion that deindividuation involves the release of destructive impulses. In the Ku Klux Klan condition, deindividuation led to an extremely small, non-significant increase in the chosen levels of shock while, in the nurses' gowns condition, deindividuation led to a significant decrease in the levels of shock selected.

Johnson and Downing (1979) suggested that the experiment provides a challenge to the notion that deindividuation *necessarily* causes anti-normative, aggressive or destructive behaviour – here, the only significant effect was a reduction in the levels of shock administered in the nurses' gowns condition. Furthermore, the experiment provides partial support for the idea that situational norms shape behaviour.

Johnson and Downing were particularly interested in the fact that – at least in the nurses' gowns condition – there was an interaction between situational norm and deindividuation. The nurses' uniform led to a sharp decrease in the levels of shock administered *in the deindividuation condition*. Deindividuated, participants wearing nurses' uniforms seemed more influenced by the norms associated with nursing than their individuated counterparts. This is interpreted by Johnson and Downing as showing when deindividuated people are more susceptible to situational norms – in this case, they were influenced by the, presumably, prosocial, helpful, non-harmful norms associated with nursing and, thus, opted to give lower levels of shock than the group control and all the other participants.

Deindividuation theory has clearly encompassed a variety of different positions. Some approaches (such as LeBon's and Zimbardo's) have emphasised the release of destructive impulses as a result of the anonymity that being in a group can provide. Other approaches (such as Festinger et.al. and Diener) have emphasised how being in a group can affect a shift in perception that can give rise to disinhibited behaviour. In quite different ways, deindividuation introduces the idea that other people – specifically the group one is in – can be an important component in explaining aggressive behaviour.

Social identity deindividuation effects (SIDE)

The work on deindividuation considered above emphasised the importance of considering groups when trying to understand aggression, but tended to emphasise the idea of loss – particularly the loss of identity – that can arise from group immersion and anonymity. Social identity deindividuation effects (see Box 9.10) echoes the idea that groups are important, but reconstrues their role, emphasising the ways in which being in a group may result in a *change*, rather than *loss*, of identity.

SIDE provides an alternative reading to most of the deindividuation literature considered above. It understands deindividuation manipulations such as group immersion and anonymity as potentially important not, as mentioned, because they cause a loss of identity but, rather, because of their effect on both identity salience and behavioural expression.

Postmes and Spears (1998) note that precursors to the idea of identity salience can be found in the work of Ziller (1964), Johnson and Downing (1979) and Diener (1980). As Postmes and Spears (1998, p. 254) note Ziller (1964) 'defined deindividuation as a closer adherence to one's group or environment'. This suggests not just a loss of personal identity but some sort of normative influence from the 'group or environment'. Similarly, as seen above, Johnson and Downing (1979) argued that, rather than causing the loss of personal identity and the release of destructive impulses, environmental conditions thought to create deindividuation (such as anonymity, reduced accountability and so on) could be seen to promote an increased sensitivity to situational cues (and possibly norms) for behaviour.

In a somewhat related vein, Diener (1980), as noted above, returned to Festinger's gestalt approach to deindividuation in emphasising the deindividuated person's shift to seeing him- or herself not so much as a separate individual but part of the group as a whole.

Taken together, these differing perspectives accept the idea of a psychological state of deindividuation, but do not see this in terms of the loss of identity and release of destructive, disinhibited and impulsive behaviour. Instead – albeit with differing emphasis – they see the state of deindividuation as increasing the influence of factors *external* to the individual – such as the situation or the group – on the behaviour of the deindividuated individual. If the environmental cues or group norms promote aggression, then the individual will be likely to act in an aggressive manner (depending on the opportunities afforded by the situation); if the cues or norms promote prosocial behaviour, then the individual will act consistently with that by undertaking prosocial actions. See Box 9.10 for a summary of SIDE and Box 9.11 for an example of a study applying the theory to an event that was in the news in 1980.

SIDE develops the ideas outlined above, placing less emphasis on an actual psychological state of deindividuation and more on the identity effects of 'deindividuating' settings. For SIDE, the settings associated with deindividuation in the research considered above – such as being in a group and anonymity – can promote not a *loss* of identity but an increase in the salience of a group identity. Thus, consistent with social identity theory (see Chapter 1), the idea here is that anonymity and being in a group may be just the sorts of conditions that lead people to shift from a *personal* to a *social* identity. In conditions promoting anonymity and one's sense of being in a group, individuals may not think of themselves in terms of their individual identities but, rather, their collective or group identities. From this perspective, as Reicher (1984a, 1984b) and Postmes and Spears (1998) note, what might appear to be 'anti-normative', 'disinhibited' or 'aggressive' behaviour may, in fact, be manifestations of the different group norms consistent with the group identity that has been made salient for the individual.

Think for a moment of a football fan within a crowd of supporters. Imagine that he or she engages in 'anti-normative' behaviour by running onto the football pitch and fighting with a rival fan. These behaviours may well be anti-normative in terms of the general prevailing societal norms, but glossing them as anti-normative misses the point that they might actually be instances of *group* normative behaviour – that is, behaviour consistent with the activated (or salient) group identity.

Box 9.11 refers to Reicher's investigation regarding the causes of and crowd behaviour associated with the St Paul's riot in Bristol in 1980. What is particularly noteworthy here is that the crowd's apparently anti-normative behaviour could be made sense of as being consistent with their social identity as members of the St Paul's community. From the perspective of their social identity, the crowd in the St Paul's riot showed not disinhibited, impulsive, anti-normative aggression but, rather, a more controlled 'social identity-consistent' repertoire of behaviours. In these ways, the SIDE model criticises the idea that situational conditions associated with deindividuation – such as anonymity and group presence – lead to a loss of identity and behaviour that is disinhibited and out of control. Instead, for SIDE, these conditions make the individual's *collective*, *group* or *social* identity salient and thereby make the norms associated with that social identity relevant for guiding the behaviour of the individual.

It is possible, however, to question how these 'situational conditions associated with deindividuation' relate to the actual expression of behaviour. That is, just because the conditions are those promoting a group identity (and norms of behaviour associated with that identity), will it inevitably follow that group members act consistently with those norms?

Klein, Spears and Reicher (2007) suggest that the situational conditions associated with deindividuation play a second role – they not only make group identity (and

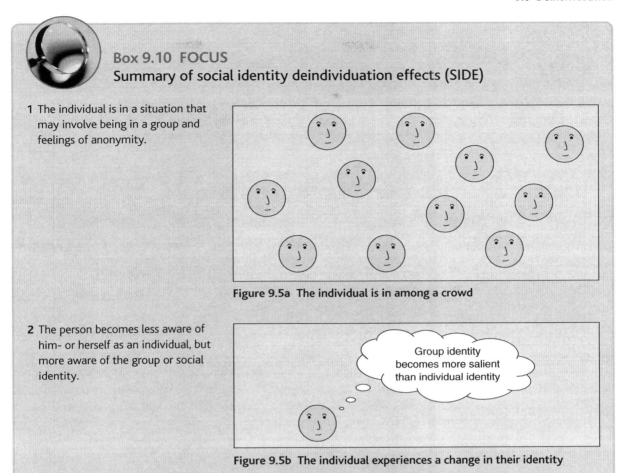

Box 9.10 FOCUS
Summary of social identity deindividuation effects (SIDE)

1 The individual is in a situation that may involve being in a group and feelings of anonymity.

Figure 9.5a The individual is in among a crowd

2 The person becomes less aware of him- or herself as an individual, but more aware of the group or social identity.

Group identity
becomes more salient
than individual identity

Figure 9.5b The individual experiences a change in their identity

3 This can result in behaviour that is consistent with the group's identity and associated norms.

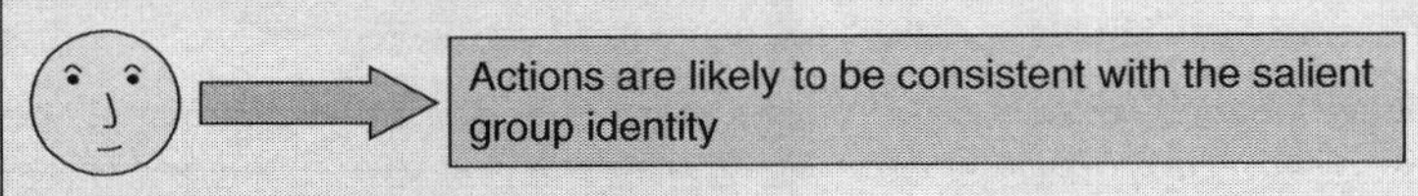

Figure 9.5c The individual's behaviour reflects the group's identity

associated norms) more salient but also, particularly with the condition of anonymity, can affect behaviour. According to Klein et al., if we examine members enacting behaviour that is consistent with their group identity, there is a distinction between behaviours that are only visible to other group members and ones visible to those outside of the group. Behaviour only visible to fellow group members may well *not* be anonymous (group members are likely to know who the others are), but, within the group, that does not matter. Behaviour that can be seen by those outside of the group is a different matter – here anonymity (being anonymous as far as the *non-group members* are concerned) becomes important. The anonymous person is more likely to freely enact behaviour consistent with their group identity, even when it is visible to those who are outside of the group, whereas, if they are not anonymous, their behaviour will be more constrained. Thus, being *in a group* and being *anonymous* can make it more likely that group identities and norms are made salient for members and are acted on even when those actions are visible to non-group members.

Critical review of deindividuation

In contrast to the research considered previously (which largely ignored the impact of co-present others), deindividuation theory introduces the idea that the presence of others – for example, being in a group – can be related

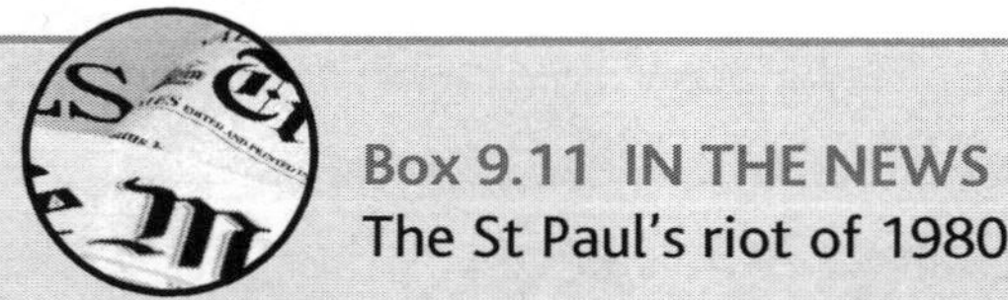

Box 9.11 IN THE NEWS
The St Paul's riot of 1980

Reicher (1984a) used a variety of interviews, official accounts and newspaper reports to analyse a riot that occurred in the St Paul's area of Bristol in 1980. While some newspaper accounts of the riot suggested that St Paul's residents were a 'mad mob', careful scrutiny of available accounts and interviews with those involved painted a very different picture.

First, the trigger for the riot was identified by some participants as the police closing down an important café – the Black and White Café – within the St Paul's community. This had been understood in terms of a threat to the identity of the St Paul's community, which triggered the riot. Second, there were geographical limits to the aggression – it did not stray beyond the boundaries of the St Paul's community. Third, there were limits regarding the targets of the violence – when one person started to attack a fire engine, that person was stopped and the 'rioters' assisted ambulances and fire engines attempting to pass along the roads where the riot was taking place.

Reicher notes, therefore, the evidence regarding the causes of the riot (a threat to the St Paul's community's identity) and the actual conduct of the riot (rioters staying within the St Paul's area and only allowing violence against certain 'illegitimate' targets) can be seen as consistent with the idea of the riot being guided by the rioters' identity as members of the St Paul's community.

Reicher's interpretation of this data is open to challenge. Gaskell (1990) suggests that the apparent causes of the St Paul's riot – threat to identity – may not explain why in certain other conflicts, such as the miners' dispute, violence is inconsistently present. Indeed, for Gaskell, some conflicts may be better explained by reference to deprivation – in particular, fraternal deprivation (where one feels deprived as a *group* rather than as an *individual*). Likewise, it is possible to ask the question, did the interviewees merely present an accountable version of their behaviour that construed it as rational, controlled and legitimate? It might be that people do not – and perhaps cannot – *objectively* report on some actual, knowable, motivational basis for their behaviour.

to aggressive behaviour. It was noted that deindividuation research encompasses a number of quite distinct approaches, some of which pay particular attention to being in a group, others emphasise conditions that give rise to anonymity and yet others (more recent approaches) are concerned with reduced self-awareness.

Postmes and Spears' (1998) meta-analysis of deindividuation research raised a number of problems for how the concept had been approached. First, while not discrediting the potential importance of deindividuating conditions – indeed, suggesting that being anonymous had some association with an increase in 'anti-normative' behaviour – they questioned the idea of a psychological state of deindividuation. That is, while situations associated with deindividuation research may be relevant for understanding anti-normative, disinhibited and (in some cases) aggressive behaviour, there may not be an identifiable and meaningful psychological experience of 'deindividuation'.

Furthermore, while deindividuation theory introduces the relevance – or potential relevance – of the group, this can be criticised on a number of fronts: groups are portrayed negatively, the emphasis is still largely on individualistic and experimentally created groups that lack the meaning and identity real-world groups have for members.

With regard to the portrayal of groups, much of the research has viewed them as if they remove a layer of protection or control that the individual in isolation has. Thus, for some researchers (such as Zimbardo), being in a group leads to the release of destructivce impulses, while, for others (such as Johnson and Downing), being in a group makes the individual more vulnerable to situational influences. This tendency to portray groups in a negative light in deindividuation research reflects the more general concerns of Spears (2010) about the ways in which groups within social psychology as a whole have been portrayed as 'bad and biasing' – which he refers to as the 'intergroup bias bias'.

In a related vein, although deindividuation theory refers, to some extent, to the group, it is, in many cases, depicted as little more than a catalyst for essentially individualistic behaviour. Thus, it is still *individual* impulses and reactions to situational cues that are understood as driving the behaviour – the group has merely been a means by which impulses can be unleashed and barriers to the effects of situational cues removed.

Finally, questions can be raised concerning how group presence and anonymity are operationalised in many deindividuation experiments. While different interventions are used to create anonymity within a group, all of them could be considered quite different from the real-life experience of being in a group or crowd outside of the laboratory. Thus, unlike experimentally contrived groups, 'real-life' groups may be meaningful in some way (such as meeting to protest or experience something together). These meaningful groups may have some shared sense of identity and their behaviour may be related to their meaning, purpose or identity. This issue has been developed in social identity deindividuation effects (SIDE) research reviewed below.

Critical recap

Deindividuation

1 Postmes and Spears' (1998) meta-analysis questioned that there was evidence to support the very existence of 'deindividuation' itself as a psychological state.

2 The group has been depicted as an entirely negative influence in much of deindividuation theory.

3 While deindividuation theory refers to being in a *group*, the theory is largely concerned with behaviour that is driven by individuals' impulses or reactions.

4 Experimentally contrived groups lack the meaning or identity that groups may have in 'real' contexts. As a consequence, the possible influence of group identity on behaviour – in particular, the way in which behaviour may be meaningfully or purposively related to such group identity – cannot be investigated.

Reflective questions

1 *Can you think of an instance of aggressive behaviour that could feasibly be explained in terms of deindividuation?*

2 *In what ways are experimentally created groups different from 'real' groups?*

9.7 Social identity theory and intergroup behaviour

We have considered something of the way in which social identity theory has been drawn on to rethink deindividuation effects, but this is one small slice of a vastly important approach within social psychology. As Chapters 2, 7 and 8 outline, social identity theory does not simply try to account for behaviour where deindividuation conditions – such as anonymity, **loss of identity,** being in a group and **group norms** – prevail. Instead, as Brown (2000a) notes, the theory argues that when people are in groups and their group identity is activated, they are likely to act in ways that are consistent with their *social identity*. This social identity is understood as shaping how group members act, how they respond to **environmental cues** and how they maintain a **positive differential** between members of their group and members of other groups. Thus (as Chapters 2, 7 and 8 illustrate), social identity theory has argued that group members' desire for a positive difference between how they perceive themselves (**ingroup**) and how they perceive members of the other group (**outgroup**) can lead them to make decisions (for example, about remuneration for the ingroup and outgroup) that reflect an **ingroup bias** (see Box 9.12).

You may at this point wonder whether ingroup bias – which could be seen as behaviour that is skewed towards the interests of the ingroup – can be equated with the more overtly negative behaviours of 'aggression' and 'conflict' that this chapter addresess. Brown

Loss of identity Losing the sense of oneself as an individual.

Group norms Group-informed ideas about how to behave towards members of one's own group (*ingroup*) and other groups (*outgroups*).

Environmental cues Aspects of the environment that might be associated with certain behaviours – for example, a gun might be a cue for aggression.

Positive differential In the above literature, this refers to the way that group members are motivated to perceive their group as different and superior to other groups and to act in ways that are consistent with this.

Ingroup, outgroup The group to which one perceives oneself as belonging (ingroup) and the group or groups to which one does not perceive oneself as belonging (outgroup).

Ingroup bias The propensity to behave in ways that favour the ingroup over one or more outgroups.

(2000b) – who has done much to advance social identity theory – warns of just this sort of conceptual blurring with some social identity theory work failing to adequately distinguish the mere presence of *intergroup bias* from the more negatively valenced phenomenon of *prejudice* against outgroup members.

Some social identity work, however, makes the case that prejudice and conflict – not just intergroup bias – can be accounted for in terms of social identity issues. Thus, Pehrson, Brown and Zagefka's (2009) longitudinal study provides an illustration of how social identity can be linked to prejudice (rather than just ingroup bias). They found that for those who defined their nationality in ethnic terms, national identification was associated with prejudice against asylum seekers. Thus, the very perception of the basis on which who is in and who is out of the ingroup (and our motivation to maintain a positive identity), they found, is associated with prejudice against the outgroup. Similarly, Reicher's study of the St Paul's riot in Bristol in 1980 (see Box 9.11) argues the case that social identity theory provides a framework by means of which sense can be made of a real-world instance of rioting, which can lead to group aggression and conflict being rendered meaningful and purposive rather than irrational and impulsive (see also Box 9.13).

Here, social identity theory's approach to understanding aggression and conflict is examined by drawing on research concerned with a long-lasting and chronic intergroup conflict (frequently associated with outbreaks of violence) – the conflict between Protestant and Catholic residents in Northern Ireland. See Box 9.12 for a summary of social identity theory and intergroup behaviour.

Social identity content and chronic conflict

Social identity theory has been drawn on to understand a number of serious, real-world conflicts. One example of this is Livingstone and Haslam's (2008) research in Northern Ireland, where conflict between some members of the Protestant and Catholic communities has been extremely intense (with many fatalities) and very enduring (lasting many decades).

Livingstone and Haslam undertook two studies with pupils aged 16–18 at schools in Northern Ireland. One of the questionnaires administered to the pupils asked them, 'If you were asked for your religious denomination, which of the following would best describe you? They were then presented with a choice of Catholic, Protestant or non-Christian. The numbers of participants identifying with these categories were, Catholic, 49, Protestant, 56, and non-Christian, 12. The participants completed questionnaires that sought to measure ingroup identification, intergroup antagonism and behavioural intentions.

The questionnaires included several item statements for each variable and participants were invited to respond by expressing the extent of their agreement or disagreement on a seven-point scale. Ingroup identification and intergroup antagonism were measured using four items. For ingroup identification, these included items such as, 'Being a (ingroup member) is an important part of who I am.' Intergroup antagonism was measured using items such as, 'In my area, there is often trouble between (ingroup members) and (outgroup members)'. Some 14 items were used to ascertain different aspects of antagonistic identity content. These included measures of avoiding the outgroup and their values – for example, 'Not living according to (outgroup) values and ideals', 'Not living in a mainly (outgroup) area'. Intergroup antagonism also included items relating to identity threat – 'When (outgroup members) express their identity, it feels like my (ingroup) identity is under threat.' It also included items relating to the incompatibility of values: 'The values of (outgroup members) are opposed to those of (ingroup members)'. Behavioural intentions were measured using three items relating to the hypothetical scenario of how the participants would respond to the ingroup/outgroup-relevant preferences of a son or daughter of theirs. Thus, participants were asked would they object if their hypothetical son or daughter married an outgroup member. They were also asked whether they would buy a football shirt if their (hypothetical) son or daughter supported Glasgow Rangers (a well-known, predominantly Protestant football team) and asked the same question again if their son or daughter supported Glasgow Celtic (a well-known, predominantly Catholic football team). In a follow-up study one year later, Livingstone and Haslam supplemented the questionnaire with qualitative data in the form of interviews in which participants were invited to comment on their behavioural intentions responses.

Livingstone and Haslam found that, first, in line with previous literature, ingroup identification – the extent to which group identity was important to the participants' sense of self – was related to behavioural intentions that showed an ingroup bias – disapproving of the son's or

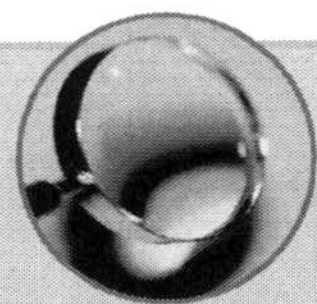

Box 9.12 FOCUS
Summary of social identity theory and intergroup behaviour

1 Individuals think of themselves in terms of their group identity.

Figure 9.6a A group identity is activated when it is salient

2 Individuals act towards other ingroup and outgroup members on the basis of their own group identity.

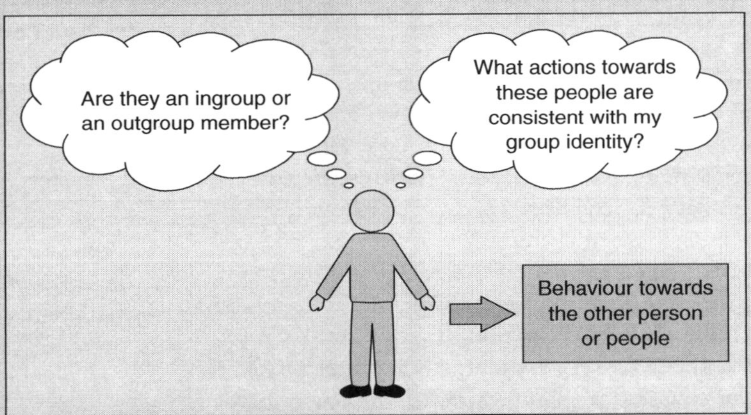

Figure 9.6b The group identity shapes intra- and intergroup behaviour

Box 9.13 IN THE NEWS
The murder of Eugene Terre'Blanche

On 3 April 2010, white supremacist leader Eugene Terre'Blanche was killed in South Africa.

Initially, the white supremacist movement linked it to provocative singing of anti-white farmer songs by some members of the ANC and promised to avenge his death by retaliating against black members of the ANC.

Subsequently, it emerged that two of his farm workers killed him in a dispute over pay. The white supremacist organisation then withdrew its threatened intergroup violence.

What is interesting for our current concerns is that when the death was construed in intergroup terms – specifically, as some sort of aggression directed at the white supremacist movement – then the promised response was in terms of intergroup conflict. When the death was subsequently attributed to an interpersonal worker–employer dispute, however, the threatened intergroup retaliation was withdrawn. The same events – when construed in intergroup and interpersonal terms – evoked dramatically different responses.

daughter's marriage to an outgroup member and expressing more willingness to buy the ingroup team's shirt than the outgroup team's shirt. Similarly, 'experiencing intergroup conflict and antagonism' also related to what Livingstone and Haslam refer to as 'negative behavioural intentions'.

What is of more significance is their findings regarding the impact of 'antagonistic forms of identity content'. Livingstone and Haslam found that the relationship between *identification* and *experience of conflict and antagonism* on the one hand and *negative behavioural intentions* on the other was moderated by 'antagonistic forms of identity content'. That is, the actual content of participants' social identities determined the extent to which identifying with the group and experiencing intergroup antagonism and conflict would determine negative behavioural intentions. If the social identity content was negative or antagonistic, then identifying with the ingroup and experiencing conflict and antagonism between the ingroup and outgroup would result in negative behavioural intentions. In a replication at a time of reduced intergroup conflict in Northern Ireland one year later, broadly similar results were obtained, suggesting that the relationship between these factors remains despite changes in manifest relations between the two groups at a societal level.

Livingstone and Haslam (2008) argue that these results suggest the content of social identities is vital to understanding the ingroups antagonistic relations with the outgroup. The findings indicate that antagonistic social identity content may both reflect *and predict* the ingroup's relationship with the outgroup. They have implications for both interventions designed to reduce intergroup conflict and intergroup research itself. First, they suggest that conflict-reducing interventions should provide the opportunity for group members to 'reconstruct and reconstrue' the ingroup–outgroup relationship in more positive terms – which, Livingstone and Haslam (2008, p. 17) admit, is 'easier said than done in settings such as Northern Ireland'. Second, Livingstone and Haslam (2008, p. 18) argue that attention to 'generic' processes should not detract attention from the actual specific content of social identities:

> More generally, the present studies warn against theorizing intergroup relations solely in terms of the generic processes that make group life possible (e.g. categorization, identification) to the neglect of the specific content that makes group life meaningful. Instead it may be suggested that social identities are meaningful self-definitions *precisely because* of their content, and abstracting the generic processes and constructs that make group life possible from the specific content that makes it meaningful tells only part of the story of what social identity actually is.

See Box 9.14 for an insight into another key researcher's work in this area.

Critical review of social identity theory and intergroup behaviour

Social identity theory can be understood as giving groups a prominent role in understanding human behaviour – in this case, aggression and intergroup conflict. Here, groups are not merely reduced to being conditions that promote anonymity, nor mere catalysts for individualistic behaviour – instead, group members' sense of shared identity is thought to inform their behaviour. From this perspective, instances of intergroup conflict and aggression can be seen as – at least potentially – meaningful rather than purely reactive and mindless. Aggression and conflict might be informed and perhaps curtailed by how individuals see themselves as members of relevant groups. Perhaps, as in the case of the St Paul's riot that Reicher (1984a) documents, discussed earlier in this chapter, they are triggered by a threat to identity and guided by identity-relevant concerns.

It is possible to ask, however, to what extent has social identity research demonstrated that it is relevant to more than just ingroup bias? That is, while there is substantial experimental data concerning some form of ingroup favouritism, there is rather less to suggest that group identity can account for aggression – or aggressive intent. In Livingstone and Haslam's (2008a) research, also discussed earlier, for example, one measure of 'negative behavioural intentions' included the willingness of participants to allow their children to wear outgroup-identifiable football shirts, such as a Rangers shirt in a predominantly Catholic neighbourhood. It could be argued that a reluctance to do so could, at best (for social identity theory), reflect an ingroup bias and, at worse (for the theory), merely a concern for the children's safety.

Attempts to read real-world conflict in terms of social identity theory have also been questioned. Gaskell (1990, p. 260), while admiring Reicher's contribution to challenging assumptions about the loss of identity in crowds, asks; 'what of crowds where identity is not an issue?' Gaskell(1990, p. 260) suggests that social identity theory needs to take into account 'contextual and

Box 9.14 KEY RESEARCHER
Professor Rupert Brown: intergroup relations and prejudice

How did you become interested in intergroup relations and prejudice?

Many years ago (more than I care to remember!), after a few false starts with my PhD, I became interested in why some groups seemed to find it difficult to cooperate with one another, despite some obvious shared goals. This also happened to coincide with my becoming more politically active and observing much factionalism and division within the Labour movement. My supervisor was Henri Tajfel, who had just developed social identity theory with John Turner, who also happened to be my line manager at the time. This theory seemed to offer some insights into why such intergroup divisions might persist, even in the face of common material interests. The combination of working closely with these two inspirational people and my growing political involvement instigated an interest in intergroup relations that has endured to this day.

Tell us about your research into intergroup relations and prejudice?

For many years, I was fascinated by the role that social identification played in instigating and maintaining intergroup divisions. Very much influenced by social identity theory, I explored such questions as when does similarity between groups promote and when does it inhibit positive intergroup attitudes and behaviour? What is the link between having a strong identification with a group and showing ingroup bias in its favour? Do we always see the outgroup as internally more homogeneous than the ingroup (the so-called outgroup homogeneity effect) or do we sometimes do the reverse (see the ingroup as more homogeneous)? Do social identity processes work in the same way in all types of groups or might they be influenced by cultural and group-specific factors? Is the search for distinctiveness (a key idea in social identity theory) the only reason why people identify with groups?

In the late 1980s, another issue began to concern me and this has assumed an increasingly important part of my research programme ever since. This is the question of how to reduce prejudice between groups. Together with Miles Hewstone, I have been looking for ways of developing and improving the contact hypothesis – then, as now, the single most effective means of prejudice reduction that is open to social psychologists. Again influenced by social identity theory, we realised that there will often be good reasons *not* to try and eliminate all vestiges of group difference and salience in intergroup encounters. This is partly because some groups may resist such attempts to de-emphasise their cultural identities, but also because it can make it more difficult for the positive attitude change engendered by contact to generalise beyond the few outgroup individuals whom one knows. Maintaining some group salience in intergroup contact situations permits a link to be made between those individuals and the outgroup as a whole. A further goal of this work has been to understand better *why* contact works, to identify the mediating processes. We have shown in a number of studies that such variables as intergroup anxiety, empathy and trust are all influenced by intergroup contact and, in turn, these affect prejudice.

This interest in the conditions under which maintaining group diversity can be beneficial for intergroup relations instigated a further line of research that I am now actively pursuing. This is known as acculturation, or, how different cultural groups that encounter each other in society, perhaps as a consequence of migration of one of them, mutually interact with and accommodate to each other. An influential theory by Berry suggests that an acculturation strategy of 'integration', in which aspects of *both* group cultures are simultaneously maintained, has the most favourable psychosocial consequences. We are exploring the validity of this hypothesis in a number of different settings (for example, immigration contexts, indigenous and non-indigenous groups, young ethnic minority and majority children) and are investigating its implications for intergroup relations also (it turns out that integration promotes more favourable intergroup relations, as well as better individual mental health outcomes). What we are trying to do here is understand the *dynamics* of acculturation, both over time and between groups.

I have also become increasingly interested in intergroup emotions. The affective side of intergroup relationships was always rather underdeveloped in social identity theory. In the past decade or two, researchers have come to realise that this is a critical weakness because much of how and why people relate to each other as group members is governed by the emotions that they feel on behalf of their group. I am particularly interested in the so-called *self-conscious emotions* of

Box 9.14 continued

collective guilt and shame. These are the emotions that may be felt when one realises that other members of one's group may have done something heinous or immoral to another group (for example, confiscating their lands, destroying their culture or even committing some genocidal act). What happens if one feels guilty or ashamed of one's own group because of this? We have been investigating this question in such diverse contexts as Chile (and the near destruction of the main indigenous culture there) and Bosnia Herzegovina (in the aftermath of the bloody war there, 1992–1995). A related question is what are the factors that can lead 'victim' groups to begin to forgive the perpetrators of such deeds and to engage in the process of intergroup reconciliation.

How does your approach compare and contrast with others'?

I suppose there are three things that have always characterised my work. The first is a theoretical eclecticism. As I noted above, I was trained very much within the social identity theory tradition and that influence has certainly persisted. One thing that always greatly impressed me about Tajfel, however, was his intellectual curiosity. Although he could be pretty intolerant of some kinds of social psychology, he was never one to restrict his thinking to one particular framework or approach. I think that some of that theoretical 'catholicism' (in its non-religious sense!) may have rubbed off on me. I don't much care what a theory is or where it comes from, so long as it proves useful in making sense of important social phenomena. A second feature of my work is its methodological diversity. I like to do laboratory experiments, sometimes of the most artificial kind; I also do a lot of field research, exploring people's intergroup attitudes and emotions in naturalistic settings where a multiplicity of powerful processes may be in play simultaneously; I mainly prefer to use quantitative techniques whenever I can, but I am not opposed to qualitative methods on any grounds of principle and have even published a couple of qualitative pieces. Again, whatever works! I remember Tajfel once commenting that an obsession with methodological correctness and purity is like endlessly packing your bags for a journey you'll never make. I couldn't agree more. Finally, I have always wanted my research to be fruitfully applied in some socially progressive way, although I would be the first to admit that that has mostly remained an unfulfilled aspiration. I am not someone given to dwelling on the past, regretting what I might have done differently, but I do sometimes wish that I had devoted more of my time and energy to the social *applications* of my work.

Whether this approach is especially different from or better/worse than those taken by others I am not sure; probably others are in a better position than me to judge.

What things helped or hindered your research?

The main hindrances have been the usual ones: a shortage of financial and human resources to support my research and also a shortage of time to disseminate it as widely as I might have wished. The main assistance has been a continuous stream of fantastic colleagues and research students whom I have worked with. It is a bit of a truism to say that science is a collective enterprise, but, truism or not, it has certainly been my very great good fortune to have worked with so many clever and industrious people who have, in their different ways, cajoled or inspired me to investigate the things that I have.

What points of interest would you like to explore in the future? What further questions would you like to explore in the future?

More of the above! There is still so much we don't really understand about how groups relate to one another and how we can make those relationships peaceful or tolerant instead of murderous or distrustful.

Finally, considering research in this area, what do you recommend to people wanting to start to research this topic?

Follow your nose! Find a problem that bugs you and use whatever theoretical and methodological tools you want to find a solution.

interactional dimensions of collective behaviour' and be able to account for why (as in the miners' strike) violence is inconsistently present. As noted in Chapter 2, Drury and Reicher's (2000) work on the elaborated social identity theory – in which the protesters' social identity was depicted as both shaping and being shaped by the unfolding events of a protest – could be seen as a development in this respect.

Furthermore, social identity theory research has paid particular attention to the identity basis for intergroup behaviour and often sought to distinguish this from the groups' material interests. This distinction might not be quite so clear-cut, however. The St Paul's riot – which was triggered by the closure of a community café – arguably involved a threat to people's material interests as well as the identity of the St Paul's community. Using semantic differentials to measure identity versus material concerns may do little to resolve the issue. Thus, Tausch, Tam, Hewstone, Kenworthy and Cairns (2007, p. 547) attempted to measure realistic (material) threat using items such as, 'The other community has more political power in Northern Ireland than they should' and, to measure symbolic (identity) threat, they used, 'The two communities in Northern Ireland have very different values'. It is likely that responses to items attempting to distinguish material and identity issues will be responded to on the basis of the rhetorical stance of the participant – for example, an overt complaint about the other group might involve claims about their preferential treatment, while 'subtle' prejudice may involve reference to the ways in which the other group is 'different'. What is less clear is that participants themselves have a clear and consistent cognitive position that distinguishes these identity and material issues.

Finally, Billig (1995, p. 67) raises issues regarding the way in which social identity researchers explicitly or implicitly adhere to some sense of equivalence across vastly different groups – seeking the 'psychological similarities behind the different forms of group identity'. Yet, as noted below, this move towards a generic understanding of groups and group processes, while enabling a wide-reaching model to be created, is at the expense of particular details. In the case of national identities, the very act of claiming membership of a particular group can be seen as a discursive act that has implications reaching far beyond the individual's sense of identity. As Billig notes, the grammatically similar identity statements 'I am a sociologist' (uttered to anthropologists) and Kennedy's 'Ich bin ein Berliner' are very different discursive actions despite them both *appearing* to reflect identification with a social group.

Critical recap

Social identity theory and intergroup behaviour

1 It is possible to question the extent to which evidence supports the idea that social identity is related to serious intergroup conflict rather than simply ingroup bias.

2 Attempts to draw on social identity theory to make sense of real-world intergroup conflict can also be questioned concerning how representative they are and the extent to which they account for the fluidity of behaviour in intergroup encounters.

3 For social identity theory, there is an important distinction between identity and material issues, yet it may be more less clear-cut than has been envisaged.

4 Social identity theory has paid attention to psychological commonalities at the expense of examining what specific instances of identity construction might accomplish.

Reflective questions

1 *What groups do you identify with as a member? How do you think being a member of a group shapes your behaviour?*

2 *What are the empirical limitations of the social identity research considered above?*

9.8 Realistic conflict theory

For a moment, just stop and consider a case of serious aggression and intergroup conflict that you have perhaps heard about on the news (see also Box 9.15). It is quite likely that it involves – among other things – fighting for scarce resources (such as power or land). The approaches that we have considered so far certainly would not deny that competition for scarce resources can play a part in aggression and intergroup conflict, but none of them emphasise this factor as much as realistic conflict theory does.

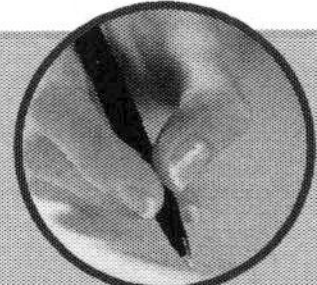

Box 9.15 TRY IT OUT
Intergroup conflict

Write down the first three cases of intergroup conflict that come to mind.

What sorts of examples do you have – are they groups at an international or more local level, do they reflect sporting affiliations, are religious or political identities relevant?

Which of the theories covered in this chapter best accounts for the intergroup conflicts you have identified? Does one theory work best for all of these examples or do different theories suit different cases of intergroup conflict?

As we shall see, realistic conflict theory shares with social identity theory an interest in how intergroup conflict can be linked to group members' sense of belonging to different groups. Crucially for realistic conflict theory, however, it emphasises the nature of the conditions of contact between those groups – are they competing for scarce resources or cooperating to achieve a shared goal? It is the answer to this question that, for this conflict theory, shapes the nature of intergroup relationships.

Muzafer Sherif's summer camp studies

While social identity theory is perhaps currently the most prominent approach to understanding intergroup behaviour within social psychology, it is certainly not the only one.

One of the earliest approaches to understanding intergroup conflict was developed by Muzafer Sherif in a series of studies at an American summer camp for boys. Sherif's approach shares with social identity theory something of the emphasis on individuals' sense of identity with a group as shaping their behaviour. Sherif, however, seeks to emphasise not only the importance of the sense of being in a distinct group but also the actual (or real) *conditions of contact between the groups*. That is, for Sherif, a vital factor when determing whether or not two (or more) groups are aggressive to each other is if the conditions under which the groups operate and meet one another promote cooperation or conflict between them.

Sherif's name, while not confined to intergroup research (see, for example, Chapter 10 for details of his work on the autokinetic effect), is largely associated with a series of three extremely significant field experiments. Each of the experiments took the form of a 2- to 3-week long summer camp for 11- and 12-year-old boys in rural America. The first of these – based in northern Connecticut in 1949 – was designed to investigate intergroup conflict. The second experiment was intended to assess both intergroup conflict and conflict reduction, but 'had to be terminated after the rise of intergroup hostility,' (Sherif 1967, p. 72). The third experiment – based at Robber's Cave, Oklahoma and which also intended to investigate both intergroup conflict and conflict reduction – was able to run to completion.

The boys were deliberately selected so that they did not know each other prior to the study and were rated as healthy and well-adjusted. Furthermore, some effort was made to ensure that they shared a relatively similar background – all boys being described as coming from 'stable, white Protestant families from the middle socioeconomic level' (1967, p. 73). These inclusion criteria may well seem problematic and certainly raise ethical issues, but, for Sherif, they were necessary for him to be sure that it was the manipulations that he introduced *in the experiment* that created the hostility and subsequent conflict resolution, rather than some characteristics of the participants or their prior history. Sherif was interested in how the **conditions of contact** between the groups could influence both within-group (intragroup) and between-group (intergroup) behaviour.

Sherif 's studies involved different stages, in which the conditions of contact were varied – the interest being in how changing these conditions might change the behaviour within and between the groups. Sherif's first study, for example, began with stage 1 – lasting 3 days – in which the 24 boys were housed in a single large bunkhouse and free to engage with whomever they wished throughout the day. Stage 2 – the stage of 'experimental ingroup formation' – involved assigning the boys to one of two groups, with a deliberate attempt to separate any newly formed friends as much as possible. This resulted in two groups, the individual members of which had approximately two-thirds of their friends in the other group. The two groups had separate bunkhouses, formed their own names – 'the Bulldogs' and 'the Red Devils' – and ate and played separately throughout the day. Sherif notes that, during this phase, leaders emerged in the groups and the group to which individuals belonged (the ingroup) became a reference group – that is, the emerging norms of each group started to shape the behaviour of individual members. Although at this stage there was little overt conflict between the two groups, group members identified with their group and showed loyalty to it – most now identifying around 90 per cent of their friends as being within their own group. Those perceived as being too friendly to outgroup members were called 'traitors' and, in some cases, threatened unless they saw less of them.

After five days of Stage 2, Sherif changed the conditions again, with the commencement of Stage 3 – 'intergroup relations'. This involved a series of competitive games between the two groups, with members of the winning group each set to receive a four-bladed penknife. It was during this stage that intergroup conflict was observed. During this period of approximately five days, each group received points for winning at tug of war, softball, soccer,

Conditions of contact In the above literature, this refers to the context (cooperative *or* competitive) in which two or more groups meet.

football and other activities – the group accumulating the greatest number of points being the overall winning group. Sherif had intended to use several planned frustrations, in which one group would suffer apparently because of the actions of the other group – for example, one group arriving to find that the members of the other group appeared to have interfered with their food, when actually the experimental team had done so. In the event, however, Sherif only used *one* such planned frustration once – the food interference one. It was effective in itself and a chain of frustrating circumstances arose from it.

The conflict between the groups during this 'intergroup relations' phase was evident everywhere. Whereas initially a sense of cordial 'sportsmanship' prevailed, soon the positive chants of 'Who do we appreciate?' turned to the somewhat less positive 'Who do we appreci-*hate?*'. Each group produced derogatory pictures of the other, raided the other group's dormitory and engaged in direct violence. In one instance, what began as a food fight escalated to the point where saucers and table knives were thrown at each other. Sherif reports that the experimenters intervened and stopped the fight, but only 'with considerable effort' (Sherif, 1967, p. 280). The violence escalated to such an extent that Sherif (1967, pp. 280, 281) reports, it was 'quickly decided' to stop the intensive intergroup conflict 'by any means necessary'. Despite various appeals from the experimenters for the fighting to stop, however, further skirmishes between the two groups continued, with groups going to considerable lengths – such as waking at 2 a.m. and 6 a.m. – to launch an attack on the other group. Sherif used a series of interventions that mixed groups up at mealtimes, encouraged individual rather than intergroup competitions and involved a softball competition between boys from both groups against a group coming from outside the camp in order to reduce intergroup conflict. Eventually, these led to a reduction in conflict between the Bulldogs and Red Devils, although, as Sherif notes, the most effective of these – the softball competition with 'outsiders' – actually resulted in a transfer of hostilities towards this new enemy.

What Sherif's initial experiment clearly demonstrated was the ease with which genuine, violent conflict could be generated, even between those who had formed friendships when the conditions of their contact were arranged to encourage this. Specifically, if the conditions of contact involve **mutually incompatible goals** – that is, the success of one group in achieving their goals results in the inevitable failure of the other group – then there will be heightened solidarity within each group and hostility between the groups. The issue that Sherif's initial experiment raised for subsequent research was what conditions of contact between hostile groups might most effectively reduce intergroup conflict. Sherif's third experiment, conducted at Robbers Cave, Oklahoma, examined precisely this issue – investigating the role of **superordinate goals** in reducing intergroup conflict. Sherif's (1967, p. 89, italics from original) concept was, '*if conflict develops from mutually incompatible goals,* ***common goals*** should promote co-operation.'

The early phases of Sherif's third experiment shared many features of his initial experiment, described above. Most crucially – by means of a series of intergroup competitions for the mutually incompatible goal of a penknife for members of the victorious group – Sherif created conditions that promoted strong intergroup hostility between the two groups (the 'Rattlers' and the 'Eagles'). Once again, there were food fights, raids on each other's dormitories and situations where the experimenters needed to step in, such as when the Eagles waited for the Rattlers with socks filled with stones. In this third experiment, however, there was another phase – superordinate goals. These goals were such that their achievement would benefit *all* members of *both* groups, - but both groups would need to cooperate in order to be successful.

Sherif created what he refers to as a series of 'urgent and natural' situations that would create the conditions for superordinate goals. One of these involved the water supply breaking down – both groups were summoned and informed of the problem and both together located the source of the problem in the water supply pipe. Sherif (1967, p. 89) notes that, 'despite the good spirits aroused, the groups fell back on their old recriminations once the immediate crisis was over'.

This was followed by another intervention in which the groups were informed that the camp could not pay for their movie choice – both groups chose a film by common vote and shared the necessary contribution to its costs before watching it together.

A third situation was created by the (experimenter-assisted) 'breakdown' of a truck that was to collect food for the boys. In a poetic twist, the boys used the very rope they has previously used for an antagonistic tug of war

Mutually incompatible goals A context in which groups have antagonistic goals and the success of one group necessitates failure or loss for the other.

Common goals, superordinate goals A context in which the groups share the same goal and success in achieving it benefits all.

Source: Wesleyan University Press

Participants in one of Sherif's summer camp studies

competition – each pulling against the other group – to 'pull together' in order to start the truck.

Sherif notes that, while there was not an immediate effect of the interventions, gradually – across a series of these contact situations involving superordinate goals – intergroup hostility was reduced. Sherif (1967, p. 90) notes, 'The boys stopped shoving each other in the meal line. They no longer called each other names and began to sit together at the table. New friendships developed, cutting across group lines.'

In another highly symbolic situation, the groups were given the choice of returning home in either separate buses or one, shared bus and – with the exception of 'a few *die-hards*' – chose to return together. Perhaps more surprisingly, on the way home, one group – which had won five dollars – spent this money on refreshments for members of *both* groups. While, there remained some element of negativity towards the outgroup – particularly from the group that was victorious at the intergroup stage – there was a marked increase in friendships and positive ratings of others that cut across the previously impermeable group lines.

Critical review of realistic conflict theory

Sherif's approach, again, provides a group perspective on conflict and aggression. Sherif's (1966, p. 15) stance was very much opposed to the more individualistic ones of other theories, such as the frustration–aggression hypothesis: 'We cannot legitimately explain behaviour in groups by extrapolating from information about each individual's motivational urges and frustrations.' For Sherif, instead, the group is a particularly relevant unit for the analysis of conflict and aggression because the impacts of intergroup conflicts are so vast. Indeed, Sherif (1966, p. 1) describes intergroup relations as 'the most overriding, the most anxiety-ridden, and therefore the most challenging of human problems in the modern world'. For Sherif (1967), intergroup conflict should not be understood in terms of individual deficiencies or characteristics but, rather, in terms of the conditions of contact between the groups. He argues that the sufficient condition for intergroup conflict is that of *mutually incompatible goals* – that is, a situation in which the groups each seek to attain goals that only one group can attain. By contrast, conditions of contact that involve *superordinate goals* – where both groups seek and can attain the same goals and need to cooperate in order to do so – can, over time, be effective in reducing intergroup conflict.

In referring to intergroup relations, Sherif's (1966, p. 1) scope could scarely be broader:

> Intergroup relations include the vexing problems of minority peoples in various nations who are struggling to achieve equal rights against prevailing arrangements based on supremacy premises. They encompass labor–management friction, and the search for more lasting solutions to prevent their recurrence. They encompass alignments and non-alignments between political parties, factions and ideological camps. Towering above all intergroup problems are those raised by the alignments, non-alignments, and counter-alignments among various nations.

Sherif's approach thus sought to provide a generic account for intergroup relations – one that would be relevant for all intergroup behaviour, however localised or vast the groups involved may be.

Brown (2000a) raises questions regarding both planks of Sherif's theory – that competition between groups is a *necessary* condition for intergroup conflict and cooperation between groups is a *sufficient* condition for the reduction of intergroup conflict. Brown refers to Sherif's own research as providing evidence that the boys wanted to 'best' the other group – even before any competition for scarce resources was introduced. Zagefka, Brown, Broquard and Leventoglu's (2007) surveys suggested that material factors – in this case, perceived economic competition – were less important as a predictor of the participants' preferences for integration with different ethnic groups than participants' desire for cultural maintenance (valuing their distinct identity). With regard to cooperation, Brown (2000a) argues that ingroup bias does not immediately disappear with cooperation. Furthermore, Worchel, Andreoli and Folger (1977) found that where there had been prior competition, *unsuccessful* cooperation resulted in *decreased* liking for the outgroup.

As noted above, Sherif – perhaps more than most other researchers considered in this chapter – seeks the broadest definition of groups. For Billig (1995), though, there is something problematic with such a generic approach. Treating all groups as equivalent and seeking to build a theory that accounts for all group behaviour runs the risk of taking attention away from the sense making particulars of a given group's context. Thus, for the sake of a generic process model in which certain broadly defined variables are understood to have a causal relationship with the measured factor (for our current concerns, aggression and conflict), much of the particular contextual and historical detail – which can make the behaviour understandable and, perhaps, meaningful – is removed.

Sherif's emphasis – as Brown (2000a) notes – is on the *actual* material conflicts of interest rather than *perceived* conflicts of interest. It could be that *perceptions* of antagonistic or mutual interests are even more important determiners of intergroup relations. Similarly, some conflicts that, at first, seem to be well accounted for by realistic conflict theory can be made sense of by taking into account how things are constructed rather than how they 'really are'. Conflicts in the Middle East, for example, can be read in terms of competition for scarce land resources, but ideologies held by all sides to the conflict could be seen as giving a sense of entitlement and legitimacy to the various territory claims. Thus, rather than accurately perceiving real material conflicts for scarce resources and acting in our rational best interest, it may be that our behaviour is shaped by ideologies that give us a sense of entitlement regarding scarce resources and legitimise our actions towards those who come to be defined as 'others'.

Critical recap

Realistic conflict theory

1 It is possible to question that intergroup competition is necessary for intergroup conflict to occur.

2 Similarly, the idea that cooperation between (previously competitive) groups will remove intergroup conflict has not been consistently supported.

3 Material competition in some research appears to be less pre-eminent in determining intergroup relations than realistic conflict theory would suggest.

4 The perception of groups' interests – and the extent to which they are in conflict – may be more important than the 'reality'.

5 Ideologies may shape our sense of entitlement to material resources, our definitions and may legitimise the aggressive treatment of 'outgroups'.

6 Groups have been defined in the broadest possible terms. Can these vastly different 'groups' be understood as meaningfully related and do we lose meaning when we move to generic models?

Reflective questions

1. *If you had to design an intervention to reduce conflict between two groups, in what ways could research into realistic conflict theory help?*

2. *In what ways could Sherif's focus on actual material conflicts of interest be critiqued?*

9.9 Aggression and intergroup conflict – a critical appraisal

Across the different theories covered in this chapter, there are a number of recurrent issues concerning how aggression and groups have been understood in theory and research concerned with aggression and intergroup conflict. Some of these issues are briefly outlined here.

Are groups a negative influence on social behaviour?

In this chapter, groups have been explored within the context of conflict and aggression, but is this part of a wider issue in social psychology, from Le Bon onwards, of perpetuating a skewed understanding of groups that emphasises irrationality and bias at the expense of other ways of understanding groups? Spears (2010) argues that, rather than there being overwhelming evidence for universal intergroup bias, its occurrence might be considered as 'constrained' and 'proportionate' and, if considered at the group level, may even appear to be 'functional and rational'. Within the laboratory context, classic ingroup bias in minimal group experiments (see Chapter 2) can be understood as a means by which participants differentiate their (meaningless) group from the other and, according to Spears (2010), this disappears when the groups are made meaningful. In real-world situations, Spears notes that there is a remarkable rationality and also a lack of conflict, even in situations where status, power or competition might predict it. Scheepers, Spears, Doosje and Manstead (2003, p. 8) cite the example of Ajax football supporters who reported that, in a finely balanced game, they would 'chose chants that would inspire their own team rather than ones that would insult and provoke the opposition, inspiring them to fight harder'. Furthermore, Smith and Spears (1996) reported that, in some cases, becoming aware of and acting consistently with one's group identity led to individualistic self-interest and bias being transcended. For Spears (2010, p. 16), then, the social psychology of 'group bias' and 'intergroup conflict' provides a narrow and one-sided conception of groups: 'While there is no denying that groups can be agents (as well as targets) of oppression and discrimination, they can also be vehicles of social change and liberation.'

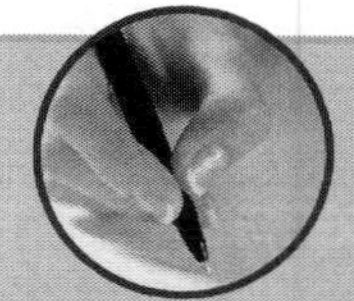

Box 9.16 TRY IT OUT Implicit definitions of aggression

Try using an online news service, such as Reuters (www.reuters.com), to search for stories about aggression.

What sorts of actions are defined as aggression? Are the sorts of instances of aggression you find in these stories similar to those that social psychology seeks to explain or do they differ in some way?

Defining aggression

Earlier, some discussion was had regarding the different ways in which aggression has been operationally defined in experiments. It is worth considering more generally, however, the way in which social psychology understands aggression.

Lubek (1995) referred to the idea that social psychology tends to define aggression as 'two men fighting' – it is as if this image is just the sort of aggressive act that all of the theories considered above are principally concerned with. It is considered 'problematic', 'illegitimate' aggressive behaviour and social psychology seeks to understand and, hopefully, ameliorate it – but we do not have to look at the news for long to find all sorts of *other* aggressive behaviours. Is someone killing another in warfare exhibiting aggression or does it depend on whether the war is 'just', what side they are on or if military protocols were adhered to? If we exclude warfare, should we exclude all forms of institutionally sanctioned aggression, such as that enacted by executioners, hit squads or interrogators?

One difficulty with restricting our definition of aggression to just those seemingly more individual acts of two men fighting is that we ignore the vast majority of the most serious aggressive acts throughout human history. A brief and unpalatable reflection on genocides in the last 80 years – the Holocaust, the genocides of Bosnia, Rwanda – reveals that, whether enacted by soldiers or civilians, all had a strong, institutionally sanctioned dimension; all were supported by at least some of those in power. If our theories do not seriously encompass these numerous acts of extreme aggression, then they are arguably skewed towards trying to explain just *facets* of aggression rather than the *totality* of human aggression (see also Box 9.16).

Process versus content

While only one approach considered in this chapter is explicitly called a general model – the General Model of Aggression – most of the approaches to aggression and intergroup conflict have attempted to account for aggression and intergroup content in terms of models of psychological processes that are general in nature. Thus, the different theories of aggression reviewed (the evolutionary approach, frustration–aggression hypothesis, situational cue theory, excitation transfer, general aggression model and deindividuation theory) and the intergroup approaches (social identity theory and realistic conflict theory) all seek to go beyond the surface particulars to the *underlying* psychological processes. In many cases, this quest for generic psychological process has meant that little attention has been paid to the specifics of content. Thus, for research concerned with media effects, attention has tended to be given to whether or not a film includes an instance of violence rather than on the specific way in which violence is legitimated or made sense of within the film. Social identity theory has been concerned with how identification with a group can shape the behaviour of the individual rather than the ways in which ingroups and outgroups are constructed and how these constructions might be used to legitimate violence against the outgroup.

While discursive and critical perspectives have been especially keen to develop attention to content – focusing on, for example, discursive constructions that might support aggression and intergroup conflict – it would be wrong to suggest that these concerns are limited to these approaches. In their research examining anti-immigration prejudice, Pehrson, Brown and Zagefka (2009, p. 74) – while supporting a broadly social identity theory approach – raise the issue that content rather than process alone is important:

> In the case of nationality, identity content is crucial because it determines how nationalist projects of autonomy, unity and identity ... are either realized or hindered by a given outgroup. This adds further weight to the argument that social identity *processes* should not be treated as independent from *content*, as they often are.

Similarly, Haslam (2006), Haslam and Bain (2007), Haslam, Loughnan, Reynolds and Wilson (2007) and Haslam and Reicher (2007) emphasise content in their argument for a social cognitive understanding of the dehumanisation of outgroups. For Haslam (Haslam, 2006,

Haslam & Bain, 2007), it is important to specify the recurrent content of manifestations of dehumanisation – the different ways in which outgroups are denied 'uniquely human attributes' in portrayals that depict them as *animalistic* or *mechanistic*. Both Pehrson et al. (2009) and Haslam (Haslam, 2006, Haslam & Bain, 2007) demonstrate that researchers within a broadly social identity theory framework have increasingly emphasised content rather than process alone in understanding intergroup conflict and, particularly, outgroup denigration. The issue of content rather than simply process is absolutely central to the ideological approaches considered below.

Ideologies that justify aggression

Some social constructionist work has been particularly interested in shared constructions in the form of ideologies. One relevant aspect of ideologies for our current concern is the way in which ideologies about the victim group or the perpetrators may denigrate the target or targets of aggression. In Chapter 7 (ingroup), reference was made to the ways in which Jews in the Holocaust were described by Nazi ideology as a 'virus', while Tutsis were described by 'Hutu Power' as 'cockroaches'. These derogatory constructions of the targets of aggression could be understood as being part of a wider framework of understanding – or ideology – that provided some form of permission or justification for acts of violence against them.

Finlay (2007) notes that extremist rhetoric can be found to construct identities for the ingroup and outgroup – defining who are the ingroup and outgroup, constructing the 'threat' that the outgroup purportedly poses and how the outgroup is to be perceived and treated. It is in such rhetoric that ideologies dehumanising the outgroup and denigrating those who support them are found. These ideologies, in turn, provide the legitimisation for terrible acts of violence against the denigrated groups. Thus, when Goebbels argued that 'This is a racial war. The Jews started it and they direct it. Their goal is to destroy and exterminate our people' (cited in Finlay, 2007, p. 327), he was constructing an ideology in which the Jews were the greatest threat to the German people and, in turn, sought to legitimise the most terrible racial violence against them.

These instances of manifestations of violence – though horrific in their scale and nature – may seem quite distinct from seemingly more sporadic acts of aggression that are not targeted at a culturally denigrated group of people. Even with these more localised acts of aggression, however, ideologies may be at work in the form of shared constructions of what it is to be male. Courtenay (2000, p. 1391) reports on research in which males who had been involved in repeated violence talked about it as an important aspect of their masculinity:

> I have been shot and stabbed. Each time I wore bandages like a badge of honor ... Each situation made me feel a little more tougher than the next guy ... Being that I had survived, these things made me feel bigger because I could imagine that the average person couldn't go through a shoot out or a knife fight, survive and get right back into the action like it was nothing.

For Courtenay (2000, p. 1391) this construction of masculinity as involving being aggressive and prepared to enter and stay in aggressive confrontations is particularly prominent for men who might otherwise be understood as lacking power or status:

> Physical dominance and violence are easily accessible resources for structuring, negotiating and sustaining masculinities, particularly among men who because of their social positioning lack less dangerous means.

These widely held versions of masculinity are often referred to as ***hegemonic masculinity*** – a phrase that runs the risk, as Burkitt (2008 p. 134) notes, of understating not only the variation of currently 'honoured' forms of masculinity but also the way in which these privileged versions of being male 'draw from and mix with more peripheral types of masculinity'.

Summary

- Aggression and intergroup conflict covers a vast area of social psychological research. This chapter considered several approaches to understanding aggression (evolutionary, frustration–aggression hypothesis, situational cue, excitation transfer, general aggression model and deindividuation) and two prominent approaches to understanding intergroup conflict (social identity theory and realistic conflict theory).
- The evolutionary approach considered the way in which we may have an instinct to aggress, which developed from the adaptive benefit of aggression, particularly for increasing the likelihood of passing on our genes.
- The frustration–aggression hypothesis suggested that aggression was linked to our desires and/or needs being blocked or frustrated. Early statements of this approach suggested that frustration was a necessary and sufficient cause for aggression – later versions suggested that, while it was necessary, it was not sufficient. Thus, while frustration was always a causal factor for instances of aggression, the presence of frustration alone would not be sufficient to *always* result in aggression.

- Situational cue theory argued that aversive stimuli might provide the impetus to aggress, while certain cues associated with aggression could be the trigger that results in aggression being enacted in specific situations.
- The excitation transfer theory accounted for aggression by arguing that it is a consequence of a physiological state of arousal, which is attributed to a person, who then becomes the target of the aroused person's aggression. The theory is particularly concerned with the misattribution of such arousal – that is, cases where there is a residual state of arousal from a prior experience that is then misattributed to another person, who then becomes the target of an act of aggression.
- The general aggression model sought to incorporate the above approaches – and others – into a model that could explain all instances of aggression. It has been particularly concerned with the way in which aggression can involve more than a single, isolated act – any one act of aggression may create new conditions that can influence immediate subsequent actions. Longer term, the general aggression model suggests that repeated experiences of aggressive situations and/or acting aggressively can create a repertoire of behaviours that inform subsequent aggressive (or non-aggressive) responses.
- Deindividuation theory introduced the idea that group presence and/or the anonymity that co-present others create could lead to impulsive, disinhibited and aggressive behaviour. A reworked version of deindividuation theory (social identity deindividuation effects, or, SIDE) was concerned with the way in which conditions such as being in a group and anonymity could result in the increased salience of a person's group identity and that identity might then shape behaviour, which would only include acts of aggression if this was consistent with the group identity.
- Social identity theory suggested that our identity as members of a group could shape our behaviour towards both ingroup and outgroup members. From this perspective, aggression towards outgroup members can potentially arise because group members want to perceive their own group as positively differentiated from other groups. Furthermore, social identity theory suggests that group identity itself may encourage some negative behaviour towards other groups.
- Realistic conflict theory argues that intergroup conflict arises where there is a material conflict of interest between groups – such as when they are competing for scarce resources. Sherif's studies generated some aggression between rival groups during a competition phase, but later interventions requiring cooperation for the mutual benefit of both groups reduced aggression and increased liking between groups.
- Research into aggression and intergroup conflict can be critiqued in a number of ways. First, much of the research has implicitly or explicitly proffered a rather negative view of groups, in which they are typically associated with aggression rather than more positive, prosocial behaviour. Second, the way in which aggression has been conceptualised can be criticised – attention has tended to focus on aggression as largely unstructured, relatively spontaneous individual behaviour caused by the individual's cognitions. This definition leaves some of the most horrific examples of mass aggression – such as genocide – out of the frame. Finally, the research considered in this chapter has tended to seek to identify causal processes at the expense of considering content. Thus, while several models have attempted to map how cognitions may lead to aggressive behaviour, fewer have been concerned with how constructions of others – for example, in ideologies about members of certain groups – may support aggressive behaviour towards them.

Review questions

1. *In what ways might aggression be linked to issues such as survival and passing on of genes?*
2. *What is the evidence for an evolutionary perspective on human aggression?*
3. *What are the theoretical limitations of the frustration–aggression hypothesis?*
4. *What are the problems – if any – with how aggression has been measured in experimental research?*
5. *To what extent do factors in the environment shape aggressive behaviour?*
6. *What are the empirical limitations of research into the misattribution of arousal?*
7. *What is meant by the idea that deindividuation could be thought of as a change rather than a loss of identity?*
8. *What evidence (empirical and anecdotal) supports the idea that our group identities are related to aggressive behaviour or conflict?*
9. *Why might a focus on realistic conditions of contact between groups miss important aspects that could shape relationships between the groups?*
10. *What are the limitations of research into aggression and intergroup conflict and how should future work proceed?*

Recommended reading

Anderson, C. A., & Bushman, B. J. (2002). Human aggression. *Annual Review of Psychology*, *53*, 27–51. An important outline of the general aggression model.

Berkowitz, L. (1990). On the formation and regulation of anger and aggression: A cognitive-neoassociationistic analysis. *American Psychologist*, *45*(4), 494–503. Len Berkowitz's outline of his developing perspective on aggression.

Billig, M. (1995). *Banal nationalism*. London: Sage. Billig's social constructionist critique of much of our understanding of groups and national identity.

Brown, R. J. (2000a). *Group processes* (2nd ed.). Oxford: Blackwell. Rupert Brown's clear and authoritative overview of inter- and intragroup research, with a particular focus on social identity and self-categorisation theory.

Livingstone, A. G., & Haslam, S. A. (2008). The importance of social identity content in a setting of chronic social conflict: Understanding intergroup relations in Northern Ireland. *British Journal of Social Psychology*, *47*, 1–21. A social identity study within the context of a situation of chronic real-world conflict.

Postmes, T., and Spears, R. (1998). Deindividuation and anti-normative behavior: A meta-analysis. *Psychological Bulletin*, *123*, 238–259. A meta-analysis of deindividuation research and review of some of the different ways that deindividuation theory has been understood.

Sherif, M. (1967). *Group conflict and co-operation*. London: Routledge & Kegan Paul. Sherif's own account of his influential theory, written with an appealing sense of honesty and directness.

Useful weblinks

http://homepage.psy.utexas.edu/homepage/Group/BussLAB/publications.htm David Buss' website with resources and publications relating to evolutionary psychology.

http://psychclassics.yorku.ca/FrustAgg/ A classic paper based on a symposium on the frustration–aggression hypothesis.

www.psychology.iastate.edu/faculty/caa/recpub.html Craig Anderson' publications. This site features many downloadable papers relating to the general aggression model.

www.zimbardo.com/zimbardo.html Philip Zimbardo's website – includes links to publications addressing aggression and deindividuation.

http://portal.st-andrews.ac.uk/research-expertise/researcher/sdr/publications A great resource for publications (many downloadable) by Steve Reicher.

www.sussex.ac.uk/psychology/people/peoplelists/person/92858/ A great resource for publications by John Drury, with a particular emphasis on crowd psychology.

www.sussex.ac.uk/migration/profile95042.html Recent publications (some downloadable) by Rupert Brown.

http://psychclassics.yorku.ca/Sherif/ One of Sherif's publications on his classic series of summer camp experiments is available here.

www.psychology.iastate.edu/faculty/caa/ An impressively comprehensive resource for Craig Anderson's research, which develops the general aggression model.

www.comm.ohio-state.edu/people/faculty/userprofile/67.html Brad Bushman's research, which develops the general aggression model – particularly strong in features and podcasts relating to popular coverage of Bushman's work.

10

Social influence and intragroup processes

Learning outcomes

By the end of this chapter you should be able to:

- understand what is meant by majority influence
- appreciate the contribution that experiments by Asch and others have made regarding how majorities can exercise social influence within a group
- understand what is meant by minority influence
- appreciate the contribution that experiments by Moscovici and others have made to the issue of minority influence within groups
- critically evaluate the developments relating to ideas of majority and minority influence
- explain the contribution of experiments by Milgram and others relating to the influence of authority on individuals and groups
- criticially evaluate developments relating to ideas of authority influence
- understand the contribution of experiments by Zimbardo and others relating to the influence of situational factors on behaviour
- analyse a selection of the important criticisms and developments relating to Zimbardo's ideas regarding situational influences on behaviour
- reflect on and analyse some of the ways in which the construction of reality may relate to issues of power and influence.

On 1 April 2009, in the midst of a large demonstration in London regarding the G20 summit, a newspaper seller, Ian Tomlinson, was struck and pushed to the ground by a member of the Metropolitan Police's Territorial Support Group. After struggling to his feet and stumbling off, he subsequently collapsed and died. This tragic event was all the more shocking as a mobile phone video emerged that showed Tomlinson was struck from behind as he walked along with his hands in his pockets.

How can we understand the behaviour of the police officer concerned? Should we think in terms of the possible influence of fellow officers or the briefing given by senior officers before the protests? Were features of the situation, such as the role of the Territorial Support Group or the identity of that group relevant? Was it relevant that the officer concerned was dressed in a way that meant they were not easily identifiable?

Source: Guardian News and Media Ltd

Ian Tomlinson is pushed to the ground by a member of the Metropolitan Police's Territorial Support Group. Was the officer concerned aggressive because of his role, briefing from authority figures or his anonymity in full riot gear uniform? Does this incident raise questions about our ideologies concerning protest and policing?

Introduction

This chapter investigates some of the different ways in which social psychologists (and others) have tried to understand how our behaviour might be shaped by others and the situation we find ourselves in. It explores research into the ways in which peers and authority figures as well as features of the situation – such as the role we have and whether or not we are anonymous – might lead us to engage in behaviour that we would otherwise never contemplate.

In reviewing some of the key literature in this area, we will come across the most famous (and, for some, notorious) social psychology experiments. The chances are that you have heard of Milgram's obedience experiments and Zimbardo's Stanford prison experiment – perhaps you have also heard of Asch's conformity studies and Tajfel's minimal group experiments – but there are other important approaches to power and influence that you may be less familiar with. If you are studying single honours psychology, you might not have come across the work of Foucault – despite him having provided one of the most profound analyses of power in any discipline. Furthermore, each of the classic experiments referred to above has attracted further studies that critique or develop them in different ways.

This chapter endeavours to review the classic research of the stars from social psychology's 'hall of fame', as well as research from those who are less well known or whose work has been peripheral to social psychology. Covering these different approaches is not meant to confuse you, nor simply give you another list of names and ideas to remember, but, instead, provide some starting points for *your* critical thinking about the area of social influence and groups and the work that has attempted to provide an understanding of it.

Chapter overview

This chapter focuses on four dominant approaches to social influence within social psychology – Asch's conformity, Moscovici's minority influence, Milgram's obedience to authority and Zimbardo's role and deindividuation research. Each of these approaches is linked to research that (perhaps ironically) has had incredible influence within social psychology. This research is reviewed and critiqued in some detail before considering the very different understandings that the work of both Foucault and Butler raises for our thinking about this topic.

First, Asch's conformity experiments are considered. Attention is paid to the idea that these demonstrate conformity – with consideration given to the different types of conformity that have been identified. Here, the work of Deutsch and Gerard (1955), which distinguishes between informational influence and normative influence, is addressed – along with relevant empirical examples. Consideration is also given to alternative understandings of Asch's experiments – including some touched on by

Asch himself – that suggest, most of the time, participants showed notable resistance to conformity pressures when they were directly contradicted by perceptual information. Limitations of the empirical research typically used in classic conformity research is addressed – including the idea that these classic experiments typically only ever allow for the possibility of majority influence (as the majority in these experiments are confederates exerting influence on the real, naïve participants).

Second, Moscovici's work on minority influence is reviewed. One particular focus is on research that suggests minority influence, while having a smaller immediate effect than majority influence, can have a longer-lasting and wider influence (affecting not just the specific focus of the influence but related issues also). Attention will also be given to some of the shortcomings of much of this research – for example, in terms of external validity – which the empirical procedures typically used (for example, confederates in colour perception experiments) have given rise to.

Third, Milgram's obedience to authority research is examined. Careful attention is given to the detail of the experiments and some of the different variations that Milgram devised. Milgram's work to address several popular alternative explanations for his results is considered (for example, concerning gender, nationality, inherent aggression and so on). Critical perspectives on Milgram are reviewed that, in different ways, question Milgram's core idea that the results can be explained in terms of obedience to authority – that participants experience a shift in their sense of agency, feeling responsible *to* the authority rather than responsible *for* their actions. Among the critical issues addressed, attention is given to research by Russell (2011) and Reicher and Haslam (2011), which, in different ways, draws attention to the, often understated, role that the *scientific rationale* for the study ('an experiment about the role of pain in human learning') may have played in enabling participants to show the levels of 'obedience' that they did.

Fourth, attention is given to Zimbardo's Stanford prison experiment. Zimbardo's research is examined in the light of his long-held commitments to both role and deindividuation, in which participants are understood to be acting as they do because they have seen the enactment of specific behaviour (for example, aggression), as defined by their role, and separate from their own individual identity. The situation that developed in the experiment was all the more acute as participants often had a reduced awareness of themselves as individuals. Zimbardo's more recent reflections on the role of ideology, the system and dehumanisation are examined, and the issues raised by Reicher and Haslam's (2006a, 2006b) own prison experiment are also considered.

Finally, there are two brief glimpses at the work of Foucault (1984/1992) and Butler (2004), both of whom, in quite different ways, offer the theoretical resources for questioning how we think about the relationship between social influence and the individual. In particular, rather than seeing social influence as something separate from and targeted at the individual, attention is given to the idea that individuals may, at one and the same time, define and form who they are *using the very resources* that may constrain and curtail what they can do and who they can be.

10.1 Conformity

Pretty early on in your psychology career you will have come across the work of Asch (see Figure 10.1) and, even prior to that, the concept of **conformity**. Most of us tend to link the two – that is, think of Asch as having found something about how, within a group of people, individuals can be persuaded to conform to – or act in accordance with – the majority. Just think of a group of younger teenagers who share a common look and way of dressing – each member of the group might experience conformity pressures to look and dress the same way that the others in the group do. Despite the familiarity of the idea of conformity, Asch's research is important because he found that individuals could conform not just to other members of established groups, but also others they had

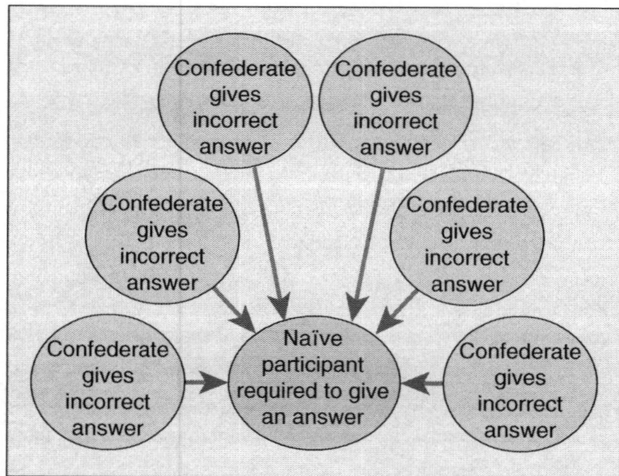

Figure 10.1 Conformity pressure in an Asch-style experiment

Conformity The influence that those of a similar status (peers) may have on an individual.

not met before. Furthermore, Asch found people would sometimes conform even if it meant that it involved publicly making an obviously incorrect judgement. There is a third reason why it is important to consider Asch – even if we are familiar with both the idea of conformity and Asch's research – and that is that, Asch's research might not be quite the convincing evidence of conformity it has often been interpreted as being.

Solomon Asch

If you had been a participant in Solomon Asch's study, you would have been in a situation that you might most closely have associated with having your eyes examined by an optician. In Asch's experiments, however (unlike most opticians), you are not saying what you can see on your own – there is a group of other people doing the same thing.

The first thing that happens to you as a participant is you are (mis)informed that the experiment is about visual perception and arrive in a room along with (typically) between six and nine others. You assume these are other participants and all sit down, facing towards the experimenter, who informs you that you need to look at various charts, which have vertical lines drawn on them. One line is labelled 'standard line' and three lines marked '1' '2' and '3' respectively are labelled 'comparison lines'. Your job is to select which of the three comparison lines is the same length as the standard line.

As each chart is revealed, you, along with the other participants, are to call out in turn the number 1, 2 or 3, as corresponds with the line that you think is the same length as the standard line. Unknown to you, the other participants are working with the experimenter (as confederates) and they have moved into seats in such a way that you are sitting over on one side, so, when the experimenter asks each of you in turn to say which comparison line is the same length as the standard line, you have to wait until several others have responded before you respond (typically there was either just one, or no, confederate participants who responded after you did). Each of these turns of the chart being presented and answers being given is called a trial and, in each experiment, there is a fairly large number of trials.

The first two charts are really obvious – unless you had some pretty significant visual impairment, you could easily tell which comparison line was the same as the standard line. You would probably have been surprised that the task was this easy and perhaps expected that it was about to get quite a lot tougher. It does *not* get harder, though – throughout the whole experiment, it ends up being really obvious which line is the same length as the standard line. You are all sitting close enough to easily see the huge differences between the comparison lines and, in an instant, which of them is the same length as the standard line.

In the first trial, everyone announces the correct response in turn – the experimenter does not comment on the answers – and the same occurs for the second trial. Then something odd happens. In the third trial, the first participant calls out the wrong answer and so does the second – in fact, all of the other participants call out the *same* wrong answer (for example, they all say line 1 when really it should be line 3). This is not some tricky perception task where they *might* be right – they are all calling out the same obviously wrong answer on trial number three and, in fact, on about a third of all of the trials. What do you do – do you call out the right answer or join in with the group's response?

We probably tend to think that we would call out the right answer in spite of the others in the group of participants calling out the wrong answers. Asch, of course, was only interested in what he called the 'critical trials' – those trials where the confederates all called out the same wrong answer. In all of the critical trials, the participants gave the *wrong* response – that is, made a 'conformity-induced error' – typically 32 per cent (approximately, one-third) of the time. You might wonder whether everyone made at least one conformity-induced error – the answer is that some participants made no errors, but 76 per cent (approximately three-quarters) made at least one.

Asch's classic study involved several confederates calling out the same incorrect answer in certain 'critical trials', thereby exerting a conformity pressure on the naïve (genuine) participant.

You might just be concerned that there was some confounding factor in Asch's experiment – perhaps there was some ambiguity in the task or some visual difficulties for some participants. In order to address *just* these sorts of issues, Asch conducted some control studies in which all participants privately wrote down their responses for each trial – errors dropped to just 1 per cent (whereas in the critical trials they had been 32 per cent). This suggests that there is something about the public announcement of errors by other participants in the experimental group that dramatically increases the chance of others giving an erroneous, conformity-induced response.

You may wonder if the participants actually believed their own responses in these critical trials. That is, when they produced a conformity-induced error, did they actually report what they at the time believed to be true?

After the trials, participants were interviewed – partly to ascertain if they really believed the responses that they had given were true when they made 'conformity-induced errors' in the critical trials. Asch (1952) notes that there was one participant who, despite making such errors, maintained that they simply reported what they saw, but, overwhelmingly, participants referred to the pressure from the group of participants. Participants also referred to how awkward they felt when they gave a correct, but minority, response – that is, when they called out the right answer on a critical trial but everyone else agreed on a different wrong answer. In cases where they did conform, they made clear that they knew the answer was incorrect, but felt under pressure to comply with the group response.

For Asch (1951, 1956, 1966), then, the fear of social repercussions from within a group can be sufficient to influence individuals to comply – even against their better judgement. Asch chose a visual perception task not because he was especially interested in how conformity pressure may cause us to make conformity-induced errors on issues such as size perception but, rather, because he wanted a task that could reveal a universal process and for which the correct answer was obvious. It is worth considering these issues in turn.

First, in looking for a universal process, Asch (1951, 1956, 1966) both reflects and anticipates other research – that is, much of the research concerning social influence within groups of people has required individuals to report what they see (movement, size, colour) rather than, say, report attitudes on a given topic. If Asch had got people to announce their attitudes on a given topic in turn – for example, a matter of political controversy – then he would have been concerned about how much of what he found was tied to the topics he had chosen and which, if any, topics most accurately revealed the fundamental process of conformity. By using visual stimuli, a number of researchers have hoped to isolate a fundamental process that would be relevant to a whole range of other (non-visual settings) – that is, if we conform regarding line length, then we might conform on all sorts of other issues.

Second, in being concerned to investigate the effects of influence where the correct answer is obvious, Asch wanted to take his research further than earlier work by Sherif (1936). Sherif had taken advantage of a relatively little known perceptual phenomenon, which is, if you look at a single point of light without any point of reference (in an entirely unlit room, for example) the light appears to move in an erratic pattern. Assuming that you did not know the light was stationary, trying to estimate how far it has moved is extremely difficult. If a group of participants are requested to call out their movement estimates in turn, what do you think will happen to their estimates? You may well have guessed that the estimates are typically influenced by each other and converge over time. Asch's experiment took this idea further by seeing how people might be susceptible to the influence of others within a group *in a situation where there was no ambiguity* – where the right answer was obvious.

In the wake of this, Deutsch and Gerard (1955) set about describing two distinct forms of conformity influence: *informational influence* and *normative influence* (see Box 10.1). Sherif's (1936) ambiguous task left participants needing to rely on others for information in order to make the right response – they were influenced by others because they had looked to them in order to inform their perception-based judgement. This **informational influence** contrasts with what Asch found. In Asch's experiments, participants knew what the correct answer was, but were influenced by others because they did not want to be the 'odd one out' – this is **normative influence**. Deutsch and Gerard argued that, while informational influence involved some sort of genuine change of perception on the part of the individual (sometimes referred to as conversion), normative influence involved no such change and those who experienced it would go along with the group merely out of a desire to avoid social sanctions – that is, they just complied.

John Turner

Deutsch and Gerard's (1955) distinction between normative and informational influences was added to by Turner, Hogg, Oakes, Reicher and Wetherell (1987) and Turner (1991), who argued that a further, third type of influence can occur within groups, which he called **referent informational influence** (see Figure 10.4). This idea relates to Turner et al's (1987) and Turner's (1991) work on self-categorisation, which was addressed in Chapter 2, but it is worth briefly noting here what Turner meant by 'referent informational influence'.

Informational influence A type of influence (usually used to further define a type of conformity influence) in which an individual is influenced by others because they look to them for information.

Normative influence A type of influence (usually used to further define a type of conformity influence) in which an individual is influenced by others because they are concerned about their social relationship with them.

Referent informational influence A type of influence where the individual's sense of group identity is relevant. Referent informational influence occurs where the individual shapes their behaviour to be consistent with a group identity that has become salient for them.

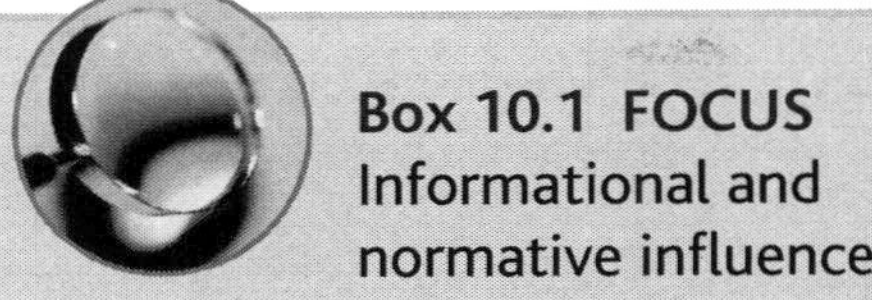

Box 10.1 FOCUS Informational and normative influences

Deutsch and Gerard (1955) distinguished between informational influence and normative influence.

Informational influence

This is most likely to occur in situations where a person is required to make a judgement in an ambiguous situation and others' views are available to the person. Here, others may influence the judgement made because of the information they are thought to provide.

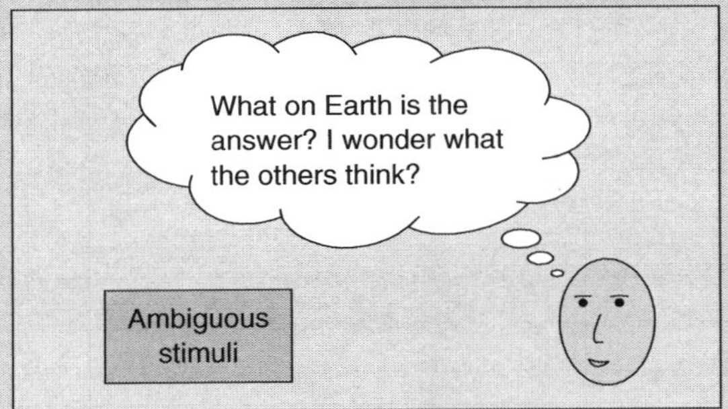

Figure 10.2 Informational influence

Normative influence

This is most likely to occur in situations where a person is required to make a judgement in a non-ambiguous situation. The judgement that they make, however, will be available for others to observe and those others have revealed that their response (which is uniform) differs from what appears to be the obviously correct one. Here, conformity may exert a pressure because of the norm to conform and the perceived costs of not conforming.

Figure 10.3 Normative influence

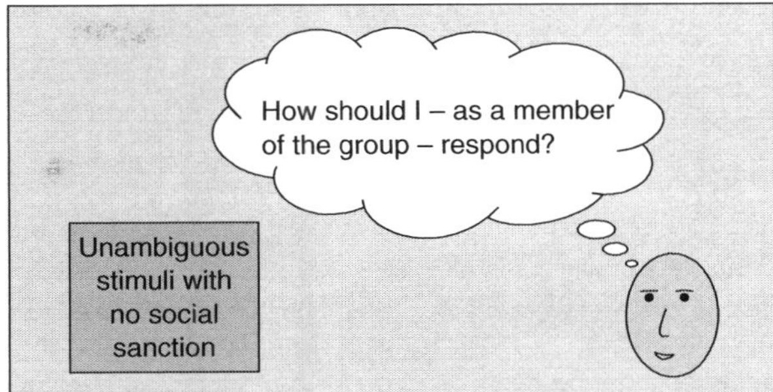

Figure 10.4 Referent informational influence

Turner noted that sometimes, even in situations where there is low ambiguity (the judgement required is easy) and there is no chance of social sanction (responses are anonymous), participants may still sometimes make errors that replicate the responses of other group members. He suggested that these errors arise because the participants see (or categorise) themselves as a group member, along with the other participants, and try to act in accordance with what they see as the group way of responding, even if this sometimes involves making erroneous judgements.

According to categorisation theory, the more closely we identify with other group members – placing them in the same category as us – the more influence they might have on our behaviour.

Subsequent research by Abrams, Wetherell, Cochrane and Hogg (1990) endorsed this finding in an Asch-style experiment where participants made both public and private judgements. In this research, participants perceived the confederates to be either students studying the same degree – psychology – or students studying a different degree – ancient history. As you would expect, conformity was always found to be greater in cases where responses were made publicly (where the risk of publicly appearing to be the odd one out is greatest). In both the public and private conditions, however, the psychology student participants were more influenced by fellow psychology students – *whom they might categorise as belonging to an important shared group* – than ancient history students (who are perhaps perceived as less closely related in category terms).

This suggests that conformity can be found to occur not only in situations where we rely on others for information or where we feel some normative pressure to comply, but also where we identify with the other members of the group – the more we perceive ourselves to belong to the same category, the more likely we are to find our behaviour is influenced by theirs. Turner suggests that even when ambiguity and social sanction are removed, people may conform to what they perceive as behaviour consistent with *their* group.

Critical review of Asch's conformity experiments

Bond and Smith (1996) conducted a meta-analysis of 133 Asch-style conformity experiments. They note that reviewing just Asch- (and Crutchfield-) style experiments, while providing a good basis for comparison with Asch's original series of studies, does restrict the focus to perceptual judgements (rather than opinion) and compliance (rather than internalisation). They confirmed that larger majority groups tended to increase the likelihood of conformity. Similarly, conformity was greater where the stimuli were ambiguous. They further noted that conformity was greater among female participants and when the majority 'did not consist of outgroup members'. They also raised some critical thoughts, however, regarding some of the ways in which the implications of Asch's work might be understood.

First, Bond and Smith suggest that conformity has generally declined over time (in assessing this they paid particular attention to US studies – as Asch's original study was conducted in the USA). Second, they suggest that conformity is higher in 'collectivist' countries (such as Japan, China and Latin America) rather than 'individualist' cultures (the USA, UK and Australia). Indeed, they suggest that 'cultural variables' are the most important factors determining rates of conformity and likely to be even more important if the research is widened to consider an opinion issue and possible internalisation measures rather than just compliance in a line judgement-style task.

Hodges and Geyer (2006) argue that Asch's studies have been largely misunderstood by most psychologists as being overwhelming evidence of conformity. Asch himself referred to how misunderstood his work was (Rock, 1990) – singling out Campbell (1961, 1990) as the only American psychologist who grasped the 'moral dimension' of his work. Most textbooks that refer to Asch's studies present them as demonstrating in vivid terms participants failing to assert an obvious truth (regarding which lines were the same length) just because of perceived pressure from others. Hodges and Geyer (2006, p. 3) argue that Asch undertook his research in order to 'refute the view that people are "silly sheep", willing to believe anything others say.' As they point out, in his reports on his findings, Asch notes that the 'most compelling' force at work in his experiments is the 'clarity of perceptual information' – not conformity pressures. The results of Asch's research could be interpreted as, first, showing low levels of public conformity and, second, almost no private persuasion. That is, participants only publicly followed the group's incorrect answer approximately one-third of the time – two-thirds of the time they selected what they saw to be true for themselves despite any group consensus. Whatever pressure or influence the group may have exerted, it was only enough to result in a public show of conformity – the participants were not actually persuaded by the group. Indeed, Asch found in one variation that if a single confederate dissented from the prevailing group consensus, then 'conformity-induced errors' on the critical trials dropped even further to just 5 per cent. Thus, the prevailing tendency to see Asch as having found the most stark evidence for conformity should, according to Hodges and Geyer, be tempered by a recognition that most people, most of the time, did not even publicly conform and almost no one was actually persuaded as to the truth of the majority's perceptual judgements.

Critical recap

Conformity

1 Bond and Smith (1996) suggest that conformity can be thought of as a cultural phenomenon – with rates of conformity varying over time and across cultures.

2 Most conformity experiments have relied on visual perception tasks – an issue referred to in the critical review of majority and minority influences below. One point to note here is that Bond and Smith (1996) suggest visual perception tasks show different rates of conformity to other measures, such as attitudinal conformity.

3 The way in which Asch's work has been interpreted can be criticised. Hodges and Geyer (2006) note that Asch himself understood his studies as showing low rates of conformity – of approximately one-third of critical trials and, even then, those conforming almost always merely gave a *public* show of conforming, hardly ever actually *believing* the incorrect line length judgements of the majority.

Reflective questions

1 *Do you think that people conform to others – if so, why?*

2 *How would you set about researching conformity?*

10.2 Minority influence

As we have seen, Asch is sometimes implicitly or explicitly presented as *only* having examined conformity influences – that is, as having arranged experiments in which the confederates were in a majority and the naïve participants in a **minority**. Although this reflects the main emphasis of his work, it is worth noting that Asch did try variations on his experiment in which the confederates were a minority with a larger number of naïve participants – for example, in one case, a couple of confederates periodically called out incorrect responses to a bemused and seemingly uninfluenced majority of 16 naïve participants. It is worth reflecting in more detail, however, on just what sort of influence the minority might have.

This issue has been investigated in some detail by Moscovici (Moscovici, 1976, 1980, 1984, 1994; Moscovici & Lage, 1976; Moscovici, Lage & Naffrechoux, 1969; Moscovici & Personnaz, 1986). In designing their experiments, Moscovici and colleagues, like Asch, used a perceptual task, but one that was a little less straightforward than line length. If you have ever disagreed with someone about whether an object is green or blue, you will probably relate to the task they used – that is, participants were asked to decide whether colour slides were green or blue. It is worth bearing in mind that, in measuring the possible effect of minority influence, Moscovici and colleagues had a particular interest in not just participants' immediate public judgements but also their private and delayed judgements.

One source of Moscovici's discontent with the prevailing view that Asch and others had demonstrated how individuals conform to the majority was that it did not reflect the demonstrable social and political realities of how new and different ideas, such as Freud's psychoanalytic approach, come to be important in a given society. Brown (2000a) draws on the example of Darwin to illustrate the way that, in some cases, a minority position can eventually have a profound influence on the majority. Darwin's (1859) *On the origin of species by means of natural selection* was strongly opposed by a powerful majority at the time it first emerged. Eventually, however – and perhaps partly due to the persistence of Darwin and others promoting these ideas – the theory of evolution came to form one of the most important axioms of modern science.

While Moscovici's illustrative examples drew on real social and political occurrences, his empirical research, undertaken with colleagues, very much stayed with the prevailing experimental orthodoxy of using errors in judgements made in visual perception tasks to measure the presence and extent of social influence. As mentioned above, for Moscovici and colleagues this largely involved getting participants to judge the colour of a number of slides. Typically, a series of different shades of blue slides were shown to a group of two confederates and four naïve participants. Moscovici, Lage and Naffrechoux (1969) used three different conditions – one where the confederates responded to all slides by calling out 'green' (the consistent condition), one where they sometimes called out 'green' (the inconsistent condition) and a control group where there were no confederates. Moscovici et al. were interested in what proportion of responses involved the erroneous colour judgement of 'green' being made.

In the control condition, there were virtually no such responses. In the inconsistent condition, about 1 per cent of responses involved erroneously calling 'green'. In the consistent condition, however, this was up to 8 per cent, with one-third of participants making at least one erroneous 'green' response.

While these figures are far lower than the conformity rates that Asch found (and, indeed, Moscovici and Lage, 1976), it is perhaps noteworthy that they should occur at all. In a follow-up to their basic procedure, Moscovici, Lage and Naffrechoux (1969) investigated whether exposure to minority influence might have any impact on participants' subsequent colour judgements. Having been through the procedure outlined, participants were subsequently required to privately complete a colour threshold task. This task involved completing a standardised test of colour discrimination individually without knowing how anyone responded, nor having their own responses made known. You might recall that Asch found follow-up questions of the participants in his study revealed that almost no one was actually internally persuaded by the majority – there was just a public show of going along with the majority. Moscovici et al. (1969) found something quite different. Those participants who had been exposed to a minority who consistently called the different shades of blue 'green' were found to be significantly more likely to describe a blue slide as being green than those in the control condition (see Box 10.2). These findings suggest that, although the public effect of the minority was quite small (8 per cent is markedly less than the roughly one-third found by Asch), there was a change in subsequent private colour judgement behaviour.

Minority The effect of a smaller number of individuals on a larger number in contexts where there is no marked, relevant difference in status.

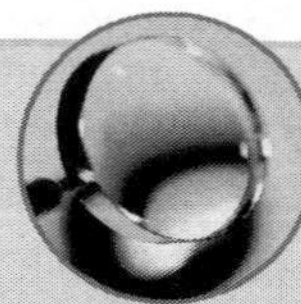

Box 10.2 FOCUS
Moscovici's minority influence research

Moscovici's research into minority influence involved exposing (usually four) participants to a minority of confederates (usually two) who would either consistently or inconsistently call blue colour slides green.

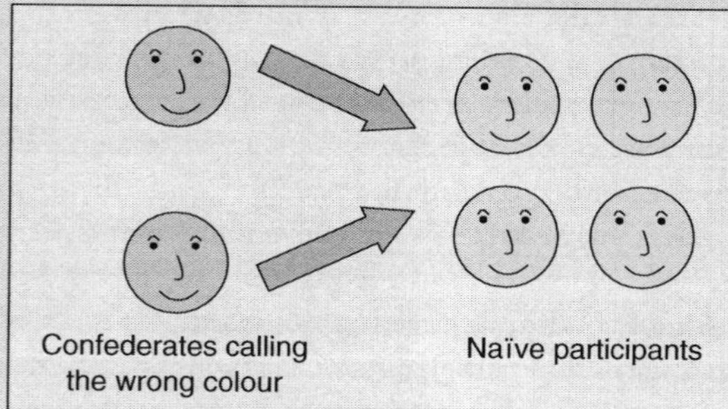

Figure 10.5 A minority attempts to influence a majority

The naïve participants were typically asked to judge slide colours publicly and privately.

Moscovici found that, while exposure to an erroneous minority led to a relatively small number of publically declared induced errors (as compared to Asch's findings), it led to more changes in participants' private colour judgements than exposure to an erroneous majority did.

These findings set up another issue to be investigated – was the change in colour judgement behaviour something that was in any sense unique to cases where participants were exposed to a minority or could it also be found to occur where majority influence had taken place? It may be worth stopping for moment to make an educated guess. Think through the last time you recall changing your mind on an issue – was any minority or majority influence at work?

Moscovici and Lage (1976) set up the usual colour slide experiment with six conditions. In one condition there were two confederates and four naïve participants and the confederates always called 'green' (consistent two confederates condition). In a second condition, there was one consistent confederate and four naïve participants (consistent single confederate condition). In a third condition, there were two inconsistent confederates and four naïve participants (inconsistent condition). There were also two majority conditions – one in which the confederate majority was consistent (consistent majority) and the other in which the confederate majority was inconsistent (inconsistent majority). Also, of course, there was a control condition with no confederates.

In terms of publicly displayed influence, the single consistent confederate, the inconsistent minority and the control group had no significant effect. By contrast, the consistent majority had the most marked effect – resulting in some 40 per cent of colour judgements being erroneous (calling the blue slide 'green'). In between these two extremes were both the non-unanimous majority and the consistent two confederates conditions, resulting in an error rate of 12 and 10 per cent respectively.

So, no real surprises so far – you would expect that the majority would bring about a larger publicly announced error judgement and such error rates would drop if the majority were inconsistent. You would probably also expect, from Moscovici et al.'s (1969) previous research, that the minority would have a relatively small influence on publicly announced judgements. Perhaps the most important aspect of Moscovici and Lage's findings, however, lies in the subsequent colour threshold tests. Only one of the experimental groups had a significantly different blue–green colour threshold than the baseline. That is, just one of the conditions found evidence that might suggest a significant shift towards calling blue slides 'green'. This private shift in colour judgements did not happen in the majority condition – it only happened in the consistent two confederates, minority, condition.

There is a twofold tale of influence that emerges from this programme of empirical research. First, those exposed to an erroneous minority are less likely to make public erroneous perceptual judgements than those exposed to an erroneous majority. Second, those exposed to an erroneous minority are more likely to display subsequent visual perception judgements in private that appear to have changed in the direction of the minority than those exposed to an erroneous majority.

One problem with the research considered so far is that it uses judgements about line lengths and colour shades as a stand-in for meaningful attitudes and behaviour. That is, if the experiments of Asch, Sherif, Moscovici and others tell us anything of importance, it is not about how we might fare in judgements made concerning visual stimuli when faced with different sources of potential social influence. Instead, the research seeks to find ingredients for influence or the inhibition of influence that can apply to attitudes and behaviours which are *meaningful and consequential*. Some research has investigated both minority and majority influence using real-world attitudinal positions on topics that have a meaning outside of those created in an experimental laboratory – for

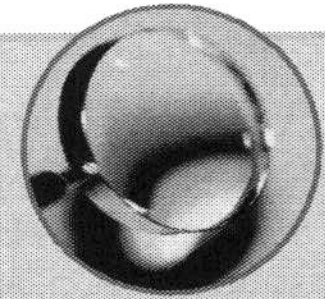

Box 10.3 FOCUS
Researching the spillover effect

Researching the spillover effect typically involves the following steps.

- Participants are presented with arguments concerning a specific issue – for example, arguments for or against gay marriages.
- Participants are informed that these arguments are a minority or a majority position.
- Participants are tested on the target attitude topic – in this case, gay marriages.
- Participants are tested on an associated attitude topic. This could be any attitudinal position that is often associated with the target attitude. If, for example, there was evidence that those in favour of gay marriages are typically in favour of affirmative action to support disadvantaged groups, then this could be the 'associated attitude' participants are tested on after being exposed to the arguments on the target topic.
- Research sometimes manipulates the following variables:
  - **time** assessing attitudes immediately after exposure to the arguments and after a delay of several weeks
  - **group identification** sometimes the message is attributed to a group the participants may identify with in one condition and to one they would be unlikely to identify with in another condition
  - **subjectivity and objectivity** sometimes the arguments are presented as objective in one condition (reflecting evidence) and subjective in another (reflecting opinion).

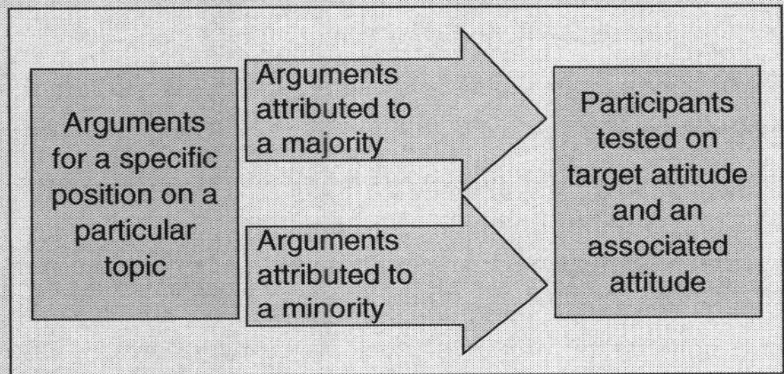

Figure 10.6 The potential spillover effect of minority influence – how minorities may influence attitudes associated with the ones that they are advocating

example, concerning abortion, capital punishment, gun ownership and deforestation.

The spillover effect of minority influence

One intriguing area of research is the ways in which minorities might have not only an immediate, and delayed, effect on the specific target of their influence (such as colour judgements), but also on associated issues. This is known as the **spillover effect** and research that has investigated it has tended to examine the effect minority influence on one attitude has on other *different, but broadly associated, attitudes* (see Box 10.3).

Perez, Mugny and Moscovici (1986) arranged for Spanish participants to be presented with arguments in favour of abortion, which were described as being either a majority or minority viewpoint. Tests of participants' attitudes on abortion and also contraception (an issue not directly addressed in the arguments participants listened to) suggested that those who were informed that the viewpoint was a majority one showed some initial movement of attitude towards being pro-abortion and pro-contraception, but this disappeared three weeks later. Those exposed to the same arguments but who were informed that the arguments represented a minority viewpoint were, by contrast, relatively unpersuaded immediately, but showed a significant movement on both issues (becoming more pro-abortion and more pro-contraception) three weeks later. Perez et al. thus highlight that minority influence might not only have a particular potency in affecting private judgements (as compared to majority influence) but also its effects may both be delayed and 'spill over' to influence other – sometimes quite loosely associated – attitudinal positions.

This issue of the spillover effect of minority influence is further investigated in Alvaro and Crano's (1997, p. 953) research, in which participants were presented

Spillover effect A term used to denote the finding in some minority influence research that the minority may have an effect on not just the specific focus of an 'influence attempt' but 'associated' issues also.

with a document entitled 'The case against gays in the military', which they describe as 'a strong persuasive message that argued against allowing homosexual soldiers in the military.' Attitude assessments by Alvaro and Crano (1997, p. 253) suggested that this message was largely counter-attitudinal – that is, they were against the participants' pre-message attitudes. Alvaro and Crano (1997) manipulated both the size of the number of supposed proponents of the message (the majority of students versus a minority of students) and whether the group proposing the message was an ingroup (members of the same university) or an outgroup (members of another, nearby university). In the majority condition, these arguments were attributed to 'representatives of the University of Arizona Student Union Association (ASUA). On the basis of a large and comprehensive survey of students, the ASUA has determined that the majority of students at U of A (the University of Arizona) strongly oppose any law that would allow gays in the military. In the 'ingroup' minority condition, the message was attributed to 'a small radical organisation of 50 University of Arizona students who strongly oppose any law that would allow gays in the military'. In the 'outgroup' minority condition, the message was attributed to 'students from Pima Community College' – which was a college near to the university.

In both minority conditions, the minority status of the message was further emphasised by the following introductory remark: 'Although the (source's) position is contrary to the beliefs of a majority of students, we would like you to read and consider their statement.' Finally, the issue was cast as either involving objective fact – 'we would like you to respond in the light of the objective evidence' – or being subjective – 'people's judgements on these issues are probably subjective. We would like you to share your feelings on this issue.' The participants' attitudes were then assessed for the direct attitude (regarding gay people in the military) and for a loosely associated, indirect, attitude regarding gun control (previous research having suggested that those opposed to gay people joining the military were against gun control).

These manipulations – majority, minority, ingroup, outgroup and objective, subjective and the two dependent variable measures of direct and indirect attitudes – made for a complex experimental design, but, the findings were surprisingly clear. The direct attitude (regarding gay people joining the military) did not significantly change under any condition. The indirect attitude (regarding gun control) only significantly changed under one condition – that is, where an ingroup minority presented the issue as a subjective one.

Alvaro and Crano (1997, p. 956) argued that the participants were more likely to be persuaded by the minority on the indirect attitude when the issue was framed as being a subjective one because 'of the relative impotence of the group as a source of threat or pressure'. In cases where we perceive an attitude as a threat, then, according to Alvaro and Crano, we are more likely to engage in effective counter-arguments and have critical or derogatory views about the source.

According to Alvaro and Crano, if the source is seen as part of an ingroup, we will be more tolerant of their divergent views and if they are a minority, expressing subjective opinions, then it is as if our argumentative defences are either turned down or switched off. This effect is exacerbated when we consider that what winds up being persuasive is another, associated attitude, not the overt content of the message at all. That is, when we do not counter-argue with the source because they are ingroup members (of whom we are pretty tolerant) and they are 'merely' expressing something as 'non-threatening' and as a minority opinion, at the very time when we feel least vulnerable to their ideas, we are most likely to find some associated attitudes have been changed. Explore this yourself a little more in Box 10.4.

Critical review of minority influence

It is worth briefly reflecting on some issues raised by the above research. As was mentioned above, much of the research into majority and minority influences within groups has tended to use visual perception tasks. This is largely because it is easier to manipulate variations (for example, making the judgement tasks harder or easier) and because, stripped of contextual factors, researchers believed it would then be easier to measure the 'pure',

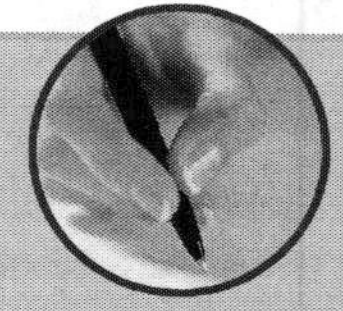

Box 10.4 TRY IT OUT Minority influence

Try to find an example of a minority trying to exert an influence on a majority – this could be a recent news event, something historical or something from your everyday life.

Does your example provide evidence for the types of influence that minority influence literature suggests? Is there evidence for a long-lasting effect? What about the spillover effect?

'context-free' effect of conformity or minority influence. Such context-free perception studies, however, were on perception tasks that participants would not have had a position on outside of the laboratory and (apart from the value placed on accurate perceptual judgements) would not, in themselves, have meant much to the participants. I am more likely to care about gay rights and gun control and have a position on these issues than on whether things seem to be blue or green.

Moving into the realm of 'real issues' has itself brought problems. First, it is perhaps worth just briefly raising the issue of ethics. Look through these studies (and others that you come across) and just reflect on whether or not you are happy with the messages being presented to participants. Is it fair for social psychologists to use any sort of persuasive message – or only if they predict that it will be unsuccessful (which was the case with Alvaro and Crano's 'Case against gays in the military' message)? Often, researchers want to use either currently debated and, therefore, controversial topics or counter-attitudinal positions. So, finding something meaningful may be difficult, but could there be repercussions for participants and others with some of the messages used?

A second problem is the way in which 'minority' and 'majority' are manipulated in the studies presenting real-world issues. With Moscovici (and Asch before him), it was easy to manipulate how widely the judgement choice was held precisely because each judgement had no existence outside of the laboratory. So, for Moscovici, if two participants out of six called the wrong colour, the size of the minority was self-evident. If we use real-world issues, having two people adopt the position does not make it a minority one because the issue – to be meaningful – has a history of debate and positions being taken on it outside of the experiment. So, instead, researchers have tended to – rather unconvincingly – *announce* the position as being a minority or a majority one. We need to ask, is it really the same to be *told* that a certain position is a minority or majority one within a given group, or within society at large, as experiencing it as such. Also, what happens when we, as participants, are being told, for example, that the majority of students at our university believe gay people should not be allowed in the military when we are pretty sure that the majority in fact hold the *opposite* view?

These concerns should create some sense of caution regarding the results – however plausible they may seem. It could be that the majority condition in Alvaro and Crano's research was particularly unpersuasive because it did not chime with participants' experience that this really *was* a majority position – if it really had been (and the students had really perceived it as such rather than just being told so), then perhaps it would have been more persuasive. Either way, it is not clear that simply informing participants an opinion is a minority or majority position will actually convince them, to the extent it overrides their own knowledge and experience of the issue outside of the laboratory.

A further criticism of these studies is that they might tell us something about how participants' public or private expressions of judgements or attitudes could be influenced (whether by majorities or minorities), but this may be quite different from how their *behaviour* is influenced – if at all. Milgram first raised this criticism with regard to Asch's conformity experiments and the many versions of it that followed, but it holds true for minority influence also. For Milgram (1964, p. 137), the contrast is between what he terms 'signal conformity' (where someone expresses a judgement or attitude) and 'action conformity' ('which refers to the elicitation of a *deed* by group forces'). Milgram was concerned that just because we may find group pressure can bring about 'signal conformity', it does not mean it can bring about 'action conformity'. Milgram was, as you may have guessed from this distinction, especially interested in how social influence could bring about *actual behaviour* on the part of others – conformity was an important part of his interest, which he investigated as part of his hugely influential series of 24 experiments focusing on obedience, discussed in the next section.

Critical recap

Minority influence

1 Most studies have investigated minority and majority influence using visual perception tasks such as line length or colour, where the correct answer is largely uncontroversial, the judgement inconsequential and regarding which participants would have no feeling or commitment outside of the experiment.

2 As an alternative to visual perception tasks, some experiments have used opinions on controversial topics, but these have also raised problems. First, there are ethical issues concerning the messages that participants have been exposed to (for example, arguments against allowing gay people into the military). Second, the manipulations may lack credibility, such as informing participants that a given opinion is either held by a minority or majority of people.

3 As Milgram (1964) asked, these experiments tend to suggest that behaviour may be affected by majority and minority influence, but usually they only measure judgement calls on visual perception tasks or opinions on controversial topics – actual behaviour is typically unexplored.

Reflective questions

1 *Do you think that minorities have a different sort of influence from that of majorities? If so, how do they differ and why?*

2 *What shortcomings can you identify in minority influence research?*

10.3 Stanley Milgram's studies of obedience

While, as we saw in the last two sections, Asch and Moscovici addressed both majority and minority influences, they did so by focusing on the influence of peers – people of a similar status within the specific situation being studied. It was another social psychologist, Stanley Milgram, who conducted a series of experiments designed to investigate the ways in which those in a position of **authority** in a particular situation may influence the behaviour of *subordinates* (those under their authority in that situation).

Milgram's studies of **obedience** are among the most famous experiments ever conducted within social psychology. The findings were disseminated not only through academic publications (Milgram, 1963, 1964, 1965a, 1965b, 2004 [1974]) but also Milgram's compelling documentary films of the studies. In addition to their influence within social psychology, Milgram's findings have, as Blass (1999) notes, had an impact on areas as diverse as philosophy, law, economics, business ethics, military psychology and Holocaust studies. Few social psychologists can claim the recognition of having a summary of their research findings appear as a Peter Gabriel song title ('We do what we're told – Milgram's 37') or be referred to in a film ('I Come I Care') – but Milgram can. The chances are, then, that you – in advance of reading this chapter – already know something of what Milgram found.

In light of this, it is worth prefacing the description of Milgram's studies and findings with a few words of caution. First, you might experience some confusion regarding the exact details of what happened in Milgram's studies. Perhaps you have already come across descriptions that seem to contradict each other – this is most likely due to the fact that Milgram himself conducted 24 different versions of the basic experiment, each slightly different from the others as he tried to pinpoint the ingredients leading to obedience and resistance.

Second, Milgram (who had studied and taught with Asch and Allport while at Harvard) had an interest in *groups* within the process of obedience and resistance (for example, Milgram, 1965a), which is often overlooked, but this chapter will address this important issue.

Third, and perhaps most important – those of us who have heard Milgram's results countless times can become immune to just how startling they really are. The more familiar you are with Milgram, the more important it is to try and suspend your knowledge for a moment and taking the findings at face value, hear them as if for the first time. One way of trying to connect with something of the dramatic nature of these studies and their findings is to imagine that you are a participant in one of Milgram's studies.

What happened in Milgram's experiments?

To understand the basic procedure, it is worth imagining that you are a participant in Milgram's (1963) study. You will have heard about the study from either a newspaper advertisement or some direct mail – either way, you understood it to be a study about memory and learning at Yale University. As soon as you arrive in the evening at the impressive campus, you are paid the fee ($4.50) and told it is yours to keep no matter what happens in the laboratory. You are met by a slightly officious laboratory experimenter wearing a grey technician's lab coat and introduced to the other volunteer – a man in his mid-forties who seems mild-mannered and likeable. The laboratory experimenter talks a bit about punishment and learning before stating the objective of the current research: 'We want to find out just what effect different people have on each other as teachers and learners, and also what effect *punishment* will have on learning in this situation.' He then continues: 'Therefore, I'm going to ask one of you to be the teacher here tonight and the other one to be the learner. Does either of you have a preference?' As neither of you expresses a preference, both you and the other participant pick a slip of paper from a hat. He announces that he is the learner and you read your slip saying 'teacher'. You then accompany the 'learner' to a room where he is strapped into a chair where he will receive electric shocks. The learner asks a question about the nature of the electric shocks, to which the experimenter impassively replies, 'Although the shocks can be extremely painful, they cause no permanent tissue damage.'

Authority For Milgram this means a person who – within the context in which an attempt at influence is made – has a greater status than the one they seek to influence.

Obedience Acting in accordance with the instructions of an 'authority' figure.

You are made aware that the learner needs to memorise word pairs (for example, 'nice day') that you will later read out to him. He will then be presented with the first word for each respective pair (such as 'nice') and need to guess the word that was paired with it from a choice of four (indicating by selecting a letter A, B, C or D) corresponding to the possible options. If the learner chooses the wrong word, then you, as the teacher, are required to administer an electric shock using the shock generator. This large piece of apparatus has 30 lever switches in a line, each of which is labelled with a specific voltage. The lowest voltage label is 15 volts and the highest 450. As well as voltage labels, there are verbal descriptions for groups of levers, starting with 'slight shock' over the first few levers, going up through 'moderate shock' and 'strong shock' and eventually arriving at 'Danger: severe shock' and, finally, just above the last two switches, the worryingly unspecified inscription 'XXX'. You are shown how the machine works and given a small demonstration shock in which the third lever of the shock generator is pressed, you experience a shock of 45 volts – enough to make you jump, but not cause lasting pain.

You are told to administer a shock to the learner each time he gives an incorrect response. You are further instructed to start with the lowest (15 volts) and 'move one level higher on the shock generator each time the learner flashes a wrong answer'. Prior to administering each shock, you are instructed to announce the relevant number of volts relating to the lever that you are about to press. You start off with a practice run of ten word pairs, so you can get used to the procedure. The learner gets three of these correct but seven wrong, so, with the final incorrect answer, you administer a shock of 105 volts (marked moderate shock).

Having familiarised yourself with the procedure and equipment, you are presented with a fresh, longer list of words and told that when you reach the end of the list, to keep repeating it and 'continue giving shocks until the learner has learned all the pairs correctly'. You are now instructed to begin the procedure starting with the first lever (15 volt shock) for the first incorrect response.

It does not take long for the learner to make incorrect responses, so you start using the machine, administering a shock each time the learner's response is wrong and increasing the shock (by 15 volts) each time. Unfortunately, the learner is only getting about one in four responses correct, so, pretty soon, you find yourself giving higher shocks than you did in the practice session. As you reach 120 volts, you may be aware that it is higher than the mains electricity that you are used to (in the USA). Pretty quickly, the shocks you are administering are marked 'strong shock'. Do you continue? Most people who do not already know this study (and most of us who do) probably like to think we would recognise the potential danger and stop. Every single participant continued. The shock levers are now labelled 'very strong shock', reaching what you might know as the potentially fatal levels of UK mains electricity – that is, 240 volts. Again, we would like to think that we would stop at this point, but no one does.

The levers you are pressing are now labelled 'intense shock' and, as you press the lever to administer 300 volts, you hear a noise – the learner is pounding on the wall in the adjacent room. At this stage you are probably worried about the learner's welfare so you turn to the experimenter, expressing your concern – perhaps you say that the learner is trying to communicate and they do not want to continue. The experimenter replies, 'Whether the learner likes it or not, you must go on until he has learned all the word pairs correctly. So please go on.' In fact, whatever protest you make, the experimenter will first respond politely but firmly, 'Please continue' or 'Please go on.' If you persist, you will be told, 'The experiment requires that you continue', 'It is absolutely essential that you continue' and 'You have no other choice, you *must* go on.' What do you imagine doing? Stopping? Some 12.5 per cent do terminate the experiment at this stage – but 87.5 per cent continue.

After this, the learner no longer gives a response to the memory test and you are instructed to wait for five to ten seconds and then treat each non-response as an incorrect answer. Let us suppose that, along with 87.5 per cent of participants, you continue. The learner refuses to answer. You might ask him if he is all right, but get no reply and – after administering 315 volts – you hear him pounding again. Perhaps you turn to the experimenter to ask if the learner is all right. The experimenter replies, 'Although the shocks may be painful, there is no permanent tissue damage, so please go on.' If you persist, the experimenter again says, 'The experiment requires that you continue' then, 'It is absolutely essential that you continue' and, if you carry on, 'You have no other choice, you *must* go on.'

At this stage, after administering an 'extreme intensity shock' of 315 volts, another 10 per cent of participants terminated the experiment – meaning that 77.5 per cent continued. After the next shock, there is no banging – no sound or response at all, just an eerie silence. Let us suppose that you are absolutely typical and respond just like 65 per cent of participants did – you continue to obey the experimenter, administering shocks (despite the silence) all the way to the very last lever on the shock generator, which is for 450 volts. After you administer the 450 volts shock three times, the experimenter ends the experiment. You probably breathe a sigh of relief (as did most participants) and perhaps display other signs of the stress you have just experienced (mopping your brow, shaking your head, fumbling for cigarettes or rubbing your eyes).

You then are requested to complete an interview, some attitude scales, projective tests and open-ended questions. Finally, you are reunited with the learner, who appears, showing himself to be unharmed by the experimental procedure. You are made aware that, although you believed yourself to be administering electric shocks, the learner did not receive any and the banging you heard was not in fact the learner but a prerecorded tape. The experiment, then, was not about whether or not punishment aided learning but about the teacher's behaviour – specifically the teacher's obedience to instructions from the experimenter. (See also Box 10.5.)

Variations in Milgram's experimental procedure

In pilot studies, Milgram had noted that where the learner victim was partly visible, participants frequently averted their eyes as they administered the shocks – not wanting to see the consequences of their actions. So, in some of the more than 20 experimental variations, Milgram wanted to see whether increasing the salience of the learner victim in different ways would decrease participants' obedience. In one variation (Experiment 2), the learner victim shouted protests that the teacher participant could clearly hear, in another variation (Experiment 3) the learner was additionally situated in the same room as the participant and, in a third, (Experiment 4), the participant was additionally required to hold down the victim's hand for him to receive the electric shock.

The results of some of these further variations will be considered in a moment, but, first, it is worth detailing what became the new baseline condition for all future variations – Experiment 5. In that variation, there were verbal protests (as in Experiment 2) and the added suggestion that the learner victim experienced a heart condition.

Participants in Experiment 5 experienced the same general procedure as described above but it differed in two respects. First, right at the beginning, the learner raised the

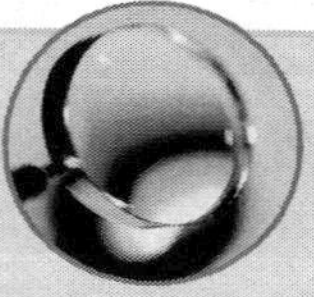

Box 10.5 FOCUS
Classic research: Overview of Milgram's obedience studies

Milgram was keen to empirically investigate how obedience worked. He devised an experiment that, while appearing to be concerned with the effects of punishment on learning actually examined participants' behaviour with regard to instructions from an 'authority figure' (usually an experimenter) regarding administering electric shocks to a 'learner', who was an experimental confederate.

The authority figure told participants the required procedure at the beginning of the experiment and requested them to continue if at any point they hesitated or questioned the procedure. The experiments used an easily measurable dependent variable – obedience was measured by the level of shock administered and the percentage of participants who chose to administer that level of shock. Total obedience was taken as being that percentage of participants who at no time disobeyed the instructions (even though they might protest) and who therefore continued to the highest level of shock available (450 volts).

In order to dissect what factors contributed most, and least, to the scenario of obedience – and thereby build a theoretical understanding of obedience – Milgram used 24 different versions of this basic experimental design. He varied many aspects of the experimental procedure, such as the characteristics of the experimenter and the 'victim' (the learner), the nature of the authority figure and setting of the experiment, the sex of participants, nature of the 'learner's' protests and proximity and physical contact with the 'learner' during the administration of shocks.

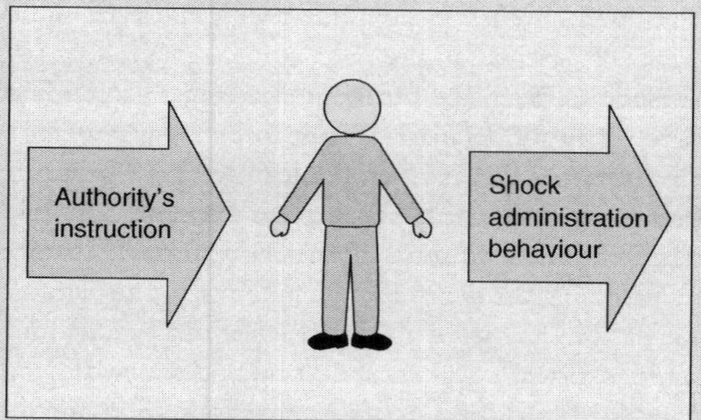

Figure 10.7 The social influence of a person in authority on a participant in Milgram's obedience experiments

fact that they had 'a slight heart condition, nothing serious' then asked if the shocks were dangerous. The experimenter replied, somewhat dismissively, that, 'Although the shocks can be painful, they cause no permanent tissue damage.' Second, throughout the experiment, there were audible protests apparently coming from the learner victim in the next room. It is worth considering these protests in a little more detail and imagining for a moment, if we possibly can, being the learner victim in this bizarre, torture-like scenario. What do the results suggest about how we might fare?

Starting at 75 volts, the learner responded to the shocks with an 'Ugh!' – getting louder as the shocks increased. At 90 volts the learner shouted, 'Ugh!' a second time. Of the 40 participants in this condition, just 1 (2.5 per cent) stopped at this point. At 120 volts, the learner victim said, 'Ugh! Hey, this really hurts.' The learner victim continued to produce vocal signs of distress ('Ugh!') at 135 volts. Then, at 150 volts, the learner victim – who had already mentioned a heart condition – shouted out, 'Ugh! Experimenter! That's all. Get me out of here. I told you I had a heart condition. My heart's starting to bother me now. Get me out of here, please. My heart's starting to bother me. I refuse to go on. Let me out.'

We would probably all like to believe that if we were the teacher participant, we would stop at this point – and if we were a genuine learner victim in some parallel situation, our appeal to the teacher participant would be responded to. Of the 39 teacher participants at this point, 33 continued (82.5 per cent of the total pool of participants). The learner victim demanded to be let out at 165 volts and at 180 volts shouted, 'Ugh! I can't stand the pain. Let me out of here!' We might hope that such a direct appeal would persuade the person who believed that they really were giving the electric shocks to stop – only one did, 32 (80 per cent) continued.

As the shocks increased the learner victim's appeals became more desperate. At 195 volts the shouted, 'Ugh! Let me out of here. Let me out of here. My heart's bothering me. Let me out of here! You have no right to keep me here! Let me out! Let me out of here! My heart's bothering me. Let me out! Let me out!' Surely if we were ever in this – admittedly unusual, to say the least – situation as a victim, we would hope that such an appeal would stop a volunteer from continuing to administer electric shocks, but, all 32 (80 per cent) continued.

At 210 volts, the learner victim directly appealed to the experimenter, 'Ugh! Experimenter! Get me out of here. I've had enough. I won't be in the experiment any more.' If this was genuine, what more could the learner victim have done? How could he have persuaded those involved to stop the experiment?

At this point, though, despite this demand to be let out and stop the experiment, 32 participants (80 per cent) continued to administer what they believed to be electric shocks to the learner victim. The cries of 'Ugh!' continued through 225 volts and 240 volts, with another demand to be let out at 255 volts – 32 participants (80 per cent) continued. At 270 volts, the learner victim let out an agonised scream and then shouted, 'Let me out of here. Let me out of here.' Again, if we were in a genuinely parallel situation to this experiment, what else could we as the learner victim have done to effect our freedom? Following the agonised scream and demand to be let out, 30 participants (75 per cent) continued.

The shocks continued to increase despite the screams and protests. At 300 volts, after another agonised scream, the learner victim shouted, 'I absolutely refuse to answer any more. Get me out of here. You can't hold me here. Get me out. Get me out of here.' The learner-victim could not have been clearer, or more insistent, that they were unable to continue and needed the teacher to stop administering the electric shocks. If we were him, what more could be said – but, on hearing this, 29 participants (72.5 per cent) continued.

At 315 volts, following what is described as 'an intensely agonized scream', the learner victim reiterated that he was no longer participating in the study and demanded to be freed: 'I told you, I refuse to answer. I'm no longer part of this experiment.' A further participant dropped out at this point, but 28 (70 per cent) continued.

At 330 volts, the learner victim made his final appeal – following an agonised scream, he shouted in increasingly hysterical tones, 'Let me out of here. Let me out of here. My heart's bothering me. Let me out I tell you. Let me out of here. You have no right to hold me here. Let me out! Let me out! Let me out! Let me out of here! Let me out! Let me out!'

Let us again – just for a moment – imagine being strapped into a chair, receiving electric shocks in some strange situation that seems to have suddenly become dangerous and sinister. What more could we do or say to appeal to the person administering the electric shocks to stop? After this, a teacher participant refused to continue, but 27 (67.5 per cent) continued.

Subsequently, the learner victim was silent and – with the exception of another single participant who stopped after administering 375 volts – the others continued to obey and administer shocks to the very end. Just as was found in Experiment 1, of the 40 participants 26 (65 per cent) showed complete obedience, administering what they believed to be shocks of 450 volts.

Milgram's results

In both Milgram's first experiment (which simply had the learner victim pounding on the wall) and his fifth (which had verbal appeals, screams and reference to a heart condition – see Table 10.1), he found that 65 per cent of participants showed total obedience. These 26 participants in each experiment continued to administer what they believed to be electric shocks, despite the pounding on the wall (Experiment 1) and the demands to be free, screams and reference to heart problems (Experiment 5). Furthermore, the shocks were not administered within the context of any sense of being deserved on the part of the learner victim – he was not guilty of any crime, for example. Indeed, from the teacher participants' perspective, *they* could have easily been learner victims had they chosen the other slip of paper from the hat. At this point, you might raise a vital question regarding the experiment – namely, did the participants really believe that they were administering electric shocks? The evidence – as Milgram presents it – suggests that they did.

Milgram (1963) notes that when asked, 'How painful to the learner were the last few shocks that you

Table 10.1 Milgram's new baseline experiment (Experiment 5)

Voltage level	What the learner victim does	What the teacher participants do
75	Cries out, 'Ugh!' (and does so until 270 volts)	100% continue
90	Cries out, 'Ugh!'	97.5% continue (1 drops out)
150	Cries out, 'Ugh! Experimenter! That's all. Get me out of here. I told you I had a heart condition. My heart's starting to bother me now. Get me out of here, please. My heart's starting to bother me. I refuse to go on. Let me out'	82.5% continue
180	Cries out, 'Ugh! I can't stand the pain. Let me out of here!'	80% continue
195	Cries out, 'Ugh! Let me out of here. Let me out of here. My heart's bothering me. Let me out of here! You have no right to keep me here! Let me out! Let me out of here! My heart's bothering me. Let me out! Let me out!'	80% continue
210	Cries out, 'Ugh! Experimenter! Get me out of here. I've had enough. I won't be in the experiment any more' (these appeals to be let out continue until 315 volts)	80% continue
270	Lets out an agonised scream and then shouts, 'Let me out of here. Let me out of here'	75% continue
300	Lets out an agonised scream and shouts, 'I absolutely refuse to answer any more. Get me out of here. You can't hold me here. Get me out. Get me out of here'	72.5% continue
315	Lets out 'an intensely agonized scream', then reiterates that he is no longer participating in the study and demands to be freed: 'I told you I refuse to answer. I'm no longer part of this experiment'	70% continue
330	Lets out an agonised scream, then shouts, in increasingly hysterical tones, 'Let me out of here. Let me out of here. My heart's bothering me. Let me out I tell you. Let me out of here. You have no right to hold me here. Let me out! Let me out! Let me out! Let me out of here! Let me out! Let me out!' (silent hereafter)	67.5% continue
375	Remains silent	65% continue to the end

administered to him?' the mean rating was 13.4 (on a 14-point scale, where 14 was 'extremely painful'). Milgram (1963, p. 375) further notes the signs of tension among teacher participants: 'Subjects were observed to sweat, tremble, stutter, bite their lips, groan and dig their fingernails into their flesh. These were characteristic rather than exceptional responses to the experiment.' While the prevalence of these behaviours is somewhat difficult to ascertain, these observations (as well as the slightly less common instances of nervous laughter) are borne out by documentaries relating to the obedience studies. Further evidence is provided by responses to interview questions and follow-up questionnaires that Milgram (2004 [1974]) reports. Milgram (2004 [1974], p. 48,) cites one teacher participant as reporting months later 'that he fully believed the learner was getting painful shocks'. Another teacher participant – who also demonstrated total obedience – is described as explaining in the interview, 'although he feels the shocks were extremely painful, he accepted the experimenter's words that they would cause no permanent damage' (2004 [1974], pp. 50, 51). Likewise, the minority of participants who disobeyed the experimenter demonstrated a belief in the experiment – some instances of which are caught in dialogue that Milgram reports, such as in Extract 10.1.

Extract 10.1

Participant R the man, he seems to be getting hurt.
Experimenter there is no permanent tissue damage.
Participant R yes, but I know what shocks do to you. I'm an electrical engineer, and I have had shocks . . .
Experimenter it is absolutely essential that you continue.
Participant R well, I won't – not with the man screaming to get out.
Experimenter you have no other choice.
Participant R I do have a choice. (Incredulous and indignant.) Why don't I have a choice? I came here of my own free will. I thought I could help in a research project. But if I have to hurt somebody to do that, or if I was in his place too, I wouldn't stay there. I can't continue. I'm very sorry. I think I've gone too far already, probably.

Source: Milgram (2004 [1974], p. 52)

Milgram (1963, p. 375) argues, 'With few exceptions subjects were convinced of the reality of the experimental situation, that they were administering shocks to another person, and the most potent shocks were extremely painful.'

Making sense of Milgram's findings

You might also wonder whether Milgram's findings were specific to men – perhaps men are more likely to be obedient, or aggressive, or both. While the majority of Milgram's obedience experiments involved entirely male participants, he did do experiments involving females – expressly for the purpose of checking whether the picture of obedience that he felt was emerging was gender-specific or not.

In Experiment 8, Milgram used 40 female participants. He found that, again (just as in Experiments 1 and 5), 26 out of the 40 participants (65 per cent) showed complete obedience, administering what they believed to be shocks to the limit of 450 volts. Milgram (2004 [1974], p. 64) reflects that 'The level of obedience was virtually identical to the performance of the men; however, the level of conflict experienced by the women was on the whole higher than that felt by our male subjects.'

Another alternative interpretation sometimes made regarding Milgram's findings is that what he really found was not obedience to authority but, rather, a high level of aggressive behaviour. As you can probably guess, Milgram devised a condition to specifically check this tendency.

In Experiment 11, the teacher participants chose their *own* shock level. If they had administered what they believed to be large electric shocks because of some disposition to aggressive behaviour, then, surely, in Experiment 11 – where they were able to select whatever shock level they wanted – a large proportion of teacher participants would rapidly gravitate towards the maximum 450-volt shock. In fact, in this condition, only 3 (7.5 per cent) went beyond 135 volts, compared to 39 (97.5 per cent) in Experiment 5 and 40 (100 per cent) in Experiments 1 and 8. Far from showing evidence of *higher* levels of shocks being administered, in Experiment 11, where teacher participants chose their own levels, only a single participant (2.5 per cent) used the 450-volt lever compared to 26 (65 per cent) in Experiments 1, 5 and 8. The evidence, then, points against some predisposition for participants to act aggressively as accounting for the shocks administered – when they could choose for themselves, the levels of shocks they administered were very considerably lower than when they were given instructions as to the levels to administer.

Prior to conducting the research, Milgram approached a number of Yale psychology students to ask them to estimate – having been given a description of the forthcoming studies – what proportion of people would be fully obedient. Milgram reports that the class mean was 1.2 per cent. This estimate of complete obedience (measured by participants administering the full 450 volts) was similar to that proposed in Milgram's (1963, p. 375) informal consultation with colleagues, who believed that 'few if any subjects would go beyond the designation "Very Strong Shock"'.

In Experiment 11, Milgram indeed found very low levels of shocking to the limit (administering 450 volts) because, as he would argue, the authority figure was not asking for any specific shock to be administered. Experiment 11, then, tells us about the effect of the absence of an authority's instruction, but it does not further specify what type of authority may result in lower levels of obedience than the (typical) figure of approximately 65 per cent of participants showing complete obedience.

In another variation (Experiment 13), Milgram investigated what would happen if 'an ordinary man' – rather than the experimenter – gave instructions to increase the voltage after each incorrect response. In this variation, the experimenter was called away (by means of a prearranged telephone call), having talked about administering shocks after incorrect responses – but not about what levels of shock should be administered. In the experimenter's absence, one of the participants (who was actually a confederate) suddenly announced that they thought the level should be increased after each incorrect response and insisted on this being followed throughout the experiment. In this condition, those obeying to the end dropped to 20 per cent.

In making sense of his startling findings, Milgram saw authority itself as crucial. Milgram reflects that a person who might be gentle and kind in everyday life could still – as a member of the military – follow orders to drop bombs on others with devastating effect. He argues that (2004 [1974], p. 148) 'In growing up, the normal individual has learned to check the expression of aggressive impulses. But the culture has failed, almost entirely, in inculcating internal controls on actions that have their origin in authority. For this reason, the latter constitutes a far greater danger to human survival.' Milgram's findings can be read as demonstrating just that, in Experiment 11 detailed above, where participants chose their own shock level, only one participant out of 40 (2.5 per cent) gave the full 450 volts, compared to 26 out of 40 (65 per cent) when the experimenter instructed them to administer increasing shock levels. This suggests that, left to their own devices, there is some limit on the administering of shocks that is far less present when in a situation where the participants are given orders. Milgram's findings considered above, however, suggest that it is not *just* orders from anyone that has such an effect. In Experiment 13, where a co-participant gave the order to increase the voltage (after the experimenter had been 'called away'), only 20 per cent of participants showed obedience to the end. Milgram argues that for high levels of obedience to occur, it has to be an authority giving the orders. The external behaviour of obedience was, for Milgram, brought about by a psychological change within the individual that was triggered and maintained by certain key situational factors.

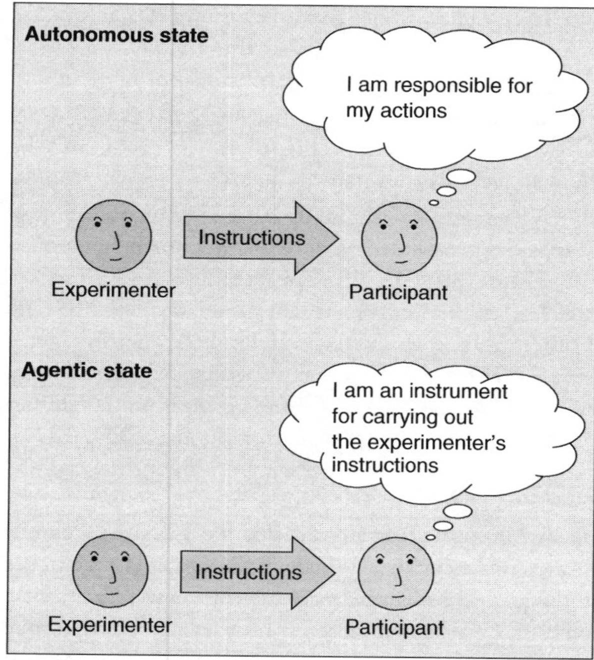

Figure 10.8 Agentic shift

Milgram's notion of the 'agentic state'

Milgram (2004 [1974], p. 135) understood the internal change that obedient participants experienced as a shift to the **agentic state**, in which a person 'no longer views himself as acting out of his own purposes but rather comes to see himself as an agent for executing the wishes of another person' (Figure 10.8).

Milgram draws on a combination of evolutionary theory and cybernetics in developing his notion of the agentic state. In terms of evolution, he argues mechanisms that facilitate individuals acting within a hierarchical structure can be seen as having evolutionary benefits – enabling

Agentic state Milgram (2004 [1974], p. 135) used this term to refer to a state in which the individual 'no longer views himself as acting out of his own purposes but rather comes to see himself as an agent for executing the wishes of another person.'

coordinated accomplishments, defence against external threats and the reduction of conflict within social groupings. Drawing on cybernetics, he suggests that, in order for an organism to function as part of a hierarchy, rather than autonomously, some shift is necessary from an autonomous mode of operating – this shift, for Milgram, is from autonomy to the agentic state.

One element of this shift involves the different way in which the person's conscience operates: 'when the individual is working *on his own*, conscience is brought into play. But when he functions in an organisational mode, directions that come from the higher-level component are not assessed against the internal standards of moral judgement. Only impulses generated within the individual, in the autonomous mode, are so checked and regulated.' (2004 [1974], p. 131). Milgram (2004 [1974]) further specifies that this is not so much a loss of conscience altogether, but a radical change. The individual's moral codes about the rights and wrongs of the behaviour they are engaged in are replaced with (or at least subdued by) a concern regarding the role that they are fulfilling in response to orders from an authority.

Milgram argues that, while in the autonomous state, individuals see themselves as acting on their own. In the agentic state, however, they see themselves as 'an agent for carrying out another person's wishes' (2004 [1974], p. 135). For Milgram (2004 [1974], p. 135) the agentic state can be understood as occurring when 'a self-regulating entity is internally modified so as to allow its functioning within a system of hierarchical control.' At a subjective level, the individual 'no longer views himself as responsible for his own actions but defines himself as an instrument for carrying out the wishes of others' (2004 [1974], p. 135). Milgram acknowledges that there is some degree of free choice regarding whether or not the individual defines themselves in this way, but situational factors can make it very likely that they do and, having done so, the possibility of redefining the situation is somewhat remote (unless the situation changes – for example, other participants start to rebel against the authority).

Milgram notes a number of situational factors that are likely to trigger and maintain the agentic state in individuals. First and foremost is the presence of a legitimate authority who issues orders that are consistent with their apparent remit. Assuming that there are no anomalies – such as rival authorities, others challenging or questioning the authority or clear questions about their legitimacy – there is a propensity to accept the authority. If someone viably presents themselves as such an authority figure, they may be readily accepted as such – especially if their appearance, manner and commands seem consistent with their authority status. For participants, finding themselves located within a physical space that appears to be within the authority's domain – the laboratory in the case of Milgram's experiments – further enhances the likelihood of obedience.

A further factor that is crucial to the triggering and maintenance of the agentic state is the definition of the situation in which individuals find themselves. Milgram notes, actions that can be seen as heinous from one perspective can be construed as warranted from alternative perspectives. In Milgram's experiment, the teacher participant pressing the lever on the shock generator could define their actions as 'administering a dangerous or even lethal shock' or 'following instructions in order to contribute to some important scientific research'. Milgram (2004 [1974], p. 147) notes the tendency for people to 'accept the definitions of actions provided by legitimate authority' and suggests that, 'although the subject performs the action, he allows authority to define its meaning'. Milgram (2004 [1974], p. 147) refers to this as 'ideological abrogation to the authority' and sees it as the main cognitive basis for obedience.

Milgram also notes some particularly important reasons for it being difficult to get out of obedience once we have entered into it. He draws on Goffman's (1959) ideas about how social situations and people's places within it are defined (implicitly) by those participating and any challenge to those definitions may be extremely uncomfortable for all involved. Thus, in a restaurant, there is a tacit agreement about who has the right to go through to the kitchen or sit and eat. Each time we visit a restaurant, our behaviour typically demonstrates an acknowledgment of this definition of who can do what in this setting. Imagine going to a restaurant and, just when the waiter or waitress comes with the pepper grinder, taking it from them and saying, 'I'll do that!' and grinding the pepper for yourself! Even to perform this simple breach would be incredibly difficult – and the regulation of it, the thing that stops us from doing it, is much more likely to be internal than external. That is, it is our sense of shame, awkwardness, embarrassment, our fear of causing offence that is likely to inhibit us rather than specific external consequences.

It is just this sort of self-regulation and concern with causing offence that Milgram argues stopped participants from disobeying the experimenter. To have disobeyed would have been to reject the experimenter's claims to 'competence and authority'. Milgram (2004 [1974],

p. 152) notes that participants were 'miserable at the prospect of having to repudiate the authority to his face'. He (2004 [1974], p. 152) mentions the paradox that this entails: 'It is a curious thing that a measure of compassion on the part of the subject, an unwillingness to "hurt" the experimenter's feelings, are part of those binding forces inhibiting disobedience.'

Indeed, the redefinition that disobedience entails raises problems for the participant's own behaviour. If their obedience up to that point is to be seen as willing participation in a legitimate experiment, then their own disobedience at any subsequent point challenges that self-definition. First, it involves changing from the role of willing volunteer and helpful participant to 'unhelpful' obstacle to the completion of the experiment (albeit for good reason). Second, if you are a participant who has obeyed and you suddenly decide to stop, you are recasting what you have done up to now as somehow questionable or less worthy than you previously believed it to be. By continuing to obey, you can stay with the more favourable definition that you are and have been following legitimate commands as part of an important scientific experiment and avoid the sense of painful realisation that your previous actions were misguided and caused harm to others.

When people disobey

Having considered the ways in which the situation may induce and maintain a state of obedience, it is worth noting that Milgram (1965a) investigated one important way in which the situation might support participants in their disobedience.

Across a number of experiments, Milgram investigated the impact that peers would have on the teacher participant's obedience. In these experiments, peers were – as far as the genuine teacher participant was concerned – others who volunteered to take part in the experiment. The three teachers in this condition had separate roles – reading the words, saying 'correct' or 'incorrect' to the learner's response and administering the electric shocks. The naïve (or genuine) participant was always allocated the task of administering the electric shocks (the only exception being Experiment 18, detailed in Milgram, 2004 [1974]). Milgram (1965a) had two variations of peer group influence – in one case it was resistant to the experimenter's orders and, in the other case, it was supportive.

The experiment proceeded as in Experiment 5, with verbal protests and screams at various pre-specified points. In contrast to earlier conditions, however, after 150 volts, one of the teachers (a confederate) rebelled and refused to participate in the experiment. At 210 volts, the second teacher (also a confederate) refused to continue.

In the original Experiment 5, at this point, only 8 teacher participants (20 per cent) refused to continue, but, with peer disobedience, 25 teacher participants (62.5 per cent) disobeyed. Similarly, whereas in the baseline Experiment 5, 26 participants (65 per cent) showed complete obedience, shocking to the limit of 450 volts, with peer rebellion, only 4 participants (10 per cent) obeyed by shocking to the maximum voltage.

In a further twist, where the two confederates teachers *obeyed* the experimenter and registered disapproval at any misgivings expressed by the naïve teacher participant, the impact was less dramatic. Against the baseline results of 26 participants (65 per cent) obeying the experimenter completely, the addition of peer pressure in *support* of the experiment continuing resulted in 29 participants (72.5 per cent) obeying the experimenter to the end.

One way of understanding these findings that introduce rebellious participants is that the rebels serve to initiate a redefinition of the situation, a challenge to the experimenter and question the legitimacy of operating in an agentic state. In reflecting on these findings, Milgram (2004 [1974]) notes that, in their act of defiance, the rebels provide an alternative way of making sense of the situation in which the participants find themselves. The rebels not only show that rebellion is possible but also their act of rebellion provides just the challenge to the definition of situation and the experimenter that the participants found so difficult to undertake themselves. Once others have, by their behaviour, challenged the definition of the situation as 'appropriate compliance to the justified demands of a legitimate authority', then the internal constraints on defiance are weakened. Then, an alternative definition of the situation – for example, that it involves 'unacceptable suffering and unreasonable demands to inflict pain' – is implied by the behaviour of the rebels. When *two* others rebel, there is actually a majority of others (two rebels to one experimenter) who implicitly define obedience within this situation as unacceptable and question the notion of trusting the demands of the experimenter. When a majority rebellion is achieved, it can be understood as seriously challenging the participant's acceptance of the experimenter's definition of the situation and, in consequence, the participant's *own* shift into an agentic state, where they see themselves as appropriately being a mere agent for the experimenter's wishes. [See Box 10.6 for a real-world example of disobeying those in authority.]

Box 10.6 IN THE NEWS
Libyan pilots who did not obey their orders

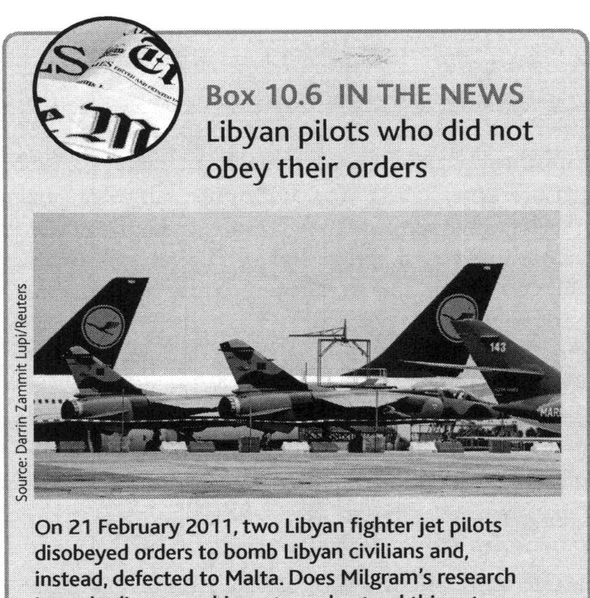

Source: Darrin Zammit Lupi/Reuters

On 21 February 2011, two Libyan fighter jet pilots disobeyed orders to bomb Libyan civilians and, instead, defected to Malta. Does Milgram's research into obedience enable us to understand this act of disobedience?

Critical review of Stanley Milgram's studies of obedience

Milgram's compelling studies have been questioned in a number of ways. One issue that Blass (1999) notes has intrigued a number of researchers is the extent to which gender influences levels of conformity. In a wide-ranging review of replications of Milgram's studies, Blass suggests that the vast majority of studies have concurred with Milgram's own findings (in Experiment 8) that the gender of the participant does not affect the level of conformity.

A second issue that Blass (1999) addresses is the idea that Milgram's high levels of conformity were a symptom of the time and culture in which they were conducted and, over time, conformity rates have decreased. Drawing on a range of replications covering more than 30 years since Milgram's original studies, he argues that there is no correlation between the date of the study and the level of conformity found. It could be noted, however, that seeking to correlate dates and conformity on a year-by-year basis could disguise the effects of larger changes across different eras. Furthermore, some of the vital ingredients that might shape obedience across time are not measured or reported. Indeed, Gergen (1973) argued that it was the increasing awareness of Milgram's findings that would make people less susceptible to authority influence, but this awareness is rarely measured or reported, making it difficult to ascertain whether just such a process is at work.

Finally, the levels of obedience varied massively in the studies, from 28 to 91 per cent, suggesting that some other significant factors are at work and raising the question of whether or not there was a like-for-like comparison over time.

A further issue that Blass raises regarding Milgram's findings is whether they are really about authority or expertise – do people obey the experimenter because they are *in* authority (in charge) or because they are *an* authority (that is, an expert)? Blass (1999) suggests that the evidence points to both as important, although some of it is drawn from the perceptions of those who did not participate in the experiment making a judgements about why the participants obeyed. This 'attributions of perceivers' evidence entailed participants watching an edited version of Milgram's documentary of his experiments, then rank ordering cards with different explanations for the participants' obedience. While this process resulted in expertise and legitimacy being given as the first and second most important reasons for obedience, the process may not tell us – if, indeed, we could ever know – what was important in the original participants' own perceptions of what it was about the experimenter that engendered obedience. Even if expertise was just as important as authority, however, it may simply question Milgram's emphasis rather than undermine his whole approach to making sense of his results. Indeed, Milgram (2004 [1974], p. 143) himself suggests that both expertise and authority are important, 'Because the experimenter issues orders in a context he is presumed to know something about, his power is increased.'

Russell (2011) undertook a careful review of Milgram's experiments that drew extensively on unpublished documents from Milgram's personal archive. Russell revealed the evolution of Milgram's ideas from early interests in national differences and group pressure on behaviour to his eventual focus on the obedience of an individual to the orders given by an experimenter. Of particular relevance for our current concerns is what Russell identifies as Milgram's development of 'strain-resolving mechanisms' – that is, features designed into the experiment that would reduce the 'strain' or tension that participants would experience in the act of inflicting harm on others, in order to maximise the likelihood of high levels of obedience. One such strain-resolving mechanism was to provide participants with a rationale for inflicting pain on others – rather than mere obedience, it was obedience within the context of a scientific investigation into human learning: 'By contributing to some greater good, Milgram had transformed the infliction of harm from "something evil" (shocking an innocent person) into something "good" (advancing human learning)' (Russell, 2011, p. 150).

This design feature does not 'invalidate' the experiments, but does raise questions about how the results of them are understood. In many accounts of Milgram's research, little, if any, attention is given to the role that the rationale of aiding scientific research into human learning may have played in leading to such high levels of obedience. Thus, the finding in Experiment 13 referred to above that only 20 per cent (rather than 65 per cent) of participants showed 'total obedience' to a co-participant giving the instructions, might be interpretable not just in terms of the 'authority' of the person giving the instructions – but also the weakening of the rationale that the increase in shocks to be administered was part of a serious scientific study. Similarly (as Reicher and Haslam, 2011, note), Experiment 10 yielded somewhat reduced levels of obedience (48 per cent) when the experiment moved from the scientifically credible Yale University to a purportedly commercial setting.

Once we do start to take into account the importance of the rationale, then, simplified understandings of the mere effect of authority alone are challenged. Also, the idea of an overarching rationale (perhaps even an ideology) become important in our accounts of apparent acts of obedience to authorities.

Finally, Reicher and Haslam (2011) develop a similar understanding within the framework of social identity theory. They suggest that participants may have come to see themselves as sharing some identity with the experimenter that the 'learner' (the supposed recipient of the shocks) did not share. Reicher and Haslam note that, in most experimental conditions, the experimenter and participant ('teacher') were physically located in a common space, while the 'learner' was separate and typically not visible (though, in most conditions, they were audible). In addition to occupying a shared space, there is the potentially more significant identity that the participant shares with the experimenter – of both being engaged with 'science' and 'scientific discovery'. From this perspective, both the participant and the experimenter may share a common identity within the experiment and common aims of being involved in scientific discovery. Objections from the 'learner' might thus be interpreted in the light of the participant's common 'part of scientific research' identity. With this (scientific) identity salient, the experimenter's instructions to 'continue' may have been adhered to because they appear to chart the course that is suited to the participants' identity in the experiment and the aims (scientific discovery) that are consistent with this identity.

Reicher and Haslam (2011) cite some dramatic evidence for this, arguing that both what can be gleaned from Milgram's original findings and a replication by Burger (2009, cited in Reicher and Haslam, 2011) suggest that, of the experimenter's four different prompts to continue, the one that was never adhered to was the one simply demanding obedience: 'You have no other choice, you must go on.' As Reicher and Haslam point out, each of the other prompts – , 'Please continue' or 'Please go on', 'The experiment requires that you continue' and 'It is absolutely essential that you continue' – do not simply demand obedience. They (2011, p. 167) note that the first of these prompts is a request, while prompts the second and third 'root the instruction in a scientific rationale' – that is, the needs of the experiment, which is the basis for shared social identity.'

What Reicher and Haslam offer, then, is the possibility of reconfiguring Milgram's findings as not simply being about an individual's act of obedience to an authority figure just because he demands obedience, but the importance of what is taking place in the active social identity of the one who is given instructions and the way in which requests that are consistent with or rooted in that identity are likely to be adhered to rather than ones which are not.

Critical recap

Stanley Milgram's studies of obedience

1 Milgram's studies have attracted numerous replications that Blass (1999) suggests are largely supportive. The rates of conformity have been found to vary enormously, however, – from 28 to 91 per cent, which raises the issue that some other factor (such as culture or precise operational details) may be especially important in determining obedience.

2 Blass (1999) also raises the point that there is a debate to be had regarding whether Milgram found a pure 'authority' effect or expertise was at work. That is, did participants obey simply because the experimenter was in authority – or was it because he might have been perceived as being an expert (what Blass refers to as 'an authority')?

3 Russell (2011) notes that Milgram developed 'strain-resolving mechanisms' – such as the scientific rationale for the research – yet these have often been ignored or downplayed in accounts of Milgram's findings.

4 Reicher and Haslam (2011) argue that Milgram's experiments can be reinterpreted in the light of social identity theory, with participants being understood as acting in accordance with their salient social identity rather than merely obeying instructions from an authority.

Box 10.7 IN THE NEWS
Prisoner abuse at Abu Ghraib

On 28 April 2004, the news broke regarding the abuse of Iraqi prisoners at the US military's Abu Ghraib prison. Images broadcast around the world showed naked Iraqi prisoners stacked on top of one another in a 'human pyramid', being pulled around on a dog lead, being tormented by vicious dogs and forced to perform sexually humiliating acts. Other images showed Iraqi prisoners hooded, forced to maintain a stress position while wired up to simulate receiving an electric shock. These, and many other images, were all the more disturbing because in each picture there would often be a member of the US military with a wide grin and each image was taken for 'entertainment' by another member of the military.

Stories about the torture, sexual abuse and, in some cases, killing of Iraqi prisoners in this (and other US and UK detention facilities) suggested that the broadcast photographs were indicative of widespread, serious prisoner abuse.

A number of trials of military personnel were conducted – particularly those whose involvement was documented by the photographs. One of these trials called on one of the most eminent social psychologists, Professor Philip Zimbardo, as an expert witness and this – and other trials – raised questions about what may have influenced these members of the military to engage in such horrific abuse.

Source: AP Photos/Press Association Images

A disturbing image of torture at Abu Ghraib – which some members of prison staff enacted and photographed. Does Zimbardo's Stanford prison experiment shed light on this behaviour? Should attention be paid to the ways in which these appalling actions relate to ideologies regarding the dehumanisation of others?

A number of people – including leading military personnel – explained these abuses in terms of the dispositions of the individuals involved – that is, a few 'bad apples' engaged in this appalling behaviour. Zimbardo (2007) notes that this type of blaming explanation can, to some extent, exonerate the situation and the wider context – indeed, it gets those responsible for the operation of Abu Ghraib itself largely 'off the hook'.

What features of the situation could be understood as influencing those who perpetrated such abuse? Was there some form of peer pressure that resulted in US military personnel following what others did – perhaps against their own better judgement? Could it have involved a minority influence in which a small number influenced others to behave in the same abusive manner that they themselves did? What role did orders from the military hierarchy have? Was the abuse somehow linked to the military personnel's sense of their role? In what ways might the wider system responsible for Abu Ghraib be responsible for the abuse within it? How might our very sense of who we and others are relate to such abuse?

These are precisely the questions that this chapter considers. In considering the different accounts that social psychologists have offered, it is worth coming back to real-life instances such as the abuse at Abu Ghraib to evaluate not just how well the theories explain specific experimental findings but also how they might explain the all too frequent real-life instances of the malign effects of social influence and power.

Reflective questions

1 *What does Milgram mean by 'agentic state' and what factors give rise to it? Can you think of a real-world example of a person or people being in this state? What were the consequences?*

2 *Why do people sometimes not obey those in authority?*

10.4 Professor Philip Zimbardo's Stanford prison experiment

In the literature reviewed so far, we have concentrated on social influence that has been brought about largely by co-present others. In the majority and minority influence experiments this typically involved two or more peers, in the obedience studies usually a single authority figure, sometimes aided or opposed by peers. We have briefly considered cases where the sources of influence might *not* be present – in two of Milgram's experiments the authority figure is not physically present and either gives instructions by phone or not at all, both of which result in substantially reduced levels of shocks being selected by participants. Zimbardo's work addresses the issue that sometimes, even in the absence of a group of peers exerting an influence or an authority figure giving instructions, people can engage in appalling behaviour towards others.

It is worth mentioning just how struck Zimbardo was (and is) by the dreadful acts that humans can commit against each other. (See Box 10.7 for an illustration of this.) Zimbardo (2007) notes some of the appalling atrocities that have occurred throughout human history. Leaving to one side those killed as a direct result of war, the twentieth century witnessed millions of individual people being 'systematically murdered by government decrees, enacted by soldiers and civilian forces willing to carry out the kill orders' (2007, p. 12) – just a handful of infamous genocides in the twentieth century left 1.5 million Armenians, more than 6 million Jews, 3 million Soviet prisoners of war, 2 million Poles, 20 million Russians, 300,000 Chinese from Nanking province, 1.7 million Cambodians, 100,000 Kurds and more than 800,000 Rwandans murdered. To these could be added the hundreds of thousands killed in the Namibian, Guatemalan and Bosnian genocides. With some horrifying details that will not be repeated here, Zimbardo illustrates just how disturbing the individual acts behind these figures really are. He illustrates how these and other acts of killing, rape and torture spared no one – adults, children, whole families, friends, neighbours and family members have all been victims of unspeakable acts of cruelty.

As if that is not disturbing enough, Zimbardo (2007, p. 15) cites Alison Des Forges of Human Rights Watch:

> The simplified accounts of genocide allow distance between us and the perpetrators of genocide. They are so evil we couldn't ever see ourselves doing the same thing. But if you consider the terrible pressure under which people were operating, then you automatically reassert their humanity – and that becomes alarming. You are forced to look at the situation and say, 'What would I have done?' Sometimes the answer is not encouraging.

It is these issues – the sickening inhumanity of human to human in institutionally sanctioned violence and the possibility that any one of us might engage in such evil acts – that Zimbardo now sees his Stanford prison experiment (SPE) as directly addressing.

What happened in the Stanford prison experiment?

If you had been a participant in Zimbardo's SPE you would have responded to an advertisement in a newspaper asking for volunteers to take part in a 'study of prison life'. You would have been offered 15 dollars a day, with the experiment due to last two weeks. You would have been randomly assigned to being either a prisoner or a guard. As one of the 12 guards, you would have been invited to attend an orientation day where the experiment would have been explained, your assignments allocated and suggestions about controlling the 'prisoners' without using physical punishment shared.

Zimbardo (2007, p. 55) reflects that he informed the guards, that while the prisoners were likely to not take the situation seriously, it was:

> Up to all of us as prison staff to produce the required psychological state in the prisoners for as long as the study lasted. We would make them feel as though they were in prison; we should never mention this as a study or an experiment.

In this orientation session, Zimbardo (2007, p. 55) also informed the guards that, while they could not use torture, they could create fear in the prisoners, create a sense of arbitrariness and lack of freedom:

> They will be able to do nothing and say nothing that we don't permit. We're going to take away their individuality in various ways . . . at no time will anybody call them by name; they will have numbers and be called only by their numbers. In general, what all this should create in them is a sense of powerlessness.

As a guard your next duty would have taken place on the following day, when the prisoners arrived. If you had been allocated to being one of the 12 prisoners, you would have been asked to make sure that you were at home on

Sunday 14 August 1971. Some time between 10 a.m. and about 2 p.m. there would have been a knock at the door and a genuine police officer in his uniform would have stood there, saying that he was going to arrest you for violating the penal code relating to either theft or burglary. He would have led you to his police car, frisked you and then put you into the police car and driven you to the makeshift prison. In many cases, neighbours looked on while these 'arrests' were made.

Arriving at the prison you would have been be blindfolded, led into the jail (named 'Stanford County Prison'), then ordered to strip and remain standing – arms outstretched against the wall and legs apart. If you wore glasses or took medication, these and all personal effects would have been removed and not returned for the duration of the experiment. You would have been left like this for some time before undergoing some 'delousing' procedure (being sprayed with talcum powder).

After enduring the guards making fun of your body, you would at last have been given your prisoners' uniform (a short woman's dress, to be worn with no undergarments), complete with a locked chain that would stay on your ankle for the duration of your time at the prison. Only after all of this had been completed would you have had your blindfold removed. As you looked around, you would have seen prison guards in uniforms, including sunglasses that obscured their eyes, brandishing batons and shouting out the prison rules. You would have been told that you must refer to each guard as 'Mr Correctional Officer' and to each other by number 'and number only'. You would then have learned that the cell lights, trips to the lavatory, receiving post and prison visits were at the guards' discretion. You would also have been informed that you must obey the guards' rules and failure to do so 'may result in punishment'.

Zimbardo (2007) notes that, initially, it was largely the prisoners' behaviour that was of interest to him, but, as the experiment progressed, some unexpected phenomena emerged. Within hours of meeting their fellow participants (who were randomly allocated to be prisoners), the guard participants began to display a sort of creative cruelty towards them. Initially, some of this involved the guards mocking the prisoners as they stood naked prior to acquiring their uniforms. Then it emerged in the 'count' – a procedure whereby prisoners were lined up and had to state their prisoner identification number in order. Prisoners were forced to perform push-ups and jumps if the guards did not approve of the way they called out their prisoner number or the way they stood to attention. Soon the demands became more arbitrary – for example, one guard demanded that prisoners sang their numbers and made one prisoner do multiple jumps for 'singing off key' and then more jumps because the prisoner's chain rattled when he did the first set of jumps. On that very first night, one guard yelled out to the prisoners, 'Did you enjoy our counts?' and one prisoner who replied, 'No sir!' was dragged out of the cell and locked in solitary confinement. This involved being locked in a cupboard known as 'the hole' – it was just 0.6 m (2 feet) square and was really made for storing a stepladder and a few cleaning materials. It could just about accommodate one prisoner standing up.

At 2.30 a.m. on the second day, when the prisoners were sound asleep, the guards suddenly let out loud shrieks from their whistles and shouted repeatedly at the prisoners to get ready for another count. For nearly an hour, prisoners were ordered to recite their prison identity numbers, with push-ups and jumps for any who were deemed not to have performed it to the guards' liking. Soon, two prisoners were made to share the dark, incredibly cramped conditions of 'the hole' and not allowed to eat breakfast.

Sensing some resistance from certain prisoners, the guards took all of the prisoners' blankets and dragged them through prickly undergrowth, leaving thousands of thorns in the cloth. When they were returned to the prisoners, they had to spend over an hour picking out the bits so that the blankets were usable.

When prisoners in one of the three cells started to barricade themselves in, the guards took the beds and clothes from the prisoners in another cell – leaving them naked and without beds. These prisoners then shouted out, 'This is an *experiment*! Leave me alone!', 'A f***ing simulation. It's a f***ing simulated experiment. It's no prison. And f*** Dr Zimbardo!' (Zimbardo, 2007, p. 61).

As one prisoner reached his hands pleadingly through the cell door bars, a guard violently smacked his club against the bars. The guards then used the 'skin chilling' carbon dioxide fire extinguisher to spray the prisoners so that they were forced back from the door.

When one prisoner refused to leave his cell, 'three guards manhandle him, throw him to the ground, handcuff his ankles, and drag him by his feet out into the yard' (2007, p. 62).

The guards created another solitary confinement 'hole' for 'rebellious prisoners'. One of the 'rebels' shouted out for Zimbardo himself: 'Hey, Zimbardo, get your ass over here!' Zimbardo (2007, p. 63) reflects that he decided 'not to intervene at this point but to watch the confrontation and the attempts to restore law and order.' Prisoners shut in solitary confinement shouted out that the rules had been violated (they were being kept there for far longer than was permitted), but to no avail.

In the days that followed, a 'divide and rule' tactic was frequently used, in which rebellion by any individual prisoner resulted in punishments for his fellow prisoners. That made it easier for the guards to exert enormous pressure on dissenting prisoners – often further exacerbated by getting all the prisoners to shout or chant abuse at the isolated prisoner. One prisoner, who was kept in 'the hole' for many hours on end, was given the chance to return to his cell if the other prisoners would sacrifice their blanket – which most, though not all, refused to do. When one prisoner refused to swear at another, the guards gave him persistent abuse and forced him to do press-ups with two prisoners sitting on his back. Prisoners were forced into sexually humiliating positions, pushed in 'the hole' while demanding to see a doctor and had food smeared into their faces if they would not succumb to forcefeeding. Even going to the toilet involved being marched there, chained together with a bag over their heads and often having their heads forced into the urinals.

Zimbardo's (2007) account is remarkably candid about how a blurring of lines between experimental simulation and reality was experienced by many – including himself. While some prisoner participants did leave early, he notes (2007, p. 69) how he had persuaded one prisoner – 8612 – to stay, mentioning the money that would be forfeited as a result: 'I had thought up the Faustian bargain on the spot. I had acted like an evil prison administrator, not the good-hearted professor I like to think I am.' He reflects, too, on how concerned he had become with a threatened 'break-in' (in which a former prisoner was to storm the prison with others), pleading with the police to transfer to a disused genuine gaol. Also, on one of the two prison visits permitted, he notes how he talked the parents of one prisoner out of having him removed from the study – despite his obvious signs of ill health.

Other officials within the study, similarly, seemed to treat the whole situation as real. Visits from a real prison chaplain, for example, were conducted with little if any differentiation between this experimental prison and real prisons. So, prisoners were asked if they wanted the chaplain to contact anyone on their behalf and he dutifully did so after leaving the pretend prison. Also, a mock parole board – involving fellow researchers and headed by the project consultant and former inmate, Carlo Prescott – took on a very realistic dimension, with those involved responding with not just the words but the emotional investment of a real parole situation.

Zimbardo notes that he halted the experiment on its sixth day – it had been scheduled to last for two weeks. Crucial to this early termination was the reaction of fellow researcher and partner Christina Maslach, who, witnessing the chained participants with bags over their heads being led to the toilet, recalls feeling 'sick to my stomach by the sight of these sad boys so totally dehumanised' (2007, p. 171). She told Zimbardo, 'What you are doing to these boys is a terrible thing!' After some initial reluctance, Zimbardo reflected that he and others had, 'internalized a set of destructive prison values that distanced them from their own humanitarian values' (2007, p. 171). Zimbardo – to the prisoner participants', and his own, delight – informed the prisoners that they were free the next morning. With considerable candour, Zimbardo (2007, p. 173) reflects:

> The power of this situation ran swiftly and deeply through most of those on this exploratory ship of human nature. Only a few were able to resist the situational temptations to yield power and dominance while maintaining some semblance of morality and decency. Obviously I was not among that noble class.

See Box 10.8 for a summary of the design of Zimbardo's experiment.

Making sense of the Stanford prison experiment

In making sense of Zimbardo's findings, it is worth first noting that Zimbardo and Haney had administered a number of psychological tests (the F-Scale, Comrey personality scales and a mood inventory, among others). These tests generally did not lend support to the idea that the guards behaved as they did because they were psychologically different from the prisoners – there were no significant differences. Nor did the guards or prisoners differ from the general population's norms – their profiles reflected the fact that all participants had been preselected on the basis of appearing 'normal' on a number of tests. Furthermore, the most abusive guards differed very little from the least abusive guards, with one exception – the two most abusive guards were highest and lowest on a scale that sought to measure how 'masculine' they were. For the prisoners, those who scored highest on 'rigid adherence to conventional values and a submissive, uncritical attitude towards authority' tended to survive longest as prisoners.

These results, collectively, do not therefore suggest that personality, mood or orientation to authority adequately explains the behaviour that became evident. A further indication that the situation – rather than the participants' relatively fixed personality traits – accounts for the findings is that much of the abusive behaviour on the part of the guards and resigned compliance on the

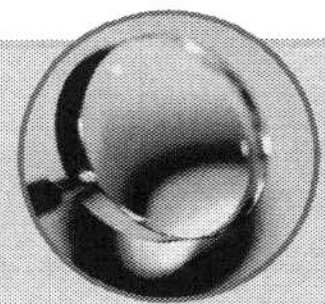

Box 10.8 FOCUS
Classic research: Professor Philip Zimbardo's Stanford prison experiment

In Zimbardo's Stanford prison experiment, participants were first allocated to being either prisoners or guards.

Those who were prisoners were dramatically arrested and taken to the simulated (but quite realistic) prison. Those who were guards attended an orientation session and worked at the prison in shifts.

Zimbardo endeavoured to include details that made the simulated prison environment as realistic as possible, so the rules, guards' uniforms and prison procedures were based largely on common prison practice at that time. Zimbardo (and his colleagues) were mainly concerned with observing the behaviour of the participants as it emerged within a relatively realistic prison environment, rather than introducing experimental manipulations or measures that might detract from the realism.

Allocated to being a prisoner

Arrested and imprisoned

Allocated to being a guard

Attend orientation day and work shifts

Figure 10.9 Participant in Zimbardo's Stanford prison experiment

What the experiment found was an extraordinary amount of violent and abusive behaviour – mainly on the part of guards towards prisoners. The levels of violence and abuse became so intense that Zimbardo stopped the experiment after six days rather than continue for the two weeks initially intended.

part of the prisoners became apparent as the experiment progressed rather than immediately. Thus, one guard reports apologising to a prisoner for pushing him on the first day and, by day four, thinking nothing of shoving and humiliating prisoners.

Zimbardo (2007, p. 211) argues that 'The primary single lesson of the Stanford Prison Experiment is that *situations matter*.' Indeed, he notes that we may be uncomfortable with just how much situations can transform individuals' behaviour. If we acknowledge that situations can effect such a massive change in individuals, then, tacitly we are forced to acknowledge that we, too, might be so affected – we, too, might abuse others over whom we have power. As Zimbardo (2007, p. 210) notes:

> The SPE, along with much other social science research . . . reveals a message we do not want to accept: that most of us can undergo significant character transformations when we are caught up in the crucible of social forces.

Specifically, Zimbardo posits that situations can engender dangerous behaviour where they present abusive or aggressive actions as permitted – via rules or the intervention of an authority – and separate from the actors' identity outside of that specific situation. That is, if someone feels they have been given permission to be abusive in a given situation (for example, because of rules or instructions) and if the situation enables them to see the abuse as linked to a specific role (such as being a guard) rather than to who they are outside of that situation, then they are quite likely to engage in abusive behaviour.

Roles

Roles emerge as one of the key factors that Zimbardo has stressed ever since first conducting the SPE in 1971 (Zimbardo, 2007). He suggests that the power of the role operated on both the guards (who became abusive in their exercise of power over prisoners) and the prisoners (who seemed to lose sight of both their freedom to leave the experiment and realities outside the mock prison).

As was noted above, Milgram saw authority figures as important in bringing about a loss of a sense of personal responsibility for one's actions. For Zimbardo, the role itself (even without a specific authority figure) could bring about some such reduced responsibility. The important point from Zimbardo's (2007, p. 218) perspective is

Role A coherent set of duties and expected behaviours often associated with a specific job, such as 'prison guard', or status, such as 'prisoner'. For Zimbardo, the roles we find ourselves in shape our behaviour in important ways.

that the role enables us to separate the actions we see as a playing out of our role from our sense of ourselves outside of that role:

> To the extent to which we can both live in the skin of a role and yet be able to separate ourselves from it when necessary, we are in a position to 'explain away' our personal responsibility for the damage we cause by our role-based actions. We abdicate responsibility for our actions, blaming them on that role, which we convince ourselves is alien to our usual nature.

In Zimbardo's account, the idea of distancing the actions from one's sense of identity outside of that situation is particularly important – and roles facilitate this because they allow us to compartmentalise different aspects of our behaviour as tied just to that specific role. Thus, the most abusive guards could separate their violent actions from their sense of self more generally, because the guard role enabled a rigid boundary between the activities seen as a part of that role and the rest of their lives. However abusive they may have been as a guard, they could assure themselves – and others – that this was a legitimate part of that highly specific (guard) role.

This provides a sort of two-way insulation – the morals and ethics of one's everyday self need not be seen as relevant to one's functioning in a separate, highly specific role and whatever one does in that clearly boundaried role need not be seen as relevant to one's sense of identity more generally.

One thing that makes Zimbardo's (2007) account particularly compelling is his reflection on his own behaviour transformation. Thus, he (2007, p. 218) notes:

> In retrospect, my role transformation from usually compassionate teacher to data-focused researcher to callous prison superintendent was most distressing . . . I did improper or bizarre things in that new, strange role.

Zimbardo goes on to illustrate how when a mother complained about the sorry state of her son, he challenged her, suggesting that if there were any problem it was a problem with her son, not 'his' prison.

Deindividuation

A second factor that has remained particularly important for Zimbardo in his reflections on the SPE is the idea of **deindividuation**. Prior to the SPE, Zimbardo had conducted an experiment that was a variant of Milgram's electric shock experiments. In Zimbardo's (1969) experiment, groups of four students were recruited to what they believed was a study of creativity under stress. They were informed that their job was to stress the two other participants, whom they could see, by administering a 75-volt shock, while the experimenter (who they could also partially see) administered a creativity rest. If any shock was administered, the two 'victims' (who were, as you probably guessed, actually confederates) acted as if they had received a painful shock.

Zimbardo found that those who were made anonymous (wearing large lab coats, hoods covering their faces and an identifying number) gave longer shocks than those who were not anonymous (wearing their normal clothes with large name tags).

For Zimbardo, the external situation of anonymity gave rise to an inner psychological state of deindividuation, in which the participants' sense of personal accountability for their behaviour was weakened. In this state, participants not only administered shocks that lasted longer than those given by the non-anonymous (individuated) participants but also they did not differentiate between victims they had previously reported they liked and those they had reported they disliked.

Zimbardo (2007) argues that the SPE was a further illustration of the power of anonymity giving rise to deindividuation and thereby weakening the individual's sense of responsibility for abusive behaviour. The reflective sunglasses of the guards, their military-style uniforms, their insistence on being referred to as 'Mr Correctional Officer' – these factors all made for the sort of anonymity that would, according to Zimbardo (2007), give rise to a deindividuated state.

Zimbardo (2007, p. 301) suggests that the destructive potential of the deindividuated state can be realised where violent, abusive behaviour is explicitly sanctioned:

> anything, or any situation that makes people feel anonymous, as though no one knows who they are or cares to know, reduces their sense of personal accountability, thereby creating the potential for evil action. This becomes especially true when a second factor is added: if the situation or some agency gives them *permission* to engage in antisocial or violent action against others.

The rules, and especially the roles associated with prison life, may have given the guards in the SPE exactly that sense of permission for the arbitrary and abusive exercise

> **Deindividuation** In the context of the research considered here, this refers to an inner psychological state in which the participants have a reduced sense of personal accountability for their behaviour and reduced awareness of themselves as individuals (see Chapter 9 for further discussion of deindividuation).

of power their deindividuated state made them especially susceptible to. Being less conscious or concerned about themselves as unique individuals may have made them enact the role more wholeheartedly without a sense of being personally responsible and, thus, with little if any restraint applied by their usual, individual, moral and ethical codes.

Dehumanisation

A third factor that Zimbardo (2007) notes in his recent reflections on the SPE is **dehumanisation**.

Dehumanisation describes the treatment (usually of others) as if they were less than human. Zimbardo (2007, p. 223) cites one of the guards as reporting, 'I made them call each other names and clean toilets out with their bare hands. I practically considered the prisoners *cattle*'. By thinking and talking of the other as an 'it' rather than a person, abuse was more easily justified and the restraints on harming another human being were reduced. Zimbardo (2007, p. 223) notes the destructive consequences of conceptualising the other as an object or non-human creature: 'Dehumanisation typically facilitates abusive and destructive actions towards those so objectified.'

Historically, it is all too easy to find examples of dehumanisation being linked to both localised and widespread abuse of others – thus, genocides from the Holocaust to Rwanda occurred in a context in which the victims had been consistently dehumanised. As noted below, dehumanisation could be seen as connected to aspects of Zimbardo's (2007) comments on the role of 'the System' in legitimating instances of the arbitrary, aggressive and abusive exercise of power.

The System

A final factor that Zimbardo (2007) raises is what he refers to as 'the System' – a concern with the people, institutions or authorities who have the power to design, maintain and justify the setting in which the behaviour to be explained occurs.

He notes that, for many years, he did not address 'system-level analysis' because the SPE was typically discussed in terms of situational versus dispositional determinants of human behaviour. That is, the SPE was drawn on to make the case for situations shaping behaviour in very profound ways – and to counter the idea of behaviour being determined by personality factors. Framed in these terms, much of the discussion of the SPE did not move to the issue of how the guards' abuse of prisoners could be traced to not just the roles, anonymity and dehumanisation arising within a given setting but also to the 'higher authority' that created and legitimised these features. In the case of the SPE, Zimbardo (2007) identifies *himself* as this authority, the one who created and sustained the situation in which the guards' abuse occurred. As he suggests, however, in more complex, real-life contexts, the matter is both more complex and more consequential.

As an expert witness in the trial of one of the members of the US military who had been involved in the abuse of Iraqi prisoners at Abu Ghraib, Zimbardo pointed out the responsibility of those (such as the military and political authorities) who did not enact the abuse directly themselves but brought about, maintained and legitimated the way in which the prison operated. Zimbardo thus highlights that, while the *situation* is of crucial importance in shaping behaviour, one should not neglect the system which has shaped, maintained and justified the situation and the responsibility it holds for any abuse occurring in it.

In discussing the power that systems have to allow situations to operate as they do, Zimbardo notes that validation often comes by means of some form of ideology or socially circulating views of the world which have implications regarding power. Thus, across the world, military aggression, the suppression of human rights and the abuse of detainees is all justified by reference to ideologies such as 'protecting national security', 'the national interest'. Indeed, Zimbardo (2007, p. 211) links such ideologies to the genocides and war crimes of recent history:

> The genocide and atrocities committed in Bosnia, Kosovo, Rwanda, Burundi, and recently in Sudan's Dafur region also provide strong evidence of people surrendering their humanity and compassion to social power and abstract ideologies of conquest and national security.

Indeed, the dehumanisation considered above could be understood as one aspect of an ideology – for example, Nazi ideology included dehumanising references to the 'Jewish virus'. These issues will be touched on again when attention is given to Foucault's perspective on power in the next section.

Thus, Zimbardo has made a sustained contribution to understanding social influence – particularly the crucial role played by situational factors – across a 40-year

Dehumanisation The representation of and treatment of others in a less than human manner. This could include dehumanising ideologies in which certain groups are represented as subhuman, as well as degrading behaviour where someone does not treat the other as a human being.

period. His work is uncomfortable, posing a profound challenge to how we think of ourselves and our capacity for evil (2007, p. 211)

> Any deed that any human being has ever committed, however horrible, is possible for any of us – under the right or wrong circumstances. That knowledge does not excuse the evil; rather it democratizes it, sharing its blame among ordinary actors rather than declaring it the province only of deviants and despots – of Them but not Us.

As noted above, in his most recent work, rather than simply stay with his original understanding of the SPE, Zimbardo (2007, p. 226) expands it to include new, broader, more systemic elements: 'The most important lesson to be derived from the SPE is that situations are created by *Systems*'.

Two elements of Zimbardo's work are perhaps worth critically reflecting on – first, a feature that was emphasised from the very beginning of his work – deindividuation – and, second, his recent emphasis on 'the System' and its ideological concomitants.

Critical review of Professor Philip Zimbardo's Stanford prison experiment

In its original form (Zimbardo, 1969), deindividuation was seen as inevitably releasing destructive impulses – indeed, the title of Zimbardo's (1969) paper suggests this: 'The human choice: individuation, reason and order versus deindividuation, impulse and chaos'.

Deindividuation – in its early form – suggested that anything promoting anonymity and, therefore, deindividuation resulted in the loss of self-regulation associated with being individuated, so giving rise to destructive, aggressive, unregulated behaviour. Because being in a group was thought to be one way of becoming anonymous (and, therefore, according to the theory 'deindividuated'), some commentators, such as Brown (2000a), have seen the idea of deindividuation as giving a very negative portrayal of group membership.

Challenges to this early conception came in the form of Gergen's (1973) finding that the anonymity provided by participants being grouped together in total darkness promoted physical displays of affection rather than aggression. Likewise, Johnson and Downing's (1979) work, rather than finding anonymity, inevitably gave rise to aggression, suggested that it increased participants' sensitivity to situational cues – where the cues were prosocial, then the behaviour that emerged was prosocial.

This last idea has been incorporated into Zimbardo's (2007, p. 301) latest reflections on deindividuation: 'If . . . the situation conveys merely a reduction of self-centredness with anonymity and encourages prosocial behaviour, people are ready to make love.'

Researchers developing the social identity theory, such as Brown (2000a, 2000b), argue against this revised position, too – at least as far as it attempts to explain the behaviour of people in groups. Brown (2000a, 2000b), instead, suggests that, in groups, rather than any loss of identity or increased situational susceptibility as a consequence of being anonymous, the behaviour of group members might be best understood as resulting from their *change* in identity, from their *individual* to their group or *social* identity (these issues are addressed in Chapters 2 and 9).

Postmes, Spears, Lee and Novak (2005) argue that anonymity can have markedly different effects depending on the type of group concerned. For groups that have a clear common identity, from which behavioural norms for individual members can be readily deduced (deduced identity), an increase in anonymity is associated with an increase in social influence. By contrast, for groups whose identity is induced from the behaviour of individual members (inductive identity), anonymity is associated with a decrease in social influence. From this perspective, what has been thought about as role-consistent behaviour might be reframed as social identity-consistent behaviour. Thus, the guards' and prisoners' behaviour in the SPE could be understood as consistent with their new social identities as guards or prisoners – had these identities been different, including a different repertoire of behaviours associated with that identity, then the behaviour of both guards and prisoners may have reflected that.

The idea that social identity is important in understanding behaviour in experiments such as Zimbardo's SPE is developed in the work of Reicher and Haslam (2006a, 2006b) (which was addressed in more detail in Chapter 1). They suggested the behaviour Zimbardo observed may have been shaped (in part) by the instructions given to the participants regarding how to behave as well as the impression the participants had that they could not leave – conditions which, for Reicher and Haslam, may have inhibited the development of a social identity among the prisoners.

In their own prison study (which Zimbardo, 2006, strongly criticises), Reicher and Haslam (2006a, 2006b) found quite different behaviour emerging – with prisoners directly challenging and overthrowing the authority of the guards because (from Reicher and Haslam's perspective) the conditions in their experiment had not inhibited the development of some of their participants' shared social identity as prisoners.

As noted above, Zimbardo's (2007) recent reflections include references to 'the System' and ideology. These wider aspects include the role of 'authorities' in setting up and maintaining the situations in which abuse occurs – for example, the political and military authorities responsible for creating Abu Ghraib and shaping how it was to operate – as well as the place of ideology in legitimising such abuse.

This very broad conception arguably introduces elements that were absent in earlier understandings of the SPE and provides a framework which seems more suited to approaching a range of destructive – institutionally sanctioned – behaviour. Thus, in reflecting on the Hutu militia's 'matter of fact' description of its terrible acts of murder and rape of Tutsi civilians, Zimbardo (2007, p. 15) notes:

> Their words force us to confront the unthinkable again and again: that human beings are capable of totally abandoning their humanity for a mindless ideology, to follow and exceed the orders of charismatic authorities to destroy everyone they label as 'The Enemy'.

It could be argued, however, that these ideas have been drawn on without considering how they relate to the literature on power and ideology or how they might reframe other ideas – such as individuation providing some measure of insulation from the social influence of the situation. It is precisely this reconfiguring of ideas of how the individual may relate to issues of relevance to social influence (such as 'norms' and 'codes') that is addressed in the next section, which touches on the work of Butler (2004) and Foucault (1985).

Critical recap

Professor Philip Zimbardo's Stanford prison experiment

1 Some of Zimbardo's work has suggested that the presence of others – including being in a group, especially where this allows for anonymity – can create a psychological state of deindividuation, where the individual loses their sense of their identity. Brown (2000a) argues that, in a group, the individual may experience a *change* rather than a *loss* of identity and the individual's behaviour need not become more destructive or impulsive.

2 Reicher and Haslam (2006a, 2006b) argue that Zimbardo's conditions may have inhibited the development of the prisoners' social identity, which, in turn, effected the observed behaviour (making the prisoners less 'resistant'). In a prison experiment that Zimbardo in turn criticises, Reicher and Haslam (2006a, 2006b) found substantial resistance from prisoners, which they explained in terms of their emergent social identity.

3 In his more recent work, Zimbardo (2007) suggests that 'the System' and 'ideology' have a role in shaping destructive role-consistent behaviour. Leading social theorists, however – such as Butler and Foucault – suggest that thorough engagement with these ideas can have far-reaching consequences. The work of Butler and also Foucault (touched on in the next section) suggests a very different way of configuring the relationship between the individual and phenomena that are related to 'social influence' – challenging the opposition of individual versus social influence that much of social psychology presumes.

Reflective questions

1. *How might deindividuation and role play a part in explaining the guards' behaviour towards prisoners in Zimbardo's experiment and real prisons?*
2. *What implications, if any, should the work of Zimbardo or Reicher and Haslam have for how we understand situations where guards are found to have abused prisoners (for example in Abu Ghraib)?*

10.5 Rethinking social influence and the individual

In much of the research considered in this chapter so far, (see Box 10.9 for an overview) social influence is positioned as a force acting on or against an individual. From this perspective, individuality is depicted as that aspect of self not touched by social influence and awareness of oneself as an individual as an important defence against 'external' influences.

Zimbardo's work illustrates these ideas particularly clearly. He suggests that being individuated or aware of ourselves as a distinct, unique individual – with all of the sense of personal responsibility for our actions that entails – is one of our best defences against the behaviour-shaping potential of certain 'all-encompassing' situations.

A number of quite distinct approaches to ideological issues provide radically different perspectives on social influence. Here, ideas from Foucault and Butler are briefly touched on to indicate some of the issues that

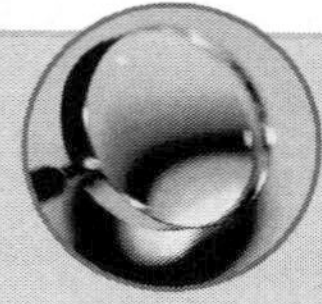

Box 10.9 FOCUS
Overview of the main types of social influence

Conformity

Asch's conformity experiments were particularly concerned with the influence of a majority of confederates (who appeared to be fellow participants or peers) on single participants. Asch was interested in the relative influence of conformity versus perception in judgements about unambiguous visual stimuli.

Minority influence

Moscovici's minority influence experiments were particularly concerned with the influence that a minority could have on a larger group. Several of the experiments involved testing for both the immediate and delayed effects of minority influence on visual perception (for example, colour judgements). Some subsequent research examined the effects that minorities might have on not just the topic of their influence but also associated attitudes – known as the 'spillover effect'.

Obedience

Milgram's obedience studies were particularly concerned with the influence not of a majority, or minority of peers but, rather, of an individual in a position of authority. Milgram was concerned with measuring obedient actions – participants doing (or not doing) what they were told – undertaken regardless of their objections or protestations. Milgram used many different versions of his basic experiment to identify the important factors in determining obedience and, in later research, considered what might happen if participants were exposed to an authority figure asking them to obey while two peers rebelled.

Situational factors – role, deindividuation, dehumanisation and the System

Zimbardo's Stanford prison experiment (SPE) investigated the effect roles (for example, of a prisoner or prison guard) – reducing their awareness of themselves as individuals (deindividuation) – had on participants' behaviour. ZImbardo was initially particularly interested in the very real aggression that seemed to arise when participants assumed their respective roles of prisoners and guards. In subsequent work, he has considered the importance of the dehumanisation of victims and how the System can legitimate abusive behaviour.

they raise for thinking about questions related to what we have called 'social influence'. Particular attention is given to some of the, perhaps, counter-intuitive ideas that Butler and Foucault propose about the relationship between what might be thought of as 'individuality' and the operation of power and influence.

Judith Butler: social norms as our horizon and resource

Judith Butler (2004) argues that there is a complex relationship between the individual person and social norms. Rather than simply suggesting that social norms constrain the person, Butler (2004, p. 33) argues for a complex relationship between the two:

> I have tried here to argue that our very sense of personhood is linked to the desire for recognition, and that desire places us outside ourselves, in a realm of social norms that we do not fully choose, but that provide the horizon and the resource for any sense of choice that we have.

For Butler, social norms are the very means by which people can come to recognise themselves and be recognised as having a life as an individual, human person. From this perspective, then, social norms enable the recognition of an individual, human life. At the same time that social norms provide a means by which the person can 'persist as a human' and have a recognisable 'individuality', however, they also limit what we can be.

Butler develops this idea with regard to her key idea about 'how one does one's gender', which was touched on in Chapter 2. She argues that there are potential ways of 'doing gender' that do not 'legitimately' or 'normatively' exist and, therefore, are not available as ways of being a *recognisable individual person*. Here, then, individuality is not the bulwark against normative or other types of what might be conceived as 'social influence' – instead, it is simultaneously constituted and constrained by it.

Michel Foucault: morality and practice of the self

In his *History of sexuality: Part two,* Michel Foucault (1985) develops a way of thinking about influence, or power, that equally reconfigures the idea that has been implied throughout this chapter – that of an *individual's interior world* (the separate, private, isolatable, individual self) being subject to the operations of *exterior social influence* (the influence of a peer group, an authority or external situations) and the *loss of part of the interior self* (responsibility for one's own actions or individual self-awareness).

From Foucault's perspective, if we were interested in, for example, how moral codes concerning sexual behaviour shape the behaviour of an individual, we would need to move beyond the notion of external peers or external authorities exerting influence on individuals and, instead, examine the very act of **formation of self**.

Using the case of sexual conduct (such as matrimonial fidelity) Foucault (1985) acknowledged that various 'prescriptive agencies' (such as family, educational institutions, churches and so on) could be important instruments in recommending values, codes of conduct and rules of action, but noted the importance of moving beyond these rather obvious 'influences' to consider what was taking place within the person and their sense of and formation of *self*. Foucault (1985, p. 29) identified the importance of:

> the way in which individuals are urged to constitute themselves as subjects of moral conduct [which involved] setting up and developing relationships with the self . . . self-reflection, self-knowledge, self-examination . . . the decipherment of self by oneself . . . the transformations that one seeks to accomplish with oneself as object.

Thus, the emphasis here is on how the person relates to themselves, forms themselves and develops practices for transforming themselves. From this perspective, the individual is operating on both themselves and the moral codes in question – they delimit the part of themselves 'that will form the object of [their] moral practice' (1985, p. 28), define themselves in relation to the codes or precepts and act on themselves, examine, monitor and reflect on themselves in relation to forming who they can, or should be, with regard to the codes in question. This, then, intricately binds together ways of knowing, being and practising *self* with moral codes. Viewed in this way, the dialectic 'code versus self' referred to above is challenged – instead, self-formation can be seen as enabled by moral codes (which shape how self is conceived, related to and acted on) and the moral codes themselves are, in turn, enabled by such self-formation.

Reflecting on Butler and Foucault

The work of Butler (2004) and Foucault (1985) touched on here has far-reaching consequences for how we make sense of power, influence and self, which have only been hinted at here. The particular strand that has been highlighted above – glossed in terms of rethinking social influence and the individual – is important because of the challenge it raises for prevalent conceptualisations of how social influence operates on, or against, the individual. While most of the research in this chapter has implicitly or explicitly pitted social influence against the individual, Butler and Foucault – in different ways – re-form that understanding, offering a self that is formed, enabled *and* constrained by the codes and norms that are culturally available.

From some perspectives, both Butler (2004) and Foucault (1985) may appear to be of limited relevance to social psychologists trying to understand social influence. The domain that they each sketch, the concepts that they develop, do not map simply on to those that are the focus of most of the social psychology of social influence. It would be misleading to suggest Butler or Foucault endeavoured to explain just the sort of phenomena that motivated Milgram's work, or their use of terms (such as Butler's, 2004, reference to 'social norms') maps readily on to the way in which Asch and others used such terms or, even, there *is* a common conceptualisation of what sort of thing we are referring to when we talk of social influence. Furthermore, notwithstanding Foucault's (1985) careful historical analyses, questions can be asked regarding the empirical evidence for the claims that both he and Butler (2004) make. While their writings have inspired an enormous amount of empirical work, their ideas may not be sufficiently empirically derived, developed, grounded or verifiable for some.

Both of these points should, perhaps, be approached with a degree of caution. It is in part the very fact that they configure the social world differently from much of the social psychology referred to in this chapter that enables them to offer such a radically different way of understanding issues of relevance to social influence – if the same terms carved up the social world in the same way, their radical alternative might not be possible.

With regard to the empirical base, the issue is not simply whether empirical evidence supports or refutes the ideas of Foucault and Butler, but rather if ideas at

Formation of self The processes of constituting self, which includes how we come to construct versions of who we are. For example, our sense of our gender, sexuality and what these categories mean are important parts of how we come to build up or construct versions of our selves.

this level, configured in these terms, *could* or indeed *should* be amenable to empirical verification. If the ideas are not verifiable, then this begs the question should this be considered a problem? If it is, then the danger is that this suggests we should avoid those types of meta-theoretical reflections which are not readily verifiable and, in consequence, social psychology may miss contact with the radical questions that such work can give rise to.

Critical recap

Rethinking social influence and the individual

1 It was noted that the work of both Foucault (1985) and Butler (2004), in different ways, provided a radical rethink of the way in which issues of relevance to social influence and the individual are conceptualised.

2 One criticism concerned the difficulties of assuming an easy fit between the concerns of Foucault and Butler and those of social psychologists concerned with social influence.

3 A second criticism concerned the relative lack of (conventional) empirical evidence to support the theoretical understandings that both Foucault and Butler develop.

4 It was noted that some of the originality and challenge of Foucault's and Butler's ideas may each rest on their different ways of conceptualising the issues of relevance to social influence that they address. Furthermore, the scope of their ideas may render them less readily amenable to conventional empirical verification.

Reflective questions

1 *In what ways might your very sense of individuality exert an 'influence' on you?*

2 *What, if anything, does the work of Butler and Foucault offer to the social psychology of social influence?*

Summary

- This chapter has reviewed work concerning social influence and intragroup processes. In doing so, it addressed the work of some of the most famous social psychologists, such as Asch, Moscovici, Milgram and Zimbardo.
- Asch's work revealed that in simple, clear-cut, visual perception tasks, participants would sometimes give a wrong answer to conform to the majority judgement. Thus, participants would, in about one-third of the trials, call out an obviously incorrect line length judgement, apparently just because a majority of others called out the same incorrect answer. For Asch, this was, almost invariably, merely a 'public show' of conformity – the participants knew that the answer they were giving in these trials was incorrect.
- Asch's research can be questioned in terms of how widely applicable such visual perception studies are – does conformity work in the same way for participants' opinions or behaviour, for example? Furthermore, there is an issue about how these studies have been interpreted. Does the fact that about one-third of participants conformed to incorrect majority responses really show conformity or non-conformity?
- Moscovici also used visual perception experiments – this time colour judgements rather than line lengths. Moscovici found that, in some cases, the minority could influence the majority and where the minority influenced participants' judgements, the influence was longer-lasting, suggesting they had caused a real change in judgement rather than a mere 'show' of agreement.
- Moscovici's work can also be critiqued in terms of it relying on visual perception judgements. Related work investigating minority influence using opinions about 'real social issues' (Alvaro & Crano, 1997) suggests a spillover effect, in which the minority has a long-lasting influence on issues related to the specific target message that participants are exposed to.
- Milgram's dramatic series of studies suggested that actual behaviour could be influenced by an authority figure who was perceived as legitimate. Milgram suggested that where the authority figure and the situation are seen as legitimate, then participants can enter the 'agentic state', in which they no longer see themselves as responsible for their own actions but, instead, as responsible for following orders as a tool or agent of the authority figure.
- Milgram's research was questioned in terms of the varying levels of obedience found in replications – some have found markedly lower rates of obedience, others very much higher rates. Blass (1999) questioned whether perceived 'expertise' rather than 'authority' alone was a factor in engendering obedience. Milgram's research also raises the question of whether or not social influence can operate in the absence of direct instructions from an authority figure. Russell (2011) and Reicher and Haslam (2011), in different ways, raise questions about the way in which the rationale that participants were given (taking part in a scientific study of learning) may have shaped their identity and their behaviour (rather than the results being due solely to the simple effect of an authority figure giving orders).

- Zimbardo's research suggests that social influence can take place even in the absence of an authority figure – or even direct instructions – as the roles in which people find themselves can shape individual behaviour. Zimbardo's famous Stanford prison experiment painted a vivid picture of prison guards abusing their power and prisoners – and prisoners largely complying. Zimbardo understood the abusive behaviour as coming about because the guards interpreted it as consistent with their role, which was further reinforced by prison rules and instructions given by those in charge of the prison. Zimbardo also saw the state of deindividuation – where participants were less aware of themselves as individuals – as increasing their susceptibility to enact what they perceived to be role-consistent behaviours. Zimbardo additionally suggested that dehumanisation of the victim – which may be supported by systems of power or ideologies – could further encourage abuse to be perpetuated.
- Zimbardo's work can be criticised in terms of how it approaches deindividation. Some (such as Brown, 2000a, 2000b) suggest that, in group situations, identity is changed rather than lost. Reicher and Haslam (2006a, 2006b), who found much more resistant prisoners in their study, argue that when social identity is allowed to flourish, it can shape the behaviour which is manifest. Furthermore, some social theorists – such as Foucault and also Butler – have developed an understanding of power and influence-related phenomena as far less external, seeing them as linked to the ways in which self is understood and formed.
- Finally, the work of both Butler and Foucault was briefly considered. In particular, the case was made that these differing theoretical positions provide the resources for questioning the relationship between social influence and the individual. Rather than the two being in potential or actual opposition to one another, both Foucault and Butler allow for a more complex understanding where *even self-formation* may be enabled and constrained by norms and codes that we might associate with 'social influence'

Review questions

1. *Did Asch find evidence for conformity or non-conformity in his experiments?*
2. *What are normative, informational and referent informational influences?*
3. *In what ways did the influence found in Moscovici's minority influence research differ from that found in majority influence research?*
4. *What is the spillover effect of minority influence?*
5. *What does Milgram mean by referring to a shift in agentic state?*
6. *What experimental manipulations were most significant in Milgram's research?*
7. *What factors does Zimbardo identify as accounting for the findings in his Stanford prison experiment?*
8. *What is ZImbardo's stance on the idea that situations shape behaviour?*
9. *What are the key differences between the main approaches covered in this chapter?*
10. *What are the ethical issues involved in research into social influence?*
11. *How has social psychology conceptualised the relationship between the individual and sources of social influence? What alternative ways of making sense of this are possible?*

Recommended reading

Butler, J. (2004). *Undoing gender.* Abingdon: Routledge. A remarkably sensitive and applied development of Butler's profoundly important work.

Haslam, S. A., & Reicher, S. (2007). Beyond the banality of evil: Three dynamics of an interactionist social psychology of tyranny. *Personality and Social Psychology Bulletin, 33*, 615–622. A paper that critiques the idea of evil actions emerging from a lack of 'care or choice' and instead emphasising the importance of group identification and the normalisation of oppression.

Milgram, S. (2004 [1974]). *Obedience to authority: An experimental view.* New York: Pinter & Martin. A fascinating and detailed presentation of data relating to Milgram's series of obedience experiments.

Postmes, T., Spears, R., Lee, A. T., & Novak, R. J. (2005). Individuality and social influence in groups: Inductive and deductive routes to group identity. *Journal of Personality and Social Psychology, 89*, 747–763. An interesting further specification of the way in which anonymity and depersonalisation may have different social influence consequences for group members depending on the nature of their group.

Reicher, S., & Haslam, S. A. (2006a). Rethinking the psychology of tyranny: The BBC prison study. *British Journal of Social Psychology*, *45*, 1–40.

Reicher, S., & Haslam, S. A. (2006b). Rethinking the psychology of tyranny: The BBC prison study. *British Journal of Social Psychology*, *45*, 55–63.

Reicher, S., & Haslam, S. A. (2011). After shock? Towards a social identity explanation of the Milgram 'obedience' studies. *British Journal of Social Psychology*, *50* 163–169. An initial, social identity-informed, response to the unprecedented access to Milgram's personal papers relating to his obedience experiments, reported in Russell (2011).

Russell, N. J. C. (2011). Milgram's obedience to authority experiments: Origins and early evolution. *British Journal of Social Psychology*, *50*, 140–162. An interesting and detailed investigation of many of Milgram's personal documents relating to his famous series of experiments.

Zimbardo, P. (2006). Commentary – On rethinking the psychology of tyranny: The BBC prison study. *British Journal of Social Psychology*, *45*, 47–53.

Zimbardo, P. (2007). *The Lucifer effect: How good people turn evil*. London: Rider. An insightful, honest and, in places, deeply disturbing account of the power of situations to shape human behaviour.

The following three references (referred to and recommended in Chapter 1 also) are papers relating to the debate between Reicher and Haslam on the one hand and Zimbardo on the other.

Useful weblinks

The following websites are grouped according to the work on social influence that they exemplify or address.

Overview of key social influence studies

www.integratedsociopsychology.net/milgram_experiment.html A useful overview of several key studies in social influence.

Asch

www.bbc.co.uk/radio4/science/mindchangers1.shtml A radio programme examining Asch's experiment.

www.youtube.com/watch?v=TYIh4MkcfJA&feature=related Asch's conformity experiment. This clip is better than some on the Web and gives a nice glimpse of how the experiment looked, but needs to be approached with caution. The commentary is a little misleading in places – for example, it 'voices' the supposed thoughts of the participant and claims at one point that the participant 'genuinely believes that the group is correct'. Asch does not make this claim.

Milgram

www.stanleymilgram.com A useful overview of Milgram's life and work with links to some related research.

Zimbardo

www.lucifereffect.com/index.html A website relating to the book of the same title and providing news links and updates related to the Stanford prison experiment.

www.zimbardo.com/zimbardo.html A great resource for Zimbardo's publications.

www.ted.com/talks/philip_zimbardo_on_the_psychology_of_evil.html An interesting talk by Zimbardo about how situations can make people 'become evil' (does include some disturbing images).

www.prisonexp.org This provides a very useful overview of Zimbardo's famous prison experiment.

www.youtube.com/watch?v=Z0jYx8nwjFQ&feature=related An overview of Zimbardo's famous Stanford prison experiment.

Reicher and Haslam

www.youtube.com/watch?v=ZaXXqrUzKHw An overview of Reicher and Haslam's prison study.

Foucault

www.dailymotion.com/video/x32axv_chomsky-vs-foucault-1971_politics This televised extract does not reflect some of Foucault's later thinking referred to in this chapter, but is interesting nonetheless as both he and Noam Chomsky raise critical points regarding the distribution and structure of power in society.

www.michel-foucault.com/index.html A useful overview of Foucault's work.

Butler

The following websites, referred to in Chapter 3 also, provide a useful introduction to the work of Judith Butler.

www.youtube.com/watch?v=Q50nQUGil3s A French documentary featuring extensive interviews with Judith Butler.

www.theory.org.uk/ctr-butl.htm A great resource for approaching the work of Judith Butler.

11

Communication and interaction

Learning outcomes

By the end of this chapter you should have a critical understanding of research concerning how talk, gesture and body movement can:

- reveal the emotions of a speaker by means of unintentional non-verbal 'leakage' or facial displays
- convey information to others by both verbal and non-verbal means
- display the level of intimacy between people and regulate or change it
- display group affiliations and identities and vary their salience
- accomplish interactional work, such as getting the attention of the person addressed, indicating who should speak next or giving account for one's actions.

In August 2009, a video (http://politiken.tv/nyheder/indland/article787913.ece) appeared on YouTube in which a Danish woman holding a baby gave a personal account of having met the baby's father one night when he visited Denmark. In the video clip the woman talked about her desire to meet the father again and appealed to him to get in touch. The video attracted nearly a million hits before it emerged that it was entirely fake – the woman was an actress and had been recruited to deliver her scripted appeal by the Danish tourist board.

Take a moment to watch the video – is there any way that you can tell this is not genuine? More specifically, is there anything about the woman's communication – such as her eye gaze, body movement, tone of voice or her words that indicates it is fake? Does being an actress mean that she is able to mask indications that this is fake in a way others cannot – if so, what are those indicators?

Source: Photolibrary.com

The Little Mermaid is a famous and non-controversial symbol of Denmark. Controversy arose, however, when *Visit Denmark* used a clip of a mother and child appealing to an absent father as part of the tourist board's strategy. Would you have spotted something unusual about that clip?

The social psychology of communication raises the possibility of identifying signs of what people really think and feel when they communicate, but can it meaningfully contribute to the detection of false communications? Are there problems with the research underpinning these ideas and, perhaps more fundamentally, is this the aspect of communication that social psychology should focus on or should communication (and interaction) be approached in a very different way?

Introduction

If we think of social psychology as concerned with understanding what happens when people meet people, then, at its heart, lies communication and interaction. The issues addressed in this chapter are so fundamental that they have received considerable popular attention. Think for a moment about any reasonable-sized bookshop – it is highly likely that there will be books about 'non-verbal communication' and 'body language'. Look at the TV schedules for the week – even though some reality TV shows may have lost their appeal, there will almost certainly be several programmes that focus mainly on showing people talking, eating and otherwise interacting with each other.

In addition to popular culture, we can see how technological development has, in part, been driven by concerns with communication and interaction. Indeed, new technology, far from reducing human interaction, has almost certainly increased it globally – albeit via different media – enabling communication and interaction by means of texting, sending e-mails, tweets and postings on Facebook.

Chapter overview

This chapter outlines some key concerns in social psychological research into communication and interaction and, in so doing, stitches together research traditions that represent markedly different approaches to social psychology. If you are able to understand, question and contrast the approaches within this chapter, you will be very well equipped for tackling any aspect of social psychology.

The first approaches that are considered are among the most widely cited aspects of social psychology and concerned with the way that our facial expressions and tone of voice may indicate – perhaps unintentionally – our 'real' feelings. Have you ever felt that you could read what someone was feeling from their face alone? Perhaps you have sometimes not trusted the words someone has said to you because their tone of voice suggested that they were insincere. It is exactly these issues of non-verbal leakage that a range of highly influential social psychological experiments have investigated.

A somewhat less well-known research tradition concerns the way in which non-verbal communication in particular may be important in conveying information. Have you ever felt the need to gesticulate when trying to describe something? It may be that your gestures are conveying information in addition to that which is available in your talk alone. Some of the research reviewed in this area suggests that both words *and* gestures are important in communicating information and, consequently, more information is communicated when both gestures and words are used rather than words alone.

The third area examined concerns the way in which our communications can not only express but also regulate our level of intimacy. What is it that enables us to tell – from conversation alone – whether two people sitting near to each other on a train have an intimate or more distant relationship. Some of the research reviewed suggests that non-vocal features, such as mutual gaze, are important, while other research emphasises the content of the talk – for example, the amount of personal disclosure. Rather than just presenting a static picture of the relationship, however, these aspects of verbal and non-verbal behaviour have been understood as helping to shape whether the relationship increases or decreases in intimacy.

The fourth area addressed examines the way in which talk is linked to identity issues. One example of this is found in the case of accents. Just imagine spending a day speaking in a different accent from your usual one. It is likely that your behaviour would attract at least as much comment as radically changing the way you dressed. If we study accents carefully, we may discover that they do, in fact, change – albeit subtly – and some sociolinguistic research suggests that, in changing their accent, the speakers align with some identities and disalign with others. Identity can also be studied from the perspective of discursive psychology, where specific identity talk can be investigated in terms of what the talk is doing in the interaction. Think about how claiming to be hopeless at remembering things might be a way of exonerating yourself for forgetting someone's birthday.

This idea that talk can be examined in terms of the interactional work that it does is considered in more detail in the final section of this chapter, which examines how we do interaction. Here, particular attention is paid to where a given verbal or non-verbal behaviour occurs in an interaction, or, its *sequential context*. The conversation analytic work reviewed considers how attention to sequences of interaction can reveal how even seemingly irrelevant aspects of speech – such as perturbations and restarts – can accomplish important interactional work, such as getting the recipient to attend to the speaker. This section also considers the relevance of a sequential orientation for research into interactions involving those deemed to be 'communicatively impaired'.

11.1 Expressing attitudes and emotions

If you walk into any bookshop that has a psychology section, you will almost certainly find books about non-verbal behaviour. Many of these books try to decode facial expressions, **mutual gaze**, body movements and gestures to reveal what people are 'really' thinking. A quick search on the Internet will reveal many communication consultants making claims such as, 'People sometimes lie, but their body language always tells the truth!' For example, if people gaze to the right, scratch their neck, filter their talk through their fingers, pull their ear lobe and shuffle awkwardly while talking they are – as well as being remarkably dextrous – taken to be lying according to many popular approaches to **body language**.

These popular ideas can be seen as related to academic work on the ways in which non-vocal channels of communication can reveal truths via **non-verbal leakage**. This popular idea is that non-verbal channels – our tone of voice, gaze, gesture and body movements – *unintentionally* communicate our true attitudes and emotions – even when we attempt to conceal these in our talk and behaviour.

Non-verbal leakage is thought to occur because, in general, we are thought to be better able to control the words we use than all of the potential non-verbal channels of communication. To take one famous example, in 1998, Bill Clinton famously stated, 'I did not have sexual relations with that woman. Miss Lewinsky'. – a version of events that was challenged by subsequent DNA evidence. Watch the video clip (at: www.youtube.com/watch?v=gV6yhEbEw9c) and see whether you think Clinton shows signs of non-verbal leakage or, being an accomplished politician, has he learned to inhibit such cues. See Box 11.4 for a further example of talk that has been subsequently seriously challenged.

Mutual gaze Where people in an interaction are gazing at each other in the region of the eyes.

Body language A popular term, typically used to refer to gaze, gestures and body movements as reflecting your thoughts and feelings.

Non-verbal leakage The idea that our 'true' feelings are expressed through our non-verbal channels because they are less easy to control than words themselves.

Social psychological research is often cited as supporting these ideas and drawn on to suggest that non-verbal behaviour better reveals our true attitudes and emotions than talk. In this section, attention is paid to some of the most popular social psychological research in this area. In investigating these classic studies, careful consideration is given to what the various findings *actually* tell us, rather than just the popular *interpretations* of what they say. The section begins by considering research that has tried to pitch verbal and non-verbal channels of communication against each other, to see what participants tend to rely on to work out speakers' attitudes or emotions. Attention then turns to work that has considered the facial expressions of emotions.

On 21 November 1989, television cameras were allowed into the UK's Parliament for the first time – meaning that MPs would be seen as well as heard. As MPs debated the televising of Parliament, one made a speech about the importance of non-verbal behaviour. The speech contained seemingly extraordinary claims regarding the importance of non-verbal communication in accounting for the impact of what we say. Thus, it was claimed that our facial expressions account for 55 percent while the actual words we use, only 7 per cent. Though surprising, these figures were not just plucked from thin air – they were actually citing the work of Mehrabian and colleagues, social psychologists who undertook some of the most popular and widely cited research into communication (Mehrabian & Ferris, 1967; Mehrabian & Weiner, 1967).

Albert Mehrabian

Albert Mehrabian was interested in the relative importance of the words used (verbal communication) and features of their delivery (**non-verbal communication**) – in particular, facial expression and tone of voice. For Mehrabian, the question was, which would be relied on to convey the liking or disliking of the speaker – the words used, tone of voice or facial expression?

It may be worth stopping to think for a moment – have you ever met someone who seemed unfriendly towards you even though you cannot pinpoint anything rude or unfriendly that they actually said? Perhaps their unfriendly facial expression, the tone of their voice or lack of eye contact made you feel that they were unfriendly despite any friendly words – for example, 'nice to see you' – that they may have spoken. Mehrabian's studies (see Box 11.1) sought to address this issue by examining how much people would rely on the actual words spoken as compared to tone of voice and facial expression when forming judgements about whether or not the speaker conveyed liking.

As Beattie (2003, p. 26) notes, Mehrabian produced the first studies that 'attempted to say exactly how much the verbal and non-verbal channels each contribute to the communication of interpersonal attitudes'. Mehrabian's findings seem so clear-cut and striking that it is hardly surprising they have had such a marked impact on popular culture (being regularly cited in advertisements, magazines, popular psychology books and on websites). Certain interpretations of these results – in particular, the idea that the words we utter only account for 7 per cent of the impact of what we say – are particularly prevalent.

Even before we consider the empirical limitations of Mehrabian's research, however, there are problems with interpreting the studies as being about the *actual* impact, power or importance of verbal versus non-verbal behaviour. The design of the studies only allows researchers to investigate the channels of communication that participants would use when being required to judge the speaker's 'liking' in a situation where very limited information was available. In this sense, in their very design, they addressed the issue of what channel participants rely on when requested to judge speaker liking in the light of sometimes contradictory verbal and non-verbal channels. This is not quite the same as asking a related but much more global question – which channel is more powerful, impactful or important?

When we consider the detail of Mehrabian's research, it is apparent that there are various ways in which it differs from situations that normally occur in everyday life – that is, it appears to lack ecological validity. Just two of these – identified by Beattie (2003) – are raised here. Other problems, which remain an issue for important research that followed Mehrabian, are addressed subsequently.

Beattie (2003) argues that Mehrabian's experiments are so unlike communication in everyday life that they may tell us little about the importance of verbal and non-verbal channels in real-life interactions. To appreciate this, it may be useful to reflect for a moment on certain key features of the experiments. In Study 1, the utterances to be judged were a series of single words, and in Study 2, facial expression was conveyed by presenting a photograph alongside an audio recording. Now try to think of

Non-verbal communication Every aspect of communication, apart from the words themselves – that is, style of talk, eye gaze, gesture and body movement. These modes of communication are sometimes referred to as non-verbal channels.

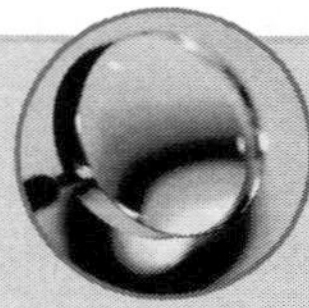

Box 11.1 FOCUS
Classic research: Non-verbal communication experiments (Mehrabian & Ferris, 1967; Mehrabian & Weiner, 1967)

Mehrabian and colleagues conducted two particularly influential studies that sought to pitch verbal communication against non-verbal communication.

Study 1

In his first study, Mehrabian sought to investigate whether tone of voice or the actual words uttered would have the most influence on participants, judgements of how much the speakers conveyed that they liked the participant. A particular interest was in how the participants would make such judgements, when the word uttered and tone of voice appeared to be contradictory.

Mehrabian and Weiner (1967) used nine words – three thought to convey liking ('honey', 'thanks' and 'dear'), three 'neutral' ('maybe', 'really' and 'oh') and three that were assumed to convey disliking ('don't', 'brute' and 'terrible'). Two female speakers read each of the nine selected words using positive, negative or neutral vocal expressions, then participants had to rate the extent to which the speakers communicated 'liking' for each delivery.

In Study 1, it was tone of voice that determined participants' assessments of the speaker's liking. Almost regardless of the words being uttered, the vocal expression (positive, neutral or negative) appeared to determine the participants' ratings of the speaker's 'liking'.

Study 2

In a second study, Mehrabian and Ferris (1967) focused their attention on one overtly neutral word – 'maybe' – and the impact of the speakers' facial expressions on participants' judgements about how much the speakers communicated that they liked the participants. The participants were shown a photograph of the speaker uttering the word 'maybe' – the facial expression shown being either positive (attempting to convey liking), negative (attempting to convey disliking) or neutral. Participants were again required to rate the extent to which the speaker communicated 'liking' – this time, for each of a series of photographs of the speaker saying the word.

In Study 2, it was found that, although the actual word uttered was neutral ('maybe'), participants' judgements of the speaker's liking varied with the facial expressions that were presented in the photographs. When the facial expression was warm and friendly, the speaker was judged to have *a more liking attitude* than when the facial expression was neutral or hostile.

Across the two studies, it would have been thought possible beforehand that words would be found to influence the judgements of liking just as much as facial expression and tone of voice – or even that words would prove *more* influential than these non-verbal features of communication – but this was not the case. Mehrabian's findings were seemingly unequivocal in displaying the *pre-eminent importance of non-verbal behaviour in communicating 'interpersonal attitudes'* such as liking. Mehrabian expressed this numerically, too, arguing that, for the communication of interpersonal attitudes, the facial and vocal channels are very important – accounting for 55 and 38 per cent, respectively, of the total impact on participants' judgements. Mehrabian further reported that words themselves – or the verbal channel – only accounted for 7 per cent of the total impact on participants' judgements of speakers' interpersonal attitudes.

any non-experimental interactions in which you communicated using just single words. If you can think of any, the interaction is likely to have been highly unusual – perhaps a game of some sort. If vocal expression is being pitched against the verbal channel to find which participants will rely on to work out the speaker's attitude or emotion, then it may be problematic to seriously curtail the verbal channel by limiting it to isolated words.

Second, with regard to Study 2, have you ever had a communication in which a single word was uttered and you had a photograph of the person as they spoke that single word? Perhaps the closest to this we could get would be some technological breakdown during a video conferencing call where both the sound and image were badly affected. Not only is this stimulus highly unusual but it also – according to Beattie (2003) – requires the participants to engage in atypical cognitive processes (integrating in their minds the static visual image with the audio message to form an overall judgement).

Michael Argyle

Argyle, Salter, Nicholson, Williams and Burgess (1970) and Argyle, Alkema and Gilmour (1971) also attempted to measure the relative importance of verbal and non-verbal channels of communication. Argyle et al. (1970, 1971) however, sought to move beyond the problems of presenting isolated words and showing photographs alongside audio recordings, (see Box 11.2).

Argyle's experiments, like Mehrabian's, also pitched verbal message against non-verbal features – in some of the combinations, the verbal message would have completely contradicted the delivery style. The question was what would participants rely on to make their judgements – would it be the words uttered or the (non-verbal) ways in which those words were uttered.

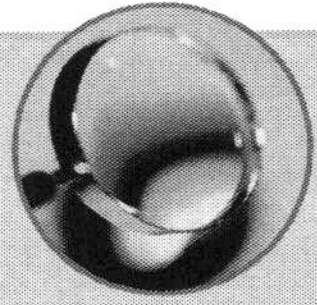

Box 11.2 FOCUS
Classic research: Message versus style of delivery (Argyle et al. 1970, 1971)

Argyle et al.'s (1970, 1971) research into the impact of message content and delivery style on participants' ratings of speakers' interpersonal attitudes involved three different verbal messages (described as 'hostile', 'neutral' and 'friendly' for one experiment and 'superior', 'neutral' and 'inferior' for another) that were delivered to groups of participants. Each message was delivered in three different vocal, postural and facial styles (again, described as 'hostile', 'neutral' and 'friendly' for one experiment and 'superior', 'neutral' and 'inferior' for another). The participants were required to rate the interpersonal attitudes of the speakers – for example, how 'hostile' or 'friendly' each speaker was – on a seven-point scale for each of these nine variations.

Examples of the messages addressed to participants

Friendly message

I enjoy meeting the subjects who take part in these experiments and I find I usually get on well with them. I hope you will be able to stay on afterwards to have a chat about the experiment. In fact, the people who have come as subjects in the past always seemed to be very pleasant.

Hostile message

I don't much enjoy meeting the subjects who take part in these experiments. I often find them rather boring and difficult to deal with. Please don't hang around too long afterwards and talk about the experiment. Some people who come as subjects are really rather disagreeable.

Descriptions of delivery styles used

Friendly style: 'warm, soft tone of voice, open posture, smiling face'

Hostile style: harsh voice, closed posture, frown with teeth showing

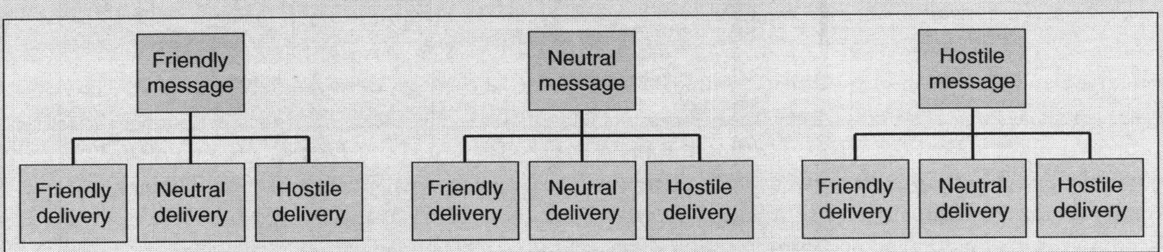

Figure 11.1 Message content (type) and the way in which the message was delivered – an outline of the way messages were communicated in experiments by Argyle, Salter, Nicholson, Williams and Burgess, 1970, and Argyle, Alkema and Gilmour, 1971

Argyle's results had two things in common with Mehrabian's – first, they unequivocally presented non-verbal features of communication as being more powerful in the communication of interpersonal attitudes than the words used and, second, versions of the results were (and still are) very widely cited in popular culture.

Where the non-verbal style *clashed* with the verbal message, participants seemed to rely on the non-verbal style to form judgements about the speaker's interpersonal attitudes. Participants made their judgements (for example, of the speaker's friendliness) using a seven-point scale, with seven being the friendliest and 1 the least friendly, and 4 being the midpoint.

What do you think you would have done as a participant – would you have rated the experimenter's friendliness on the basis of what he or she said, or the tone of voice used to say it? The hostile verbal message quoted above – despite it's highly negative content ('I don't much enjoy meeting the subjects who take part in these experiments . . .') was rated as mildly friendly (5.17, which is higher than neutral) when it was delivered in a friendly non-verbal style. Thus, the hostile *words* used appeared to be less important than the friendly non-verbal *style of delivery*.

Similarly, when the non-verbal style was hostile, the speaker's attitude was judged as hostile, however friendly the words used were. In fact, as Beattie (2003) notes, when the friendly message was delivered in an unfriendly non-verbal style, it was actually judged as marginally less friendly (1.6) than when a hostile message was delivered in a hostile non-verbal style (1.8). In all cases where the non-verbal style contradicted the verbal content, it was the non-verbal style that seemed to have greatest impact on participants' judgements of speaker attitude – it's as if participants felt, 'it's not what you say, but the way that you say it.'

Argyle interpreted the results as supporting the idea that non-verbal communication could usefully be thought of as a separate system of language better suited to the communication of interpersonal attitudes and emotions than verbal communication (which was thought of as better at communicating thinking and ideas). Argyle went so far as to argue that non-verbal communication is up to 12.5 times more powerful in the communication of interpersonal attitudes (particularly those concerning friendliness and hostility) than verbal communication. The non-verbal communication of attitudes concerning the speakers' superiority or inferiority was reported as ten times more effective than the verbal communication of these attitudes.

As with the research by Mehrabian considered above, it is worth noting that the design of Argyle's research did not set up a means of measuring how powerful the different communication channels were but, rather, something much more specific concerning what participants rely on to make judgements in very unusual circumstances. Given this design, Argyle et al.'s research does not provide information about the greater power or impact of non-verbal channels as compared to verbal channels. Instead, as Brown (1986) notes, it actually shows that *in the experimental situation created* participants relied on non-verbal channels where there was a *discrepancy* between those and the verbal channels. That is, where there was a friendly message delivered in an unfriendly way, it was perceived as unfriendly and likewise, an unfriendly message delivered in a friendly way was perceived as friendly. Even before critiquing the design of the experiment, therefore, there are problems with attempts to interpret its findings as adjudicating on the respective power of verbal and non-verbal communication.

Argyle et al.'s research – like that of Mehrabian considered above – involved participants being exposed to several combinations of verbal message and non-verbal styles of delivery. With Mehrabian's Study 1, participants were required to judge combinations of different words and vocal expressions and, in Study 2, combinations of one repeated word and different facial expressions. In the case of Argyle et al.'s research, as Beattie (2003) notes, participants watched the same person enacting nine message–delivery style combinations. As Beattie suggests, this might not only be unlike everyday life, but also actually confound the experimental results. It may be that participants quickly work out that the experiment is concerned with the different judgements of liking associated with different vocal or facial expressions and respond as they do *because they have worked out the rationale of the study*, not because that is how they would do so in a non-experimental situation.

Certain unrealistic aspects of Mehrabian's study have been considered above and Argyle et al.'s research is similarly limited. In addition to the issue of repeated exposure to different messages the combinations of words and style of delivery seem unlikely to occur in any situation outside of the laboratory – do people really tell others that they 'don't much enjoy meeting' them? Also, if this message is delivered in a friendly manner, perhaps – as Beattie (2003) suggests – it is rated as friendly because it sounds like a joke, rather than because non-verbal channels are 'more powerful' than verbal channels.

Beattie's (2003) suggested an alternative unfriendly message 'would you mind leaving' might be far less susceptible to radical reinterpretation (for example, as a joke) just for being delivered in a friendly manner. That is, by choosing words that actually *might* be uttered with mismatched styles of delivery – an unfriendly request to leave in a friendly voice – we might find that the words themselves are consequential for people's interpretations of the friendliness of the communication.

A final criticism that will be returned to later – after attention is given next to facial expression – is, if we *ever* encounter communications stripped of any surrounding context, as is the case in these experiments? Imagine someone calling on you just to say a single word or phrase or, perhaps, you are communicating using a webcam and someone simply appears to give a single word or phrase. The decontextualised experimental word and utterance presentations are so different from everyday life in important respects that it is difficult to assess what they might tell us about the *contextualised communications* of our lives outside of a social psychology laboratory.

Facial expressions

The research considered above compared verbal and non-verbal modes of communication accompanying spoken words in an effort to measure which was more important when expressing emotion. Ekman's (1980) famous series of studies, by contrast, simply used photographs of facial expressions in order to see if the emotions expressed would be culturally specific or universally recognised. For Ekman, then, the issue was not whether facial expression was more important than verbal communication but, rather, the extent to which certain facial displays would be understood as expressing the same emotion in all cultures. Naturally, it would be almost impossible to investigate how photographs of facial expressions are interpreted among literally every culture in the world, so Ekman's initial research focused on two extremely different cultures – the USA and a remote 'pre-literate' tribe, the South Fore. If Ekman found a common understanding across such diverse cultures, then that would suggest some element of cross-cultural agreement – which would be likely to include many other cultures also.

Ekman's initial study began by presenting the South Fore participants with a series of six photographs of faces. Each photograph was intended to demonstrate a different emotion – happiness, surprise, fear, anger, disgust and sadness. The task for the South Fore participants was to listen to a number of stories – each with a specific emotional content – and match the photographic display of emotion to the story that had the same emotional content. The South Fore participants were then asked to facially enact each of the six emotions, showing how their faces would look in situations associated with each emotion – for example, 'your child has died', 'you are about to fight' 'you meet friends' . Three of these are shown in Box 11.3. Photographs of these enactments were presented to US participants to see if they, too, could identify the emotions being expressed.

The South Fore participants matched each photograph with the appropriate story. Likewise, the US participants correctly identified the six emotions from photographs of the South Fore participants. These findings suggested that – for these six 'basic' emotions – there were some universally agreed facial expressions. Despite the two cultures being massively different (the South Fore were 'pre-literate' 'hunter-gathers') and almost completely separated (the South Fore had not been exposed to US culture via television or newspapers and the South Fore were not represented at all in US culture), they had a common understanding of how each of the six emotions would be facially displayed.

Some subsequent researchers, notably Russell (1994) and Carroll and Russell (1996), questioned the extent to which Ekman had discovered universal displays of fundamental emotions – both in terms of whether or not there are core emotions across cultures and whether or not there are shared practices for facially displaying them. As the title of Ekman's (1994) reply to Russell's (1994) critique suggest – 'Strong evidence for universals in facial expression: A reply to Russell's mistaken critique' – he was not entirely persuaded by Russell and, indeed, took issue with many of the issues raised. Crucial for our current purposes is that, while Ekman concedes an element of cultural variation in the facial expression of certain emotions, he strongly argues for universality for the six basic emotions. For Ekman, then, Russell does not sufficiently distinguish an element of variation that may be present in rather more peripheral emotions from the consistently verified universality in the facial expression of the six basic, or core, emotions that he identified.

An important strand of Ekman's more recent research on facial displays of emotion (Ekman & O'Sullivan, 2006; Frank & Ekman, 2003) has focused on the detection of lying. This links to the work of Argyle and Mehrabian considered above. In this work, Ekman combines earlier ideas that we might non-verbally 'leak' our true feelings with his interest in the importance of the face for displaying emotion. The idea is that, however skilled we might be at not communicating the truth in our actual words, we are likely to feel some discomfort in the attempt at deception. This discomfort will be revealed in our non-verbal behaviour.

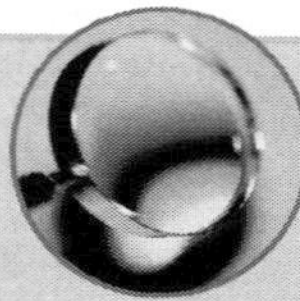

Box 11.3 FOCUS
Classic research: Cross-cultural enactments of basic emotions (Ekman, 1980)

The images below show South Fore participant's enactments of three of the six 'basic emotions' – anger, sadness and happiness. The participants were each asked to show what their face would look like if; 'you were about to fight' (a), 'you learned your child had died' (b) and 'you met friends' (c).

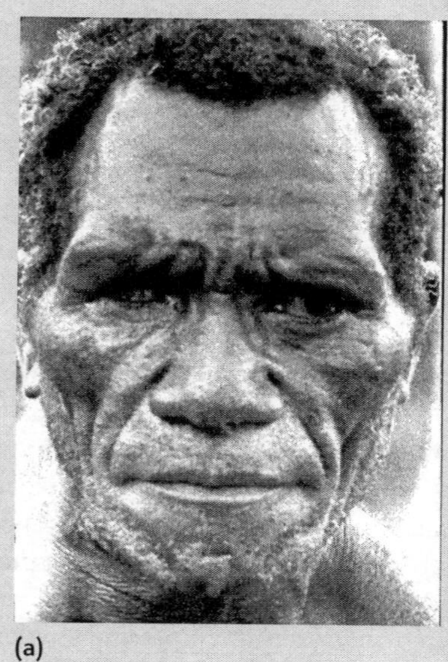
(a)

(b)

(c)

Source: Paul Ekman Group

Photographs from Ekman (1980) universal expressions of human emotions

One particularly important application of this research is in the field of forensic psychology. In police interviews with potential suspects, witnesses to a crime and even victims, it is clearly beneficial if there is some reliable means of identifying whether someone is telling the truth or not. Physiological measures have been used in some circumstances (for example, heart rate variation and increased perspiration have been taken as potential indicators of deception), but these have been criticised as imprecise. For example, the physiological signs of deception are sometimes not present at all when practised deceivers are lying, yet *are present* in the truthful talk of the innocent but anxious. Proponents of non-verbal signs of deception hope to overcome these problems. See Box 11.4 for a real-world example of the usefulness of such research.

The research considered so far has attempted to investigate how communication – in particular, non-verbal communication – might express attitudes and emotions. In doing so, it has created communications or displays of emotions that are stripped of the sorts of contexts in which we would normally find them. That is, in everyday interactions, we tend not to receive a friendly word, utterance or facial expression on its own, 'out of the blue'. Instead, our words, vocal and facial expressions are more usually placed within sequences of interaction. Our understanding of any individual word or utterance, style of delivery and facial expression is shaped by where it occurs. So, unfriendly words and/ or unfriendly styles of delivery could be seen as being quite friendly depending on the talk context in which they occur.

When we start to investigate facial expressions, words and utterances within talk contexts, then the attention to expressing attitudes and emotions may seem misplaced. It may be that, in these real-life settings, we do not use the words and expressions as windows to the speaker's psyche – we might not typically try to work out what they are 'really' thinking or feeling. Instead, perhaps, we are sensitive to what their words, style of delivery and expressions are *doing* in the present interaction. That is, in actual sequences of everyday interactions, we may be more concerned with what the word,

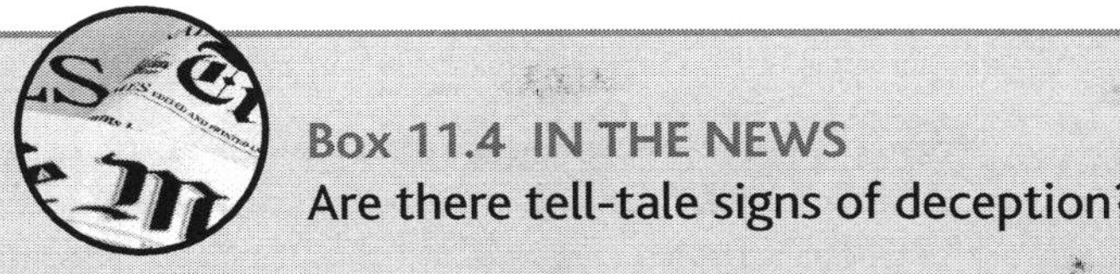

Box 11.4 IN THE NEWS
Are there tell-tale signs of deception?

In February 2008, a nine-year-old schoolgirl by the name of Shannon Matthews went missing. Her mother, Karen Matthews, called the emergency services and made televised appeals for her safe return (her call to the emergency services and some of her televised appeals can be seen at: www.youtube.com/watch?v=VSAcRbcgZgA).

Following an extensive police investigation, Shannon Matthews was found alive, but hidden, in a relative's house. Subsequent police investigations revealed that Karen Matthews had been complicit in the 'disappearance' of her daughter – in a plan that seemed to be organised to gain money for her daughter's return (a brief summary of the case can be found at: www.youtube.com/watch?v=kblZxsTA9zY&NR=1&feature=fvwp).

In the light of incriminating evidence, some attention subsequently turned to Karen Matthew's false appeals and to what, if anything, could have been detected in those televised appeals. Frank and Ekman (2003) and Ekman and O'Sullivan (2006) suggest that criminal investigations such as these can benefit from social psychological work examining non-verbal leakage. It suggests that gestures, eye gaze, posture and tone of voice may 'leak' – that is, unintentionally reveal – the truth, even when the person's words themselves do not. From this perspective, it might be possible to find in Karen Matthew's false appeals and even her call to emergency services indicators – particularly non-verbal ones – that she was lying.

Looking at the clips, can you find signs of lying? Do you think that some people – perhaps actors or pathological liars – can avoid leaking such indicators? Is it helpful to distinguish the verbal and non-verbal aspects of the communication and pay particular attention to *how* things are said rather than *what* is said when trying to detect whether or not someone is lying? What do you feel the social psychology of communication could have contributed to this investigation?

utterance or facial expression *does* rather than what we believe is the 'real' attitude or emotion that the speaker is experiencing.

Imagine for a moment that you are complaining to a friend about a rude and offensive person you met on a bus. As you tell your story, your friend might well facially display disgust and even say something very negative, such as 'disgusting'. Although this is all negative stuff, we may treat it as a sort of agreement with our assessment that the person we are talking about was rude and obnoxious. In other words, we are unlikely to be judging the 'friendliness' of our friend's utterance of the word 'disgusting' or the 'genuineness' of the emotional display of disgust. We *are* likely to be concerned, however, with *what these behaviours are doing* in the interaction. That is, we may see how their talk, tone of delivery and facial expression fit with what has been, and is being, done in the interaction. In this example, you have made a complaint about a non-present person, giving a very negative assessment of that person, and the friend you are talking to appears to be doing some form of agreement.

These ideas regarding the interactional work of verbal and non-verbal communication are addressed further below, but, first, some other dominant approaches to communication need to be considered, starting with the idea that communication is essentially about conveying information.

Critical recap

Expressing attitudes and emotions

1 Several studies report on non-verbal communication having greater 'power' than verbal communication, but the empirical studies actually do not support such generalised claims.

2 In many respects, the empirical studies that are concerned with expressing attitudes and emotions are unlike any situation encountered in life outside of a social psychology laboratory – they involve exposure to isolated words, photographs or repeated combinations of words and styles of delivery.

3 The communications, – whether words or photographs of facial displays – are delivered to participants in a decontextualised manner, which is, again, unlike life beyond the lab – there is no meaningful or realistic context in which the words or statements are produced. That is, they are 'communications as objects to be assessed by those they are addressed to' rather than meaningful, context-relevant utterances of the type that we normally encounter.

4 The experiments make it relevant for participants to 'solve the puzzle' of what the communicator or the person in the photograph is *really* thinking or feeling. Perhaps in everyday life, however, we are predominantly involved in communication not as a puzzle to be solved but as action. It may be the case that when others speak or facially display emotion, we may be involved with what that *does* and what actions it *makes relevant for us to do*, rather than some sort of decoding exercise.

Reflective questions

1 *Have you ever tried to conceal something and felt that your non-verbal behaviour might give you away?*

2 *From your experiences, do you think that the differences in communication styles between countries outweigh the similarities?*

11.2 Conveying information

The work considered so far has emphasised the idea that non-verbal channels of communication are more important (or more relied on by audiences) than verbal channels for conveying the attitudes and emotions of speakers. An important alternative approach is that both non-verbal *and* verbal channels of communication can be investigated in terms of how they *together* convey information.

Research within this tradition has paid particular attention to the information that gestures convey. If you think about how you or others use gestures, it is easy to get some sense of what this research focuses on. Suppose you were describing a character in some film you had seen. If that character had notable physical attributes – perhaps being very tall or wide – your verbal description of him or her might be matched by some accompanying gesture. A simple illustration of this is found in Extract 11.1.

Extract 11.1

```
     A  begins gesture
              ↓
12   A  Ma::n she's this wi::de.
13             (0.8)
14      And that high.
```

(In line 12, "this" is underlined; in line 14, "that" is underlined.)

Source: Goodwin (1986, p. 32)

From Extract 11.1, it can be noted that the talk about being 'wide' is accompanied by a gesture (that *also* denotes width). Both the words and the gesture convey some information relating to the observed physical environment – in this case, it is information about another person who is described as 'wide'.

It can be noted that the research considered here focuses largely on **iconic hand gestures** – that is, movements of the hand showing a close connection to the meaning within the accompanying speech. These gestures include various enactments of that meaning. McNeill (1992) and Beattie (2003) use the example of actions accompanying the phrase 'and he bends it way back' – the speaker appearing to grip something and pull it back. It is easy to contrast these with **beats,** for example, that, while co-occurring with speech, are suggestive of emphasis rather than of intrinsic semantic meaning.

In order to appreciate the idea that gestures convey information, it is worth contrasting it with two alternative positions. The first – which was discussed above – is that non-verbal channels such as gestures convey emotions and attitudes and operate separately from verbal communication. From this perspective, all non-verbal behaviour is potentially important because it may reveal attitudes and emotions on the part of the speaker that are not revealed in the speaker's talk. The second position is that non-verbal communication, particularly gestures, communicate little in themselves – their meaning being derived from the accompanying verbal content. Krauss, Morrel-Samuels and Colastante (1991) note that gestures are typically accompanied by words that convey their meaning and, they argue, people's understanding of what the gesture is communicating is largely derived from what they hear in the accompanying words rather than what they see in the gesture.

An alternative position – developed by McNeill (1985, 1992, 2000) – is that gestures do *not* operate separately from language with a special capacity for revealing emotions and attitudes. Instead, from this perspective, gesture *and* words; 'form, in the memory of the listener, a single unified system of meaning'. (1992, p. 224). Furthermore, while McNeill (2000) sees gestures as necessitating the presence of speech to convey the concept to which a gesture relates, he refutes the idea that gestures are redundant accompaniments to the words they relate to. Instead, McNeill suggests that

Iconic hand gestures Gestures that display or enact meaning – for example, stretching your hand up when describing how tall someone is (the hand gesture displaying the concept of 'tallness').

Beats Movements, typically of the hand, that capture something of the rhythm or beat of the talk – for example, banging one's fist on the table for emphasis.

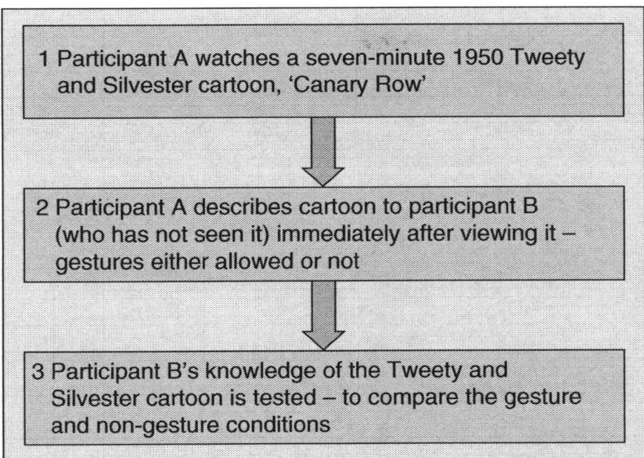

1 Participant A watches a seven-minute 1950 Tweety and Silvester cartoon, 'Canary Row'
2 Participant A describes cartoon to participant B (who has not seen it) immediately after viewing it – gestures either allowed or not
3 Participant B's knowledge of the Tweety and Silvester cartoon is tested – to compare the gesture and non-gesture conditions

Figure 11.2 McNeill's cartoon description experiments

gestures *add* to the concepts present in speech, imparting extra information that might not be present in the words on their own. In one example, McNeill (2000, p. 1) refers to the utterance, 'He grabs a big oak tree and bends it way back' which was spoken alongside a grasping and pulling gesture. For McNeill, both the speech and gesture are treated as important sources of information by recipients listening to (and watching) speakers' communications. Thus, while the words conveyed that an oak tree was bent, the gesture communicated that it was pulled – rather than pushed, for example. McNeill conducted a series of experiments to test whether or not gestures communicated information not available in speech alone. The procedure used for these experiments is shown in Figure 11.2

Using the experimental approach described in Figure 11.2, McNeill (1992) introduced a test of the recipients' knowledge of what had taken place in the cartoon that the speakers described to them. Those participants hearing about the cartoon in the non-gesture condition could then be contrasted with those in the gesture condition to see who had greater knowledge of the cartoon from the speakers' descriptions. Who do you think performed best – those who saw gestures as well as hearing the verbal description or those in the non-gesture condition?

Well, as you probably guessed, it was those who were exposed to gesture *and* speech who answered more questions correctly concerning what had happened in the cartoon.

Detailed analysis of the speakers' use of gesture revealed that important information was often present in the gestures that was not present in the talk on its own. For example, the speakers rarely described which side of the screen a character would enter on, but this information *was* typically conveyed in their gestures.

McNeill also wanted to check what recipients would do in cases where the gestures and accompanying speech did not match each other. Beattie (2003) describes how McNeill carried out experiments in which 'staged' gestures were performed alongside speech that did not match them. These posed an interesting dilemma for the recipients – should they rely on the speech or the gestures? How recipients respond to this dilemma is important for analysts also – do they give priority to one channel over the other in cases of contradiction?

Where there was a mismatch between the words and gestures, it appears that the recipients formed a single concept that took into account both the information contained in the speech *and* the information contained in the gestures. This suggests that recipients themselves treat both gesture *and* speech as conveying information – to the extent that neither channel is treated as capable of negating the other.

Beattie and Shovelton (1999a, 1999b) were interested in further investigating these findings. In one experiment, they (1999a) had participants watch a cartoon and then be filmed describing the cartoon. Other participants were then exposed to either *just* the speech or the speech *and* gestures. Questions were devised to include information that appeared to be present in the gestures used. Thus, if it was noted that some gestures indicated the speed or direction of movement, then questions concerning these details would be included – for example, 'Does the boy spin around in a clockwise direction?' The results showed that participants exposed to both speech *and* gestures answered more questions correctly than those exposed to speech alone.

In a follow-up study, Beattie and Shovelton (1999b) asked a wider range of questions by means of an interview designed to identify the type of information that gestures conveyed. Their analysis, again, suggested that participants exposed to speech *and* gestures performed markedly better than those exposed to speech alone (although, as they note, those exposed to speech alone did outperform those exposed solely to gestures). What was of particular interest, however, was the *type* of information that gestures were found to convey. Their findings suggest that gestures convey a wealth of information concerning the physical attributes, location (particularly relative position) and movement of objects and actions that were seen in the cartoon.

Beattie (2003) draws on this research to suggest that iconic gestures may have a greater role in conveying information than McNeill suggested. First, they may operate somewhat more independently of speech than McNeill thought – that they are able to convey meaning even in the absence of a unifying concept provided by the accompanying speech. Furthermore, the sheer range of information that iconic gestures can communicate may be greater than McNeill envisaged. Thus, Beattie (2003, pp. 116, 117) argues that, 'there is the possibility that even McNeill may have underestimated the range and types of information conveyed by the iconic gestures which accompany spontaneous speech.'

The research by Beattie (2003) and Beattie and Shovelton (1999a, 1999b) has, like that of McNeill (1992), tended to use the prevailing paradigm of participants watching and then recounting a cartoon to other participants. It could be argued that this is not a normal, everyday use of gestures – when is the last time you described a cartoon that you had watched to someone else? Furthermore, the types of gestures available in this environment and for this purpose (describing a cartoon) will be different from those used in many other communicative environments. Thus, they will be rich in iconic representations of exaggerated movements, but poor in more abstract (metaphoric) and indexical (pointing) gestures.

Finally, there is something unusually unilateral about the research considered above – one person talks (either with or without gesturing) and the other person listens (and is sometimes tested afterwards). In life outside of psychology experiments, we may find that our gestures (and our communications in general) are used in environments far more complex, varied and interactional than the monologues studied within such experiments.

Critical recap

Conveying information

1 The research has often used staged enactments of speech and gestures.

2 The research has predominantly relied on a highly specific and unusual context in which one person describes a cartoon that they (and not the other person) have seen.

3 The range of gestures likely to be available within this context is limited and it may even give a distorted understanding of the iconic gestures that *are* present – for example, leading to an accentuated sense of the importance of exaggerated movements, which are a feature of cartoons.

4 The context typically involves studying the gestures accompanying a monologue – for example, one participant describes to another, who attentively listens and watches, what they have seen. This contrasts with everyday interactions between people – that is, we often talk and gesture in environments where others are far more active than the passive recipients found in these studies.

Reflective questions

1 *Have you ever tried to communicate on the phone and felt that you need to see each other to fully convey a piece of information?*

2 *Have you ever watched people interacting where one is using lots of gestures – what, if anything, do you think that the gestures communicated?*

11.3 Communication and relationships

The research that we have reviewed so far in this chapter has tended to be examining aspects of communication – particularly non-verbal communication – on its own, separate from the world of relationships between people. In the next section we consider how styles of speech may relate to shared identities – such as belonging to an identifiable group – but here we will address another aspect of this by examining how gaze and speech may be connected to the intimacy between communicators.

Imagine that you are on a train and, while not specifically trying to eavesdrop, you cannot help but overhear a conversation between two other passengers. As you turn to see the people who are talking, you notice them gazing intensely into each other's eyes. You hear them both disclose quite personal experiences while talking. What impression would you get of the sort of relationship that they have? Do you think that the gaze and disclosure would increase or decrease intimacy?

Social psychologists have been particularly interested in the way in which features of our verbal and non-verbal behaviour are linked to our relationships. One aspect of this is the idea that our communication *reveals* features of our relationship – that is, how we communicate with others reflects something of the relationship that we have with them. A second aspect, receiving more sustained attention, is that our communication with others *influences* how we relate to them – our verbal and non-verbal behaviour with others shapes what our relationship with them *is*, or *will become*. Thus, a prolonged gaze into each other's eyes might not only reveal some pre-existing level of intimacy between two people, but also, may actually heighten the intimacy between them at that moment.

Michael Argyle and Janet Dean (1965)

Argyle and Dean (1965) addressed precisely this issue of how eye gaze is associated with intimacy in what was to become one of the most widely cited of all studies into communication.

Argyle and Dean had conducted preliminary studies that suggested both mutual eye gaze and physical closeness heightened the intimacy between people. Furthermore, people appeared to regulate this intimacy – that is, they would stand closer to a confederate with their eyes shut than they would with their eyes open. The idea here is that the participants were attempting to maintain a desired level of intimacy and, if the other person has their eyes shut, then there cannot be any mutual gaze, so standing closer will not uncomfortably escalate the intimacy. If, by contrast, the other person has their eyes open, then they may gaze at the participant and, therefore, by standing further away, the participant can mitigate the impact of the intimacy-escalating gaze from the other person. This attempt to maintain a particular level of intimacy is called the **equilibrium hypothesis.**

This phenomenon is just the sort of thing experienced by people who regularly commute on crowded trains, undergrounds and buses. Imagine being squeezed next to a complete stranger on a crowded train – physically, you could hardly be closer. In this situation, it is highly likely that you will avoid gazing at each other's eye regions. By contrast, you might gaze more freely at the eye regions of those whom you are much further away from. Next time you are travelling in very crowded conditions, see if this seems to reflect how others behave – do strangers thrust next to each other studiously avoid eye contact in a way that those further apart do not?

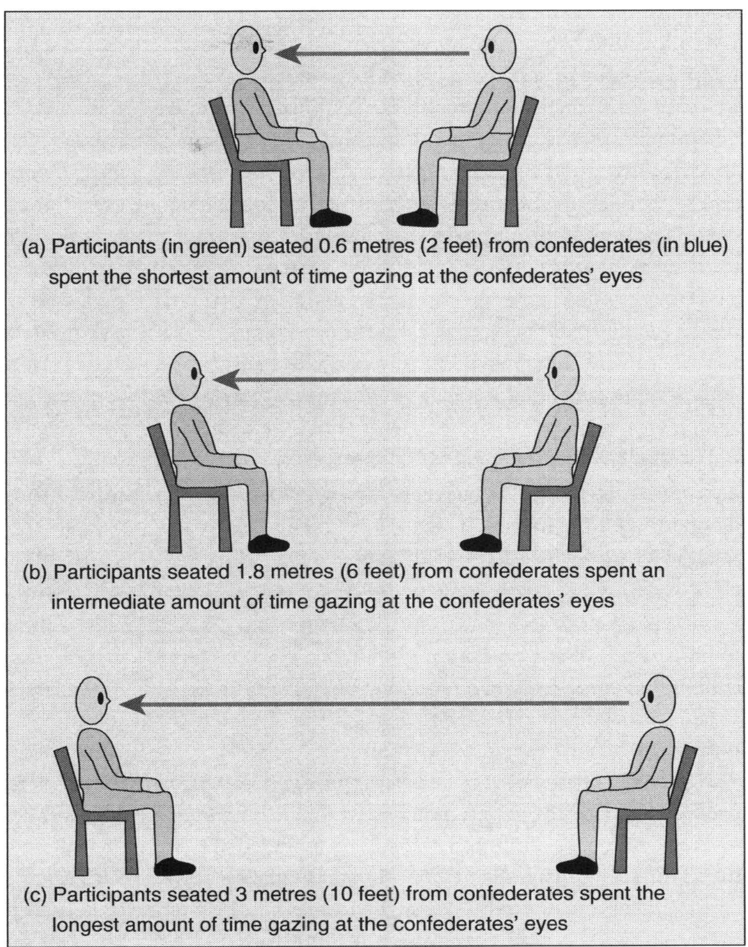

(a) Participants (in green) seated 0.6 metres (2 feet) from confederates (in blue) spent the shortest amount of time gazing at the confederates' eyes
(b) Participants seated 1.8 metres (6 feet) from confederates spent an intermediate amount of time gazing at the confederates' eyes
(c) Participants seated 3 metres (10 feet) from confederates spent the longest amount of time gazing at the confederates' eyes

Figure 11.3 (a) Close proximity – a participant seated 0.6 metres (2 feet) from a confederate, (b) Intermediate proximity – a participant seated 1.8 metres (6 feet) from a confederate and (c) Lowest proximity – a participant seated 3 metres (10 feet) from a confederate

Argyle and Dean's (1965) main study sought to provide compelling empirical evidence regarding their earlier suggestive findings. Their main experiment involved 12 men and 12 women who were asked to discuss, with either a male or female confederate, a somewhat ambiguous picture on a card. The confederate was instructed to gaze steadily at the participant – this meant that any gaze from the participant to the confederate's eye region should result in mutual gaze. The confederate and the participant were sat facing each other across a table at distances of approximately 0.6, 1.8 or 3 metres (2, 6 or 10 feet), while observers watched from behind a one-way mirror, recording the duration and frequency of the participant's gazes at the confederate.

Argyle and Dean found that, regardless of the sex of the participant or confederate, the participants spent less time gazing at the confederate's eye region when they were seated close together and more time doing so when they were seated further apart (see Figure 11.3).

Argyle and Dean's (1965) results confirmed the equilibrium hypothesis – we seek to maintain a desirable level of intimacy in our interactions and will adjust our gaze (or, in the preliminary study, our proximity) in order to

Equilibrium hypothesis The idea that we seek to maintain a desirable level of intimacy in our interactions and will adjust our gaze or proximity to do so (for example, squeezed next to a stranger on a train, we may gaze away to reduce the intimacy that the situation has thrust on us).

maintain this. If we are *forced* into very close proximity, we will mitigate the intimacy-escalating potential of this by limiting our mutual gaze; when further apart, we may increase intimacy by increasing the amount of time we gaze at the other's eye regions.

While the results bore out Argyle and Dean's hypotheses and, subsequently, had a massive influence on the psychology of communication, some problems with the empirical study were identified. Rutter (1984) argued that the experiment was not like social encounters in real life – that is, it lacked external validity. Rutter further argued that the experiment had an inbuilt error in the way in which gaze was calculated. Rutter's first point is that, in Argyle and Dean's main experiment, confederates were instructed to gaze steadily at the participants, yet this makes the social encounter bizarre and unlike any that we are likely to experience outside of a laboratory setting. Indeed, if we try to think about any scenario in which we have been continually stared at, we might be hard pressed to come up with any and, if we have, then we may well recall it as particularly strange or unusual. If the experimental scenario is so fundamentally different, *in terms of gaze behaviour*, from everyday interaction, then we may legitimately ask what it can tell us about everyday (or non-experimental) gaze behaviour.

Rutter's second point is that the observers assessing the eye gaze of the participants may have misjudged where they were gazing, being likely to make false positive claims – that is, judging a participant as gazing at the eyes of a confederate even when they were not. Further, Rutter argues that this error was not randomly distributed across the observers' judgements but systematically present. That is, the observers were most likely to judge the participants as gazing at the confederates' eyes when they were seated further apart because, in such a situation, the precise target of any gaze is more difficult to accurately discern. From Rutter's perspective, the finding that there is more mutual gaze when participants are seated further from the confederates, might simply be a product of observer error. Rather than participants *actually* gazing at the confederates more when they were seated further away from them, Rutter suggests that the observers might just have *judged* that they did in a situation where the real target of the participants' gaze was difficult to specify.

Mark Knapp's model of the stages of interaction

Knapp (1984) constructed a model of relationships that sought to identify different levels of affiliation. Knapp's model argued that there are different stages of interaction from stranger to intimate, and each stage is understood as both characterised and accomplished by different communication strategies.

One aspect of **Knapp's model of interaction stages** is that we should be able to tell how intimate a relationship is by examining the characteristic communication strategies at work. Think of the last conversation you overheard on a train or bus – did the participants merely exchange greetings (initiating) or did they talk openly about their feelings (intensifying)? It is likely that even a brief snippet of conversation was enough for you to make a tentative guess about whether the people talking were close friends or more distant acquaintances.

A second aspect of Knapp's model is that the characteristic communication strategy does not simply reflect where the relationship is but also helps to determine how intimate the relationship is. Try to think of some people with whom you have never been close – mere acquaintances. It is likely that your talk may never get past an exchange of greetings with some of these people. Now think of your talk with your closest friends – this, no doubt, has a markedly different feel, involving much more personal disclosure, intensity and support. Knapp suggests that, in addition to the current talk telling us about the current relationship, it can also *shape* the relationship. From this perspective, then, it may be that some acquaintances become friends partly because we had increasingly open, personal and supportive conversations with them. By contrast, some acquaintances may have remained just that (partly) because we never had these kinds of meaningful conversations with them. Thus, the closeness we experience in various relationships may be influenced by the extent to which we have talked about each other's interests (experimenting) and our feelings (intensifying) – factors that can lead to deeper affiliation.

One aspect of Knapp's model, indicated above, is that it accounts for the development of a relationship – from strangers, through different stages to intimates. It also seeks to account for relationships that remain at a specific level of affiliation or decline. At each stage in the relationship, according to Knapp, there could be a development on to the next level, stabilisation or decline. Thus, while initial (experimenting) talk about personal interests – 'I like watching repeats of *Friends*', 'I'm involved with Amnesty International' – might develop into (intensifying) talk about personal feelings – 'I'm worried about the amount of work I have to cope

Knapp's model of interaction stages A model of different levels of intimacy in an interaction that suggest people may both reflect and determine the intimacy of their relationship via the intimacy of their interaction with each other.

with', 'I'm having problems in ...' – it could also stabilise at the experimenting level or decline. That is, our interactions might continue to successfully focus on our common, or unique, likes and dislikes (stabilise) or it could stagnate, such that we run out of topics we are comfortable about sharing, resulting in our interactions declining towards the lower stage of initiating. If you think of interactions you have had that have felt awkward, you may recognise this. You might have found yourself with someone you did not know well and you, or the person you were talking with, felt like you were trying to keep a conversation going when you had nothing to talk about. This desperate attempt to make conversation illustrates stagnation – where the introduction of new topics starts to run dry. Once the experimenting phase gives way to stagnation, then – according to Knapp's model – the interaction decreases in affiliation and returns to the initiating stage, where talk is more superficial and involves less personal disclosure. The strained interaction between Ross and Mike (from the television show *Friends*) shown in Box 11.5 provides a vivid illustration of stagnation.

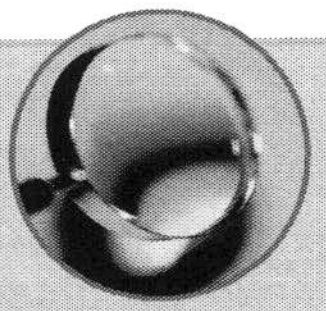

Box 11.5 FOCUS *Friends*, Season 9, Episode 9

The following dialogue between the characters Ross and Mike is a good example of the stagnation stage in interaction in Knapp's model.

Ross: OK. (They sit.) So, um, Phoebe tells me you, ah, you play piano.

Mike: Yeah.

Ross: You know, I, I used to, ah, play keyboards in college.

Mike: Ah? (pause) Do you have one here?

Ross: No.

Mike: OK. (pause)

(They clink beer bottles and drink. Then, they stare uncomfortably at their bottles.)

Ross: Um ... ah ... you know, I' m divorced. Um, Phoebe, ah ... Phoebe said you ... You' ve been divorced?

Mike: Yeah. (pause) Yeah, I' m sorry. I don' t ... I don' t really like to talk about it.

Ross: (pause) That's OK. We' ll talk about (pause) something else. (They pause. They drink.)

Mike: So, you're a palaeontologist, right?

Ross: Yeah.

Mike: My cousin's a palaeontologist.

Ross: Ah? (Mike nods. Another pause.) Well, he and I would probably have a lot to talk about.

Criticisms of Knapp's model

Two aspects of Knapp's model that have received particular critical attention are the notion that decline is simply the reverse of development and its tendency to treat self-disclosure as simply one of many strategies to increase affiliation – rather than it having some sort of primacy.

On the first of these points, Baxter (1983) argues that the decline and break-up of relationships is bound to differ from development because, after achieving a certain level of affiliation or intimacy, people have increased their shared knowledge of and mutual history with each other. Thus, we cannot simply 'retrace our steps' – returning to lower levels of affiliation in the reverse order of our relationship's development – because we are changed as a result of the level of affiliation that we attained up to that point. Our interaction with a former intimate partner is unlikely to be exactly the same as that with a complete stranger. Also, the process of breaking up is equally unlikely to be a step-by-step reversal of the increasing affiliation that occurred during the development of our relationship. Having been particularly close to someone, we have a deep knowledge of them and a catalogue of shared experiences that means we cannot, for example, decline to a stage where we are 'finding out about each other' (experimenting). Knapp's model, in suggesting a staircase of stages on which we progress or regress, one step at a time, does not account for the change that occurs during the process of increased affiliation.

The second criticism is that Knapp's model does not recognise the especially important role that self-disclosure plays in the development of relationships. Here, self-disclosure is taken to be talk that conveys information about self to the other – particularly information that is not otherwise readily available. Thus, it would hardly be self-disclosure to say 'my hair is ginger', but 'I' m wearing a wig' would be.

One reason that self-disclosure is thought to be particularly important for affiliation is what Gouldner (1960) refers to as the **norm of reciprocity**, which places a duty

Norm of reciprocity The expectation that those interacting will respond in kind to the actions of each other. Thus, if one person shares intimate personal information, the norm of reciprocity suggests that the other person should do likewise.

on those interacting to reciprocate in kind the actions of each other. Imagine talking to someone when, somewhat out of the blue, they tell you about a significant bereavement that they experienced. In this context, it is not only tricky to start talking about trivial matters such as how 'It has suddenly turned chilly again', but also difficult not to reciprocate with a disclosure that has a similar level of emotional intensity – perhaps you also had a bereavement or other significant negative experience. Altman and Taylor (1973) argue that it is because one disclosure makes it *expected* that a similar disclosure will be shared by the other that self-disclosure can initiate a step-by-step increase in the affiliation or intimacy between those in that interaction.

Critical recap

Communication and relationships

1 The most famous study in this area (Argyle & Dean, 1965) can be seen as having two major weaknesses. First, the confederates used in the experiment engaged in bizarre and *interactionally consequential* behaviour – they gazed at the participants' eyes throughout the experiment. Second, judgements about where the participants were looking were confounded by the distance between the participants and confederates (the further apart they were, the more difficult it would be to assess whether or not the participants were actually gazing into the eye region of the confederates).

2 Knapp's (1984) model of the stages of interaction has been criticised for underestimating the importance of disclosure, in particular, in increasing affiliation. Furthermore, Knapp has been criticised for treating his model of increasing affiliation and intimacy as reversible. That is, where people decrease affiliation and intimacy, Knapp suggests that they simply return to an earlier stage, implying that nothing has changed as a result of the intervening experience of heightened intimacy.

Reflective questions

1. *Have you ever found yourself increasing your distance from another person, avoiding eye contact or reducing the intimacy of the topics you are discussing when you have been in conversation with someone? Do you feel that this was linked to stopping the level of intimacy escalating?*
2. *Have you ever observed others use proximity, gaze or topic intimacy to adjust the intensity of an interaction? Which, if any, of these is most effective?*

11.4 Communication and identity

In the previous section, attention was given to the ways in which aspects of verbal and non-verbal communication may relate to the regulation of relationships between people – largely in dyads. Here we consider a related concern – which is how styles of speech (including accent) may be associated with people's relationships with others in terms of group membership. That is, how might accent (and other aspects of speech style) display, maintain or achieve certain types of group identity?

Have you ever overheard someone talking and felt able to make some sort of guess about them just from what you can hear? Perhaps their tone, accent and the words they use gives a sense of whether they are male or female, how old they are, where they are from and their socio-economic status? In other words, we might find that we can quickly place people into groups (rightly or wrongly) based solely on how they speak (see Box 11.6).

In the examples given in Box 11.6, the speakers each read out the same passage in English, yet, despite this, it is likely that your impressions of each of them is (at least partly) shaped by *how* they read it. It is easy to see, then, that, even when the same language is being used, and even when the speakers read the same words, there can be considerable variation in the dialect, which can shape the judgements we might form of the speaker. Furthermore, perceived group membership (such as social class) and what we associate with those groups (for example, power, wealth) play a significant role in this judgement. One important strand of research, which has informed the social psychology of communication and has a particular interest in how language variation relates to groups, is sociolinguistics.

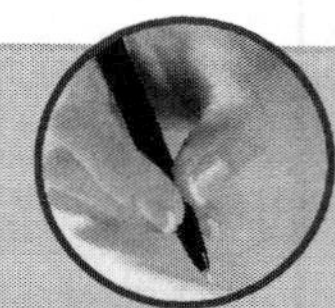

Box 11.6 TRY IT OUT
Accent and identity

Try listening to these recordings and note the impressions, if any, that you form about each speaker.

Sample 1:
http://accent.gmu.edu/searchsaa.php?function=detail&speakerid=68

Sample 2:
http://accent.gmu.edu/searchsaa.php?function=detail&speakerid=70

Comparisons of Standard English and dialects

These Dutch football supporters have a style of dress that clearly indicates their group affiliation – but can styles of talking also accentuate or attenuate specific group identities?

Source: Chris Lobina / Rex Features

Early work in sociolinguistics paid particular attention to the ways in which dialect varied within a linguistic community. In this research, 'dialect' was a broad term, used to encompass all aspects of speech variation that could be linked to social groups, times and places – such as accent, grammar and words used. Such research investigated the forms of dialect that were at work among English speakers within the USA (Labov, 2006) and UK (Trudgill, 1974).

In addition to aspects of accent, there were systematic ways in which the grammar (for example, the presence or absence of the possessive 's') of the participants differed from what might be considered 'Standard English' (or 'Standard American English'). One aspect of this work that soon emerged was the specifiable, systematic features of non-Standard (sometimes called 'regional') talk and its difference from Standard English (sometimes glossed as 'received pronunciation', or, RP – although Standard English encompasses vocabulary, grammar and accent). A second feature to arise from early research within sociolinguistics was that Standard and non-Standard language forms are often found to shape judgements made about speakers.

Returning to the speech samples given in Box 11.6, what impressions, if any, did you note concerning the two speakers? If you had to guess who had the higher socio-economic status, would you choose the non-Standard English (Sample 1) or the Standard English (Sample 2) speaker?

Lambert, Hodgson, Gardner and Fillenbaum (1960) used exactly this sort of procedure – with the same passage read in two different accents. Participants were subsequently required to rate the speaker along a number of dimensions. As Coupland (2007) notes, studies using this format have found that the speakers were rated differently according to their accents (and, although scripted, their wording and grammar still varied a little). Judgements about speakers of Standard English tended to confer status on the speaker – they were perceived as intelligent, competent and powerful. Judgements about speakers of non-Standard English were – not always, but sometimes – found to attribute solidarity to them (they were perceived as being close, friendly and warm). Some researchers studying these variations in other languages, such as Kristiansen (2004), have noted that there is not always a simple standard versus non-standard dichotomy against which speech can be mapped. He found that speech in the Danish town of Naestved orientates to three 'norm ideals' – sjaelland style, Copenhagen style and a more generic 'urban but modern 'style.

Speech accommodation

The work on Standard English and the other aspects of language considered above tends to conceptualise variations in dialect as occurring between speakers – a way of differentiating one speaker from another. You may have sometimes noted, however, that dialect can vary within the speech of a single person. Perhaps you have overheard someone at a customer service desk having one conversation and then moving to another with someone else – and maybe the switch from one conversation to another is associated with a shift in some aspect of their dialect. Perhaps their accent relates to the person with whom they are speaking in some way – being markedly similar to or different from the speech of the other.

It is exactly this phenomenon that has been of interest to Giles and colleagues (Giles, Coupland, & Coupland, 1991) in their work on developing what Giles refers to as 'communication' or 'speech accommodation' theory. Giles notes that – if we pay sufficiently close attention – we will find speakers often modify their speech, not just to different audiences (as Bell, 1984, 2001, found) but also even to the same audience. Of particular interest to Giles is not the absolute form that the speech takes but, rather, the ways in which it relates to the talk of the other person (or people). Thus, dialect can be seen as a resource that can be used to converge to, or diverge from, those the target speaker is interacting with.

Aspects of this resonate with Argyle and Dean's (1965) work on the use of gaze to regulate intimacy. With Argyle and Dean (as seen earlier in this chapter), gaze is described as a tool for regulating intimacy and with speech accommodation theory, similarity of dialect is depicted as serving a related function. Thus, Coupland (2007, p. 62) notes:

> In pursuit of being judged more likeable, for example, a speaker could be expected to *converge* her or his speech towards that of a listener in certain respects. *Divergence* could, alternatively, symbolise the desire to reduce intimacy, as could *maintenance* (implying no variation or deviation from an existing way of communicating).

It should perhaps be noted that the emphasis here is on *perceptions* of the speech styles, of others not on their *actual* styles of speech – thus, Thakerar, Giles and Cheshire (1982) show evidence of speakers modifying their speech to what they thought was characteristic for the audience, even though it was not. Similarly, Bourhis and Giles' (1977) undertook a classic experiment in a language laboratory in which people were learning Welsh. The learners were asked questions through headphones in English – the voice asking the questions having a Standard (or RP) accent. When the voice asked a provocative question about why the students were learning 'a dying language with a dismal future', what do you think happened to their accents? Do you think the 'Welshness' was accentuated, maintained or attenuated? You have probably guessed that it was accentuated – with some participants finding Welsh expletives with which to reply.

It can be noted that speech convergence is not always successful in making speakers more liked by their audiences. Genesee and Bourhis (1988) found that salespeople adopting the same dialects as their customers were perceived negatively – they attributed the salespeople's accommodation to their style as merely motivated by a desire to sell. Speech accommodation theory does, however, open up the idea that dialect variation can be considered not just as a phenomenon occurring between different people but also *within* individuals, which, in turn, opens up the issue of how speech is used to do or accomplish things in interaction.

Social identities

While speech accommodation theory, as we have seen, opens up the idea of speech variation within individuals and shows how it can be used to affiliate and disaffiliate, it does tend to imply quite a deliberately motivated use of dialect. Furthermore, variation is only considered in so far as it relates to talk directed at an audience – that is, whether it converges with, or diverges from, perceptions of how the audience speaks. Alternative strands of research, however, have explored the ways in which we might have access to different styles of speech that are associated with different identities.

Consider, for example, a Welsh woman, nearing retirement, who is a mother, working as a cleaner at a tourist attraction and interacting with the young English director of the attraction. Even from this thumbnail sketch we can envisage many possible identities at the disposal of both interactants – covering areas such as national identity, gender, socio-economic status, power relationships and age, to name but some. Coupland (2007) makes the case that, for many speakers, in an interaction, there is a host of possibly relevant identities – each of which might be indexed by different features of talk (and, indeed, all forms of communication), but only some will actually be made salient in that interaction.

One way of making sense of these different identities is to draw on self-categorisation theory (see Chapter 2). According to self-categorisation theory, we can think of ourselves in terms of a range of different group or category memberships. Thus, we might think of ourselves as being female, student, single, athletic, Buddhist, into psychology, Afro-Caribbean, Danish, in our thirties and a mother, but not all of these identity-relevant categories will necessarily be activated at once. Instead, the people and situations that we encounter may make certain category-based identities salient at the expense of others – our behaviour *and our communication* may then be consistent with these activated identities.

Palomares (2009) addressed exactly these issues, starting with the observation that a number of researchers (such as Coates, 2004) have made regarding differences between the ways in which males and females typically communicate. In order to appreciate the sorts of differences that Palomares (2009) was interested in, look at the two samples of e-mails in Box 11.7 and note any differences between them – both are on the topic of who is the best designer of high-heel shoes:

You might have noted that the communication in Sample 1 in Box 11.7 is far less tentative than that found in Sample 2. Did you see how, in Sample 2, the communicator used hedging ('probably') disclaimers ('I'm not sure') and tag questions ('doesn't he?') As Palomares (2009) notes, tentativeness is an important aspect of variation that can be found not just in speech but also all aspects of communication – including e-mails, which is the form he

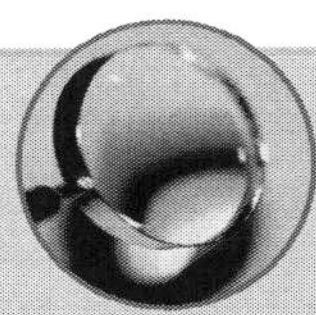

Box 11.7 FOCUS

Examples of e-mails responding to the question 'Who is the best designer of high-heel shoes' (based on Palomares, 2009)

Sample 1

Christian Louboutin is the best designer of high-heel shoes because his lovely shoes not only reflect different moods but also even represent different attitudes of life, love or hate, happy or sad. No matter what feeling you have now, there is always a pair of shoes suitable for you!!!

Sample 2

I'm not sure, but I think it's probably someone called Johnny Chow or Jimmy Choo, isn't it? I may be wrong but I think he kinda designs expensive high-heel shoes, doesn't he?

investigated. Research into the communication styles of males and females has typically suggested that one difference is that females are more tentative than males. Palomares' (2009) research raises problems for this idea.

Look again at the two samples in Box 11.7. Although Sample 1 is less tentative than Sample 2, do you think that it was written by a male? What you might have picked up on is that here is a topic (high-heel shoes) that is stereotypically feminine and – as you might have guessed – Sample 1 *was* written by a female (edited slightly here).

Palomares (2009) found that, rather than there being global differences between men and women regarding how tentative they are in their communications, tentativeness will vary enormously, depending on both the topic the individual is communicating about – and to whom they are communicating. When gender identity was made salient – by communicating with someone of the opposite sex – then tentativeness varied according to how prototypically gender-matched the topic was. In other words, Palomares (2009) argues that where participants communicated with someone of the opposite sex, they were particularly aware of themselves in terms of their own gender identity. If they were then asked to communicate about a topic that their sex was more strongly associated with (for example, high-heel shoes for female participants, cars for male participants), they were not at all tentative. If, however, participants had to communicate with members of the opposite sex on topics that were more associated with the opposite sex (males communicating on the topic of high-heel shoes, females on the topic of cars), they were far more tentative in their communications.

Before considering the further research of Palomares and Lee (2010) in this area, it is worth quickly noting one potential drawback of Palomares' conclusion as just described. It may be the case that the hesitancy in the 'gendered mismatched' communications – men communicating about high-heel shoes and women about cars – could have far less to do with the activation of gender identities than Palamores suggested. It could be that the hesitancy is a function of the perceived relative expertise, which may be based on gender stereotypes but does not presume that a gender identity has been activated.

Palomares and Lee (2010) suggested that self-categorisation theory can also account for the effect that avatars may have on communication – specifically, computer-mediated communication (CMC). They suggest that if we interact using a gendered (obviously male or female) avatar, we may – regardless of our biological sex identity – use styles of communication stereotypically associated with our *avatar's* gender. When the avatar's gender was matched, males and females conformed to *stereotypical ideas* of male and females styles of communicating (females being more emotion-focused, apologetic and tentative). When there was a gender mismatch, however – participants communicating via an avatar of the opposite sex – *the avatar's* apparent gender shaped the style of communication that participants used. This finding was particularly strong among female participants using a male avatar – their communicating being markedly less apologetic, emotion-focused and tentative when they interacted using a male (rather than a female) avatar.

For Palomares and Lee (2010), our communication styles are shaped by the gender identity that has been made salient for us and, thus, we will use a style of communication (rightly or wrongly) associated with that gender.

Multiple speech identities

Perhaps you have overheard two strangers talking and found yourself reaching certain conclusions – not only about their social class or regional identity but also what sort of conversation it is and who is in the more powerful position. If you, like me, find yourself doing this, you are using linguistic variation – the different ways that members of a speech community use language (accent, vocabulary) to index possibly relevant aspects of the speakers' identities.

One important point to note here is that these different styles of speech are available not just for those of us nosy enough to listen to other people talking – they are available for those who are interacting themselves. We can further note, as Coupland (2007) does, that people do not just have one, single, fixed identity that determines how any given person speaks. Instead people have (potentially at least) many *different* identities – only some of these may be made salient in the interaction at specific moments. Thus, if we hear two people speaking, we may hear a marked upper-class accent, talk that suggests the interaction is work-related and one person is in charge of the other. However, in a short burst of an interaction, we might not get much of a clue regarding the regional or national identities of the interactants, nor be aware of other non-work-related interests they have in common and have no clue that they are not just related as boss and employee, but intimately as well.

Furthermore, any features that *do* become salient may shift – being upper class, in a business conversation or being someone's boss may be relevant for *some* of the interaction but not *all* of it. If we listen to people speaking, we might detect that the features marking someone's accent as upper class are (literally) accentuated at some points in the interaction rather than others. Those people who seem to be engaged in some business talk might switch to talking about their children, a TV show or politics at another point in the conversation. The interaction that seemed marked by one of them being in charge of the other could switch to something more intimate. If we are sufficiently self-aware we might notice how we ourselves change our speech style, not only as we talk to different people but also even – to an extent – within one conversation to one person. The impetus for the switch between identities – reflected by marked changes in speech style – could be understood as located not *outside* of the interaction, but *in* the speech or discursive environment itself. Coupland (2007) describes these discourse environments that activate specific identities (such as social class, ethnic or regional or national identity, type of conversation and relationship between the interactants) as frames (drawing on the concept developed by Goffman, 1974).

For Coupland (2007), the many different possible frames (or discursive environments that make certain identities relevant) can be meaningfully grouped into three broad categories. There are *macro-level social frames* (sometimes called *socio-cultural framing*) – these include those frames (or discursive environments) that make identities concerned with social class, ethnicity and cultural, religious or regional identity relevant. There are also *meso-level social frames* (sometimes called *genre framing*) – these include frames that make salient the *type* of conversation (and the associated identities for that type of conversation), such as business meeting, casual chat, academic enquiry, formal complaint and so on. Finally,

Extract 11.2

(*Note:* Adapted and line numbers not from the original)

Sue	*well I've [booked them and they're all allright* (.)
Liz	[where would I get it from?
Sue	*but I can't give them ticket numbers until they [pay*
Liz	[charcoal
Sue	(closing) (breathy voice) *OK?*
Marie	Blacks
Liz	yeah camping stuff innit yeah
Marie	(and Woolies)
Sue	mm *(.) allright*
Liz	reckoned Woolies as well but I don't think so
	(1.0) I'll just g[o down to Blacks
Sue	*[that'll be great (1.0) we'll let you know if you can*
	o:h Friday morning(.)yeah that's OK the option's till Friday anyway
	(.)
	((other client conversations in the background))
Sue	*OK then fine(1.0) OK then (.) bye (.) Sue (1.0) (breathy) OK? bye*
Marie	(faint) is anyone else (.) starving?
Sue	well I was going to have one but I' m not going to now
Marie	well have one don' t pay any attention to what I say
Sue	no
Marie	I talk a load of rubbish

Source: Coupland (2007, p. 116)

there are *micro-level social frames* (sometimes called *interpersonal framing*) – these make relevant personal and relational identities, such as aspects of shared history between the interactants, the power distribution between them and the level of intimacy in the relationship.

In an analysis of interactions in a Cardiff travel agency, Coupland (2007) suggests that different frames may make different types of identities relevant (a shortened version of his data can be found in Extract 11.2.)

(Coupland (2007) notes certain contrasts between Sue's talk on the telephone (in italics) and her talk with her colleagues. One gloss on this is that Sue's telephone talk in her professional capacity is more middle-class and professional in phonological components – as well as in the more formal nature of the language used – than her talk with her travel agency assistant colleagues. Thus, aspects of Sue's pronunciation are closer to received pronunciation for English when she is on the telephone than they are when talking with Liz and Marie. Sue also uses more formal language with specific business expressions in the telephone call (for example, *'but I can't give them ticket numbers until they pay'*, Line 3) than in her talk with Liz and Marie (such as 'well I was going to have one but I' m not going to now', Line 18).

Coupland argues that the temptation to provide a class-based analysis – in which class is seen as relevant for both Sue's talk on the telephone *and* her talk with Liz and Marie – would be missing the fact that, while class may be relevant for the public discourse talk on the telephone, it is not relevant in the private (micro-level) discourse with her colleagues. The reason Coupland (2007, p. 119) gives for this is that, 'it is non-contrastive among the group of colleagues and friends'. That is, because Sue and her colleagues share a common class identity, a class-based analysis of her talk with them is misplaced. What is present in her talk with her colleagues, according to Coupland, is heavily implicit talk – 'well I was going to have one but I'm not going to now' (line 18) – that, in form and content, is a more personal and intimate style of talking than her telephone talk. Where Coupland *does* note a common dimension on which Sue's telephone talk can be contrasted with her talk with colleagues, it concerns not class but *power*. Thus, for Coupland, there is a contrast between the professional power and competence talk on the telephone (*'well I've booked them and they're all allright'*, Line 1) and the intimate, powerless, diet-related, talk with Liz and Marie ('well I was going to have one but I'm not going to now', Line 18). Coupland (2007, p. 120) goes on to suggest that, 'Sue is very audibly depressed at having been forced to confront her dieting regime. Perhaps she thinks she is a failure'.

Coupland's observations make use of both phonological features of speech delivery (such as accent) and talk content in his analysis. Furthermore, he specifically challenges the dangers – present in a large amount of **sociolinguistic** research – of misapplying structural features (such as class), which simply might not be relevant to the talk or, more subtly, may be relevant for *some* aspects (in this case, the telephone call) but not others (the talk with colleagues).

Coupland's analysis, however, perhaps shows a limitation of the idea that talk can be thought of as operating within three overarching frames – for example, one can question which frame characterises her talk with her colleagues and are the frames too crude to pick up the subtle variations present in any conversation, whatever the frame or frames? Furthermore, from a social constructionist perspective, there could be more emphasis on the turn-by-turn work that is being done through the talk, which would entail more attention being given to how the target speaker's (Sue's) talk orientates to (or takes into account) the talk of others. Finally, from a social constructionist perspective, describing the inner psychological realities experienced by the speakers involves a sudden leap into realist and essentialist thinking that is at odds with a perspective that emphasises how reality is constituted in and through talk.

The social construction of identity

Research on the social construction of identity was dealt with more comprehensively in Chapter 2, which addresses the construction of self and identity in talk. Here, a brief extract is drawn on to illustrate how **discursive psychology** has drawn upon the notion of the social construction of identity in talk to consider what is done or accomplished by identity talk in interaction.

Potter and Wetherell's (1987) landmark book made clear the relevance and implications of social constructionism and, specifically, discourse analysis for social psychology. One idea that the book demonstrated was the way in which interviewees could talk about – or construct – their identities in seemingly contradictory ways. The idea of multiple possible constructions of reality is,

Sociolinguistics An approach to communication that is particularly concerned with how styles of speech relate to different groups, categories and identities.

Discursive psychology An approach to understanding interaction and social psychology that is informed by the work of Edwards and Potter and which pays particular attention to the sort of interactional work that talk does and the implications that this has for social psychological understanding.

of course, at the heart of social constructionist thinking – and Potter and Wetherell demonstrated a form of discourse analysis that would be sensitive to such contradictory talk and analyse it to see what sort of work it was doing. One instance of this – the use of disclaimers in racist talk – has already been addressed in Chapter 7 in discussions of stereotypes and prejudice. This attention to multiple constructions of **identity** opens up the idea that identity talk is not a reporting of who the speaker is but, rather, the particular version of self that is given can be examined in terms of *what it is doing*.

From this perspective, then, instances of identity talk can be approached not in terms of what they tell us about who the speaker *really* is – or even who they *think* they are – but as *actions within interaction* – that is, the identity talk does something. In a paper inspired by Potter and Wetherell (1987), Dickerson (1996) reports an analysis of interviews in which participants were asked for their thoughts about televised politics. Extracts 11.3,11.4 and 11.5 are taken from Dickerson (1996) and illustrate the ways in which identity talk can do interactional work.

Extract 11.3

(*Note:* Line numbers from the original)

16 K I don't consider myself to be easily led

Source: Dickerson (1996, p. 70)

Extract 11.4

(*Note:* Line numbers from the original)

1 P is there ever anything that strikes you on (0.5) umm
2 the news that you think well 'hold on it's too
3 biased there' or [>can we (three syllables)<
4 K [well um I've never actually err
5 P yeah
6 K (0.5) felt (1.0)
7 P yeah
8 K (.) bias
9 P (0.5) yeah (1.0) yeah
10 K (8.0) phhh I mean I don't phh I don't know umm (2.5)
11 whether people who are more easily led phh (0.5) might
12 P (1.5) mmm (1.5) yeah
13 K (1.0) might actually be led in a biased fashion but
14 err
15 P (0.5) yeah (2.0)
16 K I don' t consider myself to be easily led

Source: Dickerson (1996, pp. 69, 70)

The brief utterance in Extract 11.3 could be understood as communicating how the speaker, 'K', thinks about themselves – that is, it could read as revealing information about the speaker's sense of self. In terms of frameworks that we have considered within this chapter so far, this utterance could be made sense of as revealing the speaker's feelings about themselves from the perjorative description 'easily led'. Alternatively, although we do not have gestural information, the talk could be seen as simply conveying information about how the speaker is, or at least how, they see themselves. From another perspective this could be seen as an example of what Knapp (1984) might consider to be self-disclosure, which might (perhaps more so in non-interview contexts) be associated with an increase in relationship intensity. Finally, without reference to the accent used, there is something about the delivery that might be marked as being the sort of formal, Standard English that is often associated with high-status talk.

For each of these observations derived from the approaches considered above, little, if any, attention needs to be paid to the surrounding talk context – that is, where in the sequence of interaction between I and K does this talk occur? For the discursive approach developed here, however, an examination of context is important, so that we can better see what any one utterance might be doing, Extracts 11.4 and 11.5 may shed more light on this.

Extract 11.5

(*Note:* Line numbers from the original)

19 K and political reporters I suppose try and be unbiased
20 but sometimes (1.0) >there is a bias<

Source: Dickerson (1996, p. 69)

Extract 11.5 precedes Extract 11.4 by approximately 30 seconds. Thus, the interviewee has claimed that sometimes '>there is a bias<' (Extract 11.5) before denying ever actually feeling bias (Extract 11.4). It can be noted that K's construction of their identity 'I don't consider myself to be easily led' (Extract 11.3) occurs at precisely this sequential location – in a position that follows both admitting and seemingly denying the presence of bias.

One reading of this is that constructing *some* people as easily led, but not the speaker, makes sense of the

Identity Any representation or idea of our specific self – including representations found in our talk.

seeming contradiction – of having said that 'there *is* bias' but, subsequently, saying they have never actually 'felt bias'. The version of self and others produced gives a way of reading the earlier assessment – 'there is bias' – indeed, this may have an impact on others who are 'easily led', but the speaker has never actually 'felt bias'. Implicitly then, unlike others, the speaker is not 'easily led'. That is, the talk about 'not being easily led' recasts 'felt bias' as meaning 'being affected by or led by bias' and, therefore, reduces any apparent contradiction in the previous talk.

The point being made here is that, from a discursive perspective, examining where identity talk occurs enables some consideration to be given to the *interaction-orientated work* that it may be doing.

Critical recap

Communication and identity

1 Some early sociolinguistics were particularly concerned with structural distinctions – such as how people from different social strata talk differently. Issues of class perhaps were, and in some cases still are, presumed to be relevant without actually seeing whether the participants display that they are.

2 Some approaches within sociolinguistics move away from considering structural differences in society to the motivated use of dialect – that is, they consider what talk is used to do. These approaches, however, often have a very narrow range of 'functions' of communication – sometimes just affiliation or disaffiliation, sometimes extending to power and status work as well.

3 Work that has emphasised how men and women talk in different styles (for example, women being more hedged, self-questioning and hesitant) has underestimated that the topic of conversation may have a bearing on the style of communication.

4 Little attention, within much of the research considered here, has been given to what identity talk *does* in interactions.

Reflective questions

1. *Have you ever found yourself adjusting your style of speech or have you seen this in others? What do you think was being done by this change in speaking style?*
2. *When is the last time you made a claim about the sort of person that you are in a conversation? What do you think this claim did – if anything?*

11.5 Doing interaction

In discussing identities and communication above, we considered some approaches that emphasised what is sometimes glossed as the pragmatic aspects of communication – that is, what it *does*. In this section, that idea is developed first by considering ideas about how features of talk, gaze and gesture might help regulate interaction (by for example, helping to determine who speaks next) and then the far-reaching idea of conversation analysis that communicative practices (such as talk, gaze and gesture) could be understood as 'action in interaction' .

Let us start by considering a much-debated aspect of communication already considered earlier in this chapter – the use of gaze. In order to set the scene for this, Extract 11.6 and its accompanying key may be helpful.

Extract 11.6

Ethyl	So they st- their clas[ses start around
Barbara	.... [X__________
Ethyl	(0.2) in
Barbara	______

Transcript key

On the left is the name of the person whose actions (talk or gaze movement) is described on the right.

The hyphen after 'st' indicates that the sound is cut off.

The square bracket '['indicates that this talk by Ethyl is overlapping something Barbara is doing – see the '['immediately below.

The dots '...' indicate that Barbara's gaze is moving.

The 'X' indicates that Barbara's gaze has arrived at Ethyl – specifically, she is gazing at her eyes.

The solid line indicates that Barbara is continuing to gaze at Ethyl.

The number in brackets indicates, in tenths of a second, the amount of silence that has elapsed in between spates of talk.

Source: Goodwin (1980, p. 278)

In Extract 11.6, Ethyl seems to stumble with her words – 'So they st- their classes start around'. What are we to make of this – should we look inside Ethyl's psyche for an explanation, is her stumble to do with her feeling awkward or stressed or is it a sign that she is lying? Perhaps we should just presume that the stumble is accidental and leave it at that. An alternative approach is to see what Barbara (the person Ethyl is talking to) does – how does she treat Ethyl's faltering or perturbated speech? In this extract and others that Goodwin (1980, 1984) examines, the person to whom the speech is addressed (Barbara in this case) will, if they are not gazing at the speaker already, bring their gaze to the speaker. In Extract 11.6, Barbara starts to move her gaze (indicated by the dots) immediately following Ethyl's cut off 'st-'.

We will return to Goodwin's analysis later in this chapter, but, for now, we can note that some otherwise easily dismissable practice – cutting off and restarting speech – could be seen as being treated by the **addressee** in a certain way as their behaviour (gazing at the speaker) appears to be associated with it. Incidentally, you can try this at home – or anywhere, within reason – some time when you are speaking and the person you are speaking to is gazing elsewhere. Try stopping right in the middle of a word and restarting what you had said – for example, 'I think it's rea- I think it's really good'. See if the person you are addressing gazes at you or, if they are visually occupied, they may nod or otherwise indicate that they are attentive. It is perhaps worth exercising a degree of caution about the circumstances in which you try this – if your addressee is busy driving, using dangerous equipment or performing surgery on you at the time, it may be best to wait for another opportunity.

The idea that various practices – such as features of our talk, gaze, gesture and body movements – could be related to what is done in interaction has received attention from a number of researchers. Such work has sought to understand how gaze and other features of vocal or non-vocal behaviour can *do* interactional work, such as indicate who should speak next. Argyle (1975), Argyle, Ingham, Alkema and McCallin (1973) and Argyle and Cook (1976) argued that many of these features of talk, body movement, gaze and gesture can deal with whose turn it is to speak (who 'has the floor'). Thus, for Argyle gaze (at the addressee), sentence completion, prosody (falling – the voice lowering in tone), a stretched final syllable, an incomplete sentence (for the addressee to complete) and various body movements and gestures can all be ways in which the current speaker indicates that they are ending their turn and giving the listener an opportunity to take the floor.

A problem with the formulation of Argyle and colleagues is that it sketches a wide range of potentially relevant resources that speakers may draw on without systematically exploring each. Thus, we are left with a list of ingredients with little sense as to how they might fit together in real sequences of conversation. Staying just with the idea of gaze initially, it could be argued that a speaker gazing at an addressee can do a range of different things, depending on exactly where it is placed in a sequence of things in an interaction. We have probably all been involved in conversations where the speaker gazes at us and we produce some appropriate response – 'He didn't!', 'Really?', 'No!', 'That's amazing!' – without the speaker relinquishing their right to carry on speaking.

One attempt to investigate in more detail how a speaker's use of gaze might relate to who has the floor is found in the work of Kendon (1967). Kendon's work is important, not least because it provides something of a stepping stone towards some of the more interactionally sensitive work considered below. Kendon's experiment – which prompted further critical empirical studies by Beattie and Rutter – is outlined in Box 11.8.

Beattie (1978) and Rutter, Stephenson, Ayling and White (1978, both cited in Rutter, 1984) both criticised Kendon (1967). Beattie drew on data from tutorials and faculty meetings at Cambridge to question Kendon. Beattie argued that if Kendon was right, then he had identified an important means by which speakers, and those about to speak, signal to their addressee what they are about to do. So, the gaze away is a signal that that person will carry on speaking and the gaze at the addressee is a signal they are stopping and the addressee can start to speak instead. Beattie suggested that, if Kendon was right, then where these signals are present, they should enable a smoother conversation than where they are absent. Evidence for this would be a shorter transition time between one person finishing speaking and the other person starting to speak (he called these 'speaker switches').

Beattie did not find that these speaker signals led to any reduction in the gap between one person ending their turn at talk and the next person starting to talks, however. Indeed, Beattie argued that the proportion of smooth, instantaneous 'switches' of speaker occurred exactly where they should not have done according to Kendon. That is, instantaneous switches occurred *most* in those cases where, instead of the current speaker gazing at the addressee, there had been no gaze from the current speaker to the addressee at all (see Box 11.9).

Addressee The person being addressed – spoken to and so on – in an interaction.

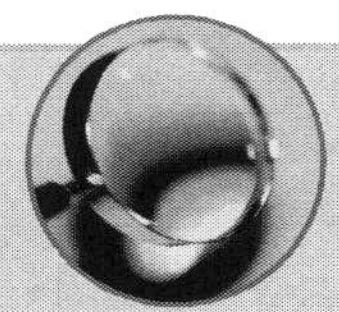

Box 11.8 FOCUS
Classic research: Gaze and speakership (Kendon, 1967)

Procedure

Kendon examined 46 minutes of recordings of meetings between seven pairs of unacquainted students in a laboratory-based 'getting to know each other' encounter. The 46 minutes were selected from various phases of the conversations and comprised 100 long (5 seconds or more) utterances.

Findings

Kendon (1967) found that, as the speaker came to the end of their utterance, they 'generally' looked up at the listener (in 70 per cent of the data fragments). Likewise, new speakers were found to generally look away when they started speaking (again, in 70 per cent of the data fragments) – see Figures 11.4a and b.

Implications

Kendon (1967) argued that the gaze placement of the speaker can thus signal that a response is required (by gazing at his or her addressee) or that they are going to carry on/start speaking (by gazing away).

(a) Current speaker (left) gazes to addressee (right) as they end their talk

(b) The new speaker (right) gazes away as they begin to talk

Figure 11.4 Gaze and speakership, based on Kendon (1967)

As seen in Box 11.9, Rutter et al. (1978, cited in Rutter, 1984) conducted two experiments that also questioned Kendon's (1967) interpretations of his data. Rutter (1984) argued that if Kendon was correct, then there should be a greater proportion of speakers looking at 'addressees' at the *ends* rather than at the *beginnings* of utterances (because the gaze at the addressee was supposed to signal that it was their turn to speak). Furthermore, there should be greater levels of eye contact at the ends of utterances (when the current speaker gazes to the addressee to hand the floor to them) and lower levels of eye contact at the beginnings of new utterances (as the new speaker gazes away). As Rutter (1984) notes, however, in the first experiment – which involved pairs of participants discussing themselves and their interests – Rutter et al. (1978) did not find support for any of these propositions derived from Kendon (1967).

Rutter et al. (1978) conducted a second experiment that involved 12 pairs of strangers and 12 pairs of friends discussing topics from a socio-political questionnaire focusing on items that revealed disagreement. Rutter's second experiment, again, failed to confirm all three conditions that he deemed crucial for Kendon's argument (although it did offer partial confirmation).

Rutter (1984) argued that gazes between speakers and addressees should not be thought of in terms of signals to deal with interaction – such as indicating whose turn it is to speak – as there just was not enough evidence for this. Instead, for Rutter, gaze was about *getting* information – people gaze to *look* at the other and to see what they are doing and how they are reacting rather than to signal anything. Periods of *mutual* gaze – where two people interacting are both gazing at each other – are, for Rutter (1984), Rutter et al.(1978) and Rutter, Stephenson, Lazzerini, Ayling and White (1977), *chance products* of two individuals looking at the other to gain information. That is, if you have two individuals who both look to gain information, you will – by chance alone – get

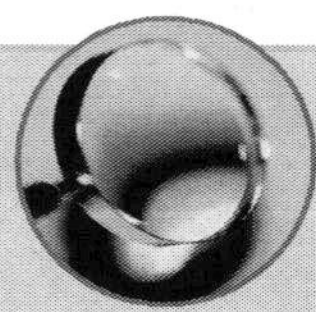

Box 11.9 FOCUS
Was Kendon (1967) right? The challenge from Beattie (1978) and Rutter et al. (1978)

Beattie (1978, cited in Rutter, 1984): does gaze reduce the gap between one speaker finishing and the next starting?

Data used:
Real tutorials and faculty meetings at Cambridge.

What Beattie argued should be found if Kendon was correct:
Shorter transitions from one speaker to another, when the current speaker gazes at the next speaker.

What Beattie actually found:
The shortest transitions actually occurred where there was *no* gaze from the current speaker to the next speaker at all.

Rutter et al. (1978): does gaze occur in the positions Kendon's research suggests it should?

Data used:
In Experiment 1, Rutter et al. made audio recordings of participants, who were *unknown* to each other, discussing themselves and their interests in pairs.

In Experiment 2, Rutter et al. made audio recordings of participants, who were *known* to each other, discussing in pairs points of disagreement arising from a socio-political questionnaire.

What Rutter argued should be found if Kendon was correct:
There should be more of a gaze at the 'listener' and greater eye contact at the ends of utterances rather than at the beginning.

What Rutter actually found:
Experiment 1 entirely failed to confirm what should have been found according to Kendon.

Experiment 2 offered only partial support.

periods when both are looking at each other and that is what Rutter argues is happening when mutual gaze occurs.

Rutter et al.'s (1978) research itself could be criticised, first, for not identifying why Experiments 1 and 2 yielded somewhat different results. Second, his research (like that of Beattie, 1978 cited in Rutter, 1984) did not use transcripts to show what happened in specific sequences of interaction – instead, we are left with statistical aggregrates. Furthermore, where we *do* find a description of the types of data that formed the analysis, this raises additional questions. Thus, Rutter (1984) reports on Rutter et al.'s (1978, p. 4) research, describing the analysis as follows: 'The analysis was based on only the most relevant data – every utterance which consisted of ten words or more, was deemed to be complete, and ended in a floor change without overlapping speech.' These steps resulted in many instances of floor change being discarded, without the possibility of investigating how gaze and other resources might be implicated.

Each of the criteria for rejecting data that Rutter identified (less than 10 words, incomplete, overlapping speech) could be especially important in interactional terms and excluding such data from analysis could distort the resulting picture of interaction. To take one example, the emphasis on utterances that were 'deemed to be complete' is likely to have involved discarding word cut-offs, **restarts** and other speech perturbations that were touched on above. If all speech perturbations are removed, then a specific resource that, as we saw above, has been identified by Goodwin (1979, 1980, 1984) as important for gaining mutual gaze is discarded in research that had hoped to clarify how gaze activity does, or does not, relate to speaker transition. Thus, **perturbations** could be one of the resources that speakers use to get their addressee to gaze at them just as they are about to end their utterance. Rutter's (1984, p. 4) ready dismissing of this and other 'contaminated' or 'inadequat' speech (short, perturbated, overlapping) means that certain

Restarts Where some bit of talk is started over again immediately after it has been uttered.

Perturbations Disturbances to our talk, such as words that are not fully articulated.

issues – which could be crucial to speakership – cannot be examined and the data left is skewed towards just certain types of talk.

While, arguably, appropriately questioning some rigidity implicit in Kendon's (1967) interpretation of his findings, Rutter (1984) perhaps too readily dismissed interactional perspectives per se. From a **conversation analytic** perspective, the speaker's gaze at the addressee at turn completion is not a context-free mechanical device that accomplishes a change in speakership regardless of its sequential position. Instead, for conversation analysis, *where* gaze or any vocal or non-vocal activity occurs is crucial to understanding exactly what sort of interactional work it is doing. Thus, where the addressee is gazing, what talk is being produced and what interactional work is being done need to inform our analysis. Indeed, to come to an understanding of how gaze operates between speakers and addressees, it is important to examine precisely how both parties orientate to each other's actions on a turn-by-turn basis.

Argyle, Ingham, Alkema and McCallin (1973), Argyle and Cook (1976) and Kendon (1967), though different, make a related point about the way in which our talk, gaze, body movements and gestures might regulate interaction – in particular, determining and signalling who is expected to speak next. Both have identified specific practices, such as gaze to, or away from, addressees, that could well play a part in speaker allocation, but their analysis is limited, from a conversation analytic perspective, because these potentially important resources are not investigated with sufficient attention to the detail of the sequential context in which they are placed.

Before returning to the extract from Goodwin considered above, it is worth just noting three fundamental aspects of conversation analysis that inform this and other conversation analytic studies.

Sacks, Schegloff and Jefferson (1974), in their landmark paper, published the first *systematic* study of how conversation is organised. They emphasised two of the fundamental aspects of all conversations – the *turn-constructional component* and the *turn-allocation component*. The turn-constructional component can be understood as the units that our talk is organised into. In advance of encountering the work of Sacks et al., we might think that our speaking and writing are both structured around sentences – that is, we speak and write in grammatically recognisable sentences. Sacks et al. demonstrated – with extensive data extracts – that sentences are, in fact, one type of turn-constructional unit for which other alternatives (such as single words or phrases) are available. In Extracts 11.7 and 11.8, Sacks et al. illustrate single-word and single-phrase turn contructional units.

Extract 11.7

	Desk	What is your last name [Loraine.
→	Caller	[Dinnis.
→	Desk	What?
→	Caller	Dinnis.

Source: Sacks, Schegloff and Jefferson (1974, p. 702)

Extract 11.8

	Anna	Was last night the first time you met Missiz Kelly?
		(1.0)
→	Bea	Met whom?
	Anna	Missiz Kelly.
	Bea	<u>Yes.</u>

Source: Sacks, Schegloff and Jefferson (1974, p. 702)

Neither of the arrowed turns at talk in Extracts 11.7 and 11.8 are formed of sentences – in Extract 11.7 a single word ('Dinnis', 'What?', 'Dinnis') is used in three of the four turns (the first being spoken overlapping the Desk's 'Loraine'). In Extract 11.8, a phrase is used in the arrowed line ('Met whom?')

Sacks et al. demonstrated that, whether our talk is organised into sentences, phrases, clauses or single words, the majority of the time, one person talks, the others remaining silent, more or less, and despite the fact that the sizes of turns vary, the transition from one speaker to the next is carefully coordinated.

Sacks et al. argue that this coordination between speakers is possible because our units of talk (whether single words, phrases, clauses or sentences) have a projectable point at which they are complete – that is, people in a conversation can tell when a particular unit of talk is complete. If you were involved in either of these conversations, you would probably be just as skilled at working out what constituted a recognisably complete unit of talk. Without knowing anything of what was being talked about, the setting or who the participants in the conversation were, you could still judge when each speaker had produced a complete turn-constructional unit and reached a transition relevance place.

These recognisably complete units of talk relate to the second fundamental aspect of conversations, which is the turn-allocation component. When turn constructional components are complete, the participants in any conversation are at just the point where a change of speaker is not inevitable but *relevant*. When a transition relevance

Conversation analytic An approach to understanding interaction informed by the work of Sacks and paying particular attention to the interactional work that is done in sequences of talk.

place is reached, participants in a conversation will address the issue of speakership (whose turn it is to talk) in one of three ways: the current speaker may carry on speaking (producing another turn-constructional unit) or may select another to speak (for example, by asking them a question, as in Extracts 11.7 and 11.8) or another addressee may select themselves to speak. The breathtaking thing about these seemingly mundane observations is that we do not have to conjure up instances where this occurs – this *is* how conversation is organised.

What Sacks et al. achieved was to produce a systematic account of how conversation *per se* is organised – their account being both *context-free* (it applies to all conversations) and *context-sensitive* (the rules they outline cope with precisely who has done what in this immediate conversation).

The third fundamental aspect of conversation to be sketched here is that there is a regular pairing of certain types or classes of utterance – referred to as *adjacency pairs* (Sacks, 1995; Sacks & Schegloff, 1973; Sacks, Schegloff & Jefferson, 1974). This is such a common feature of our everyday interactions that we may not think it worthy of our serious attention, but, from a conversation analytic perspective, it is *because* this and other features of conversation are so fundamental to our conversations, that they do merit careful investigation.

In Extracts 11.7 and 11.8, a question was followed by a response. Often the response to a question is an answer, but it need not be – for example, in Extract 11.8, the first question – 'Was last night the first time you met Missiz Kelly?' – is responded to not with an answer but another question. Thus, another question–response sequence is inserted in between the first question about meeting 'Missiz Kelly' and the later response 'Yes'.

Greetings and greeting responses, invitations and offers and acceptances/declinations can be seen as similarly paired. How many times a day do you find that when you say 'Hi' or 'Hello' to someone, they respond with a greeting? Likewise, if someone invites you somewhere or offers you something, you will typically produce some talk that accepts, declines or relates to that in some way (for example, one of my own favourite responses is 'I'll have to just check').

You might now be thinking of somewhat rare examples where you greeted someone who did *not* return a greeting or you were invited and you did *not* accept or decline. Conversation analytic research into adjacency pairs suggests that sometimes the paired response will not be given, but, in these cases where an expected paired response is missing, it will be 'accountably' or 'notably' absent. That is, its absence will be treated in a different

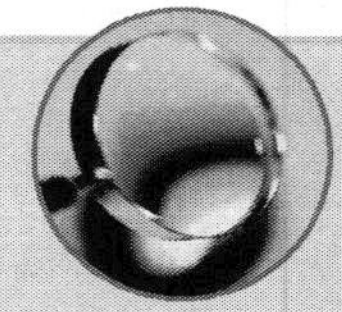

Box 11.10 FOCUS
Goodwin (1980) speech perturbation and addressee gaze. Returning to Extract 11.6 (Goodwin, 1980, p. 278)

Ethyl So they st- their clas[ses start around
Barbara . . . . . . [X__________
Ethyl (0.2) in
Barbara ______

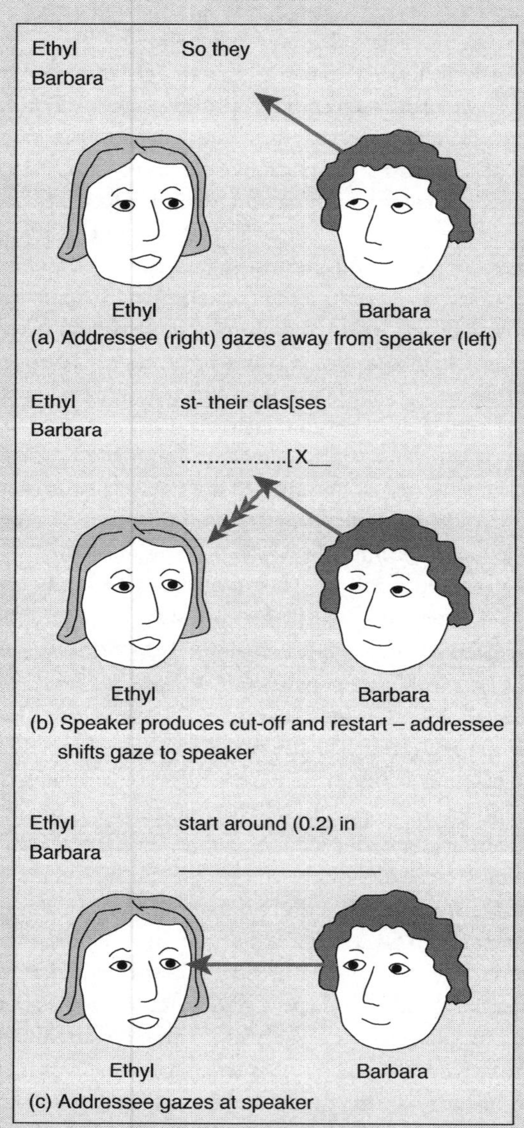

Figure 11.5 Speech perturbation and addressee gaze, based on Goodwin (1980)

way from its presence. If we say 'Hi' and get no response, we might say 'Hi' again, in pursuit of some response – somehow or other the lack of a response raises issues regarding why the person did not respond that just do not occur if we *do* get a response. The person who does not respond to our question, give a greeting response to our greeting or accept or decline our invitation may well have the question, greeting or invitation reissued. Furthermore, they may have to account for (or explain) themselves if they still do not produce the expected paired response.

Let us briefly return to the example from Goodwin (1980) cited in Extract 11.6 at the beginning of this section. It is repeated, together with a diagrammatic version, in Box 11.10. See also Box 11.11 to learn more about Goodwin's work.

It was noted above that Ethyl's speech has a cut-off, – 'st-' (a word that is stopped before being fully articulated) – and, immediately following this, Barbara starts to move her gaze to Ethyl. What is crucial here, though, is not just the gross point that speakers' perturbations tend to be followed by addressees shifting their gaze to the speaker but also, this happens in a specific location sequence.

In Extract 11.6, there are two especially important aspects to the sequential environment in which Ethyl's speech perturbation occurs. First, it occurs *within* a recognisably complete unit of talk a (turn-constructional unit) – it does not occur at a transition relevance place. Second, Ethyl's perturbation occurs at a place in the interaction where the person she is addressing (Barbara) is not gazing at her. In this specific sequential environment, Ethyl's perturbation does or accomplishes something that it would not do if it was placed elsewhere. The crucial point being illustrated here is that it is not just the 'communicative practice' (the talk, gaze, body movement or gesture) that emerges as important but also *the sequential location* of such practices which is absolutely key. Talk, gestures, body movements and gaze only do what they do because of *where they are placed in sequences of interaction.*

The conversation analytic framework considered here provides a perspective that differs from several of the other approaches described earlier. Take a look at the following two samples of actual talk:

1 I'm running an ad in the paper
2 that's awfully sweet of you

Sample 1 seems to simply convey information – the speaker appears to be informing the addressee about something that they are involved with at present (running an advertisement in a newspaper). We do not have the accompanying gestures – if there were any – but the talk itself seems to fit with the 'conveying information' approach considered above.

Sample 2 could be understood from a number of the perspectives that were addressed above. We do not have access to the accent the speaker used, but it could be that the choice of words reveals something of the identity work being done – the use of 'awfully' as an intensifier is sometimes associated with received pronunciation, the 'high-status' dialect considered above. Thus, in Sample 2, the speaker may be doing some type of status work in their talk.

From another perspective – examined above when discussing the expressing of attitudes and emotions – the utterance in Sample 2 may reveal positive feelings ('sweet') about whatever the speaker is referring to. Researchers from this tradition might want to check if the *spoken* feelings matched those revealed in the gestures, gaze and body movements of the speaker.

Finally, researchers interested in communication and relationships might consider how the talk of Sample 2 about feelings of appreciation towards the addressee, might increase the intimacy of the relationship. These researchers might also be interested in the accompanying body movements, gaze and gestures, to see whether they, too, suggest an increase in intimacy (such as prolonged gaze at the addressee's eyes) or if they perhaps were used to maintain equilibrium by decreasing intimacy (less gaze at the addressee's eyes).

From a conversation analytic perspective, interesting though these observations are, attention needs to turn not to the abstracted bits of utterance in isolation but, rather, to the sequence in which Samples 1 and 2 were found. This sequence is given in Extract 11.9.

Extract 11.9

1 B Uh if you'd care to come over and visit a little while
2 this morning I'll give you a cup of coffee
3 A hehh
4 Well
5 that's awfully sweet of you,
6 I don't think I can make it this morning .hh uhm
7 I'm running an ad in the paper and-and uh I have to
8 stay near the phone

Source: Atkinson and Drew (1979, p. 58)

The two snippets of talk – Samples 1 and 2 – considered above can now be seen as fitting into a very specific

Sequential context The context of ongoing interaction in which a specific gaze, gesture, body movement, utterance or other vocalisation is positioned.

Box 11.11 KEY RESEARCHER
Professor Charles Goodwin: non-vocal interaction

How did you become interested in communication and social interaction?

I chose the field of communications and, specifically, the Annenberg School of Communications at the University of Pennsylvania, because I felt that communications – then a new academic discipline – offered exciting new perspectives for thinking about a range of interesting phenomena, including human social life. At the time I was most influenced by people such as Marshall McLuhan and film as an art form. When I actually got to graduate school I was quite unhappy with both the methodological and theoretical frameworks in social psychology and related fields that informed much of my coursework. I did, however, have a quite brilliant and exceptional adviser – the cybernetician Klaus Krippendorff – who introduced me to the work of Gregory Bateson, which I found very exciting. At the same time I began to sit in on classes with Erving Goffman. His approach, with its focus on looking at the details of actual interaction, seemed relevant, appropriate and exciting in ways that the experimental methods and topics of the social psychology I was being taught never did. I learned that people who had worked with Bateson on his Palo Alto project on human communication were now at the Philadelphia Child Guidance Clinic where they were helping to create the field of family therapy. I very much wanted to have an opportunity to work with them. However, because of budget cuts the only job available in the summer of 1969 was typing the plastic identification cards used by patients at the clinic. I took the job because I really wanted to at least have a toe in an environment focused on systematically looking at human interaction. For this work they also hired a young anthropologist who had been doing fieldwork studying the daily lives of African-American families in South Philadelphia. While working, we talked together about many things, including with passion how one might study human interaction. Candy has been my partner and intellectual companion ever since.

Shortly after we got together, Erving Goffman phoned Candy (whose written identity is Marjorie Harness Goodwin) and offered to fund her PhD research through the Center for Urban Ethnography in Philadelphia. For her fieldwork, she studied the daily lives, talk and social organisation of preadolescent African American children on the street, a project that was published in 1990 as *He Said She Said*. In class, Goffman told us that you could not do ethnography with a tape recorder. He mentioned someone I had never heard of, called Harvey Sacks, and said we should not be misled by what he was doing. However, he gave Candy's several tape recorders as part of her research package. I reminded Candy of what Goffman had said in class and argued that she should not use the tape recorders. However, she refused to listen to me. The tapes she made opened important new domains of analysis, which would have been impossible without them.

Sometime after this, I got a job at the Philadelphia Child Guidance Clinic and worked as part of the team that recorded family therapy sessions and used some of them to make training films about how to do therapy. I was thus in the position of studying videotapes of human interaction – albeit in a very special situation – all day long. Moreover, I was deeply influenced by the work of the clinic, which stressed how psychological phenomena were constituted through interactive practices.

Meanwhile, Candy spent approximately two months writing detailed transcripts of children's street talk then took them and her ideas to Bill Labov. He was very enthusiastic and told her about the work of Harvey Sacks. At the time, Labov did not know me or of my own interest in human interaction – I was simply Candy's boyfriend. Candy went to Labov's office regularly and made copies of one or two lectures at a time and brought them home for me to read. Both of us were blown away by them. I now realise we were in an ideal position to read the Sacks lectures. Working with different, though related materials (video and audio recordings of people's activities in consequential natural settings) both of us were grappling with the question of how to describe the practices of interaction that human beings used to build talk and embodied action in concert with each other. The brilliance and insight of Sacks' lectures were immediately clear to us and extraordinarily illuminating. We could immediately use what he said to try to see patterning and structure in our own data. In working with the Sacks lectures, we were not reading literature but using powerful materials that helped us to think through the issues we were facing in our own work. Moreover, instead of being faced with what later appear as a gigantic tome, we only had one or two lectures at a time and looked forward to each next instalment as a special treat.

I had planned to do my dissertation using as data the family therapy sessions I was recording at the

Box 11.11 continued

clinic. However, I began to realise that there were some serious problems with this. The work of the clinic put a particular analytic focus on everything that was happening. I would be expected to analyse what was happening as family therapy, using their theoretical frameworks, rather than as basic mundane interaction.

Though we had very little money, Candy and I bought the first consumer video recorder – the Sony Portapak – and began to videotape whatever events we could find. Shortly after we began recording our own video, Gail Jefferson came to the Center for Urban Ethnography. Because of our deep immersion in the Sacks lectures, we got in touch with her immediately. This quickly led to weekly informal seminars focused on video in our home that were attended by the three of us (Gail, Chuck and Candy) and Malcah Yeager-Dror. Gail was a truly extraordinary teacher and the seminars with her were the greatest intellectual experience of my life. In these seminars, we first looked with others at the materials, such as the cigarette utterance, that would form the basis for my dissertation and 1981 book. Gail is best known for her extraordinary work on audio materials. However, I would like to emphasise her central importance in the development of video analysis as well. My ability to work systematically with video materials was formed through interaction with her in these seminars. Despite the fact that she was not on either of our committees, Gail was the primary intellectual mentor for both myself and Candy. I would also like to emphasise the uniqueness of Gail's theoretical contributions to the study of human interaction.

With Gail, we went to the 1973 Summer Institute of Linguistics at Ann Arbor. There we had the opportunity to take classes with Sacks and Schegloff and to continue our most important weekly seminars at our apartment with the three of them, ourselves, and Malcah. On weekends, we recorded more data, including the tape now known as Auto Discussion.

In later years, two events led me to think about interaction in ways that I hadn' t before. First, Lucy Suchman invited us to study workplace interaction at Xerox Parc. That, in conjunction with work I had started to do with archaeologists as they excavated in the field, led me to see that, while I had done analysis of both language and the body in situated human interaction, I had drawn an invisible barrier at the skin of the actors and not taken into account analytically the structure of the environments they were working within. Second, my father had a stroke that left him with a three-word vocabulary. When I visited him the night after the stroke, I could see from the placement of his eye movements that he was acting as a hearer to what I was saying (the doctors thought he had no understanding whatsoever). However, for a number of years, I did not want to record his interactions, though I found them enormously interesting because of my prior work with the organisation of embodied face-to-face interaction. I eventually realised the importance of showing people the competence of someone such as Chil and, with a growing body of other researchers, the importance of analysing phenomena such as aphasia from a perspective that focused on the organisation of interaction rather than exclusively on events inside the individual brain.

My immersion in the study of talk and human interaction occurred during the years in the late 1960s and early 1970s that are now known as the Sixties. What I recall most from this time is taking extraordinary ideas, art and events for granted. A new recording by Bob Dylan would be followed almost immediately by something like Sgt Pepper from the Beatles and, in addition to generational engagement and political events, such as opposition to the Vietnam War, there were also amazing revelations, such as learning that Richard Nixon was recording all of his conversations. I accepted this richness as normal, just the way things were. Only in retrospect do I appreciate how special that time was. A similar extraordinary environment shaped my development as a scholar. When the work of Gregory Bateson led me to the study of human interaction, I could both begin to work with video with some of his former colleagues, and start to sit in on classes with Erving Goffman. I could meet someone else who shared my passion for human interaction and together we could begin to make recordings that opened up talk and embodied action in the mundane social world in ways that we couldn't imagine when we began them. Once we got interested in this, people such as William Labov, who inspired Candy's fieldwork recording natural conversations on the street, were generous enough to lead us to the Sacks lectures at a time when almost none of his work had been published. Shortly after we began to immerse ourselves in them, while pursuing our own analysis of recorded interaction, Gail Jefferson appeared and turned our little living room into a site for extraordinary intellectual growth and, indeed laid the foundations for the kinds of video analysis I do. We then got the opportunity to actually work with Harvey Sacks and Emmanuel Schegloff - indeed, during the summer when they were doing the final revisions

Box 11.11 continued

to the turn-taking paper. When we returned to the University of Pennsylvania, we sat in on the seminars where Erving Goffman was working out his model of the speaker that appeared in *Footing* and had graduate student data seminars that included Goffman, Labov and Gail Jefferson. In reply to the question asked here, my interest in communication and social interaction was shaped by the opportunity to grow through encounters with an extraordinary set of stimulating creative minds.

How does your approach compare and contrast with others?

My early work differed from much other contemporary analysis of talk-in-interaction because of its use of video and focus on embodiment. However, even at that early period there was most important work on these phenomena being done by people such Adam Kendon, Christian Heath and later Jürgen Streeck. I am not trying to be exhaustive and apologise for names not included. However, this work was, and is, treated by mainstream conversation analysis as different from its focus. I am very happy to now have a host of younger colleagues all over the world who share my interests in video analysis of embodiment and interaction in a range of different settings, including scientific, medical and work settings (including research that grew independently from fields such as ethnomethodology), others who are doing groundbreaking research on the lives of people with aphasia, autism and other disabilities, and new, very important work, on how units are constructed through cooperative action between speakers and hearers in languages such as Japanese and Korean. I feel there are strong ties between what I do and work in fields such as linguistic anthropology, cognitive science of the type pioneered by Ed Hutchins and his colleagues, functional grammar in the United States and interactional linguistics in Europe, the very exciting work being done on prosody in interaction, etc. There is an incredible amount of important and exciting work now happening that I find most relevant to my own interests.

I am not happy with trying to set up comparisons and contrasts. On the surface my own work spans many different kinds of phenomena: face-to-face interaction in conversation, the work of archaeologists doing excavations, chemists in the lab, oceanographers at sea, lawyers in the courtroom and others in workplace settings, interaction with a person with severe aphasia, etc. However, I do not think of these as distinct and different lines of research. They all shed different but complementary light on how human beings build the actual worlds they inhabit with others through situated interaction. Basically, I make recordings of what people are doing in the settings that are relevant to their work and lives and try to systematically describe the practices they use to build in concert with each other the events that constitute the activities that make up those settings.

What do you recommend to people wanting to start to research this topic?

I do the kind of work I do (with video and particular kinds of interests) and not everyone has to do that. For me, what I find most valuable is getting a recording of people performing some activity and then really looking at it, even if, and perhaps especially if, it appears too simple to be interesting (for example, pointing at something in a bit of dirt, someone saying they have stopped smoking, etc.). Listen carefully to precisely how words are spoken (Gail again), what people are doing with their bodies, how they are attending to each other and relevant phenomena in their surrounding, etc. Then try to figure out and describe what practices participants use to construct that event and what has to be in place for what you are looking at to seem obvious and uninteresting and how it is in fact organised. Don't start with a predefined set of categories or focus exclusively on what can be written down as words spoken. For example, don't let noticing of a pointing lead to an exclusive focus on the gesture. Is the world being pointed at also part of the organisation of what is happening here, etc. Initially, follow the trails indicated by the materials you are working with. What do the participants themselves treat as important? Then, try to describe systematic practices, which leads to collections of similar and contrasting phenomena.

sequential context. How would you gloss what is going on in Extract 11.9?

This possibly quite familiar format is an invitation (Lines 1 and 2), followed by a declination (Lines 3–8). We have already considered above how invitations are the first of a pair of utterances that, once issued, make an acceptance or declination interactionally relevant. Here, we see a declination – but we can also notice that it is produced with a delay (Line 4), appreciation of the invitation (Line 5), a statement about availability rather than choice (Line 6) and a reason for the restricted availability (Lines 7 and 8). As you may have experienced yourself, turning down an invitation can be a delicate thing to do and you may recognise the features here in your own talk when you have had to do this sort of thing. In declining, typically people produce hesitation or delay, an appreciation of the invitation, a comment on their availability and an account for their non-availability, regardless of who they are, who is inviting them and whatever it is they are being invited to.

The point here is that the sample bits of talk – 1 and 2 – can be seen as *doing interactional work* – Sample 1 is giving an account for lack of availability and Sample 2 is doing an appreciation of the invitation. These utterances can be considered in terms of what they are doing – but an appreciation of this is only possible by examining them *within the sequential context* in which they occurred.

From the perspective of conversation analysis, all talk, gaze, body movements and gestures can be considered as action in interaction or **doing interaction** in a sequentially sensitive manner. In this way, it shares something of the emphasis on action found in the social constructionist approaches to talk (specifically identity talk) considered earlier. Both conversation analysis and social constructionist approaches do not consider talk as simply a medium for conveying information or inner emotions and attitudes. Likewise, talk is not understood as a tool for achieving some psychologically determined equilibrium in relationships. Instead, for conversation and social constructionist approaches, talk is a resource (sometimes 'practice') for *interactionally relevant work.*

Unlike social constructionist approaches (such as discourse analysis), however, conversation analysis includes non-talk resources, such as gaze, body movements and gestures, as well as talk (each of these are considered as resources that can be used to *do* interactional work). Furthermore, for conversation analysis there is less emphasis on how features of the world (such as identity) are constructed. Finally, conversation analysis tends to place even more emphasis on sequential position than many, though not all, social constructionist approaches. These last two distinctive features are sometimes glossed by saying conversation analysis emphasises position (where things are) rather than composition (how things are constructed).

Before leaving conversation analysis, it is worth noting that it is sometimes dismissed as merely preoccupied with everyday, mundane interactions. One strand of this criticism is that it seems to focus on data derived from everyday interactions – such as telephone calls and mealtime interactions. A second strand is that it always interprets the data in terms of the interactional work that is being done – sometimes at the expense of the topic being discussed or relevant aspects of the wider social context in which the conversation is taking place (Billig, 1999a).

Perhaps a four-fold response to this is worth considering. First, yes, it does pay attention to the sorts of everyday interactions that we are all very familiar with. This can make it feel less exotic than other approaches, with their promise of revealing hidden thoughts and feelings, but this is to miss the fact that our everyday interactions are important precisely because they are ubiquitous and thus merit the systematic analysis they receive in conversation analytic work (Sacks, 1995; Sacks & Schegloff, 1973).

Second, conversation analysis has not been *restricted* to everyday conversations, but been drawn on to understand a wide range of interactions (Drew, 1992), including doctor–patient interactions, courtroom cross-examinations, political interviews, research interviews, assessment interviews, focus groups and interactions involving those who are **communicatively impaired**.

Third, conversation analysis emphasises those features of context that the participants themselves treat as relevant. By focusing on the immediate interactional context, conversation analysts would expect to see participants make relevant in their interaction, those aspects of 'wider context' that are important for their conversations and it is those aspects analysts need to consider. If we try to second guess what other aspects of wider context may be relevant, then we can wind up with a near infinite range of possibly relevant contextual factors that may tell us more about the analyst than the sequence we are supposed to be analysing (Schegloff, 1997, 1999).

Fourth, the disciplined attention to how resources are drawn on to undertake actions in interaction has not cut conversation anlaysis off from applied implications. Conversation analysis has been important in the development of automated systems, humanoid robots and for the better understanding of interactions involving those who are deemed to be communicatively impaired. Work on automated systems such as automated flight information (Wooffitt, Fraser, Gilbert, & McGlashan, 1997)

Doing interaction The actions that our communications might accomplish, such as blaming others, exonerating ourselves or justifying something we have said or are about to say.

Communicatively impaired Those who have, or are deemed to have, deficits that include difficulty with communication as a major symptom – for example, autism or aphasia.

benefited from conversation analysis' detailing of how calls to human information centres are organised – such as how misunderstandings are identified and corrected (or repaired). People involved in the development of humanoid robots have been interested in features of skilful human interaction, such as turn organisation and gaze, with a view to learning from empirically based descriptions of what humans *actually* do in order to design human-like robots. Research that has involved 'communicatively impaired' participants has tended to focus on aphasia and, more recently, autism. Goodwin (1995, 2003) has demonstrated the ways in which an aphasic man capable of only three words – 'and', 'yes' and 'no' – can initiate and maintain complex interactions. A particular emphasis has been on the ways in which the use of gestures, objects in the environment and the conversational sequence itself can act as resources that enable far more complex interactions than measures of his lexical ability would suggest. In a similar fashion, Dickerson, Rae, Stribling, Dautenhahn and Werry (2005) and Dickerson, Stribling and Rae (2007) have argued that autistic children can be found to use gaze and gestures in a remarkably sophisticated way if we consider the *specific sequential location in which they are used* rather than just crude summaries (such as the total amount of gaze and gestures used).

Critical recap

Doing interaction

1 Some approaches (Argyle et al., 1973; Argyle, 1975; Argyle & Cook, 1976) have outlined a list of 'standalone' resources for 'doing' interactional work – such as allocating the floor – without considering the importance of the interaction context in which these resources are placed. That is, what they do might be shaped by exactly where they are placed rather than in some inherent property they have *independent* of that placement.

2 Kendon's (1967) work had some sense of where the interactional resource of interest – in his case, gaze placement – is located, but this was crudely glossed (at the end or beginning of utterances). This resulted in aggregated claims (for example, new speakers gaze away 70 per cent of the time) rather than highly precise observations based on careful scrutiny of the detailed sequential context.

3 Both Argyle and Kendon made use of experimentally generated data that could be understood as highly specific and rarely encountered forms of interaction in the real world, so they might not tell us how *everyday* interactions are organised.

4 Critical appraisals of Kendon's work (Beattie, 1978, cited in Rutter, 1984; Rutter, 1984;) have themselves suffered from the analytic procedures they employed – for example, discarding incomplete, perturbated speech may have involved discarding instances of what Goodwin (1980) argued are vital interactional resources (cut-offs, restarts and perturbations) that get the addressee to gaze at the speaker.

5 Conversation analytic research has been criticised for treating interaction as the *whole* of communication and losing both topic and context. That is, what people are speaking about recedes from view as attention turns to what is being done through their talk. Furthermore, as Billig (1999a, 1999b) argues, conversation analysis has tended to ignore the wider context (an argument that has attracted rebuttals from Schegloff, 1997, 1999).

Reflective questions

1 *How is gaze treated in conversations? What would happen if, for no obvious reason, you did* **not** *gaze at someone you were in a face-to-face conversation with? Would they use the perturbations and restarts that Goodwin refers to?*

2 *Can you think of a case when an almost insignificant element of a conversation – perhaps even silence – somehow became important? Is the sequential position – where it occurs – significant?*

Summary

- Communication can be approached in many quite different ways. This chapter has focused on five ways of thinking about how we communicate and interact.
- Communication can be considered in terms of how emotions and attitudes are expressed, particularly through non-verbal channels and facial expressions. There is a debate about whether or not research supports the idea that non-verbal channels are more powerful than verbal ones in communicating emotions and attitudes. There is also a debate about how culturally specific our universal expressions of emotions are.
- A quite different approach to communication is to consider how it conveys information. Particular attention has been given to how a speaker's gestures may do this and how they may relate to the information conveyed by the speaker's words. A further question is how do audiences make use of these different sources of information and how do they deal with any contradiction between the two?

- Another way of thinking about communication and interaction is to consider how it can reveal and regulate the relationship between those who are communicating with each other. Some research has considered how gaze may reflect the level of intimacy and control in a relationship, while other research has explored the role that topic intimacy may have in this regard.
- A very different way of making sense of research into communication and interaction is to think of it in terms of identity. One element of this is how styles of speech convey and modify or change the speaker's identity – accent perhaps being the most obvious example of this. A second quite different perspective on identity and talk is provided by discursive work, which suggests our constructions of self – or identity talk – can be examined in terms of what is being done by the speaker when they talk about themselves in a specific way.
- The final approach to communication and interaction that was considered was concerned with 'doing interaction' – that is, how all of our potentially 'communicative' behaviour (talk, style of talk, gaze, gestures and body language) can be investigated in terms of what it does within an interaction. One example considered here was the way in which apparent speaker slips in speech – perturbations and restarts – can be seen as interactionally significant to the addressee, who might suddenly turn their gaze to the speaker when these occur. A more general issue that was touched on regarding the conversation analytic approach was that it is the position within a sequence of interaction that is important in understanding what is done by a given utterance, gaze, gesture, body movement or other potentially communicative acts.

Review questions

1. *What is meant by the idea of non-verbal leakage?*
2. *What evidence is there to support the idea that non-verbal channels are more powerful in communicating emotions and attitudes than verbal channels?*
3. *Are expressions of emotion universal?*
4. *What evidence is there to support the idea that gaze can regulate the level of intimacy between people?*
5. *What did McNeill (1985, 1992, 2000) argue regarding the role of gestures in communication?*
6. *How might speech style be related to identity?*
7. *What is meant by the idea that we construct our self or identity via our talk?*
8. *What did Goodwin (1980) argue regarding speech perturbations and restarts?*

Recommended reading

Argyle, M., & Dean, J. (1965). Eye-contact, distance and affiliation. *Sociometry, 28*, 289–304. This is the classic, and extremely well-cited, paper in which Argyle and Dean develop the idea that eye gaze is used to regulate levels of intimacy.

Coupland, N. (2007). *Style: Language variation and identity*. Cambridge: Cambridge University Press. In this book, Coupland examines the way in which styles of speech (including features such as accents and speech lexicon) are linked to issues of identity.

Edwards, D. (2006). Discourse, cognition and social practices: The rich surface of language and social interaction. *Discourse Studies*, *8*, 41–49. A clear, crisp outline of a conversation analysis-informed discursive psychology.

Goodwin, C. (1980). Restarts, pauses, and the achievement of mutual gaze at turn-beginning. *Sociological Inquiry, 50* (3–4), 272–302. This carefully argued paper involves a detailed examination of the easily missed interactional relevance of various forms of perturbations and restarts in conversation.

Goodwin, C. (Ed.) (2003). *Conversation and brain damage*. Oxford: Oxford University Press. This book brilliantly demonstrates the ways in which conversation analysis can be applied to understanding interactions in which one or more parties are deemed to have some form of organic communication impairment.

McNeill, D. (2005). *Gesture and thought*. Chicago, IL: University of Chicago Press. In this book, McNeill draws on and develops his ideas about the communicative importance of gestures.

Sacks, H. Jefferson, G., Ed. (1995). Lectures on conversation, (Vols I and II). Oxford: Blackwell. With an introduction by Schegloff, these are Sack's classic lectures in which conversation analysis was conceived. They have had a vast impact and are eminently readable.

Useful webLinks

The following websites provide a great resource for research publications relating to specific academics and include a number of downloadable references.

http://mcneilllab.uchicago.edu David McNeill's website, addressing issues concerned with the communication of information via gestures.

www.sscnet.ucla.edu/soc/faculty/schegloff/ Emmanuel Schegloff's conversation analytic publications and data archive.

www.sscnet.ucla.edu/clic/cgoodwin/publish.htm Charles Goodwin's conversation analytic publications.

www.soc.ucsb.edu/faculty/lerner/pub/publications.htm Gene Lerner's conversation analytic publications.

www.utexas.edu/coc/cms/faculty/streeck/profile/Links.html A useful site for links to several sites touching on issues covered in this chapter – such as the work of McNeill and conversation analytic sites.

www2.fmg.uva.nl/emca/resource.htm Very useful for links to other conversation analytic sites and it provides a useful overview of people and events connected to conversation analytic (and ethnomethodological) research.

www.paulekman.com Paul Ekman's website addressing the issue of the universality of the facial expressions of emotions.

www-staff.lboro.ac.uk/~ssjap/JP%20Articles/jparticles.htm Jonathan Potter's discursive website.

Glossary

Actor–observer difference The idea that people explain the causes of their own behaviour in a different way from the behaviour of others. Specifically, the concept of actor–observer difference suggests that I will tend to attribute my behaviour or experiences to external or situational causes, whereas I will attribute the behaviour or experiences of others to internal factors. Imagine seeing someone trip as they walk along a pavement. We may be quick to attribute their stumbling to carelessness, yet if *we* trip, we may well attribute it to the pavement being uneven.

Adaptive, functional These terms refer to the idea that an instinct – such as the aggression instinct – has evolved because it had some usefulness in terms of the survival and transfer of genes for our evolutionary ancestors.

Addressee The person being addressed – spoken to and so on – in an interaction.

Adjacency pairs Paired turns of talk that typically come together, such that one part of the pair is usually uttered (or are treated as being expected) in response to the first part of the pair. Common examples include greetings and greeting responses ('Hi' – 'Hi') and questions and question responses ('Do you have the time?' – 'Yes, it's seven minutes past ten.')

Affective response The emotional responses or the feelings that a person may experience.

Affective state A person's emotional state or feelings at a given time.

Agentic state Milgram (2004 [1974], p. 135) used this term to refer to a state in which the individual 'no longer views himself as acting out of his own purposes but rather comes to see himself as an agent for executing the wishes of another person.'

Aggregated behaviours A collection of comparable behaviours – for example, all environmentally friendly behaviours (such as recycling, energy consumption, not burning fossil fuels, steps to reduce carbon footprint) – rather than just one (such as recycling). The emphasis on aggregated behaviours is thought to be important where the attitude being measured is at a relatively broad level.

Altruisim The word altruism comes from Auguste Comte who distinguished 'altruism' from 'egotistic' helping. This distinction – which, as Batson (1991) and Dovidio et al. (2006) note, is still important today – raises three important issues for thinking about altruism. First, for many researchers, definitions of altruism emphasise the motivation or intent driving the 'helping' behaviour, second, the idea that altruisitic behaviour is driven by the intent to benefit others and, third, that altruistic helping can be contrasted with other (more selfishly driven) helping behaviour.

Anonymity, anonymous This refers to the external conditions under which a person is not readily identified as an individual and/or their actions cannot readily be attributed to them as an individual.

Appeal to rhetorical commonplaces This refers to the ways in which talk can mobilise points of consensus by seeking to place the position being argued as a natural consequence of adopting some consensual point or commonplace.

Arousal: cost-reward model – An account of prosocial behaviour that suggests the process begins with some observed stimuli (for example, seeing someone in distress) creating a state of arousal, which then leads to a weighing up of the costs and benefit (to self and other) of helping versus not helping.

Arousal, excitation These are both used to describe states of heightened nervous system activation – often associated with an increased heartbeat – that include pleasurable and aversive states. There is a commonality at a physiological level across the seemingly different states of fear, sexual arousal, anger and exercise-induced arousal. For the physiological state to have a particular meaning, it needs to be labelled or attributed to some specific cause.

Assessment Used in the conversation analytic literature to mean evaluative descriptions of any aspect of the world.

Assortative mating The idea that people seek out partners who share certain characteristics with themselves. From this perspective, similarity between couples is a consequence of each partner seeking out and selecting another who shares similar traits to themselves.

Attitudes as action-orientated versus expressive This distinction is between an understanding of attitudes in terms of what they do (particularly in interactional terms) and what underlying cognitive and affective states they express. Thus, if someone says 'I hate being late!' should we think about that as a stand-alone expression of some underlying cognitive or affective reality - or in terms of what sort of interactional work it could be doing (perhaps chivvying others along) at the moment and in the interactional context where it is uttered?

Attributional semantics An area of attribution research that is concerned with the ways in which our verbal descriptions can have causal implications. A particular emphasis of attributional semantics research has been on the identification of the different sorts of causal implications that different verbs may have.

Attributional This is often used to refer to research concerned with the impact and applications of attributions – such as how attributions can affect our close relationships, how therapeutic techniques have been developed in the light of attribution research.

Attribution bias Distortions or errors that occur in the process of making an attribution.

Attributions The way in which behaviours are explained in terms of what caused them. If I think that my partner's bad mood is caused by their stress at work, then I have made an attribution regarding the cause of their bad mood. Some attribution literature suggests that attributing negative partner behaviour to certain types of causes – for example, causes 'external' to the partner – is associated with the health and longevity of the relationship. More specifically, if – as in the above example – -negative partner behaviour (bad mood) is attributed to an external cause (stress at work), then the relationship is, it is argued, more likely to flourish.

Attribution The process of identifying a cause or causes for an outcome – for example, my thinking about why I got a low grade for my last essay.

Attribution This refers to the process of locating a cause for a given phenomenon. In the context of prosocial behaviour, attribution is relevant in terms of how potential helpers make attributions about what brought about the difficulties experienced by 'the potential recipients of help'. If an individual thinks about how it is a person has fallen to the floor or the inhabitants of a country are experiencing starvation, then they could be thought of as making an attribution that might, potentially, shape whether, and how, they help.

Authority For Milgram this means a person who – within the context in which an attempt at influence is made – has a greater status than the one they seek to influence.

Available discourses The culturally available constructions about how things are – or how or who we can be. In the context of the work outlined here, consideration was given to how a culture might have certain constructions or versions of how to be a man or woman or how to have a certain sexuality.

Aversive Anything that could be perceived or experienced as unpleasant, which can include frustration, but may also include other unpleasant affect (anger, sadness) or sensations (pain or discomfort).

Balance theory A theory that suggests we seek consistency between our liking of people and common targets of our attitudes. We are in balance when we agree with those we like and disagree with those we dislike. From this perspective, similarity between partners can – in part – be understood as a consequence of having greater liking for those with similar attitudes towards things.

Base rates Expectations concerning the frequency with which any attribute might occur in a specific category, such as what proportion of males and females might be thought of as 'assertive'. These expectations might be derived from information (or misinformation) including schemas, that the person making the judgement may hold.

Beats Movements, typically of the hand, that capture something of the rhythm or beat of the talk – for example, banging one's fist on the table for emphasis.

Behavioural intention The decision to engage in a particular action.

Bias Aspects of our thinking that are not rational nor objective, but, instead, influenced by our cognitive imitations or our motivations to think in a certain way – such as I blame my failure on others so that I can feel good about myself.

Body language A popular term, typically used to refer to gaze, gestures and body movements as reflecting thoughts and feelings.

Bundle theory The idea that what we are is simply the totality of our conscious experiences, with no essential self lying beyond this stream of consciousness.

Bystander Anyone who could be considered to be aware of another person in need of any form of helping intervention. Thus, if you observe someone collapsed on a train, struggling with a heavy load or searching for something they have lost, you could be defined as a bystander, whether you know them or not and whether you help them or not.

Categorisation In the cognitive social psychology literature, this refers to the way in which we think of people (and things) in terms of common groupings or categories. This may include ethnic categories, sex categories and occupational categories among others.

Causal schema Kelley (1972, p. 151) defined this as 'a general conception that a person has about how certain kinds of causes interact to produce a specific kind of effect.' It is the person's sense of what sort of causal arrangement might explain the thing they are trying to explain.

Cognition Thinking or mental processes.

Cognitively appraise The process of thinking about and making sense of our selves, experience or our environment. This can include thinking about states of arousal and may involve trying to attribute them to particular causes.

Cognitive miser An important idea concerning what schemas are used for that stresses their function in saving (or being miserly with) thinking effort on the part of the person using them.

Cognitive response The amount of cognitive involvement with, or response to, a stimuli such as a persuasive attempt.

Common goals, superordinate goals A context in which the groups share the same goal and success in achieving it benefits all.

Communicated accounts versus real reasons This distinction is between the explanation (or account) that is given – for example, the reason that you *said* you were unable to pop round for a coffee when asked by the shifty-looking stranger at the bus stop (for example, 'Too busy right now') – and the real reason you declined the invitation (for example, they gave you the creeps).

Communicatively impaired Those who have deficits that include difficulty with communication as a major symptom – for example, autism or aphasia.

Conditions of contact This refers to the context (cooperative *or* competitive) in which members from two or more groups meet.

Conformity The influence that those of a similar status (peers) may have on an individual.

Constructing events This refers to the idea that events may be talked about or constructed in different ways and any one version can be investigated in terms of the sort of interactional or ideological work that it may do.

Constructions of difference This refers to the ways in which differences – in this case, between groups of people – can be built up and used in talk. One example is the way in which constructions of gender differences can be used to justify inequality between men and women.

Constructions of prosocial behaviour This refers to the ways in which we come to define and talk about certain actions as being 'prosocial'. One strand of this is concerned with culturally shared definitions – how do people in a given culture at a given time come to share certain ideas of what is or is not prosocial behaviour? A second strand concerns how we may construct the behaviour of self and others as prosocial or not in our talk and interaction.

Conversational model An approach to attribution that emphasises the way requests for explanations may shape the explanations they ellicit. One particular focus has been on the implict (sometimes explict) contrast between the actual and possible states of affairs that are being asked about – for example, the question, 'Why are you late?' requires an explanation that is relevant for lateness, but not punctuality. Researchers in this field tend to make use of hypothetical sentences rather than the careful examination of sequence of interaction.

Conversation analysis Easily confused with the conversational model because of its name, but very different. Conversation analysis is a term used to describe an approach that cuts across several disciplinary boundaries and involves the careful analysis of real-world sequences of interaction with an emphasis on the ways in which people build interaction conjointly – with each turn of interaction both orientating to and reshaping the immediate sequential context.

Conversation analytic An approach to understanding interaction informed by the work of Sacks and paying particular attention to the interactional work that is done in sequences of talk.

Core identity A person's relatively stable sense of who they are, being formed from recurrent features of several *sub-identities*. This can change according to symbolic interactionist ideas, but is likely to change less readily than a sub-identity.

Cycles, episodes of aggression This refers to the idea that an instance of aggression may not end with the aggressive act, but, instead, the aggressive act (and responses to it) may feed into the cognitions and affective response of the person who aggressed (and others) and can result in other aggressive or non-aggressive behaviour.

Dehumanisation The representation of and treatment of others in a less than human manner. This could include dehumanising ideologies in which certain groups are represented as subhuman, as well as degrading behaviour where someone does not treat the other as a human being.

Deindividuation This is used in different ways in the literature but, generally, denotes a psychological state of decreased awareness of oneself as an individual and/or a lessened sense of accountability for one's own behaviour.

Desensitisation The idea that we may – through familiarity – become less responsive (sometimes measured physiologically) to stimuli – such as aggressive images – which we frequently encounter.

Dialogic self This term is used here almost synonymously with ensembled individualism and the relational self and contrasts with self-contained individualism. Where it does differ from ensembled individualism and the relational self is that it suggests dialogue between people in interaction is where self is constructed.

Diffusion of responsibility Within the context of prosocial research, diffusion of responsibility refers to a (theoretically defined) phenomenon of a reduced sense of a personal responsibility to help, occurring in situations where the potential helper perceives that others are available to do so. This has been incorporated into models of prosocial behaviour that suggest where people perceive others are available to offer help, individuals will experience their own 'responsibility for helping' to be spread or diffused among these others and, therefore, be less likely to help themselves.

Disclaimers Utterances that deny the accountability an utterance might otherwise entail. Disclaimers often preface potentially accountable talk and provide a way for recipients to interpret what follows.

Discursive formations These are culturally and historically located constructions of all aspects of our social world.

Discursive psychology An approach to understanding interaction and social psychology that is informed by the work of Edwards and Potter and which pays particular attention to the sort of interactional work that talk does and the implications that this has for social psychological understanding.

Doing interaction This refers to the idea that talk does things, such as blaming others, exonerating ourselves or justifying something we have said or are about to say, which are relevant in, and for interaction.

Dual processing models Models that describe two different processes for responding to a persuasive attempt, one of which (the central or systematic route) typically entails greater involvement with the message itself and the other (the peripheral or heuristic route) more attention to the source.

Dynamic self-concept The idea that a self-concept has consequences for cognition and behaviour, is fluid and open to change.

Ego theory The idea that there is some essence beyond our conscious experiences – we are more than just the bundle of our stream of conscious experiences – and this something is *self*.

Empathic attribution This is the idea that if we feel empathy for another person, our attributions for their behaviour will be different. Specifically, we will make more external or situational attributions (meaning that our attributions for their behaviour takes a similar form to what the actor–observer difference bias suggests is typical of our attributions for our own behaviour).

Ensembled individualism This refers to a view of the individual person widely held in non-Western (and particularly non-English-speaking) cultures. According to ensemble individualism, a 'self' includes others and relationships with others and cannot be so readily separated from them as 'self-contained individualism' assumes.

Environmental cues Aspects of the environment that might be associated with certain behaviours – for example, a gun might be a cue for aggression.

Epistemic identity An identity that is relevant to a knowledge state about a given target. This is particularly relevant where there are different epistemic identities for people involved in an interaction, such as a grandmother talking about her own grandchild with a friend.

Equilibrium hypothesis The idea that we seek to maintain a desirable level of intimacy in our interactions and will adjust our gaze or proximity to do so (for example, squeezed next to a stranger on a train, we may gaze away to reduce the intimacy that the situation has thrust on us).

Equity theory The idea that people are motivated by a concern with both maximising their outcomes (like exchange theory) and (unlike exchange theory) with fairness (which considers how much profit each party in the relationship deserves). The concern with fairness is understood as a particularly important issue for understanding partners' satisfaction or distress within a relationship.

Exchange theory The idea that our motivation to enter and remain in relationships is driven by our assessment of the profit (rewards 2 costs) of doing so. Our behaviour is thus driven by seeking to maximise our profit. Profit, in this context, can include any perceived net benefits, not just financial ones.

Excitation transfer This term describes the process of *misattributing* and/or *mislabelling* a state of arousal or excitation. More specifically, this term denotes a model within social psychology that has sought to explain phenomena such as aggression, prosocial behaviour and relationships.

Excuses versus justifications Excuses deny agency (it was not my choice or fault) – for example, an excuse for arriving late at a dinner party could be, 'The train was late'. Justifications, by contrast, accept responsibility and give a rationale for the action, so a justification for lateness could be, 'I thought it would be nice for you if people staggered their arrival – some coming early and some, like myself, later.'

Exonerating explanations Explanations that account for why we did something others might not approve of or we did not do something others wanted us to do – 'I would have tidied the place, but I had to make an important call', for example.

Explanation The process of communicating an attribution – such as telling someone why you can't come to their party.

Explanatory relevance of 'descriptive' talk This refers to the way in which simple descriptions can *do* interactional work, such as accounting for or holding someone else to account for why something was (or was not done). Thus, 'It's so untidy in here!' may hold someone to account for the mess, while, 'It's been non-stop since you left!' may account for the untidiness.

External and situational These terms identify the location for the cause as outside of the outcome to be explained – for example, I was nervous in the interview because of the spotlight pointed at my face and the aggressive style of questioning.

Formation of self The processes of constituting self, which includes how we come to construct versions of who we are. For example, our sense of our gender, sexuality and what these categories mean are important parts of how we come to build up, or construct, versions of our selves.

Frustration Any situation in which the individual does not get what they want – sometimes referred to as their goal response being blocked.

Fundamental attribution error A specific bias towards making attributions to internal causes – that is, causes thought to be 'within' the person whose behaviour (or experience) we are trying to explain. An example would be to attribute someone's examination failure to their lack of effort or ability (internal causes) rather than to the difficulty of the paper (an external cause).

Group aspects of prosocial behaviour This refers to the various ways in which prosocial behaviour may be shaped by our own perceived group identities (for example, our religious, political or activist identities may shape our prosocial behaviour) and/or those of others (for instance, perceiving others as belonging to the same or a different group than us may shape our prosocial behaviour towards them).

Group norms Group-informed ideas about how to behave towards members of one's own group (*ingroup*) and other groups (*outgroups*).

Group selection An account of prosocial behaviour that is consistent with evolutionary theory. Group selection suggests that, because altruistic behaviour increases the probability of survival for groups where it is found, those groups where it is present are more likely to successfully pass on their pool of genes (including genes associated with altruistic behaviour).

Helping Could be understood as, 'an action that has the consequence of providing some benefit to or improving the well-being of another person. The definition of helping is not particularly stringent; as long as the well-being of one or more people is improved by the actions of another' (Dovidio et al., 2006, p. 22).

Iconic hand gestures Gestures that display or enact meaning – for example, stretching your hand up when describing how tall someone is (the hand gesture displaying the concept of 'tallness').

Ideal self A representation of a self that one desires to be.

Identity Identity broadly refers to anything that can be considered a 'representation' of self such as talk or thoughts about who one is.

Ideological implications These are the power-relevant implications of a given construction. Thus, certain constructions of 'being female' have emphasised a relative passivity in contrast to 'active males'. Versions of the world or constructions such as these could be understood as having power implications – empowering men – at the expense of depowering women.

Implicit attitude measures These are indirect measures of attitudes that are thought to avoid problems anticipated if a more explicit (such as a self-report) measure were to be used. Implicit attitude measures are often used where it is thought the participants might be reluctant to admit their 'real' attitudes – for example, research into prejudice. Often reaction times to stimuli presented on a computer screen are used for this sort of measure.

Individualistic perspectives This phrase refers to ways of understanding self that emphasise self as an individual rather than self in relation to others.

Informational influence A type of influence (usually used to further define a type of conformity influence) in which an individual is influenced by others because they look to them for information.

Ingroup A group to which we belong or perceive ourselves belonging to.

Ingroup bias The propensity to behave in ways that favour the ingroup over one or more outgroups.

Instinct In the above literature, a genetically transmitted tendency towards certain types of behaviour.

Interactional context This refers not to the physical setting but, rather, the sequence of vocal and nonvocal communication. Thus, any single utterance could be analysed in terms of its place within a sequence of interaction.

Interactional implications These are the implications within an immediate interaction. Thus, constructing gender, sexuality and relationships in a certain way may do things that are relevant for my immediate interaction – for example, doing agreement, blaming, exonerating.

Interactionally relevant work The things done by talk (such as accounting, blaming and exonerating) that are relevant or consequential for the interaction.

Intergroup bias The idea that our attributions for group-relevant outcomes (or things to be explained) may be shaped by our sense of our own and others' group identities. We might, therefore, attribute the success of a football team we support differently (perhaps to the skill of the group) from the success of a rival team (where luck or poor refereeing may be emphasised).

Internal, actor and person These terms identify the cause as being *within* the person doing or experiencing the behaviour to be explained – 'my boyfriend is jealous because of their personality', 'I failed an exam because I didn't revise', for example.

Internal states Any cognitions and feeling that we may have – for example, anger.

Invoking commonplaces, rhetorically self-sufficient arguments and categories in talk This refers to some of the different ways that talk may draw credibility or warrant itself through an appeal to common understandings about the way the world is.

Just world hypothesis This refers to the idea that may be more or less common in certain populations – that the world is essentially fair. According to this hypothesis, bad things happen to bad people and good things happen to good people. The just world hypothesis predicts both *not* helping (the onlooker thinks the 'victim' deserves what has happened to them) and *helping* (the onlooker thinks that, by helping, good things will happen to them).

Kin selection theory An account of prosocial behaviour that is consistent with evolutionary theory. Kin selection theory suggests that we will show a preference for helping those who are most closely genetically related to us and, thereby, increase the likelihood of our common genes being passed on.

Knapp's model of interaction stages A model of different levels of intimacy in an interaction that suggest people may both reflect and determine the intimacy of their relationship via the intimacy of their interaction with each other.

Levels of specificity This term refers to a concern that the specificity of the attitude measures and the behaviour measure are compatible – that is, either both are highly specific or both are quite general.

Likert scale An attitude scale that requires participants to indicate the extent of their agreement or disagreement with attitude-valanced statements – that is, they are required to mark on a scale their agreement or disagreement with distinct attitudinal positions.

Loss of identity Losing the sense of oneself as an individual.

Market forces The idea that people have a certain 'market value' as a potential mate. Similarity between couples can thus be explained in terms of them having similar traits because those matched traits have the same market value.

Membership categories, membership categorisation The categories that people use in their talk to do internationally relevant work.

Membership categorisation devices (MCDs) The categories that people use to do interactionally relevant work.

Minimal group A group that has a minimal basis for being thought of as a group, usually created by social psychologists who deliberately use the most spurious basis for distinguishing one minimal group from another. The minimal group will, however, have some characterising label (such as high estimators, Kandinsky group) and members will be made aware that they belong to that specific group and not another named group.

Minority influence The effect of a smaller number of individuals on a larger number in contexts where there is no marked, relevant difference in status.

Misattribute(d) or mislabel(led) arousal These terms refer to a process that may take place once a state of arousal has been experienced – and usually when the initial stimulus (or cause of it) is no longer present. Our labelling of what we are feeling, and/or what caused us to feel it, is where we make sense of our arousal or excitation. If we undergo a frightening experience – and then have some lingering state of arousal – we could mislabel that arousal as sexual attraction or aggression, for example, and attribute it to a person we happen to be with.

Multiple necessary cause schema This is a schema in which many causes are anticipated as being needed to explain an unusual, or difficult to achieve, phenomenon.

Multiple sufficient cause schema This is a schema in which any one of a number of possible causes are anticipated as being adequate or sufficient to explain a regular or easy to achieve phenomenon.

Mutual gaze Where people in an interaction are gazing at each other in the region of the eyes.

Mutually incompatible goals A context in which groups have antagonistic goals and the success of one group necessitates failure or loss for the other.

Negative affect Any unpleasant feelings, such as anger, sadness or depression.

Neo-associationist A theoretical position informed, partly, by behaviourist concerns with associations between environmental stimuli. In the case of aggression literature, it specifically refers to the idea that negative affect is associated with anger-related feelings and aggressive thoughts and intentions.

Non-verbal communication Every aspect of communication, apart from the words themselves – that is, style of talk, eye gaze, gesture and body movement. These modes of communication are sometimes referred to as non-verbal channels.

Non-verbal leakage The idea that our 'true' feelings are expressed through our non-verbal channels because they are less easy to control than words themselves.

Normative influence A type of influence (usually used to further define a type of conformity influence) in which an individual is influenced by others because they are concerned about their social relationship with them.

Norm of reciprocity The expectation that those interacting will respond in kind to the actions of each other. Thus, if one person shares intimate personal information, the norm of reciprocity suggests that the other person should do likewise.

Noun phrase positioning This refers to the position that nouns have within (usually quite simple) sentences. Some research within this field has suggested that changing the order of nouns can change the causal implications of the sentence. Thus, a passive sentence such as, 'Student shouted at by lecturer' may suggest that the first noun (the student) at least partly brought it on him- or herself, whereas the active alternative, 'Lecturer shouted at student' might imply that it was entirely the lecturer's fault.

Obedience Acting in accordance with the instructions of an 'authority' figure.

Observed actual aggression This is a measure of aggression in which attention is given to what people would conventionally define as aggression – the direct infliction of physical pain or discomfort on another.

Observed direct verbal aggression This is a measure of aggression in which attention is given to aggressive and domineering ways of talking and interacting – it includes 'interactional dominance', interruption and 'ignoring others'.

Outcome The happening, behaviour or event for which a cause is sought – for example, my friend seems to act coldly towards me, I have failed an exam, I did not laugh at the comedian.

Outgroup A group to which we do not belong or do not perceive ourselves as belonging to.

'Out there' reality Within the current context, this refers to the ways in which speakers may try to construct their talk or stance as a reflection of the 'real world' rather than as a subjective or partisan stance for which equally credible alternatives exist.

Perceived control This refers to how easy or difficult the target behaviour is thought to be by the individual.

Personal evaluation The way in which an individual believes that they are perceived by another. In the context of this literature, the focus is on how being perceived in a positive or negative way affects attraction towards, and cognitive evaluation of, the person whose evaluations are being considered.

Person factors Any characteristics of our personality or gender, it can include factors that have been modified by the current, or other, cycles of aggression.

Perturbations Disturbances to our talk, such as words that are not fully articulated.

Planned helping This refers to the non-ad hoc help that we might offer by, for example, giving our time or money to a charity or providing other forms of regular help to others (such as visiting or assisting them on a regular basis).

Positive differential This refers to the way that group members are motivated to perceive their group as different and superior to other groups and to act in ways that are consistent with this.

Prejudice Any instance in which judgements about another are made in advance of adequate scrutiny of the relevant facts (particular attention is given to racist and sexist forms of prejudice). While many researchers would see stereotypes as being the cause of prejudice, the term 'prejudice' (unlike stereotypes) does not make a presumption about the importance of various types of cognitive activity. Thus, many researchers drawing on approaches that are not cognitively orientated (for example, discourse analysts) might refer to prejudice rather than schemas or stereotypes.

Prosocial behaviour Following Dovidio et al. (2006), this is used to refer to a broad range of 'beneficial' behaviours. Usually these behaviours would benefit others, though the person engaging in the prosocial behaviour may also benefit.

Questionnaire evaluations A measure of aggression that relies on how positively or negatively the participant evaluates someone else (often an experimenter) on a questionnaire.

Rational actor The idea that human behaviour can be made sense of in terms of individuals rationally pursuing what they perceive to be their own self-interest.

Reciprocal altruism An account of prosocial behaviour that is consistent with evolutionary theory. Reciprocal altruism suggests that people engage in altruistic behaviour because it increases the likelihood of themselves receiving help at some point.

Reciprocal liking Mutual liking between two people. In the context of this literature, the interest is in how such mutual liking is an important factor in attraction.

Referent informational influence A type of influence where the individual's sense of group identity is relevant. Referent informational influence occurs where the individual shapes their behaviour to be consistent with a group identity that has become salient for them.

Relational self The idea that self is interdependent and interconnected and necessarily, includes us being 'in relation' to others.

Reproductive fitness The extent to which a potential mate is likely to maximise the chance of passing on one's genes to future offspring. Someone with high reproductive fitness is more likely to be able to have offspring (and thereby pass on genes) than someone with low reproductive fitness.

Restarts Where some bit of talk is started over again immediately after it has been uttered.

Rhetorical approach This refers to Billig's work, which emphasises how attitudes are argumentatively shaped, being formed on matters that are up for debate and designed to argue against other stances on these argued-about issues.

Role A coherent set of duties and expected behaviours often associated with a specific job, such as 'prison guard', or status, such as 'prisoner'. For Zimbardo (2007), the roles we find ourselves in shape our behaviour in important ways.

Schema A cognitive structure that represents the information and misinformation we have about any form of category. A particularly important form being those that relate to social positions known as *role schemas*. Role schemas include both *achieved roles*, which involve and reflect some choice (such as job, educational status, sports groups, political or religious affiliation), and *ascribed roles* that do not (such as age, sex and ethnicity). Some work considers the ways in which, once a person being perceived has been categorised, the relevant schema then has an influence on the thinking about that person.

Schematic (aschematic) Issues and topics that are relevant (irrelevant) to our self-schema.

Self Self is difficult to define – not least because of the different ways in which it is used in social psychological literature. At its broadest, self can be thought of as referring to any aspect of who or what the individual is – or is considered to be.

Self-concept The version or idea about self that someone holds. It is very similar to self-schema (but is not only used by cognitive social psychologists).

Self-construal Almost synonymous with self-concept – the ways in which an individual construes or thinks about self.

Self-contained individualism This predominantly Western understanding of the individual – also the perspective that is most common in psychology stresses self as being separable from others.

Self-regulation The means by which we manage or regulate ourselves – particularly our behaviour and our emotions.

Self-schema The collection of ideas that a person holds about themselves; tends to be used by cognitive social psychologists.

Self-serving bias A distortion in the attribution process affecting our attributions for our own behaviour and experiences. The self-serving bias suggests that we will tend to explain our successes in terms of internal causes (such as attributing our exam success to our ability and effort) and our failures in terms of external factors (attributing our exam failure to difficulty of the paper or the external stresses in our life, for example).

Semantic differential An attitude scale that requires participants to indicate where they are positioned on scales labelled with mutually incompatible adjectives at opposite ends to each other.

Sequential context The context of ongoing interaction in which a specific gaze, gesture, body movement, utterance or vocalisation is positioned.

Sex-linked preferences This refers to the idea that what is thought to be desirable in a mate is linked to the sex of the person making the judgement. This strand of evolutionary psychology suggests that men and women have different positions regarding ideal partner attributes and this difference can be explained in evolutionary terms.

Social comparison Comparisons made between the attributes of one's own self and those of others in a given domain (or on shared dimensions), such as comparing your own intelligence with that of someone else.

Social context This refers to the wider setting within which real instances of behaviour take place. By considering the specifics of the social context, aggressive behaviour, for example, may be seen as having a meaning or purpose in some cases that cannot be appreciated when issues of social context are ignored.

Social identity deindividuation effects (SIDE) Emphasises the way in which situations of group immersion and anonymity can give rise to, not a loss of, identity but, rather, a change of identity, with a particular emphasis on the group identities that may become salient in such situations.

Social identity Our sense of ourselves as being a member of a group or groups – our shared, collective or group identity.

Social representations The definition of this term is the subject of some debate and discussion, but, broadly, it is used to refer to socially shared understandings that may change over time or differ for certain groups. One concept that could be thought of in these terms is 'mental illness' – an idea that has been defined in incredibly different terms across time and cultures, yet, within some groups has certain shared or consensual properties.

Sociolinguistics An approach to communication that is particularly concerned with how styles of speech, including accents, relate to different groups, categories and identities.

Speaker's own interests This refers to the ways in which speakers construct the interests of themselves and others (particularly those they find themselves arguing with). Speakers may position their own talk as unconnected to or even running counter to their own vested interests, while constructing the talk of their argumentative opponents as simply a reflection of their opponents' own self-interest.

Spillover effect A term used to denote the finding in some minority influence research that the minority may have an effect on not just the specific focus of an 'influence attempt' but 'associated' issues also.

Stereotype A type of role schema that is relatively rigid. Once a person being perceived has a stereotype applied to them, then, however accurate or inaccurate it may be, our perception is likely to be significantly affected by the content of that stereotype.

Stereotype content The specific characteristics (intelligent, aggressive, antisocial, gregarious) people attribute to different groups or categories of people. Research within this tradition has paid particular attention to the ways in which the stereotype content associated with certain groups changes over time.

Stereotype process This refers to the ways in which having a stereotype shapes cognitive processes such as encoding, retrieval and evaluation.

Stimulus conditions This refers to factors in the environment – such as aversive conditions – that may bring about a given behavioural response – such as aggression.

Stripped-down stimulus sentences This refers to the made-up sentences given to participants in -experiments – without any surrounding context – in order to assess the causal implications of the verb, the noun and/or the sentence structure. The phrase is usually used to highlight how different these experimental conditions are from the way in which causal sentences and explanations are encountered in non-experimental contexts.

Sub-identity A relatively specific identity arising from a specific role relationship. See also *core identity*.

Subject As used by Foucault, this term refers to the modern individual and is deliberately used to suggest that the individual is not free, but, instead, tied to their own sense of who they are as well as being subject to others.

Subjective norm The individual's perception of what people who are important to him or her think about the target behaviour and how motivated the individual is to comply with those perceptions.

Subject positions These are the various selves that we might inhabit – the different ways of being a person within a given socio-historical context.

Symbolic interactionism A collection of approaches particularly concerned with the ways in which a sense of self is socially based, being dependent, in various ways, on the perceptions made by others and interactions with them.

Sympathetic denigration This refers to the ways in which talk may denigrate or disempower others, while appearing to be sympathetic towards them.

Thurstone scale An attitude scale that involves the participants selecting preweighted statements they agree with on a given topic. Unlike the other popular scales, the participants do not have to indicate their position on a linear scale (such as the extent of their agreement or disagreement).

Victim empathy The extent to which participants express empathy (usually in questionnaire responses) for victims (often presented as summaries of a case where someone has been the victim of a crime).

Wider argumentative context The idea that attitudes can be considered in terms of their relation to the sorts of things that are argued or debated at a given place and time. This is suggestive of a move from attitudes as simply the cognitive and/or affective products of individual minds operating in isolation from one another.

Working self-concept The currently active or salient collection of self-concepts – the idea being that these are just a selection from a wider pool of all possible self-concepts.

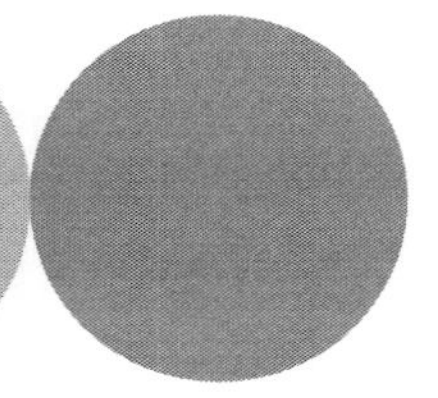

References

Abell, J., & Walton, C. (2010). Imagine: Towards an integrated and applied social psychology. *British Journal of Social Psychology, 49*, 685–690.

Abrams, D., Wetherell, M., Cochrane, S., & Hogg, M. A. (1990). Knowing what to think by knowing who you are: Self-categorization and the nature of norm formation, conformity and group polarization. *British Journal of Social Psychology, 29*(2), 97–119.

Adams, J. S. (1965). Inequity in social exchange. In L. Berkowitz (Ed.), *Advances in experimental social psychology* (pp. 267–299). New York: Academic Press.

Adorno, T. W., Frenkel-Brunswik, E., Levinson, D. J., & Sanford, R. M. (1950). *The authoritarian personality*. New York: Harper.

Ajzen, I. (1985). From intentions to actions: A theory of planned behavior. In J. Kuhi & J. Beckmann (Eds.), *Action–control: From cognition to behavior* (pp. 11–39). Heidelberg: Springer.

Ajzen, I. (1988). *Attitudes, personality and behavior*. Milton Keynes, England: Open University Press & Chicago, IL: Dorsey Press.

Ajzen, I. (1991). The theory of planned behavior. *Organizational Behavior and Human Decision Processes, 50*, 179–211.

Ajzen, I. (1998). *Attitudes, personality and behavior*. Chicago, IL: The Dorsey Press.

Allegranti, B. (2011). *Embodied performances: Sexuality, gender, bodies*. London: Palgrave Macmillan.

Allport, G. W. (1935). Attitudes. In C. Murchison (Ed.), *Handbook of social psychology* (pp. 798–844). Worcester, MA: Clark University Press.

Allport, G. W. (1950). *The nature of personality: Selected papers*. Cambridge, MA: Addison-Wesley.

Allport, G. W. (1954). *The nature of prejudice*. Reading, MA: Addison-Wesley.

Altman, I., & Taylor, D. A. (1973). *Social penetration*. New York: Holst, Rinehart & Winston.

Alvaro, E. M., & Crano, W. D. (1997). Indirect minority influence: Evidence for leniency in source evaluation and counter-argumentation. *Journal of Personality and Social Psychology, 72*, 949–965.

Anderson, C. A. (1989). Temperature and aggression: Ubiquitous effects of heat on the occurrence of human violence. *Psychological Bulletin, 106*, 74–96.

Anderson. C. A., & Bushman, B. J. (1997). External validity of 'trivial' experiments: The case of laboratory aggression. *Review of General Psychology, 1*, 19–41.

Anderson, C. A., & Bushman, B. J. (2002). Human aggression. *Annual Review of Psychology, 53*, 27–51.

Anderson, E. (2008a). 'Being masculine is not about who you sleep with ...': Heterosexual athletes contesting masculinity and the one-time rule of homosexuality. *Sex Roles: A Journal of Research, 58*(1–2), 104–115.

Anderson, E. (2008b). Inclusive masculinity in a fraternal setting. *Men and Masculinities, 10*(5), 604–620.

Anderson, E. (2008c). 'I used to think women were weak': Orthodox masculinity, gender-segregation and sport. *Sociological Forum, 23*(2), 257–280.

Antaki, C. (1994). *Explaining and arguing: The social organisation of accounts*. London: Sage.

Argyle, M. (1975). *Bodily communication*. London: Methuen.

Argyle, M., Alkema, F., & Gilmour, R. (1971). The communication of friendly and hostile attitudes by verbal and non-verbal signals. *European Journal of Social Psychology, 1*, 385–402.

Argyle, M., & Cook, M. (1976). *Gaze and mutual gaze*. London: Cambridge University Press.

Argyle, M., & Dean, J. (1965). Eye-contact, distance and affiliation. *Sociometry, 28*, 289–304.

Argyle, M., Ingham, R., Alkema, F., & McCallin, M. (1973). The different functions of gaze. *Semiotica, 7*, 19–32.

Argyle, M., Salter, V., Nicholson, H., Williams, M., & Burgess, P. (1970). The communication of inferior and superior attitudes by verbal and non-verbal signals. *British Journal of Social and Clinical Psychology, 9*, 221–231.

Arkes, H. R., & Tetlock, P. E. (2004). Attributions of implicit prejudice, or 'Would Jesse Jackson "Fail" the implicit association test?' *Psychological Inquiry. 15*, (4), 257–278.

Asch, S. E. (1946) Forming impressions of personality. *Journal of Abnormal and Social Psychology, 41*, 258–290.

Asch, S. E. (1951). Effects of group pressure upon the modification and distortion of judgement. In H. Guetzkow (Ed.), *Groups, leadership and men*. Pittsburgh, PA: Carnegie Press.

Asch, S. E. (1952). *Social psychology*. Englewood Cliffs, NJ: Prentice Hall.

Asch, S. E. (1956). Studies of independence and conformity: A minority of one against a unanimous majority. *Psychological Monographs, 70*, 1–70.

Asch, S. E. (1966). Opinions and social pressure. In A. P. Hare, E. F. Borgatta, & R. F. Bales (Eds.), *Small groups: Studies in social interaction* (pp. 318–324). New York: Alfred A. Knopf.

Atkinson, J. M., & Drew, P. (1979). *Order in court: The organization of verbal interaction in juridical settings*. London: Macmillan.

Au, T. K. (1986). A verb is worth a thousand words: The causes and consequences of interpersonal events implicit in language. *Journal of Memory and Language, 25*, 104–122.

Augoustinos, M., Hastie, B., & Wright, M. (2011). Apologizing for historical injustice: Emotion, truth, and identity in political discourse. *Discourse & Society, 22*, 507–531.

Augoustinos, M., LeCouteur, A., & Soyland, J. (2002). Self-sufficient arguments in political rhetoric: Constructing reconciliation and apologising to the stolen generations. *Discourse and Society, 13*, 105–142.

Augoustinos, M., Tuffin, K., & Rapley, M. (1999). Genocide or a failure to gel? Racism, history and nationalism in Australian talk. *Discourse & Society, 10*, 351–378.

Augoustinos, M., Walker, I., & Donaghue, N. (2006). *Social cognition: An integrated introduction*. London: Sage.

Aumer-Ryan, K., Hatfield, E., & Frey, R. (2007). Examining equity theory across cultures. *Interpersona: An International Journal on Personal Relationships, 1*(1), 61–75.

Austin, W., & Walster, E. (1975). Equity with the world: An investigation of the trans-relational effects of equity and inequity. *Sociometry, 38*, 474–496.

Axsom, D., Yates, S., & Chaiken, S. (1987). Audience response as a heuristic cue in persuasion. *Journal of Personality and Social Psychology, 53*, 30–40.

Bagozzi, R. P., & Burnkrant, R. E. (1979). Attitude organization and the attitude–behavior relationship. *Journal of Personality and Social Psychology, 37*, 913–929.

Bagozzi, R. P., & Burnkrant, R. E. (1980). Single component versus multicomponent models of attitude: Some cautions and contingencies for their use. *Advances in Consumer Research, 7*, 339–344.

Bakhtin. M. (1981 [1935]). Discourse in the novel. In M. Holquist (Ed.), *The dialogic imagination: Four essays by M. Bakhtin* (C. Emerson & M. Holquist, Trans., pp. 259–422). Austin, TX: University of Texas Press.

Bakhtin, M. (1986 [1952]). The problem of speech genres. In C. Emerson and M. Holquist (Eds.), *Speech genres and other late essays* (V. W. McGee, Trans., pp. 60–102). Austin, TX: University of Texas Press.

Baron, R. A. (1997). The sweet smell of ... helping: effects of pleasant ambient fragrance on prosocial behavior in shopping malls. *Personality and Social Psychology Bulletin, 23*, 498–503.

Bartholow, B. D., Bushman, B. J., & Sestir, M. A. (2006). Chronic violent video game exposure and desensitization to violence: Behavioral and event-related brain potential data. *Journal of Experimental Social Psychology, 42*, 532–539.

Batson, C. D. (1991). *The altruism question: Toward a social-psychological answer*. Hillsdale, NJ: Erlbaum.

Batson, C. D., Batson, J. G., Todd, R. M., Brummett, B. H., Shaw, L. L., & Aldeguer, C.M.R. (1995). Empathy and the collective good: Caring for one of the others in a social dilemma, *Journal of Personality and Social Psychology, 68*, 619–631.

Batson, C. D., Duncan, B. D., Ackerman, P., Buckley, T., & Birch, K. (1981). Is empathic emotion a source of altruistic motivation? *Journal of Personality and Social Psychology, 40*, 290–302.

Batson, C. D., Klein, T. R., Highberger, L., & Shaw, L. L. (1995). Immorality from empathy-induced altruism: When compassion and justice conflict. *Journal of Personality and Social Psychology, 68*, 1042–1054.

Batson, C. D., & Oleson, K. C. (1991). Current status of the empathy–altruism hypothesis. In M. S. Clark (Ed.), *Review of personality and social psychology* (Vol. 12, pp. 62–85). Newbury Park, CA: Sage.

Batson, C. D., O'Quin, K., Fultz, J., Vanderplas, M., & Isen, A. M. (1983). Influence of self-reported distress and empathy on egoistic versus altruistic motivation to help. *Journal of Personality and Social Psychology, 45*, 706–718.

Baumeister, R. F. (1987). How the self became a problem: A psychological review of historical research. *Journal of Personality and Social Psychology, 52*, 163–176.

Baumeister, R. F., DeWall, C. N., Ciarocco, N. J., & Twenge, J. M. (2005). Social exclusion impairs self-regulation. *Journal of Personality and Social Psychology, 88*, 589–604.

Baxter, J. (2002). Competing discourses in the classroom: A post-structuralist discourse analysis of girls' and boys' speech in public contexts. *Discourse and Society, 13*, 827–842.

Baxter, L. A., (1983). Relationship disengagement: An examination of reversal hypothesis, *Western Journal of Speech Communication, 47*, 85–98.

Baxter, L. A., & West, L. (2003). Couple perceptions of their similarities and differences: A dialectical perspective. *Journal of Social and Personal Relationships, 20*(4), 491–514.

Beattie, G. (2003). *Visible thought: The new psychology of body language*. Abingdon: Routledge.

Beattie, G. W., & Shovelton, H. K. (1999a). Do iconic hand gestures really contribute anything to the semantic information conveyed by speech? An experimental investigation. *Semiotica, 123*, 1–30.

Beattie, G. W., & Shovelton, H. K. (1999b). Mapping the range of information contained in the iconic hand gestures that accompany spontaneous speech. *Journal of Language and Social Psychology, 18*, 438–62.

Bell, A. (1984). Language style as audience design. *Language in Society, 13*, 145–204.

Bell, A. (2001). Back in style: Reworking audience design. In P. Eckert, & D. Rickford, (Eds.), *Style and sociolinguistic variation* (pp. 139–169). Cambridge: Cambridge University Press.

Bem, D. J. (1972). Self-perception theory. In L. Berkowitz (Ed.), *Advances in experimental social psychology* (Vol. 6, pp. 11–62). New York: Academic Press.

Benwell, B. M., & Stokoe, E. (2006). *Discourse and identity*. Edinburgh: Edinburgh University Press.

Benwell, B. M., & Stokoe, E. (2010). Identity in social action: Conversation, narratives and genealogies. In M. Wetherell & C. T. Mohanty (Eds.), *The Sage handbook of identities* (pp. 56–77). London: Sage.

Berkowitz, L. (1962). *Aggression: A social psychological analysis*. New York: McGraw-Hill.

Berkowitz L. (1965). Some aspects of observed aggression. *Journal of Personality and Social Psychology, 12*, 359–369.

Berkowitz, L. (1984). Some effects of thoughts on anti- and prosocial influences of media events: A cognitive-neoassociationistic analysis. *Psychological Bulletin, 95*, 410–427.

Berkowitz, L. (1989). The frustration–aggression hypothesis: Examination and reformulation. *Psychological Bulletin, 106*, 59–73.

Berkowitz, L. (1990). On the formation and regulation of anger and aggression: A cognitive-neoassociationistic analysis. *American Psychologist, 45*(4), 494–503.

Berkowitz, L. (1993). Pain and aggression: Some findings and implications. *Motivation and Emotion, 17*, 277–293.

Berkowitz, L., & Alioto, J. T. (1973). The meaning of an observed event as a determinant of its aggressive consequences. *Journal of Personality and Social Psychology, 28*, 206–217.

Berkowitz, L., Cochran, S. T., & Embree, M. C. (1981). Physical pain and the goal of aversively stimulated aggression. *Journal of Personality and Social Psychology, 40*, 687–700.

Berkowitz, L., & Donnerstein, E. (1982). External validity is more than skin deep: Some answers to criticism of laboratory experiments. *American Psychologist, 37*, 245–257.

Berkowitz, L., & Geen, R. G. (1967). The stimulus qualities of the target of aggression: A further study. *Journal of Personality and Social Psychology, 5*, 364–368.

Berkowitz, L., & LePage, A. (1967). Weapons as aggression-eliciting stimuli. *Journal of Personality and Social Psychology, 7*, 202–207.

Berkowitz, L., Lepinski, J. P., & Angulo, E. J. (1969). Awareness of own anger level and subsequent aggression. *Journal of Personality and Social Psychology, 11*, 293–300.

Berkowitz, L., & Troccoli, B. T. (1990). Feelings, direction of attention, and expressed evaluations of others. *Cognition and Emotion, 4*, 305–325.

Bierhoff, H. W., Klein, R., & Kramp, P. (1991). Evidence for the altruistic personality from data on accident research. *Journal of Personality, 59*, 263–280.

Billig, M. (1985). Prejudice, categorization and particularization: From a perceptual to a rhetorical approach. *European Journal of Social Psychology, 15*, 79–103.

Billig, M. (1987). *Arguing and thinking: A rhetorical approach to social psychology*. Cambridge: Cambridge University Press.

Billig, M. (1991). *Ideology and opinions. Studies in rhetorical psychology*. London: Sage.

Billig, M. (1995). *Banal nationalism*. London: Sage Publications.

Billig, M. (1996). *Arguing and thinking: A rhetorical approach to social psychology* (Rev. Ed.). Cambridge: Cambridge University Press.

Billig, M. (1999a). Whose terms? Whose ordinariness?: Rhetoric and ideology in conversation analysis. *Discourse & Society, 10*, 543–558.

Billig, M. (1999b). Conversation analysis and the claims of naivety. *Discourse & Society, 10*, 572–576.

Billig, M. (2001). Humour and hatred: The racist jokes of the Ku Klux Klan. *Discourse & Society, 12*, 291–313.

Billig, M. (2002). Henri Tajfel's cognitive aspects of prejudice. *British Journal of Social Psychology, 41*, 171–188.

Billig, M. (2008). *The hidden roots of critical psychology: Understanding the impact of Locke, Shaftesbury and Reid*. London: Sage.

Billig, M. (2011). Writing social psychology: Fictional things and unpopulated texts. *British Journal of Social Psychology, 50*, 4–35.

Blackmore, S. (2003). *Consciousness: An introduction*. London: Hodder Education.

Blackmore, S. (2010). *Consciousness: An introduction* (2nd ed.). London: Hodder Education.

Blanton, H. (2001). Evaluating the self in the context of another: The three-selves model of social comparison assimilation and contrast. In G. B. Moskowitz (Ed.), *Cognitive social psychology: The Princeton symposium on the legacy and future of social cognition* (pp. 75–87). Mahwah, NJ: Erlbaum.

Blanton, H., & Stapel, D. (2008). Unconscious and spontaneous and ... complex: The three selves model of social comparison assimilation and contrast. *Journal of Personality and Social Psychology, 94*(6), 1018–1032.

Blass, T. (1999). The Milgram paradigm after 35 years: Some things we now know about obedience to authority. *Journal of Applied Social Psychology, 29*, (51), 955–978.

Block, J. and Funder, D. C. (1986). Social roles and social perception: Individual differences in attribution and 'error'. *Journal of Personality and Social Psychology, 51*, 1200–1207.

Blumstein, P. W., Carssow, K. G., Hall, J., Hawkins, B., Hoffman, R., Ishem, E., Maurer, C. P., Spens, D., Taylor, J., & Zimmerman, D. L. (1974). The honoring of accounts. *American Sociological Review, 39*, 551–566.

Bond, R., & Smith, P. B. (1996). Culture and conformity: A meta-analysis of studies using Asch's (1952, 1956) line judgment task. *Psychological Bulletin, 119*, 11–137.

Boonzaier, F. (2008). 'If the man says you must sit, then you must sit': The relational construction of woman abuse: Gender, subjectivity and violence. *Feminism & Psychology, 18*, 183.

Bornstein, R. F. (1989). Exposure and affect: Overview and meta-analysis of research, 1968–1987. *Psychological Bulletin, 106*, 265–289.

Bornstein, R. F., & D'Agostino, P. R. (1992). Stimulus recognition and the mere exposure effect. *Journal of Personality and Social Psychology, 63*, 545–552.

Bourhis, R. Y. & Giles, H. (1977). The language of intergroup distinctiveness. In H. Giles (Ed.), *Language, ethnicity and intergroup relations* (pp. 119–135). London: Academic Press.

Breckler, S. J. (1984). Empirical validation of affect, behavior and cognition as distinct components of attitude. *Journal of Personality and Social Psychology, 47*, 1191–1205.

Broadbent, D. (1958). *Perception and communication*. London: Pergamon.

Brock, T. E. (1965). Communicator–recipient similarity and decision change. *Journal of Personality and Social Psychology, 1*, 650–654.

Brown, R. J. (1978). Divided we fall: An analysis of relations between sections of a factory workforce. In H. Tajfel (Ed.), *Differentiation between social groups: Studies in the social psychology of intergroup relations* (pp. 395–430). London: Academic Press.

Brown, R. (1986). *Social psychology* (2nd ed.). New York: Free Press.

Brown, R. J. (2000a). *Group processes* (2nd ed.). Oxford: Blackwell.

Brown, R. (2000b). Social identity theory: Past achievements, current problems and future challenges. *European Journal of Social Psychology, 30*, 745–778.

Brown, R. J. (2010). *Prejudice: Its social psychology* (2nd ed.). Chichester: Wiley-Blackwell.

Brown, R., & Fish, D. (1983). The psychological causality implicit in language. *Cognition, 14*, 237–273.

Bruner, J. S., & Goodman, C. C. (1947). Value and need as organizing factors in perception. *Journal of Abnormal and Social Psychology, 42*, 33–44.

Burkitt, I. (2008). *Social selves: Theories of self and society* (2nd ed.). London: Sage.

Burnstein, E., Crandall, C., & Kitayama, S. (1994). Some neo-Darwinian decision rules for altruism: Weighing cues for inclusive fitness as a function of the biological importance of the decision. *Journal of Personality and Social Psychology, 67*, 773–789.

Bushman, B. J., & Anderson, C. A. (2002). Violent video games and hostile expectations: A test of the general aggression model. *Personality and Social Psychology Bulletin, 28*, 1679–1689.

Bushman, B. J., Baumeister, R. F., Thomaes, S., Ryu, E., Begeer, S., & West, S. G. (2009). Looking again, and harder, for a link between low self-esteem and aggression. *Journal of Personality, 77*(2), 427–446.

Bushman, B. J., Bonacci, A. M., van Dijk, M., & Baumeister, R. F. (2003). Narcissism, sexual refusal, and aggression: Testing a narcissistic reactance model of sexual coercion. *Journal of Personality and Social Psychology, 84*, 1027–1040.

Bushman, B. J., Wang, M. C., & Anderson, C. A. (2005). Is the curve relating temperature to aggression linear or curvilinear? Assaults and temperature in Minneapolis re-examined. *Journal of Personality and Social Psychology, 89*, 62–66.

Buss, D. M. (1989). Sex differences in human mate preferences: Evolutionary hypotheses tested in 37 cultures. *Behavioral and Brain Sciences, 12*, 1–49.

Buss, D. M. (2005). *The handbook of evolutionary psychology*. Hoboken, NJ: Wiley.

Buss, D. M. (2006). Strategies of human mating. *Psychological Topics, 15*, 239–260.

Buss, D. M. (2007). The evolution of human mating. *Acta Psychologica Sinica, 39*, 502–512.

Buss, D. M., & Barnes, M. (1986). Preferences in human mate selection. *Journal of Personality and Social Psychology, 50*, 559–570.

Buston, P. M., & Emlen, S. T. (2003). Cognitive processes underlying human mate choice: The relationship between self-perception and mate preference in Western society. *Proceedings of the National Academy of Sciences of the USA, 100*, 8805–8810.

Butler, J. (1999). *Gender trouble, feminism and the subversion of identity*. New York: Routledge.

Butler, J. (2004). *Undoing gender*. Abingdon: Routledge.

Buunk, B. P., Oldersma, F. L., De Dreu, K. W. (2001). Enhancing satisfaction through downward comparison: The role of relational discontent and individual, differences in social comparison orientation. *Journal of Experimental Social Psychology, 37*, 1–16.

Byrne, D. (1971). *The attraction paradigm*. New York: Academic Press.

Calder, B. J., Insko, C. A., & Yandell, B. (1974). The relation of cognitive and memorial processes to persuasion in a simulated jury trial. *Journal of Applied Social Psychology, 4*, 62–93.

Campbell, D. T. (1961). Conformity in psychology's theories of acquired behavioral dispositions. In I. A. Berg & B. M. Bass (Eds.), *Conformity and deviation* (pp. 101–142). New York: Harper & Row.

Campbell, D. T. (1990). Asch's moral epistemology for socially shared knowledge. In I. Rock (Ed.), *The legacy of Solomon Asch: Essays in cognition and social psychology* (pp. 39–52). Hillsdale, NJ: Erlbaum.

Carnagey, N. L., Anderson. C. A., & Bushman, B. J. (2007). The effect of video game violence on physiological desensitization to real life violence. *Journal of Experimental Social Psychology, 43*, 489–496.

Carroll, J. M. and Russell, J. A. (1996). Do facial expressions signal specific emotions? Judging the face in context. *Journal of Personality and Social Psychology, 70*, 205–218.

Chaiken, S. (1979). Communicator physical attractiveness and persuasion. *Journal of Personality and Social Psychology, 37*(8), 1387–1397.

Chaiken, S. (1980). Heuristic versus systematic information processing and the use of source versus message cues in persuasion. *Journal of Personality and Social Psychology, 39*, 752–756.

Chapman, L. J. (1967). Illusory correlation in observational report. *Journal of Verbal Learning and Verbal Behavior, 5*, 151–155.

Cheng, P. W., & Holyoak, K. J. (1989). On the natural selection of reasoning theories. *Cognition, 33*, 285–313.

Cherry, F. (1995). *The stubborn particulars of social psychology: Essays on the research process*. London: Routledge.

Choi, I., & Nisbett, R. E. (1998). Situational salience and cultural differences in the correspondence bias and actor–observer bias. *Personality and Social Psychology Bulletin, 24*, 949–960.

Choi, I., Nisbett, R. E., & Norenzayan, A. (1999). Causal attribution across cultures: Variation and universality. *Psychological Bulletin, 125*, 47–63.

Chomsky, N. (1959). A review of verbal behavior by B. F. Skinner. *Language, 35*, 26–58.

Chu, S., Hardaker, R., & Lycett, J. E. (2007). Too good to be 'true'? The handicap of high socio-economic status in attractive males. *Personality and Individual Differences, 42*, 1291–1300.

Cialdini, R. B., Darby, B. L., & Vincent, J. E. (1973). Transgression and altruism: A case for hedonism. *Journal of Personality and Social Psychology, 9*, 502–516.

Clayman, S. E. (1992). 'Footing in the achievement of neutrality: The case of news–interview discourse', In P. Drew & J. Heritage (Eds.) *Talk at work* (pp. 163–198). Cambridge: Cambridge University Press.

Coates, J. (2004). *Women, men and language: A sociolinguistic account of gender differences in language* (3rd ed.). Harlow: Pearson.

Cohen, C. E. (1981) Person categories and social perception: Testing some boundary conditions of the processing effects of prior knowledge. *Journal of Personality and Social Psychology, 40*, 441–452.

Cohen, B. A., & Waugh, G. W. (1989). Assessing computer anxiety. *Psychological Reports, 65*, 735–738.

Condor, S. (2000). Pride and prejudice: Identity management in English people's talk about 'this country'. *Discourse and Society, 11*, 163–193.

Condor, S., & Figgou, L. (2011). Rethinking the prejudice problematic: A collaborative cognition approach. In J. Dixon & M. Levine (Eds), *Beyond prejudice: Extending the social psychology of intergroup conflict, inequality and social change*. Cambridge: Cambridge University Press.

Condor, S., Figgou, L., Abell, J., Gibson, S., & Stevenson, C. (2006). 'They're not racist': Prejudice mitigation and suppression in dialogue. *British Journal of Social Psychology, 45*, 441–462.

Confer, J. C., Easton, J. E., Fleischman, D. S., Goetz, C., Lewis, D. M., Perilloux, C., & Buss, D. M. (2010). Evolutionary psychology: Controversies, questions, prospects, and limitations. *American Psychologist, 65*, 110–126.

Cooke, R., & Sheeran, P. (2004). Moderation of cognition–intention and cognition–behaviour relations: A meta-analysis of properties of variables from the theory of planned behaviour. *British Journal of Social Psychology, 43*, 159–186.

Cook, G. I., Marsh, R. L., & Hicks, J. L. (2003). Halo and devil effects demonstrate valenced-based influences on source-monitoring decisions. *Consciousness & Cognition, 12*, 257–278.

Corcoran, T. (2009). Second nature. *British Journal of Social Psychology, 48*, 375–388.

Corneille, O., Klein, O. Lambert, S., & Judd, C. M. (2002). On the role of familiarity with units of measurement in categorical accentuation: Tajfel and Wilkes (1963) revisted and replicated. *Psychological Science, 13*(4), 380–383.

Cosmides, L., & Tooby, J. (1992). Cognitive adaptations for social exchange. In J. H. Barkow and L. Cosmides (Eds.), *The adapted mind: Evolutionary psychology and the generation of culture* (pp. 193–228). Oxford: Oxford University Press.

Coupland, N. (2007). *Style: Language variation and identity*. Cambridge: Cambridge University Press.

Courtenay, W. H. (2000). Constructions of masculinity and their influence on men's well-being: A theory of gender and health. *Social Science & Medicine, 50*(10), 1385–1401.

Crinean, M., & Garnham, A. (2006). Implicit causality, implicit consequentiality and semantic roles. *Language and Cognitive Processes, 21*, 636–648.

Crossley, M. L. (2009). Breastfeeding as a moral imperative: An autoethnographic study. *Feminism & Psychology, 19*(1), 71–87.

Cuddy, A. J. C., Fiske, S. T., Kwan, V. S. Y., Glick, P., Demoulin, S., Leyens, J. P., Bond, M. H., Croizet, J. C., Ellemers, N., Sleebos, E., Htun, T. T., Kim, H. J., Maio, G., Perry, J., Petkova, K., Todorov, V., Rodriguez-Bailon, R., Morales, E., Moya, M., Palacios, M., Smith, V., Perez, R., Vala, J., & Ziegler, R. (2009). Stereotype content model across cultures: Towards universal similarities and some differences. *British Journal of Social Psychology, 48*, 1–33.

Curry, R. L. (1988). Influence of kinship on helping behaviour in Galapagos mockingbirds. *Behavioral Ecology and Sociobiology, 22*, 141–152.

Cutrona, C. E., Russell, D., & Jones, R. D. (1985). Cross-situational consistency in causal attribution: Does attributional style exist? *Journal of Personality and Social Psychology, 47*, 1043–1058.

Darley, J. M., & Batson, C. D., (1973). 'From Jerusalem to Jericho': A study of situational and dispositional variables in helping behavior. *Journal of Personality and Social Psychology, 27*, 100–108.

Darley, B., & Latané, J. (1968). Bystander interventions in emergencies: Diffusion of responsibility. *Journal of Personality and Social Psychology, 8*, 377–383.

Darwin, C. (1859). *On the origin of species by means of natural selection, or the preservation of favoured races in the struggle for life*. London: John Murray.

Davey, A., Fincham, F. D., Beach, S. R. H., & Brody, G. H. (2001). Attributions in marriage: Examining the entailment model in dyadic context. *Journal of Family Psychology, 15*, 721–734.

Deaux, K. (1976). Sex: A perspective on the attribution process. In J. H. Harvey, W. J. Ickes & R. F. Kidd (Eds.), *New directions in attribution research* (Vol. 1). Hillsdale, NJ: Erlbaum.

Deaux, K., & Farris, E. (1977). Attributing causes for one's own performance: The effects of sex, norms and outcome. *Journal of Research in Personality, 11*, 59–72.

Deutsch, M., & Gerard, H. B. (1955). A study of normative and informational social influences upon individual judgment. *Journal of Abnormal and Social Psychology, 51*, 629–636.

Devine, P. G. (1989). Stereotypes and prejudice: Their automatic and controlled components. *Journal of Personality and Social Psychology. 56*, 5–18.

DeWall, C. N., Baumeister, R. F., Mead, N. L., & Vohs, K. D. (2011). How leaders self-regulate their task performance: Evidence that power promotes diligence, depletion, and disdain. *Journal of Personality and Social Psychology. 100*(1), 47–65.

Dickerson, P. (1996). 'Let me tell us who I am': The discursive construction of viewer identity. *European Journal of Communication, 11*, 57–82.

Dickerson, P. (1997a). 'It's not just me who's saying this ...': The deployment of cited others in televised political discourse. *British Journal of Social Psychology, 36*, 33–48.

Dickerson, P. (1997b). Humpty Dumpty meets Mikhail Bakhtin. *Journal of Pragmatics, 27*, 527–530.

Dickerson, P. (1998). 'I did it for the nation': Repertoires of intent in televised political discourse. *British Journal of Social Psychology, 37*, 477–494.

Dickerson, P. (2001). Disputing with care: Analysing interviewees' treatment of interviewers' prior turns in televised political interviews. *Discourse Studies, 3*, 203–222.

Dickerson, P., Rae, J., Stribling, P., Dautenhahn, K., & Werry, I. (2005). Autistic children's co-ordination of gaze and talk: Re-examining the 'asocial' autist. In K. Richards and P. Seedhouse (Eds.), *Applying conversation analysis* (pp. 19–37). Basingstoke: Palgrave Macmillan.

Dickerson, P., Stribling, P. & Rae, J. (2007). Tapping into interaction: How children with autistic spectrum disorders design and place tapping in relation to activities in progress. *Gesture, 7*, 271–303.

Diener, E. (1976). Effects of prior destructive behavior, anonymity, and group presence on deindividuation and aggression. *Journal of Personality and Social Psychology, 33*, 497–507.

Diener, E. (1979). Deindividuation, self-awareness and disinhibition. *Journal of Personality and Social Psychology, 37*, 1160–1171.

Diener, E. (1980). Deindividuation: The absence of self-awareness and self-regulation in group members. In P. B. Paulus (Ed.), *The psychology of group influence* (pp. 209–242). Hillsdale, NJ: Lawrence Erlbaum.

Diener, E., Lusk, R., DeFour, D., & Flax, R. (1980). Deindividuation: Effects of group size, density, number of observers, and group member similarity on self-consciousness and disinhibited behavior. *Journal of Personality and Social Psychology, 39*(3), 449–459.

van Dijk, T. (1993). *Elite discourse and racism*. Newbury Park, CA: Sage.

van Dijk, T. (2002). Discourse and racism. In David T. Goldberg & John Solomos (Eds.), *A companion to racial and ethnic studies* (pp. 145–159). Oxford: Blackwell.

Di Pellegrino, G., Fadiga, L., Fogassi, L., Gallese, V., & Rizzolatti, G. (1992). Understanding motor events: A neurophysiological study. *Experimental Brain Research, 91*, 176–180.

Dittmar, H., Long, K., & Bond, R. (2007). When a better self is only a button click away: Associations between materialistic values, emotional and identity-related buying motives, and compulsive buying tendency online. *Journal of Social and Clinical Psychology, 26*(3), 334–361.

Dixon, J., & Levine, M. (Eds.) (2011). *Beyond prejudice: Extending the social psychology of intergroup conflict, inequality and social change.* Cambridge: Cambridge University Press.

Dodson, C. S., Darragh, J., & Williams, A. (2008). Stereotypes and retrieval-provoked illusory source recollections. *Journal of Experimental Psychology: Learning, Memory & Cognition, 34,* 460–477.

Dollard, J., Doob, L., Miller, N. E., Mowrer, O. H., & Sears, R. R. (1939). *Frustration and aggression.* New Haven, CT: Yale University Press.

Donnerstein, E., & Berkowitz, L. (1981). Victim reactions in aggressive erotic films as a factor in violence against women. *Journal of Personality and Social Psychology, 41,* 710–724.

Donnerstein, E., Donnerstein, M., & Evans, R. (1975). Erotic stimuli and aggression: Facilitation or inhibition. *Journal of Personality and Social Psychology, 32,* 237–244.

Donnerstein, E., Donnerstein, M., Simon, S., & Ditrichs, R. (1972). Variables in interracial aggression: Anonymity, expected retaliation, and a riot. *Journal of Personality and Social Psychology, 22*: 236–245.

Dovidio, J. F., Evans, N., & Tyler, R. B. (1986). Racial stereotypes: The contents of their cognitive representations. *Journal of Experimental Social Psychology, 22*(1), 22–37.

Dovidio, J. F., Kawakami, K., & Gaertner, S. L. (2002). Implicit and explicit prejudice and interracial interaction. *Journal of Personality and Social Psychology, 82,* 62–68.

Dovidio, J. F. Piliavin, J. A., Gaertner, S. L. Schroeder, D. A., & Clark, R. D. (1991). The arousal:cost–reward model and the process of intervention: A review of the evidence. In M. S. Clark (Ed.), *Review of personality and social psychology:* 12: *Prosocial behaviour* (pp. 86–118). Newbury Park, CA: Sage.

Dovidio, J. F., Piliavin, J. A., Schroeder, D. A., & Penner, L. A. (2006). *The social psychology of prosocial behaviour.* Mahwah, NJ: Erlbaum.

Drew, P. (1992). Contested evidence in a courtroom cross-examination: The case of a trial for rape. In P. Drew & J. Heritage (Eds.), *Talk at work: Social interaction in institutional settings* (pp. 470–520). Cambridge: Cambridge University Press.

Drew, P., & Walker, T. (2009). Going too far: Complaining, escalating and disaffiliation. *Journal of Pragmatics, 41*(12), 2400–2414.

Druian, P., & Catrambone, R. (1986). *Cognitive accessibility of the self-concept in person perception.* Behavioural Science Research Foundation. Unpublished.

Drury, J., & Reicher, S. (1999). The intergroup dynamics of collective empowerment: Substantiating the social identity model of crowd behaviour. *Group Processes and Intergroup Relations, 2,* 381–402.

Drury J., & Reicher, S. (2000) Collective action and psychological change: The emergence of new social identities. *British Journal of Social Psychology, 39,* 579–604.

Duncan, B. L. (1976). Differential social perception and attribution of intergroup violence: Testing the lower limits of stereotyping of blacks. *Journal of Personality and Social Psychology, 34,* 590–598.

Durkheim, E. (1898). Representations individuelles et representations collectives. *Revue de Metaphysique et de Morale, 6,* 273–302.

Dutton, D. G., & Aron, A. P. (1974). Some evidence for heightened sexual attraction under conditions of high anxiety. *Journal of Personality and Social Psychology, 30*(4), 510–517.

Duval, S., & Wicklund, R. A. (1972). *A theory of objective self awareness [by] Shelley Duval and Robert A. Wicklund.* New York: Academic Press.

Eagly, A. H. (1992). Uneven progress: Social psychology and the study of attitudes. *Journal of Personality and Social Psychology, 63,* 693–710.

Eagly, A., & Chaiken, S. (1993). *The psychology of attitudes.* Fort Worth, TX: Harcourt Brace Jovanovich.

Eagly, A. H., Chaiken, S., & Wood, W. (1981). An attribution analysis of persuasion. In J. H. Harvey, W. J. Ickes, & R. F. Kidd (Eds.), *New directions in attribution research* (Vol. 3, pp. 37–62). Hillsdale, NJ: Erlbaum.

Eagly, A., Mladinic, A., & Otto, S. (1994). Cognitive and affective bases of attitudes toward social groups and social policies. *Journal of Experimental Social Psychology, 30,* 113–137.

Eckes, T. (1994). Features of men, features of women: Assessing stereotypic beliefs about gender subtypes. *British Journal of Social Psychology, 33,* 107–123.

Edley, N., & Wetherell, M. (1997). Jockeying for position: The construction of masculine identities. *Discourse & Society, 8*(2), 203–217.

Edley, N., & Wetherell, M. (1999). Imagined futures: Young men's talk about fatherhood and domestic life. *British Journal of Social Psychology, 38*(2), 181–194.

Edwards, D. (1994). Script formulations: A study of event descriptions in conversation. *Journal of Language and Social Psychology, 13*(3), 211–247.

Edwards, D. (1995). Two to tango: Script formulations, dispositions, and rhetorical symmetry in relationship troubles talk. *Research on Language and Social Interaction, 28*(4), 319–350.

Edwards, D. (1998). The relevant thing about her: Social identity categories in use. In C. Antaki & S. Widdicombe (Eds.), *Identities in talk* (pp. 15–33). London: Sage.

Edwards, D. (2006). Discourse, cognition and social practices: The rich surface of language and social interaction. *Discourse Studies, 8,* 41–49.

Edwards, D., & Potter, J. (1992). *Discursive psychology.* London: Sage.

Edwards, D., & Potter, J. (1993). Language and causation: A discursive action model of description and attribution. *Psychological Review, 100*(1), 23–41.

Ekman, P. (1980). *The face of man: Expression of universal emotion in a New Guinea village.* New York: Garland Press.

Ekman, P. (1994). Strong evidence for universals in facial expression: A reply to Russell's mistaken critique. *Psychological Bulletin, 115,* 268–287.

Ekman, P., & O'Sullivan, M. (2006). From flawed self-assessment to blatant whoppers: The utility of voluntary and involuntary behavior in detecting deception. *Behavioral Sciences and the Law, 24,* 673–686.

Eliot, M. A., Armitage C. J., Baughan C. J., (2007). Using the theory of planned behaviour to predict observed driving behaviour. *British Journal of Social Psychology, 46*, 69–90.

Evans, A., Riley, S., & Shankar, A. (2010). Technologies of sexiness: Theorizing women's engagement in the sexualisation of culture. *Feminism & Psychology, 20*(1), 1–18.

Every, D., & Augoustinos, M. (2008). Constructions of Australia in pro- and anti-asylum seeker discourse. *Nations and Nationalism, 14*(3), 562–580.

Fabbri-Destro, M., & Rizzolatti, G. (2008). Mirror neurons and mirror systems in monkeys and humans. *Physiology, 23*, 171–179.

Fazio, R. H., & Williams, C. J. (1986). Attitude accessibility as a moderator of the attitude–perception and attitude–behavior relations: An investigation of the 1984 presidential election. *Journal of Personality and Social Psychology, 51*, 505–514.

Feeney, J. A. (2006). Studying close relationships: Methodological challenges and advances. In P. Noller & J. A. Feeney (Eds.), *Close relationships: Functions, forms and processes*. Hove: Psychology Press.

Ferstl, E. C., Garnham, A., & Manouilidou, C. (2011). Implicit causality bias in English: A corpus of 300 verbs. *Behavior Research Methods, 43*(1), 124–135.

Festinger, L. (1958). The motivating effect of cognitive dissonance. In G. Lindsey (Ed.), *Assessment of human motives*. New York: Holt, Rinehart & Winston.

Festinger, L., Pepitone, A., & Newcomb, T. (1952). Some consequences of de-individuation in a group. *Journal of Abnormal and Social Psychology, 47*, 382–389.

Festinger, L., Riecken, H. W., & Schachter, S. (1956). *When prophecy fails: A social and psychological study of a modern group that predicted the end of the world*. Minneapolis, MN: University of Minnesota Press.

Festinger, L., Schachter, S., & Back, K. W. (1950). *Social pressures in informal groups: A study of human factors in housing*. New York: Harper.

Fincham, F. D. (1985). Attribution processes in distressed and nondistressed couples: 2. Responsibility for marital problems. *Journal of Abnormal Psychology, 94*, 183–190.

Fincham, F. D., Beach, S. R., & Nelson. G. (1987). Attributional processes in distressed and nondistressed couples: 3. Causal and responsibility attributions for spouse behavior. *Cognitive Therapy and Research, 11*, 71–86.

Fincham, F. D., Beach, S. R., & Baucom, D. H. (1987). Attribution processes in distressed and nondistressed couples: 4. Self–partner attribution differences. *Journal of Personality and Social Psychology, 52*, 739–748.

Fincham, F. D., Harold, G. T., & Gano-Phillips, S. (2000). The longitudinal association between attributions and marital satisfaction: Direction of effects and role of efficacy expectations. *Journal of Family Psychology, 14*(2), 267–285.

Fincham, F. D., & O'Leary, K. D. (1983). Causal inferences for spouse behavior in maritally distressed and nondistressed couples. *Journal of Social and Clinical Psychology, 1*, 42–57.

Finlay, W. M. L. (2007). The propaganda of extreme hostility: Denunciation and the regulation of the group. *British Journal of Social Psychology, 46*, 323–341.

Fishbein, M., & Ajzen, I. (1974). Attitudes towards objects as predictors of single and multiple behavioural criteria. *Psychological Review, 81*(1), 29–74.

Fishbein, M., & Ajzen, I. (1975). *Belief, attitude, intention, and behavior: An introduction to theory and research*. Reading, MA: Addison-Wesley.

Fishman, P. (1978). Interaction: The work women do. *Social Problems, 25*, 397–406.

Fiske, J. (1987). *Television culture*. London: Methuen.

Fiske, S. T., & Cox, M. G. (1979). Describing others: Person impressions as person concepts. *Journal of Personality, 47*, 136–161.

Fiske, S. T., & Neuberg, S. L. (1990). A continuum of impression formation, from category-based to individuating processes: Influences of information and motivation on attention and interpretation. In M. P. Zanna (Ed.), *Advances in experimental social psychology* (Vol. 23, pp. 1–74). New York: Academic Press.

Fiske, S. T., & Taylor, S. E. (1984). *Social cognition*. New York: McGraw-Hill.

Fiske, S. T., & Taylor, S. E. (1991). *Social cognition* (2nd ed.). New York: McGraw-Hill.

Fiske, S. T., & Taylor, S. E. (2008). *Social cognition: From brains to culture*. London: McGraw-Hill.

Flynn, F. J., Reagans R. E., Amanatullah, E. T., & Ames, D. R. (2006). Helping one's way to the top: Self-monitors achieve status by helping others and knowing who helps whom. *Journal of Personality and Social Psychology, 91*(6), 1123–1137.

Fogarty, K., & Augoustinos, M. (2008). Feckless fathers and monopolising mothers: Motive, identity and fundamental truths in the Australian Public Inquiry into Child Custody. *British Journal of Social Psychology, 22*, 535–556.

Försterling, F., Preikschas, S., & Agthe, M. (2007). Ability, luck, and looks: An evolutionary look at achievement ascriptions and the sexual attribution bias. *Journal of Personality and Social Psychology, 92*, 775–788.

Foucault, M. (1967). *Madness and civilization: A history of insanity in the age of reason*. London: Routledge.

Foucault, M. (1970). *The order of things: An archaeology of the human sciences*. London: Taristock.

Foucault, M. (1977). *Discipline and punish: The birth of the prison*. London: Penguin.

Foucault, M. (1978). *The history of sexuality (Vol. 1): An introduction: The will to knowledge*. New York: Pantheon Books.

Foucault, M. (1983). *This is not a pipe*. Berkeley, CA: University of California Press.

Foucault, M. (1985). *The history of sexuality (Vol. 2): The use of pleasure*. New York: Pantheon Books.

Foucault, M. (1986). *The history of sexuality (Vol. 3): The care of the self*. New York: Pantheon Books.

Fowler, R. (1991). *Language in the news*. London: Routledge.

Fox, D. R. (1985). Psychology, ideology, utopia and the commons. *American Psychologist, 40*, 48–58.

Fox, D. R., & Prilleltensky, I. (1996). The inescapable nature of politics in psychology. *New Ideas In Psychology, 14*, 21–26.

Frank, M. G., & Ekman, P. (2003). *Nonverbal detection of deception in forensic contexts: Handbook of forensic psychology*. New York: Academic Press.

Freud, S. (1930) *Civilization and its discontents*, trans. and ed., James Strachey, 1961, New York: W.W. Norton.

Funder, D. C. (1987). Errors and mistakes: Evaluating the accuracy of social judgment. *Psychological Bulletin, 101*: 75–90.

Furnham, A. (1995). The just world, charitable giving, and attitudes to disability. *Personality and Individual Differences, 19*, 577–583.

Gaertner, S. L., & Dovidio, J. F. (1977). The subtlety of white racism, arousal, and helping behaviour. *Journal of Personality and Social Psychology, 35*, 691–707.

Gallese V., Keysers C., & Rizzolatti, G. (2004). A unifying view of the basis of social cognition. *Trends in Cognitive Sciences, 8*, 396–403.

Gansberg, M. (1964). 37 who saw murder didn't call the police. *The New York Times*, 27 March, p. 1.

Garfinkel, H. (1967). *Studies in ethnomethodology*. Englewood Cliffs, NJ: Prentice Hall.

Garvey, C., & Caramazza, A. (1974). Implicit causality in verbs. *Linguistic Inquiry, 5*, 459–464.

Gaskell, G. (1990) Collective behavior in a societal context. In H. Himmelweit & G. Gaskell (Eds.), *Societal psychology* (pp. 252–272). Newbury Park, CA: Sage.

Geary, D. C., Vigil, J., & Byrd-Craven, J. (2004). Evolution of human mate choice. *Journal of Sex Research, 41*, 27–42.

Geer, J. H., & Jarmecky, L. (1973). The effect of being responsible for reducing another's pain on subjects' response and arousal. *Journal of Personality and Social Psychology, 26*, 232–237.

Genesee, F., & Bourhis, R. Y. (1988). Evaluative reactions to language choice strategies: The role of factors. *Language and Communication, 8*, 229–250.

Gergen, K. J. (1973). Social psychology as history. *Journal of Personality and Social Psychology, 26*(2), 309–320.

Gergen, K. J. (1991) *The saturated self: Dilemmas of identity in contemporary life*. New York: Basic Books.

Gergen, K. J. (1994). *Realities and relationships*. Cambridge, MA: Harvard University Press.

Gergen, K. J. (2009a). *Relational being: Beyond self and community*. New York: Oxford University Press.

Gergen, K. J. (2009b). *An invitation to social construction* (2nd ed.) London: Sage.

Gilbert, G. M. (1951). Stereotype persistence and change among college students. *Journal of Abnormal and Social Psychology, 46*, 245–254.

Giles, H., Coupland, J., & Coupland, N. (1991). *Contexts of accommodation: Developments in applied sociolinguistics*. Cambridge: Cambridge University Press.

Gill, R. (1993). Justifying injustice: Broadcasters' accounts of inequality in radio. In E. Burman & I. Parker (Eds.), *Discourse analytic research: Repertoires and readings of texts in action* (pp. 75–93). London: Routledge.

Goffman, E. (1959). *The presentation of self in everyday life*. New York: Doubleday/Anchor Books.

Goffman, E. (1974). *Frame analysis: An essay on the organization of experience*. New York: Harper & Row.

Goodwin, C. (1979). The interactive construction of a sentence in natural conversation. In G. Psathas (Ed.), *Everyday language: Studies in ethnomethodology* (pp. 97–121). New York: Irvington Publishers.

Goodwin, C. (1980). Restarts, pauses, and the achievement of mutual gaze at turn-beginning. *Sociological Inquiry, 50*(3–4), 272–302.

Goodwin, C. (1984). Notes on story structure and the organization of participation. In M. Atkinson and J. Heritage (Eds.), *Structures of social action* (pp. 225–246). Cambridge: Cambridge University Press.

Goodwin, C. (1986). Gesture as a resource for the organization of mutual orientation. *Semiotica, 62*(1–2), 29–49.

Goodwin, C. (1995). Co-constructing meaning in conversations with an aphasic man. *Research on Language and Social Interaction, 28*(3), 233–260.

Goodwin, C. (Ed.) (2003). *Conversation and brain damage*. Oxford: Oxford University Press.

Goodwin, R. (2008). *Changing relations: Achieving intimacy in a time of social transition*. Cambridge: Cambridge University Press.

Gottman, J. M., & Driver, J. L. (2005). Dysfunctional marital conflict and everyday marital interaction. *Journal of Divorce & Remarriage, 43*(3–4), 63–78.

Gough, H. G., & Heilbrun, A. B. (1983). In O. K. Buros (Ed.), *The adjective checklist manual*. Palo Alto, CA: Consulting Psychologists Press.

Gouldner, A. W. (1960). The norm of reciprocity: A preliminary statement. *American Sociological Review, 25*(2), 161–178.

Greenwald, A. G., McGhee, D. E., Schwartz, J. L. K. (1998). Measuring individual differences in implicit cognition: The implicit association test. *Journal of Personality and Social Psychology, 74*(6), 1464–1480.

Greenwood, J. D. (2004a). What happened to the social in social psychology? *Journal for the Theory of Social Behaviour, 34*, 19–34.

Greenwood, J. D. (2004b). The *disappearance of the social in American social psychology*. Cambridge: Cambridge University Press.

Greitmeyer, T., & Rudolph, U. (2003). Help, giving and aggression from an attributional perspective: Why and when we help or retaliate. *Journal of Applied Social Psychology, 33*, 1069–1087.

Grice, H. P. (1975). Logic and conversation. In A.P. Martinich, (Ed.), *Philosophy of language* (pp. 165–175). New York: Oxford University Press.

Guimelli, C. (1998). Differentiation between the central core elements of social representations: Normative vs. functional elements. *Swiss Journal of Psychology, 57*(4), 209–224.

Haddock, G., Maio, G. R., Arnold, K., & Huskinson, T. L. (2008). Should persuasion be affective or cognitive? The moderating effects of need for affect and need for cognition. *Personality and Social Psychology Bulletin, 34*, 769–778.

Hale, C. L. (1987). A comparison of accounts: When is a failure not a failure? *Journal of Language and Social Psychology, 66*, 117–132.

Halliday, M. A. K. (1985). *Spoken and written language*. Oxford: Oxford University Press.

Hamilton, D. L. (1979). A cognitive attributional analysis of stereotyping. In L. Berkowitz (Ed.), *Advances in experimental social psychology* (12th ed.), (pp. 53–84). New York: Academic Press.

Hamilton, D. L., & Gifford, R. K. (1976). Illusory correlation in interpersonal perception: A cognitive basis of stereotypic judgments. *Journal of Experimental Social Psychology, 12*, 392–407.

Hamilton, W. D. (1964). The genetic evolution of social behaviour. *Journal of Theoretical Biology, 7*, 1–52.

Hanson-Easey, S., & Augoustinos, M. (2010). Out of Africa: Accounting for refugee policy and the language of causal attribution. *Discourse & Society, 21*, 295–323.

Hardy, C., & van Vugt, M. (2006). Nice guys finish first: The competitive altruism hypothesis. *Personality and Social Psychology Bulletin, 32*, 1402–1413.

Hareli, S. (2005). Accounting for one's behaviour: What really determines its effectiveness? Its type or its content? *Journal for the Theory of Social Behavior, 35*, 359–372.

Haslam, N. (2006). Dehumanization: An integrative review. *Personality and Social Psychology Review, 10*, 252–264.

Haslam, N., & Bain, P. (2007). Humanizing the self: Moderators of the attribution of lesser humanness to others. *Personality and Social Psychology Bulletin, 33*, 57–68.

Haslam, N., Loughnan, S., Reynolds, C., & Wilson, S. (2007). Dehumanization: A new perspective. *Social and Personality Psychology Compass, 1*, 409–422.

Haslam, S. A., & Reicher, S. (2007). Beyond the banality of evil: Three dynamics of an interactionist social psychology of tyranny. *Personality and Social Psychology Bulletin, 33*, 615–622.

Hatfield, E. (2005). *Love and sex: Cross-cultural perspectives*. Lanham, MD: University Press of America.

Hatfield, E., Berscheid, E., & Walster, G. W. (1976). New directions in equity research. In L. Berkowitz & E. Hatfield (Eds.), *Advances in experimental social psychology, Vol. 9: Equity theory: Toward a general theory of social interaction* (pp. 1–42). New York: Academic Press.

Hatfield, E., Rapson, R. L., & Aumer-Ryan, K. (2007). Equity theory. In R. F. Baumeister & K. D. Vohs (Eds.), *Encyclopedia of social psychology*. New York: Sage.

Hatfield, E., Traupmann-Pillemer, J., & Sprecher, S. (1984). Older women's perception of their intimate relationships. *Journal of Social and Clinical Psychology, 2*, 108–124.

Hatfield, E., Utne, M. K., & Traupmann, J. (1979). Equity theory and intimate relationships. In R. L. Burgess & T. L. Huston (Eds.), *Social exchange in developing relationships* (pp. 99–133). New York: Academic Press.

Hatfield, E., Walster, G. W., & Traupmann, J. (1979). Equity and premarital sex. *Journal of Personality and Social Psychology, 37*, 82–92.

Heider, F. (1944). Social perception and phenomenal causality. *Psychological Review, 51*, 358–374.

Heider, F. (1958). *The psychology of interpersonal relations*. New York: John Wiley.

Heider, F., & Simmel, M. (1944). An experimental study of apparent behavior. *American Journal of Psychology, 57*, 243–259.

Henry, P. J., Reyna, C., & Weiner, B. (2004). Hate welfare but help the poor: How the attributional content of stereotypes explains the paradox of reactions to the destitute in America. *Journal of Applied Social Psychology, 34*, 34–58.

Hepburn, A. (2003). *An introduction to critical social psychology*. London: Sage.

Herder, J. G. (1969 [1784]). Ideas for a philosophy of the history of mankind. In F. M. Barnard (trans. & Ed.), *J. G. Herder on social and political culture* (pp. 253–326). Cambridge: Cambridge University Press.

Heritage, J., & Greatbatch, D. (1991). On the institutional character of institutional talk: The case of news interviews. In D. Boden and D. Zimmerman (Eds.), *Talk and social structure: Studies in ethnomethodology and conversation analysis* (pp. 93–137). Cambridge: Polity.

Herzlich, C., & Pierret, J. (1987). *Illness in self and society* (E. Foster, Trans.). Baltimore, MD: Johns Hopkins University Press.

Hewstone, M. (1988). Attributional bases of intergroup conflict. In W. Stroebe, A. W. Kruglanski, D. Bar-Tal & M. Hewstone (Eds.), *The social psychology of intergroup conflict: Theory, research and applications*. New York: Springer.

Hewstone, M. (1989). *Causal attribution: From cognitive processes to collective beliefs*. Oxford: Blackwell.

Hewstone, M. (1990). The 'ultimate attribution error'? A review of the literature on intergroup causal attribution. *European Journal of Social Psychology, 20*, 311–335.

Hicks, J. L., & Cockman, D. (2003). The effect of general knowledge on source memory and decision process. *Journal of Memory and Language, 48*, 489–511.

Higgins, E. T. (1987). Self-discrepancy: A theory relating self and affect. *Psychological Review, 94*(3), 319–340.

Hilton, D. J. (1990). Conversational processes and causal explanation. *Psychological Bulletin, 107*, 65–81.

Hilton, D. J. (1991). A conversational model of causal explanation. In W. Stroebe & M. Hewstone (Eds.), *European review of social psychology* (Vol. 2, pp. 52–81). London: Wiley.

Hilton, D. J. (1995). The social context of reasoning: Conversational inference and rational judgment. *Psychological Bulletin, 118*, 248–271.

Hilton, N. Z., Harris, G. T., & Rice, M. E. (2000). The functions of aggression by male teenagers. *Journal of Personality and Social Psychology, 79*(6), 988–994.

Hinkle, S., & Brown, R. J. (1990). Intergroup differentiation and social identity: Some links and lacunae. In D. Abrams & M. A. Hogg (Eds.), *Social identity theory: Constructive and critical advances* (pp. 48–70). New York: Springer-Verlag.

Hodges, B. H., & Geyer, A. (2006). A nonconformist account of the Asch experiments: Values, pragmatics, and moral dilemmas. *Personality and Social Psychology Review, 10*, 2–19.

Homans, G. C. (1958). Social behaviour as exchange. *American Journal of Sociology, 63*(6), 597–606.

Honess, T. & Yardley, K. (Eds.) (1987). *Self and identity: Perspectives across the lifespan*. London: Routledge & Kegan Paul.

Holtgraves, R. (1989). The form and function of remedial moves. *Journal of Language and Social Psychology, 8*, 1–16.

Hovland, C. I., Janis, I. L., & Kelley, H. H. (1953). *Communications and persuasion: Psychological studies in opinion change*. New Haven, CT: Yale University Press.

Hovland, C. I., & Weiss W. (1951). The influence of source credibility on communication effectiveness. *Public Opinion Quarterly, 15*, 635–650.

Howitt, D. & Owusu-Bempah, J. (1994). *The racism of psychology: Time for change*. Hemel Hempstead: Harvester WheatSheaf.

Huesmann, L. R., & Eron, L. D. (1986). *Television and the aggressive child: A cross-national comparison*. Mahwah, NJ: Erlbaum.

Ichheiser, G. (1943a). Misinterpretations of personality in everyday life and the psychologist's frame of reference. *Character and Personality, 12*, 145–160.

Ichheiser, G. (1943b). Why psychologists tend to overlook certain 'obvious' facts. *Philosophy of Science, 10*, 204–207.

Ichheiser, G. (1949). Misunderstandings in human relations: A study of false social perception. *American Journal of Sociology, 55*, 1–70.

Jacobson, N. S., McDonald, D. W., Follette, W. C., & Berley, R. A. (1985). Attribution processes in distressed and nondistressed married couples. *Cognitive Therapy and Research, 9*, 35–50.

Jain, S. P., & Maheswaran, D. (2000). Motivated reasoning: A depth-of-processing perspective. *Journal of Consumer Research, 26*, 358–371.

James, W. (1890). *The principles of psychology* (Vol. 1). New York: Henry Holt.

Jaspal, R., & Cinnirella, M. (2010). Coping with potentially incompatible group norms: The overlooked role of social identification in deviance. *British Journal of Social Psychology, 49*, 849–870.

Jefferson, G. (2004). Glossary of transcript symbols with an introduction. In G. H. Lerner (Ed.), *Conversation analysis: Studies from the first generation* (pp. 13–31). Amsterdam/Philadelphia, PA: John Benjamins Publishing Company.

Jodelet, D. (1991). *Madness and social representations*. Hemel Hempstead: Harvester Wheatsheaf.

Johnson, C., Mullen, B., Carlson, D., & Southwick, S. (2001). The affective and memorial components of distinctiveness-based illusory correlations. *British Journal of Social Psychology, 40*, 337–358.

Johnson, D. W., & Downing, L. L. (1979). Deindividuation and valence of cues: Effects on prosocial or antisocial behaviour. *Journal of Personality and Social Psychology, 37*, 1532–1538.

Jonas, E., Schimel, J., Greenberg, J., & Pyszczynski, T. (2002). The Scrooge effect: Evidence that mortality salience increases prosocial attitudes and behavior. *Personality and Social Psychology Bulletin, 28*, 1342–1353.

Jones, E. E., & Davis, K. E. (1965). From acts to dispositions: The attribution process in person perception. In L. Berkowitz (Ed.), *Advances in experimental social psychology* (Vol. 2, pp. 219–266). New York: Academic Press.

Jones, E. E., & Harris, V. A. (1967). The attribution of attitudes. *Journal of Experimental Social Psychology, 3*, 1–24.

Jones, E. E., & Nisbett, R. E. (1972). The actor and the observer: Divergent perceptions of the causes of the behavior. In E. E. Jones, D. E. Kanouse, H. H. Kelley, R. E. Nisbett, S. Valins & B. Weiner (Eds.), *Attribution: Perceiving the causes of behavior* (pp. 79–94). Morristown, NJ: General Learning Press.

Jones, J. T., Pelham, B. W., Carvallo, M., & Mirenberg, M. C. (2004). How do I love thee? Let me count the js: Implicit egotism and interpersonal attraction. *Journal of Personality and Social Psychology, 87*, 665–683.

Kahneman, D., & Tversky, A. (1973). On the psychology of prediction. *Psychology Review, 80*, 237–251.

Kaplan, K. J. (1972). On the ambivalence–indifference problem in attitude theory and measurement: A suggested modification of the semantic differential technique. *Psychological Bulletin, 77*(5), 361–372.

Karlins, M., Coffman, T. L., & Walters, G. (1969). On the fading of social stereotypes: Studies in three generations of college students. *Journal of Personality and Social Psychology, 13*, 1–16.

Katz, D., & Braly, K. W. (1933). Racial stereotypes of one-hundred college students. *Journal of Abnormal and Social Psychology, 28*, 280–290.

Kelley, H. H. (1967). Attribution theory in social psychology. In D. Levine (Ed.), *Nebraska symposium on motivation* (pp. 192–238). Lincoln, NE: University of Nebraska Press.

Kelley, H. H. (1972). Causal schemata and the attribution process. In E. E. Jones, D. Kanouse, H. H. Kelley, R. E. Nisbett, S. Valins & B. Weiner (Eds.), *Attribution: Perceiving the causes of behaviour*. Morristown, NJ: General Learning Press.

Kelley, H. H., & Thibaut, J. (1978). *Interpersonal relations: A theory of interdependence*. New York: Wiley.

Kendon, A. (1967). Some functions of gaze-direction in social interaction. *Acta Psychologica, 26*, 22–63.

Kenny, D. A. (1985). Quantitative methods for social psychology. In G. Lindzey & E. Aronson (Eds.), *Handbook of social psychology* (Vol. 1, 3rd ed., pp. 487–508). New York: Random House.

Kingdon, J. W. (1967). Politicians' beliefs about voters. *The American Political Science Review, 61*(1), 137–145.

Kitzinger, C., & Frith, H. (1999). Just say no? The use of conversation analysis in developing a feminist perspective on sexual refusal. *Discourse and Society, 10*, 293–316.

Klatzky, R. L., Martin, G. L., & Kane, R. A. (1982). Influence of social-category activation on processing of visual information. *Social Cognition, 1*, 95–109.

Klein, O., Spears, R., & Reicher, S. D. (2007). Social identity performance: Extending the strategic side of SIDE. *Personality and Social Psychology Review, 11*(1), 28–45.

Klohnen, E. C., & Luo, S. (2003). Interpersonal attraction and personality: What is attractive: Self similarity, ideal similarity, complementarity, or attachment security? *Journal of Personality and Social Psychology, 85*, 706–722.

Knapp, M. L. (1984). *Interpersonal communication and human relationships*. Boston, MA: Allyn & Bacon.

Koborov, N., & Thorne, A. (2009). The negotiation of compulsory romance in young women friend's stories about romantic heterosexual experience. *Feminism & Psychology, 19*, 49–70.

Konijn, E. A., Nije Bijvank, M., & Bushman, B. J. (2007). I wish I were a warrior: The role of wishful identification in effects of violent video games on aggression in adolescent boys. *Developmental Psychology, 43*, 1038–1044.

Konrath, S., Bushman, B. J., & Campbell, W. K. (2006). Attenuating the link between threatened egotism and aggression. *Psychological Science, 17*, 995–1001.

Kraft, P., Rise, J., Sutton, S., & Røysamb, E. (2005). Perceived difficulty in the theory of planned behaviour: Perceived behavioural control or affective attitude? *British Journal of Social Psychology, 44*(3), 479–496.

Krauss, R., Morrel-Samuels, P., & Colasante, C. (1991). Do conversational hand gestures communicate? *Journal of Personality and Social Psychology, 61*, 743–754.

Kristiansen, T. (2004). Social meaning and norm-ideals for speech in a Danish community. In A. Jaworski, N. Coupland & D. Galasinski (Eds), *Metalanguage: Social and ideological perspectives* (pp. 67–92). Berlin/New York: Mouton de Gruyter.

Kruger, D. J., & Fisher, M. L. (2008). Women's life history attributes are associated with preferences in mating relationships. *Evolutionary Psychology, 6*(2), 289–302.

Kuhn, M. H., & McPartland, T. S. (1954). An empirical investigation of self-attitude. *American Sociological Review, 19*, 68–76.

Kuhn, T. S. (1996). *The structure of scientific revolutions* (3rd ed.). Chicago, IL: University of Chicago Press.

Kurz, T., Augoustinos, M., & Crabb, S. (2010). Fighting the 'climate change election': A discursive analysis of Australian political rhetoric around climate change. *British Journal of Social Psychology, 49*, 601–625.

Labov, W. (2006). *The social stratification of English in New York City* (2nd ed.). Cambridge: Cambridge University Press.

Lalljee, M. (1981). Attribution theory and the analysis of explanation. In C. Antaki (Ed.), *The psychology of ordinary explanations of human behaviour* (pp. 119–138). London: Academic Press.

Lambert, W., Hodgson, R. C., Gardner, R. C., & Fillenbaum, S. (1960). Evaluational reactions to spoken languages. *Journal of Abnormal and Social Psychology, 60*, 44–51.

Langer, E., Blank, A., & Chanowitz, B. (1978). The mindlessness of ostensibly thoughtful action: The role of 'placebic' information in interpersonal interaction. *Journal of Personality and Social Psychology, 36*(6), 635–642.

LaPiere, R.T. (1934). Attitudes vs. actions. *Social Forces, 13*, 230–237.

Latané, B., & Darley, J. M. (1970). *The unresponsive bystander: Why doesn't he help?* New York: Appleton-Century-Crofts.

Leahey, T. H. (2004). *A history of psychology: Main currents in psychological thought* (6th ed.). Upper Saddle River, NJ: Prentice Hall.

LeBon, G. (1896). *The crowd: A study of the popular mind*. London: Macmillan.

LeCouteur, A., & Augoustinos, M. (2001). Apologising to the stolen generations: Argument, rhetoric and identity in public reasoning. *Australian Psychologist, 36*, 51–61.

LeCouteur, A., & Oxlad, M. (2011). Managing accountability for domestic violence: Identities, membership categories and morality in perpetrators' talk. *Feminism & Psychology, 21*, 5–28.

LeCouteur, A., Rapley, M., & Augoustinos, M. (2001). 'This very difficult debate about Wik': Stake, voice and the management of category memberships in race politics. *British Journal of Social Psychology, 40*, 35–57.

Lerner, M. L. (1980). *The belief in a just world: A fundamental delusion*. New York: Plenum.

Levin, P., & Isen, A. (1975). Further studies on the effect of feeling good on helping. *Sociometry, 38*, 141–147.

Levine, M., Prosser, A., Evans, D., & Reicher, S. (2005). Identity and emergency intervention: How social group membership and inclusiveness of group boundaries shapes helping behaviour. *Personality and Social Psychology Bulletin, 31*(4), 443–453.

Lewin, K. (1943). Defining the 'field at a given time'. *Psychological Review, 50*(3), 292–310.

Leyens, J.-P., Camino, L., Parke, R. D., & Berkowitz, L. (1975). Effects of movie violence on aggression in a field setting as a function of group dominance and cohesion. *Journal of Personality and Social Psychology, 32*(2), 346–360.

Linville, P. W. (1982). The complexity–extremity effect and age-based stereotyping. *Journal of Personality and Social Psychology, 42*, 193–210.

Linville, P. W., Fischer, G. W., & Salovey, P. (1989). Perceived distributions of the characteristics of in-group and out-group members: Empirical evidence and a computer simulation. *Journal of Personality and Social Psychology, 57*(2), 165–188.

Linz, D., Donnerstein, E., & Penrod, S. (1988). Long-term exposure to violent and sexually degrading depictions of women. *Journal of Personality and Social Psychology, 55*, 758–768.

Lippmann, W. (1922). *Public opinion*. New York: Macmillan.

Livingstone, A. G., & Haslam, S. A. (2008). The importance of social identity content in a setting of chronic social conflict: Understanding intergroup relations in Northern Ireland. *British Journal of Social Psychology, 47*, 1–21.

Locksley, A., Borgida, E., Brekke, N., & Hepburn, C. (1980). Sex stereotypes and social judgment. *Journal of Personality and Social Psychology, 39*, 821–831.

Locksley, A. Hepburn, C., & Ortiz, V. (1982). Social stereotypes and judgments of individuals: An instance of the base rate fallacy. *European Journal of Experimental Social Psychology, 18*, 23–42.

Loftus, E. F. (1975). Leading questions and the eyewitness report. *Cognitive Psychology, 7*, 550–572.

Loftus, E. F., & Zanni, G. (1975). Eyewitness testimony: The influence of the wording of a question. *Bulletin of Psychonomic Society, 5*, 19–31.

Lorenz, K. (1966). *On aggression*. London: Methuen.

Lubek, I. (1995). Aggression research: A critical-historical, multilevel approach. *Theory & Psychology, 5*, 99–129.

Macrae, C. N., & Bodenhausen, G. V. (2000). Social cognition: Thinking categorically about others. *Annual Review of Psychology, 51*, 93–120.

Maddux, J. E., & Rogers, R. W. (1980). Effects of source expertness, physical attractiveness, and supporting arguments on persuasion: A case of brains over beauty. *Journal of Personality and Social Psychology, 39*(2), 235–244.

Madon, S., Guyll, M., Aboufadel, K., Montiel, E., Smith, A., Palumbo, P., & Jussim, L. (2001). Ethnic and national stereotypes: The Princeton trilogy revisited and revised. *Personality and Social Psychology Bulletin, 27*, 996–1010.

Malamuth, N. M., & Check, J. V. P. (1980). Penile tumescence and perceptual responses to rape as a function of victim's perceived reactions. *Journal of Applied Social Psychology, 10*, 528–547.

Malle, B. F., Knobe, J., & Nelson, S. (2007). Actor–observer asymmetries in behaviour explanations: New answers to an old question. *Journal of Personality and Social Psychology, 93*, 491–514.

Mandelbaum, J. (1987). Couples sharing stories. *Communication Quarterly, 35*(2), 144–171.

Mandelbaum, J. (2003). Interactive methods for constructing relationships. In P. Glenn, C. LeBaron, & J. Mandelbaum (Eds.), *Studies in language and social interaction: In honour of Robert Hopper* (pp. 207–220). Mahwah, NJ: Erlbaum.

Manicas, P. T. (1987). *A history and philosophy of the social sciences*. London: Blackwell.

Manning, R., Levine, M., & Collins, A. (2007). The Kitty Genovese murder and the social psychology of helping: The parable of the 38 witnesses. *American Psychologist, 62*, 555–562.

Manucia, G. K., Baumann, D. J., & Cialdini R. B. (1984). Mood influences on helping: Direct effects or side effects? *Journal of Personality and Social Psychology, 46*, 357–364.

Markus, H. R. (1977). Self-schemata and processing information about the self. *Journal of Personality and Social Psychology, 35*, 63–78.

Markus H. R., & Kitayama, S. (1991). Culture and the self: Implications for cognition, emotion and motivation. *Psychological Review, 98*, 224–253.

Markus, H., & Wurf, E. (1987). The dynamic self-concept: A social psychological perspective. *Annual Review of Psychology, 38*, 299–337.

McAndrew, F. T. (2002). New evolutionary perspectives on altruism: Multilevel-selection and costly-signalling theories. *Current Directions in Psychological Science, 11*, 79–82.

McArthur, L. A. (1972). The how and what of why: Some determinants and consequences of causal attribution. *Journal of Personality and Social Psychology, 22*, 171–193.

McDougall, W. (1908). *An introduction to social psychology*. London: Methuen.

McGuire, W. J. (1968). Personality and attitude change: An information processing theory. In A. G. Greenwald, T. C. Brock, & T. M. Ostrom (Eds.), *Psychological foundations of attitudes* (pp. 171–196). San Diego, CA: Academic Press.

McMillen, D. L., Sanders, D. Y., & Solomon, G. S. (1977). Self-esteem, attentiveness and helping behavior. *Personality and Social Psychology Bulletin, 3*(2), 257–261.

McNeill, D. (1985). So you think gestures are nonverbal? *Psychological Review, 92*, 350–371.

McNeill, D. (1992). *Hand and mind: What gestures reveal about thought*. Chicago, IL: University of Chicago Press.

McNeill, D. (Ed.) (2000). *Language and gesture: Window into thought and action*. Cambridge: Cambridge University Press.

McNeill, D. (2005). *Gesture and thought*. Chicago, IL: University of Chicago Press.

Mead, G. H. (1934). *Mind, self and society from the standpoint of a social behaviorist* (Charles W. Morris, Ed.). Chicago, IL: University of Chicago.

Medvene, L. (1992). Self-help groups, peer helping and social comparison. In S. Spacapan & S. Oskamp (Eds.), *Helping and being helped: Naturalistic studies* (pp. 49–82). Newbury Park, CA: Sage.

Mehrabian, A. (1967). Substitute for apology: Manipulations of cognitions to reduce negative attitude toward self. *Psychological Reports, 20*, 687–692.

Mehrabian, A., and Ferris, S. R. (1967). Inference of attitudes from nonverbal communication in two channels. *Journal of Consulting Psychology, 31*, 248–252.

Mehrabian, A., & Wiener, M. (1967). Decoding of inconsistent communications. *Journal of Personality and Social Psychology, 6*, 109–114.

Menon, T., Morris, M. W., Chiu, C. Y., & Hong, Y. Y. (1999). Culture and the construal of agency: Attribution to individual versus group dispositions. *Journal of Personality and Social Psychology, 76*(5), 701–717.

Meston, C. M., & Frohlich, P. F. (2003). Love at first fright: Partner salience moderates roller coaster-induced excitation transfer. *Archives of Sexual Behavior, 32*, 537–544.

Mezulis, A. H., Abramson, L. Y., Hyde, J. S., & Hankin, B. L. (2004). Is there a universal positivity bias in attributions? A meta-analytic review of individual, developmental, and cultural differences in the self-serving attributional bias. *Psychological Bulletin, 130*, 711–747.

Michotte, A. (1962). *The perception of causality*. Andover, MA: Methuen.

Milgram, S. (1963). Behavioral study of obedience. *Journal of Abnormal and Social Psychology, 67*, 371–378.

Milgram. S. (1964). Issues in the study of obedience: A reply to Baumrind. *American Psychologist, 19*, 848–852.

Milgram, S. (1965a). Liberating effects of group pressure. *Journal of Personality and Social Psychology, 1*, 127–134.

Milgram, S. (1965b). Some conditions of obedience and disobedience to authority. *Human Relations, 18*, 57–76.

Milgram, S. (2004[1974]). *Obedience to authority: An experimental view*. New York: Pinter & Martin.

Millar, M. G., & Tesser, A. (1990). Attitudes and behavior: The cognitive–affective mismatch hypothesis. *Advances in Consumer Research, 17*, 86–90.

Miller, D. T. (1977). Altruism and threat to belief in a just world. *Journal of Experimental Social Psychology, 13*, 113–124.

Miller, D. T., & Ross, M. (1975). Self-serving biases in the attribution of causality: Fact or fiction? *Psychological Bulletin, 82*, 213–225.

Miller, G. A. (1956). The magical number seven, plus or minus two: Some limits on our capacity for processing information. *Psychological Review, 63*(2), 81–97.

Miller, J. G. (1984). Culture and the development of everyday social explanation. *Journal of Personality and Social Psychology, 46*, 961–978.

Miller, N. E. (1941). The frustration–aggression hypothesis [1] (with Robert R. Sears, O. H. Mowrer, Leonard W. Doob & John Dollard). *Psychological Review, 48*, 337–342.

Milnes, K. (2010). Challenging the sexual double standard: Constructing sexual equality narratives as a strategy of resistance. *Feminism & Psychology, 20*, 255–259.

Mohiyeddini, C., Pauli, R., & Bauer, S. (2009). The role of emotion in bridging the intention–behaviour gap: The case of sports participation. *Psychology of Sport and Exercise, 10*, 226–234.

Moloney, G., and Walker, I. (2002). Talking about transplants. Social representations and the dialectical, dilemmatic nature of organ donation and transplantation. *British Journal of Social Psychology, 41*, 299–320.

Mook, D. G. (1983). In defense of external invalidity. *American Psychologist, 38*, 379–387.

Moore, J. (1984). The evolution of reciprocal sharing. *Ethology and Sociobiology, 5*, 4–14.

Morant, N. (2006). Social representations and professional knowledge: The representations of mental illness among mental health practitioners. *British Journal of Social Psychology, 45*, 817–838.

Moreland, R. L., & Beach, S. (1992). Exposure effects in the classroom: The development of affinity among students. *Journal of Experimental Social Psychology, 28*, 255–276.

Morley, D. (1980). *The 'Nationwide' audience: Structure and decoding*. London: BFI.

Morley, D. (1992). *Television, audiences and cultural studies*. London: Routledge.

Moscovici, S. (1976). *Social influence and social change*. London: Academic Press.

Moscovici, S. (1980). Toward a theory of conversion behaviour. In L. Berkowitz (Ed.), *Advances in experimental social psychology* (13th ed.) (pp. 209–239). San Diego, CA: Academic Press.

Moscovici, S. (1984). The phenomenon of social representations. In R. M. Farr & S. Moscovici (Eds.), *Social representations* (pp. 71–100). Cambridge: Cambridge University Press.

Moscovici, S. (1985). Social influence and conformity. In G. Lindzey & E. Aronson (Eds.), *Handbook of social psychology* (Vol. 2, pp. 347–412). New York: McGraw-Hill.

Moscovici, S. (1988). Notes towards a description of social representations. *European Journal of Social Psychology, 18*, 211–250.

Moscovici, S. (1994). Three concepts: Minority, conflict and behavioral style. In S. Moscovici, A. Mucchi-Faina & A. Maass (Eds.), *Minority influence* (pp. 233–251), Chicago, IL: Nelson-Hall.

Moscovici, S., & Lage, E. (1976). Studies in social influence: III. Majority vs minority influence in a group. *European Journal of Social Psychology, 6*, 149–174.

Moscovici, S., Lage, E., & Naffrechoux, M. (1969). Influence of a consistent minority on the responses of a majority in a colour perception task. *Sociometry, 32*, 365–379.

Moscovici, S., & Personnaz, B. (1986). Studies on latent influence by the spectrometer method: I. The impact of psychologization in the case of conversion by a minority or a majority. *European Journal of Social Psychology, 16*, 345–360.

Mulac, A., Jansma, L. G., & Linz, D. (2002). Men's behavior toward women after viewing sexually explicit films: Degradation makes a difference. *Communication Monographs, 69*(4), 311–328.

Mullen, B., & Johnson, C. (1990). Distinctiveness-based illusory correlations and stereotyping: A meta-analytic integration. *British Journal of Social Psychology, 29*, 11–28.

Mullin, C. R., & Linz, D. (1995). Desensitization and resensitization to violence against women: Effects of exposure to sexually violent films on judgments of domestic violence victims. *Journal of Personality and Social Psychology, 69*(3), 449–459.

Mummendey, A, Klink, A, & Brown, R. (2001). Nationalism and patriotism: National identification and out-group rejection. *The British Journal of Social Psychology, 40*(Pt 2), 159–172.

Newell, A., Shaw, J. C., & Simon, H. A. (1957). Empirical explorations of the logic theory machine: A case study in heuristics. IRE-AIEE-ACM '57 (Western), Papers presented at the February 26–28, 1957, western joint computer conference: Techniques for reliability.

Newman, L. S. (2009). Was Walter Lippmann interested in stereotyping? Public opinion and cognitive social psychology. *History of Psychology, 12*, 7–18.

Nisbett, R. E., Caputo, C., Legant, P., & Maracek, J. (1973). Behaviour as seen by the actor and as seen by the observer. *Journal of Personality and Social Psychology, 27*, 154–164.

Nisbett, R. E., & Ross, L. (1980). *Human inference: Strategies and shortcomings of social judgment*. Englewood Cliffs, NJ: Prentice Hall.

O'Keefe, D. J., & Jackson, S. (1995). Argument quality and persuasive effects: A review of current approaches. In S. Jackson (Ed.), *Argumentation and values: Proceedings of the ninth Alta conference on argumentation* (pp. 88–92). Annandale, VA: Speech Communication.

Onorato, R. S., & Turner, J. C. (2004). Fluidity in the self-concept: The shift from personal to social identity. *European Journal of Social Psychology, 34*, 257–278.

Ouellette, J. A., & Wood, W. (1998). Habit and intention in everyday life: The multiple processes by which past behavior predicts future behavior. *Psychological Bulletin, 124*, 54–74.

Palomares, N. A. (2009). Women are sort of more tentative than men, aren't they? How men and women use tentative language differently, similarly, and counter-stereotypically as a function of gender salience. *Communication Research, 36*, 538–560.

Palomares, N. A., & Lee, E.-J. (2010). Virtual gender identity: The linguistic assimilation to gendered avatars in computer-mediated communication. *Journal of Language and Social Psychology, 29*, 5–23.

Parker, I. (1999). Critical psychology: Critical links. *Annual Review of Critical Psychology, 1*, 3–18.

Pavlov, I. I. (1927) *Conditioned reflexes* (G.V. Anrep, Trans.) Oxford: Oxford University Press.

Pehrson, S., Brown, R., & Zagefka, H. (2009). When does national identification lead to the rejection of immigrants? Cross-sectional and longitudinal evidence for the role of essentialist ingroup definitions. *British Journal of Social Psychology, 48*, 61–76.

Penner, L. A., Brannick, M., Connell, P., & Webb, S. (2005). The effects of the September 11 attacks on volunteering: An archival analysis. *Journal of Applied Social Psychology, 35*, 1333–1360.

Perez, J. A., Mugny, G., & Moscovici, S. (1986). Les effets pardoxaux du deni dans l'influence sociale. *Cahiers de Psychologie Sociale, 32*, 1–14.

Peterson, C. (1980). Memory and the 'dispositional shift'. *Social Psychology Quarterly, 43*, 372–380.

Peterson, C., Semmel, A., von Baeyer, C., Abramson, L. Y., Metalsky, G. I., & Seligman, M. E. P. (1982). The attributional style questionnaire. *Cognitive Therapy and Research, 6*, 287–300.

Pettigrew, T. F. (1979). The ultimate attribution error: Extending Allport's cognitive analysis of prejudice. *Personality and Social Psychology Bulletin, 5*, 461–476.

Petty, R. E., Cacioppo, J. T., & Goldman, R. (1981). Personal involvement as a determinant of argument-based persuasion. *Journal of Personality and Social Psychology, 41*, 847–855.

Piliavin, I. M., Rodin, J., & Piliavin, J. A. (1969). Good Samaritanism: An underground phenomenon? *Journal of Personality and Social Psychology, 13*, 289–299.

Piliavin, J. A., & Callero, P. L. (1991). *Giving blood: The development of an altruistic identity*. Baltimore, MD: Johns Hopkins University Press.

Piliavin, J. A., Dovidio, J. F., Gaertner, S. L., & Clark, R. D. III (1981). *Emergency intervention*. New York: Academic Press.

Piliavin, J. A., & Piliavin, I. M. (1972). The effects of blood on reactions to a victim. *Journal of Personality and Social Psychology, 23*, 253–261.

Pillemer, J., Hatfield, E., & Sprecher, S. (2008). The importance of fairness and equity for the marital satisfaction of older women. *Journal of Women and Aging, 20*, 215–230.

Pomerantz, A. (1984). Agreeing and disagreeing with assessments: Some features of preferred/dispreferred turn-shapes. In J. M. Atkinson & J. Heritage (Eds.), *Structures of social action: Studies in conversation analysis* (pp. 79–112). Cambridge: Cambridge University Press.

Pomerantz, A., & Mandelbaum, J. (2005). A conversation analytic approach to relationships: Their relevance for interactional conduct. In K. Fitch & R.E. Sanders (Eds.), *Handbook of language and social interaction* (pp. 149–171). Mahwah, NJ: Erlbaum.

Postmes, T., & Spears, R. (1998). Deindividuation and anti-normative behavior: A meta-analysis. *Psychological Bulletin, 123*, 238–259.

Postmes, T., Spears, R., Lee, A. T., & Novak, R. J. (2005). Individuality and social influence in groups: Inductive and deductive routes to group identity. *Journal of Personality and Social Psychology, 89*, 747–763.

Potter, J. (1996). *Representing reality: Discourse, rhetoric and social construction*. London: Sage.

Potter, J. (1998). Discursive social psychology: From attitudes to evaluations. *European Review of Social Psychology, 9*, 233–266.

Potter, J. (2010). Contemporary discursive psychology: Issues, prospects and Corcoran's awkward ontology. *British Journal of Social Psychology, 49*, 657–678.

Potter, J., & Hepburn, A. (2005). Qualitative interviews in psychology: Problems and possibilities. *Qualitative Research in Psychology, 2*, 281–307.

Potter, J., & Wetherell, M., (1987). *Discourse and social psychology: Beyond attitudes and behaviour*. London: Sage.

Prentice-Dunn, S., & Rogers, R. W. (1983). Deindividuation in aggression. In R. G. Geen & E. I. Donnerstein (Eds.), *Aggression: Theoretical and emprical reviews: Vol. 2: Issues in research* (pp. 155–171). New York: Academic Press.

Prentice-Dunn, S., & Rogers, R. W. (1989). Deindividuation and the self-regulation of behavior. In P. B. Paulus (Ed.), *Psychology of group influence* (2nd ed., pp. 87–109). Hillsdale, NJ: Erlbaum.

Prilleltensky, I. (1989). Psychology and the status quo. *American Psychologist, 44*, 795–802.

Puchta, C., & Potter, J. (2002). Manufacturing individual opinions: Market research focus groups and the discursive psychology of attitudes. *British Journal of Social Psychology, 41*, 345–363.

de Quervain, D. J.-F., Fischbacher U., Treyer, V., Schellhammer, M., Schnyder, U., Buck, A., & Fehr, E. (2004). The neural basis of altruistic punishment. *Science, 305*, 1254–1258.

Rabinow, P. (1984). *The Foucault reader: An introduction to Foucault's thought*. London: Penguin.

Ramirez, J., Bryant, J., & Zillmann, D. (1982). Effects of erotica on retaliatory behaviour as a function of level of prior provocation. *Journal of Personality and Social Psychology, 43*, 971–978.

Raymond, G., & Heritage, J. (2006). The epistemics of social relations: Owning grandchildren. *Language in Society, 35*, 677–705.

Regan, D., & Totten, J. (1975). Empathy and attribution: Turning observers into actors. *Journal of Personality and Social Psychology, 32*, 850–856.

Regan, D. T., Williams, M., & Sparling, S. (1972). Voluntary expiation of guilt: A field experiment. *Journal of Personality and Social Psychology, 24*(1), 42–45.

Reicher, S. D. (1984a). St Paul's: A study in the limits of crowd behaviour. In J. Murphy, M. John, & H. Brown (Eds), *Dialogues and debates in social psychology* (pp. 187–205). London: Erlbaum/Open University.

Reicher, S. D. (1984b). Social influence in the crowd: Attitudinal and behavioural effects of de-individuation in conditions of high and low group salience. *British Journal of Social Psychology, 23*, 341–350.

Reicher, S. (1996). The crowd century: Reconciling practical success with theoretical failure. *British Journal of Social Psychology, 35*, 535–553.

Reicher, S., & Haslam, S. A. (2006a). Rethinking the psychology of tyranny: The BBC prison study. *British Journal of Social Psychology, 45*, 1–40.

Reicher, S., & Haslam, S. A. (2006b). Rethinking the psychology of tyranny: The BBC prison study. *British Journal of Social Psychology, 45*, 55–63.

Reicher, S., & Haslam, S. A. (2011) After shock? Towards a social identity explanation of the Milgram 'obedience' studies. *British Journal of Social Psychology, 50* 163–169.

Reicher, S., & Hopkins, N. (2001). *Self and nation*. London: Sage.

Rholes, W. S., & Pryor, J. B. (1982). Cognitive accessibility and causal attributions. *Personality and Social Psychology Bulletin, 8*, 719–727.

Riela, S., Rodriguez, G., Aron, A., Xu, X., & Acevedo, B. (2010). Experiences of falling in love: Investigating culture, ethnicity, gender and speed. *Journal of Social and Personal Relationships, 27*, 473–493.

Rock, I., (Ed.) (1990). *The legacy of Solomon Asch: Essays in cognition and social psychology*. Hillsdale, NJ: Erlbaum.

Rose, D., Efraim, D., Gervais, M., Joffe, H., Jovchelovitch, S., & Morant, N. (1995). Questioning consensus in social representations theory. *Papers on Social Representations, 4*(2), 150–176.

Rose, N. (1998). *Inventing our selves: Psychology, power and personhood*. Cambridge: Cambridge University Press.

Rosenthal, A. M. (1964). *Thirty-eight witnesses*. New York: McGraw-Hill.

Ross, L. (1977). The intuitive psychologist and his shortcomings: Distortions in the attribution process. In L. Berkowitz (Ed.), *Advances in experimental social psychology* (Vol. 10) (pp. 173–220). New York: Academic Press.

Ross, L, Amabile, T. M., & Steinmetz, J. L. (1977). Social roles, social control and biases in social perception processes. *Journal of Personality and Social Psychology, 35*, 485–494.

Rossan, S. (1987). Identity and its development in adulthood. In T. Honess & K. Yardley (Eds.), *Self and identity: Perspectives across the lifespan* (pp. 304–319). New York: Routledge.

Rothstein, S. I., & Pierotti, R. (1988). Distinctions among reciprocal altruism, kin selection, and co-operation and a model for the initial evolution of beneficent behaviour. *Ethology and Sociobiology, 9*, 189–209.

Rudolph, U., & Fosterling, F. (1997). The psychological causality implicit in verbs: A review. *Psychological Bulletin, 121*, 192–218.

Russell, J. A. (1994). Is there universal recognition of emotion from facial expressions? A review of cross-cultural studies. *Psychological Bulletin, 115*, 102–141.

Russell, N. J. C. (2011). Milgram's obedience to authority experiments: Origins and early evolution. *British Journal of Social Psychology, 50*, 140–162.

Rutter, D. R. (1984). *Looking and seeing: The role of visual communication in social interaction*. Chichester: Wiley.

Rutter, D. R., Stephenson, G. M., Ayling, K., & White, P. A. (1978). The timing of looks in dyadic conversation. *British Journal of Social and Clinical Psychology, 17*, 17–21.

Rutter, D. R., Stephenson, G. M., Lazzerini, A., Ayling, K., & White, P. A. (1977). Eye-contact: A chance product of individual looking. *British Journal of Social and Clinical Psychology, 16*, 191–192.

Sacks, H. (1984). Notes on methodology. In J. M. Atkinson & J. Heritage. (Eds.), *Structures of social action: Studies in conversation analysis* (pp. 21–27). Cambridge: Cambridge University Press.

Sacks, H. (Jefferson, G., Ed.) (1995). *Lectures on conversation* (Vols I and II). Oxford: Blackwell.

Sacks, H., & Schegloff, E. (1973). Opening and closing. *Semiotica, 8*, 289–327.

Sacks, H., Schegloff, E., & Jefferson, G. (1974). A simplest systematics for the organization of turn-taking for conversation. *Language, 50*(4), 696–735.

Sampson, E. E. (1988). The debate on individualism: Indigenous psychologies of the individual and their role in personal and societal functioning. *American Psychologist, 43*, 15–22.

Sampson, E. E. (1993). *Celebrating the other: A dialogic account of human nature*. Hemel Hempstead: Harvester Wheatsheaf.

Saucier, D. A., Miller, C. T., & Doucet, N. (2005). Differences in helping whites and blacks: A meta-analysis. *Personality and Social Psychology Review, 9*, 2–16.

Schachter, S., & Singer, J. E. (1962). Cognitive, social and physiological determinants of emotional state. *Psychological Review, 69*, 379–399.

Scheepers, D., Spears, R., Doosje, B., & Manstead, A. S. (2003). Two functions of inter-group discrimination: Identity and instrumental motives as a result of group identification and threat. *Personality and Social Psychology Bulletin, 29*, 568–577.

Schegloff, E. A. (1988). Goffman and the analysis of conversation. In P. Drew & A. Wootton (Eds.), *Erving Goffman: Exploring the interaction order*. Cambridge: Cambridge University Press.

Schegloff, E. A. (1995). Introduction. In Harvey Sacks (Gail Jefferson, Ed.), *Lectures on conversation* (Vol. 1, p. xviii). Cambridge, MA: Blackwell.

Schegloff, E. A. (1997). Whose text? Whose context? *Discourse Society, 8*, 165–187.

Schegloff, E. A. (1999). 'Schegloff's texts' as 'Billig's data': A critical reply. *Discourse and Society, 8*, 558–575.

Schifter, D. B., & Ajzen, I. (1985). Intention, perceived control, and weight loss: An application of the theory of planned behavior. *Journal of Personality and Social Psychology, 49*, 843–851.

Schlenker, B. R., & Darby, B. W. (1981). The use of apologies in social predicaments. *Social Psychology Quarterly, 44*, 271–278.

Schmidt, G., & Weiner, B. (1988). An attribution–affect–action theory of behavior: Replications of judgments of help-giving. *Personality and Social Psychology Bulletin, 14*, 610–621.

Scott, M. L., & Lyman, S. M. (1968). Accounts. *American Sociological Review*, (33), 46–62.

Sedikides, C. (1993). Assessment, enhancement, and verification determinants of the self-evaluation process. *Journal of Personality and Social Psychology, 65*, 317–338.

Sedikides, C., Campbell, W. K., Reeder, G. D., & Elliot, A. J. (1998). The self-serving bias in relational context. *Journal of Personality and Social Psychology, 74*, 378–386.

Sedikides, C., & Green, J. D. (2000). On the self-protective nature of inconsistency–negativity management: Using the person memory paradigm to examine self-referent memory. *Journal of Personality and Social Psychology. 79*, 906–922.

Seligman, M. E., Abramson, L. Y., Semmel, A., von Baeyer, C. (1979). Depressive attributional style. *Journal of Abnormal Psychology, 88*, 242–247.

Semin, G. R., & Manstead, A. S. R. (1983). *The accountability of conduct: A social psychological analysis*. London: Academic Press.

Shackelford, T. K., Schmitt, D. P., & Buss, D. M. (2005). Mate preferences of married persons in the newlywed year and four years later. *Cognition and Emotion, 19*, 1262–1270.

Shaw, J. C., Wild, E., & Colquitt, J. A. (2003). To justify or excuse? A meta-analytic review of the effects of explanations. *Journal of Applied Psychology, 88*, 444–458.

Sheeran, P., Aarts, H., Custers, R., Rivis, A., Webb, T. L., & Cooke, R. (2005). The goal-dependent automaticity of drinking habits. *British Journal of Social Psychology, 44*, 47–64.

Sherif, M. (1936). *The psychology of social norms*. New York: Harper Collins.

Sherif, M. (1937). An experimental approach to the study of attitudes. *Sociometry: A Journal of Research in Social Psychology, 1*, 90–98.

Sherif, M. (1966). *In common predicament: Social psychology of inter-group conflict and cooperation*. Boston, MA: Houghton-Mifflin.

Sherif, M. (1967). *Group conflict and co-operation*. London: Routledge & Kegan Paul.

Sherman, P. W. (1981). Kinship demography, and Belding's ground squirrel nepotism. *Behavioral Ecology and Sociology, 8*, 604–606.

Sherman, P. W. (1985). Alarm calls of Belding's ground squirrels to aerial predators. *Behavioral Ecology and Sociobiology, 17*, 313–323.

Sherman, J. W., & Bessenoff, G. R. (1999). Stereotypes as source-monitoring cues: On the interaction between episodic and semantic memory. *Psychological Science, 10*(2), 106–110.

Shotland, R. L., & Straw, M. (1976). Bystander response to an assault: When a man attacks a woman. *Journal of Personality and Social Psychology, 34*, 990–999.

Shotter, J. (1995). In conversation: Joint action, shared intentionality and ethics. *Theory & Psychology, 5*, 49–73.

Shrauger, J. S., and Schoeneman , T. J. (1979). Symbolic interactionist view of self-concept: Through the looking glass darkly. *Psychological Bulletin, 86*, 549–573.

Simon, H. (1950). A behavioral model of rational choice. *Quarterly Journal of Economics, 69*, 99–118.

Singh, R., & Ho, S. Y. (2000). Attitudes and attraction: A new test of the attraction, repulsion and similarity–dissimilarity asymmetry hypotheses. *British Journal of Social Psychology, 39*, 197–211.

Singh, R., Ho, L. J., Tan, H. L., & Bell, P. A. (2007). Attitudes, personal evaluations, cognitive evaluation and interpersonal attraction: On the direct, indirect and reverse-causal effects. *British Journal of Social Psychology, 46*, 19–42.

Smail, D. (1978). *Psychotherapy: A personal approach*. London: Dent.

Smail, D. (2002). Psychology and power: Understanding human action. *Journal of Critical Psychology, Counselling and Psychotherapy, 2*, 1–10.

Smail, D. (2004). Therapeutic psychology and the ideology of privilege. *Clinical Psychology, 38*, 9–14.

Smail, D. (2006a). Implications for practice. *Clinical Psychology Forum, 162*, 17–20.

Smail, D. (2006b). Is clinical psychology selling its soul (again)? *Clinical Psychology Forum, 168*, 17–20.

Smail, D. (2010). The rocky path from clinical to community psychology–a personal view. *Journal of Community and Applied Social Psychology, 20*, 455–461.

Smith, K. D., Keating, J. P., & Stotland, E. (1989). Altruism reconsidered: The effect of denying feedback on a victim's status to empathic witnesses. *Journal of Personality and Social Psychology, 57*(4), 641–650.

Smith, H. J., & Spears, R. (1996). Evaluating performance and desire as a function of personal and collective (dis)advantage: A group escape from individual bias. *Personality and Social Psychology Bulletin, 22*, 690–704.

Son Hing, L. S., Chung-Yan, G., Hamilton, L., & Zanna, M. (2008). A two-dimensional model that employs explicit and implicit attitudes to characterize prejudice. *Journal of Personality and Social Psychology, 94*, 971–987.

Spears, R. (2010). Group rationale, collective sense: Beyond intergroup bias. Invited position paper. *British Journal of Social Psychology, 49*, 1–20.

Spence, A., & Townsend, E. (2007). Predicting behaviour towards genetically modified food using implicit and explicit attitudes. *British Journal of Social Psychology, 46*(2), 437–457.

Stander, V. A., Hsiung, P. C., MacDermid, S. (2001). The relationship of attributions to marital distress: A comparison of mainland Chinese and U.S. couples. *Journal of Family Psychology, 15*(1), 124–134.

Stapel, D. A., & Blanton, H. (2004). From seeing to believing: Subliminal social comparisons affect implicit and explicit self-evaluations. *Journal of Personality and Social Psychology, 87*(4), 468–481.

Staske, S. A. (1996). Talking feelings: The collaborative construction of emotion in talk between close relational partners. *Symbolic Interaction, 19*, 111–135.

Staske, S. A. (1998). The normalization of problematic emotion in conversations between close relational partners: Interpersonal emotion work. *Symbolic Interaction, 21*, 59–86.

Stivers, T. (2008). Stance, alignment, and affiliation during storytelling: When nodding is a token of affiliation. *Research on Language and Social Interaction, 41*(1), 31–57.

Stokoe, E. (2006). Public intimacy in neighbour relationships and complaints. *Sociological Research Online, 11*(3). (Available online at: www.socresonline.org.uk/11/3/stokoe.html).

Stokoe, E. (2008). Categories and sequences: Formulating gender in talk-in-interaction. In L. Litosseliti, H. Saunston, K. Segall, & J. Sunderland (Eds.), *Language and Gender Research Methodologies*. London: Palgrave Macmillan.

Stokoe, E. (2009). Doing actions with identity categories: Complaints and denials in neighbor disputes. *Text and Talk, 29*, 75–97.

Stokoe, E. (2010a). 'Have you been married, or ...?' Eliciting and accounting for relationship histories in speed-dating encounters. *Research on Language and Social Interaction, 43*(3), 260–282.

Stokoe, E. (2010b). Gender, conversation analysis, and the anatomy of membership categorization practices. *Social and Personality Psychology Compass, 4*(7), 428–438.

Stokoe, E. (2010c). 'I'm not gonna hit a lady': Conversation analysis, membership categorization and men's denials of violence towards women. *Discourse and Society, 21*(1), 59–82.

Stokoe, E. (2012, in press). 'You know how men are': The anatomy of a categorical practice. *Gender and Language, 6*(1).

Stokoe, E., & Edwards, D. (2009). Accomplishing social action with identity categories: Mediating neighbour complaints. In M. Wetherell (Ed.), *Theorizing identities and social action* (pp. 95–115). London: Sage.

Stokoe, E., & Edwards, D. (2010). Asking ostensibly silly questions in police interrogations. In A. F. Freed & S. Ehrlich (Eds.), *Why do you ask? The function of questions in institutional discourse* (pp. 108–132). Oxford: Oxford University Press.

Stokoe, E., & Hepburn, A. (2005). 'You can hear a lot through the walls': Noise formulations in neighbour complaints. *Discourse & Society, 16*(5), 647–673.

Stokoe, E. H., & Wallwork, J. (2003). Space invaders: The moral–spatial order in neighbour dispute discourse. *British Journal of Social Psychology, 42*, 551–569.

Stone, E., Shackelford, T. K., & Buss, D. M. (2008). Socioeconomic development and shifts in mate preferences. *Evolutionary Psychology, 6*, 447–455.

Stone, M. (2011). Excerpts from the LAPD Officers' trial. Available online at: http://law2.umkc.edu/faculty/projects/ftrials/lapd/kingtranscript.html.

Storms, M. (1973). Videotape and the attribution process: Reversing actors' and observers' points of view. *Journal of Personality and Social Psychology, 27*, 165–175.

Stuermer, S., Snyder, M., & Omoto, A. M. (2005). Prosocial emotions and helping: The moderating role of group membership. *Journal of Personality and Social Psychology, 88*, 532–546.

Summers, M. (2007). Rhetorically self-sufficient arguments in Western Australian parliamentary debates on lesbian and gay law reform. *British Journal of Social Psychology, 46*, 839–858.

Tajfel, H. (1957). Value and the perceptual judgment of magnitude. *Psychological Review, 64*, 192–204.

Tajfel, H. (1959). Quantitative judgment in social perception. *British Journal of Psychology, 50*, 16–29.

Tajfel, H. (1969). Cognitive aspects of prejudice. *Journal of Social Issues, 25*, 79–97.

Tajfel, H. (1970). Experiments in intergroup discrimination. *Scientific American, 223*, 96–102.

Tajfel, H. (Ed.). (1978). *Differentiation between social groups: Studies in the social psychology of intergroup relations*. London: Academic Press.

Tajfel, H., & Wilkes, A. L. (1963). Classification and quantitative judgment. *British Journal of Psychology, 54*, 101–114.

Tausch, N., Tam, T., Hewstone, M., Kenworthy, J. B., & Cairns, E. (2007). Individual-level and group-level mediators of contact effects in Northern Ireland: The moderating role of social identification. *British Journal of Social Psychology, 46*, 541–556.

Taylor, D. M., & Jaggi, V. (1974). Ethnocentrism and causal attribution in a South Indian context. *Journal of Cross-Cultural Psychology, 5*, 162–171.

Tedeschi, J. T. & Rosenfeld, P. (1981). Impression management and the forced compliance situation. In J. T. Tedeschi, (Ed.), *Impression management and social psychological research*. (pp. 147–180). New York: Academic Press.

Terry, D. J., & O'Leary, J. E. (1995). The theory of planned behavior: The effects of perceived behavioral control and self-efficacy. *British Journal of Social Psychology, 34*, 199–220.

Tesser, A. (1988). Toward a self-evaluative maintenance model of social behavior. In L. Berkowitz (Ed.), *Advances in experimental social psychology* (Vol. 21, pp. 181–227), Orlando, FL: Academic Press.

Thakerar, J. N., Giles, H., & Cheshire, J. (1982). Psychological and linguistic parameters of speech accommodation theory. In C. Fraser and K. R. Scherer (Eds.) *Advances in the social psychology of language* (pp. 205–255). New York: Cambridge University Press.

Thibaut, J. W., & Kelley, H. H. (1959). *The social psychology of groups*. New York: Wiley.

Thurstone, L. L. (1931). The measurement of attitudes. *Journal of Abnormal Psychology, 26*, 249–269.

Trafimow, D., Sheeran, P., Lombardo, B., Finlay, K. A., Brown, J., & Armitage, C. J. (2004). Affective and cognitive control of persons and behaviors. *British Journal of Social Psychology, 43*, 207–224.

Traupmann, J., Hatfield, E., & Wexler, P. (1983). Equity and sexual satisfaction in dating couples. *British Journal of Social Psychology, 22*, 33–40.

Traupmann, J., Petersen, R., Utne, M., & Hatfield, E. (1981). Measuring equity in intimate relations. *Applied Psychological Measurement, 5*, 467–480.

Traverso, V. (2009). The dilemmas of third-party complaints in conversation between friends. *Journal of Pragmatics, 41*(12), 2385–2399.

Trivers, R. (1971). The evolution of reciprocal altruism. *Quarterly Review of Biology*, 46, 35–57.

Trivers, R. L. (1972). Parental investment and sexual selection. In B. Campbell (Ed.), *Sexual selection and the descent of man* (pp. 136–179). Chicago: Aldine-Atherton.

Trudgill, P. (1974). *The social differentiation of English in Norwich*. Cambridge: Cambridge University Press.

Turner, J. C. (1991). *Social influence*. Belmont, CA: Thomson Brooks/Cole Publishing.

Turner, J. C., Hogg, M. A., Oakes, P. J., Reicher, S. D., & *Wetherell, M. S. (1987). Rediscovering the social group: A self-categorisation theory*. Oxford: Blackwell.

Tversky, A., & Kahneman, D. (1974). Judgement under uncertainty: Heuristics and biases. *Science, 185*, 1124–1130.

Tversky, A., & Kahneman, D. (1980). Causal schemata in judgments under uncertainty. In M. Fishbein (Ed.), *Progress in social psychology* (Vol. 1, pp. 49–72). Hillsdale, NJ: Erlbaum.

Tversky, A., & Kahneman, D. (1981). The framing of decisions and psychology of choice. *Science, 211*, 453–458.

Tversky, A., & Kahneman, D. (1983). Extension versus intuitive reasoning: The conjunction fallacy in probability judgment. *Psychological Review, 90*, 293–315.

Vaughan, K. B., & Lanzetta, J. T. (1980). Vicarious instigation and conditioning of facial expressive and automatic responses to a model's expressive display of pain. *Journal of Personality and Social Psychology, 38*, 909–923.

Verplanken, B., Hofstee, G., & Janssen, H. J. W. (1998). Accessibility of affective versus cognitive components of attitude. *European Journal of Social Psychology, 28*, 23–35.

Vico, G. (1975[1725]). *The life of Giambattista Vico: Written by himself* (M. H. Fisch & T. G. Bergin, Eds. & Trans.). Ithaca, NY: Cornell University Press.

Vico, G. (1975[1744]). *Principles of new science of Giambattista Vico concerning the common nature of the nations* (3rd ed., T. G. Bergin & M. H. Fisch, Eds. & Trans.). Ithaca, NY: Cornell University Press.

Vignoles, V. L., Chryssochoou, X., & Breakwell, G. M. (2004). Combining uniqueness and relationships: Representations of the person among the Anglican clergy. *British Journal of Social Psychology, 43*, 113–132.

Watson, D. (1982). The actor and the observer: How are their perceptions of causality divergent? *Psychological Bulletin, 92*, 682–700.

Watson, J. B. (1913). Psychology as a behaviorist views it. *Psychological Review, 20*, 158–177.

Watson, J. B., & Rayner, R. (1920). Conditioned emotional reactions. *Journal of Experimental Psychology, 3*(1), 1–14.

Weatherall, A., & Walton, M. (1999). The metaphorical construction of sexual experience in a speech community of New Zealand university students. *British Journal of Social Psychology, 38*, 479–498.

Weiner, B., Amirkhan, J., Folkes, V. S., & Verette, J. A. (1987). An attributional analysis of excuse-giving: Studies of a naive theory of emotion. *Journal of Personality and Social Psychology, 52*, 316–324.

Weiner, B., Perry, R. P., & Magnusson, J. (1988). An attributional analysis of reactions to stigma. *Journal of Personality and Social Psychology, 55*(5), 738–748.

Wertheimer, M. (1938[1923]). Laws of organization in perceptual forms (first published as Untersuchungen zur lehre von der gestalt II, *Psycologische Forschung, 4*, 301–350). In W. Ellis, (1938). *A source book of Gestalt psychology* (pp. 71–88). London: Routledge & Kegan Paul.

Wetherell, M. (1998). Positioning and interpretative repertoires: Conversation analysis and post-structuralism in dialogue. *Discourse & Society, 9*, 387–412.

Wetherell, M., & Edley, N. (1999). Negotiating hegemonic masculinity: Imaginary positions and psycho-discursive practices. *Feminism & Psychology, 9*(3), 335–356.

Wetherell, M., & Potter, J. (1992). *Mapping the language of racism: Discourse and the legitimation of exploitation*. Hemel Hempstead: Harvester Wheatsheaf.

Wheeler, L., & Kim, Y. (1997). What is beautiful is culturally good: The physical attractiveness stereotype has different content in collectivistic cultures. *Personality and Social Psychology Bulletin, 23*, 795–800.

Wicker, A. W. (1969), Attitudes versus actions: The relationship of verbal and overt behavioral responses to attitude objects. *Journal of Social Issues, 25*, 41–78.

Wiggins, S., & Potter, J. (2003). Attitudes and evaluative practices: Category vs. item and subjective vs. objective constructions in everyday food assessments. *British Journal of Social Psychology, 42*, 513–531.

Wildschut, T., Sedikides, C., Arndt, J., & Routledge, C. (2006). Nostalgia: Content, triggers, functions. *Journal of Personality and Social Psychology, 91*, 975–993.

Wilke, H., & Lanzetta, J. T. (1970). The obligation to help: The effects of amount of prior help on subsequent helping behavior. *Journal of Experimental Social Psychology, 6*, 488–493.

Wilkinson, S., & Kitzinger, C. (1995). *Feminism and discourse: Psychological perspectives*. London: Sage.

Wills, T.A. (1992). The helping process in the context of personal relationships. In S. Spacapanand & S. Oskamp (Eds.), *New directions in helping: Vol. 2: Help seeking* (pp. 109–142). New York: Academic Press.

Wilson, A. N. (2004). *London: A short history*. New York: Modern Library.

Wirtz, P. H., von Kanel, R., Mohiyeddini, C., Emini, L., Ruedisueli, K., Groessbauer, S., & Ehlert, U. (2006). Low social support and poor emotional regulation are associated with increased stress hormone reactivity to mental stress in systemic hypertension. *Journal of Clinical Endocrinology and Metabolism, 91*(10), 3857–3865.

Wong, S., & Goodwin, R. (2009). Experiencing marital satisfaction across three cultures: A qualitative study. *Journal of Social and Personal Relationships, 26*, 1011–1028.

Wood, D., and Brumbaugh, C. C. (2009). Using revealed mate preferences to evaluate market force and differential preference explanations for mate selection. *Journal of Personality and Social Psychology, 96*, 1226–1244.

Wooffitt, R. (1992). *Telling tales of the unexpected: The organisation of factual discourse*. Hemel Hempstead: Harvester Wheatsheaf.

Wooffitt, R. (2007). Communication and laboratory performance in parapsychology experiments: Demand characteristics and the social organisation of interaction. *British Journal of Social Psychology, 46*, 477–498.

Wooffitt, R. C., Fraser, N., Gilbert, N., & McGlashan, S. (1997). *Humans, computers and wizards: Studying human (simulated) computer interaction*. London: Routledge.

Worchel, S., Andreoli, V. A., & Folger, R. (1977). Intergroup cooperation and attraction: The effect of previous interaction and outcome of combined effort. *Journal of Experimental Social Psychology, 13*, 131–140.

Wundt, W. (1904[1873–1874]). *Principles of physiological psychology* (Edward Titchener, Trans). London: Swan Sonnenschein.

Zagefka, H., Brown, R., Broquard, M., & Leventoglu, S. (2007). Predictors and consequences of negative attitudes toward immigrants in Belgium and Turkey: The role of acculturation preferences and economic competition. *British Journal of Social Psychology, 46*, 153–169.

Zajonc, R. B. (1968). Attitudinal effects of mere exposure. *Journal of Personality and Social Psychology, 9*, 1–27.

Ziller, R. C. (1964) Individuation and socialization. *Human Relations, 17*, 341–360.

Zillmann, D. (1983). Transfer of excitation in emotional behavior. In J. T. Cacioppo & R. E. Petty (Eds.), *Social psychophysiology: A sourcebook* (pp. 215–240). New York: Guilford Press.

Zillmann, D. (1996). Sequential dependencies in emotional experience and behavior. In R. D. Kavanaugh, B. Zimmerberg, & S. Fein (Eds.), *Emotion: Interdisciplinary perspectives* (pp. 243–272). Mahwah, NJ: Erlbaum.

Zillmann, D. (1998). *Connections between sexuality and aggression* (2nd ed.). Mahwah, NJ: Erlbaum.

Zillmann, D., & Bryant, J. (1974). Effect of residual excitation on the emotional response to provocation and delayed aggressive behavior. *Journal of Personality and Social Psychology, 30*, 782–791.

Zillmann, D., & Sapolsky, B. S. (1977). What mediates the effect of mild erotica on annoyance and hostile behavior in males? *Journal of Personality and Social Psychology, 35*, 587–596.

Zimbardo, P. (1969). The human choice: Individuation, reason and order versus deindividuation, impulse and chaos. In J. Arnold and D. Levine (Eds), *Nebraska symposium on motivation, 17*. Lincoln, NB: University of Nebraska Press.

Zimbardo, P. (2006). Commentary – on rethinking the psychology of tyranny: The BBC prison study. *British Journal of Social Psychology, 45*, 47–53.

Zimbardo, P. (2007). *The Lucifer effect: How good people turn evil*. London: Rider.

Zuckerman, M. (1975). Belief in a just world and altruistic behaviour. *Journal of Personality and Social Psychology, 31*, 972–976.

Zuckerman, M. (1979). Attribution of success and failure revisited, or: The motivational bias is alive and well in attribution theory. *Journal of Personality, 47*, 245–287.

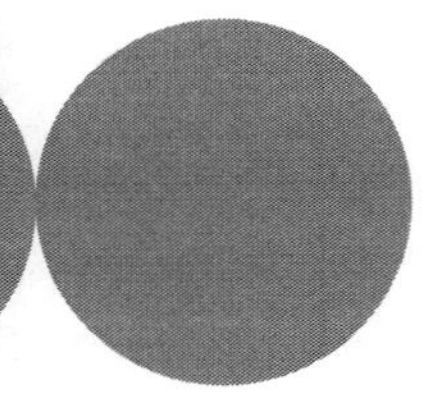

Name index

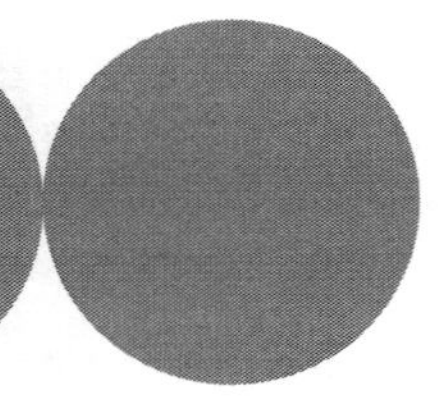

Subject index

Note: References in **bold** are to the Glossary.